Longer pipelines and wider superscalar issue put even more pressure ~~on the per-~~ formance potential of the hardware. But data and control dependenc~~es, along with instruc-~~ tion latencies, offer an upper limit on delivered performance because the processor must sometimes wait for a dependency to be resolved, such as with mispredicted branch. *(page 514)*

7 Large and Fast: Exploiting Memory Hierarchy

A memory hierarchy uses smaller and faster memory technologies close to the processor. Thus accesses that hit in the highest level of the hierarchy can be processed quickly. Accesses that miss go to lower levels of the hierarchy, which are larger but slower. If the hit rate is high enough, the memory hierarchy has an effective access time close to that of the highest (and fastest) level and a size equal to that of the lowest (and largest) level. *(page 544)*

While *caches, translation lookaside buffers*, and *virtual memory* may initially look very different, they can be understood by looking at how they deal with four questions: (1) Where can a block be placed? (2) How is a block found? (3) What block is replaced on a miss? (4) How are writes handled? *(page 608)*

The challenge in designing memory hierarchies is that every change that potentially improves the *miss rate* can also negatively affect overall performance: Increasing size decreases *capacity misses* but may also increase *access time*; increasing *associativity* decreases miss rate due to *conflict misses* but may also increase access time; and increasing *block size* may decrease miss rate yet also increase *miss penalty. (page 611)*

8 Interfacing Processors and Peripherals

Different bus characteristics allow the creation of buses optimized for a wide range of demands. In general, higher-cost systems use wider and faster buses that are *synchronous*. In contrast, low-cost systems favor buses that are narrower, do not require intelligence among the devices (hence a single master), and are *asynchronous* so that low-speed devices can interface inexpensively. *(page 671)*

The performance of an I/O system, whether measured by bandwidth or latency, depends on all the elements in the path between the device and memory, including the operating system that generates the I/O commands. *(page 691)*

9 Microprocessors

In comparing cost performance of a bus-connected UMA multiprocessor to that of a network-connected NUMA multiprocessor, the network-connected NUMA has consistent performance per unit cost, while the bus-connected machine has a "sweet spot" plateau. The plateau suggest that customers need to be more selective with bus-connected than with network-connected multiprocessors, and that bus designers need to be careful to pick a sweet spot that matches the needs of most customers. *(page 732)*

A key characteristic of programs for parallel machines is frequency of *synchronization* and *communication*. Large-scale parallel machines have *distributed physical memory;* the higher bandwidth and lower overhead of local memory compared with that of nonlocal memory strongly rewards parallel processing programmers who utilize *locality. (page 742)*

A P P E N D I C E S

A Assemblers, Linkers, and the SPIM Simulator

Assembly language is a programming language. Its principal difference from high-level languages is that it provides only a few, simple types of data and control flow. Assembly language programs do not specify the type of value held in a variable, leaving it to the programmer to apply the appropriate operations. In addition, programs must implement all control flow with *go tos. (page A-12)*

B The Basics of Logic Design

C Mapping Control to Hardware

Independent of whether the control is represented as a finite state diagram or as a microprogram, the translation to hardware is similar: Each state or microinstruction asserts a set of control outputs and specifies how to choose the next state. Next-state function may be encoded in a finite state machine or with an explicit sequencer; control logic may be either ROMs or PLAs. *(page C-32)*

SECOND EDITION

Computer Organization and Design

THE HARDWARE/SOFTWARE INTERFACE

T R A D E M A R K S

The following trademarks are the property of the following organizations:

TeX is a trademark of Americal Mathematical Society.

Apple II and Macintosh are trademarks of Apple Computers, Inc.

CDC 6600, CDC 7600, CDC STAR-100, CYBER-180, CYBER-180/990, and CYBER-205 are trademarks of Control Data Corporation.

The Cosmic Cube is a trademark of California Institute of Technology.

CP3100 is a trademark of Conner Peripherals.

Cray, CRAY-1, CRAY J90, CRAY T90, CRAY X-MP/416, and CRAY Y-MP are trademarks of Cray Research.

Alpha, AlphaServer, AlphaStation, DEC, DECsystem, DECsystem 3100, DECstation, PDP-8, PDP-11, Unibus, VAX, VAX 8700, and VAX11/780 are trademarks of Digital Equipment Corporation.

MP2361A, Super Eagle, VP100, VP200, and VPP300 are trademarks of Fujitsu Corporation.

Gnu C Compiler is a trademark of Free Software Foundation.

Goodyear MPP is a trademark of Goodyear Tire and Rubber Co., Inc.

Apollo DN 300, Apollo DN 10000, Convex, HP, HP Precision Architecture, HPPA, HP850, HP 3000, HP 300/70, PA-RISC, and Precision are registered trademarks of Hewlet-Packard Company.

432, 960 CA, 4004, 8008, 8080, 8086, 8087, 8088, 80186, 80286, 80386, 80486, Delta, iAPX 432, i860, Intel, Intel486, Intel Hypercube, iPSC/2, MMX, Multibus, Multibus II, Paragon, and Pentium are trademarks of Intel Corporation. Intel Inside is a registered trademark of Intel Corporation.

360, 360/30, 360/40, 360/50, 360/65, 360/85, 360/91, 370, 370/158, 370/165, 370/168, 370-XA, ESA/370, 701, 704, 709, 801, 3033, 3080, 3080 series, 3080 VF, 3081, 3090, 3090/100, 3090/200, 3090/400, 3090/600, 3090/600S, 3090 VF, 3330, 3380, 3380D, 3380 Disk Model AK4, 3380J, 3390, 3880-23, 3990, 7090, 7094, IBM, IBM PC, IBM PC-AT, IBM SVS, ISAM, MVS, PL.8, PowerPC, POWERstation, RT-PC, RAMAC, RS/6000, Sage, Stretch, System/360, Vector Faility, and VM are trademarks of International Business Machines Corporation. POWERserver, RISC System/6000, and SP2 are registered trademarks of International Business Machines Corporation.

ICL DAP is a trademark of International Computers Limited.

Inmos and Transputer are trademarks of Inmos.

FutureBus is a trademark of the Institute of Electrical and Electronic Engineers.

KSR-1 is a trademark of Kendall Square Research.

MASPAR MP-1 and MASPAR MP-2 are trademarks of MasPar Corporation.

MIPS, R2000, R3000, and R10000 are registered trademarks of MIPS Technology, Inc.

Windows is a trademark of Microsoft Corporation.

NuBus is a trademark of Massachusetts Institute of Technology.

Delta Series 8608, System V/88 R32V1, VME bus, 6809, 68000, 68010, 68020, 68030, 68881, 68882, 88000, 88000 1.8.4m14, 88100, and 88200 are trademarks of Motorola Corporation.

Ncube and nCube/ten are trademarks of Ncube Corporation.

NEC is a registered trademark of NEC Corporation.

Network Computer is a trademark of Oracle Corporation.

Parsytec GC is a trademark of Parsytec, Inc.

Imprimis, IPI-2, Sabre, Sabre 97209, Seagate, and Wren IV are trademarks of Seagate Technology, Inc.

NUMA-Q, Sequent, and Symmetry are trademarks of Sequent Computers.

Power Challenge, Silicon Graphics, Silicon Graphics 43/240, Silicon Graphics 4D/60, Silicon Graphics 4D/240, and Silicon Graphics 4D Series are trademarks of Silicon Graphics. Origin2000 is a registered trademark of Silicon Graphics.

SPEC is a registered trademark of the Standard Performance Evaluation Corporation.

Spice is a trademark of University of California at Berkeley.

Enterprise, Java, Sun, Sun Ultra, Sun Microsystems, and Ultra are trademarks of Sun Microsystems, Inc. SPARC and UltraSPARC are registered trademarks of SPARC International, Inc., licensed to Sun Microsystems, Inc.

Connection Machine, CM-2, and CM-5 are trademarks of Thinking Machines.

Burroughs 6500, B5000, B5500, D-machine, UNIVAC, UNIVAC I, and UNIVAC 1103 are trademarks of UNISYS.

Alto, PARC, Palo Alto Research Center, and Xerox are trademarks of Xerox Corporation.

The UNIX trademark is licensed exclusively through X/Open Company Ltd.

All other product names are trademarks or registered trademarks of their respective companies. Where trademarks appear in this book and Morgan Kaufmann Publishers was aware of a trademark claim, the trademarks have been printed in initial caps or all caps.

SECOND EDITION

Computer Organization and Design

THE HARDWARE/SOFTWARE INTERFACE

John L. Hennessy
Stanford University

David A. Patterson
University of California, Berkeley

With a contribution by
James R. Larus
University of Wisconsin

Morgan Kaufmann Publishers, Inc.
San Francisco, California

Sponsoring Editor   Denise Penrose
Production Manager   Yonie Overton
Production Editor   Julie Pabst
Editorial Coordinator   Jane Elliott
Text and Cover Design   Ross Carron Design
Illustration   Alexander Teshin Associates, with second edition modifications by Dartmouth
    Publishing, Inc.
Chapter Opener Illustrations   Canary Studios
Copyeditor   Ken DellaPenta
Composition   Nancy Logan
Proofreader   Jennifer McClain
Indexer   Steve Rath
Printer   Courier Corporation

Morgan Kaufmann Publishers, Inc.
Editorial and Sales Office:
340 Pine Street, Sixth Floor
San Francisco, CA 94104-3205
USA

Telephone   415/392-2665
Facsimile   415/982-2665
Email   *mkp@mkp.com*
WWW   *http://www.mkp.com*
Order toll free   800/745-7323

Advice, Praise, and Errors: Any correspondence related to this publication or intended for the authors
should be sent electronically to *mkp@mkp.com.* Information regarding error sightings is encouraged. Any
error sightings that are accepted for correction in subsequent printings will be rewarded by the authors
with a payment of $1.00 (U.S.) per correction at the time of their implementation in a reprint.

Library of Congress Cataloging-in-Publication Data
Patterson, David A.
        Computer organization and design : the hardware/software interface
        / David A. Patterson, John L. Hennessy.—2nd ed.
              p.   cm.
        Includes bibliographical references and index.
        ISBN 1-55860-428-6 (cloth).—ISBN 1-55860-491-X (paper)
        1. Computer organization. 2. Computers—Design and construction.
              3. Computer interfaces.   I. Hennessy, John L.   II. Title
              QA76.9.C643H46   1997
              004.2'2—dc21   97-16050

TO LINDA AND ANDREA

Foreword

by John H. Crawford
Intel Fellow, Director of Microprocessor Architecture
Intel Corporation, Santa Clara, California

Computer design is an exciting and competitive discipline. The microprocessor industry is on a treadmill where we double microprocessor performance every 18 months and double microprocessor complexity—measured by the number of transistors per chip—every 24 months. This unprecedented rate of change has been evident for the entire 25-year history of the microprocessor, and it promises to continue for many years to come as the creativity and energy of many people are harnessed to drive innovation ahead in spite of the challenge of ever-smaller dimensions. This book trains the student with the concepts needed to lay a solid foundation for joining this exciting field. More importantly, this book provides a framework for thinking about computer organization and design that will enable the reader to continue the lifetime of learning necessary for staying at the forefront of this competitive discipline.

The text focuses on the boundary between hardware and software and explores the levels of hardware in the vicinity of this boundary. This boundary is captured in a computer's architecture specification. It is a critical boundary for a successful computer product: an architect must define an interface that can be efficiently implemented by hardware and efficiently targeted by compilers. The interface must be able to retain these efficiencies for many generations of hardware and compiler technology, much of which will be unknown at the time the architecture is specified. This boundary is central to the discipline of computer design: it is where compilation (in software) ends and interpretation (in hardware) begins.

This book builds on introductory programming skills to introduce the concepts of assembly language programming and the tools needed for this task: the assembler, linker, and loader. Once these prerequisites are completed, the remainder of the book explores the first few levels of hardware below the architectural interface. The basic concepts are motivated and introduced with clear and intuitive examples, then elaborated into the "real stuff" used in today's modern microprocessors. For example, doing the laundry is used as an analogy in Chapter 6 to explain the basic concepts of pipelining, a key technique used in all modern computers. In Chapter 4, algorithms for the basic floating-point arithmetic operators such as addition, multiplication, and division are first explained in decimal, then in binary, and finally they are elaborated into the best-known methods used for high-speed arithmetic in today's computers.

New to this edition are sections in each chapter entitled "Real Stuff." These sections describe how the concepts from the chapter are implemented in commercially successful products. These provide relevant, tangible examples of the concepts and reinforce their importance. As an example, the Real Stuff in Chapter 6, Enhancing Performance with Pipelining, provides an overview of a dynamically scheduled pipeline as implemented in both the IBM/Motorola PowerPC 604 and Intel's Pentium Pro microprocessor.

The history of computing is woven as a thread throughout the book to reward the reader with a glimpse of key successes from the brief history of this young discipline. The other side of history is reported in the Fallacies and Pitfalls section of each chapter. Since we can learn more from failure than from success, these sections provide a wealth of learning!

The authors are two of the most admired teachers, researchers, and practitioners of the art of computer design today. John Hennessy has straddled both sides of the hardware/software boundary, providing technical leadership for the legendary MIPS compiler as well as the MIPS hardware products through many generations. David Patterson was one of the original RISC proponents: he coined the acronym RISC, evangelized the case for RISC, and served as a key consultant on Sun Microsystem's SPARC line of processors. Continuing his talent for marketable acronyms, his next breakthrough was RAID (Redundant Arrays of Inexpensive Disks), which revolutionized the disk storage industry for large data servers, and then NOW (Networks of Workstations).

Like other great "software" products, this second edition went through an extensive beta testing program: 13 beta sites tested the draft manuscript in classes to "debug" the text. Changes from this testing have been incorporated into the "production" version.

Patterson and Hennessy have succeeded in taking the first edition of their excellent introductory textbook on computer design and making it even better. This edition retains all of the good points of the original, yet adds significant new content and some minor enhancements. What results is an outstanding introduction to the exciting field of computer design.

Contents

Foreword   vi
by John H. Crawford

Worked Examples   xiii

Computer Organization and Design Online   xvi

Preface   xix

C H A P T E R S

1   **Computer Abstractions and Technology**   2

   1.1   Introduction   3
   1.2   Below Your Program   5
   1.3   Under the Covers   10
   1.4   Integrated Circuits: Fueling Innovation   21
   1.5   Real Stuff: Manufacturing Pentium Chips   24
   1.6   Fallacies and Pitfalls   29
   1.7   Concluding Remarks   30
   1.8   Historical Perspective and Further Reading   32
   1.9   Key Terms   44
  1.10   Exercises   45

2   **The Role of Performance**   52

   2.1   Introduction   54
   2.2   Measuring Performance   58
   2.3   Relating the Metrics   60
   2.4   Choosing Programs to Evaluate Performance   66
   2.5   Comparing and Summarizing Performance   69
   2.6   Real Stuff: The SPEC95 Benchmarks and Performance of Recent Processors   71
   2.7   Fallacies and Pitfalls   75
   2.8   Concluding Remarks   82

2.9   Historical Perspective and Further Reading 83
2.10 Key Terms 89
2.11 Exercises 90

3   **Instructions: Language of the Machine** 104

3.1   Introduction 106
3.2   Operations of the Computer Hardware 107
3.3   Operands of the Computer Hardware 109
3.4   Representing Instructions in the Computer 116
3.5   Instructions for Making Decisions 122
3.6   Supporting Procedures in Computer Hardware 132
3.7   Beyond Numbers 142
3.8   Other Styles of MIPS Addressing 145
3.9   Starting a Program 156
3.10 An Example to Put It All Together 163
3.11 Arrays versus Pointers 171
3.12 Real Stuff: PowerPC and 80x86 Instructions 175
3.13 Fallacies and Pitfalls 185
3.14 Concluding Remarks 187
3.15 Historical Perspective and Further Reading 189
3.16 Key Terms 196
3.17 Exercises 196

4   **Arithmetic for Computers** 208

4.1   Introduction 210
4.2   Signed and Unsigned Numbers 210
4.3   Addition and Subtraction 220
4.4   Logical Operations 225
4.5   Constructing an Arithmetic Logic Unit 230
4.6   Multiplication 250
4.7   Division 265
4.8   Floating Point 275
4.9   Real Stuff: Floating Point in the PowerPC and 80x86 301
4.10 Fallacies and Pitfalls 304
4.11 Concluding Remarks 308
4.12 Historical Perspective and Further Reading 312
4.13 Key Terms 322
4.14 Exercises 322

5   **The Processor: Datapath and Control** 336

5.1   Introduction 338
5.2   Building a Datapath 343
5.3   A Simple Implementation Scheme 351

5.4   A Multicycle Implementation   377
5.5   Microprogramming: Simplifying Control Design   399
5.6   Exceptions   410
5.7   Real Stuff: The Pentium Pro Implementation   416
5.8   Fallacies and Pitfalls   419
5.9   Concluding Remarks   421
5.10   Historical Perspective and Further Reading   423
5.11   Key Terms   426
5.12   Exercises   427

6 Enhancing Performance with Pipelining   434

6.1   An Overview of Pipelining   436
6.2   A Pipelined Datapath   449
6.3   Pipelined Control   466
6.4   Data Hazards and Forwarding   476
6.5   Data Hazards and Stalls   489
6.6   Branch Hazards   496
6.7   Exceptions   505
6.8   Superscalar and Dynamic Pipelining   510
6.9   Real Stuff: PowerPC 604 and Pentium Pro Pipelines   517
6.10   Fallacies and Pitfalls   520
6.11   Concluding Remarks   521
6.12   Historical Perspective and Further Reading   525
6.13   Key Terms   529
6.14   Exercises   529

7 Large and Fast: Exploiting Memory Hierarchy   538

7.1   Introduction   540
7.2   The Basics of Caches   545
7.3   Measuring and Improving Cache Performance   564
7.4   Virtual Memory   579
7.5   A Common Framework for Memory Hierarchies   603
7.6   Real Stuff: The Pentium Pro and PowerPC 604 Memory Hierarchies   611
7.7   Fallacies and Pitfalls   615
7.8   Concluding Remarks   618
7.9   Historical Perspective and Further Reading   621
7.10   Key Terms   627
7.11   Exercises   628

8 Interfacing Processors and Peripherals   636

8.1   Introduction   638
8.2   I/O Performance Measures: Some Examples from Disk and File
       Systems   641
8.3   Types and Characteristics of I/O Devices   644

8.4   **Buses: Connecting I/O Devices to Processor and Memory** 655
8.5   **Interfacing I/O Devices to the Memory, Processor, and Operating System** 673
8.6   **Designing an I/O System** 684
8.7   **Real Stuff: A Typical Desktop I/O System** 687
8.8   **Fallacies and Pitfalls** 688
8.9   **Concluding Remarks** 690
8.10 **Historical Perspective and Further Reading** 694
8.11 **Key Terms** 700
8.12 **Exercises** 700

9 **Multiprocessors** 710

9.1   **Introduction** 712
9.2   **Programming Multiprocessors** 714
9.3   **Multiprocessors Connected by a Single Bus** 717
9.4   **Multiprocessors Connected by a Network** 727
9.5   **Clusters** 734
9.6   **Network Topologies** 736
9.7   **Real Stuff: Future Directions for Multiprocessors** 740
9.8   **Fallacies and Pitfalls** 743
9.9   **Concluding Remarks—Evolution versus Revolution in Computer Architecture** 746
9.10 **Historical Perspective and Further Reading** 748
9.11 **Key Terms** 756
9.12 **Exercises** 756

A P P E N D I C E S

A **Assemblers, Linkers, and the SPIM Simulator** A-2

by James R. Larus, University of Wisconsin

A.1   **Introduction** A-3
A.2   **Assemblers** A-10
A.3   **Linkers** A-17
A.4   **Loading** A-19
A.5   **Memory Usage** A-20
A.6   **Procedure Call Convention** A-22
A.7   **Exceptions and Interrupts** A-32
A.8   **Input and Output** A-36
A.9   **SPIM** A-38
A.10 **MIPS R2000 Assembly Language** A-49
A.11 **Concluding Remarks** A-75
A.12 **Key Terms** A-76
A.13 **Exercises** A-76

B **The Basics of Logic Design**   B-2

B.1 **Introduction** B-3
B.2 **Gates, Truth Tables, and Logic Equations** B-4
B.3 **Combinational Logic** B-8
B.4 **Clocks** B-18
B.5 **Memory Elements** B-21
B.6 **Finite State Machines** B-35
B.7 **Timing Methodologies** B-39
B.8 **Concluding Remarks** B-44
B.9 **Key Terms** B-45
B.10 **Exercises** B-45

C **Mapping Control to Hardware**   C-2

C.1 **Introduction** C-3
C.2 **Implementing Combinational Control Units** C-4
C.3 **Implementing Finite State Machine Control** C-8
C.4 **Implementing the Next-State Function with a Sequencer** C-21
C.5 **Translating a Microprogram to Hardware** C-28
C.6 **Concluding Remarks** C-31
C.7 **Key Terms** C-32
C.8 **Exercises** C-32

Glossary G-1

Index I-1

Worked Examples

Chapter 2: The Role of Performance

Throughput and Response Time 56
Relative Performance 57
Improving Performance 60
Using the Performance Equation 62
Comparing Code Segments 64
MIPS as a Performance Measure 78

Chapter 3: Instructions: Language of the Machine

Compiling Two C Assignment Statements into MIPS 108
Compiling a Complex C Assignment into MIPS 109
Compiling a C Assignment Using Registers 110
Compiling an Assignment When an Operand Is in Memory 112
Compiling Using Load and Store 113
Compiling Using a Variable Array Index 114
Translating a MIPS Assembly Instruction into a Machine Instruction 117
Translating MIPS Assembly Language into Machine Language 119
Compiling an *If* Statement into a Conditional Branch 123
Compiling *if-then-else* into Conditional Branches 124
Compiling a Loop with Variable Array Index 126
Compiling a *while* Loop 127
Compiling a Less Than Test 128
Compiling a *switch* Statement by Using a Jump Address Table 129
Compiling a Procedure that Doesn't Call Another Procedure 134
Compiling a Recursive Procedure, Showing Nested Procedure Linking 136
Compiling a String Copy Procedure, Showing How to Use C Strings 143
Translating Assembly Constants into Machine Language 145
Loading a 32-Bit Constant 147
Showing Branch Offset in Machine Language 149
Branching Far Away 150
Decoding Machine Code 154
Linking Object Files 160
Compiling an Assignment Statement into Accumulator Instructions 190
Compiling an Assignment Statement into Memory-Memory Instructions 192
Compiling an Assignment Statement into Stack Instructions 193

Chapter 4: Arithmetic for Computers

ASCII versus Binary Numbers 212
Binary to Decimal Conversion 214
Signed versus Unsigned Comparison 215
Negation Shortcut 216
Sign Extension Shortcut 217
Binary-to-Hexadecimal Shortcut 218

Binary Addition and Subtraction 220
C Bit Fields 229
Both Levels of the Propagate and Generate 247
Speed of Ripple Carry versus Carry Lookahead 248
First Multiply Algorithm 253
Second Multiply Algorithm 256
Third Multiply Algorithm 257
Booth's Algorithm 261
Multiply by $2i$ via Shift 262
First Divide Algorithm 268
Third Divide Algorithm 271
Floating-Point Representation 279
Converting Binary to Decimal Floating Point 280
Decimal Floating-Point Addition 282
Decimal Floating-Point Multiplication 287
Compiling a Floating-Point C Program into MIPS Assembly Code 293
Compiling Floating-Point C Procedure with Two-Dimensional Matrices into MIPS 294
Rounding with Guard Digits 297

Chapter 5: The Processor: Datapath and Control

Composing Datapaths 351
Implementing Jumps 370
Performance of Single-Cycle Machines 373
Performance of a Single-Cycle CPU with Floating-Point Instructions 375
CPI in a Multicycle CPU 397

Chapter 6: Enhancing Performance with Pipelining

Single-Cycle versus Pipelined Performance 438
Stall on Branch Performance 442
Forwarding with Two Instructions 446
Reordering Code to Avoid Pipeline Stalls 447
Labeled Pipeline Execution, Including Control 471
Dependency Detection 479
Forwarding 485
Pipelined Branch 498
Loops and Prediction 501
Comparing Performance of Several Control Schemes 504
Exception in a Pipelined Computer 507
Simple Superscalar Code Scheduling 513
Loop Unrolling for Superscalar Pipelines 513

Chapter 7: Large and Fast: Exploiting Memory Hierarchy

Bits in a Cache 550
Mapping an Address to a Multiword Cache Block 556
Calculating Cache Performance 565
Cache Performance with Increased Clock Rate 567
Associativity in Caches 571
Size of Tags versus Set Associativity 575
Performance of Multilevel Caches 576
Overall Operation of a Memory Hierarchy 595

Chapter 8: Interfacing Processors and Peripherals

Impact of I/O on System Performance 639
Disk Read Time 648

Performance of Two Networks 654
FSM Control for I/O 662
Performance Analysis of Synchronous versus Asynchronous Buses 662
Performance Analysis of Two Bus Schemes 665
Overhead of Polling in an I/O System 676
Overhead of Interrupt-Driven I/O 679
Overhead of I/O Using DMA 681
I/O System Design 685

Chapter 9: Multiprocessors

Speedup Challenge 715
Speedup Challenge, Bigger Problem 716
Parallel Program (Single Bus) 718
Parallel Program (Message Passing) 729

Appendix A: Assemblers, Linkers, and the SPIM Simulator

Local and Global Labels A-11
String Directive A-15
Macros A-15
Stack in Recursive Procedure A-28
Interrupt Handler A-34

Appendix B: The Basics of Logic Design

Truth Tables B-5
Logic Equations B-6
Sum of Products B-11
PLAs B-13
Don't Cares B-16

Appendix C: Mapping Control to Hardware

Logic Equations for Next-State Outputs C-12
Control ROM Entries C-17

Computer Organization and Design Online

All of the following resources are available at *http://www.mkp.com/cod2e.htm.*

Web Extensions

These materials are extensions of the book's content.

Web Extension I: Survey of RISC Architectures

Supplies current detailed information for several RISC architectures.

- Desktop RISC Architectures (Alpha, PA-RISC, MIPS, PowerPC, SPARC)
- Embedded RISC Architectures (ARM, Hitachi SH4, MIT M32R, MIPS 16, Thumb)

Web Extension II: Introducing C to Pascal Programmers

Provides Pascal programmers with a quick reference for understanding the C code in the text.

- Variable Declarations
- Assignment Statements
- Relational Expressions and Conditional Statements
- Loops
- Examples to Put It All Together
- Exercises

Web Extension III: Another Approach to Instruction Set Architecture—VAX

Presents an example of a CISC computer architecture for comparison with the MIPS architecture described in the text.

- VAX Operands and Addressing Modes
- Encoding VAX Instructions
- VAX Operations
- An Example to Put it All Together: swap

- A Longer Example: sort
- Fallacies and Pitfalls
- Historical Perspective and Further Reading
- Exercises

Supplements

This electronic support package includes files that can be viewed and down-loaded in a number of formats.

Lecture slides

Electronic versions of text figures

Instructors Manual

Links to course home pages from selected schools

Instructions for using new DOS and Windows versions of PCspim simulators

Links to SPIM simulators (see page xviii)

Resources

Multiprocessors Page

Extends Chapter 9's coverage of real machines by providing links to companies that manufacture current multiprocessor machines.

Discussion Group

Provides readers with the opportunity to exchange ideas and information related to the book.

The SPIM Simulator

Developed by James R. Larus, the SPIM S20 is a software simulator that runs assembly language programs for the MIPS R2000/R3000 RISC computers. It can read and run MIPS a.out files (when compiled and running on a system containing a MIPS processor). SPIM is a self-contained system that contains a debugger and an interface to the operating system.

SPIM is portable; it has run on a DECStation 31000/51000, Sun 3, Sun 4, PC/RT, IBM RS/6000, HP Bobcat, HP Snake, and Sequent. Students can generate code for a simple, clean, orthogonal computer, regardless of the machine used. SPIM comes with complete source code and documentation of all instructions.

SPIM can be downloaded in versions for DOS, Windows, and UNIX, either from *www.mkp.com/cod2e.htm* or by direct ftp.

Retrieval of SPIM by ftp

SPIM is available for anonymous ftp from *ftp.cs.wisc.edu* in the file *pub/spim/spim.tar.Z* (this is a compressed tar file).

For those who are unfamiliar with command-line anonymous ftp, here are the steps to follow to get a copy of your preferred version of SPIM.

1. ftp to *ftp.cs.wisc.edu* from your computer:

    ```
    % ftp ftp.cs.wisc.edu
    ```

2. The ftp server will respond and ask you to log in. Log in as anonymous and use your email address as a password:

    ```
    Name (ftp.cs.wisc.edu:larus): anonymous
    331 Guest login ok, send login or email address as password
    Password:
    ```

3. The server will then print a welcome message. Change to the directory containing spim:

    ```
    ftp> cd pub/spim
    ```

4. Set binary mode for the transfer (since the file is compressed):

    ```
    ftp> binary
    ```

5. Choose the file appropriate for your machine and copy:

    ```
    ftp> get spim.tar.Z (UNIX)
    ftp> get PCspim.zip (Windows)
    ftp> get PCspim-dos.zip (DOS)
    ```

6. Exit the ftp program:

    ```
    ftp> quit
    ```

7. Uncompress and untar the file:

    ```
    % uncompress spim.tar.Z
    % tar xvf spim.tar
    ```

    If the uncompression fails, you probably forgot to set binary (step 4). Try again. There are directions in the file README.

Preface

The most beautiful thing we can experience is the mysterious.
It is the source of all true art and science.

Albert Einstein, *What I Believe*, 1930

About This Book

We believe that learning in computer science and engineering should reflect the current state of the field, as well as introduce the principles that are shaping computing. We also feel that readers in every specialty of computing need to appreciate the organizational paradigms that determine the capabilities, performance, and, ultimately, the success of computer systems.

Modern computer technology requires professionals of every computing specialty to understand both hardware and software. The interaction between hardware and software at a variety of levels also offers a framework for understanding the fundamentals of computing. Whether your primary interest is computer science or electrical engineering, the central ideas in computer organization and design are the same. Thus, our emphasis in this book is to show the relationship between hardware and software and to focus on the concepts that are the basis for current computers.

Traditionally, the competing influences of assembly language, organization, and design have encouraged books that consider each area as a distinct subset. In our view, such distinctions have increasingly lost meaning as computer technology has advanced. To truly understand the breadth of our field, it is important to understand the interdependencies among these topics.

The audience for this book includes those with little experience in assembly language or logic design who need to understand basic computer organization as well as readers with backgrounds in assembly language and/or logic design who want to learn how to design a computer or understand how a system works and why it performs as it does.

Changes for the Second Edition

We had six major goals for the second edition: tie the ideas from the book more closely to the real world; enhance how well the book works for beginners; extend the book material using the World Wide Web; improve quality; improve pedagogy; and finally, update the technical content to reflect changes in the industry since the publication of the first edition in 1994—the conventional reason for a new edition.

First, to make the examples in the book even more concrete and connected with the real world, in each chapter we explained how the ideas were realized in the latest microprocessors from Intel or from IBM/Motorola. Hence you can learn how the mechanisms discussed are used in the computer on your desktop. Each chapter has a new section called "Real Stuff" that ties the ideas you read about to the machine you probably use everyday.

Second, we wanted the book to work better for readers interested in an overview of computer organization. Each chapter now has a list of the key terms discussed in the chapter, and we added a glossary of more than 300 definitions. We also rely on analogies from everyday life to explain subtleties of computers:

- commercial airplanes to show how performance differs if measured as bandwidth or latency

- the stealth of spies to explain procedure invocation and nesting

- plumbing to show how carry-lookahead logic works

- the laundry room to explain pipeline execution and hazards

- a desk in a library to demonstrate principles of memory hierarchy

- the management overhead as committees grow to illustrate the difficulty of achieving high performance in large-scale multiprocessors

More specifically, we added more assembly language programming examples and more explanation in each example to help the beginner understand assembly language programming in Chapters 3 and 4. We also added an introductory section to the pipelining chapter (Chapter 6) that allows understanding of the important ideas and issues in pipeline design without having to delve into the details of a pipelined datapath and control.

Our third goal was to go beyond the limitations of a printed book by adding descriptions and links on the World Wide Web. Throughout this book, you will often see the "Web Enhanced" icon shown at the left. Wherever this icon appears, you can go to *http://www.mkp.com/cod2e.htm* to find materials related to the text.

The WWW lets us give examples of recent, relevant machines so that you can see the latest versions of the ideas in the book. For example, we've added a new online appendix (Web Extension I) comparing RISC architectures. Other examples include links for specific references in the book to other sites; instructions on how to use PCspim, the new DOS and Windows versions of the SPIM simulator, as well as links to all the versions of SPIM; access to all the figures from the book; lecture slides; links to instructors' home pages; and an online Instructors Manual. We also included some appendices from the first edition (Web Extensions II and III) that you may find valuable. We intend to update these pages periodically to make new and better links.

Fourth, we wanted to significantly reduce the flaws that creep into a book during the revision process. The first edition of the book used beta testing to see which ideas worked well and which did not, and we were very happy with the improvements as a result. We did the same with the second edition. To further reduce the chances of bugs in the book, we gave ourselves a longer development cycle and involved many more computer architects in its preparation. First, Tod Amon completely revised all exercises, in part based on suggestions of exercises by a dozen instructors. The book now has 30% new exercises and another 30% that have been reworked for a total of 400. We believe that they are much more clearly worded than before and that there is sufficient variety for a broader group of students. Second, Kent Wilken carefully read the beta edition, suggesting hundreds of improvements. After we revised the beta edition, George Adams gave another very careful read of our revision, again making hundreds of useful suggestions. Finally, we reviewed the copyedit and read the page proof to try to catch mistakes that can creep in during the book production process. Although we are sure there must still be bugs for which you can get rewards, we believe this edition is far cleaner than the first.

The fifth goal was to improve the exposition of the ideas in the book, based on difficulties mentioned by readers of the first edition. We expanded the section of Chapter 3 explaining procedures, showing the procedure infrastructure in a longer sequence of examples. Chapter 4 has a longer description of carry lookahead and carry save adders. We simplified the explanation of the multicycle datapath in Chapter 5 by adding several registers. Chapter 6 actually got a good deal shorter by adding an overview section, since it allowed us to reduce the number of examples in the detailed pipelining sections. We also made numerous changes in the pipeline diagrams to make them easier to understand and more consistent. Chapter 7 was reorganized to put all caches together before moving to virtual memory and then translation buffers, coming back to the commonalities at the end. We also changed the emphasis from virtual memory as simply another level of the hierarchy to the hardware enforcer of protection. Chapter 8 was refocused to be more quantitative and design oriented. Chapter 9 was completely rewritten and retitled, reflecting the dramatic change in the parallel processing industry since 1994.

Finally, in the interval since the first edition of this book, a computer has run a program at the rate of 1 teraFLOPS—a trillion floating-point operations per second or a million floating-point operations per *microsecond*, another computer has played better chess than the best human being, and the whole world is more closely connected thanks to the World Wide Web. These events occurred in part because computer designers have first improved performance of a single computer by a factor of 100 in the last 10 years and then harnessed together many of them to achieve even greater performance. We have included descriptions of new ideas that helped make these miracles occur, such as branch prediction and out-of-order execution in Chapter 6, multilevel and nonblocking caches in Chapter 7, switched networks and new buses in Chapter 8, and nonuniform-memory-access, shared-memory multiprocessors and clusters in Chapter 9.

Supplements and Web Extensions

A directory of the Web supplements, extensions, and resources appears on page xvi. In it you'll find a complete electronic supplements package, as well as a variety of materials and resources designed to support this text, that you can access on the publisher's World Wide Web site at *www.mkp.com/ cod2e.htm*. Included in the supplements package is an online Instructors Manual. The Instructors Manual contents are available from the Web site with the exception of the solutions. Instructors should contact the publisher directly to obtain access to solutions.

If they prefer, instructors may choose a printed Instructors Manual that includes chapter objectives, teaching hints, and critical points for each chapter as well as solutions to the exercises. Instructors should contact the publisher directly to obtain the printed Instructors Manual.

Relationship to CA:AQA

Some readers may be familiar with *Computer Architecture: A Quantitative Approach*. Our motivation in writing that book was to describe the principles of computer architecture using solid engineering fundamentals and quantitative cost/performance trade-offs. We used an approach that combined examples and measurements, based on commercial systems, to create realistic design experiences. Our goal was to demonstrate that computer architecture could be learned using scientific methodologies instead of a descriptive approach.

A majority of the readers for *Computer Organization and Design: The Hardware/Software Interface* do not plan to become computer architects. The performance of future software systems will be dramatically affected, however, by how well software designers understand the basic hardware techniques at work in a system. Thus, compiler writers, operating system designers, database programmers, and most other software engineers need a firm grounding in the principles presented in this book. Similarly, hardware designers must understand clearly the effects of their work on software applications.

Thus, we knew that this book had to be much more than a subset of the material in *Computer Architecture*. We've approached every topic in a new way. Topics shared between the books were written anew for this effort, while many other topics are presented here for the first time. To further ensure the uniqueness of *Computer Organization and Design*, we exchanged the writing responsibilities we assigned to ourselves for *Computer Architecture*. The topics that Hennessy covered in the first book were written by Patterson in this one, and vice versa. Several of our reviewers suggested that we call this book "Computer Organization: A Conceptual Approach" to emphasize the significant differences from our other book. It is our hope that the reader will find new insights in every section, as well as a more tractable introduction to the abstractions and principles at work in a modern computer.

We were so happy with *Computer Organization and Design* that the second edition of *Computer Architecture* was revised to remove most of the introductory material, hence the there is much less overlap today than with the first editions of both books.

Learning by Evolution

It is tempting for authors to present the latest version of a hardware concept and spend considerable time explaining how these often sophisticated ideas work. We decided instead to present each idea from its first principles, emphasizing the simplest version of an idea, how it works, and how it came to be. We believe that presenting the fundamental concepts first offers greater insight into why machines look the way they do today, as well as how they might evolve as technology changes.

To facilitate this approach, we have based the book upon the MIPS processor. It offers an easy-to-understand instruction set and can be implemented in a simple, straightforward manner. This allows readers to grasp an entire machine organization and to follow exactly how the machine implements its instructions. Throughout the text, we present the concepts before the details, building from simpler versions of ideas to more complex ones. Examples of this approach can be found in almost every chapter. Chapter 3 builds up to MIPS assembly language starting with one simple instruction type. The concepts and algorithms used in modern computer arithmetic are built up starting from the familiar grade school algorithms in Chapter 4. Chapters 5 and 6 start from the simplest possible implementation of a MIPS subset and build to a fully pipelined version. Chapter 7 illustrates the abstractions and concepts in memory hierarchies by starting with the simplest possible cache, then extending it, and then covering virtual memory and TLBs using the same ideas.

This evolutionary process is used extensively in Chapters 5 and 6, where the complete datapath and control for a processor are presented. Since learning is a visual process, we have included sequences of figures that contain progressively more detail or show a sequence of events within the machine. We have also used a second color to help readers follow the figures and sequences of figures.

Learning from this Book

Our objective of demonstrating first principles through the interrelationship of hardware and software is enhanced by several features found in each chapter. The Hardware/Software Interface sections are used to highlight these relationships. We've also included Big Picture sections for each chapter to remind readers of the major insights. And as mentioned above, each chapter has a Real Stuff section to tie concepts to mechanisms found in current desktop computers. We hope that these elements reinforce our goal of making this book equally valuable as a foundation for further study in both hardware and software courses.

To illustrate the relationship between high-level language and machine language and to describe the hardware algorithms, we have chosen C. It is widely used in compiler and operating system courses, it is widely used by computer professionals, and several facilities in the language make it suitable for describing hardware algorithms. For those who are familiar with Pascal rather than C, Web Extension II, found at *www.mkp.com/cod2e.htm* provides a quick introduction to C for Pascal programmers and should be sufficient to understand the code sequences in the text.

We have tried to manage the pace of the presentation for readers of varying experience. Ideas that are not essential to a newcomer, but which may be of interest to the more advanced reader, are set off from the main text and presented as elaborations. When appropriate, advanced concepts have been saved for the exercise sets and enhanced with additional discussion as In More Depth sections. In addition, we found that the extent of background that students have in logic design varies widely. Thus, Appendix B provides all the necessary background for those readers not versed in the basics of logic design, as well as some slightly more sophisticated material for the more advanced student. Within a course, this material can be used in supplementary lectures or incorporated into the mainstream of the course, depending on the background of the students and the goals of the instructor.

We have also found that readers enjoy learning the history of the field, so the Historical Perspective sections include many photographs of important machines and little known stories about the ideas behind them. We hope that the perspective offered by these anecdotes and photographs will add a new dimension for our readers.

Course Syllabi and this Book

One particularly difficult issue facing instructors is the balance of assembly language programming with computer organization. We have written this book so that readers will learn more about organization and design, while still providing a complete introduction to assembly language. By using a RISC architecture, students can learn the basics of an instruction set and assembly language programming in less time than is typically reserved in the curriculum for CISC-based assembly courses. Many instructors have also found that using a simulator, rather than running in native mode on a real machine, provides the experience of assembly language programming in substantially less time (and with less pain for the student).

SPIM is the simulator of the MIPS processor developed by James R. Larus. The publisher's Web site at *www.mkp.com/cod2e.htm* has links to spim and xspim, which were developed by Larus to run on UNIX, and to PCspim (DOS) and PCspim (Windows), which were adapted from the Unix versions by David Carley. Although not identical to the Unix versions, the DOS and Windows versions offer the same general functionality. PCspim (Windows) will run under Windows 3.1, Windows 95, and Windows NT. We feel this will enhance student opportunities for learning about computer organization (see Appendix A). Finally, stepwise derivation of assembly from a high-level language takes less study time than learning it from the ground up. Chapter 3 and Appendix A may be used together or separately, depending upon the reader's background. Chapter 3 provides the basics and can be supplemented with additional detail from Appendix A for a complete introduction to modern assembly language programming. In the end, we hope this approach offers a more efficient treatment of assembly for most readers, while being sufficiently broad to support detailed lecture or laboratory coverage if an instructor wants more emphasis on assembly language programming.

For those courses intended to expose students to the important principles of computer organization, the chapters from 4 to 9 explain the key ideas. Chapter 4 explains the idea of number representation for both integers and floating-point numbers and shows how arithmetic algorithms work. Chapters 5 and 6 introduce key ideas in control and pipelining and can be covered at several levels. Chapter 7 introduces the principles of memory hierarchies, unifying the ideas of caching and virtual memory. Chapter 8 shows how I/O systems are organized and controlled, explaining the cooperative relationship between the hardware and the operating system. Finally, Chapter 9 uses examples to introduce the key principles used in multiprocessors.

For readers who want a greater emphasis on computer design, Chapters 4 through 8, together with Appendices B and C, provide that opportunity. For example, Chapter 4 explains a number of techniques used by computer designers to speed up addition and multiplication. Chapters 5 and 6 derive complete implementations of a MIPS subset using the arithmetic elements from Chapter 4 and a number of common datapath elements (such as register files and memories) that are explained in detail in Appendix B. Chapter 5 starts with a very simple implementation; a complete datapath and control unit are constructed for this organization. The implementation is then modified to derive a faster version where each instruction can take differing numbers of clock cycles. The control for this multicycle implementation is designed using two different methods in Chapter 5. Appendix C shows in detail how the control specifications are implemented using structured logic blocks. Chapter 6 builds on the single-clock cycle implementation created in Chapter 5 to show how pipelined machines are designed. The design is extended to show how hazards can be handled and how control for interrupts works. The student interested in computer design is not only exposed to three different designs for the same instruction set, but can also see how these designs compare in terms of advantages and disadvantages.

Chapter Organization and Overview

Using these plans as the core, we developed the other chapters to introduce and support that core.

Many students remarked that they appreciated learning about the continuing rapid change in speed and capacity of hardware, as well as some of the history of computer development. This material is the focus of Chapter 1. It provides a perspective on how software or hardware will need to scale during the coming decades. Chapter 1 also introduces topics to be covered in later chapters.

Chapter 2 shows that time is the only safe measure of computer performance. It also relates common measurements used by hardware and software designers to the reliable measurement of time. The material in this chapter motivates the techniques discussed in Chapters 5, 6, and 7 and provides a framework for evaluating them.

Chapter 3 builds on the knowledge of a programming language to derive an assembly language, offering several rules of thumb that guide the designer of the assembly language. We chose the instruction set of a real computer, in this case MIPS, so that real compilers could be used by students to see the code that would be generated. We hide the delayed branch and load until Chapter 6 for pedagogical reasons. Fortunately, the MIPS assembler schedules both delayed branches and loads so the assembly language programmer can ignore these complexities without danger. Readers can see a very different approach to instruction set design in the Intel 80x86, which is covered in this chapter as well.

Although there is no consensus on what should be covered or what should be skipped in learning about computer arithmetic, we couldn't write Chapter 4 without reaching some conclusions of our own! Our solution is to introduce all the central ideas in the chapter and to provide some additional background for more advanced topics in the exercises. This allows one instructor to cover more advanced topics and assign exercises based on them, while another instructor may skip the material.

Chapters 5 and 6 show a realistic example of a processor in detail. Most readers appreciate having a real example to study, and a complete example provides the insight needed to see how all the pieces of a processor fit together for a pipelined and nonpipelined machine. To facilitate skipping some details on hardware implementation of control, we have included much of this material in Appendix C.

Just as Chapters 2 through 6 provide important background for readers with an interest in compilers, Chapters 7 and 8 provide vital background to anyone pursuing further work in operating systems or databases. Chapter 7 describes the principles of memory hierarchies, focusing on the commonality between virtual memory and caching. Chapter 7 also emphasizes the role of the operating system and its interaction with the memory system.

Topics as diverse as operating systems, databases, graphics, and networking require an understanding of I/O systems organization as well as the major technical characteristics of devices that influence this organization. Chapter 8 focuses on the topic of how I/O systems are organized starting with bus organizations, working up to communication between the processor and I/O device, and finally to the management role of the operating system. While we emphasize the interfacing issues, especially between hardware and software, several other important topics are introduced. Many of these topics are useful not only in computer organization but as background in other areas. For example, the handshaking protocol, used to interface asynchronous I/O devices, has applications in any distributed system.

For some readers, this book may be their only overview of computer systems, so we have included a survey of multiprocessing. Rather than the traditional catalog of characteristics for many parallel machines, we have tried to describe the underlying principles that will drive the designs of parallel processors for the next decade. This section includes a small running example to show different versions of the same program for different parallel architectures. And as mentioned above, we have linked many example multiprocessors from the real world on the book's WWW page at *www.mkp.com/cod2e.htm*.

Because the book is intended as an introduction for readers with a variety of interests, we tried to keep the presentation flexible. The appendices on assembly language and logic design are one of the principle vehicles to allow such flexibility, as these are easily skipped by more advanced readers. The presence of the appendices has made it possible to use this book in a course that mixes EE and CS majors with fairly different backgrounds in logic design and software.

Assembly language programming is best learned by doing and in many cases will be done with the use of the simulator available with this book. Because of this, we invited Jim Larus, the creator of the SPIM simulator, to join us as contributor of Appendix A. Appendix A describes the SPIM simulator and provides further details of the MIPS assembly language. In addition, it describes assemblers and linkers, which handle the translation of assembly language programs to executable machine language.

The logic design appendix is intended as a supplement to the material on computer organization rather than a comprehensive introduction to logic design. While many EE students in a computer organization course will have already had a course on logic design or digital electronics, we have found that CS majors in many institutions have not had much exposure to this area. The first few sections of Appendix B provide the necessary background. We include some material, such as the organization of memories and finite state machine control of a processor, in the mainstream material, since it is crucial to understanding computer organization.

Selection of Material

If you had no prior background and wanted to read from cover-to-cover, the following order makes sense: Chapters 1 and 2, Web Extension III (if needed),

Chapter 3, Chapter 4, Appendix A and Web Extension II (if interested), Appendix B, Chapter 5, Appendix C, Chapters 6, 7, 8, and 9. Clearly, most readers skip material. We have worked to provide readers with flexibility in their approach to the material, without making the discussions redundant. The chapters have been written as self-contained units with cross-references to other chapters when related text or figures should be considered. The book has been used successfully in a variety of courses with different goals and student backgrounds.

Concluding Remarks

In *Computer Architecture* we alternated the gender of a pronoun chapter by chapter. In this book we believe we have removed all such pronouns, except of course for specific people.

If you read the following acknowledgments section, you will see that we went to great lengths to correct mistakes. Since a book goes through many printings, we have the opportunity to make even more corrections. If you uncover any remaining, resilient bugs, please contact the publisher by electronic mail at *mkp@mkp.com* or by low-tech mail using the address found on the copyright page. The first person to report a technical error will be awarded a $1.00 bounty upon its implementation in future printings of the book!

Finally, like the last book, there is no strict ordering of the authors' names. About half the time you will see Hennessy and Patterson, both in this book and in advertisements, and half the time you will see Patterson and Hennessy. You'll even find it listed both ways in bibliographic publications such as *Books In Print*. This again reflects the true collaborative nature of this book: Together we brainstormed about the ideas and method of presentation, then individually wrote about one-half of the chapters and acted as reviewer for every draft of the other. The page count suggests we again wrote almost exactly the same number of pages. Thus, we equally share the blame for what you are about to read.

Acknowledgments for the Second Edition

We'd like to again express our appreciation to **Jim Larus** for his willingness in contributing his expertise on assembly language programming, as well as for welcoming readers of this book to use the simulator he developed and maintains at the University of Wisconsin. PCspim (DOS) and PCspim (Windows) versions of the simulator were developed by **David Carley**.

Tod Amon of Southwest Texas University was the exercise editor, creating and editing many new exercises. He also incorporated exercises donated by

> **Doug Clark**, Princeton; **Richard Fateman**, University of California, Berkeley; **Max Hailperin**, Gustavus Adolphus College; **Robert Kline**, West Chester University; **Gandhi Puvvada**, University of Southern California; **Hamzeh Roumani**, York University; **Mike Smith**, Harvard University; and **Gregory Weber**, Indiana University.

The following people helped with solutions of the exercises:

> **George Adams,** Purdue University, and the following students: **Pritpal Ahuja**, Princeton; **Alan Alpert**, Southwest Texas State University; **Charles Farleigh**, Stanford; **Bob Heath**, University of Kentucky; **Scott Karlin**, Princeton; **Bill Poucher**, Stanford; **Xiang Yu**, Princeton.

Marc Zimmerman, a student of Kent Wilken at the University of California at Davis, worked out solutions to the exercises to help Tod Amon evaluate the clarity of the exercise text. Thanks to the good work by all these people, we have a much richer and more clearly written set of exercises.

The beta edition was released for class testing in the fall of 1996 by the following instructors and institutions:

> **Mike Clancy**, University of California, Berkeley; **Doug Clark**, Princeton; **David Culler**, University of California, Berkeley; **Max Hailperin**, Gustavus Adolphus College; **Richard Hughey**, University of California at Santa Cruz; **Mary Jane Irwin**, Pennsylvania State University; **Truman Joe**, Stanford University; **Robert Kline**, West Chester University; **Everald Mills** and **Kosuke Imamura**, Seattle University; **Gandhi Puvvada**, University of Southern California; **Mike Smith**, Harvard University; **Steve Taylor**, Worcester Polytechnical University; and **Bob Wood**, Florida State University.

We would like to thank these instructors and their students for their help.

We would especially like to acknowledge the careful reviewing by **Kent Wilken** of University of California at Davis and **George Adams** of Purdue University. We are grateful to both for their efforts in making this edition as clean and clear as possible.

We wish to thank the extended Morgan Kaufmann family for agreeing to publish this book again, this time under the able leadership of **Denise Penrose**. She found imaginative ways to balance our workload, had excellent ideas for realizing the goals of the second edition, and kept our feet to the fire of a demanding schedule. **Julie Pabst** managed the entire book production process, from the beta edition to the final second edition that you hold today. **Jane Elliott** coordinated the beta test, ran and still runs the bug extermination program, and created the first draft of the glossary among many other tasks. **Jennifer Mann** started the development process by surveying users of the first edition and finding beta testers. We thank also the many freelance vendors who contributed to this volume, especially **Nancy Logan**, our compositor.

The contributions of the scores of people we mentioned here and hundreds of others who participated in the beta testing and surveys have made this second edition our best book yet. Enjoy!

David A. Patterson   **John L. Hennessy**

1

Computer
Abstractions
and Technology

*Civilization advances by extending
the number of important operations
which we can perform without
thinking about them.*

Alfred North Whitehead
An Introduction to Mathematics, 1911

1.1   **Introduction**   3

1.2   **Below Your Program**   5

1.3   **Under the Covers**   10

1.4   **Integrated Circuits: Fueling Innovation**   21

1.5   **Real Stuff: Manufacturing Pentium Chips**   24

1.6   **Fallacies and Pitfalls**   29

1.7   **Concluding Remarks**   30

1.8   **Historical Perspective and Further Reading**   32

1.9   **Key Terms**   44

1.10 **Exercises**   45

1.1 Introduction

Welcome to this book! We're delighted to have this opportunity to convey the excitement of the world of computer systems. This is not a dry and dreary field, where progress is glacial and where new ideas atrophy from neglect. No! Computer systems have a vital and synergistic relationship to an important industry—responsible for 5% to 10% of the gross national product of the United States—and this unusual industry embraces innovation at a breathtaking rate. Since 1985 there have been a half-dozen new machines whose introduction appeared to revolutionize the computing industry; these revolutions were cut short only because someone else built an even better computer.

This race to innovate has led to unprecedented progress since computing's inception in the late 1940s. Had the transportation industry kept pace with the computer industry, for example, today we could travel coast to coast in 5 seconds for 50 cents. Take just a moment to contemplate how such an improvement would change society—living in Tahiti while working in San Francisco, going to Moscow for an evening at the Bolshoi Ballet—and you can appreciate the implications of such a change.

Computers have led to a third revolution for civilization, with the information revolution taking its place alongside the agricultural and the industrial revolutions. The resulting multiplication of humankind's intellectual strength and reach naturally has affected the sciences as well. There is now a new vein of scientific investigation, with computational scientists joining theoretical and experimental scientists in the exploration of new frontiers in astronomy, biology, chemistry, physics, . . .

The computer revolution continues. Each time the cost of computing improves by another factor of 10, the opportunities for computers multiply. Applications that were economically infeasible suddenly become practical. In the recent past, the following applications were "computer science fiction."

- *Automatic teller machines:* A computer placed in the wall of banks to distribute and collect cash was a ridiculous concept in the 1950s, when the cheapest computer cost at least $500,000 and was the size of a car.

- *Computers in automobiles:* Until microprocessors improved dramatically in price and performance in the early 1980s, computer control of cars was ludicrous. Today, computers reduce pollution and improve fuel efficiency via engine controls and increase safety through the prevention of dangerous skids and through the inflation of air bags to protect occupants in a crash.

- *Laptop computers:* Who would have dreamed that advances in computer systems would lead to laptop computers, allowing students to bring computers to coffeehouses and on airplanes?

- *Human genome project:* The cost of computer equipment to map human DNA sequences will be hundreds of millions of dollars. It's unlikely that anyone would have considered this project had the computer costs been 10 to 100 times higher, as they would have been 10 to 20 years ago.

- *World Wide Web:* Not in existence at the time of the first edition of this book, currently the World Wide Web is transforming our society. Among its uses are distributing news, sending flowers, buying from online catalogues, taking electronic tours to help pick vacation spots, finding others who share your esoteric interests, and even more mundane topics like finding the lecture notes of the authors of your textbooks.

Clearly, advances in this technology now affect almost every aspect of our society. Hardware advances have allowed programmers to create wonderfully useful software, and explain why computers are omnipresent. Tomorrow's science fiction computer applications are the cashless society, automated intelligent highways, and genuinely ubiquitous computing: no one carries computers because they are available everywhere.

Successful programmers have always been concerned about the performance of their programs because getting results to the user quickly is critical in creating successful software. In the 1960s and 1970s, a primary constraint on computer performance was the size of the computer's memory. Thus programmers often followed a simple credo: Minimize memory space to make programs fast. In the last decade, advances in computer design and memory technology have greatly reduced the importance of small memory size. Programmers interested in performance now need to understand the issues that have replaced the simple memory model of the 1960s: the hierarchical nature of memories and the parallel nature of processors. Programmers who seek to build competitive versions of compilers, operating systems, databases, and even applications will therefore need to increase their knowledge of computer organization.

We are honored to have the opportunity to explain what's inside this revolutionary machine, unraveling the software below your program and the hardware under the covers of your computer. By the time you finish this book, you will understand the secrets of programming a computer in its native tongue, the internal organization of computers and how it affects performance of your programs, and even how you could go about designing a computer of your very own.

This first chapter lays the foundation for the rest of the book. It introduces the basic ideas and definitions, places the major components of software and hardware in perspective, and introduces integrated circuits, the technology that fuels the computer revolution.

1.2 Below Your Program

In Paris they simply stared when I spoke to them in French; I never did succeed in making those idiots understand their own language.

Mark Twain, *The Innocents Abroad,* 1869

To actually speak to an electronic machine, you need to send electrical signals. The easiest signals for machines to understand are *on* and *off*, and so the machine alphabet is just two letters. Just as the 26 letters of the English alphabet do not limit how much can be written, the two letters of the computer alphabet do not limit what computers can do. The two symbols for these two letters are the numbers 0 and 1, and we commonly think of the machine language as numbers in base 2, or *binary numbers*. We refer to each "letter" as a *binary digit* or *bit*. Computers are slaves to our commands; hence, the name for an individual command is *instruction*. Instructions, which are just collections of bits that the computer understands, can be thought of as numbers. For example, the bits

1000110010100000

tell one computer to add two numbers. Chapter 3 explains why we use numbers for instructions *and* data; we don't want to steal that chapter's thunder, but using numbers for both instructions and data is a foundation of computing.

The first programmers communicated to computers in binary numbers, but this was so tedious that they quickly invented new notations that were closer to the way humans think. At first these notations were translated to binary by hand, but this process was still tiresome. Using the machine to help program the machine, the pioneers invented programs to translate from symbolic notation to binary. The first of these programs was named an *assembler*. This program translates a symbolic version of an instruction into the binary version. For example, the programmer would write

```
add A,B
```

and the assembler would translate this notation into

```
1000110010100000
```

This instruction tells the computer to add the two numbers A and B. The name coined for this symbolic language, still used today, is *assembly language*.

Although a tremendous improvement, assembly language is still far from the notation a scientist might like to use to simulate fluid flow or that an accountant might use to balance the books. Assembly language requires the programmer to write one line for every instruction that the machine will follow, forcing the programmer to think like the machine.

Such low-level thinking inspired a simple question: If we can write a program to translate from assembly language to binary instructions to simplify programming, what prevents us from writing a program that translates from some higher-level notation down to assembly language?

The answer was: nothing. Although more challenging to create than an assembler, this higher-level translator was plausible.

Programmers today owe their productivity—and their sanity—to this observation. Programs that accept this more natural notation are called *compilers*, and the languages they *compile* are called *high-level programming languages*. They enable a programmer to write this high-level language expression:

```
A + B
```

The compiler would compile it into this assembly language statement:

```
add A,B
```

The assembler would translate this statement into the binary instruction that tells the computer to add the two numbers A and B:

```
1000110010100000
```

Figure 1.1 shows the relationships among these programs and languages.

High-level
language
program
(in C)

```
swap(int v[], int k)
{int temp;
    temp = v[k];
    v[k] = v[k+1];
    v[k+1] = temp;
}
```

C compiler

Assembly
language
program
(for MIPS)

```
swap:
    muli $2, $5,4
    add  $2, $4,$2
    lw   $15, 0($2)
    lw   $16, 4($2)
    sw   $16, 0($2)
    sw   $15, 4($2)
    jr   $31
```

Assembler

Binary machine
language
program
(for MIPS)

```
00000000101000010000000000011000
00000000100011100001100000100001
10001100011000100000000000000000
10001100111100100000000000000100
10101100111100100000000000000000
10101100011000100000000000000100
00000011111000000000000000001000
```

FIGURE 1.1 C program compiled into assembly language and then assembled into binary machine language. Although the translation from high-level language to binary machine language is shown in two steps, some compilers cut out the middleman and produce binary machine language directly. These languages and this program are examined in more detail in Chapter 3. (Web Extension III, available at *www.mkp.com/cod2e.htm*, explains C to Pascal programmers.)

High-level programming languages offer several important benefits. First, they allow the programmer to think in a more natural language, using English words and algebraic notation, resulting in programs that look much more like text than like tables of cryptic symbols (see Figure 1.1). Moreover, they allow languages to be designed according to their intended use. Hence, Fortran was designed for scientific computation, Cobol for business data processing, Lisp for symbol manipulation, and so on.

The second advantage of programming languages is improved programmer productivity. One of the few areas of widespread agreement in software development is that it takes less time to develop programs when they are written in languages that require fewer lines to express an idea. Conciseness is a clear advantage of high-level languages over assembly language.

The final advantage is that programming languages allow programs to be independent of the computer on which they were developed, since compilers and assemblers can translate high-level language programs to the binary instructions of any machine. These three advantages are so strong that today little programming is done in assembly language.

As programming matured, many of its practitioners saw that reusing programs was much more efficient than writing everything from scratch. Hence programmers began to pool potentially widely used routines into libraries. One of the first of these *subroutine libraries* was for inputting and outputting data, which included, for example, routines to control printers, such as ensuring paper is in the printer before printing can begin. Such software controlled other input/output devices, such as magnetic disks, magnetic tapes, and displays.

It soon became apparent that a set of programs could be run more efficiently if there was a separate program that supervised running those programs. As soon as one program completed, the supervising program would start the next program in the queue, thereby avoiding delays. These supervising programs, which soon included the input/output subroutine libraries, are the basis for what we call *operating systems* today. Operating systems are programs that manage the resources of a computer for the benefit of the programs that run on that machine.

Software came to be categorized by its use. Software that provides services that are commonly useful is called *systems software*. Operating systems, compilers, and assemblers are examples of systems software. In contrast to programs aimed at programmers, *applications software*, or just *applications,* is the name given to programs aimed at computer users, such as spreadsheets or text editors. Figure 1.2 shows the classical drawing mapping the hierarchical layers of software and hardware.

This simplified view has some problems. Should we really place compilers in the systems software level in Figure 1.2? Compilers produce programs at both the applications *and* the systems level, and applications programs don't normally call on the compiler while they are running. A more realistic view of the nature of systems appears in Figure 1.3. It shows that software does not consist of monolithic layers, but is composed of many programs that build on one another. Like the strands of a thick rope, each time you look carefully at what appears to be a single strand, you find it is really composed of many finer components.

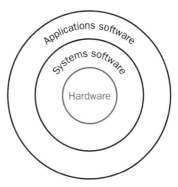

FIGURE 1.2 A simplified view of hardware and software as hierarchical layers, classically shown as concentric rings building up from the core of hardware to the software closest to the user.

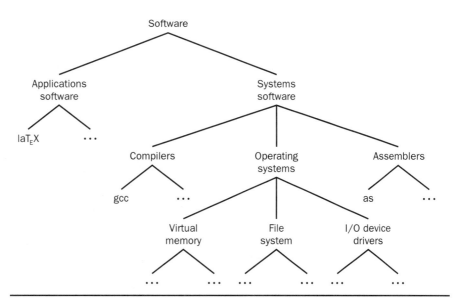

FIGURE 1.3 An example of the decomposability of computer systems. The terms in the middle of the chart, such as laT$_E$X and gcc, are examples of Unix programs. The terms lower in the chart, such as virtual memory, will be introduced in Chapters 7 and 8.

1.3   ## Under the Covers

Now that we have looked below your program to uncover the underlying software, let's open the covers of the computer to learn about the underlying hardware.

Figure 1.4 shows a typical desktop computer with keyboard, mouse, screen, and a box containing even more hardware. What is not visible in the photograph is a network that connects the computer to printers and disks. This photograph reveals two of the key components of computers: *input devices*, such as the keyboard and mouse, and *output devices*, such as the screen and printers. As the names suggest, input feeds the computer and output is the result of computation sent to the user. Some devices, such as networks and disks, provide both input and output to the computer.

Chapter 8 describes input/output (I/O) devices in more detail, but let's take an introductory tour through the computer hardware, starting with the external I/O devices.

FIGURE 1.4   A desktop computer. The cathode ray tube (CRT) screen is the primary output device, and the keyboard and mouse are the primary input devices.

Anatomy of a Mouse

I got the idea for the mouse while attending a talk at a computer conference. The speaker was so boring that I started daydreaming and hit upon the idea.

Doug Engelbart

Although many users now take mice for granted, the idea of a pointing device such as a mouse was invented 30 years ago. Engelbart showed the first demonstration of a system with a mouse on a research prototype in 1967. The Alto, which was the inspiration for all workstations as well as for the Macintosh, included a mouse as its pointing device in 1973. By the 1980s, all workstations and many personal computers included this device, and new user interfaces based on graphics displays and mice became popular. The mouse is actually quite simple, as the photograph in Figure 1.5 shows.

The mechanical version consists of a large ball that is mounted in such a way that it makes contact with a pair of wheels, one positioned on the x-axis and the other on the y-axis. These wheels either turn mechanical counters or turn a slotted wheel, through which a light-emitting diode (LED) shines on a photosensor. In either scheme, moving the mouse rolls the large ball, which turns the x-wheel or the y-wheel or both, depending on whether the mouse is moved in the vertical, horizontal, or diagonal direction. Although there are many styles of interfaces for these pointing devices, moving each wheel essentially increments or decrements counters somewhere in the system. The counters serve to record how far the mouse has moved and in which direction.

FIGURE 1.5 The inside of a mechanical mouse. Mouse courtesy of Logitech.

Through the Looking Glass

Through computer displays I have landed an airplane on the deck of a moving carrier, observed a nuclear particle hit a potential well, flown in a rocket at nearly the speed of light and watched a computer reveal its innermost workings.

Ivan Sutherland, the "father" of computer graphics, quoted in
"Computer Software for Graphics," *Scientific American*, 1984

The most fascinating I/O device is probably the graphics display. Based on television technology, a *raster cathode ray tube* (CRT) *display* scans an image one line at a time, 30 to 75 times per second (Figure 1.6). At this *refresh rate*, people don't notice a flicker on the screen.

The image is composed of a matrix of picture elements, or *pixels*, which can be represented as a matrix of bits, called a *bit map*. Depending on the size of the screen and the resolution, the display matrix ranges in size from 512×340 to 1560×1280 pixels. The simplest display has 1 bit per pixel, allowing it to be black or white. For displays that support 256 different shades of black and white, sometimes called *gray-scale* displays, 8 bits per pixel are required. A color display might use 8 bits for each of the three primary colors (red, blue, and green), for 24 bits per pixel, permitting millions of different colors to be displayed.

Portable computers often use *liquid crystal displays* (LCDs) instead of CRTs to get a thin, low-power display. The main difference is that the LCD pixel is not the source of light. A typical LCD includes rod-shaped molecules in a liquid that form a twisting helix that bends light entering the display, typically from a light source behind the display. The rods straighten out when a current is applied and no longer bend the light. The active matrix LCD has a tiny switch at each pixel to precisely control current and thus make sharper images.

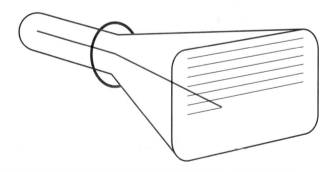

FIGURE 1.6 A CRT display. A beam is shot by an electronic gun through the vacuum onto a phosphor-coated screen. The steering coil at the neck of the CRT aims the gun. Raster scan systems, used in television and in almost all computers, paint the screen a line at a time as a series of dots, or pixels. The screen is refreshed 30 to 70 times per second.

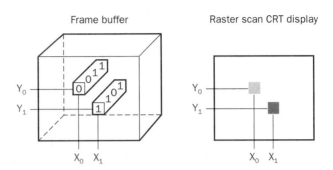

FIGURE 1.7 Each coordinate in the frame buffer on the left determines the shade of the corresponding coordinate for the raster scan CRT display on the right. Pixel (X_0, Y_0) contains the bit pattern 0011, which is a lighter shade of gray on the screen than the bit pattern 1101 in pixel (X_1, Y_1).

No matter what the display, the computer hardware support for graphics consists mainly of a *raster refresh buffer*, or *frame buffer*, to store the bit map. The image to be represented on-screen is stored in the frame buffer, and the bit pattern per pixel is read out to the graphics display at the refresh rate. Figure 1.7 shows a frame buffer with 4 bits per pixel.

The goal of the bit map is to faithfully represent what is on the screen. The challenges in graphics systems arise because the human eye is very good at detecting even subtle changes on the screen. For example, when the screen is being updated, the eye can detect the inconsistency between the portion of the screen that has changed and that which hasn't.

Opening the Box

If we open the box containing the computer, we see a fascinating board of thin green plastic, covered with dozens of small gray or black rectangles. Figure 1.8 shows the contents of the desktop computer in Figure 1.4. This *motherboard* is shown vertically in the back, with a floppy disk drive and power supplies shown on the left.

The small rectangles on the motherboard contain the devices that drive our advancing technology, *integrated circuits* or *chips*. The board is composed of three pieces: the piece connecting to the I/O devices mentioned above, the memory, and the processor. The I/O devices are connected via the two large boards attached perpendicularly to the motherboard toward the middle on the right-hand side.

The *memory* is where the programs are kept when they are running; it also contains the data needed by the running programs. In Figure 1.8, memory is found on the two small boards that are attached perpendicularly toward the middle of the motherboard. Each small memory board contains eight integrated circuits.

FIGURE 1.8   Inside a personal computer. The vertical board in the back is a printed circuit board (PC board), called the *motherboard* in a PC, that contains most of the electronics of the computer; Figure 1.11 is an overhead photograph of that board, rotated 90 degrees. The processor is the large black rectangle in the lower-right corner of the board. (Figure 1.19 is a photograph of the processor before it is placed in the black package.) The two large boards attached perpendicularly in the top third of the motherboard on the right contain input/output interfaces to the Ethernet local area network and a video card for a CRT. The two small boards attached perpendicularly to the middle of the motherboard contain the memory chips. The large box to the lower left contains the power supply, and above it are a hard magnetic disk drive and a floppy disk drive.

The *processor* is the active part of the board, following the instructions of a program to the letter. It adds numbers, tests numbers, signals I/O devices to activate, and so on. The processor is the large square below the memory boards in the lower-right corner of Figure 1.8. Occasionally, people call the processor the *CPU,* for the more bureaucratic-sounding *central processor unit.*

Descending even lower into the hardware, Figure 1.9 reveals details of the processor in Figure 1.8. The processor comprises two main components: datapath and control, the respective brawn and brain of the processor. The *datapath* performs the arithmetic operations, and *control* tells the datapath, memory, and I/O devices what to do according to the wishes of the instructions of the program. Chapter 5 explains the datapath and control for a straightforward implementation, and Chapter 6 describes the changes needed for a higher-performance design.

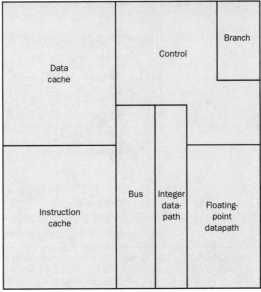

FIGURE 1.9 Inside the processor chip used on the board shown in Figure 1.8. This chip is the Intel Pentium: the upper photo is a close-up of the chip and the lower drawing identifies major blocks. The die area is 91 mm², and it contains about 3.3 million transistors. Cache memory occupies almost 1 million of those transistors. Chapter 7 explains why so much of the resources are spent on caches. Other components of the chip are described in later chapters: branch prediction is covered in Chapter 6 and buses in Chapter 8. Photo courtesy of Intel.

We have now identified the major components of any computer. When we come to an important point in this book, a point so important that we hope you will remember it forever, we emphasize it by identifying it as a "Big Picture" item. We have about a dozen Big Pictures in this book, with the first being the five components of a computer.

The Big Picture

The five classic components of a computer are input, output, memory, datapath, and control, with the last two sometimes combined and called the processor. Figure 1.10 shows the standard organization of a computer. This organization is independent of hardware technology: You can place every piece of every computer, past and present, into one of these five categories. To help you keep all this in perspective, the five components of a computer are shown on the front page of the following chapters, with the portion of interest to that chapter highlighted.

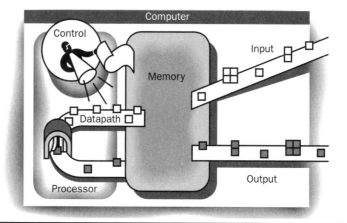

FIGURE 1.10 The organization of a computer, showing the five classic components. The processor gets instructions and data from memory; input writes data to memory and output reads data from memory. Control sends the signals that determine the operations of the datapath, memory, input, and output.

Descending into the depths of any component of the hardware reveals insights into the machine. We have done this for the processor, so let's try memory. The board in Figure 1.11 contains two kinds of memories: DRAM and cache. *DRAM* stands for *dynamic random access memory*. Several DRAMs are used together to contain the instructions and data of a program. In contrast to sequential access memories such as magnetic tapes, the *RAM* portion of the

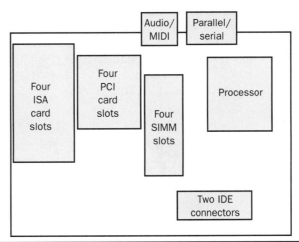

FIGURE 1.11 Close-up of PC motherboard. This board uses the Intel Pentium Pro processor, which is located on the right upper edge of the board. It is covered by tall black metal points, called *heat sinks*, which help cool the chip. The Pentium Pro package contains high-speed cache memories. The main memory is contained on the two small boards that are perpendicular to the motherboard in the middle. The DRAM chips are mounted on these boards (called *SIMMs*, for single inline memory modules) and then plugged into the connectors. Much of the rest of the board comprises connectors for external I/O devices: audio/MIDI and parallel/serial at the top edge, four PCI card slots below them, four ISA card slots to the left, and two IDE connectors on the lower right. Such cards connect the board to printers, speakers, CRTs, local area networks, disks, and so on.

term DRAM means that memory accesses take the same amount of time no matter what portion of the memory is read. *Cache memory* consists of a small, fast memory that acts as a buffer for the DRAM memory. (The nontechnical definition of *cache* is a safe place for hiding things.)

You may have noticed a common theme in both the software and the hardware descriptions: delving into the depths of hardware or software reveals more information or, conversely, lower-level details are hidden to offer a simpler model at higher levels. The use of such layers, or *abstractions,* is a principal technique for designing very sophisticated computer systems.

One of the most important abstractions is the interface between the hardware and the lowest-level software. Because of its importance, it is given a special name: the *instruction set architecture,* or simply *architecture,* of a machine. The instruction set architecture includes anything programmers need to know to make a binary machine language program work correctly, including instructions, I/O devices, and so on. (The components of an architecture are discussed in Chapters 3, 4, 7, and 8.)

This standardized interface allows computer designers to talk about functions independently from the hardware that performs them. For example, we can talk about the functions of a digital clock (keeping time, displaying the time, setting the alarm) independently from the clock hardware (quartz crystal, LED displays, plastic buttons). Computer designers distinguish architecture from an *implementation* of an architecture along the same lines: an implementation is hardware that obeys the architecture abstraction. These ideas bring us to another Big Picture.

> **The Big Picture**
>
> Both hardware and software consist of hierarchical layers, with each lower layer hiding details from the level above. This principle of *abstraction* is the way both hardware designers and software designers cope with the complexity of computer systems. One key interface between the levels of abstraction is the *instruction set architecture*: the interface between the hardware and low-level software. This abstract interface enables many *implementations* of varying cost and performance to run identical software.

Macintosh users understand the impact of changing instruction set architectures: programs designed for the PowerPC architecture do not run on the 68000-based machines, and 68000-based programs do not run well on the PowerPC. The Intel 80x86 family, in contrast, offers several implementations of the same architecture: programs written for the original 8086 in 1978 can be run on the latest Pentium Pro. As Chapter 3 points out, Intel has added features over the years, but all succeeding generations are still constrained to run old programs and run them well.

A Safe Place for Data

I think Silicon Valley was misnamed. If you look back at the dollars shipped in products in the last decade, there has been more revenue from magnetic disks than from silicon. They ought to rename the place Iron Oxide Valley.

Al Hoagland, one of the pioneers of magnetic disks, 1982

Thus far we have seen how to input data, compute using the data, and display data. If we were to lose power to the computer, however, everything would be lost because the memory inside the computer is *volatile*; that is, when it loses power, it forgets. In contrast, a cassette tape for a stereo doesn't forget the recorded music when you turn off the power because the tape is magnetic and is thus a *nonvolatile* memory technology.

To distinguish between the memory used to hold programs while they are running and this nonvolatile memory used to store programs between runs, the term *primary memory* or *main memory* is used for the former, and *secondary memory* for the latter. DRAMs have dominated main memory since 1975, but magnetic disks have dominated secondary memory since 1965.

There are two major types of magnetic disks: floppy disks and hard disks. The basic concept at work in these disks is the same: a rotating platter coated with a magnetic recording material. The primary differences arise because the floppy disk is made of a mylar substance that is flexible, while the hard disk uses metal. Floppy disks can be removed and carried around, while most hard disks today are not removable. Floppy disk capacity ranges from 1.44 MB in low-cost floppy disks to 100 MB in the Zip floppy disks.

Another removable medium is the optical compact disk, or CD, which can be cheaper but slower than magnetic disk. At the bottom of the performance barrel is magnetic tape, used for backing up disks; it can take seconds to find data on a magnetic tape.

As Figure 1.12 shows, a magnetic hard disk consists of a collection of platters, which rotate on a spindle at 3600 to 7200 revolutions per minute. The metal platters are covered with magnetic recording material on both sides, similar to the material found on a cassette tape. To read and write information on a hard disk, a movable *arm* containing a small electromagnetic coil called a *read/write head* is located just above each surface. By borrowing disk heads and media stabilization from hard disk technology, Zip drives come closer to the performance and capacity of hard disks than of traditional floppy disks.

Diameters of hard disks vary by about a factor of 5 today, from 1.3 to 5.25 inches, and have been shrunk over the years to fit into new products; workstation servers, personal computers, laptops, and palmtops have all inspired new disk form factors. Traditionally, the widest disks have the highest performance, the smallest disks have the lowest unit cost, and the best cost per megabyte is usually a disk in between.

FIGURE 1.12   A disk showing 10 disk platters and the read/write heads. Photo courtesy of Storage Technology Corp.

The use of mechanical components means that access times for magnetic disks are much slower than for DRAMs: disks typically take 5 to 20 milliseconds, while DRAMs take 50 to 100 nanoseconds—making DRAMs about 100,000 times faster. Yet disks have much lower costs than DRAM for the same storage capacity because the production costs for a given amount of disk storage are lower than for the same amount of integrated circuit. In 1997, the cost per megabyte of disk is about 50 times less expensive than DRAM's cost per megabyte.

Thus there are three primary differences between magnetic disks and main memory: disks are nonvolatile because they are magnetic; they have a slower access time because they are mechanical devices; and they are cheaper per megabyte because they have very high storage capacity at a modest cost.

Communicating to Other Computers

We've explained how we can input, compute, display, and save data, but there is still one missing item found in today's computers: computer networks. Just as the processor shown in Figure 1.10 on page 16 is connected to memory and I/O devices, networks connect whole computers, allowing computer users to extend the power of computing by including communication. Networks have become so popular that they are the backbone of current computer systems; a new machine without an optional network interface would be ridiculed. Networked computers have several major advantages:

- *Communication:* Information is exchanged between computers at high speeds.

- *Resource sharing:* Rather than each machine having its own I/O devices, devices can be shared by computers on the network.

- *Nonlocal access:* By connecting computers over long distances, users need not be near the computer they are using.

Networks vary in length and performance, with the cost of communication increasing according to both the speed of communication and the distance that information travels. Perhaps the most popular network is the *Ethernet*. Its length is limited to about a kilometer, and the most popular version takes at least a second to send 1 million bytes of data. Its length and speed make the Ethernet useful to connect computers on the same floor of a building; hence, it is an example of what is generically called a *local area network*. *Wide area networks*, which cross continents, are the backbone of the Internet, which supports the World Wide Web. They are typically based on optical fibers and are leased from telecommunication companies.

1.4   Integrated Circuits: Fueling Innovation

I thought [computers] would be a universally applicable idea, like a book is. But I didn't think it would develop as fast as it did, because I didn't envision we'd be able to get as many parts on a chip as we finally got. The transistor came along unexpectedly. It all happened much faster than we expected.

J. Presper Eckert, co-inventor of ENIAC, speaking in 1991

Processors and memory have improved at an incredible rate because computer designers have long embraced the latest in electronic technology to try to win the race of designing a better computer. Figure 1.13 shows the technologies that have been used over time, with an estimate of the relative

Year	Technology used in computers	Relative performance/unit cost
1951	Vacuum tube	1
1965	Transistor	35
1975	Integrated circuit	900
1995	Very large-scale integrated circuit	2,400,000

FIGURE 1.13   Relative performance per unit cost of technologies used in computers over time. Source: Computer Museum, Boston.

performance per unit cost for each technology. This section explores the technology that has fueled the computer industry since 1975 and will continue to do so for the foreseeable future. Since this technology shapes what computers will be able to do and how quickly they will evolve, we believe all computer professionals should be familiar with the basics of integrated circuits.

A *transistor* is simply an on/off switch controlled by electricity. The *integrated circuit* combined dozens to hundreds of transistors into a single chip. To describe the tremendous increase in the number of transistors from hundreds to millions, the adjective *very large scale* is added to the term, creating the abbreviation *VLSI*, for *very large-scale integrated circuit*.

This rate of increasing integration has been remarkably stable. Figure 1.14 shows the growth in DRAM capacity since 1977. The industry has consistently quadrupled capacity every 3 years, resulting in an increase in excess of 16,000 times in just over 20 years! This remarkable rate of advance in cost/ performance and capacity of integrated circuits governs the design of hardware *and* software, underscoring the need to understand this technology.

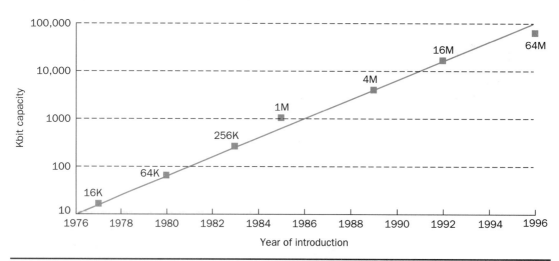

FIGURE 1.14   Growth of capacity per DRAM chip over time. The y-axis is measured in Kbits, where K = 1024 (2^{10}). The DRAM industry has quadrupled capacity every 3 years, a 60% increase per year, for almost 20 years. One exception was the 1-Mbit DRAM, which arrived a year earlier than expected; another was the 64-Mbit DRAM, which arrived a year late. This "four times every three years" rule of thumb is called the *DRAM growth rule*.

Let's start at the beginning. The manufacture of a chip begins with *silicon*, a substance found in sand. Because silicon does not conduct electricity well, it is called a *semiconductor*. With a special chemical process, it is possible to add materials to silicon that allow tiny areas to transform into one of three devices:

- Excellent conductors of electricity (similar to copper or aluminum wire)

- Excellent insulators from electricity (like plastic sheathing or glass)

- Areas that can conduct *or* insulate under special conditions (as a switch)

Transistors fall in the last category. A VLSI circuit, then, is just millions of combinations of conductors, insulators, and switches manufactured in a single, small package.

The manufacturing process for integrated circuits is critical to the cost of the chips and hence important to computer designers. Figure 1.15 shows that process. The process starts with a silicon crystal ingot, which looks like a giant sausage. Today, ingots are 6–12 inches in diameter and about 12–24 inches long. An ingot is finely sliced into *wafers* no more than 0.1 inch thick. These wafers then go through a series of processing steps, during which patterns of chemicals are placed on each wafer, creating the transistors, conductors, and insulators discussed above.

A single microscopic flaw in the wafer itself or in one of the dozens of patterning steps can result in that area of the wafer failing. These *defects*, as they are called, make it virtually impossible to manufacture a perfect wafer. To cope with imperfection, several strategies have been used, but the simplest is to place many independent components on a single wafer. The patterned wafer is then chopped up, or *diced,* into these components, called *dies* and more informally known as *chips*. Dicing enables you to discard only those dies that were unlucky enough to contain the flaws, rather than the whole wafer. This concept is quantified by the *yield* of a process, which is defined as the percentage of good dies from the total number of dies on the wafer.

Once you've found good dies, they are connected to the input/output pins of a package, using a process called *bonding*. These packaged parts are tested a final time, since mistakes can occur in packaging, and then they are shipped to customers.

Elaboration: We occasionally insert elaborations to include ideas that are not essential to the newcomer, but which may be of interest if you are more advanced.

One new issue in computer design is energy efficiency. Not only is it vital for computers used in portable applications to extend battery life, it is a consideration for desktop computers as single-chip computers increase in clock rate. For example, the Alpha 21264 microprocessor dissipates an amazing 72 watts at 600 MHz. Power may become an issue that limits performance.

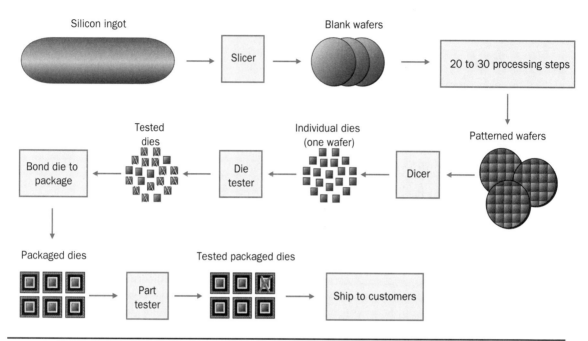

FIGURE 1.15 The chip manufacturing process. After being sliced from the silicon ingot, blank wafers are put through 20 to 30 steps to create patterned wafers (see Figure 1.17). These patterned wafers are then diced into dies (see Figure 1.18) and each die is tested. In this figure, one wafer produced 20 dies, of which only 6 passed testing. (*X* means the die is bad.) The yield of good dies in this case was 6/20, or 30%. These good dies are then bonded into packages (see Figure 1.19) and tested one more time before shipping the packaged parts to customers. One bad packaged part was found in this final test.

1.5 Real Stuff: Manufacturing Pentium Chips

Each chapter has a section entitled "Real Stuff" that ties the concepts in the book with the computer you may use every day. These sections always cover the technology underlying the IBM PC and will often include the technology of the Apple Macintosh as well. For this chapter, we tie the integrated circuit concepts of the prior section to the chips that drive the IBM PC.

Figure 1.16 is a photograph of a wafer containing single-chip processors before they have been diced. It contains copies of the chip shown in the close-up in Figure 1.9. Figure 1.17 is a photograph of a wafer of Pentium Pros, the Pentium's successor. Figure 1.18 shows an individual die of the Pentium Pro.

Note that there are many more of the smaller dies per wafer than the larger dies: there are 196 Pentium dies in the 8-inch diameter wafer in Figure 1.16 but

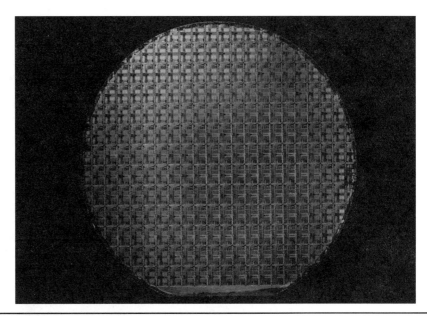

FIGURE 1.16 An 8-inch (200-mm) diameter wafer containing Intel Pentium processors. The number of Pentium dies per wafer at 100% yield is 196. The die area is 91 mm^2, and it contains about 3.3 million transistors. Figure 1.9 on page 15 is a photomicrograph of one of these Pentium dies. The several dozen partially rounded chips at the boundaries of the wafer are useless; they are included because it's easier to create the masks used to pattern the silicon. Photo courtesy of Intel.

only 78 of the larger Pentium Pro dies in the wafer in Figure 1.17. Since a wafer costs about the same no matter what is on it, fewer dies mean higher costs. Costs are increased further because a larger die is much more likely to contain a defect and thus fail to work.

Hence die costs rise very fast with increasing die area. (Exercises 1.46 through 1.53 explore die costs in more detail.) Clearly, computer designers must be familiar with the technology they are using to be sure that the added cost of larger chips is justified by enhanced performance.

FIGURE 1.17   An 8-inch (200-mm) diameter wafer containing Intel Pentium Pro processors. The number of Pentium Pro dies per wafer at 100% yield is 78. The die is 306 mm^2, and it contains about 5.5 million transistors. Figure 1.18 is a photomicrograph of one of these dies. Wafer courtesy of Intel.

Figure 1.19 shows the packaged parts for both dies. Note that the Pentium Pro package actually contains two dies! Rather than have an even larger die size for the Pentium Pro, Intel engineers decided to go with a second die. As the exercises show, two small dies can be cheaper than one large die. The second die is an external cache chip, described in Chapter 7.

Computer designers must know both hardware *and* software technologies to build competitive computers. Silicon is the medium in which computer designers work, so they must understand the foundations of integrated circuit costs and performance. Designers must also learn the principles of the software that most strongly affects computer hardware, namely, compilers and operating systems.

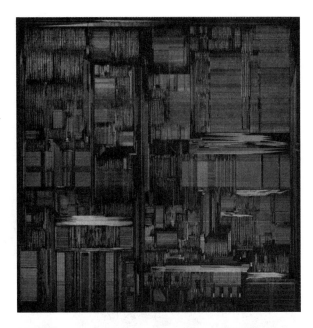

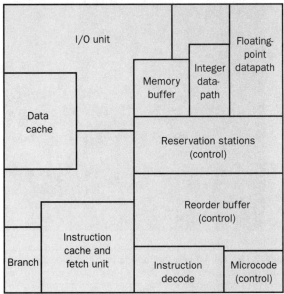

FIGURE 1.18 A Pentium Pro die: the photo (top) is a close-up of the chip, and the drawing (bottom) identifies major blocks. The die area is 306 mm², and it contains about 5.5 million transistors. Cache memory is a smaller fraction of the die area—just 1 million of 5.5 million transistors—because the Pentium Pro is packaged with an external cache with 31 million transistors. The blocks in the Pentium Pro die are described in later chapters: microcode is described in Chapter 5; instruction decode, reservation stations, reorder buffer, and branch prediction in Chapter 6; and caches and memory buffers in Chapter 7. Photo courtesy of Intel.

a.

b.

FIGURE 1.19   A package containing the Pentium die (a) and a package of the Pentium Pro die (b). The Pentium uses 296 pins and the Pentium Pro uses 387 pins. The extra pins allow a wider path between the main memory and the processor, allowing faster transfers of data and the addressing of larger memories. The second die in the Pentium Pro package is an external cache (see Figure 7.32 on page 612 for another view). Photos courtesy of Intel.

1.6   Fallacies and Pitfalls

Science must begin with myths, and the criticism of myths.

Sir Karl Popper, *The Philosophy of Science*, 1957

The purpose of a section on fallacies and pitfalls, which will be found in every chapter, is to explain some commonly held misconceptions that you might encounter. We call such misbeliefs *fallacies*. When discussing a fallacy, we try to give a counterexample. We also discuss *pitfalls*, or easily made mistakes. Often pitfalls are generalizations of principles that are true in a limited context. The purpose of these sections is to help you avoid making these mistakes in the machines you may design or use.

Fallacy: Computers have been built in the same, old-fashioned way for far too long, and this antiquated model of computation is running out of steam.

For an antiquated model of computation, it surely is improving quickly. Figure 1.20 plots the top performance per year of workstations between 1987 and 1997. (Chapter 2 explains the proper way to measure performance.) The graph shows a line indicating an improvement of 54% per year, or doubling performance approximately every 18 months. In contrast to the statement above, computers are improving in performance faster today than at any time in their history—a hundredfold improvement between 1987 and 1997!

Pitfall: Ignoring the inexorable progress of hardware when planning a new machine.

Suppose you plan to introduce a machine in three years, and you claim the machine will be a terrific seller because it's three times as fast as anything available today. Unfortunately, the machine will probably sell poorly because the average performance growth rate for the industry will yield machines with the same performance. For example, assuming a 50% yearly growth rate in performance, a machine with performance x today can be expected to have performance $1.5^3 x = 3.4x$ in three years. Your machine would have no performance advantage! Many projects within computer companies are canceled, either because they ignore this rule or because the project is completed late and the performance of the delayed machine is below the industry average. This phenomenon may occur in any industry, but rapid improvements in cost/performance make it a major concern in the computer industry.

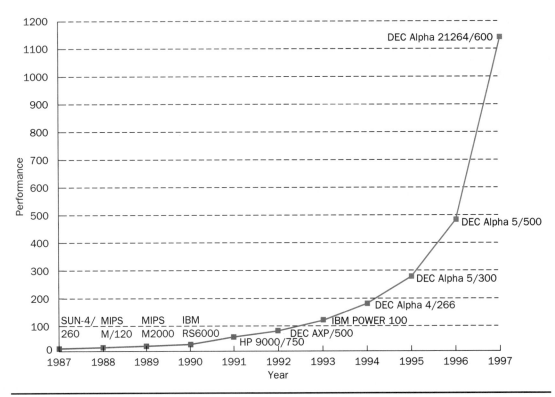

FIGURE 1.20   Performance increase of workstations, 1987–1997. Here performance is given as approximately the number of times faster than the VAX-11/780, which was a commonly used yardstick. The rate of performance improvement is about 1.54 per year, or doubling every 1.6 years. These performance numbers are for the integer SPEC92 benchmarks (SPECbase_int92); see Chapter 2, section 2.6 for more details on SPEC. As these points are becoming more difficult to see over time, here are the machines, with performance ratings in parentheses, starting in 1987: Sun-4/260 (9), MIPS M/120 (13), MIPS M2000 (18), IBM RS6000/540 (24), HP 9000/750 (51), Digital 3000 AXP/500 (80), IBM POWERstation 100 (117), Digital Alphastation 4/266 (183), Digital Alphastation 5/300 (280), Digital Alphastation 5/500 (481), and a machine based on the 600-MHz Alpha 21264 microprocessor (1140). The later two machines were based on SPECin95base and multiplied by a factor to estimate SPECbase92 performance.

1.7   Concluding Remarks

Where . . . the ENIAC is equipped with 18,000 vacuum tubes and weighs 30 tons, computers in the future may have 1,000 vacuum tubes and perhaps weigh just 1 1/2 tons.

Popular Mechanics, March 1949

Although it is difficult to predict exactly what level of cost/performance computers will have in the future, it's a safe bet that they will be much better than they are today. To participate in these advances, computer designers and programmers must understand a wider variety of issues.

Both hardware and software designers construct computer systems in hierarchical layers, with each lower layer hiding details from the level above. This principle of abstraction is fundamental to understanding today's computer systems, but it does not mean that designers can limit themselves to knowing a single technology. Perhaps the most important example of abstraction is the interface between hardware and low-level software, called the *instruction set architecture*. Maintaining the instruction set architecture as a constant enables many implementations of that architecture—presumably varying in cost and performance—to run identical software. On the downside, the architecture may preclude introducing innovations that require the interface to change.

Key technologies for modern processors are compilers and silicon. Clearly, to participate you must understand some of the characteristics of both. Equal in importance to an understanding of integrated circuit technology is an understanding of the expected rates of technological change. One example of this relationship is the DRAM tradition of a fourfold capacity increase every three years. While silicon fuels the rapid advance of hardware, new ideas in the organization of computers have improved price/performance. Two of the key ideas are exploiting parallelism in the processor, typically via pipelining, and exploiting locality of accesses to a memory hierarchy, typically via caches.

Road Map for This Book

At the bottom of these abstractions are the five classic components of a computer: datapath, control, memory, input, and output (refer back to Figure 1.10). These five components also serve as the framework for the rest of the chapters in this book:

- *Datapath:* Chapters 4, 5, and 6
- *Control:* Chapters 5 and 6
- *Memory:* Chapter 7
- *Input:* Chapter 8
- *Output:* Chapter 8

Chapter 6 describes how processor pipelining exploits parallelism, and Chapter 7 describes how the memory hierarchy exploits locality. The remaining chapters provide the introduction and the conclusion to this material. Chapter 2 covers performance and thus describes how to evaluate the whole computer. Chapter 3 describes instruction sets—the interface between compilers and the machine—and emphasizes the role of compilers and programming languages in using the features of the instruction set. Chapter 9 concludes this coverage with a discussion on multiprocessors.

Historical Perspective and Further Reading

An active field of science is like an immense anthill; the individual almost vanishes into the mass of minds tumbling over each other, carrying information from place to place, passing it around at the speed of light.

Lewis Thomas, "Natural Science," in *The Lives of a Cell*, 1974

A section devoted to a historical perspective closes each chapter in the text. We may trace the development of an idea through a series of machines or describe some important projects, and we provide references in case you are interested in probing further. This section provides historical background on some of the key ideas presented in this opening chapter. Its purpose is to give you the human story behind the technological advances and to place achievements in their historical context. By understanding the past, you may be better able to understand the forces that will shape computing in the future.

The First Electronic Computers

J. Presper Eckert and John Mauchly at the Moore School of the University of Pennsylvania built what is widely accepted to be the world's first operational electronic, general-purpose computer. This machine, called ENIAC (Electronic Numerical Integrator and Calculator), was funded by the United States Army and became operational during World War II, but was not publicly disclosed until 1946. ENIAC was a general-purpose machine used for computing artillery firing tables. This U-shaped computer was 80 feet long by 8.5 feet high and several feet wide (Figure 1.21). Each of the 20 10-digit registers was 2 feet long. In total, ENIAC used 18,000 vacuum tubes.

In size, ENIAC was two orders of magnitude bigger than machines built today, yet it was more than four orders of magnitude slower, performing 1900 additions per second. ENIAC provided conditional jumps and was programmable, clearly distinguishing it from earlier calculators. Programming was done manually by plugging cables and setting switches, and data was entered on punched cards. Programming for typical calculations required from half an hour to a whole day. ENIAC was a general-purpose machine, limited primarily by a small amount of storage and tedious programming.

In 1944, John von Neumann was attracted to the ENIAC project. The group wanted to improve the way programs were entered and discussed storing programs as numbers; von Neumann helped crystallize the ideas and wrote a memo proposing a stored-program computer called EDVAC (Electronic Discrete Variable Automatic Computer). Herman Goldstine distributed the

FIGURE 1.21   ENIAC, the world's first general-purpose electronic computer. Note the court tag in the lower-right corner; this is from the patent case mentioned on page 34. Photo courtesy of Charles Babbage Institute, University of Minnesota.

memo and put von Neumann's name on it, much to the dismay of Eckert and Mauchly, whose names were omitted. This memo has served as the basis for the commonly used term *von Neumann computer*. Several early pioneers in the computer field believe that this term gives too much credit to von Neumann, who wrote up the ideas, and too little to the engineers, Eckert and Mauchly, who worked on the machines. For this reason, the term does not appear elsewhere in this book.

In 1946, Maurice Wilkes of Cambridge University visited the Moore School to attend the latter part of a series of lectures on developments in electronic computers. When he returned to Cambridge, Wilkes decided to embark on a project to build a stored-program computer named EDSAC (for Electronic Delay Storage Automatic Calculator). EDSAC, shown in Figure 1.22, became operational in 1949 and was the world's first full-scale, operational, stored-program computer [Wilkes 1985]. (A small prototype called the Mark-I, built at the University of Manchester in 1948, might be called the first operational stored-program machine.) Section 3.4 in Chapter 3 explains the stored-program concept.

FIGURE 1.22   EDSAC in 1949 was the first full-scale stored-program computer. Wilkes is the person in the front, kneeling and wearing glasses. Photo courtesy of the Computer Museum, Boston.

In 1947, Eckert and Mauchly applied for a patent on electronic computers. The dean of the Moore School, by demanding that the patent be turned over to the university, may have helped Eckert and Mauchly conclude that they should leave. Their departure crippled the EDVAC project, delaying completion until 1952.

Goldstine left to join von Neumann at the Institute for Advanced Study (IAS) at Princeton in 1946. Together with Arthur Burks, they issued a report based on the memo written earlier [Burks, Goldstine, and von Neumann 1946]. The paper was incredible for the period; reading it today, you would never guess this landmark paper was written more than 50 years ago because it discusses most of the architectural concepts seen in modern computers. This paper led to the IAS machine built by Julian Bigelow. It had a total of 1024 40-bit words and was roughly 10 times faster than ENIAC. The group thought about uses for the machine, published a set of reports, and encouraged visitors. These reports and visitors inspired the development of a number of new computers.

Recently, there has been some controversy about the work of John Atanasoff, who built a small-scale electronic computer in the early 1940s. His machine, designed at Iowa State University, was a special-purpose computer that was never completely operational. Mauchly briefly visited Atanasoff before he built ENIAC. The presence of the Atanasoff machine, together with delays in filing the ENIAC patents (the work was classified and patents could not be filed until after the war) and the distribution of von Neumann's EDVAC paper, were used to break the Eckert-Mauchly patent. Though controversy still rages over Atanasoff's role, Eckert and Mauchly are usually given credit for building the first working, general-purpose, electronic computer [Stern 1980].

Another early machine that deserves some credit was a special-purpose machine built by Konrad Zuse in Germany in the late 1930s and early 1940s. Although Zuse had the design for a programmable computer ready, the German government decided not to fund scientific investigations taking more than two years because the bureaucrats expected the war would be won by that deadline.

Across the English Channel, during World War II special-purpose electronic computers were built to decrypt the intercepted German messages. A team at Bletchley Park, including Alan Turing, built the Colossus in 1943. The machines were kept secret until 1970; after the war, the group had little impact on commercial British computers.

While work on ENIAC went forward, Howard Aiken was building an electromechanical computer called the Mark-I at Harvard (a name that Manchester later adopted for its machine). He followed the Mark-I with a relay machine, the Mark-II, and a pair of vacuum tube machines, the Mark-III and Mark-IV. In contrast to earlier machines like EDSAC, which used a single memory for instructions and data, the Mark-III and Mark-IV had separate memories for instructions and data. The machines were regarded as reactionary by the advocates of stored-program computers; the term *Harvard architecture* was coined to describe machines with separate memories. Paying respect to history, this term is used today in a different sense to describe machines with a single main memory but with separate caches for instructions and data.

The Whirlwind project was begun at MIT in 1947 and was aimed at applications in real-time radar signal processing. Although it led to several inventions, its most important innovation was magnetic core memory. Whirlwind had 2048 16-bit words of magnetic core. Magnetic cores served as the main memory technology for nearly 30 years.

Commercial Developments

In December 1947, Eckert and Mauchly formed Eckert-Mauchly Computer Corporation. Their first machine, the BINAC, was built for Northrop and was shown in August 1949. After some financial difficulties, their firm was acquired by Remington-Rand, where they built the UNIVAC I (Universal Automatic Computer), designed to be sold as a general-purpose computer (Figure 1.23). First delivered in June 1951, UNIVAC I sold for about $1 million and was the first successful commercial computer—48 systems were built! This early machine, along with many other fascinating pieces of computer lore, may be seen at the Computer Museum in Boston, Massachusetts, and the Computer History Center in Mountain View, California.

IBM had been in the punched card and office automation business but didn't start building computers until 1950. The first IBM computer, the IBM 701, shipped in 1952, and eventually 19 units were sold. In the early 1950s, many people were pessimistic about the future of computers, believing that the market and opportunities for these "highly specialized" machines were quite limited.

FIGURE 1.23 UNIVAC I, the first commercial computer in the United States. It correctly predicted the outcome of the 1952 presidential election, but its initial forecast was withheld from broadcast because experts doubted the use of such early results. Photo courtesy of the Charles Babbage Institute, University of Minnesota.

In 1964, after investing $5 billion, IBM made a bold move with the announcement of the System/360. An IBM spokesman said the following at the time:

> We are not at all humble in this announcement. This is the most important product announcement that this corporation has ever made in its history. It's not a computer in any previous sense. It's not a product, but a line of products ... that spans in performance from the very low part of the computer line to the very high.

Moving the idea of the architecture abstraction into commercial reality, IBM announced six implementations of the System/360 architecture that varied in price and performance by a factor of 25. Figure 1.24 shows four of these

a.

c.

b.

d.

FIGURE 1.24 IBM System/360 computers: models 40, 50, 65, and 75 were all introduced in 1964. These four models varied in cost and performance by a factor of almost 10; it grows to 25 if we include models 20 and 30 (not shown). The clock rate, range of memory sizes, and approximate price for only the processor and memory of average size: (a) Model 40, 1.6 MHz, 32 KB–256 KB, and $225,000; (b) Model 50, 2.0 MHz, 128 KB–256 KB, and $550,000; (c) Model 65, 5.0 MHz, 256 KB–1 MB, and $1,200,000; and (d) Model 75, 5.1 MHz, 256 KB–1 MB, $1,900,000. Adding I/O devices typically increased the price by factors of 1.8 to 3.5, with higher factors for cheaper models. Photos courtesy of IBM.

models. IBM bet its company on the success of a *computer family*, and IBM won. The System/360 and its successors dominated the large computer market.

About a year later Digital Equipment Corporation (DEC) unveiled the PDP-8, the first commercial *minicomputer*, shown in Figure 1.25. This small machine was a breakthrough in low-cost design, allowing DEC to offer a computer for under $20,000. Minicomputers were the forerunners of microprocessors, with Intel inventing the first microprocessor in 1971—the Intel 4004, shown in Figure 1.26 as a microphotograph.

FIGURE 1.25   The DEC PDP-8, the first commercial minicomputer, announced in 1965.
Among other uses, the PDP-8 was used to stage the musical *A Chorus Line*. Photo courtesy of Digital Equipment Corporation, Corporate Photo Library.

FIGURE 1.26 Microphotograph of the Intel 4004 from 1971, the first microprocessor. Contrast this microprocessor, with just 2300 transistors and 0.3 by 0.4 cm in size, with the microprocessor in Figure 1.18 on page 27. Photo courtesy of Intel.

In 1963 came the announcement of the first *supercomputer*. This announcement came not from the large companies nor even from the high tech centers. Seymour Cray led the design of the Control Data Corporation CDC 6600 in Minnesota. This machine included many ideas that are beginning to be found in the latest microprocessors. Cray later left CDC to form Cray Research, Inc., in Wisconsin. In 1976 he announced the Cray-1 (Figure 1.27). This machine was simultaneously the fastest in the world, the most expensive, and the computer with the best cost/performance for scientific programs. But 1996 saw the passing of Cray Research into the hands of Silicon Graphics, which means there are no longer any stand-alone supercomputer companies.

FIGURE 1.27 Cray-1, the first commercial vector supercomputer, announced in 1976. This machine had the unusual distinction of being both the fastest computer for scientific applications and the computer with the best price/performance for those applications. Viewed from the top, the computer looks like the letter C. Seymour Cray passed away in 1996 as a result of injuries sustained in an automobile accident. At the time of his death, this 70-year-old computer pioneer was working on his vision of the next generation of supercomputers. (See the Cray link at *www.mkp.com/books_catalog/cod/links.htm* for more details.) Photo courtesy of Cray Research, Inc.

While Seymour Cray was creating the world's most expensive computer, other designers around the world were looking at using the microprocessor to create a computer so cheap that you could have it at home. There is no single fountainhead for the *personal computer*, but in 1977 the Apple II (Figure 1.28) of Steve Jobs and Steve Wozniak set standards for low cost, high volume, and high reliability that defined the personal computer industry. But even with a four-year head start, Apple's personal computers finished second in popularity. The IBM Personal Computer, announced in 1981, became the best-selling computer of any kind; its success gave Intel the most popular microprocessor and Microsoft the most popular operating system. Today, the most popular CD is the Microsoft operating system, even though it costs many times more than a music CD!

FIGURE 1.28 The Apple IIC. Designed by Steve Wozniak, its success defined the personal computer industry in 1977 and set standards of cost and reliability for the industry. Photo courtesy of Apple Computer, Inc.

While the general-purpose computer is the focus of attention in this book, computers are used as well inside other products without the owner being aware what is inside. These embedded processors are increasingly popular. For example, the table below shows the most popular microprocessors in 1995. For MIPS, only 300,000 of the 5,500,000 are used in computers: the rest of the microprocessors are embedded in video games, laser printers, and so on.

Instruction set	Number
80x86	50,000,000
MIPS	5,500,000
PowerPC	3,300,000
SPARC	700,000
HP PA-RISC	300,000
DEC Alpha	200,000

Computer Generations

Since 1952, there have been thousands of new computers using a wide range of technologies and having widely varying capabilities. To put these developments in perspective, the industry has tended to group computers into generations. This classification is often based on the implementation technology used in each generation, as shown in Figure 1.29. Traditionally, each *computer generation* is 8 to 10 years in length, although the length and birth years—especially of recent generations—are debated. By convention, the first generation is taken to be commercial electronic computers, rather than the mechanical or electromechanical machines that preceded them.

The success of the microprocessor has considerably extended the fourth generation, to almost as long as the prior three. Success has been sustained by rapid but evolutionary improvements. Computer generations aren't commonly mentioned today as a result of the long-standing domination of the industry by the VLSI microprocessor. With no revolutionary technology on the horizon, it is unclear when a fifth generation will appear.

Figure 1.30 summarizes the key characteristics of some machines mentioned in this section. After adjusting for inflation, price/performance has improved by about 240 million in 45 years, or about 54% per year.

Readers interested in computer history should consult *Annals of the History of Computing,* a journal devoted to the history of computing. Several books describing the early days of computing have also appeared, many written by the pioneers themselves.

Generation	Dates	Technology	Principal new product
1	1950–1959	Vacuum tubes	Commercial electronic computer
2	1960–1968	Transistors	Cheaper computers
3	1969–1977	Integrated circuit	Minicomputer
4	1978–?	LSI and VLSI	Personal computers and workstations

FIGURE 1.29   Computer generations are usually determined by the change in dominant implementation technology. Typically, each generation offers the opportunity to create a new class of computers and to create new computer companies.

Year	Name	Size (cu. ft.)	Power (watts)	Performance (adds/sec)	Memory (KB)	Price	Price/ performance vs. UNIVAC	Adjusted price (1996 $)	Adjusted price/ performance vs. UNIVAC
1951	UNIVAC I	1000	124,500	1,900	48	$1,000,000	1	$4,996,749	1
1964	IBM S/360 model 50	60	10,000	500,000	64	$1,000,000	263	$4,140,257	318
1965	PDP-8	8	500	330,000	4	$16,000	10,855	$66,071	13,135
1976	Cray-1	58	60,000	166,000,000	32,768	$4,000,000	21,842	$8,459,712	51,604
1981	IBM PC	1	150	240,000	256	$3,000	42,105	$4,081	154,673
1991	HP 9000/ model 750	2	500	50,000,000	16,384	$7,400	3,556,188	$8,156	16,122,356
1996	Intel PPro PC (200 MHz)	2	500	400,000,000	16,384	$4,400	47,846,890	$4,400	239,078,908

FIGURE 1.30   Characteristics of key commercial computers since 1950, in actual dollars and in 1996 dollars adjusted for inflation. In contrast to Figure 1.24, in this figure the price of the IBM S/360 model 50 includes I/O devices. Source: The Computer Museum, Boston, and Producer Price Index for Industrial Commodities.

To Probe Further

Bell, C. G. [1984]. "The mini and micro industries," *IEEE Computer* 17:10 (October) 14–30.

An insider's personal view of the computing industry, including computer generations.

Bell, C. G. [1996]. *Computer Pioneers and Pioneer Computers*, ACM and the Computer Museum, videotapes.

Two videotapes on the history of computing, produced by Gordon and Gwen Bell, including the following machines and their inventors: Harvard Mark-I, ENIAC, EDSAC, IAS machine, and many others.

Burks, A. W., H. H. Goldstine, and J. von Neumann [1946]. "Preliminary discussion of the logical design of an electronic computing instrument," Report to the U.S. Army Ordnance Department, p. 1; also appears in *Papers of John von Neumann*, W. Aspray and A. Burks, eds., MIT Press, Cambridge, MA., and Tomash Publishers, Los Angeles, 1987, 97–146.

A classic paper explaining computer hardware and software before the first stored-program computer was built. We quote extensively from it in Chapter 3. It simultaneously explained computers to the world and was a source of controversy because the first draft did not give credit to Eckert and Mauchly.

Campbell-Kelly, M., and W. Aspray [1996]. *Computer: A History of the Information Machine*, Basic Books, New York.

Two historians chronicle the dramatic story. The New York Times *calls it well written and authoritative.*

Goldstine, H. H. [1972]. *The Computer: From Pascal to von Neumann*, Princeton University Press, Princeton, NJ.

A personal view of computing by one of the pioneers who worked with von Neumann.

Hennessy, J. L., and D. A. Patterson [1996]. Sections 1.4 and 1.5 of *Computer Architecture: A Quantitative Approach*, second edition, Morgan Kaufmann Publishers, San Francisco.

These sections contain much more detail on the cost of integrated circuits and explain the reasons for the difference between price and cost.

Public Broadcasting System [1992]. *The Machine that Changed the World*, videotapes.

These five one-hour programs include rare footage and interviews with pioneers of the computer industry.

Slater, R. [1987]. *Portraits in Silicon*, MIT Press, Cambridge, MA.

Short biographies of 31 computer pioneers.

Stern, N. [1980]. "Who invented the first electronic digital computer?" *Annals of the History of Computing* 2:4 (October) 375–76.

A historian's perspective on Atanasoff vs. Eckert and Mauchly.

Wilkes, M. V. [1985]. *Memoirs of a Computer Pioneer*, MIT Press, Cambridge, MA.

A personal view of computing by one of the pioneers.

1.9   Key Terms

A list of key terms appears at the end of each chapter and appendix. These terms reflect the key ideas discussed in each chapter or appendix. If you're unsure of the meaning of any of the terms listed below, please refer to the Glossary at the back of the book. Each key term is fully defined there.

abstraction
assembler
assembly language
binary digit or bit
cache memory
central processor unit (CPU)
chip
compiler
computer generation
control
datapath
defect
die
die area
dynamic random access
    memory (DRAM)
floppy disk
general-purpose electronic
    computer
gigabyte
hard disk

high-level programming
    language
implementation
input device
instruction set architecture
integrated circuit
kilobyte
magnetic disk
megabyte
memory
motherboard
nonvolatile memory
operating system
output device
personal computer
pipelining
pixel
primary or main memory
raster cathode ray tube (CRT)
    display
secondary memory

semiconductor
sequential access memory
silicon
silicon crystal ingot
single in-line memory module
    (SIMM)
subroutine library
supercomputer
systems software
terabyte
transistor
vacuum tube
vector supercomputer
very large-scale integrated
    circuit (VLSI)
volatile memory
wafer
wide area network
yield

1.10 Exercises

The relative time ratings of exercises are shown in square brackets after each exercise number. On average, an exercise rated [10] will take you twice as long as one rated [5]. Sections of the text that should be read before attempting an exercise will be given in angled brackets; for example, <§1.4> means you should have read section 1.4, "Integrated Circuits: Fueling Innovation," to help you solve this exercise. If the solution to an exercise depends on others, they will be listed in curly brackets; for example, {Ex. 1.51} means that you should answer Exercise 1.51 before trying this exercise.

Exercises 1.1 through 1.26 Find the word or phrase from the list below that best matches the description in the following questions. Use the letters to the left of words in the answer. Each answer should be used only once.

a	abstraction	n	DRAM (dynamic random access memory)
b	assembler	o	implementation
c	binary number	p	instruction
d	bit	q	instruction set architecture
e	cache	r	integrated circuit
f	central processor unit (CPU)	s	memory
g	chip	t	operating system
h	compiler	u	processor
i	computer family	v	semiconductor
j	control	w	supercomputer
k	datapath	x	transistor
l	defect	y	VLSI (very large-scale integrated circuit)
m	die	z	yield

1.1 [2] Specific abstraction that the hardware provides the low-level software.

1.2 [2] Active part of the computer, following the instructions of the programs to the letter. It adds numbers, tests numbers, and so on.

1.3 [2] Another name for processor.

1.4 [2] Approach to the design of hardware or software. The system consists of hierarchical layers, with each lower layer hiding details from the level above.

1.5 [2] Base 2 number.

1.6 [2] Binary digit.

1.7 [2] Collection of implementations of the same instruction set architecture. They are available at the same time and vary in price and performance.

1.8 [2] Component of the processor that performs arithmetic operations.

1.9 [2] Component of the processor that tells the datapath, memory, and I/O devices what to do according to the instructions of the program.

1.10 [2] Hardware that obeys the instruction set architecture abstraction.

1.11 [2] High-performance machine, costing more than $1 million.

1.12 [2] Individual command to a computer.

1.13 [2] Integrated circuit commonly used to construct main memory.

1.14 [2] Integrates dozens to hundreds of transistors into a single chip.

1.15 [2] Integrates hundreds of thousands to millions of transistors into a single chip.

1.16 [2] Location of programs when they are running, containing the data needed as well.

1.17 [2] Microscopic flaw in a wafer.

1.18 [2] Nickname for a die or integrated circuit.

1.19 [2] On/off switch controlled by electricity.

1.20 [2] Percentage of good dies from the total number of dies on the wafer.

1.21 [2] Program that manages the resources of a computer for the benefit of the programs that run on that machine.

1.22 [2] Program that translates a symbolic version of an instruction into the binary version.

1.23 [2] Program that translates from a higher-level notation to assembly language.

1.24 [2] Rectangular component that results from dicing a wafer.

1.25 [2] Small, fast memory that acts as a buffer for the main memory.

1.26 [2] Substance that does not conduct electricity well.

Exercises 1.36 through 1.44 Using the categories in the list below, classify the following examples. Use the letters to the left of the words in the answer. Unlike the previous exercises, answers in this group may be used more than once.

a	applications software	f	output device
b	high-level programming language	g	personal computer
c	input device	h	semiconductor
d	integrated circuit	i	supercomputer
e	minicomputer	j	systems software

1.27 [1] Assembler

1.28 [1] C++

1.29 [1] Cathode ray tube display

1.30 [1] Compiler

1.31 [1] Cray-1

1.32 [1] DEC Alpha

1.33 [1] DRAM

1.34 [1] IBM PC

1.35 [1] Keyboard

1.36 [1] Macintosh

1.37 [1] Microprocessor

1.38 [1] Mouse

1.39 [1] Operating system

1.40 [1] Pascal

1.41 [1] Printer

1.42 [1] Silicon

1.43 [1] Spreadsheet

1.44 [1] Text editor

1.45 [10] <§1.3> In a magnetic disk, the disks containing the data are constantly rotating. On average it should take half a revolution for the desired data on the disk to spin under the read/write head. Assuming that the disk is rotating at 5400 revolutions per minute, what is the average time for the data to rotate under the disk head? What is the average time if the disk is spinning at 7200 revolutions per minute?

1.46 [5] <§§1.4, 1.5> Assume that wafer A has twice as many dies on it as wafer B and that the same fabrication process is used for both wafers (thus, defects per unit area is a constant). Will one of the dies be likely to cost twice as much as the other one, or will the difference be greater? Provide an informal explanation of your answer (do not rely on the formulas used for Exercises 1.48 through 1.53).

1.47 [5] <§§1.4, 1.5> Estimate the number of transistors that could be placed in the period at the end of this sentence using the fabrication processes that produced the dies in Figures 1.9 and 1.18.

In More Depth

Integrated Circuit Cost

Our approach in this book is to include optional sections—called "In More Depth"—in the exercises, leaving it up to the instructor whether to cover the material in class, have students read it on their own, or skip the material altogether. This first such section gives more information on the cost of integrated circuits and is used in Exercises 1.48 through 1.53.

The cost of an integrated circuit can be expressed in three simple equations:

$$\text{Cost per die} = \frac{\text{Cost per wafer}}{\text{Dies per wafer} \times \text{yield}}$$

$$\text{Dies per wafer} \approx \frac{\text{Wafer area}}{\text{Die area}}$$

$$\text{Yield} = \frac{1}{(1 + (\text{Defects per area} \times \text{Die area}/2))^2}$$

The first equation is straightforward to derive. The second is an approximation, since it does not subtract the area near the border of the round wafer that cannot accommodate the rectangular dies. The final equation is based on years of empirical observations of yields at integrated circuit factories, with the exponent related to the number of critical processing steps in the manufacturing process.

1.48 [5] <§§1.4, 1.5> What is the approximate relationship between cost and die area? The approximate relationship can be described as

Cost = $f((\text{Die area})^x)$

for some x. You don't have to determine f, but you can determine x by first writing

Dies per wafer = $f((\text{Die area})^y)$

Yield = $f((\text{Die area})^z)$

and then examining how these two equations impact the first one (you need to figure out what y and z are). What implications does this have for designers?

1.49 [15] <§§1.4, 1.5> Compare the estimate of the number of dies per wafer calculated in the formula above to the actual number given in the caption of Figure 1.16 on page 25. Propose a formula that gives a more accurate estimate of the number of dies per wafer, and give an explanation of your formula.

1.50 [10] <§§1.4, 1.5> What is the approximate cost of a die in the wafer shown in Figure 1.16 on page 25? Assume that an 8-inch wafer costs $1000 and that the defect density is 1 per square centimeter. Use the number of dies per wafer given in the figure caption.

Exercises 1.51 through 1.53 DRAM chips have significantly increased in die size with each generation, yet yields have stayed about the same (43% to 48%). Figure 1.31 shows key statistics for DRAM production over the years.

Year	Capacity (Kbits)	Die area (sq. cm)	Wafer diameter (inches)	Yield
1980	64	0.16	5	48%
1983	256	0.24	5	46%
1985	1024	0.42	6	45%
1989	4096	0.65	6	43%
1992	16384	0.97	8	48%

FIGURE 1.31 History of DRAM capacity, die size, wafer size, and yield. Source: Howard Dicken of DM Data Inc., of Scottsdale, Arizona.

1.51 [5] <§§1.4, 1.5> Given the increase in die area of DRAMs, what parameter (see the equations) must improve to maintain yield?

1.52 [10] <§§1.4, 1.5> {Ex. 1.51} Derive a formula for the improving parameter found in Exercise 1.51 from the other parameters.

1.53 [10] <§§1.4, 1.5> {Ex. 1.51, 1.52} Using the formula in the answer to Exercise 1.52, what is the calculated improvement in that parameter between 1980 and 1992?

1.54 [8] <§§1.1–1.5> This book covers abstractions for computer systems at many different levels of detail. Pick another system with which you are familiar and write one or two paragraphs describing some of the many different levels of abstraction inherent in that system. Some possibilities include automobiles, homes, airplanes, geometry, the economy, and the government. Be sure to identify both high-level and low-level abstractions.

1.55 [15] <§§1.1–1.5> A less technically inclined friend has asked you to explain how computers work. Write a detailed, one-page description for your friend.

1.56 [10] <§§1.1–1.5> In what ways do you lack a clear understanding of how computers work? Are there levels of abstraction with which you are particularly unfamiliar? Are there levels of abstraction with which you are familiar but still have specific questions about? Write at least one paragraph addressing each of these questions.

2

The Role of
Performance

Time discovers truth.

Seneca
Moral Essays, 22 A.D.

2.1   **Introduction**   54

2.2   **Measuring Performance**   58

2.3   **Relating the Metrics**   60

2.4   **Choosing Programs to Evaluate Performance**   66

2.5   **Comparing and Summarizing Performance**   69

2.6   **Real Stuff: The SPEC95 Benchmarks and Performance of Recent Processors**   71

2.7   **Fallacies and Pitfalls**   75

2.8   **Concluding Remarks**   82

2.9   **Historical Perspective and Further Reading**   83

2.10   **Key Terms**   89

2.11   **Exercises**   90

The Five Classic Components of a Computer

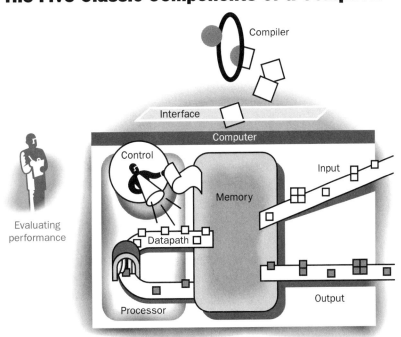

Introduction

This chapter discusses how to measure, report, and summarize performance and describes the major factors that determine the performance of a computer. A primary reason for examining performance is that hardware performance is often key to the effectiveness of an entire system of hardware and software.

Assessing the performance of such a system can be quite challenging. The scale and intricacy of modern software systems, together with the wide range of performance improvement techniques employed by hardware designers, have made performance assessment much more difficult. It is simply impossible to sit down with an instruction set manual and a significant software system and determine how fast the software will run on the machine. In fact, for different types of applications, different performance metrics may be appropriate and different aspects of a computer system may be the most significant in determining overall performance.

Of course, in trying to choose among different computers, performance is almost always an important attribute. Accurately measuring and comparing different machines is critical to purchasers, and therefore to designers. The people selling computers know this as well. Often, salespeople would like you to see their machine in the best possible light, whether or not this light accurately reflects the needs of the purchaser's application. In some cases, claims are made about computers that don't provide useful insight for any real applications. Hence, understanding how best to measure performance and the limitations of performance measurements is important in selecting a machine.

Our interest in performance, however, goes beyond issues of assessing performance only from the outside of a machine. To understand why a piece of software performs as it does, why one instruction set can be implemented to perform better than another, or how some hardware feature affects performance, we need to understand what determines the performance of a machine. For example, to improve the performance of a software system, we may need to understand what factors in the hardware contribute to the overall system performance and the relative importance of these factors. These factors may include how well the program uses the instructions of the machine, how well the underlying hardware implements the instructions, and how well the memory and I/O systems perform. Understanding how to determine the performance impact of these factors is crucial to understanding the motivation behind the design of particular aspects of the machine, as we will see in the chapters that follow.

Airplane	Passenger capacity	Cruising range (miles)	Cruising speed (m.p.h.)	Passenger throughput (passengers x m.p.h.)
Boeing 777	375	4630	610	228,750
Boeing 747	470	4150	610	286,700
BAC/Sud Concorde	132	4000	1350	178,200
Douglas DC-8-50	146	8720	544	79,424

FIGURE 2.1 The capacity, range, and speed for a number of commercial airplanes. The last column shows the rate at which the airplane transports passengers, which is the capacity times the cruising speed (ignoring range and takeoff and landing times).

The rest of this section describes different ways in which performance can be determined. In section 2.2, we describe the metrics for measuring performance from the viewpoint of both a computer user and a designer. In section 2.3, we look at how these metrics are related and present the classical processor performance equation, which we will use throughout the text. Sections 2.4 and 2.5 describe how best to choose benchmarks to evaluate machines and how to accurately summarize the performance of a group of programs. Section 2.6 describes one set of commonly used CPU benchmarks and examines measurements for a variety of Intel processors using those benchmarks. Finally, in section 2.7, we'll examine some of the many pitfalls that have trapped designers and those who analyze and report performance.

Defining Performance

When we say one computer has better performance than another, what do we mean? Although this question might seem simple, an analogy with passenger airplanes shows how subtle the question of performance can be. Figure 2.1 shows some typical passenger airplanes, together with their cruising speed, range, and capacity. If we wanted to know which of the planes in this table had the best performance, we would first need to define performance. For example, considering different measures of performance, we see that the plane with the highest cruising speed is the Concorde, the plane with the longest range is the DC-8, and the plane with the largest capacity is the 747.

Let's suppose we define performance in terms of speed. This still leaves two possible definitions. You could define the fastest plane as the one with the highest cruising speed, taking a single passenger from one point to another in the least time. If you were interested in transporting 450 passengers from one point to another, however, the 747 would clearly be the fastest, as the last column of the figure shows. Similarly, we can define computer performance in several different ways.

If you were running a program on two different workstations, you'd say that the faster one is the workstation that gets the job done first. If you were running a computer center that had two large timeshared computers running jobs submitted by many users, you'd say that the faster computer was the one that completed the most jobs during a day. As an individual computer user, you are interested in reducing *response time*—the time between the start and completion of a task—also referred to as *execution time*. Computer center managers are often interested in increasing *throughput*—the total amount of work done in a given time.

Throughput and Response Time

Example

To illustrate the application of new ideas, specific examples are used throughout this text. We highlight the example and then provide an answer. Try working out the answer yourself, or—if you feel unsure about the material—just follow along. The examples that appear are similar in type to the problems that you will have an opportunity to tackle in the exercises at the end of each chapter. Here's our first example:

Do the following changes to a computer system increase throughput, decrease response time, or both?

1. Replacing the processor in a computer with a faster version

2. Adding additional processors to a system that uses multiple processors for separate tasks—for example, handling an airline reservations system

Answer

Decreasing response time almost always improves throughput. Hence, in case 1, both response time and throughput are improved. In case 2, no one task gets work done faster, so only throughput increases. If, however, the demand for processing in the second case was almost as large as the throughput, the system might force requests to queue up. In this case, increasing the throughput could also improve response time, since it would reduce the waiting time in the queue. Thus, in many real computer systems, changing either execution time or throughput often affects the other.

In discussing the performance of machines, we will be primarily concerned with response time for the first few chapters. (In Chapter 8, on input/output systems, we will discuss throughput-related measures.) To maximize performance, we want to minimize response time or execution time for some task. Thus we can relate performance and execution time for a machine X:

$$\text{Performance}_X = \frac{1}{\text{Execution time}_X}$$

This means that for two machines X and Y, if the performance of X is greater than the performance of Y, we have

$$\text{Performance}_X > \text{Performance}_Y$$

$$\frac{1}{\text{Execution time}_X} > \frac{1}{\text{Execution time}_Y}$$

$$\text{Execution time}_Y > \text{Execution time}_X$$

That is, the execution time on Y is longer than that on X, if X is faster than Y.

In discussing a computer design, we often want to relate the performance of two different machines quantitatively. We will use the phrase "X is n times faster than Y" to mean

$$\frac{\text{Performance}_X}{\text{Performance}_Y} = n$$

If X is n times faster than Y, then the execution time on Y is n times longer than it is on X:

$$\frac{\text{Performance}_X}{\text{Performance}_Y} = \frac{\text{Execution time}_Y}{\text{Execution time}_X} = n$$

Relative Performance

Example

If machine A runs a program in 10 seconds and machine B runs the same program in 15 seconds, how much faster is A than B?

Answer

We know that A is n times faster than B if

$$\frac{\text{Performance}_A}{\text{Performance}_B} = n$$

or

$$\frac{\text{Execution time}_B}{\text{Execution time}_A} = n$$

Thus the performance ratio is

$$\frac{15}{10} = 1.5$$

and A is therefore 1.5 times faster than B.

In the above example, we could also say that machine B is 1.5 times *slower than* machine A, since

$$\frac{\text{Performance}_A}{\text{Performance}_B} = 1.5$$

means that

$$\frac{\text{Performance}_A}{1.5} = \text{Performance}_B$$

For simplicity, we will normally use the terminology *faster than* when we try to compare machines quantitatively. Because performance and execution time are reciprocals, increasing performance requires decreasing execution time. To avoid the potential confusion between the terms *increasing* and *decreasing*, we usually say "improve performance" or "improve execution time" when we mean "increase performance" and "decrease execution time."

2.2   Measuring Performance

Time is the measure of computer performance: the computer that performs the same amount of work in the least time is the fastest. Program *execution time* is measured in seconds per program. But time can be defined in different ways, depending on what we count. The most straightforward definition of time is called *wall-clock time*, *response time*, or *elapsed time*. These terms mean the total time to complete a task, including disk accesses, memory accesses, input/output (I/O) activities, operating system overhead—everything.

Computers are often timeshared, however, and a processor may work on several programs simultaneously. In such cases, the system may try to optimize throughput rather than attempt to minimize the elapsed time for one program. Hence, we often want to distinguish between the elapsed time and the time that the processor is working on our behalf. *CPU execution time* or simply *CPU time*, which recognizes this distinction, is the time the CPU spends computing for this task and does not include time spent waiting for I/O or running other programs. (Remember, though, that the response time experienced by the user will be the elapsed time of the program, not the CPU time.) CPU time can be further divided into the CPU time spent in the program, called *user CPU time*, and the CPU time spent in the operating system performing tasks on behalf of the program, called *system CPU time*. Differentiating between system and user CPU time is difficult to do accurately because it is often hard to assign responsibility for operating system activities to one user program rather than another.

The breakdown of the elapsed time for a task is reflected in the Unix `time` command, which, for example, might return the following:

`90.7u 12.9s 2:39 65%`

User CPU time is 90.7 seconds, system CPU time is 12.9 seconds, elapsed time is 2 minutes and 39 seconds (159 seconds), and the percentage of elapsed time that is CPU time is

$$\frac{90.7 + 12.9}{159} = 0.65$$

or 65%. More than a third of the elapsed time in this example was spent waiting for I/O, running other programs, or both.

Sometimes we ignore system CPU time when examining CPU execution time because of the inaccuracy of operating systems' self-measurement and the inequity of including system CPU time when comparing performance between machines with different operating systems. On the other hand, system code on some machines is user code on others, and no program runs without some operating system running on the hardware, so a case can be made for using the sum of user CPU time and system CPU time as the measure of program execution time.

For consistency, we maintain a distinction between performance based on elapsed time and that based on CPU execution time. We will use the term *system performance* to refer to elapsed time on an unloaded system, and use *CPU performance* to refer to user CPU time. We will concentrate on CPU performance in this chapter, although our discussions of how to summarize performance can be applied to either elapsed time or to CPU time measurements.

Although as computer users we care about time, when we examine the details of a machine it's convenient to think about performance in other metrics. In particular, computer designers may want to think about a machine by using a measure that relates to how fast the hardware can perform basic functions. Almost all computers are constructed using a clock that runs at a constant rate and determines when events take place in the hardware. These discrete time intervals are called *clock cycles* (or ticks, clock ticks, clock periods, clocks, cycles). Designers refer to the length of a *clock period* both as the time for a complete *clock cycle* (e.g., 2 nanoseconds, or 2 ns) and as the *clock rate* (e.g., 500 megahertz, or 500 MHz), which is the inverse of the clock period. In the next section, we will formalize the relationship between the clock cycles of the hardware designer and the seconds of the computer user.

2.3   Relating the Metrics

Users and designers often examine performance using different metrics. If we could relate these different metrics, we could determine the effect of a design change on the performance as seen by the user. Since we are confining ourselves to CPU performance at this point, the bottom-line performance measure is CPU execution time. A simple formula relates the most basic metrics (clock cycles and clock cycle time) to CPU time:

$$\text{CPU execution time for a program} = \text{CPU clock cycles for a program} \times \text{Clock cycle time}$$

Alternatively, because clock rate and clock cycle time are inverses,

$$\text{CPU execution time for a program} = \frac{\text{CPU clock cycles for a program}}{\text{Clock rate}}$$

This formula makes it clear that the hardware designer can improve performance by reducing either the length of the clock cycle or the number of clock cycles required for a program. As we will see in this chapter and later in Chapters 5, 6, and 7, the designer often faces a trade-off between the number of clock cycles needed for a program and the length of each cycle. Many techniques that decrease the number of clock cycles also increase the clock cycle time.

Improving Performance

Example

Our favorite program runs in 10 seconds on computer A, which has a 400-MHz clock. We are trying to help a computer designer build a machine, B, that will run this program in 6 seconds. The designer has determined that a substantial increase in the clock rate is possible, but this increase will affect the rest of the CPU design, causing machine B to require 1.2 times as many clock cycles as machine A for this program. What clock rate should we tell the designer to target?

Answer

Let's first find the number of clock cycles required for the program on A:

$$\text{CPU time}_A = \frac{\text{CPU clock cycles}_A}{\text{Clock rate}_A}$$

$$10 \text{ seconds} = \frac{\text{CPU clock cycles}_A}{400 \times 10^6 \frac{\text{cycles}}{\text{second}}}$$

$$\text{CPU clock cycles}_A = 10 \text{ seconds} \times 400 \times 10^6 \frac{\text{cycles}}{\text{second}} = 4000 \times 10^6 \text{cycles}$$

CPU time for B can be found using this equation:

$$\text{CPU time}_B = \frac{1.2 \times \text{CPU clock cycles}_A}{\text{Clock rate}_B}$$

$$6 \text{ seconds} = \frac{1.2 \times 4000 \times 10^6 \text{cycles}}{\text{Clock rate}_B}$$

$$\text{Clock rate}_B = \frac{1.2 \times 4000 \times 10^6 \text{cycles}}{6 \text{ seconds}} = \frac{800 \times 10^6 \text{cycles}}{\text{second}} = 800 \text{ MHz}$$

Machine B must therefore have twice the clock rate of A to run the program in 6 seconds.

Hardware Software Interface

Throughout this text, you will see sections called "Hardware Software Interface." These sections highlight major interactions between some aspect of the software (typically a program, a compiler, or an operating system) and some hardware aspect of a computer. In addition to highlighting such interactions, these sections are reminders that hardware and software design interact in many ways.

The equations in our previous examples do not include any reference to the number of instructions needed for the program. However, since the compiler clearly generated instructions to execute, and the machine had to execute the instructions to run the program, the execution time must depend on the number of instructions in a program. One way to think about execution time is that it equals the number of instructions executed multiplied by the average time per instruction. Therefore, the number of clock cycles required for a program can be written as

$$\text{CPU clock cycles} = \text{Instructions for a program} \times \frac{\text{Average clock cycles}}{\text{per instruction}}$$

The term *clock cycles per instruction*, which is the average number of clock cycles each instruction takes to execute, is often abbreviated as CPI. Since different instructions may take different amounts of time depending on what they do, CPI is an average of all the instructions executed in the program. CPI provides one way of comparing two different implementations of the same instruction set architecture, since the instruction count required for a program will, of course, be the same.

Using the Performance Equation

Example

Suppose we have two implementations of the same instruction set architecture. Machine A has a clock cycle time of 1 ns and a CPI of 2.0 for some program, and machine B has a clock cycle time of 2 ns and a CPI of 1.2 for the same program. Which machine is faster for this program, and by how much?

Answer

We know that each machine executes the same number of instructions for the program; let's call this number I. First, find the number of processor clock cycles for each machine:

$$\text{CPU clock cycles}_A = I \times 2.0$$

$$\text{CPU clock cycles}_B = I \times 1.2$$

Now we can compute the CPU time for each machine:

$$\text{CPU time}_A = \text{CPU clock cycles}_A \times \text{Clock cycle time}_A$$

$$= I \times 2.0 \times 1 \text{ ns} = 2 \times I \text{ ns}$$

Likewise, for B:

$$\text{CPU time}_B = I \times 1.2 \times 2 \text{ ns} = 2.4 \times I \text{ ns}$$

Clearly, machine A is faster. The amount faster is given by the ratio of the execution times:

$$\frac{\text{CPU performance}_A}{\text{CPU performance}_B} = \frac{\text{Execution time}_B}{\text{Execution time}_A} = \frac{2.4 \times I \text{ ns}}{2 \times I \text{ ns}} = 1.2$$

We can conclude that machine A is 1.2 times faster than machine B for this program.

We can now write this basic performance equation in terms of instruction count (the number of instructions executed by the program), CPI, and clock cycle time:

$$\text{CPU time} = \text{Instruction count} \times \text{CPI} \times \text{Clock cycle time}$$

or

$$\text{CPU time} = \frac{\text{Instruction count} \times \text{CPI}}{\text{Clock rate}}$$

These formulas are particularly useful because they separate the three key factors that affect performance. We can use these formulas to compare two different implementations or to evaluate a design alternative if we know its impact on these three parameters.

The Big Picture

Figure 2.2 shows the basic measurements at different levels in the computer and what is being measured in each case. We can see how these factors are combined to yield execution time measured in seconds:

$$\text{Time} = \frac{\text{Instructions}}{\text{Program}} \times \frac{\text{Clock cycles}}{\text{Instruction}} \times \frac{\text{Seconds}}{\text{Clock cycle}}$$

Always bear in mind that the only complete and reliable measure of computer performance is time. For example, changing the instruction set to lower the instruction count may lead to an organization with a slower clock cycle time that offsets the improvement in instruction count. Similarly, because CPI depends on instruction mix, the code that executes the fewest number of instructions may not be the fastest.

Components of performance	Units of measure
CPU execution time for a program	Seconds for the program
Instruction count	Instructions executed for the program
Clock cycles per instruction (CPI)	Average number of clock cycles per instruction
Clock cycle time	Seconds per clock cycle

FIGURE 2.2 The basic components of performance and how each is measured.

How can we determine the value of these factors in the performance equation? We can measure the CPU execution time by running the program, and the clock cycle time is usually published as part of the documentation for a machine. The instruction count and CPI can be more difficult to obtain. Of course, if we know the clock rate and CPU execution time, we need only one of the instruction count or the CPI to determine the other.

We can measure the instruction count by using software tools that profile the execution or by using a simulator of the architecture. Alternatively, we can use hardware counters, which have been included on some processors, to record a variety of measurements, including the number of instructions executed. Since the instruction count depends on the architecture, but not on the exact implementation, we can measure the instruction count without knowing all the details of the implementation. The CPI, however, depends on a wide variety of design details in the machine, including both the memory system and the processor structure (as we will see in Chapters 5, 6, and 7), as well as on the mix of instruction types executed in an application. Thus CPI varies by application, as well as among implementations with the same instruction set.

Designers often obtain CPI by a detailed simulation of an implementation or by combining hardware counters and simulation. Sometimes it is possible to compute the CPU clock cycles by looking at the different types of instructions and using their individual clock cycle counts. In such cases, the following formula is useful:

$$\text{CPU clock cycles} = \sum_{i=1}^{n} (\text{CPI}_i \times \text{C}_i)$$

where C_i is the count of the number of instructions of class i executed, CPI_i is the average number of cycles per instruction for that instruction class, and n is the number of instruction classes. Remember that overall CPI for a program will depend on both the number of cycles for each instruction type and the frequency of each instruction type in the program execution.

Comparing Code Segments

Example

A compiler designer is trying to decide between two code sequences for a particular machine. The hardware designers have supplied the following facts:

Instruction class	CPI for this instruction class
A	1
B	2
C	3

For a particular high-level-language statement, the compiler writer is considering two code sequences that require the following instruction counts:

Code sequence	Instruction counts for instruction class		
	A	B	C
1	2	1	2
2	4	1	1

Which code sequence executes the most instructions? Which will be faster? What is the CPI for each sequence?

Answer

Sequence 1 executes $2 + 1 + 2 = 5$ instructions. Sequence 2 executes $4 + 1 + 1 = 6$ instructions. So sequence 1 executes fewer instructions.

We can use the equation for CPU clock cycles based on instruction count and CPI to find the total number of clock cycles for each sequence:

$$\text{CPU clock cycles} = \sum_{i=1}^{n}(\text{CPI}_i \times C_i)$$

This yields

$$\text{CPU clock cycles}_1 = (2 \times 1) + (1 \times 2) + (2 \times 3) = 2 + 2 + 6 = 10 \text{ cycles}$$

$$\text{CPU clock cycles}_2 = (4 \times 1) + (1 \times 2) + (1 \times 3) = 4 + 2 + 3 = 9 \text{ cycles}$$

So code sequence 2 is faster, even though it actually executes one extra instruction. Since code sequence 2 takes fewer overall clock cycles but has more instructions, it must have a lower CPI. The CPI values can be computed by

$$\text{CPI} = \frac{\text{CPU clock cycles}}{\text{Instruction count}}$$

$$\text{CPI}_1 = \frac{\text{CPU clock cycles}_1}{\text{Instruction count}_1} = \frac{10}{5} = 2$$

$$\text{CPI}_2 = \frac{\text{CPU clock cycles}_2}{\text{Instruction count}_2} = \frac{9}{6} = 1.5$$

The above example shows the danger of using only one factor (instruction count) to assess performance. When comparing two machines, you must look at all three components, which combine to form execution time. If some of the factors are identical, like the clock rate in the above example, performance can be determined by comparing all the nonidentical factors. Since CPI varies by instruction mix, both instruction count and CPI must be compared, even if clock rates are identical. Exercises 2.18 through 2.24 explore this further by asking you to evaluate a series of machine and compiler enhancements that affect clock rate, CPI, and instruction count. In the next section, we'll examine a common performance measurement that does not incorporate all the terms and can thus be misleading.

2.4 | Choosing Programs to Evaluate Performance

A computer user who runs the same programs day in and day out would be the perfect candidate to evaluate a new computer. The set of programs run would form a *workload*. To evaluate two computer systems, a user would simply compare the execution time of the workload on the two machines. Most users, however, are not in this situation. Instead, they must rely on other methods that measure the performance of a candidate machine, hoping that the methods will reflect how well the machine will perform with the user's workload. This alternative is usually followed by evaluating the machine using a set of *benchmarks*, which are programs specifically chosen to measure performance. The benchmarks form a workload that the user hopes will predict the performance of the actual workload.

Today, it is widely understood that the best type of programs to use for benchmarks are real applications. These may be applications that the user employs regularly or simply applications that are typical. For example, in an environment where the users are primarily engineers, you might use a set of benchmarks containing several typical engineering or scientific applications. If the user community were primarily software development engineers, the best benchmarks would probably include such applications as a compiler or document processing system. Using real applications as benchmarks makes it much more difficult to find trivial ways to speed up the execution of the benchmark. Furthermore, when techniques are found to improve performance, such techniques are much more likely to help other programs in addition to the benchmark.

The use of benchmarks whose performance depends on very small code segments encourages optimizations in either the architecture or compiler that target these segments. The compiler optimizations might recognize special code fragments and generate an instruction sequence that is particularly efficient for this code fragment. Likewise, a designer might try to make some sequence of instructions run especially fast because the sequence occurs in a benchmark. Recently, several companies have introduced compilers with special-purpose optimizations targeted at specific benchmarks. Often these optimizations must be explicitly enabled with a specific compiler option, which would not be used when compiling other programs. Whether the compiler would produce good code, or even *correct* code, if a real application program used these switches, is unclear. Sometimes in the quest to produce highly optimized code for benchmarks, engineers introduce erroneous optimizations. For example, in late 1995, Intel published a new performance rating for the integer SPEC benchmarks (see sections 2.6 and 2.9 for a further discussion of SPEC) running on a Pentium processor and using an internal compiler, not used outside of Intel. Unfortunately, the code produced for one of the benchmarks was wrong, a fact that was discovered when a competitor read through the binary to understand how Intel had sped up one of the programs in the benchmark suite so dramatically. In January of 1996, Intel admitted the error and restated the performance.

Small programs or programs that spend almost all their execution time in a very small code fragment are especially vulnerable to such efforts. For example, the SPEC processor benchmark suite was chosen to use primarily real applications. Unfortunately, the first release of the SPEC suite in 1989 included a benchmark called matrix300, which consists solely of a series of matrix multiplications. In fact, 99% of the execution time is in a single line of this benchmark. The fact that so much time is spent in one line doing the same computation many times has led several companies to purchase or develop special compiler technology to improve the running time of this benchmark. Figure 2.3 shows the performance ratios (inverse to execution time) for one machine with two different compilers. The enhanced compiler has essentially no effect on the running time of 8 of the 10 benchmarks, but it improves performance on matrix300 by a factor of more than nine. On matrix300, the program runs 729.8 times faster using the enhanced compiler than the reference time obtained from a VAX-11/780—but the more typical performance of the machine is much slower. The other programs run from just over 30 times faster to just over 140 times faster. A user expecting a program to run 700 times faster than it does on a VAX-11/780 would likely be very disappointed! In the 1992 release of the SPEC benchmark suite, matrix300 was dropped.

So why doesn't everyone run real programs to measure performance? One reason is that small benchmarks are attractive when beginning a design, since they are small enough to compile and simulate easily, sometimes by hand. They are especially tempting when designers are working on a novel machine because compilers may not be available until much later in the design. Small benchmarks are also more easily standardized than large programs; hence numerous published performance results are available for small benchmarks.

Although the use of such small benchmarks early in the design process may be justified, there is no valid rationale for using them to evaluate working computer systems. In the past, it was hard to obtain large applications that could

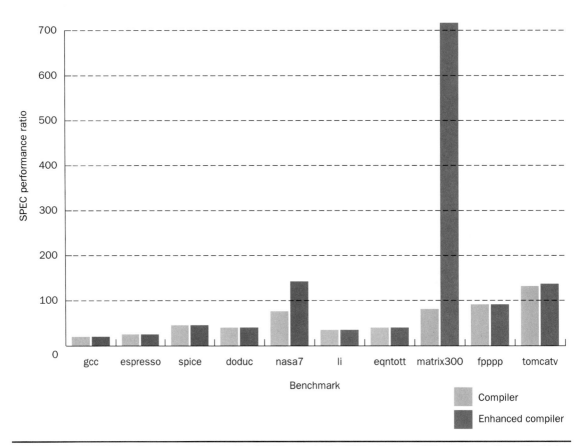

FIGURE 2.3 SPEC89 performance ratios for the IBM Powerstation 550 using two different compilers. The higher numbers on matrix300 (and nasa7) result from applying an optimization technique to these two kernel-oriented benchmarks. For the enhanced compiler, special flags are passed to the compiler for both nasa7 and matrix300, which are not used for the other benchmarks. In both programs, the compiler transforms the program by blocking the matrix operations that are in the inner loops. These blocking transformations substantially lower the number of memory accesses required and transform the inner loops from having high cache miss rates to having almost negligible cache miss rates. Interestingly, the original motivation for including matrix300 was to exercise the computer's memory system; however, this optimization basically reorganizes the program to minimize memory usage. This data appeared in two SPEC reports during the fall and winter of 1991. The susceptibility of this benchmark to compiler optimization, and the relatively uninteresting behavior of the benchmark after optimization, led to the elimination of matrix300 from the 1992 release of the SPEC benchmarks.

be easily ported to a machine, but this is no longer true. Using small programs as benchmarks was an attempt to make fair comparisons among different machines, but use of anything less than real programs after initial design studies is likely to give misleading results and lure the designer astray.

Once we have selected a set of suitable benchmarks and obtained performance measurements, we can write a performance report. The guiding principle in reporting performance measurements should be *reproducibility*—we should list everything another experimenter would need to duplicate the results. This list must include the version of the operating system, compilers, and the input, as well as the machine configuration. As an example, we include the system description section of a SPEC benchmark report in Figure 2.4.

Hardware	
Model number	Powerstation 550
CPU	41.67-MHz POWER 4164
FPU	Integrated
Number of CPUs	1
Cache size per CPU	64K data/8K instruction
Memory	64 MB
Disk subsystem	2 400-MB SCSI
Network interface	NA
Software	
OS type and rev	AIX v3.1.5
Compiler rev	AIX XL C/6000 Ver. 1.1.5
	AIX XL Fortran Ver. 2.2
Other software	None
File system type	AIX
Firmware level	NA
System	
Tuning parameters	None
Background load	None
System state	Multiuser (single-user login)

FIGURE 2.4 System description of the machine used to obtain the higher performance results in Figure 2.3. A footnote attached to the entry for the Fortran compiler states: "AIX XL Fortran Alpha Version 2.2 used for testing." Although no tuning parameters are indicated, additional footnotes describe a number of special flags passed to the compilers for the benchmarks.

2.5 Comparing and Summarizing Performance

Once we have selected programs to use as benchmarks and agreed on whether we are measuring response time or throughput, you might think that performance comparison would be straightforward. However, we must still decide how to summarize the performance of a group of benchmarks.

	Computer A	Computer B
Program 1 (seconds)	1	10
Program 2 (seconds)	1000	100
Total time (seconds)	1001	110

FIGURE 2.5   Execution times of two programs on two different machines. Taken from Figure 1 of Smith [1988].

Although summarizing a set of measurements results in less information, marketers and even users often prefer to have a single number to compare performance. The key question is, How should a summary be computed? Figure 2.5, which is abstracted from an article about summarizing performance, illustrates some of the difficulties facing such efforts.

Using our definition of *faster*, the following statements hold for the program measurements in Figure 2.5:

- A is 10 times faster than B for program 1.

- B is 10 times faster than A for program 2.

Taken individually, each of these statements is true. Collectively, however, they present a confusing picture—the relative performance of computers A and B is unclear.

Total Execution Time: A Consistent Summary Measure

The simplest approach to summarizing relative performance is to use total execution time of the two programs. Thus

$$\frac{\text{Performance}_B}{\text{Performance}_A} = \frac{\text{Execution time}_A}{\text{Execution time}_B} = \frac{1001}{110} = 9.1$$

That is, B is 9.1 times faster than A for programs 1 and 2 together.

This summary is directly proportional to execution time, our final measure of performance. If the workload consists of running programs 1 and 2 an equal number of times, this statement would predict the relative execution times for the workload on each machine.

The average of the execution times that is directly proportional to total execution time is the *arithmetic mean* (AM):

$$AM = \frac{1}{n}\sum_{i=1}^{n} Time_i$$

where $Time_i$ is the execution time for the ith program of a total of n in the workload. Since it is the mean of execution times, a smaller mean indicates a smaller average execution time and thus improved performance.

The arithmetic mean is proportional to execution time, assuming that the programs in the workload are each run an equal number of times. Is that the right workload? If not, we can assign a weighting factor w_i to each program to indicate the frequency of the program in that workload. If, for example, 20% of the tasks in the workload were program 1 and 80% of the tasks in the workload were program 2, then the weighting factors would be 0.2 and 0.8. By summing the products of weighting factors and execution times, we can obtain a clear picture of the performance of the workload. This sum is called the *weighted arithmetic mean*. One method of weighting programs is to choose weights so that the execution time of each benchmark is equal on the machine used as the base. The standard arithmetic mean is a special case of the weighted arithmetic mean where all weights are equal. We explore the weighted mean in more detail in Exercises 2.29 and 2.30.

2.6   Real Stuff: The SPEC95 Benchmarks and Performance of Recent Processors

The most popular and comprehensive set of CPU benchmarks is the SPEC (System Performance Evaluation Cooperative) suite of benchmarks. SPEC was created by a set of computer companies in 1989 to improve the measurement and reporting of CPU performance through a better controlled measurement process and the use of more realistic benchmarks. A more detailed history is contained in section 2.9.

The latest release of the SPEC benchmarks is the SPEC95 suite, which consists of 8 integer and 10 floating-point programs, as shown in Figure 2.6. Separate summaries are reported for each set. The execution time measurements are first normalized by dividing the execution time on a Sun SPARCstation 10/40 by the execution time on the measured machine; this normalization yields a measure, called the *SPEC ratio*, which has the advantage that bigger numeric results indicate faster performance (i.e., SPEC ratio is the inverse of execution time). A SPECint95 or SPECfp95 summary measurement is obtained by taking the geometric mean of the SPEC ratios. (See the fallacy on page 81 of the next section for a discussion of trade-offs in using geometric mean.)

Benchmark	Description
go	Artificial intelligence; plays the game of Go
m88ksim	Motorola 88K chip simulator; runs test program
gcc	The Gnu C compiler generating SPARC code
compress	Compresses and decompresses file in memory
li	Lisp interpreter
ijpeg	Graphic compression and decompression
perl	Manipulates strings and prime numbers in the special-purpose programming language Perl
vortex	A database program
tomcatv	A mesh generation program
swim	Shallow water model with 513 x 513 grid
su2cor	Quantum physics; Monte Carlo simulation
hydro2d	Astrophysics; Hydrodynamic Naiver Stokes equations
mgrid	Multigrid solver in 3-D potential field
applu	Parabolic/elliptic partial differential equations
turb3d	Simulates isotropic, homogeneous turbulence in a cube
apsi	Solves problems regarding temperature, wind velocity, and distribution of pollutant
fpppp	Quantum chemistry
wave5	Plasma physics; electromagnetic particle simulation

FIGURE 2.6   The SPEC95 CPU benchmarks. The 8 integer benchmarks in the top half of the table are written in C, while the 10 floating-point benchmarks in the bottom half are written in Fortran 77. For more information on SPEC and on the SPEC benchmarks, see the link to the SPEC Web pages at *www.mkp.com/books_catalog/cod/links.htm.*

For a given instruction set architecture, increases in CPU performance can come from three sources:

1. Increases in clock rate

2. Improvements in processor organization that lower the CPI

3. Compiler enhancements that lower the instruction count or generate instructions with a lower average CPI (e.g., by using simpler instructions)

To illustrate such performance improvements, Figures 2.7 and 2.8 show the SPECint95 and SPECfp95 measurements for a series of Intel Pentium processors (as implemented in the Intel XXpress system) and Pentium Pro processors (as implemented in the Intel Alder system). Since SPEC requires that the benchmarks be run on real hardware and the memory system has a significant effect on performance, other systems with these processors may produce different performance levels. The Intel machines measured here have aggressive memory systems and compilers (as opposed to the standard third-party compilers in broad use), and most systems delivered with these processors will have lower performance for the SPEC benchmarks.

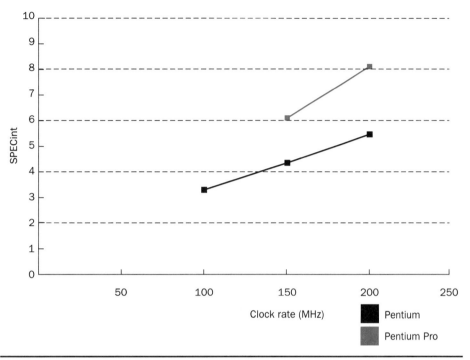

FIGURE 2.7 The SPECint95 ratings for the Pentium and Pentium Pro processors at different clock speeds. SPEC requires two sets of measurements: one that allows aggressive optimization with benchmark-specific switches, and one that allows only the standard optimization switches (called SPECint_base95). For the integer benchmarks on these processors, the results are the same. The link to these results can be found at *www.mkp.com/books_catalog/cod/links.htm.*

There are several important observations from these two performance graphs. The most obvious is the performance enhancement offered by the Pentium Pro over the Pentium: at the same clock rate the SPECint95 measure shows that the Pentium Pro is 1.4 to 1.5 times faster, and the SPECfp95 measure shows that the Pentium Pro is 1.7 to 1.8 times faster. Although there are specific compiler enhancements for each processor, the majority of the performance improvement comes from organizational enhancements to the Pentium Pro; we will see some of these enhancements when we examine pipelining in Chapter 6 and the memory system in Chapter 7.

The other major observation is that when the clock rate is increased by a certain factor, the processor performance increases by a lower factor. For example, when the clock rate of the Pentium doubles from 100 MHz to 200 MHz, the SPECint95 performance improves by only 1.7 and the SPECfp95 performance improves by only 1.4! The reason for this is performance loss in the memory

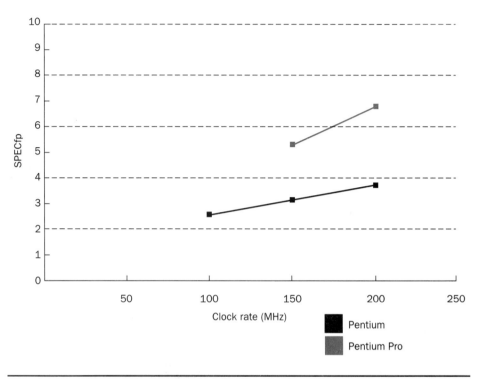

FIGURE 2.8   The SPECfp95 ratings for the Pentium and Pentium Pro processors at different clock speeds. These results can be found via the link to SPEC at
www.mkp.com/books_cataog/cod/links.htm.

system. In general, since the speed of the main memory is not increased, increasing the processor speed will exacerbate the bottleneck at the memory system. This effect is most acute on the floating-point benchmarks, since they are
larger. This behavior is an example of a general principle, called *Amdahl's law,*
which we examine in more detail in the next section.

In comparison, the Pentium Pro processor performance scales somewhat
better with increases in clock rate, though still not as fast as the clock rate. For
example, the SPECfp95 improvement in going from 150 MHz to 200 MHz is
1.24, while the Pentium processor shows a smaller improvement of 1.18 for the
same increase in clock rate.

In Chapter 7, we will see how the memory systems on these processors are
designed and how designers minimize the memory system losses as processor
performance improves. Section 7.6 describes some techniques that the Pentium Pro uses to reduce performance lost in the memory system, which explain
why its performance scales better with clock rate than a Pentium.

2.7 Fallacies and Pitfalls

Cost/performance fallacies and pitfalls have ensnared many a computer architect, including us. Accordingly, this section suffers no shortage of relevant examples. We start with a pitfall that has trapped many designers and reveals an important relationship in computer design.

Pitfall: Expecting the improvement of one aspect of a machine to increase performance by an amount proportional to the size of the improvement.

This pitfall has visited designers of both hardware and software. A simple design problem illustrates it well. Suppose a program runs in 100 seconds on a machine, with multiply operations responsible for 80 seconds of this time. How much do I have to improve the speed of multiplication if I want my program to run five times faster?

The execution time of the program after I make the improvement is given by the following simple equation:

Execution time after improvement

$$= \left(\frac{\text{Execution time affected by improvement}}{\text{Amount of improvement}} + \text{Execution time unaffected} \right)$$

For this problem:

$$\text{Execution time after improvement} = \frac{80 \text{ seconds}}{n} + (100 - 80 \text{ seconds})$$

Since we want the performance to be five times faster, the new execution time should be 20 seconds, giving

$$20 \text{ seconds} = \frac{80 \text{ seconds}}{n} + 20 \text{ seconds}$$

$$0 = \frac{80 \text{ seconds}}{n}$$

That is, there is no amount by which we can enhance multiply to achieve a fivefold increase in performance, if multiply accounts for only 80% of the workload. The performance enhancement possible with a given improvement is limited by the amount that the improved feature is used. This concept is referred to as *Amdahl's law* in computing, or the law of diminishing returns in everyday life. We'll see some other implications of this relationship in Exercises 2.41 through 2.46.

A common theme in hardware design is a corollary of Amdahl's law: *Make the common case fast.* This simple guideline reminds us that in many cases the frequency with which one event occurs may be much higher than another. Amdahl's law reminds us that the opportunity for improvement is affected by how much time the event consumes. Thus making the common case fast will tend to enhance performance better than optimizing the rare case. Ironically, the common case is often simpler than the rare case and hence is often easier to enhance.

Fallacy: Hardware-independent metrics predict performance.

Because accurately predicting and comparing performance is so difficult, many designers and researchers have tried to devise methods to assess performance that do not rely on measurements of execution time. These methods are frequently employed when designers compare different instruction sets to factor out the effects of different implementations or software systems and arrive at conclusions about the performance obtainable for different instruction sets.

One such method, which has been used in the past, is to use code size as a measure of speed. With this method, the instruction set architecture with the smallest program is fastest. The size of the compiled program is, of course, important when memory space is at a premium, but it is not the same as performance. In fact, today, the fastest machines tend to have instruction sets that lead to larger programs but can be executed faster with less hardware.

Evidence of the fallacy of using code size to measure speed can be found on the cover of a book published in 1973, shown in Figure 2.9. The figure clearly shows the lack of a direct relationship between code size and execution time. For example, the CDC 6600's programs are over three times as big as those on the Burroughs B5500, yet the CDC machine runs Algol 60 programs almost six times *faster* than the B5500, a machine designed specifically for Algol 60.

Compiler writers sometimes use code size to choose between two different code segments on the same architecture. While this is less misleading than trying to compare code size across architectures, the accuracy of predicting performance from code size can vary widely.

Pitfall: Using MIPS as a performance metric.

A number of popular measures have been devised in attempts to create a standard and easy-to-use measure of computer performance. One result has been that simple metrics, valid in a limited context, have been heavily misused. All proposed alternatives to the use of time as the performance metric have led eventually to misleading claims, distorted results, or incorrect interpretations.

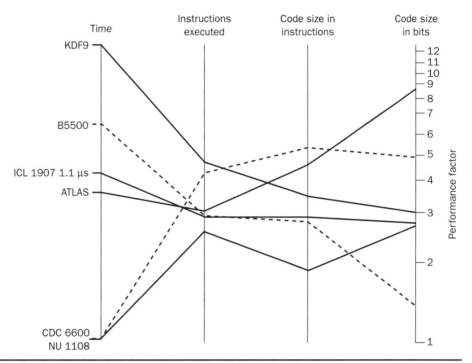

FIGURE 2.9 This graph is from the cover of *Algol 60 Compilation and Assessment* by B. A. Wichmann (published in 1973). The graph shows relative execution time, instructions executed, and code size in both instructions and bits for a set of programs written in Algol 60 and run on six different machines. The results are normalized to a reference machine, with a higher number indicating more execution time, larger instruction counts, or larger code size. The graph clearly shows that abstract measures such as code size bear little relationship to performance measures such as execution time or instructions executed. Despite the evidence that code size and execution time could be totally unrelated, many designers continued to emphasize code size throughout the 1980s. Graph redrawn with permission from Academic Press.

One alternative to time as the metric is MIPS (million instructions per second). For a given program, MIPS is simply

$$\text{MIPS} = \frac{\text{Instruction count}}{\text{Execution time} \times 10^6}$$

This MIPS measurement is also called *native MIPS* to distinguish it from some alternative definitions of MIPS that we discuss in section 2.9.

Since MIPS is an instruction execution rate, MIPS specifies performance inversely to execution time; faster machines have a higher MIPS rating. The good news about MIPS is that it is easy to understand, and faster machines mean bigger MIPS, which matches intuition.

There are three problems with using MIPS as a measure for comparing machines. First, MIPS specifies the instruction execution rate but does not take into account the capabilities of the instructions. We cannot compare computers with different instruction sets using MIPS, since the instruction counts will certainly differ. Second, MIPS varies between programs on the same computer; thus a machine cannot have a single MIPS rating for all programs. Finally and most importantly, MIPS can vary inversely with performance! There are many examples of this anomalous behavior; one is given below.

MIPS as a Performance Measure

Example

Consider the machine with three instruction classes and CPI measurements from the last example on page 64. Now suppose we measure the code for the same program from two different compilers and obtain the following data:

Code from	Instruction counts (in billions) for each instruction class		
	A	B	C
Compiler 1	5	1	1
Compiler 2	10	1	1

Assume that the machine's clock rate is 500 MHz. Which code sequence will execute faster according to MIPS? According to execution time?

Answer

First we find the execution time for the two different compilers using the following equation:

$$\text{Execution time} = \frac{\text{CPU clock cycles}}{\text{Clock rate}}$$

We can use an earlier formula for CPU clock cycles:

$$\text{CPU clock cycles} = \sum_{i=1}^{n} (\text{CPI}_i \times C_i)$$

$$\text{CPU clock cycles}_1 = (5 \times 1 + 1 \times 2 + 1 \times 3) \times 10^9 = 10 \times 10^9$$

$$\text{CPU clock cycles}_2 = (10 \times 1 + 1 \times 2 + 1 \times 3) \times 10^9 = 15 \times 10^9$$

Now, we find the execution time for the two compilers:

$$\text{Execution time}_1 = \frac{10 \times 10^9}{500 \times 10^6} = 20 \text{ seconds}$$

$$\text{Execution time}_2 = \frac{15 \times 10^9}{500 \times 10^6} = 30 \text{ seconds}$$

So, we conclude that compiler 1 generates the faster program, according to execution time. Now, let's compute the MIPS rate for each version of the program, using

$$\text{MIPS} = \frac{\text{Instruction count}}{\text{Execution time} \times 10^6}$$

$$\text{MIPS}_1 = \frac{(5 + 1 + 1) \times 10^9}{20 \times 10^6} = 350$$

$$\text{MIPS}_2 = \frac{(10 + 1 + 1) \times 10^9}{30 \times 10^6} = 400$$

So, the code from compiler 2 has a higher MIPS rating, but the code from compiler 1 runs faster!

As examples such as this show, MIPS can fail to give a true picture of performance—even when comparing two versions of the same program on the same machine. In section 2.9, we discuss other uses of the term *MIPS*, and how such usages can also be misleading.

Fallacy: Synthetic benchmarks predict performance.

Synthetic benchmarks are artificial programs that are constructed to try to match the characteristics of a large set of programs. The goal is to create a single benchmark program where the execution frequency of statements in the benchmark matches the statement frequency in a large set of benchmarks. Whetstone and Dhrystone are the most popular synthetic benchmarks. Whetstone was based on measurements of Algol programs in a scientific and engineering environment. It was later converted to Fortran and became popular. Dhrystone, which was inspired by Whetstone, was created as a benchmark for systems programming environments and was based on a set of published frequency measurements. Dhrystone was originally written in Ada and later converted to C, after which it became popular.

One major drawback of synthetic benchmarks is that no user would ever run a synthetic benchmark as an application because these programs don't compute anything a user would find remotely interesting. Furthermore, because synthetic benchmarks are not real programs, they usually do not reflect program behavior, other than the behavior considered when they were created. Finally, compiler and hardware optimizations can inflate performance of these benchmarks, far beyond what the same optimizations would achieve on real programs. Of course, because these benchmarks are not natural programs, they may not reward optimizations of behavior that occur in real programs. Here are some examples of how Dhrystone may distort the importance of various optimizations:

- Optimizing compilers can easily discard 25% of the Dhrystone code; examples include loops that are executed only once, making the loop overhead instructions unnecessary. To address these problems, the authors of the benchmark "require" both optimized and unoptimized code to be reported. In addition, they "forbid" the practice of inline procedure expansion optimization because Dhrystone's simple procedure structure allows elimination of all procedure calls at almost no increase in code size.

- One C compiler appears to include optimizations targeted just for Dhrystone. If the proper option flag is set at compile time, the compiler turns the portion of the C version of this benchmark that copies a variable-length string of bytes (terminated by an end-of-string symbol) into a loop that transfers a fixed number of words. The compiler also assumes that the source and destination of the string is word-aligned in memory. Although an estimated 99.70% to 99.98% of typical string copies could *not* use this optimization, this single change can make a 20% to 30% improvement in Dhrystone's overall performance.

The small size and simplistic structure of synthetic benchmarks makes them especially vulnerable to this type of activity.

Pitfall: Using the arithmetic mean of normalized execution times to predict performance.

This pitfall has trapped many researchers, including one of the authors of this book. An inviting method of presenting machine performance is to normalize execution times to a reference machine, just as is done to obtain a SPEC ratio, and then take the average of the normalized execution times. However, if we average the normalized execution time values with an arithmetic mean, the result will depend on the choice of the machine we use as the reference. For example, in Figure 2.10, the execution times from Figure 2.5 are normalized to both A and B, and the arithmetic mean is computed. When we normalize to A, the arithmetic mean indicates that A is faster than B by 5.05/1, which is the inverse ratio of the execution times. When we normalize to B, we conclude that *B is faster by exactly the same ratio.* Clearly, both these results cannot be correct!

			Normalized to A		Normalized to B	
	Time on A	Time on B	A	B	A	B
Program 1	1	10	1	10	0.1	1
Program 2	1000	100	1	0.1	10	1
Arithmetic mean of time or normalized time	500.5	55	1	5.05	5.05	1
Geometric mean of time or normalized time	31.6	31.6	1	1	1	1

FIGURE 2.10   Execution times from Figure 2.5 normalized to each machine. The means are computed for each column. While the arithmetic means vary when we normalize to either A or B, the geometric means are consistent, independent of normalization.

The difficulty arises from the use of the arithmetic mean of ratios. Instead, normalized results should be combined with the *geometric* mean. The formula for the geometric mean is

$$\sqrt[n]{\prod_{i=1}^{n} \text{Execution time ratio}_i}$$

where Execution time ratio$_i$ is the execution time, normalized to the reference machine, for the *i*th program of a total of n in the workload, and

$$\prod_{i=1}^{n} a_i \text{ means the product } a_1 \times a_2 \times \ldots \times a_n$$

The geometric mean is independent of which data series we use for normalization because it has the property

$$\frac{\text{Geometric mean}(X_i)}{\text{Geometric mean}(Y_i)} = \text{Geometric mean}\left(\frac{X_i}{Y_i}\right)$$

meaning that taking either the ratio of the means or the means of the ratios produces the same results. Thus the geometric mean produces the same relative result whether we normalize to A or B, as we can see in the bottom row of Figure 2.10. When execution times are normalized, only a geometric mean can be used to consistently summarize the normalized results. Unfortunately, as we show in the exercises, geometric means do not track total execution time and thus cannot be used to predict relative execution time for a workload.

Fallacy: The geometric mean of execution time ratios is proportional to total execution time.

The advantage of the geometric mean is that it is independent of the running times of the individual programs, and it doesn't matter which machine is used for normalization. The drawback to using geometric means of execution times is that they violate our fundamental principle of performance measurement—they do not predict execution time. The geometric means in Figure 2.10 suggest that for programs 1 and 2 the performance is the same for machines A and B. Yet, the arithmetic mean of the execution times, which we know is proportional to total execution time, suggests that machine B is 9.1 times faster than machine A! If we use total execution time as the performance measure, A and B would have the same performance only for a workload that ran the first program 100 times more often than the second program!

In general, no workload for three or more machines will match the performance predicted by the geometric mean of normalized execution times. The ideal solution is to measure a real workload and weight the programs according to their frequency of execution. If this can't be done, normalizing so that equal time is spent on each program on some machine at least makes the relative weightings explicit and predicts execution time of a workload with that mix. If results must be normalized to a specific machine, first summarize performance with the proper weighted measure, and then do the normalizing.

The Big Picture

Execution time is the only valid and unimpeachable measure of performance. Many other metrics have been proposed and found wanting. Sometimes these metrics are flawed from the start by not reflecting execution time; other times a metric valid in a limited context is extended and used beyond that context or without the additional clarification needed to make it valid.

Similarly, any measure that summarizes performance should reflect execution time. Weighted arithmetic means summarize performance while tracking execution time. Through the use of weights, a weighted arithmetic mean can adjust for different running times, balancing the contribution of each benchmark to the summary.

2.8 Concluding Remarks

Although we have focused on performance and how to evaluate it in this chapter, designing only for performance without considering cost is unrealistic. All computer designers must balance performance and cost. Of course, there exists a domain of *high-performance design,* in which performance is the primary goal and cost is secondary. Much of the supercomputer industry designs in this fashion. At the other extreme is *low-cost design,* where cost takes precedence over performance. Computers like the low-end IBM PC clones belong here, as do most embedded computers. Between these extremes is *cost/performance design*, in which the designer balances cost against performance. Examples from the workstation industry typify the kinds of trade-offs that designers in this region must live with.

We have seen in this chapter that there is a reliable method of determining and reporting performance, using the execution time of real programs as the metric. This execution time is related to other important measurements we can make by the following equation:

$$\frac{\text{Seconds}}{\text{Program}} = \frac{\text{Instructions}}{\text{Program}} \times \frac{\text{Clock cycles}}{\text{Instruction}} \times \frac{\text{Seconds}}{\text{Clock cycle}}$$

We will use this equation and its constituent factors many times. Remember, though, that individually the factors do not determine performance: Only the product, which equals execution time, is a reliable measure of performance.

Of course, simply knowing this equation is not enough to guide the design or evaluation of a computer. We must understand how the different aspects of a design affect each of these key parameters. This insight involves a wide variety of issues, from the effects of instruction set design on dynamic instruction count, to the impact of pipelining and memory systems on CPI, to the interaction between the technology and organization that determine the clock rate. The art of computer design lies not in plugging numbers into a performance equation, but in accurately determining how design alternatives will affect performance and cost.

Most computer users care about both cost and performance. While understanding the relationship among aspects of a design and its performance is challenging, determining the cost of various design features is often a more difficult problem. The cost of a machine is affected not only by the cost of the components, but by the costs of labor to assemble the machine, of research and development overhead, of sales and marketing, and of the profit margin. Finally, because of the rapid change in implementation technologies, the most cost-effective choice today is often suboptimal in six months or a year.

Computer designs will always be measured by cost and performance, and finding the best balance will always be the art of computer design, just as in any engineering task.

2.9   Historical Perspective and Further Reading

From the earliest days of computing, designers have specified performance goals—ENIAC was to be 1000 times faster than the Harvard Mark-I, and the IBM Stretch (7030) was to be 100 times faster than the fastest machine then in existence. What wasn't clear, though, was how this performance was to be measured.

The original measure of performance was the time required to perform an individual operation, such as addition. Since most instructions took the same execution time, the timing of one was the same as the others. As the execution times of instructions in a machine became more diverse, however, the time required for one operation was no longer useful for comparisons.

To take these differences into account, an *instruction mix* was calculated by measuring the relative frequency of instructions in a computer across many programs. Multiplying the time for each instruction by its weight in the mix gave the user the *average instruction execution time*. (If measured in clock cycles, average instruction execution time is the same as average CPI.) Since instruction sets were similar, this was a more precise comparison than add times. From average instruction execution time, then, it was only a small step to MIPS. MIPS had the virtue of being easy to understand; hence it grew in popularity.

MIPS, MOPS, and Other FLOPS

One particularly misleading definition of MIPS that has been occasionally popular is *peak MIPS*. Peak MIPS is obtained by choosing an instruction mix that minimizes the CPI, even if that instruction mix is totally impractical. In the example above, the peak MIPS ratings are the same for both machines: 500 MIPS. To achieve a 500-MIPS rating with a 500-MHz clock, the CPI for the program must be 1. But the only program that can have a CPI of 1 is a program consisting solely of type A instructions!

In practice, processors are sometimes marketed by touting the peak MIPS rating, which can distort the real picture of performance. When the Intel i860 was announced in February 1989, the product announcement used the peak performance of the processor to compare performance against other machines. The i860 was able to execute up to two floating-point operations and one integer operation per clock. With a clock rate target of 50 MHz, the i860 was claimed to offer 100 MFLOPS and 150 MOPS (millions of operations per second). The first i860-based systems (using 40-MHz parts) became available for benchmarking during the first quarter of 1991. By comparison, a MIPS machine based on a 33-MHz R3000 processor, available at about the same time, had a peak performance of about 16 MFLOPS and 33 MOPS. Although the peak performance claims might suggest that the i860-based machine was more than five times faster than the R3000-based machine, the SPEC benchmarks showed that the R3000-based machine was actually about 15% faster! Although peak MIPS is an essentially useless measure, computer manufacturers still occasionally announce products using peak MIPS as a metric, often neglecting to include the word "peak"!

One attempt to retain the use of the term MIPS, but to make it useful among different instruction sets, was to choose a definition of MIPS that is relative to some agreed-upon reference machine, similar to the SPEC ratio measurement. *Relative MIPS*, the term used for this measure, has been defined as follows:

$$\text{Relative MIPS} = \frac{\text{Time}_{\text{reference}}}{\text{Time}_{\text{unrated}}} \times \text{MIPS}_{\text{reference}}$$

where

$\text{Time}_{\text{reference}}$ = Execution time of a program on the reference machine

$\text{Time}_{\text{unrated}}$ = Execution time of the same program on machine to be rated

$\text{MIPS}_{\text{reference}}$ = Agreed-upon MIPS rating of the reference machine

Relative MIPS is proportional to execution time *only* for a given program and a given input. Even when these are identified, it becomes harder to find a reference machine on which to run programs as the machine ages. (In the 1980s the dominant reference machine was the VAX-11/780, which was called a 1-MIPS machine, for a reason we will discuss shortly, and is now hard to find in operation.) Moreover, should the older machine be run with the newest release of the compiler and operating system, or should the software be fixed so the reference machine does not become faster over time? There is also the temptation to generalize from a relative MIPS rating obtained using one benchmark to a general statement about relative performance, even though there can be wide variations in performance of two machines across a complete set of benchmarks.

The development of relative MIPS as a popular performance measurement demonstrates that benchmarking does not necessarily evolve in a logical fashion. In the 1970s, MIPS was being used as a way to compare the performance of IBM 360/370 implementations. Because the measure was used to compare identical architectures (and hence identical instruction counts), it was a valid metric. The notion of relative MIPS came along as a way to extend the easily understandable MIPS rating. In 1977, when the VAX-11/780 was ready to be announced, DEC ran small benchmarks that were also run on an IBM 370/158. IBM marketing referred to the 370/158 as a 1-MIPS computer and, since the programs ran at the same speed, DEC marketing called the VAX-11/780 a 1-MIPS computer.

The popularity of the VAX-11/780 made it a popular reference machine for relative MIPS, especially since relative MIPS for a 1-MIPS reference machine is easy to calculate. If a machine was five times faster than the VAX-11/780, its rating for that benchmark would be 5 relative MIPS. The 1-MIPS rating was widely believed for four years, until Joel Emer of DEC measured the VAX-11/780 under a timesharing load. Emer found that the actual VAX-11/780 MIPS rate was 0.5. Subsequent VAXs that run 3 million VAX instructions per second for some benchmarks were therefore called 6-MIPS machines because they run six times faster than the VAX-11/780.

The 1970s and 1980s marked the growth of the supercomputer industry, which was defined by high performance on floating-point-intensive programs. Average instruction time and MIPS were clearly inappropriate metrics for this industry—hence the invention of MFLOPS (millions of floating-point operations per second). Unfortunately, customers quickly forgot the program used for the rating, and marketing groups decided to start quoting peak MFLOPS in the supercomputer performance wars. The usage of MFLOPS and problems associated with it are discussed starting on page 99 in the exercises.

The Quest for an Average Program

As processors were becoming more sophisticated and relied on memory hierarchies (the topic of Chapter 7) and pipelining (the topic of Chapter 6), a single execution time for each instruction no longer existed; neither execution time nor MIPS, therefore, could be calculated from the instruction mix and the manual. While it might seem obvious today that the right thing to do would have been to develop a set of real applications that could be used as standard benchmarks, this was a difficult task until relatively recent times. Variations in operating systems and language standards made it hard to create large programs that could be moved from machine to machine simply by recompiling. Instead, the next step was benchmarking using synthetic programs. The Whetstone synthetic program was created by measuring scientific programs written in Algol 60 (see Curnow and Wichmann's [1976] description). This program was converted to Fortran and was widely used to characterize scientific program performance. Whetstone performance is typically quoted in Whetstones per second—the number of executions of one iteration of the Whetstone benchmark! Dhrystone was developed much more recently (see Weicker's [1984] description and methodology).

About the same time Whetstone was developed, the concept of *kernel benchmarks* gained popularity. Kernels are small, time-intensive pieces from real programs that are extracted and then used as benchmarks. This approach was developed primarily for benchmarking high-end machines, especially supercomputers. Livermore Loops and Linpack are the best-known examples. The Livermore Loops consist of a series of 21 small loop fragments. Linpack consists of a portion of a linear algebra subroutine package. Kernels are best used to isolate the performance of individual features of a machine and to explain the reasons for differences in the performance of real programs. Because scientific applications often use small pieces of code that execute for a long period of time, characterizing performance with kernels is most popular in this application class. Although kernels help illuminate performance, they often overstate the performance on real applications. For example, today's supercomputers often achieve a high percentage of their peak performance on such kernels. However, when executing real applications, the performance often is only a small fraction of the peak performance.

The Quest for a Simple Program

Another misstep on the way to developing better benchmarking methods was the use of toy programs as benchmarks. Such programs typically have between 10 and 100 lines of code and produce a result the user already knows before running the toy program. Programs like Sieve of Erastosthenes, Puzzle, and Quicksort were popular because they are small, easy to compile, and run on almost any computer. These programs became quite popular in the early 1980s, when universities were engaged in designing the early RISC machines. The small size of these programs made it easy to compile and run them on simulators. Unfortunately, we have to admit that we played a role in popularizing such benchmarks, by using them to compare performance and even collecting sets of such programs for distribution. Even more unfortunately, some people continue to use such benchmarks—much to our embarrassment! However, we can report that we have learned our lesson and we now understand that the best use of such programs is as beginning programming assignments.

Summarizing Can Be Tricky

Almost every issue that involves measuring and reporting performance has been controversial, including the question of how to summarize performance. The methods used have included the arithmetic mean of normalized performance, the harmonic mean of rates, the geometric mean of normalized execution time, and the total execution time. Several references listed at the end of this section discuss this question, including Smith's [1988] article, whose proposal is the approach used in section 2.5.

SPECulating about Performance

An important advance in performance evaluation was the formation of the System Performance Evaluation Cooperative (SPEC) group in 1988. SPEC comprises representatives of many computer companies—the founders being Apollo/Hewlett-Packard, DEC, MIPS, and Sun—who have agreed on a set of real programs and inputs that all will run. It is worth noting that SPEC couldn't have come into being before portable operating systems and the popularity of high-level languages. Now compilers, too, are accepted as a proper part of the performance of computer systems and must be measured in any evaluation.

History teaches us that while the SPEC effort may be useful with current computers, it will not meet the needs of the next generation without changing. In 1991, a throughput measure was added, based on running multiple versions of the benchmark. It is most useful for evaluating timeshared usage of a uni-processor or a multiprocessor. Other system benchmarks that include OS-intensive and I/O-intensive activities have also been added. Another change, motivated in part by the kind of results shown in Figure 2.3, was the decision to drop matrix300 and to add more benchmarks. One result of the difficulty in finding benchmarks was that the initial version of the SPEC benchmarks (called SPEC89) contained six floating-point benchmarks but only four integer benchmarks. Calculating a single summary measurement using the geometric mean of execution times normalized to a VAX-11/780 meant that this measure favored machines with strong floating-point performance.

In 1992, a new benchmark set (called SPEC92) was introduced. It incor-porated additional benchmarks, dropped matrix300, and provided separate means (SPECint and SPECfp) for integer and floating-point programs. In addition, the SPECbase measure, which disallows program-specific optimiza-tion flags, was added to provide users with a performance measurement that would more closely match what they might experience on their own programs. The SPECfp numbers show the largest increase versus the base SPECfp mea-surement, typically ranging from 15% to 30% higher.

In 1995, the benchmark set was once again updated, adding some new inte-ger and floating-point benchmarks, as well as removing some benchmarks that suffered from flaws or had running times that had become too small given the factor of 20 or more performance improvement since the first SPEC release. SPEC95 also changed the base machine for normalization to a Sun SPARC-station 10/40, since operating versions of the original base machine were be-coming difficult to find!

SPEC has also added additional benchmark suites beyond the original suites targeted at CPU performance. The SDM (Systems Development Multi-tasking) benchmark contains two benchmarks that are synthetic versions of development workloads (edits, compiles, executions, system commands). The SFS (System-level File Server) benchmark set is a synthetic workload for test-ing performance as a file server. Both these benchmark sets include significant I/O and operating systems components, unlike the CPU tests. The most recent addition to SPEC is the SPEChpc96 suite, two benchmarks aimed at testing performance on high-end scientific workloads. For the future, SPEC is explor-ing benchmarks for new functions, such as Web servers.

Creating and developing such benchmark sets has become difficult and time consuming. Although SPEC was initially created as a good faith effort by a group of companies, it became important to competitive marketing and sales efforts. The selection of benchmarks and the rules for running them are made by representatives of the companies that compete by advertising test results.

Conflicts between the companies' perspectives and those of consumers naturally arise. Perhaps in the future the decisions about such performance benchmarks should be made by, or at least include, a more representative group.

To Probe Further

Curnow, H. J., and B. A. Wichmann [1976]. "A synthetic benchmark," *The Computer J.* 19 (1):80.

Describes the first major synthetic benchmark, Whetstone, and how it was created.

Flemming, P. J., and J. J. Wallace [1986]. "How not to lie with statistics: The correct way to summarize benchmark results," *Comm. ACM* 29:3 (March) 218–21.

Describes some of the underlying principles in using different means to summarize performance results.

McMahon, F. M. [1986]. "The Livermore FORTRAN kernels: A computer test of numerical performance range," Tech. Rep. UCRL-55745, Lawrence Livermore National Laboratory, Univ. of California, Livermore (December).

Describes the Livermore Loops—a set of Fortran kernel benchmarks.

Smith, J. E. [1988]. "Characterizing computer performance with a single number," *Comm. ACM* 31:10 (October) 1202–06.

Describes the difficulties of summarizing performance with just one number and argues for total execution time as the only consistent measure.

SPEC [1989]. *SPEC Benchmark Suite Release 1.0*, SPEC, Santa Clara, CA, October 2.

Describes the SPEC benchmark suite. For up-to-date information, see the SPEC Web page via a link at www.mkp.com/books_catalog/cod/links.htm.

Weicker, R. P. [1984]. "Dhrystone: A synthetic systems programming benchmark," *Comm. ACM* 27:10 (October) 1013–30.

Describes the Dhrystone benchmark and its construction.

2.10   Key Terms

This chapter has introduced the basics of performance evaluation, measurement, and analysis. A variety of new terms were introduced, and they are listed below. These key terms are defined in the Glossary at the back of the book.

Amdahl's law
arithmetic mean
clock cycle or tick, clock tick, clock period, clock, cycle
clock cycles per instruction (CPI)
clock rate
CPU execution time
geometric mean

harmonic mean of rates
instruction mix
kernel benchmark
million floating-point operations per second (MFLOPS)
million instructions per second (MIPS)
response or execution time

speedup
system CPU time
System Performance Evaluation Cooperative (SPEC) benchmark
user CPU time
weighted arithmetic mean
workload

2.11   Exercises

2.1 [5] <§2.1> We wish to compare the performance of two different machines: M1 and M2. The following measurements have been made on these machines:

Program	Time on M1	Time on M2
1	10 seconds	5 seconds
2	3 seconds	4 seconds

Which machine is faster for each program and by how much?

2.2 [5] <§2.1> Consider the two machines and programs in Exercise 2.1. The following additional measurements were made:

Program	Instructions executed on M1	Instructions executed on M2
1	200×10^6	160×106

Find the instruction execution rate (instructions per second) for each machine when running program 1.

2.3 [5] <§§2.2–2.3> If the clock rates of machines M1 and M2 in Exercise 2.1 are 200 MHz and 300 MHz, respectively, find the clock cycles per instruction (CPI) for program 1 on both machines using the data in Exercises 2.1 and 2.2.

2.4 [5] <§§2.2–2.3> {Ex. 2.3} Assuming the CPI for program 2 on each machine in Exercise 2.1 is the same as the CPI for program 1 found in Exercise 2.3, find the instruction count for program 2 running on each machine using the execution times from Exercise 2.1.

2.5 [5] <§2.1> Suppose that M1 in Exercise 2.1 costs $10,000 and M2 costs $15,000. If you needed to run program 1 a large number of times (i.e., if you were concerned with throughput instead of response time), which machine would you buy in large quantities? Why?

2.6 [10] <§2.1> Suppose you had many more machines to consider besides M1 and M2 described in Exercises 2.1 and 2.5 (each with a cost and an execution time for program 1, which you need to run a large number of times). Could you use the cost divided by the execution time as a metric to help you in your purchasing decision? How about the cost multiplied by the execution time? If either of the two formulas cannot be used, present a simple example that demonstrates why not.

2.7 [5] <§2.1> {Ex. 2.6} If we wanted our metric (call it cost-effectiveness) to be similar to performance in that a larger number should indicate a better cost-effectiveness, what formula would we use?

2.8 [5] <§2.1> Another user is concerned with the throughput of the machine in Exercise 2.1, as measured with an equal workload of programs 1 and 2. Which machine has better performance for this workload? By how much? Which machine is more cost-effective for this workload? By how much?

2.9 [10] <§2.1> Yet another user has the following requirements for the machines discussed in Exercise 2.1: program 1 must be executed 200 times each hour. Any remaining time can be used for running program 2. If the machine has enough performance to execute program 1 the required number of times per hour, performance is measured by the throughput for program 2. Which machine is faster for this workload? Which machine is more cost-effective?

2.10 [5] <§§2.2–2.3> Consider two different implementations, M1 and M2, of the same instruction set. There are four classes of instructions (A, B, C, and D) in the instruction set.

M1 has a clock rate of 500 MHz. The average number of cycles for each instruction class on M1 is as follows:

Class	CPI for this class
A	1
B	2
C	3
D	4

M2 has a clock rate of 750 MHz. The average number of cycles for each instruction class on M2 is as follows:

Class	CPI for this class
A	2
B	2
C	4
D	4

Assume that peak performance is defined as the fastest rate that a machine can execute an instruction sequence chosen to maximize that rate. What are the peak performances of M1 and M2 expressed as instructions per second?

2.11 [10] <§§2.2–2.3> If the number of instructions executed in a certain program is divided equally among the classes of instructions in Exercise 2.10, how much faster is M2 than M1?

2.12 [5] <§§2.2–2.3> {Ex. 2.11} Assuming the CPI values from Exercise 2.10 and the instruction distribution from Exercise 2.11, at what clock rate would M1 have the same performance as the 750-MHz version of M2?

2.13 [10] <§§2.2–2.3> Consider two different implementations, M1 and M2, of the same instruction set. There are three classes of instructions (A, B, and C) in the instruction set. M1 has a clock rate of 400 MHz, and M2 has a clock rate of 200 MHz. The average number of cycles for each instruction class on M1 and M2 is given in the following table:

Class	CPI on M1	CPI on M2	C1 usage	C2 usage	Third-party usage
A	4	2	30%	30%	50%
B	6	4	50%	20%	30%
C	8	8	20%	50%	20%

The table also contains a summary of how three different compilers use the instruction set. C1 is a compiler produced by the makers of M1, C2 is a compiler produced by the makers of M2, and the other compiler is a third-party product. Assume that each compiler uses the same number of instructions for a given program but that the instruction mix is as described in the table. Using C1 on both M1 and M2, how much faster can the makers of M1 claim that M1 is compared with M2? Using C2 on both M2 and M1, how much faster can the makers of M2 claim that M2 is compared with M1? If you purchase M1, which compiler would you use? If you purchase M2, which compiler would you use? Which machine would you purchase if we assume that all other criteria are identical, including costs?

2.14 [5] <§§2.2, 2.3, 2.7> For the following set of variables, identify all of the subsets that can be used to calculate execution time. Each subset should be minimal; that is, it should not contain any variable that is not needed.

{CPI, clock rate, cycle time, MIPS, number of instructions in program, number of cycles in program}

2.15 [10] <§§2.2, 2.3, 2.7> We are interested in two implementations of a machine, one with and one without special floating-point hardware.

Consider a program, P, with the following mix of operations:

floating-point multiply	10%
floating-point add	15%
floating-point divide	5%
integer instructions	70%

Machine MFP (Machine with Floating Point) has floating-point hardware and can therefore implement the floating-point operations directly. It requires the following number of clock cycles for each instruction class:

floating-point multiply	6
floating-point add	4
floating-point divide	20
integer instructions	2

Machine MNFP (Machine with No Floating Point) has no floating-point hardware and so must emulate the floating-point operations using integer instructions. The integer instructions all take 2 clock cycles. The number of integer instructions needed to implement each of the floating-point operations is as follows:

floating-point multiply	30
floating-point add	20
floating-point divide	50

Both machines have a clock rate of 1000 MHz. Find the native MIPS ratings for both machines.

2.16 [10] <§§2.2, 2.3, 2.7> If the machine MFP in Exercise 2.15 needs 300 million instructions for this program, how many integer instructions does the machine MNFP require for the same program?

2.17 [5] <§§2.2, 2.3, 2.7> {Ex. 2.16} Assuming the instruction counts from Exercise 2.16, what is the execution time (in seconds) for the program in Exercise 2.15 run on MFP and MNFP?

2.18 [10] <§§2.2–2.3> You are the lead designer of a new processor. The processor design and compiler are complete, and now you must decide whether to produce the current design as it stands or spend additional time to improve it.

You discuss this problem with your hardware engineering team and arrive at the following options:

a. *Leave the design as it stands.* Call this base machine *Mbase*. It has a clock rate of 500 MHz, and the following measurements have been made using a simulator:

Instruction class	CPI	Frequency
A	2	40%
B	3	25%
C	3	25%
D	5	10%

b. *Optimize the hardware.* The hardware team claims that it can improve the processor design to give it a clock rate of 600 MHz. Call this machine *Mopt*. The following measurements were made using a simulator for Mopt:

Instruction class	CPI	Frequency
A	2	40%
B	2	25%
C	3	25%
D	4	10%

What is the CPI for each machine?

2.19 [5] <§§2.2, 2.3, 2.7> {Ex. 2.18} What are the native MIPS ratings for Mbase and Mopt in Exercise 2.18?

2.20 [10] <§§2.2–2.3> {Ex. 2.18} How much faster is Mopt than Mbase in Exercise 2.18?

2.21 [5] <§§2.2–2.3> The compiler team has heard about the discussion to enhance the machine discussed in Exercises 2.18 through 2.20. The compiler team proposes to improve the compiler for the machine to further enhance performance. Call this combination of the improved compiler and the base machine *Mcomp*. The instruction improvements from this enhanced compiler have been estimated as follows:

Instruction class	Percentage of instructions executed vs. base machine
A	90%
B	90%
C	85%
D	95%

For example, if the base machine executed 500 class A instructions, Mcomp would execute $0.9 \times 500 = 450$ class A instructions for the same program. What is the CPI for Mcomp?

2.22 [5] <§§ 2.2–2.3> {Ex. 2.18, 2.21} Using the data of Exercise 2.18, how much faster is Mcomp than Mbase?

2.23 [10] <§§2.2–2.3> {Ex. 2.18, 2.21, 2.22} The compiler group points out that it is possible to implement both the hardware improvements of Exercise 2.18 and the compiler enhancements described in Exercise 2.21. If *both* the hardware and compiler improvements are implemented, yielding machine *Mboth*, how much faster is Mboth than Mbase?

2.24 [10] <§§2.2–2.3> {Ex. 2.18, 2.21, 2.22, 2.23} You must decide whether to incorporate the hardware enhancements suggested in Exercise 2.18 or the compiler enhancements of Exercise 2.21 (or both) to the base machine described in Exercise 2.18. You estimate that the following time would be required to implement the optimizations described in Exercises 2.18, 2.21, and 2.23:

Optimization	Time to implement	Machine name
Hardware	6 months	Mopt
Compiler	6 months	Mcomp
Both	8 months	Mboth

Recall from Chapter 1 that CPU performance improves by approximately 50% per year, or about 3.4% per month. Assuming that the base machine has performance equal to that of its competitors, which optimizations (if any) would you choose to implement?

2.25 [10] <§§2.4, 2.6> Look at the current list of SPEC programs in Figure 2.6 on page 72. Does it include applications that match the ways you typically use your computer? What classes of programs are irrelevant or missing? Why do you think they were or were not included in SPEC? What would have to be done to include/exclude such programs in the next SPEC release?

2.26 [5] <§2.5> The table below shows the number of floating-point operations executed in two different programs and the runtime for those programs on three different machines:

Program	Floating-point operations	Execution time in seconds		
		Computer A	Computer B	Computer C
Program 1	10,000,000	1	10	20
Program 2	100,000,000	1000	100	20

Which machine is fastest according to total execution time? How much faster is it than the other two machines?

2.27 [5] <§§2.5, 2.7> You wonder how the performance of the three machines in Exercise 2.26 would compare using other means to normalize performance. Which machine is fastest by the geometric mean?

2.28 [15] <§§2.5, 2.7> {Ex. 2.27} Find a workload for the two programs of Exercise 2.26 that will produce the same performance summary using total execution time of the workload as the geometric mean of performance, as computed in Exercise 2.27. Give the workload as a percentage of executions of each program for the pairs of machines: A and B, B and C, and A and C.

2.29 [15] <§§2.5, 2.7> One user has told you that the two programs in Exercise 2.26 constitute the bulk of his workload, but he does not run them equally. The user wants to determine how the three machines compare when the workload consists of different mixes of these two programs. (You know you can use the arithmetic mean to find the relative performance.)

Suppose the total number of FLOPS executed in the workload is equally divided among the two programs. That is, program 1 is run 10 times as often as program 2. Find which machine is fastest for this workload and by how much. How does this compare with the total execution time for a workload with equal numbers of program executions?

2.30 [15] <§§2.5, 2.7> An alternative weighting to that of Exercise 2.29 is to assume that equal amounts of time will be spent running each program on some machine. Which machine is fastest using the data of Exercise 2.26 and assuming a weighting that generates equal execution time for each benchmark on machine A? Which machine is fastest if we assume a weighting that generates equal execution time for each benchmark on machine B? How do these results compare with the unweighted performance summaries?

2.31 [5] <§2.7> Assume that multiply instructions take 12 cycles and account for 10% of the instructions in a typical program and that the other 90% of the instructions require an average of 4 cycles for each instruction. What percentage of time does the CPU spend doing multiplication?

2.32 [5] <§2.7> {Ex. 2.31} Your hardware engineering team has indicated that it would be possible to reduce the number of cycles required for multiplication to 6 in Exercise 2.31, but this will require a 20% increase in the cycle time. Nothing else will be affected. Should they proceed with the modification?

2.33 [10] <§§2.1–2.7> Consider the following hypothetical news release:

"The company will unveil the industry's first 800-MHz version of the chip, which offers a 20% performance boost over the company's former speed champ, which runs at 666 MHz. The new chip can be plugged into system boards for the older original chip (which ran at 400 MHz) to provide a 70% performance boost."

Comment on the definition (or definitions) of performance that you believe the company used. Do you think the news release is misleading?

2.34 [3 hours] <§2.5> Pick two computers, A and B, and run the Dhrystone benchmark and some substantial C program, such as the C compiler, calling this program P. Try running the two programs using no optimization and maximum optimization. Then calculate the following performance ratios:

a. Unoptimized Dhrystone on machine A versus unoptimized Dhrystone on machine B.

b. Unoptimized P on A versus unoptimized P on B.

c. Optimized Dhrystone on A versus optimized Dhrystone on B.

d. Optimized P on A versus optimized P on B.

e. Unoptimized Dhrystone versus optimized Dhrystone on machine A.

f. Unoptimized P versus optimized P on A.

g. Unoptimized Dhrystone versus optimized Dhrystone on B.

h. Unoptimized P versus optimized P on B.

We want to explore whether Dhrystone accurately predicts the performance of other C programs. If Dhrystone does predict performance, then the following equations should be true about the ratios:

(a) = (b) and (c) = (d)

If Dhrystone accurately predicts the value of compiler optimizations for real programs, then

(e) = (f) and (g) = (h)

Determine which of the above relationships hold. For the situations where the relationships are not close, try to find the explanation. Do features of the machines, the compiler optimizations, or the differences between P and Dhrystone explain the answer?

2.35 [3 hours] <§2.5> Perform the same experiment as in Exercise 2.34, replacing Dhrystone with Whetstone and choosing a floating-point program written in Fortran to replace P.

2.36 [4 hours] <§§2.4, 2.7> Devise a program in C or Pascal that determines the peak MIPS rating for a computer. Run it on two machines to calculate the peak MIPS. Now run a real C or Pascal program such as a compiler on the two machines. How well does peak MIPS predict performance of the real program?

2.37 [indefinite] <§§2.1–2.7> Collect a set of articles that you believe contain incorrect analyses of performance or use misleading performance metrics to try to persuade readers. For example, an article in the *New York Times* (April 20, 1994, p. D1) described a video game player "that will surpass the computing power of even the most powerful personal computers" and presented the following chart to support the argument that "video game machines may be the supercomputers of tomorrow":

Machine	Approximate number of instructions per second	Price
1975 IBM Mainframe	10,000,000	$10,000,000
1976 Cray-1	160,000,000	$20,000,000
1979 Digital VAX	1,000,000	$200,000
1981 IBM PC	250,000	$3,000
1984 Sun 2	1,000,000	$10,000
1994 Pentium-chip PC	66,000,000	$3,000
1995 Sony PCX video game	500,000,000	$500
1995 Microunity set-top	1,000,000,000	$500

The article never discussed how the nature of the instructions should impact the definition of "powerful." For each article you collect, describe why you think it is misleading or incorrect. Good places to look for material include the business or technology sections of newspapers, magazines (both articles and ads), and the Internet (newsgroups and the Web).

In More Depth

MFLOPS as a Performance Metric

Another popular alternative to execution time is *million floating-point operations per second*, abbreviated *megaFLOPS* or *MFLOPS* but always pronounced "megaflops." The formula for MFLOPS is simply the definition of the acronym:

$$\text{MFLOPS} = \frac{\text{Number of floating-point operations in a program}}{\text{Execution time} \times 10^6}$$

A *floating-point operation* is an addition, subtraction, multiplication, or division operation applied to a number in a single or double precision floating-point representation. Such data items are heavily used in scientific calculations and are specified in programming languages using key words like *float*, *real*, *double*, or *double precision*.

Clearly, a MFLOPS rating is dependent on the program. Different programs require the execution of different numbers of floating-point operations (see Exercise 2.38 for an example). Since MFLOPS were intended to measure floating-point performance, they are not applicable outside that range. Compilers, as an extreme example, have a MFLOPS rating near 0 no matter how fast the machine is, because compilers rarely use floating-point arithmetic.

Because it is based on operations in the program rather than on instructions, MFLOPS has a stronger claim than MIPS to being a fair comparison between different machines. The key to this claim is that the same program running on different computers may execute a different number of instructions but will always execute the same number of floating-point operations. Unfortunately, MFLOPS is not dependable because the set of floating-point operations is not consistent across machines, and the number of actual floating-point operations performed may vary. For example, the Cray-2 has no divide instruction, while the Motorola 68882 has divide, square root, sine, and cosine. Thus several floating-point operations are needed on the Cray-2 to perform a floating-point division, whereas on the Motorola 68882, a call to the sine routine, which would require performing several floating-point operations on most machines, would require only one operation.

Another potential problem is that the MFLOPS rating changes according not only to the mixture of integer and floating-point operations but to the mixture of fast and slow floating-point operations. For example, a program with 100% floating-point adds will have a higher rating than a program with 100% floating-point divides. The solution to both these problems is to define a method of counting the number of floating-point operations in a high-level language program. This counting process can also weight the operations, giving more complex operations larger weights, allowing a machine to achieve a high MFLOPS rating even if the program contains many floating-point divides. These MFLOPS might be called *normalized MFLOPS*. Of course, because of the counting and weighting, these normalized MFLOPS may be very different from the actual rate at which a machine executes floating-point operations.

Like any other performance measure, the MFLOPS rating for a single program cannot be generalized to establish a single performance metric for a computer. The use of the same term to refer to everything from peak performance (the maximum MFLOPS rate possible for any code segment), to the MFLOPS rate for one benchmark, to a normalized MFLOPS rating, only increases the confusion. The worst of these variants of MFLOPS, peak MFLOPS, is unrelated to actual performance; the best variant is redundant with execution time, our principal measure of performance. Yet, unlike execution time, it is tempting to characterize a machine with a single MFLOPS rating without naming the program or input.

2.38 [5] <§2.2> Find the MFLOPS ratings for each of the two programs on each machine in Exercise 2.26, assuming that each floating-point operation counts as 1 FLOP. How do the MFLOPS ratings for programs 1 and 2 compare for each machine? Does the example illustrate one of the problems discussed above?

2.39 [15] <§2.5> If performance is expressed as a rate, such as MFLOPS, then a higher rating and a higher average indicate better performance. When performance is expressed as a rate, the average that tracks total execution time is the *harmonic mean* (HM):

$$HM = \frac{n}{\sum_{i=1}^{n} \frac{1}{Rate_i}}$$

Each Rate$_i$ is $1/$Time$_i$, where Time$_i$ is the execution time for the ith of n programs in the workload. Prove that the harmonic mean of a set of rates tracks execution time by showing that it is the inverse of the arithmetic mean of the corresponding execution times.

2.40 [4 hours] <§2.4> Devise a program in C or Fortran that determines the peak MFLOPS rating for a computer. Run it on two machines to calculate the peak MFLOPS. Now run a real floating-point program on both machines. How well does peak MFLOPS predict performance of the real floating-point program?

In More Depth

Amdahl's Law

Amdahl's law is sometimes given in another form that yields the speedup. *Speedup* is the measure of how a machine performs after some enhancement relative to how it performed previously. Thus, if some feature yields a speedup ratio of 2, performance with the enhancement is twice what it was before the enhancement. Hence, we can write

$$\text{Speedup} = \frac{\text{Performance after improvement}}{\text{Performance before improvement}}$$

$$= \frac{\text{Execution time before improvement}}{\text{Execution time after improvement}}$$

The earlier version of Amdahl's law was given as

Execution time after improvement

$$= \left(\frac{\text{Execution time affected by improvement}}{\text{Amount of improvement}} + \text{Execution time unaffected} \right)$$

2.41 [5] <§2.7> Suppose we enhance a machine to make all floating-point instructions run five times faster. Let's look at how speedup behaves when we incorporate the faster floating-point hardware. If the execution time of some benchmark before the floating-point enhancement is 10 seconds, what will the speedup be if half of the 10 seconds is spent executing floating-point instructions?

2.42 [10] <§2.7> We are looking for a benchmark to show off the new floating-point unit described in Exercise 2.41, and we want the overall benchmark to show a speedup of 3. One benchmark we are considering runs for 100 seconds with the old floating-point hardware. How much of the initial execution time would floating-point instructions have to account for to show an overall speedup of 3 on this benchmark?

2.43 [10] <§2.7> Assuming that we enhance the floating-point unit as described in Exercise 2.41, plot the speedup obtained, versus the fraction of time in the original program spent doing floating-point operations, on a graph of the following form:

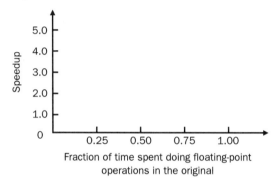

Fraction of time spent doing floating-point operations in the original

2.44 [5] <§2.7> You are going to enhance a machine, and there are two possible improvements: either make multiply instructions run four times faster than before, or make memory access instructions run two times faster than before. You repeatedly run a program that takes 100 seconds to execute. Of this time, 20% is used for multiplication, 50% for memory access instructions, and 30% for other tasks. What will the speedup be if you improve only multiplication? What will the speedup be if you improve only memory access? What will the speedup be if both improvements are made?

2.45 [5] <§2.7> {Ex. 2.44} You are going to change the program described in Exercise 2.44 so that the percentages are not 20%, 50%, and 30% anymore. Assuming that none of the new percentages is 0, what sort of program would result in a tie (with regard to speedup) between the two individual improvements? Provide both a formula and some examples.

2.46 [20] <§2.7> Amdahl's law is often written in terms of overall speedup as a function of two variables: the size of the enhancement (or amount of improvement) and the fraction of the original execution time that the enhanced feature is being used. Derive this form of the equation from the two equations above.

3

Instructions: Language of the Machine

I speak Spanish to God,
Italian to women,
French to men,
and German to my horse.

Charles V, King of France
1337–1380

3.1   **Introduction**   106

3.2   **Operations of the Computer Hardware**   107

3.3   **Operands of the Computer Hardware**   109

3.4   **Representing Instructions in the Computer**   116

3.5   **Instructions for Making Decisions**   122

3.6   **Supporting Procedures in Computer Hardware**   132

3.7   **Beyond Numbers**   142

3.8   **Other Styles of MIPS Addressing**   145

3.9   **Starting a Program**   156

3.10   **An Example to Put It All Together**   163

3.11   **Arrays versus Pointers**   171

3.12   **Real Stuff: PowerPC and 80x86 Instructions**   175

3.13   **Fallacies and Pitfalls**   185

3.14   **Concluding Remarks**   187

3.15   **Historical Perspective and Further Reading**   189

3.16   **Key Terms**   196

3.17   **Exercises**   196

The Five Classic Components of a Computer

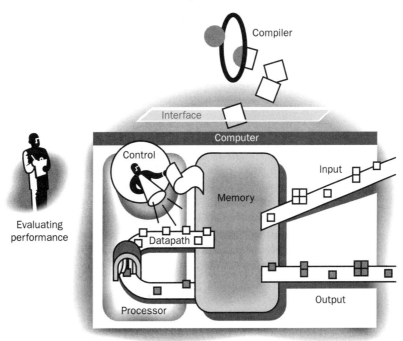

3.1   Introduction

To command a computer's hardware, you must speak its language. The words of a machine's language are called *instructions*, and its vocabulary is called an *instruction set*. In this chapter you will see the instruction set of a real computer, both in the form written by humans and in the form read by the machine. Starting from a notation that looks like a restricted programming language, we refine it step-by-step until you see the real language of a real computer.

You might think that the languages of machines would be as diverse as those of humans, but in reality machine languages are quite similar, more like regional dialects than like independent languages. Hence once you learn one, it is easy to pick up others. This similarity occurs because all computers are constructed from hardware technologies based on similar underlying principles and because there are a few basic operations that all machines must provide. Moreover, computer designers have a common goal: to find a language that makes it easy to build the hardware and the compiler while maximizing performance and minimizing cost. This goal is time-honored; the following quote was written before you could buy a computer, and it is as true today as it was in 1947.

> *It is easy to see by formal-logical methods that there exist certain [instruction sets] that are in abstract adequate to control and cause the execution of any sequence of operations. . . . The really decisive considerations from the present point of view, in selecting an [instruction set], are more of a practical nature: simplicity of the equipment demanded by the [instruction set], and the clarity of its application to the actually important problems together with the speed of its handling of those problems.*

> Burks, Goldstine, and von Neumann, 1947

The "simplicity of the equipment" is as valuable a consideration for the machines of the 2000s as it was for those of the 1950s. The goal of this chapter is to teach an instruction set that follows this advice, showing both how it is represented in the hardware and the relationship between high-level programming languages and this more primitive one. We are using the C programming language. (If you are familiar with Pascal, you may wish to refer to Web Extension III, available at *www.mkp.com/cod2e.htm*, for a short comparison of C with Pascal.)

By learning how instructions are represented, you will also discover the secret of computing: the stored-program concept. And you will exercise your "foreign language" skills by writing programs in the language of the machine and running them on the simulator that comes with this book. We conclude with a look at the historical evolution of instruction sets and an overview of other machine dialects.

The chosen instruction set comes from MIPS, used by NEC, Nintendo, Silicon Graphics, and Sony, among others, and is typical of instruction sets designed since the early 1980s. We reveal the MIPS instruction set a piece at a time, giving the rationale along with the machine structures. This step-by-step tutorial weaves the components with their explanations, making assembly language more palatable. To keep the overall picture in mind, each section ends with a figure summarizing the MIPS instruction set revealed thus far, highlighting the portions presented in that section.

3.2 Operations of the Computer Hardware

There must certainly be instructions for performing the fundamental arithmetic operations.

Burks, Goldstine, and von Neumann, 1947

Every computer must be able to perform arithmetic. The MIPS assembly language notation

```
add a, b, c
```

instructs a computer to add the two variables b and c and to put their sum in a.

This notation is rigid in that each MIPS arithmetic instruction performs only one operation and must always have exactly three variables. For example, suppose we want to place the sum of variables b, c, d, and e into variable a. (In this section we are being deliberately vague about what a "variable" is; in the next section we'll give a more detailed and realistic picture.)

The following sequence of instructions adds the variables:

```
add a, b, c   # The sum of b and c is placed in a.
add a, a, d   # The sum of b, c, and d is now in a.
add a, a, e   # The sum of b, c, d, and e is now in a.
```

Thus it takes three instructions to take the sum of four variables.

The words to the right of the sharp symbol (#) on each line above are *comments* for the human reader, and they are ignored by the computer. Note that unlike other programming languages, each line of this language can contain at most one instruction. Another difference is that comments always terminate at the end of a line.

The natural number of operands for an operation like addition is three: the two numbers being added together and a place to put the sum. Requiring every instruction to have exactly three operands, no more and no less, conforms to the philosophy of keeping the hardware simple: hardware for a variable number of operands is more complicated than hardware for a fixed number. This situation illustrates the first of four underlying principles of hardware design:

Design Principle 1: Simplicity favors regularity.

We can now show, in the two examples that follow, the relationship of programs written in higher-level programming languages to programs in this more primitive notation. Figure 3.1 summarizes the portions of MIPS assembly language described in this section.

Compiling Two C Assignment Statements into MIPS

Example

This segment of a C program contains the five variables a, b, c, d, and e:

```
a = b + c;
d = a - e;
```

The translation from C to MIPS assembly language instructions is performed by the *compiler*. Show the MIPS code produced by a C compiler.

Answer

A MIPS instruction operates on two source operands and places the result in one destination operand. Hence the two simple C statements above compile directly into these two MIPS assembly language instructions:

```
add a, b, c
sub d, a, e
```

MIPS assembly language

Category	Instruction	Example	Meaning	Comments
Arithmetic	add	add a,b,c	a = b + c	Always three operands
	subtract	sub a,b,c	a = b - c	Always three operands

FIGURE 3.1   MIPS architecture revealed in section 3.2. The real machine operands will be unveiled in the next section. Highlighted portions in such summaries show MIPS assembly language structures introduced in this section; for this first figure, all is new.

Compiling a Complex C Assignment into MIPS

Example

A somewhat complex C statement contains the five variables f, g, h, i, and j:

```
f = (g + h) - (i + j);
```

What would a C compiler produce?

Answer

The compiler must break this C statement into several assembly instructions since only one operation is performed per MIPS instruction. The first MIPS instruction calculates the sum of g and h. We must place the result somewhere, so the compiler creates a temporary variable, called t0:

```
add t0,g,h  # temporary variable t0 contains g + h
```

Although the next C operation is subtract, we need to calculate the sum of i and j before we can subtract. Thus the second instruction places the sum i and j in another temporary variable created by the compiler, called t1:

```
add t1,i,j  # temporary variable t1 contains i + j
```

Finally, the subtract instruction subtracts the second sum from the first and places the result in the variable f, completing the compiled code:

```
sub f,t0,t1 # f gets t0 - t1, which is (g + h)-(i + j)
```

These instructions are symbolic representations of what the MIPS processor actually understands. In the next few sections we will evolve this symbolic representation into the real language of MIPS, with each step making the symbolic representation more concrete.

3.3

Operands of the Computer Hardware

Unlike programs in high-level languages, the operands of arithmetic instructions cannot be any variables; they must be from a limited number of special locations called *registers*. Registers are the bricks of computer construction, for registers are primitives used in hardware design that are also visible to the programmer when the computer is completed. The size of a register in the MIPS architecture is 32 bits; groups of 32 bits occur so frequently that they are given the name *word* in the MIPS architecture.

One major difference between the variables of a programming language and registers is the limited number of registers, typically 32 on current computers. MIPS has 32 registers. (See section 3.15 for the history of the number of registers.) Thus, continuing in our stepwise evolution of the symbolic representation of the MIPS language, in this section we have added the restriction that the three operands of MIPS arithmetic instructions must each be chosen from one of the 32 32-bit registers.

The reason for the limit to 32 registers may be found in the second of our four underlying design principles of hardware technology:

Design Principle 2: Smaller is faster.

A very large number of registers would increase the clock cycle time simply because it takes electronic signals longer when they must travel farther.

Guidelines such as "smaller is faster" are not absolutes; 31 registers may not be faster than 32. Yet the truth behind such observations causes computer designers to take them seriously. In this case, the designer must balance the craving of programs for more registers with the designer's desire to keep the clock cycle fast.

Chapters 5 and 6 show the central role that registers play in hardware construction; as we shall see in this chapter, effective use of registers is key to program performance.

Although we could simply write instructions using numbers for registers, from 0 to 31, the MIPS convention is to use two character names following a dollar sign to represent a register. Section 3.6 will explain the reasons behind these names. For now we will use $s0, $s1, . . . for registers that correspond to variables in C programs and $t0, $t1, . . . for temporary registers needed to compile the program into MIPS instructions.

Compiling a C Assignment Using Registers

Example

It is the compiler's job to associate program variables with registers. Take, for instance, the C assignment statement from our earlier example:

```
f = (g + h) - (i + j);
```

The variables f, g, h, i, and j can be assigned to the registers $s0, $s1, $s2, $s3, and $s4, respectively. What is the compiled MIPS assembly code?

Answer

The compiled program is very similar to the prior example, except we replace the variables with the registers mentioned above plus two temporary registers, $t0 and $t1, which correspond to the temporary variables above:

```
add $t0,$s1,$s2   # register $t0 contains g + h
add $t1,$s3,$s4   # register $t1 contains i + j
sub $s0,$t0,$t1   # f gets $t0 - $t1, which is (g + h)-(i + j)
```

Programming languages have simple variables that contain single data elements as in these examples, but they also have more complex data structures such as arrays. These complex data structures can contain many more data elements than there are registers in a machine. How can a computer represent and access such large structures?

Recall the five components of a computer introduced in Chapter 1 and depicted on page 105. The processor can keep only a small amount of data in registers, but computer memory contains millions of data elements. Hence data structures, such as arrays, are kept in memory.

As explained above, arithmetic operations occur only on registers in MIPS instructions; thus MIPS must include instructions that transfer data between memory and registers. Such instructions are called *data transfer* instructions. To access a word in memory, the instruction must supply the memory *address*. Memory is just a large, single-dimensional array, with the address acting as the index to that array, starting at 0. For example, in Figure 3.2, the address of the third data element is 2, and the value of Memory[2] is 10.

The data transfer instruction that moves data from memory to a register is traditionally called *load*. The format of the load instruction is the name of the operation followed by the register to be loaded, then a constant and register used to access memory. The memory address is formed by the sum of the constant portion of the instruction and the contents of the second register. The actual MIPS name for this instruction is lw, standing for *load word*.

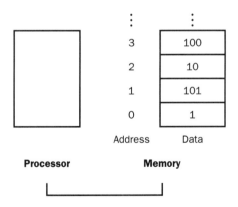

FIGURE 3.2 Memory addresses and contents of memory at those locations. This is a simplification of the MIPS addressing; Figure 3.3 shows MIPS addressing for sequential words in memory.

Compiling an Assignment When an Operand Is in Memory

Example

Let's assume that A is an array of 100 words and that the compiler has associated the variables g and h with the registers $s1 and $s2 as before. Let's also assume that the starting address, or *base address,* of the array is in $s3. Translate this C assignment statement:

```
g = h + A[8];
```

Answer

Although there is a single operation in this C assignment statement, one of the operands is in memory, so we must first transfer A[8] to a register. The address of this array element is the sum of the base of the array A, found in register $s3, plus the number to select element 8. The data should be placed in a temporary register for use in the next instruction. Thus the first compiled instruction is

```
lw    $t0,8($s3) # Temporary reg $t0 gets A[8]
```

The following instruction can operate on the value in $t0 (which equals A[8]) since it is in a register. The instruction must add h ($s2) to A[8] ($t0) and put the sum in the register corresponding to g ($s1):

```
add   $s1,$s2,$t0 # g = h + A[8]
```

The constant in a data transfer instruction is called the *offset,* and the register added to form the address is called the *base register.*

Hardware Software Interface

In addition to associating variables with registers, the compiler allocates data structures like arrays and structures to locations in memory. The compiler can then place the proper starting address into the data transfer instructions.

Since 8-bit *bytes* are useful in many programs, most architectures address individual bytes. Therefore the address of a word matches the address of one of the 4 bytes within the word. Hence, addresses of sequential words differ by 4. For example, Figure 3.3 shows the actual MIPS addresses for Figure 3.2; the byte address of the third word is 8.

Words must always start at addresses that are multiples of 4 in MIPS. This requirement is called an *alignment restriction,* and many architectures have it. (Chapter 5 suggests why alignment leads to faster data transfers.)

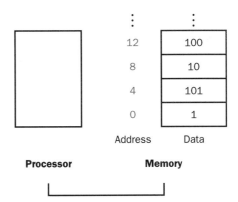

FIGURE 3.3 Actual MIPS memory addresses and contents of memory for those words.
The changed addresses are highlighted to contrast with Figure 3.2. Since MIPS addresses each byte, word addresses are multiples of four (there are four bytes in a word).

Machines with byte addresses are split into those that use the address of the leftmost or "big end" byte as the word address versus those that use the rightmost or "little end" byte. MIPS is in the *Big Endian* camp. (Appendix A, section A.9 on page A-38, shows the two options to number bytes in a word.)

Byte addressing also affects the array index. To get the proper byte address in the code above, the offset to be added to the base register $\$s3$ must be 4×8, or 32, so that the load address will select A[8] and not A[8/4].

The instruction complementary to load is traditionally called *store*; it transfers data from a register to memory. The format of a store is similar to that of a load: the name of the operation, followed by the register to be stored, then offset to select the array element, and finally the base register. Once again, the MIPS address is specified in part by a constant and in part by the contents of a register. The actual MIPS name is sw, standing for *store word*.

Compiling Using Load and Store

Example

Assume variable h is associated with register $\$s2$ and the base address of the array A is in $\$s3$. What is the MIPS assembly code for the C assignment statement below?

    A[8] = h + A[8];

Answer

Although there is a single operation in the C statement, now two of the operands are in memory, so we need even more MIPS instructions. The first two instructions are the same as the prior example, except this time we use the proper offset for byte addressing in the load word instruction to select A[8], and the add instruction places the sum in $t0:

```
lw    $t0,32($s3)    # Temporary reg $t0 gets A[8]
add   $t0,$s2,$t0    # Temporary reg $t0 gets h + A[8]
```

The final instruction stores the sum into A[12], using 48 as the offset and register $s3 as the base register.

```
sw    $t0,48($s3)    # Stores h + A[8] back into A[12]
```

Arrays are often accessed with variables instead of constants, so that the array element being selected can change while the program is running.

Compiling Using a Variable Array Index

Example

Here is an example of an array with a variable index:

```
g = h + A[i];
```

Assume A is an array of 100 elements whose base is in register $s3 and that the compiler associates the variables g, h, and i with the registers $s1, $s2, and $s4. What is the MIPS assembly code corresponding to this C segment?

Answer

Before we can load A[i] into a temporary register, we need to have its address. Before we can add i to the base of array A to form the address, we must multiply the index i by 4 due to the byte addressing problem. We will see a multiply instruction in the next chapter; for now we will get the effect of multiplying i by 4 by first adding i to itself (i + i = 2i) and then adding that sum to itself (2i + 2i = 4i):

```
add $t1,$s4,$s4    # Temp reg $t1 = 2 * i
add $t1,$t1,$t1    # Temp reg $t1 = 4 * i
```

To get the address of A[i], we need to add $t1 and the base of A in $s3:

```
add $t1,$t1,$s3    # $t1 = address of A[i] (4 * i + $s3)
```

Now we can use that address to load A[i] into a temporary register:

```
lw   $t0,0($t1)  # Temporary reg $t0 = A[i]
```

The final instruction adds A[i] and h, and places the sum in g:

```
add  $s1,$s2,$t0 # g = h + A[i]
```

Hardware Software Interface

Many programs have more variables than machines have registers. Consequently, the compiler tries to keep the most frequently used variables in registers and places the rest in memory, using loads and stores to move variables between registers and memory. The process of putting less commonly used variables (or those needed later) into memory is called *spilling* registers.

The hardware principle relating size and speed suggests that memory must be slower than registers since registers are smaller. This is indeed the case; data accesses are faster if data is kept in registers instead of memory.

Moreover, data is more useful when in a register. A MIPS arithmetic instruction can read two registers, operate on them, and write the result. A MIPS data transfer instruction only reads one operand or writes one operand, without operating on it.

Thus MIPS registers take both less time to access *and* have higher throughput than memory—a rare combination—making data in registers both faster to access and simpler to use. To achieve highest performance, MIPS compilers must use registers efficiently.

Figure 3.4 summarizes the portions of the symbolic representation of the MIPS instruction set described in this section. Load word and store word are the instructions that transfer words between memory and registers in the MIPS architecture. Other brands of computers use instructions in addition to load and store to transfer data. An architecture with such alternatives is the Intel 80x86, described in section 3.12.

Elaboration: The offset plus base register addressing is an excellent match to structures as well, since the register can point to the beginning of the structure and the offset can select the desired element. We'll see such an example in section 3.10.

The register in the data transfer instructions was originally invented to hold an index of an array with the offset used for the starting address of an array. Thus the base register is also called the *index register*. Today's memories are much larger and the software model of data allocation is more sophisticated, so the base address of the array is normally passed in a register since it won't fit in the offset, as we shall see.

MIPS operands

Name	Example	Comments
32 registers	$s0, $s1, . . . , $t0, $t1, . . .	Fast locations for data. In MIPS, data must be in registers to perform arithmetic.
2^{30} memory words	Memory[0], Memory[4], . . . , Memory[4294967292]	Accessed only by data transfer instructions in MIPS. MIPS uses byte addresses, so sequential words differ by 4. Memory holds data structures, such as arrays, and spilled registers.

MIPS assembly language

Category	Instruction	Example	Meaning	Comments
Arithmetic	add	add $s1,$s2,$s3	$s1 = $s2 + $s3	three operands; data in registers
	subtract	sub $s1,$s2,$s3	$s1 = $s2 – $s3	three operands; data in registers
Data transfer	load word	lw $s1,100($s2)	$s1 = Memory[$s2 + 100]	Data from memory to register
	store word	sw $s1,100($s2)	Memory[$s2 + 100] = $s1	Data from register to memory

FIGURE 3.4   MIPS architecture revealed through section 3.3. Highlighted portions show MIPS assembly language structures introduced in section 3.3.

3.4   Representing Instructions in the Computer

We are now ready to explain the difference between the way humans instruct machines and the way machines see instructions. But first, let's quickly review how a machine represents numbers.

Humans are taught to think in base 10, but numbers may be represented in any base. For example, 123 base 10 = 1111011 base 2.

Numbers are kept in computer hardware as a series of high and low electronic signals, and so they are considered base 2 numbers. (Just as base 10 numbers are called *decimal* numbers, base 2 numbers are called *binary* numbers.) A single digit of a binary number is thus the "atom" of computing, since all information is composed of binary digits or *bits*. This fundamental building block can be one of two values, which can be thought of as several alternatives: high or low, on or off, true or false, or 1 or 0.

Instructions are also kept in the computer as a series of high and low electronic signals and may be represented as numbers. In fact, each piece of an instruction can be considered as an individual number, and placing these numbers side by side forms the instruction.

Since registers are part of almost all instructions, there must be a convention to map register names into numbers. In MIPS assembly language, registers $s0 to $s7 map onto registers 16 to 23, and registers $t0 to $t7 map onto registers 8 to 15. Hence $s0 means register 16, $s1 means register 17, $s2 means register 18, . . . , $t0 means register 8, $t1 means register 9, and so on. We'll describe the convention for the rest of the 32 registers in the following sections.

Translating a MIPS Assembly Instruction into a Machine Instruction

Example

Let's do the next step in the refinement of the MIPS language as an example. We'll show the real MIPS language version of the instruction represented symbolically as

```
add $t0,$s1,$s2
```

first as a combination of decimal numbers and then of binary numbers.

Answer

The decimal representation is

0	17	18	8	0	32

Each of these segments of an instruction is called a *field*. The first and last fields (containing 0 and 32 in this case) in combination tell the MIPS computer that this instruction performs addition. The second field gives the number of the register that is the first source operand of the addition operation (17 = $s1) and the third field gives the other source operand for the addition (18 = $s2).The fourth field contains the number of the register that is to receive the sum (8 = $t0). The fifth field is unused in this instruction, so it is set to 0. Thus this instruction adds register $s1 to register $s2 and places the sum in register $t0.

This instruction can also be represented as fields of binary numbers as opposed to decimal:

000000	10001	10010	01000	00000	100000
6 bits	5 bits	5 bits	5 bits	5 bits	6 bits

To distinguish it from assembly language, we call the numeric version of instructions *machine language* and a sequence of such instructions *machine code*.

This layout of the instruction is called the *instruction format*. As you can see from counting the number of bits, this MIPS instruction takes exactly 32 bits— the same size as a data word. In keeping with our design principle that simplicity favors regularity, all MIPS instructions are 32 bits long.

MIPS Fields

MIPS fields are given names to make them easier to discuss:

op	rs	rt	rd	shamt	funct
6 bits	5 bits	5 bits	5 bits	5 bits	6 bits

Here is the meaning of each name of the fields in MIPS instructions:

- *op*: Basic operation of the instruction, traditionally called the *opcode*.
- *rs*: The first register source operand.
- *rt*: The second register source operand.
- *rd*: The register destination operand, it gets the result of the operation.
- *shamt*: Shift amount. (This term is explained in Chapter 4 when we see the shift instructions; it will not be used until then, and hence the field contains zero.)
- *funct*: Function. This field selects the specific variant of the operation in the op field, and is sometimes called the *function code*.

A problem occurs when an instruction needs longer fields than those shown above. For example, the load word instruction must specify two registers and a constant. If the address were to use one of the 5-bit fields in the format above, the constant within the load word instruction would be limited to only 2^5 or 32. This constant is used to select elements from large arrays or data structures, and it often needs to be much larger than 32. This 5-bit field is too small to be useful.

Hence we have a conflict between the desire to keep all instructions the same length and the desire to have a single instruction format. This leads us to the third hardware design principle:

Design Principle 3: Good design demands good compromises.

The compromise chosen by the MIPS designers is to keep all instructions the same length, thereby requiring different kinds of instruction formats for different kinds of instructions. For example, the format above is called *R-type* (for register) or *R-format*. A second type of instruction format is called *I-type* or *I-format* and is used by the data transfer instructions. The fields of I-format are

op	rs	rt	address
6 bits	5 bits	5 bits	16 bits

The 16-bit address means a load word instruction can load any word within a region of $\pm 2^{15}$ or 32,768 bytes (2^{13} or 8192 words) of the address in the base register rs.

Let's take a look at the load word instruction from page 114:

```
lw    $t0,32($s3)      # Temporary reg $t0 gets A[8]
```

Here, 19 (for $s3) is placed in the rs field, 8 (for $t0) is placed in the rt field, and 32 is placed in the address field. Note that the meaning of the rt field has changed for this instruction: in a load word instruction, the rt field specifies the *destination* register, which receives the result of the load.

Although multiple formats complicate the hardware, we can reduce the complexity by keeping the formats similar. For example, the first three fields of the R-type and I-type formats are the same size and have the same names; the fourth field in I-type is equal to the length of the last three fields of R-type.

In case you were wondering, the formats are distinguished by the values in the first field: each format is assigned a distinct set of values in the first field (op) so that the hardware knows whether to treat the last half of the instruction as three fields (R-type) or as a single field (I-type). Figure 3.5 shows the numbers used in each field for the MIPS instructions covered through section 3.3.

Instruction	Format	op	rs	rt	rd	shamt	funct	address
add	R	0	reg	reg	reg	0	32	n.a.
sub (subtract)	R	0	reg	reg	reg	0	34	n.a.
lw (load word)	I	35	reg	reg	n.a.	n.a.	n.a.	address
sw (store word)	I	43	reg	reg	n.a.	n.a.	n.a.	address

FIGURE 3.5 MIPS instruction encoding. In the table above, "reg" means a register number between 0 and 31, "address" means a 16-bit address, and "n.a." (not applicable) means this field does not appear in this format. Note that add and sub instructions have the same value in the op field; the hardware uses the funct field to decide the variant of the operation: add (32) or subtract (34).

Translating MIPS Assembly Language into Machine Language

Example

We can now take an example all the way from what the programmer writes to what the machine executes. Assuming that $t1 has the base of the array A and that $s2 corresponds to h, the C assignment statement

```
A[300] = h + A[300];
```

is compiled into

```
lw    $t0,1200($t1) # Temporary reg $t0 gets A[300]
add   $t0,$s2,$t0   # Temporary reg $t0 gets h + A[300]
sw    $t0,1200($t1) # Stores h + A[i] back into A[300]
```

What is the MIPS machine language code for these three instructions?

Answer   For convenience, let's first represent the machine language instructions using decimal numbers. From Figure 3.5 we can determine the three machine language instructions:

op	rs	rt	rd	address/shamt	funct
35	9	8		1200	
0	18	8	8	0	32
43	9	8		1200	

The lw instruction is identified by 35 (see Figure 3.5) in the first field (op). The base register 9 ($t1) is specified in the second field (rs), and the destination register 8 ($t0) is specified in the third field (rt). The offset to select A[300] (1200 = 300 × 4) is found in the final field (address).

The add instruction that follows is specified with 0 in the first field (op) and 32 in the last field (funct). The three register operands ($18, $8, and $8) are found in the second, third, and fourth fields and correspond to $s2, $t0, and $t0.

The sw instruction is identified with 43 in the first field. The rest of this final instruction is identical to the lw instruction.

The binary equivalent to the decimal form is the following (1200 in base 10 is 0000 0100 1011 0000 base 2):

100011	01001	01000	0000 0100 1011 0000		
000000	10010	01000	01000	00000	100000
101011	01001	01000	0000 0100 1011 0000		

Note the similarity of the binary representations of the first and last instructions. The only difference is found in the third bit from the left.

Figure 3.6 summarizes the portions of MIPS assembly language described in this section. As we shall see in Chapters 5 and 6, the similarity of the binary representations of related instructions simplifies hardware design. These instructions are another example of regularity in the MIPS architecture.

Elaboration: Representing decimal numbers in base 2 gives an easy way to represent positive integers in computer words. Chapter 4 explains how negative numbers can be represented, but for now take it on faith that a 32-bit word can represent integers between -2^{31} and $+2^{31} -1$ or $-2,147,483,648$ to $+2,147,483,647$. Such integers are called *two's complement* numbers.

MIPS operands

Name	Example	Comments
32 registers	$s0, $s1, ..., $s7 $t0, $t1, ..., $t7	Fast locations for data. In MIPS, data must be in registers to perform arithmetic. Registers $s0–$s7 map to 16–23 and $t0–$t7 map to 8–15.
2^{30} memory words	Memory[0], Memory[4], . . . , Memory[4294967292]	Accessed only by data transfer instructions in MIPS. MIPS uses byte addresses, so sequential words differ by 4. Memory holds data structures, such as arrays, and spilled registers.

MIPS assembly language

Category	Instruction	Example	Meaning	Comments
Arithmetic	add	add $s1,$s2,$s3	$s1 = $s2 + $s3	Three operands; data in registers
	subtract	sub $s1,$s2,$s3	$s1 = $s2 - $s3	Three operands; data in registers
Data transfer	load word	lw $s1,100($s2)	$s1 = Memory[$s2 + 100]	Data from memory to register
	store word	sw $s1,100($s2)	Memory[$s2 + 100] = $s1	Data from register to memory

MIPS machine language

Name	Format	Example						Comments
add	R	0	18	19	17	0	32	add $s1,$s2,$s3
sub	R	0	18	19	17	0	34	sub $s1,$s2,$s3
lw	I	35	18	17	100			lw $s1,100($s2)
sw	I	43	18	17	100			sw $s1,100($s2)
Field size		6 bits	5 bits	5 bits	5 bits	5 bits	6 bits	All MIPS instructions 32 bits
R-format	R	op	rs	rt	rd	shamt	funct	Arithmetic instruction format
I-format	I	op	rs	rt	address			Data transfer format

FIGURE 3.6   MIPS architecture revealed through section 3.4. Highlighted portions show MIPS machine language structures introduced in section 3.4. The two MIPS instruction formats so far are R and I. The first 16 bits are the same: both contain an *op* field, giving the base operation; an *rs* field, giving one of the sources; and the *rt* field, which specifies the other source operand, except for load word, where it specifies the destination register. R-format divides the last 16 bits into an *rd* field, specifying the destination register; *shamt* field, which is unused in Chapter 3 and hence always is 0; and the *funct* field, which specifies the specific operation of R-format instructions. I-format keeps the last 16 bits as a single *address* field.

The Big Picture

Today's computers are built on two key principles:

1. Instructions are represented as numbers.
2. Programs can be stored in memory to be read or written just like numbers.

These principles lead to the *stored-program* concept; its invention let the computing genie out of its bottle. Figure 3.7 shows the power of the concept; specifically, memory can contain the source code for an editor program, the corresponding compiled machine code, the text that the compiled program is using, and even the compiler that generated the machine code.

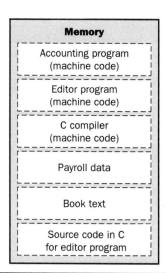

FIGURE 3.7   The stored-program concept. Stored programs allow a computer that performs accounting to become, in the blink of an eye, a computer that helps an author write a book. The switch happens simply by loading memory with programs and data and then telling the computer to begin executing at a given location in memory. Treating instructions in the same way as data greatly simplifies both the memory hardware and the software of computer systems. Specifically, the memory technology needed for data can also be used for programs, and programs like compilers, for instance, can translate code written in a notation far more convenient for humans into code that the machine can understand.

3.5   Instructions for Making Decisions

The utility of an automatic computer lies in the possibility of using a given sequence of instructions repeatedly, the number of times it is iterated being dependent upon the results of the computation. When the iteration is completed a different sequence of [instructions] is to be followed, so we must, in most cases, give two parallel trains of [instructions] preceded by an instruction as to which routine is to be followed. This choice can be made to depend upon the sign of a number (zero being reckoned as plus for machine purposes). Consequently, we introduce an [instruction] (the conditional transfer [instruction]) which will, depending on the sign of a given number, cause the proper one of two routines to be executed.

Burks, Goldstine, and von Neumann, 1947

What distinguishes a computer from a simple calculator is its ability to make decisions. Based on the input data and the values created during the computation, different instructions are executed. Decision making is commonly represented in programming languages using the *if* statement, sometimes combined with *go to* statements and labels. MIPS assembly language includes two decision-making instructions, similar to an *if* statement with a *go to*. The first instruction is

```
beq register1, register2, L1
```

This instruction means go to the statement labeled L1 if the value in register1 equals the value in register2. The mnemonic beq stands for *branch if equal*. The second instruction is

```
bne register1, register2, L1
```

It means go to the statement labeled L1 if the value in register1 does *not* equal the value in register2. The mnemonic bne stands for *branch if not equal*. These two instructions are traditionally called *conditional branches*.

Compiling an *If* Statement into a Conditional Branch

Example

In the following C code segment, f, g, h, i, and j are variables:

```
        if (i == j) go to L1;
        f = g + h;
L1:     f = f - i;
```

Assuming that the five variables f through j correspond to the five registers $s0 through $s4, what is the compiled MIPS code?

Answer

The first C statement compares for equality and then branches to the subtract operation. Since both the operands are in registers, this maps exactly to a branch if equal instruction (we'll define the label L1 later):

```
beq $s3,$s4, L1  # go to L1 if i equals j
```

The following C assignment statement performs a single operation, and if all the operands are allocated to registers, it is just one instruction:

```
add $s0,$s1,$s2  # f = g + h (skipped if i equals j)
```

The final statement can again be compiled into a single instruction. The problem is how to specify its address so that the conditional branch can skip the add instruction above.

Instructions are stored in memory in stored-program computers; hence instructions must have memory addresses just like other words in memory. The last instruction simply appends the label L1 that was forward-referenced by the beq instruction.

```
L1:      sub $s0,$s0,$s3  # f = f - i (always executed)
```

The label L1 thus corresponds to the address of the subtract instruction.

Notice that the assembler relieves the compiler or the assembly language programmer from the tedium of calculating addresses for branches, just as it does for calculating data addresses for loads and stores (see section 3.9).

Hardware Software Interface

Compilers frequently create branches and labels where they do not appear in the programming language. Avoiding the burden of writing explicit labels and branches is one benefit of writing in high-level programming languages and is a reason coding is faster at that level.

Compiling *if-then-else* into Conditional Branches

Example

Using the same variables and registers from the previous example, compile this C *if* statement:

```
if (i == j) f = g + h; else f = g - h;
```

Answer

Figure 3.8 is a flowchart of what the MIPS code should do. The first C expression compares for equality, so it would seem that we would want the beq as before. In general the code will be more efficient if we test for the opposite condition to branch over the code that performs the subsequent *then* part of the *if* (the label Else is defined below):

```
bne $s3,$s4,Else  # go to Else if i ≠ j
```

The next C assignment statement performs a single operation, and if all the operands are allocated to registers, it is just one instruction:

```
add $s0,$s1,$s2   # f = g + h (skipped if i ≠ j)
```

We now need to go to the end of the *if* statement. This example introduces another kind of branch, often called an *unconditional branch*. This instruction says that the machine always follows the branch. To distinguish between conditional and unconditional branches, the MIPS name for this type of instruction is *jump*, abbreviated as j (the label Exit is defined below).

```
j Exit          # go to Exit
```

The assignment statement in the *else* portion of the *if* statement can again be compiled into a single instruction. We just need to append the label Else to this instruction. We also show the label Exit that is after this instruction, showing the end of the *if-then-else* compiled code:

```
Else:   sub $s0,$s1,$s2 # f = g - h (skipped if i = j)
Exit:
```

Loops

Decisions are important both for choosing between two alternatives—found in *if* statements—and for iterating a computation—found in loops. The same assembly instructions are the building blocks for both cases.

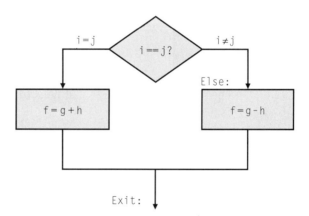

FIGURE 3.8   Illustration of the options in the *if* statement above. The left box corresponds to the *then* part of the *if* statement, and the right box corresponds to the *else* part.

Compiling a Loop with Variable Array Index

Here is a loop in C:

```
Loop:    g = g + A[i];
         i = i + j;
         if (i != h) go to Loop;
```

Assume A is an array of 100 elements and that the compiler associates the variables g, h, i, and j to the registers $s1, $s2, $s3, and $s4, respectively. Let's assume that the base of the array A is in $s5. What is the MIPS assembly code corresponding to this C loop?

The first step is to load A[i] into a temporary register. We borrow the code from the similar example that starts on page 114. We need only add the label Loop to the first instruction so that we can branch back to that instruction at the end of the loop:

```
Loop:    add $t1,$s3,$s3     # Temp reg $t1 = 2 * i
         add $t1,$t1,$t1     # Temp reg $t1 = 4 * i
         add $t1,$t1,$s5     # $t1 = address of A[i]
         lw  $t0,0($t1)      # Temporary reg $t0 = A[i]
```

The next two instructions add A[i] to g and then j to i:

```
         add $s1,$s1,$t0     # g = g + A[i]
         add $s3,$s3,$s4     # i = i + j
```

The final instruction branches back to Loop if i ≠ h:

```
         bne $s3,$s2, Loop   # go to Loop if i ≠ h
```

Since the body of the loop modifies i, we must multiply its value by 4 each time through the loop. (Section 3.11 shows how to avoid these "multiplies" when writing loops like this one.)

Hardware Software Interface

Such sequences of instructions that end in a branch are so fundamental to compiling that they are given their own buzzword: a *basic block* is a sequence of instructions without branches, except possibly at the end, and without branch targets or branch labels, except possibly at the beginning. One of the first early phases of compilation is breaking the program into basic blocks.

Compiling a *while* Loop

Example

Of course, programmers don't normally write loops with *go to* statements, so it is up to the compiler to translate traditional loops into MIPS language. Here is a traditional loop in C:

```
while (save[i] == k)
       i = i + j;
```

Assume that i, j, and k correspond to registers $s3, $s4, and $s5 and the base of the array save is in $s6. What is the MIPS assembly code corresponding to this C segment?

Answer

The first step is to load save[i] into a temporary register. It starts with code similar to the prior example:

```
Loop:    add $t1,$s3,$s3      # Temp reg $t1 = 2 * i
         add $t1,$t1,$t1      # Temp reg $t1 = 4 * i
         add $t1,$t1,$s6      # $t1 = address of save[i]
         lw  $t0,0($t1)       # Temp reg $t0 = save[i]
```

The next instruction performs the loop test, exiting if save[i] ≠ k:

```
         bne  $t0,$s5, Exit   # go to Exit if save[i] ≠ k
```

The next instruction adds j to i:

```
         add  $s3,$s3,$s4     # i = i + j
```

The end of the loop branches back to the *while* test at the top of the loop. We just add the Exit label after it, and we're done:

```
         j    Loop            # go to Loop
Exit:
```

(See Exercise 3.9 for an optimization of this sequence.)

The test for equality or inequality is probably the most popular test, but sometimes it is useful to see if a variable is less than another variable. For example, a *for* loop may want to test to see if the index variable is less than 0. Such comparisons are accomplished in MIPS assembly language with an instruction that compares two registers and sets a third register to 1 if the first is less than the second; otherwise, it is set to 0. The MIPS instruction is called *set on less than,* or slt. For example,

```
slt    $t0, $s3, $s4
```

means that register $t0 is set to 1 if the value in register $s3 is less than the value in register $s4; otherwise, register $t0 is set to 0.

Hardware Software Interface

MIPS compilers use the slt, beq, bne, and the fixed value of 0 always available by reading register $zero to create all relative conditions: equal, not equal, less than, less than or equal, greater than, greater than or equal. (As you might expect, register $zero maps to register 0.)

Compiling a Less Than Test

Example

What is the code to test if variable a (corresponding to register $s0) is less than variable b (register $s1) and then branch to label Less if the condition holds?

Answer

The first step is to use the set on less than instruction and a temporary register:

```
slt $t0,$s0,$s1          # $t0 gets 1 if $s0 < $s1 (a < b)
```

Register $t0 is set to 1 if a is less than b. Hence, a branch to see if register $t0 is not equal to 0 will give us the effect of branching if a is less than b. Register $zero always contains 0, so this final test is accomplished using the bne instruction and comparing register $t0 to register $zero:

```
bne $t0,$zero, Less      # go to Less if $t0 ≠ 0
                         #  (that is, if a < b)
```

This pair of instructions, slt and bne, implements branch on less than.

Heeding von Neumann's warning about the simplicity of the "equipment," the MIPS architecture doesn't include branch on less than because it is too complicated; either it would stretch the clock cycle time or this instruction would take extra clock cycles per instruction. Two faster instructions are more useful.

Case/Switch Statement

Most programming languages have a *case* or *switch* statement that allows the programmer to select one of many alternatives depending on a single value. One way to implement *switch* is via a sequence of conditional tests, turning the *switch* statement into a chain of *if-then-else* statements. But sometimes the alternatives may be efficiently encoded as a table of addresses of alternative instruction sequences, called a *jump address table*, and the program needs only to index into the table and then jump to the appropriate sequence. The jump table is then just an array of words containing addresses that correspond to labels in the code.

To support such situations, computers like MIPS include a *jump register* instruction (jr), meaning an unconditional jump to the address specified in a register. The program loads the appropriate entry from the jump table into a register, and then it jumps to the proper address using a jump register.

Compiling a *switch* Statement by Using a Jump Address Table

Example

This C version of a *case* statement is called a *switch* statement. The following C code chooses among four alternatives depending on whether k has the value 0, 1, 2, or 3.

```
switch (k) {
        case 0:   f = i + j; break; /* k = 0 */
        case 1:   f = g + h; break; /* k = 1 */
        case 2:   f = g - h; break; /* k = 2 */
        case 3:   f = i - j; break; /* k = 3 */
}
```

Assume the six variables f through k correspond to six registers $s0 through $s5 and that register $t2 contains 4. What is the corresponding MIPS code?

Answer

We use the *switch* variable k to index a jump address table, and then jump via the value loaded. We first test k to be sure it matches one of the cases (0 ≤ k ≤3); if not, the code exits the *switch* statement.

```
slt   $t3,$s5,$zero     # Test if k < 0
bne   $t3,$zero,Exit    # if k < 0, go to Exit
slt   $t3,$s5,$t2       # Test if k < 4
beq   $t3,$zero,Exit    # if k >= 4, go to Exit
```

Since we are using the variable k to index into this table of words, we must first multiply by 4 to turn k into its byte address:

```
add  $t1,$s5,$s5      # Temp reg $t1 = 2 * k
add  $t1,$t1,$t1      # Temp reg $t1 = 4 * k
```

Assume that four sequential words in memory, starting at an address contained in $t4, have addresses corresponding to the labels L0, L1, L2, and L3. We can now load the proper jump address this way:

```
add  $t1,$t1,$t4      # $t1 = address of JumpTable[k]
lw   $t0,0($t1)       # Temp reg $t0 = JumpTable[k]
```

A jump register instruction jumps via the register to the address from the jump table.

```
jr   $t0              # jump based on register $t0
```

The first three *switch* cases in this example are the same: a label, a single instruction performing the *case* statement, and then a jump to exit the *switch* statement:

```
L0: add  $s0,$s3,$s4   # k = 0 so f gets i + j
    j    Exit          # end of this case so go to Exit
L1: add  $s0,$s1,$s2   # k = 1 so f gets g + h
    j    Exit          # end of this case so go to Exit
L2: sub  $s0,$s1,$s2   # k = 2 so f gets g - h
    j    Exit          # end of this case so go to Exit
```

A more complex example might have several instructions for each case.

For the final case we drop the jump to exit (since this is the last instruction of the switch code) and append an Exit label afterwards to mark the end of the switch statement:

```
L3: sub  $s0,$s3,$s4   # k = 3 so f gets i - j
Exit:                  # end of switch statement
```

Figure 3.9 summarizes the portions of MIPS assembly language described in this section. This step along the evolution of the MIPS language has added branches and jumps to our symbolic representation, and fixes the useful value 0 permanently in a register.

Elaboration: If you have heard about *delayed branches*, covered in Chapter 6, don't worry: The MIPS assembler makes them invisible to the assembly language programmer. Also, for C programmers not familiar with the infinitely abusable go to statement, it transfers control from wherever it appears to the label.

MIPS operands

Name	Example	Comments
32 registers	$s0, $s1, ..., $s7 $t0, $t1, ...,$t7, $zero	Fast locations for data. In MIPS, data must be in registers to perform arithmetic. Registers $s0–$s7 map to 16–23 and $t0–$t7 map to 8–15. MIPS register $zero always equals 0.
2^{30} memory words	Memory[0], Memory[4], ..., Memory[4294967292]	Accessed only by data transfer instructions in MIPS. MIPS uses byte addresses, so sequential words differ by 4. Memory holds data structures, such as arrays, and spilled registers.

MIPS assembly language

Category	Instruction	Example	Meaning	Comments
Arithmetic	add	add $s1,$s2,$s3	$s1 = $s2 + $s3	Three operands; data in registers
	subtract	sub $s1,$s2,$s3	$s1 = $s2 – $s3	Three operands; data in registers
Data transfer	load word	lw $s1,100($s2)	$s1 = Memory[$s2 + 100]	Data from memory to register
	store word	sw $s1,100($s2)	Memory[$s2 + 100] = $s1	Data from register to memory
Conditional branch	branch on equal	beq $s1,$s2,L	if ($s1 == $s2) go to L	Equal test and branch
	branch on not equal	bne $s1,$s2,L	if ($s1 != $s2) go to L	Not equal test and branch
	set on less than	slt $s1,$s2,$s3	if ($s2 < $s3) $s1 = 1; else $s1 = 0	Compare less than; used with beq, bne
Unconditional jump	jump	j 2500	go to 10000	Jump to target address
	jump register	jr $t1	go to $t1	For *switch* statements

MIPS machine language

Name	Format	Example						Comments	
add	R	0	18	19	17	0	32	add	$s1,$s2,$s3
sub	R	0	18	19	17	0	34	sub	$s1,$s2,$s3
lw	I	35	18	17	100			lw	$s1,100($s2)
sw	I	43	18	17	100			sw	$s1,100($s2)
beq	I	4	17	18	25			beq	$s1,$s2,100
bne	I	5	17	18	25			bne	$s1,$s2,100
slt	R	0	18	19	17	0	42	slt	$s1,$s2,$s3
j	J	2	2500					j 10000 (see section 3.8)	
jr	R	0	9	0	0	0	8	jr	$t1
Field size		6 bits	5 bits	5 bits	5 bits	5 bits	6 bits	All MIPS instructions 32 bits	
R-format	R	op	rs	rt	rd	shamt	funct	Arithmetic instruction format	
I-format	I	op	rs	rt	address			Data transfer, branch format	

FIGURE 3.9   MIPS architecture revealed through section 3.5. Highlighted portions show MIPS structures introduced in section 3.5. The J-format, used for jump instructions, is explained in section 3.8. Section 3.8 also explains the proper values in address fields of branch instructions.

3.6   Supporting Procedures in Computer Hardware

A procedure or subroutine is one tool programmers use to structure programs, both to make them easier to understand and to allow code to be reused. Procedures allow the programmer to concentrate on just one portion of the task at a time, with parameters acting as a barrier between the procedure and the rest of the program and data, allowing it to be passed values and return results.

You can think of a procedure like a spy who leaves with a secret plan, acquires resources, performs the task, covers his tracks, and then returns to the point of origin with the desired result. Nothing else should be perturbed once the mission is complete. Moreover, a spy operates on only a "need to know" basis, so the spy can't make assumptions about his employer.

Similarly, in the execution of a procedure, the program must follow these six steps:

1. Place parameters in a place where the procedure can access them.

2. Transfer control to the procedure.

3. Acquire the storage resources needed for the procedure.

4. Perform the desired task.

5. Place the result value in a place where the calling program can access it.

6. Return control to the point of origin.

As mentioned above, registers are the fastest place to hold data in a computer, so we want to use them as much as possible. Hence MIPS software allocates the following of its 32 registers for procedure calling:

- $a0–$a3: four argument registers in which to pass parameters

- $v0–$v1: two value registers in which to return values

- $ra: one return address register to return to the point of origin

In addition to allocating these registers, MIPS assembly language includes an instruction just for the procedures: it jumps to an address and simultaneously saves the address of the following instruction in register $ra. The *jump-and-link* instruction (jal) is simply written

```
jal ProcedureAddress
```

The *link* portion of the name means that an address or link is formed that points to the calling site to allow the procedure to return to the proper address. This "link," stored in register $ra, is called the *return address*. The return address is needed because the same procedure could be called from several parts of the program.

Implicit in the stored-program idea is the need to have a register to hold the address of the current instruction being executed. For historical reasons, this register is almost always called the *program counter*, abbreviated *PC* in the MIPS architecture, although a more sensible name would have been *instruction address register*. The jal instruction saves PC + 4 in register $ra to link to the following instruction to set up the procedure return.

We already have an instruction to do the return jump:

```
jr   $ra
```

The jump register instruction, which we used above in the *switch* statement, jumps to the address stored in register $ra—which is just what we want. Thus the calling program, or *caller*, puts the parameter values in $a0–$a3, and uses jal X to jump to procedure X (sometimes named the *callee*). The callee then performs the calculations, places the results in $v0–$v1, and returns control to the caller using jr $ra.

Using More Registers

Suppose a compiler needs more registers for a procedure than the four argument and two return value registers. Since we are supposed to cover our tracks after our mission is complete, any registers needed by the caller must be restored to the values that they contained *before* the procedure was invoked. This situation is an example in which we need to spill registers to memory, as mentioned in the Hardware Software Interface section on page 115.

The ideal data structure for spilling registers is a *stack*—a last-in-first-out queue. A stack needs a pointer to the most recently allocated address in the stack to show where the next procedure should place the registers to be spilled or where old register values can be found. The stack pointer is adjusted by one word for each register that is saved or restored. Stacks are so popular that they have their own buzzwords for transferring data to and from the stack: placing data onto the stack is called a *push*, and removing data from the stack is called a *pop*.

MIPS software allocates another register just for the stack: the *stack pointer* ($sp), used to save the registers needed by the callee. By historical precedent, stacks "grow" from higher addresses to lower addresses. This convention means that you push values onto the stack by subtracting from the stack pointer. Adding to the stack pointer shrinks the stack, thereby popping values off the stack.

Compiling a Procedure that Doesn't Call Another Procedure

Example

Let's turn the example on page 109 into a procedure:

```
int leaf_example (int g, int h, int i, int j)
{
        int f;

        f = (g + h) - (i + j);
        return f;
}
```

For the rest of this section we assume we can add or subtract constants like 4, 8, or 12. (Section 3.8 reveals how constants are handled in MIPS assembly anguage.) What is the compiled MIPS assembly code?

Answer

The parameter variables g, h, i, and j correspond to the argument registers $a0, $a1, $a2, and $a3, and f corresponds to $s0. The compiled program starts with the label of the procedure:

```
leaf_example:
```

The next step is to save the registers used by the procedure. The C assignment statement in the procedure body is identical to the example on page 109, which uses two temporary registers. Thus we need to save three registers: $s0, $t0, and $t1. We create space for three words on the stack and then store the old values:

```
sub $sp,$sp,12   # adjust stack to make room for 3 items
sw  $t1, 8($sp)  # save register $t1 for use afterwards
sw  $t0, 4($sp)  # save register $t0 for use afterwards
sw  $s0, 0($sp)  # save register $s0 for use afterwards
```

Figure 3.10 shows the stack before, during, and after the procedure call. The next three statements correspond to the body of the procedure, which follows the example on page 109:

```
add $t0,$a0,$a1  # register $t0 contains g + h
add $t1,$a2,$a3  # register $t1 contains i + j
sub $s0,$t0,$t1  # f = $t0 - $t1, which is (g + h)-(i + j)
```

To return the value of f, we copy it into a return value register:

```
add $v0,$s0,$zero  # returns f ($v0 = $s0 + 0)
```

Before returning, we restore the old values of the registers we saved and then "pop" the stack to its original value:

```
lw   $s0, 0($sp)    # restore register $s0 for caller
lw   $t0, 4($sp)    # restore register $t0 for caller
lw   $t1, 8($sp)    # restore register $t1 for caller
add $sp,$sp,12      # adjust stack to delete 3 items
```

The procedure ends with a jump register using the return address:

```
jr   $ra            # jump back to calling routine
```

In the example above we used temporary registers and assumed their old values must be saved and restored. To avoid saving and restoring a register whose value is never used, which might happen with a temporary register, MIPS software offers two classes of registers:

- $t0–$t9: 10 temporary registers that are *not* preserved by the callee (called procedure) on a procedure call

- $s0–$s7: 8 saved registers that must be preserved on a procedure call (if used, the callee saves and restores them)

This simple convention reduces register spilling. In the example above, since the caller (procedure doing the calling) does not expect registers $t0 and $t1 to be preserved across a procedure call, we can drop two stores and two loads from the code. We still must save and restore $s0, since the callee must assume that the caller needs its value.

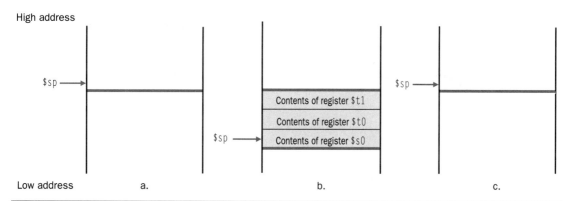

FIGURE 3.10   The values of the stack pointer and the stack (a) before, (b) during, and (c) after the procedure call. The stack pointer always points to the "top" of the stack, or the last word in the stack in this drawing.

Nested Procedures

Procedures that do not call others are called *leaf* procedures. Life would be simple if all procedures were leaf procedures, but they aren't. Just as a spy might employ other spies as part of a mission, who in turn might use even more spies, so do procedures invoke other procedures. Moreover, recursive procedures even invoke "clones" of themselves. Just as we need to be careful when using registers in procedures, more care must also be taken when invoking non-leaf procedures.

For example, suppose that the main program calls procedure A with an argument of 3, by placing the value 3 into register $a0 and then using jal A. Then suppose that procedure A calls procedure B via jal B with an argument of 7, also placed in $a0. Since A hasn't finished its task yet, there is a conflict over the use of register $a0. Similarly, there is a conflict over the return address in register $ra, since it now has the return address for B. Unless we take steps to prevent the problem, this conflict will eliminate procedure A's ability to return to its caller.

One solution is to push all the other registers that must be preserved onto the stack, just as we did with the saved registers. The caller pushes any argument registers ($a0–$a3) or temporary registers ($t0–$t9) that are needed after the call. The callee pushes the return address register $ra and any saved registers ($s0–$s7) used by the callee. The stack pointer $sp is adjusted to account for the number of registers placed on the stack. Upon the return, the registers are restored from memory and the stack pointer is readjusted.

Compiling a Recursive Procedure, Showing Nested Procedure Linking

Example   Let's tackle a recursive procedure that calculates factorial:

```
int fact (int n)
{
    if (n < 1) return (1);
        else return (n * fact(n-1));
}
```

Assume that you can add or subtract constants like 1 or 8, as we will show in section 3.8. What is the MIPS assembly code?

Answer
The parameter variable n corresponds to the argument register $a0. The compiled program starts with the label of the procedure and then saves two registers on the stack, the return address and $a0:

```
fact:
        sub     $sp,$sp,8    # adjust stack for 2 items
        sw      $ra, 4($sp)  # save the return address
        sw      $a0, 0($sp)  # save the argument n
```

The first time fact is called, sw saves an address in the program that called fact. The next two instructions test if n is less than 1, going to L1 if n ≥ 1.

```
        slt     $t0,$a0,1    # test for n < 1
        beq     $t0,$zero,L1 # if n >= 1, go to L1
```

If n is less than 1, fact returns 1 by putting 1 into a value register: it adds 1 to 0 and places that sum in $v0. It then pops the two saved values off the stack and jumps to the return address:

```
        add     $v0,$zero,1  # return 1
        add     $sp,$sp,8    # pop 2 items off stack
        jr      $ra          # return to after jal
```

Before popping two items off the stack, we could have loaded $a0 and $ra. Since $a0 and $ra don't change when n is less than 1, we skip those instructions.

If n is not less than 1, the argument n is decremented and then fact is called again with the decremented value:

```
L1:     sub     $a0,$a0,1    # n >= 1: argument gets (n - 1)
        jal     fact         # call fact with (n - 1)
```

The next instruction is where fact returns. Now the old return address and old argument are restored, along with the stack pointer:

```
        lw      $a0, 0($sp)  # return from jal: restore argument n
        lw      $ra, 4($sp)  # restore the return address
        add     $sp, $sp,8   # adjust stack pointer to pop 2 items
```

Next, the value register $v0 gets the product of old argument $a0 and the current value of the value register. We assume a multiply instruction is available, even though it is not covered until Chapter 4:

```
        mult    $v0,$a0,$v0  # return n * fact (n - 1)
```

Finally, fact jumps again to the return address:

```
        jr      $ra          # return to the caller
```

Preserved	Not preserved
Argument registers: $a0–$a3	Return value registers: $v0–$v1
Saved registers: $s0–$s7	Temporary registers: $t0–$t9
Stack pointer register: $sp	
Return address register: $ra	
Stack above the stack pointer	Stack below the stack pointer

FIGURE 3.11   What is and what is not preserved across a procedure call. If the software relies on the frame pointer register or on the global pointer register, discussed in the following sections, they are also preserved.

Figure 3.11 summarizes what is preserved across a procedure call. Note that several schemes are used to preserve the stack. The stack above $sp is preserved simply by making sure the callee does not write above $sp; $sp is itself preserved by the callee adding exactly the same amount that was subtracted from it, and the other registers are preserved by saving them on the stack (if they are used) and restoring them from there. These actions also guarantee that the caller will get the same data back on a load from the stack as it put into the stack on a store: because the callee promises to preserve $sp and because the callee also promises not to modify the caller's portion of the stack, that is, the area above the $sp at the time of the call.

Allocating Space for New Data

The final complexity is that the stack is also used to store variables that are local to the procedure that do not fit in registers, such as local arrays or structures. The segment of the stack containing a procedure's saved registers and local variables is called a *procedure frame* or *activation record*. Figure 3.12 shows the state of the stack before, during, and after the procedure call.

Some MIPS software uses a *frame pointer* ($fp) to point to the first word of the frame of a procedure. A stack pointer might change during the procedure, and so references to a local variable in memory might have different offsets depending on where they are in the procedure, making the procedure harder to understand. Alternatively, a frame pointer offers a stable base register within a procedure for local memory references. Note that an activation record appears on the stack whether or not an explicit frame pointer is used. We've been avoiding $fp by avoiding changes to $sp within a procedure: in our examples, the stack is adjusted only on entry and exit of the procedure.

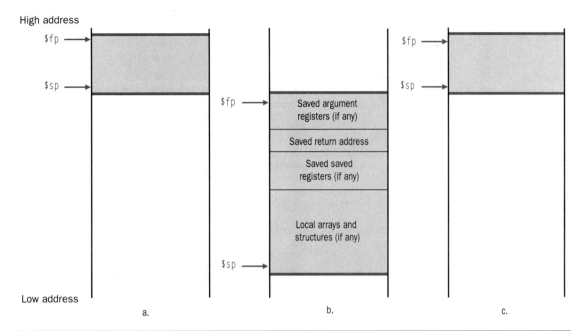

High address

Low address

a.   b.   c.

FIGURE 3.12   Illustration of the stack allocation (a) before, (b) during, and (c) after the procedure call. The frame pointer ($fp) points to the first word of the frame, often a saved argument register, and the stack pointer ($sp) points to the top of the stack. The stack is adjusted to make room for all the saved registers and any memory-resident local variables. Since the stack pointer may change during program execution, it's easier for programmers to reference variables via the stable frame pointer, although it could be done just with the stack pointer and a little address arithmetic. If there are no local variables on the stack within a procedure, the compiler will save time by *not* setting and restoring the frame pointer. When a frame pointer is used, it is initialized using the address in $sp on a call, and $sp is restored using $fp.

Figure 3.13 summarizes the register conventions for the MIPS assembly language, and Figure 3.14 summarizes the parts of the MIPS instruction set described so far.

Elaboration: What if there are more than four parameters? The MIPS convention is to place the extra parameters on the stack just above the frame pointer. The procedure then expects the first four parameters to be in registers $a0 through $a3 and the rest in memory, addressable via the frame pointer.

As mentioned in the caption of Figure 3.12, the frame pointer is convenient because all references to variables in the stack within a procedure will have the same offset. The frame pointer is not necessary, however. The GNU MIPS C compiler uses a frame pointer, but the C compiler from MIPS/Silicon Graphics does not; it uses register 30 as another save register ($s8).

Elaboration: jal actually saves the address of the instruction that *follows* jal into register $ra, thereby allowing a procedure return to be simply jr $ra.

**Hardware
Software
Interface**

A C variable is a location in storage, and its interpretation depends both on its *type* and *storage class*. Types are discussed in detail in Chapter 4, but examples include integers and characters. C has two storage classes: *automatic* and *static*. Automatic variables are local to a procedure and are discarded when the procedure exits. Static variables exist across exits from and entries to procedures. C variables declared outside all procedures are considered static, as are any variables declared using the keyword static. The rest are automatic. To simplify access to static data, MIPS software reserves another register, called the *global pointer*, or $gp.

We will see where in memory the static data is allocated in section 3.9.

Name	Register number	Usage	Preserved on call?
$zero	0	the constant value 0	n.a.
$v0–$v1	2–3	values for results and expression evaluation	no
$a0–$a3	4–7	arguments	yes
$t0–$t7	8–15	temporaries	no
$s0–$s7	16–23	saved	yes
$t8–$t9	24–25	more temporaries	no
$gp	28	global pointer	yes
$sp	29	stack pointer	yes
$fp	30	frame pointer	yes
$ra	31	return address	yes

FIGURE 3.13   MIPS register convention. Register 1, called $at, is reserved for the assembler (see section 3.9), and registers 26–27, called $k0–$k1, are reserved for the operating system.

MIPS operands

Name	Example	Comments
32 registers	$s0–$s7, $t0–$t9, $zero, $a0–$a3, $v0–$v1, $gp, $fp, $sp, $ra	Fast locations for data. In MIPS, data must be in registers to perform arithmetic. MIPS register $zero always equals 0. $gp (28) is the global pointer, $sp (29) is the stack pointer, $fp (30) is the frame pointer, and $ra (31) is the return address.
2^{30} memory words	Memory[0], Memory[4], . . . , Memory[4294967292]	Accessed only by data transfer instructions. MIPS uses byte addresses, so sequential words differ by 4. Memory holds data structures, such as arrays, and spilled registers, such as those saved on procedure calls.

MIPS assembly language

Category	Instruction	Example	Meaning	Comments
Arithmetic	add	add $s1,$s2,$s3	$s1 = $s2 + $s3	Three operands; data in registers
	subtract	sub $s1,$s2,$s3	$s1 = $s2 – $s3	Three operands; data in registers
Data transfer	load word	lw $s1,100($s2)	$s1 = Memory[$s2 + 100]	Data from memory to register
	store word	sw $s1,100($s2)	Memory[$s2 + 100] = $s1	Data from register to memory
Conditional branch	branch on equal	beq $s1,$s2,L	if ($s1 == $s2) go to L	Equal test and branch
	branch on not equal	bne $s1,$s2,L	if ($s1 != $s2) go to L	Not equal test and branch
	set on less than	slt $s1,$s2,$s3	if ($s2 < $s3) $s1=1; else $s1 = 0	Compare less than; for beq, bne
Unconditional jump	jump	j 2500	go to 10000	Jump to target address
	jump register	jr $ra	go to $ra	For switch, procedure return
	jump and link	jal 2500	$ra = PC + 4; go to 10000	For procedure call

MIPS machine language

Name	Format	Example						Comments
add	R	0	18	19	17	0	32	add $s1,$s2,$s3
sub	R	0	18	19	17	0	34	sub $s1,$s2,$s3
lw	I	35	18	17	100			lw $s1,100($s2)
sw	I	43	18	17	100			sw $s1,100($s2)
beq	I	4	17	18	25			beq $s1,$s2,100
bne	I	5	17	18	25			bne $s1,$s2,100
slt	R	0	18	19	17	0	42	slt $s1,$s2,$s3
j	J	2	2500					j 10000 (see section 3.8)
jr	R	0	31	0	0	0	8	jr $ra
jal	J	3	2500					jal 10000 (see section 3.8)
Field size		6 bits	5 bits	5 bits	5 bits	5 bits	6 bits	All MIPS instructions 32 bits
R-format	R	op	rs	rt	rd	shamt	funct	Arithmetic instruction format
I-format	I	op	rs	rt	address			Data transfer, branch format

FIGURE 3.14   MIPS architecture revealed through section 3.6. Highlighted portions show MIPS assembly language structures introduced in section 3.6. The J-format, used for jump and jump-and-link instructions, is explained in section 3.8. This section also explains why putting 25 in the address field of beq and bne machine language instructions is equivalent to 100 in assembly language.

3.7   Beyond Numbers

Computers were invented to crunch numbers, but as soon as they became commercially viable they were used to process text. Most computers today use 8-bit bytes to represent characters, with the American Standard Code for Information Interchange (ASCII) being the representation that nearly everyone follows. Figure 3.15 summarizes ASCII.

A series of instructions can be used to extract a byte from a word, so load word and store word are sufficient for transferring bytes as well as words. Because of the popularity of text in some programs, however, MIPS provides special instructions to move bytes. Load byte (lb) loads a byte from memory, placing it in the rightmost 8 bits of a register. Store byte (sb) takes a byte from the rightmost 8 bits of a register and writes it to memory. Thus we copy a byte with the sequence

```
lb $t0,0($sp)   # Read byte from source
sb $t0,0($gp)   # Write byte to destination
```

ASCII value	Char-acter	ASCII value	Char-acter	ASCII value	Char-acter	ASCII value	Char-acter	ASCII value	Char-acter	ASCII value	Char-acter
32	space	48	0	64	@	80	P	96	`	112	p
33	!	49	1	65	A	81	Q	97	a	113	q
34	"	50	2	66	B	82	R	98	b	114	r
35	#	51	3	67	C	83	S	99	c	115	s
36	$	52	4	68	D	84	T	100	d	116	t
37	%	53	5	69	E	85	U	101	e	117	u
38	&	54	6	70	F	86	V	102	f	118	v
39	'	55	7	71	G	87	W	103	g	119	w
40	(	56	8	72	H	88	X	104	h	120	x
41	)	57	9	73	I	89	Y	105	i	121	y
42	*	58	:	74	J	90	Z	106	j	122	z
43	+	59	;	75	K	91	[	107	k	123	{
44	,	60	<	76	L	92	\	108	l	124		
45	-	61	=	77	M	93	]	109	m	125	}
46	.	62	>	78	N	94	^	110	n	126	~
47	/	63	?	79	O	95	_	111	o	127	DEL

FIGURE 3.15   ASCII representation of characters. Note that upper- and lowercase letters differ by exactly 32; this observation can lead to shortcuts in checking or changing upper- and lowercase. Values not shown include formatting characters. For example, 9 represents a tab character and 13 represents a carriage return. Other useful ASCII values are 8 for backspace and 0 for Null, the value the programming language C uses to mark the end of a string.

Characters are normally combined into strings, which have a variable number of characters. There are three choices for representing a string: (1) the first position of the string is reserved to give the length of a string, (2) an accompanying variable has the length of the string (as in a structure), or (3) the last position of a string is indicated by a character used to mark the end of a string. C uses the third choice, terminating a string with a byte whose value is 0 (named Null in ASCII). Thus the string "Cal" is represented in C by the following 4 bytes, shown as decimal numbers: 67, 97, 108, 0.

Compiling a String Copy Procedure, Showing How to Use C Strings

Example

The procedure `strcpy` copies string `y` to string `x` using the null byte termination convention of C:

```
void strcpy (char x[], char y[])
{
    int i;

    i = 0;
    while ((x[i] = y[i]) != 0) /* copy and test byte */
        i = i + 1;
}
```

What is the MIPS assembly code?

Answer

Below is the basic MIPS assembly code segment. We again assume we can add or subtract constants like 1 or 4, which we cover in section 3.8. Assume that base addresses for arrays `x` and `y` are found in `$a0` and `$a1`, while `i` is in `$s0`. `strcpy` adjusts the stack pointer and then saves the saved register `$s0` on the stack:

```
strcpy:
    sub    $sp,$sp,4     # adjust stack for 1 more item
    sw     $s0, 4($sp)   # save $s0
```

To initialize `i` to 0, the next instruction sets `$s0` to 0 by adding 0 to 0 and placing that sum in `$s0`:

```
    add    $s0,$zero,$zero   # i = 0 + 0
```

This is the beginning of the loop. The address of `y[i]` is first formed by adding `i` to `y[]`:

```
    L1: add    $t1,$a1,$s0  # address of y[i] in $t1
```

Note that we don't have to multiply `i` by four since `y` is an array of *bytes* and not of words, as in prior examples.

To load the character in y[i], we use load byte, which puts the character into $t2:

```
lb      $t2, 0($t1)  # $t2 = y[i]
```

A similar address calculation puts the address of x[i] in $t3, and then the character in $t2 is stored at that address.

```
add     $t3,$a0,$s0  # address of x[i] in $t3
sb      $t2, 0($t3)  # x[i] = y[i]
```

Next we increment i, and loop back if the character was not 0; that is, if this is not the last character of the string.

```
add     $s0,$s0,1    # i = i + 1
bne     $t2,$zero,L1 # if y[i] != 0, go to L1
```

If we don't loop back, it was the last character of the string, we restore $s0 and the stack pointer, and then return.

```
lw      $s0, 4($sp)  # y[i] == 0: end of string;
                     # restore old s0
add     $sp,$sp,4    # pop 1 word off stack
jr      $ra          # return
```

String copies are usually done with pointers instead of arrays in C to avoid the operations on i in the code above. See section 3.11 for an explanation of arrays versus pointers.

Since the procedure strcpy above is a leaf procedure, the compiler could allocate i to a temporary register and avoid saving and restoring $s0. Hence, instead of thinking of the $t registers as being just for temporaries, we can think of them as registers that the callee should use whenever convenient. When a compiler finds a leaf procedure, it exhausts all temporary registers before using the registers it must save.

Elaboration: There is a universal encoding of the characters of most human languages called *Unicode*, which needs 16 bits to represent a character. The programming language Java, for example, uses Unicode. The full MIPS instruction set has explicit instructions to load and store 16-bit quantities, called *halfwords*. We skip halfword instructions in this book to keep the instruction set as easy to understand as possible, although section A.10 starting on page A-49 includes the full instruction set.

Also, MIPS software tries to keep the stack aligned to word addresses, allowing the program to always use lw and sw (whlch must be aligned) to access the stack. This convention means that a char variable allocated on the stack will be allocated 4 bytes, even though it needs just 1 byte. A string variable or an array of bytes *will* pack 4 bytes per word, however.

3.8 | Other Styles of MIPS Addressing

Designers of the MIPS architecture provided two more ways of accessing operands. The first is to make it faster to access small constants, and the second is to make branches more efficient.

Constant or Immediate Operands

Many times a program will use a constant in an operation—for example, incrementing an index to point to the next element of an array, counting iterations of a loop, or adjusting the stack in a nested procedure call. In fact, in two programs, more than half of the arithmetic instructions have a constant as an operand: in the C compiler gcc, 52% of arithmetic operations involve constants; in the circuit simulation program spice, it is 69%.

Using only the instructions in Figure 3.14, we would have to load a constant from memory to use it. (The constants would have been placed in memory when the program was loaded.) For example, to add the constant 4 to register $sp, we could use the code

```
lw      $t0, AddrConstant4($zero)  # $t0 = constant 4
add     $sp,$sp,$t0                # $sp = $sp + $t0 ($t0 == 4)
```

assuming that AddrConstant4 is the memory address of the constant 4.

An alternative that avoids memory accesses is to offer versions of the arithmetic instructions in which one operand is a constant, with the novel constraint that this constant is kept inside the *instruction* itself. Following the recommendation urging regularity, we use the same format for these instructions as for the data transfer and branch instructions. In fact, the *I* in the name of the I-type format is for *immediate*, the traditional name for this type of operand. The MIPS field containing the constant is 16 bits long.

Translating Assembly Constants into Machine Language

Example

The add instruction that has one constant operand is called *add immediate* or addi. To add 4 to register $sp, we just write

```
addi      $sp,$sp,4    # $sp = $sp + 4
```

The op field value for addi is 8. Try to guess the rest of the corresponding MIPS machine instruction.

Answer   This instruction is the following machine code (using decimal numbers):

op	rs	rt	immediate
8	29	29	4

(Figure 3.13 on page 140 shows that register 29 corresponds to $sp.) In binary addi is

001000	11101	11101	0000 0000 0000 0100

Immediate or constant operands are also popular in comparisons. Since register $zero always has 0, we can already compare to 0. To compare to other values, there is an immediate version of the set on less than instruction. To test if register $s2 is less than the constant 10, we can just write

    slti $t0,$s2,10   # $t0 = 1 if $s2 < 10

Similar to the earlier example on page 128 (Hardware Software Interface), this instruction can be followed by bne $t0,$zero to branch if register $s2 is less than the constant 10.

Immediate addressing illustrates the final hardware design principle, first mentioned in Chapter 2:

Design Principle 4: Make the common case fast.

Constant operands occur frequently, and by making constants part of arithmetic instructions, they are much faster than if they were loaded from memory.

Although constants are frequently short and fit into the 16-bit field, sometimes they are bigger. The MIPS instruction set includes the instruction *load upper immediate* (lui) specifically to set the upper 16 bits of a constant in a register, allowing a subsequent instruction to specify the lower 16 bits of the constant. Figure 3.16 shows the operation of lui.

The machine language version of lui $t0, 255   # $t0 is register 8:

001111	00000	01000	0000 0000 1111 1111

Contents of register $t0 after executing lui $t0, 255:

0000 0000 1111 1111	0000 0000 0000 0000

FIGURE 3.16   The effect of the lui instruction. The instruction lui transfers the 16-bit immediate constant field value into the leftmost 16 bits of the register, filling the lower 16 bits with 0s. As we shall see in Chapter 4, this instruction is like multiplying the constant by 2^{16} before loading it into the register.

Loading a 32-Bit Constant

Example

What is the MIPS assembly code to load this 32-bit constant into register $s0?

```
0000 0000 0011 1101 0000 1001 0000 0000
```

Answer

First we would load the upper 16 bits, which is 61 in decimal, using lui:

```
lui $s0, 61   # 61 decimal = 0000 0000 0011 1101 binary
```

The value of register $s0 afterward is

```
0000 0000 0011 1101 0000 0000 0000 0000
```

The next step is to add the lower 16 bits, whose decimal value is 2304:

```
addi $s0, $s0, 2304 # 2304 decimal = 0000 1001 0000 0000
```

The final value in register $s0 is the desired value:

```
0000 0000 0011 1101 0000 1001 0000 0000
```

Hardware Software Interface

Either the compiler or the assembler must break large constants into pieces and then reassemble them into a register. As you might expect, the immediate field's size restriction may be a problem for memory addresses in loads and stores as well as for constants in immediate instructions. If this job falls to the assembler, as it does for MIPS software, then the assembler must have a temporary register available in which to create the long values. This is a reason for the register $at, which is reserved for the assembler.

Hence the symbolic representation of the MIPS machine language is no longer limited by the hardware, but to whatever the creator of an assembler chooses to include (see section 3.9). We stick close to the hardware to explain the architecture of the machine, noting when we use the enhanced language of the assembler that is not found in the machine.

Elaboration: We need to be careful about creating 32-bit constants. The instruction addi will copy the leftmost bit of the 16-bit immediate field of the instruction into the upper 16 bits of a word. An instruction we will see in the next chapter, ori, for *logical or immediate*, loads 0s into the upper 16 bits and hence is used by the assembler in conjunction with lui to create 32-bit constants.

Addressing in Branches and Jumps

The simplest addressing is found in the MIPS jump instructions. They use the final MIPS instruction format, called the *J-type*, which consists of 6 bits for the operation field and the rest of the bits for the address field. Thus,

```
j    10000   # go to location 10000
```

is assembled into this format:

2	10000
6 bits	26 bits

where the value of the jump opcode is 2 and the jump address is 10000.

Unlike the jump instruction, the conditional branch instruction must specify two operands in addition to the branch address. Thus,

```
bne $s0,$s1,Exit      # go to Exit if $s0 ≠ $s1
```

is assembled into this instruction, leaving only 16 bits for the branch address:

5	16	17	Exit
6 bits	5 bits	5 bits	16 bits

If addresses of the program had to fit in this 16-bit field, it would mean that no program could be bigger than 2^{16}, which is far too small to be a realistic option today. An alternative would be to specify a register that would always be added to the branch address, so that a branch instruction would calculate the following:

$$\text{Program counter} = \text{Register} + \text{Branch address}$$

This sum allows the program to be as large as 2^{32} and still be able to use conditional branches, solving the branch address size problem. The question is then, which register?

The answer comes from seeing how conditional branches are used. Conditional branches are found in loops and in *if* statements, so they tend to branch to a nearby instruction. For example, almost half of all conditional branches in gcc and spice go to locations less than 16 instructions away. Since the program counter (PC) contains the address of the current instruction, we can branch within $\pm 2^{15}$ words of the current instruction if we use the PC as the register to be added to the address. Almost all loops and *if* statements are much smaller than 2^{16} words, so the PC is the ideal choice.

This form of branch addressing is called *PC-relative addressing*. As we shall see in Chapter 5, it is convenient for the hardware to increment the PC early to point to the next instruction. Hence the MIPS address is actually relative to the address of the following instruction (PC + 4) as opposed to the current instruction (PC).

Like most recent machines, MIPS uses PC-relative addressing for all conditional branches because the destination of these instructions is likely to be close to the branch. On the other hand, jump-and-link instructions invoke procedures that have no reason to be near the call, and so they normally use other forms of addressing. Hence the MIPS architecture offers long addresses for procedure calls by using the J-type format for both jump and jump-and-link instructions.

Showing Branch Offset in Machine Language

Example

The *while* loop on page 127 was compiled into this MIPS assembler code:

```
Loop:   add $t1,$s3,$s3     # Temp reg $t1 = 2 * i
        add $t1,$t1,$t1     # Temp reg $t1 = 4 * i
        add $t1,$t1,$s5     # $t1 = address of save[i]
        lw  $t0,0($t1)      # Temp reg $t0 = save[i]
        bne $t0,$s5, Exit   # go to Exit if save[i] ≠ k
        add $s3,$s3,$s4     # i = i + j
        j   Loop            # go to Loop
Exit:
```

If we assume that the loop is placed starting at location 80000 in memory, what is the MIPS machine code for this loop?

Answer

The assembled instructions and their addresses would look like this:

80000	0	19	19	9	0	32
80004	0	9	9	9	0	32
80008	0	9	21	9	0	32
80012	35	9	8	0		
80016	5	8	21	8		
80020	0	19	20	19	0	32
80024	2			80000		
80028	...					
80012	35	9	8	0		

Remember that MIPS instructions use byte addresses, so addresses of sequential words differ by four, the number of bytes in a word. The bne instruction on the fifth line adds 8 bytes to the address of the *following* instruction (80020), specifying the branch destination relative to that instruction (8) instead of the current instruction (12) or using the full destination address (80028). The jump instruction on the last line does use the full address (80000), corresponding to the label Loop.

Since all MIPS instructions are 4 bytes long, MIPS stretches the distance of the branch by having PC-relative addressing refer to the number of *words* to the next instruction instead of the number of bytes. Thus the 16-bit field can branch four times as far by interpreting the field as a relative word address rather than as a relative byte address. Hence the address field in the bne instruction at location 80016 in the example above should have 2 instead of 8. (Relative word addressing is the reason that the machine language versions of beq and bne in Figures 3.9 and 3.14 have 25 in their address fields instead of 100, as in the assembly language versions.)

Hardware Software Interface

Nearly every conditional branch is to a nearby location, but occasionally it branches far away, farther than can be represented in the 16 bits of the conditional branch instruction. The assembler comes to the rescue just as it did with large addresses or constants: it inserts an unconditional jump to the branch target, and the condition is inverted so that the branch decides whether to skip the jump.

Branching Far Away

Example

Given a branch on register $s0 being equal to register $s1,

```
        beq    $s0,$s1, L1
```

replace it by a pair of instructions that offers a much greater branching distance.

Answer

It can be replaced by these instructions:

```
        bne    $s0,$s1, L2
        j      L1
L2:
```

Elaboration: The 26-bit field in jump instructions is also a word address, meaning that it represents a 28-bit byte address. Since the PC is 32 bits, 4 bits must come from someplace else. The MIPS jump instruction replaces only the lower 28 bits of the PC, leaving the upper 4 bits of the PC unchanged. The loader and linker (section 3.9) must be careful to avoid placing a program across an address boundary of 256 MB (64 million instructions), for otherwise a jump must be replaced by a jump register instruction preceded by other instructions to load the full 32-bit address into a register.

MIPS Addressing Mode Summary

We have seen two new forms of addressing in this section. Multiple forms of addressing are generically called *addressing modes*. The MIPS addressing modes are the following:

1. *Register addressing*, where the operand is a register

2. *Base* or *displacement addressing*, where the operand is at the memory location whose address is the sum of a register and a constant in the instruction

3. *Immediate addressing*, where the operand is a constant within the instruction itself

4. *PC-relative addressing*, where the address is the sum of the PC and a constant in the instruction

5. *Pseudodirect addressing*, where the jump address is the 26 bits of the instruction concatenated with the upper bits of the PC

Note that a single operation can use more than one addressing mode. Add, for example, uses both immediate (addi) and register (add) addressing. Figure 3.17 shows how operands are identified for each addressing mode. Section 3.12 expands this list to show addressing modes found in other styles of computers.

| **Hardware Software Interface** | Although we show the MIPS architecture as having 32-bit addresses, nearly all microprocessors (including MIPS) have 64-bit address extensions. (See Web Extension I at *www.mkp.com/cod2e.htm*.) These extensions were in response to the needs of software for larger programs. The process of instruction set extension allows architectures to be expanded in a way that lets software move compatibly |

upward to the next generation of architecture.

Decoding Machine Language

Sometimes you are forced to reverse-engineer machine language to create the original assembly language. One example is when looking at a core dump. Figure 3.18 shows the MIPS encoding of the fields for the MIPS machine language. This figure can be used to translate by hand between assembly language and machine language.

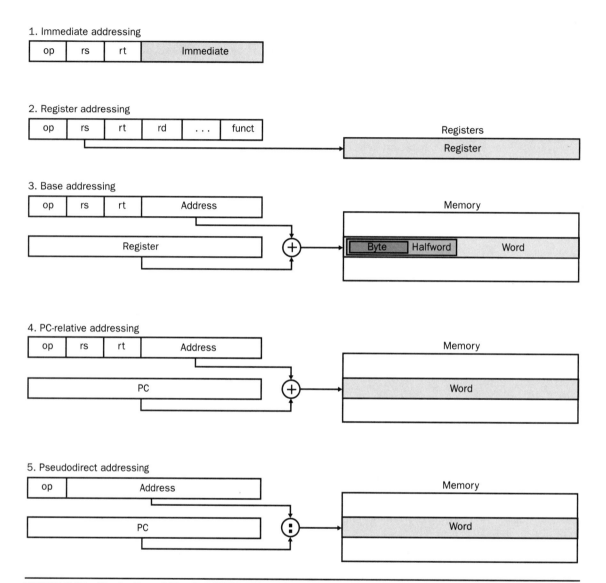

FIGURE 3.17   Illustration of the five MIPS addressing modes. The operands are shaded in color. The operand of mode 3 is in memory, whereas the operand for mode 2 is a register. Note that versions of load and store access bytes, half-words, or words. For mode 1 the operand is 16 bits of the instruction itself. Modes 4 and 5 are used to address instructions in memory, with mode 4 adding a 16-bit address to the PC and mode 5 concatenating a 26-bit address with the upper bits of the PC.

op(31:26)								
28–26 31–29	0(000)	1(001)	2(010)	3(011)	4(100)	5(101)	6(110)	7(111)
0(000)	R-format	Bltz/gez	jump	jump & link	branch eq	branch ne	blez	bgtz
1(001)	add immediate	addiu	set less than imm.	sltiu	andi	ori	xori	load upper imm
2(010)	TLB	FlPt						
3(011)								
4(100)	load byte	lh	lwl	load word	lbu	lhu	lwr	
5(101)	store byte	sh	swl	store word			swr	
6(110)	lwc0	lwc1						
7(111)	swc0	swc1						

op(31:26)=010000 (TLB), rs(25:21)								
23–21 25–24	0(000)	1(001)	2(010)	3(011)	4(100)	5(101)	6(110)	7(111)
0(00)	mfc0		cfc0		mtc0		ctc0	
1(01)								
2(10)								
3(11)								

op(31:26)=000000 (R-format), funct(5:0)								
2–0 5–3	0(000)	1(001)	2(010)	3(011)	4(100)	5(101)	6(110)	7(111)
0(000)	sll		srl	sra	sllv		srlv	srav
1(001)	jump reg.	jalr			syscall	break		
2(010)	mfhi	mthi	mflo	mtlo				
3(011)	mult	multu	div	divu				
4(100)	add	addu	subtract	subu	and	or	xor	nor
5(101)			set l.t.	sltu				
6(110)								
7(111)								

FIGURE 3.18 MIPS instruction encoding. This notation gives the value of a field by row and by column. For example, in the top portion of the figure load word is found in row number 4 (100_{two} for bits 31–29 of the instruction) and column number 3 (011_{two} for bits 28–26 of the instruction), so the corresponding value of the op field (bits 31–26) is 100011_{two}. Underscore means the field is used elsewhere. For example, R-format in row 0 and column 0 (op = 000000_{two}) is defined in the bottom part of the figure. Hence subtract in row 4 and column 2 of the bottom section means that the funct field (bits 5–0) of the instruction is 100010_{two} and the op field (bits 31–26) is 000000_{two}. The FlPt value in row 2, column 1 is defined in Figure 4.48 on page 292 in Chapter 4. Bltz/gez is the opcode for four instructions found in Appendix A: bltz, bgez, bltzal, and bgezal. Instructions given in full name using color are described in Chapter 3, while instructions given in mnemonics using color are described in Chapter 4. Appendix A covers all instructions.

Decoding Machine Code

Example

What is the assembly language corresponding to this machine instruction?

(Bits: 31 28 26   5   2 0)*

```
0000 0000 1010 1111 1000 0000 0010 0000
```

Answer

The first step is to look at the op field to determine the operation. Referring to Figure 3.18, when bits 31–29 are 000 and bits 28–26 are 000, it is an R-format instruction. Let's reformat the binary instruction into R-format fields, listed in Figure 3.19:

op	rs	rt	rd	shamt	funct
000000	00101	01111	10000	00000	100000

The bottom portion of Figure 3.18 determines the operation of an R-format instruction. In this case, bits 5–3 are 100 and bits 2–0 are 000, which means this binary pattern represents an `add` instruction.

We decode the rest of the instruction by looking at the field values. The decimal values are 5 for the rs field, 15 for rt, 16 for rd (shamt is unused). Figure 3.13 on page 140 says these numbers represent registers $a1, $t7, and $s0. Now we can show the assembly instruction:

```
add $s0,$a1,$t7
```

Figure 3.20 shows the MIPS assembly language revealed in Chapter 3; the remaining hidden portion of MIPS instructions deals mainly with arithmetic, covered in the next chapter.

Name	Fields						Comments
Field size	6 bits	5 bits	5 bits	5 bits	5 bits	6 bits	All MIPS instructions 32 bits
R-format	op	rs	rt	rd	shamt	funct	Arithmetic instruction format
I-format	op	rs	rt	address/immediate			Transfer, branch, imm. format
J-format	op	target address					Jump instruction format

FIGURE 3.19 MIPS instruction formats in Chapter 3. Highlighted portions show instruction formats introduced in this section.

MIPS operands

Name	Example	Comments
32 registers	$s0–$s7, $t0–$t9, $zero, $a0–$a3, $v0–$v1, $gp, $fp, $sp, $ra, $at	Fast locations for data. In MIPS, data must be in registers to perform arithmetic. MIPS register $zero always equals 0. Register $at is reserved for the assembler to handle large constants.
2^{30} memory words	Memory[0], Memory[4], . . . , Memory[4294967292]	Accessed only by data transfer instructions. MIPS uses byte addresses, so sequential words differ by 4. Memory holds data structures, such as arrays, and spilled registers, such as those saved on procedure calls.

MIPS assembly language

Category	Instruction	Example	Meaning	Comments
Arithmetic	add	add $s1,$s2,$s3	$s1 = $s2 + $s3	Three operands; data in registers
	subtract	sub $s1,$s2,$s3	$s1 = $s2 - $s3	Three operands; data in registers
	add immediate	addi $s1,$s2,100	$s1 = $s2 + 100	Used to add constants
Data transfer	load word	lw $s1,100($s2)	$s1 = Memory[$s2 + 100]	Word from memory to register
	store word	sw $s1,100($s2)	Memory[$s2 + 100] = $s1	Word from register to memory
	load byte	lb $s1,100($s2)	$s1 = Memory[$s2 + 100]	Byte from memory to register
	store byte	sb $s1,100($s2)	Memory[$s2 + 100] = $s1	Byte from register to memory
	load upper immediate	lui $s1,100	$s1 = 100 * 2^{16}	Loads constant in upper 16 bits
Conditional branch	branch on equal	beq $s1,$s2,25	if ($s1 == $s2) go to PC + 4 + 100	Equal test; PC-relative branch
	branch on not equal	bne $s1,$s2,25	if ($s1 != $s2) go to PC + 4 + 100	Not equal test; PC-relative
	set on less than	slt $s1,$s2,$s3	if ($s2 < $s3) $s1 = 1; else $s1 = 0	Compare less than; for beq, bne
	set less than immediate	slti $s1,$s2,100	if ($s2 < 100) $s1 = 1; else $s1 = 0	Compare less than constant
Unconditional jump	jump	j 2500	go to 10000	Jump to target address
	jump register	jr $ra	go to $ra	For switch, procedure return
	jump and link	jal 2500	$ra = PC + 4; go to 10000	For procedure call

FIGURE 3.20   MIPS assembly language revealed in Chapter 3. Highlighted portions show portions from sections 3.7 and 3.8.

3.9   Starting a Program

This section describes the four steps in transforming a C program in a file on disk into a program running on a computer. Figure 3.21 shows the translation hierarchy. Some systems combine these steps to reduce translation time, but these are the logical four phases that all programs go through. This section follows this translation hierarchy.

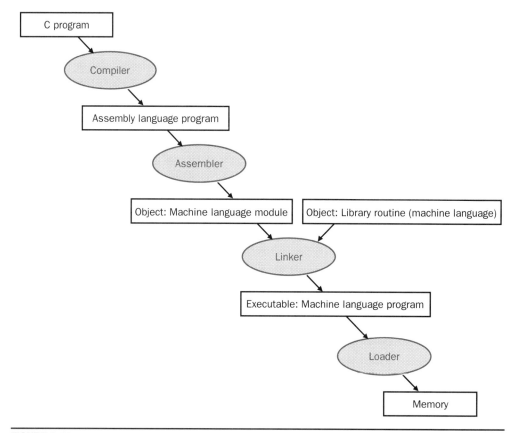

FIGURE 3.21   A translation hierarchy. A high-level-language program is first compiled into an assembly language program and then assembled into an object module in machine language. The linker combines multiple modules with library routines to resolve all references. The loader then places the machine code into the proper memory locations for execution by the processor. To speed up the translation process, some steps are skipped or combined together. Some compilers produce object modules directly, and some systems use linking loaders that perform the last two steps. To identify the type of file, Unix follows a suffix convention for files: C source files are named x.c, assembly files are x.s, object files are named x.o, and an executable file by default is called a.out. MS-DOS uses the suffixes .TXT, .ASM, .OBJ, and .EXE to the same effect.

Compiler

The compiler transforms the C program into an *assembly language program*, a symbolic form of what the machine understands. High-level-language programs take many fewer lines of code than assembly language, so programmer productivity is much higher.

In 1975 many operating systems and assemblers were written in assembly language because memories were small and compilers were inefficient. The 16,000-fold increase in memory capacity per DRAM chip has reduced program size concerns, and optimizing compilers today can produce assembly language programs nearly as good as an assembly language expert, and sometimes even better for large programs.

Assembler

As mentioned on page 147, since assembly language is the interface to higher-level software, the assembler can also treat common variations of machine language instructions as if they were instructions in their own right. These instructions need not be implemented in hardware; however, their appearance in assembly language simplifies translation and programming. Such instructions are called *pseudoinstructions*.

For example, the MIPS hardware makes sure that register $zero always has the value 0. That is, whenever register $zero is used, it supplies a 0, and the programmer cannot change the value of register $zero. Register $zero is used to create the assembly language instruction move that copies the contents of one register to another. Thus the MIPS assembler accepts this instruction even though it is not found in the MIPS architecture:

```
move $t0,$t1        # register $t0 gets register $t1
```

The assembler converts this assembly language instruction into the machine language equivalent of the following instruction:

```
add  $t0,$zero,$t1 # register $t0 gets 0 + register $t1
```

The MIPS assembler also converts blt (branch on less than) into the two instructions slt and bne mentioned in the example on page 128. Other examples include bgt, bge, and ble. It also converts branches to faraway locations into a branch and jump. As mentioned above, the MIPS assembler can even allow 32-bit constants to be loaded into a register despite the 16-bit limit of the immediate instructions.

In summary, pseudoinstructions give MIPS a richer set of assembly language instructions than those implemented by the hardware. The only cost is reserving one register, $at, for use by the assembler. If you are going to write assembly programs, use pseudoinstructions to simplify your task. To understand the MIPS architecture and to be sure to get best performance, however, study the real MIPS instructions found in Figures 3.18 and 3.20.

Assemblers will also accept numbers in a variety of bases. In addition to binary and decimal, they usually accept a base that is more succinct than binary yet can easily be converted to a bit pattern. MIPS assemblers use base 16, called *hexadecimal*; we use the subscript "hex" to indicate a hexadecimal number. The hexadecimal digits are 0 to 9 for the first 10 digits and then the letters *a* to *f* for the last 6 digits. For example, the bit pattern from the example on page 154 is shown as both binary and hexadecimal numbers:

$$0000\ 0000\ 1010\ 1111\ 1000\ 0000\ 0010\ 0000_{two} = 00af\ 8020_{hex}$$

Such features are convenient, but the primary task of an assembler is assembly into machine code. The assembler turns the assembly language program into an *object file*, which is a combination of *machine language* instructions, data, and information needed to place instructions properly in memory.

To produce the binary version of each instruction in the assembly language program, the assembler must determine the addresses corresponding to all labels. Assemblers keep track of labels used in branches and data transfer instructions in a *symbol table*. As you might expect, the table contains pairs of symbol and address.

The object file for Unix systems typically contains six distinct pieces:

- The *object file header* describes the size and position of the other pieces of the object file.

- The *text segment* contains the machine language code.

- The *data segment* contains whatever data that comes with the program: either *static data*, which is allocated throughout the program, or *dynamic data*, which can grow or shrink as needed by the program.

- The *relocation information* identifies instructions and data words that depend on absolute addresses when the program is loaded into memory.

- The *symbol table* contains the remaining labels that are not defined, such as external references.

- The *debugging information* contains a concise description of how the modules were compiled so that a debugger can associate machine instructions with C source files and make data structures readable.

The next subsection shows how to attach such routines that have already been assembled, such as library routines.

Linker

What we have presented so far suggests that a single change to one line of one procedure requires compiling and assembling the whole program. Complete retranslation is a terrible waste of computing resources. This repetition is particularly wasteful for standard library routines because programmers would be compiling and assembling routines that by definition almost never change. An alternative is to compile and assemble each procedure independently, so that a change to one line would require compiling and assembling only one procedure. This alternative requires a new systems program, called a *link editor* or *linker*, that takes all the independently assembled machine language programs and "stitches" them together.

There are three steps for the linker:

1. Place code and data modules symbolically in memory.

2. Determine the addresses of data and instruction labels.

3. Patch both the internal and external references.

The linker uses the relocation information and symbol table in each object module to resolve all undefined labels. Such references occur in branch instructions, jump instructions, and data addresses, so the job of this program is much like that of an editor: It finds the old addresses and replaces them with the new addresses. Editing is the origin of the name "link editor," or linker for short. The reason a linker makes sense is that it is much faster to patch code than it is to recompile and reassemble.

If all external references are resolved, the linker next determines the memory locations each module will occupy. Figure 3.22 shows the MIPS convention for allocation of program and data to memory. Since the files were assembled in isolation, the assembler could not know where a module's instructions and data will be placed relative to other modules. When the linker places a module in memory, all *absolute* references, that is, memory addresses that are not relative to a register, must be *relocated* to reflect its true location.

The linker produces an *executable file* that can be run on a computer. Typically, this file has the same format as an object file, except that it contains no unresolved references, relocation information, symbol table, or debugging information. It is possible to have partially linked files, such as library routines, which still have unresolved addresses and hence result in object files.

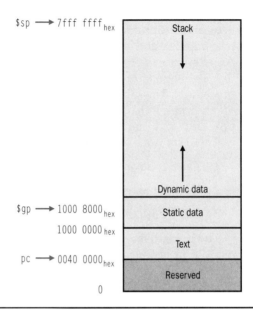

$sp → 7fff ffff_hex

$gp → 1000 8000_hex

1000 0000_hex

pc → 0040 0000_hex

0

Stack

Dynamic data

Static data

Text

Reserved

FIGURE 3.22 The MIPS memory allocation for program and data. Starting top down, the stack pointer is initialized to $7fff\ ffff_{hex}$ and grows down toward the data segment. At the other end, the program code ("text") starts at $0040\ 0000_{hex}$. The static data starts at $1000\ 0000_{hex}$. Dynamic data, allocated by malloc in C, is next and grows up toward the stack. The global pointer, $gp, is set to an address to make it easy to access data. It is initialized to $1000\ 8000_{hex}$ so that it can access from $1000\ 0000_{hex}$ to $1000\ ffff_{hex}$ using the positive and negative 16-bit offsets from $gp (see two's complement addressing in Chapter 4).

Linking Object Files

Example

Link the two object files below. Show updated addresses of the first few instructions of the completed executable file. We show the instructions in assembly language just to make the example understandable; in reality, the instructions would be numbers.

Note that in the object files we have highlighted the addresses and symbols that must be updated in the link process: the instructions that refer to the addresses of procedures A and B and the instructions that refer to the addresses of data words X and Y.

Object file header			
	Name	Procedure A	
	Text size	100_{hex}	
	Data size	20_{hex}	
Text segment	Address	Instruction	
	0	lw $a0, 0($gp)	
	4	jal 0	
	...	...	
Data segment	0	(X)	
	...	...	
Relocation information	Address	Instruction type	Dependency
	0	lw	X
	4	jal	B
Symbol table	Label	Address	
	X	–	
	B	–	
Object file header			
	Name	Procedure B	
	Text size	200_{hex}	
	Data size	30_{hex}	
Text segment	Address	Instruction	
	0	sw $a1, 0($gp)	
	4	jal 0	
	...	...	
Data segment	0	(Y)	
	...	...	
Relocation information	Address	Instruction type	Dependency
	0	lw	Y
	4	jal	A
Symbol table	Label	Address	
	Y	–	
	A	–	

Answer   Procedure A needs to find the address for the variable labeled X to put in the load instruction and to find the address of procedure B to place in the jal instruction. Procedure B needs the address of the variable labeled Y for the store instruction and the address of procedure A for its jal instruction.

Executable file header		
	Text size	300_{hex}
	Data size	50_{hex}
Text segment	Address	Instruction
	$0040\ 0000_{hex}$	lw $a0, 8000_{hex}($gp)
	$0040\ 0004_{hex}$	jal 40 0100_{hex}
	...	...
	$0040\ 0100_{hex}$	sw $a1, 8020_{hex}($gp)
	$0040\ 0104_{hex}$	jal 40 0000_{hex}
	...	...
Data segment	Address	
	$1000\ 0000_{hex}$	(X)
	...	...
	$1000\ 0020_{hex}$	(Y)
	...	...

From Figure 3.22 we know that the text segment starts at address $40\ 0000_{hex}$ and the data segment at $1000\ 0000_{hex}$. The text of procedure A is placed at the first address and its data at the second. The object file header for procedure A says that its text is 100_{hex} bytes and its data is 20_{hex} bytes, so the starting address for procedure B text is $40\ 0100_{hex}$, and its data starts at $1000\ 0020_{hex}$.

Now the linker updates the address fields of the instructions. It uses the instruction type field to know the format of the address to be edited. We have two types here:

1.   The jals are easy because they use pseudodirect addressing. The jal at address $40\ 0004_{hex}$ gets $40\ 0100_{hex}$ (the address of procedure B) in its address field, and the jal at $40\ 0104_{hex}$ gets $40\ 0000_{hex}$ (the address of procedure A) in its address field.

2.   The load and store addresses are harder because they are relative to a base register. In this example, the global pointer is used as the base register. Figure 3.22 shows that $gp is initialized to $1000\ 8000_{hex}$. To get the address $1000\ 0000_{hex}$ (the address of word X), we place 8000_{hex} in the address field of lw at address $40\ 0000_{hex}$. Chapter 4 explains 16-bit two's complement computer arithmetic, which is why 8000_{hex} in the address field yields $1000\ 0000_{hex}$ as the address. Similarly, we place 8020_{hex} in the address field of sw at address $40\ 0100_{hex}$ to get the address $1000\ 0020_{hex}$ (the address of word Y).

Loader

Now that the executable file is on disk, the operating system reads it to memory and starts it. It follows these steps in Unix systems:

1. Reads the executable file header to determine size of the text and data segments.

2. Creates an address space large enough for the text and data.

3. Copies the instructions and data from the executable file into memory.

4. Copies the parameters (if any) to the main program onto the stack.

5. Initializes the machine registers and sets the stack pointer to the first free location.

6. Jumps to a start-up routine that copies the parameters into the argument registers and calls the main routine of the program. When the main routine returns, the start-up routine terminates the program with an `exit` system call.

Sections A.3 and A.4 in Appendix A describe linkers and loaders in more detail.

3.10 An Example to Put It All Together

One danger of showing assembly language code in snippets is that you will have no idea what a full assembly language program looks like. In this section and the next, we derive the MIPS code from two procedures written in C: one to swap array elements and one to sort them.

The Procedure `swap`

Let's start with the code for the procedure `swap` in Figure 3.23. This procedure simply swaps two locations in memory. When translating from C to assembly language, we follow these general steps:

1. Allocate registers to program variables.

2. Produce code for the body of the procedure.

3. Preserve registers across the procedure invocation.

This section describes the `swap` procedure in these three pieces, concluding by putting all the pieces together.

```
swap(int v[], int k)
{
  int temp;
  temp = v[k];
  v[k] = v[k+1];
  v[k+1] = temp;
}
```

FIGURE 3.23   A C procedure that swaps two locations in memory. This procedure will be used in the sorting example in the next section. Web Extension III at *www.mkp.com/cod2e.htm* shows the C and Pascal versions of this procedure side by side.

Register Allocation for swap

As mentioned on page 132, the MIPS convention on parameter passing is to use registers $a0, $a1, $a2, and $a3. Since swap has just two parameters, v and k, they will be found in registers $a0 and $a1. The only other variable is temp, which we associate with register $t0 since swap is a leaf procedure (see page 144). This register allocation corresponds to the variable declarations in the first part of the swap procedure in Figure 3.23.

Code for the Body of the Procedure swap

The remaining lines of C code in swap are

```
temp = v[k];
v[k] = v[k+1];
v[k+1] = temp;
```

Recall that the memory address for MIPS refers to the *byte* address, and so words are really 4 bytes apart. Hence we need to multiply the index k by 4 before adding it to the address. *Forgetting that sequential word addresses differ by 4 instead of by 1 is a common mistake in assembly language programming.* Hence the first step is to get the address of v[k] by multiplying k by 4:

```
add    $t1, $a1,$a1    # reg $t1 = k * 2
add    $t1, $t1,$t1    # reg $t1 = k * 4
add    $t1, $a0,$t1    # reg $t1 = v + (k * 4)
                       # reg $t1 has the address of v[k]
```

Now we load v[k] using $t1, and then v[k+1] by adding 4 to $t1:

```
lw     $t0, 0($t1)     # reg $t0 (temp) = v[k]
lw     $t2, 4($t1)     # reg $t2 = v[k + 1]
                       # refers to next element of v
```

Next we store $t0 and $t2 to the swapped addresses:

```
sw     $t2, 0($t1)     # v[k] = reg $t2
sw     $t0, 4($t1)     # v[k+1] = reg $t0 (temp)
```

Procedure body		
swap: add	$t1, $a1, a1	# reg $t1 = k * 2
add	$t1, $t1, t1	# reg $t1 = k * 4
add	$t1, $a0, $t1	# reg $t1 = v + (k * 4)
		# reg $t1 has the address of v[k]
lw	$t0, 0($t1)	# reg $t0 (temp) = v[k]
lw	$t2, 4($t1)	# reg $t2 = v[k + 1]
		# refers to next element of v
sw	$t2, 0($t1)	# v[k] = reg $t2
sw	$t0, 4($t1)	# v[k+1] = reg $t0 (temp)

Procedure return		
jr	$ra	# return to calling routine

FIGURE 3.24 MIPS assembly code of the procedure swap **in Figure 3.23.**

Now we have allocated registers and written the code to perform the operations of the procedure. The only missing code is the code that preserves for the caller the saved registers that are used within swap. Since we are not using saved registers in this leaf procedure, there is nothing to preserve.

The Full swap Procedure

We are now ready for the whole routine, which includes the procedure label and the return jump. To make it easier to follow, we identify in Figure 3.24 each block of code with its purpose in the procedure.

The Procedure sort

To ensure that you appreciate the rigor of programming in assembly language, we'll try a second, longer example. In this case, we'll build a routine that calls the swap procedure. This program sorts an array of integers. Figure 3.25 shows the C version of the program. Once again we present this procedure in several steps, concluding with the full procedure.

Register Allocation for sort

The two parameters of the procedure sort, v and n, are in the parameter registers $a0 and $a1, and we assign register $s0 to i and register $s1 to j.

Code for the Body of the Procedure sort

The procedure body consists of two nested *for* loops and a call to swap that includes parameters. Let's unwrap the code from the outside to the middle.

The first translation step is the first *for* loop:

```
for (i = 0; i < n; i = i + 1) {
```

```
sort (int v[], int n)
{
    int i, j;
    for (i = 0; i < n; i = i + 1) {
        for (j = i - 1; j >= 0 && v[j] > v[j + 1]; j = j - 1) { swap(v,j);
        }
    }
}
```

FIGURE 3.25   A C procedure that performs a sort on the array v. In case you are unfamiliar with C, the three parts of the first *for* statement are the initialization that happens before the first iteration (i = 0), the test if the loop should iterate again (i < n), and the operation that happens at the end of each iteration (i = i + 1). Web Extension II at *www.mkp.com/cod2e.htm* shows the C and Pascal versions of this procedure side by side.

Recall that the C *for* statement has three parts: initialization, loop test, and iteration increment. It takes just one instruction to initialize i to 0, the first part of the *for* statement:

```
        move  $s0, $zero    # i = 0
```

(Remember that move is a pseudoinstruction provided by the assembler for the convenience of the assembly language programmer; see page 157.) It also takes just one instruction to increment i, the last part of the *for* statement:

```
        addi  $s0, $s0, 1    # i = i + 1
```

The loop should be exited if i < n is *not* true, or, said another way, should be exited if i ≥ n. The set on less than instruction sets register $t0 to 1 if $s0 < $a1 and 0 otherwise. Since we want to test if $s0 ≥ $a1, we branch if register $t0 is 0. This test takes two instructions:

```
for1tst: slt  $t0, $s0, $a1   # reg $t0 = 0 if $s0 ≥ $a1 (i≥n)
         beq  $t0, $zero,exit1 # go to exit1 if $s0≥$a1 (i≥n)
```

The bottom of the loop just jumps back to the loop test:

```
         j    for1tst         # jump to test of outer loop
exit1:
```

The skeleton code of the first *for* loop is then

```
         move $s0, $zero    # i = 0
for1tst: slt  $t0, $s0, $a1 # reg $t0 = 0 if $s0 ≥ $a1 (i≥n)
         beq  $t0, $zero,exit1 # go to exit1 if $s0≥$a1 (i≥n)
         . . .
         (body of first for loop)
         . . .
         addi $s0, $s0, 1   # i = i + 1
         j    for1tst       # jump to test of outer loop
exit1:
```

Voila! Exercise 3.9 explores writing faster code for similar loops.

The second *for* loop looks like this in C:

```
for (j = i - 1; j >= 0 && v[j] > v[j + 1]; j = j - 1) {
```

The initialization portion of this loop is again one instruction:

```
addi    $s1, $s0, -1        # j = i - 1
```

The decrement of j at the end of the loop is also one instruction:

```
addi    $s1, $s1, -1        # j = j - 1
```

The loop test has two parts. We exit the loop if either condition fails, so the first test must exit the loop if it fails ($j < 0$):

```
for2tst: slti   $t0, $s1, 0 # reg $t0 = 1 if $s1 < 0 (j < 0)
         bne    $t0, $zero, exit2 # go to exit2 if $s1<0 (j < 0)
```

This branch will skip over the second condition test. If it doesn't skip, $j \geq 0$.

The second test exits if v[j] > v[j + 1] is *not* true, or exits if v[j] ≤ v[j + 1]. First we create the address by multiplying j by 4 (since we need a byte address) and add it to the base address of v:

```
add     $t1, $s1,$s1        # reg $t1 = j * 2
add     $t1, $t1,$t1        # reg $t1 = j * 4
add     $t2, $a0,$t1        # reg $t2 = v + (j * 4)
```

Now we load v[j]:

```
lw      $t3, 0($t2)         # reg $t3   = v[j]
```

Since we know that the second element is just the following word, we add 4 to the address in register $t2 to get v[j + 1]:

```
lw      $t4, 4($t2)         # reg $t4   = v[j + 1]
```

The test of v[j] ≤ v[j + 1] is the same as v[j + 1] ≥ v[j], so the two instructions of the exit test are

```
slt     $t0, $t4, $t3       # reg $t0 = 0 if $t4   ≥ $t3
beq     $t0, $zero,exit2    # go to exit2 if $t4   ≥ $t3
```

The bottom of the loop jumps back to the inner loop test:

```
j       for2tst             # jump to test of inner loop
```

Combining the pieces together, the skeleton of the second *for* loop looks like this:

```
addi    $s1, $s0, -1        # j = i - 1
for2tst: slti $t0, $s1, 0   #  reg $t0 = 1 if $s1 < 0 (j<0)
bne     $t0, $zero,exit2    # go to exit2 if $s1 < 0 (j<0)
add     $t1, $s1,$s1        # reg $t1 = j * 2
```

```
add     $t1, $t1,$t1      # reg $t1 = j * 4
add     $t2, $a0,$t1      # reg $t2 = v + (j * 4)
lw      $t3, 0($t2)       # reg $t3   = v[j]
lw      $t4, 4($t2)       # reg $t4   = v[j + 1]
slt     $t0, $t4, $t3     #  reg $t0 = 0 if $t4  ≥ $t3
beq     $t0, $zero,exit2  # go to exit2 if $t4   ≥ $t3
        . . .
        (body of second for loop)
        . . .
addi    $s1, $s1, -1      # j = j - 1
j       for2tst           # jump to test of inner loop
exit2:
```

The Procedure Call in sort

The next step is the body of the second *for* loop:

```
swap(v,j);
```

Calling swap is easy enough:

```
jal    swap
```

Passing Parameters in sort

The problem comes when we want to pass parameters because the sort procedure needs the values in registers $a0 and $a1, yet the swap procedure needs to have its parameters placed in those same registers. One solution is to copy the parameters for sort into other registers earlier in the procedure, making registers $a0 and $a1 available for the call of swap. (This copy is faster than saving and restoring on the stack.) We first copy $a0 and $a1 into $s2 and $s3 during the procedure:

```
move    $s2, $a0    # copy parameter $a0 into $s2
move    $s3, $a1    # copy parameter $a1 into $s3
```

Then we pass the parameters to swap with these two instructions:

```
move    $a0, $s2    # first swap parameter is v
move    $a1, $s1    # second swap parameter is j
```

Preserving Registers in sort

The only remaining code is the saving and restoring of registers. Clearly we must save the return address in register $ra, since sort is a procedure and is called itself. The sort procedure also uses the saved registers $s0, $s1, $s2, and $s3, so they must be saved. The prologue of the sort procedure is then

```
addi   $sp,$sp,-20   # make room on stack for 5 regs
sw     $ra,16($sp)   # save $ra on stack
sw     $s3,12($sp)   # save $s3 on stack
sw     $s2, 8($sp)   # save $s2 on stack
sw     $s1, 4($sp)   # save $s1 on stack
sw     $s0, 0($sp)   # save $s0 on stack
```

The tail of the procedure simply reverses all these instructions, then adds a jr to return.

The Full Procedure sort

Now we put all the pieces together in Figure 3.26, being careful to replace references to registers $a0 and $a1 in the *for* loops with references to registers $s2 and $s3. Once again to make the code easier to follow, we identify each block of code with its purpose in the procedure. In this example, 9 lines of the sort procedure in C became the 35 lines in the MIPS assembly language.

Elaboration: One optimization that would work well in this example is *procedure inlining*. Instead of passing arguments in parameters and invoking the code with a jal instruction, the compiler would copy the code from the body of the swap procedure where the call to swap appears in the code. Inlining would avoid four instructions in this example. The downside of the inlining optimization is that the compiled code would be bigger, assuming that the inlined procedure is called from several locations. Such a code expansion might turn into *lower* performance if it increased the cache miss rate; see Chapter 7.

The MIPS compilers always save room on the stack for the arguments in case they need to be stored, so in reality they always increment $sp by 16 to make room for all 4 argument registers (16 bytes). One reason is that C provides a vararg option that allows a pointer to pick, say, the third argument to a procedure. When the compiler encouters the rare vararg, it copies the registers onto the stack into the reserved locations.

Saving registers				
	sort:	addi	$sp,$sp, -20	# make room on stack for 5 registers
		sw	$ra, 16($sp)	# save $ra on stack
		sw	$s3,12($sp)	# save $s3 on stack
		sw	$s2, 8($sp)	# save $s2 on stack
		sw	$s1, 4($sp)	# save $s1 on stack
		sw	$s0, 0($sp)	# save $s0 on stack
Procedure body				
Move parameters		move	$s2, $a0	# copy parameter $a0 into $s2 (save $a0)
		move	$s3, $a1	# copy parameter $a1 into $s3 (save $a1)
Outer loop		move	$s0, $zero	# i = 0
	for1tst:slt		$t0, $s0, $s3	# reg $t0 = 0 if $s0 ≥ $s3 (i ≥ n)
		beq	$t0, $zero, exit1	# go to exit1 if $s0 ≥ $s3 (i ≥ n)
Inner loop		addi	$s1, $s0, -1	# j = i - 1
	for2tst:slti		$t0, $s1, 0	# reg $t0 = 1 if $s1 < 0 (j < 0)
		bne	$t0, $zero, exit2	# go to exit2 if $s1 < 0 (j < 0)
		add	$t1, $s1, $s1	# reg $t1 = j * 2
		add	$t1, $t1, $t1	# reg $t1 = j * 4
		add	$t2, $s2, $t1	# reg $t2 = v + (j * 4)
		lw	$t3, 0($t2)	# reg $t3 = v[j]
		lw	$t4, 4($t2)	# reg $t4 = v[j + 1]
		slt	$t0, $t4, $t3	# reg $t0 = 0 if $t4 ≥ $t3
		beq	$t0, $zero, exit2	# go to exit2 if $t4 ≥ $t3
Pass parameters and call		move	$a0, $s2	# 1st parameter of swap is v (old $a0)
		move	$a1, $s1	# 2nd parameter of swap is j
		jal	swap	# swap code shown in Figure 3.24
Inner loop		addi	$s1, $s1, -1	# j = j - 1
		j	for2tst	# jump to test of inner loop
Outer loop	exit2:	addi	$s0, $s0, 1	# i = i + 1
		j	for1tst	# jump to test of outer loop
Restoring registers				
	exit1:	lw	$s0, 0($sp)	# restore $s0 from stack
		lw	$s1, 4($sp)	# restore $s1 from stack
		lw	$s2, 8($sp)	# restore $s2 from stack
		lw	$s3,12($sp)	# restore $s3 from stack
		lw	$ra,16($sp)	# restore $ra from stack
		addi	$sp,$sp, 20	# restore stack pointer
Procedure return				
		jr	$ra	# return to calling routine

FIGURE 3.26   MIPS assembly version of procedure sort **in Figure 3.25 on page 166.**

3.11   Arrays versus Pointers

A challenging topic for any new programmer is understanding pointers. Comparing assembly code that uses arrays and array indices to the assembly code that uses pointers offers insight into that difference. This section shows C and MIPS assembly versions of two procedures to clear a sequence of words in memory: one using array indices and one using pointers. Figure 3.27 shows the two C procedures.

> **Hardware Software Interface**
>
> People used to be taught to use pointers in C to get greater efficiency than available with arrays: "Use pointers, even if you can't understand the code." The procedure clear2 in Figure 3.27 is such an example. Modern optimizing compilers can produce just as good code for the array version of the code. The purpose of this section is to show how pointers map into MIPS instructions, and not to endorse a questionable style.

```
clear1(int array[], int size)
{
  int i;
  for (i = 0; i < size; i = i + 1)
      array[i] = 0;
}


clear2(int *array, int size)
{
  int *p;
  for (p = &array[0]; p < &array[size]; p = p + 1)
      *p = 0;
}
```

FIGURE 3.27   Two C procedures for setting an array to all zeros. Clear1 uses indices, while clear2 uses pointers. The second procedure needs some explanation for those unfamiliar with C. The address of a variable is indicated by & and referring to the object pointed to by a pointer is indicated by *. The declarations declare that array and p are pointers to integers. The first part of the *for* loop in clear2 assigns the address of the first element of array to the pointer p. The second part of the *for* loop tests to see if the pointer is pointing beyond the last element of array. Incrementing a pointer by one, in the last part of the *for* loop, means moving the pointer to the next sequential object of its declared size. Since p is a pointer to integers, the compiler will generate MIPS instructions to increment p by four, the number of bytes in a MIPS integer. The assignment in the loop places 0 in the object pointed to by p.

Array Version of Clear

Let's start with the array version, clear1, focusing on the body of the loop and ignoring the procedure linkage code. We assume that the two parameters array and size are found in the registers $a0 and $a1, and that i is allocated to register $t0.

The initialization of i, the first part of the *for* loop, is straightforward:

```
move  $t0,$zero       # i = 0 (register $t0 = 0)
```

To set array[i] to 0 we must first get its address. Start by multiplying i by 4 to get the byte address:

```
loop1: add   $t1,$t0,$t0     # $t1 = i * 2
       add   $t1,$t1,$t1     # $t1 = i * 4
```

Since the starting address of the array is in a register, we must add it to the index to get the address of array[i] using an add instruction:

```
add   $t2,$a0,$t1     # $t2 = address of array[i]
```

(This example is an ideal situation for indexed addressing; see page 175.) Finally we can store 0 in that address:

```
sw    $zero, 0($t2)   # array[i] = 0
```

This instruction is the end of the body of the loop, so the next step is to increment i:

```
addi  $t0,$t0,1       # i = i + 1
```

The loop test checks if i is less than size:

```
slt   $t3,$t0,$a1     # $t3 = (i < size)
bne   $t3,$zero,loop1 # if (i < size) go to loop1
```

We have now seen all the pieces of the procedure. Here is the MIPS code for clearing an array using indices:

```
       move  $t0,$zero       # i = 0
loop1: add   $t1,$t0,$t0     # $t1 = i * 2
       add   $t1,$t1,$t1     # $t1 = i * 4
       add   $t2,$a0,$t1     # $t2 = address of array[i]
       sw    $zero, 0($t2)   # array[i] = 0
       addi  $t0,$t0,1       # i = i + 1
       slt   $t3,$t0,$a1     # $t3 = (i < size)
       bne   $t3,$zero,loop1 # if (i < size) go to loop1
```

(This code works as long as size is greater than 0.)

Pointer Version of Clear

The second procedure that uses pointers allocates the two parameters array
and size to the registers $a0 and $a1 and allocates p to register $t0. The code
for the second procedure starts with assigning the pointer p to the address of
the first element of the array:

```
        move    $t0,$a0     # p = address of array[0]
```

The next code is the body of the *for* loop, which simply stores 0 into p:

```
 loop2:  sw      $zero,0($t0) # Memory[p] = 0
```

This instruction implements the body of the loop, so the next code is the iteration increment, which changes p to point to the next word:

```
        addi    $t0,$t0,4   # p = p + 4
```

Incrementing a pointer by 1 means moving the pointer to the next sequential
object in C. Since p is a pointer to integers, each of which use 4 bytes, the compiler increments p by 4.

   The loop test is next. The first step is calculating the address of the last element of array. Start with multiplying size by 4 to get its byte address:

```
        add   $t1,$a1,$a1     # $t1 = size * 2
        add   $t1,$t1,$t1     # $t1 = size * 4
```

and then we add the product to the starting address of the array to get the
address of the first word *after* the array:

```
        add   $t2,$a0,$t1     # $t2 = address of array[size]
```

The loop test is simply to see if p is less than the last element of array:

```
        slt   $t3,$t0,$t2     # $t3 = (p<&array[size])
        bne   $t3,$zero,loop2# if (p<&array[size]) go to loop2
```

   With all the pieces completed, we can show a pointer version of the code to
zero an array:

```
        move $t0,$a0         # p = address of array[0]
 loop2:  sw   $zero,0($t0)    # Memory[p] = 0
        addi $t0,$t0,4       # p = p + 4
        add  $t1,$a1,$a1      # $t1 = size * 2
        add  $t1,$t1,$t1      # $t1 = size * 4
        add  $t2,$a0,$t1      # $t2 = address of array[size]
        slt  $t3,$t0,$t2      # $t3 = (p<&array[size])
        bne  $t3,$zero,loop2# if (p<&array[size]) go to loop2
```

As in the first example, this code assumes size is greater than 0.

Note that this program calculates the address of the end of the array every iteration of the loop, even though it does not change. A faster version of the code moves this calculation outside the loop:

```
        move $t0,$a0          # p = address of array[0]
        add  $t1,$a1,$a1      # $t1 = size * 2
        add  $t1,$t1,$t1      # $t1 = size * 4
        add  $t2,$a0,$t1      # $t2 = address of array[size]
loop2:  sw   $zero,0($t0)     # Memory[p] = 0
        addi $t0,$t0,4        # p = p + 4
        slt  $t3,$t0,$t2      # $t3 = (p<&array[size])
        bne  $t3,$zero,loop2  # if (p<&array[size]) go to loop2
```

Comparing the Two Versions of Clear

Comparing the two code sequences side by side illustrates the difference between array indices and pointers (the changes introduced by the pointer version are highlighted):

```
        move $t0,$zero    # i = 0              move $t0,$a0      # p = & array[0]
loop1:  add  $t1,$t0,$t0  # $t1 = i * 2        add  $t1,$a1,$a1  # $t1 = size * 2
        add  $t1,$t1,$t1  # $t1 = i * 4        add  $t1,$t1,$t1  # $t1 = size * 4
        add  $t2,$a0,$t1  # $t2 = &array[i]    add  $t2,$a0,$t1  # $t2 = &array[size]
        sw   $zero, 0($t2)# array[i] = 0  loop2: sw $zero,0($t0)# Memory[p] = 0
        addi $t0,$t0,1    # i = i + 1          addi $t0,$t0,4    # p = p + 4
        slt  $t3,$t0,$a1  # $t3 = (i < size)   slt  $t3,$t0,$t2  # $t3=(p<&array[size])
        bne  $t3,$zero,loop1# if () go to loop1 bne $t3,$zero,loop2# if () go to loop2
```

The version on the left must have the "multiply" and add inside the loop because i is incremented and each address must be recalculated from the new index; the memory pointer version on the right increments the pointer p directly. The pointer version reduces the instructions executed per iteration from 7 to 4. Many modern compilers will optimize the C code in clear1 to produce code similar to the assembly code above on the right-hand side.

Elaboration: The C compiler would add a test to be sure that size is greater than 0. One way would be to add a jump just before the first instruction of the loop to the slt instruction.

3.12

Real Stuff: PowerPC and 80x86 Instructions

Beauty is in the eye of the beholder.

American saying

Designers of instruction sets sometimes provide more powerful operations than those found in MIPS. The goal is generally to reduce the number of instructions executed by a program. The danger is that this reduction can occur at the cost of simplicity, increasing the time a program takes to execute because the instructions are slower. This slowness may be the result of a slower clock cycle time or of requiring more clock cycles than a simpler sequence (see section 2.8 on page 82).

The path toward operation complexity is thus fraught with peril. To avoid these problems, designers have moved toward simpler instructions. Section 3.13 demonstrates the pitfalls of complexity.

The IBM/Motorola PowerPC

The PowerPC, made by IBM and Motorola and used in the Apple Macintosh, shares many similarities to MIPS: both have 32 integer registers, instructions are all 32 bits long, and data transfer is possible only with loads and stores. The primary difference is two more addressing modes plus a few operations.

Indexed Addressing

In the examples above we saw cases where we needed one register to hold the base of the array and the other to hold the index of the array. PowerPC provides an addressing mode, often called *indexed addressing*, that allows two registers to be added together. The MIPS code

```
add     $t0,$a0,$s3  # $a0 has base of an array, $s3 is index
lw      $t1,0($t0)   # reg $t1 gets Memory[$a0+$s3]
```

could be replaced by the following single instruction in PowerPC:

```
lw      $t1,$a0+$s3  # reg $t1 gets Memory[$a0+$s3]
```

Using the same notation as Figure 3.17, Figure 3.28 shows indexed addressing. It is available with both loads and stores.

Update Addressing

Imagine the case of a code sequence marching through an array of words in memory, such as in the array version of clear1 on page 172. A frequent pair

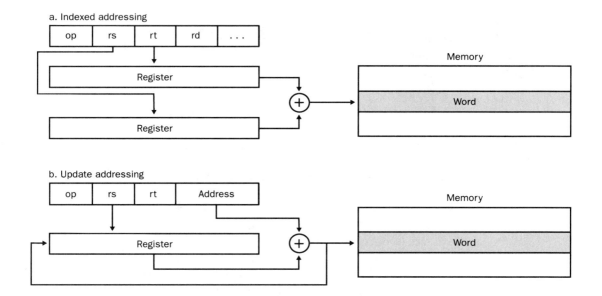

FIGURE 3.28   Illustration of indexed and update addressing mode. The operand is shaded in color.

of operations would be loading a word and then incrementing the base register to point to the next word. The idea of *update addressing* is to have a new version of data transfer instructions that will automatically increment the base register to point to the next word each time data is transferred. Since the MIPS architecture uses byte addresses and words are 4 bytes, this new form would be equivalent to this pair of MIPS instructions:

```
lw      $t0,4($s3)    # reg $t0 gets Memory[$s3+4]
addi    $s3,$s3,4     # $s3 = $s3 + 4
```

The PowerPC includes an instruction like this:

```
lwu     $t0,4($s3)    # reg $t0=Memory[$s3+4]; $s3 = $s3+4
```

That is, the register is updated with the address calculated as part of the load. Figure 3.28 also shows update addressing. PowerPC has update addressing options for both base and indexed addressing, and for both loads and stores.

Unique PowerPC Instructions

The PowerPC instructions follow the same architecture style as MIPS, largely relying on fast execution of simple instructions for performance. Here are a few exceptions.

The first is load multiple and store multiple. These can transfer up to 32 words of data in a single instruction and are intended to make fast copies of locations in memory by using load multiple and store multiple back to back. They also save code size when saving or restoring registers.

A second example is loops. The PowerPC has a special counter register, separate from the other 32 registers, to try to improve performance of a *for* loop.

Suppose we wanted to execute the following C code:

```
for (i = n; i != 0; i = i - 1)
    {. . .};
```

If we want to decrement a register, compare to 0, and then branch as long as the register is not 0, we could use the following MIPS instructions:

```
Loop:  ...
       addi    $t0,$t0,-1      # $t0 = $t0 - 1
       bne     $t0,$zero, Loop # if $t0 != 0 go to Loop
```

In PowerPC we could use a single instruction instead:

```
       bc      Loop,ctr!=0     # $ctr = $ctr - 1;
                               # if $ctr != 0 go to Loop
```

**Hardware
Software
Interface**

In addition to going against the advice of simplicity, such sophisticated operations may not *exactly* match what the compiler needs to produce. For example, suppose that instead of decrementing by one, the compiler wanted to increment by four, or instead of branching on not equal zero, the compiler wanted to branch if the index was less than or equal to the limit. Then the instruction just described would be a mismatch. When faced with such objections, the instruction set designer might then generalize the operation, adding another operand to specify the increment and perhaps an option on which branch condition to use. Then the danger is that a common case, say, incrementing by one, will be slower than a sequence of simple operations.

The Intel 80x86

MIPS was the vision of a single small group in 1985; the pieces of this architecture fit nicely together, and the whole architecture can be described succinctly. Such is not the case for the 80x86; it is the product of several independent groups who evolved the architecture over almost 20 years, adding new features to the original instruction set as someone might add clothing to a packed bag. Here are important 80x86 milestones:

- **1978**: The Intel 8086 architecture was announced as an assembly-language-compatible extension of the then-successful Intel 8080, an 8-bit microprocessor. The 8086 is a 16-bit architecture, with all internal registers 16 bits wide. Unlike MIPS, the registers have dedicated uses, and hence the 8086 is not considered a *general-purpose register* architecture.

- **1980**: The Intel 8087 floating-point coprocessor is announced. This architecture extends the 8086 with about 60 floating-point instructions. Instead of using registers, it relies on a stack (see section 3.15 and section 4.9).

- **1982**: The 80286 extended the 8086 architecture by increasing the address space to 24 bits, by creating an elaborate memory-mapping and protection model (see Chapter 7), and by adding a few instructions to round out the instruction set and to manipulate the protection model.

- **1985**: The 80386 extended the 80286 architecture to 32 bits. In addition to a 32-bit architecture with 32-bit registers and a 32-bit address space, the 80386 added new addressing modes and additional operations. The added instructions make the 80386 nearly a general-purpose register machine. The 80386 also added paging support in addition to segmented addressing (see Chapter 7). Like the 80286, the 80386 has a mode to execute 8086 programs without change.

- **1989–95**: The subsequent 80486 in 1989, Pentium in 1992, and Pentium Pro in 1995 were aimed at higher performance, with only four instructions added to the user-visible instruction set: three to help with multiprocessing (Chapter 9) and a conditional move instruction.

- **1997**: After the Pentium and Pentium Pro were shipping, Intel announced that it would expand the Pentium and the Pentium Pro architectures with MMX. This new set of 57 instructions uses the floating-point stack to accelerate multimedia and communication applications. MMX instructions typically operate on multiple short data elements at a time, in the tradition of single instruction, multiple data (SIMD) architectures (see Chapter 9).

This history illustrates the impact of the "golden handcuffs" of compatibility on the 80x86, as the existing software base at each step was too important to jeopardize with significant architectural changes.

Whatever the artistic failures of the 80x86, keep in mind that there are more instances of this architectural family than of any other in the world, perhaps 300 million in 1997. Nevertheless, this checkered ancestry has led to an architecture that is difficult to explain and impossible to love.

Brace yourself for what you are about to see! Do *not* try to read this section with the care you would need to write 80x86 programs; the goal instead is to give you familiarity with the strengths and weaknesses of the world's most popular architecture.

Rather than show the entire 16-bit and 32-bit instruction set, in this section we concentrate on the 32-bit subset that originated with the 80386, as this portion of the architecture will be increasingly dominant over time. We start our explanation with the registers and addressing modes, move on to the integer operations, and conclude with an examination of instruction encoding.

80x86 Registers and Data Addressing Modes

The evolution of the instruction set can be seen in the registers of the 80386 (Figure 3.29). The 80386 basically extended all 16-bit registers (except the segment registers) to 32 bits, prefixing an *E* to their name to indicate the 32-bit version. We'll refer to them generically as GPRs (general-purpose registers). With only eight 80386 GPRs, mean MIPS programs can use four times as many.

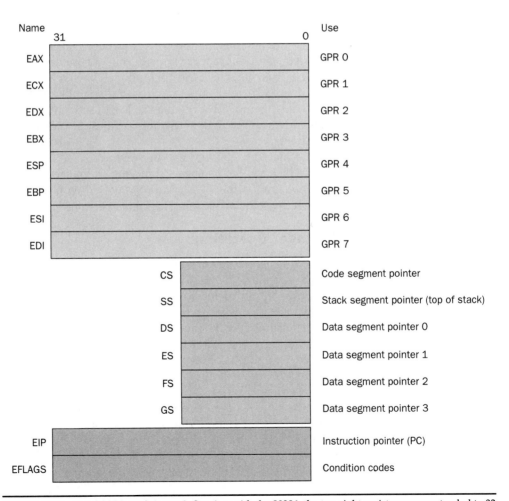

FIGURE 3.29   The 80386 register set. Starting with the 80386, the top eight registers were extended to 32 bits and could also be used as general-purpose registers.

Source/destination operand type	Second source operand
Register	Register
Register	Immediate
Register	Memory
Memory	Register
Memory	Immediate

FIGURE 3.30   Instruction types for the arithmetic, logical, and data transfer instructions. The 80x86 allows the combinations shown. The only restriction is the absence of a memory-memory mode. Immediates may be 8, 16, or 32 bits in length; a register is any one of the 14 major registers in Figure 3.29 (not EIP or EFLAGS).

The arithmetic, logical, and data transfer instructions are two-operand instructions that allow the combinations shown in Figure 3.30. There are two important differences here. The 80x86 arithmetic and logical instructions must have one operand act as both a source and a destination; MIPS allows separate registers for source and destination. This restriction puts more pressure on the limited registers, since one source register must be modified. The second important difference is that one of the operands can be in memory. Thus virtually any instruction may have one operand in memory, unlike MIPS and PowerPC.

The seven data memory-addressing modes, described in detail below, offer two sizes of addresses within the instruction. These so-called *displacements* can be 8 bits or 32 bits.

Although a memory operand can use any addressing mode, there are restrictions on which *registers* can be used in a mode. Figure 3.31 shows the 80x86 addressing modes and which GPRs cannot be used with that mode, plus how you would get the same effect using MIPS instructions.

80x86 Integer Operations

The 8086 provides support for both 8-bit (*byte*) and 16-bit (*word*) data types. The 80386 adds 32-bit addresses and data (*double words*) in the 80x86. The data type distinctions apply to register operations as well as memory accesses. Almost every operation works on both 8-bit data and on one longer data size. That size is determined by the mode, and is either 16 bits or 32 bits.

Clearly some programs want to operate on data of all three sizes, so the 80386 architects provide a convenient way to specify each version without expanding code size significantly. They decided that most programs would be dominated by either 16-bit or 32-bit data, and so it made sense to be able to set a default large size. This default data size is set by a bit in the code segment register. To override the default data size, an 8-bit *prefix* is attached to the instruction to tell the machine to use the other large size for this instruction.

The prefix solution was borrowed from the 8086, which allows multiple prefixes to modify instruction behavior. The three original prefixes override the

Mode	Description	Register restrictions	MIPS equivalent
Register indirect	Address is in a register.	not ESP or EBP	`lw $s0,0($s1)`
Based mode with 8- or 32-bit displacement	Address is contents of base register plus displacement.	not ESP or EBP	`lw $s0,100($s1) # ≤16-bit` `# displacement`

Base plus scaled index	The address is
	Base + (2^Scale x Index)
	where Scale has the value 0, 1, 2, or 3.
		Base: any GPR
		Index: not ESP
			`mul $t0,$s1,4`
			`add $t0,$t0,$s1`
			`lw  $s0,0($t0)`

Base plus scaled index with 8- or 32-bit displacement	The address is
	Base + (2^Scale x Index) + displacement
	where Scale has the value 0, 1, 2, or 3.
		Base: any GPR
		Index: not ESP
			`mul $t0, $s1,4`
			`add $t0, $t0,$s1`
			`lw  $s0, 100($t0) # ≤16-bit`
			`# displacement`

FIGURE 3.31   80x86 32-bit addressing modes with register restrictions and the equivalent MIPS code. The Base plus Scaled Index addressing mode, not found in MIPS or the PowerPC, is included to avoid the multiplies by four (scale factor of 2) to turn an index in a register into a byte address (see Figures 3.24 and 3.26). A scale factor of 1 is used for 16-bit data, and a scale factor of 3 for 64-bit data. Scale factor of 0 means the address is not scaled. If the displacement is longer than 16 bits in the second or fourth modes, then the MIPS equivalent mode would need two more instructions: a `lui` to load the upper 16 bits of the displacement and an `add` to sum the upper address with the base register $s1. (Intel gives two different names to what is called Based addressing mode—Based and Indexed—but they are essentially identical and we combine them here.)

default segment register, lock the bus to support a semaphore (see Chapter 9), or repeat the following instruction until the register ECX counts down to 0. This last prefix was intended to be paired with a byte move instruction to move a variable number of bytes. The 80386 also added a prefix to override the default address size.

The 80x86 integer operations can be divided into four major classes:

1. Data movement instructions, including move, push, and pop

2. Arithmetic and logic instructions, including test and integer and decimal arithmetic operations

3. Control flow, including conditional branches, unconditional jumps, calls, and returns

4. String instructions, including string move and string compare

The first two categories are unremarkable, except that the arithmetic and logic instruction operations allow the destination to either be a register or a memory location. Figure 3.32 shows some typical 80x86 instructions and their functions.

Conditional branches on the PowerPC and the 80x86 are based on *condition codes* or *flags*. Condition codes are set as a side effect of an operation; most are used to compare the value of a result to 0. Branches then test the condition codes. The argument for condition codes is that they occur as part of normal operations and are faster to test than it is to compare registers as MIPS does for

Instruction	Function
JE name	if equal(condition code) {EIP=name}; EIP-128 ≤ name < EIP+128
JMP name	EIP=name
CALL name	SP=SP-4; M[SP]=EIP+5; EIP=name;
MOVW EBX,[EDI+45]	EBX=M[EDI+45]
PUSH ESI	SP=SP-4; M[SP]=ESI
POP EDI	EDI=M[SP]; SP=SP+4
ADD EAX,#6765	EAX= EAX+6765
TEST EDX,#42	Set condition code (flags) with EDX and 42_{hex}
MOVSL	M[EDI]=M[ESI]; EDI=EDI+4; ESI=ESI+4

FIGURE 3.32   Some typical 80x86 instructions and their functions. A list of frequent operations appears in Figure 3.33. The CALL saves the EIP of the next instruction on the stack. (EIP is the Intel PC.)

beq and bne. The argument against condition codes is that the compare to 0 extends the time of the operation, since it uses extra hardware after the operation, and that often the programmer must use compare instructions to test a value that is not the result of an operation. Also, PC-relative branch addresses must be specified in the number of bytes, since unlike MIPS, 80386 instructions are not all 4 bytes in length.

String instructions are part of the 8080 ancestry of the 80x86 and are not commonly executed in most programs. They are often slower than equivalent software routines (see the fallacy on page 185).

Figure 3.33 lists some of the integer 80x86 instructions. Many of the instructions are available in both byte and word formats.

80x86 Instruction Encoding

Saving the worst for last, the encoding of instructions in the 8086 is complex, with many different instruction formats. Instructions for the 80386 may vary from 1 byte, when there are no operands, up to 17 bytes.

Figure 3.34 shows the instruction format for several of the example instructions in Figure 3.32. The opcode byte usually contains a bit saying whether the operand is 8 bits or 32 bits. For some instructions the opcode may include the addressing mode and the register; this is true in many instructions that have the form "register = register op immediate." Other instructions use a "postbyte" or extra opcode byte, labeled "mod, reg, r/m," which contains the addressing mode information. This postbyte is used for many of the instructions that address memory. The base plus scaled index mode uses a second postbyte, labeled "sc, index, base."

Instruction	Meaning
Control	**Conditional and unconditional branches**
JNZ, JZ	Jump if condition to EIP + 8-bit offset; JNE (for JNZ), JE (for JZ) are alternative names
JMP	Unconditional jump—8-bit or 16-bit offset
CALL	Subroutine call—16-bit offset; return address pushed onto stack
RET	Pops return address from stack and jumps to it
LOOP	Loop branch—decrement ECX; jump to EIP + 8-bit displacement if ECX ≠ 0
Data transfer	**Move data between registers or between register and memory**
MOV	Move between two registers or between register and memory
PUSH, POP	Push source operand on stack; pop operand from stack top to a register
LES	Load ES and one of the GPRs from memory
Arithmetic, logical	**Arithmetic and logical operations using the data registers and memory**
ADD, SUB	Add source to destination; subtract source from destination; register-memory format
CMP	Compare source and destination; register-memory format
SHL, SHR, RCR	Shift left; shift logical right; rotate right with carry condition code as fill
CBW	Convert byte in 8 rightmost bits of EAX to 16-bit word in right of EAX
TEST	Logical AND of source and destination sets condition codes
INC, DEC	Increment destination, decrement destination; register-memory format
OR, XOR	Logical OR; exclusive OR; register-memory format
String	**Move between string operands; length given by a repeat prefix**
MOVS	Copies from string source to destination by incrementing ESI and EDI; may be repeated
LODS	Loads a byte, word, or double word of a string into the EAX register

FIGURE 3.33   Some typical operations on the 80x86. Many operations use register-memory format, where either the source or the destination may be memory and the other may be a register or immediate operand.

Figure 3.35 shows the encoding of the two postbyte address specifiers for both 16-bit and 32-bit mode. Unfortunately, to fully understand which registers and which addressing modes are available, you need to see the encoding of all addressing modes and sometimes even the encoding of the instructions.

80x86 Conclusion

Intel had a 16-bit microprocessor two years before its competitors' more elegant architectures, such as the Motorola 68000, and this head start led to the selection of the 8086 as the CPU for the IBM PC. Intel engineers generally acknowledge that the 80x86 is more difficult to build than machines like MIPS, but the much larger market means Intel can afford more resources to help overcome the added complexity. What the 80x86 lacks in style is made up in quantity, making it beautiful from the right perspective.

The saving grace is that the most frequently used 80x86 architectural components are not too difficult to implement, as Intel has demonstrated by rapidly improving performance of integer programs since 1978. To get that performance, compilers must avoid the portions of the architecture that are hard to implement fast.

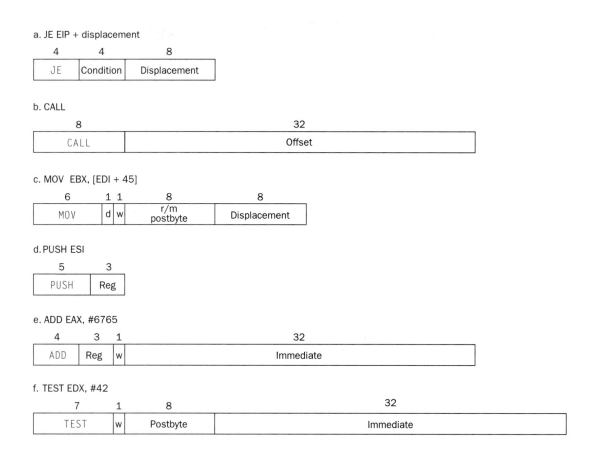

FIGURE 3.34 Typical 80x86 instruction formats. The encoding of the postbyte is shown in Figure 3.35. Many instructions contain the 1-bit field w, which says whether the operation is a byte or double word. The d field in MOV is used in instructions that may move to or from memory and shows the direction of the move. The ADD instruction requires 32 bits for the immediate field because in 32-bit mode the immediates are either 8 bits or 32 bits. The immediate field in the TEST is 32 bits long because there is no 8-bit immediate for test in 32-bit mode. Overall, instructions may vary from 1 to 17 bytes in length. The long length comes from extra 1-byte prefixes, having both a 4-byte immediate and a 4-byte displacement address, using an opcode of 2 bytes, and using the scaled index mode specifier, which adds another byte.

reg	w = 0	w = 1		r/m	mod = 0		mod = 1		mod = 2		mod = 3
		16b	32b		16b	32b	16b	32b	16b	32b	
0	AL	AX	EAX	0	addr=BX+SI	=EAX	*same*	*same*	*same*	*same*	*same*
1	CL	CX	ECX	1	addr=BX+DI	=ECX	*addr as*	*addr as*	*addr as*	*addr as*	*as*
2	DL	DX	EDX	2	addr=BP+SI	=EDX	*mod=0*	*mod=0*	*mod=0*	*mod=0*	*reg*
3	BL	BX	EBX	3	addr=BP+SI	=EBX	*+ disp8*	*+ disp8*	*+ disp16*	*+ disp32*	*field*
4	AH	SP	ESP	4	addr=SI	=(sib)	SI+disp8	(sib)+disp8	SI+disp8	(sib)+disp32	"
5	CH	BP	EBP	5	addr=DI	=disp32	DI+disp8	EBP+disp8	DI+disp16	EBP+disp32	"
6	DH	SI	ESI	6	addr=disp16	=ESI	BP+disp8	ESI+disp8	BP+disp16	ESI+disp32	"
7	BH	DI	EDI	7	addr=BX	=EDI	BX+disp8	EDI+disp8	BX+disp16	EDI+disp32	"

FIGURE 3.35 The encoding of the first address specifier of the 80x86, "mod, reg, r/m." The first four columns show the encoding of the 3-bit reg field, which depends on the w bit from the opcode and whether the machine is in 16-bit mode (8086) or 32-bit mode (80386). The remaining columns explain the mod and r/m fields. The meaning of the 3-bit r/m field depends on the value in the 2-bit mod field and the address size. Basically, the registers used in the address calculation are listed in the sixth and seventh columns, under mod = 0, with mod = 1 adding an 8-bit displacement and mod = 2 adding a 16-bit or 32-bit displacement, depending on the address mode. The exceptions are r/m = 6 when mod = 1 or mod = 2 in 16-bit mode selects BP plus the displacement; r/m = 5 when mod = 1 or mod = 2 in 32-bit mode selects EBP plus displacement; and r/m = 4 in 32-bit mode when mod ≠ 3, where (sib) means use the scaled index mode shown in Figure 3.31 on page 181. When mod = 3, the r/m field indicates a register, using the same encoding as the reg field combined with the w bit.

3.13 Fallacies and Pitfalls

Fallacy: More powerful instructions mean higher performance.

Part of the power of the Intel 80x86 is the prefixes that can modify the execution of the following instruction. One prefix can repeat the following instruction until a counter counts down to 0. Thus, to move data in memory, it would seem that the natural instruction sequence is to use move with the repeat prefix to perform 32-bit memory-to-memory moves. On a 133-MHz Pentium (with the Triton chip set, 60-ns EDO DRAM, 256-KB cache), this user-level program can move data at about 40 MB/sec.

An alternative method, which uses the standard instructions found in all computers, is to load the data into the registers and then store the registers back to memory. This second version of this program, with the code replicated so as to reduce loop overhead, copies at about 60 MB/sec on the same machine, or 1.5 times faster. A third version, which used the larger floating-point registers instead of the integer registers of the 80x86, copies at about 80 MB/sec, or 2.0 times faster than the complex instruction.

Fallacy: Write in assembly language to obtain the highest performance.

At one time compilers for programming languages produced naive instruction sequences; the increasing sophistication of compilers means the gap between compiled code and code produced by hand is closing fast. In fact, to compete with current compilers, the assembly language programmer needs to thoroughly understand the concepts in Chapters 6 and 7 on processor pipelining and memory hierarchy.

This battle between compilers and assembly language coders is one situation in which humans are losing ground. For example, C offers the programmer a chance to give a hint to the compiler about which variables should be kept in registers versus spilled to memory. When compilers were poor at register allocation, such hints were vital to performance. In fact, some C textbooks spent a fair amount of time giving examples that effectively use register hints. Today's C compilers generally ignore such hints because the compiler does a better job at allocation than the programmer.

As a specific counterexample, we ran the MIPS assembly language programs in Figures 3.24 and 3.26 to compare performance to the C programs in Figures 3.23 and 3.25. Figure 3.36 shows the results. As you can see, the compiled program is 1.5 times faster than the assembled program. The compiler generally was able to create assembly language code that was tailored exactly to these conditions, while the assembly language program was written in a slightly more general fashion to make it easier to modify and understand. The specific improvements of the C compiler were a more streamlined procedure linkage convention and changing the address calculations to move the multiply outside the inner loop.

Even *if* writing by hand resulted in faster code, the dangers of writing in assembly language are longer time spent coding and debugging, the loss in portability, and the difficulty of maintaining such code. One of the few widely accepted axioms of software engineering is that coding takes longer if you write more lines, and it clearly takes many more lines to write a program in assembly language than in C. And once it is coded, the next danger is that it will become a popular program. Such programs always live longer than expected, meaning that someone will have to update the code over several years and make it work with new releases of operating systems and new models of ma-

Language	Time
Assembly	37.9 seconds
C	25.3 seconds

FIGURE 3.36 Performance comparison of the C and assembly language versions of the sort **and** swap **procedures in section 3.10.** The size of the array to be sorted was increased to 10,000 elements. The programs were run on a DECsystem 5900 with 128 MB of main memory and a 40-MHz R3000 processor using version 4.2a (Revision 47) of the Ultrix operating system. The C compiler was run with the −O option.

chines. Writing in higher-level language instead of assembly language not only allows future compilers to tailor the code to future machines, it also makes the software easier to maintain and allows the program to run on more brands of computers.

Pitfall: Forgetting that sequential word addresses in machines with byte addressing do not differ by one.

Many an assembly language programmer has toiled over errors made by assuming that the address of the next word can be found by incrementing the address in a register by one instead of by the word size in bytes. Forewarned is forearmed!

Pitfall: Using a pointer to an automatic variable outside its defining procedure.

A common mistake in dealing with pointers is to pass a result from a procedure that includes a pointer to an array that is declared local to that procedure. Following the stack discipline, in Figure 3.12 on page 139, the memory that contains the local array will be reused as soon as the procedure returns. Pointers to automatic variables can lead to chaos.

3.14 Concluding Remarks

Less is more.

Robert Browning, *Andrea del Sarto*, 1855

The two principles of the *stored-program* computer are the use of instructions that are indistinguishable from numbers and the use of alterable memory for programs. These principles allow a single machine to aid environmental scientists, financial advisers, and novelists in their specialties. The selection of a set of instructions that the machine can understand demands a delicate balance among the number of instructions needed to execute a program, the number of clock cycles needed by an instruction, and the speed of the clock. Four design principles guide the authors of instruction sets in making that delicate balance:

1. *Simplicity favors regularity.* Regularity motivates many features of the MIPS instruction set: keeping all instructions a single size, always requiring three register operands in arithmetic instructions, and keeping the register fields in the same place in each instruction format.

2. *Smaller is faster.* The desire for speed is the reason that MIPS has 32 registers rather than many more.

3. *Good design demands good compromises.* One MIPS example was the compromise between providing for larger addresses and constants in instructions and keeping all instructions the same length.

4. *Make the common case fast.* Examples of making the common MIPS case fast include PC-relative addressing for conditional branches and immediate addressing for constant operands.

Above this machine level is assembly language, a language that humans can read. The assembler translates it into the binary numbers that machines can understand, and it even "extends" the instruction set by creating symbolic instructions that aren't in the hardware. For instance, constants or addresses that are too big are broken into properly sized pieces, common variations of instructions are given their own name, and so on. The MIPS instructions we have covered so far (both real and pseudo) are listed in Figure 3.37.

These instructions are not born equal; the popularity of the few dominates the many. For example, Figure 3.38 shows the popularity of each class of instructions for two programs, gcc and spice. The varying popularity of instructions plays an important role in the chapters on performance, datapath, control, and pipelining.

Each category of MIPS instructions is associated with constructs that appear in programming languages:

- The arithmetic instructions correspond to the operations found in assignment statements.

- Data transfer instructions are most likely to occur when dealing with data structures like arrays or structures.

- The conditional branches are used in *if* statements and in loops.

- The unconditional jumps are used in procedure calls and returns and also for *case/switch* statements.

More of the MIPS instruction set is revealed in Chapter 4, after we explain computer arithmetic.

MIPS instructions	Name	Format	Pseudo MIPS	Name	Format
add	add	R	move	move	R
subtract	sub	R	multiply	mult	R
add immediate	addi	I	multiply immediate	multi	I
load word	lw	I	load immediate	li	I
store word	sw	I	branch less than	blt	I
load byte	lb	I	branch less than or equal	ble	I
store byte	sb	I	branch greater than	bgt	I
load upper immediate	lui	I	branch greater than or equal	bge	I
branch on equal	beq	I			
branch on not equal	bne	I			
set less than	slt	R			
set less than immediate	slti	I			
jump	j	J			
jump register	jr	R			
jump and link	jal	J			

FIGURE 3.37 The MIPS instruction set covered so far, with the real MIPS instructions on the left and the pseudoinstructions on the right. Appendix A (section A.10 on page A-49) describes the full MIPS architecture. Figure 3.18 on page 153 shows more details of the MIPS architecture revealed in this chapter.

Instruction class	MIPS examples	HLL correspondence	Frequency	
			gcc	spice
Arithmetic	add, sub, addi	operations in assignment statements	48%	50%
Data transfer	lw, sw, lb, sb, lui	references to data structures, such as arrays	33%	41%
Conditional branch	beq, bne, slt, slti	*if* statements and loops	17%	8%
Jump	j, jr, jal	procedure calls, returns, and *case/switch* statements	2%	1%

FIGURE 3.38 MIPS instruction classes, examples, correspondence to high-level program language constructs, and percentage of MIPS instructions executed by category for two programs, gcc and spice. Figure 4.54 on page 311 shows the percentage of the individual MIPS instructions executed.

3.15   Historical Perspective and Further Reading

accumulator: Archaic term for register. On-line use of it as a synonym for "register" is a fairly reliable indication that the user has been around quite a while.

Eric Raymond, *The New Hacker's Dictionary*, 1991

Accumulator Architectures

Hardware was precious in the earliest stored-program computers. As a consequence, computer pioneers could not afford the number of registers found in today's machines. In fact, these machines had a single register for arithmetic instructions. Since all operations would accumulate in a single register, it was called the *accumulator*, and this style of instruction set is given the same name. For example, EDSAC in 1949 had a single accumulator.

The three-operand format of MIPS suggests that a single register is at least two registers shy of our needs. Having the accumulator as both a source operand *and* as the destination of the operation fills part of the shortfall, but it still leaves us one operand short. That final operand is found in memory. Accumulator machines have the memory-based operand-addressing mode suggested earlier. It follows that the add instruction of an accumulator instruction set would look like this:

```
add    200
```

This instruction means add the accumulator to the word in memory at address 200 and place the sum back into the accumulator. No registers are specified because the accumulator is known to be both a source and a destination of the operation.

Compiling an Assignment Statement into Accumulator Instructions

Example

What is the accumulator-style assembly code for this C code?

```
A = B + C;
```

Answer

It would be translated into the following instructions in an accumulator instruction set:

```
load   AddressB  # Acc = Memory[AddressB], or Acc = B
add    AddressC  # Acc = B + Memory[AddressC],or Acc = B + C
store  AddressA  # Memory[AddressA] = Acc, or A = B + C
```

All variables in a program are allocated to memory in accumulator machines, instead of normally to registers as we saw for MIPS. One way to think about this is that variables are always spilled to memory in this style of machine. As you may imagine, it takes many more instructions to execute a program with a single-accumulator architecture. (See Exercise 3.19 for another example.)

The next step in the evolution of instruction sets was the addition of registers dedicated to specific operations. Hence, registers might be included to act as indices for array references in data transfer instructions, to act as separate accumulators for multiply or divide instructions, and to serve as the top-of-stack pointer. Perhaps the best-known example of this style of instruction set is found in the Intel 8086, the computer at the core of the IBM Personal Computer. This style of instruction set is labeled *extended accumulator, dedicated register,* or *special-purpose register.* Like the single-register accumulator machines, one operand may be in memory for arithmetic instructions. Like the MIPS architecture, however, there are also instructions where all the operands are registers.

General-Purpose Register Architectures

The generalization of the dedicated-register machine allows all the registers to be used for any purpose, hence the name *general-purpose register.* MIPS is an example of a general-purpose register machine. This style of instruction set may be further divided into those that allow one operand to be in memory as found in accumulator machines, called a *register-memory* architecture, and those that demand that operands always be in registers, called either a *load-store* or a *register-register* machine. Figure 3.39 shows a history of the number of registers in some popular computers.

Machine	Number of general-purpose registers	Architectural style	Year
EDSAC	1	accumulator	1949
IBM 701	1	accumulator	1953
CDC 6600	8	load-store	1963
IBM 360	16	register-memory	1964
DEC PDP-8	1	accumulator	1965
DEC PDP-11	8	register-memory	1970
Intel 8008	1	accumulator	1972
Motorola 6800	2	accumulator	1974
DEC VAX	16	register-memory, memory-memory	1977
Intel 8086	1	extended accumulator	1978
Motorola 68000	16	register-memory	1980
Intel 80386	8	register-memory	1985
MIPS	32	load-store	1985
HP PA-RISC	32	load-store	1986
SPARC	32	load-store	1987
PowerPC	32	load-store	1992
DEC Alpha	32	load-store	1992

FIGURE 3.39 Number of general-purpose registers in popular machines over the years.

The first load-store machine was the CDC 6600 in 1963, considered by many to be the first supercomputer. MIPS is a more recent example of a load-store machine.

The 80386 is Intel's attempt to transform the 80x86 into a general-purpose register-memory instruction set. Perhaps the best-known register-memory instruction set is the IBM 360 architecture, first announced in 1964. This instruction set is still at the core of IBM's mainframe computers—responsible for a large part of the business of the largest computer company in the world. Register-memory architectures were the most popular in the 1960s and the first half of the 1970s.

Digital Equipment Corporation's VAX architecture took memory operands one step further in 1977. It allowed any combination of registers and memory operands to be used in an instruction. A style of machine in which all operands can be in memory is called *memory-memory*. (In truth the VAX instruction set, like almost all other instruction sets since the IBM 360, is a hybrid since it also has general-purpose registers.)

Compiling an Assignment Statement into Memory-Memory Instructions

Example   What is the memory-memory style assembly code for this C code?

```
A = B + C;
```

Answer   It would be translated into the following instructions in a memory-memory instruction set:

```
add     AddressA,AddressB,AddressC
```

(See Exercise 3.19 for another example.)

Although MIPS has a single add instruction with 32-bit operands, the Intel 80x86 has many versions of a 32-bit add to specify whether an operand is in memory or is in a register. In addition, the memory operand can be accessed with more than seven addressing modes. This combination of address modes and register/memory operands means that there are dozens of variants of an 80x86 add instruction. Clearly this variability makes 80x86 implementations more challenging.

Compact Code and Stack Architectures

When memory is scarce, it is also important to keep programs small, so machines like the Intel 80x86, IBM 360, and VAX had variable-length instructions, both to match the varying operand specifications and to minimize code size. Intel 80x86 instructions are from 1 to 17 bytes long; IBM 360 instructions are 2, 4, or 6 bytes long; and VAX instruction lengths are anywhere from 1 to 54 bytes. If instruction memory space becomes precious once again, such techniques could return to popularity.

In the 1960s, a few companies followed a radical approach to instruction sets. In the belief that it was too hard for compilers to utilize registers effectively, these companies abandoned registers altogether! Instruction sets were based on a *stack model* of execution, like that found in the older Hewlett-Packard handheld calculators. Operands are pushed on the stack from memory or popped off the stack into memory. Operations take their operands from the stack and then place the result back onto the stack. In addition to simplifying compilers by eliminating register allocation, stack machines lent themselves to compact instruction encoding, thereby removing memory size as an excuse not to program in high-level languages.

Compiling an Assignment Statement into Stack Instructions

Example What is the stack-style assembly code for this C code?

```
A = B + C;
```

Answer It would be translated into the following instructions in a stack instruction set:

```
push  AddressC  # Top=Top+4;Stack[Top]=Memory[AddressC]
push  AddressB  # Top=Top+4;Stack[Top]=Memory[AddressB]
add             # Stack[Top-4]=Stack[Top]
                # + Stack[Top-4];Top=Top-4;
pop   AddressA  # Memory[AddressA]=Stack[Top];
                #    Top=Top-4;
```

To get the proper byte address, we adjust the stack by 4. The downside of stacks as compared to registers is that it is hard to reuse data that has been fetched or calculated without repeatedly going to memory. (See Exercise 3.19 for another example.)

Memory space may be precious again for the heralded Network Computer (NC), both because memory space is limited to keep costs low and because programs must be downloaded over the Internet, and smaller programs take less time to transmit. Hence compactness in instruction set encoding is desired for the NC. Such arguments have been used to justify building a hardware interpreter for the Java intermediate language, which is based on a stack. Time will tell whether these arguments have technical versus marketing merit.

High-Level-Language Computer Architectures

In the 1960s, systems software was rarely written in high-level languages. For example, virtually every commercial operating system before Unix was programmed in assembly language, and more recently even OS/2 was originally programmed at that same low level. Some people blamed the code density of the instruction sets rather than the programming languages and the compiler technology.

Hence a machine-design philosophy called *high-level-language computer architecture* was advocated, with the goal of making the hardware more like the programming languages. More efficient programming languages and compilers, plus expanding memory, doomed this movement to a historical footnote. The Burroughs B5000 was the commercial fountainhead of this philosophy, but today there is no significant commercial descendent of this 1960s radical.

Reduced Instruction Set Computer Architectures

This language-oriented design philosophy was replaced in the 1980s by *RISC (reduced instruction set computer)*. Improvements in programming languages, compiler technology, and memory cost meant that less programming was being done at the assembly level, so instruction sets could be measured by how well compilers used them as opposed to how well assembly language programmers used them.

Virtually all new instruction sets since 1982 have followed this RISC philosophy of fixed instruction lengths, load-store instruction sets, limited addressing modes, and limited operations. MIPS, Sun SPARC, Hewlett-Packard PA-RISC, IBM PowerPC, and DEC Alpha are all examples of RISC architectures.

A Brief History of the 80x86

The ancestors of the 80x86 were the first microprocessors, produced late in the first half of the 1970s. The Intel 4004 and 8008 were extremely simple 4-bit and 8-bit accumulator-style machines. Morse et al. [1980] describe the evolution of the 8086 from the 8080 in the late 1970s in an attempt to provide a 16-bit machine with better throughput. At that time, almost all programming for microprocessors was done in assembly language—both memory and compilers were in short supply. Intel wanted to keep its base of 8080 users, so the 8086 was designed to be "compatible" with the 8080. The 8086 was *never* object-code compatible with the 8080, but the machines were close enough that translation of assembly language programs could be done automatically.

In early 1980, IBM selected a version of the 8086 with an 8-bit external bus, called the 8088, for use in the IBM PC. They chose the 8-bit version to reduce the cost of the machine. This choice, together with the tremendous success of the IBM PC, has made the 8086 architecture ubiquitous. The success of the IBM

PC was due in part because IBM opened the architecture of the PC and enabled the PC-clone industry to flourish. As discussed in section 3.12, the 80286, 80386, 80486, Pentium, and Pentium Pro have extended the architecture and provided a series of performance enhancements.

Although the 68000 was chosen for the Macintosh, the Mac was never as pervasive as the PC, partly because Apple did not allow Mac clones based on the 68000, and the 68000 did not acquire the same software leverage that the 8086 enjoys. The Motorola 68000 may have been more significant *technically* than the 8086, but the impact of the selection by IBM and IBM's open architecture strategy dominated the technical advantages of the 68000 in the market.

Some argue that the inelegance of the 80x86 instruction set is unavoidable, the price that must be paid for rampant success by any architecture. We reject that notion. Obviously no successful architecture can jettison features that were added in previous implementations, and over time some features may be seen as undesirable. The awkwardness of the 80x86 begins at its core with the 8086 instruction set, and was exacerbated by the architecturally inconsistent expansions found in the 8087, 80286, 80386, and MMX.

A counterexample is the IBM 360/370 architecture, which is much older than the 80x86. It dominates the mainframe market just as the 80x86 dominates the PC market. Due undoubtedly to a better base and more compatible enhancements, this instruction set makes much more sense than the 80x86 more than 30 years after its first implementation.

Hewlett-Packard and Intel will announce a new, common instruction set architecture in about 1998. It will be upwards compatible with the 80x86, and thus the 80x86 instruction will be available in some form in computers of the next century.

Instruction set anthropologists of the 21st century will peel off layer after layer from such machines until they uncover artifacts from the first microprocessor. Given such a find, how will they judge 20th-century computer architecture?

To Probe Further

Bayko, J. [1996]. "Great Microprocessors of the Past and Present," available at *www.mkp.com/books_catalog/cod/links.htm*.

A personal view of the history of representative or unusual microprocessors, from the Intel 4004 to the Patriot Scientific ShBoom!

Kane, G., and J. Heinrich [1992]. *MIPS RISC Architecture*, Prentice Hall, Englewood Cliffs, NJ.

This book describes the MIPS architecture in greater detail than Appendix A.

Levy, H., and R. Eckhouse [1989]. *Computer Programming and Architecture: The VAX*, Digital Press, Boston.

This book concentrates on the VAX, but also includes descriptions of the Intel 80x86, IBM 360, and CDC 6600.

Morse, S., B. Ravenal, S. Mazor, and W. Pohlman [1980]. "Intel Microprocessors—8080 to 8086," *Computer* 13:10 (October).

The architecture history of the Intel from the 4004 to the 8086, according to the people who participated in the designs.

Wakerly, J. [1989]. *Microcomputer Architecture and Programming*, Wiley, New York.

The Motorola 680x0 is the main focus of the book, but it covers the Intel 8086, Motorola 6809, TI 9900, and Zilog Z8000.

3.16   Key Terms

The terms listed below reflect the key ideas discussed in this chapter. If you're unsure of the meaning of any of these terms, refer to the Glossary for a full definition.

activation record	general-purpose register	opcode
address	(GPR)	PC-relative addressing
addressing mode	global pointer	procedure
base or displacement	immediate addressing	procedure frame
addressing	instruction format	program counter (PC)
basic block	instruction set	pseudoinstruction
callee	jump address table	register addressing
caller	jump-and-link instruction	return address
conditional branch	linker or link editor	stack
data transfer instruction	load-store or register-register	stack pointer
executable file	machine	stored-program computer
frame pointer	loader	stored-program concept
	object program	word

3.17   Exercises

Appendix A describes the MIPS simulator, which is helpful for these exercises. Although the simulator accepts pseudoinstructions, try not to use pseudoinstructions for any exercises that ask you to produce MIPS code. Your goal should be to learn the real MIPS instruction set, and if you are asked to count instructions, your count should reflect the actual instructions that will be executed and not the pseudoinstructions.

There are some cases where pseudoinstructions must be used (for example, the la instruction when an actual value is not known at assembly time). In many cases they are quite convenient and result in more readable code (for example, the `li` and `move` instructions). If you choose to use pseudoinstructions for these reasons, please add a sentence or two to your solution stating which pseudoinstructions you have used and why.

3.1 [5] <§§3.3, 3.5, 3.8> Add comments to the following MIPS code and describe in one sentence what it computes. Assume that $a0 is used for the input and initially contains n, a positive integer. Assume that $v0 is used for the output.

```
begin:   addi $t0, $zero, 0
         addi $t1, $zero, 1
loop:    slt  $t2, $a0, $t1
         bne  $t2, $zero, finish
         add  $t0, $t0, $t1
         addi $t1, $t1, 2
         j    loop
finish:  add  $v0, $t0, $zero
```

3.2 [12] <§§3.3, 3.5, 3.8> The following code fragment processes an array and produces two important values in registers $v0 and $v1. Assume that the array consists of 5000 words indexed 0 through 4999, and its base address is stored in $a0 and its size (5000) in $a1. Describe in one sentence what this code does. Specifically, what will be returned in $v0 and $v1?

```
         add  $a1, $a1, $a1
         add  $a1, $a1, $a1
         add  $v0, $zero, $zero
         add  $t0, $zero, $zero
outer:   add  $t4, $a0, $t0
         lw   $t4, 0($t4)
         add  $t5, $zero, $zero
         add  $t1, $zero, $zero
inner:   add  $t3, $a0, $t1
         lw   $t3, 0($t3)
         bne  $t3, $t4, skip
         addi $t5, $t5, 1
skip:    addi $t1, $t1, 4
         bne  $t1, $a1, inner
         slt  $t2, $t5, $v0
         bne  $t2, $zero, next
         add  $v0, $t5, $zero
         add  $v1, $t4, $zero
next:    addi $t0, $t0, 4
         bne  $t0, $a1, outer
```

3.3 [10] <§§3.3, 3.5, 3.8> Assume that the code from Exercise 3.2 is run on a machine with a 500-MHz clock that requires the following number of cycles for each instruction:

Instruction	Cycles
add,addi,slt	1
lw, bne	2

In the worst case, how many seconds will it take to execute this code?

3.4 [5] <§3.8> Show the single MIPS instruction or minimal sequence of instructions for this C statement:

```
a = b + 100;
```

Assume that a corresponds to register $t0 and b corresponds to register $t1.

3.5 [10] <§3.8> Show the single MIPS instruction or minimal sequence of instructions for this C statement:

```
x[10] = x[11] + c;
```

Assume that c corresponds to register $t0 and the array x has a base address of $4{,}000{,}000_{ten}$.

3.6 [10] <§§ 3.3, 3.5, 3.8> The following program tries to copy words from the address in register $a0 to the address in register $a1, counting the number of words copied in register $v0. The program stops copying when it finds a word equal to 0. You do not have to preserve the contents of registers $v1, $a0, and $a1. This terminating word should be copied but not counted.

```
loop:   lw      $v1,0($a0)      # Read next word from source
        addi    $v0,$v0,1       # Increment count words copied
        sw      $v1,0($a1)      # Write to destination
        addi    $a0,$a0,1       # Advance pointer to next source
        addi    $a1,$a1,1       # Advance pointer to next dest
        bne     $v1,$zero,loop  # Loop if word copied ≠ zero
```

There are multiple bugs in this MIPS program; fix them and turn in a bug-free version. Like many of the exercises in this chapter, the easiest way to write MIPS programs is to use the simulator described in Appendix A. (Go to *www.mkp.com/cod2e.htm* to get a copy of this program.)

3.7 [15] <§3.4> Using the MIPS program in Exercise 3.6 (with bugs intact), determine the instruction format for each instruction and the decimal values of each instruction field.

3.8 [10] <§§3.2, 3.3, 3.5, 3.8> {Ex. 3.7} Starting with the corrected program in the answer to Exercise 3.6, write the C code segment that might have produced this code. Assume that variable `source` corresponds to register `$a0`, variable `destination` corresponds to register `$a1`, and variable `count` corresponds to register `$v0`. Show variable declarations, but assume that `source` and `destination` have been initialized to the proper addresses.

3.9 [10] <§3.5> The C segment

```
while (save[i] == k)
    i = i + j;
```

on page 127 uses both a conditional branch and an unconditional jump each time through the loop. Only poor compilers would produce code with this loop overhead. Rewrite the assembly code so that it uses at most one branch or jump each time through the loop. How many instructions are executed before and after the optimization if the number of iterations of the loop is 10 (i.e., `save[i + 10 * j]` equals `k` and `save[i], . . . , save[i + 9 * j]` do not equal `k`)?

3.10 [25] <§3.9> As discussed on page 157 and summarized in Figure 3.37, pseudoinstructions are not part of the MIPS instruction set but often appear in MIPS programs. For each pseudoinstruction in the following table, produce a minimal sequence of actual MIPS instructions to accomplish the same thing. You may need to use `$at` for some of the sequences. In the following table, `big` refers to a specific number that requires 32 bits to represent and `small` to a number that can be expressed using 16 bits.

Pseudoinstruction	What it accomplishes
`move $t5, $t3`	`$t5 = $t3`
`clear $t5`	`$t5 = 0`
`li $t5, small`	`$t5 = small`
`li $t5, big`	`$t5 = big`
`lw $t5, big($t3)`	`$t5 = Memory[$t3 + big]`
`addi $t5, $t3, big`	`$t5 = $t3 + big`
`beq $t5, small, L`	`if ($t5 = small) go to L`
`beq $t5, big, L`	`if ($t5 = big) go to L`
`ble $t5, $t3, L`	`if ($t5 <= $t3) go to L`
`bgt $t5, $t3, L`	`if ($t5 > $t3) go to L`
`bge $t5, $t3, L`	`if ($t5 >= $t3) go to L`

3.11 [30] <§3.5> Consider the following fragment of C code:

```
for (i=0; i<=100; i=i+1) {a[i] = b[i] + c;}
```

Assume that a and b are arrays of words and the base address of a is in $a0 and the base address of b is in $a1. Register $t0 is associated with variable i and register $s0 with c. Write the code for MIPS. How many instructions are executed during the running of this code? How many memory data references will be made during execution?

3.12 [5] <§§3.8, 3.9> Given your understanding of PC-relative addressing, explain why an assembler might have problems directly implementing the branch instruction in the following code sequence:

```
here:    beq $t1, $t2, there
 . . .
there:   add $t1, $t1, $t1
```

Show how the assembler might rewrite this code sequence to solve these problems.

3.13 [10] <§3.12> Consider an architecture that is similar to MIPS except that it supports update addressing (like the PowerPC) for data transfer instructions. If we run gcc using this architecture, some percentage of the data transfer instructions shown in Figure 3.38 on page 189 will be able to make use of the new instructions, and for each instruction changed, one arithmetic instruction can be eliminated. If 25% of the data transfer instructions can be changed, which will be faster for gcc, the modified MIPS architecture or the unmodified architecture? How much faster? (You can assume that both architectures have CPI values as given in Exercise 3.16 and that the modified architecture has its cycle time increased by 10% in order to accommodate the new instructions.)

3.14 [10] <§3.14> When designing memory systems, it becomes useful to know the frequency of memory reads versus writes as well as the frequency of accesses for instructions versus data. Using the average instruction-mix information for MIPS for the program gcc in Figure 3.38 on page 189, find the following:

a. The percentage of *all* memory accesses that are for data (vs. instructions).

b. The percentage of *all* memory accesses that are reads (vs. writes). Assume that two-thirds of data transfers are loads.

3.15 [10] <§3.14> Perform the same calculations as for Exercise 3.14, but replace the program gcc with spice.

3.16 [15] <§3.14> Suppose we have made the following measurements of average CPI for instructions:

Instruction	Average CPI
Arithmetic	1.0 clock cycles
Data transfer	1.4 clock cycles
Conditional branch	1.7 clock cycles
Jump	1.2 clock cycles

Compute the effective CPI for MIPS. Average the instruction frequencies for gcc and spice in Figure 3.38 on page 189 to obtain the instruction mix.

3.17 [20] <§3.10> In this exercise, we'll examine quantitatively the pros and cons of adding an addressing mode to MIPS that allows arithmetic instructions to directly access memory, as is found on the 80x86. The primary benefit is that fewer instructions will be executed because we won't have to first load a register. The primary disadvantage is that the cycle time will have to increase to account for the additional time to read memory. Consider adding a new instruction:

```
addm $t2, 100($t3)  # $t2 = $t2 + Memory[$t3+100]
```

Assume that the new instruction will cause the cycle time to increase by 10%. Use the instruction frequencies for the gcc benchmark from Figure 3.38 on page 189, and assume that two-thirds of the data transfers are loads and the rest are stores. Assume that the new instruction affects only the clock speed, not the CPI. What percentage of loads must be eliminated for the machine with the new instruction to have at least the same performance?

3.18 [10] <§3.10> Using the information in Exercise 3.17, write a multiple-instruction sequence in which a load of $t0 followed immediately by the use of $t0—in, say, an add—could *not* be replaced by a single instruction of the form proposed.

In More Depth

Comparing Instruction Sets of Different Styles

For the next two exercises, your task is to compare the memory efficiency of four different styles of instruction sets for two code sequences. The architecture styles are the following:

- *Accumulator.*
- *Memory-memory*: All three operands of each instruction are in memory.

- *Stack*: All operations occur on top of the stack. Only push and pop access memory, and all other instructions remove their operands from the stack and replace them with the result. The implementation uses a stack for the top two entries; accesses that use other stack positions are memory references.

- *Load-store*: All operations occur in registers, and register-to-register instructions have three operands per instruction. There are 16 general-purpose registers, and register specifiers are 4 bits long.

Consider the following C code:

```
a = b + c;    # a, b, and c are variables in memory
```

Section 3.15 contains the equivalent assembly language code for the different styles of instruction sets. For a given code sequence, we can calculate the instruction bytes fetched and the memory data bytes transferred using the following assumptions about all four instruction sets:

- The opcode is always 1 byte (8 bits).

- All memory addresses are 2 bytes (16 bits).

- All data operands are 4 bytes (32 bits).

- All instructions are an integral number of bytes in length.

- There are no optimizations to reduce memory traffic.

For example, a register load will require four instruction bytes (one for the opcode, one for the register destination, and two for a memory address) to be fetched from memory along with four data bytes. A memory-memory add instruction will require seven instruction bytes (one for the opcode and two for each of the three memory addresses) to be fetched from memory and will result in 12 data bytes being transferred (eight from memory to the processor and four from the processor back to memory). The following table displays a summary of this information for each of the architectural styles for the code appearing above and in section 3.15:

Style	Instructions for a = b + c	Code bytes	Data bytes
Accumulator	3	3 + 3 + 3	4 + 4 + 4
Memory-memory	1	7	12
Stack	4	3 + 3 + 1 + 3	4 + 4 + 0 + 4
Load-store	4	4 + 4 + 3 + 4	4 + 4 + 0 + 4

3.19 [20] <§3.15> For the following C code, write an equivalent assembly language program in each architectural style (assume all variables are initially in memory):

```
a = b + c;
b = a + c;
d = a - b;
```

For each code sequence, calculate the instruction bytes fetched and the memory data bytes transferred (read or written). Which architecture is most efficient as measured by code size? Which architecture is most efficient as measured by total memory bandwidth required (code + data)? If the answers are not the same, why are they different?

3.20 [5] <§3.15> Sometimes architectures are characterized according to the typical number of memory addresses per instruction. Commonly used terms are 0, 1, 2, and 3 addresses per instruction. Associate the names above with each category.

3.21 [10] <§3.7> Compute the decimal byte values that form the null-terminated ASCII representation of the following string:

```
A byte is 8 bits
```

3.22 [30] <§§3.6, 3.7> Write a program in MIPS assembly language to convert an ASCII decimal string to an integer. Your program should expect register $a0 to hold the address of a null-terminated string containing some combination of the digits 0 through 9. Your program should compute the integer value equivalent to this string of digits, then place the number in register $v0. Your program need not handle negative numbers. If a nondigit character appears anywhere in the string, your program should stop with the value –1 in register $v0. For example, if register $a0 points to a sequence of three bytes 50_{ten}, 52_{ten}, 0_{ten} (the null-terminated string "24"), then when the program stops, register $v0 should contain the value 24_{ten}. (The subscript "ten" means base 10.)

3.23 [20] <§§3.6, 3.7> Write a procedure, bfind, in MIPS assembly language. The procedure should take a single argument that is a pointer to a null-terminated string in register $a0. The bfind procedure should locate the first b character in the string and return its address in register $v0. If there are no b's in the string, then bfind should return a pointer to the null character at the end of the string. For example, if the argument to bfind points to the string "imbibe," then the return value will be a pointer to the third character of the string.

3.24 [20] <§§3.6, 3.7> {Ex. 3.23} Write a procedure, bcount, in MIPS assembly language. The bcount procedure takes a single argument, which is a pointer to a string in register $a0, and it returns a count of the total number of b characters in the string in register $v0. You must use your bfind procedure in Exercise 3.23 in your implementation of bcount.

3.25 [30] <§§3.6, 3.7> Write a procedure, itoa, in MIPS assembly language that will convert an integer argument into an ASCII decimal string. The procedure should take two arguments: the first is an integer in register $a0; the second is the address at which to write a result string in register $a1. Then itoa should convert its first argument to a null-terminated decimal ASCII string and store that string at the given result location. The return value from itoa, in register $v0, should be a count of the number of non-null characters stored at the destination.

In More Depth

Tail Recursion

Some recursive procedures can be implemented iteratively without using recursion. Iteration can significantly improve performance by removing the overhead associated with procedure calls. For example, consider a procedure used to accumulate a sum:

```
int sum (int n, int acc) {
   if (n > 0)
       return sum(n - 1, acc + n);
   else
       return acc;
}
```

Consider the procedure call sum(3,0). This will result in recursive calls to sum(2,3), sum(1,5), and sum(0,6), and then the result 6 will be returned four times. This recursive call of sum is referred to as a *tail call*, and this example use of tail recursion can be implemented very efficiently (assume $a0 = n and $a1 = acc):

```
sum:    beq $a0, $zero, sum_exit # go to sum_exit if n is 0
        add $a1, $a1, $a0        # add n to acc
        addi $a0, $a0, -1        # subtract 1 from n
        j sum                    # go to sum
sum_exit:
        move $v0, $a1            # return value acc
        jr   $ra                 # return to caller
```

3.26 [30] <§3.6> Write a MIPS procedure to compute the nth Fibonacci number F(n) where

```
F(n) = 0,      if n = 0;
       1,      if n = 1;
       F(n-1) + F(n-2), otherwise.
```

Base your algorithm on the straightforward but hopelessly inefficient procedure below, which generates a recursive process:

```
int fib(int n){
   if (n == 0)
      return 0;
   else if (n == 1)
      return 1;
   else
return fib(n-1) + fib(n-2);
```

3.27 [30] <§3.6> Write a program as in Exercise 3.26, except this time base your program on the following procedure and optimize the tail call so as to make your implementation efficient:

```
int fib_iter (int a, int b, int count) {
   if (count == 0)
      return b;
   else
      return fib_iter(a + b, a, count - 1);
```

Here, the first two parameters keep track of the previous two Fibonacci numbers computed. To compute F(n) you have to make the procedure call fib_iter(1, 0, n).

3.28 [20] <§3.6> Estimate the difference in performance between your solution to Exercise 3.26 and your solution to Exercise 3.27.

In More Depth

The Single Instruction Computer

The computer architecture used in this book, MIPS, has one of the simpler instruction sets in existence. However, it is possible to imagine even simpler instruction sets. In this assignment, you are to consider a hypothetical machine called SIC, for Single Instruction Computer. As its name implies, SIC has only one instruction: subtract and branch if negative, or `sbn` for short. The `sbn` instruction has three operands, each consisting of the address of a word in memory:

```
sbn a,b,c # Mem[a] = Mem[a] - Mem[b];if (Mem[a]<0) go to c
```

The instruction will subtract the number in memory location b from the number in location a and place the result back in a, overwriting the previous value. If the result is greater than or equal to 0, the computer will take its next instruction from the memory location just after the current instruction. If the result is less than 0, the next instruction is taken from memory location c. SIC has no registers and no instructions other than `sbn`.

Although it has only one instruction, SIC can imitate many of the operations of more complex instruction sets by using clever sequences of `sbn` instructions. For example, here is a program to copy a number from location a to location b:

```
start:  sbn temp,temp,.+1    # Sets temp to zero
        sbn temp,a,.+1       # Sets temp to -a
        sbn b,b,.+1          # Sets b to zero
        sbn b,temp,.+1       # Sets b to -temp, which is a
```

In the program above, the notation .+1 means "the address after this one," so that each instruction in this program goes on to the next in sequence whether or not the result is negative. We assume temp to be the address of a spare memory word that can be used for temporary results.

3.29 [10] <§3.15> Write a SIC program to add a and b, leaving the result in a and leaving b unmodified.

3.30 [20] <§3.15> Write a SIC program to multiply a by b, putting the result in c. Assume that memory location one contains the number 1. Assume that a and b are greater than 0 and that it's OK to modify a or b. (Hint: What does this program compute?)

```
c = 0; while (b > 0) {b = b - 1; c = c + a;}
```

4

Arithmetic for Computers

Numerical precision is the very soul of science.

Sir D'arcy Wentworth Thompson
On Growth and Form, 1917

4.1   **Introduction**   210

4.2   **Signed and Unsigned Numbers**   210

4.3   **Addition and Subtraction**   220

4.4   **Logical Operations**   225

4.5   **Constructing an Arithmetic Logic Unit**   230

4.6   **Multiplication**   250

4.7   **Division**   265

4.8   **Floating Point**   275

4.9   **Real Stuff: Floating Point in the PowerPC and 80x86**   301

4.10   **Fallacies and Pitfalls**   304

4.11   **Concluding Remarks**   308

4.12   **Historical Perspective and Further Reading**   312

4.13   **Key Terms**   322

4.14   **Exercises**   322

The Five Classic Components of a Computer

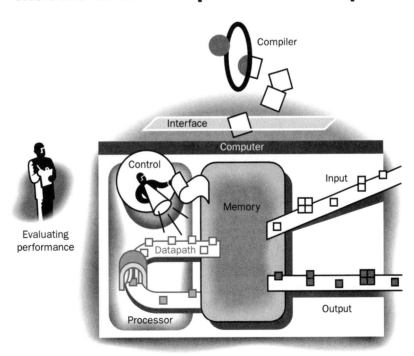

Introduction

Computer words are composed of bits; thus words can be represented as binary numbers. Although the natural numbers 0, 1, 2, and so on can be represented either in decimal or binary form, what about the other numbers that commonly occur? For example:

- How are negative numbers represented?

- What is the largest number that can be represented in a computer word?

- What happens if an operation creates a number bigger than can be represented?

- What about fractions and real numbers?

We could also ask, What is the inside story about the infamous bug in the Pentium? And underlying all these questions is a mystery: How does hardware really add, subtract, multiply, or divide numbers?

The goal of this chapter is to unravel this mystery, including representation of numbers, arithmetic algorithms, hardware that follows these algorithms, and the implications of all this for instruction sets. These insights may even explain quirks that you have already encountered with computers. (If you are familiar with signed binary numbers, you may wish to skip the next section and go to section 4.3 on page 220.)

Signed and Unsigned Numbers

Numbers can be represented in any base; humans prefer base 10 and, as we examined in Chapter 3, base 2 is best for computers. Because we will frequently be dealing with both decimal and binary numbers, to avoid confusion we will subscript decimal numbers with *ten* and binary numbers with *two*.

In any number base, the value of *i*th digit *d* is

$$d \times \text{Base}^i$$

where *i* starts at 0 and increases from right to left. This leads to an obvious way to number the bits in the word: Simply use the power of the base for that bit. For example,

1011_{two}

represents

$$(1 \times 2^3) + (0 \times 2^2) + (1 \times 2^1) + (1 \times 2^0)_{ten}$$
$$= (1 \times 8) + (0 \times 4) + (1 \times 2) + (1 \times 1)_{ten}$$
$$= \quad 8 \quad + \quad 0 \quad + \quad 2 \quad + \quad 1_{ten}$$
$$= 11_{ten}$$

Hence the bits are numbered 0, 1, 2, 3, ... from *right to left* in a word. The drawing below shows the numbering of bits within a MIPS word and the placement of the number 1011_{two}:

31 30 29 28	27 26 25 24	23 22 21 20	19 18 17 16	15 14 13 12	11 10 9 8	7 6 5 4	3 2 1 0
0 0 0 0	0 0 0 0	0 0 0 0	0 0 0 0	0 0 0 0	0 0 0 0	0 0 0 0	1 0 1 1

(32 bits wide)

Since words are drawn vertically as well as horizontally, leftmost and rightmost may be unclear. Hence, the phrase *least significant bit* is used to refer to the rightmost bit (bit 0 above) and *most significant bit* to the leftmost bit (bit 31).

The MIPS word is 32 bits long, so we can represent 2^{32} different 32-bit patterns. It is natural to let these combinations represent the numbers from 0 to $2^{32} - 1$ ($4{,}294{,}967{,}295_{ten}$):

$$
\begin{aligned}
&0000\ 0000\ 0000\ 0000\ 0000\ 0000\ 0000\ 0000_{two} &=& \quad 0_{ten}\\
&0000\ 0000\ 0000\ 0000\ 0000\ 0000\ 0000\ 0001_{two} &=& \quad 1_{ten}\\
&0000\ 0000\ 0000\ 0000\ 0000\ 0000\ 0000\ 0010_{two} &=& \quad 2_{ten}\\
&\ldots && \ldots\\
&1111\ 1111\ 1111\ 1111\ 1111\ 1111\ 1111\ 1101_{two} &=& 4{,}294{,}967{,}293_{ten}\\
&1111\ 1111\ 1111\ 1111\ 1111\ 1111\ 1111\ 1110_{two} &=& 4{,}294{,}967{,}294_{ten}\\
&1111\ 1111\ 1111\ 1111\ 1111\ 1111\ 1111\ 1111_{two} &=& 4{,}294{,}967{,}295_{ten}
\end{aligned}
$$

Hardware Software Interface

Base 2 is not natural to human beings; we have 10 fingers and so find base 10 natural. Why didn't computers use decimal? In fact, the first commercial computer *did* offer decimal arithmetic. The problem was that the computer still used on and off signals, so a decimal digit was simply represented by several binary digits. Decimal proved so inefficient that subsequent machines reverted to all binary, converting to base 10 only for the infrequent input/output events.

ASCII versus Binary Numbers

Example

We could represent numbers as strings of ASCII digits instead of as two's complement integers (see Figure 3.15 on page 142). What is the expansion in storage if the number 1 billion is represented in ASCII versus a 32-bit integer?

Answer

One billion is 1 000 000 000, so it would take 10 ASCII digits, each 8 bits long. Thus the storage expansion would be $(10 \times 8)/32$ or 2.5. In addition to the expansion in storage, the hardware to add, subtract, multiply, and divide such numbers is also difficult. Such difficulties explain why computing professionals are raised to believe that binary is natural and that the occasional decimal machine is bizarre.

Keep in mind that the binary bit patterns above are simply *representatives* of numbers. Numbers really have an infinite number of digits, with almost all being 0 except for a few of the rightmost digits. We just don't normally show leading 0s.

As we shall see in sections 4.5 through 4.7, hardware can be designed to add, subtract, multiply, and divide these binary bit patterns. If the number that is the proper result of such operations cannot be represented by these rightmost hardware bits, *overflow* is said to have occurred. It's up to the operating system and program to determine what to do if overflow occurs.

Computer programs calculate both positive and negative numbers, so we need a representation that distinguishes the positive from the negative. The most obvious solution is to add a separate sign, which conveniently can be represented in a single bit; the name for this representation is *sign and magnitude*.

Alas, sign and magnitude representation has several shortcomings. First, it's not obvious where to put the sign bit. To the right? To the left? Early machines tried both. Second, adders for sign and magnitude may need an extra step to set the sign because we can't know in advance what the proper sign will be. Finally, a separate sign bit means that sign and magnitude has both a positive and negative zero, which can lead to problems for inattentive programmers. As a result of these shortcomings, sign and magnitude was soon abandoned.

In the search for a more attractive alternative, the question arose as to what would be the result for unsigned numbers if we tried to subtract a large number from a small one. The answer is that it would try to borrow from a string of leading 0s, so the result would have a string of leading 1s.

Given that there was no obvious better alternative, the final solution was to pick the representation that made the hardware simple: leading 0s mean positive, and leading 1s mean negative. This convention for representing signed binary numbers is called *two's complement* representation:

$$
\begin{aligned}
0000\ 0000\ 0000\ 0000\ 0000\ 0000\ 0000\ 0000_{two} &= & 0_{ten} \\
0000\ 0000\ 0000\ 0000\ 0000\ 0000\ 0000\ 0001_{two} &= & 1_{ten} \\
0000\ 0000\ 0000\ 0000\ 0000\ 0000\ 0000\ 0010_{two} &= & 2_{ten}
\end{aligned}
$$

. . .   . . .

$$
\begin{aligned}
0111\ 1111\ 1111\ 1111\ 1111\ 1111\ 1111\ 1101_{two} &= & 2{,}147{,}483{,}645_{ten} \\
0111\ 1111\ 1111\ 1111\ 1111\ 1111\ 1111\ 1110_{two} &= & 2{,}147{,}483{,}646_{ten} \\
0111\ 1111\ 1111\ 1111\ 1111\ 1111\ 1111\ 1111_{two} &= & 2{,}147{,}483{,}647_{ten} \\
1000\ 0000\ 0000\ 0000\ 0000\ 0000\ 0000\ 0000_{two} &= & -2{,}147{,}483{,}648_{ten} \\
1000\ 0000\ 0000\ 0000\ 0000\ 0000\ 0000\ 0001_{two} &= & -2{,}147{,}483{,}647_{ten} \\
1000\ 0000\ 0000\ 0000\ 0000\ 0000\ 0000\ 0010_{two} &= & -2{,}147{,}483{,}646_{ten}
\end{aligned}
$$

. . .   . . .

$$
\begin{aligned}
1111\ 1111\ 1111\ 1111\ 1111\ 1111\ 1111\ 1101_{two} &= & -3_{ten} \\
1111\ 1111\ 1111\ 1111\ 1111\ 1111\ 1111\ 1110_{two} &= & -2_{ten} \\
1111\ 1111\ 1111\ 1111\ 1111\ 1111\ 1111\ 1111_{two} &= & -1_{ten}
\end{aligned}
$$

The positive half of the numbers, from 0 to $2{,}147{,}483{,}647_{ten}$ ($2^{31}-1$), use the same representation as before. The following bit pattern ($1000\ldots0000_{two}$) represents the most negative number $-2{,}147{,}483{,}648_{ten}$ (-2^{31}). It is followed by a declining set of negative numbers: $-2{,}147{,}483{,}647_{ten}$ ($1000\ldots0001_{two}$) down to -1_{ten} ($1111\ldots1111_{two}$).

Two's complement does have one negative number, $-2{,}147{,}483{,}648_{ten}$, that has no corresponding positive number. Such imbalance was a worry to the inattentive programmer, but sign and magnitude had problems for both the programmer *and* the hardware designer. Consequently, every computer today uses two's complement binary representations for signed numbers.

Two's complement representation has the advantage that all negative numbers have a 1 in the most significant bit. Consequently, hardware needs to test only this bit to see if a number is positive or negative (with 0 considered positive). This particular bit is often called the *sign bit*. By recognizing the role of the sign bit, we can represent positive and negative numbers in terms of the bit value times a power of 2 (here xi means the ith bit of x):

$$(x31 \times -2^{31}) + (x30 \times 2^{30}) + (x29 \times 2^{29}) + \ldots + (x1 \times 2^{1}) + (x0 \times 2^{0})$$

The sign bit is multiplied by -2^{31}, and the rest of the bits are then multiplied by positive versions of their respective base values.

Binary to Decimal Conversion

Example

What is the decimal value of this 32-bit two's complement number?

$$1111\ 1111\ 1111\ 1111\ 1111\ 1111\ 1111\ 1100_{two}$$

Answer

Substituting the number's bit values into the formula above:

$$(1 \times -2^{31}) + (1 \times 2^{30}) + (1 \times 2^{29}) + \ldots + (1 \times 2^{2}) + (0 \times 2^{1}) + (0 \times 2^{0})$$
$$= -2^{31} + 2^{30} + 2^{29} + \ldots + 2^{2} + 0 + 0$$
$$= -2{,}147{,}483{,}648_{ten} + 2{,}147{,}483{,}644_{ten}$$
$$= -4_{ten}$$

We'll see a shortcut to simplify conversion soon.

Hardware Software Interface

Signed versus unsigned applies to loads as well as to arithmetic. The *function* of a signed load is to copy the sign repeatedly to fill the rest of the register—called *sign extension*—but its *purpose* is to place a correct representation of the number within that register. Unsigned loads simply fill with 0s to the left of the data, since the number represented by the bit pattern is unsigned.

When loading a 32-bit word into a 32-bit register, the point is moot; signed and unsigned loads are identical. MIPS does offer two flavors of byte loads: *load byte* (lb) treats the byte as a signed number and thus sign extends to fill the 24 leftmost bits of the register, while *load byte unsigned* (lbu) works with unsigned integers. Since programs almost always use bytes to represent characters rather than consider bytes as short signed integers, lbu is used practically exclusively for byte loads.

Just as an operation on unsigned numbers can overflow the capacity of hardware to represent the result, so can an operation on two's complement numbers. Overflow occurs when the leftmost retained bit of the binary bit pattern is not the same as the infinite number of digits to the left (the sign bit is incorrect): a 0 on the left of the bit pattern when the number is negative or a 1 when the number is positive.

Hardware Software Interface

Unlike the numbers discussed above, memory addresses naturally start at 0 and continue to the largest address. Put another way, negative addresses make no sense. Thus, programs want to deal sometimes with numbers that can be positive or negative and sometimes with numbers that can be only positive. Programming languages reflect this distinction. C, for example, names the former *integers* (declared as int in the program) and the latter *unsigned integers* (unsigned int).

Comparison instructions must deal with this dichotomy. Sometimes a bit pattern with a 1 in the most significant bit represents a negative number and, of course, is less than any positive number, which must have a 0 in the most significant bit. With unsigned integers, on the other hand, a 1 in the most significant bit represents a number that is *larger* than any that begins with a 0.

MIPS offers two versions of the set on less than comparison to handle these alternatives. *Set on less than* (slt) and *set on less than immediate* (slti) work with signed integers. Unsigned integers are compared using *set on less than unsigned* (sltu) and *set on less than immediate unsigned* (sltiu).

Signed versus Unsigned Comparison

Example

Suppose register $s0 has the binary number

$$1111\ 1111\ 1111\ 1111\ 1111\ 1111\ 1111\ 1111_{two}$$

and that register $s1 has the binary number

$$0000\ 0000\ 0000\ 0000\ 0000\ 0000\ 0000\ 0001_{two}$$

What are the values of registers $t0 and $t1 after these two instructions?

```
slt     $t0, $s0, $s1 # signed comparison
sltu    $t1, $s0, $s1 # unsigned comparison
```

Answer

The value in register $s0 represents -1 if it is an integer and $4,294,967,295_{ten}$ if it is an unsigned integer. The value in register $s1 represents 1 in either case. Then register $t0 has the value 1, since $-1_{ten} < 1_{ten}$, and register $t1 has the value 0, since $4,294,967,295_{ten} > 1_{ten}$.

Before going on to addition and subtraction, let's examine a few useful shortcuts when working with two's complement numbers.

The first shortcut is a quick way to negate a two's complement binary number. Simply invert every 0 to 1 and every 1 to 0, then add one to the result. This shortcut is based on the observation that the sum of a number and its inverted representation must be $111 \ldots 111_{two}$, which represents –1. Since $x + \bar{x} \equiv -1$, therefore $x + \bar{x} + 1 = 0$ or $\bar{x} + 1 = -x$.

Negation Shortcut

Example

Negate 2_{ten}, and then check the result by negating -2_{ten}.

Answer

2_{ten} = 0000 0000 0000 0000 0000 0000 0000 0010$_{two}$

Negating this number by inverting the bits and adding one,

$$
\begin{array}{rl}
 & 1111\ 1111\ 1111\ 1111\ 1111\ 1111\ 1111\ 1101_{two} \\
+ & 1_{two} \\
\hline
= & 1111\ 1111\ 1111\ 1111\ 1111\ 1111\ 1111\ 1110_{two} \\
= & {-2}_{ten}
\end{array}
$$

Going the other direction,

$$1111\ 1111\ 1111\ 1111\ 1111\ 1111\ 1111\ 1110_{two}$$

is first inverted and then incremented:

$$
\begin{array}{rl}
 & 0000\ 0000\ 0000\ 0000\ 0000\ 0000\ 0000\ 0001_{two} \\
+ & 1_{two} \\
\hline
= & 0000\ 0000\ 0000\ 0000\ 0000\ 0000\ 0000\ 0010_{two} \\
= & 2_{ten}
\end{array}
$$

The second shortcut tells us how to convert a binary number represented in n bits to a number represented with more than n bits. For example, the immediate field in the load, store, branch, add, and set on less than instructions contains a two's complement 16-bit number, representing $-32{,}768_{ten}$ (-2^{15}) to $32{,}767_{ten}(2^{15}{-}1)$. To add the immediate field to a 32-bit register, the machine must convert that 16-bit number to its 32-bit equivalent. The shortcut is to take the most significant bit from the smaller quantity—the sign bit—and replicate it to fill the new bits of the larger quantity. The old bits are simply copied into the right portion of the new word. This shortcut is commonly called *sign extension*.

Sign Extension Shortcut

Example Convert 16-bit binary versions of 2_{ten} and -2_{ten} to 32-bit binary numbers.

Answer The 16-bit binary version of the number 2 is

$$0000\,0000\,0000\,0010_{two} = 2_{ten}$$

It is converted to a 32-bit number by making 16 copies of the value in the most significant bit (0) and placing that in the left-hand half of the word. The right half gets the old value:

$$0000\,0000\,0000\,0000\,0000\,0000\,0000\,0010_{two} = 2_{ten}$$

Let's negate the 16-bit version of 2 using the earlier shortcut. Thus,

$$0000\,0000\,0000\,0010_{two}$$

becomes

$$1111\,1111\,1111\,1101_{two}$$
$$+ \qquad\qquad\qquad\qquad 1_{two}$$
$$\overline{}$$
$$= \qquad 1111\,1111\,1111\,1110_{two}$$

Creating a 32-bit version of the negative number means copying the sign bit 16 times and placing it on the left:

$$1111\,1111\,1111\,1111\,1111\,1111\,1111\,1110_{two} = {}^-2_{ten}$$

This trick works because positive two's complement numbers really have an infinite number of 0s on the left and those that are negative two's complement numbers have an infinite number of 1s. The binary bit pattern representing a number hides leading bits to fit the width of the hardware; sign extension simply restores some of them.

A final shortcut, which we previewed in Chapter 3, is that we can save reading and writing long binary numbers by using a higher base than binary that converts easily into binary. Since almost all computer data sizes are multiples of 4, *hexadecimal* (base 16) numbers are popular. Since base 16 is a power of 2, we can trivially convert by replacing each group of four binary digits by a single hexadecimal digit, and vice versa. Figure 4.1 shows the hexadecimal Rosetta stone. We will use either the subscript *hex* or the C notation, which uses 0x*nnnn*, for hexadecimal numbers.

Hexadecimal	Binary	Hexadecimal	Binary	Hexadecimal	Binary	Hexadecimal	Binary
0_{hex}	0000_{two}	4_{hex}	0100_{two}	8_{hex}	1000_{two}	c_{hex}	1100_{two}
1_{hex}	0001_{two}	5_{hex}	0101_{two}	9_{hex}	1001_{two}	d_{hex}	1101_{two}
2_{hex}	0010_{two}	6_{hex}	0110_{two}	a_{hex}	1010_{two}	e_{hex}	1110_{two}
3_{hex}	0011_{two}	7_{hex}	0111_{two}	b_{hex}	1011_{two}	f_{hex}	1111_{two}

FIGURE 4.1 The hexadecimal-binary conversion table. Just replace one hexadecimal digit by the corresponding four binary digits, and vice versa. If the length of the binary number is not a multiple of four, go from right to left.

Binary-to-Hexadecimal Shortcut

Example   Convert the following hexadecimal and binary numbers into the other base:

$$\text{eca8 } 6420_{hex}$$
$$0001\ 0011\ 0101\ 0111\ 1001\ 1011\ 1101\ 1111_{two}$$

Answer   Just a table lookup one way:

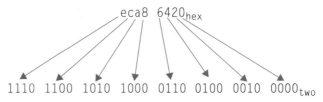

And then the other direction:

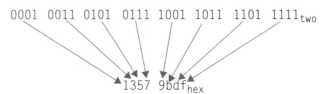

Summary

The main point of this section is that we need to represent both positive and negative integers within a computer word, and although there are pros and cons to any option, the overwhelming choice since 1965 has been two's complement. Figure 4.2 shows the additions to the MIPS assembly language revealed in this section. (The MIPS machine language is also illustrated on the back endpapers of this book.)

MIPS operands

Name	Example	Comments
32 registers	$s0–$s7, $t0–$t9, $gp, $fp, $zero, $sp, $ra, $at	Fast locations for data. In MIPS, data must be in registers to perform arithmetic. MIPS register $zero always equals 0. Register $at is reserved for the assembler to handle large constants.
2^{30} memory words	Memory[0], Memory[4], . . . , Memory[4294967292]	Accessed only by data transfer instructions. MIPS uses byte addresses, so sequential words differ by 4. Memory holds data structures, such as arrays, and spilled registers, such as those saved on procedure calls.

MIPS assembly language

Category	Instruction	Example	Meaning	Comments
Arithmetic	add	add $s1,$s2,$s3	$s1 = $s2 + $s3	Three operands
	subtract	sub $s1,$s2,$s3	$s1 = $s2 − $s3	Three operands
	add immediate	addi $s1,$s2,100	$s1 = $s2 + 100	+ constant
Data transfer	load word	lw $s1,100($s2)	$s1 = Memory[$s2 + 100]	Word from memory to register
	store word	sw $s1,100($s2)	Memory[$s2 + 100] = $s1	Word from register to memory
	load byte unsigned	lbu $s1,100($s2)	$s1 = Memory[$s2 + 100]	Byte from memory to register
	store byte	sb $s1,100($s2)	Memory[$s2 + 100] = $s1	Byte from register to memory
	load upper immediate	lui $s1,100	$s1 = 100 * 2^{16}	Loads constant in upper 16 bits
Conditional branch	branch on equal	beq $s1,$s2,25	if ($s1 == $s2) go to PC + 4 + 100	Equal test; PC-relative branch
	branch on not equal	bne $s1,$s2,25	if ($s1 != $s2) go to PC + 4 + 100	Not equal test; PC-relative
	set on less than	slt $s1,$s2,$s3	if ($s2 < $s3) $s1 = 1; else $s1 = 0	Compare less than; two's complement
	set less than immediate	slti $s1,$s2,100	if ($s2 < 100) $s1 = 1; else $s1 = 0	Compare < constant; two's complement
	set less than unsigned	sltu $s1,$s2,$s3	if ($s2 < $s3) $s1 = 1; else $s1 = 0	Compare less than; unsigned numbers
	set less than immediate unsigned	sltiu $s1,$s2,100	if ($s2 < 100) $s1 = 1; else $s1 = 0	Compare < constant; unsigned numbers
Unconditional jump	jump	j 2500	go to 10000	Jump to target address
	jump register	jr $ra	go to $ra	For switch, procedure return
	jump and link	jal 2500	$ra = PC + 4; go to 10000	For procedure call

FIGURE 4.2 MIPS architecture revealed thus far. Color indicates portions from this section added to the MIPS architecture revealed in Chapter 3 (Figure 3.20 on page 155). MIPS machine language is listed in the back endpapers of this book.

Elaboration: Two's complement gets its name from the rule that the unsigned sum of an n-bit number and its negative is 2^n, hence the complement or negation of a two's complement number x is $2^n - x$.

A third alternative representation is called *one's complement.* The negative of a one's complement is found by inverting each bit, from 0 to 1 and from 1 to 0, which helps explain its name since the complement of x is $2^n - x - 1$. It was also an attempt to be a better solution than sign and magnitude, and several scientific computers did use the notation. This representation is similar to two's complement except that it also has two 0s: $00 \ldots 00_{two}$ is positive 0 and $11 \ldots 11_{two}$ is negative 0. The most negative number $10 \ldots 000_{two}$ represents $-2{,}147{,}483{,}647_{ten}$, and so the positives and negatives are balanced. One's complement adders did need an extra step to subtract a number, and hence two's complement dominates today.

A final notation, which we will look at when we discuss floating point, is to represent the most negative value by $00 \ldots 000_{two}$ and the most positive value represented by $11 \ldots 11_{two}$, with 0 typically having the value $10 \ldots 00_{two}$. This is called a *biased* notation, for it biases the number such that the number plus the bias has a nonnegative representation.

4.3   Addition and Subtraction

Subtraction: Addition's Tricky Pal

No. 10, Top Ten Courses for Athletes at a Football Factory,
David Letterman et al., *Book of Top Ten Lists*, 1990

Addition is just what you would expect in computers. Digits are added bit by bit from right to left, with carries passed to the next digit to the left, just as you would do by hand. Subtraction uses addition: The appropriate operand is simply negated before being added.

Binary Addition and Subtraction

Let's try adding 6_{ten} to 7_{ten} in binary and then subtracting 6_{ten} from 7_{ten} in binary.

$$
\begin{array}{rll}
  & 0000\ 0000\ 0000\ 0000\ 0000\ 0000\ 0000\ 0111_{two} & = \quad 7_{ten} \\
+ & 0000\ 0000\ 0000\ 0000\ 0000\ 0000\ 0000\ 0110_{two} & = \quad 6_{ten} \\
\hline
= & 0000\ 0000\ 0000\ 0000\ 0000\ 0000\ 0000\ 1101_{two} & = \quad 13_{ten}
\end{array}
$$

The 4 bits to the right have all the action; Figure 4.3 shows the sums and carries. The carries are shown in parentheses, with the arrows showing how they are passed.

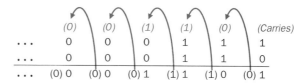

FIGURE 4.3   Binary addition, showing carries from right to left. The rightmost bit adds 1 to 0, resulting in the sum of this bit being 1 and the carry out from this bit being 0. Hence, the operation for the second digit to the right is $0 + 1 + 1$. This generates a 0 for this sum bit and a carry out of 1. The third digit is the sum of $1 + 1 + 1$, resulting in a carry out of 1 and a sum bit of 1. The fourth bit is $1 + 0 + 0$, yielding a 1 sum and no carry.

Subtracting 6_{ten} from 7_{ten} can be done directly:

$$
\begin{aligned}
& \ \text{0000 0000 0000 0000 0000 0000 0000 0111}_{two} \ = \ 7_{ten} \\
- & \ \text{0000 0000 0000 0000 0000 0000 0000 0110}_{two} \ = \ 6_{ten} \\
\hline
= & \ \text{0000 0000 0000 0000 0000 0000 0000 0001}_{two} \ = \ 1_{ten}
\end{aligned}
$$

or via addition using the two's complement representation of −6:

$$
\begin{aligned}
& \ \text{0000 0000 0000 0000 0000 0000 0000 0111}_{two} \ = \ 7_{ten} \\
+ & \ \text{1111 1111 1111 1111 1111 1111 1111 1010}_{two} \ = \ {-6}_{ten} \\
\hline
= & \ \text{0000 0000 0000 0000 0000 0000 0000 0001}_{two} \ = \ 1_{ten}
\end{aligned}
$$

We said earlier that overflow occurs when the result from an operation cannot be represented with the available hardware, in this case a 32-bit word. When can overflow occur in addition? When adding operands with different signs, overflow cannot occur. The reason is the sum must be no larger than one of the operands. For example, $-10 + 4 = -6$. Since the operands fit in 32 bits and the sum is no larger than an operand, the sum must fit in 32 bits as well. Therefore no overflow can occur when adding positive and negative operands.

There are similar restrictions to the occurrence of overflow during subtract, but it's just the opposite principle: When the signs of the operands are the *same*, overflow cannot occur. To see this, remember that $x - y = x + (-y)$ because we subtract by negating the second operand and then add. So, when we subtract operands of the same sign we end up by *adding* operands of *different* signs. From the prior paragraph, we know that overflow cannot occur in this case either.

Having examined when overflow cannot occur in addition and subtraction, we still haven't answered how to detect when it does occur. Overflow occurs when adding two positive numbers and the sum is negative, or vice versa. Clearly, adding or subtracting two 32-bit numbers can yield a result that needs

33 bits to be fully expressed. The lack of a 33rd bit means that when overflow occurs the sign bit is being set with the *value* of the result instead of the proper sign of the result. Since we need just one extra bit, only the sign bit can be wrong. This means a carry out occurred into the sign bit.

Overflow occurs in subtraction when we subtract a negative number from a positive number and get a negative result, or when we subtract a positive number from a negative number and get a positive result. This means a borrow occurred from the sign bit. Figure 4.4 shows the combination of operations, operands, and results that indicate an overflow. (Exercise 4.42 gives a shortcut for detecting overflow more simply in hardware.)

We have just seen how to detect overflow for two's complement numbers in a machine. What about unsigned integers? Unsigned integers are commonly used for memory addresses where overflows are ignored.

The machine designer must therefore provide a way to ignore overflow in some cases and to recognize it in others. The MIPS solution is to have two kinds of arithmetic instructions to recognize the two choices:

- Add (add), add immediate (addi), and subtract (sub) cause exceptions on overflow.

- Add unsigned (addu), add immediate unsigned (addiu), and subtract unsigned (subu) do *not* cause exceptions on overflow.

Because C ignores overflows, the MIPS C compilers will always generate the unsigned versions of the arithmetic instructions addu, addiu, and subu no matter what the type of the variables. The MIPS Fortran compilers, however, pick the appropriate arithmetic instructions, depending on the type of the operands.

Operation	Operand A	Operand B	Result
$A + B$	≥ 0	≥ 0	< 0
$A + B$	< 0	< 0	≥ 0
$A - B$	≥ 0	< 0	< 0
$A - B$	< 0	≥ 0	≥ 0

FIGURE 4.4   Overflow conditions for addition and subtraction.

Hardware Software Interface

The machine designer must decide how to handle arithmetic overflows. Although some languages like C leave the decision up to the machine designer, languages like Ada and Fortran require that the program be notified. The programmer or the programming environment must then decide what to do when overflow occurs.

MIPS detects overflow with an *exception*, also called an *interrupt* on many computers. An exception or interrupt is essentially an unscheduled procedure call. The address of the instruction that overflowed is saved in a register, and the computer jumps to a predefined address to invoke the appropriate routine for that exception. The interrupted address is saved so that in some situations the program can continue after corrective code is executed. (Section 5.6 covers exceptions in more detail; Chapters 7 and 8 describe other situations where exceptions and interrupts occur.)

MIPS includes a register called the *exception program counter* (EPC) to contain the address of the instruction that caused the exception. The instruction *move from system control* (mfc0) is used to copy EPC into a general-purpose register so that MIPS software has the option of returning to the offending instruction via a jump register instruction.

Summary

The main point of this section is that, independent of the representation, the finite word size of computers means that arithmetic operations can create results that are too large to fit in this fixed word size. It's easy to detect overflow in unsigned numbers, although these are almost always ignored because programs don't want to detect overflow for address arithmetic, the most common use of natural numbers. Two's complement presents a greater challenge, yet some software systems require detection of overflow, so today all machines have a way to detect it. Figure 4.5 shows the additions to the MIPS architecture from this section.

Elaboration: MIPS can trap on overflow, but unlike many other machines there is no conditional branch to test overflow. A sequence of MIPS instructions can discover overflow. For signed addition, the sequence is the following (see the In More Depth section on page 329 for the definition of the xor and nor instructions):

```
addu $t0, $t1,  $t2          # $t0 = sum, but don't trap
xor  $t3, $t1,  $t2          # Check if signs differ
slt  $t3, $t3,  $zero        # $t3 = 1 if signs differ
bne  $t3, $zero, No_overflow # $t1, $t2 signs ≠, so no overflow
xor  $t3, $t0,  $t1          # signs =; sign of sum match too?
                             # $t3 negative if sum sign different
slt  $t3, $t3,  $zero        # $t3 = 1 if sum sign different
bne  $t3, $zero, Overflow    # All three signs ≠; go to overflow
```

MIPS operands

Name	Example	Comments
32 registers	`$s0–$s7, $t0–$t9, $gp, $fp, $zero, $sp, $ra, $at`	Fast locations for data. In MIPS, data must be in registers to perform arithmetic. MIPS register `$zero` always equals 0. Register `$at` is reserved for the assembler to, for example, handle large constants.
2^{30} memory words	Memory[0], Memory[4], . . . , Memory[4294967292]	Accessed only by data transfer instructions. MIPS uses byte addresses, so sequential words differ by 4. Memory holds data structures, such as arrays, and spilled registers, such as those saved on procedure calls.

MIPS assembly language

Category	Instruction	Example		Meaning	Comments
Arithmetic	add	`add`	`$s1,$s2,$s3`	$s1 = $s2 + $s3	Three operands; overflow detected
	subtract	`sub`	`$s1,$s2,$s3`	$s1 = $s2 – $s3	Three operands; overflow detected
	add immediate	`addi`	`$s1,$s2,100`	$s1 = $s2 + 100	+ constant; overflow detected
	add unsigned	`addu`	`$s1,$s2,$s3`	$s1 = $s2 + $s3	Three operands; overflow undetected
	subtract unsigned	`subu`	`$s1,$s2,$s3`	$s1 = $s2 – $s3	Three operands; overflow undetected
	add immediate unsigned	`addiu`	`$s1,$s2,100`	$s1 = $s2 + 100	+ constant; overflow undetected
	move from coprocessor register	`mfc0`	`$s1,$epc`	$s1 = $epc	Used to copy Exception PC plus other special registers
Data transfer	load word	`lw`	`$s1,100($s2)`	$s1 = Memory[$s2 + 100]	Word from memory to register
	store word	`sw`	`$s1,100($s2)`	Memory[$s2 + 100] = $s1	Word from register to memory
	load byte unsigned	`lbu`	`$s1,100($s2)`	$s1 = Memory[$s2 + 100]	Byte from memory to register
	store byte	`sb`	`$s1,100($s2)`	Memory[$s2 + 100] = $s1	Byte from register to memory
	load upper immediate	`lui`	`$s1,100`	$s1 = 100 * 2^{16}	Loads constant in upper 16 bits
Conditional branch	branch on equal	`beq`	`$s1,$s2,25`	if ($s1 == $s2) go to PC + 4 + 100	Equal test; PC-relative branch
	branch on not equal	`bne`	`$s1,$s2,25`	if ($s1 != $s2) go to PC + 4 + 100	Not equal test; PC-relative
	set on less than	`slt`	`$s1,$s2,$s3`	if ($s2 < $s3) $s1 = 1; else $s1 = 0	Compare less than; two's complement
	set less than immediate	`slti`	`$s1,$s2,100`	if ($s2 < 100) $s1 = 1; else $s1 = 0	Compare < constant; two's complement
	set less than unsigned	`sltu`	`$s1,$s2,$s3`	if ($s2 < $s3) $s1 = 1; else $s1 = 0	Compare less than; unsigned numbers
	set less than immediate unsigned	`sltiu`	`$s1,$s2,100`	if ($s2 < 100) $s1 = 1; else $s1 = 0	Compare < constant; unsigned numbers
Uncondi-tional jump	jump	`j`	`2500`	go to 10000	Jump to target address
	jump register	`jr`	`$ra`	go to $ra	For switch, procedure return
	jump and link	`jal`	`2500`	$ra = PC + 4; go to 10000	For procedure call

FIGURE 4.5 MIPS architecture revealed thus far. Color indicates the portions revealed since Figure 4.2 on page 219. MIPS machine language is also listed on the back endpapers of this book.

For unsigned addition ($t0 = $t1 + $t2), the test is

```
addu $t0, $t1, $t2      # $t0 = sum
nor  $t3, $t1, $zero    # $t3 = NOT $t1
                        # (2's comp - 1: 2³² - $t1 - 1)
sltu $t3, $t3, $t2      # (2³² - $t1 - 1) < $t2
                        # ⟹ 2³² - 1 < $t1 + $t2
bne  $t3,$zero, Overflow # if (2³² - 1 < $t1 + $t2) go to overflow
```

Elaboration: In the preceding text, we said that you copy EPC into a register via mfc0 and then return to the interrupted code via jump register. This leads to an interesting question: Since you must first transfer EPC to a register to use with jump register, how can jump register return to the interrupted code *and* restore the original values of *all* registers? You either restore the old registers first, thereby destroying your return address from EPC that you placed in a register for use in jump register, or you restore all registers but the one with the return address so that you can jump—meaning an exception would result in changing that one register at any time during program execution! Neither option is satisfactory.

To rescue the hardware from this dilemma, MIPS programmers agreed to reserve registers $k0 and $k1 for the operating system; these registers are *not* restored on exceptions. Just as the MIPS compilers avoid using register $at so that the assembler can use it as a temporary register (see the Hardware Software Interface section on page 147 in Chapter 3), compilers also abstain from using registers $k0 and $k1 to make them available for the operating system. Exception routines place the return address in one of these registers and then use jump register to restore the instruction address.

4.4   Logical Operations

> *"Contrariwise," continued Tweedledee, "if it was so, it might be; and if it were so, it would be; but as it isn't, it ain't. That's logic."*
>
> Lewis Carroll, *Alice's Adventures in Wonderland,* 1865

Although the first computers concentrated on full words, it soon became clear that it was useful to operate on fields of bits within a word or even on individual bits. Examining characters within a word, each of which are stored as 8 bits, is one example of such an operation. It follows that instructions were added to simplify, among other things, the packing and unpacking of bits into words.

One class of such operations is called *shifts*. They move all the bits in a word to the left or right, filling the emptied bits with 0s. For example, if register $s0 contained

0000 0000 0000 00000 000 0000 0000 0000 1101$_{two}$

and the instruction to shift left by eight was executed, the new value would look like this:

0000 0000 0000 0000 0000 0000 1101 0000 0000$_{two}$

The dual of a shift left is a shift right. The actual name of the two MIPS shift instructions are called *shift left logical* (sll) and *shift right logical* (srl). The following instruction performs the operation above, assuming that the result should go in register $t2:

    sll $t2,$s0,8 # reg $t2 = reg $s0 << 8 bits

We delayed explaining the *shamt* field in the R-format in Chapter 3. It stands for *shift amount* and is used in shift instructions. Hence, the machine language version of the instruction above is

op	rs	rt	rd	shamt	funct
0	0	16	10	8	0

The encoding of sll is 0 in both the op and funct fields, rd contains $t2, rt contains $s0, and shamt contains 8. The rs field is unused, and thus is set to 0.

Another useful operation that isolates fields is *AND*. (We capitalize the word to avoid confusion between the operation and the English conjunction.) AND is a bit-by-bit operation that leaves a 1 in the result only if both bits of the operands are 1. For example, if register $t2 still contains

0000 0000 0000 0000 0000 1101 0000 0000$_{two}$

and register $t1 contains

0000 0000 0000 0000 0011 1100 0000 0000$_{two}$

then, after executing the MIPS instruction

    and $t0,$t1,$t2 # reg $t0 = reg $t1 & reg $t2

the value of register $t0 would be

0000 0000 0000 0000 0000 1100 0000 0000$_{two}$

As you can see, AND can be used to apply a bit pattern to a set of bits to force 0s where there is a 0 in the bit pattern. Such a bit pattern in conjunction with AND is traditionally called a *mask*, since the mask "conceals" some bits.

To place a value into one of these seas of 0s, there is the dual to AND, called *OR*. It is a bit-by-bit operation that places a 1 in the result if *either* operand bit is a 1. To elaborate, if the registers $t1 and $t2 are unchanged from the preceding example, the result of the MIPS instruction

```
or $t0,$t1,$t2 # reg $t0 = reg $t1 | reg $t2
```

is this value in register $t0:

0000 0000 0000 0000 0011 1101 0000 0000$_{two}$

Figure 4.6 shows the logical C operations and the corresponding MIPS instructions. Constants are useful in logical operations as well as in arithmetic operations, so MIPS also provides the instructions *and immediate* (andi) and *or immediate* (ori). This section describes the logical operations AND, OR, and shift found in every computer today. The logical instructions are highlighted in Figure 4.7, which summarizes the MIPS instructions seen thus far.

Logical operations	C operators	MIPS instructions
Shift left	<<	sll
Shift right	>>	srl
Bit-by-bit AND	&	and, andi
Bit-by-bit OR	|	or, ori

FIGURE 4.6 Logical operations and their corresponding operations in C and MIPS.

Hardware Software Interface

C allows *bit fields* or *fields* to be defined within words, both allowing objects to be packed within a word *and* to match an externally enforced interface such as an I/O device. All fields must fit within a single word. Fields are unsigned integers that can be as short as 1 bit. C compilers insert and extract fields using logical instructions in MIPS: and, or, sll, and srl.

MIPS operands

Name	Example	Comments
32 registers	$s0–$s7, $t0–$t9, $gp, $fp, $zero, $sp, $ra, $at	Fast locations for data. In MIPS, data must be in registers to perform arithmetic. MIPS register $zero always equals 0. Register $at is reserved for the assembler to handle large constants.
2^{30} memory words	Memory[0], Memory[4], . . . , Memory[4294967292]	Accessed only by data transfer instructions. MIPS uses byte addresses, so sequential words differ by 4. Memory holds data structures, such as arrays, and spilled registers, such as those saved on procedure calls.

MIPS assembly language

Category	Instruction	Example	Meaning	Comments
Arithmetic	add	add $s1,$s2,$s3	$s1 = $s2 + $s3	Three operands; overflow detected
	subtract	sub $s1,$s2,$s3	$s1 = $s2 − $s3	Three operands; overflow detected
	add immediate	addi $s1,$s2,100	$s1 = $s2 + 100	+ constant; overflow detected
	add unsigned	addu $s1,$s2,$s3	$s1 = $s2 + $s3	Three operands; overflow undetected
	subtract unsigned	subu $s1,$s2,$s3	$s1 = $s2 – $s3	Three operands; overflow undetected
	add immediate unsigned	addiu $s1,$s2,100	$s1 = $s2 + 100	+ constant; overflow undetected
	move from coprocessor register	mfc0 $s1,$epc	$s1 = $epc	Used to copy Exception PC plus other special registers
Logical	and	and $s1,$s2,$s3	$s1 = $s2 & $s3	Three reg. operands; bit-by-bit AND
	or	or $s1,$s2,$s3	$s1 = $s2 | $s3	Three reg. operands; bit-by-bit OR
	and immediate	andi $s1,$s2,100	$s1 = $s2 & 100	Bit-by-bit AND reg with constant
	or immediate	ori $s1,$s2,100	$s1 = $s2 | 100	Bit-by-bit OR reg with constant
	shift left logical	sll $s1,$s2,10	$s1 = $s2 << 10	Shift left by constant
	shift right logical	srl $$s1,$s2,10	$s1 = $s2 >> 10	Shift right by constant
Data transfer	load word	lw $s1,100($s2)	$s1 = Memory[$s2 + 100]	Word from memory to register
	store word	sw $s1,100($s2)	Memory[$s2 + 100] = $s1	Word from register to memory
	load byte unsigned	lbu $s1,100($s2)	$s1 = Memory[$s2 +100]	Byte from memory to register
	store byte	sb $s1,100($s2)	Memory[$s2 + 100] = $s1	Byte from register to memory
	load upper immediate	lui $s1,100	$s1 = 100 * 2^{16}	Loads constant in upper 16 bits
Conditional branch	branch on equal	beq $s1,$s2,25	if ($s1 != $s2) go to PC + 4 + 100	Equal test; PC-relative branch
	branch on not equal	bne $s1,$s2,25	if ($s1 == $s2) go to PC + 4 + 100	Not equal test; PC-relative
	set on less than	slt $s1,$s2,$s3	if ($s2 < $s3) $s1 = 1; else $s1 = 0	Compare less than; two's complement
	set less than immediate	slti $s1,$s2,100	if ($s2 < 100) $s1 = 1; else $s1 = 0	Compare < constant; two's complement
	set less than unsigned	sltu $s1,$s2,$s3	if ($s2 < $s3) $s1 = 1; else $s1 = 0	Compare less than; natural numbers
	set less than immediate unsigned	sltiu $s1,$s2,100	if ($s2 < 100) $s1 = 1; else $s1 = 0	Compare < constant; natural numbers
Unconditional jump	jump	j 2500	go to p10000	Jump to target address
	jump register	jr $ra	go to $ra	For switch, procedure return
	jump and link	jal 2500	$ra = PC + 4; go to 10000	For procedure call

FIGURE 4.7 MIPS architecture revealed thus far. Color indicates the portions since Figure 4.5 on page 224. MIPS machine language is also listed on the back endpapers of this book.

C Bit Fields

The following C code allocates three fields with a word labeled receiver: a 1-bit field named ready, a 1-bit field named enable, and an 8-bit field named receivedByte. It copies receivedByte into data, sets ready to 0, and sets enable to 1.

```
int data;
struct
{
    unsigned int ready:        1;
    unsigned int enable:       1;
    unsigned int receivedByte: 8;
}receiver;
    ...
    data = receiver.receivedByte;
    receiver.ready = 0;
    receiver.enable = 1;
```

What is the compiled MIPS code? Assume data and receiver are allocated to $s0 and $s1.

The fields look like this in a word (C right-aligns fields):

31 ... 10	9 2	1	0
	receivedByte	enable	ready

The first step is to isolate the 8-bit field (receivedByte) by first shifting it as far to the left as possible and then as far to the right as possible:

```
sll     $s0, $s1, 22 # move 8-bit field to left end
srl     $s0, $s0, 24 # move 8-bit field to right end
```

The third instruction clears the least significant bit with the mask $fffe_{hex}$ and the last instruction sets its neighbor bit to 1:

```
andi    $s1, $s1, fffehex # bit 0 set to 0
ori     $s1, $s1, 0002hex # bit 1 set to 1
```

Elaboration: In the example this alternative sequence works as well:

```
srl     $s0, $s1, 2
andi    $s0, $s0, 0x00ff
```

The field is in the lower 16 bits of the word and we want 0s in the upper bits of the result of the `andi`. In general, a shift left of $32 - (n + m)$ followed by a shift right by $32 - n$ will isolate any n-bit field whose least significant bit is in bit m.

Since `addi` and `slti` are intended for signed numbers, it is not surprising that their immediate fields are sign-extended before use. Branch and data transfer address fields are sign-extended as well.

Perhaps it *is* surprising that `addiu` and `sltiu` also sign-extend their immediates, but they do. The `u` stands for unsigned, but in reality `addiu` is often used simply as an `add` instruction that cannot overflow, and hence we often want to add negative numbers. It's much harder to come up for an excuse that `sltiu` does not sign extend its immediate.

Since `andi` and `ori` normally work with unsigned integers, the immediates are treated as unsigned integers as well, meaning that they are expanded to 32 bits by padding with leading 0s instead of sign extension. Thus if the bit fields in the third line of the example above extended beyond the 16 least significant bits, the `andi` instruction would need a 32-bit constant to avoid clearing the upper portion of the fields.

The MIPS assembler creates 32-bit constants with the pair of instructions `lui` and `ori`; see Chapter 3, page 147 for an example of creating 32-bit constants using `lui` and `addi`.

4.5   Constructing an Arithmetic Logic Unit

*ALU n. [**A**rthritic **L**ogic **U**nit or (rare) **A**rithmetic **L**ogic **U**nit] A random-number generator supplied as standard with all computer systems.*

Stan Kelly-Bootle, *The Devil's DP Dictionary*, 1981

The *arithmetic logic unit* or *ALU* is the brawn of the computer, the device that performs the arithmetic operations like addition and subtraction or logical operations like AND and OR. This section constructs an ALU from the four hardware building blocks shown in Figure 4.8 (see Appendix B for more details on these building blocks). Cases 1, 2, and 4 in Figure 4.8 all have two inputs. We will sometimes use versions of these components with more than two inputs, confident that you can generalize from this simple example. In any case, Appendix B provides examples with more inputs. (You may wish to review sections B.1 through B.3 before proceeding further.)

Because the MIPS word is 32 bits wide, we need a 32-bit-wide ALU. Let's assume that we will connect 32 1-bit ALUs to create the desired ALU. We'll therefore start by constructing a 1-bit ALU.

A 1-Bit ALU

The logical operations are easiest, because they map directly onto the hardware components in Figure 4.8.

1. AND gate (c = a · b)

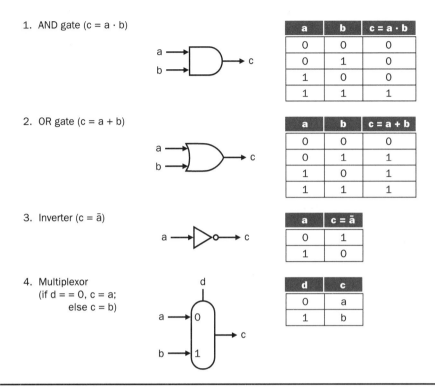

a	b	c = a · b
0	0	0
0	1	0
1	0	0
1	1	1

2. OR gate (c = a + b)

a	b	c = a + b
0	0	0
0	1	1
1	0	1
1	1	1

3. Inverter (c = $\bar{a}$)

a	c = $\bar{a}$
0	1
1	0

4. Multiplexor
   (if d = = 0, c = a;
        else c = b)

d	c
0	a
1	b

FIGURE 4.8 Four hardware building blocks used to construct an arithmetic logic unit.
The name of the operation and an equation describing it appear on the left. In the middle is the symbol for the block we will use in the drawings. On the right are tables that describe the outputs in terms of the inputs. Using the notation from Appendix B, a • b means "a AND b," a + b means "a OR b," and a line over the top (e.g., $\bar{a}$) means invert.

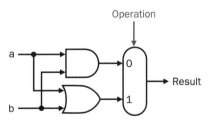

FIGURE 4.9 The 1-bit logical unit for AND and OR.

The 1-bit logical unit for AND and OR looks like Figure 4.9. The multiplexor on the right then selects a AND b or a OR b, depending on whether the value of *Operation* is 0 or 1. The line that controls the multiplexor is shown in color to distinguish it from the lines containing data. Notice that we have renamed the control and output lines of the multiplexor to give them names that reflect the function of the ALU.

The next function to include is addition. From Figure 4.3 on page 221 we can deduce the inputs and outputs of a single-bit adder. First, an adder must have two inputs for the operands and a single-bit output for the sum. There must be a second output to pass on the carry, called *CarryOut*. Since the CarryOut from the neighbor adder must be included as an input, we need a third input. This input is called *CarryIn*. Figure 4.10 shows the inputs and the outputs of a 1-bit adder. Since we know what addition is supposed to do, we can specify the outputs of this "black box" based on its inputs, as Figure 4.11 demonstrates.

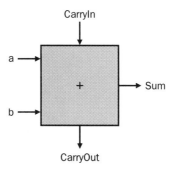

FIGURE 4.10   A 1-bit adder. This adder is called a full adder; it is also called a (3,2) adder because it has 3 inputs and 2 outputs. An adder with only the a and b inputs is called a (2,2) adder or half adder.

Inputs			Outputs		
a	**b**	**CarryIn**	**CarryOut**	**Sum**	**Comments**
0	0	0	0	0	$0 + 0 + 0 = 00_{two}$
0	0	1	0	1	$0 + 0 + 1 = 01_{two}$
0	1	0	0	1	$0 + 1 + 0 = 01_{two}$
0	1	1	1	0	$0 + 1 + 1 = 10_{two}$
1	0	0	0	1	$1 + 0 + 0 = 01_{two}$
1	0	1	1	0	$1 + 0 + 1 = 10_{two}$
1	1	0	1	0	$1 + 1 + 0 = 10_{two}$
1	1	1	1	1	$1 + 1 + 1 = 11_{two}$

FIGURE 4.11   Input and output specification for a 1-bit adder.

From Appendix B, we know that we can express the output functions Carry-Out and Sum as logical equations, and these equations can in turn be implemented with the building blocks in Figure 4.8. Let's do CarryOut. Figure 4.12 shows the values of the inputs when CarryOut is a 1.

We can turn this truth table into a logical equation, as explained in Appendix B. (Recall that a + b means "a OR b" and that a · b means "a AND b.")

$$CarryOut = (b \cdot CarryIn) + (a \cdot CarryIn) + (a \cdot b) + (a \cdot b \cdot CarryIn)$$

If a · b · CarryIn is true, then one of the other three terms must also be true, so we can leave out this last term corresponding to the fourth line of the table. We can thus simplify the equation to

$$CarryOut = (b \cdot CarryIn) + (a \cdot CarryIn) + (a \cdot b)$$

Figure 4.13 shows that the hardware within the adder black box for CarryOut consists of three AND gates and one OR gate. The three AND gates correspond exactly to the three parenthesized terms of the formula above for CarryOut, and the OR gate sums the three terms.

Inputs		
a	b	CarryIn
0	1	1
1	0	1
1	1	0
1	1	1

FIGURE 4.12 Values of the inputs when CarryOut is a 1.

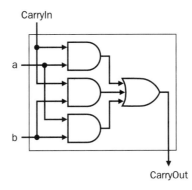

CarryOut

FIGURE 4.13 Adder hardware for the carry out signal. The rest of the adder hardware is the logic for the Sum output given in the equation above.

The Sum bit is set when exactly one input is 1 or when all three inputs are 1. The Sum results in a complex Boolean equation (recall that $\bar{a}$ means NOT a):

$$\text{Sum} = (a \cdot \bar{b} \cdot \overline{\text{CarryIn}}) + (\bar{a} \cdot b \cdot \overline{\text{CarryIn}}) + (\bar{a} \cdot \bar{b} \cdot \text{CarryIn}) + (a \cdot b \cdot \text{CarryIn})$$

The drawing of the logic for the Sum bit in the adder black box is left as an exercise (see Exercise 4.43).

Figure 4.14 shows a 1-bit ALU derived by combining the adder with the earlier components. Sometimes designers also want the ALU to perform a few more simple operations, such as generating 0. The easiest way to add an operation is to expand the multiplexor controlled by the Operation line and, for this example, to connect 0 directly to the new input of that expanded multiplexor.

A 32-Bit ALU

Now that we have completed the 1-bit ALU, the full 32-bit ALU is created by connecting adjacent "black boxes." Using xi to mean the ith bit of x, Figure 4.15 shows a 32-bit ALU. Just as a single stone can cause ripples to radiate to the shores of a quiet lake, a single carry out of the least significant bit (Result0) can ripple all the way through the adder, causing a carry out of the most significant bit (Result31). Hence, the adder created by directly linking the carries of 1-bit adders is called a *ripple carry* adder. We'll see a faster way to connect the 1-bit adders starting on page 241.

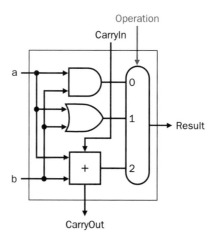

FIGURE 4.14   A 1-bit ALU that performs AND, OR, and addition (see Figure 4.13).

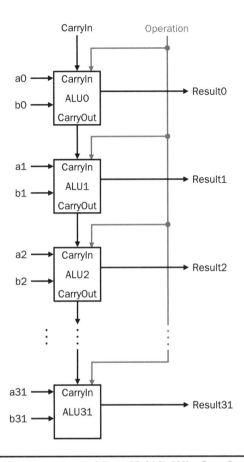

FIGURE 4.15 A 32-bit ALU constructed from 32 1-bit ALUs. CarryOut of the less significant bit is connected to the CarryIn of the more significant bit. This organization is called ripple carry.

Subtraction is the same as adding the negative version of an operand, and this is how adders perform subtraction. Recall that the shortcut for negating a two's complement number is to invert each bit (sometimes called the *one's complement* as explained in the elaboration on page 219) and then add 1. To invert each bit, we simply add a 2:1 multiplexor that chooses between b and $\overline{b}$, as Figure 4.16 shows.

Suppose we connect 32 of these 1-bit ALUs, as we did in Figure 4.15. The added multiplexor gives the option of b or its inverted value, depending on Binvert, but this is only one step in negating a two's complement number. Notice that the least significant bit still has a CarryIn signal, even though it's unnecessary for addition. What happens if we set this CarryIn to 1 instead of 0?

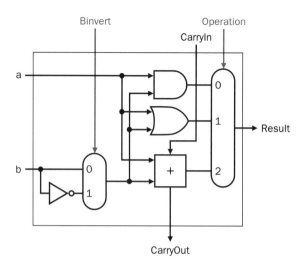

FIGURE 4.16   A 1-bit ALU that performs AND, OR, and addition on a and b or a and $\overline{b}$. By selecting b (Binvert = 1) and setting CarryIn to 1 in the least significant bit of the ALU, we get two's complement subtraction of b from a instead of addition of b to a.

The adder will then calculate a + b + 1. By selecting the inverted version of b, we get exactly what we want:

$$a + \overline{b} + 1 = a + (\overline{b} + 1) = a + (-b) = a - b$$

The simplicity of the hardware design of a two's complement adder helps explain why two's complement representation has become the universal standard for integer computer arithmetic.

Tailoring the 32-Bit ALU to MIPS

This set of operations—add, subtract, AND, OR—is found in the ALU of almost every computer. If we look at Figure 4.7 on page 228, we see that the operations of most MIPS instructions can be performed by this ALU. But the design of the ALU is incomplete.

One instruction that still needs support is the set on less than instruction (slt). Recall that the operation produces 1 if rs < rt, and 0 otherwise. Consequently, slt will set all but the least significant bit to 0, with the least significant bit set according to the comparison. For the ALU to perform slt, we first need to expand the three-input multiplexor in Figure 4.16 to add an input for the slt result. We call that new input *Less,* and use it only for slt.

The top drawing of Figure 4.17 shows the new 1-bit ALU with the expanded multiplexor. From the description of `slt` above, we must connect 0 to the Less input for the upper 31 bits of the ALU, since those bits are always set to 0. What remains to consider is how to compare and set *the least significant bit* for set on less than instructions.

What happens if we subtract b from a? If the difference is negative, then a < b since

$$(a - b) < 0 \Rightarrow ((a - b) + b) < (0 + b)$$
$$\Rightarrow a < b$$

We want the least significant bit of a set on less than operation to be a 1 if a < b; that is, a 1 if a − b is negative and a 0 if it's positive. This desired result corresponds exactly to the sign-bit values: 1 means negative and 0 means positive. Following this line of argument, we need only connect the sign bit from the adder output to the least significant bit to get set on less than.

Unfortunately, the Result output from the most significant ALU bit in the top of Figure 4.17 for the `slt` operation is *not* the output of the adder; the ALU output for the `slt` operation is obviously the input value Less.

Thus, we need a new 1-bit ALU for the most significant bit that has an extra output bit: the adder output. The bottom drawing of Figure 4.17 shows the design, with this new adder output line called *Set*, and used only for `slt`. As long as we need a special ALU for the most significant bit, we added the overflow detection logic since it is also associated with that bit.

Alas, the test of less than is a little more complicated than just described because of overflow; Exercise 4.23 on page 326 explores what must be done. Figure 4.18 shows the 32-bit ALU.

Notice that every time we want the ALU to subtract, we set both CarryIn and Binvert to 1. For adds or logical operations, we want both control lines to be 0. We can therefore simplify control of the ALU by combining the CarryIn and Binvert to a single control line called *Bnegate*.

To further tailor the ALU to the MIPS instruction set, we must support conditional branch instructions. These instructions branch either if two registers are equal or if they are unequal. The easiest way to test equality with the ALU is to subtract b from a and then test to see if the result is 0 since

$$(a - b = 0) \Rightarrow a = b$$

Thus, if we add hardware to test if the result is 0, we can test for equality. The simplest way is to OR all the outputs together and then send that signal through an inverter:

$$\text{Zero} = \overline{(\text{Result31} + \text{Result30} + \ldots + \text{Result2} + \text{Result1} + \text{Result0})}$$

Figure 4.19 shows the revised 32-bit ALU. We can think of the combination of the 1-bit Bnegate line and the 2-bit Operation lines as 3-bit control lines for

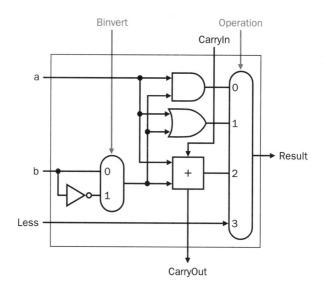

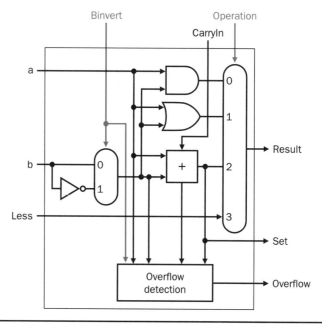

FIGURE 4.17   (Top) A 1-bit ALU that performs AND, OR, and addition on a and b or b̄, and (bottom) a 1-bit ALU for the most significant bit. The top drawing includes a direct input that is connected to perform the set on less than operation (see Figure 4.18); the bottom has a direct output from the adder for the less than comparison called Set. (Refer to Exercise 4.42 to see how to calculate overflow with fewer inputs.)

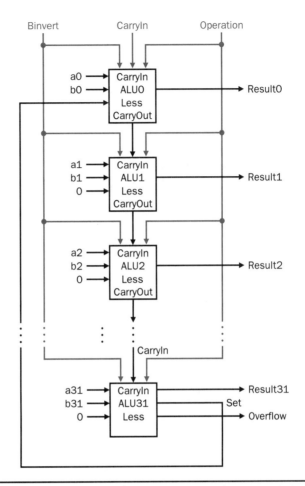

FIGURE 4.18   A 32-bit ALU constructed from the 31 copies of the 1-bit ALU in the top of Figure 4.17 and one 1-bit ALU in the bottom of that figure. The Less inputs are connected to 0 except for the least significant bit, and that is connected to the Set output of the most significant bit. If the ALU performs a − b and we select the input 3 in the multiplexor in Figure 4.17, then Result = 0 . . . 001 if a < b, and Result = 0 . . . 000 otherwise.

the ALU, telling it to perform add, subtract, AND, OR, or set on less than. Figure 4.20 shows the ALU control lines and the corresponding ALU operation.

Finally, now that we have seen what is inside a 32-bit ALU, we will use the universal symbol for a complete ALU, as shown in Figure 4.21.

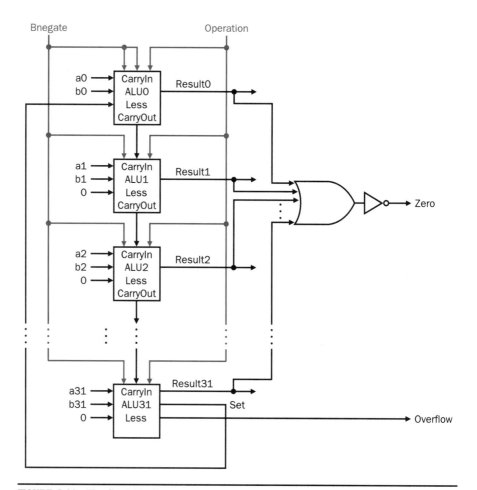

FIGURE 4.19   The final 32-bit ALU. This adds a Zero detector to Figure 4.18.

ALU control lines	Function
000	and
001	or
010	add
110	subtract
111	set on less than

FIGURE 4.20   The values of the three ALU control lines Bnegate and Operation and the corresponding ALU operations.

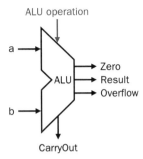

FIGURE 4.21 The symbol commonly used to represent an ALU, as shown in Figure 4.19. This symbol is also used to represent an adder, so it is normally labeled either with ALU or Adder.

Carry Lookahead

The next question is, How quickly can this ALU add two 32-bit operands? We can determine the a and b inputs, but the CarryIn input depends on the operation in the adjacent 1-bit adder. If we trace all the way through the chain of dependencies, we connect the most significant bit to the least significant bit, so the most significant bit of the sum must wait for the *sequential* evaluation of all 32 1-bit adders. This sequential chain reaction is too slow to be used in time-critical hardware.

There are a variety of schemes to anticipate the carry so that the worst-case scenario is a function of the $\log_2$ of the number of bits in the adder. These anticipatory signals are faster because they go through fewer gates in sequence, but it takes many more gates to anticipate the proper carry.

A key to understanding fast carry schemes is to remember that, unlike software, hardware executes in parallel whenever inputs change.

Fast Carry Using "Infinite" Hardware

Appendix B mentions that any equation can be represented in two levels of logic. Since the only external inputs are the two operands and the CarryIn to the least significant bit of the adder, in theory we could calculate the CarryIn values to all the remaining bits of the adder in just two levels of logic.

For example, the CarryIn for bit 2 of the adder is exactly the CarryOut of bit 1, so the formula is

$$\text{CarryIn2} = (\text{b1} \cdot \text{CarryIn1}) + (\text{a1} \cdot \text{CarryIn1}) + (\text{a1} \cdot \text{b1})$$

Similarly, CarryIn1 is defined as

$$\text{CarryIn1} = (\text{b0} \cdot \text{CarryIn0}) + (\text{a0} \cdot \text{CarryIn0}) + (\text{a0} \cdot \text{b0})$$

Using the shorter and more traditional abbreviation of ci for CarryIni, we can rewrite the formulas as

$$c2 = (b1 \cdot c1) + (a1 \cdot c1) + (a1 \cdot b1)$$
$$c1 = (b0 \cdot c0) + (a0 \cdot c0) + (a0 \cdot b0)$$

Substituting the definition of c1 for the first equation results in this formula:

$$c2 = (a1 \cdot a0 \cdot b0) + (a1 \cdot a0 \cdot c0) + (a1 \cdot b0 \cdot c0)$$
$$+ (b1 \cdot a0 \cdot b0) + (b1 \cdot a0 \cdot c0) + (b1 \cdot b0 \cdot c0) + (a1 \cdot b1)$$

You can imagine how the equation expands as we get to higher bits in the adder; it grows exponentially with the number of bits. This complexity is reflected in the cost of the hardware for fast carry, making this simple scheme prohibitively expensive for wide adders.

Fast Carry Using the First Level of Abstraction: Propagate and Generate

Most fast carry schemes limit the complexity of the equations to simplify the hardware, while still making substantial speed improvements over ripple carry. One such scheme is a *carry-lookahead adder*. In Chapter 1, we said computer systems cope with complexity by using levels of abstraction. A carry-lookahead adder relies on levels of abstraction in its implementation.

Let's factor our original equation as a first step:

$$ci+1 = (bi \cdot ci) + (ai \cdot ci) + (ai \cdot bi)$$
$$= (ai \cdot bi) + (ai + bi) \cdot ci$$

If we were to rewrite the equation for c2 using this formula, we would see some repeated patterns:

$$c2 = (a1 \cdot b1) + (a1 + b1) \cdot ((a0 \cdot b0) + (a0 + b0) \cdot c0)$$

Note the repeated appearance of $(ai \cdot bi)$ and $(ai + bi)$ in the formula above. These two important factors are traditionally called *generate* (gi) and *propagate* (pi):

$$gi = ai \cdot bi$$
$$pi = ai + bi$$

Using them to define $ci+1$, we get

$$ci+1 = gi + pi \cdot ci$$

To see where the signals get their names, suppose gi is 1. Then

$$ci+1 = gi + pi \cdot ci = 1 + pi \cdot ci = 1$$

That is, the adder *generates* a CarryOut ($ci+1$) independent of the value of CarryIn (ci). Now suppose that gi is 0 and pi is 1. Then

$$ci+1 \; = \; gi + pi \cdot ci \; = \; 0 + 1 \cdot ci \; = \; ci$$

That is, the adder *propagates* CarryIn to a CarryOut. Putting the two together, CarryIn$i+1$ is a 1 if either gi is 1 or both pi is 1 and CarryIni is 1.

As an analogy, imagine a row of dominoes set on edge. The end domino can be tipped over by pushing one far away provided there are no gaps between the two. Similarly, a carry out can be made true by a generate far away provided all the propagates between them are true.

Relying on the definitions of propagate and generate as our first level of abstraction, we can express the CarryIn signals more economically. Let's show it for 4 bits:

$$c1 \; = \; g0 + (p0 \cdot c0)$$

$$c2 \; = \; g1 + (p1 \cdot g0) + (p1 \cdot p0 \cdot c0)$$

$$c3 \; = \; g2 + (p2 \cdot g1) + (p2 \cdot p1 \cdot g0) + (p2 \cdot p1 \cdot p0 \cdot c0)$$

$$c4 \; = \; g3 + (p3 \cdot g2) + (p3 \cdot p2 \cdot g1) + (p3 \cdot p2 \cdot p1 \cdot g0)$$
$$+ \, (p3 \cdot p2 \cdot p1 \cdot p0 \cdot c0)$$

These equations just represent common sense: CarryIni is a 1 if some earlier adder generates a carry and all intermediary adders propagate a carry. Figure 4.22 uses plumbing to try to explain carry lookahead.

Even this simplified form leads to large equations and, hence, considerable logic even for a 16-bit adder. Let's try moving to two levels of abstraction.

Fast Carry Using the Second Level of Abstraction

First we consider this 4-bit adder with its carry-lookahead logic as a single building block. If we connect them in ripple carry fashion to form a 16-bit adder, the add will be faster than the original with a little more hardware.

To go faster, we'll need carry lookahead at a higher level. To perform carry lookahead for 4-bit adders, we need propagate and generate signals at this higher level. Here they are for the four 4-bit adder blocks:

$$P0 = p3 \cdot p2 \cdot p1 \cdot p0$$
$$P1 = p7 \cdot p6 \cdot p5 \cdot p4$$
$$P2 = p11 \cdot p10 \cdot p9 \cdot p8$$
$$P3 = p15 \cdot p14 \cdot p13 \cdot p12$$

That is, the "super" propagate signal for the 4-bit abstraction (Pi) is true only if each of the bits in the group will propagate a carry.

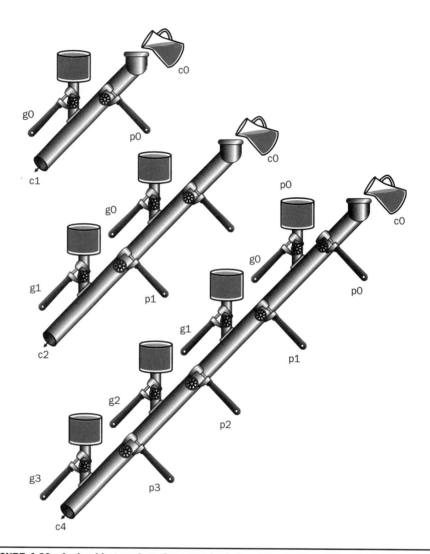

FIGURE 4.22   A plumbing analogy for carry lookahead for 1 bit, 2 bits, and 4 bits using water, pipes, and valves. The wrenches are turned to open and close valves. Water is shown in color. The output of the pipe (c_{i+1}) will be full if either the nearest generate value (g_i) is turned on or if the i propagate value (p_i) is on and there is water further upstream, either from an earlier generate, or propagate with water behind it. CarryIn (c_0) can result in a carry out without the help of any generates, but with the help of *all* propagates.

For the "super" generate signal (G_i), we care only if there is a carry out of the most significant bit of the 4-bit group. This obviously occurs if generate is true for that most significant bit; it also occurs if an earlier generate is true *and* all the intermediate propagates, including that of the most significant bit, are also true:

$$G0 = g3 + (p3 \cdot g2) + (p3 \cdot p2 \cdot g1) + (p3 \cdot p2 \cdot p1 \cdot g0)$$

$$G1 = g7 + (p7 \cdot g6) + (p7 \cdot p6 \cdot g5) + (p7 \cdot p6 \cdot p5 \cdot g4)$$

$$G2 = g11 + (p11 \cdot g10) + (p11 \cdot p10 \cdot g9) + (p11 \cdot p10 \cdot p9 \cdot g8)$$

$$G3 = g15 + (p15 \cdot g14) + (p15 \cdot p14 \cdot g13) + (p15 \cdot p14 \cdot p13 \cdot g12)$$

Figure 4.23 updates our plumbing analogy to show P0 and G0.

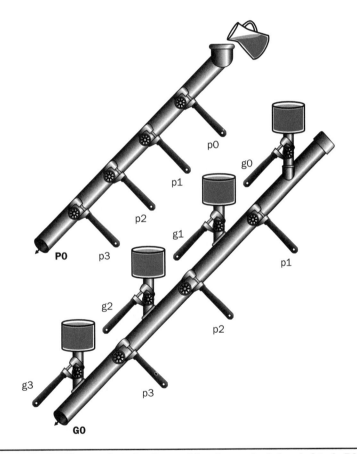

FIGURE 4.23   A plumbing analogy for the next-level carry-lookahead signals P0 and G0.
P0 is open only if all four propagates (pi) are open, while water flows in G0 only if at least one generate (gi) is open and all the propagates downstream from that generate are open.

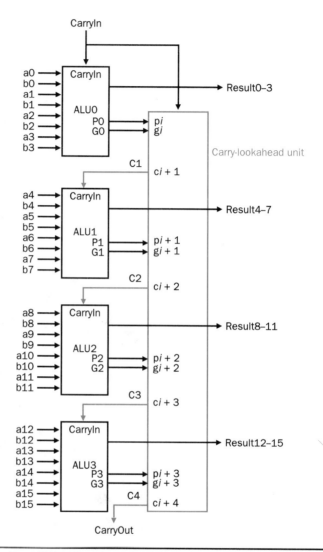

FIGURE 4.24   Four 4-bit ALUs using carry lookahead to form a 16-bit adder. Note that the carries come from the carry-lookahead unit, not from the 4-bit ALUs.

Then the equations at this higher level of abstraction for the carry in for each 4-bit group of the 16-bit adder (C1, C2, C3, C4 in Figure 4.24) are very similar to the carry out equations for each bit of the 4-bit adder (c1, c2, 3, c4) on page 243:

$$C1 = G0 + (P0 \cdot c0)$$

$$C2 = G1 + (P1 \cdot G0) + (P1 \cdot P0 \cdot c0)$$

$$C3 = G2 + (P2 \cdot G1) + (P2 \cdot P1 \cdot G0) + (P2 \cdot P1 \cdot P0 \cdot c0)$$

$$C4 = G3 + (P3 \cdot G2) + (P3 \cdot P2 \cdot G1) + (P3 \cdot P2 \cdot P1 \cdot G0)$$
$$+ (P3 \cdot P2 \cdot P1 \cdot P0 \cdot c0)$$

Figure 4.24 shows 4-bit adders connected with such a carry lookahead unit. Exercises 4.44 through 4.48 explore the speed differences between these carry schemes, different notations for multibit propagate and generate signals, and the design of a 64-bit adder.

Both Levels of the Propagate and Generate

Example

Determine the gi, pi, Pi, and Gi values of these two 16-bit numbers:

```
a:      0001 1010 0011 0011 two
b:      1110 0101 1110 1011 two
```

Also, what is CarryOut15 (C4)?

Answer

Aligning the bits makes it easy to see the values of generate gi ($ai \cdot bi$) and propagate pi ($ai + bi$):

```
a:      0001 1010 0011 0011
b:      1110 0101 1110 1011
gi:     0000 0000 0010 0011
pi:     1111 1111 1111 1011
```

where the bits are numbered 15 to 0 from left to right. Next, the "super" propagates (P3, P2, P1, P0) are simply the AND of the lower-level propagates:

$$P3 = 1 \cdot 1 \cdot 1 \cdot 1 = 1$$

$$P2 = 1 \cdot 1 \cdot 1 \cdot 1 = 1$$

$$P1 = 1 \cdot 1 \cdot 1 \cdot 1 = 1$$

$$P0 = 1 \cdot 0 \cdot 1 \cdot 1 = 0$$

The "super" generates are more complex, so use the followinge quations:

$$G0 = g3 + (p3 \cdot g2) + (p3 \cdot p2 \cdot g1) + (p3 \cdot p2 \cdot p1 \cdot g0)$$
$$= 0 + (1 \cdot 0) + (1 \cdot 0 \cdot 1) + (1 \cdot 0 \cdot 1 \cdot 1) = 0 + 0 + 0 + 0 = 0$$

$$G1 = g7 + (p7 \cdot g6) + (p7 \cdot p6 \cdot g5) + (p7 \cdot p6 \cdot p5 \cdot g4)$$
$$= 0 + (1 \cdot 0) + (1 \cdot 1 \cdot 1) + (1 \cdot 1 \cdot 1 \cdot 0) = 0 + 0 + 1 + 0 = 1$$

$$G2 = g11 + (p11 \cdot g10) + (p11 \cdot p10 \cdot g9) + (p11 \cdot p10 \cdot p9 \cdot g8)$$
$$= 0 + (1 \cdot 0) + (1 \cdot 1 \cdot 0) + (1 \cdot 1 \cdot 1 \cdot 0) = 0 + 0 + 0 + 0 = 0$$

$$G3 = g15 + (p15 \cdot g14) + (p15 \cdot p14 \cdot g13) + (p15 \cdot p14 \cdot p13 \cdot g12)$$
$$= 0 + (1 \cdot 0) + (1 \cdot 1 \cdot 0) + (1 \cdot 1 \cdot 1 \cdot 0) = 0 + 0 + 0 + 0 = 0$$

Finally, CarryOut15 is

$$C4 = G3 + (P3 \cdot G2) + (P3 \cdot P2 \cdot G1) + (P3 \cdot P2 \cdot P1 \cdot G0)$$
$$+ (P3 \cdot P2 \cdot P1 \cdot P0 \cdot c0)$$
$$= 0 + (1 \cdot 0) + (1 \cdot 1 \cdot 1) + (1 \cdot 1 \cdot 1 \cdot 0) + (1 \cdot 1 \cdot 1 \cdot 0 \cdot 0)$$
$$= 0 + 0 + 1 + 0 + 0 = 1$$

Hence there *is* a carry out when adding these two 16-bit numbers.

The reason carry lookahead can make carries faster is that all logic begins evaluating the moment the clock cycle begins, and the result will not change once the output of each gate stops changing. By taking a shortcut of going through fewer gates to send the carry in signal, the output of the gates will stop changing sooner, and hence the time for the adder can be less.

To appreciate the importance of carry lookahead, we need to calculate the relative performance between it and ripple carry adders.

Speed of Ripple Carry versus Carry Lookahead

Example One simple way to model time for logic is to assume each AND or OR gate takes the same time for a signal to pass through it. Time is estimated by simply counting the number of gates along the longest path through a piece of logic. Compare the number of *gate delays* for the critical paths of two 16-bit adders, one using ripple carry and one using two-level carry lookahead.

Answer Figure 4.13 on page 233 shows that the carry out signal takes two gate delays per bit. Then the number of gate delays between a carry in to the least significant bit and the carry out of the most significant is $16 \times 2 = 32$.

For carry lookahead, the carry out of the most significant bit is just C4, defined in the example. It takes two levels of logic to specify C4 in terms of Pi and Gi (the OR of several AND terms). Pi is specified in one level of logic (AND) using pi, and Gi is specified in two levels using pi and gi, so the worst case for this next level of abstraction is two levels of logic. pi and gi are each one level of logic, defined in terms of ai and bi. If we assume one gate delay for each level of logic in these equations, the worst case is $2 + 2 + 1 = 5$ gate delays.

Hence for 16-bit addition a carry-lookahead adder is six times faster, using this simple estimate of hardware speed.

Summary

The primary point of this section is that the traditional ALU can be constructed from a multiplexor and a few gates that are replicated 32 times. To make it more useful to the MIPS architecture, we expand the traditional ALU with hardware to test if the result is 0, detect overflow, and perform the basic operation for set on less than.

Carry lookahead offers a faster path than waiting for the carries to ripple through all 32 1-bit adders. This faster path is paved by two signals, generate and propagate. The former creates a carry regardless of the carry input, and the other passes a carry along. Carry lookahead also gives another example of how abstraction is important in computer design to cope with complexity.

Elaboration: We have now accounted for all but one of the arithmetic and logical operations for the core MIPS instruction set: the ALU in Figure 4.21 omits support of shift instructions. It would be possible to widen the ALU multiplexor to include a left shift by 1 bit or right shift by 1 bit. But hardware designers have created a circuit called a *barrel shifter*, which can shift from 1 to 31 bits in no more time than it takes to add two 32-bit numbers, so shifting is normally done outside the ALU.

Elaboration: The logic equation for the Sum output of the full adder on page 234 can be expressed more simply by using a more powerful gate than AND and OR. An *exclusive OR* gate is true if the two operands disagree; that is,

$$x \neq y \Rightarrow 1 \text{ and } x == y \Rightarrow 0$$

In some technologies, exclusive OR is more efficient than two levels of AND and OR gates. Using the symbol $\oplus$ to represent exclusive OR, here is the new equation:

$$\text{Sum} = a \oplus b \oplus \text{CarryIn}$$

Also, we have drawn the ALU the traditional way, using gates. Computers are designed today in CMOS transistors, which are basically switches. CMOS ALU and barrel shifters take advantage of these switches and have many fewer multiplexors than shown in our designs, but the design principles are similar.

4.6   Multiplication

Multiplication is vexation,
Division is as bad;
The rule of three doth puzzle me,
And practice drives me mad.

Anonymous, Elizabethan manuscript, 1570

With the construction of the ALU and explanation of addition, subtraction, and shifts, we are ready to build the more vexing operation of multiply.

But first let's review the multiplication of decimal numbers in longhand to remind ourselves of the steps and the names of the operands. For reasons that will become clear shortly, we limit this decimal example to using only the digits 0 and 1. Multiplying 1000_{ten} by 1001_{ten}:

$$
\begin{array}{rr}
\text{Multiplicand} & 1000_{ten} \\
\text{Multiplier} \qquad \times & 1001_{ten} \\
\hline
& 1000 \\
& 0000 \\
& 0000 \\
& 1000 \\
\hline
\text{Product} & 1001000_{ten}
\end{array}
$$

The first operand is called the *multiplicand* and the second the *multiplier*. The final result is called the *product*. As you may recall, the algorithm learned in grammar school is to take the digits of the multiplier one at a time from right to left, multiplying the multiplicand by the single digit of the multiplier and shifting the intermediate product one digit to the left of the earlier intermediate products.

The first observation is that the number of digits in the product is considerably larger than the number in either the multiplicand or the multiplier. In fact, if we ignore the sign bits, the length of the multiplication of an n-bit multiplicand and an m-bit multiplier is a product that is $n + m$ bits long. That is, $n + m$ bits are required to represent all possible products. Hence, like add, multiply must cope with overflow because we frequently want a 32-bit product as the result of multiplying two 32-bit numbers.

In this example we restricted the decimal digits to 0 and 1. With only two choices, each step of the multiplication is simple:

1. Just place a copy of the multiplicand (1 × multiplicand) in the proper place if the multiplier digit is a 1, or

2. Place 0 (0 × multiplicand) in the proper place if the digit is 0.

Although the decimal example above happened to use only 0 and 1, multiplication of binary numbers must always use 0 and 1, and thus always offers only these two choices.

Now that we have reviewed the basics of multiplication, the traditional next step is to provide the highly optimized multiply hardware. We break with tradition in the belief that you will gain a better understanding by seeing the evolution of the multiply hardware and algorithm through three generations. The rest of this section presents successive refinements of the hardware and the algorithm until we have a version used in some computers. For now, let's assume that we are multiplying only positive numbers.

First Version of the Multiplication Algorithm and Hardware

The initial design mimics the algorithm we learned in grammar school; the hardware is shown in Figure 4.25. We have drawn the hardware so that data flows from top to bottom to more closely resemble the paper-and-pencil method.

Let's assume that the multiplier is in the 32-bit Multiplier register and that the 64-bit Product register is initialized to 0. From the paper-and-pencil example above, it's clear that we will need to move the multiplicand left one digit each step as it may be added to the intermediate products. Over 32 steps a

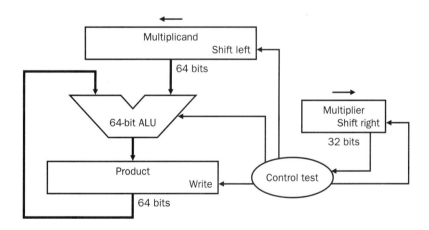

FIGURE 4.25 First version of the multiplication hardware. The Multiplicand register, ALU, and Product register are all 64 bits wide, with only the Multiplier register containing 32 bits. The 32-bit multiplicand starts in the right half of the Multiplicand register, and is shifted left 1 bit on each step. The multiplier is shifted in the opposite direction at each step. The algorithm starts with the product initialized to 0. Control decides when to shift the Multiplicand and Multiplier registers and when to write new values into the Product register.

32-bit multiplicand would move 32 bits to the left. Hence we need a 64-bit Multiplicand register, initialized with the 32-bit multiplicand in the right half and 0 in the left half. This register is then shifted left 1 bit each step to align the multiplicand with the sum being accumulated in the 64-bit Product register.

Figure 4.26 shows the three basic steps needed for each bit. The least significant bit of the multiplier (Multiplier0) determines whether the multiplicand is

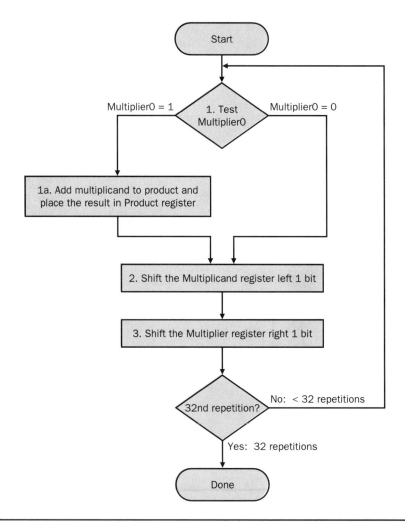

FIGURE 4.26 The first multiplication algorithm, using the hardware shown in Figure 4.25. If the least significant bit of the multiplier is 1, add the multiplicand to the product. If not, go to the next step. Shift the multiplicand left and the multiplier right in the next two steps. These three steps are repeated 32 times.

added to the Product register. The left shift in step 2 has the effect of moving the intermediate operands to the left, just as when multiplying by hand. The shift right in step 3 gives us the next bit of the multiplier to examine in the following iteration. These three steps are repeated 32 times to obtain the product.

First Multiply Algorithm

Example

Using 4-bit numbers to save space, multiply $2_{ten} \times 3_{ten}$, or $0010_{two} \times 0011_{two}$.

Answer

Figure 4.27 shows the value of each register for each of the steps labeled according to Figure 4.26, with the final value of $0000\ 0110_{two}$ or 6_{ten}. Color is used to indicate the register values that change on that step, and the bit circled is the one examined to determine the operation of the next step.

Iteration	Step	Multiplier	Multiplicand	Product
0	Initial values	0011	0000 0010	0000 0000
1	1a: 1 ⇒ Prod = Prod + Mcand	0011	0000 0010	0000 0010
	2: Shift left Multiplicand	0011	0000 0100	0000 0010
	3: Shift right Multiplier	0001	0000 0100	0000 0010
2	1a: 1 ⇒ Prod = Prod + Mcand	0001	0000 0100	0000 0110
	2: Shift left Multiplicand	0001	0000 1000	0000 0110
	3: Shift right Multiplier	0000	0000 1000	0000 0110
3	1: 0 ⇒ no operation	0000	0000 1000	0000 0110
	2: Shift left Multiplicand	0000	0001 0000	0000 0110
	3: Shift right Multiplier	0000	0001 0000	0000 0110
4	1: 0 ⇒ no operation	0000	0001 0000	0000 0110
	2: Shift left Multiplicand	0000	0010 0000	0000 0110
	3: Shift right Multiplier	0000	0010 0000	0000 0110

FIGURE 4.27 Multiply example using first algorithm in Figure 4.26. The bit examined to determine the next step is circled in color.

If each step took a clock cycle, this algorithm would require almost 100 clock cycles to multiply. The relative importance of arithmetic operations like multiply varies with the program, but addition and subtraction may be anywhere from 5 to 100 times more popular than multiply. Accordingly, in many applications, multiply can take multiple clock cycles without significantly affecting performance. Yet Amdahl's law (see Chapter 2, page 75) reminds us that even a moderate frequency for a slow operation can limit performance.

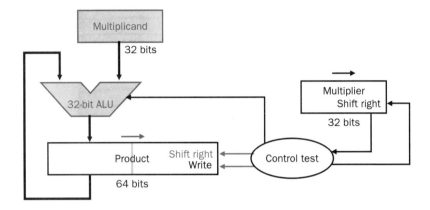

FIGURE 4.28   Second version of the multiplication hardware. Compare with the first version in Figure 4.25. The Multiplicand register, ALU, and Multiplier register are all 32 bits wide, with only the Product register left at 64 bits. Now the product is shifted right. These changes are highlighted in color.

Second Version of the Multiplication Algorithm and Hardware

Computer pioneers recognized that half of the bits of the multiplicand in the first algorithm were always 0, so only half could contain useful bit values. A full 64-bit ALU thus seemed wasteful and slow since half of the adder bits were adding 0 to the intermediate sum.

The original algorithm shifts the multiplicand left with 0s inserted in the new positions, so the multiplicand cannot affect the least significant bits of the product after they settle down. Instead of shifting the multiplicand left, they wondered, what if we shift the *product right*? Now the multiplicand would be fixed relative to the product, and since we are adding only 32 bits, the adder need be only 32 bits wide. Figure 4.28 shows how this change halves the widths of both the ALU and the multiplicand.

Figure 4.29 shows the multiply algorithm inspired by this observation. This algorithm starts with the 32-bit Multiplicand and 32-bit Multiplier registers set to their named values and the 64-bit Product register set to 0. This algorithm only forms a 32-bit sum, so only the left half of the 64-bit Product register is changed by the addition.

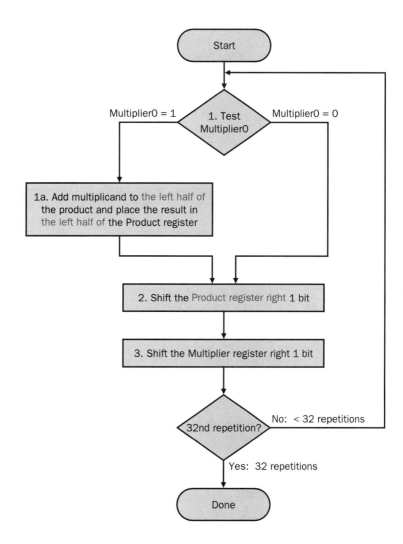

FIGURE 4.29 The second multiplication algorithm, using the hardware in Figure 4.28. In this version, the Product register is shifted right instead of shifting the multiplicand. Color type shows the changes from Figure 4.26.

Second Multiply Algorithm

Example

Multiply $0010_{two} \times 0011_{two}$ using the algorithm in Figure 4.29.

Answer

Figure 4.30 shows the revised 4-bit example, again giving a product of $0000\ 0110_{two}$.

Iteration	Step	Multiplier	Multiplicand	Product
0	Initial values	001①	0010	0000 0000
1	1a: 1 => Prod = Prod + Mcand	0011	0010	0010 0000
	2: Shift right Product	0011	0010	0001 0000
	3: Shift right Multiplier	000①	0010	0001 0000
2	1a: 1 => Prod = Prod + Mcand	0001	0010	0011 0000
	2: Shift right Product	0001	0010	0001 1000
	3: Shift right Multiplier	0000	0010	0001 1000
3	1: 0 => no operation	0000	0010	0001 1000
	2: Shift right Product	0000	0010	0000 1100
	3: Shift right Multiplier	0000	0010	0000 1100
4	1: 0 => no operation	0000	0010	0000 1100
	2: Shift right Product	0000	0010	0000 0110
	3: Shift right Multiplier	0000	0010	0000 0110

FIGURE 4.30 Multiply example using second algorithm in Figure 4.29. The bit examined to determine the next step is circled in color.

Final Version of the Multiplication Algorithm and Hardware

The final observation of the frugal computer pioneers was that the Product register had wasted space that matched exactly the size of the multiplier: As the wasted space in the product disappears, so do the bits of the multiplier. In response, the third version of the multiplication algorithm combines the rightmost half of the product with the multiplier. Figure 4.31 shows the hardware. The least significant bit of the 64-bit Product register (Product0) now is the bit to be tested.

The algorithm starts by assigning the multiplier to the right half of the Product register, placing 0 in the upper half. Figure 4.32 shows the new steps.

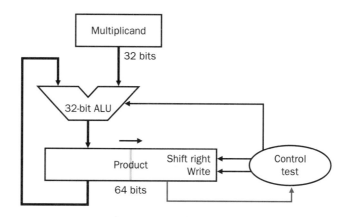

FIGURE 4.31   Third version of the multiplication hardware. Comparing with the second version in Figure 4.28 on page 254, the separate Multiplier register has disappeared. The multiplier is placed instead in the right half of the Product register.

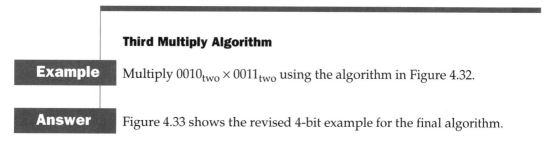

Third Multiply Algorithm

Example   Multiply $0010_{two} \times 0011_{two}$ using the algorithm in Figure 4.32.

Answer   Figure 4.33 shows the revised 4-bit example for the final algorithm.

Signed Multiplication

So far we have dealt with positive numbers. The easiest way to understand how to deal with signed numbers is to first convert the multiplier and multiplicand to positive numbers and then remember the original signs. The algorithms should then be run for 31 iterations, leaving the signs out of the calculation. As we learned in grammar school, we need negate the product only if the original signs disagree.

It turns out that the last algorithm will work for signed numbers provided that we remember that the numbers we are dealing with have infinite digits, and that we are only representing them with 32 bits. Hence the shifting steps would need to extend the sign of the product for signed numbers. When the algorithm completes, the lower word would have the 32-bit product.

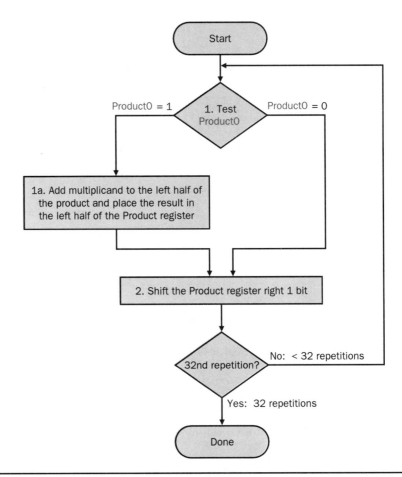

FIGURE 4.32   The third multiplication algorithm. It needs only two steps because the Product and Multiplier registers have been combined. Color type shows changes from Figure 4.29.

Iteration	Step	Multiplicand	Product
0	Initial values	0010	0000 0011
1	1a: 1 => Prod = Prod + Mcand	0010	0010 0011
	2: Shift right Product	0010	0001 0001
2	1a: 1 => Prod = Prod + Mcand	0010	0011 0001
	2: Shift right Product	0010	0001 1000
3	1: 0 => no operation	0010	0001 1000
	2: Shift right Product	0010	0000 1100
4	1: 0 => no operation	0010	0000 1100
	2: Shift right Product	0010	0000 0110

FIGURE 4.33   Multiply example using third algorithm in Figure 4.32. The bit examined to determine the next step is circled in color.

Booth's Algorithm

A more elegant approach to multiplying signed numbers than above is called *Booth's algorithm*. It starts with the observation that with the ability to both add and subtract there are multiple ways to compute a product. Suppose we want to multiply 2_{ten} by 6_{ten}, or 0010_{two} by 0110_{two}:

```
            0010 two
  x         0110 two

  +      0000   shift (0 in multiplier)
  +      0010   add   (1 in multiplier)
  +      0010   add   (1 in multiplier)
  +      0000   shift (0 in multiplier)

       00001100 two
```

Booth observed that an ALU that could add or subtract could get the same result in more than one way. For example, since

$$6_{ten} \quad\quad = -\ 2_{ten} + 8_{ten}$$

or

$$0110_{two} \quad\quad = -\ 0010_{two} + 1000_{two}$$

we could replace a string of 1s in the multiplier with an initial subtract when we first see a 1 and then later add when we see the bit *after* the last 1. For example,

```
            0010 two
  x         0110 two

  +      0000 shift (0 in multiplier)
  -      0010 sub (first 1 in multiplier)
  +      0000 shift (middle of string of 1s)
  +      0010 add (prior step had last 1)

       00001100 two
```

Booth invented this approach in a quest for speed because in machines of his era shifting was faster than addition. Indeed, for some patterns his algorithm would be faster; it's our good fortune that it handles signed numbers as well, and we'll prove this later. The key to Booth's insight is in his classifying groups of bits into the beginning, the middle, or the end of a run of 1s:

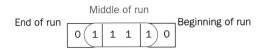

Of course, a string of 0s already avoids arithmetic, so we can leave these alone.

If we are limited to looking at just 2 bits, we can then try to match the situation in the preceding drawing, according to the value of these 2 bits:

Current bit	Bit to the right	Explanation	Example
1	0	Beginning of a run of 1s	0000**1**111000$_{two}$
1	1	Middle of a run of 1s	000011**1**1000$_{two}$
0	1	End of a run of 1s	00001111**0**00$_{two}$
0	0	Middle of a run of 0s	0000**0**111000$_{two}$

Booth's algorithm changes the first step of the algorithm in Figure 4.32—looking at 1 bit of the multiplier and then deciding whether to add the multiplicand—to looking at 2 bits of the multiplier. The new first step, then, has four cases, depending on the values of the 2 bits. Let's assume that the pair of bits examined consists of the current bit and the bit to the right—which was the current bit in the previous step. The second step is still to shift the product right. The new algorithm is then the following:

1. Depending on the current and previous bits, do one of the following:

   00: Middle of a string of 0s, so no arithmetic operation.

   01: End of a string of 1s, so add the multiplicand to the left half of the product.

   10: Beginning of a string of 1s, so subtract the multiplicand from the left half of the product.

   11: Middle of a string of 1s, so no arithmetic operation.

2. As in the previous algorithm, shift the Product register right 1 bit.

Now we are ready to begin the operation, shown in Figure 4.34. It starts with a 0 for the mythical bit to the right of the rightmost bit for the first stage. Figure 4.34 compares the two algorithms, with Booth's on the right. Note that

Itera-tion	Multi-plicand	Original algorithm		Booth's algorithm	
		Step	Product	Step	Product
0	0010	Initial values	0000 011⓪	Initial values	0000 011⓪ ⓪
1	0010	1: 0 ⟹ no operation	0000 0110	1a: 00 ⟹ no operation	0000 0110 0
	0010	2: Shift right Product	0000 001①	2: Shift right Product	0000 001① ⓪
2	0010	1a: 1 ⟹ Prod = Prod + Mcand	0010 0011	1c: 10 ⟹ Prod = Prod − Mcand	1110 0011 0
	0010	2: Shift right Product	0001 000①	2: Shift right Product	1111 000① ①
3	0010	1a: 1 ⟹ Prod = Prod + Mcand	0011 0001	1d: 11 ⟹ no operation	1111 0001 1
	0010	2: Shift right Product	0001 100⓪	2: Shift right Product	1111 100⓪ ①
4	0010	1: 0 ⟹ no operation	0001 1000	1b: 01 ⟹ Prod = Prod + Mcand	0001 1000 1
	0010	2: Shift right Product	0000 1100	2: Shift right Product	0000 1100 0

FIGURE 4.34 Comparing algorithm in Figure 4.32 and Booth's algorithm for positive numbers. The bit(s) examined to determine the next step is circled in color.

Booth's operation is now identified according to the values in the 2 bits. By the fourth step, the two algorithms have the same values in the Product register.

The one other requirement is that shifting the product right must preserve the sign of the intermediate result, since we are dealing with signed numbers. The solution is to extend the sign when the product is shifted to the right. Thus, step 2 of the second iteration turns $1110\ 0011\ 0_{two}$ into $1111\ 0001\ 1_{two}$ instead of $0111\ 0001\ 1_{two}$. This shift is called an *arithmetic right shift* to differentiate it from a logical right shift.

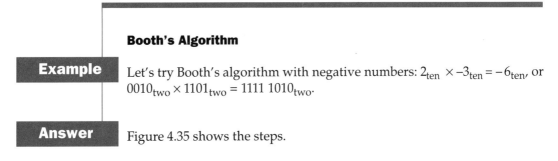

Booth's Algorithm

Example

Let's try Booth's algorithm with negative numbers: $2_{ten} \times -3_{ten} = -6_{ten}$, or $0010_{two} \times 1101_{two} = 1111\ 1010_{two}$.

Answer

Figure 4.35 shows the steps.

Our example multiplies one bit at a time, but it is possible to generalize Booth's algorithm to generate multiple bits for faster multiplies (see Exercise 4.53).

Iteration	Step	Multiplicand	Product
0	Initial values	0010	0000 1101 0
1	1c: 10 $\Rightarrow$ Prod = Prod – Mcand	0010	1110 1101 0
	2: Shift right Product	0010	1111 0110 1
2	1b: 01 $\Rightarrow$ Prod = Prod + Mcand	0010	0001 0110 1
	2: Shift right Product	0010	0000 1011 0
3	1c: 10 $\Rightarrow$ Prod = Prod – Mcand	0010	1110 1011 0
	2: Shift right Product	0010	1111 0101 1
4	1d: 11 $\Rightarrow$ no operation	0010	1111 0101 1
	2: Shift right Product	0010	1111 1010 1

FIGURE 4.35   Booth's algorithm with negative multiplier example. The bits examined to determine the next step are circled in color.

Hardware Software Interface

Replacing arithmetic by shifts can also occur when multiplying by constants. Some compilers replace multiplies by short constants with a series of shifts, adds, and subtracts. Because one bit to the left represents a number twice as large in base 2, shifting the bits left has the same effect as multiplying by a power of 2, so almost every compiler will substitute a left shift for a multiply by a power of 2.

Multiply by 2^i via Shift

Example

Let's multiply 5_{ten} by 2_{ten} using a left shift by 1.

Answer

Given that
$$101_{two} = (1 \times 2^2) + (0 \times 2^1) + (1 \times 2^0)_{ten} = 4 + 0 + 1_{ten} = 5_{ten}$$
if we shift left 1 bit, we get
$$1010_{two} = (1 \times 2^3) + (0 \times 2^2) + (1 \times 2^1) + (0 \times 2^0)_{ten}$$
$$= 8 + 0 + 2 + 0_{ten} = 10_{ten}$$
and
$$5 \times 2^1{}_{ten} = 10_{ten}$$
Hence the MIPS sll instruction can be used for multiplies by powers of 2.

Now that we have seen Booth's algorithm work, we are ready to see *why* it works for two's complement signed integers. Let a be the multiplier and b be the multiplicand and we'll use a_i to refer to bit i of a. Recasting Booth's algorithm in terms of the bit values of the multiplier yields this table:

a_i	a_{i-1}	Operation
0	0	Do nothing
0	1	Add b
1	0	Subtract b
1	1	Do nothing

Instead of representing Booth's algorithm in tabular form, we can represent it as the expression

$$(a_{i-1} - a_i)$$

where the value of the expression means the following actions:

$$\begin{aligned} 0:\quad &\text{do nothing} \\ +1:\quad &\text{add } b \\ -1:\quad &\text{subtract } b \end{aligned}$$

Since we know that shifting of the multiplicand left with respect to the Product register can be considered multiplying by a power of 2, Booth's algorithm can be written as the sum

$$\begin{aligned} &(a_{-1} - a_0)\ \times b \times 2^0 \\ +\ &(a_0\ \ - a_1)\ \times b \times 2^1 \\ +\ &(a_1\ \ - a_2)\ \times b \times 2^2 \\ \ldots&\ldots \\ +\ &(a_{29} - a_{30}) \times b \times 2^{30} \\ +\ &(a_{30} - a_{31}) \times b \times 2^{31} \end{aligned}$$

We can simplify this sum by noting that

$$-a_i \times 2^i + a_i \times 2^{i+1} = (-a_i + 2a_i) \times 2^i = (2a_i - a_i) \times 2^i = a_i \times 2^i$$

recalling that $a_{-1} = 0$ and by factoring out b from each term:

$$b \times ((a_{31} \times -2^{31}) + (a_{30} \times 2^{30}) + (a_{29} \times 2^{29}) + \ldots + (a_1 \times 2^1) + (a_0 \times 2^0))$$

The long formula in parentheses to the right of the first multiply operation is simply the two's complement representation of a (see page 213.) Thus the sum is further simplified to

$$b \times a$$

Hence Booth's algorithm does in fact perform two's complement multiplication of a and b.

Multiply in MIPS

MIPS provides a separate pair of 32-bit registers to contain the 64-bit product, called *Hi* and *Lo*. To produce a properly signed or unsigned product, MIPS has two instructions: multiply (`mult`) and multiply unsigned (`multu`). To fetch the integer 32-bit product, the programmer uses *move from lo* (`mflo`). The MIPS assembler generates a pseudoinstruction for multiply that specifies three general-purpose registers, generating `mflo` and `mfhi` instructions to place the product into registers.

Hardware Software Interface	Both MIPS multiply instructions ignore overflow, so it is up to the software to check to see if the product is too big to fit in 32 bits. To avoid overflow, Hi must be 0 for `multu` or must be the replicated sign of Lo for `mult`. The instruction *move from hi* (`mfhi`) can be used to transfer Hi to a general-purpose register to test for overflow.

Summary

Multiplication is accomplished by simple shift and add hardware, derived from the paper-and-pencil method learned in grammar school. Compilers even use shift instructions for multiplications by powers of two. Signed multiplication is more challenging, with Booth's algorithm rising to the challenge with essentially a clever factorization of the two's complement number representation of the multiplier.

Elaboration: The original reason for Booth's algorithm was speed because early machines could shift faster than they could add. The hope was that this encoding scheme would increase the number of shifts. This algorithm is sensitive to particular bit patterns, however, and may actually increase the number of adds or subtracts. For example, bit patterns that alternate 0 and 1, called *isolated 1s*, will cause the hardware to add or subtract at each step. Looking at more bits to carefully avoid isolated 1s can reduce the number of adds in the worst case. Greater advantage comes from performing multiple bits per step, which we explore in Exercise 4.53.

Even faster multiplications are possible by essentially providing one 32-bit adder for each bit of the multiplier: one input is the multiplicand ANDed with a multiplier bit and the other is the output of a prior adder. When adding such a large column of numbers, a *carry save adder* is useful (see Exercises 4.49 to 4.52).

Elaboration: The replacement of a multiply by a shift, as in the example on page 262, is an instance of a general compiler optimization strategy called *strength reduction*.

4.7   Division

Divide et impera.

Latin for "Divide and rule," ancient political maxim cited by Machiavelli, 1532

The reciprocal operation of multiply is divide, an operation that is even less frequent and even more quirky. It even offers the opportunity to perform a mathematically invalid operation: dividing by 0.

Let's start with an example of long division using decimal numbers to recall the names of the operands and the grammar school division algorithm. For reasons similar to those in the previous section, we limit the decimal digits to just 0 or 1. The example is dividing $1{,}001{,}010_{ten}$ by 1000_{ten}:

$$
\begin{array}{r}
1001_{ten} \quad \text{Quotient} \\
\text{Divisor } 1000_{ten}\ \overline{)\,1001010_{ten}} \quad \text{Dividend} \\
-1000 \qquad\qquad\quad \\
\overline{10\qquad\qquad\quad} \\
101 \qquad\qquad\quad \\
1010 \qquad\qquad\quad \\
-1000 \qquad\qquad\quad \\
\overline{10_{ten}} \quad \text{Remainder}
\end{array}
$$

The two operands *(dividend* and *divisor)* and the result *(quotient)* of divide are accompanied by a second result called the *remainder*. Here is another way to express the relationship between the components:

$$\text{Dividend} = \text{Quotient} \times \text{Divisor} + \text{Remainder}$$

where the remainder is smaller than the divisor. Infrequently, programs use the divide instruction just to get the remainder, ignoring the quotient.

The basic grammar school division algorithm tries to see how big a number can be subtracted, creating a digit of the quotient on each attempt. Our carefully selected decimal example uses only the numbers 0 and 1, so it's easy to figure out how many times the divisor goes into the portion of the dividend: it's either 0 times or 1 time. Binary numbers contain only 0 or 1, so binary division is restricted to these two choices, thereby simplifying binary division.

Let's assume that both the dividend and divisor are positive and hence the quotient and the remainder are nonnegative. The division operands and both results are 32-bit values, and we will ignore the sign for now. Rather than make

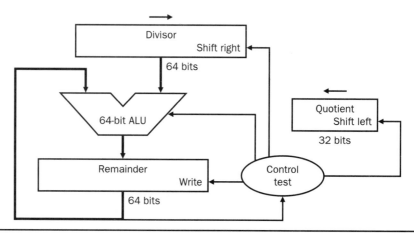

FIGURE 4.36 First version of the division hardware. The Divisor register, ALU, and Remainder register are all 64 bits wide, with only the Quotient register being 32 bits. The 32-bit divisor starts in the left half of the Divisor register and is shifted right 1 bit on each step. The remainder is initialized with the dividend. Control decides when to shift the Divisor and Quotient registers and when to write the new value into the Remainder register.

each of the three evolutionary steps explicit with drawings and examples, as we did for multiply, we will save space by giving a sketch for the two intermediate steps and then give the final algorithm in detail.

First Version of the Division Algorithm and Hardware

Figure 4.36 shows hardware to mimic our grammar school algorithm. We start with the 32-bit Quotient register set to 0. Each step of the algorithm needs to move the divisor to the right one digit, so we start with the divisor placed in the left half of the 64-bit Divisor register and shift it right 1 bit each step to align it with the dividend. The Remainder register is initialized with the dividend.

Figure 4.37 shows three steps of the first division algorithm. Unlike a human, the computer isn't smart enough to know in advance whether the divisor is smaller than the dividend. It must first subtract the divisor in step 1; remember that this is how we performed the comparison in the set on less than instruction. If the result is positive, the divisor was smaller or equal to the dividend, so we generate a 1 in the quotient (step 2a). If the result is negative, the next step is to restore the original value by adding the divisor back to the remainder and generate a 0 in the quotient (step 2b). The divisor is shifted right and then we iterate again. The remainder and quotient will be found in their namesake registers after the iterations are complete.

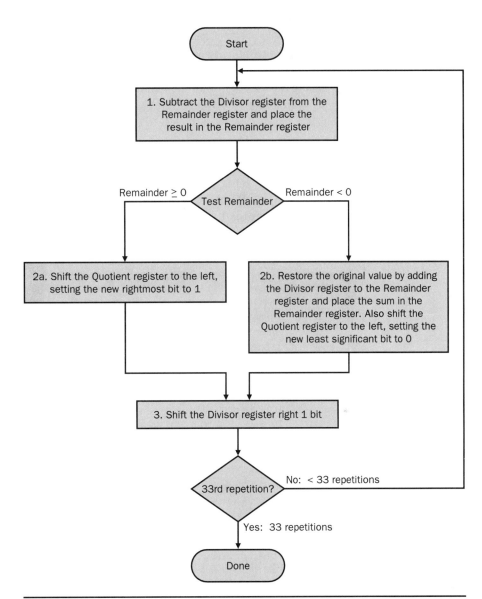

FIGURE 4.37 The first division algorithm, using the hardware in Figure 4.36. If the Remainder is positive, the divisor did go into the dividend, so step 2a generates a 1 in the quotient. A negative Remainder after step 1 means that the divisor did not go into the dividend, so step 2b generates a 0 in the quotient and adds the divisor to the remainder, thereby reversing the subtraction of step 1. The final shift, in step 3, aligns the divisor properly, relative to the dividend for the next iteration. These steps are repeated 33 times; the reason for the apparent extra step will become clear in the next version of the algorithm.

First Divide Algorithm

Example

Using a 4-bit version of the algorithm to save pages, let's try dividing 7_{ten} by 2_{ten}, or $0000\ 0111_{two}$ by 0010_{two}.

Answer

Figure 4.38 shows the value of each register for each of the steps, with the quotient being 3_{ten} and the remainder 1_{ten}. Notice that the test in step 2 of whether the remainder is positive or negative simply tests whether the sign bit of the Remainder register is a 0 or 1. The surprising requirement of this algorithm is that it takes $n + 1$ steps to get the proper quotient and remainder.

Iteration	Step	Quotient	Divisor	Remainder
0	Initial values	0000	0010 0000	0000 0111
1	1: Rem = Rem − Div	0000	0010 0000	ⓛ110 0111
	2b: Rem < 0 ⟹ +Div, sll Q, Q0 = 0	0000	0010 0000	0000 0111
	3: Shift Div right	0000	0001 0000	0000 0111
2	1: Rem = Rem − Div	0000	0001 0000	ⓛ111 0111
	2b: Rem < 0 ⟹ +Div, sll Q, Q0 = 0	0000	0001 0000	0000 0111
	3: Shift Div right	0000	0000 1000	0000 0111
3	1: Rem = Rem − Div	0000	0000 1000	ⓛ111 1111
	2b: Rem < 0 ⟹ +Div, sll Q, Q0 = 0	0000	0000 1000	0000 0111
	3: Shift Div right	0000	0000 0100	0000 0111
4	1: Rem = Rem − Div	0000	0000 0100	⓪000 0011
	2a: Rem ≥ 0 ⟹ sll Q, Q0 = 1	0001	0000 0100	0000 0011
	3: Shift Div right	0001	0000 0010	0000 0011
5	1: Rem = Rem − Div	0001	0000 0010	⓪000 0001
	2a: Rem ≥ 0 ⟹ sll Q, Q0 = 1	0011	0000 0010	0000 0001
	3: Shift Div right	0011	0000 0001	0000 0001

FIGURE 4.38   Division example using first algorithm in Figure 4.37. The bit examined to determine the next step is circled in color.

Second Version of the Division Algorithm and Hardware

Once again the frugal computer pioneers recognized that, at most, half of the divisor has useful information, and so both the divisor and ALU could potentially be cut in half. Shifting the remainder to the left instead of shifting the divisor to the right produces the same alignment and accomplishes the goal of simplifying the hardware necessary for the ALU and the divisor. Figure 4.39 shows the simplified hardware for the second version of the algorithm.

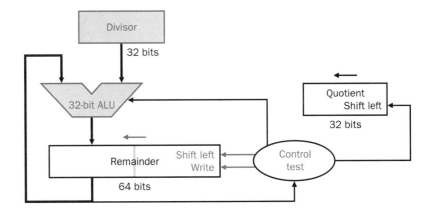

FIGURE 4.39 Second version of the division hardware. The Divisor register, ALU, and Quotient register are all 32 bits wide, with only the Remainder register left at 64 bits. Compared to Figure 4.36, the ALU and Divisor registers are halved and the remainder is shifted left. These changes are highlighted.

Another change comes from noticing that the first step of the current algorithm cannot produce a 1 in the quotient bit; if it did, then the quotient would be too large for the register. By switching the order of the operations to shift and then subtract, one iteration of the algorithm can be removed. When the algorithm terminates, the remainder will be found in the left half of the Remainder register.

Final Version of Division Algorithm and Hardware

With the same insight and motivation as in the third version of the multiplication algorithm, computer pioneers saw that the Quotient register could be eliminated by shifting the bits of the quotient into the Remainder instead of shifting in 0s as in the preceding algorithm. Figure 4.40 shows the third version of the algorithm.

We start the algorithm by shifting the Remainder left as before. Thereafter, the loop contains only two steps because the shifting of the Remainder register shifts both the remainder in the left half and the quotient in the right half (see Figure 4.41). The consequence of combining the two registers and the new order of the operations in the loop is that the remainder will be shifted left one time too many. Thus the final correction step must shift back only the remainder in the left half of the register.

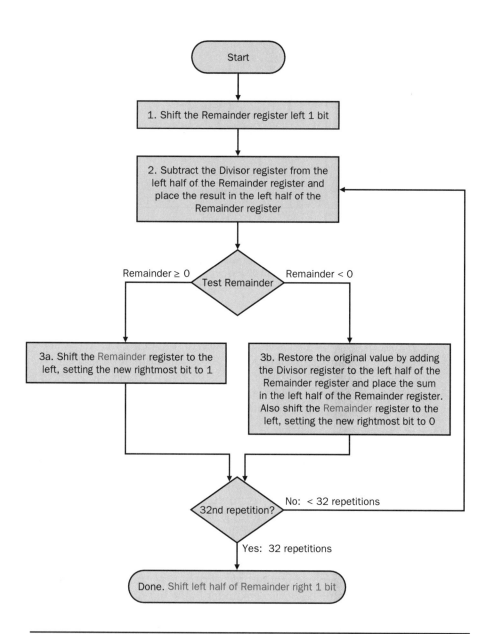

FIGURE 4.40   The third division algorithm has just two steps. The Remainder register shifts left.

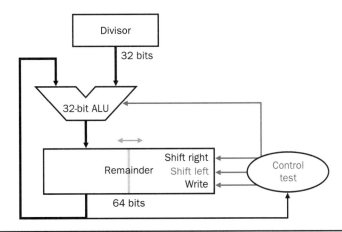

FIGURE 4.41 Third version of the division hardware. This version combines the Quotient register with the right half of the Remainder register.

Third Divide Algorithm

Example

Use the third version of the algorithm to divide $0000\ 0111_{two}$ by 0010_{two}.

Answer

Figure 4.42 shows how the quotient is created in the bottom of the Remainder register and how both are shifted left in a single operation.

Iteration	Step	Divisor	Remainder
0	Initial values	0010	0000 0111
	Shift Rem left 1	0010	0000 1110
1	2: Rem = Rem – Div	0010	⓪110 1110
	3b: Rem < 0 ⟹ + Div, sll R, R0 = 0	0010	0001 1100
2	2: Rem = Rem – Div	0010	⓪111 1100
	3b: Rem < 0 ⟹ + Div, sll R, R0 = 0	0010	0011 1000
3	2: Rem = Rem – Div	0010	⓪001 1000
	3a: Rem ≥ 0 ⟹ sll R, R0 = 1	0010	0011 0001
4	2: Rem = Rem – Div	0010	⓪001 0001
	3a: Rem ≥ 0 ⟹ sll R, R0 = 1	0010	0010 0011
	Shift left half of Rem right 1	0010	0001 0011

FIGURE 4.42 Division example using third algorithm in Figure 4.40. The bit examined to determine the next step is circled in color.

Signed Division

So far we have ignored signed numbers in division. The simplest solution is to remember the signs of the divisor and dividend and then negate the quotient if the signs disagree.

The one complication is that we must also set the sign of the remainder. Remember that the following equation must always hold:

$$\text{Dividend} = \text{Quotient} \times \text{Divisor} + \text{Remainder}$$

To understand how to set the sign of the remainder, let's look at the example of dividing all the combinations of $\pm 7_{ten}$ by $\pm 2_{ten}$. The first case is easy:

$$+7 \div +2: \text{ Quotient} = +3, \text{Remainder} = +1$$

Checking the results:

$$7 = 3 \times 2 + (+1) = 6 + 1$$

If we change the sign of the dividend, the quotient must change as well:

$$-7 \div +2: \text{ Quotient} = -3$$

Rewriting our basic formula to calculate the remainder:

$$\text{Remainder} = (\text{Dividend} - \text{Quotient} \times \text{Divisor})$$
$$= -7 - (-3 \times +2) = -7 - (-6) = -1$$

So,

$$-7 \div +2: \text{ Quotient} = -3, \text{Remainder} = -1$$

Checking the results again:

$$-7 = -3 \times 2 + (-1) = -6 - 1$$

The reason the answer isn't a quotient of -4 and a remainder of $+1$, which would also fit this formula, is that the absolute value of the quotient would then change depending on the sign of the dividend and the divisor! Clearly if

$$-(x \div y) \neq (-x) \div y$$

programming would be an even greater challenge. This anomalous behavior is avoided by following the rule that the dividend and remainder must have the same signs, no matter what the signs of the divisor and quotient.

We calculate the other combinations by following the same rule:

$$+7 \div -2: \text{ Quotient} = -3, \text{Remainder} = +1$$

$$-7 \div -2: \text{ Quotient} = +3, \text{Remainder} = -1$$

Thus the correctly signed division algorithm negates the quotient if the signs of the operands are opposite and makes the sign of the nonzero remainder match the dividend.

Divide in MIPS

You may have already observed that the same hardware can be used for both multiply and divide. The only requirement is a 64-bit register that can shift left or right and a 32-bit ALU that adds or subtracts. For example, MIPS uses the 32-bit Hi and 32-bit Lo registers for both multiply and divide. As we might expect from the algorithm above, Hi contains the remainder, and Lo contains the quotient after the divide instruction completes.

To handle both signed integers and unsigned integers, MIPS has two instructions: *divide* (div) and *divide unsigned* (divu). The MIPS assembler allows divide instructions to specify three registers, generating the mflo or mfhi instructions to place the desired result into a general-purpose register.

Hardware Software Interface MIPS divide instructions ignore overflow, so software must determine if the quotient is too large. In addition to overflow, division can also result in an improper calculation: division by 0. Some machines distinguish these two anomalous events. MIPS software must check the divisor to discover division by 0 as well as overflow.

Summary

The common hardware support for multiply and divide allows MIPS to provide a single pair of 32-bit registers that are used both for multiply and divide. Figure 4.43 summarizes the additions to the MIPS architecture for the last two sections.

Elaboration: The reason for needing an extra iteration for the first algorithm and the early shift in the second and third algorithms involves the placement of the dividend in the Remainder register. We expect to have a 32-bit quotient and a 32-bit divisor, but each is really a 31-bit integer plus a sign bit. The product would be 31+31, or 62 bits plus a single sign bit; the hardware can then support only a 63-bit dividend. Given that registers are normally powers of 2, this means we must place the 63-bit dividend properly in the 64-bit Remainder register. If we place the 63 bits to the right, we need to run the algorithm for an extra step to get to that last bit. A better solution is to shift early, thereby saving a step of the algorithm.

An even faster algorithm does not immediately add the dividend back if the remainder is negative. It simply *adds* the dividend to the shifted remainder in the following step since $(r + d) \times 2 - d = r \times 2 + d \times 2 - d = r \times 2 + d$. This *nonrestoring* division algorithm, which takes 1 clock per step, is explored further in Exercise 4.54; the algorithm here is called *restoring* division.

MIPS operands

Name	Example	Comments
32 registers	$s0–$s7, $t0–$t9, $gp, $fp, $zero, $sp, $ra, $at, Hi, Lo	Fast locations for data. In MIPS, data must be in registers to perform arithmetic. MIPS register $zero always equals 0. Register $at is reserved for the assembler to handle large constants. Hi and Lo contain the results of multiply and divide.
2^{30} memory words	Memory[0], Memory[4], . . . , Memory[4294967292]	Accessed only by data transfer instructions. MIPS uses byte addresses, so sequential words differ by 4. Memory holds data structures, such as arrays, and spilled registers, such as those saved on procedure calls.

MIPS assembly language

Category	Instruction	Example		Meaning	Comments
Arithmetic	add	add	$s1,$s2,$s3	$s1 = $s2 + $s3	Three operands; overflow detected
	subtract	sub	$s1,$s2,$s3	$s1 = $s2 – $s3	Three operands; overflow detected
	add immediate	addi	$s1,$s2,100	$s1 = $s2 + $s3	+ constant; overflow detected
	add unsigned	addu	$s1,$s2,$s3	$s1 = $s2 + $s3	Three operands; overflow undetected
	subtract unsigned	subu	$s1,$s2,$s3	$s1 = $s2 – $s3	Three operands; overflow undetected
	add immediate unsigned	addiu	$s1,$s2,100	$s1 = $s2 + $s3	+ constant; overflow undetected
	move from coprocessor register	mfc0	$s1,$epc	$s1 = $epc	Used to copy Exception PC plus other special registers
	multiply	mult	$s2,$s3	Hi, Lo = $s2 × $s3	64-bit signed product in Hi, Lo
	multiply unsigned	multu	$s2,$s3	Hi, Lo = $s2 × $s3	64-bit unsigned product in Hi, Lo
	divide	div	$s2,$s3	Lo = $s2 / $s3, Hi = $s2 mod $s3	Lo = quotient, Hi = remainder
	divide unsigned	divu	$s2,$s3	Lo = $s2 / $s3, Hi = $s2 mod $s3	Unsigned quotient and remainder
	move from Hi	mfhi	$s1	$s1 = Hi	Used to get copy of Hi
	move from Lo	mflo	$s1	$s1 = Lo	Used to get copy of Lo
Logical	and	and	$s1,$s2,$s3	$s1 = $s2 & $s3	Three reg. operands; logical AND
	or	or	$s1,$s2,$s3	$s1 = $s2 | $s3	Three reg. operands; logical OR
	and immediate	andi	$s1,$s2,100	$s1 = $s2 & 100	Logical AND reg, constant
	or immediate	ori	$s1,$s2,100	$s1 = $s2 | 100	Logical OR reg, constant
	shift left logical	sll	$s1,$s2,10	$s1 = $s2 << 10	Shift left by constant
	shift right logical	srl	$s1,$s2,10	$s1 = $s2 >> 10	Shift right by constant
Data transfer	load word	lw	$s1,100($s2)	$s1 = Memory[$s2+100]	Word from memory to register
	store word	sw	$s1,100($s2)	Memory[$s2 + 100] = $s1	Word from register to memory
	load byte unsigned	lbu	$s1,100($s2)	$s1 = Memory[$s2 + 100]	Byte from memory to register
	store byte	sb	$s1,100($s2)	Memory[$s2 + 100] = $s1	Byte from register to memory
	load upper immediate	lui	$s1,100	$s1 = 100 * 2^{16}	Loads constant in upper 16 bits
Conditional branch	branch on equal	beq	$s1,$s2,25	if ($s1 == $s2) go to PC + 4 + 100	Equal test; PC-relative branch
	branch on not equal	bne	$s1,$s2,25	if ($s1 != $s2) go to PC + 4 + 100	Not equal test; PC-relative
	set on less than	slt	$s1,$s2,$s3	if ($s2 < $s3) $s1 = 1; else $s1 = 0	Compare less than; two's complement
	set less than immediate	slti	$s1,$s2,100	if ($s2 < 100) $s1 = 1; else $s1=0	Compare < constant; two's complement
	set less than unsigned	sltu	$s1,$s2,$s3	if ($s2 < $s3) $s1 = 1; else $s1=0	Compare less than; natural numbers
	set less than immediate unsigned	sltiu	$s1,$s2,100	if ($s2 < 100) $s1 = 1; else $s1 = 0	Compare < constant; natural numbers
Unconditional jump	jump	j	2500	go to 10000	Jump to target address
	jump register	jr	$ra	go to $ra	For switch, procedure return
	jump and link	jal	2500	$ra = PC + 4; go to 10000	For procedure call

FIGURE 4.43 MIPS architecture revealed thus far. Color indicates the portions revealed since Figure 4.7 on page 228. MIPS machine language is listed on the back endpapers of this book. *(page 274)*

4.8 Floating Point

Speed gets you nowhere if you're headed the wrong way.

American proverb

In addition to signed and unsigned integers, programming languages support numbers with fractions, which are called *reals* in mathematics. Here are some examples of reals:

$3.14159265\ldots_{ten}$ (π)

$2.71828\ldots_{ten}$ (e)

0.000000001_{ten} or $1.0_{ten} \times 10^{-9}$ (seconds in a nanosecond)

$3{,}155{,}760{,}000_{ten}$ or $3.15576_{ten} \times 10^{9}$ (seconds in a typical century)

Notice that in the last case, the number didn't represent a small fraction, but it was bigger than we could represent with a 32-bit signed integer. The alternative notation for the last two numbers is called *scientific notation*, which has a single digit to the left of the decimal point. A number in scientific notation that has no leading 0s is called a *normalized* number, which is the usual way to write it. For example, $1.0_{ten} \times 10^{-9}$ is in normalized scientific notation, but $0.1_{ten} \times 10^{-8}$ and $10.0_{ten} \times 10^{-10}$ are not.

Just as we can show decimal numbers in scientific notation, we can also show binary numbers in scientific notation:

$1.0_{two} \times 2^{-1}$

To keep a binary number in normalized form, we need a base that we can increase or decrease by exactly the number of bits the number must be shifted to have one nonzero digit to the left of the decimal point. Only a base of 2 fulfills our need. Since the base is not 10, we also need a new name for decimal point; *binary point* will do fine.

Computer arithmetic that supports such numbers is called *floating point* because it represents numbers in which the binary point is not fixed, as it is for integers. The programming language C uses the name *float* for such numbers. Just as in scientific notation, numbers are represented as a single nonzero digit to the left of the binary point. In binary, the form is

$1.xxxxxxxxx_{two} \times 2^{yyyy}$

(Although the computer represents the exponent in base 2 as well as the rest of the number, to simplify the notation we'll show the exponent in decimal.)

A standard scientific notation for reals in normalized form offers three advantages. It simplifies exchange of data that includes floating-point numbers; it simplifies the floating-point arithmetic algorithms to know that numbers will always be in this form; and it increases the accuracy of the numbers that can be stored in a word, since the unnecessary leading 0s are replaced by real digits to the right of the binary point.

Floating-Point Representation

The designer of a floating-point representation must find a compromise between the size of the significand and the size of the exponent because a fixed word size means you must take a bit from one to add a bit to the other. This trade-off is between accuracy and range: Increasing the size of the significand enhances the accuracy of the significand, while increasing the size of the exponent increases the range of numbers that can be represented. As our design guideline from Chapter 3 reminds us, good design demands good compromises.

Floating-point numbers are usually a multiple of the size of a word. The representation of a MIPS floating-point number is shown below, where s is the sign of the floating-point number (1 meaning negative), *exponent* is the value of the 8-bit exponent field (including the sign of the exponent), and *significand* is the 23-bit number in the fraction. This representation is called *sign and magnitude*, since the sign has a separate bit from the rest of the number.

31	30	29	28	27	26	25	24	23	22	21	20	19	18	17	16	15	14	13	12	11	10	9	8	7	6	5	4	3	2	1	0
s					exponent									significand																	

1 bit   8 bits   23 bits

In general, floating-point numbers are of the form

$$(-1)^S \times F \times 2^E$$

F involves the value in the significand field and E involves the value in the exponent field; the exact relationship to these fields will be spelled out soon.

These chosen sizes of exponent and significand give MIPS computer arithmetic an extraordinary range. Fractions as small as $2.0_{ten} \times 10^{-38}$ and numbers as large as $2.0_{ten} \times 10^{38}$ can be represented in a computer. Alas, extraordinary differs from infinite, so it is still possible for numbers to be too large. Thus, overflow interrupts can occur in floating-point arithmetic as well as in integer arithmetic. Notice that *overflow* here means that the exponent is too large to be represented in the exponent field.

Floating point offers a new kind of exceptional event as well. Just as programmers will want to know when they have calculated a number that is too large to be represented, they will want to know if the nonzero fraction they are calculating has become so small that it cannot be represented; either event could result in a program giving incorrect answers. This situation occurs when the negative exponent is too large to fit in the exponent field. To distinguish it from overflow, people call this event *underflow*.

One way to reduce chances of underflow or overflow is to use a notation that has a larger exponent. In C this is called *double*, and operations on doubles are called *double precision* floating-point arithmetic; *single precision* floating point is the name of the earlier format.

The representation of a double precision floating-point number takes two MIPS words, as shown below, where *s* is still the sign of the number, *exponent* is the value of the 11-bit exponent field, and *significand* is the 52-bit number in the fraction.

31	30	29	28	27	26	25	24	23	22	21	20	19	18	17	16	15	14	13	12	11	10	9	8	7	6	5	4	3	2	1	0
s					exponent												significand														
1 bit			11 bits														20 bits														

significand (continued)
32 bits

MIPS double precision allows numbers almost as small as $2.0_{ten} \times 10^{-308}$ and almost as large as $2.0_{ten} \times 10^{308}$. Although double precision does increase the exponent range, its primary advantage is its greater accuracy because of the large significand.

These formats go beyond MIPS. They are part of the *IEEE 754 floating-point standard*, found in virtually every computer invented since 1980. This standard has greatly improved both the ease of porting floating-point programs and the quality of computer arithmetic.

To pack even more bits into the significand, IEEE 754 makes the leading 1 bit of normalized binary numbers implicit. Hence, the significand is actually 24 bits long in single precision (implied 1 and a 23-bit fraction), and 53 bits long in double precision (1+52). Since 0 has no leading 1, it is given the reserved exponent value 0 so that the hardware won't attach a leading 1 to it.

Thus $00 \ldots 00_{two}$ represents 0; the representation of the rest of the numbers uses the form from before with the hidden 1 added:

$$(-1)^S \times (1 + \text{Significand}) \times 2^E$$

where the bits of the significand represent the fraction between 0 and 1 and E specifies the value in the exponent field, to be given in detail shortly. If we number the bits of the significand from *left to right* s1, s2, s3, . . . , then the value is

$$(-1)^S \times (1 + (s1 \times 2^{-1}) + (s2 \times 2^{-2}) + (s3 \times 2^{-3}) + (s4 \times 2^{-4}) + \ldots) \times 2^E$$

The designers of IEEE 754 also wanted a floating-point representation that could be easily processed by integer comparisons, especially for sorting. This desire is why the sign is in the most significant bit, allowing a test of less than, greater than, or equal to 0 to be performed quickly.

Placing the exponent before the significand also simplifies sorting of floating-point numbers using integer comparison instructions, since numbers with bigger exponents look larger than numbers with smaller exponents, as long as both exponents have the same sign. (It's a little more complicated than a simple integer sort, since this notation is essentially sign and magnitude rather than two's complement.)

Negative exponents pose a challenge to simplified sorting. If we use two's complement or any other notation in which negative exponents have a 1 in the most significant bit of the exponent field, a negative exponent will look like a big number. For example, $1.0_{two} \times 2^{-1}$ would be represented as

31	30	29	28	27	26	25	24	23	22	21	20	19	18	17	16	15	14	13	12	11	10	9	8	7	6	5	4	3	2	1	0
0	1	1	1	1	1	1	1	1	0	0	0	0	0	0	0	0	0	0	0	0	0	0	0	0	0	0	0	.	.	.

(Remember that the leading 1 is implicit in the significand.) The value $1.0_{two} \times 2^{+1}$ would look like the smaller binary number

31	30	29	28	27	26	25	24	23	22	21	20	19	18	17	16	15	14	13	12	11	10	9	8	7	6	5	4	3	2	1	0
0	0	0	0	0	0	0	1	0	0	0	0	0	0	0	0	0	0	0	0	0	0	0	0	0	0	0	0	.	.	.

The desirable notation must therefore represent the most negative exponent as $00 \ldots 00_{two}$ and the most positive as $11 \ldots 11_{two}$. This convention is called *biased notation*, with the bias being the number subtracted from the normal, un-signed representation to determine the real value.

IEEE 754 uses a bias of 127 for single precision, so −1 is represented by the bit pattern of the value $-1 + 127_{ten}$, or $126_{ten} = 0111\ 1110_{two}$, and +1 is represented by 1 + 127, or $128_{ten} = 1000\ 0000_{two}$. Biased exponent means that the value represented by a floating-point number is really

$$(-1)^S \times (1 + \text{Significand}) \times 2^{(\text{Exponent} - \text{Bias})}$$

The exponent bias for double precision is 1023.

Thus IEEE 754 notation can be processed by integer compares to accelerate sorting of floating-point numbers. Let's show the representation.

Floating-Point Representation

Example

Show the IEEE 754 binary representation of the number -0.75_{ten} in single and double precision.

Answer

The number -0.75_{ten} is also

$$-3/4_{ten} \text{ or } -3/2^2{}_{ten}$$

It is also represented by the binary fraction:

$$-11_{two}/2^2{}_{ten} \text{ or } -0.11_{two}$$

In scientific notation, the value is

$$-0.11_{two} \times 2^0$$

and in normalized scientific notation, it is

$$-1.1_{two} \times 2^{-1}$$

The general representation for a single precision number is

$$(-1)^S \times (1 + \text{Significand}) \times 2^{(\text{Exponent} - 127)}$$

and so when we add the bias 127 to the exponent of $-1.1_{two} \times 2^{-1}$, the result is

$$(-1)^1 \times (1 + .1000\ 0000\ 0000\ 0000\ 0000\ 000_{two}) \times 2^{(126 - 127)}$$

The single precision binary representation of -0.75_{ten} is then

31	30	29	28	27	26	25	24	23	22	21	20	19	18	17	16	15	14	13	12	11	10	9	8	7	6	5	4	3	2	1	0
1	0	1	1	1	1	1	1	0	1	0	0	0	0	0	0	0	0	0	0	0	0	0	0	0	0	0	0	0	0	0	0

1 bit   8 bits   23 bits

The double precision representation is

$$(-1)^1 \times (1 + .1000\ 0000\ 0000\ 0000\ 0000\ 0000\ 0000\ 0000\ 0000\ 0000\ 0000\ 0000\ 0000_{two}) \times 2^{(1022-1023)}$$

31	30	29	28	27	26	25	24	23	22	21	20	19	18	17	16	15	14	13	12	11	10	9	8	7	6	5	4	3	2	1	0
1	0	1	1	1	1	1	1	1	1	1	0	1	0	0	0	0	0	0	0	0	0	0	0	0	0	0	0	0	0	0	0

1 bit   11 bits   20 bits

0	0	0	0	0	0	0	0	0	0	0	0	0	0	0	0	0	0	0	0	0	0	0	0	0	0	0	0	0	0	0	0

32 bits

Now let's try going the other direction.

Converting Binary to Decimal Floating Point

Example

What decimal number is represented by this word?

31	30	29	28	27	26	25	24	23	22	21	20	19	18	17	16	15	14	13	12	11	10	9	8	7	6	5	4	3	2	1	0
1	1	0	0	0	0	0	0	1	0	1	0	0	0	0	0	0	0	0	0	0	0	0	0	0	0	0	0	0	0	0	0 . . .

Answer

The sign bit is 1, the exponent field contains 129, and the significand field contains $1 \times 2^{-2} = 1/4$, or 0.25. Using the basic equation,

$$
\begin{aligned}
(-1)^S \times (1 + \text{Significand}) \times 2^{(\text{Exponent} - \text{Bias})} &= (-1)^1 \times (1 + 0.25) \times 2^{(129 - 127)} \\
&= -1 \times 1.25 \times 2^2 \\
&= -1.25 \times 4 \\
&= -5.0
\end{aligned}
$$

In the next sections we will give the algorithms for floating-point addition and multiplication. At their core, they use the corresponding integer operations on the significands, but extra bookkeeping is necessary to handle the exponents and normalize the result. We first give an intuitive derivation of the algorithms in decimal, and then give a more detailed, binary version in the figures.

Elaboration: In an attempt to increase range without removing bits from the significand, some computers before the IEEE 754 standard used a base other than 2. For example, the IBM 360 and 370 mainframe computers use base 16. Since changing the IBM exponent by one means shifting the significand by 4 bits, "normalized" base 16 numbers can have up to 3 leading bits of 0s! Hence hexadecimal digits mean that up to 3 bits must be dropped from the significand, which leads to surprising problems in the accuracy of floating-point arithmetic, as noted in section 4.12.

Floating-Point Addition

Let's add numbers in scientific notation by hand to illustrate the problems in floating-point addition: $9.999_{\text{ten}} \times 10^1 + 1.610_{\text{ten}} \times 10^{-1}$. Assume that we can store only four decimal digits of the significand and two decimal digits of the exponent.

Step 1.   To be able to add these numbers properly, we must align the decimal point of the number that has the smaller exponent. Hence, we need a form of the smaller number, $1.610_{ten} \times 10^{-1}$, that matches the larger exponent. We obtain this by observing that there are multiple representations of an unnormalized floating-point number in scientific notation:

$$1.610_{ten} \times 10^{-1} = 0.1610_{ten} \times 10^{0} = 0.01610_{ten} \times 10^{1}$$

The number on the right is the version we desire, since its exponent matches the exponent of the larger number, $9.999_{ten} \times 10^{1}$. Thus the first step shifts the significand of the smaller number to the right until its corrected exponent matches that of the larger number. But we can represent only four decimal digits so, after shifting, the number is really:

$$0.016_{ten} \times 10^{1}$$

Step 2.   Next comes the addition of the significands:

$$
\begin{array}{r}
9.999_{ten} \\
+ \quad 0.016_{ten} \\
\hline
10.015_{ten}
\end{array}
$$

The sum is $10.015_{ten} \times 10^{1}$.

Step 3.   This sum is not in normalized scientific notation, so we need to correct it. Again, there are multiple representations of this number; we pick the normalized form:

$$10.015_{ten} \times 10^{1} = 1.0015_{ten} \times 10^{2}$$

Thus, after the addition we may have to shift the sum to put it into normalized form, adjusting the exponent appropriately. This example shows shifting to the right, but if one number were positive and the other were negative, it would be possible for the sum to have many leading 0s, requiring left shifts. Whenever the exponent is increased or decreased, we must check for overflow or underflow—that is, we must make sure that the exponent still fits in its field.

Step 4.   Since we assumed that the significand can be only four digits long (excluding the sign), we must round the number. In our grammar school algorithm, the rules truncate the number if the digit to the right of the desired point is between 0 and 4 and add 1 to the digit if the number to the right is between 5 and 9. The number

$$1.0015_{ten} \times 10^{2}$$

is rounded to four digits in the significand to

$$1.002_{ten} \times 10^{2}$$

since the fourth digit to the right of the decimal point was between 5 and 9. Notice that if we have bad luck on rounding, such as adding 1 to a string of 9s, the sum may no longer be normalized and we would need to perform step 3 again.

Figure 4.44 shows the algorithm for binary floating-point addition that follows this decimal example. Steps 1 and 2 are similar to the example just discussed: adjust the significand of the number with the smaller exponent and then add the two significands. Step 3 normalizes the results, forcing a check for overflow or underflow. The test for overflow and underflow in step 3 depends on the precision of the operands. Recall that the pattern of all zero bits in the exponent is reserved and used for the floating-point representation of zero. Also, the pattern of all one bits in the exponent is reserved for indicating values and situations outside the scope of normal floating-point numbers (see the elaboration on page 300). Thus, for single precision, the maximum exponent is 127 and the minimum exponent is –126. The limits for double precision are 1023 and –1022.

For simplicity, we assume truncation in step 4, one of four rounding options in IEEE 754 floating point. The accuracy of floating-point calculations depends a great deal on the accuracy of rounding, so although it is easy to follow, truncation leads away from accuracy.

Decimal Floating-Point Addition

Example

Try adding the numbers 0.5_{ten} and -0.4375_{ten} in binary using the algorithm in Figure 4.44.

Answer

Let's first look at the binary version of the two numbers in normalized scientific notation, assuming that we keep 4 bits of precision:

$$0.5_{ten} = 1/2_{ten} = 1/2^1{}_{ten}$$
$$= 0.1_{two} = 0.1_{two} \times 2^0 = 1.000_{two} \times 2^{-1}$$
$$-0.4375_{ten} = -7/16_{ten} = -7/2^4{}_{ten}$$
$$= -0.0111_{two} = -0.0111_{two} \times 2^0 = -1.110_{two} \times 2^{-2}$$

Now we follow the algorithm:

Step 1. The significand of the number with the lesser exponent ($-1.11_{two} \times 2^{-2}$) is shifted right until its exponent matches the larger number:

$$-1.110_{two} \times 2^{-2} = -0.111_{two} \times 2^{-1}$$

Step 2. Add the significands:

$$1.0_{two} \times 2^{-1} + (-0.111_{two} \times 2^{-1}) = 0.001_{two} \times 2^{-1}$$

Step 3. Normalize the sum, checking for overflow or underflow:

$$0.001_{two} \times 2^{-1} = 0.010_{two} \times 2^{-2} = 0.100_{two} \times 2^{-3}$$
$$= 1.000_{two} \times 2^{-4}$$

Since $127 \geq -4 \geq -126$, there is no overflow or underflow. (The biased exponent would be $-4 + 127$, or 123, which is between 1 and 254, the smallest and largest unreserved biased exponents.)

Step 4. Round the sum:

$$1.000_{two} \times 2^{-4}$$

The sum already fits exactly in 4 bits, so there is no change to the bits due to rounding.

This sum is then

$$1.000_{two} \times 2^{-4} = 0.0001000_{two} = 0.0001_{two}$$
$$= 1/2^4{}_{ten} = 1/16_{ten} = 0.0625_{ten}$$

This sum is what we would expect from adding 0.5_{ten} to -0.4375_{ten}.

Many machines dedicate hardware to run floating-point operations as fast as possible. Figure 4.45 sketches the basic organization of hardware for floating-point addition.

Floating-Point Multiplication

Now that we have explained floating-point addition, let's try floating-point multiplication. We start by multiplying decimal numbers in scientific notation by hand: $1.110_{ten} \times 10^{10} \times 9.200_{ten} \times 10^{-5}$. Assume that we can store only four digits of the significand and two digits of the exponent.

Step 1. Unlike addition, we calculate the exponent of the product by simply adding the exponents of the operands together:

New exponent = $10 + (-5) = 5$

Let's do this with the biased exponents as well to make sure we obtain the same result: $10 + 127 = 137$, and $-5 + 127 = 122$, so

New exponent = $137 + 122 = 259$

This result is too large for the 8-bit exponent field, so something is amiss! The problem is with the bias because we are adding the biases as well as the exponents:

New exponent = $(10 + 127) + (-5 + 127) = (5 + 2 \times 127) = 259$

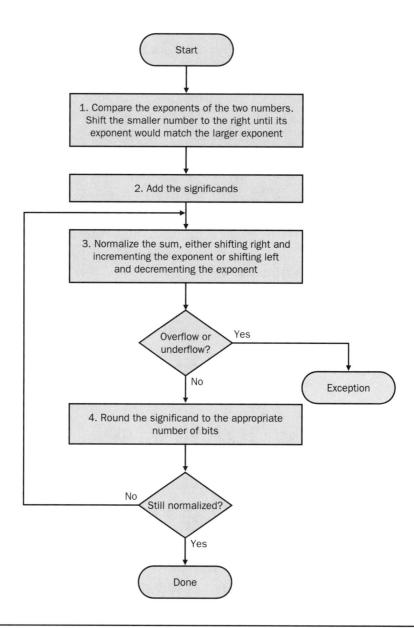

FIGURE 4.44   Floating-point addition. The normal path is to execute steps 3 and 4 once, but if rounding causes the sum to be unnormalized, we must repeat step 3.

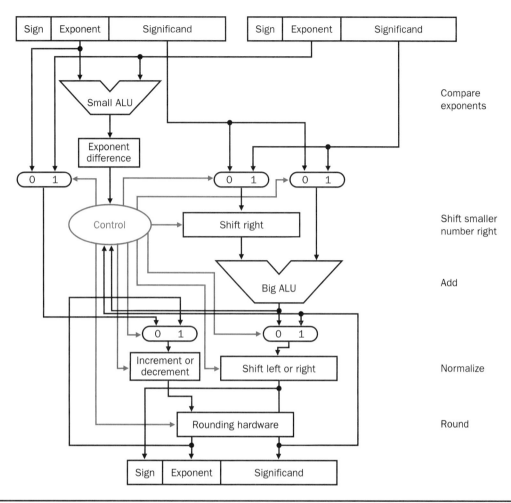

FIGURE 4.45 Block diagram of an arithmetic unit dedicated to floating-point addition. The steps of Figure 4.44 correspond to each block, from top to bottom. First the exponent of one operand is subtracted from the other using the small ALU to determine which is larger and by how much. This difference controls the three multiplexors; from left to right, they select the larger exponent, the significand of the smaller number, and the significand of the larger number. The smaller significand is shifted right and then the significands are added together using the big ALU. The normalization step then shifts the sum left or right and increments or decrements the exponent. Rounding then creates the final result, which may require normalizing again to produce the final result.

Accordingly, to get the correct biased sum when we add biased numbers, we must subtract the bias from the sum:

New exponent = 137 + 122 – 127 = 259 – 127 = 132 = (5 + 127)

and 5 is indeed the exponent we calculated initially.

Step 2. Next comes the multiplication of the significands:

$$1.110_{ten}$$
$$\times \qquad 9.200_{ten}$$
$$\overline{\qquad 0000 \qquad}$$
$$0000$$
$$2220$$
$$9990$$
$$\overline{10212000_{ten}}$$

There are three digits to the right of the decimal for each operand, so the decimal point is placed six digits from the right in the product significand:

$$10.212000_{ten}$$

Assuming that we can keep only three digits to the right of the decimal point, the product is 10.212×10^5.

Step 3. This product is unnormalized, so we need to correct it. Again, there are multiple representations of this number, so we must pick the normalized form:

$$10.212_{ten} \times 10^5 = 1.0212_{ten} \times 10^6$$

Thus, after the multiplication, the product can be shifted right one digit to put it in normalized form, adding 1 to the exponent. At this point, we can check for overflow and underflow. Underflow may occur if both operands are small—that is, if both have large negative exponents.

Step 4. We assumed that the significand is only four digits long (excluding the sign), so we must round the number. The number

$$1.0212_{ten} \times 10^6$$

is rounded to four digits in the significand to

$$1.021_{ten} \times 10^6$$

Step 5. The sign of the product depends on the signs of the original operands. If they are both the same, the sign is positive; otherwise it's negative. Hence the product is

$$+1.021_{ten} \times 10^6$$

The sign of the sum in the addition algorithm was determined by addition of the significands, but in multiplication the sign of the product is determined by the signs of the operands.

Once again, as Figure 4.46 shows, multiplication of binary floating-point numbers is quite similar to the steps we have just completed. We start with calculating the new exponent of the product by adding the biased exponents, being sure to subtract one bias to get the proper result. Next is multiplication of significands, followed by an optional normalization step. The size of the exponent is checked for overflow or underflow, and then the product is rounded. If rounding leads to further normalization, we once again check for exponent size. Finally, set the sign bit to 1 if the signs of the operands were different (negative product) or to 0 if they were the same (positive product).

Decimal Floating-Point Multiplication

Example

Let's try multiplying the numbers 0.5_{ten} and -0.4375_{ten} using the steps in Figure 4.46.

Answer

In binary, the task is multiplying $1.000_{two} \times 2^{-1}$ by $-1.110_{two} \times 2^{-2}$.

Step 1. Adding the exponents without bias:

$$-1 + (-2) = -3$$

or, using the biased representation:

$$(-1 + 127) + (-2 + 127) - 127 = (-1 - 2) + (127 + 127 - 127)$$
$$= -3 + 127 = 124$$

Step 2. Multiplying the significands:

```
          1.000two
   ×      1.110two
         ────────
          0000
         1000
        1000
       1000
      ────────
      1110000two
```

The product is $1.110000_{two} \times 2^{-3}$, but we need to keep it to 4 bits, so it is $1.110_{two} \times 2^{-3}$.

Step 3. Now we check the product to make sure it is normalized, and then check the exponent for overflow or underflow. The product is already normalized and, since $127 \geq -3 \geq -126$, there is no overflow or underflow. (Using the biased representation, $254 \geq 124 \geq 1$, so the exponent fits.)

Step 4.   Rounding the product makes no change:

$$1.110_{two} \times 2^{-3}$$

Step 5.   Since the signs of the original operands differ, make the sign of the product negative. Hence the product is

$$-1.110_{two} \times 2^{-3}$$

Converting to decimal to check our results:

$$-1.110_{two} \times 2^{-3} = -0.001110_{two} = -0.00111_{two}$$
$$= -7/2^5{}_{ten} = -7/32_{ten} = -0.21875_{ten}$$

The product of 0.5_{ten} and -0.4375_{ten} is indeed -0.21875_{ten}.

Floating-Point Instructions in MIPS

MIPS supports the IEEE 754 single-precision and double-precision formats with these instructions:

- Floating-point *addition, single* (add.s) and *addition, double* (add.d)

- Floating-point *subtraction, single* (sub.s) and *subtraction, double* (sub.d)

- Floating-point *multiplication, single* (mul.s) and *multiplication, double* (mul.d)

- Floating-point *division, single* (div.s) and *division, double* (div.d)

- Floating-point *comparison, single* (c.x.s) and *comparison, double* (c.x.d), where x may be *equal* (eq), *not equal* (neq), *less than* (lt), *less than or equal* (le), *greater than* (gt), or *greater than or equal* (ge)

- Floating-point *branch, true* (bc1t) and *branch, false* (bc1f)

Floating-point comparison sets a bit to true or false, depending on the comparison condition, and a floating-point branch then decides whether or not to branch, depending on the condition.

The MIPS designers decided to add separate floating-point registers—called $f0, $f1, $f2, . . .—used either for single precision or double precision. Hence they included separate loads and stores for floating-point registers: lwc1 and swc1. The base registers for floating-point data transfers remain integer registers. The MIPS code to load two single precision numbers from memory, add them, and then store the sum might look like this:

```
lwc1    $f4,x($sp)    # Load 32 bit F.P. number into F4
lwc1    $f6,y($sp)    # Load 32-bit F.P. number into F6
add.s   $f2,$f4,$f6   # F2 = F4 + F6 single precision
swc1    $f2,z($sp)    # Store 32-bit F.P. number from F2
```

A double precision register is really an even-odd pair of single precision registers, using the even register number as its name.

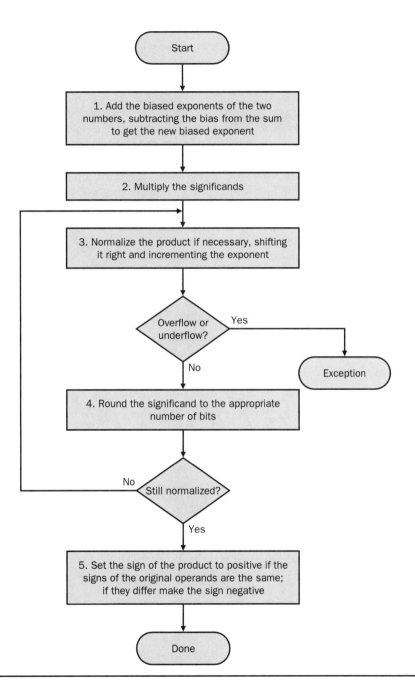

FIGURE 4.46 Floating-point multiplication. The normal path is to execute steps 3 and 4 once, but if rounding causes the sum to be unnormalized, we must repeat step 3.

Hardware Software Interface

One issue that computer designers face in supporting floating-point arithmetic is whether to use the same registers used by the integer instructions or to add a special set for floating point. Because programs normally perform integer operations and floating-point operations on different data, separating the registers will only slightly increase the number of instructions needed to execute a program. The major impact is to create a separate set of data transfer instructions to move data between floating-point registers and memory.

The benefits of separate floating-point registers are having twice as many registers without using up more bits in the instruction format, having twice the register bandwidth by having separate integer and floating-point register sets, and being able to customize registers to floating point; for example, some machines convert all sized operands in registers into a single internal format.

Figure 4.47 summarizes the floating-point portion of the MIPS architecture revealed in Chapter 4, with the additions to support floating point shown in color. Similar to Figure 3.18 on page 153 in Chapter 3, we show the encoding of these instructions in Figure 4.48.

MIPS floating-point operands

Name	Example	Comments
32 floating-point registers	$f0, $f1, $f2, . . . , $f31	MIPS floating-point registers are used in pairs for double precision numbers.
2^{30} memory words	Memory[0], Memory[4], . . . , Memory[4294967292]	Accessed only by data transfer instructions. MIPS uses byte addresses, so sequential words differ by 4. Memory holds data structures, such as arrays, and spilled registers, such as those saved on procedure calls.

MIPS floating-point assembly language

Category	Instruction	Example		Meaning	Comments
Arithmetic	FP add single	add.s	$f2,$f4,$f6	$f2 = $f4 + $f6	FP add (single precision)
	FP subtract single	sub.s	$f2,$f4,$f6	$f2 = $f4 − $f6	FP sub (single precision)
	FP multiply single	mul.s	$f2,$f4,$f6	$f2 = $f4 × $f6	FP. multiply (single precision)
	FP divide single	div.s	$f2,$f4,$f6	$f2 = $f4 / $f6	FP divide (single precision)
	FP add double	add.d	$f2,$f4,$f6	$f2 = $f4 + $f6	FP add (double precision)
	FP subtract double	sub.d	$f2,$f4,$f6	$f2 = $f4 − $f6	FP sub (double precision)
	FP multiply double	mul.d	$f2,$f4,$f6	$f2 = $f4 × $f6	FP multiply (double precision)
	FP divide double	div.d	$f2,$f4,$f6	$f2 = $f4 / $f6	FP divide (double precision)
Data transfer	load word copr. 1	lwc1	$f1,100($s2)	$f1 = Memory[$s2 + 100]	32-bit data to FP register
	store word copr. 1	swc1	$f1,100($s2)	Memory[$s2 + 100] = $f1	32-bit data to memory
Conditional branch	branch on FP true	bc1t	25	if (cond == 1) go to PC + 4 + 100	PC-relative branch if FP cond.
	branch on FP false	bc1f	25	if (cond == 0) go to PC + 4 + 100	PC-relative branch if not cond.
	FP compare single (eq,ne,lt,le,gt,ge)	c.lt.s $f2,$f4		if ($f2 < $f4) cond = 1; else cond = 0	FP compare less than single precision
	FP compare double (eq,ne,lt,le,gt,ge)	c.lt.d $f2,$f4		if ($f2 < $f4) cond = 1; else cond = 0	FP compare less than double precision

MIPS floating-point machine language

Name	Format	Example						Comments	
add.s	R	17	16	6	4	2	0	add.s	$f2,$f4,$f6
sub.s	R	17	16	6	4	2	1	sub.s	$f2,$f4,$f6
mul.s	R	17	16	6	4	2	2	mul.s	$f2,$f4,$f6
div.s	R	17	16	6	4	2	3	div.s	$f2,$f4,$f6
add.d	R	17	17	6	4	2	0	add.d	$f2,$f4,$f6
sub.d	R	17	17	6	4	2	1	sub.d	$f2,$f4,$f6
mul.d	R	17	17	6	4	2	2	mul.d	$f2,$f4,$f6
div.d	R	17	17	6	4	2	3	div.d	$f2,$f4,$f6
lwc1	I	49	20	2	100			lwc1	$f2,100($s4)
swc1	I	57	20	2	100			swc1	$f2,100($s4)
bc1t	I	17	8	1	25			bc1t	25
bc1f	I	17	8	0	25			bc1f	25
c.lt.s	R	17	16	4	2	0	60	c.lt.s	$f2,$f4
c.lt.d	R	17	17	4	2	0	60	c.lt.d	$f2,$f4
Field size		6 bits	5 bits	5 bits	5 bits	5 bits	6 bits	All MIPS instructions 32 bits	

FIGURE 4.47 MIPS floating-point architecture revealed thus far. See Appendix A, section A.10, on page A-49, for more detail.

op(31:26):							
28–26 / 31–29	0(000)	1(001)	2(010)	3(011)	4(100)	5(101)	6(110)	7(111)
0(000)	Rfmt	Bltz/gez	j	jal	beq	bne	blez	bgtz
1(001)	addi	addiu	slti	sltiu	andi	ori	xori	lui
2(010)	TLB	FlPt						
3(011)								
4(100)	lb	lh	lwl	lw	lbu	lhu	lwr	
5(101)	sb	sh	swl	sw			swr	
6(110)	lwc0	lwc1						
7(111)	swc0	swc1						

op(31:26) = 010001 (FlPt), (rt(16:16) = 0 => c = f, rt(16:16) = 1 => c = t), rs(25:21):							
32–21 / 25–24	0(000)	1(001)	2(010)	3(011)	4(100)	5(101)	6(110)	7(111)
0(00)	mfc1		cfc1		mtc1		ctc1	
1(01)	bc1.c							
2(10)	f = single	f = double						
3(11)								

op(31:26) = 010001 (FlPt), (f above: 01000 => f = s, 01001 => f = d), funct(5:0):							
2–0 / 5–3	0(000)	1(001)	2(010)	3(011)	4(100)	5(101)	6(110)	7(111)
0(000)	add f	sub f	mul f	div f		abs f	mov f	neg f
1(001)								
2(010)								
3(011)								
4(100)	cvt.s f	cvt.d f			cvt.w f			
5(101)								
6(110)	c.f f	c.un f	c.eq f	c.ueq f	c.olt f	c.ult f	c.ole f	c.ule f
7(111)	c.sf f	c.ngle f	c.seq f	c.ngl f	c.lt f	c.nge f	c.le f	c.ngt f

FIGURE 4.48   MIPS floating-point instruction encoding. This notation gives the value of a field by row and by column. For example, in the top portion of the figure lw is found in row number 4 (100_{two} for bits 31–29 of the instruction) and column number 3 (011_{two} for bits 28–26 of the instruction), so the corresponding value of the op field (bits 31–26) is 100011_{two}. Underscore means the field is used elsewhere. For example, FlPt in row 2 and column 1 (op = 010001_{two}) is defined in the bottom part of the figure. Hence sub.t in row 0 and column 1 of the bottom section means that the funct field (bits 5–0) of the instruction) is 000001_{two} and the op field (bits 31–26) is 010001_{two}. Note that the 5-bit rs field, specified in the middle portion of the figure, determines whether the operation is single precision (f = s so rs = 10000) or double precision (f = d so rs = 10001). Similarly, bit 16 of the instruction determines if the bc1.c instruction tests for true (bit 16 = 1 =>bc1.t) or false (bit 16 = 0 =>bc1.f). Rfmt and TLB instruction encodings are found in Figure 3.18 on page 153. Instructions in color are described in Chapters 3 or 4, with Appendix A covering all instructions.

Compiling a Floating-Point C Program into MIPS Assembly Code

Example

Let's convert a temperature in Fahrenheit to Celsius:

```
float f2c (float fahr)
    {
        return ((5.0/9.0) * (fahr - 32.0));
    }
```

Assume that the floating-point argument `fahr` is passed in $f12 and the result should go in $f0. (Unlike integer registers, floating-point register 0 can contain a number.) What is the MIPS assembly code?

Answer

We assume that the compiler places the three floating-point constants in memory within easy reach of the global pointer $gp. The first two instructions load the constants 5.0 and 9.0 into floating-point registers:

```
f2c:
    lwc1  $f16,const5($gp)   # $f16 = 5.0 (5.0 in memory)
    lwc1  $f18,const9($gp)   # $f18 = 9.0 (9.0 in memory)
```

They are then divided to get the fraction 5.0/9.0:

```
    div.s $f16, $f16, $f18  # $f16 = 5.0 / 9.0
```

(Many compilers would divide 5.0 by 9.0 at compile time and save the single constant 5.0/9.0 in memory, thereby avoiding the divide at runtime.) Next we load the constant 32.0 and then subtract it from `fahr` ($f12):

```
    lwc1  $f18, const32($gp)# $f18 = 32.0
    sub.s $f18, $f12, $f18  # $f18 = fahr - 32.0
```

Finally, we multiply the two intermediate results, placing the product in $f0 as the return result, and then return:

```
    mul.s $f0, $f16, $f18  # $f0 = (5/9)*(fahr - 32.0)
    jr    $ra              # return
```

Now let's perform floating-point operations on matrices, code commonly found in scientific programs.

Compiling Floating-Point C Procedure with Two-Dimensional Matrices into MIPS

Example

Most floating-point calculations are performed in double precision. Let's perform matrix multiply of X = Y * Z. Let's assume X, Y, and Z are all square matrices with 32 elements in each dimension.

```
void mm (double x[][], double y[][], double z[][])
{
    int i, j, k;

    for (i = 0; i! = 32; i = i + 1)
        for (j = 0; j! = 32; j = j + 1)
            for (k = 0; k! = 32; k = k + 1)
                x[i][j] = x[i][j] + y[i][k] * z[k][j];
}
```

The array starting addresses are parameters, so they are in $a0, $a1, and $a2. Assume that the integer variables are in $s0, $s1, and $s2, respectively. What is the MIPS assembly code for the body of the procedure?

Answer

Note that x[i][j] is used in the innermost loop above. Since the loop index is k, the index does not affect x[i][j], so we can avoid loading and storing x[i][j] each iteration. Instead, the compiler loads x[i][j] into a register outside the loop, accumulates the sum of the products of y[i][k] and z[k][j] in that same register, and then stores the sum into x[i][j] upon termination of the innermost loop.

We keep the code simpler by using the assembly language pseudoinstructions li (which loads a constant into a register), and l.d and s.d (which the assembler turns into a pair of data transfer instructions, lwc1 or swc1, to a pair of floating-point registers).

The body of the procedure starts with saving the loop termination value of 32 in a temporary register and then initializing the three *for* loop variables:

```
mm:...
        li      $t1, 32     # $t1 = 32 (row size/loop end)
        li      $s0, 0      # i = 0; initialize 1st for loop
L1:     li      $s1, 0      # j = 0; restart 2nd for loop
L2:     li      $s2, 0      # k = 0; restart 3rd for loop
```

To calculate the address of x[i][j], we need to know how a 32×32, two-dimensional array is stored in memory. As you might expect, its layout is the same as if there were 32 single-dimension arrays, each with 32 elements. So the first step is to skip over the i "single-dimensional arrays," or rows, to get the one we want. Thus we multiply the index in the first dimension by the size of the row, 32. Since 32 is a power of 2, we can use a shift instead (see page 262):

```
sll    $t2, $s0, 5    # $t2 = i * 2^5 (size of row of x)
```

Now we add the second index to select the jth element of the desired row:

```
addu   $t2, $t2, $s1  # $t2 = i * size(row) + j
```

To turn this sum into a byte index, we multiply it by the size of a matrix element in bytes. Since each element is 8 bytes for double precision, we can instead shift left by 3:

```
sll    $t2, $t2, 3    # $t2 = byte offset of [i][j]
```

Next we add this sum to the base address of x, giving the address of x[i][j], and then load the double precision number x[i][j] into $f4:

```
addu   $t2, $a0, $t2  # $t2 = byte address of x[i][j]
l.d    $f4, 0($t2)    # $f4 = 8 bytes of x[i][j]
```

The following five instructions are virtually identical to the last five: calculate the address and then load the double precision number z[k][j].

```
L3:  sll    $t0, $s2, 5    # $t0 = k * 2^5 (size of row of z)
     addu   $t0, $t0, $s1  # $t0 = k * size(row) + j
     sll    $t0, $t0, 3    # $t0 = byte offset of [k][j]
     addu   $t0, $a2, $t0  # $t0 = byte address of z[k][j]
     l.d    $f16, 0($t0)   # $f16 = 8 bytes of z[k][j]
```

Similarly, the next five instructions are like the last five: calculate the address and then load the double precision number y[i][k].

```
sll    $t2, $s0, 5    # $t0 = i * 2^5 (size of row of y)
addu   $t0, $t0, $s2  # $t0 = i * size(row) + k
sll    $t0, $t0, 3    # $t0 = byte offset of [i][k]
addu   $t0, $a1, $t0  # $t0 = byte address of y[i][k]
l.d    $f18, 0($t0)   # $f18 = 8 bytes of y[i][k]
```

Now that we have loaded all the data, we are finally ready to do some floating-point operations! We multiply elements of y and z located in registers $f18 and $f16, and then accumulate the sum in $f4.

```
mul.d $f16, $f18, $f16# $f16 = y[i][k] * z[k][j]
add.d $f4, $f4, $f16  # f4 = x[i][j] + y[i][k] * z[k][j]
```

The final block increments the index k and loops back if the index is not 32. If it is 32, and thus the end of the innermost loop, we need to store the sum accumulated in $f4 into x[i][j].

```
addiu  $s2, $s2, 1      # $k k + 1
bne    $s2, $t1, L3     # if (k != 32) go to L3
s.d    $f4, 0($t2)      # x[i][j] = $f4
```

Similarly, these final four instructions increment the index variable of the middle and outermost loops, looping back if the index is not 32 and exiting if the index is 32.

```
addiu  $s1, $s1, 1      # $j = j + 1
bne    $s1, $t1, L2     # if (j != 32) go to L2
addiu  $s0, $s0, 1      # $i = i + 1
bne    $s0, $t1, L1     # if (i != 32) go to L1
. . .
```

Elaboration: The array layout discussed in the example, called *row major order,* is used by C and many other programming languages. Fortran instead uses *column major order,* whereby the array is stored column by column.

Only 16 of the 32 MIPS floating-point registers can be used for single precision operations: $f0, $f2, $f4, . . . , $f30. Double precision is computed using pairs of these registers. The odd-numbered floating-point registers are used only to load and store the right half of 64-bit floating-point numbers. A later version of the MIPS instruction set, MIPS II, added l.d and s.d to the hardware instruction set. An even later version, MIPS IV, added indexed addressing for floating-point data transfers, removing the need for the fourth instruction of the five-instruction load sequences above.

Another reason for separate integers and floating-point registers is that microprocessors in the 1980s didn't have enough transistors to put the floating-point unit on the same chip as the integer unit. Hence the floating-point unit, including the floating-point registers, were optionally available as a second chip. Such optional accelerator chips are called *coprocessors,* and explain the acronym for floating-point loads in MIPS: lwc1 means load word to coprocessor 1, the floating-point unit. (Coprocessor 0 deals with virtual memory, described in Chapter 7.) Since the early 1990s, microprocessors have integrated floating point (and just about everything else) on chip, and hence the term "coprocessor" joins "accumulator" and "core memory" as quaint terms that date the speaker.

Elaboration: Although there are many ways to throw hardware at floating-point multiply to make it go fast, floating-point division is considerably more challenging to make fast and accurate. Slow divides in early computers led to removal of divides from many algorithms, but parallel computers have inspired rediscovery of divide-intensive algorithms that work better on these machines. Hence we may need faster divides.

One technique to leverage a fast multiplier is *Newton's iteration,* where division is recast as finding the zero of a function to find the reciprocal $1/x$, which is then multiplied by the other operand. Iteration techniques *cannot* be rounded properly without calculating many extra bits. A TI chip solves this problem by calculating an extra-precise reciprocal, and IBM relies on fused multiply-add to solve it (see section 4.9).

The *SRT division* technique instead tries to guess several quotient bits per step, using a table lookup based on the upper bits of the dividend and remainder, relying on subsequent steps to correct wrong guesses. A Cyrix chip uses this technique to generate 16 bits per step!

Accurate Arithmetic

Unlike integers, which can represent exactly every number between the smallest and largest number, floating-point numbers are normally approximations for a number they can't really represent. The reason is that an infinite variety of real numbers exists between, say, 0 and 1, but no more than 2^{53} can be represented exactly in double precision floating point. The best we can do is get the floating-point representation close to the actual number. Thus, IEEE 754 offers several modes of rounding to let the programmer pick the desired approximation.

Rounding sounds simple enough, but to round accurately requires the hardware to include extra bits in the calculation. In the preceding examples, we were vague on the number of bits that an intermediate representation can occupy, but clearly if every intermediate result had to be truncated to the exact number of digits, there would be no opportunity to round. IEEE 754, therefore, always keeps 2 extra bits on the right during intermediate calculations, called *guard* and *round*, respectively. Let's do a decimal example to illustrate the value of these extra digits.

Rounding with Guard Digits

Example

Add $2.56_{ten} \times 10^0$ to $2.34_{ten} \times 10^2$, assuming that we have three significant decimal digits. Round to the nearest decimal number with three significant decimal digits, first with guard and round digits, and then without them.

Answer

First we must shift the smaller number to the right to align the exponents, so $2.56_{ten} \times 10^0$ becomes $0.0256_{ten} \times 10^2$. Since we have guard and round digits, we are able to represent the two least significant digits when we align exponents. The guard digit holds 5 and the round digit holds 6. The sum is

$$
\begin{array}{r}
2.3400_{ten} \\
+ \quad 0.0256_{ten} \\
\hline
2.3656_{ten}
\end{array}
$$

Thus the sum is $2.3656_{ten} \times 10^2$. Since we have two digits to round, we want values 0 to 49 to round down and 51 to 99 to round up, with 50 being the tiebreaker. Rounding the sum up with three significant digits yields $2.37_{ten} \times 10^2$.

Doing this *without* guard and round digits drops two digits from the calculation. The new sum is then

$$
\begin{array}{r}
2.34_{ten} \\
+ \quad 0.02_{ten} \\
\hline
2.36_{ten}
\end{array}
$$

The answer is $2.36_{ten} \times 10^2$, off by 1 in the last digit from the sum obtained above.

Since the worst case for rounding would be when the actual number is half-way between two floating-point representations, accuracy in floating point is normally measured in terms of the number of bits in error in the least significant bits of the significand; the measure is called the number of *units in the last place,* or *ulp.* If a number was off by 2 in the least significant bits, it would be called off by 2 ulps. Provided there is no overflow, underflow, or invalid operation exceptions, IEEE 754 guarantees that the computer uses the number that is within one-half ulp.

Elaboration: Although the example above really needed just one extra bit, multiply can need two. A binary product may have one leading 0 bit, hence the normalizing step must shift the product 1 bit left. This shifts the guard digit into the least significant bit of the product, leaving the round bit to help accurately round the product.

The goal of the extra rounding bits is to allow the machine to get the same results as if the intermediate results were calculated to infinite precision and then rounded. Thus the standard has a third bit in addition to guard and round; it is set whenever there are nonzero bits to the right of the round bit. This *sticky bit* allows the computer to see the difference between $0.50 \ldots 00_{ten}$ and $0.50 \ldots 01_{ten}$ when rounding. The sticky bit may be set, for example, during addition, when the smaller number is shifted to the right.

Summary

The Big Picture below reinforces the stored-program concept from Chapter 3; the meaning of the information cannot be determined just by looking at the bits, for the same bits can represent a variety of objects. This section shows that computer arithmetic is finite and thus can disagree with natural arithmetic. For example, the IEEE 754 standard floating-point representation

$$(-1)^S \times (1 + \text{Significand}) \times 2^{(\text{Exponent} - \text{bias})}$$

is almost always an approximation of the real number. Computer systems must take care to minimize this gap between computer arithmetic and arithmetic in the real world, and programmers at times need to be aware of the implications of this approximation.

The Big Picture

Bit patterns have no inherent meaning. They may represent signed integers, unsigned integers, floating-point numbers, instructions, and so on. What is represented depends on the instruction that operates on the bits in the word.

The major difference between computer numbers and numbers in the real world is that computer numbers have limited size, hence limited precision; it's possible to calculate a number too big or too small to be represented in a word. Programmers must remember these limits and write programs accordingly.

Hardware Software Interface

In the last chapter we presented the storage classes of the programming language C (see the Hardware Software Interface section on page 140). The following table shows some of the C data types together with the MIPS data transfer instructions and instructions that operate on those types that appear in Chapters 3 and 4.

C type	Data transfers	Operations
int	lw, sw, lui	addu, addiu, subu, mult, div, and, andi, or, ori, slt, slti
unsigned int	lw, sw, lui	addu, addiu, subu, multu, divu, and, andi, or, ori, sltu, sltiu
char	lb, sb, lui	addu, addiu, subu, multu, divu, and, andi, or, ori, sltu, sltiu
bit field	lw, sw, lui	and, andi, or, ori, sll, srl
float	lwc1, swc1	add.s, sub.s, mult.s, div.s, c.eq.s, c.lt.s, c.le.s
double	lwc1, swc1	add.d, sub.d, mult.d, div.d, c.eq.d, c.lt.d, c.le.d

Elaboration: The IEEE 754 floating-point standard is filled with little widgets to help the programmer try to maintain accuracy. We'll cover a few here, but take a look at the references at the end of section 4.12 to learn more.

There are four rounding modes: always round up (toward $+\infty$), always round down (toward $-\infty$), truncate, and round to nearest even. The final mode determines what to do if the number is exactly halfway in between. The Internal Revenue Service always rounds 0.50 dollars up, possibly to the benefit of the IRS. A more equitable way would be to round up this case half the time and round down the other half. IEEE 754 says that if the least significant bit retained in a halfway case would be odd, add one; if it's even, truncate. This method always creates a 0 in the least significant bit, giving the rounding mode its name. This mode is the most commonly used.

Other features of IEEE 754 are special symbols to represent unusual events. For example, instead of interrupting on a divide by 0, software can set the result to a bit pattern representing $+\infty$ or $-\infty$; the largest exponent is reserved for these special symbols. When the programmer prints the results, the program will print an infinity symbol. (For the mathematically trained, the purpose of infinity is to form topological closure of the reals.)

IEEE 754 even has a symbol for the result of invalid operations, such as 0/0 or subtracting infinity from infinity. This symbol is *NaN*, for *Not a Number*. The purpose of NaNs is to allow programmers to postpone some tests and decisions to a later time in the program when it is convenient. To accommodate comparisons that may include NaNs, the standard includes *ordered* and *unordered* as options for compares. Hence the full MIPS instruction set has many flavors of compares to support NaNs.

Finally, in an attempt to squeeze every last bit of precision from a floating-point operation, the standard allows some numbers to be represented in unnormalized form. Rather than having a gap between 0 and the smallest normalized number, IEEE allows *denormalized numbers* (also known as *denorms* or *subnormals*). They have the same exponent as zero but a nonzero significand. They allow a number to degrade in significance until it becomes 0, called *gradual underflow*. For example, the smallest single precision normalized number is

$$1.0000\ 0000\ 0000\ 0000\ 0000\ 000_{two} \times 2^{-126}$$

but the smallest single precision denormalized number is

$$0.0000\ 0000\ 0000\ 0000\ 0000\ 001_{two} \times 2^{-126}, \text{ or } 1.0_{two} \times 2^{-149}$$

For double precision, the denorm gap goes from 1.0×2^{-1022} to 1.0×2^{-1074}.

The possibility of an occasional unnormalized operand has given headaches to floating-point designers who are trying to build fast floating-point units. Hence many computers cause an exception if an operand is denormalized, letting software complete the operation. Although software implementations are perfectly valid, their lower performance has lessened the popularity of denorms in portable floating-point software. Also, if programmers do not expect denorms, their programs may be surprised.

Here are the encodings of IEEE 754 floating-point numbers, with the sign bit determining the sign:

Single precision		Double precision		Object represented
Exponent	Significand	Exponent	Significand	
0	0	0	0	0
0	nonzero	0	nonzero	± denormalized number
1–254	anything	1–2046	anything	± floating-point number
255	0	2047	0	± infinity
255	nonzero	2047	nonzero	NaN (Not a Number)

4.9 Real Stuff: Floating Point in the PowerPC and 80x86

Both the PowerPC and 80x86 have regular multiply and divide instructions that operate entirely on registers, unlike the reliance on Hi and Lo in MIPS. (In fact, later versions of the MIPS instruction set have added similar instructions.)

The main differences are found in floating-point instructions. PowerPC is like MIPS except for one novel instruction and twice as many registers: PowerPC offers 32 single precision and 32 double precision floating-point registers. The 80x86 floating-point architecture, on the other hand, is completely different from all other computers in the world.

The Multiply-Add Instruction of the PowerPC

The matrix multiply on page 294 relied on a multiply operation and an add operation, which is typical of many matrix and vector operations. Hence the PowerPC has a "fused" multiply-add instruction: a single instruction reads three operands, multiplies two operands and adds the third to the product, and writes the sum in the result operand. Hence the two MIPS floating-point instructions in the matrix multiply example would be replaced by one in PowerPC. This instruction can increase peak floating-point performance.

Fused multiply-add also performs the two operations and *then* rounds, unlike separate multiply and add instructions, which would round after each operation. The instructions also calculate extra bits for intermediate results to improve accuracy. Besides being potentially faster, the extra accuracy of fused multiply-add can also be helpful for calculating divide and square root, and in software libraries that calculate at higher precision than 64 bits. In fact, PowerPC hardware uses fused multiply-add hardware to calculate divide, and accurate division was the motivation for skipping the round between the two operations.

The 80x86 Floating-Point Architecture

The Intel 8087 floating-point coprocessor was announced in 1980. This architecture extended the 8086 with about 60 floating-point instructions.

Intel provided a stack architecture with its floating-point instructions: loads push numbers onto the stack, operations find operands in the two top elements of the stacks, and stores can pop elements off the stack. Intel supplemented this stack architecture with instructions and addressing modes that allow the architecture to have some of the benefits of a register-memory model. In addition to finding operands in the top two elements of the stack, one operand can be in memory or in one of the seven registers on-chip below the top of the stack. Thus a complete stack instruction set is supplemented by a limited set of register-memory instructions.

This hybrid is still a restricted register-memory model, however, in that loads always move data to the top of the stack while incrementing the top-of-stack pointer and stores can only move the top of stack to memory. Intel uses the notation ST to indicate the top of stack, and ST(i) to represent the ith register below the top of stack.

Another novel feature of this architecture is that the operands are wider in the register stack than they are stored in memory, and all operations are performed at this wide internal precision. Unlike the maximum of 64 bits on the MIPS and PowerPC, the 80x86 floating-point operands on the stack are 80 bits wide. Numbers are automatically converted to the internal 80-bit format on a load and converted back to the appropriate size on a store. This *double extended precision* is not supported by programming languages, although it has been useful to programmers of mathematical software.

Memory data can be 32-bit (single precision) or 64-bit (double precision) floating-point numbers. The register-memory version of these instructions will then convert the memory operand to this Intel 80-bit format before performing the operation. The data transfer instructions also will automatically convert 16- and 32-bit integers to floating point, and vice versa, for integer loads and stores.

The 80x86 floating-point operations can be divided into four major classes:

1. Data movement instructions, including load, load constant, and store

2. Arithmetic instructions, including add, subtract, multiply, divide, square root, and absolute value

3. Comparison, including instructions to send the result to the integer processor so that it can branch

4. Transcendental instructions, including sine, cosine, log, and exponentiation

Figure 4.49 shows some of the 60 floating-point operations. We use the curly brackets { } to show optional variations of the basic operations: {I} means there is an integer version of the instruction, {P} means this variation will pop one operand off the stack after the operation, and {R} means reverse the order of the operands in this operation.

Not all combinations suggested by the notation are provided. Hence

F{I}SUB{R}{P}

represents these instructions found in the 80x86:

FSUB, FISUB, FSUBR, FISUBR, FSUBP, FSUBRP

For the integer subtract instructions, there is no pop (FISUBP) or reverse pop (FISUBRP).

Note that we get even more combinations when including the operand modes for these operations. Figure 4.50 shows the many options for floating-point add, even ignoring the integer and pop versions of the instruction.

The floating-point instructions are encoded using the ESC opcode of the 8086 and the postbyte address specifier (see Figure 3.35 on page 185). The memory operations reserve 2 bits to decide whether the operand is a 32- or 64-bit floating point or a 16- or 32-bit integer. Those same 2 bits are used in versions that do not access memory to decide whether the stack should be popped after the operation and whether the top of stack or a lower register should get the result.

Data transfer	Arithmetic	Compare	Transcendental
F{I}LD mem/ST(i)	F{I}ADD{P} mem/ST(i)	F{I}COM{P}{P}	FPATAN
F{I}ST{P} mem/ST(i)	F{I}SUB{R}{P} mem/ST(i)	F{I}UCOM{P}{P}	F2XM1
FLDPI	F{I}MUL{P} mem/ST(i)	FSTSW AX/mem	FCOS
FLD1	F{I}DIV{R}{P} mem/ST(i)		FPTAN
FLDZ	FSQRT		FPREM
	FABS		FSIN
	FRNDINT		FYL2X

FIGURE 4.49 The floating-point instructions of the 80x86. The first column shows the data transfer instructions, which move data to memory or to one of the registers below the top of the stack. The last three operations in the first column push constants on the stack: pi, 1.0, and 0.0. The second column contains the arithmetic operations described above. Note that the last three operate only on the top of stack. The third column is the compare instructions. Since there are no special floating-point branch instructions, the result of the compare must be transferred to the integer CPU via the FSTSW instruction, either into the AX register or into memory, followed by an SAHF instruction to set the condition codes. The floating-point comparison can then be tested using integer branch instructions. The final column gives the higher-level floating-point operations.

Instruction	Operands	Comment
FADD		Both operands in stack; result replaces top of stack.
FADD	ST(i)	One source operand is ith register below the top of stack; result replaces the top of stack.
FADD	ST(i), ST	One source operand is the top of stack; result replaces ith register below the top of stack.
FADD	mem32	One source operand is a 32-bit location in memory; result replaces the top of stack.
FADD	mem64	One source operand is a 64-bit location in memory; result replaces the top of stack.

FIGURE 4.50   The variations of operands for floating-point add in the 80x86.

Floating-point performance of the 80x86 family has traditionally lagged far behind other computers. It is hard to tell whether it is simply a lack of attention by Intel engineers, a disinterest by customers of PCs, if the fault lies with its architecture, or most likely some combination. We can say that many new architectures have been announced since 1980, and none have followed in Intel's footsteps.

4.10   Fallacies and Pitfalls

Thus mathematics may be defined as the subject in which we never know what we are talking about, nor whether what we are saying is true.

Bertrand Russell, *Recent Words on the Principles of Mathematics*, 1901

Arithmetic fallacies and pitfalls generally stem from the difference between the limited precision of computer arithmetic and the unlimited precision of natural arithmetic.

Fallacy: Floating-point addition is associative; that is, $x + (y + z) = (x + y) + z$.

Given the great range of numbers that can be represented in floating point, problems occur when adding two large numbers of opposite signs plus a small number. For example, suppose $x = -1.5_{ten} \times 10^{38}$, $y = 1.5_{ten} \times 10^{38}$, and $z = 1.0$, and that these are all single precision numbers. Then

$$x + (y + z) = -1.5_{ten} \times 10^{38} + (1.5_{ten} \times 10^{38} + 1.0)$$
$$= -1.5_{ten} \times 10^{38} + (1.5_{ten} \times 10^{38}) = 0.0$$
$$(x + y) + z = (-1.5_{ten} \times 10^{38} + 1.5_{ten} \times 10^{38}) + 1.0$$
$$= (0.0_{ten}) + 1.0$$
$$= 1.0$$

Since floating-point numbers have limited precision and result in approximations of real results, $1.5_{ten} \times 10^{38}$ is so much larger than 1.0_{ten} that $1.5_{ten} \times 10^{38} + 1.0$ is still $1.5_{ten} \times 10^{38}$. That is why the sum of x, y, and z is 0.0 or 1.0, depending on the order of the floating-point additions, and hence floating-point add is *not* associative.

Fallacy: Just as a left shift instruction can replace an integer multiply by a power of 2, a right shift is the same as an integer division by a power of 2.

Recall that a binary number x, where xi means the ith bit, represents the number

$$\ldots + (x3 \times 2^3) + (x2 \times 2^2) + (x1 \times 2^1) + (x0 \times 2^0)$$

Shifting the bits of x right by n bits would seem to be the same as dividing by 2^n. And this *is* true for unsigned integers. The problem is with signed integers. For example, suppose we want to divide -5_{ten} by 4_{ten}; the quotient should be -1_{ten}. The two's complement representation of -5_{ten} is

1111 1111 1111 1111 1111 1111 1111 1011_{two}

According to this fallacy, shifting right by two should divide by 4_{ten} (2^2):

0011 1111 1111 1111 1111 1111 1111 1110_{two}

With a 0 in the sign bit, this result is clearly wrong. The value created by the shift right is actually $1,073,741,822_{ten}$ instead of -1_{ten}.

A solution would be to have an arithmetic right shift (see page 261) that extends the sign bit instead of shifting in 0s. A 2-bit arithmetic shift right of -5_{ten} produces

1111 1111 1111 1111 1111 1111 1111 1110_{two}

The result is -2_{ten} instead of -1_{ten}; close, but no cigar.

The PowerPC, however, does have a fast shift instruction (*shift right algebraic*) that in conjunction with a special add (add with carry) gives the same answer as dividing by a power of 2.

Pitfall: The MIPS instruction add immediate unsigned addiu *sign-extends its 16-bit immediate field.*

Despite its name, addiu is used to add constants to signed integers when we don't care about overflow. MIPS has no subtract immediate instruction and negative numbers need sign extension, so the MIPS architects decided to sign-extend the immediate field.

Fallacy: Only theoretical mathematicians care about floating-point accuracy.

Newspaper headlines of November 1994 prove this statement is a fallacy (see Figure 4.51). The following is the inside story behind the headlines.

The Pentium uses a standard floating-point divide algorithm that generates multiple quotient bits per step, using the most significant bits of divisor and dividend to guess the next 2 bits of the quotient. The guess is taken from a look-

FIGURE 4.51   A sampling of newspaper and magazine articles from November 1994, including the _New York Times, San Jose Mercury News, San Francisco Chronicle,_ and _Infoworld._ The Pentium floating-point divide bug even made the "Top 10 List" of the _David Letterman Late Show_ on television. Intel eventually took a $300 million write-off to replace the buggy chips.

up table containing −2, −1, 0, +1, or +2. The guess is multiplied by the divisor and subtracted from the remainder to generate a new remainder. Like nonrestoring division (see Exercise 4.54), if a previous guess gets too large a remainder, the partial remainder is adjusted in a subsequent pass.

Evidently there were five elements of the table from the 80486 that Intel thought could never be accessed, and they optimized the PLA to return 0 instead of 2 in these situations on the Pentium. Intel was wrong: while the first 11 bits were always correct, errors would show up occasionally in bits 12 to 52, or the 4th to 15th decimal digits.

The following is a time line of the Pentium bug morality play:

- _July 1994:_ Intel discovers the bug in the Pentium. The actual cost to fix the bug was several hundred thousand dollars. Following normal bug fix procedures, it will take months to make the change, reverify, and put the corrected chip into production. Intel planned to put good chips into production in January 1995, estimating that 3 to 5 million Pentiums would be produced with the bug.

- *September 1994:* A math professor at Lynchburg College in Virginia, Thomas Nicely, discovers the bug. After calling Intel technical support and getting no official reaction, he posts his discovery on the Internet. It quickly gained a following, and some pointed out that even small errors become big when multiplying by big numbers: the fraction of people with a rare disease times the population of Europe, for example, might lead to the wrong estimate of the number of sick people.

- *November 7, 1994: Electronic Engineering Times* puts the story on its front page, which is soon picked up by other newspapers.

- *November 22, 1994:* Intel issues a press release, calling it a "glitch." The Pentium "can make errors in the ninth digit. . . . Even most engineers and financial analysts require accuracy only to the fourth or fifth decimal point. Spreadsheet and word processor users need not worry. . . . There are maybe several dozen people that this would affect. So far, we've only heard from one. . . . [Only] theoretical mathematicians (with Pentium machines purchased before the summer) should be concerned." What irked many was that customers were told to describe their application to Intel, and then *Intel* would decide whether or not their application merited a new Pentium without the divide bug.

- *December 5, 1994:* Intel claims the flaw happens once in 27,000 years for the typical spreadsheet user. Intel assumes a user does 1000 divides per day and multiplies the error rate assuming floating-point numbers are random, which is one in 9 billion, and then gets 9 million days, or 27,000 years. Things begin to calm down, despite Intel neglecting to explain why a typical customer would access floating-point numbers randomly.

- *December 12, 1994:* IBM Research Division disputes Intel's calculation of the rate of errors (you can access this article by visiting *www.mkp.com/books_catalog/cod/links.htm*). IBM claims that common spreadsheet programs, recalculating for 15 minutes a day, could produce Pentium-related errors as often as once every 24 days. IBM assumes 5000 divides per second, 15 minutes, yielding 4.2 million divides per day, and does not assume random distribution of numbers, instead calculating the chances as one in 100 million. As a result, IBM immediately stops shipment of all IBM personal computers based on the Pentium. Things heat up again for Intel.

- *December 21, 1994:* Intel releases the following, signed by Intel's president, chief executive officer, chief operating officer, and chairman of the board: "We at Intel wish to sincerely apologize for our handling of the recently publicized Pentium processor flaw. The Intel Inside symbol means that your computer has a microprocessor second to none in quality and performance. Thousands of Intel employees work very hard to ensure that this is true. But no microprocessor is ever perfect. What Intel continues to believe is technically an extremely minor problem has taken on a life of its own. Although Intel firmly stands behind the quality of the current version of the Pentium processor, we recognize that many users have concerns. We want to resolve these concerns. Intel will exchange the current version of the Pentium processor for an updated version, in which this floating-point divide flaw is corrected, for any owner who requests it, free of charge anytime during the life of their computer." Analysts estimate that this recall cost Intel $300 million.

This story brings up a few points for everyone to ponder. How much cheaper would it have been to fix the bug in July 1994? What was the cost to repair the damage to Intel's reputation? And what is the corporate responsibility in disclosing bugs in a product so widely used and relied upon as a microprocessor?

In April 1997 another floating-point bug was revealed in the Pentium Pro and Pentium II microprocessors. When the floating-point-to-integer store instructions (`fist`, `fistp`) encounter a negative floating-point number that is too large to fit in a 16- or 32-bit word after being converted to integer, they set the wrong bit in the FPO status word (precision exception instead of invalid operation exception). To Intel's credit, this time they publicly acknowledged the bug and offered a software patch to get around it—quite a different reaction from what they did in 1994.

4.11 Concluding Remarks

Computer arithmetic is distinguished from paper-and-pencil arithmetic by the constraints of limited precision. This limit may result in invalid operations through calculating numbers larger or smaller than the predefined limits. Such anomalies, called "overflow" or "underflow," may result in exceptions or interrupts, emergency events similar to unplanned subroutine calls. Chapter 5 discusses exceptions in more detail.

Floating-point arithmetic has the added challenge of being an approximation of real numbers, and care needs to be taken to ensure that the computer number selected is the representation closest to the actual number. The challenges of imprecision and limited representation are part of the inspiration for the field of numerical analysis.

Over the years, computer arithmetic has become largely standardized, greatly enhancing the portability of programs. Two's complement binary integer arithmetic and IEEE 754 binary floating-point arithmetic are found in the vast majority of computers sold today. For example, every desktop computer sold since this book was first printed follows these conventions.

A side effect of the stored-program computer is that bit patterns have no inherent meaning. The same bit pattern may represent a signed integer, unsigned integer, floating-point number, instruction, and so on. It is the instruction that operates on the word that determines its meaning.

With the explanation of computer arithmetic in this chapter comes a description of much more of the MIPS instruction set. One point of confusion is the instructions covered in these chapters versus instructions executed by MIPS chips versus the instructions accepted by MIPS assemblers. The next two figures try to make this clear.

Figure 4.52 lists the MIPS instructions covered in Chapters 3 and 4. We call the set of instructions on the left-hand side of the figure the *MIPS core*. The instructions on the right we call the *MIPS arithmetic core*. On the left of Figure 4.53 are the instructions the MIPS processor executes that are not found in Figure 4.52. We call the full set of hardware instructions *MIPS I*. On the right of Figure 4.53 are the instructions accepted by the assembler that are not part of MIPS I. We call this set of instructions *Pseudo MIPS*.

MIPS core instructions	Name	Format	MIPS arithmetic core	Name	Format
add	add	R	multiply	mult	R
add immediate	addi	I	multiply unsigned	multu	R
add unsigned	addu	R	divide	div	R
add immediate unsigned	addiu	I	divide unsigned	divu	R
subtract	sub	R	move from Hi	mfhi	R
subtract unsigned	subu	R	move from Lo	mflo	R
and	and	R	move from system control (EPC)	mfc0	R
and immediate	andi	I	floating-point add single	add.s	R
or	or	R	floating-point add double	add.d	R
or immediate	ori	I	floating-point subtract single	sub.s	R
shift left logical	sll	R	floating-point subtract double	sub.d	R
shift right logical	srl	R	floating-point multiply single	mul.s	R
load upper immediate	lui	I	floating-point multiply double	mul.d	R
load word	lw	I	floating-point divide single	div.s	R
store word	sw	I	floating-point divide double	div.d	R
load byte unsigned	lbu	I	load word to floating-point single	lwc1	I
store byte	sb	I	store word to floating-point single	swc1	I
branch on equal	beq	I	branch on floating-point true	bc1t	I
branch on not equal	bne	I	branch on floating-point false	bc1f	I
jump	j	J	floating-point compare single	c.x.s	R
jump and link	jal	J	(x = eq, neq, lt, le, gt, ge)		
jump register	jr	R	floating-point compare double	c.x.d	R
set less than	slt	R	(x = eq, neq, lt, le, gt, ge)		
set less than immediate	slti	I			
set less than unsigned	sltu	R			
set less than immediate unsigned	sltiu	I			

FIGURE 4.52 The MIPS instruction set covered so far. This book concentrates on the instructions in the left column.

Figure 4.54 gives the popularity of the MIPS instructions for two programs: gcc and spice. All instructions are listed that were responsible for at least 0.5% of the instructions executed. The table following summarizes that information:

Instruction subset	gcc	spice
MIPS core	95%	45%
MIPS arithmetic core	0%	49%
Remaining MIPS I	5%	6%

Note that although programmers and compiler writers may use MIPS I to have a richer menu of options, MIPS core instructions dominate gcc execution, and the integer core plus arithmetic core dominate spice.

Remaining MIPS I	Name	Format	Pseudo MIPS	Name	Format
exclusive or ($rs \oplus rt$)	xor	R	move	move	rd,rs
exclusive or immediate	xori	I	absolute value	abs	rd,rs
nor ($\neg(rs \vee rt)$)	nor	R	not ($\neg rs$)	not	rd,rs
shift right arithmetic	sra	R	negate (signed or unsigned)	neg$s$	rd,rs
shift left logical variable	sllv	R	rotate left	rol	rd,rs,rt
shift right logical variable	srlv	R	rotate right	ror	rd,rs,rt
shift right arith. variable	srav	R	mult. & don't check oflw (signed or uns.)	mul$s$	rd,rs,rt
shift right arith. variable	srav	R	multiply & check oflw (signed or uns.)	mulo$s$	rd,rs,rt
move to Hi	mthi	R	divide and check overflow	div	rd,rs,rt
move to Lo	mtlo	R	divide and don't check overflow	divu	rd,rs,rt
load halfword	lh	I	remainder (signed or unsigned)	rem$s$	rd,rs,rt
load halfword unsigned	lhu	I	load immediate	li	rd,imm
store halfword	sh	I	load address	la	rd,addr
load word left (unaligned)	lwl	I	load double	ld	rd,addr
load word right (unaligned)	lwr	I	store double	sd	rd,addr
store word left (unaligned)	swl	I	unaligned load word	ulw	rd,addr
store word right (unaligned)	swr	I	unaligned store word	usw	rd,addr
branch on less than zero	bltz	I	unaligned load halfword (signed or uns.)	ulh$s$	rd,addr
branch on less or equal zero	blez	I	unaligned store halfword	ush	rd,addr
branch on greater than zero	bgtz	I	branch	b	Label
branch on $\geq$ zero	bgez	I	branch on equal zero	beqz	rs,L
branch on $\geq$ zero and link	bgezal	I	branch on $\geq$ (signed or unsigned)	bge$s$	rs,rt,L
branch on < zero and link	bgezal	I	branch on > (signed or unsigned)	bgt$s$	rs,rt,L
jump and link register	jalr	R	branch on $\leq$ (signed or unsigned)	ble$s$	rs,rt,L
return from exception	rfe	R	branch on < (signed or unsigned)	blt$s$	rs,rt,L
system call	syscall	R	set equal	seq	rd,rs,rt
break (cause exception)	break	R	set not equal	sne	rd,rs,rt
move from FP to integer	mfc1	R	set greater or equal (signed or unsigned)	sge$s$	rd,rs,rt
move to FP from integer	mtc1	R	set greater than (signed or unsigned)	sgt$s$	rd,rs,rt
FP move (s or d)	mov$f$	R	set less or equal (signed or unsigned)	sle$s$	rd,rs,rt
FP absolute value (s or d)	abs$f$	R	set less than (signed or unsigned)	sle$s$	rd,rs,rt
FP negate (s or d)	neg$f$	R	load to floating point (s or d)	lf	rd,addr
FP convert (w, s, or d)	cvtff	R	store from floating point (s or d)	sf	rd,addr
FP compare un (s or d)	c.xn$f$	R			

FIGURE 4.53   Remaining MIPS I and "Pseudo MIPS" instruction sets. Appendix A describes all these instructions. f means single (s) and double precision (d) versions of the floating-point instruction, and s means signed and unsigned (u) versions.

Core MIPS	Name	gcc	spice	Arithmetic core + MIPS I	Name	gcc	spice
add	add	0%	0%	FP add double	add.d	0%	4%
add immediate	addi	0%	0%	FP subtract double	sub.d	0%	3%
add unsigned	addu	9%	10%	FP multiply double	mul.d	0%	5%
add immediate unsigned	addiu	17%	1%	FP divide double	div.d	0%	2%
subtract unsigned	subu	0%	1%	load word to FP single	l.s	0%	24%
and	and	1%	0%	store word to FP single	s.s	0%	9%
and immediate	andi	2%	1%	branch on FP true	bc1t	0%	1%
shift left logical	sll	5%	5%	branch on FP false	bc1f	0%	1%
shift right logical	srl	0%	1%	FP compare double	c.x.d	0%	1%
load upper immediate	lui	2%	6%	move to FP	mtc1	0%	2%
load word	lw	21%	7%	move from FP	mfc2	0%	2%
store word	sw	12%	2%	convert float integer	cut	0%	1%
load byte	lb	1%	0%	shift right arithmetic	sra	2%	0%
store byte	sb	1%	0%	load half	lh	1%	0%
branch on equal (zero)	beq	9%	3%	branch less than zero	bltz	1%	0%
branch on not equal (zero)	bne	8%	2%	branch greater or equal zero	bgez	1%	0%
jump and link	jal	1%	1%	branch less or equal zero	blez	0%	1%
jump register	jr	1%	1%				
set less than	slt	2%	0%				
set less than immediate	slti	1%	0%				
set less than unsigned	sltu	1%	0%				
set less than imm. uns.	sltiu	1%	0%				

FIGURE 4.54 The frequency of the MIPS instructions for two programs, gcc and spice. Calculated from "pixie" output of the full MIPS I. (Pixie is an instruction measurement tool from MIPS.) All instructions that accounted for at least 0.5% of the instructions executed in either gcc or spice are included in the table. Thus the integer multiply and divide instructions are not listed because they were responsible for less than 0.5% of the instructions executed. Pseudoinstructions are converted into MIPS I before execution, and hence do not appear here.

For the rest of the book, we concentrate on the MIPS core instructions—the integer instruction set excluding multiply and divide—to make the explanation of computer design easier. As we can see, the MIPS core includes the most popular MIPS instructions, and be assured that understanding a computer that runs the MIPS core will give you sufficient background to understand even more ambitious machines.

4.12 Historical Perspective and Further Reading

Gresham's Law ("Bad money drives out Good") for computers would say, "The Fast drives out the Slow even if the Fast is wrong."

W. Kahan, 1992

At first it may be hard to imagine a subject of less interest than the correctness of computer arithmetic or its accuracy, and harder still to understand why a subject so old and mathematical should be so controversial. Computer arithmetic is as old as computing itself, and some of the subject's earliest notions, like the economical reuse of registers during serial multiplication and division, still command respect today. Maurice Wilkes [1985] recalled a conversation about that notion during his visit to the United States in 1946, before the earliest stored-program machine had been built:

> . . . a project under von Neumann was to be set up at the Institute of Advanced Studies in Princeton. . . . Goldstine explained to me the principal features of the design, including the device whereby the digits of the multiplier were put into the tail of the accumulator and shifted out as the least significant part of the product was shifted in. I expressed some admiration at the way registers and shifting circuits were arranged . . . and Goldstine remarked that things of that nature came very easily to von Neumann.

There is no controversy here; it can hardly arise in the context of exact integer arithmetic so long as there is general agreement on what integer the correct result should be. However, as soon as approximate arithmetic enters the picture, so does controversy, as if one person's "negligible" must be another's "everything."

The First Dispute

Floating-point arithmetic kindled disagreement before it was ever built. John von Neumann was aware of Konrad Zuse's proposal for a computer in Germany in 1939 that was never built, probably because the floating point made it appear too complicated to finish before the Germans expected World War II to end. Hence von Neumann refused to include it in the machine he built at Princeton. In an influential report coauthored in 1946 with H. H. Goldstine and A. W. Burks, he gave the arguments for and against floating point. In favor:

> . . . to retain in a sum or product as many significant digits as possible and . . . to free the human operator from the burden of estimating and inserting into a problem "scale factors"—multiplication constants which serve to keep numbers within the limits of the machine.

Floating point was excluded for several reasons:

> *There is, of course, no denying the fact that human time is consumed in arranging for the introduction of suitable scale factors. We only argue that the time consumed is a very small percentage of the total time we will spend in preparing an interesting problem for our machine. The first advantage of the floating point is, we feel, somewhat illusory. In order to have such a floating point, one must waste memory capacity which could otherwise be used for carrying more digits per word. It would therefore seem to us not at all clear whether the modest advantages of a floating binary point offset the loss of memory capacity and the increased complexity of the arithmetic and control circuits.*

The argument seems to be that most bits devoted to exponent fields would be bits wasted. Experience has proved otherwise.

One software approach to accommodate reals without floating-point hardware was called *floating vectors*; the idea was to compute at runtime one scale factor for a whole array of numbers, choosing the scale factor so that the array's biggest number would barely fill its field. By 1951, James H. Wilkinson had used this scheme extensively for matrix computations. The problem proved to be that a program might encounter a very large value, and hence the scale factor must accommodate these rare large numbers. The common numbers would thus have many leading 0s, since all numbers had to use a single scale factor. Accuracy was sacrificed because the least significant bits had to be lost on the right to accommodate leading 0s. This wastage became obvious to practitioners on early machines that displayed all their memory bits as dots on cathode ray tubes (like TV screens) because the loss of precision was visible. Where floating point deserved to be used, no practical alternative existed.

Thus true floating-point hardware became popular because it was useful. By 1957, floating-point hardware was almost ubiquitous. A decimal floating-point unit was available for the IBM 650; and soon the IBM 704, 709, 7090, 7094 . . . series would offer binary floating-point hardware for double as well as single precision.

As a result, everybody had floating point, but every implementation was different.

Diversity versus Portability

Since roundoff introduces some error into almost all floating-point operations, to complain about another bit of error seems picayune. So for 20 years nobody complained much that those operations behaved a little differently on different machines. If software required clever tricks to circumvent those idiosyncrasies and finally deliver results correct in all but the last several bits, such tricks were deemed part of the programmer's art. For a long time, matrix computations mystified most people who had no notion of error analysis; perhaps this continues to be true. That may be why people are still surprised that numerically stable matrix computations depend upon the quality of arithmetic in so few places, far fewer than are generally supposed. Books by Wilkinson and widely used software packages like Linpack and Eispack sustained a false impression, widespread in the early 1970s, that a modicum of skill sufficed to produce *portable* numerical software.

Portable here means that the software is distributed as source code in some standard language to be compiled and executed on practically any commercially significant machine, and that it will then perform its task as well as any other program performs that task on that machine. Insofar as numerical software has often been thought to consist entirely of machine-independent mathematical formulas, its portability has often been taken for granted; the mistake in that presumption will become clear shortly.

Packages like Linpack and Eispack cost so much to develop—over a hundred dollars per line of Fortran delivered—that they could not have been developed without U.S. government subsidy; their portability was a precondition for that subsidy. But nobody thought to distinguish how various components contributed to their cost. One component was algorithmic—devise an algorithm that deserves to work on at least one computer despite its roundoff and over/underflow limitations. Another component was the software engineering effort required to achieve and confirm portability to the diverse computers commercially significant at the time; this component grew more onerous as ever more diverse floating-point arithmetics blossomed in the 1970s.

And yet scarcely anybody realized how much that diversity inflated the cost of such software packages.

A Backward Step

Early evidence that somewhat different arithmetics could engender grossly different software development costs was presented in 1964. It happened at a meeting of SHARE, the IBM mainframe users' group, at which IBM announced System/360, the successor to the 7094 series. One of the speakers described the tricks he had been forced to devise to achieve a level of quality for the S/360 library that was not quite so high as he had previously achieved for the 7094.

Part of the trouble could have been foretold by von Neumann had he still been alive. In 1948 he and Goldstine had published a lengthy error analysis so difficult and so pessimistic that hardly anybody paid attention to it. It did predict correctly, however, that computations with larger arrays of data would probably fall prey to roundoff more often. IBM S/360s had bigger memories than 7094s, so data arrays could grow bigger, and they did. To make matters worse, the S/360s had narrower single precision words (32 bits versus 36) and used a cruder arithmetic (hexadecimal or base 16 versus binary or base 2) with consequently poorer worst-case precision (21 significant bits versus 27) than old 7094s. Consequently, software that had almost always provided (barely) satisfactory accuracy on 7094s too often produced inaccurate results when run on S/360s. The quickest way to recover adequate accuracy was to replace old codes' single precision declarations with double precision before recompilation for the S/360. This practice exercised S/360 double precision far more than had been expected.

The early S/360s' worst troubles were caused by lack of a guard digit in double precision. This lack showed up in multiplication as a failure of identities like $1.0 * x = x$ because multiplying x by 1.0 dropped x's last hexadecimal digit (4 bits). Similarly, if x and y were very close but had different exponents, subtraction dropped off the last digit of the smaller operand before computing $x - y$. This last aberration in double precision undermined a precious theorem that single precision then (and now) honored: If $1/2 \leq x/y \leq 2$, then no rounding error can occur when $x - y$ is computed; it must be computed exactly.

Innumerable computations had benefited from this minor theorem, most often unwittingly, for several decades before its first formal announcement and proof. We had been taking all this stuff for granted.

The identities and theorems about exact relationships that persisted, despite roundoff, with reasonable implementations of approximate arithmetic were not appreciated until they were lost. Previously, all that had been thought to matter were precision (how many significant digits were carried) and range (the spread between over/underflow thresholds). Since the S/360s' double precision had more precision and wider range than the 7094s', software was expected to continue to work at least as well as before. But it didn't.

Programmers who had matured into program managers were appalled at the cost of converting 7094 software to run on S/360s. A small subcommittee of SHARE proposed improvements to the S/360 floating point. This committee was surprised and grateful to get a fair part of what they asked for from IBM, including all-important guard digits. By 1968, these had been retrofitted to S/360s in the field at considerable expense; worse than that was customers' loss of faith in IBM's infallibility (a lesson learned by Intel 30 years later). IBM employees who can remember the incident still shudder.

The People Who Built the Bombs

Seymour Cray was associated for decades with the CDC and Cray computers that were, when he built them, the world's biggest and fastest. He always understood what his customers wanted most: *speed*. And he gave it to them even if, in so doing, he also gave them arithmetics more "interesting" than anyone else's. Among his customers have been the great government laboratories like those at Livermore and Los Alamos, where nuclear weapons were designed. The challenges of "interesting" arithmetics were pretty tame to people who had to overcome Mother Nature's challenges.

Perhaps all of us could learn to live with arithmetic idiosyncrasy if only one computer's idiosyncrasies had to be endured. Instead, when accumulating different computers' different anomalies, software dies the Death of a Thousand Cuts. Here is an example from Cray's machines:

```
if (x == 0.0)   y = 17.0 else y = z/x
```

Could this statement be stopped by a divide-by-zero error? On a CDC 6600 it could. The reason was a conflict between the 6600's adder, where x was compared with 0.0, and the multiplier and divider. The adder's comparison examined x's leading 13 bits, which sufficed to distinguish zero from normal nonzero floating-point numbers x. The multiplier and divider examined only 12 leading bits. Consequently, tiny numbers existed that were nonzero to the adder but zero to the multiplier and divider! To avoid disasters with these tiny numbers, programmers learned to replace statements like the one above by

```
if (1.0*x == 0.0)   y = 17.0 else y = z/x
```

But this statement is unsafe to use in would-be portable software because it malfunctions obscurely on other computers designed by Cray, the ones marketed by Cray Research, Inc. If x is so huge that 2.0 * x would overflow, then 1.0 * x may overflow too! Overflow happens because Cray computers check the product's exponent *before* the product's exponent has been normalized, just to save the delay of a single AND gate.

In case you think the statement above is safe to use now for portable software, since computers of the CDC 6600 era are no longer commercially significant, you should be warned that it can lead to overflow on a Cray computer even if z is almost as tiny as x; the trouble here is that the Cray computes not z/x but z * (1/x), and the reciprocal can overflow even though the desired quotient is unexceptionable. A similar difficulty troubles the Intel i860s used in its massively parallel computers. The would-be programmer of portable code faces countless dilemmas like these whenever trying to program for the full range of existing computers.

Rounding error anomalies that are far worse than the over/underflow anomaly just discussed also affect Cray computers. The worst error comes from the lack of a guard digit in add/subtract, an affliction of IBM S/360s. Further bad luck for software is occasioned by the way Cray economized his multiplier; about one-third of the bits that normal multiplier arrays generate have been left out of his multipliers because they would contribute less than a unit to the last place of the final Cray-rounded product. Consequently, a Cray's multiplier errs by almost a bit more than might have been expected. This error is compounded when division takes three multiplications to improve an approximate reciprocal of the divisor and then multiply the numerator by it. Square root compounds a few more multiplication errors.

The fast way drove out the slow, even though the fast was occasionally slightly wrong.

Making the World Safe for Floating Point, or Vice Versa

William Kahan was an undergraduate at the University of Toronto in 1953 when he learned to program its Ferranti-Manchester Mark-I computer. Because he entered the field early, Kahan became acquainted with a wide range of devices and a large proportion of the personalities active in computing; the numbers of both were small at that time. He has performed computations on slide rules, desktop mechanical calculators, tabletop analog differential analyzers, and so on; he used all but the earliest electronic computers and calculators mentioned in this book.

Kahan's desire to deliver reliable software led to an interest in error analysis that intensified during two years of postdoctoral study in England, where he became acquainted with Wilkinson. In 1960, he resumed teaching at Toronto, where an IBM 7090 had been acquired, and was granted free rein to tinker with its operating system, Fortran compiler, and runtime library. (He denies that he ever came near the 7090 hardware with a soldering iron but admits asking to do so.) One story from that time illuminates how misconceptions and numerical anomalies in computer systems can incur awesome hidden costs.

A graduate student in aeronautical engineering used the 7090 to simulate the wings he was designing for short takeoffs and landings. He knew such a wing would be difficult to control if its characteristics included an abrupt onset of stall, but he thought he could avoid that. His simulations were telling him otherwise. Just to be sure that roundoff was not interfering, he had repeated many of his calculations in double precision and gotten results much like those in single; his wings had stalled abruptly in both precisions. Disheartened, the student gave up.

Meanwhile Kahan replaced IBM's logarithm program (ALOG) with one of his own, which he hoped would provide better accuracy. While testing it, Kahan reran programs using the new version of ALOG. The student's results changed significantly; Kahan approached him to find out what had happened.

The student was puzzled. Much as the student preferred the results produced with the new ALOG—they predicted a gradual stall—he knew they must be wrong because they disagreed with his double precision results. The discrepancy between single and double precision results disappeared a few days later when a new release of IBM's double precision arithmetic software for the 7090 arrived. (The 7090 had no double precision hardware.) He went on to write a thesis about it and to build the wings; they performed as predicted. But that is not the end of the story.

In 1963, the 7090 was replaced by a faster 7094 with double precision floating-point hardware but with otherwise practically the same instruction set as the 7090. Only in double precision and only when using the new hardware did the wing stall abruptly again. A lot of time was spent to find out why. The 7094 hardware turned out, like the superseded 7090 software and the subsequent early S/360s, to lack a guard bit in double precision. Like so many programmers on those machines and on Cray's, the student discovered a trick to compensate for the lack of a guard digit; he wrote the expression $(0.5 - x)$ $+ 0.5$ in place of $1.0 - x$. Nowadays we would blush if we had to explain why such a trick might be necessary, but it solved the student's problem.

Meanwhile the lure of California was working on Kahan and his family; they came to Berkeley and he to the University of California. An opportunity presented itself in 1974 when accuracy questions induced Hewlett-Packard's calculator designers to call in a consultant. The consultant was Kahan, and his work dramatically improved the accuracy of HP calculators, but that is another story. Fruitful collaboration with congenial co-workers, however, fortified him for the next and crucial opportunity.

It came in 1976, when John F. Palmer at Intel was empowered to specify the "best possible" floating-point arithmetic for all of Intel's product line. The 8086 was imminent, and an 8087 floating-point coprocessor for the 8086 was contemplated. (A *coprocessor* is simply an additional chip that accelerates a portion of the work of a processor; in this case, it accelerated floating-point computation.)

Palmer had obtained his Ph.D. at Stanford a few years before and knew whom to call for counsel of perfection—Kahan. They put together a design that obviously would have been impossible only a few years earlier and looked not quite possible at the time. But a new Israeli team of Intel employees led by Rafi Navé felt challenged to prove their prowess to Americans and leaped at an opportunity to put something impossible on a chip—the 8087.

By now, floating-point arithmetics that had been merely diverse among mainframes had become chaotic among microprocessors, one of which might be host to a dozen varieties of arithmetic in ROM firmware or software. Robert G. Stewart, an engineer prominent in IEEE activities, got fed up with this anarchy and proposed that the IEEE draft a decent floating-point standard. Simultaneously, word leaked out in Silicon Valley that Intel was going to put on one chip some awesome floating point well beyond anything its competitors had in mind. The competition had to find a way to slow Intel down, so they formed a committee to do what Stewart requested.

Meetings of this committee began in late 1977 with a plethora of competing drafts from innumerable sources and dragged on into 1985 when IEEE Standard 754 for Binary Floating Point was made official. The winning draft was very close to one submitted by Kahan, his student Jerome T. Coonen, and Harold S. Stone, a professor visiting Berkeley at the time. Their draft was based on the Intel design, with Intel's permission of course, as simplified by Coonen. Their harmonious combination of features, almost none of them new, had at the outset attracted more support within the committee and from outside experts like Wilkinson than any other draft, but they had to win nearly unanimous support within the committee to win official IEEE endorsement, and that took time.

The First IEEE 754 Chips

In 1980, Intel became tired of waiting and released the 8087 for use in the IBM PC. The floating-point architecture of the companion 8087 had to be retro-fitted into the 8086 opcode space, making it inconvenient to offer two operands per instruction as found in the rest of the 8086. Hence the decision for one operand per instruction using a stack: "The designer's task was to make a Virtue of this Necessity." (Kahan's [1990] history of the stack architecture selection for the 8087 is entertaining reading.)

Rather than the classical stack architecture, which has no provision for avoiding common subexpressions from being pushed and popped from memory into the top of the stack found in registers, Intel tried to combine a flat register file with a stack. The reasoning was that the restriction of the top of stack as one operand was not so bad since it only required the execution of an FXCH instruction (which swapped registers) to get the same result as a two-operand instruction, and FXCH was much faster than the floating-point operations of the 8087.

Since floating-point expressions are not that complex, Kahan reasoned that eight registers meant that the stack would rarely overflow. Hence he urged that the 8087 use this hybrid scheme with the provision that stack overflow or stack underflow would interrupt the 8086 so that interrupt software could give the illusion to the compiler writer of an unlimited stack for floating-point data.

The Intel 8087 was implemented in Israel, and 7500 miles and 10 time zones made communication difficult from California. According to Palmer and Morse (*The 8087 Primer*, J. Wiley, New York, 1984, p. 93):

Unfortunately, nobody tried to write a software stack manager until after the 8087 was built, and by then it was too late; what was too complicated to perform in hardware turned out to be even worse in software. One thing found lacking is the ability to conveniently determine if an invalid operation is indeed due to a stack overflow. . . . Also lacking is the ability to restart the instruction that caused the stack overflow . . .

The result is that the stack exceptions are too slow to handle in software. As Kahan [1990] says:

Consequently, almost all higher-level languages' compilers emit inefficient code for the 80x87 family, degrading the chip's performance by typically 50% with spurious stores and loads necessary simply to preclude stack over/underflow. . . .

I still regret that the 8087's stack implementation was not quite so neat as my original intention. . . . If the original design had been realized, compilers today would use the 80x87 and its descendents more efficiently, and Intel's competitors could more easily market faster but compatible 80x87 imitations.

In 1982, Motorola announced its 68881, which found a place in Sun 3s and Macintosh IIs; Apple had been a supporter of the proposal from the beginning. Another Berkeley graduate student, George S. Taylor, had soon designed a high-speed implementation of the proposed standard for an early supermini-computer (ELXSI 6400). The standard was becoming de facto before its final draft's ink was dry.

An early rush of adoptions gave the computing industry the false impression that IEEE 754, like so many other standards, could be implemented easily by following a standard recipe. Not true. Only the enthusiasm and ingenuity of its early implementors made it look easy.

In fact, to implement IEEE 754 correctly demands extraordinarily diligent attention to detail; to make it run fast demands extraordinarily competent ingenuity of design. Had the industry's engineering managers realized this, they might not have been so quick to affirm that, as a matter of policy, "We conform to all applicable standards."

IEEE 754 Today

Today the computing industry is enmeshed in a host of standards that evolve continuously as technology changes. The floating-point standards IEEE 754/854 (they are practically the same) stand in somewhat splendid isolation only because nobody wishes to repeat the protracted wrangling that surrounded their birth, when, with unprecedented generosity, the representatives of hardware interests acceded to the demands of those few who represented the interests of mathematical and numerical software.

Unfortunately, the compiler-writing community was not represented adequately in the wrangling, and some of the features didn't balance language and compiler issues against other points. That community has been slow to make IEEE 754's unusual features available to the applications programmer. Humane exception handling is one such unusual feature; directed rounding another. Without compiler support, these features have atrophied.

The successful parts of IEEE 754 are that it is a widely implemented standard with a common floating-point format, it requires minimum accuracy to one-half ulp in the least significant bit, and that operations must be commutative.

At present, IEEE 754/854 have been implemented to a considerable degree of fidelity in at least part of the product line of every North American computer manufacturer. The only significant exceptions are the DEC VAX, IBM S/370 descendants, and Cray Research vector supercomputers, and all three are being replaced by compliant machines. Even Cray Research, now a division of Silicon Graphics, announced that successors to the T90 vector computer will conform "to some degree" to ease the transfer of data files and portable software between Crays and the desktop computers through which Cray users have come to access their machines nowadays.

In 1989, the Association for Computing Machinery, acknowledging the benefits conferred upon the computing industry by IEEE 754, honored Kahan with the Turing Award. On accepting it, he thanked his many associates for their diligent support, and his adversaries for their blunders.

So . . . not all errors are bad.

To Probe Further

If you are interested in learning more about floating point, two publications by David Goldberg [1991, 1995] are good starting points; they abound with pointers to further reading. Several of the stories told above come from Kahan [1972, 1983]. The latest word on the state of the art in computer arithmetic is often found in the *Proceedings* of the latest IEEE-sponsored Symposium on Computer Arithmetic, held every two years; the 13th was held in 1997.

Burks, A. W., H. H. Goldstine, and J. von Neumann [1946]. "Preliminary discussion of the logical design of an electronic computing instrument," *Report to the U.S. Army Ordnance Dept.*, p. 1; also in *Papers of John von Neumann*, W. Aspray and A. Burks, eds., MIT Press, Cambridge, MA, and Tomash Publishers, Los Angeles, 97–146, 1987.

This classic paper includes arguments against floating-point hardware.

Goldberg, D. [1991]. "What every computer scientist should know about floating-point arithmetic," *ACM Computing Surveys* 23(1), 5–48.

Another good introduction to floating-point arithmetic by the same author, this time with emphasis on software.

Goldberg, D. [1995]. "Computer arithmetic," *Appendix A of Computer Architecture: A Quantitative Approach*, second edition, J. L. Hennessy and D. A. Patterson, Morgan Kaufmann Publishers, San Francisco.

A more advanced introduction to integer and floating-point arithmetic, with emphasis on hardware. It covers sections 4.6–4.8 of this book in just 10 pages, leaving another 45 pages for advanced topics.

Kahan, W. [1972]. "A survey of error-analysis," in *Info. Processing 71* (Proc. IFIP Congress 71 in Ljubljana), vol. 2, pp. 1214–39, North-Holland Publishing, Amsterdam.

This survey is a source of stories on the importance of accurate arithmetic.

Kahan, W. [1983]. "Mathematics written in sand," *Proc. Amer. Stat. Assoc. Joint Summer Meetings of 1983, Statistical Computing Section*, pp. 12–26.

The title refers to silicon and is another source of stories illustrating the importance of accurate arithmetic.

Kahan, W. [1990]. "On the advantage of the 8087's stack," unpublished course notes, Computer Science Division, University of California at Berkeley.

What the 8087 floating-point architecture could have been.

Kahan, W. [1997]. Available via a link to Kahan's homepage at *www.mkp.com/books_catalog/ cod/links.htm*.

A collection of memos related to floating point, including "Beastly Numbers" (another less famous Pentium bug)," Notes on the IEEE Floating Point Arithmetic" (including comments on how some features are atrophying), and "The Baleful Effects of Computing Benchmarks" (on the unhealthy preoccupation on speed versus correctness, accuracy, ease of use, flexibility, . . .).

Koren, I. [1993]. *Computer Arithmetic Algorithms*, Prentice Hall, Englewood Cliffs, NJ.

A textbook aimed at seniors and first-year graduate students that explains fundamental principles of basic arithmetic, as well as complex operations such as logarithmic and trigonometric functions.

Wilkes, M. V. [1985]. *Memoirs of a Computer Pioneer*, MIT Press, Cambridge, MA.

This computer pioneer's recollections include the derivation of the standard hardware for multiply and divide developed by von Neumann.

4.13   Key Terms

These terms reflect the key ideas in the chapter. Check the Glossary for definitions of the terms you are unsure of.

AND gate	floating point	round
AND operation	guard	scientific notation
arithmetic logic unit (ALU)	hexadecimal	significand
biased notation	least significant bit	single precision
Booth's algorithm	most significant bit	sticky bit
divisor	normalized	underflow
double precision	overflow	units in the last place (ulp)
exclusive OR gate	quotient	
exponent	remainder	

4.14   Exercises

Never give in, never give in, never, never, never—in nothing, great or small, large or petty—never give in.

Winston Churchill, address at Harrow School, 1941

4.1 [3] <§4.2> Convert 512_{ten} into a 32-bit two's complement binary number.

4.2 [3] <§4.2> Convert $-1,023_{ten}$ into a 32-bit two's complement binary number.

4.3 [5] <§4.2> Convert $-4,000,000_{ten}$ into a 32-bit two's complement binary number.

4.4 [5] <§4.2> What decimal number does this two's complement binary number represent: $1111\ 1111\ 1111\ 1111\ 1111\ 1110\ 0000\ 1100_{two}$?

4.5 [5] <§4.2> What decimal number does this two's complement binary number represent: $1111\ 1111\ 1111\ 1111\ 1111\ 1111\ 1111\ 1111_{two}$?

4.6 [5] <§4.2> What decimal number does this two's complement binary number represent: $0111\ 1111\ 1111\ 1111\ 1111\ 1111\ 1111\ 1111_{two}$?

4.7 [5] <§4.2> What binary number does this hexadecimal number represent: $7fff\ fffa_{hex}$? What decimal number does it represent?

4.8 [5] <§4.2> What hexadecimal number does this binary number represent: $1100\ 1010\ 1111\ 1110\ 1111\ 1010\ 1100\ 1110_{two}$?

4.9 [5] <§4.2> Why doesn't MIPS have a subtract immediate instruction?

4.10 [10] <§4.2> Find the shortest sequence of MIPS instructions to determine the absolute value of a two's complement integer. Convert this instruction (accepted by the MIPS assembler):

```
abs    $t2,$t3
```

This instruction means that register $t2 has a copy of register $t3 if register $t3 is positive, and the two's complement of register $t3 if $t3 is negative. (Hint: It can be done with three instructions.)

4.11 [10] <§4.2> Two friends, Harry and David, are arguing. Harry says, "All integers greater than zero and exactly divisible by six have exactly two 1s in their binary representation." David disagrees. He says, "No, but all such numbers have an even number of 1s in their representation." Do you agree with Harry or with David, or with neither? (Hint: Look for counterexamples.)

4.12 [15] <§4.4> Consider the following code used to implement the instruction

```
sllv $s0, $s1, $s2
```

which uses the least significant 5 bits of the value in register $s2 to specify the amount register $s1 should be shifted left:

```
         .data
mask:    .word  0xffffff83f
         .text
start:   lw     $t0, mask
         lw     $s0, shifter
         and    $s0,$s0,$t0
         andi   $s2,$s2,0x1f
         sll    $s2,$s2,6
         or     $s0,$s0,$s2
         sw     $s0, shifter
shifter: sll    $s0,$s1,0
```

Add comments to the code and write a paragraph describing how it works. Note that the two `lw` instructions are pseudoinstructions that use a label to specify a memory address that contains the word of data to be loaded. Why do you suppose that writing "self-modifying code" such as this is a bad idea (and oftentimes not actually allowed)?

4.13 [10] <§4.2> If A is a 32-bit address, typically an instruction sequence such as

```
lui $t0, A_upper
ori $t0, $t0, A_lower
lw $s0, 0($t0)
```

can be used to load the word at A into a register (in this case, $s0). Consider the following alternative, which is more efficient:

```
lui $t0, A_upper_adjusted
lw $s0, A_lower($t0)
```

Describe how A_upper is adjusted to allow this simpler code to work. (Hint: A_upper needs to be adjusted because A_lower will be sign-extended.)

4.14 [15] <§§3.4, 4.2, 4.8> The Big Picture on page 299 mentions that bits have no inherent meaning. Given the bit pattern:

1000 1111 1110 1111 1100 0000 0000 0000

what does it represent, assuming that it is

   a. a two's complement integer?

   b. an unsigned integer?

   c. a single precision floating-point number?

   d. a MIPS instruction?

You may find Figures 3.18 (page 153), 4.48 (page 292), and A.18 (page A-50) useful.

4.15 [10] <§§4.2, 4.4, 4.8> This exercise is similar to Exercise 4.14, but this time use the bit pattern

0000 0000 0000 0000 0000 0000 0000 0000

4.16 [10] <§4.3> One of the differences between Sun's SPARC architecture and the MIPS architecture we've been studying is that the load word instruction on the SPARC can specify the address either as the sum of two registers'

contents or as one register's contents plus a constant offset (i.e., the way MIPS does). The paper "An analysis of MIPS and SPARC instruction set utilization on the SPEC benchmarks" (R. F. Cmelik, S. I. Kong, D. R. Ditzel, and E. J. Kelly, *Fourth International Conference on Architectural Support for Programming Languages and Operating Systems*, Santa Clara, CA, April 1991) reports that on the SPARC, the gcc benchmark has 15% of its loads use the register + register version (with neither register being $zero). Assume that the same would be true on the MIPS, if it were modified to have this extra addressing option for lw instructions. Using the data from Figure 4.54, what percentage of gcc's instructions could be eliminated with this architectural modification? Why?

4.17 [10] <§4.3> Find the shortest sequence of MIPS instructions to determine if there is a carry out from the addition of two registers, say, registers $t3 and $t4. Place a 0 or 1 in register $t2 if the carry out is 0 or 1, respectively. (Hint: It can be done in two instructions.)

4.18 [15] <§4.3> {Ex. 4.17} Find the shortest sequence of MIPS instructions to perform double precision integer addition. Assume that one 64-bit, two's complement integer is in registers $t4 and $t5 and another is in registers $t6 and $t7. The sum is to be placed in registers $t2 and $t3. In this example, the most significant word of the 64-bit integer is found in the even-numbered registers, and the least significant word is found in the odd-numbered registers. (Hint: It can be done in four instructions.)

4.19 [15] <§4.3> Suppose that all of the conditional branch instructions except beq and bne were removed from the MIPS instruction set along with slt and all of its variants (slti, sltu, sltui). Show how to perform

```
slt $t0, $s0, $s1
```

using the modified instruction set in which slt is not available. (Hint: It requires more than two instructions.)

4.20 [10] <§4.4> The following MIPS instruction sequence could be used to implement a new instruction that has two register operands. Give the instruction a name and describe what it does. Note that register $t0 is being used as a temporary.

```
srl $s1, $s1, 1    #
sll $t0, $s0, 31   # These 4 instructions accomplish
srl $s0, $s0, 1    # "new $s0 $s1"
or  $s1, $s1, $t0  #
```

4.21 [5] <§4.4> Instead of using a special hardware multiplier, it is possible to multiply using shift and add instructions. This is particularly attractive when multiplying by small constants. Suppose we want to put five times the value of $s0 into $s1, ignoring any overflow that may occur. Show a minimal sequence of MIPS instructions for doing this without using a multiply instruction.

4.22 [15] <§4.4> Some computers have explicit instructions to extract an arbitrary field from a 32-bit register and to place it in the least significant bits of a register. The figure below shows the desired operation:

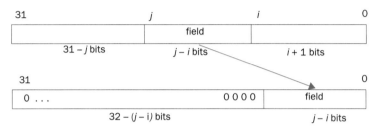

Find the shortest sequence of MIPS instructions that extracts a field for the constant values $i = 7$ and $j = 19$ from register $s0 and places it in register $s1. (Hint: It can be done in two instructions.)

4.23 [15] <§4.5> The ALU supported set on less than (slt) using just the sign bit of the adder. Let's try a set on less than operation using the values -7_{ten} and 6_{ten}. To make it simpler to follow the example, let's limit the binary representations to 4 bits: 1001_{two} and 0110_{two}.

$$1001_{two} - 0110_{two} = 1001_{two} + 1010_{two} = 0011_{two}$$

This result would suggest that $-7 > 6$, which is clearly wrong. Hence we must factor in overflow in the decision. Modify the 1-bit ALU in Figure 4.17 on page 238 to handle slt correctly. Make your changes on a photocopy of this figure to save time.

4.24 [20] <§4.6> Find the shortest sequence of MIPS instructions to perform double precision integer multiplication. Try to do it in 35 instructions or less. Assume that one 64-bit, *unsigned* integer is in registers $t4 and $t5 and another is in registers $t6 and $t7. The 128-bit product is to be placed in registers $t0, $t1, $t2, and $t3. In this example, the most significant word is found in the lower-numbered registers, and the least significant word is found in the higher-numbered registers. (Hint: Write out the formula for $(a \times 2^{32} + b) \times (c \times 2^{32} + d)$.)

4.25 [5] <§4.8> Show the IEEE 754 binary representation for the floating-point number 10_{ten} in single and double precision.

4.26 [5] <§4.8> This exercise is similar to Exercise 4.25, but this time replace the number 10_{ten} with 10.5_{ten}.

4.27 [10] <§4.8> This exercise is similar to Exercise 4.25, but this time replace the number 10_{ten} with 0.1_{ten}.

4.28 [10] <§4.8> This exercise is similar to Exercise 4.25, but this time replace the number 10_{ten} with the decimal fraction $-2/3$.

4.29 [10] <§4.8> Write a simple C program that inputs a floating-point number and shows its bit representation in hexadecimal.

4.30 [10] <§4.8> Write a simple C++ program that inputs a floating-point number and shows its bit representation in hexadecimal.

4.31 [10] <§4.8> A single precision IEEE number is stored in memory at address X. Write a sequence of MIPS instructions to multiply the number at X by 2 and store the result back at X. Accomplish this without using any floating-point instructions (don't worry about overflow).

4.32 [10] <§4.11> For the program gcc (Figure 4.54 on page 311), find the 10 most frequently executed MIPS instructions. List them in order of popularity, from most used to least used. Show the rank, name, and percentage of instructions executed for each instruction. If there is a tie for a given rank, list all instructions that tie with the same rank, even if this results in more than 10 instructions.

4.33 [10] <§4.11> This exercise is similar to Exercise 4.32, but this time replace the program gcc with the program spice.

4.34 <§4.11> {Ex. 4.32, 4.33} These questions examine the relative frequency of instructions in different programs.

    a. [5] Which instructions are found both in the answer to Exercise 4.32 and in the answer to Exercise 4.33?

    b. [5] What percentage of gcc instructions executed is due to the instructions identified in Exercise 4.34a?

    c. [5] What percentage of gcc instructions executed is due to the instructions identified in Exercise 4.32?

    d. [5] What percentage of spice instructions executed is due to the instructions identified in Exercise 4.34a?

    e. [5] What percentage of spice instructions executed is due to the instructions identified in Exercise 4.33?

4.35 [10] <§4.11> {Ex. 4.32–4.34} If you were designing a machine to execute the MIPS instruction set, what are the five instructions that you would try to make as fast as possible, based on the answers to Exercises 4.32 through 4.34? Give your rationale.

4.36 [15] <§§2.3, 4.11> Using Figure 4.54 on page 311, calculate the average clock cycles per instruction (CPI) for the program gcc. Figure 4.55 gives the average CPI per instruction category, taking into account cache misses and other effects. Assume that instructions omitted from the table have a CPI of 1.0.

Instruction category	Average CPI
Loads and stores	1.4
Conditional branch	1.8
Jumps	1.2
Integer multiply	10.0
Integer divide	30.0
Floating-point add and subtract	2.0
Floating-point multiply, single precision	4.0
Floating-point multiply, double precision	5.0
Floating-point divide, single precision	12.0
Floating-point divide, double precision	19.0

FIGURE 4.55   CPI for MIPS instruction categories.

4.37 [15] <§§2.3, 4.11> This exercise is similar to Exercise 4.36, but this time replace the program gcc with the program spice.

4.38 [2 weeks] Write a simulator for a subset of the MIPS instruction set using MIPS instructions and the SPIM simulator described in Appendix A. Your simulator should execute hand-assembled programs that are located in the data segment of the SPIM simulator and should use $v0 and $v1 for input and output. Other portions of the data segment can be used for storing the memory contents and register values of your virtual machine. Your implementation can use any of the MIPS instructions, but your simulator need only support a smaller subset of the instruction set (e.g., the instructions appearing in Chapters 5 and 6). (Additional details regarding this assignment are available at *www.mkp.com/cod2e.htm.*)

4.39 [1 week] {Ex. 4.38} Add an exception handler to the simulator you developed for Exercise 4.38. Your simulator should generate a simulated exception if a misaligned word is accessed via an lw, sw, or jr instruction. The exception handler should print out an error message identifying the offending address (within the simulation) and then realign the access, perform the instruction, and resume executing the simulated program. (Additional details regarding this assignment are available at *www.mkp.com/cod2e.htm.*)

In More Depth

Logical Instructions

The full MIPS instruction set has two more logical operations not mentioned thus far: xor and nor. The operation xor stands for exclusive OR, and nor stands for not OR. The table that follows defines these operations on a bit-by-bit basis. These instructions will be useful in the following two exercises.

A	B	A xor B	A nor B
0	0	0	1
0	1	1	0
1	0	1	0
1	1	0	0

4.40 [15] <§4.4> Show the minimal MIPS instruction sequence for a new instruction called swap that exchanges two registers. After the sequence completes, the Destination register has the original value of the Source register, and the Source register has the original value of the Destination register. Convert this instruction:

```
swap $s0,$s1
```

The hard part is that this sequence *must use only these two registers!* (Hint: It can be done in three instructions if you use the new logical instructions. What is the value of (A xor B xor A)?)

4.41 [5] <§4.4> Show the minimal MIPS instruction sequence for a new instruction called not that takes the one's complement of a Source register and places it in a Destination register. Convert this instruction (accepted by the MIPS assembler):

```
not $s0,$s1
```

(Hint: It can be done in two instructions if you use the new logical instructions.)

4.42 [20] <§4.5> A simple check for overflow during addition is to see if the CarryIn to the most significant bit is *not* the same as the CarryOut of the most significant bit. Prove that this check is the same as in Figure 4.4 on page 222.

4.43 [10] <§4.5> Draw the gates for the Sum bit of an adder, given the equation on page 234.

4.44 [5] <§4.5> Rewrite the equations on page 242 for a carry-lookahead logic for a 16-bit adder using a new notation. First use the names for the CarryIn signals of the individual bits of the adder. That is, use c4, c8, c12, . . . instead of C1, C2, C3, ... Also, let $P_{i,j}$ mean a propagate signal for bits i to j, and $G_{i,j}$ mean a generate signal for bits i to j. For example, the equation

$$C2 = G1 + (P1 \cdot G0) + (P1 \cdot P0 \cdot c0)$$

can be rewritten as

$$c8 = G_{7,4} + (P_{7,4} \cdot G_{3,0}) + (P_{7,4} \cdot P_{3,0} \cdot c0)$$

This more general notation is useful in creating wider adders.

4.45 [15] <§4.5> {Ex. 4.44} Write the equations for the carry-lookahead logic for a *64-bit* adder using the new notation from Exercise 4.44 and using 16-bit adders as building blocks. Include a drawing similiar to Figure 4.24 in your solution.

4.46 [10] <§4.5> Now calculate the relative performance of adders. Assume that hardware corresponding to any equation containing only OR or AND terms, such as the equations for *pi* and *gi* on page 242, takes one time unit T. Equations that consist of the OR of several AND terms, such as the equations for c1, c2, c3, and c4 on page 243, would thus take two time units, 2T, because it would take T to produce the AND terms and then an additional T to produce the result of the OR. Calculate the numbers and performance ratio for 4-bit adders for both ripple carry and carry lookahead. If the terms in equations are further defined by other equations, then add the appropriate delays for those intermediate equations, and continue recursively until the actual input bits of the adder are used in an equation. Include a drawing of each adder labeled with the calculated delays and the path of the worst-case delay highlighted.

4.47 [15] <§4.5> This exercise is similar to Exercise 4.46, but this time calculate the relative speeds of a 16-bit adder using ripple carry only, ripple carry of 4-bit groups that use carry lookahead, and the carry-lookahead scheme on page 242.

4.48 [15] <§4.5> {Ex. 4.45} This exercise is similar to Exercises 4.46 and 4.47, but this time calculate the relative speeds of a 64-bit adder using ripple carry only, ripple carry of 4-bit groups that use carry lookahead, ripple carry of 16-bit groups that use carry lookahead, and the carry-lookahead scheme from Exercise 4.45.

4.49 [10] <§4.5> There are times when we want to add a collection of numbers together. Suppose you wanted to add four 4-bit numbers (A,B, E, F) using 1-bit full adders. Let's ignore carry lookahead for now. You would likely connect the 1-bit adders in the organization in the top of Figure 4.56. Below the traditional organization is a novel organization of full adders. Try adding four numbers using both organizations to convince yourself that you get the same answer.

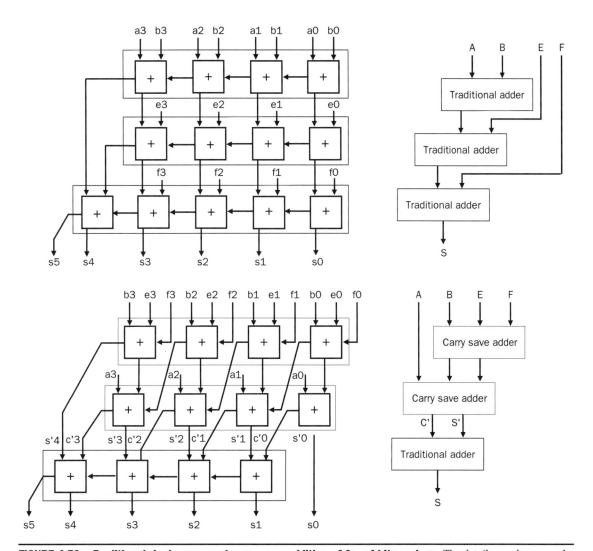

FIGURE 4.56   Traditional ripple carry and carry save addition of four 4-bit numbers. The details are shown on the left, with the individual signals in lowercase, and the corresponding higher-level blocks are on the right, with collective signals in uppercase. Note that the sum of four n-bit numbers can take $n+2$ bits.

4.50 [5] <§4.5> {Ex. 4.49} Assume that the time delay through each 1-bit adder is 2T. Calculate the time of adding four 4-bit numbers to the organization at the top versus the organization in the bottom in Figure 4.56.

In More Depth

Carry Save Adders

Exercises 4.49 and 4.50 motivate an organization that uses the 1-bit adder in Figure 4.10 on page 232 in a way it was not intended. Although this piece of hardware is simple and fast, the problem comes from trying to get the CarryIn signal calculated in a timely fashion across several adders.

We can think of the adder instead as a hardware device that can add three inputs together (ai, bi, ci) and produce two outputs (s, $ci+1$). When we are just adding two numbers together, there is little we can do with this observation, but when we are adding more than two operands, it is possible to reduce the cost of the carry. The idea is to form two independent sums, called S' (sum bits) and C' (carry bits). At the end of the process, we need to add C' and S' together using a normal adder. This technique of delaying carry propagation until the end of a sum of numbers is called *carry save addition*. The block drawing on the lower right of Figure 4.56 shows the organization, with two levels of carry save adders connected by a single normal adder.

4.51 [10] <§4.5> {Ex. 4.47, 4.50} Calculate the delays to add four 16-bit numbers using full carry-lookahead adders versus carry save with a carry-lookahead adder forming the final sum. (The time unit T in Exercises 4.46 and 4.50 is the same.)

4.52 [20] <§4.5, 4.6> {Ex. 4.47} Perhaps the most likely case of adding many numbers at once in a computer would be when trying to multiply more quickly by using many adders to add many numbers in a single clock cycle. Compared to the multiply algorithm in Figure 4.32 on page 258, a carry save scheme with many adders could multiply more than 10 times faster.

This exercise estimates the cost and speed of a combinational multiplier to multiply two positive 16-bit numbers. Assume that you have 16 intermediate terms M15, M14, . . . , M0, called *partial products*, that contain the multiplicand ANDed with multiplier bits m15, m14, . . . , m0.

The idea is to use carry save adders to reduce the n operands into $2/3n$ in parallel groups of three, and do this repeatedly until you get two large numbers to add together with a traditional adder.

First show the block organization of the 16-bit carry save adders to add these 16 terms, as shown on the right in Figure 4.56. Then calculate the delays to add these 16 numbers. Compare this time to the iterative multiplication scheme in Figure 4.32 on page 258 but only assume 16 iterations using a 16-bit adder that has full carry lookahead whose speed was calculated in Exercise 4.47.

4.53 [30] <§4.6> The original reason for Booth's algorithm was to reduce the number of operations by avoiding operations when there were strings of 0s and 1s. Revise the algorithm on page 260 to look at 3 bits at a time and compute the multiplicand 2 bits at a time. Fill in the following table to determine the 2-bit Booth encoding:

Current bits		Previous bit	Operation	Reason
a_{i+1}	a_i	a_{i-1}		
0	0	0		
0	0	1		
0	1	0		
0	1	1		
1	0	0		
1	0	1		
1	1	0		
1	1	1		

Assume that you have both the multiplicand and $2 \times$ multiplicand already in registers. Explain the reason for the operation on each line, and show a 6-bit example that runs faster using this algorithm. (Hint: Try dividing to conquer; see what the operations would be in each of the eight cases in the table using a 2-bit Booth algorithm, and then optimize the pair of operations.)

4.54 [30] <§4.6, 4.7> The division algorithm in Figure 4.40 on page 270 is called *restoring division*, since each time the result of subtracting the divisor from the dividend is negative you must add the divisor back into the dividend to restore the original value. Recall that shift left is the same as multiplying by two. Let's look at the value of the left half of the Remainder again, starting with step 3b of the divide algorithm and then going to step 2:

$$(\text{Remainder} + \text{Divisor}) \times 2 - \text{Divisor}$$

This value is created from restoring the Remainder by adding the Divisor, shifting the sum left, and then subtracting the Divisor. Simplifying the result we get

$$\text{Remainder} \times 2 + \text{Divisor} \times 2 - \text{Divisor} = \text{Remainder} \times 2 + \text{Divisor}$$

Based on this observation, write a *nonrestoring division* algorithm using the notation of Figure 4.40 that does not add the Divisor to the Remainder in step 3b. Show that your algorithm works by dividing $0000\ 0111_{two}$ by 0010_{two}.

4.55 [5] <§4.8> Add $6.42_{ten} \times 10^1$ to $9.51_{ten} \times 10^2$, assuming that you have only three significant digits, first with guard and round digits and then without them.

4.56 [5] <§4.8> This exercise is similar to Exercise 4.55, but this time use the numbers $8.76_{ten} \times 10^1$ and $1.47_{ten} \times 10^2$.

4.57 [25] <§4.8> Derive the floating-point algorithm for division as we did for addition and multiplication on pages 280 through 288. First divide $1.110_{ten} \times 10^{10}$ by $1.100_{ten} \times 10^{-5}$, showing the same steps that we did in the example starting on page 282. Then derive the floating-point division algorithm using a format similar to the multiplication algorithm in Figure 4.46 on page 289.

4.58 [30] <§4.8> The elaboration on page 300 explains the four rounding modes of IEEE 754 and the extra bit, called the *sticky bit*, needed in addition to the 2 bits called *guard* and *round*. Guard is the first bit, round is the second bit, and sticky represents whether the remaining bits are 0 or not. Fill in the following table with logical equations that are functions of guard (g), round (r), and sticky (s) for the result of a floating-point addition that creates Sum. Let p be the proper number of bits in the significand for a given precision and Sum_p be the pth most significant bit of Sum. A blank box means that the p most significant bits of the sum are correctly rounded. If you place an equation in a box, a false equation means that the p bits are correctly rounded; a true equation means add 1 to the pth most significant bit of Sum.

Rounding mode	Sum ≥ 0	Sum < 0
Toward $-\infty$		
Toward $+\infty$		
Truncate		
Nearest even		

4.59 [30] <§4.8> The elaboration on page 300 mentions that IEEE 754 has two special symbols that are floating-point operands: infinity and Not a Number (NaN). There are also small numbers called *denorms,* which are not normalized. Because these special symbols and numbers are not used very frequently, implementations that employ a mix of both hardware and software techniques are sometimes used. For example, instead of using complicated hardware to handle these special cases, an exception is generated and they are handled in software. Many implementation options exist, each of which has unique performance characteristics. Your task is to benchmark several different machines for floating-point operations as the operands vary from normal numbers to these special cases. Be sure to state your conclusions by comparing the performance of different machines with one another and describing their similarities and differences. What impact are your results likely to have on software designers who must choose whether or not to make use of the special features in the IEEE 754 standard?

4.60 [30] <§4.5> If you have access to a computer containing a MIPS processor, write a loop in assembly language that sets registers $k0 ($26) and $k1 ($27) to an initial value, and then loop for several seconds, checking the contents of these registers. Print the values if they change. See the elaboration on page 225 for an explanation of why they change. Can you find a reason for the particular values you observe?

5

The Processor:
Datapath
and Control

In a major matter,
no details are small.

French Proverb

5.1   **Introduction**   338

5.2   **Building a Datapath**   343

5.3   **A Simple Implementation Scheme**   351

5.4   **A Multicycle Implementation**   377

5.5   **Microprogramming: Simplifying Control Design**   399

5.6   **Exceptions**   410

5.7   **Real Stuff: The Pentium Pro Implementation**   416

5.8   **Fallacies and Pitfalls**   419

5.9   **Concluding Remarks**   421

5.10   **Historical Perspective and Further Reading**   423

5.11   **Key Terms**   426

5.12   **Exercises**   427

The Five Classic Components of a Computer

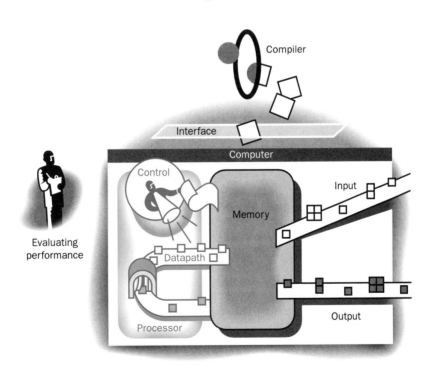

5.1 Introduction

In Chapter 2, we saw that the performance of a machine was determined by three key factors: instruction count, clock cycle time, and clock cycles per instruction (CPI). The compiler and the instruction set architecture, which we examined in Chapters 3 and 4, determine the instruction count required for a given program. However, both the clock cycle time and the number of clock cycles per instruction are determined by the implementation of the processor. In this chapter, we construct the datapath and control unit for two different implementations of the MIPS instruction set.

We will be designing an implementation that includes a subset of the core MIPS instruction set:

- The memory-reference instructions load word (`lw`) and store word (`sw`)

- The arithmetic-logical instructions `add`, `sub`, `and`, `or`, and `slt`

- The instructions branch equal (`beq`) and jump (`j`), which we add last

This subset does not include all the integer instructions (for example, multiply and divide are missing), nor does it include any floating-point instructions. However, the key principles used in creating a datapath and designing the control will be illustrated. The implementation of the remaining instructions is similar.

In examining the implementation, we will have the opportunity to see how the instruction set architecture determines many aspects of the implementation, and how the choice of various implementation strategies affects the clock rate and CPI for the machine. Many of the key design principles introduced in Chapter 3 can be illustrated by looking at the implementation, such as the guidelines *Make the common case fast* and *Simplicity favors regularity*. In addition, most concepts used to implement the MIPS subset in this chapter and the next are the same basic ideas that are used to construct a broad spectrum of computers, from high-performance machines to general-purpose microprocessors to special-purpose processors, which are used increasingly in products ranging from VCRs to automobiles.

An Overview of the Implementation

In Chapters 3 and 4, we looked at the core MIPS instructions, including the integer arithmetic-logical instructions, the memory-reference instructions, and the branch instructions. Much of what needs to be done to implement these instructions is the same, independent of the exact class of instruction. For every instruction, the first two steps are identical:

1. Send the program counter (PC) to the memory that contains the code and fetch the instruction from that memory.

2. Read one or two registers, using fields of the instruction to select the registers to read. For the load word instruction we need to read only one register, but most other instructions require that we read two registers.

After these two steps, the actions required to complete the instruction depend on the instruction class. Fortunately, for each of the three instruction classes (memory-reference, arithmetic-logical, and branches), the actions are largely the same, independent of the exact opcode.

Even across different instruction classes there are some similarities. For example, all instruction classes use the arithmetic-logical unit (ALU) after reading the registers. The memory-reference instructions use the ALU for an address calculation, the arithmetic-logical instructions for the operation execution, and branches for comparison. As we can see, the simplicity and regularity of the instruction set simplifies the implementation by making the execution of many of the instruction classes similar.

After using the ALU, the actions required to complete the different instruction classes differ. A memory-reference instruction will need to access the memory either to write data for a store or read data for a load. An arithmetic-logical instruction must write the data from the ALU back into a register. Lastly, for a branch instruction, we may need to change the next instruction address based on the comparison.

Figure 5.1 shows the high-level view of a MIPS implementation. In the remainder of the chapter, we refine this view to fill in the details, which requires that we add further functional units, increase the number of connections between units, and, of course, add a control unit to control what actions are taken for different instruction classes. Before we begin to create a more complete implementation, we need to discuss a few principles of logic design.

A Word about Logic Conventions and Clocking

To discuss the design of a machine, we must decide how the logic implementing the machine will operate and how the machine is clocked. This section reviews a few key ideas in digital logic that we will use extensively in this chapter. If you have little or no background in digital logic, you will find it helpful to read through Appendix B before continuing. Section B.9 presents the key terms introduced in Appendix B and is useful as a quick check-up if you want to review your logic design background.

When designing logic, it is often convenient for the designer to change the mapping between a logically true or false signal and the high or low voltage level. Thus, in some parts of a design, a signal that is logically asserted may actually be an electrically low signal, while in others an electrically high signal is asserted. To maintain consistency, we will use the word *asserted* to indicate a signal that is logically high and *assert* to specify that a signal should be driven logically high.

The functional units in the MIPS implementation consist of two different types of logic elements: elements that operate on data values and elements that contain state. The elements that operate on data values are all *combinational*, which means that their outputs depend only on the current inputs. Given the same input, a combinational element always produces the same output. The ALU shown in Figure 5.1 and discussed in detail in Chapter 4 is a combinational element. Given a set of inputs, it always produces the same output because it has no internal storage.

Other elements in the design are not combinational, but instead contain *state*. An element contains state if it has some internal storage. We call these elements *state elements* because, if we pulled the plug on the machine, we could restart it by loading the state elements with the values they contained before

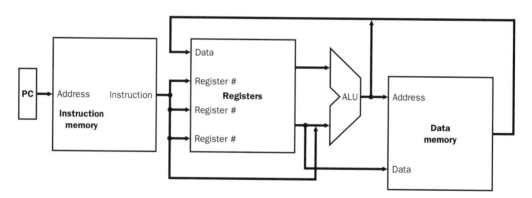

FIGURE 5.1   An abstract view of the implementation of the MIPS subset showing the major functional units and the major connections between them. All instructions start by using the program counter to supply the instruction address to the instruction memory. After the instruction is fetched, the register operands used by an instruction are specified by fields of that instruction. Once the register operands have been fetched, they can be operated on to compute a memory address (for a load or store), to compute an arithmetic result (for an integer arithmetic-logical instruction), or a compare (for a branch). If the instruction is an arithmetic-logical instruction, the result from the ALU must be written to a register. If the operation is a load or store, the ALU result is used as an address to either store a value from the registers or load a value from memory into the registers. The result from the ALU or memory is written back into the register file. Branches require the use of the ALU output to determine the next instruction address, which requires some control logic, as we will see.

we pulled the plug. Furthermore, if we saved and restored the state elements, it would be as if the machine had never lost power. Thus, these state elements completely characterize the machine. In Figure 5.1, the instruction and data memories as well as the registers are all examples of state elements.

A state element has at least two inputs and one output. The required inputs are the data value to be written into the element, and the clock, which determines when the data value is written. The output from a state element provides the value that was written in an earlier clock cycle. For example, one of the logically simplest state elements is a D-type flip-flop (see Appendix B), which has exactly these two inputs (a value and a clock) and one output. In addition to flip-flops, our MIPS implementation also uses two other types of state elements: memories and registers, both of which appear in Figure 5.1. The clock is used to determine when the state element should be written; a state element can be read at any time.

Logic components that contain state are also called *sequential* because their outputs depend on both their inputs and the contents of the internal state. For example, the output from the functional unit representing the registers depends both on the register numbers supplied and on what was written into the registers previously. The operation of both the combinational and sequential elements and their construction are discussed in more detail in Appendix B.

Clocking Methodology

A *clocking methodology* defines when signals can be read and when they can be written. It is important to specify the timing of reads and writes because, if a signal is written at the same time it is read, the value of the read could correspond to the old value, the newly written value, or even some mix of the two! Needless to say, computer designs cannot tolerate such unpredictability. A clocking methodology is designed to prevent this circumstance.

For simplicity, we will assume an *edge-triggered* clocking methodology. An edge-triggered clocking methodology means that any values stored in the machine are updated only on a clock edge. Thus, the state elements all update their internal storage on the clock edge. Because only state elements can store a data value, any collection of combinational logic must have its inputs coming from a set of state elements and its outputs written into a set of state elements. The inputs are values that were written in a previous clock cycle, while the outputs are values that can be used in a following clock cycle.

Figure 5.2 shows the two state elements surrounding a block of combinational logic, which operates in a single clock cycle: All signals must propagate from state element 1, through the combinational logic, and to state element 2 in the time of one clock cycle. The time necessary for the signals to reach state element 2 defines the length of the clock cycle.

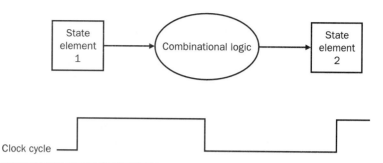

FIGURE 5.2 Combinational logic, state elements, and the clock are closely related. In a synchronous digital system, the clock determines when elements with state will write values into internal storage. Any inputs to a state element must reach a stable value (that is, have reached a value from which they will not change until after the clock edge) before the active clock edge causes the state to be updated. All state elements, including memory, are assumed to be edge-triggered.

For simplicity, we do not show a write control signal when a state element is written on every active clock edge. In contrast, if a state element is not updated on every clock, then an explicit write control signal is required. Both the clock signal and the write control signal are inputs, and the state element is changed only when the write control signal is asserted and a clock edge occurs.

An edge-triggered methodology allows us to read the contents of a register, send the value through some combinational logic, and write that register in the same clock cycle, as shown in Figure 5.3. It doesn't matter whether we assume that all writes take place on the rising clock edge or on the falling clock edge, since the inputs to the combinational logic block cannot change except on the chosen clock edge. With an edge-triggered timing methodology, there is *no* feedback within a single clock cycle, and the logic in Figure 5.3 works correctly. In Appendix B we briefly discuss additional timing constraints (such as set-up and hold times) as well as other timing methodologies.

Nearly all of these state and logic elements will have inputs and outputs that are 32 bits wide, since that is the width of most of the data handled by the processor. We will make it clear whenever a unit has an input or output that is other than 32 bits in width. The figures will indicate *buses*, which are signals wider than 1 bit, with thicker lines. At times we will want to combine several buses to form a wider bus; for example, we may want to obtain a 32-bit bus by combining two 16-bit buses. In such cases, labels on the bus lines will make it clear that we are concatenating buses to form a wider bus. Arrows are also added to help clarify the direction of the flow of data between elements. Finally, color indicates a control signal as opposed to a signal that carries data; this distinction will become clearer as we proceed through this chapter.

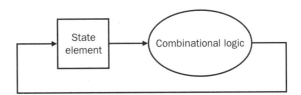

FIGURE 5.3   An edge-triggered methodology allows a state element to be read and written in the same clock cycle without creating a race that could lead to indeterminate data values. Of course, the clock cycle still must be long enough so that the input values are stable when the active clock edge occurs. Feedback cannot occur within 1 clock cycle because of the edge-triggered update of the state element. If feedback were possible, this design could not work properly. Our designs in this chapter and the next rely on the edge-triggered timing methodology and structures like the one shown in this figure.

The MIPS Subset Implementation

We will start with a simple implementation that uses a single long clock cycle for every instruction and follows the general form of Figure 5.1. In this first design, every instruction begins execution on one clock edge and completes execution on the next clock edge.

While easier to understand, this approach is not practical, since it would be slower than an implementation that allows different instruction classes to take different numbers of clock cycles, each of which could be much shorter. After designing the control for this simple machine, we will look at an implementation that uses multiple clock cycles for each instruction. This implementation is more realistic but also requires more complex control.

In this chapter, we will take the specification of the control to the level of logic equations or finite state machine specifications. From either representation, a modern computer-aided design (CAD) system can synthesize a hardware implementation; Appendix C shows how this is done. Before closing the chapter, we will discuss how exceptions, mentioned in Chapter 4, are implemented.

5.2   Building a Datapath

A reasonable way to start a datapath design is to examine the major components required to execute each class of MIPS instruction. Let's start by looking at which datapath elements each instruction needs and build up the sections of the datapath for each instruction class from these elements. When we show the datapath elements, we will also show their control signals.

The first element we will need is a place to store the instructions of a program. A memory unit, which is a state element, is used to hold and supply instructions given an address, as shown in Figure 5.4. The address of the instruction must also be kept in a state element, which we call the *program counter* (PC), also shown in Figure 5.4. Lastly, we will need an adder to increment the PC to the address of the next instruction. This adder, which is combinational, can be built from the ALU we designed in the last chapter simply by wiring the control lines so that the control always specifies an add operation. We will draw such an ALU with the label *Add*, as in Figure 5.4, to indicate that it has been permanently made an adder and cannot perform the other ALU functions.

To execute any instruction, we must start by fetching the instruction from memory. To prepare for executing the next instruction, we must also increment the program counter so that it points at the next instruction, 4 bytes later. The datapath for this step, shown in Figure 5.5, uses the three elements from Figure 5.4.

Now let's consider the R-format instructions (see Figure 3.19 on page 154). They all read two registers, perform an ALU operation on the contents of the registers, and write the result. We call these instructions either *R-type instructions* or *arithmetic-logical instructions* (since they perform arithmetic or logical

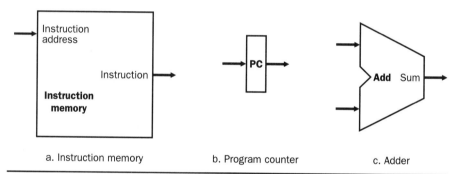

a. Instruction memory   b. Program counter   c. Adder

FIGURE 5.4 Two state elements are needed to store and access instructions, and an adder is needed to compute the next instruction address. The state elements are the instruction memory and the program counter. The instruction memory need only provide read access because the datapath does not write instructions. Since the instruction memory is only reads, we treat it as combinational logic: the output at any time reflects the contents of the location specified by the address input, and no read control signal is needed. (We will need to write the instruction memory when we load the program; this is not hard to add, and we ignore it for simplicity.) Since the instruction memory unit can only be read, we do not include a read control signal; this simplifies the design. The program counter is a 32-bit register that will be written at the end of every clock cycle and thus does not need a write control signal. The adder is an ALU wired to always perform an add of its two 32-bit inputs and place the result on its output.

operations). This instruction class includes add, sub, and slt, which were introduced in Chapter 3, as well as and and or, which were introduced in Chapter 4. Recall that a typical instance of such an instruction is add $t1,$t2,$t3, which reads $t2 and $t3 and writes $t1.

The processor's 32 registers are stored in a structure called a *register file*. A register file is a collection of registers in which any register can be read or written by specifying the number of the register in the file. The register file contains the register state of the machine. In addition, we will need an ALU to operate on the values read from the registers.

Because the R-format instructions have three register operands, we will need to read two data words from the register file and write one data word into the register file for each instruction. For each data word to be read from the registers, we need an input to the register file that specifies the register number to be read and an output from the register file that will carry the value that has been read from the registers. To write a data word, we will need two inputs: one to specify the *register number* to be written and one to supply the *data* to be written into the register. The register file always outputs the contents of whatever register numbers are on the Read register inputs. Writes, however, are controlled by the write control signal, which must be asserted for a write to occur at the clock edge. Thus, we need a total of four inputs (three for register

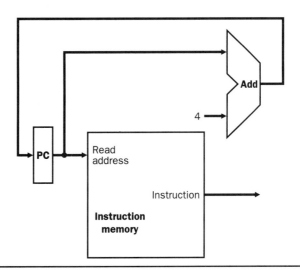

FIGURE 5.5 A portion of the datapath used for fetching instructions and incrementing the program counter. The fetched instruction is used by other parts of the datapath.

numbers and one for data) and two outputs (both for data), as shown in Figure 5.6. The register number inputs are 5 bits wide to specify one of 32 registers ($32 = 2^5$), whereas the data input and two data output buses are each 32 bits wide.

The ALU, shown in Figure 5.6, is controlled by the 3-bit signal described in Chapter 4. The ALU takes two 32-bit inputs and produces a 32-bit result.

The datapath for these R-type instructions, which uses the register file and the ALU of Figure 5.6, is shown in Figure 5.7. Since the register numbers come from fields of the instruction, we show the instruction, which comes from Figure 5.5, as connected to the register number inputs of the register file.

Next, consider the MIPS load word and store word instructions, which have the general form: `lw $t1,offset_value($t2)` or `sw $t1,offset_value ($t2)`. These instructions compute a memory address by adding the base reg-

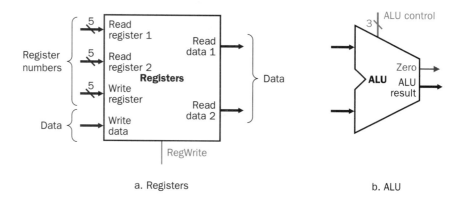

a. Registers   b. ALU

FIGURE 5.6   The two elements needed to implement R-format ALU operations are the register file and the ALU. The register file contains all the registers and has two read ports and one write port. The design of multiported register files is discussed in section B.5 of Appendix B. The register file always outputs the contents of the registers corresponding to the Read register inputs on the outputs; no other control inputs are needed. In contrast, a register write must be explicitly indicated by asserting the write control signal. Remember that writes are edge-triggered, so that all the write inputs (i.e., the value to be written, the register number, and the write control signal) must be valid at the clock edge. Since writes to the register file are edge-triggered, our design can legally read and write the same register within a clock cycle: the read will get the value written in an earlier clock cycle, while the value written will be available to a read in a subsequent clock cycle. The inputs carrying the register number to the register file are all 5 bits wide, whereas the lines carrying data values are 32 bits wide. The operation to be performed by the ALU is controlled with the ALU operation signal, which will be 3 bits wide, using the ALU designed in the previous chapter (see Figure 4.19 on page 240). We will use the Zero detection output of the ALU shortly to implement branches. The overflow output will not be needed until section 5.6, when we discuss exceptions; we omit it until then.

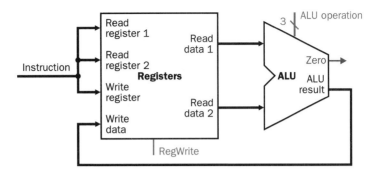

FIGURE 5.7 The datapath for R-type instructions. The ALU discussed in Chapter 4 can be controlled to provide all the basic ALU functions required for R-type instructions.

ister, which is $t2, to the 16-bit signed offset field contained in the instruction. If the instruction is a store, the value to be stored must also be read from the register file where it resides in $t1. If the instruction is a load, the value read from memory must be written into the register file in the specified register, which is $t1. Thus, we will need both the register file and the ALU shown in Figure 5.6.

In addition, we will need a unit to sign-extend the 16-bit offset field in the instruction to a 32-bit signed value, and a data memory unit to read from or write to. The data memory must be written on store instructions; hence, it has both read and write control signals, an address input, as well as an input for the data to be written into memory. Figure 5.8 shows these two elements.

Figure 5.9 shows how to combine these elements to build the datapath for a load word or a store word instruction, assuming that the instruction has already been fetched. The register number inputs for the register file come from fields of the instruction, as does the offset value, which after sign extension becomes the second ALU input.

The beq instruction has three operands, two registers that are compared for equality, and a 16-bit offset used to compute the branch target address relative to the branch instruction address. Its form is beq $t1,$t2,offset. To implement this instruction, we must compute the branch target address by adding the sign-extended offset field of the instruction to the PC. There are two details in the definition of branch instructions (see Chapter 3) to which we must pay attention:

■ The instruction set architecture specifies that the base for the branch address calculation is the address of the instruction following the branch.

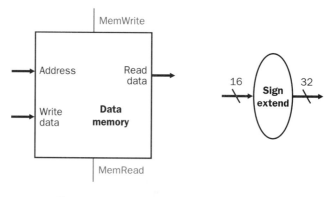

a. Data memory unit

b. Sign-extension unit

FIGURE 5.8   The two units needed to implement loads and stores, in addition to the register file and ALU of Figure 5.6, are the data memory unit and the sign extension unit. The memory unit is a state element with inputs for the address and the write data, and a single output for the read result. There are separate read and write controls, although only one of these may be asserted on any given clock. The sign extension unit has a 16-bit input that is sign-extended into a 32-bit result appearing on the output (see Chapter 4, page 216). We assume the data memory is edge-triggered for writes. Standard memory chips actually have a write enable signal that is used for writes. Although the write enable is not edge-triggered, our edge-triggered design could easily be adapted to work with real memory chips. See section B.5 of Appendix B for a further discussion of how real memory chips work.

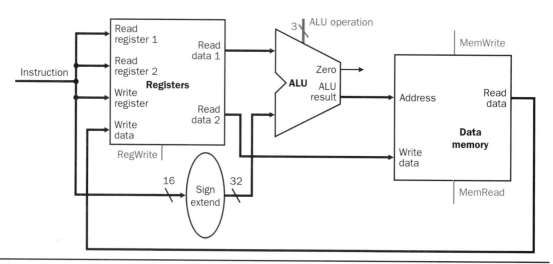

FIGURE 5.9   The datapath for a load or store does a register access, followed by a memory address calculation, then a read or write from memory, and a write into the register file if the instruction is a load.

Since we compute PC + 4 (the address of the next instruction) in the instruction fetch datapath, it is easy to use this value as the base for computing the branch target address.

■ The architecture also states that the offset field is shifted left 2 bits so that it is a word offset; this shift increases the effective range of the offset field by a factor of four.

To deal with the latter complication, we will need to shift the offset field by two.

In addition to computing the branch target address, we must also determine whether the next instruction is the instruction that follows sequentially or the instruction at the branch target address. When the condition is true (i.e., the operands are equal), the branch target address becomes the new PC, and we say that the branch is *taken*. If the operands are not equal, the incremented PC should replace the current PC (just as for any other normal instruction); in this case, we say that the branch is *not taken*.

Thus, the branch datapath must do two operations: compute the branch target address and compare the register contents. (Branches also require that we modify the instruction fetch portion of the datapath, which we will deal with shortly.) Figure 5.10 shows the branch datapath. To compute the branch target address, the branch datapath includes a sign extension unit, just like that in Figure 5.8, and an adder. To perform the compare, we need to use the register file shown in Figure 5.6 to supply the two register operands (although we will not need to write into the register file). In addition, the comparison can be done using the ALU we designed in Chapter 4. Since that ALU provides an output signal that indicates whether the result was 0, we can send the two register operands to the ALU with the control set to do a subtract. If the Zero signal out of the ALU unit is asserted, we know that the two values are equal. Although the Zero output always signals if the result is 0, we will be using it only to implement the equal test of branches. Later, we will show exactly how to connect the control signals of the ALU for use in the datapath.

The jump instruction operates by replacing the lower 28 bits of the PC with the lower 26 bits of the instruction shifted left by 2 bits. This shift is accomplished simply by concatenating 00 to the jump offset (as described in the elaboration in Chapter 3, page 150).

Now that we have examined the datapaths needed for the individual instruction classes, we can combine them into a single datapath and add the control to complete the implementation. The datapaths shown in Figures 5.5, 5.7, 5.9, and 5.10 will be the building blocks for two different implementations. In the next section, we will create an implementation that uses a single long clock cycle for every instruction. In section 5.4, we will look at an implementation that uses multiple shorter clock cycles for every instruction.

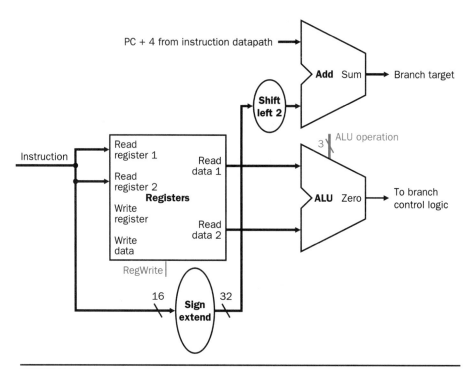

FIGURE 5.10   The datapath for a branch uses the ALU to evaluate the branch condition and a separate adder to compute the branch target as the sum of the incremented PC and the sign-extended, lower 16 bits of the instruction (the branch displacement), shifted left 2 bits. The unit labeled *Shift left 2* is simply a routing of the signals between input and output that adds 00_{two} to the low-order end of the sign-extended offset field; no actual shift hardware is needed, since the amount of the "shift" is constant. Since we know that the offset was sign-extended from 16 bits, the shift will throw away only "sign bits." Control logic is used to decide whether the incremented PC or branch target should replace the PC, based on the Zero output of the ALU.

Elaboration: In the MIPS instruction set, branches are *delayed*, meaning that the instruction immediately following the branch is always executed, *independent* of whether the branch condition is true or false. When the condition is false, the execution looks like a normal branch. When the condition is true, a delayed branch first executes the instruction immediately following the branch before jumping to the specified branch target address. The motivation for delayed branches arises from how pipelining affects branches (see section 6.6). For simplicity, we ignore delayed branches in this chapter and implement a nondelayed `beq` instruction.

A Simple Implementation Scheme

In this section, we look at what might be thought of as the simplest possible implementation of our MIPS subset. We build this simple datapath and its control by assembling the datapath segments of the last section and adding control lines as needed. This simple implementation covers load word (lw), store word (sw), branch equal (beq), and the arithmetic-logical instructions add, sub, and, or, and set on less than. We will later enhance the design to include a jump instruction (j).

Creating a Single Datapath

Suppose we were going to build a datapath from the pieces we looked at in Figures 5.5, 5.7, 5.9, and 5.10. The simplest datapath might attempt to execute all instructions in 1 clock cycle. This means that no datapath resource can be used more than once per instruction, so any element needed more than once must be duplicated. We therefore need a memory for instructions separate from one for data. Although some of the functional units will need to be duplicated when the individual datapaths of the previous section are combined, many of the elements can be shared by different instruction flows.

To share a datapath element between two different instruction classes, we may need to allow multiple connections to the input of an element and have a control signal select among the inputs. This selection is commonly done with a device called a *multiplexor*, although this device might better be called a *data selector*. The multiplexor, which was introduced in the last chapter (Figure 4.8 on page 231), selects from among several inputs based on the setting of its control lines.

Composing Datapaths

Example   The arithmetic-logical (or R-type) instruction datapath of Figure 5.7 on page 347 and the memory instruction datapath of Figure 5.9 on page 348 are quite similar. The key differences are the following:

- The second input to the ALU unit is either a register (if it's an R-type instruction) or the sign-extended lower half of the instruction (if it's a memory instruction).

- The value stored into a destination register comes from the ALU (for an R-type instruction) or the memory (for a load).

Show how to combine the two datapaths using multiplexors, without duplicating the functional units that are in common in Figures 5.7 and 5.9. Ignore the control of the multiplexors.

Answer

To combine the two datapaths and use only a single register file and an ALU, we must support two different sources for the second ALU input, as well as two different sources for the data stored into the register file. Thus one multiplexor is placed at the ALU input and another at the data input to the register file. Figure 5.11 shows the combined datapath.

The instruction fetch portion of the datapath, shown in Figure 5.5 on page 345, can easily be added to the datapath in Figure 5.11. Figure 5.12 shows the result. The combined datapath includes a memory for instructions and a separate memory for data. This combined datapath requires both an adder and an ALU, since the adder is used to increment the PC while the other ALU is used for executing the instruction in the same clock cycle.

Now we can combine all the pieces to make a simple datapath for the MIPS architecture by adding the datapath for branches from Figure 5.10 on page 350. Figure 5.13 on page 354 shows the datapath we obtain by composing the separate pieces. The branch instruction uses the main ALU for comparison of the register operands, so we must keep the adder in Figure 5.10 for computing the branch target address. An additional multiplexor is required to select either the sequentially following instruction address (PC + 4) or the branch target address to be written into the PC.

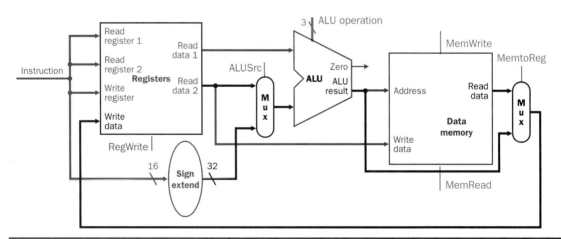

FIGURE 5.11   Combining the datapaths for the memory instructions and the R-type instructions. This example shows how a single datapath can be assembled from the pieces in Figures 5.7 and 5.9 by adding multiplexors. The added multiplexors and connections have been highlighted. The control lines for the multiplexors are also shown.

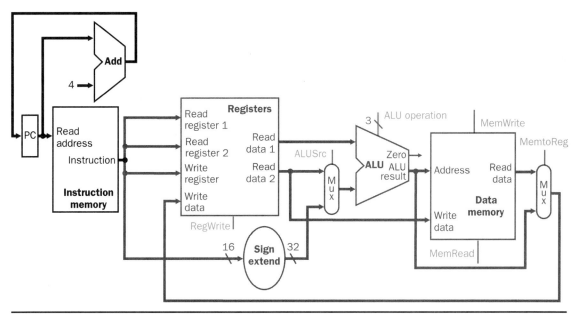

FIGURE 5.12 The instruction fetch portion of the datapath from Figure 5.5 is appended to the datapath of Figure 5.11 that handles memory and ALU instructions. The addition is highlighted. The result is a datapath that supports many operations of the MIPS instruction set—branches and jumps are the major missing pieces.

Now that we have completed this simple datapath, we can add the control unit. The control unit must be able to take inputs and generate a write signal for each state element, the selector control for each multiplexor, and the ALU control. The ALU control is different in a number of ways, and it will be useful to design it first before we design the rest of the control unit.

The ALU Control

Recall from Chapter 4 that the ALU has three control inputs. Only five of the possible eight input combinations are used. Figure 4.20 on page 240 showed the five following combinations:

ALU control input	Function
000	AND
001	OR
010	add
110	subtract
111	set on less than

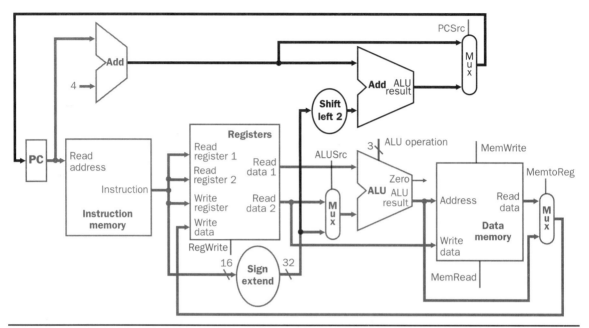

FIGURE 5.13 The simple datapath for the MIPS architecture combines the elements required by different instruction classes. This datapath can execute the basic instructions (load/store word, ALU operations, and branches) in a single clock cycle. The additions to Figure 5.12, which are all highlighted, are used to implement branches. The datapath components for branches come from Figure 5.10. A multiplexor is also needed, since the value written into the PC can be either the sequentially incremented PC or the branch target PC. The support for jumps will be added later.

Depending on the instruction class, the ALU will need to perform one of these five functions. For load word and store word instructions, we use the ALU to compute the memory address by addition. For the R-type instructions, the ALU needs to perform one of the five actions (AND, OR, subtract, add, or set on less than), depending on the value of the 6-bit funct (or function) field in the low-order bits of the instruction (see Chapter 3, page 118). For branch equal, the ALU must perform a subtraction.

We can generate the 3-bit ALU control input using a small control unit that has as inputs the function field of the instruction and a 2-bit control field, which we call ALUOp. ALUOp indicates whether the operation to be performed should be add (00) for loads and stores, subtract (01) for beq, or determined by the operation encoded in the funct field (10). The output of the ALU control unit is a 3-bit signal that directly controls the ALU by generating one of the five 3-bit combinations shown previously.

In Figure 5.14, we show how to set the ALU control inputs based on the 2-bit ALUOp control and the 6-bit function code. For completeness, the relationship between the ALUOp bits and the instruction opcode is also shown. Later in this chapter we will see how the ALUOp bits are generated from the main control unit.

This style of using multiple levels of decoding (i.e., the main control unit generates the ALUOp bits, which then are used as input to the ALU control that generates the actual signals to control the ALU unit) is a common implementation technique. Using multiple levels of control can reduce the size of the main control unit. Using several smaller control units may also potentially increase the speed of the control unit. Such optimizations are important, since the control unit is often performance-critical.

There are several different ways to implement the mapping from the 2-bit ALUOp field and the 6-bit funct field to the three ALU operation control bits. Because only a small number of the 64 possible values of the function field are of interest and the function field is used only when the ALUOp bits equal 10, we can use a small piece of logic that recognizes the subset of possible values and causes the correct setting of the ALU control bits.

As a step in designing this logic, it is useful to create a truth table for the interesting combinations of the function code field and the ALUOp bits, as we've done in Figure 5.15; this truth table shows how the 3-bit ALU control is set depending on these two input fields. Since the full truth table is very large ($2^8 = 256$ entries) and we don't care about the value of the ALU control for many of these input combinations, we show only the truth table entries for which the ALU control must have a specific value. Throughout this chapter, we will use

Instruction opcode	ALUOp	Instruction operation	Funct field	Desired ALU action	ALU control input
LW	00	load word	XXXXXX	add	010
SW	00	store word	XXXXXX	add	010
Branch equal	01	branch equal	XXXXXX	subtract	110
R-type	10	add	100000	add	010
R-type	10	subtract	100010	subtract	110
R-type	10	AND	100100	and	000
R-type	10	OR	100101	or	001
R-type	10	set on less than	101010	set on less than	111

FIGURE 5.14 How the ALU control bits are set depends on the ALUOp control bits and the different function codes for the R-type instruction. The opcode, listed in the first column, determines the setting of the ALUOp bits. All the encodings are shown in binary. Notice that when the ALUOp code is 00 or 01, the output fields do not depend on the function code field; in this case, we say that we "don't care" about the value of the function code, and the funct field is shown as XXXXXX. When the ALUOp value is 10, then the function code is used to set the ALU control input.

ALUOp		Funct field						Operation
ALUOp1	**ALUOp0**	**F5**	**F4**	**F3**	**F2**	**F1**	**F0**	
0	0	X	X	X	X	X	X	010
X	1	X	X	X	X	X	X	110
1	X	X	X	0	0	0	0	010
1	X	X	X	0	0	1	0	110
1	X	X	X	0	1	0	0	000
1	X	X	X	0	1	0	1	001
1	X	X	X	1	0	1	0	111

FIGURE 5.15   The truth table for the three ALU control bits (called Operation). The inputs are the ALUOp and function code field. Only the entries for which the ALU control is asserted are shown. Some don't-care entries have been added. For example, the ALUOp does not use the encoding 11, so the truth table can contain entries 1X and X1, rather than 10 and 01. Also, when the function field is used, the first two bits (F5 and F4) of these instructions are always 10, so they are don't-care terms and are replaced with XX in the truth table.

this practice of showing only the truth table entries that must be asserted and not showing those that are all zero or don't care. (This practice has a disadvantage, which we discuss in section C.2 of Appendix C.)

Because in many instances we do not care about the values of some of the inputs and to keep the tables compact, we also include "don't-care" terms. A don't-care term in this truth table (represented by an X in an input column) indicates that the output does not depend on the value of the input corresponding to that column. For example, when the ALUOp bits are 00, as in the first line of the table in Figure 5.15, we always set the ALU control to 010, independent of the function code. In this case, then, the function code inputs will be don't cares in this line of the truth table. Later, we will see examples of another type of don't-care term. If you are unfamiliar with the concept of don't-care terms, see Appendix B for more information.

Once the truth table has been constructed, it can be optimized and then turned into gates. This process is completely mechanical. Thus, rather than show the final steps here, we describe the process and the result in section C.2 of Appendix C.

Designing the Main Control Unit

Now that we have described how to design an ALU that uses the function code and a 2-bit signal as its control inputs, we can return to looking at the rest of the control. To start this process, let's identify the fields of an instruction and the control lines that are needed for the datapath we constructed in Figure 5.13 on page 354. To understand how to connect the fields of an instruction to the datapath, it is useful to review the formats of the three instruction classes: the R-type, branch, and load/store instructions. These formats are shown in Figure 5.16.

Field	0	rs	rt	rd	shamt	funct
Bit positions	31–26	25–21	20–16	15–11	10–6	5–0

a.   R-type instruction

Field	35 or 43	rs	rt	address	
Bit positions	31–26	25–21	20–16	15–0	

b.   Load or store instruction

Field	4	rs	rt	address	
Bit positions	31–26	25–21	20–16	15–0	

c.   Branch instruction

FIGURE 5.16   The three instruction classes (R-type, load and store, and branch) use two different instruction formats. The jump instructions use another format, which we will discuss shortly. (a) Instruction format for R-format instructions, which all have an opcode of 0. These instructions have three register operands: rs, rt, and rd. Fields rs and rt are sources, and rd is the destination. The ALU function is in the funct field and is decoded by the ALU control design in the previous section. The R-type instructions that we implement are add, sub, and, or, and slt. The shamt field is used only for shifts; we will ignore it in this chapter. (b) Instruction format for load (opcode = 35_{ten}) and store (opcode = 43_{ten}) instructions. The register rs is the base register that is added to the 16-bit address field to form the memory address. For loads, rt is the destination register for the loaded value. For stores, rt is the source register whose value should be stored into memory. (c) Instruction format for branch equal (opcode = 4). The registers rs and rt are the source registers that are compared for equality. The 16-bit address field is sign-extended, shifted, and added to the PC to compute the branch target address.

There are several major observations about this instruction format that we will rely on:

- The op field, also called the *opcode*, is always contained in bits 31–26. We will refer to this field as Op[5-0].

- The two registers to be read are always specified by the rs and rt fields, at positions 25–21 and 20–16. This is true for the R-type instructions, branch equal, and for store.

- The base register for load and store instructions is always in bit positions 25–21 (rs).

- The 16-bit offset for branch equal, load, and store is always in positions 15–0.

- The destination register is in one of two places. For a load it is in bit positions 20–16 (rt), while for an R-type instruction it is in bit positions 15–11 (rd). Thus we will need to add a multiplexor to select which field of the instruction is used to indicate the register number to be written.

Using this information, we can add the instruction labels and extra multiplexor (for the Write register number input of the register file) to the simple datapath. Figure 5.17 shows these additions plus the ALU control block, the write signals for state elements, the read signal for the data memory, and the

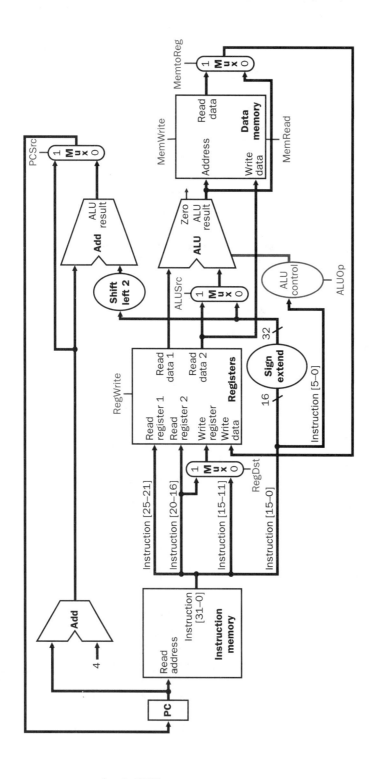

FIGURE 5.17 The datapath of Figure 5.13 with all necessary multiplexors and all control lines identified. The control lines are shown in color. The ALU control block has also been added. The PC does not require a write control, since it is written once at the end of every clock cycle; the branch control logic determines whether it is written with the incremented PC or the branch target address.

Signal name	Effect when deasserted	Effect when asserted
RegDst	The register destination number for the Write register comes from the rt field (bits 20–16).	The register destination number for the Write register comes from the rd field (bits 15–11).
RegWrite	None	The register on the Write register input is written with the value on the Write data input.
ALUSrc	The second ALU operand comes from the second register file output (Read data 2).	The second ALU operand is the sign-extended, lower 16 bits of the instruction.
PCSrc	The PC is replaced by the output of the adder that computes the value of PC + 4.	The PC is replaced by the output of the adder that computes the branch target.
MemRead	None	Data memory contents designated by the address input are put on the Read data output.
MemWrite	None	Data memory contents designated by the address input are replaced by the value on the Write data input.
MemtoReg	The value fed to the register Write data input comes from the ALU.	The value fed to the register Write data input comes from the data memory.

FIGURE 5.18 The effect of each of the seven control signals. When the 1-bit control to a two-way multiplexor is asserted, the multiplexor selects the input corresponding to 1. Otherwise, if the control is deasserted, the multiplexor selects the 0 input. Remember that the state elements all have the clock as an implicit input and that the clock is used in controlling writes. The clock is never gated externally to a state element, since this can create timing problems. (See Appendix B for further discussion of this problem.)

control signals for the multiplexors. Since all the multiplexors have two inputs, they each require a single control line.

Figure 5.17 shows seven single-bit control lines plus the 2-bit ALUOp control signal. We have already defined how the ALUOp control signal works, and it is useful to define what the seven other control signals do informally before we determine how to set these control signals during instruction execution. Figure 5.18 describes the function of these seven control lines.

Now that we have looked at the function of each of the control signals, we can look at how to set them. The control unit can set all but one of the control signals based solely on the opcode field of the instruction. The PCSrc control line is the exception. That control line should be set if the instruction is branch on equal (a decision that the control unit can make) *and* the Zero output of the ALU, which is used for equality comparison, is true. To generate the PCSrc signal, we will need to AND together a signal from the control unit, which we call *Branch*, with the Zero signal out of the ALU.

These nine control signals (seven from Figure 5.18 and two for ALUOp) can now be set on the basis of six input signals to the control unit, which are the opcode bits. The datapath with the control unit and the control signals are shown in Figure 5.19.

Before we try to write a set of equations or a truth table for the control unit, it will be useful to try to define the control function informally. Because the setting of the control lines depends only on the opcode, we define whether each control signal should be 0, 1, or don't care (X), for each of the opcode values.

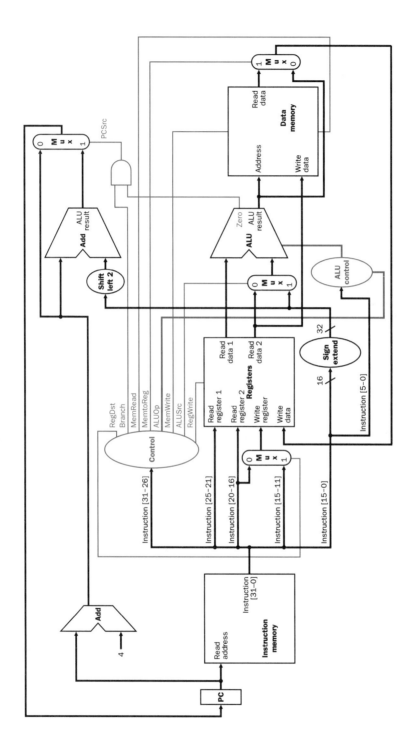

FIGURE 5.19 **The simple datapath with the control unit.** The input to the control unit is the 6-bit opcode field from the instruction. The outputs of the control unit consist of three 1-bit signals that are used to control multiplexors (RegDst, ALUSrc, and MemtoReg), three signals for controlling reads and writes in the register file and data memory (RegWrite, MemRead, and MemWrite), a 1-bit signal used in determining whether to possibly branch (Branch), and a 2-bit control signal for the ALU (ALUOp). An AND gate is used to combine the branch control signal and the Zero output from the ALU; the AND gate output controls the selection of the next PC. Notice that PCSrc is now a derived signal, rather than one coming directly from the control unit. Thus we drop the signal name in subsequent figures.

(page 360)

Figure 5.20 defines how the control signals should be set for each opcode; this information follows directly from Figures 5.14, 5.18, and 5.19.

Operation of the Datapath

With the information contained in Figures 5.18 and 5.20, we can design the control unit logic, but before we do that, let's look at how each instruction uses the datapath. In the next few figures, we show the flow of three different instruction classes through the datapath. The asserted control signals and active datapath elements are highlighted in each of these. Note that a multiplexor whose control is 0 has a definite action, even if its control line is not highlighted. Multiple-bit control signals are highlighted if any constituent signal is asserted.

Let's begin with an R-type instruction, such as add $t1,$t2,$t3. Rather than looking at the entire datapath as one piece of combinational logic, it is easier to think of an instruction executing in a series of steps, focusing our attention on the portion of the datapath associated with each step. There are four steps to execute an R-type instruction:

1. An instruction is fetched from the instruction memory and the PC is incremented. Figure 5.21 shows this first step. The active units and asserted control lines are highlighted; those that are asserted in later steps of an R-type instruction are in gray, and those in light gray are those not active for an R-type instruction in any step. The same format is followed for the next three steps.

Instruction	RegDst	ALUSrc	Memto-Reg	Reg Write	Mem Read	Mem Write	Branch	ALUOp1	ALUOp0
R-format	1	0	0	1	0	0	0	1	0
lw	0	1	1	1	1	0	0	0	0
sw	X	1	X	0	0	1	0	0	0
beq	X	0	X	0	0	0	1	0	1

FIGURE 5.20   The setting of the control lines is completely determined by the opcode fields of the instruction. The first row of the table corresponds to the R-format instructions (add, sub, and, or, and slt). For all these instructions, the source register fields are rs and rt and the destination register field is rd; this defines how the signals ALUSrc and RegDst are set. Furthermore, an R-type instruction writes a register (RegWrite = 1), but neither reads nor writes data memory. When the Branch control signal is 0, the PC is unconditionally replaced with PC + 4; otherwise, the PC is replaced by the branch target if the Zero output of the ALU is also high. The ALUOp field for R-type instructions is set to 10 to indicate that the ALU control should be generated from the funct field. The second and third rows of this table give the control signal settings for lw and sw. These ALUSrc and ALUOp fields are set to perform the address calculation. The MemRead and MemWrite are set to perform the memory access. Finally, RegDst and RegWrite are set for a load to cause the result to be stored into the rt register. The branch instruction is similar to an R-format operation, since it sends the rs and rt registers to the ALU. The ALUOp field for branch is set for a subtract (ALU control = 01), which is used to test for equality. Notice that the MemtoReg field is irrelevant when the RegWrite signal is 0—since the register is not being written, the value of the data on the register data write port is not used. Thus, the entry MemtoReg in the last two rows of the table is replaced with X for don't care. Don't cares can also be added to RegDst when RegWrite is 0. This type of don't care must be added by the designer, since it depends on knowledge of how the datapath works.

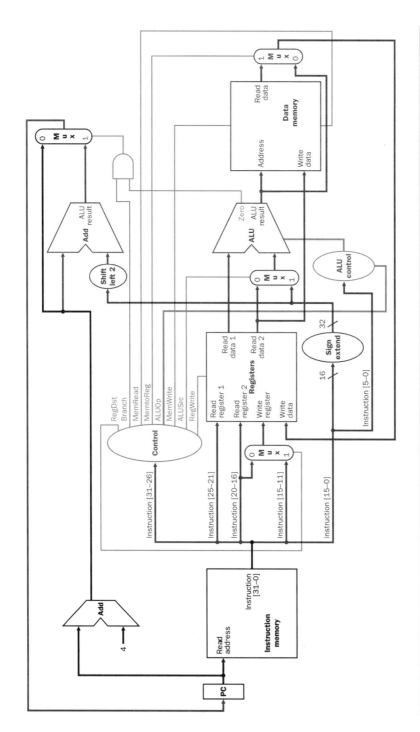

FIGURE 5.21 The first step of an R-type instruction performs a fetch from instruction memory and increments the PC. The portions active in this step are highlighted; the light portions are not active at this step, though some will be active later in the cycle.

2. Two registers, $t2 and $t3, are read from the register file as shown in Figure 5.22 on page 364. The main control unit computes the setting of the control lines during this step also.

3. The ALU operates on the data read from the register file, using the function code (bits 5–0, which is the funct field, of the instruction) to generate the ALU function. Figure 5.23 on page 365 shows the operation of this step.

4. The result from the ALU is written into the register file using bits 15–11 of the instruction to select the destination register ($t1). Figure 5.24 on page 366 shows the final step added to the previous three.

Remember that this implementation is combinational. That is, it is not really a series of four distinct steps. The datapath really operates in a single clock cycle, and the signals within the datapath can vary unpredictably during the clock cycle. The signals stabilize roughly in the order of the steps given above because the flow of information follows this order. Thus, Figure 5.24 shows not only the action of the last step, but essentially the operation of the entire datapath when the clock cycle actually ends.

We can illustrate the execution of a load word, such as

```
lw $t1, offset($t2)
```

in a style similar to Figure 5.24. Figure 5.25 on page 368 shows the active functional units and asserted control lines for a load. We can think of a load instruction as operating in five steps (similar to the R-type executed in four):

1. An instruction is fetched from the instruction memory and the PC is incremented.

2. A register ($t2) value is read from the register file.

3. The ALU computes the sum of the value read from the register file and the sign-extended, lower 16 bits of the instruction (offset).

4. The sum from the ALU is used as the address for the data memory.

5. The data from the memory unit is written into the register file; the register destination is given by bits 20–16 of the instruction ($t1).

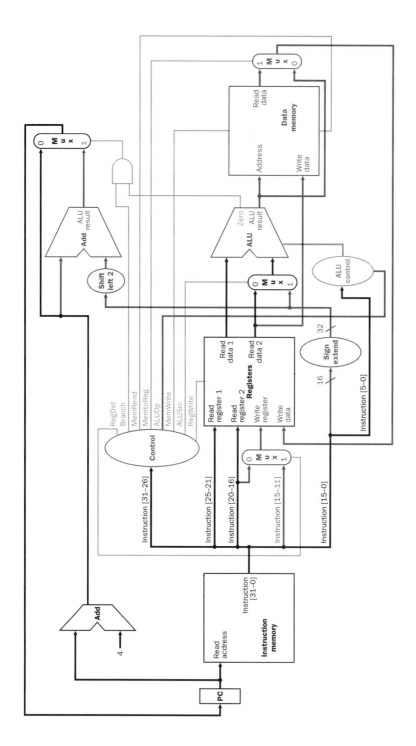

FIGURE 5.22 The second phase in the execution of R-type instructions reads the two source registers from the register file. The main control unit also uses the opcode field to determine the control line setting. These units become active in addition to the units active during the instruction fetch portion, shown in Figure 5.21.

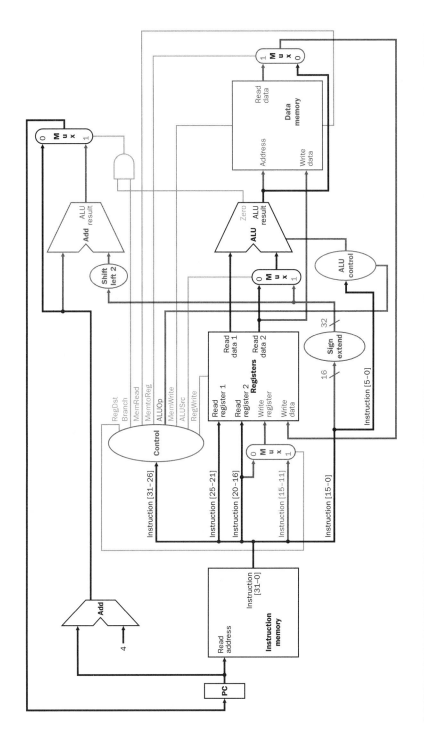

FIGURE 5.23 The third phase of execution for R-type instructions involves the ALU operating on the register data operands. The control line values are all set, and the ALU control has been computed. The ALU operates on the data.

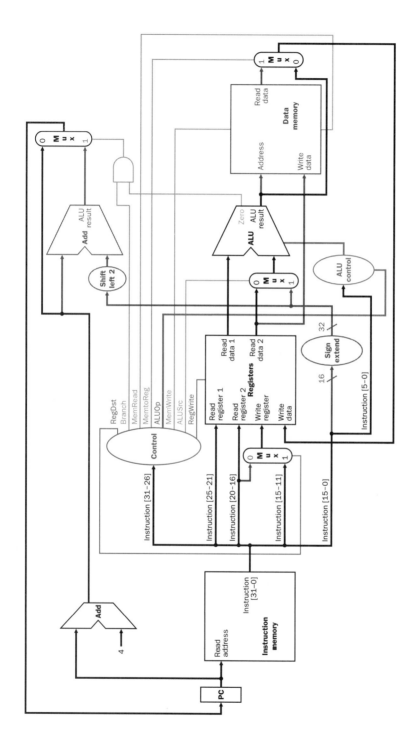

FIGURE 5.24 The final step in an R-type instruction, writing the result, is added to the active units shown for the previous three steps in Figure 5.23. The PC is also updated at the end of this phase. Because the datapath is combinational, this step shows all the active units and asserted control lines when they are stable. Observe that if the instruction is one that uses the same register as both an input and output (such as add R1, R1, R1) it works correctly: the value read from the registers is the value of R1 written at the end of some earlier clock cycle, while the value to be written into the registers by the instruction is not actually written into the register until the clock edge at the end of the current clock cycle.

Finally, we can show the operation of the branch-on-equal instruction, such as `beq $t1,$t2,offset`, in the same fashion. It operates much like an R-format instruction, but the ALU output is used to determine whether the PC is written with PC + 4 or the branch target address. Figure 5.26 shows the four steps in execution:

1. An instruction is fetched from the instruction memory and the PC is incremented.

2. Two registers, `$t1` and `$t2`, are read from the register file.

3. The ALU performs a subtract on the data values read from the register file. The value of PC + 4 is added to the sign-extended, lower 16 bits of the instruction (`offset`) shifted left by two; the result is the branch target address.

4. The Zero result from the ALU is used to decide which adder result to store into the PC.

In the next section, we will examine machines that are truly sequential, namely, those in which each of these steps is a distinct clock cycle.

Finalizing the Control

Now that we have seen how the instructions operate in steps, let's continue with the control implementation. The control function can be precisely defined using the contents of Figure 5.20 on page 361. The outputs are the control lines, the input is the 6-bit opcode field, Op [5–0]. Thus we can create a truth table for each of the outputs. Before doing so, let's write down the encoding for each of the opcodes of interest in Figure 5.20, both as a decimal number and as a series of bits that are input to the control unit:

Name	Opcode in decimal	Opcode in binary					
		Op5	Op4	Op3	Op2	Op1	Op0
R-format	0_{ten}	0	0	0	0	0	0
lw	35_{ten}	1	0	0	0	1	1
sw	43_{ten}	1	0	1	0	1	1
beq	4_{ten}	0	0	0	1	0	0

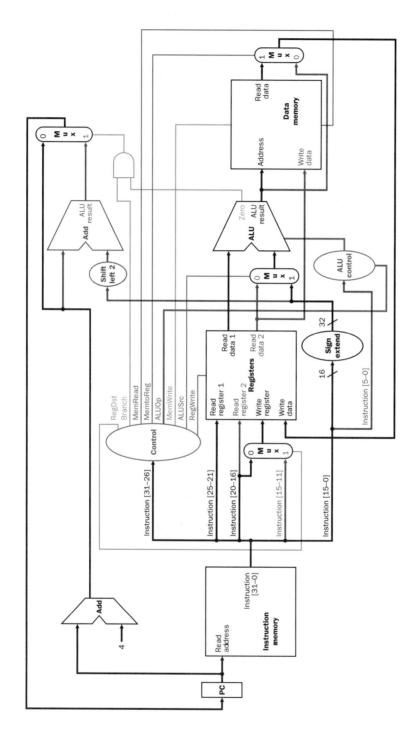

FIGURE 5.25 The operation of a load instruction with the simple datapath control scheme. A store instruction would operate very similarly. The main difference would be that the memory control would indicate a write rather than a read, the second register value read would be used for the data to store, and the operation of writing the data memory value to the register file would not occur.

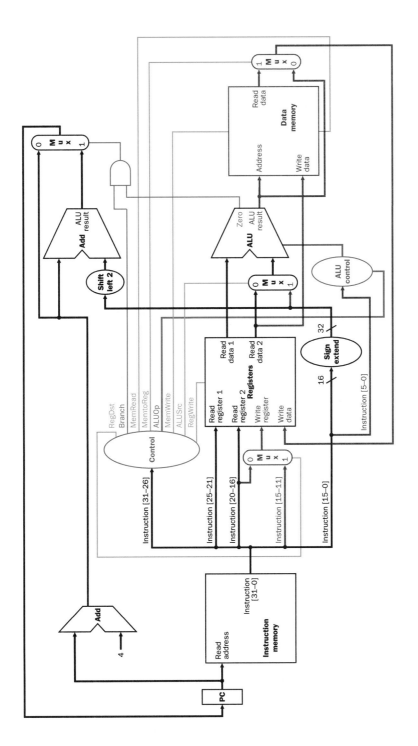

FIGURE 5.26 The datapath in operation for a branch equal instruction. After using the register file and ALU to perform the compare, the Zero output is used to select the next program counter from between the two candidates.

Input or output	Signal name	R-format	lw	sw	beq
Inputs	Op5	0	1	1	0
	Op4	0	0	0	0
	Op3	0	0	1	0
	Op2	0	0	0	1
	Op1	0	1	1	0
	Op0	0	1	1	0
Outputs	RegDst	1	0	X	X
	ALUSrc	0	1	1	0
	MemtoReg	0	1	X	X
	RegWrite	1	1	0	0
	MemRead	0	1	0	0
	MemWrite	0	0	1	0
	Branch	0	0	0	1
	ALUOp1	1	0	0	0
	ALUOp0	0	0	0	1

FIGURE 5.27 The control function for the simple single-cycle implementation is completely specified by this truth table. The top half of the table gives the combinations of input signals that correspond to the four opcodes that determine the control output settings. (Remember that Op [5–0] corresponds to bits 31–26 of the instruction, which is the op field.) The bottom portion of the table gives the outputs. Thus, the output RegWrite is asserted for two different combinations of the inputs. If we consider only the four opcodes shown in this table, then we can simplify the truth table by using don't cares in the input portion. For example, we can detect an R-format instruction with the expression $\overline{Op5} \cdot \overline{Op2}$, since this is sufficient to distinguish the R-format instructions from lw, sw, and beq. We do not take advantage of this simplification, since the rest of the MIPS opcodes are used in a full implementation.

Using this information, we can now describe the logic in the control unit in one large truth table that combines all the outputs, as in Figure 5.27. It completely specifies the control function, and we can implement it directly in gates in an automated fashion. We show this final step in section C.2 in Appendix C.

Now, let's add the jump instruction to show how the basic datapath and control can be extended to handle other instructions in the instruction set.

Implementing Jumps

Example

Figure 5.19 on page 360 shows the implementation of many of the instructions we looked at in Chapter 3. One class of instructions missing is that of the jump instruction. Extend the datapath and control of Figure 5.19 to include the jump instruction. Describe how to set any new control lines.

Field	2	address
Bit positions	31–26	25–0

FIGURE 5.28 Instruction format for the jump instruction (opcode = 2). The destination address for a jump instruction is formed by concatenating the upper 4 bits of the current PC + 4 to the 26-bit address field in the jump instruction and adding 00 as the 2 low-order bits.

Answer

The jump instruction looks somewhat like a branch instruction but computes the target PC differently and is not conditional. Like a branch, the low-order 2 bits of a jump address are always 00_{two}. The next lower 26 bits of this 32-bit address come from the 26-bit immediate field in the instruction, as shown in Figure 5.28. The upper 4 bits of the address that should replace the PC come from the PC of the jump instruction plus four. Thus, we can implement a jump by storing into the PC the concatenation of

- the upper 4 bits of the current PC + 4 (these are bits 31–28 of the sequentially following instruction address)

- the 26-bit immediate field of the jump instruction

- the bits 00_{two}

Figure 5.29 shows the addition of the control for jump added to Figure 5.19. An additional multiplexor is used to select the source for the new PC value, which is either the incremented PC (PC + 4), the branch target PC, or the jump target PC. One additional control signal is needed for the additional multiplexor. This control signal, called *Jump*, is asserted only when the instruction is a jump—that is, when the opcode is 2.

Why a Single-Cycle Implementation Is Not Used

Although the single-cycle design will work correctly, it would not be used in modern designs because it is inefficient. To see why this is so notice that the clock cycle must have the same length for every instruction in this single-cycle design, and the CPI (see Chapter 2) will therefore be 1. Of course, the clock cycle is determined by the longest possible path in the machine. This path is almost certainly a load instruction, which uses five functional units in series: the instruction memory, the register file, the ALU, the data memory, and the register file. Although the CPI is 1, the overall performance of a single-cycle implementation is not likely to be very good, since several of the instruction classes could fit in a shorter clock cycle.

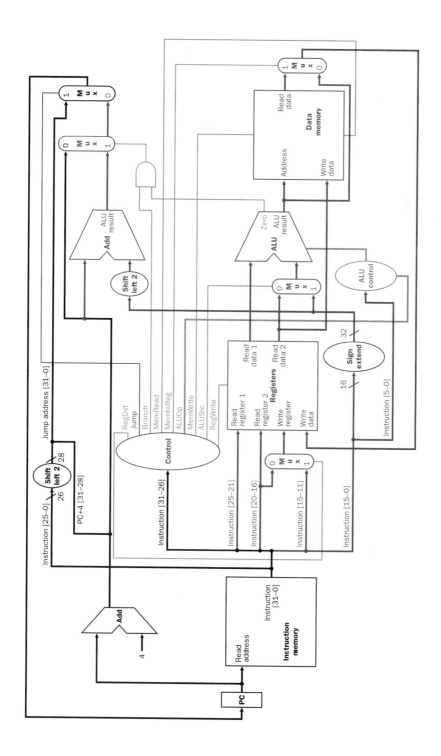

FIGURE 5.29 The simple control and datapath are extended to handle the jump instruction. An additional multiplexor (at the upper right) is used to choose between the jump target and either the branch target or the sequential instruction following this one. This multiplexor is controlled by the jump control signal. The jump target address is obtained by shifting the lower 26 bits of the jump instruction left 2 bits, effectively adding 00 as the low-order bits, and then concatenating the upper 4 bits of PC + 4 as the high-order bits, thus yielding a 32-bit address.

Performance of Single-Cycle Machines

Example

Assume that the operation time for the major functional units in this implementation are the following:

- Memory units: nanoseconds (ns)
- ALU and adders: 2 ns
- Register file (read or write): 1 ns

Assuming that the multiplexors, control unit, PC accesses, sign extension unit, and wires have no delay, which of the following implementations would be faster and by how much?

1. An implementation in which every instruction operates in 1 clock cycle of a fixed length.

2. An implementation where every instruction executes in 1 clock cycle using a variable-length clock, which for each instruction is only as long as it needs to be. (Such an approach is not terribly practical, but it will allow us to see what is being sacrificed when all the instructions must execute in a single clock of the same length.)

To compare the performance, assume the following instruction mix: 24% loads, 12% stores, 44% R-format instructions, 18% branches, and 2% jumps.

Answer

Let's start by comparing the CPU execution times. Recall from Chapter 2 that

$$\text{CPU execution time} = \text{Instruction count} \times \text{CPI} \times \text{Clock cycle time}$$

Since CPI must be 1, we can simplify this to

$$\text{CPU execution time} = \text{Instruction count} \times \text{Clock cycle time}$$

We need only find the clock cycle time for the two implementations, since the instruction count and CPI are the same for both implementations. The critical path for the different instruction classes is as follows:

Instruction class	Functional units used by the instruction class				
R-format	Instruction fetch	Register access	ALU	Register access	
Load word	Instruction fetch	Register access	ALU	Memory access	Register access
Store word	Instruction fetch	Register access	ALU	Memory access	
Branch	Instruction fetch	Register access	ALU		
Jump	Instruction fetch				

Using these critical paths, we can compute the required length for each instruction class:

Instruction class	Instruction memory	Register read	ALU operation	Data memory	Register write	Total
R-format	2	1	2	0	1	6 ns
Load word	2	1	2	2	1	8 ns
Store word	2	1	2	2		7 ns
Branch	2	1	2			5 ns
Jump	2					2 ns

The clock cycle for a machine with a single clock for all instructions will be determined by the longest instruction, which is 8 ns. (This timing is approximate, since our timing model is quite simplistic. In reality, the timing of modern digital systems is complex, often allowing time to be borrowed from one clock cycle for use in the next.)

A machine with a variable clock will have a clock cycle that varies between 2 ns and 8 ns. We can find the average clock cycle length for a machine with a variable-length clock using the information above and the instruction frequency distribution.

Thus, the average time per instruction with a variable clock is

$$\text{CPU clock cycle} = 8 \times 24\% + 7 \times 12\% + 6 \times 44\% + 5 \times 18\% + 2 \times 2\%$$

$$= 6.3 \text{ ns}$$

Since the variable clock implementation has a shorter average clock cycle, it is clearly faster. Let's find the performance ratio:

$$\frac{\text{CPU performance}_{\text{variable clock}}}{\text{CPU performance}_{\text{single clock}}} = \frac{\text{CPU execution time}_{\text{single clock}}}{\text{CPU execution time}_{\text{variable clock}}}$$

$$= \frac{\text{IC} \times \text{CPU clock cycle}_{\text{single clock}}}{\text{IC} \times \text{CPU clock cycle}_{\text{variable clock}}}$$

$$= \frac{\text{CPU clock cycle}_{\text{single clock}}}{\text{CPU clock cycle}_{\text{variable clock}}}$$

$$= \frac{8}{6.3} = 1.27$$

The variable clock implementation would be 1.27 times faster. Unfortunately, implementing a variable-speed clock for each instruction class is extremely difficult, and the overhead for such an approach could be larger than any advantage gained. As we will see in the next section, an alternative is to use a shorter clock cycle that does less work and then vary the number of clock cycles for the different instruction classes.

The penalty for using the single-cycle design with a fixed clock cycle is significant, but might be considered acceptable for this small instruction set. However, if we tried to implement the floating-point unit or an instruction set with more complex instructions, this single-cycle design wouldn't work well at all. Let's look at an example with floating point.

Performance of a Single-Cycle CPU with Floating-Point Instructions

Example

Suppose we have a floating-point unit that requires 8 ns for a floating-point add and 16 ns for a floating-point multiply. All the other functional unit times are as in the previous example, and a floating-point instruction is like an arithmetic-logical instruction, except that it uses the floating-point ALU rather than the main ALU. Using the instruction distribution for spice from Chapter 4, Figure 4.54 on page 311, find the performance ratio between an implementation in which the clock cycle is different for each instruction class and an implementation in which all instructions have the same clock cycle time. Assume the following:

- All loads take the same time and comprise 31% of the instructions.
- All stores take the same time and comprise 21% of the instructions.
- R-format instructions comprise 27% of the mix.
- Branches comprise 5% of the instructions, while jumps comprise 2%.
- FP add and subtract take the same time and together total 7% of the instructions.
- FP multiply and divide take the same time and together total 7% of the instructions.

Answer   From the previous example, we know that

$$\frac{\text{CPU performance}_{\text{variable clock}}}{\text{CPU performance}_{\text{single clock}}} = \frac{\text{CPU clock cycle}_{\text{single clock}}}{\text{CPU clock cycle}_{\text{variable clock}}}$$

The cycle time for the single-cycle machine will be equal to the longest instruction time, which is floating-point multiply. The time for a floating-point multiply, and thus the clock cycle, is $2 + 1 + 16 + 1 = 20$ ns.

Consider a machine whose instructions have different cycle times. The time for a floating-point add instruction is $2 + 1 + 8 + 1 = 12$ ns. Multiplying the cycle times by the instruction frequencies tells us that the average clock length will be

$$\text{CPU clock cycle} = 8 \times 31\% + 7 \times 21\% + 6 \times 27\% + 5 \times 5\%$$

$$+ 2 \times 2\% + 20 \times 7\% + 12 \times 7\% = 7.0 \text{ ns}$$

The improvement in performance is

$$\frac{\text{CPU performance}_{\text{variable clock}}}{\text{CPU performance}_{\text{single clock}}} = \frac{\text{CPU clock cycle}_{\text{single clock}}}{\text{CPU clock cycle}_{\text{variable clock}}}$$

$$= \frac{20}{7} = 2.9$$

A variable clock would allow us to improve performance by 2.9 times.

Similarly, if we had a machine with more powerful operations and addressing modes, instructions could vary from three or four functional unit delays to tens or even hundreds of functional unit delays. In addition, because we must assume that the clock cycle is equal to the worst-case delay for all instructions, we can't use implementation techniques that reduce the delay of the common case but do not improve the worst-case cycle time. A single-cycle implementation thus violates our key design principle of making the common case fast.

In addition, with this single-cycle implementation, each functional unit can be used only once per clock; therefore, some functional units must be duplicated, raising the cost of the implementation. A single-cycle design is inefficient both in its performance and in its hardware cost!

We can avoid these difficulties by using implementation techniques that have a shorter clock cycle—derived from the basic functional unit delays—and that require multiple clock cycles for each instruction. The next section explores this alternative implementation scheme. In Chapter 6, we'll look at another implementation technique, called pipelining, that uses a datapath very similar to the single-cycle datapath, but is much more efficient. Pipelining gains efficiency by overlapping the execution of multiple instructions, increasing hardware utilization and improving performance.

5.4 A Multicycle Implementation

In an earlier example, we broke each instruction into a series of steps corresponding to the functional unit operations that were needed. We can use these steps to create a *multicycle implementation*. In a multicycle implementation, each *step* in the execution will take 1 clock cycle. The multicycle implementation allows a functional unit to be used more than once per instruction, as long as it is used on different clock cycles. This sharing can help reduce the amount of hardware required. The ability to allow instructions to take different numbers of clock cycles and the ability to share functional units within the execution of a single instruction are the major advantages of a multicycle design. Figure 5.30 shows the abstract version of the multicycle datapath. Comparing this to the datapath for the single-cycle version shown in Figure 5.13 on page 354, we can see the following differences:

- A single memory unit is used for both instructions and data.

- There is a single ALU, rather than an ALU and two adders.

- One or more registers are added after every major functional unit to hold the output of that unit until the value is used in a subsequent clock cycle.

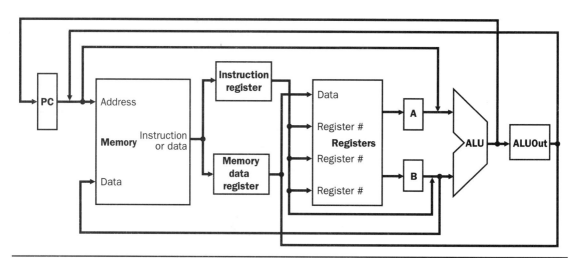

FIGURE 5.30   The high-level view of the multicycle datapath. This picture shows the key elements of the datapath: a shared memory unit, a single ALU shared among instructions, and the connections among these shared units. The use of shared functional units requires the addition or widening of multiplexors as well as new temporary registers that hold data between clock cycles of the same instruction. The additional registers are the Instruction register (IR), the Memory data register (MDR), A, B, and ALUOut.

At the end of a clock cycle, all data that are used in subsequent clock cycles must be stored in a state element. Data used by *subsequent instructions* in a later clock cycle is stored into one of the programmer-visible state elements (i.e., the register file, the PC, or the memory). In contrast, data used by the *same instruction* in a later cycle must be stored into one of these additional registers.

Thus the position of the additional registers is determined by the two factors: what combinational units will fit in a clock cycle and what data are needed in later cycles implementing the instruction. In this multicycle design, we assume that the clock cycle can accommodate at most one of the following operations: a memory access, a register file access (two reads or one write), or an ALU operation. Thus any data produced by one of these three functional units (the memory, the register file, or the ALU) must be saved into a temporary register for use on a later cycle.

The following temporary registers are added to meet these requirements:

- The Instruction register (IR) and the Memory data register (MDR) are added to save the output of the memory for an instruction read and a data read, respectively. Two separate registers are used, since, as will be clear shortly, both values are needed during the same clock cycle.

- The A and B registers are used to hold the register operand values read from the register file.

- The ALUOut register holds the output of the ALU.

All the registers except the IR hold data only between a pair of adjacent clock cycles and will thus not need a write control signal. The IR needs to hold the instruction until the end of execution of that instruction, and thus will require a write control signal. This distinction will become more clear when we show the individual clock cycles for each instruction.

Because several functional units are shared for different purposes, we need both to add multiplexors and to expand existing multiplexors. For example, since one memory is used for both instructions and data, we need a multiplexor to select between the two sources for a memory address, namely the PC (for instruction access) and ALUOut (for data access).

Replacing the three ALUs of the single-cycle datapath by a single ALU means that the single ALU must accommodate all the inputs that used to go to the three different ALUs. Handling the additional inputs requires two changes to the datapath:

1. An additional multiplexor is added for the first ALU input. The multiplexor chooses between the A register and the PC.

2. The multiplexor on the second ALU input is changed from a two-way to a four-way multiplexor. The two additional inputs to the multiplexor are the constant 4 (used to increment the PC) and the sign-extended and shifted offset field (used in the branch address computation).

Figure 5.31 shows the details of the datapath with these additional multiplexors. By introducing a few registers and multiplexors, we are able to reduce the number of memory units from two to one and eliminate two adders. Since registers and multiplexors are fairly small, this could yield a substantial reduction in the hardware cost.

Because the datapath shown in Figure 5.31 takes multiple clock cycles per instruction, it will require a different set of control signals. The programmer-visible state units (the PC, the memory, and the registers) as well as the IR will need write control signals. The memory will also need a read signal. We can use the ALU control unit from the single-cycle datapath (see Figures 5.15 and Appendix C) to control the ALU here as well. Finally, each of the two-input multiplexors requires a single control line, while the four-input multiplexor requires two control lines. Figure 5.32 shows the datapath of Figure 5.31 with these control lines added.

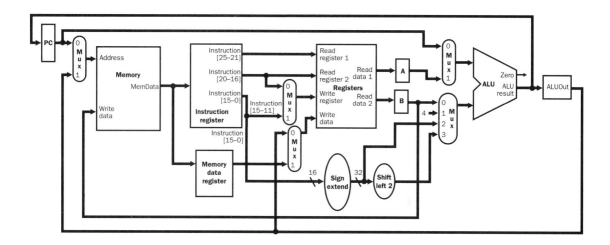

FIGURE 5.31   Multicycle datapath for MIPS handles the basic instructions. Although this datapath supports normal incrementing of the PC, a few more connections and a multiplexor will be needed for branches and jumps; we will add these shortly. The additions versus the single-clock datapath include several registers (IR, MDR, A, B, ALUOut), a multiplexor for the memory address, a multiplexor for the top ALU input, and expanding the multiplexor on the bottom ALU input into a four-way selector. These small additions allow us to remove two adders and a memory unit.

The multicycle datapath still requires additions to support branches and jumps; after these additions, we will see how the instructions are sequenced and then generate the datapath control.

With the jump instruction and branch instruction, there are three possible sources for the value to be written into the PC:

1. The output of the ALU, which is the value PC + 4 during instruction fetch. This value should be stored directly into the PC.

2. The register ALUOut, which is where we will store the address of the branch target after it is computed.

3. The lower 26 bits of the Instruction register (IR) shifted left by two and concatenated with the upper 4 bits of the incremented PC, which is the source when the instruction is a jump.

As we observed when we implemented the single-cycle control, the PC is written both unconditionally and conditionally. During a normal increment and jumps, the PC is written unconditionally. If the instruction is a conditional branch, the incremented PC is replaced with the value in ALUOut only if the two designated registers are equal. Thus the control needs two PC write signals, which we will call PCWrite and PCWriteCond.

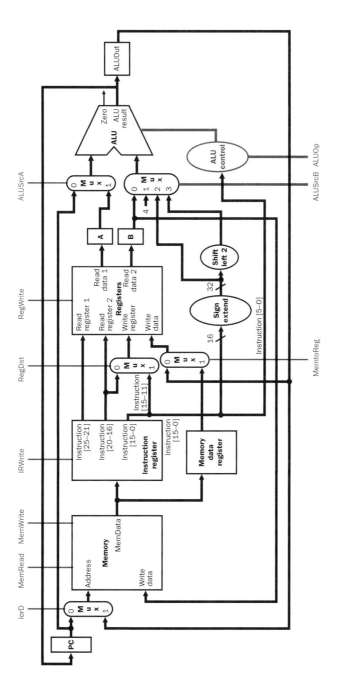

FIGURE 5.32 The multicycle datapath from Figure 5.31 with the control lines shown. The signals ALUOp and ALUSelB are 2-bit control signals, while all the other control lines are 1-bit signals. Neither register A nor B require a write signal, since their contents are only read on the cycle immediately after it is written. The memory data register has been added to hold the data from a load when the data returns from memory. Data from a load returning from memory cannot be written directly into the register file since the clock cycle cannot accommodate the time required for both the memory access and the register file write. The MemRead signal has been moved to the top of the memory unit to simplify the figures. The full set of datapaths and control lines for branches will be added shortly.

We need to connect these two control signals to the PC write control. Just as we did in the single-cycle datapath, we will use a few gates to derive the PC write control signal from PCWrite, PCWriteCond, and the Zero signal of the ALU, which is used to detect if the two register operands of a `beq` are equal. To determine whether the PC should be written during a conditional branch, we AND together the Zero signal of the ALU with the PCWriteCond. The output of this AND gate is then ORed with PCWrite, which is the unconditional PC write signal. The output of this OR gate is connected to the write control signal for the PC.

Figure 5.33 shows the complete multicycle datapath and control unit, including the additional control signals and multiplexor for implementing the PC updating.

Before examining the steps to execute each instruction, let us informally examine the effect of all the control signals (just as we did for the single-cycle design in Figure 5.18 on page 359). Figure 5.34 shows what each control signal does when asserted and deasserted.

Elaboration: To reduce the number of signal lines interconnecting the functional units, designers can use *shared buses*. A shared bus is a set of lines that connect multiple units; in most cases, they include multiple sources that can place data on the bus and multiple readers of the value. Just as we reduced the number of functional units for the datapath, we can reduce the number of buses interconnecting these units by sharing the buses. For example, there are six sources coming to the ALU; however, only two of them are needed at any one time. Thus, a pair of buses can be used to hold values that are being sent to the ALU. Rather than placing a large multiplexor in front of the ALU, a designer can use a shared bus and then ensure that only one of the sources is driving the bus at any point. Although this saves signal lines, the same number of control lines will be needed to control what goes on the bus. The major drawback to using such bus structures is a potential performance penalty, since a bus is unlikely to be as fast as a point-to-point connection.

Breaking the Instruction Execution into Clock Cycles

Given the datapath in Figure 5.33, we now need to look at what should happen in each clock cycle of the multicycle execution, since this will determine what additional control signals may be needed, as well as the setting of the control signals. Our goal in breaking the execution into clock cycles should be to balance the amount of work done in each cycle, so that we minimize the clock cycle time. We can begin by breaking the execution of any instruction into a series of steps, each taking 1 clock cycle, which will be roughly balanced in length. For example, we will restrict each step to contain at most one

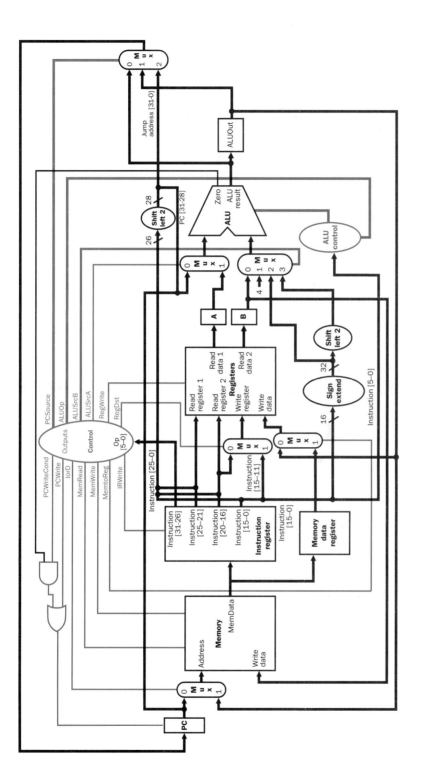

FIGURE 5.33 The complete datapath for the multicycle implementation together with the necessary control lines. The control lines of Figure 5.32 are attached to the control unit, and the control and datapath elements needed to effect changes to the PC are included. The major additions from Figure 5.32 include the multiplexor used to select the source of a new PC value (at the top right); two gates used to combine the PC write signals (top left); and the control signals PCSource, PCWrite, and PCWriteCond. The PCWriteCond signal is ANDed with the Zero output of the ALU to decide whether a branch should be taken; the resulting signal is ORed with the control signal PCWrite to generate the actual write control signal for the PC. In addition, the output of the IR is rearranged to send the lower 26 bits (the jump address) to the logic used to select the next PC. These 26 bits are shifted to the left by two, adding 2 low-order 0 bits; these 28 bits are then concatenated with the high-order 4 bits of the PC, which has already been incremented.

Actions of the 1-bit control signals

Signal name	Effect when deasserted	Effect when asserted
RegDst	The register file destination number for the Write register comes from the rt field.	The register file destination number for the Write register comes from the rd field.
RegWrite	None	The general-purpose register selected by the Write register number is written with the value of the Write data input.
ALUSrcA	The first ALU operand is the PC.	The first ALU operand comes from the A register.
MemRead	None	Content of memory at the location specified by the Address input is put on Memory data output.
MemWrite	None	Memory contents at the location specified by the Address input is replaced by value on Write data input.
MemtoReg	The value fed to the register file Write data input comes from ALUOut.	The value fed to the register file Write data input comes from the MDR.
IorD	The PC is used to supply the address to the memory unit.	ALUOut is used to supply the address to the memory unit.
IRWrite	None	The output of the memory is written into the IR.
PCWrite	None	The PC is written; the source is controlled by PCSource.
PCWriteCond	None	The PC is written if the Zero output from the ALU is also active.

Actions of the 2-bit control signals

Signal name	Value	Effect
ALUOp	00	The ALU performs an add operation.
	01	The ALU performs a subtract operation.
	10	The funct field of the instruction determines the ALU operation.
ALUSrcB	00	The second input to the ALU comes from the B register.
	01	The second input to the ALU is the constant 4.
	10	The second input to the ALU is the sign-extended, lower 16 bits of the IR.
	11	The second input to the ALU is the sign-extended, lower 16 bits of the IR shifted left 2 bits.
PCSource	00	Output of the ALU (PC + 4) is sent to the PC for writing.
	01	The contents of ALUOut (the branch target address) are sent to the PC for writing.
	10	The jump target address (IR[25–0] shifted left 2 bits and concatenated with PC + 4[31–28]) is sent to the PC for writing.

FIGURE 5.34   The action caused by the setting of each control signal in Figure 5.33 on page 383. The top table describes the 1-bit control signals, while the bottom table describes the 2-bit signals. Only those control lines that affect multiplexors have an action when they are deasserted. This information is similar to that in Figure 5.18 on page 359 for the single-cycle datapath, but adds several new control lines (IRWrite, PCWrite, PCWriteCond, ALUSrcB, and PCSource) and removes control lines that are no longer used or have been replaced (PCSrc, Branch, and Jump).

ALU operation, or one register file access, or one memory access. With this restriction, the clock cycle could be as short as the longest of these operations.

Recall that at the end of every clock cycle any data values that will be needed on a subsequent cycle must be stored into a register, which can be either one of the major state elements (e.g., the PC, the register file, or the memory), a temporary register written on every clock cycle (e.g., A, B, MDR, or ALUOut), or a temporary register with write control (e.g., IR). Also remember that because our design is edge-triggered, we can continue to read the current value of a register; the new value does not appear until the next clock cycle.

In the single-cycle datapath, each instruction uses a set of datapath elements to carry out its execution. Many of the datapath elements operate in series, using the output of another element as an input. Some datapath elements operate in parallel; for example, the PC is incremented and the instruction is read at the same time. A similar situation exists in the multicycle datapath. All the operations listed in one step occur in parallel within 1 clock cycle, while successive steps operate in series in different clock cycles. The limitation of one ALU operation, one memory access, and one register file access determines what can fit in one step.

Notice that we distinguish between reading from or writing into the PC or one of the stand-alone registers and reading from or writing into the register file. In the former case, the read or write is part of a clock cycle, while reading or writing a result into the register file takes an additional clock cycle. The reason for this distinction is that the register file has additional control and access overhead compared to the single stand-alone registers. Thus keeping the clock cycle short motivates dedicating separate clock cycles for register file accesses.

The potential execution steps and their actions are given below. Each instruction needs from three to five of these steps:

1. Instruction fetch step

Fetch the instruction from memory and compute the address of the next sequential instruction:

```
IR = Memory[PC];
PC = PC + 4;
```

Operation: Send the PC to the memory as the address, perform a read, and write the instruction into the Instruction register (IR), where it will be stored. Also, increment the PC by four. To implement this step, we will need to assert the control signals MemRead and IRWrite, and set IorD to 0 to select the PC as the source of the address. We also increment the PC by four in this stage, which requires setting the ALUSrcA signal to 0 (sending the PC to the ALU), the ALUSrcB signal to 01 (sending 4 to the ALU), and ALUOp to 00 (to make the ALU add). Finally, we will also want to store the incremented instruction address back into the PC, which requires setting PCWrite. The increment of the PC and the instruction memory access can occur in parallel. The new value of the PC is not visible until the next clock cycle. (The incremented PC will also be stored into ALUOut, but this action is benign.)

2. Instruction decode and register fetch step

In the previous step and in this one, we do not yet know what the instruction is, so we can perform only actions that are either applicable to all instructions (such as fetching the instruction in step 1) or are not harmful, in case the instruction isn't what we think it might be. Thus, in this step we can read the two registers indicated by the rs and rt instruction fields, since it isn't harmful to read them even if it isn't necessary. The values read from the register file may be needed in later stages, so we read them from the register file and store the values into the temporary registers A and B.

We will also compute the branch target address with the ALU, which also is not harmful because we can ignore the value if the instruction turns out not to be a branch. The potential branch target is saved in ALUOut.

Performing these "optimistic" actions early has the benefit of decreasing the number of clock cycles needed to execute an instruction. We can do these optimistic actions early because of the regularity of the instruction formats. For instance, if the instruction has two register inputs, they are always in the rs and rt fields; and if the instruction is a branch, the offset is always the low-order 16 bits:

```
A = Reg[IR[25-21]];
B = Reg[IR[20-16]];
ALUOut = PC + (sign-extend (IR[15-0]) << 2);
```

Operation: Access the register file to read registers rs and rt and store the results into the registers A and B. Since A and B are overwritten on every cycle, the register file can be read on every cycle with the values stored into A and B. This step also computes the branch target address and stores the address in ALUOut, where it will be used on the next clock cycle if the instruction is a branch. This requires setting ALUSrcA to 0 (so that the PC is sent to the ALU), ALUSrcB to the value 11 (so that the sign-extended and shifted offset field is sent to the ALU), and ALUOp to 00 (so the ALU adds). The register file accesses and computation of branch target occur in parallel.

After this clock cycle, determining the action to take can depend on the instruction contents.

3. Execution, memory address computation, or branch completion

This is the first cycle during which the datapath operation is determined by the instruction class. In all cases, the ALU is operating on the operands prepared in the previous step, performing one of three functions, depending on the instruction class. We specify the action to be taken depending on the instruction class:

Memory reference:

```
ALUOut = A + sign-extend (IR[15-0]);
```

Operation: The ALU is adding the operands to form the memory address. This requires setting ALUSrcA to 1 (so that the first ALU input is register A) and setting ALUSrcB to 10 (so that the output of the sign extension unit is used for the second ALU input). The ALUOp signals will need to be set to 00 (causing the ALU to add).

Arithmetic-logical instruction (R-type):

```
ALUOut = A op B;
```

Operation: The ALU is performing the operation specified by the function code on the two values read from the register file in the previous cycle. This requires setting ALUSrcA = 1 and setting ALUSrcB = 00 (together causing the registers A and B to be used as the ALU inputs). The ALUOp signals will need to be set to 10 (so that the funct field is used to determine the ALU control signal settings).

Branch:

```
if (A == B) PC = ALUOut;
```

Operation: The ALU is used to do the equal comparison between the two registers read in the previous step. The Zero signal out of the ALU is used to determine whether or not to branch. This requires setting ALUSrcA = 1 and setting ALUSrcB = 00 (so that the register file outputs are the ALU inputs). The ALUOp signals will need to be set to 01 (causing the ALU to subtract) for equality testing. The PCCondWrite signal will need to be asserted to update the PC if the Zero output of the ALU is asserted. By setting PCSource to 01, the value written into the PC will come from ALUOut, which holds the branch target address computed in the previous cycle. For conditional branches that are taken, we actually write the PC twice: once from the output of the ALU (during the Instruction decode/register fetch) and once from ALUOut (during the Branch completion step). The value written into the PC last is the one used for the next instruction fetch.

Jump:

```
PC = PC [31-28] || (IR[25-0]<<2)
```

Operation: The PC is replaced by the jump address. PCSource is set to direct the jump address to the PC, and PCWrite is asserted to write the jump address into the PC.

4. Memory access or R-type instruction completion step

During this step, a load or store instruction accesses memory and an arithmetic-logical instruction writes its result. When a value is retrieved from memory it is stored into the memory data register (MDR), where it must be used on the next clock cycle.

Memory reference:

```
MDR = Memory [ALUOut];
```

or

```
Memory [ALUOut] = B;
```

Operation: If the instruction is a load, a data word is retrieved from memory and is written into the MDR. If the instruction is a store, then the data is written into memory. In either case, the address used is the one computed during the previous step and stored in ALUOut. For a store, the source operand is saved in B. (B is actually read twice, once in step 2 and once in step 3. Luckily, the same value is read both times, since the register number—which is stored in IR and used to read from the register file—does not change.) The signal MemRead (for a load) or MemWrite (for store) will need to be asserted. In addition, for loads, the signal IorD is set to 1 to force the memory address to come from the ALU, rather than the PC. Since MDR is written on every clock cycle, no explicit control signal need be asserted.

Arithmetic-logical instruction (R-type):

```
Reg[IR[15-11]] = ALUOut;
```

Operation: Place the contents of ALUOut, which corresponds to the output of the ALU operation in the previous cycle, into the Result register. The signal RegDst must be set to 1 (to force the rd (bits 15–11) field to be used to select the register file entry to write). RegWrite must be asserted, and MemtoReg must be set to 0 (so that the output of the ALU is written, as opposed to the memory data output).

5. Memory read completion step

During this step, loads complete by writing back the value from memory.

Load:

```
Reg[IR[20-16]] = MDR;
```

Operation: Write the load data, which was stored into MDR in the previous cycle, into the register file. To do this, we set MemtoReg = 1 (to write the result from memory), assert RegWrite (to cause a write), and we make RegDst = 0 to choose the rt (bits 20–16) field as the register number.

Step name	Action for R-type instructions	Action for memory-reference instructions	Action for branches	Action for jumps
Instruction fetch	IR = Memory[PC] PC = PC + 4			
Instruction decode/register fetch	A = Reg [IR[25–21]] B = Reg [IR[20–16]] ALUOut = PC + (sign-extend (IR[15–0]) << 2)			
Execution, address computation, branch/ jump completion	ALUOut = A op B	ALUOut = A + sign-extend (IR[15–0])	if (A == B) then PC = ALUOut	PC = PC [31–28] ‖ (IR[25–0]<<2)
Memory access or R-type completion	Reg [IR[15–11]] = ALUOut	Load: MDR = Memory[ALUOut] or Store: Memory [ALUOut] = B		
Memory read completion		Load: Reg[IR[20–16]] = MDR		

FIGURE 5.35 Summary of the steps taken to execute any instruction class. Instructions take from three to five execution steps. The first two steps are independent of the instruction class. After these steps, an instruction takes from one to three more cycles to complete, depending on the instruction class. The empty entries for the Memory access step or the Memory read completion step indicate that the particular instruction class takes fewer cycles. In a multicycle implementation, a new instruction will be started as soon as the current instruction completes, so these cycles are not idle or wasted. As mentioned earlier, the register file actually reads every cycle, but as long as the IR does not change, the values read from the register file are identical. In particular, the value read into register B during the Instruction decode stage, for a branch or R-type instruction, is the same as the value stored into B during the Execution stage and then used in the Memory access stage for a store word instruction.

This five-step sequence is summarized in Figure 5.35. From this sequence we can determine what the control must do on each clock cycle.

Defining the Control

Now that we have determined what the control signals are and when they must be asserted, we can implement the control unit. To design the control unit for the single-cycle datapath, we used a set of truth tables that specified the setting of the control signals based on the instruction class. For the multicycle datapath, the control is more complex because the instruction is executed in a series of steps. The control for the multicycle datapath must specify both the signals to be set in any step and the next step in the sequence.

In this subsection and in section 5.5, we will look at two different techniques to specify the control. The first technique is based on finite state machines that are usually represented graphically. The second technique, called *microprogramming*, uses a programming representation for control. Both of these techniques represent the control in a form that allows the detailed implementation—using gates, ROMs, or PLAs—to be synthesized by a CAD system. In this chapter, we will focus on the design of the control and its representation in these two forms. If you are interested in how these control specifications are translated into actual hardware, Appendix C continues the development of this chapter, translating the multicycle control unit to a detailed hardware implementation. The key ideas of control can be grasped from this chapter without examining the material in Appendix C. However, if you want to get down to the bits, Appendix C can show you how to do it!

The first method we use to specify the multicycle control is a *finite state machine*. A finite state machine consists of a set of states and directions on how to change states. The directions are defined by a *next-state function*, which maps the current state and the inputs to a new state. When we use a finite state machine for control, each state also specifies a set of outputs that are asserted when the machine is in that state. The implementation of a finite state machine usually assumes that all outputs that are not explicitly asserted are deasserted. The correct operation of the datapath depends on the fact that a signal that is not explicitly asserted is deasserted, rather than acting as a don't care. For example, the RegWrite signal should be asserted only when a register file entry is to be written; when it is not explicitly asserted, it must be deasserted.

Multiplexor controls are slightly different, since they select one of the inputs whether they are 0 or 1. Thus, in the finite state machine, we always specify the setting of all the multiplexor controls that we care about. When we implement the finite state machine with logic, setting a control to 0 may be the default and thus may not require any gates. A simple example of a finite state machine appears in Appendix B, and if you are unfamiliar with the concept of a finite state machine, you may want to examine Appendix B before proceeding.

The finite state control essentially corresponds to the five steps of execution shown on pages 385 through 388; each state in the finite state machine will take 1 clock cycle. The finite state machine will consist of several parts. Since the first two steps of execution are identical for every instruction, the initial two states of the finite state machine will be common for all instructions. Steps 3 through 5 differ, depending on the opcode. After the execution of the last step for a particular instruction class, the finite state machine will return to the initial state to begin fetching the next instruction.

Figure 5.36 shows this abstracted representation of the finite state machine. To fill in the details of the finite state machine, we will first expand the instruction fetch and decode portion, then we will show the states (and actions) for the different instruction classes.

We show the first two states of the finite state machine in Figure 5.37 using a traditional graphic representation. We number the states to simplify the explanation, though the numbers are arbitrary. State 0, corresponding to step 1, is the starting state of the machine.

The signals that are asserted in each state are shown within the circle representing the state. The arcs between states define the next state and are labeled

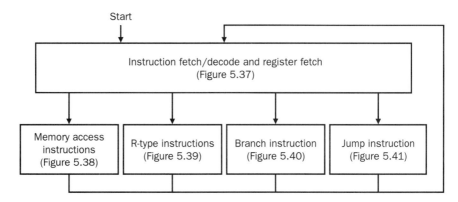

FIGURE 5.36 The high-level view of the finite state machine control. The first steps are independent of the instruction class; then a series of sequences that depend on the instruction opcode are used to complete each instruction class. After completing the actions needed for that instruction class, the control returns to fetch a new instruction. Each box in this figure may represent one to several states. The arc labeled *Start* marks the state in which to begin when the first instruction is to be fetched.

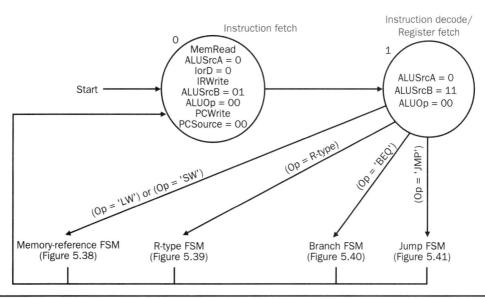

FIGURE 5.37 The instruction fetch and decode portion of every instruction is identical. These states correspond to the top box in the abstract finite state machine in Figure 5.36. In the first state we assert two signals to cause the memory to read an instruction and write it into the Instruction register (MemRead and IRWrite), and we set IorD to 0 to choose the PC as the address source. The signals ALUSrcA, ALUSrcB, ALUOp, PCWrite, and PCSource are set to compute PC + 4 and store it into the PC. (It will also be stored into ALUOut, but never used from there.). In the next state, we compute the branch target address by setting ALUSrcB to 11 (causing the shifted and sign-extended lower 16 bits of the IR to be sent to the ALU), setting ALUSrcA to 0 and ALUOp to 00; we store the result in the ALUOut register, which is written on every cycle. There are four next states that depend on the class of the instruction, which is known during this state. The control unit input, called Op, is used to determine which of these arcs to follow.

with conditions that select a specific next state when multiple next states are possible. After state 1, the signals asserted depend on the class of instruction. Thus, the finite state machine has four arcs exiting state 1, corresponding to the four instruction classes: memory reference, R-type, branch on equal, and jump. This process of branching to different states depending on the instruction is called *decoding*, since the choice of the next state, and hence the actions that follow, depend on the instruction class.

Figure 5.38 shows the portion of the finite state machine needed to implement the memory-reference instructions. For the memory-reference instructions, the first state after fetching the instruction and registers computes the memory address (state 2). To compute the memory address, the ALU input multiplexors must be set so that the first input is the A register, while the second input is the sign-extended displacement field; the result is written into the ALUOut register. After the memory address calculation, the memory should be read or written; this requires two different states. If the instruction opcode is lw, then state 3 (corresponding to the step Memory access) does the memory read (MemRead is asserted). The output of the memory is always written into MDR. If it is sw, state 5 does a memory write (MemWrite is asserted). In states 3 and 5, the signal IorD is set to 1 to force the memory address to come from the ALU. (This is not needed for stores, since the write address uses a different input into the memory.) After performing a write, the instruction sw has completed execution, and the next state is state 0. If the instruction is a load, however, another state (state 4) is needed to write the result from the memory into the register file. Setting the multiplexor controls MemtoReg = 1 and RegDst = 0 will send the loaded value in the MDR to be written into the register file, using rt as the register number. After this state, corresponding to the Memory read completion step, the next state is state 0.

To implement the R-type instructions requires two states corresponding to steps 3 (Execute) and 4 (R-type completion). Figure 5.39 shows this two-state portion of the finite state machine. State 6 asserts ALUSrcA and sets the ALUSrcB signals to 00; this forces the two registers that were read from the register file to be used as inputs to the ALU. Setting ALUOp to 10 causes the ALU control unit to use the function field to set the ALU control signals. In state 7, RegWrite is asserted to cause the register file to write, RegDst is asserted to cause the rd field to be used as the register number of the destination, and MemtoReg is deasserted to select ALUOut as the source of the value to write into the register file.

For branches, only a single additional state is necessary, because they complete execution during the third step of instruction execution. During this state, the control signals that cause the ALU to compare the contents of registers A and B must be set, and the signals that cause the PC to be written conditionally with the address in the ALUOut register are also set. To perform the

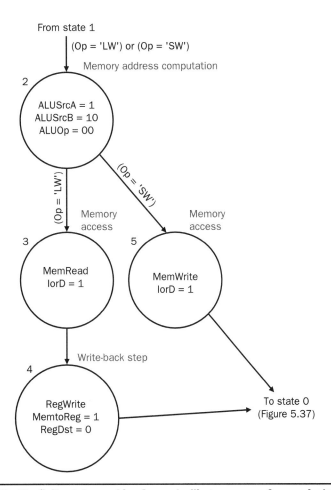

From state 1

(Op = 'LW') or (Op = 'SW')

Memory address computation

2

ALUSrcA = 1
ALUSrcB = 10
ALUOp = 00

(Op = 'LW')

(Op = 'SW')

Memory access

Memory access

3

MemRead
IorD = 1

5

MemWrite
IorD = 1

Write-back step

4

RegWrite
MemtoReg = 1
RegDst = 0

To state 0
(Figure 5.37)

FIGURE 5.38 The finite state machine for controlling memory-reference instructions has four states. These states correspond to the box labeled "Memory access instructions" in Figure 5.36. After performing a memory address calculation, a separate sequence is needed for load and for store. The setting of the control signals ALUSrcA, ALUSrcB, and ALUOp is used to cause the memory address computation in state 2. Loads require an extra state to write the result from the MDR (where the result is written in state 3) into the register file.

comparison requires that we assert ALUSrcA and set ALUSrcB to 00, and set the ALUOp value to 01 (forcing a subtract). (We use only the Zero output of the ALU, not the result of the subtraction.) To control the writing of the PC, we assert PCWriteCond and set PCSource = 01, which will cause the value in the

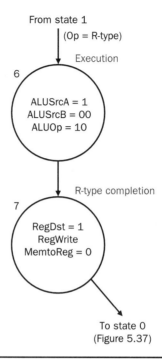

From state 1
(Op = R-type)

Execution

6

ALUSrcA = 1
ALUSrcB = 00
ALUOp = 10

R-type completion

7

RegDst = 1
RegWrite
MemtoReg = 0

To state 0
(Figure 5.37)

FIGURE 5.39 R-type instructions can be implemented with a simple two-state finite state machine. These states correspond to the box labeled "R-type instructions" in Figure 5.36. The first state causes the ALU operation to occur, while the second state causes the ALU result (which is in ALUOut) to be written in the register file. The three signals asserted during state 7 cause the contents of ALUOut to be written into the register file in the entry specified by the rd field of the Instruction register.

ALUOut register (containing the branch address calculated in state 1, Figure 5.37 on page 391) to be written into the PC if the Zero bit out of the ALU is asserted. Figure 5.40 shows this single state.

The last instruction class is jump; like branch, it requires only a single state (shown in Figure 5.41) to complete its execution. In this state, the signal PCWrite is asserted to cause the PC to be written. By setting PCSource to 10, the value supplied for writing will be the lower 26 bits of the Instruction register with 00_{two} added as the low-order bits concatenated with the upper 4 bits of the PC.

We can now put these pieces of the finite state machine together to form a specification for the control unit, as shown in Figure 5.42. In each state, the signals that are asserted are shown. The next state depends on the opcode bits of the instruction, so we label the arcs with a comparison for the corresponding instruction opcodes.

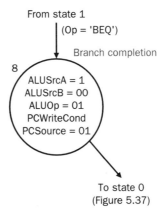

From state 1

(Op = 'BEQ')

Branch completion

8

ALUSrcA = 1
ALUSrcB = 00
ALUOp = 01
PCWriteCond
PCSource = 01

To state 0
(Figure 5.37)

FIGURE 5.40 The branch instruction requires a single state. The first three outputs that are asserted cause the ALU to compare the registers (ALUSrcA, ALUSrcB, and ALUOp), while the signals PCSource and PCWriteCond perform the conditional write if the branch condition is true. Notice that we do not use the value written into ALUOut; instead, we use only the Zero output of the ALU. The branch target address is read from ALUOut, where it was saved at the end of state 1.

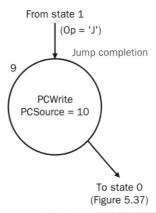

From state 1

(Op = 'J')

Jump completion

9

PCWrite
PCSource = 10

To state 0
(Figure 5.37)

FIGURE 5.41 The jump instruction requires a single state that asserts two control signals to write the PC with the lower 26 bits of the Instruction register shifted left 2 bits and concatenated to the upper 4 bits of the PC of this instruction.

Given this implementation, and the knowledge that each state requires 1 clock cycle, we can find the CPI for a typical instruction mix.

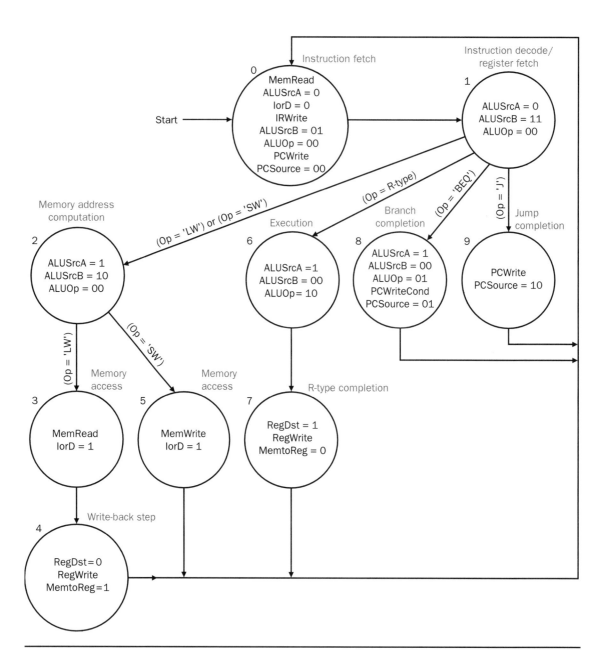

FIGURE 5.42   The complete finite state machine control for the datapath shown in Figure 5.33. The labels on the arcs are conditions that are tested to determine which state is the next state; when the next state is unconditional, no label is given. The labels inside the nodes indicate the output signals asserted during that state; we always specify the setting of a multiplexor control signal if the correct operation requires it. Hence, in some states a multiplexor control will be set to 0. In Appendix C, we examine how to turn this finite state machine into logic equations and look at how to implement those logic equations.

CPI in a Multicycle CPU

Example

Using the control shown in Figure 5.42 and the gcc instruction mix shown in the example starting on page 373, what is the CPI, assuming that each state requires 1 clock cycle?

Answer

The mix is 22% loads, 11% stores, 49% R-format operations, 16% branches, and 2% jumps. From Figure 5.42, the number of clock cycles for each instruction class is the following:

- Loads: 5
- Stores: 4
- R-format instructions: 4
- Branches: 3
- Jumps: 3

The CPI is given by the following:

$$\text{CPI} = \frac{\text{CPU clock cycles}}{\text{Instruction count}} = \frac{\sum \text{Instruction count}_i \times \text{CPI}_i}{\text{Instruction count}}$$

$$= \sum \frac{\text{Instruction count}_i}{\text{Instruction count}} \times \text{CPI}_i$$

The ratio

$$\frac{\text{Instruction count}_i}{\text{Instruction count}}$$

is simply the instruction frequency for the instruction class i. We can therefore substitute to obtain

$$\text{CPI} = 0.22 \times 5 + 0.11 \times 4 + 0.49 \times 4 + 0.16 \times 3 + 0.02 \times 3$$

$$= 1.1 + 0.44 + 1.96 + 0.48 + 0.06 = 4.04$$

This CPI is better than the worst-case CPI would have been if all the instructions took the same number of clock cycles (5).

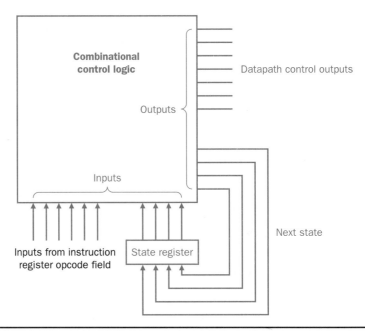

FIGURE 5.43   Finite state machine controllers are typically implemented using a block of combinational logic and a register to hold the current state. The outputs of the combinational logic are the next-state number and the control signals to be asserted for the current state. The inputs to the combinational logic are the current state and any inputs used to determine the next state. In this case, the inputs are the instruction register opcode bits. Notice that in the finite state machine used in this chapter, the outputs depend only on the current state, not on the inputs. The following elaboration explains this in more detail.

A finite state machine can be implemented with a temporary register that holds the current state and a block of combinational logic that determines both the datapath signals to be asserted as well as the next state. Figure 5.43 shows how such an implementation might look. Appendix C describes in detail how the finite state machine is implemented using this structure. In section C.3, the combinational control logic for the finite state machine of Figure 5.42 is implemented both with a ROM (read-only memory) and a PLA (programmable logic array). (Also see Appendix B for a description of these logic elements.) In the next section of this chapter, we consider another way to represent control. Both of these techniques are simply different representations of the same control information.

Elaboration: The style of finite state machine in Figure 5.43 is called a Moore machine, after Edward Moore. Its identifying characteristic is that the output depends only on the current state. For a Moore machine, the box labeled combinatorial control logic can be split into two pieces. One piece has the control output and only the state input, while the other has only the next-state output.

An alternative style of machine is a Mealy machine, named after George Mealy. The Mealy machine allows both the input and the current state to be used to determine the output. Moore machines have potential implementation advantages in speed and size of the control unit. The speed advantages arise because the control outputs, which are needed early in the clock cycle, do not depend on the inputs, but only on the current state. In Appendix C, when the implementation of this finite state machine is taken down to logic gates, the size advantage can be clearly seen. The potential disadvantage of a Moore machine is that it may require additional states. For example, in situations where there is a one-state difference between two sequences of states, the Mealy machine may unify the states by making the outputs depend on the inputs.

5.5 | Microprogramming: Simplifying Control Design

For the control of our simple MIPS subset, a graphical representation of the finite state machine, as in Figure 5.42, is certainly adequate. We can draw such a diagram on a single page and translate it into equations (see Appendix C) without generating too many errors. Consider instead an implementation of the full MIPS instruction set, which contains over 100 instructions (see Appendix A). In one implementation, instructions take from 1 clock cycle to over 20 clock cycles. Clearly, the control function will be much more complex. Or consider an instruction set with more instructions of widely varying classes: The control unit could easily require thousands of states with hundreds of different sequences. For example, the Intel 80x86 instruction set has many more addressing mode combinations, as well as a much larger set of opcodes.

In such cases, specifying the control unit with a graphical representation will be cumbersome, since the finite state machine can contain hundreds to thousands of states, and even more arcs! The graphical representation—although useful for a small finite state machine—will not fit on a page, let alone be understandable, when it becomes very large. Programmers know this phenomenon quite well: As programs become large, additional structuring techniques (for example, procedures and modules) are needed to keep the programs comprehensible. Of course, specifying complex control functions directly as equations, without making any mistakes, becomes essentially impossible.

Can we use some of the ideas from programming to help create a method of specifying the control that will make it easier to understand as well as to design? Suppose we think of the set of control signals that must be asserted in a state as an instruction to be executed by the datapath. To avoid confusing the instructions of the MIPS instruction set with these low-level control instructions, the latter are called *microinstructions*. Each microinstruction defines the set of datapath control signals that must be asserted in a given state. Executing a microinstruction has the effect of asserting the control signals specified by the microinstruction.

In addition to defining which control signals must be asserted, we must also specify the sequencing—what microinstruction should be executed next? In the finite state machine shown in Figure 5.42 on page 396, the next state is determined in one of two different ways. Sometimes a single next state follows the current state unconditionally. For example, state 1 always follows state 0, and the only way to reach state 1 is via state 0. In other cases, the choice of the next state depends on the input. This is true in state 1, which has four different successor states.

When we write programs, we also have an analogous situation. Sometimes a group of instructions should be executed sequentially, and sometimes we need to branch. In programming, the default is sequential execution, while branching must be indicated explicitly. In describing the control as a program, we also assume that microinstructions written sequentially are executed in sequence, while branching must be indicated explicitly. The default sequencing mechanism can still be implemented using a structure like the one in Figure 5.43 on page 398; however, it is often more efficient to implement the default sequential state using a counter. We will see how such an implementation looks at the end of this section.

Designing the control as a program that implements the machine instructions in terms of simpler microinstructions is called *microprogramming*. The key idea is to represent the asserted values on the control lines symbolically, so that the microprogram is a representation of the microinstructions, just as assembly language is a representation of the machine instructions. In choosing a syntax for an assembly language, we usually represent the machine instructions as a series of fields (opcode, registers, and offset or immediate field); likewise, we will represent a microinstruction syntactically as a sequence of fields whose functions are related.

Defining a Microinstruction Format

The microprogram is a symbolic representation of the control that will be translated by a program to control logic. In this way, we can choose how many fields a microinstruction should have and what control signals are affected by each field. The format of the microinstruction should be chosen so as to simplify the representation, making it easier to write and understand the microprogram. For example, it is useful to have one field that controls the ALU and a set of three fields that determine the two sources for the ALU operation as well as the destination of the ALU result. In addition to readability, we would also like the microprogram format to make it difficult or impossible to write inconsistent microinstructions. A microinstruction is inconsistent if it requires that a given control signal be set to two different values. We will see an example of how this could happen shortly.

To avoid a format that allows inconsistent microinstructions, we can make each field of the microinstruction responsible for specifying a nonoverlapping set of control signals. To choose how to make this partition of the control signals for this implementation into microinstruction fields, it is useful to re-examine two previous figures:

- Figure 5.33, on page 383, which shows all the control signals and how they affect the datapath
- Figure 5.34, on page 384, which shows the function of each datapath control signal

Signals that are never asserted simultaneously may share the same field. Figure 5.44 shows how the microinstruction can be broken into seven fields and defines the general function of each field. The first six fields of the micro-instruction control the datapath, while the Sequencing field (the seventh field) specifies how to select the next microinstruction.

Microinstructions are usually placed in a ROM or a PLA (both described in Appendix B and used to implement control in Appendix C), so we can assign addresses to the microinstructions. The addresses are usually given out se-quentially, in the same way that we chose sequential numbers for the states in the finite state machine. Three different methods are available to choose the next microinstruction to be executed:

1. Increment the address of the current microinstruction to obtain the address of the next microinstruction. This sequential behavior is indi-cated in the microprogram by putting Seq in the Sequencing field. Since sequential execution of instructions is encountered often, many micro-programming systems make this the default.

Field name	Function of field
ALU control	Specify the operation being done by the ALU during this clock; the result is always written in ALUOut.
SRC1	Specify the source for the first ALU operand.
SRC2	Specify the source for the second ALU operand.
Register control	Specify read or write for the register file, and the source of the value for a write.
Memory	Specify read or write, and the source for the memory. For a read, specify the destination register.
PCWrite control	Specify the writing of the PC.
Sequencing	Specify how to choose the next microinstruction to be executed.

FIGURE 5.44 Each microinstruction contains these seven fields. The values for each field are shown in Figure 5.45.

2. Branch to the microinstruction that begins execution of the next MIPS instruction. We will label this initial microinstruction (corresponding to state 0) as `Fetch` and place the indicator `Fetch` in the Sequencing field to indicate this action.

3. Choose the next microinstruction based on the control unit input. Choosing the next microinstruction on the basis of some input is called a *dispatch*. Dispatch operations are usually implemented by creating a table containing the addresses of the target microinstructions. This table is indexed by the control unit input and may be implemented in a ROM or in a PLA. There are often multiple dispatch tables; for this implementation, we will need two dispatch tables, one to dispatch from state 1 and one to dispatch from state 2. We indicate that the next microinstruction should be chosen by a dispatch operation by placing `Dispatch i`, where `i` is the dispatch table number, in the Sequencing field.

Figure 5.45 gives a description of the values allowed for each field of the microinstruction and the effect of the different field values. Remember that the microprogram is a symbolic representation. This microinstruction format is just one example of many potential formats.

Elaboration: The basic microinstruction format may allow combinations that cannot be supported within the datapath. Typically, a microassembler will perform checks on the microinstruction fields to ensure that such inconsistencies are flagged as errors and corrected. An alternative is to structure the microinstruction format to avoid this, but this might make the microinstruction harder to read. Most microprogramming systems choose readability and require the microcode assembler to detect inconsistencies.

Creating the Microprogram

Now let's create the microprogram for the control unit. We will label the instructions in the microprogram with symbolic labels, which can be used to specify the contents of the dispatch tables (see section C.5 in Appendix C for a discussion of how the dispatch tables are defined and assembled). In writing the microprogram, there are two situations in which we may want to leave a field of the microinstruction blank. When a field that controls a functional unit or that causes state to be written (such as the Memory field or the ALU dest field) is blank, no control signals should be asserted. When a field *only* specifies the control of a multiplexor that determines the input to a functional unit, such as the SRC1 field, leaving it blank means that we do not care about the input to the functional unit (or the output of the multiplexor).

Field name	Values for field	Function of field with specific value
Label	Any string	Used to specify labels to control microcode sequencing. Labels that end in a 1 or 2 are used for dispatching with a jump table that is indexed based on the opcode. Other labels are used as direct targets in the microinstruction sequencing. Labels do not generate control signals directly but are used to define the contents of dispatch tables and generate control for the Sequencing field.
ALU control	Add	Cause the ALU to add.
	Subt	Cause the ALU to subtract; this implements the compare for branches.
	Func code	Use the instruction's funct field to determine ALU control.
SRC1	PC	Use the PC as the first ALU input.
	A	Register A is the first ALU input.
SRC2	B	Register B is the second ALU input.
	4	Use 4 for the second ALU input.
	Extend	Use output of the sign extension unit as the second ALU input.
	Extshft	Use the output of the shift-by-two unit as the second ALU input.
Register control	Read	Read two registers using the rs and rt fields of the IR as the register numbers, putting the data into registers A and B.
	Write ALU	Write the register file using the rd field of the IR as the register number and the contents of ALUOut as the data.
	Write MDR	Write the register file using the rt field of the IR as the register number and the contents of the MDR as the data.
Memory	Read PC	Read memory using the PC as address; write result into IR (and the MDR).
	Read ALU	Read memory using ALUOut as address; write result into MDR.
	Write ALU	Write memory using the ALUOut as address; contents of B as the data.
PCWrite control	ALU	Write the output of the ALU into the PC.
	ALUOut-cond	If the Zero output of the ALU is active, write the PC with the contents of the register ALUOut.
	Jump address	Write the PC with the jump address from the instruction.
Sequencing	Seq	Choose the next microinstruction sequentially.
	Fetch	Go to the first microinstruction to begin a new instruction.
	Dispatch i	Dispatch using the ROM specified by i (1 or 2).

FIGURE 5.45 Each field of the microinstruction has a number of values that it can take on. The second column gives the possible values that are legal for the field, and the third column defines the effect of that value. Each field value, other than the label field, is mapped to a particular setting of the datapath control lines; this mapping is described in Appendix C, section C.5. That section also shows how the label field is used to generate the dispatch tables. As we will see, the microcode implementation will differ slightly from the finite state machine control, but only in ways that do not affect instruction semantics.

The easiest way to understand the microprogram is to break it into pieces that deal with each component of instruction execution, just as we did when we designed the finite state machine.

The first component of every instruction execution is to fetch the instructions, decode them, and compute both the sequential PC and branch target PC. These actions correspond directly to the first two steps of execution described on pages 385 through 388. The two microinstructions needed for these first two steps are shown below:

Label	ALU control	SRC1	SRC2	Register control	Memory	PCWrite control	Sequencing
Fetch	Add	PC	4		Read PC	ALU	Seq
	Add	PC	Extshft	Read			Dispatch 1

To understand what each microinstruction does, it is easiest to look at the effect of a group of fields. In the first microinstruction, the fields asserted and their effects are the following:

Fields	Effect
ALU control, SRC1, SRC2	Compute PC + 4. (The value is also written into ALUOut, though it will never be read from there.)
Memory	Fetch instruction into IR.
PCWrite control	Causes the output of the ALU to be written into the PC.
Sequencing	Go to the next microinstruction.

The label field, containing the label Fetch, will be used in the Sequencing field when the microprogram wants to start the execution of the next instruction.

For the second microinstruction, the operations controlled by the microinstruction are the following:

Fields	Effect
ALU control, SRC1, SRC2	Store PC + sign extension (IR[15–0]) << 2 into ALUOut.
Register control	Use the rs and rt fields to read the registers placing the data in A and B.
Sequencing	Use dispatch table 1 to choose the next microinstruction address.

We can think of the dispatch operation as a *case* or *switch* statement with the opcode field and the dispatch table 1 used to select one of four different microinstruction sequences with one of four different labels (all ending in "1"):

- Mem1 for memory-reference instructions
- Rformat1 for R-type instructions
- BEQ1 for the branch equal instruction
- JUMP1 for the jump instruction

The microprogram for memory-reference instructions has four microinstructions, as shown below. The first instruction does the memory address calculation. A two-instruction sequence is needed to complete a load (memory read followed by register file write), while the store requires only one microinstruction after the memory address calculation:

Label	ALU control	SRC1	SRC2	Register control	Memory	PCWrite control	Sequencing
Mem1	Add	A	Extend				Dispatch 2
LW2					Read ALU		Seq
				Write MDR			Fetch
SW2					Write ALU		Fetch

Let's look at the fields of the first microinstruction in this sequence:

Fields	Effect
ALU control, SRC1, SRC2	Compute the memory address: Register (rs) + sign-extend (IR[15–0]), writing the result into ALUOut.
Sequencing	Use the second dispatch table to jump to the microinstruction labeled either LW2 or SW2.

The first microinstruction in the sequence specific to lw is labeled LW2, since it is reached by a dispatch through table 2. This microinstruction has the following effect:

Fields	Effect
Memory	Read memory using the ALU output as the address and writing the data into the MDR.
Sequencing	Go to the next microinstruction.

The next microinstruction completes execution with a microinstruction that has the following effects:

Fields	Effect
Register control	Write the contents of the MDR into the register file entry specified by rt.
Sequencing	Go to the microinstruction labeled Fetch.

The store microinstruction, labeled SW2, operates similarly to the load micro-instruction labeled LW2:

Fields	Effect
Memory	Write memory using contents of ALUOut as the address and the contents of B as the value.
Sequencing	Go to the microinstruction labeled Fetch.

The microprogram sequence for R-type instructions consists of two microinstructions: the first does the ALU operation (and is labeled Rformat1 for dispatch purposes), while the second writes the result into the register file:

Label	ALU control	SRC1	SRC2	Register control	Memory	PCWrite control	Sequencing
Rformat1	Func code	A	B				Seq
				Write ALU			Fetch

You might think that because the fields of these two microinstructions do not conflict (i.e., each uses different fields), you could combine them into one. Indeed, microcode optimizers perform such operations when compiling microcode. In this case, however, the result of the ALU instruction is written into the register ALUOut, and the written value cannot be read until the next clock cycle; hence we cannot combine them into one microinstruction. (If you did combine them, you'd end up writing the wrong thing into the register file!) You could try to remove the ALUOut register to allow the two microinstructions to be combined, but this would require lengthening the clock cycle to allow the register file write to occur in the same clock cycle as the ALU operation.

The first microinstruction initiates the ALU operation:

Fields	Effect
ALU control, SRC1, SRC2	The ALU operates on the contents of the A and B registers, using the function field to specify the ALU operation.
Sequencing	Go to the next microinstruction.

The second microinstruction causes the ALU output to be written in the register file:

Fields	Effect
Register control	The value in ALUOut is written into the register file entry specified by the rd field.
Sequencing	Go to the microinstruction labeled Fetch.

Because the immediately previously executed microinstruction computed the branch target address, the microprogram sequence for branch, labeled with BEQ, requires just one microinstruction:

Label	ALU control	SRC1	SRC2	Register control	Memory	PCWrite control	Sequencing
BEQ1	Subt	A	B			ALUOut-cond	Fetch

The asserted fields of this microinstruction are the following:

Fields	Effect
ALU control, SRC1, SRC2	The ALU subtracts the operands in A and B to generate the Zero output.
PCWrite control	Causes the PC to be written using the value already in ALUOut, if the Zero output of the ALU is true.
Sequencing	Go to the microinstruction labeled Fetch.

The jump microcode sequence also consists of one microinstruction:

Label	ALU control	SRC1	SRC2	Register control	Memory	PCWrite control	Sequencing
JUMP1						Jump address	Fetch

Only two fields of this microinstruction are asserted:

Fields	Effect
PCWrite control	Causes the PC to be written using the jump target address.
Sequencing	Go to the microinstruction labeled Fetch.

The entire microprogram appears in Figure 5.46. It consists of the 10 microinstructions appearing above. This microprogram matches the 10-state finite state machine we designed earlier, since they were both derived from the same five-step execution sequence for the instructions. In more complex machines, the microprogram sequence might consist of hundreds or thousands of microinstructions and would be the representation of choice for the control. Datapaths of more complex machines typically require additional scratch registers used for holding intermediate results when implementing complex multicycle instructions. Registers A and B are like such scratch registers, but datapaths for more complex instruction sets often have a larger number of such registers

Label	ALU control	SRC1	SRC2	Register control	Memory	PCWrite control	Sequencing
Fetch	Add	PC	4		Read PC	ALU	Seq
	Add	PC	Extshft	Read			Dispatch 1
Mem1	Add	A	Extend				Dispatch 2
LW2					Read ALU		Seq
				Write MDR			Fetch
SW2					Write ALU		Fetch
Rformat1	Func code	A	B				Seq
				Write ALU			Fetch
BEQ1	Subt	A	B			ALUOut-cond	Fetch
JUMP1						Jump address	Fetch

FIGURE 5.46 The microprogram for the control unit. Recall that the labels are used to determine the targets for the dispatch operations. Dispatch 1 does a jump based on the IR to a label ending with a 1, while Dispatch 2 does a jump based on the IR to a label ending with 2.

with a richer set of interconnections to other datapath elements. These registers are available to the microprogrammer and make the analogy of implementing the control as a programming task even stronger.

Implementing the Microprogram

Translating a microprogram into hardware involves two aspects: deciding how to implement the sequencing function and choosing a method of storing the main control function. The microprogram can be thought of as a text representation of a finite state machine, and implemented in exactly the same way we would implement a finite state machine: using a PLA to encode both the sequencing function as well as the main control (see Figure 5.43 on page 398). Often, however, both the implementation of the sequencing function, as well as the implementation of the main control function, are done differently, especially for large microprograms.

The alternative form of implementation involves storing the control function in a read-only memory (ROM) and implementing the sequencing function separately. Figure 5.47 shows this different way to implement the sequencing function: using an incrementer to choose the next control instruction. In this type of implementation, the microcode store would determine the value of the datapath control lines, as well as *how to select* the next state (as opposed to *specifying* the next state, as in our finite state machine implementation). The address select logic would contain the dispatch tables, implemented in ROMs or PLAs, and would, under the control of the address select outputs, determine the next microinstruction to execute. The advantage of this implementation of the sequencing function is that it removes the logic to implement normal

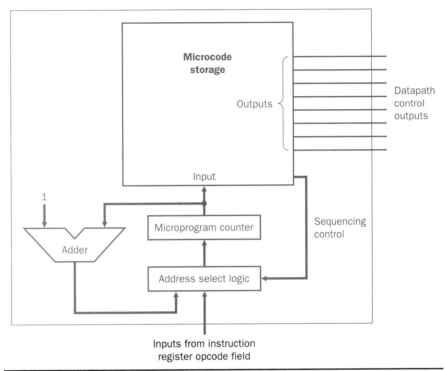

FIGURE 5.47 A typical implementation of a microcode controller would use an explicit incrementer to compute the default sequential next state and would place the microcode in a read-only memory. The microinstructions, used to set the datapath control, are assembled directly from the microprogram. The microprogram counter, which replaces the state register of a finite state machine controller, determines how the next microinstruction is chosen. The address select logic contains the dispatch tables as well as the logic to select from among the alternative next states; the selection of the next microinstruction is controlled by the sequencing control outputs from the control logic. The combination of the current microprogram counter, incrementer, dispatch tables, and address select logic forms a sequencer that selects the next microinstruction. The microcode storage may consist either of read-only memory (ROM) or may be implemented by a PLA. PLAs may be more efficient in VLSI implementations, while ROMs may be easier to change. Further discussions of the advantages of these two alternatives can be found in section 5.9 and in Appendix C.

sequencing of microinstructions, implementing such sequencing with a counter. Thus, in cases where there are long sequences of microinstructions, the explicit sequencer can result in less logic in the microcode controller.

In Figure 5.47, the main control function could be implemented in ROM, rather than implemented in a PLA. With a ROM implementation, the microprogram is assembled and stored in microcode storage and is addressed by the microprogram counter, in much the same way as a normal program is stored in program memory and the next instruction is chosen by the program counter.

This analogy with programming is both the origin of the terminology (microcode, microprogramming, etc.) and the initial method by which microprograms were implemented (see section 5.10).

Although the type of sequencer shown in Figure 5.47 is typically used to implement a microprogram control specification, it can also be used to implement a finite state specification. Section C.4 of Appendix C describes how to generate such a sequencer in more detail. Section C.5 describes how a microprogram can be translated to such an implementation. Similarly, Appendix C shows how the control function can be implemented in either a ROM or a PLA and discusses the trade-offs. In total, Appendix C shows how to go from the symbolic representations of finite state machines or microprograms shown in this chapter to either bits in a memory or entries in a PLA. If you are interested in detailed implementation or the translation process, you may want to proceed to Appendix C.

The choice of which way to represent the control (finite state diagram versus microprogram) and how to implement control (PLA versus ROM and encoded state versus explicit sequencer) are independent decisions, affected by both the structure of the control function and the technology used to implement the control. We return to these issues briefly in section 5.9, but before we do that we need to look at one of the hardest aspects of control: exceptions.

5.6   Exceptions

Control is the most challenging aspect of processor design: it is both the hardest part to get right and the hardest part to make fast. One of the hardest parts of control is implementing *exceptions* and *interrupts*—events other than branches or jumps that change the normal flow of instruction execution. An exception is an unexpected event from within the processor; arithmetic overflow is an example of an exception. An interrupt is an event that also causes an unexpected change in control flow but comes from outside of the processor. Interrupts are used by I/O devices to communicate with the processor, as we will see in Chapter 8.

Many architectures and authors do not distinguish between interrupts and exceptions, often using the older name *interrupt* to refer to both types of events. We follow the MIPS convention, using the term *exception* to refer to *any* unexpected change in control flow without distinguishing whether the cause is internal or external; we use the term *interrupt* only when the event is externally caused. The Intel 80x86 architecture uses the word *interrupt* for all these events, while the PowerPC architecture uses the word *exception* to indicate that an unusual event has occurred and *interrupt* to indicate the change in control flow.

Interrupts were initially created to handle unexpected events like arithmetic overflow and to signal requests for service from I/O devices. The same basic mechanism was extended to handle internally generated exceptions as well. Here are some examples showing whether the situation is generated internally by the processor or externally generated:

Type of event	From where?	MIPS terminology
I/O device request	External	Interrupt
Invoke the operating system from user program	Internal	Exception
Arithmetic overflow	Internal	Exception
Using an undefined instruction	Internal	Exception
Hardware malfunctions	Either	Exception or interrupt

Many of the requirements to support exceptions come from the specific situation that causes an exception to occur. Accordingly, we will return to this topic in Chapter 7, when we discuss memory hierarchies, and in Chapter 8, when we discuss I/O, and we better understand the motivation for additional capabilities in the exception mechanism. In this section, we deal with the control implementation for detecting two types of exceptions that arise from the portions of the instruction set and implementation that we have already discussed.

Detecting exceptional conditions and taking the appropriate action is often on the critical timing path of a machine, which determines the clock cycle time and thus performance. Without proper attention to exceptions during design of the control unit, attempts to add exceptions to a complicated implementation can significantly reduce performance, as well as complicate the task of getting the design correct.

How Exceptions Are Handled

The two types of exceptions that our current implementation can generate are execution of an undefined instruction and an arithmetic overflow. The basic action that the machine must perform when an exception occurs is to save the address of the offending instruction in the exception program counter (EPC) and then transfer control to the operating system at some specified address.

The operating system can then take the appropriate action, which may involve providing some service to the user program, taking some predefined action in response to an overflow, or stopping the execution of the program and reporting an error. After performing whatever action is required because of the exception, the operating system can terminate the program or may continue its execution, using the EPC to determine where to restart the execution of the program. In Chapter 7, we will look more closely at the issue of restarting the execution.

For the operating system to handle the exception, it must know the reason for the exception, in addition to the instruction that caused it. There are two main methods used to communicate the reason for an exception. The method used in the MIPS architecture is to include a status register (called the *Cause register*), which holds a field that indicates the reason for the exception.

A second method is to use *vectored interrupts*. In a vectored interrupt, the address to which control is transferred is determined by the cause of the exception. For example, to accommodate the two exception types listed above, we might define the following:

Exception type	Exception vector address (in hex)
Undefined instruction	C0 00 00 00$_{hex}$
Arithmetic overflow	C0 00 00 20$_{hex}$

The operating system knows the reason for the exception by the address at which it is initiated. The addresses are separated by 32 bytes or 8 instructions, and the operating system must record the reason for the exception and may perform some limited processing in this sequence. When the exception is not vectored, a single entry point for all exceptions can be used, and the operating system decodes the status register to find the cause.

We can perform the processing required for exceptions by adding a few extra registers and control signals to our basic implementation and by slightly extending the finite state machine. Let's assume that we are implementing the exception system used in the MIPS architecture. (Implementing vectored exceptions is no more difficult.) We will need to add two additional registers to the datapath:

- *EPC:* A 32-bit register used to hold the address of the affected instruction. (Such a register is needed even when exceptions are vectored.)

- *Cause:* A register used to record the cause of the exception. In the MIPS architecture, this register is 32 bits, although some bits are currently unused. Assume that the low-order bit of this register encodes the two possible exception sources mentioned above: undefined instruction = 0 and arithmetic overflow = 1.

We will need to add two control signals to cause the EPC and Cause registers to be written; call these *EPCWrite* and *CauseWrite*. In addition, we will need a 1-bit control signal to set the low-order bit of the Cause register appropriately; call this signal *IntCause*. Finally, we will need to be able to write the *exception address*, which is the operating system entry point for exception handling, into the PC; let's assume that this address is C0000000$_{hex}$. Currently, the PC is fed from the output of a three-way multiplexor, which is controlled by the signal

PCSource (see Figure 5.33 on page 383). We can change this to a four-way multiplexor, with additional input wired to the constant value C0000000$_{hex}$. Then PCSource can be set to 11$_{two}$ to select this value to be written into the PC.

Because the PC is incremented during the first cycle of every instruction, we cannot just write the value of the PC into the EPC, since the value in the PC will be the instruction address plus four. However, we can use the ALU to subtract four from the PC and write the output into the EPC. This requires no additional control signals or paths, since we can use the ALU to subtract, and the constant 4 is already a selectable ALU input. The data write port of the EPC, therefore, is connected to the ALU output. Figure 5.48 shows the multicycle datapath with these additions needed for implementing exceptions.

Using the datapath of Figure 5.48, the action to be taken for each different type of exception can be handled in one state apiece. In each case, the state sets the Cause register, computes and saves the original PC into the EPC, and writes the exception address into the PC. Thus, to handle the two exception types we are considering, we will need to add only the two states shown in Figure 5.49.

To connect this finite state machine to the finite state machine of the main control unit, we must determine how to detect exceptions and add arcs that transfer control from the main execution machine to this exception-handling finite state machine.

How Control Checks for Exceptions

Now we have to design a method to detect these exceptions and to transfer control to the appropriate state in the exception states shown in Figure 5.49. Each of the two possible exceptions is detected differently:

- *Undefined instruction*: This is detected when no next state is defined from state 1 for the op value. We handle this exception by defining the next-state value for all op values other than lw, sw, 0 (R-type), j, and beq as state 10. We show this by symbolically using *other* to indicate that the op field does not match any of the opcodes that label arcs out of state 1. A modified finite state diagram is shown in Figure 5.50.

- *Arithmetic overflow*: Chapter 4 included logic in the ALU to detect overflow, and a signal called *Overflow* is provided as an output from the ALU. This signal is used in the modified finite state machine to specify an additional possible next state for state 7, as shown in Figure 5.50.

Figure 5.50 represents a complete specification of the control for this MIPS subset with two types of exceptions. Remember that the challenge in designing the control of a real machine is to handle the variety of different interactions between instructions and other exception-causing events in such a way that

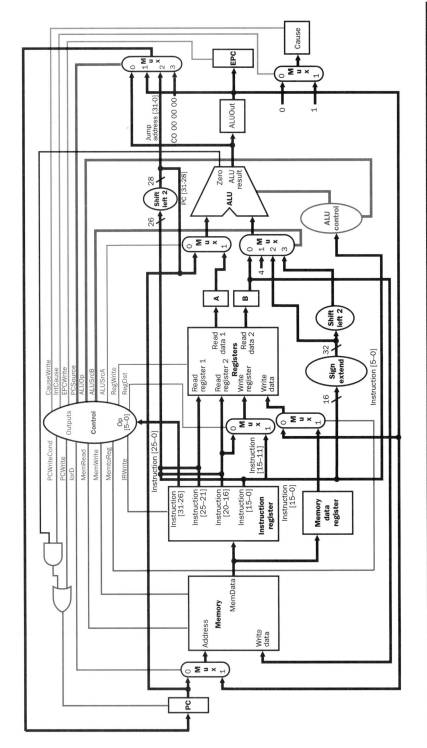

FIGURE 5.48 The multicycle datapath with the addition needed to implement exceptions. The specific additions include the Cause and EPC registers, a multiplexor to control the value sent to the Cause register, an expansion of the multiplexor controlling the value written into the PC, and control lines for the added multiplexor and registers.

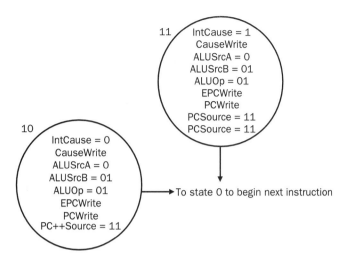

State 11:
IntCause = 1
CauseWrite
ALUSrcA = 0
ALUSrcB = 01
ALUOp = 01
EPCWrite
PCWrite
PCSource = 11
PCSource = 11

State 10:
IntCause = 0
CauseWrite
ALUSrcA = 0
ALUSrcB = 01
ALUOp = 01
EPCWrite
PCWrite
PC++Source = 11

To state 0 to begin next instruction

FIGURE 5.49 This pair of states handles the necessary actions for the two different exceptions we are considering. Each state provides control for three actions: setting the Cause register, getting the address of the offending instruction into the EPC, and setting the PC to the exception vector address. Both state 10 and state 11 represent the starting point for an exception. Control is transferred to one of these two states when an exception occurs. After either state 10 or state 11 is completed, control is transferred to state 0, and a new instruction is fetched.

the control logic remains both small and fast. The complex interactions that are possible are what make the control unit the most challenging aspect of hardware design.

Elaboration: If you examine the finite state machine in Figure 5.50 closely, you can see that some problems could occur in the way the exceptions are handled. For example, in the case of arithmetic overflow, the instruction causing the overflow completes writing its result because the overflow branch is in the state when the write completes. However, it's possible that the architecture defines the instruction as having no effect if the instruction causes an exception; this is what the MIPS instruction set architecture specifies. In Chapter 7, we will see that certain classes of exceptions require us to prevent the instruction from changing the machine state, and that this aspect of handling exceptions becomes complex and potentially limits performance.

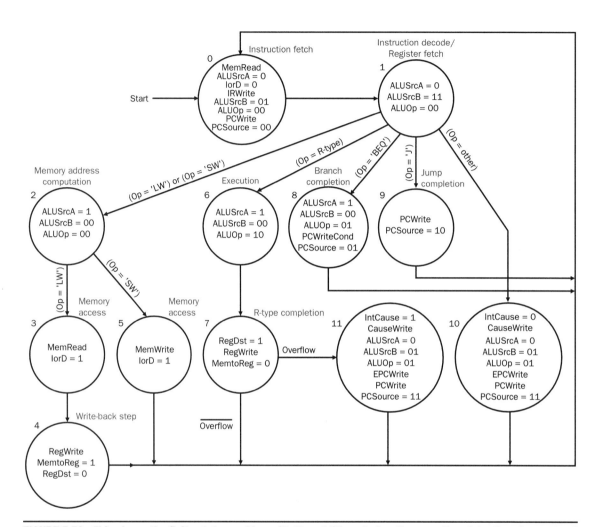

FIGURE 5.50 This shows the finite state machine with the additions to handle exception detection. States 10 and 11 come from Figure 5.49 on page 415. The branch out of state 1 labeled (*Op = other*) indicates the next state when the input does not match the opcode of any of lw, sw, 0 (R-type), j, or beq. The branch out of state 7 labeled *Overflow* indicates the action to be taken when the ALU signals an overflow.

5.7   Real Stuff: The Pentium Pro Implementation

The techniques described in this chapter for building datapaths and control units are at the heart of every computer. All recent computers, however, go beyond the techniques of this chapter and use pipelining. *Pipelining,* which is the subject of the next chapter, improves performance by overlapping the execution of multiple instructions, achieving throughput close to one instruction per clock cycle (like our single-cycle implementation) with a clock cycle time determined by the delay of individual functional units rather than the entire execution path of an instruction (like our multicycle design). The last Intel 80x86 processor without pipelining was the 80386 introduced in 1985; the very first MIPS processor, the R2000, also introduced in 1985, was pipelined.

Recent Intel 80x86 processors (the 80486, Pentium, and Pentium Pro) employ successively more sophisticated pipelining approaches. These processors, however, are still faced with the challenge of implementing control for the complex 80x86 instruction set, described in Chapter 3. The basic functional units and datapaths in use in modern processors, while significantly more complex than those described in this chapter, have the same basic functionality and similar types of control signals. Thus the task of designing a control unit builds on the same principles used in this chapter.

Challenges Implementing More Complex Architectures

Unlike the MIPS architecture, the 80x86 architecture contains instructions that are very complex and can take tens, if not hundreds, of cycles to execute. For example, the string move instruction (MOVS) requires calculating and updating two different memory addresses as well as loading and storing a byte of the string. The larger number and greater complexity of addressing modes in the 80x86 architecture complicates implementation of even simple instructions similar to those on MIPS. Fortunately, a multicycle datapath is well structured to adapt to variations in the amount of work required per instruction that are inherent in 80x86 instructions. This adaptability comes from two capabilities:

1. A multicycle datapath allows instructions to take varying numbers of clock cycles. Simple 80x86 instructions that are similar to those in the MIPS architecture can execute in three or four clock cycles, while more complex instructions can take tens of cycles.

2. A multicycle datapath can use the datapath components more than once per instruction. This is critical to handling more complex addressing modes, as well as implementing more complex operations, both of which are present in the 80x86 architecture. Without this capability the datapath would need to be extended to handle the demands of the more complex instructions without reusing components, which would be completely impractical. For example, a single-cycle datapath, which doesn't reuse components, for the 80x86 would require several data memories and a very large number of ALUs.

Using the multicycle datapath and a microprogrammed controller provides a framework for implementing the 80x86 instruction set. The challenging task, however, is creating a high-performance implementation, which requires dealing with the diversity of the requirements arising from different instructions. Simply put, a high-performance implementation needs to ensure that the simple instructions execute quickly, and that the burden of the complexities of the instruction set penalize primarily the complex, less frequently used, instructions.

To accomplish this goal, every Intel implementation of the 80x86 architecture since the 486 has used a combination of hardwired control to handle simple instructions, and microcoded control to handle the more complex instructions. For those instructions that can be executed in a single pass through the datapath (i.e., those with complexity similar to a MIPS instruction), the hardwired control generates the control information and executes the instruction in one pass through the datapath that takes a small number of clock cycles. Those instructions that require multiple datapath passes and complex sequencing are handled by the microcoded controller that takes a larger number of cycles and multiple passes through the datapath to complete the execution of the instruction. The benefit of this approach is that it enables the designer to achieve low cycle counts for the simple instructions without having to build the enormously complex datapath that would be required to handle the full generality of the most complex instructions.

The Structure of the Pentium Pro Implementation

Both the Pentium and Pentium Pro processors are capable of executing more than one instruction per clock, using an advanced pipelining technique, called *superscalar*. We describe how a superscalar processor works in the next chapter. The important thing to understand here is that executing more than one instruction per clock requires duplicating the datapath resources. The simplest way to think about this is that the processor has multiple datapaths, though these are tailored to handle one class of instructions: say, loads and stores, ALU operations, or branches. In this way, the processor is able to execute a load or store in the same clock cycle that it is also executing a branch and an ALU operation. The Pentium allows up to two such instructions to be executed in a clock cycle, while the Pentium Pro allows up to four.

The datapaths of the Pentium Pro actually execute simple microinstructions (or microoperations in Intel terminology), similar to MIPS instructions. These microinstructions are fully self-contained operations that are initially 72 bits wide. The control of datapath to implement these microinstructions is completely hardwired. This last level of control expands up to four 72-bit microinstructions into 120 control lines for the integer datapaths and 285 control lines for the floating-point datapath. This last step of expanding the microinstructions into control lines is very similar to the control generation for the single-cycle datapath or for the ALU control.

These microinstructions are generated from the 80x86 instructions either by hardwired control or by microprogrammed control. For 80x86 instructions that require less than four microinstructions to implement the 80x86 instruction, the 80x86 instruction is directly decoded into one to four microinstructions by a set of PLAs. These PLAs can generate a total of 1200 different microinstructions. If an 80x86 instruction requires more than four microinstructions, the control dispatches to a microcode control store and uses a traditional microcode sequencer to generate a sequence of five or more microinstructions. The microcode ROM provides a total of about 8000 microinstructions, with a number of sequences being shared among 80x86 instructions.

The use of simple low-level hardwired control and simple datapaths for handling the microinstructions allows the Pentium Pro to achieve impressive clock rates, similar to those for microprocessors implementing simpler instruction set architectures. Furthermore, the translation process, which combines direct hardwired control for simple instructions with microcoded control for complex instructions, allows the Pentium Pro to execute the simple, high-frequency instructions in the 80x86 instruction set at a high rate, yielding a low, and very competitive, CPI for integer instructions.

5.8 Fallacies and Pitfalls

Pitfall: Implementing a complex instruction with microcode may not be faster than a sequence using simpler instructions.

Most machines with a large and complex instruction set are implemented, at least in part, using a microcode stored in ROM. Surprisingly, on such machines, sequences of individual simpler instructions are sometimes as fast as or even faster than the custom microcode sequence for a particular instruction.

How can this possibly be true? At one time, microcode had the advantage of being fetched from a much faster memory than instructions in the program. Since caches came into use in 1968, microcode no longer has such a consistent edge in fetch time. Microcode does, however, still have the advantage of using internal temporary registers in the computation, which can be helpful on machines with few general-purpose registers. The disadvantage of microcode is that the algorithms must be selected before the machine is announced and can't be changed until the next model of the architecture. The instructions in a program, on the other hand, can utilize improvements in its algorithms at any time during the life of the machine. Along the same lines, the microcode sequence is probably not optimal for all possible combinations of operands.

One example of such an instruction in the 80x86 implementations is the move string instruction (MOVS) used with a repeat prefix that we discussed in Chapter 3. This instruction is often slower than a loop that moves words at a time, as we saw earlier in the Fallacies and Pitfalls (see page 185).

Another example involves the LOOP instruction, which decrements a register and branches to the specified label if the decremented register is not equal to zero. This instruction is similar to the PowerPC instruction "branch conditional to count register" (bcctr) discussed in Chapter 3. These instructions are designed to be used as the branch at the bottom of loops that have a fixed number of iterations (e.g., many *for* loops). Such an instruction, in addition to packing in some extra work, has benefits in minimizing the potential losses from the branch in pipelined machines (as we will see when we discuss branches in the next chapter).

Unfortunately, on all recent Intel 80x86 implementations, the LOOP instruction is always slower than the macrocode sequence consisting of simpler individual instructions (assuming that the small code size difference is not a factor). Thus, optimizing compilers focusing on speed never generate the LOOP instruction. This, in turn, makes it hard to motivate making LOOP fast in future implementations, since it is so rarely used!

Fallacy: If there is space in control store, new instructions are free of cost.

One of the benefits of a microprogrammed approach is that control store implemented in ROM is not very expensive, and as transistor budgets grew, extra ROM was practically free. The analogy here is that of building a house and discovering, near completion, that you have enough land and materials left to add a room. This room wouldn't be free, however, since there would be the costs of labor and maintenance for the life of the home. The temptation to add "free" instructions can occur only when the instruction set is not fixed, as is likely to be the case in the first model of a computer. Because upward compatibility of binary programs is a highly desirable feature, all future models of this machine will be forced to include these so-called free instructions, even if space is later at a premium.

During the design of the 80286, many instructions were added to the instruction set. The availability of more silicon resource and the use of microprogrammed implementation made such additions seem painless. Possibly the largest addition was a sophisticated protection mechanism, which is largely unused, but still must be implemented in newer implementations. This addition was motivated by a perceived need for such a mechanism and the desire to enhance microprocessor architectures to provide functionality equal to that of larger computers. Likewise, a number of decimal instructions were added to provide decimal arithmetic on bytes. Such instructions are rarely used today because using binary arithmetic on 32 bits and converting back and forth to decimal representation is considerably faster. Like the protection mechanisms, the decimal instructions must be implemented in newer processors even if only rarely used.

5.9 Concluding Remarks

As we have seen in this chapter, both the datapath and control for a processor can be designed starting with the instruction set architecture and an understanding of the basic characteristics of the technology. In section 5.2, we saw how the datapath for a MIPS processor could be constructed based on the architecture and the decision to build a single-cycle implementation. Of course, the underlying technology also affects many design decisions by dictating what components can be used in the datapath, as well as whether a single-cycle implementation even makes sense. Along the same lines, in the first portion of section 5.4, we saw how the decision to break the clock cycle into a series of steps led to the revised multicycle datapath. In both cases, the top-level organization—a single-cycle or multicycle machine—together with the instruction set, prescribed many characteristics of the datapath design.

Similarly, the control is largely defined by the instruction set architecture, the organization, and the datapath design. In the single-cycle organization, these three aspects essentially define how the control signals must be set. In the multicycle design, the exact decomposition of the instruction execution into cycles, which is based on the instruction set architecture, together with the datapath, define the requirements on the control.

Control is one of the most challenging aspects of computer design. A major reason is that designing the control requires an understanding of how all the components in the processor operate. To help meet this challenge, we examined two techniques for specifying control: finite state diagrams and microprogramming. These control representations allow us to abstract the specification of the control from the details of how to implement it. Using abstraction in this fashion is the major method we have to cope with the complexity of computer designs.

Once the control has been specified, we can map it to detailed hardware. The exact details of the control implementation will depend on both the structure of the control and on the underlying technology used to implement it. Abstracting the specification of control is also valuable because the decisions of how to implement the control are technology-dependent and likely to change over time.

Trade-offs in Control Approaches

Much has changed since Wilkes [1953] wrote the first paper on microprogramming. The most important changes are the following:

- Control units are implemented as integral parts of the processor, often on the same silicon die. They cannot be changed independent of the rest of the processor. Furthermore, given the right computer-aided design tools, the difficulty of implementing a ROM or a PLA is the same.

- ROM, which was used to hold the microinstructions, is no longer faster than RAM, which holds the machine language program. A PLA implementation of a control function is often much smaller than the ROM implementation, which may have many duplicate or unused entries. If the PLA is smaller, it is usually faster.

- Instruction sets have become much simpler than they were in the 1960s and 1970s, leading to reduced complexity in the control.

- Computer-aided design tools have improved so that control can be specified symbolically and, by using much faster computers, thoroughly simulated before hardware is constructed. This improvement makes it plausible to get the control logic correct without the need for fixes later.

These changes have blurred the distinctions among different implementation choices. Certainly, using an abstract specification of control is helpful. How that control is then implemented depends on its size, the underlying technology, and the available CAD tools.

The Big Picture   Control may be designed using one of several initial representations. The choice of sequence control, and how logic is represented, can then be determined independently; the control can then be implemented with one of several methods using a structured logic technique. Figure 5.51 shows the variety of methods for specifying the control and moving from the specification to an implementation using some form of structured logic.

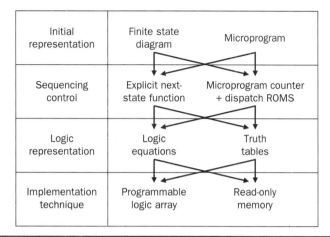

Initial representation	Finite state diagram	Microprogram
Sequencing control	Explicit next-state function	Microprogram counter + dispatch ROMS
Logic representation	Logic equations	Truth tables
Implementation technique	Programmable logic array	Read-only memory

FIGURE 5.51 Alternative methods for specifying and implementing control. The arrows indicate possible design paths: any path from the initial representation to the final implementation technology is viable. Traditionally, "hardwired control" means that the techniques on the left-hand side are used, and "microprogrammed control" means that the techniques on the right-hand side are used.

5.10 Historical Perspective and Further Reading

Maurice Wilkes learned computer design in a summer workshop from Eckert and Mauchly and then went on to build the first full-scale, operational, stored-program computer—the EDSAC. From that experience he realized the difficulty of control. He thought of a more centralized control using a diode matrix and, after visiting the Whirlwind computer in the United States, wrote [Wilkes 1985]:

> *I found that it did indeed have a centralized control based on the use of a matrix of diodes. It was, however, only capable of producing a fixed sequence of eight pulses— a different sequence for each instruction, but nevertheless fixed as far as a particular instruction was concerned. It was not, I think, until I got back to Cambridge that I realized that the solution was to turn the control unit into a computer in miniature by adding a second matrix to determine the flow of control at the microlevel and by providing for conditional micro-instructions.*

Wilkes [1953] was ahead of his time in recognizing that problem. Unfortunately, the solution was also ahead of its time: To provide control, microprogramming relies on fast memory that was not available in the 1950s. Thus Wilkes's ideas remained primarily academic conjecture for a decade, although he did construct the EDSAC 2 using microprogrammed control in 1958 with ROM made from magnetic cores.

IBM brought microprogramming into the spotlight in 1964 with the IBM 360 family. Before this event, IBM saw itself as a cluster of many small businesses selling different machines with their own price and performance levels, but also with their own instruction sets. (Recall that little programming was done in high-level languages, so that programs written for one IBM machine would not run on another.) Gene Amdahl, one of the chief architects of the IBM 360, said that managers of each subsidiary agreed to the 360 family of computers only because they were convinced that microprogramming made it feasible. To be sure of the viability of microprogramming, the IBM vice president of engineering even visited Wilkes surreptitiously and had a "theoretical" discussion of the pros and cons of microcode. IBM believed that the idea was so important to its plans that it pushed the memory technology inside the company to make microprogramming feasible.

Stewart Tucker of IBM was saddled with the responsibility of porting software from the IBM 7090 to the new IBM 360. Thinking about the possibilities of microcode, he suggested expanding the control store to include simulators, or interpreters, for older machines. Tucker [1967] coined the term *emulation* for this, meaning full simulation at the microprogrammed level. Occasionally, emulation on the 360 was actually faster than on the original hardware.

Once the giant of the industry began using microcode, the rest soon followed. (IBM was over half of the computer industry in 1964, measured in revenue.) One difficulty in adopting microcode was that the necessary memory technology was not widely available, but that was soon solved by semiconductor ROM and later RAM. The microprocessor industry followed the same history, with the limited resources of the earliest chips forcing hardwired control. But as the resources increased, the advantages of simpler design, ease of change, and the ability to use a wide variety of underlying implementations persuaded many to use microprogramming.

In the 1960s and 1970s, microprogramming was one of the most important techniques used in implementing machines. Through most of that period, machines were implemented with discrete components or MSI (medium-scale integration—fewer than 1000 gates per chip), and designers had to choose between two types of implementations: *hardwired control* or *microprogrammed control*. Hardwired control was characterized by finite state machines using an explicit next state and implemented primarily with random logic. In this era, microprogrammed control used microcode to specify control that was then implemented with a microprogram sequencer (a counter) and ROMs. Hardwired control received its name because the control was implemented in hardware and could not be easily changed. Microprograms implemented in ROM were also called *firmware* because they could be changed somewhat more easily than hardware, but not nearly as easily as software.

The reliance on standard parts of low- to medium-level integration made these two design styles radically different. Microprogrammed approaches were attractive because implementing the control with a large collection of low-density gates was extremely costly. Furthermore, the popularity of relatively complex instruction sets demanded a large control unit, making a ROM-based implementation much more efficient. The hardwired implementations were faster, but too costly for most machines. Furthermore, it was very difficult to get the control correct, and changing ROMs was easier than replacing a random logic control unit. Eventually, microprogrammed control was implemented in RAM, to allow changes late in the design cycle, and even in the field after a machine shipped.

With the increasing popularity of microprogramming came more sophisticated instruction sets. Over the years, most microarchitectures became more and more dedicated to support the intended instruction set, so that reprogramming for a different instruction set failed to offer satisfactory performance. With the passage of time came much larger control stores, and it became possible to consider a machine as elaborate as the VAX with more than 300 different instruction opcodes and more than a dozen memory-addressing modes. The use of RAM to store the microcode also made it possible to debug the microcode and even fix some bugs once machines were in the field. The VAX architecture represented the high-water mark for instruction set architectures based on microcode implementations. Typical implementations of the full VAX instruction set required 400 to 500 Kbits of control store.

The VAX architecture has been laid to rest and replaced by the Alpha architecture. This new architecture is based on the same principles of design used in other RISC architectures, including the MIPS, SPARC, IBM PowerPC, and the HP Precision architecture. With the disappearance of the VAX, traditional microprogramming, in which the control is implemented with one major control store, will largely disappear from conventional microprocessor designs. Even processors such as the Intel Pentium and Pentium Pro are employing large amounts of hardwired control, at least for the central core of the processor.

Of course, control unit design will continue to be a major aspect of all computers, and the best way to specify and implement the control will vary, just as computers will vary, from streamlined RISC architectures with simple control, to special-purpose processors with potentially large amounts of more complex and specialized control. One recent movement in this direction is an announcement by Sun that they will build processors designed to interpret Java. Whether such an approach is competitive with compilation, whether there is a significant market for more specialized processors, and what role microcode will play are questions that will be answered in the next few years.

To Probe Further

Kidder, T. [1981]. *Soul of a New Machine*, Little, Brown, and Co., New York.

Describes the design of the Data General Eclipse series that replaced the first DG machines such as the Nova. Kidder records the intimate interactions among architects, hardware designers, microcoders, and project management.

Levy, H. M., and R. H. Eckhouse, Jr. [1989]. *Computer Programming and Architecture: The VAX*, Second ed., Digital Press, Bedford, MA.

Good description of the VAX architecture and several different microprogrammed implementations.

Patterson, D. A. [1983]. "Microprogramming," *Scientific American* 248:3 (March) 36–43.

Overview of microprogramming concepts.

Tucker, S. G. [1967]. "Microprogram control for the System/360," *IBM Systems J.* 6:4, 222–41.

Describes the microprogrammed control for the 360, the first microprogrammed commercial machine.

Wilkes, M. V. [1985]. *Memoirs of a Computer Pioneer*, MIT Press, Cambridge, MA.

Intriguing biography with many stories about industry pioneers and the trials and successes in building early machines.

Wilkes, M. V., and J. B. Stringer [1953]. "Microprogramming and the design of the control circuits in an electronic digital computer," *Proc. Cambridge Philosophical Society* 49:230–38. Also reprinted in D. P. Siewiorek, C. G. Bell, and A. Newell, *Computer Structures: Principles and Examples*, McGraw-Hill, New York, 158–63, 1982, and in "The Genesis of Microprogramming," in *Annals of the History of Computing* 8:116.

These two classic papers describe Wilkes's proposal for microcode.

5.11   Key Terms

This section lists the variety of major new terms introduced in this chapter, which range from elements of the datapath, to clocking methodologies, to control mechanisms, to logic structures used for control. These terms are defined in the Glossary.

branch not taken	exception or interrupt	multicycle or multiple clock
branch taken	firmware	cycle implementation
branch target address	hardwired control	sign-extend
control signal	macroinstruction	single-cycle implementation
datapath element	microcode	superscalar
delayed branch	microinstruction	vectored interrupt
dispatch	microprogram	
don't-care term	microprogrammed control	

5.12 Exercises

5.1 [5] <§5.3> Describe the effect that a single stuck-at-0 fault (i.e., regardless of what it should be, the signal is always 0) would have on the multiplexors in the single-cycle datapath in Figure 5.19 on page 360. Which instructions, if any, would still work? Consider each of the following faults separately: RegDst = 0, ALUSrc = 0, MemtoReg = 0, Zero = 0.

5.2 [5] <§5.3> This exercise is similar to Exercise 5.1, but this time consider stuck-at-1 faults (the signal is always 1).

5.3 [5] <§5.4> This exercise is similar to Exercise 5.1, but this time consider the effect that the stuck-at-0 faults would have on the multiplexors in the multiple-cycle datapath in Figure 5.32 on page 381. Consider each of the following faults: RegDst = 0, MemtoReg = 0, IorD = 0, ALUSrcA = 0.

5.4 [5] <§5.3> This exercise is similar to Exercise 5.3, but this time consider stuck-at-1 faults (the signal is always 1).

5.5 [15] <§5.3> We wish to add the instruction addi (add immediate) to the single-cycle datapath described in this chapter. Add any necessary datapaths and control signals to the single-cycle datapath of Figure 5.19 on page 360 and show the necessary additions to Figure 5.20 on page 361. You can photocopy these figures or download them from *www.mkp.com/cod2e.htm* to make it faster to show the additions.

5.6 [15] <§5.3> This question is similar to Exercise 5.5 except that we wish to add the instruction jal (jump and link), which is described in Chapter 3 on page 132. You may find it easier to modify the datapath in Figure 5.29 on page 372.

5.7 [8] <§5.3> This question is similar to Exercise 5.5 except that we wish to add the instruction bne (branch if not equal), which is described in Chapter 3.

5.8 [15] <§5.3> This question is similar to Exercise 5.5 except that we wish to add a variant of the lw (load word) instruction, which sums two registers to obtain the address of the data to be loaded (see Exercise 4.16) and uses the R-format.

5.9 [5] <§5.3> Explain why it is not possible to modify the single-cycle implementation to implement the swap instruction described in Exercise 4.40 without modifying the register file.

5.10 [5] <§§5.3, 5.4> A friend is proposing that the control signal MemtoReg be eliminated. The multiplexor that has MemtoReg as an input will instead use the control signal MemRead. Will your friend's modification work? Consider both datapaths.

5.11 [10] <§5.3> This exercise is similar to Exercise 5.10 but more general. Determine whether any of the control signals (other than MemtoReg) in the single-cycle implementation can be eliminated and replaced by another existing control signal. Why or why not?

5.12 [15] <§5.3> Consider the following idea: Let's modify the instruction set architecture and remove the ability to specify an offset for memory access instructions. Specifically, all load-store instructions with nonzero offsets would become pseudoinstructions and would be implemented using two instructions. For example:

```
addi    $at, $t1, 104   # add the offset to a temporary
lw      $t0, $at        # new way of doing lw $t0, 104 ($t1)
```

What changes would you make to the single-cycle datapath and control if this simplified architecture were to be used?

5.13 [10] <§5.3> {Ex. 5.12} If the modifications described in Exercise 5.12 are implemented, there are some definite trade-offs with regard to performance. Specifically, the cycle time may be affected, and all load-store instructions with nonzero offsets would now require an extra addi instruction (a good compiler might find ways to reduce the need for extra addi instructions, but you can ignore this). If there are too many load-store instructions with nonzero offsets, it is likely that the modification would not improve performance. Assuming delays as specified on page 373, what is the highest percentage of load-store instructions with offsets that could be tolerated (i.e., that would still result in the modification having a positive impact on performance)?

5.14 [10] <§5.3> In estimating the performance of the single-cycle implementation, we assumed that only the major functional units had any delay (i.e., the delay of the multiplexors, control unit, PC access, sign extension unit, and wires was considered to be negligible). Assume that we change the delays specified on page 373 such that we use a different type of adder for simple addition:

- ALU: 2 ns
- adder for PC + 4: X ns
- adder for branch address computation: Y ns

a. What would the cycle time be if $X = 3$ and $Y = 3$?

b. What would the cycle time be if $X = 5$ and $Y = 5$?

c. What would the cycle time be if $X = 1$ and $Y = 8$?

5.15 [15] <§5.4> We wish to add the instruction addi (add immediate) to the multicycle datapath described in this chapter. This instruction is described in Chapter 4 on page 223. Add any necessary datapaths and control signals to the multicycle datapath of Figure 5.33 on page 383 and show the necessary modifications to the finite state machine of Figure 5.42 on page 396. You may find it helpful to examine the execution steps shown on pages 385 through 388 and consider the steps that will need to be performed to execute the new instruction. You can photocopy existing figures or download figures from *www.mkp.com/cod2e.htm* to make it easier to show your modifications. Try to find a solution that minimizes the number of clock cycles required for the new instruction. Please explicitly state how many cycles it takes to execute the new instruction on your modified datapath and finite state machine.

5.16 [5] <§§5.5, 5.8> {Ex. 5.15} Write the microcode sequences for the addi instruction. If you need to make any changes to the microinstruction format or field contents, indicate how the new format and fields will set the control outputs.

5.17 [15] <§5.4> This question is similar to Exercise 5.15 except that we wish to add the instruction jal (jump and link), which is described in Chapter 3.

5.18 [15] <§5.4> This question is similar to Exercise 5.15 except that we wish to add the swap instruction described in Exercise 4.40. Do not modify the register file. Since the instruction format for swap has not yet been defined, you are free to define it however you wish.

5.19 [15] <§5.4> This question is similar to Exercise 5.15 except that we wish to add a new instruction, wai (where am I), which puts the instruction's location (the value of the PC when the instruction was fetched) into a register specified by the *rt* field of the machine language instruction. Assume that the datapath hasn't changed and that, as usual, the clock cycle is too short to allow an ALU operation and a register file access in a single clock cycle if one of them is dependent on the results of the other.

5.20 [15] <§5.4> This question is similar to Exercise 5.15 except that we wish to add a new instruction, jm (jump memory). Its instruction format is similar to that of load word except that the rt field is not used because the data loaded from memory is put in the PC instead of the target register.

5.21 [20] <5.4> This question is similar to Exercise 5.15 except that we wish to add support for four-operand arithmetic instructions such as add3, which adds three numbers together instead of two:

```
add3 $t5, $t6, $t7, $t8    # $t5 = $t6 + $t7 + $t8
```

Assume that the ISA is modified by introducing a new instruction format similar to the R-format except that bits [0–4] are used to specify the additional register (we still use rs, rt, and rd) and of course a new opcode is used. Your solution should not rely on adding additional read ports to the register file, nor should a new ALU be used.

5.22 [10] <§5.4> Show how the jump register instruction (described on pages 129 and A-65) can be implemented simply by making changes to the finite state machine of Figure 5.42 on page 396. (It may help you to remember that $0 = \$zero = 0$.)

5.23 [15] <§5.4> Consider a change to the multiple-cycle implementation that alters the register file so that it has only one read port. Describe (via a diagram) any additional changes that will need to be made to the datapath in order to support this modification. Modify the finite state machine to indicate how the instructions will work, given your new datapath.

5.24 [15] <§§5.1–5.4> For this problem, use the gcc data from Figure 4.54 on page 311. Assume that there are three machines:

- M1: The multicycle datapath of Chapter 5 with a 500-MHz clock.

- M2: A machine like the multicycle datapath of Chapter 5, except that register updates are done in the same clock cycle as a memory read or ALU operation. Thus, in Figure 5.42 on page 396, states 6 and 7 and states 3 and 4 are combined. This machine has a 400-MHz clock, since the register update increases the length of the critical path.

- M3: A machine like M2, except that effective address calculations are done in the same clock cycle as a memory access. Thus, states 2, 3, and 4 can be combined, as can 2 and 5, as well as 6 and 7. This machine has a 250-MHz clock because of the long cycle created by combining address calculation and memory access.

Find out which machine is fastest. Are there instruction mixes that would make another machine faster, and if so, what are they?

5.25 [20] <§5.4> Your friends at C^3 (Creative Computer Corporation) have determined that the critical path that sets the clock cycle length of the multicycle datapath is memory access for loads and stores (*not* for instructions). This has caused their newest implementation of the MIPS 30000 to run at a clock rate of 500 MHz rather than the target clock rate of 750 MHz. However, Clara at C^3 has a solution. If all the cycles that access memory are broken into two clock cycles, then the machine can run at its target clock rate. Using the gcc mixes shown in Chapter 4 (Figure 4.54 on page 311), determine how much faster the machine with the two-cycle memory accesses is compared with the 500-MHz machine with single-cycle memory access. Assume that all jumps and branches take the same number of cycles and that the set instructions and arithmetic immediate instructions are implemented as R-type instructions.

5.26 [20] <§5.4> Suppose there were a MIPS instruction, called bcp, that copied a block of words from one address to another. Assume that this instruction requires that the starting address of the source block is in register $t1 and the destination address is in $t2, and that the number of words to copy is in $t3 (which is ≥ 0). Furthermore, assume that the values of these registers as well as register $t4 can be destroyed in executing this instruction (so that the registers can be used as temporaries to execute the instruction).

Write the MIPS assembly language program to implement block copy. How many instructions will be executed to perform a 100-word block copy? Using the CPI of the instructions in the multicycle implementation, how many cycles are needed for the 100-word block copy?

5.27 [30] <§5.5> {Ex 5.26} Microcode has been used to add more powerful instructions to an instruction set; let's explore the potential benefits of this approach. Devise a strategy for implementing the bcp instruction described in Exercise 5.26 using the multicycle datapath and microcode. You will probably need to make some changes to the datapath in order to efficiently implement the bcp instruction. Provide a description of your proposed changes and describe how the bcp instruction will work. Are there any advantages that can be obtained by adding internal registers to the datapath to help support the bcp instruction? Estimate the improvement in performance that you can achieve by implementing the instruction in hardware (as opposed to the software solution you obtained in Exercise 5.26) and explain where the performance increase comes from.

5.28 [30] <§5.5> {Ex. 5.27} Using the strategy you developed in Exercise 5.27, modify the MIPS microinstruction format described in Figure 5.45 on page 403 and provide the complete microprogram for the bcp instruction. Describe in detail how you extended the microcode so as to support the creation of more complex control structures (such as a loop) within the microcode. Has support for the bcp instruction changed the size of the microcode? Will other instructions besides bcp be affected by the change in the microinstruction format?

5.29 [15] <§5.6> We wish to add the instruction rfe (return from exception) to the multicycle datapath described in this chapter. A primary task of the rfe instruction is to copy the contents of the EPC to the PC (the exception mechanisms require several additional capabilities that we will discuss in Chapter 7). Add any necessary datapaths and control signals to the multicycle datapath of Figure 5.48 on page 414 and show the necessary modifications to the finite state machine of Figures 5.49 and 5.50 on pages 415 and 416. You can photocopy the figures or download them from *www.mkp.com/cod2e.htm* to make it easier to show your modifications.

5.30 [1 week] <§§5.2, 5.3> Using a hardware simulation language such as Verilog, implement a functional simulator for the single-cycle version. Build your simulator using an existing library of parts, if such a library is available. If the parts contain timing information, determine what the cycle time of your implementation will be.

5.31 [1 week] <§§5.2, 5.4, 5.5> Using a hardware simulation language such as Verilog, implement a functional simulator for the multicycle version of the design. Build your simulator using an existing library of parts, if such a library is available. If the parts contain timing information, determine what the cycle time of your implementation will be.

5.32 [2–3 months] <§§5.1–5.3> Using standard parts, build a machine that implements the single-cycle machine in this chapter.

5.33 [2–3 months] <§§5.1–5.8> Using standard parts, build a machine that implements the multicycle machine in this chapter.

5.34 [Discussion] <§§5.5, 5.8, 5.9> Hypothesis: If the first implementation of an architecture uses microprogramming, it affects the instruction set architecture. Why might this be true? Can you find an architecture that will probably always use microcode? Why? Which machines will never use microcode? Why? What control implementation do you think the architect had in mind when designing the instruction set architecture?

5.35 [Discussion] <§§5.5, 5.10> Wilkes invented microprogramming in large part to simplify construction of control. Since 1980, there has been an explosion of computer-aided design software whose goal is also to simplify construction of control. This has made control design much easier. Can you find evidence, based either on the tools or on real designs, that supports or refutes this hypothesis?

5.36 [Discussion] <§5.10> The MIPS instructions and the MIPS microinstructions have many similarities. What would make it difficult for a compiler to produce MIPS microcode rather than macrocode? What changes to the microarchitecture would make the microcode more useful for this application?

6

Enhancing Performance with Pipelining

Thus times do shift,
each thing his turn does hold;
New things succeed,
as former things grow old.

Robert Herrick
Hesperides: Ceremonies for Christmas Eve, 1648

6.1 **An Overview of Pipelining** 436

6.2 **A Pipelined Datapath** 449

6.3 **Pipelined Control** 466

6.4 **Data Hazards and Forwarding** 476

6.5 **Data Hazards and Stalls** 489

6.6 **Branch Hazards** 496

6.7 **Exceptions** 505

6.8 **Superscalar and Dynamic Pipelining** 510

6.9 **Real Stuff: PowerPC 604 and Pentium Pro Pipelines** 517

6.10 **Fallacies and Pitfalls** 520

6.11 **Concluding Remarks** 521

6.12 **Historical Perspective and Further Reading** 525

6.13 **Key Terms** 529

6.14 **Exercises** 529

The Five Classic Components of a Computer

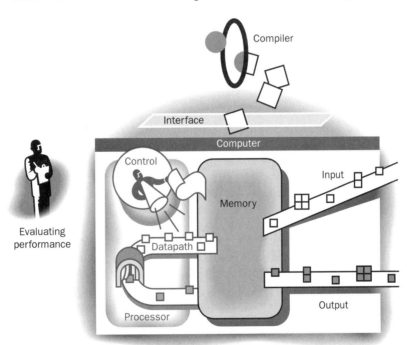

6.1   An Overview of Pipelining

Never waste time.

American proverb

Pipelining is an implementation technique in which multiple instructions are overlapped in execution. Today, pipelining is key to making processors fast.

This section relies heavily on one analogy to give an overview of the pipelining terms and issues. If you are interested in just the big picture, you should concentrate on this section and then skip to section 6.8 to see how pipelining works and its implications on program performance. If you are interested in exploring the anatomy of a pipelined computer, you will find this section referred to repeatedly in sections 6.2 through 6.7.

Anyone who has done a lot of laundry has intuitively used pipelining. The *nonpipelined* approach to laundry would be:

1.   Place one dirty load of clothes in the washer.

2.   When the washer is finished, place the wet load in the dryer.

3.   When the dryer is finished, place the dry load on a table and fold.

4.   When folding is finished, ask your roommate to put the clothes away.

When your roommate is done, then start over with the next dirty load.

The *pipelined* approach takes much less time, as Figure 6.1 shows. As soon as the washer is finished with the first load and placed in the dryer, you load the washer with the second dirty load. When the first load is dry, you place it on the table to start folding, move the wet load to the dryer, and the next dirty load into the washer. Next you have your roommate put the first load away, you start folding the second load, the dryer has the third load, and you put the fourth load into the washer. At this point all steps—called *stages* in pipelining—are operating concurrently. As long as we have separate resources for each stage, we can pipeline the tasks.

The pipelining paradox is that the time from placing a single dirty sock in the washer until it is dried, folded, and put away is not shorter for pipelining; the reason pipelining is faster for many loads is that everything is working in parallel, so more loads are finished per hour. If all the stages take about the same amount of time and there is enough work to do, then the speedup due to pipelining is equal to the number of stages in the pipeline.

Pipelined laundry is potentially four times faster than nonpipelined: 20 loads would take about 5 times as long as 1 load, while 20 loads of sequential laundry takes 20 times as long as 1 load. It's only 2.3 times faster in Figure 6.1 because we only show 4 loads.

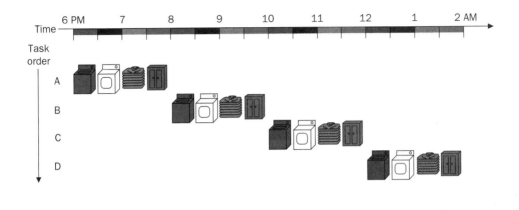

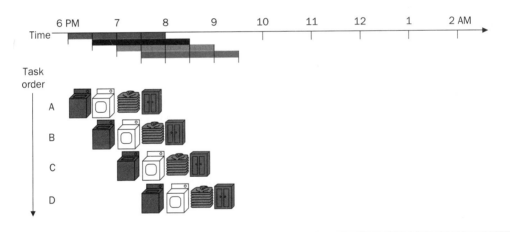

FIGURE 6.1 The laundry analogy for pipelining. Ann, Brian, Cathy, and Don each have dirty clothes to be washed, dried, folded, and put away. The washer, dryer, "folder," and "storer" each take 30 minutes for their task. Sequential laundry takes 8 hours for four loads of wash, while pipelined laundry takes just 3.5 hours. We show the pipeline stage of different loads over time by showing copies of the four resources on this two-dimensional timeline, but we really have just one of each resource.

The same principles apply to processors where we pipeline instruction execution. MIPS instructions classically take five steps:

1. Fetch instruction from memory.

2. Read registers while decoding the instruction (the format of MIPS instructions allows reading and decoding to occur simultaneously).

3. Execute the operation or calculate an address.

4. Access an operand in data memory.

5. Write the result into a register.

Hence the MIPS pipeline we explore in this chapter has five stages. The following example shows that pipelining speeds up instruction execution just as it speeds up the laundry.

Single-Cycle versus Pipelined Performance

Example

To make this discussion concrete, let's create a pipeline. In this example, and in the rest of this chapter, we limit our attention to eight instructions: load word (lw), store word (sw), add (add), subtract (sub), and (and), or (or), set-less-than (slt), and branch-on-equal (beq).

Compare the average time between instructions of a single-cycle implementation, in which all instructions take 1 clock cycle, to a pipelined implementation. The operation times for the major functional units in this example are 2 ns for memory access, 2 ns for ALU operation, and 1 ns for register file read or write. (As we said in Chapter 5, in the single-cycle model every instruction takes exactly 1 clock cycle, so the clock cycle must be stretched to accommodate the slowest instruction.)

Answer

The time required for each of the eight instructions is shown in Figure 6.2. The single-cycle design must allow for the slowest instruction— in Figure 6.2 it is lw—so the time required for every instruction is 8 ns. Similarly to Figure 6.1, Figure 6.3 compares nonpipelined and pipelined execution of three load word instructions. Thus, the time between the first and fourth instructions in the nonpipelined design is 3×8 ns or 24 ns.

All the pipeline stages take a single clock cycle, so the clock cycle must be long enough to accommodate the slowest operation. Just as the single-cycle design must take the worst-case clock cycle of 8 ns even though some instructions can be as fast as 5 ns, the pipelined execution clock cycle must have the worst-case clock cycle of 2 ns even though some stages take only 1 ns. Pipelining still offers a fourfold performance improvement: the time between the first and fourth instructions is 3×2 ns or 6 ns.

We can turn the pipelining speedup discussion above into a formula. If the stages are perfectly balanced, then the time between instructions on the pipelined machine—assuming ideal conditions—is equal to

$$\text{Time between instructions}_{\text{pipelined}} = \frac{\text{Time between instructions}_{\text{nonpipelined}}}{\text{Number of pipe stages}}$$

Instruction class	Instruction fetch	Register read	ALU operation	Data access	Register write	Total time
Load word (lw)	2 ns	1 ns	2 ns	2 ns	1 ns	8 ns
Store word (sw)	2 ns	1 ns	2 ns	2 ns		7 ns
R-format (add, sub, and, or, slt)	2 ns	1 ns	2 ns		1 ns	6 ns
Branch (beq)	2 ns	1 ns	2 ns			5 ns

FIGURE 6.2 Total time for eight instructions calculated from the time for each component. This calculation assumes that the multiplexors, control unit, PC accesses, and sign extension unit have no delay.

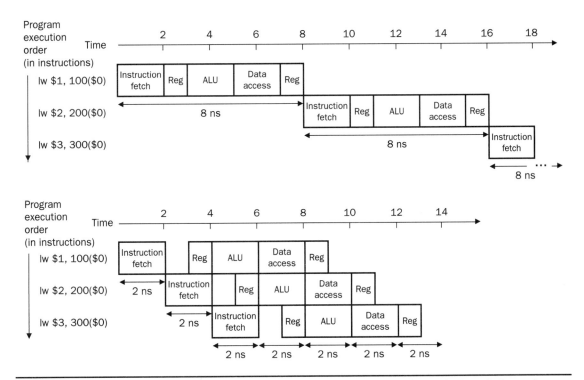

FIGURE 6.3 Single-cycle, nonpipelined execution in top vs. pipelined execution in bottom. Both use the same hardware components, whose time is listed in Figure 6.2. In this case we see a fourfold speedup on average time between instructions, from 8 ns down to 2 ns. Compare this figure to Figure 6.1. For the laundry, we assumed all stages were equal. If the dryer were slowest, then the dryer stage would set the stage time. The computer pipeline stage times are limited by the slowest resource, either the ALU operation or the memory access. We assume the write to the register file occurs in the first half of the clock cycle and the read from the register file occurs in the second half. We use this assumption throughout this chapter.

Under ideal conditions, the speedup from pipelining equals the number of pipe stages; a five-stage pipeline is five times faster.

The formula suggests that a five-stage pipeline should offer a fivefold improvement over the 8 ns nonpipelined time, or a 1.6-ns clock cycle. The example shows, however, that the stages may be imperfectly balanced. In addition, pipelining involves some overhead. Thus the time per instruction in the pipelined machine will exceed the minimum possible, and speedup will be less than the number of pipeline stages.

Moreover, even our claim of fourfold improvement for our example is not reflected in the total execution time for the three instructions: it's 14 ns versus 24 ns. To see why total execution time is less important, what would happen if we increased the number of instructions? We start by extending the previous figures to 1003 instructions. We would add 1000 instructions in the pipelined example; each instruction adds 2 ns to the total execution time. The total execution time would be 1000×2 ns + 14 ns, or 2,014 ns. In the nonpipelined example, we would add 1000 instructions, each taking 8 ns, so total execution time would be 1000×8 ns + 24 ns, or 8,024 ns. Under these ideal conditions, the ratio of total execution times for real programs on nonpipelined to pipelined machines is close to the ratio of times between instructions:

$$\frac{8{,}024 \text{ ns}}{2{,}014 \text{ ns}} = 3.98 \approx \frac{8 \text{ ns}}{2 \text{ ns}}$$

Pipelining improves performance by *increasing instruction throughput, as opposed to decreasing the execution time of an individual instruction,* but instruction throughput is the important metric because real programs execute billions of instructions.

Designing Instruction Sets for Pipelining

Even with this simple explanation of pipelining, we can get insight into the design of the MIPS instruction set, which was designed for pipelined execution.

First, all MIPS instructions are the same length. This restriction makes it much easier to fetch instructions in the first pipeline stage and to decode them in the second stage. In an instruction set like the 80x86, where instructions vary from 1 byte to 17 bytes, pipelining is considerably more challenging.

Second, MIPS has only a few instruction formats, with the source register fields being located in the same place in each instruction. This symmetry means that the second stage can begin reading the register file at the same time that the hardware is determining what type of instruction was fetched. If MIPS instruction formats were not symmetric, we would need to split stage 2, resulting in six pipeline stages. (We will shortly see the downside of longer pipelines.)

Third, memory operands only appear in loads or stores in MIPS. This restriction means we can use the execute stage to calculate the memory address and then access memory in the following stage. If we could operate on the operands in memory, as in the 80x86, stages 3 and 4 would expand to an address stage, memory stage, and then execute stage.

Fourth, operands must be aligned in memory (see the Hardware/Software Interface section on page 112 in Chapter 3). Hence we need not worry about a single data transfer instruction requiring two data memory accesses; the requested data can be transferred between processor and memory in a single pipeline stage.

Pipeline Hazards

There are situations in pipelining when the next instruction cannot execute in the following clock cycle. These events are called *hazards*. We explain the three types of hazards, using our analogy first, and then give the computer equivalent problem and solution.

Structural Hazards

The first hazard is called a *structural hazard*. It means that the hardware cannot support the combination of instructions that we want to execute in the same clock cycle. A structural hazard in the laundry room would occur if we used a washer-dryer combination instead of a separate washer and dryer, or if our roommate was busy doing something else and wouldn't put clothes away. Our carefully scheduled pipeline plans would then be foiled.

As we said above, the MIPS instruction set was designed to be pipelined, making it fairly easy for designers to avoid structural hazards when designing a pipeline. Suppose, however, that we had a single memory instead of two memories. If the pipeline in Figure 6.3 had a fourth instruction, we would see that in 1 clock cycle that the first instruction is accessing data from memory while the fourth instruction is fetching an instruction from that same memory. Without two memories, our pipeline could have a structural hazard.

Control Hazards

The second hazard is called a *control hazard*, arising from the need to make a decision based on the results of one instruction while others are executing.

Suppose our laundry crew was given the happy task of cleaning the uniforms of a football team. Given how filthy the laundry is, we need to determine whether the detergent and water temperature setting we select is strong enough to get the uniforms clean but not so strong that the uniforms wear out sooner. In our laundry pipeline, we have to wait until the second stage to examine the dry uniform to see if we need to change the washer setup or not. What to do?

Here are two solutions to control hazards in the laundry room and two computer equivalents.

Stall: Just operate sequentially until the first batch is dry and then repeat until you have the right formula. This conservative option certainly works, but it is slow.

The equivalent decision task in a computer is the branch instruction. If the computer were to stall on a branch, then it would have to pause before continuing the pipeline. Let's assume that we put in enough extra hardware so that we can test registers, calculate the branch address, and update the PC during the second stage (see section 6.6 for details). Even with this extra hardware, the pipeline involving conditional branches would look like Figure 6.4. The lw instruction, executed if the branch fails, is stalled one extra 2-ns clock cycle before starting. This figure shows an important pipeline concept, officially called a *pipeline stall*, but often given the nickname *bubble*. We shall see stalls elsewhere in the pipeline.

Stall on Branch Performance

Example

Estimate the impact on the clock cycles per instruction (CPI) of stalling on branches. Assume all other instructions have a CPI of 1.

Answer

Figure 3.38 on page 189 in Chapter 3 shows conditional branches being 17% of the instructions executed for gcc. Since other instructions run have a CPI of 1 and branches took one extra clock cycle for the stall, then we would see a CPI of 1.17 and hence a slowdown of 1.17 versus the ideal case. (Since Figure 3.38 includes slt and slti as branch instructions, and they would not stall, this CPI result is appproximate.)

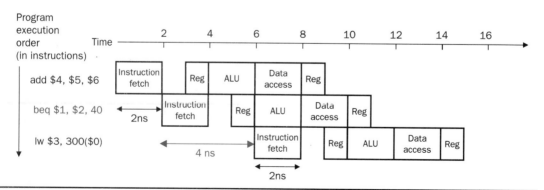

FIGURE 6.4   Pipeline showing stalling on every conditional branch as solution to control hazards. There is a one-stage pipeline stall, or bubble, after the branch.

If we cannot resolve the branch in the second stage, as is often the case for longer pipelines, then we'd see an even larger slowdown if we stall on branches. The cost of this option is too high for most computers to use and motivates a second solution to the control hazard:

> *Predict*: If you're pretty sure you have the right formula to wash uniforms, then just predict that it will work and wash the second load while waiting for the first load to dry. This option does not slow down the pipeline when you are correct. When you are wrong, however, you need to redo the load that was washed while guessing the decision.

Computers do indeed use prediction to handle branches. One simple approach is to always predict that branches will fail. When you're right, the pipeline proceeds at full speed. Only when branches succeed does the pipeline stall. Figure 6.5 shows such an example.

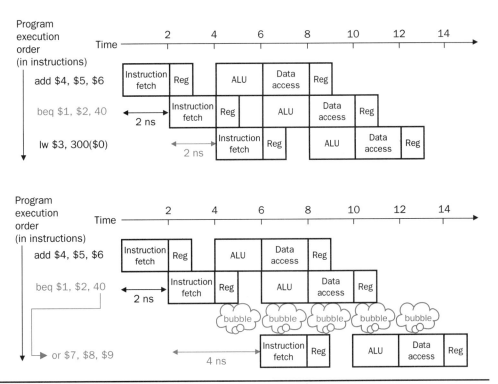

FIGURE 6.5 Predicting that branches are not taken as a solution to control hazard. The top drawing shows the pipeline when the branch is not taken. The bottom drawing shows a taken branch.

A more sophisticated version of branch prediction would have some predicted as branching (*taken*) and some not branching (*untaken*). In our analogy, the dark or home uniforms might take one formula while the light or road uniforms might take another. As a computer example, at the bottom of loops are branches that jump back to the top of the loop. Since they are likely to be taken and they branch backwards, we could always predict taken for branches that jump to an earlier address.

Such rigid approaches to branch prediction rely on stereotypical behavior and don't account for the individuality of a specific branch instruction. *Dynamic* hardware predictors, in stark contrast, make their guesses depending on the behavior of each branch and may change predictions for a branch over the life of a program. Following our analogy, in dynamic prediction a person would look at how dirty the uniform was and guess at the formula, adjusting the next guess depending on the success of recent guesses. One popular approach to dynamic prediction in computers is keeping a history for each branch as taken or untaken, and then using the past to predict the future. Such hardware has about a 90% accuracy (see section 6.6). When the guess is wrong, the pipeline control must ensure that the instructions following the wrongly guessed branch have no effect and must restart the pipeline from the proper branch address.

As in the case of all other solutions to control hazards, longer pipelines exacerbate the problem, in this case by raising the cost of misprediction. Solutions to control hazards are described in more detail in section 6.6.

Elaboration: There is a third approach to the control hazard, called *delayed decision*. In our analogy, whenever you are going to make such a decision about laundry, just place a load of nonfootball clothes in the washer while waiting for football uniforms to dry. As long as you have enough dirty clothes that are not affected by the test, this solution works fine.

Called the *delayed branch* in computers, this is the solution actually used by the MIPS architecture. The delayed branch always executes the next sequential instruction, with the branch taking place *after* that one instruction delay. It is hidden from the MIPS assembly language programmer because the assembler can automatically arrange the instructions to get the branch behavior desired by the programmer. MIPS software will place an instruction immediately after the delayed branch instruction that is not affected by the branch, and a taken branch changes the address of the instruction that *follows* this safe instruction. In our example, the add instruction before the branch in Figure 6.4 does not affect the branch, so in Figure 6.6 we move it to the *delayed branch slot* following the branch.

Compilers typically fill about 50% of the branch delay slots with useful instructions. If the pipeline is longer than five stages, then we may get more branch delay slots, which are even harder to fill.

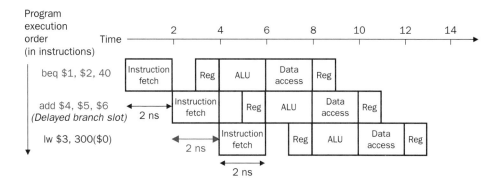

FIGURE 6.6 Pipeline delayed branch as solution to control hazard. The pipe bubble has been replaced by add.

Data Hazards

Returning to the laundry room, suppose that you are folding a load that is mostly socks. You realize that through bad luck the mate of every sock in this load is in another load that is still in the washer. You can't match the socks and put them away until that load is done. Hence you must stall the pipeline. This problem in computers is called a *data hazard*: an instruction depends on the results of a previous instruction still in the pipeline.

For example, suppose we have an add instruction followed immediately by a subtract instruction that uses the sum:

```
add    $s0, $t0, $t1
sub    $t2, $s0, $t3
```

Without intervention, a data hazard could severely stall the pipeline. The add instruction doesn't write its result until the fifth stage, meaning that we would have to add three bubbles to the pipeline.

Although we could try to rely on compilers to avoid such data hazards, we would fail. These dependencies happen just too often and the delay is just too long to expect the compiler to rescue us from this dilemma.

The primary solution is based on the observation that we don't need to wait for the instruction to complete before trying to resolve the data hazard. For the code sequence above, as soon as the ALU creates the sum for the add, we can supply it as an input for the subtract. Getting the missing item early from the internal resources is called *forwarding* or *bypassing*.

Forwarding with Two Instructions

Example

For the two instructions above, show what pipeline stages would be connected by forwarding. Use the drawing in Figure 6.7 to represent the datapath during the five stages of the pipeline. Align a copy of the datapath for each instruction, similar to the laundry pipeline in Figure 6.1.

Answer

Figure 6.8 shows the connection to forward the value in $s0 after the execution stage of the add instruction as input to the execution stage of the sub instruction.

In this graphical representation of events, forwarding paths are valid only if the destination stage is later in time than the source stage. For example, there cannot be a valid forwarding path from the output of the memory access stage in the first instruction to the input of the execution stage of the following, since that would mean going backwards in time.

Forwarding works very well, and is described in detail in section 6.4. It cannot prevent all pipeline stalls, however. For example, suppose the first instruction were a load of $s0 instead of an add. As we can imagine from looking at Figure 6.8, the desired data would be available only *after* the fourth stage of the first instruction in the dependence, which is too late for the *input* of the third stage of sub. Hence, even with forwarding, we would have to stall one stage for a *load-use data hazard*, as Figure 6.9 shows. Section 6.5 shows how pipelining hardware handles hard cases like these.

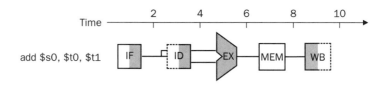

FIGURE 6.7 Graphical representation of the instruction pipeline, similar in spirit to the laundry pipeline in Figure 6.1 on page 437. Here we use symbols representing the physical resources with the abbreviations for pipeline stages used throughout the chapter. The symbols for the five stages: *IF* for the instruction fetch stage, with the box representing instruction memory; *ID* for the instruction decode/register file read stage, with the drawing showing the register file being read; *EX* for the execution stage, with the drawing representing the ALU; *MEM* for the memory access stage, with the box representing data memory; and *WB* for the write back stage, with the drawing showing the register file being written. The shading indicates the element is used by the instruction. Hence MEM has a white background because add does not access the data memory. Shading on the right half of the register file or memory means the element is read in that stage, and shading of the left half means it is written in that stage. Hence the right half of ID is shaded in the second stage because the register file is read, and the left half of WB is shaded in the fifth stage because the register file is written.

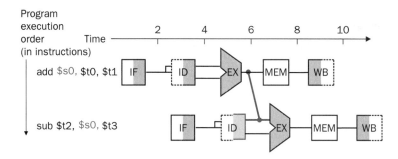

FIGURE 6.8 Graphical representation of forwarding. The connection shows the forwarding path from the output of the EX stage of add to the input of the EX stage for sub, replacing the value from register $s0 read in the second stage of sub.

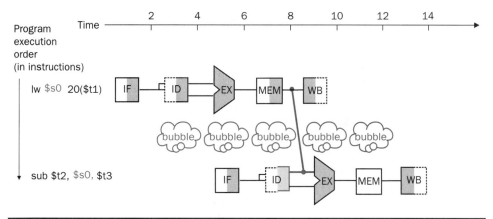

FIGURE 6.9 We need a stall even with forwarding when an R-format instruction following a load tries to use the data. Without the stall, the path from memory access stage output to execution stage input would be going backwards in time, which is impossible.

Reordering Code to Avoid Pipeline Stalls

Example

Find the hazard in this code from the body of the swap procedure, from Figure 3.23 on page 164:

```
            # reg $t1 has the address of v[k]
lw    $t0, 0($t1)    # reg $t0 (temp) = v[k]
lw    $t2, 4($t1)    # reg $t2 = v[k+1]
sw    $t2, 0($t1)    # v[k] = reg $t2
sw    $t0, 4($t1)    # v[k+1] = reg $t0 (temp)
```

Reorder the instructions to avoid pipeline stalls.

Answer

The hazard occurs on register $t2 between the second lw and the first sw. Swapping the two sw instructions removes this hazard:

```
            # reg $t1 has the address of v[k]
lw   $t0, 0($t1)   # reg $t0 (temp) = v[k]
lw   $t2, 4($t1)   # reg $t2 = v[k+1]
sw   $t0, 4($t1)   # v[k+1] = reg $t0 (temp)
sw   $t2, 0($t1)   # v[k] = reg $t2
```

Note that we do not create a new hazard because there is still one instruction between the write of register $t0 by the load and the read of register $t0 in the store. Thus, on a machine with forwarding, the reordered sequence takes 4 clock cycles.

Hardware Software Interface

In an example of the trade-off between compiler and hardware complexity, the original MIPS processors avoided hardware to stall the pipeline by requiring software to follow a load with an instruction independent of that load. Such loads are called *delayed loads*.

Forwarding yields another insight into the MIPS architecture, in addition to the four mentioned on page 440. Each MIPS instruction writes a single result and does so at the end of its execution. Forwarding is harder if there are multiple results to forward per instruction or they need to write before the end of the instruction. For example, the PowerPC's load instructions may use update addressing (page 175 in Chapter 3), so the processor must be able to forward two results per load instruction.

Pipeline Overview Summary

Pipelining is a technique that exploits parallelism among the instructions in a sequential instruction stream. It has the substantial advantage that, unlike some speedup techniques (see Chapter 9), it is fundamentally invisible to the programmer.

In the next sections of this chapter, we cover the concept of pipelining using the MIPS instruction subset lw, sw, add, sub, and, or, slt, and beq (same as Chapter 5) and a simplified version of its pipeline. We then look at the problems that pipelining introduces and the performance attainable under typical situations.

> **The Big Picture**
>
> Pipelining increases the number of simultaneously executing instructions and the rate at which instructions are started and completed. Pipelining does not reduce the time it takes to complete an individual instruction: the five-stage pipeline still takes 5 clock cycles for the instruction to complete. In the terms used in Chapter 2, page 56, pipelining improves instruction *throughput* rather than individual instruction *execution time*.
>
> Instruction sets can either simplify or make life harder for pipeline designers, who must already cope with structural, control, and data hazards. Branch prediction, forwarding, and stalls help make a computer fast while still getting the right answers.

If you wish to take a more casual approach, we believe that after finishing this section, you have sufficient background to skip to sections 6.8 and 6.9 to familiarize yourself with advanced pipelining concepts, such as superscalar and dynamic pipelining, and to see how pipelining works in recent microprocessors.

Or if you are more dedicated, after finishing this section and Chapter 5, you are ready to understand the changes needed for pipelining in the datapath, explained in section 6.2, and the control lines, explained in section 6.3. You should be able to follow the datapath and control modifications for forwarding in section 6.4, and similar changes for stalls to resolve load-use hazards in section 6.5. You can then read section 6.6 to learn more details about solutions to branch hazards, and then see how exceptions are handled in section 6.7.

Elaboration: The name "forwarding" comes from the idea that the result is passed forward from an earlier instruction to a later instruction. "Bypassing" comes from passing the result by the register file to the desired unit.

6.2   A Pipelined Datapath

Figure 6.10 shows the single-cycle datapath from Chapter 5. The division of an instruction into five stages means a five-stage pipeline, which in turn means that up to five instructions will be in execution during any single clock cycle. Thus we must separate the datapath into five pieces, with each piece named corresponding to a stage of instruction execution:

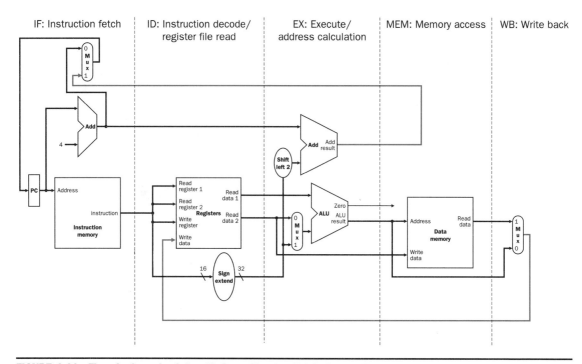

FIGURE 6.10 The single-cycle datapath from Chapter 5 (similar to Figure 5.17 on page 358). Each step of the instruction can be mapped onto the datapath from left to right. The only exceptions are the update of the PC and the write-back step, shown in color, which sends either the ALU result or the data from memory to the left to be written into the register file. (Normally we use color lines for control, but these are data lines.)

1. IF: Instruction fetch

2. ID: Instruction decode and register file read

3. EX: Execution or address calculation

4. MEM: Data memory access

5. WB: Write back

In Figure 6.10, these five components correspond roughly to the way the datapath is drawn; instructions and data move generally from left to right through the five stages as they complete execution. Going back to our laundry analogy, clothes get cleaner, drier, and more organized as they move through the line, and they never move backwards.

There are, however, two exceptions to this left-to-right flow of instructions:

■ The write-back stage, which places the result back into the register file in the middle of the datapath

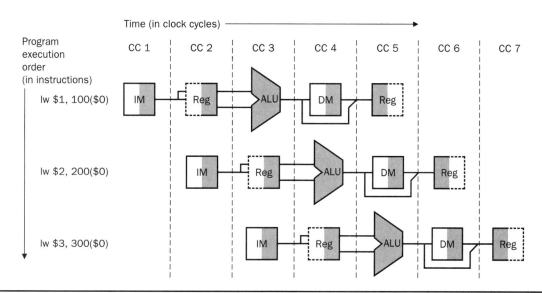

FIGURE 6.11 Instructions being executed using the single-cycle datapath in Figure 6.10, assuming pipelined execution. Similar to Figures 6.7 through 6.9, this figure pretends that each instruction has its own datapath, and shades each portion according to use. Unlike those figures, each stage is labeled by the physical resource used in that stage, corresponding to the portions of the datapath in Figure 6.10. *IM* represents the instruction memory and the PC in the instruction fetch stage, *Reg* stands for the register file and sign extender in the instruction decode/register file read stage (ID), and so on. To maintain proper time order, this stylized datapath breaks the register file into two logical parts: registers read during register fetch (ID) and registers written during write back (WB). This dual use is represented by drawing the unshaded left half of the register file using dashed lines in the ID stage, when it is not being written, and the unshaded right half in dashed lines in the WB stage, when it is not being read. As before, we assume the register file is written in the first half of the clock cycle and the register file is read during the second half.

- The selection of the next value of the PC, choosing between the incremented PC and the branch address from the MEM stage

Data flowing from right to left does not affect the current instruction; only later instructions in the pipeline are influenced by these reverse data movements. Note that the first right-to-left arrow can lead to data hazards and the second leads to control hazards.

One way to show what happens in pipelined execution is to pretend that each instruction has its own datapath, and then to place these datapaths on a timeline to show their relationship. Figure 6.11 shows the execution of the instructions in Figure 6.3 by displaying their private datapaths on a common timeline. We use a stylized version of the datapath in Figure 6.10 to show the relationships in Figure 6.11.

Figure 6.11 seems to suggest that three instructions need three datapaths. In Chapter 5, we added registers to hold data so that portions of the datapath

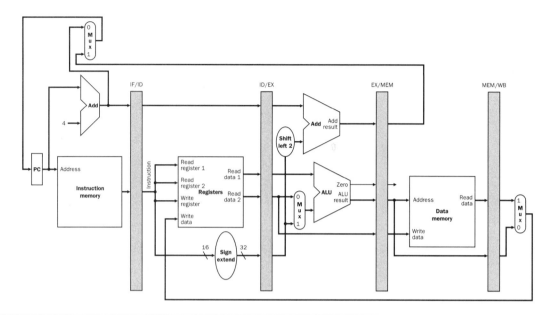

FIGURE 6.12 The pipelined version of the datapath in Figure 6.10. The pipeline registers, in color, separate each pipeline stage. They are labeled by the stages that they separate; for example, the first is labeled *IF/ID* because it separates the instruction fetch and instruction decode stages. The registers must be wide enough to store all the data corresponding to the lines that go through them. For example, the IF/ID register must be 64 bits wide because it must hold both the 32-bit instruction fetched from memory and the incremented 32-bit PC address. We will expand these registers over the course of this chapter, but for now the other three pipeline registers contain 128, 97, and 64 bits, respectively.

could be shared during instruction execution; we use the same technique here to share the multiple datapaths. For example, as Figure 6.11 shows, the instruction memory is used during only one of the five stages of an instruction, allowing it to be shared by other instructions during the other four stages.

To retain the value of an individual instruction for its other four stages, the value read from instruction memory must be saved in a register. Similar arguments apply to every pipeline stage, so we must place registers wherever there are dividing lines between stages in Figure 6.10. (This change is similar to the registers added in Chapter 5 when we went from a single-cycle to a multicycle datapath.) Returning to our laundry analogy, we might have a basket between each stage to hold the clothes for the next step.

Figure 6.12 shows the pipelined datapath with the pipeline registers highlighted. All instructions advance during each clock cycle from one pipeline register to the next. The registers are named for the two stages separated by that register. For example, the pipeline register between the IF and ID stages is called IF/ID.

Notice that there is no pipeline register at the end of the write-back stage. All instructions must update some state in the machine—the register file, memory, or the PC—so a separate pipeline register is redundant to the state that is updated. For example, a load instruction will place its result in 1 of the 32 registers, and any later instruction that needs that data will simply read the appropriate register. (Sections 6.4 and 6.5 describe what happens when there are data hazards between pipelined instructions; ignore them for now.)

To show how the pipelining works, throughout this chapter we show sequences of figures to demonstrate operation over time. These extra pages would seem to require much more time for you to understand. Fear not; the sequences take much less time than it might appear because you can compare them to see what changes in each clock cycle.

Figures 6.13 through 6.15, our first sequence, show the active portions of the datapath highlighted as a load instruction goes through the five stages of pipelined execution. We show a load first because it is active in all five stages. As in Figures 6.7 through 6.12, we highlight the *right half* of registers or memory when they are being *read* and highlight the *left half* when they are being *written*. We show the instruction abbreviation lw with the name of the pipe stage that is active in each figure. The five stages are the following:

1. *Instruction fetch:* The top portion of Figure 6.13 shows the instruction being read from memory using the address in the PC and then placed in the IF/ID pipeline register. (The IF/ID pipeline register is similar to the Instruction register in Figure 5.30 on page 378.) The PC address is incremented by 4 and then written back into the PC to be ready for the next clock cycle. This incremented address is also saved in the IF/ID pipeline register in case it is needed later for an instruction, such as beq. The computer cannot know which type of instruction is being fetched, so it must prepare for any instruction, passing potentially needed information down the pipeline.

2. *Instruction decode and register file read:* The bottom portion of Figure 6.13 shows the instruction portion of the IF/ID pipeline register supplying the 16-bit immediate field, which is sign-extended to 32 bits, and the register numbers to read the two registers. All three values are stored in the ID/EX pipeline register, along with the incremented PC address. We again transfer everything that might be needed by any instruction during a later clock cycle.

3. *Execute or address calculation:* Figure 6.14 shows that the load instruction reads the contents of register 1 and the sign-extended immediate from the ID/EX pipeline register and adds them using the ALU. That sum is placed in the EX/MEM pipeline register.

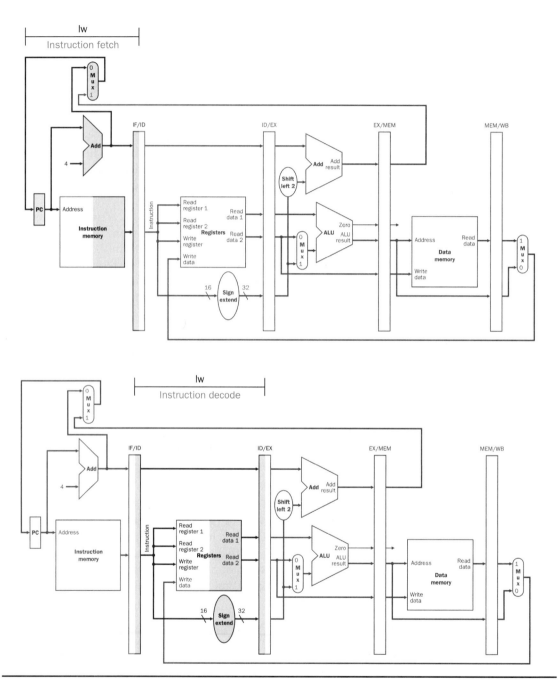

FIGURE 6.13   IF and ID: first and second pipe stages of an instruction, with the active portions of the datapath in Figure 6.12 highlighted. The highlighting convention is the same as that used in Figure 6.7. As in Chapter 5, there is no confusion when reading and writing registers because the contents change only on the clock edge. Although the load needs only the top register in stage 2, the processor doesn't know what instruction is being decoded, so it sign-extends the 16-bit constant and reads both registers into the ID/EX pipeline register. We don't need all three operands, but it simplifies control to keep all three.

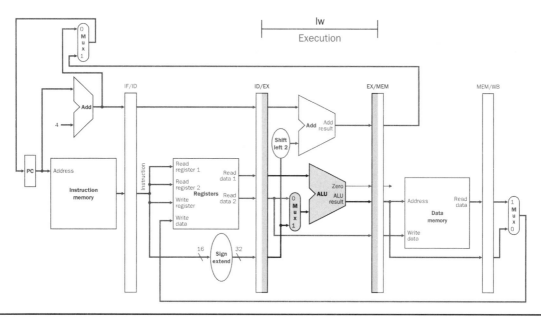

FIGURE 6.14 EX: the third pipe stage of a load instruction, highlighting the portions of the datapath in Figure 6.12 used in this pipe stage. The register is added to the sign-extended immediate, and the sum is placed in the EX/MEM pipeline register.

4. *Memory access:* The top portion of Figure 6.15 shows the load instruction reading the data memory using the address from the EX/MEM pipeline register and loading the data into the MEM/WB pipeline register.

5. *Write back:* The bottom portion of Figure 6.15 shows the final step: reading the data from the MEM/WB pipeline register and writing it into the register file in the middle of the figure.

This walk-through of the load instruction shows that any information needed in a later pipe stage must be passed to that stage via a pipeline register. Walking through a store instruction shows the similarity of instruction execution, as well as passing the information for later stages. Here are the five pipe stages of the store instruction:

1. *Instruction fetch:* The instruction is read from memory using the address in the PC and then is placed in the IF/ID pipeline register. This stage occurs before the instruction is identified, so the top portion of Figure 6.13 works for store as well as load.

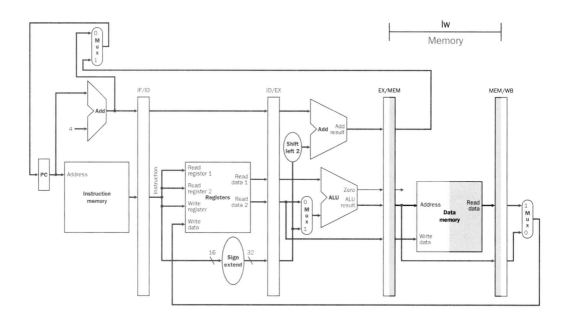

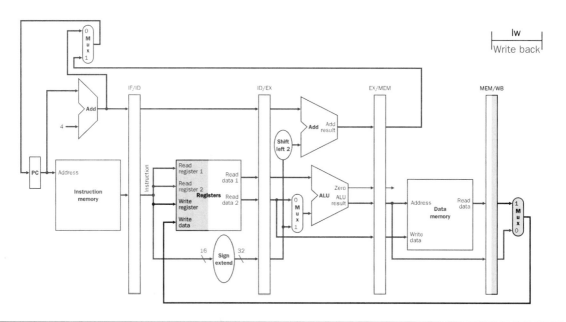

FIGURE 6.15   MEM and WB: the fourth and fifth pipe stages of a load instruction, highlighting the portions of the datapath in Figure 6.12 used in this pipe stage. Data memory is read using the address in the EX/MEM pipeline registers, and the data is placed in the MEM/WB pipeline register. Next, data is read from the MEM/WB pipeline register and written into the register file in the middle of the datapath.

2. *Instruction decode and register file read:* The instruction in the IF/ID pipe-line register supplies the register numbers for reading two registers and extends the sign of the 16-bit immediate. These three 32-bit values are all stored in the ID/EX pipeline register. The bottom portion of Figure 6.13 for load instructions also shows the operations of the second stage for stores. These first two stages are executed by all instructions, since it is too early to know the type of the instruction.

3. *Execute and address calculation:* Figure 6.16 shows the third step; the effective address is placed in the EX/MEM pipeline register.

4. *Memory access:* The top portion of Figure 6.17 shows the data being written to memory. Note that the register containing the data to be stored was read in an earlier stage and stored in ID/EX. The only way to make the data available during the MEM stage is to place the data into the EX/MEM pipeline register in the EX stage, just as we stored the effective address into EX/MEM.

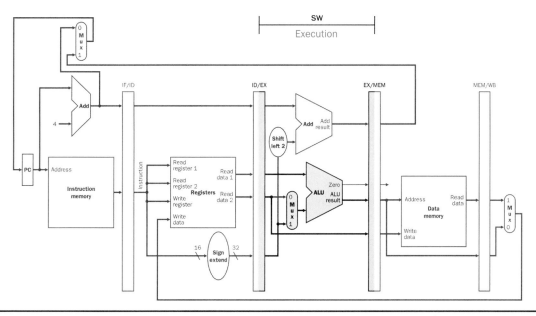

FIGURE 6.16 EX: the third pipe stage of a store instruction. Unlike the third stage of the load instruction in Figure 6.14, the second register value is loaded into the EX/MEM pipeline register to be used in the next stage. Although it wouldn't hurt to always write this second register into the EX/MEM pipeline register, we write the second register only on a store instruction to make the pipeline easier to understand.

5. *Write back:* The bottom portion of Figure 6.17 shows the final step of the store. For this instruction, nothing happens in the write-back stage. Since every instruction behind the store is already in progress, we have no way to accelerate those instructions. Hence an instruction passes through a stage even if there is nothing to do because later instructions are already progressing at the maximum rate.

The store instruction again illustrates that to pass something from an early pipe stage to a later pipe stage, the information must be placed in a pipeline register; otherwise, the information is lost when the next instruction enters that pipeline stage. For the store instruction we needed to pass one of the registers read in the ID stage to the MEM stage, where it is stored in memory. The data was first placed in the ID/EX pipeline register and then passed to the EX/MEM pipeline register.

Load and store illustrate a second key point: each logical component of the datapath—such as instruction memory, register read ports, ALU, data memory, and register write port—can be used only within a *single* pipeline stage. Otherwise we would have a *structural hazard* (see page 441). Hence these components, and their control, can be associated with a single pipeline stage.

Now we can uncover a bug in the design of the load instruction. Did you see it? Which register is changed in the final stage of the load? More specifically, which instruction supplies the write register number? The instruction in the IF/ID pipeline register supplies the write register number, yet this instruction occurs considerably *after* the load instruction!

Hence, we need to preserve the destination register number in the load instruction. Just as store passed the register *contents* from the ID/EX to the EX/MEM pipeline registers for use in the MEM stage, load must pass the register *number* from the ID/EX through EX/MEM to the MEM/WB pipeline register for use in the WB stage. Another way to think about the passing of the register number is that, in order to share the pipelined datapath, we needed to preserve the instruction read during the IF stage, so each pipeline register contains a portion of the instruction needed for that stage and later stages.

Figure 6.18 shows the correct version of the datapath, passing the write register number first to the ID/EX register, then to the EX/MEM register, and finally to the MEM/WB register. The register number is used during the WB stage to specify the register to be written. Figure 6.19 is a single drawing of the corrected datapath, highlighting the hardware used in all five stages of the load word instruction in Figures 6.13 through 6.15. (See section 6.6 for an explanation of how to make the branch instruction work as expected.)

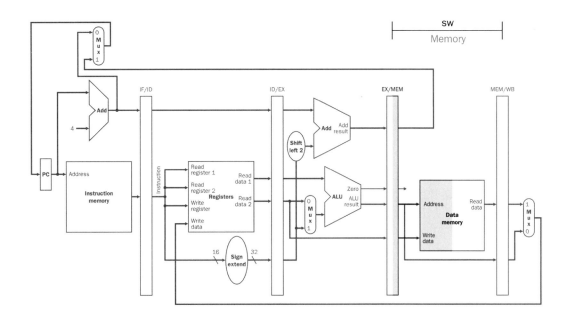

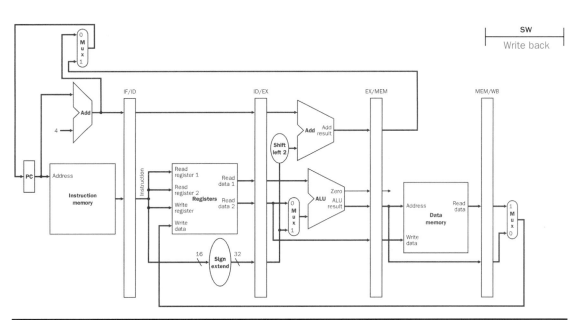

FIGURE 6.17 MEM and WB: the fourth and fifth pipe stage of a store instruction. In the fourth stage, the data is written into data memory for the store. Note that the data comes from the EX/MEM pipeline register and that nothing is changed in the MEM/WB pipeline register. Once the data is written in memory, there is nothing left for the store instruction to do, so nothing happens in stage 5.

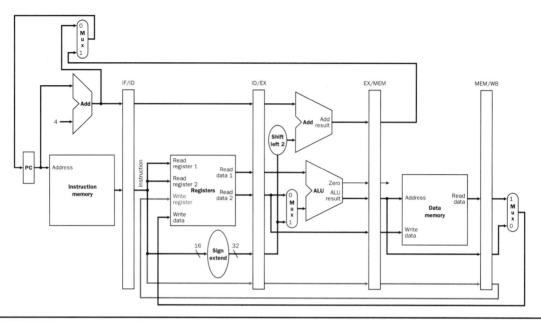

FIGURE 6.18 The corrected pipelined datapath to properly handle the load instruction. The write register number now comes from the MEM/WB pipeline register along with the data. The register number is passed from the ID pipe stage until it reaches the MEM/WB pipeline register, adding 5 more bits to the last three pipeline registers. This new path is shown in color.

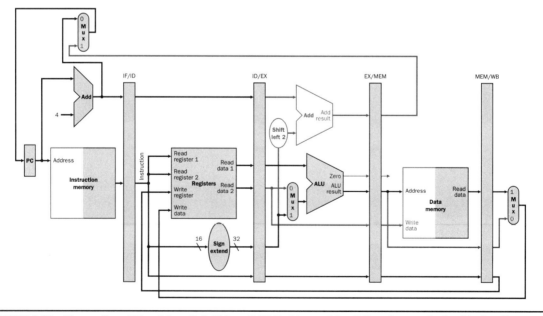

FIGURE 6.19 The portion of the datapath in Figure 6.18 that is used in all five stages of a load instruction.

Graphically Representing Pipelines

Pipelining can be difficult to understand, since many instructions are simultaneously executing in a single datapath in every clock cycle. To aid understanding, there are two basic styles of pipeline figures: *multiple-clock-cycle pipeline diagrams*, such as Figure 6.11 on page 451, and *single-clock-cycle pipeline diagrams*, such as Figures 6.13 through 6.17. Let's try showing a sequence of instructions using both styles of pipeline diagrams for this two-instruction sequence:

```
lw   $10, 20($1)
sub  $11, $2, $3
```

Figure 6.20 shows the multiple-clock-cycle pipeline diagram for these instructions. Time advances from left to right across the page in these diagrams, and instructions advance from the top to the bottom of the page, similar to the laundry pipeline in Figure 6.1 on page 437. A representation of the pipeline stages is placed in each portion along the instruction axis, occupying the proper clock cycles. These stylized datapaths represent the five stages of our pipeline, but a rectangle naming each pipe stage works just as well. Figure 6.21 shows the more traditional version of the multiple-clock-cycle pipeline diagram. Note that Figure 6.20 shows the physical resources used at each stage, while Figure 6.21 uses the *name* of each stage. We use multiple-clock-cycle diagrams to give overviews of pipelining situations.

Single-clock-cycle pipeline diagrams show the state of the entire datapath during a single clock cycle, and usually all five instructions in the pipeline are identified by labels above their respective pipeline stages. We use this type of figure to show the details of what is happening within the pipeline during each clock cycle; typically, the drawings appear in groups to show pipeline operation over a sequence of clock cycles. Figures 6.22 through 6.24 show the single-clock-cycle pipeline diagrams for these two instructions.

These two views of the pipeline are equivalent, of course. One confusing aspect is the order of instructions in the two diagrams: the newest instruction is at the *bottom and to the right* of the multiple-clock-cycle pipeline diagram, and it is on the *left* in the single-clock-cycle pipeline diagram.

Taking a one-clock vertical slice from a multiple-clock-cycle diagram shows the state of the pipeline in a single-clock-cycle diagram. Converting from a sequence of single-clock-cycle pipeline diagrams to one multiple-clock-cycle pipeline diagram is harder. Because the newest instruction must be on the bottom, you rotate each single-clock drawing 90 degrees counterclockwise. The rotated diagrams are then placed side-by-side, each offset by one clock cycle, so that the datapaths of all five stages of each instruction are aligned to occupy a single horizontal line. (See Exercise 6.8.)

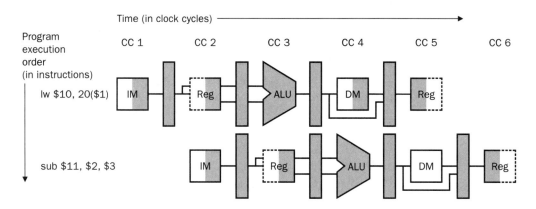

FIGURE 6.20 Multiple-clock-cycle pipeline diagram of two instructions. This style of pipeline representation shows the complete execution of instructions in a single figure. Instructions are listed in instruction execution order from top to bottom, and clock cycles move from left to right. Unlike Figure 6.7, here we show the pipeline registers between each stage. Figure 6.21 shows the traditional way to draw this diagram.

Program execution order (in instructions)	Time (in clock cycles)					
	CC 1	CC 2	CC 3	CC 4	CC 5	CC 6
lw $10, $20($1)	Instruction fetch	Instruction decode	Execution	Data access	Write back	
sub $11, $2, $3		Instruction fetch	Instruction decode	Execution	Data access	Write back

FIGURE 6.21 Traditional multiple-clock-cycle pipeline diagram of two instructions in Figure 6.20.

Elaboration: Because the program counter communicates information between two instructions, as opposed to within a single instruction, diagrams such as Figure 6.22 show the PC as an explicit register. You could consider it as a pipeline register before the instruction fetch stage, or equivalently between the write-back stage of one instruction and the instruction fetch of the next instruction. The PC would then be drawn as an elongated rectangle, like the other pipeline registers.

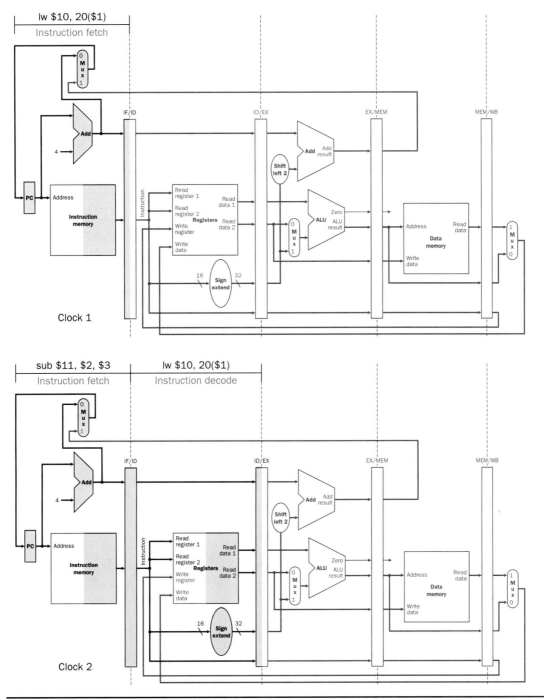

FIGURE 6.22 Single-cycle pipeline diagrams for clock cycles 1 (top diagram) and 2 (bottom diagram). This style of pipeline representation is a snapshot of every instruction executing during 1 clock cycle. Our example has but two instructions, so at most two stages are identified in each clock cycle; normally, all five stages are occupied. The highlighted portions of the datapath are active in that clock cycle. The load is fetched in clock cycle 1 and decoded in clock cycle 2, with the subtract fetched in the second clock cycle. To make the figures easier to understand, the other pipeline stages are empty, but normally there is an instruction in every pipeline stage. *(page 463)*

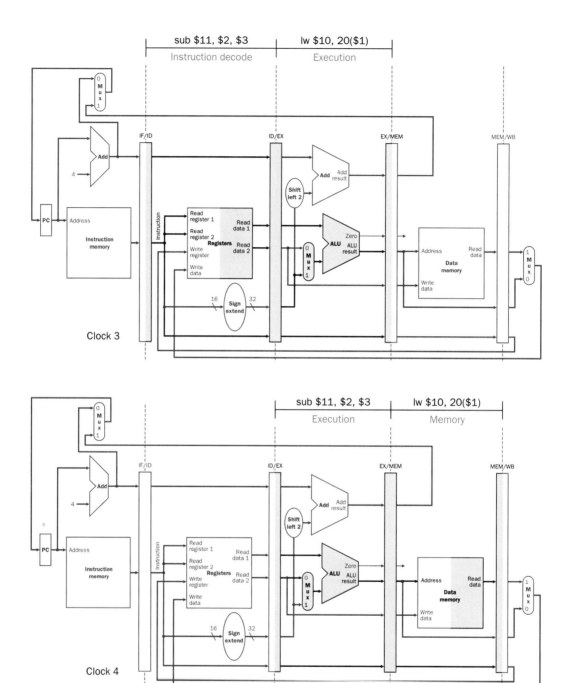

FIGURE 6.23 Single-cycle pipeline diagrams for clock cycles 3 (top diagram) and 4 (bottom diagram). In the third clock cycle in the top diagram, lw enters the EX stage. At the same time, sub enters ID. In the fourth clock cycle (bottom datapath), lw moves into MEM stage, reading memory using the address found in EX/MEM at the beginning of clock cycle 4. At the same time, the ALU subtracts and then places the difference into EX/MEM at the end of the clock cycle. *(page 464)*

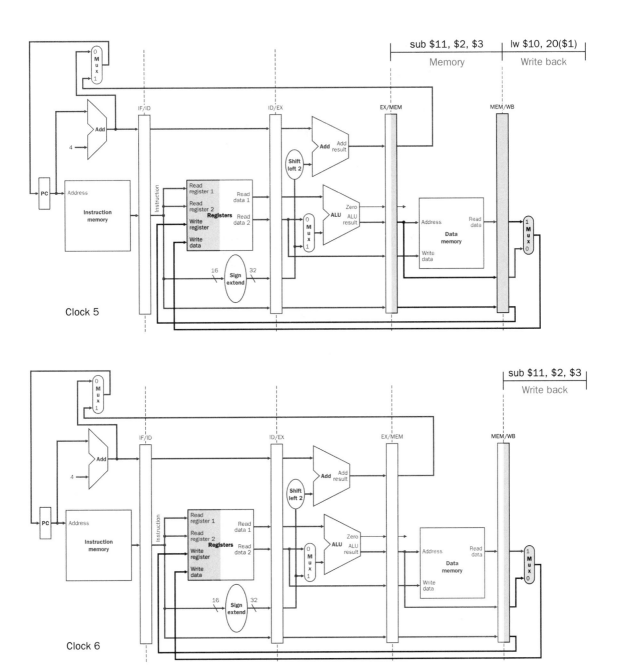

FIGURE 6.24 Single-cycle pipeline diagrams for clock cycles 5 (top diagram) and 6 (bottom diagram). In clock cycle 5, lw completes by writing the data in MEM/WB into register 10, and sub sends the difference in EX/MEM to MEM/WB. In the next clock cycle, sub writes the value in MEM/WB to register 11.

6.3   Pipelined Control

In the 6600 Computer, perhaps even more than in any previous computer, the control system is the difference.

James Thornton, *Design of a Computer:*
The Control Data 6600, 1970

Just as we added control to the simple datapath in section 5.2, we now add control to the pipelined datapath. We start with a simple design that views the problem through rose-colored glasses; in sections 6.4 through 6.8, we remove these glasses to reveal the hazards of the real world.

The first step is to label the control lines on the existing datapath. (Figure 6.25 shows those lines.) We borrow as much as we can from the control for the simple datapath in Figure 5.17 on page 358. In particular, we use the same ALU control logic, branch logic, destination-register-number multiplexor, and control lines. These functions are defined in Figure 5.14 on page 355, Figure 5.18 on page 359, and Figure 5.20 on page 361. (We reproduce the key information in Figures 6.26 through 6.28 to make the remaining text easier to follow.)

As for the single-cycle implementation discussed in Chapter 5, we assume that the PC is written on each clock cycle, so there is no separate write signal for the PC. By the same argument, there are no separate write signals for the pipeline registers (IF/ID, ID/EX, EX/MEM, and MEM/WB), since the pipeline registers are also written during each clock cycle.

To specify control for the pipeline, we need only set the control values during each pipeline stage. Because each control line is associated with a component active in only a single pipeline stage, we can divide the control lines into five groups according to the pipeline stage:

1. *Instruction fetch:* The control signals to read instruction memory and to write the PC are always asserted, so there is nothing special to control in this pipeline stage.

2. *Instruction decode/register file read:* As in the previous stage, the same thing happens at every clock cycle, so there are no optional control lines to set.

3. *Execution/address calculation:* The signals to be set are RegDst, ALUOp, and ALUSrc (see Figures 6.26 and 6.27). The signals select the Result register, the ALU operation, and either Read data 2 or a sign-extended immediate for the ALU.

4. *Memory access:* The control lines set in this stage are Branch, MemRead,

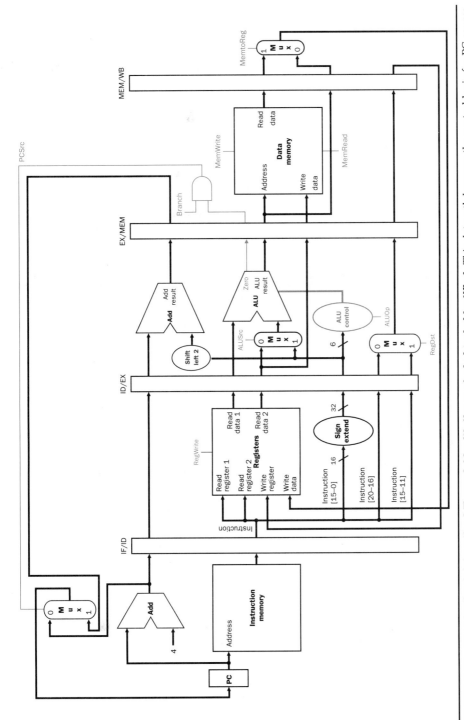

FIGURE 6.25 **The pipelined datapath of Figure 6.18 with the control signals identified.** This datapath borrows the control logic for PC source, register destination number, and ALU control from Chapter 5. Note that we now need the 6-bit funct field (function code) of the instruction in the EX stage as input to ALU control, so these bits must also be included in the ID/EX pipeline register. Recall that these 6 bits are also the 6 least significant bits of the immediate field in the instruction, so the ID/EX pipeline register can supply them from the immediate field since sign extension leaves these bits unchanged.

Instruction opcode	ALUOp	Instruction operation	Function code	Desired ALU action	ALU control input
LW	00	load word	XXXXXX	add	010
SW	00	store word	XXXXXX	add	010
Branch equal	01	branch equal	XXXXXX	subtract	110
R-type	10	add	100000	add	010
R-type	10	subtract	100010	subtract	110
R-type	10	AND	100100	and	000
R-type	10	OR	100101	or	001
R-type	10	set on less than	101010	set on less than	111

FIGURE 6.26   A copy of Figure 5.14 from page 355. This figure shows how the ALU control bits are set depending on the ALUOp control bits and the different function codes for the R-type instruction.

Signal name	Effect when deasserted (0)	Effect when asserted (1)
RegDst	The register destination number for the Write register comes from the rt field (bits 20–16).	The register destination number for the Write register comes from the rd field (bits 15–11).
RegWrite	None	The register on the Write register input is written with the value on the Write data input.
ALUSrc	The second ALU operand comes from the second register file output (Read data 2).	The second ALU operand is the sign-extended, lower 16 bits of the instruction.
PCSrc	The PC is replaced by the output of the adder that computes the value of PC + 4.	The PC is replaced by the output of the adder that computes the branch target.
MemRead	None	Data memory contents designated by the address input are put on the Read data output.
MemWrite	None	Data memory contents designated by the address input are replaced by the value on the Write data input.
MemtoReg	The value fed to the register Write data input comes from the ALU.	The value fed to the register Write data input comes from the data memory.

FIGURE 6.27   A copy of Figure 5.18 from page 359. The function of each of seven control signals is defined. The ALU control lines (ALUOp) are defined in the second column of Figure 6.26. When a 1-bit control to a two-way multiplexor is asserted, the multiplexor selects the input corresponding to 1. Otherwise, if the control is deasserted, the multiplexor selects the 0 input. Note that PCSrc is controlled by an AND gate in Figure 6.25. If the Branch signal and the ALU Zero signal are both set, then PCSrc is 1; otherwise, it is 0. Control sets the Branch signal only during a `beq` instruction; otherwise, PCSrc is set to 0.

and MemWrite. These signals are set by the branch equal, load, and store instructions, respectively. Recall that PCSrc in Figure 6.27 selects the next sequential address unless control asserts Branch and the ALU result was zero.

5. *Write back*: The two control lines are MemtoReg, which decides between sending the ALU result or the memory value to the register file, and RegWrite, which writes the chosen value.

Instruction	Execution/Address Calculation stage control lines				Memory access stage control lines			Write-back stage control lines	
	Reg Dst	ALU Op1	ALU Op0	ALU Src	Branch	Mem Read	Mem Write	Reg Write	Mem to Reg
R-format	1	1	0	0	0	0	0	1	0
lw	0	0	0	1	0	1	0	1	1
sw	X	0	0	1	0	0	1	0	X
beq	X	0	1	0	1	0	0	0	X

FIGURE 6.28 The values of the control lines are the same as in Figure 5.20 on page 361, but they have been shuffled into three groups corresponding to the last three pipeline stages.

Since pipelining the datapath leaves the meaning of the control lines unchanged, we can use the same control values as before. Figure 6.28 has the same values as in Chapter 5, but now the nine control lines are grouped by pipeline stage.

Implementing control means setting the nine control lines to these values in each stage for each instruction. The simplest way to do this is to extend the pipeline registers to include control information.

Since the control lines start with the EX stage, we can create the control information during instruction decode. Figure 6.29 shows that these control signals are then used in the appropriate pipeline stage as the instruction moves down the pipeline, just as the destination register number for loads moves down the pipeline in Figure 6.18 on page 460. Figure 6.30 shows the full datapath with the extended pipeline registers and with the control lines connected to the proper stage.

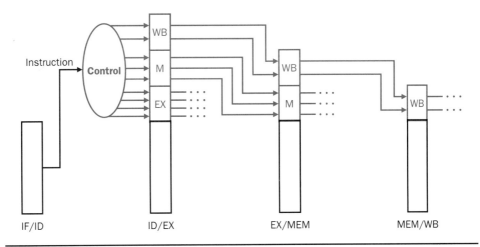

FIGURE 6.29 The control lines for the final three stages. Note that four of the nine control lines are used in the EX phase, with the remaining five control lines passed on to the EX/MEM pipeline register extended to hold the control lines; three are used during the MEM stage, and the last two are passed to MEM/WB for use in the WB stage.

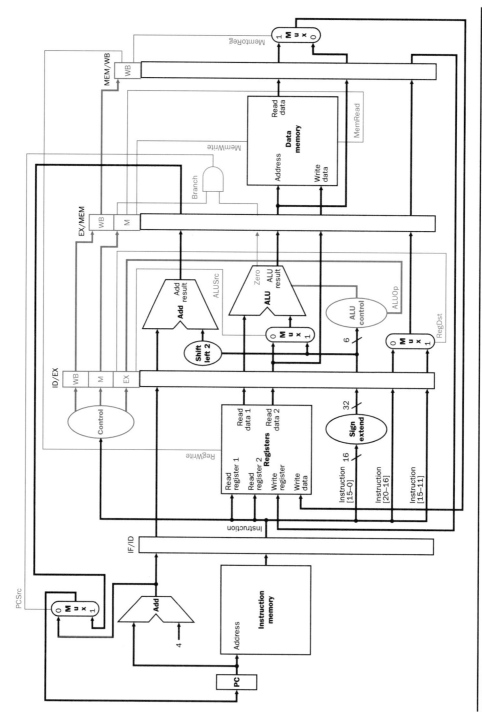

FIGURE 6.30 The pipelined datapath of Figure 6.25, with the control signals connected to the control portions of the pipeline registers. The control values for the last three stages are created during the instruction decode stage and then placed in the ID/EX pipeline register. The control lines for each pipe stage are used, and remaining control lines are then passed to the next pipeline stage.

Labeled Pipeline Execution, Including Control

Example Show these five instructions going through the pipeline:

```
lw     $10, 20($1)
sub    $11, $2, $3
and    $12, $4, $5
or     $13, $6, $7
add    $14, $8, $9
```

Label the instructions in the pipeline that precede the lw as before <1>, before <2>, ..., and the instructions after the add as after <1>, after <2>,....

Answer Figures 6.31 through 6.35 show these instructions proceeding through the nine clock cycles it takes them to complete execution, highlighting what is active in a stage and identifying the instruction associated with each stage during a clock cycle.

Reviewing these figures carefully will give you insight into how pipelines work. A few items you may notice:

■ In Figure 6.33 you can see the sequence of the destination register numbers from left to right at the bottom of the pipeline registers. The numbers advance to the right during each clock cycle, with the MEM/WB pipeline register supplying the number of the register written during the WB stage.

■ When a stage is inactive, the values of control lines that are deasserted, are shown as 0 or X (for don't care).

■ In contrast to Chapter 5, where sequencing of control required special hardware, sequencing of control is embedded in the pipeline structure itself. First, all instructions take the same number of clock cycles, so there is no special control for instruction duration. Second, all control information is computed during instruction decode, and then passed along by the pipeline registers.

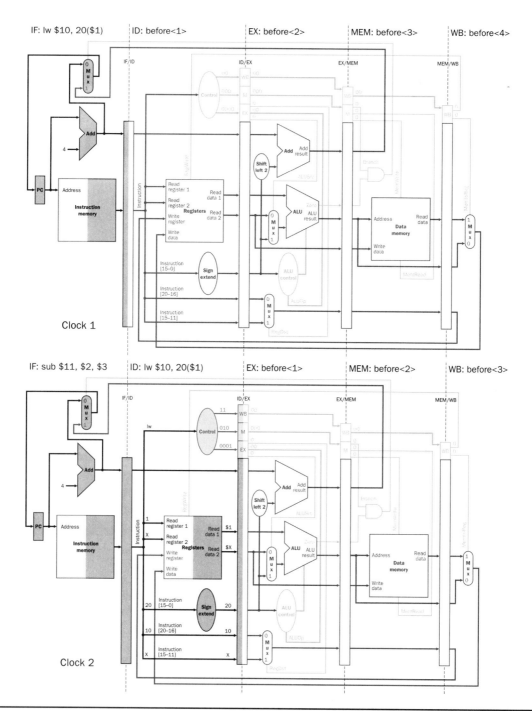

FIGURE 6.31 Clock cycles 1 and 2. The phrase "before<*i*>" means the *i*th instruction before lw. The lw instruction in the top datapath is in the IF stage. At the end of the clock cycle, the lw instruction is in the IF/ID pipeline registers. In the second clock cycle, seen in the bottom datapath, the lw moves to the ID stage, and sub enters in the IF stage. Note that the values of the instruction fields and the selected source registers are shown in the ID stage. Hence register $1 and the constant 20, the operands of lw, are written into the ID/EX pipeline register. The number 10, representing the destination register number of lw, is also placed in ID/EX. Bits 15–11 are 0, but we use X to show that a field plays no role in a given instruction. The top of the ID/EX pipeline register shows the control values for lw to be used in the remaining stages. These control values can be read from the lw row of the table in Figure 6.28 on page 469. *(page 472)*

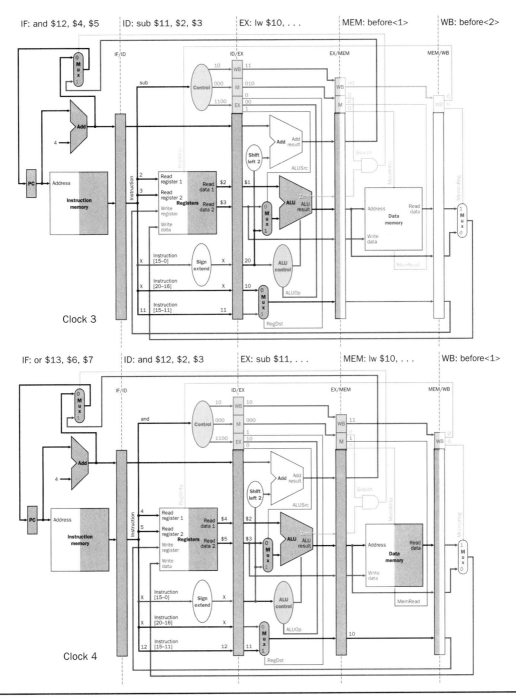

FIGURE 6.32 Clock cycles 3 and 4. In the top diagram, lw enters the EX stage in the third clock cycle, adding $1 and 20 to form the address in the EX/MEM pipeline register. (The lw instruction is written lw $10, . . . upon reaching EX because the identity of instruction operands is not needed by EX or the subsequent stages. In this version of the pipeline, the actions of EX, MEM, and WB depend only on the instruction and its destination register or its target address.) At the same time, sub enters ID, reading registers $2 and $3, and the and instruction starts IF. In the fourth clock cycle (bottom datapath), lw moves into MEM stage, reading memory using the value in EX/MEM as the address. In the same clock cycle, the ALU subtracts $3 from $2 and places the difference into EX/MEM, and reads registers $4 and $5 during ID, and the or instruction enters IF. The two diagrams show the control signals being created in the ID stage and peeled off as they are used in subsequent pipe stages. *(page 473)*

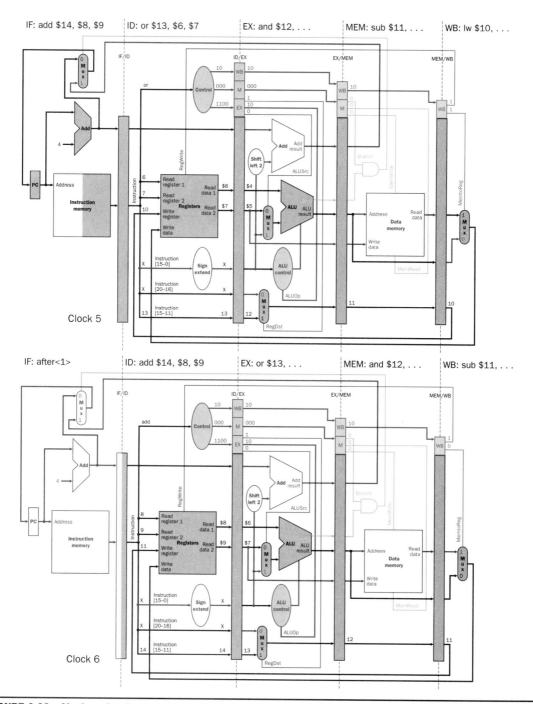

FIGURE 6.33 Clock cycles 5 and 6. With add, the final instruction in this example, entering IF in the top datapath, all instructions are engaged. By writing the data in MEM/WB into register 10, lw completes; both the data and the register number are in MEM/WB. In the same clock cycle sub sends the difference in EX/MEM to MEM/WB, and the rest of the instructions move forward. In the next clock cycle, sub selects the value in MEM/WB to write to register number 11, again found in MEM/WB. The remaining instructions play follow-the-leader: the ALU calculates the OR of $6 and $7 for the or instruction in the EX stage, and registers $8 and $9 are read in the ID stage for the add instruction. The instructions after add are shown as inactive just to emphasize what occurs for the five instructions in the example. The phrase "after<*i*>" means the *i*th instruction after add. *(page 474)*

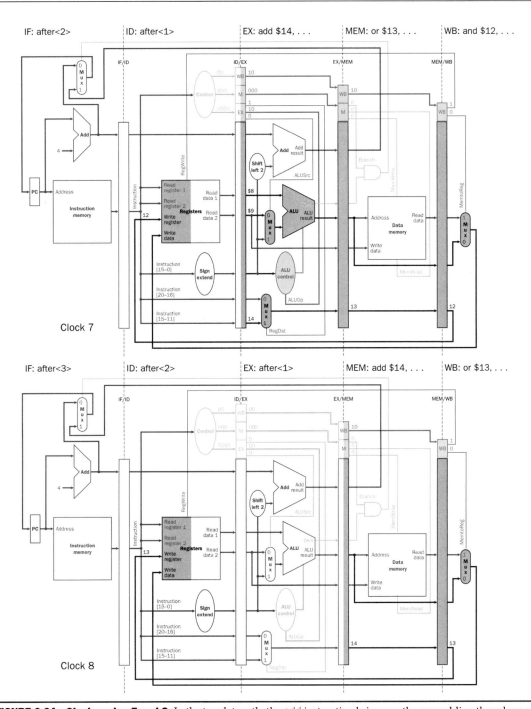

FIGURE 6.34 Clock cycles 7 and 8. In the top datapath, the add instruction brings up the rear, adding the values corresponding to registers $8 and $9 during the EX stage. The result of the or instruction is passed from EX/MEM to MEM/WB in the MEM stage, and the WB stage writes the result of the and instruction in MEM/WB to register $12. Note that the control signals are deasserted (set to 0) in the ID stage, since no instruction is being executed. In the following clock cycle (lower drawing), the WB stage writes the result to register $13, thereby completing or, and the MEM stage passes the sum from the add in EX/MEM to MEM/WB. The instructions after add are shown as inactive for pedagogical reasons.

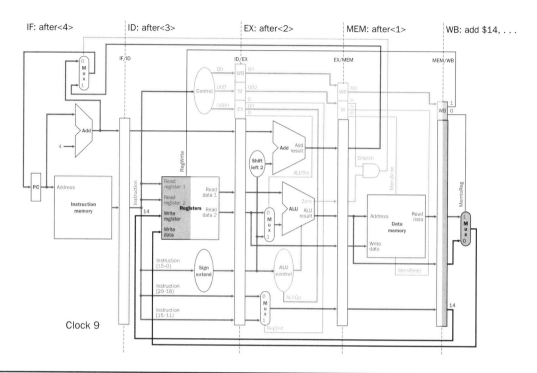

FIGURE 6.35   Clock cycle 9. The WB stage writes the sum in MEM/WB into register $14, completing add and the five-instruction sequence. The instructions after add are shown as inactive for pedagogical reasons.

6.4   Data Hazards and Forwarding

There is less in this than meets the eye.

Tallulah Bankhead, remark to Alexander Wollcott, 1922

The examples in the previous section show the power of pipelined execution and how the hardware performs the task. It's now time to take off the rose-colored glasses and look at what happens with real programs. The instructions in Figures 6.31 through 6.35 were independent; none of them used the results calculated by any of the others. Yet in section 6.1 we saw that data hazards are obstacles to pipelined execution.

Let's look at a sequence with many dependencies, shown in color:

```
sub   $2, $1,    $3     # Register $2 written by sub
and   $12,$2,    $5     # 1st operand($2) depends on sub
or    $13,$6,    $2     # 2nd operand($2) depends on sub
add   $14,$2,    $2     # 1st($2) & 2nd($2) depend on sub
sw    $15,100($2)       # Base ($2) depends on sub
```

The last four instructions are all dependent on the result in register $2 of the first instruction. If register $2 had the value 10 before the subtract instruction and –20 afterwards, the programmer intends that –20 will be used in the following instructions that refer to register $2.

How would this sequence perform with our pipeline? Figure 6.36 illustrates the execution of these instructions using a multiple-clock-cycle pipeline representation. To demonstrate the execution of this instruction sequence in our current pipeline, the top of Figure 6.36 shows the value of register $2 at the beginning of each clock cycle.

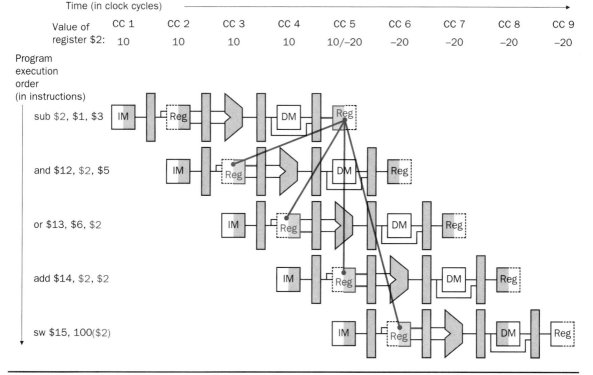

FIGURE 6.36 Pipelined dependencies in a five-instruction sequence using simplified datapaths to show the dependencies. All the dependent actions are shown in color, and "CC *i*" at the top of the figure means clock cycle *i*. The first instruction writes into $2, and all the following instructions read $2. This register is written in clock cycle 5, so the proper value is unavailable before clock cycle 5. (Our register file will read the value written in that clock cycle.) The colored lines from the top datapath to the lower ones show the dependencies. Those that must go backwards in time are *pipeline data hazards*.

One potential hazard can be resolved by the design of the register file hardware: what happens when a register is read and written in the same clock cycle? We assume that the write is in the first half of the clock cycle and the read is in the second half, so the read delivers what is written. As is the case for many implementations of register files, we have no data hazard in this case.

Figure 6.36 shows that the values read for register $2 would *not* be the result of the sub instruction unless the read occurred during clock cycle 5 or later. The instructions that would get the correct value of –20 are add and sw; and and or would get the incorrect value 10. Using this style of drawing, such problems become apparent when a dependence line goes backwards in time. Thus, in Figure 6.36, we see problems with and and or instructions because they are dependent on a value written later.

Hardware Software Interface

We'll shortly see hardware schemes for resolving data hazards. One alternative strategy is to legislate data hazards out of existence: the compiler is forbidden to generate sequences such as the five instructions above. For example, the compiler would insert two independent instructions between the sub and the and instructions, thereby making the hazard disappear. When no such instructions can be found, the compiler inserts instructions guaranteed to be independent: nop instructions. The abbreviation stands for "no operation," because nop neither modifies data nor writes a result. The code below uses nop instructions to get the proper result:

```
sub   $2,   $1, $3
nop
nop
and   $12, $2, $5
or    $13, $6, $2
add   $14, $2, $2
sw    $15, 100($2)
```

Although this code works properly for this pipeline, these two nops occupy 2 clock cycles that do no useful work. As we said in section 6.1, these dependencies happen too often to rely on compilers to come to the rescue.

We must first detect a hazard and then *forward* the proper value to resolve the hazard (see page 446). On closer inspection, when an instruction tries to read a register in its EX stage that an earlier instruction intends to write in its WB stage, we actually need the values as inputs to the ALU.

A notation that names the fields of the pipeline registers allows for a more precise notation of dependencies. For example, "ID/EX.RegisterRs" refers to the number of one register whose value is found in the pipeline register ID/EX; that is, the one from the first read port of the register file. The first part of the name, to the left of the period, is the name of the pipeline register; the second part is the name of the field in that register. Using this notation, the two pairs of hazard conditions are

1a. EX/MEM.RegisterRd = ID/EX.RegisterRs
1b. EX/MEM.RegisterRd = ID/EX.RegisterRt
2a. MEM/WB.RegisterRd = ID/EX.RegisterRs
2b. MEM/WB.RegisterRd = ID/EX.RegisterRt

The first hazard in the sequence on page 477 is on register $2, between the result of sub $2,$1,$3 and the first read operand of and $12,$2,$5. This hazard can be detected when the and instruction is in the EX stage and the prior instruction is in the MEM stage, so this is hazard 1a:

EX/MEM.RegisterRd = ID/EX.RegisterRs = $2.

Dependency Detection

Example Classify the dependencies in this sequence from page 477:

```
sub     $2,     $1, $3   # Register $2 set by sub
and     $12,    $2, $5   # 1st operand($2) set by sub
or      $13,    $6, $2   # 2nd operand($2) set by sub
add     $14,    $2, $2   # 1st($2) & 2nd($2) set by sub
sw      $15,    100($2)  # Index($2) set by sub
```

Answer As mentioned above, the sub-and is a type 1a hazard. The remaining hazards are

■ The sub-or is a type 2b hazard:

MEM/WB.RegisterRd = ID/EX.RegisterRt = $2;

■ The two dependencies on sub-add are not hazards because the register file supplies the proper data during the ID stage of add.

■ There is no data hazard between sub and sw because sw reads $2 the clock cycle *after* sub writes $2.

Because some instructions do not write registers, this policy is inaccurate; sometimes it would forward when it was unnecessary. One solution is simply to check to see if the RegWrite signal will be active: examining the WB control field of the pipeline register during the EX and MEM stages determines if Reg-Write is asserted. Also, MIPS requires that every use of $0 as an operand must yield an operand value of zero. In the event that an instruction in the pipeline has $0 as its destination (for example, s11 $0, $1, 2), we want to avoid forwarding its possibly nonzero result value. Not forwarding results destined for $0 frees the assembly programmer and the compiler of any requirement to avoid using $0 as a destination. The conditions above thus work properly as long we add EX/MEM.RegisterRd ≠ 0 to the first hazard condition and MEM/WB.RegisterRd ≠ 0 to the second.

Now that we can detect hazards, half of the problem is resolved—but we must still forward the proper data.

Figure 6.37 shows the dependencies between the pipeline registers and the inputs to the ALU for the same code sequence as in Figure 6.36. The change is that the dependency begins from a *pipeline* register rather than waiting for the WB stage to write the register file. Thus the required data exists in time for later instructions, with the pipeline registers holding the data to be forwarded.

If we can take the inputs to the ALU from *any* pipeline register rather than just ID/EX, then we can forward the proper data. By adding multiplexors to the input of the ALU and with the proper controls, we can run the pipeline at full speed in the presence of these data dependencies.

For now, we will assume the only instructions we need to forward are the four R-format instructions: add, sub, and, and or. Figure 6.38 shows a close-up of the ALU and pipeline register before and after adding forwarding. Figure 6.39 shows the values of the control lines for the ALU multiplexors that select either the register file values or one of the forwarded values.

This forwarding control will be in the EX stage, because the ALU forwarding multiplexors are found in that stage. Thus we must pass the operand register numbers from the ID stage via the ID/EX pipeline register to determine whether to forward values. We already have the rt field (bits 20–16). Before forwarding, the ID/EX register had no need to include space to hold the rs field. Hence rs (bits 25–21) is added to ID/EX.

Let's now write both the conditions for detecting hazards and the control signals to resolve them (we highlight the small differences):

1. EX hazard:

   if (EX/MEM.RegWrite
   and (EX/MEM.RegisterRd ≠ 0)
   and (EX/MEM.RegisterRd = ID/EX.RegisterRs)) ForwardA = 10

   if (EX/MEM.RegWrite
   and (EX/MEM.RegisterRd ≠ 0)
   and (EX/MEM.RegisterRd = ID/EX.RegisterRt)) ForwardB = 10

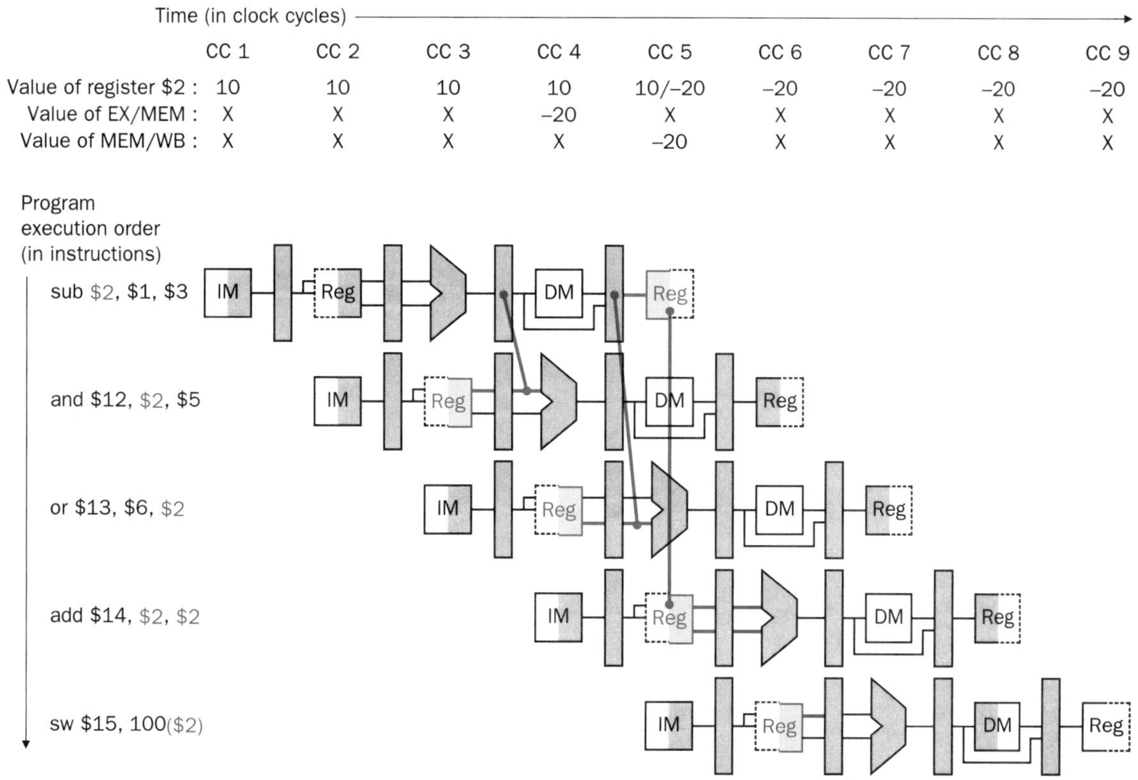

Time (in clock cycles)

	CC 1	CC 2	CC 3	CC 4	CC 5	CC 6	CC 7	CC 8	CC 9
Value of register $2 :	10	10	10	10	10/−20	−20	−20	−20	−20
Value of EX/MEM :	X	X	X	−20	X	X	X	X	X
Value of MEM/WB :	X	X	X	X	−20	X	X	X	X

Program
execution order
(in instructions)

sub $2, $1, $3

and $12, $2, $5

or $13, $6, $2

add $14, $2, $2

sw $15, 100($2)

FIGURE 6.37 The dependencies between the pipeline registers move forward in time, so it is possible to supply the inputs to the ALU needed by the and **instruction and** or **instruction by forwarding the results found in the pipeline registers.** The values in the pipeline registers show that the desired value is available before it is written into the register file. We assume that the register file forwards values that are read and written during the same clock cycle, so the add does not stall, but the values come from the register file instead of a pipeline register. Register file "forwarding"—that is, the read gets the value of the write in that clock cycle—is why clock cycle 5 shows register $2 having the value 10 at the beginning and −20 at the end of the clock cycle.

This case forwards the result from the previous instruction to either input of the ALU. If the previous instruction is going to write to the register file and the write register number matches the read register number of ALU inputs A or B, provided it is not register 0, then steer the multiplexor to pick the value instead from the pipeline register EX/MEM.

2. MEM hazard:

if (MEM/WB.RegWrite
and (MEM/WB.RegisterRd ≠ 0)
and (MEM/WB.RegisterRd = ID/EX.RegisterRs)) ForwardA = 01

if (MEM/WB.RegWrite
and (MEM/WB.RegisterRd ≠ 0)
and (MEM/WB.RegisterRd = ID/EX.RegisterRt)) ForwardB = 01

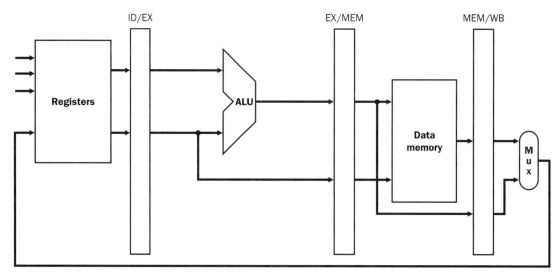

a. No forwarding

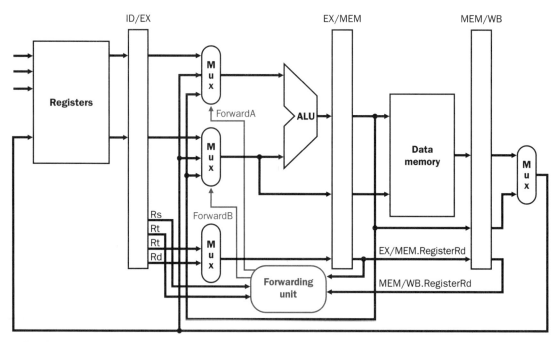

b. With forwarding

FIGURE 6.38   On the top are the ALU and pipeline registers before adding forwarding. On the bottom, the multi-plexors have been expanded to add the forwarding paths, and we show the forwarding unit. The new hardware is shown in color. This figure is a stylized drawing, however, leaving out details from the full datapath such as the sign extension hardware. Note that the ID/EX.RegisterRt field is shown twice, once to connect to the mux and once to the forwarding unit, but it is a single signal.

Mux control	Source	Explanation
ForwardA = 00	ID/EX	The first ALU operand comes from the register file.
ForwardA = 10	EX/MEM	The first ALU operand is forwarded from the prior ALU result.
ForwardA = 01	MEM/WB	The first ALU operand is forwarded from data memory or an earlier ALU result.
ForwardB = 00	ID/EX	The second ALU operand comes from the register file.
ForwardB = 10	EX/MEM	The second ALU operand is forwarded from the prior ALU result.
ForwardB = 01	MEM/WB	The second ALU operand is forwarded from data memory or an earlier ALU result.

FIGURE 6.39   The control values for the forwarding multiplexors in Figure 6.38. The signed immediate that is another input to the ALU is described in the elaboration at the end of this section.

As mentioned above, there is no hazard in the WB stage, because we assume that the register file supplies the correct result if the instruction in the ID stage reads the same register written by the instruction in the WB stage. Such a register file performs another form of forwarding, but it occurs within the register file.

One complication is potential data hazards between the result of the instruction in the WB stage, the result of the instruction in the MEM stage, and the source operand of the instruction in the ALU stage. For example, when summing a vector of numbers in a single register, a sequence of instructions will all read and write to the same register:

```
add $1,$1,$2;
add $1,$1,$3;
add $1,$1,$4;
 . . .
```

In this case, the result is forwarded from the MEM stage because the result in the MEM stage is the more recent result. Thus the control for the MEM hazard would be (with the additions highlighted)

if (MEM/WB.RegWrite
and (MEM/WB.RegisterRd ≠ 0)
and (EX/MEM.RegisterRd ≠ ID/EX.RegisterRs)
and (MEM/WB.RegisterRd = ID/EX.RegisterRs)) ForwardA = 01

if (MEM/WB.RegWrite
and (MEM/WB.RegisterRd ≠ 0)
and (EX/MEM.RegisterRd ≠ ID/EX.RegisterRt)
and (MEM/WB.RegisterRd = ID/EX.RegisterRt)) ForwardB = 01

Figure 6.40 shows the hardware necessary to support forwarding.

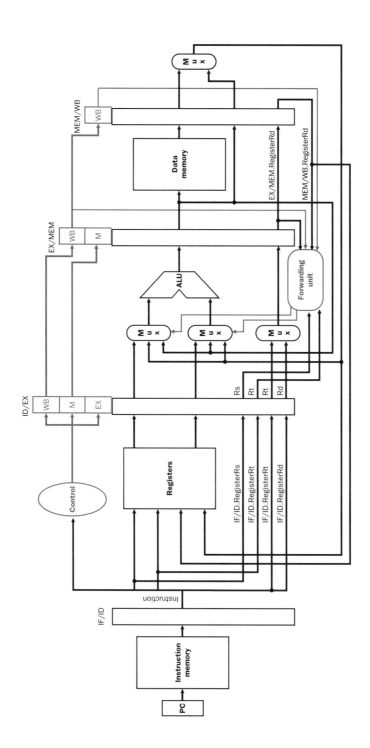

FIGURE 6.40 The datapath modified to resolve hazards via forwarding. Compared with the datapath in Figure 6.30 on page 470, the additions are the multiplexors to the inputs to the ALU. This figure is a more stylized drawing, however, leaving out details from the full datapath such as the branch hardware and the sign extension hardware.

(page 484)

Forwarding

Example

Show how forwarding works with this instruction sequence (with dependencies highlighted):

```
sub     $2, $1, $3
and     $4, $2, $5
or      $4, $4, $2
add     $9, $4, $2
```

Answer

Figures 6.41 and 6.42 show the events in clock cycles 3–6 in the execution of these instructions. In clock cycle 4, the forwarding unit sees the writing by the sub instruction of register $2 in the MEM stage, while the and instruction in the EX stage is reading register $2. The forwarding unit selects the EX/MEM pipeline register instead of the ID/EX pipeline register as the upper input to the ALU to get the proper value for register $2. The following or instruction reads register $4, which is written by the and instruction, and register $2, which is written by the sub instruction. Thus in clock cycle 5 the forwarding unit selects the EX/MEM pipeline register for the upper input to the ALU and the MEM/WB pipeline register for the lower input to the ALU. The following add instruction reads both register $4, the target of the and instruction, and register $2, which the sub instruction has already written. Notice that the prior two instructions both write register $4, so the forwarding unit must pick the immediately preceding one (MEM stage). In clock cycle 6, the forwarding unit thus selects the EX/MEM pipeline register, containing the result of the or instruction, for the upper ALU input but uses the non-forwarding register value for the lower input to the ALU.

Elaboration: Because hazards are officially defined with respect to a particular hardware datapath, instruction sequences with result dependencies are no longer considered hazards when forwarding resolves the dependencies. Hence the name is forwarding unit rather than hazard forwarding unit.

A second point is that an alternative to the explanation of forwarding in this section is to determine the control of the multiplexors on the ALU inputs during the ID stage, setting those values in new control fields of the ID/EX pipeline register. The hardware may then be faster because the time to select the ALU inputs is likely to be on the critical path.

The MIPS nop instruction mentioned on page 478 is represented by all 0s. It represents sll $0, $0, 0, which shifts the register 0 left 0 places. It does nothing to register 0, which can't be changed in any case, and hence is used as a nop by MIPS software.

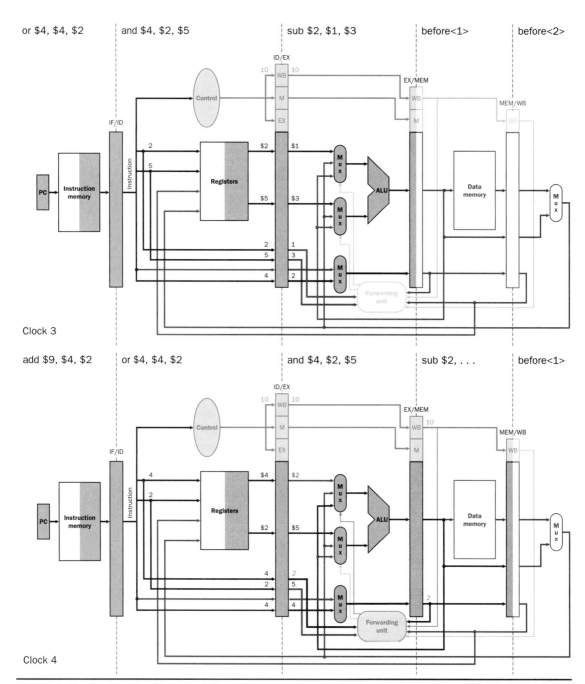

FIGURE 6.41   Clock cycles 3 and 4 of the instruction sequence in the example on page 485. The bold lines are those active in a clock cycle, and the italicized register numbers in color indicate a hazard. The forwarding unit is highlighted by shading it when it is forwarding data to the ALU. The instructions before sub are shown as inactive just to emphasize what occurs for the four instructions in the example. Operand names are used in EX for control of forwarding, thus they are included in the instruction label for EX. Operand names are not needed in MEM or WB, so . . . is used. Compare this with Figures 6.32 through 6.35 showing the datapath without forwarding where ID is the last stage to need operand information.

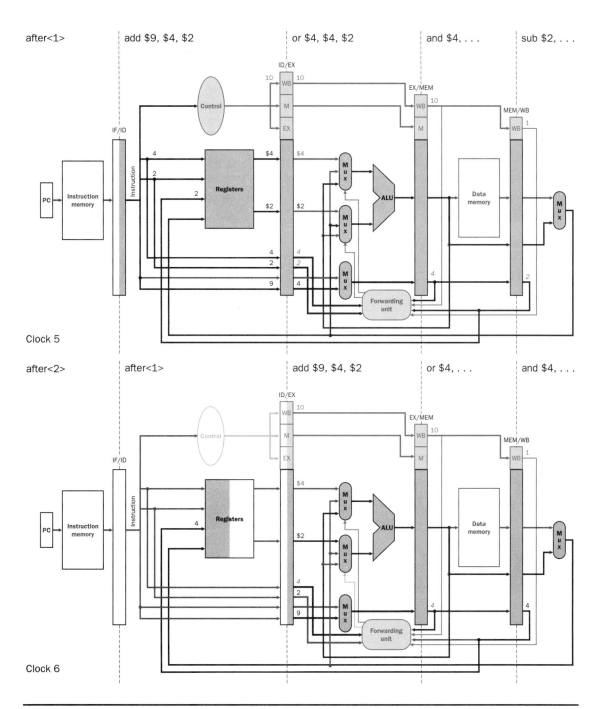

FIGURE 6.42 Clock cycles 5 and 6 of the instruction sequence in the example on page 485. The forwarding unit is highlighted when it is forwarding data to the ALU. The two instructions after add are shown as inactive just to emphasize what occurs for the four instructions in the example. The bold lines are those active in a clock cycle, and the italicized register numbers in color indicate a hazard.

Elaboration: Forwarding can also help with hazards when store instructions are dependent on other instructions. Since they use just one data value during the MEM stage, forwarding is easy. But consider loads immediately followed by stores. We need to add more forwarding hardware to make memory-to-memory copies run faster. If we were to redraw Figure 6.37 on page 481, replacing the sub and and instruction by lw with an sw, we would see that it is possible to avoid a stall, since the data exists in the MEM/WB register of a load instruction in time for its use in the MEM stage of a store instruction. We would need to add forwarding into the memory access stage for this option. Exercise 6.17 examines the changes to the datapath to avoid this hazard.

The signed-immediate input to the ALU, needed by loads and stores, is missing from the datapath in Figure 6.40 on page 484. Since central control decides between register and immediate, and since the forwarding unit chooses the pipeline register for a register input to the ALU, the easiest solution is to add a 2:1 multiplexor that chooses between the ForwardB multiplexor output and the signed immediate. Figure 6.43 shows this addition. Note that this solution differs from what we learned in Chapter 5, where the multiplexor controlled by line ALUSelB was expanded to include the immediate input. This solution also solves store forwarding by connecting the forwarding multiplexor output—containing store data in this case—to the EX/MEM pipeline register.

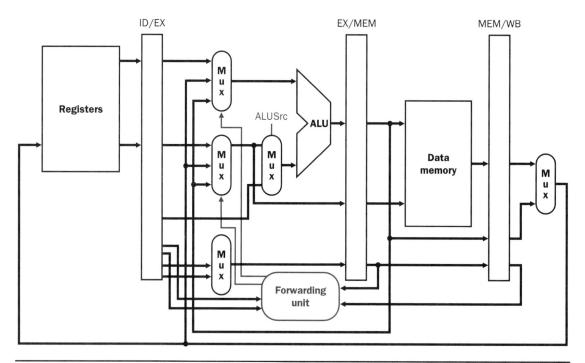

FIGURE 6.43   A close-up of the datapath in Figure 6.38 on page 482 shows a 2:1 multiplexor, which has been added to select the signed immediate as an ALU input.

6.5 Data Hazards and Stalls

If at first you don't succeed, redefine success.

Anonymous

As we said in section 6.1, one case where forwarding cannot save the day is when an instruction tries to read a register following a load instruction that writes the same register. Figure 6.44 illustrates the problem. The data is still being read from memory in clock cycle 4 while the ALU is performing the operation for the following instruction. Something must stall the pipeline for the combination of load followed by an instruction that reads its result.

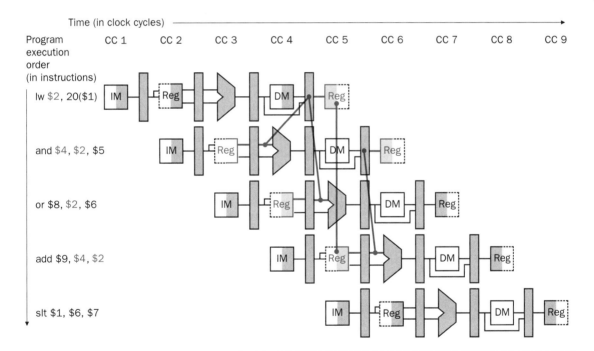

FIGURE 6.44 A pipelined sequence of instructions. Since the dependence between the load and the following instruction (and) goes backwards in time, this hazard cannot be solved by forwarding. Hence, this combination must result in a stall by the hazard detection unit.

Hence, in addition to a forwarding unit, we need a *hazard detection unit*. It operates during the ID stage so that it can insert the stall between the load and its use. Checking for load instructions, the control for the hazard detection unit is this single condition:

> if (ID/EX.MemRead and
>   ((ID/EX.RegisterRt = IF/ID.RegisterRs) or
>   (ID/EX.RegisterRt = IF/ID.RegisterRt)))
>   stall the pipeline

The first line tests to see if the instruction is a load: the only instruction that reads data memory is a load. The next two lines check to see if the destination register field of the load in the EX stage matches either source register of the instruction in the ID stage. If the condition holds, the instruction stalls 1 clock cycle. After this 1-cycle stall, the forwarding logic can handle the dependency and execution proceeds. (If there were no forwarding, then the instructions in Figure 6.44 would need another stall cycle.)

If the instruction in the ID stage is stalled, then the instruction in the IF stage must also be stalled; otherwise, we would lose the fetched instruction. Preventing these two instructions from making progress is accomplished simply by preventing the PC register and the IF/ID pipeline register from changing. Provided these registers are preserved, the instruction in the IF stage will continue to be read using the same PC, and the registers in the ID stage will continue to be read using the same instruction fields in the IF/ID pipeline register. Returning to our favorite analogy, it's as if you restart the washing machine with the same clothes and let the dryer continue tumbling empty.

To stall the pipeline, we need to get the same effect as inserting nop instructions, as in the Hardware/Software Interface section on page 478, but this time the nop "instructions" begin in the EX pipeline stage. In Figure 6.28 on page 469, we see that deasserting all nine control signals (setting them to 0) in the EX, MEM, and WB stages will create a "do nothing" instruction. By identifying the hazard in the ID stage, we can insert a bubble into the pipeline by changing the EX, MEM, and WB control fields of the ID/EX pipeline register to 0. These benign control values are percolated forward at each clock cycle with the proper effect: no registers or memories are written if the control values are all 0.

Figure 6.45 shows what really happens in the hardware. The hazard forces the and and or instructions to repeat in clock cycle 4 what they did in clock cycle 3: and reads registers and decodes, and or is refetched from instruction memory. Such repeated work is what a stall looks like, but its effect is to stretch the time of the and and or instructions and delay the fetch of the add instruction. Like an air bubble in a water pipe, a stall bubble delays everything behind it and proceeds down the instruction pipe until it exits at the end.

Figure 6.46 highlights the pipeline connections for both the hazard detection unit and the forwarding unit. As before, the forwarding unit controls the

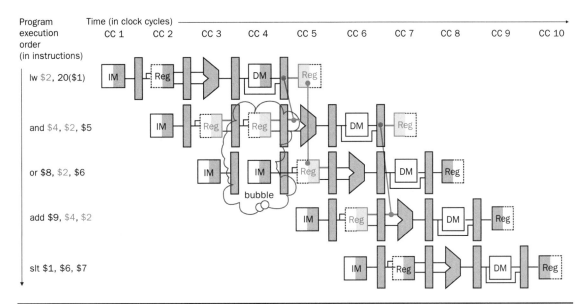

Program execution order (in instructions)

Time (in clock cycles)

lw $2, 20($1)

and $4, $2, $5

or $8, $2, $6

add $9, $4, $2

slt $1, $6, $7

FIGURE 6.45 The way stalls are really inserted into the pipeline. Since the dependencies go forward in time, there are no data hazards.

ALU multiplexors to replace the value from a general-purpose register with the value from the proper pipeline register. The hazard detection unit controls the writing of the PC and IF/ID registers plus the multiplexor that chooses between the real control values and all 0s. The hazard detection unit stalls and deasserts the control fields if the load-use hazard test above is true.

Figures 6.47 to 6.49 show the single-cycle diagram for clocks 2 to 7 for the same example as before, but this time a load replacing the subtract instruction.

The Big Picture

Although the hardware may or may not rely on the compiler to resolve hazard dependencies to ensure correct execution, the compiler must understand the pipeline to achieve the best performance. Otherwise, unexpected stalls will reduce the performance of the compiled code.

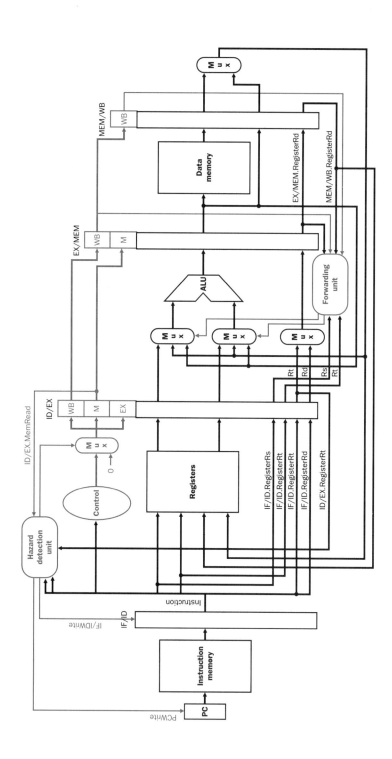

FIGURE 6.46 Pipelined control overview, showing the two multiplexors for forwarding, the hazard detection unit, and the forwarding unit. Although the ID and EX stages have been simplified—the sign-extended immediate and branch logic are missing—this drawing gives the essence of the forwarding hardware requirements.

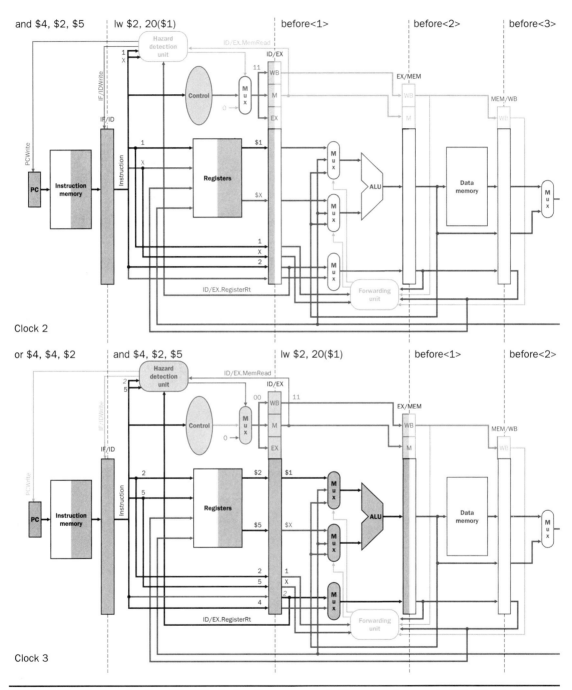

FIGURE 6.47 Clock cycles 2 and 3 of the instruction sequence in the example on page 485 with a load replacing sub. The bold lines are those active in a clock cycle, the italicized register numbers in color indicate a hazard, and the ... in the place of operands means that their identity is information not needed by that stage. The values of the significant control lines, registers, and register numbers are labeled in the figures. The and instruction wants to read the value created by the lw instruction in clock cycle 3, so the hazard detection unit stalls the and and or instructions. Hence the hazard detection unit is highlighted. *(page 493)*

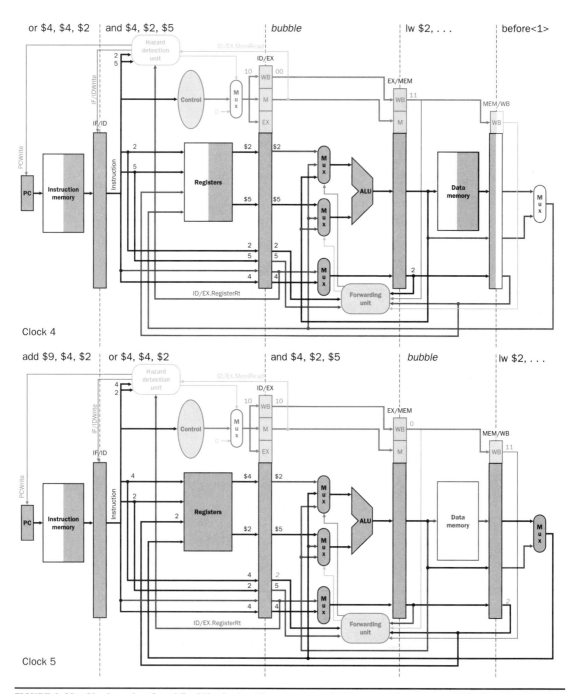

FIGURE 6.48   Clock cycles 4 and 5 of the instruction sequence in the example on page 485 with a load replacing sub**.** The bubble is inserted in the pipeline in clock cycle 4, and then the and instruction is allowed to proceed in clock cycle 5. The forwarding unit is highlighted in clock cycle 5 because it is forwarding data from lw to the ALU. Note that in clock cycle 4 the forwarding unit forwards the address of the lw as if it were the contents of register $2; this is rendered harmless by the insertion of the bubble. The bold lines are those active in a clock cycle, and the italicized register numbers in color indicate a hazard.

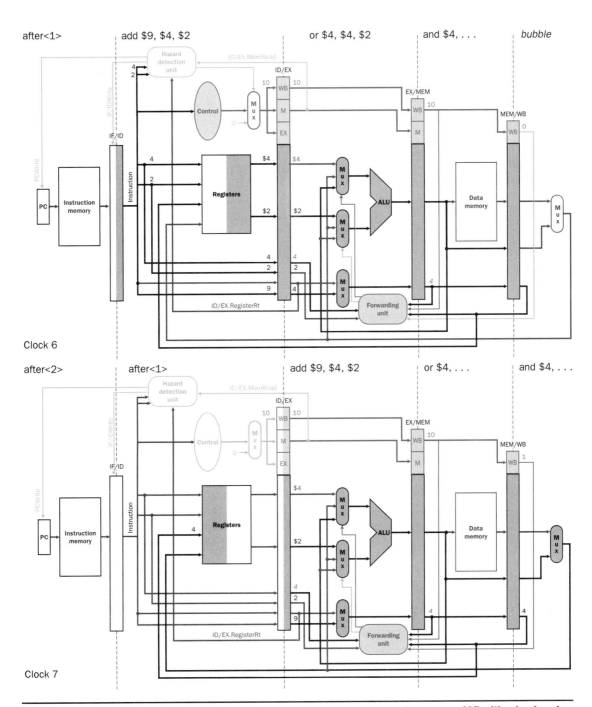

FIGURE 6.49 Clock cycles 6 and 7 of the instruction sequence in the example on page 485 with a load replacing sub**.** Note that unlike in Figure 6.42, the stall allows the lw to complete, and so there is no forwarding from MEM/WB in clock cycle 6. Register $4 for the add in the EX stage still depends on the result from or in EX/MEM so the forwarding unit passes the result to the ALU. The bold lines show ALU input lines active in a clock cycle, and the italicized register numbers indicate a hazard. The instructions after add are shown as inactive for pedagogical reasons.

Elaboration: Regarding the remark earlier about setting control lines to 0 to avoid writing registers or memory: only the signals RegWrite and MemWrite need be 0, while the other control signals can be don't cares.

6.6   Branch Hazards

There are a thousand hacking at the branches of evil to one who is striking at the root.

Henry David Thoreau, *Walden*, 1854

Thus far we have limited our concern to hazards involving arithmetic operations and data transfers. But as we saw in section 6.1, there are also pipeline hazards involving branches. Figure 6.50 shows a sequence of instructions and indicates when the branch would occur in this pipeline. An instruction must be fetched at every clock cycle to sustain the pipeline, yet in our design the decision about whether to branch doesn't occur until the MEM pipeline stage. As mentioned in section 6.1, this delay in determining the proper instruction to fetch is called a *control hazard* or *branch hazard*, in contrast to the *data hazards* we have just examined.

This section on control hazards is shorter than the previous sections on data hazards. The reasons are that control hazards are relatively simple to understand, they occur much less frequently than data hazards, and there is nothing as effective against control hazards as forwarding is for data hazards. Hence we use simpler schemes. We look at two schemes for resolving control hazards and one optimization to improve these schemes.

Assume Branch Not Taken

As we saw in section 6.1, stalling until the branch is complete is too slow. A common improvement over branch stalling is to assume that the branch will not be taken and thus continue execution down the sequential instruction stream. If the branch is taken, the instructions that are being fetched and decoded must be discarded. Execution continues at the branch target. If branches are untaken half the time, and if it costs little to discard the instructions, this optimization halves the cost of control hazards.

To discard instructions, we merely change the original control values to 0s, much as we did to stall for a load-use data hazard. The difference is that we must also change the three instructions in the IF, ID, and EX stages when the branch reaches the MEM stage; for load-use stalls, we just changed control to

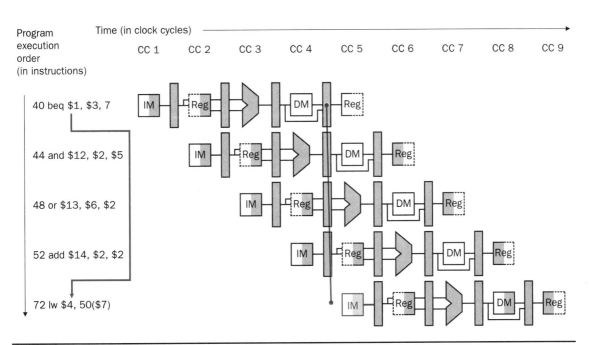

FIGURE 6.50 The impact of the pipeline on the branch instruction. The numbers to the left of the instruction (40, 44, . . .) are the addresses of the instructions. Since the branch instruction decides whether to branch in the MEM stage—clock cycle 4 for the `beq` instruction above—the three sequential instructions that follow the branch will be fetched and begin execution. Without intervention, those three following instructions will begin execution before `beq` branches to `lw` at location 72. (Figure 6.4 on page 442 assumed extra hardware to reduce the control hazard to 1 clock cycle; Figure 6.50 uses the non-optimized datapath.)

0 in the ID stage and let them percolate through the pipeline. Discarding instructions, then, means we must be able to flush instructions in the IF, ID, and EX stages of the pipeline.

Reducing the Delay of Branches

One way to improve branch performance is to reduce the cost of the taken branch. If we move the branch execution earlier in the pipeline, then fewer instructions need be flushed.

Thus far we have assumed the next PC for a branch is selected in the MEM stage. We could save 1 clock cycle of penalty by selecting the branch address at the end of the EX stage instead: if we move the branch decision even earlier in the pipeline, then only one instruction need be flushed. Many MIPS implementations move the branch execution to the ID stage.

The easy part of this change is to move up the branch address calculation. We already have the PC value and the immediate field in the IF/ID pipeline register, so we just move the branch adder from the MEM stage to the ID stage.

The harder part is the branch decision itself. For branch equal, we would compare the two registers read during the ID stage to see if they are equal. Equality can be tested by first exclusive-ORing their respective bits and then ANDing all the results. This approach is much faster than using the ALU to subtract and then test if the output is zero, since there are no carries for exclusive-OR. By moving the branch execution to the ID stage, there is only one instruction to flush if the branch is taken, the one currently being fetched.

To flush instructions in the IF stage, we add a control line, called IF.Flush, that zeros the instruction field of the IF/ID pipeline register. Clearing the register transforms the fetched instruction into a nop, an instruction that does no operation to change state (see the Elaboration on 485). Figure 6.51 shows the revised datapath.

Pipelined Branch

Example

Show what happens when the branch is taken in this instruction sequence, assuming the pipeline is optimized for branches that are not taken and that we moved the branch execution to the ID stage:

```
36    sub $10, $4, $8
40    beq  $1, $3,  7 # PC-relative branch to 40 + 4 + 7*4 = 72
44    and $12, $2, $5
48    or  $13, $2, $6
52    add $14, $4, $2
56    slt $15, $6, $7
. . .
72    lw  $4, 50($7)
```

Answer

Figure 6.52 shows what happens when a branch is taken. Unlike Figure 6.50, there is only one pipeline bubble on a taken branch.

Dynamic Branch Prediction

Assuming a branch is not taken is one crude form of *branch prediction*. In that case, we predict that branches are untaken, flushing the pipeline when we are wrong. As we mentioned in section 6.1, with more hardware it is possible to try other schemes of branch prediction.

One approach is to look up the address of the instruction to see if a branch was taken the last time this instruction was executed, and, if so, to begin fetching new instructions from the same place as the last time.

One implementation of that approach is a *branch prediction buffer* or *branch history table*. A branch prediction buffer is a small memory indexed by the

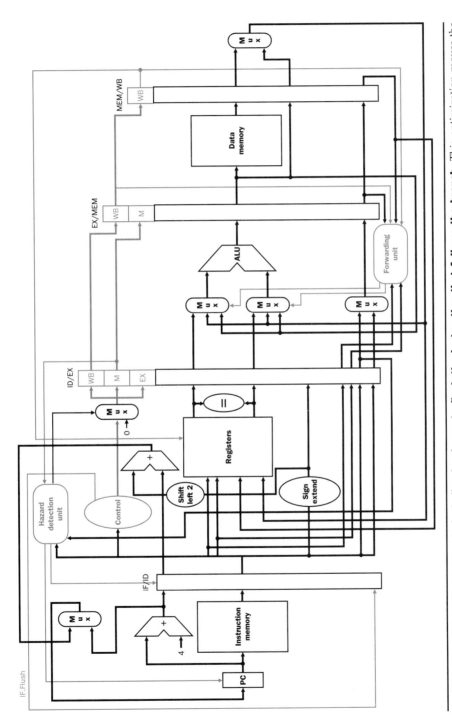

FIGURE 6.51 Datapath for branch, including hardware to flush the instruction that follows the branch. This optimization moves the branch decision from the fourth pipeline stage to the second; only one instruction that follows the branch will be in the pipe at that time. The control lines IF.Flush turns the fetched instruction into a `nop` by zeroing the IF/ID pipeline register. Although the flush line is shown coming from the control unit in this figure, in reality it comes from hardware that determines if a branch is taken, labeled with an equal sign to the right of the registers in the ID stage.

(page 499)

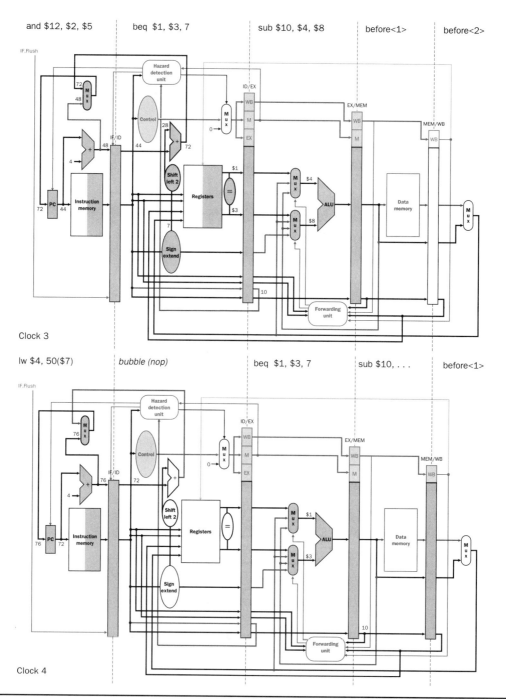

FIGURE 6.52   The ID stage of clock cycle 3 determines that a branch must be taken, so it selects 72 as the next PC address and zeros the instruction fetched for the next clock cycle. Clock cycle 4 shows the instruction at location 72 being fetched and the single bubble or nop instruction in the pipeline as a result of the taken branch. (Since the nop is really or $0, $0, 0, it's arguable whether or not the ID stage in clock 4 should be highlighted.)

lower portion of the address of the branch instruction. The memory contains a bit that says whether the branch was recently taken or not.

This is the simplest sort of buffer; we don't know, in fact, if the prediction is the right one—it may have been put there by another branch that has the same low-order address bits. But this doesn't affect correctness. Prediction is just a hint that is assumed to be correct, so fetching begins in the predicted direction. If the hint turns out to be wrong, the prediction bit is inverted and stored back, and the proper sequence is executed.

This simple 1-bit prediction scheme has a performance shortcoming: even if a branch is almost always taken, we will likely predict incorrectly twice, rather than once, when it is not taken. The following example shows this dilemma.

Loops and Prediction

Example

Consider a loop branch that branches nine times in a row, then is not taken once. What is the prediction accuracy for this branch, assuming the prediction bit for this branch remains in the prediction buffer?

Answer

The steady-state prediction behavior will mispredict on the first and last loop iterations. Mispredicting the last iteration is inevitable since the prediction bit will say taken: the branch has been taken nine times in a row at that point. The misprediction on the first iteration happens because the bit is flipped on prior execution of the last iteration of the loop, since the branch was not taken on that exiting iteration. Thus, the prediction accuracy for this branch that is taken 90% of the time is only 80% (two incorrect predictions and eight correct ones).

Ideally, the accuracy of the predictor would match the taken branch frequency for these highly regular branches. To remedy this weakness, 2-bit prediction schemes are often used. In a 2-bit scheme, a prediction must be wrong twice before it is changed. Figure 6.53 shows the finite state machine for a 2-bit prediction scheme.

A branch prediction buffer can be implemented as a small, special buffer accessed with the instruction address during the IF pipe stage. If the instruction is predicted as taken, fetching begins from the target as soon as the PC is known; as mentioned on page 497, it can be as early as the ID stage. Otherwise, sequential fetching and executing continue. If the prediction turns out to be wrong, the prediction bits are changed as shown in Figure 6.53.

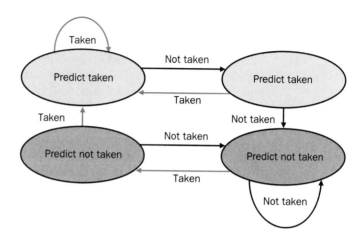

FIGURE 6.53 The states in a 2-bit prediction scheme. By using 2 bits rather than 1, a branch that strongly favors taken or not taken—as many branches do—will be mispredicted only once. The 2 bits are used to encode the four states in the system.

Elaboration: As we described in section 6.1, in a five-stage pipeline we can make the control hazard a feature by redefining the branch. A delayed branch always executes the following instruction, but the second instruction following the branch will be affected by the branch.

Compilers and assemblers try to place an instruction that always executes after the branch in the *branch delay slot.* The job of the software is to make the successor instructions valid and useful. Figure 6.54 shows the three ways in which the branch delay slot can be scheduled.

The limitations on delayed-branch scheduling arise from (1) the restrictions on the instructions that are scheduled into the delay slots and (2) our ability to predict at compile time whether a branch is likely to be taken or not.

Delayed branching is losing popularity. As machines go both to longer pipelines and toward issuing multiple instructions per clock cycle (see section 6.8), a single delay slot does not offer much help. Moreover, dynamic predictors increase in popularity as the transistors per chip increase.

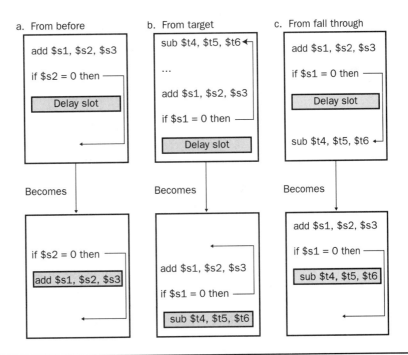

FIGURE 6.54   Scheduling the branch delay slot. The top box in each pair shows the code before scheduling; the bottom box shows the scheduled code. In (a), the delay slot is scheduled with an independent instruction from before the branch. This is the best choice. Strategies (b) and (c) are used when (a) is not possible. In the code sequences for (b) and (c), the use of $s1 in the branch condition prevents the add instruction (whose destination is $s1) from being moved into the branch delay slot. In (b) the branch-delay slot is scheduled from the target of the branch; usually the target instruction will need to be copied because it can be reached by another path. Strategy (b) is preferred when the branch is taken with high probability, such as a loop branch. Finally, the branch may be scheduled from the not-taken fall-through as in (c). To make this optimization legal for (b) or (c), it must be OK to execute the sub instruction when the branch goes in the unexpected direction. By "OK" we mean that the work is wasted, but the program will still execute correctly. This is the case, for example, if $t4 were an unused temporary register when the branch goes in the unexpected direction.

Pipeline Summary

Thus far we have seen three models of execution: single cycle, multicycle, and pipelined. Pipelined control strives for 1 clock cycle per instruction, like single cycle, but also for a fast clock cycle, like multicycle. Let's revisit the example from page 375.

Comparing Performance of Several Control Schemes

Example

Compare performance for single-cycle, multicycle, and pipelined control using the instruction mix for gcc from Figure 4.54. The operation times for the major functional units in this example are 2 ns for memory access, 2 ns for ALU operation, and 1 ns for register file read or write. For pipelined execution, assume that half of the load instructions are immediately followed by an instruction that uses the result, that the branch delay on misprediction is 1 clock cycle, and that one-quarter of the branches are mispredicted. Assume that jumps always pay 1 full clock cycle of delay, so their average time is 2 clock cycles.

Answer

The instruction mix for gcc is 22% loads, 11% stores, 49% R-format operations, 16% branches, and 2% jumps (see Answer on page 376). For the pipelined design, loads take 1 clock cycle when there is no load-use dependency and 2 when there is. Hence the average clock cycles per load instruction is 1.5. Stores take 1 clock cycle, as do the R-format instructions. Branches take 1 when predicted correctly and 2 when not, so the average clock cycles per branch instruction is 1.25. The jump CPI is 2. Hence the average CPI is

$$1.5 \times 22\% + 1 \times 11\% + 1 \times 49\% + 1.25 \times 16\% + 2 \times 2\% = 1.17$$

We multiply 1.17 by the 2-ns clock cycle time of a pipelined machine to get the average instruction time in nanoseconds, yielding 2.34 ns. From before, we know that the average instruction time for the multicycle is 4.04 ns, and 8 ns for single cycle. Hence pipelined control is 1.7 times faster than multicycle and 3.4 times faster than single-cycle control.

6.7 Exceptions

To make a computer with automatic program-interruption facilities behave [sequentially] was not an easy matter, because the number of instructions in various stages of processing when an interrupt signal occurs may be large.

Fred Brooks Jr., *Planning a Computer System: Project Stretch*, 1962

Another form of control hazard involves exceptions. For example, suppose the following instruction

```
add  $1,$2,$1
```

has an arithmetic overflow. We need to transfer control to the exception routine at location $4000\ 0040_{hex}$ (see Chapter 5, page 385) immediately after this instruction because we wouldn't want this invalid value to contaminate other registers or memory locations.

Just as we did for the taken branch in the previous section, we must flush the instructions that follow the add instruction from the pipeline and begin fetching instructions from the new address. We will use the same mechanism we used for taken branches, but this time the exception causes the deasserting of control lines.

We already saw how to flush the instruction in the IF stage by turning it into a nop. To flush instructions in the ID stage, we use the multiplexor already in the ID stage that zeros control signals for stalls. A new control signal, called ID.Flush, is ORed with the stall signal from the Hazard Detection Unit to flush during ID. To flush the instruction in the EX phase, we use a new signal called EX.Flush to cause new multiplexors to zero the control lines. To start fetching instructions from location $4000\ 0040_{hex}$, we simply add an additional input to the PC multiplexor that sends $4000\ 0040_{hex}$ to the PC. Figure 6.55 shows these changes.

This example points out a problem with exceptions: If we do not stop execution in the middle of the instruction, the programmer will not be able to see the original value of register $1 that helped cause the overflow because it will be clobbered as the destination register of the add instruction. Because of careful planning, the overflow exception is detected during the EX stage; hence we can use the EX.Flush signal to prevent the instruction in the EX stage from writing its result in the WB stage.

The final step is to save the address of the offending instruction in the Exception Program Counter (EPC), as we did in Chapter 5. In reality, we save the address + 4, so the exception handling routine must first subtract 4 from the saved value. Figure 6.55 shows a stylized version of the datapath, including the branch hardware and necessary accommodations to handle exceptions.

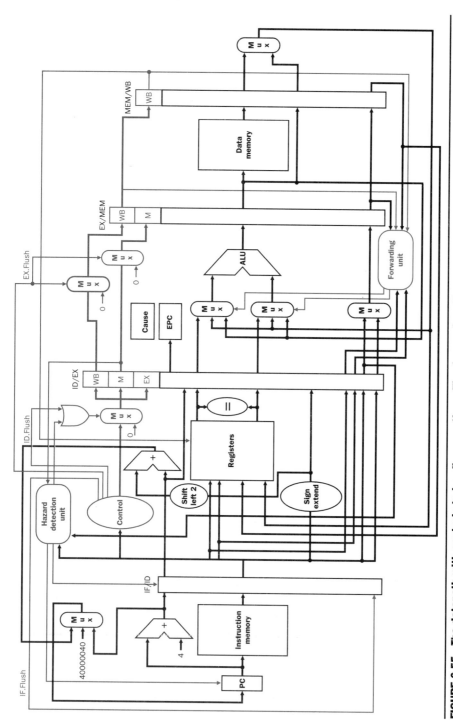

FIGURE 6.55 The datapath with controls to handle exceptions. The changes from Figure 6.51 include a new input, with the value 4000 0040$_{hex}$ in the multiplexor that supplies the new PC value; a Cause register to record the cause of the exception; and an Exception PC register to save the address of the instruction that caused the exception. The 4000 0040$_{hex}$ input to the multiplexor is the initial address to begin fetching instructions in the event of an exception. Although not shown, the ALU overflow signal is an input to the control unit.

Exception in a Pipelined Computer

Example

Given this instruction sequence,

```
40hex   sub    $11, $2, $4
44hex   and    $12, $2, $5
48hex   or     $13, $2, $6
4Chex   add     $1, $2, $1
50hex   slt    $15, $6, $7
54hex   lw     $16, 50($7)
. . .
```

assume the instructions to be invoked on an exception begin like this:

```
40000040hex   sw    $25, 1000($0)
40000044hex   sw    $26, 1004($0)
. . .
```

Show what happens in the pipeline if an overflow exception occurs in the add instruction.

Answer

Figure 6.56 shows the events, starting with the add instruction in the EX stage. The overflow is detected during that phase, and 4000 0040$_{hex}$ is forced into the PC. Clock cycle 6 shows that the add and following instructions are flushed, and the first instruction of the exception code is fetched. Note that the address of the instruction *following* the add is saved: 4C$_{hex}$ + 4 = 50$_{hex}$.

Chapter 5 lists some other causes of exceptions:

- I/O device request
- Invoking an operating system service from a user program
- Using an undefined instruction
- Hardware malfunction

With five instructions active in any clock cycle, the challenge is to associate an exception with the appropriate instruction. Moreover, multiple exceptions can occur simultaneously in a single clock cycle. The normal solution is to prioritize the exceptions so that it is easy to determine which is serviced first; this strategy works for pipelined machines as well. In most MIPS implementations, the hardware sorts exceptions so that the earliest instruction is interrupted.

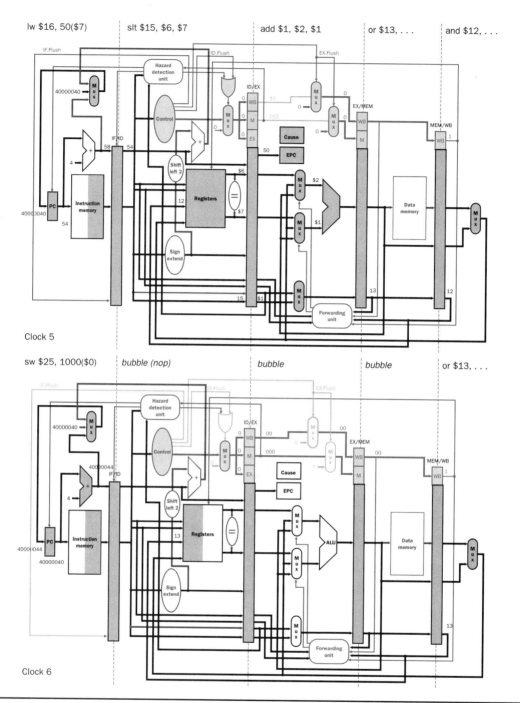

FIGURE 6.56 The result of an exception due to arithmetic overflow in the add instruction. The overflow is detected during the EX stage of clock 5, saving the address following the add in the EPC register ($4C + 4 = 50_{hex}$). Overflow causes all the Flush signals to be set near the end of this clock cycle, deasserting control values (setting them to 0) for the add. Clock cycle 6 shows the instructions converted to bubbles in the pipeline plus the fetching of the first instruction of the exception routine—sw $25,1000($0)—from instruction location $4000\ 0040_{hex}$. Note that the and and or instructions, which are prior to the add, still complete. Although not shown, the ALU overflow signal is an input to the control unit.

(*page 508*)

I/O device requests and hardware malfunctions are not associated with a specific instruction, so the implementation has some flexibility as to when to interrupt the pipeline. The hardware should pick the simplest instruction to associate with the I/O exception, but because the hardware is unstable when a malfunction happens, it may be wise to stop as soon as possible.

The EPC captures the address of the interrupted instructions, and the MIPS Cause register records all possible exceptions in a clock cycle, so the exception software must match the exception to the instruction. An important clue is knowing in which pipeline stage a type of exception can occur. For example, an undefined instruction is discovered in the ID stage, and invoking the operating system occurs in the EX stage. Exceptions are collected in the Cause register so that the hardware can interrupt based on later exceptions, once the earliest one has been serviced.

Hardware Software Interface The machine and the operating system must work in conjunction so that exceptions behave as you would expect. The hardware contract is normally to stop the offending instruction in midstream, let all prior instructions complete, flush all following instructions, set a register to show the cause of the exception, save the address of the offending instruction, and then jump to a prearranged address. The operating system contract is to look at the cause of the exception and act appropriately. For an undefined instruction, hardware malfunction, or arithmetic overflow exception, the operating system normally kills the program and returns an indicator of the reason. For an I/O device request or an operating system service call, the operating system saves the state of the program, performs the desired task, and then restores the program to continue execution.

The difficulty of always associating the correct exception with the correct instruction in pipelined computers has led some computer designers to relax this requirement in noncritical cases. Such machines are said to have *imprecise interrupts* or *imprecise exceptions*. In the example above, PC would normally have 58_{hex} at the start of the clock cycle after the exception is detected, even though the offending instruction is at address $4C_{hex}$. A machine with imprecise exceptions might put 58_{hex} into EPC and leave it up to the operating system to determine which instruction caused the problem. MIPS and the vast majority of machines today support *precise interrupts* or *precise exceptions*. (One reason is to support virtual memory, which we shall see in Chapter 7.)

6.8   Superscalar and Dynamic Pipelining

Be forewarned that sections 6.8 and 6.9 are brief overviews of fascinating but advanced topics. If you want to learn more details, you should consult our more advanced book, *Computer Architecture: A Quantitative Approach,* second edition.

In the interest of even faster processors, there have been three major directions in which the simple pipelines of this chapter have been extended. The first is sometimes called *superpipelining,* but it simply means longer pipelines. Since the ideal maximum speedup from pipelining is related to the number of pipeline stages, some recent microprocessors have gone to pipelines with eight or more stages.

Using our laundry analogy, we could divide our washer into three machines that perform the wash, rinse, and spin steps of a traditional machine. We would then move from a four-stage to a six-stage pipeline. To get the full speedup, we need to rebalance the remaining steps so they are the same length, in processors or in laundry.

The second trend is to replicate the internal components of the computer so that it can launch multiple instructions in every pipeline stage. The buzzword *superscalar* is applied to this technique. A superscalar laundry would replace our household washer and dryer with, say, three washers and three dryers. You would also have to recruit more assistants to fold and put away three times as much laundry in the same amount of time. The downside is the extra work to keep all the machines busy and transferring the loads to the next pipeline stage.

Launching multiple instructions per stage allows the instruction execution rate to exceed the clock rate or, stated alternatively, for the CPI to be less than 1. (Some wags have even flipped the metric, calling it *IPC,* or *instructions per clock cycle!*) Hence a 1000-MHz four-way superscalar microprocessor can execute a peak rate of four billion instructions per second, and have a best case CPI of 0.25. Today's superscalar machines try to find two to six instructions to execute in every pipeline stage. If the instructions in the instruction stream are dependent or don't meet certain criteria, however, only the first few instructions in the sequence are issued, or perhaps even just the first instruction.

The third trend is *dynamic pipeline scheduling* or *dynamic pipelining* by the hardware to avoid pipeline hazards. So far, our pipeline stalls when waiting for a hazard to be resolved, even if the later instructions are ready to go. For example, in the code sequence

```
lw     $t0, 20($s2)
addu   $t1, $t0, $t2
sub    $s4, $s4, $t3
slti   $t5, $s4, 20
```

even though the sub and slti instructions are ready to execute, they must wait for the lw and addu to complete first, which might take many clock cycles if memory is slow. (Chapter 7 explains caches, the reason that memory accesses are sometimes very slow.) Dynamic pipelining is normally combined with extra hardware resources so later instructions can proceed in parallel.

The cost is much more complicated pipeline control, and a more complicated instruction execution model than the simple linear timeline in Figure 6.1.

Superscalar MIPS

What would a MIPS machine look like as a superscalar implementation? Let's assume that two instructions are issued per clock cycle. One of the instructions could be an integer ALU operation or branch, and the other could be a load or store.

Issuing two instructions per cycle will require fetching and decoding 64 bits of instructions. To keep the decoding simple, we could require that the instructions be paired and aligned on a 64-bit boundary, with the ALU or branch portion appearing first. The alternative is to examine the instructions and possibly swap them before they are sent to the ALU or memory unit; however, this introduces additional requirements for hazard detection. In either case, the second instruction can be issued only if the first instruction can be issued. Figure 6.57 shows how the instructions look as they go into the pipeline in pairs. Remember that the hardware makes this decision dynamically, issuing only the first instruction if the conditions are not met.

To issue an ALU and a data transfer operation in parallel, the first need for additional hardware—beyond the usual hazard detection logic—is extra ports in the register file (see Figure 6.58). In 1 clock cycle we may need to read two

Instruction type	Pipe stages							
ALU or branch instruction	IF	ID	EX	MEM	WB			
Load or store instruction	IF	ID	EX	MEM	WB			
ALU or branch instruction		IF	ID	EX	MEM	WB		
Load or store instruction		IF	ID	EX	MEM	WB		
ALU or branch instruction			IF	ID	EX	MEM	WB	
Load or store instruction			IF	ID	EX	MEM	WB	
ALU or branch instruction				IF	ID	EX	MEM	WB
Load or store instruction				IF	ID	EX	MEM	WB

FIGURE 6.57 Superscalar pipeline in operation. The ALU and data transfer instructions are issued at the same time.

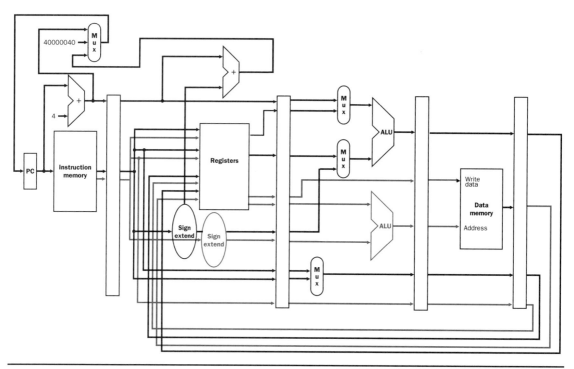

FIGURE 6.58 A superscalar datapath. The superscalar additions are highlighted: another 32 bits from instruction memory, two more read ports and one more write port on the register file, and another ALU. Assume the bottom ALU handles address calculations for data transfers and the top ALU handles everything else.

registers for the ALU operation and two more for a store, and also one write port for an ALU operation and one write port for a load. Since the ALU is tied up for the ALU operation, we also need a separate adder to calculate the effective address for data transfers. Without these extra resources, our superscalar pipeline would be hindered by structural hazards.

There is another difficulty that may limit the effectiveness of a superscalar pipeline. In our simple MIPS pipeline, loads have a latency of 1 clock cycle, which prevents one instruction from using the result without stalling. In the superscalar pipeline, the result of a load instruction cannot be used on the next *clock cycle*. This means that the next *two* instructions cannot use the load result without stalling. To effectively exploit the parallelism available in a superscalar processor, more ambitious compiler or hardware scheduling techniques are needed, as well as more complex instruction decoding.

Simple Superscalar Code Scheduling

Example

How would this loop be scheduled on a superscalar pipeline for MIPS?

```
Loop:   lw      $t0, 0($s1)     # $t0=array element
        addu    $t0,$t0,$s2     # add scalar in $s2
        sw      $t0, 0($s1)     # store result
        addi    $s1,$s1,-4      # decrement pointer
        bne     $s1,$zero,Loop  # branch $s1!=0
```

Reorder the instructions to avoid as many pipeline stalls as possible.

Answer

The first three instructions have data dependencies, and so do the last two. Figure 6.59 shows the best schedule for these instructions. Notice that just one pair of instructions executes in superscalar mode. It takes 4 clocks per loop iteration; at 4 clocks to execute 5 instructions, we get the disappointing CPI of 0.8 versus the best case of 0.5.

	ALU or branch instruction	Data transfer instruction	Clock cycle
Loop:		lw $t0, 0($s1)	1
	addi $s1,$s1,-4		2
	addu $t0,$t0,$s2		3
	bne $s1,$zero,Loop	sw $t0, 4($s1)	4

FIGURE 6.59 The scheduled code as it would look on a superscalar MIPS.

One technique to get more performance from loops that access arrays is *loop unrolling;* as the name suggests, multiple copies of the loop body are made, and instructions from different iterations are scheduled together.

Loop Unrolling for Superscalar Pipelines

Example

See how well loop unrolling and scheduling work in the example above. Assume that the loop index is a multiple of four.

Answer

To schedule the loop without any delays, it turns out that we need to make four copies of the loop body. After unrolling, the loop will contain four copies each of `lw`, `addu`, and `sw`, plus one `addi` and one `bne`. The unrolled and scheduled code is shown in Figure 6.60.

Notice now that 12 of the 14 instructions in the loop execute in superscalar mode. It takes 8 clocks for four loop iterations, or 2 clocks per iteration. Loop unrolling and scheduling with superscalar execution gave us a factor of two improvement, partly from reducing the loop control instructions and partly from superscalar execution. The cost of this performance improvement is using four temporary registers rather than one.

	ALU or branch instruction		Data transfer instruction		Clock cycle
Loop:	addi	$s1,$s1,-16	lw	$t0, 0($s1)	1
			lw	$t1,12($s1)	2
	addu	$t0,$t0,$s2	lw	$t2, 8($s1)	3
	addu	$t1,$t1,$s2	lw	$t3, 4($s1)	4
	addu	$t2,$t2,$s2	sw	$t0, 0($s1)	5
	addu	$t3,$t3,$s2	sw	$t1,12($s1)	6
			sw	$t2, 8($s1)	7
	bne	$s1,$zero,Loop	sw	$t3, 4($s1)	8

FIGURE 6.60   The unrolled and scheduled code of Figure 6.59 as it would look on a superscalar MIPS. Since the first pair decrements $s1 by 16, the addresses loaded are the original value of $s1, then that address minus 4, minus 8, and minus 12.

The Big Picture

Both pipelining and superscalar execution increase peak instruction throughput. Longer pipelines and wider superscalar issue put even more pressure on the compiler to deliver on the performance potential of the hardware. But data and control dependencies in programs, together with instruction latencies, offer an upper limit on delivered performance because the processor must sometimes wait for a dependency to be resolved, such as with mispredicted branch.

While striving for the highest performance, hardware designers must also ensure correct execution of all instruction sequences. Compiler writers may or may not be asked to participate by limiting the types of sequences generated, but they *must* understand the pipeline to achieve best performance, and then to generate the appropriate code.

Dynamic Pipeline Scheduling

Dynamic pipeline scheduling goes past stalls to find later instructions to execute while waiting for the stall to be resolved. Typically, the pipeline is divided into three major units: an instruction fetch and issue unit, execute units, and a commit unit. Figure 6.61 shows the model. The first unit fetches instructions, decodes them, and sends each instruction to a corresponding functional unit of the execute stage. There might be 5 to 10 functional units. Each functional unit has buffers, called *reservation stations*, that hold the operands and the operation. As soon as the buffer contains all its operands and the functional unit is ready to execute, the result is calculated. It is then up to the commit unit to decide when it is safe to put the result into the register file or (for a store) into memory.

The basic model is multiple independent state machines performing instruction execution: one unit fetching and decoding instructions, several functional units performing the operations, and one unit deciding when instructions are complete so that the results can be committed. To make programs behave as if they were running on a simple nonpipelined computer, the instruction fetch and decode unit is required to issue instructions in order, and the commit unit is required to write results to registers and memory in

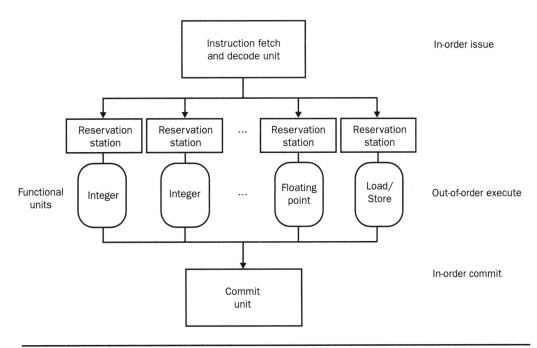

FIGURE 6.61 The three primary units of a dynamically scheduled pipeline.

program execution order. This conservative mode is called *in-order completion*. Hence, if an exception occurs, the computer can point to the last instruction executed, and the only registers updated will be all those written by instructions before the exceptional instruction. The functional units, however, are free to start and finish whenever they want. A more radical approach, which typically introduces imprecise interrupts, is to allow the commit to be out of order. This liberal mode is called *out-of-order completion*.

Dynamic pipelining is more complicated than the traditional or *static pipelining*, and getting the bugs out of such hardware is a challenge. Part of the difficulty is that dynamic scheduling is normally combined with branch prediction, so the commit unit must be able to discard all the results in the execution unit that were due to instructions executed after a mispredicted branch. Combining dynamic scheduling with branch prediction is called *speculative execution*. A second reason for complexity is that dynamic scheduling is also typically combined with superscalar execution, so each unit may be issuing or committing four to six instructions each clock cycle.

In summary, such dynamic machines are predicting program flow, looking at the instructions in multiple segments to see which to execute next, and then speculatively executing instructions based on the prediction and the instruction dependencies. The motivations for dynamic execution are threefold:

1. Hide memory latency, a major issue for computers described in Chapter 7.

2. Avoid stalls that the compiler could not schedule, often due to potential dependencies between store and load.

3. Speculatively execute instructions while waiting for hazards to be resolved.

A microprocessor that follows all three trends—deep pipelines, superscalar, and dynamic pipelining—is the DEC Alpha 21264. This superscalar machine fetches four instructions per clock cycle—but can issue up to six instructions—and uses out-of-order execution and in-order completion. The pipeline takes nine stages for simple integer and floating-point operations, yielding a clock rate of 600 MHz in 1997.

Putting this rate into perspective, the 1997 clock rate of the Cray T-90 supercomputer is just 455 MHz. Chapter 2 reminds us that clock rate is only one of three key performance parameters, but this is still an impressive achievement.

Elaboration: A commit unit controls updates to the register file *and* memory. Some dynamically scheduled machines update the register file immediately during execution. Other machines have a copy of the register file, and the actual update to the register file occurs later as part of the commit. For memory, there is normally a *store buffer*, also called a *write buffer* (see Chapter 7). The commit unit allows the store to write to memory from the buffer when the buffer has a valid address and valid data, and when the store is no longer dependent on predicted branches.

Elaboration: Memory accesses benefit from *nonblocking caches*, which continue servicing cache accesses during a cache miss (see Chapter 7). Out-of-order execution processors need nonblocking caches to allow instructions to execute during a miss.

6.9 Real Stuff: PowerPC 604 and Pentium Pro Pipelines

Dynamically scheduled pipelines are used in both the PowerPC 604 and the Pentium Pro. They have such similar pipeline organizations that we use a single generic drawing, Figure 6.62, to describe both. Figure 1.18 on page 27 shows the silicon area required by dynamic pipelining in the Pentium Pro.

The instruction cache fetches 16 bytes of instructions and sends them to an instruction queue: four instructions for the PowerPC and a variable number of instructions for the Pentium Pro. Next, several instructions are fetched and decoded. Both processors use a 512-entry branch history table to predict branches and speculatively execute instructions after the predicted branch. The dispatcher unit sends each instruction and its operands to the reservation station of one of the six functional units. The dispatcher also places an entry for the instruction in the reorder buffer of the commit unit. Thus an instruction cannot issue unless there is space available in both an appropriate reservation station and in the reorder buffer.

With so many instructions executing at the same time, we can run out of places to keep results. Both processors have extra internal registers, called *rename buffers* or *rename registers*, that are used to hold results while waiting for the commit unit to commit the result to one of the real registers. The decode unit is where rename buffers get assigned, thereby reducing hazards on register numbers. Whenever an entry in the reservation station has all its operands and the associated functional unit is available, the operation is performed.

The commit unit keeps track of all the pending instructions in its reorder buffer. Because both machines use branch prediction, an instruction isn't finished until the commit unit says it is. When the branch functional unit determines whether or not a branch was taken, it informs both the branch prediction unit, so that it can update its state machine, and the commit unit, so that it can decide the fate of pending instructions. If the prediction was accurate, the results of the instructions after the branch are marked valid and thus can be placed in the programmer-visible registers and memory. If a misprediction occurred, then all the instructions after the branch are marked invalid and discarded from the reservation stations and reorder buffer.

The commit unit can commit several instructions per clock cycle. To provide precise behavior during exceptions, the commit unit makes sure the instruc-

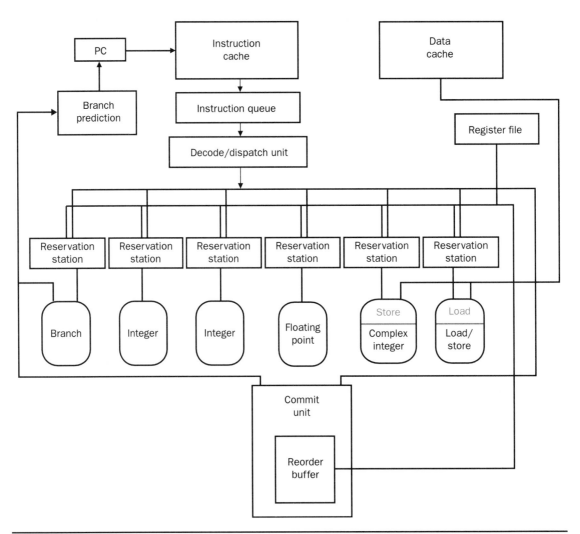

FIGURE 6.62   The generic pipeline organization of the Intel Pentium Pro and the PowerPC 604. Both have six functional units, and the first four have the same responsibilities. For the Pentium Pro, the last two functional units are Store and Load (in color), and the PowerPC 604 has Complex Integer and Load/Store functional units. The figure shows that every functional unit has its own path to a reservation station, but the Pentium Pro has a single central reservation station that can be used for any functional units with one bus shared by the branch and one of the integer units, one bus shared by the other integer unit and floating-point unit, and separate buses for the rest of the functional units. The names for the major units on the Pentium Pro are Fetch/Decode Unit, Dispatch/Execute Unit, and Retire Unit, and the functional units are called Jump Execution Unit (EU), Integer EU, Floating Point EU, Store Address Generation Unit (AGU), and Load AGU. The real names for the major units on the PowerPC are Instruction Unit, Functional Units, and Completion Unit, and the functional units are called Branch Processing Unit, Single-Cycle Integer Unit, Floating Point Unit, Multi-Cycle Integer Unit, and Load/Store Unit.

tions commit in the order they were issued. Thus the commit unit cannot commit an instruction until the operation is finished in the functional unit, all branches on which it might depend are resolved, and all instructions issued before it have committed.

Figure 6.63 lists the specific parameters for the PowerPC 604 and Pentium Pro pipelines. Many of the differences between the Pentium Pro and the PowerPC 604 are cosmetic. The largest difference, not surprisingly, is in decode and dispatch. As described in section 5.7, rather than try to pipeline variable-length 80x86 instructions, the Pentium Pro decode unit translates the Intel instructions into 72-bit, fixed-length microoperations, and then sends these microoperations to the reorder buffer and reservation stations. This translation takes 1 clock cycle to determine the length of the 80x86 instructions and then 2 more to create the microoperations.

As discussed in Chapter 5, these microoperations have two source registers and one destination register, and are similar to MIPS instructions. Most 80x86 instructions are translated into one to four microoperations, but the really complex 80x86 instructions are executed by a conventional microprogram that issues long sequences of microoperations.

Parameter name	PowerPC 604	Pentium Pro
Maximum number of instructions issued per clock cycle	4	3
Maximum number of instructions completing execution per clock cycle	6	5
Maximum number of instructions committed per clock cycle	6	3
Number of bytes fetched from instruction cache	16	16
Number of bytes in instruction queue	32	32
Number of instructions in reorder buffer	16	40
Number of entries in branch table buffer	512	512
Number of history bits per entry in branch history buffer	2	4
Number of rename buffers	12 integer + 8 FP	40
Total number of reservation stations	12	20
Total number of functional units	6	6
Number of integer functional units	2	2
Number of complex integer operation functional units	1	0
Number of floating-point functional units	1	1
Number of branch functional units	1	1
Number of memory functional units	1 for both load and store	1 for load + 1 for store

FIGURE 6.63 Specific parameters of the PowerPC 604 and Pentium Pro in Figure 6.62.

6.10   Fallacies and Pitfalls

Fallacy: Pipelining is easy.

Our books testify to the subtlety of correct pipeline execution. Our advanced book had a pipeline bug in its first edition, despite its being reviewed by more than 100 people and being class-tested at 18 universities. The bug was uncovered only when someone tried to build the computer in that book. Similarly, the alpha version of the first edition of this book had a bug involving forwarding and store instructions, and this bug escaped the scrutiny of many reviewers and students. Beware!

Fallacy: Pipelining ideas can be implemented independent of technology.

When the number of transistors on-chip and speed of transistors made a five-stage pipeline the best solution, then the delayed branch (see elaborations on pages 444 and 502) was a simple solution to control hazards. With longer pipelines, superscalar execution, and dynamic branch prediction, it is now redundant. In the early 1990s, dynamic pipeline scheduling took too many resources and was not required for high performance, but as transistor budgets continued to double and logic became much faster than memory, then multiple functional units and dynamic pipelining made more sense.

Pitfall: Failure to consider instruction set design can adversely impact pipelining.

Many of the difficulties of pipelining arise because of instruction set complications. Here are some examples:

- Widely variable instruction lengths and running times can lead to imbalance among pipeline stages, causing other stages to back up. They can also severely complicate hazard detection and the maintenance of precise exceptions.

- Sophisticated addressing modes can lead to different sorts of problems. Addressing modes that update registers, such as update addressing (see page 175 in Chapter 3), complicate hazard detection. Other addressing modes that require multiple memory accesses substantially complicate pipeline control and make it difficult to keep the pipeline flowing smoothly.

Perhaps the best example is the DEC Alpha and the DEC NVAX. In comparable technology, the new instruction set architecture of the Alpha allowed an implementation whose performance is more than twice as fast as NVAX. In another example, Bhandarkar and Clark [1991] compared the MIPS M/2000 and the VAX 8700 by counting clock cycles of the SPEC benchmarks; they

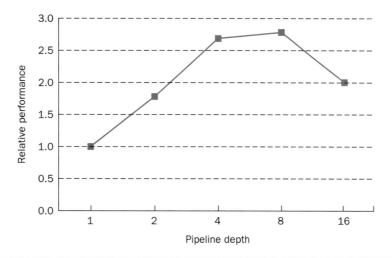

FIGURE 6.64 The depth of pipelining versus the speedup obtained. The *x* axis shows the number of stages in the EX portion of the floating-point pipeline. A single-stage pipeline corresponds to 32 levels of logic, which might be appropriate for a single FP operation. This data is based on Table 2 in S. R. Kunkel and J. E. Smith, "Optimal pipelining in supercomputers," *Proc. 13th Symposium on Computer Architecture* (June 1986), pages 404–414.

concluded that, although the MIPS M/2000 executes more instructions, the VAX on average executes 2.7 times as many clock cycles, so the MIPS is faster.

Fallacy: Increasing the depth of pipelining always increases performance.

Three factors combine to limit the performance improvement gained by pipelining. First, data hazards in the code mean that increasing the pipeline depth increases the time per instruction because a larger percentage of the cycles become stalls. Second, control hazards mean that increasing pipeline depth results in slower branches, thereby increasing the clock cycles for the program. Finally, pipeline register overhead can limit the decrease in clock period obtained by further pipelining. Figure 6.64 shows the trade-off between pipeline depth and performance for a floating-point pipeline.

6.11 Concluding Remarks

Nine-tenths of wisdom consists of being wise in time.

American proverb

This chapter started in the laundry room, showing principles of pipelining in an everyday setting. Using that analogy as a guide, we explain instruction pipelining step by step, starting with the single-cycle datapath and then adding pipeline registers, forwarding paths, data hazard detection, branch prediction, and flushing instructions on exceptions. Figure 6.65 shows the final evolved datapath and control.

Pipelining improves the average execution time per instruction. Depending on whether you start with a single-cycle or multiple-cycle datapath, this reduction can be thought of as decreasing the clock cycle time or as decreasing the number of clock cycles per instruction (CPI). We started with the simple single-cycle datapath, so pipelining was presented as reducing the clock cycle time of the simple datapath. Figure 6.66 shows the effect on CPI and clock rate for each of the datapaths from Chapters 5 and 6, with pipelining offering both a low CPI and a fast clock rate.

Pipelining improves throughput, but not the inherent execution time, or *latency*, of instructions; the latency is similar in length to the multi-cycle approach. Unlike that approach, which uses the same hardware repeatedly during instruction execution, pipelining starts an instruction every clock cycle by having dedicated hardware. Figure 6.67 shows the datapaths from Figure 6.66 placed according to the amount of sharing of hardware and instruction latency.

Latency introduces difficulties due to dependencies in programs because a dependency means the machine must wait the full instruction latency for the hazard to be resolved. The cost of data dependencies can be reduced through the use of forwarding hardware, and the frequency of control dependencies can be reduced through both branch prediction hardware and compiler scheduling.

The switch to longer pipelines, superscalar instruction issue, and dynamic scheduling has recently sustained the 60% per year processor performance increase that we have benefited from since 1986. In the past, it appeared that the choice was between the highest clock rate processors and the most sophisticated superscalar processors. The Alpha 21264—which issues six instructions per clock cycle, does out-of-order execution, and in 1997 has a 600-MHz clock rate—proved that it is possible to do both. Not surprisingly, this 15-million-transistor chip also has the best SPEC95 performance.

With remarkable advances in processing, Amdahl's law suggests that another part of the system will become the bottleneck. That bottleneck is the topic of the next chapter: the memory system.

An alternative to pushing uniprocessors to automatically exploit parallelism at the instruction level is trying multiprocessors, which exploit parallelism at much coarser levels. Parallel processing is the topic of Chapter 9.

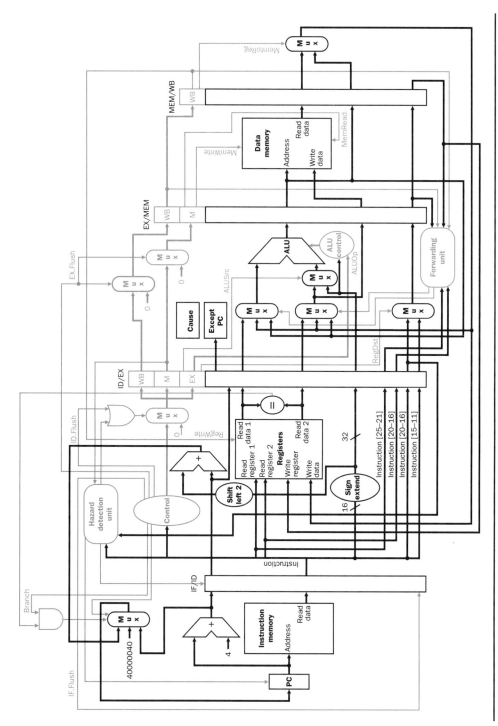

FIGURE 6.65   The final datapath and control for this chapter.

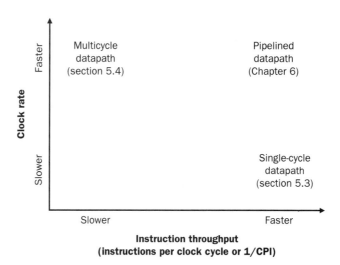

FIGURE 6.66 The performance consequences of simple (single-cycle) datapath and multicycle datapath from Chapter 5 and the pipelined execution model in Chapter 6. Although the instructions per clock cycle (instruction throughput) is slightly larger in the simple datapath, the pipelined datapath is close and it uses a clock rate as fast as the multicycle datapath.

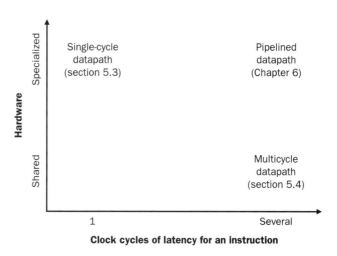

FIGURE 6.67 The basic relationship between the datapaths in Figure 6.66. The pipelined datapath is shown as multiple clock cycles for instruction latency because the execution time of an instruction is not shorter; it's the instruction throughput that is improved.

6.12 Historical Perspective and Further Reading

supercomputer: Any machine still on the drawing board.

Stan Kelly-Bootle, *The Devil's DP Dictionary*, 1981

This section describes some of the major advances in pipelining. It is generally agreed that one of the first general-purpose pipelined machines was Stretch, the IBM 7030 (Figure 6.68). Stretch followed the IBM 704 and had a goal of being 100 times faster than the 704. The goals were a "stretch" of the state of the art at that time—hence the nickname. The plan was to obtain a factor of 1.6 from overlapping fetch, decode, and execute, using a four-stage pipeline; apparently the rest was to come from much more hardware and faster logic. Stretch was also a training ground for both the architects of the IBM 360, Gerrit Blaauw and Fred Brooks Jr., and the architect of the IBM RS/6000, John Cocke.

FIGURE 6.68 The Stretch computer, one of the first pipelined computers. Photo courtesy of IBM.

Control Data Corporation (CDC) delivered what is considered to be the first supercomputer, the CDC 6600, in 1964 (Figure 6.69). The core instructions of Cray's subsequent computers have many similarities to those of the original CDC 6600. The CDC 6600 was unique in many ways. The interaction between pipelining and instruction set design was understood, and the instruction set was kept simple to promote pipelining. The CDC 6600 also used an advanced packaging technology. Thornton's book [1970] provides an excellent description of the entire machine, from technology to architecture, and includes a foreword by Seymour Cray. (Unfortunately, this book is currently out of print.) Both Cray and Thorton have won the ACM Eckert-Mauchly Award.

The IBM 360/91 introduced many new concepts, including dynamic detection of memory hazards, generalized forwarding, and reservation stations (Figure 6.70). The approach is normally named *Tomasulo's algorithm*, after an engineer who worked on the project. The team that created the 360/91 was led by Michael Flynn, who was given the 1992 ACM Eckert-Mauchly Award, in part for his contributions to the IBM 360/91, and in 1997 the same award went to Robert Tomasulo, for his pioneering work on out-of-order processing.

The internal organization of the 360/91 shares many features with the PowerPC 604 and the Pentium Pro. One major difference was that there was no branch prediction and hence no speculation. Another major difference was

FIGURE 6.69 The CDC 6600, the first supercomputer. Photo courtesy of Charles Babbage Institute, University of Minnesota.

FIGURE 6.70 The IBM 360/91 pushed the state of the art in pipelined execution when it was unveiled in 1966. Photo courtesy of IBM.

that there was no commit unit, so once the instructions finished execution, they updated the registers. Out-of-order instruction commit led to *imprecise interrupts*, which proved to be unpopular and led to the commit units in dynamically scheduled pipelined machines since that time.

The RISC machines refined the notion of compiler-scheduled pipelines in the early 1980s. The concepts of delayed branches and delayed loads—common in microprogramming—were extended into the high-level architecture. In fact, the Stanford machine that led to the commercial MIPS architecture was called Microprocessor without Interlocked Pipelined Stages because it was up to the assembler or compiler to avoid data hazards.

IBM did pioneering work on multiple issue. In the 1970s, a project called ACS was underway. It included multiple-instruction issue concepts, but never reached product stage. The earliest proposal for a superscalar processor that dynamically makes issue decisions was by John Cocke; he described the key ideas in several talks in the mid-1980s and coined the name *superscalar*. This original design was named America. The IBM Power-1 architecture, used in the RS/6000 line, is based on these ideas, and the PowerPC is a variation of the Power-1 architecture. Cocke won the Turing Award for his architecture work, the highest award in computer science and engineering.

An approach that predated superscalar that relies on similar compiler technology is called *long instruction word* (LIW) or sometimes *very long instruction word* (VLIW). In this approach, several instructions are issued during each clock cycle as in the superscalar case, but in LIW the compiler guarantees that there are no dependencies between instructions that issue at the same time and that there are sufficient hardware resources to execute them, thereby simplifying the instruction decoding and issuing logic. A very practical advantage of superscalar over LIW designs is that superscalar processors can run without changing binary machine programs that run on more traditional architectures; LIW works well when the source code for the programs is available so that the programs can be recompiled.

To Probe Further

Bhandarkar, D., and D. W. Clark [1991]. "Performance from architecture: Comparing a RISC and a CISC with similar hardware organizations," *Proc. Fourth Conf. on Architectural Support for Programming Languages and Operating Systems,* IEEE/ACM (April), Palo Alto, 310–19.

A quantitative comparison of RISC and CISC written by scholars who argued for CISCs as well as built them; they conclude that MIPS is between 2 and 4 times faster than a VAX built with similar technology, with a mean of 2.7.

Hennessy, J. L., and D. A. Patterson [1996]. *Computer Architecture: A Quantitative Approach,* Second Edition, Morgan Kaufmann, San Francisco.

Chapters 3 and 4 go into considerably more detail about pipelined machines, including dynamic hardware scheduling and superscalar machines.

Jouppi, N. P., and D. W. Wall [1989]. "Available instruction-level parallelism for superscalar and superpipelined machines," *Proc. Third Conf. on Architectural Support for Programming Languages and Operating Systems,* IEEE/ACM (April), Boston, 272–82.

A comparison of superpipelined and superscalar systems.

Kogge, P. M. [1981]. *The Architecture of Pipelined Computers,* McGraw-Hill, New York.

A formal text on pipelined control, with emphasis on underlying principles.

Russell, R. M. [1978]. "The CRAY-1 computer system," *Comm. of the ACM* 21:1 (January) 63–72.

A short summary of a classic computer, which uses vectors of operations to remove pipeline stalls.

Smith, A., and J. Lee [1984]. "Branch prediction strategies and branch target buffer design," *Computer* 17:1 (January) 6–22.

An early survey on branch prediction.

Smith, J. E., and A. R. Plezkun [1988]. "Implementing precise interrupts in pipelined processors," *IEEE Trans. on Computers* 37:5 (May) 562–73.

Covers the difficulties in interrupting pipelined computers.

Thornton, J. E. [1970]. *Design of a Computer: The Control Data 6600,* Scott, Foresman, Glenview, IL.

A classic book describing a classic machine, considered the first supercomputer.

6.13 Key Terms

These terms reflect the key ideas discussed in the chapter. Please refer to the Glossary at the back of the book for definitions of any terms you might be unsure of.

branch delay slot
branch or control hazard
branch prediction
branch prediction buffer or
    branch history table
commit unit
data dependencies
data hazard or pipeline data
    hazard
delayed load
dynamic pipeline scheduling
flush (instructions)

forwarding or bypassing
imprecise interrupt or
    exception
in-order commit
in-order execution
instruction latency
latency (pipeline)
load-use data hazard
loop unrolling
multiple-instruction issue
nop
out-of-order commit

out-of-order execution
pipeline stall
pipelining stage
precise interrupt or exception
rename buffer or register
reorder buffer
reservation station
speculative execution
structural hazard
superpipelining
superscalar pipelining

6.14 Exercises

6.1 [5] <§6.1> If the time for an ALU operation were actually 4 ns instead of 2 ns (as described in Figure 6.2 on page 439), how would this affect the speedup obtained from pipelining a single-cycle implementation?

6.2 [5] <§6.1> Using a drawing similar to Figure 6.8 on page 447, show the forwarding paths needed to execute the following three instructions:

```
add $2, $3, $4
add $4, $5, $6
add $5, $3, $4
```

6.3 [5] <§6.1> How could we modify the following code to make use of a delayed branch slot?

```
Loop:  lw   $2, 100($3)
       addi $3, $3, 4
       beq  $3, $4, Loop
```

6.4 [10] <§6.1> Identify all of the data dependencies in the following code. Which dependencies are data hazards that will be resolved via forwarding?

```
add $2, $5, $4
add $4, $2, $5
sw  $5, 100($2)
add $3, $2, $4
```

6.5 [5] <§6.2> For each pipeline register in Figure 6.25 on page 467, label each portion of the pipeline register with the name of the value that is loaded into the register. Determine the length of each field in bits. For example, the IF/ID pipeline register contains two fields, one of which is an instruction field that is 32 bits wide.

6.6 [15] <§§4.8, 6.2> Using Figure 4.42 on page 271 as your foundation, figure out a reasonable pipelined datapath structure for floating-point addition, and integrate the floating-point registers and the data memory into your picture to produce a figure similar to Figure 6.12 on page 452, except that your diagram should also contain an alternative pipeline for floating-point add instructions. Don't worry too much about the delays associated with each of the functions in Figure 4.42. You should simply assume that the sum of the delays is fairly large, and thus requires you to use 2 or 3 cycles to perform floating-point addition. The addition should be pipelined so that a new floating-point add instruction can be started every cycle, assuming that there are no dependencies (you can ignore dependencies for this problem).

6.7 [10] <§6.2> Using Figure 6.25 on page 467 as a guide, use colored pens or markers to show which portions of the datapath are active and which are inactive in each of the five stages of the add instruction. We suggest that you use five photocopies of Figure 6.25 to answer this exercise. (We hereby grant you permission to violate the Copyright Protection Act in doing the exercises in Chapters 5 and 6!) You could also download the figure from *www.mkp.com/cod2e.htm*. Be sure to include a legend to explain your color scheme.

6.8 [15] <§6.3> To be sure you understand the relationship between the two styles of drawing pipelines, draw the information in Figures 6.31 through 6.35 on pages 472 through 476 in the style of Figure 6.36 on page 477. Be sure to highlight the active portions of the datapaths in this simpler figure.

6.9 [20] <§6.3> Figure 6.71 is similar to Figure 6.33 on page 474, but the instructions are unidentified. Your task is to determine as much as you can about the five instructions in the five pipeline stages. If you cannot fill in a field of an instruction, state why. For some fields it will be easier to decode the machine instructions into assembly language, using Figure 3.18 on page 153 and Figure A.18 on page A-50 as references. For other fields it will be easier to look at the

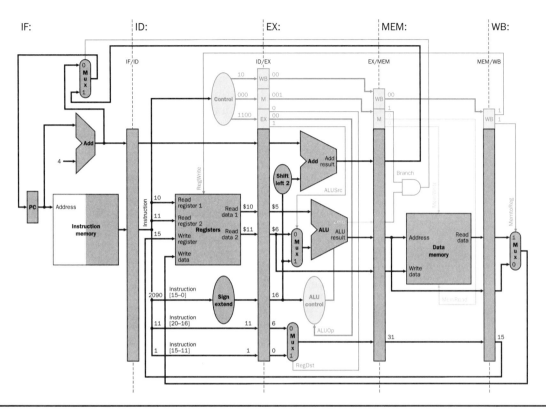

FIGURE 6.71 The pipelined datapath for Exercise 6.9. Use the numeric labels to determine as many fields of each of the five instructions in the pipeline as possible.

values of the control signals, using Figures 6.26 through 6.28 on pages 468 and 469 as references. You may need to carefully examine Figures 6.31 through 6.35 to understand how collections of control values are presented (i.e., the leftmost bit in one cycle will become the uppermost bit in another cycle). For example, the EX control value for the subtract instruction, 1100, computed during the ID stage of cycle 3 in Figure 6.32, becomes three separate values specifying RegDst (1), ALUOp (10), and ALUSrc (0) in cycle 4.

6.10 [40] <§6.3> Using Figure 6.33 on page 474, determine the value of *every* field in the four pipeline registers in clock cycle 5. (These are the values at the beginning of the clock cycle.) Assume that before the instructions are executed, the state of the machine was as follows:

- The PC has the value 500$_{ten}$, the address of the lw instruction.
- Every register has the initial value 10$_{ten}$ plus the register number (e.g., register $8 has the initial value 18$_{ten}$).

- Every memory word accessed as data has the initial value 1000_{ten} plus the byte address of the word (e.g., Memory[8] has the initial value 1008_{ten}).

Determine the value of every field, including those unidentified in the figure and those unnecessary for a specific instruction. If you believe a field value is impossible to determine from the information provided, explain why.

6.11 [5] <§§6.4, 6.5> Consider executing the following code on the pipelined datapath of Figure 6.46 on page 492:

```
add    $1,  $2,  $3
add    $4,  $5,  $6
add    $7,  $8,  $9
add    $10, $11, $12
add    $13, $14, $15
```

At the end of the fifth cycle of execution, which registers are being read and which register will be written?

6.12 [5] <§§6.4, 6.5> {Ex. 6.11} With regard to the program in Exercise 6.11, explain what the forwarding unit is doing during the fifth cycle of execution. If any comparisons are being made, mention them.

6.13 [5] <§§6.4, 6.5> {Ex. 6.11} With regard to the program in Exercise 6.11, explain what the hazard detection unit is doing during the fifth cycle of execution. If any comparisons are being made, mention them.

6.14 [5] <§6.5> Consider a program consisting of 100 lw instructions (don't worry about whether this is good code) and in which each instruction is dependent upon the instruction before it. What would the actual CPI be if the program were run on the pipelined datapath of Figure 6.45 on page 491?

6.15 [5] <§6.4, 6.5> Consider executing the following code on the pipelined datapath of Figure 6.46 on page 492:

```
add    $5, $6, $7
lw     $6, 100($7)
sub    $7, $6, $8
```

How many cycles will it take to execute this code? Draw a diagram like that of Figure 6.44 on page 489 that illustrates the dependencies that need to be resolved, and provide another diagram like that of Figure 6.45 on page 491 that illustrates how the code will actually be executed (incorporating any stalls or forwarding) so as to resolve the identified problems.

6.16 [15] <§6.5> List all the inputs and outputs of the forwarding unit in Figure 6.46 on page 492. Give the names and the number of bits for each input and output.

6.17 [30] <§6.5, Appendix C> {Ex. 6.16} Using Appendix C and the answer to Exercise 6.16, design the hardware to implement the forwarding unit. (Hint: To decide if register numbers are equal, try using an exclusive OR gate. See the elaboration on page 249 of Chapter 4 or the In More Depth section on page 329 of Chapter 4.)

6.18 [20] <§6.5> The forwarding unit could be moved to the ID stage and forwarding decisions could be made earlier. The results of these decisions would need to be passed along with the instruction and used in the EX stage when actual forwarding would take place. This modification would speed up the EX stage and might allow for possible cycle-time improvement. Perform the modification. Provide a revised datapath and a description of the necessary changes. How has the ID/EX register changed? Provide new forwarding equations to replace those appearing on pages 480–483.

6.19 [10] <§§6.4, 6.5> The following code contains a "read after write" data hazard that is resolved by forwarding:

```
add    $2, $3, $4
add    $5, $2, $6
```

Consider the similar situation in which a memory read occurs after a memory write:

```
sw     $7, 100($2)
lw     $8, 100($2)
```

Write a paragraph describing how this situation differs from the one involving registers, and describe how the potential "read after write" problem is resolved.

6.20 [20] <§§6.4, 6.5> Consider an instruction sequence used for a memory-to-memory copy:

```
lw     $2, 100($5)
sw     $2, 200($6)
```

The elaboration starting on page 488 of the text discusses this situation and states that additional forwarding hardware can improve its performance. Show the necessary additions to the datapath of Figure 6.43 to allow code like this to run without stalling. Include forwarding equations (such as the ones appearing on pages 480–483) for all of the control signals for any new or modified multiplexors in your datapath. Finally, rewrite the stall formula on page 490 so that this code sequence won't stall.

6.21 [15] <§§6.2–6.5> In Exercise 5.15, the ability to specify an offset for load and store instructions was removed. How would this modification to the instruction set architecture affect a pipelined implementation? Describe changes to the datapath and how performance would be impacted. Be sure to include a discussion of forwarding in your answer.

6.22 [10] <§§6.2–6.5> Exercise 3.23 described an instruction, `addm`, that allows arithmetic instructions to directly access memory, as is found in the 80x86. Write a paragraph or two explaining why it would be hard to add this instruction to the MIPS pipeline described in this chapter.

6.23 [10] <§§6.4–6.6> The example on page 447 shows how to *maximize* performance on our pipelined datapath with forwarding and stalls on a use following a load. Rewrite the following code to *minimize* performance on this datapath—that is, reorder the instructions so that this sequence takes the *most* clock cycles to execute while still obtaining the same result.

```
lw    $3,    0($5)
lw    $4,    4($5)
add   $7,    $7,    $3
add   $8,    $8,    $4
add   $10,   $7,    $8
sw    $6,    0($5)
beq   $10,   $11,   Loop
```

6.24 [15] <§6.6> Using the example on page 498, rewrite the code to be as fast as possible using a new instruction `beqd`, which means a branch equal instruction with a single-branch delay slot.

6.25 [10] <§6.6> {Ex. 6.24} Using the answer to Exercise 6.24, draw the execution of the instructions as in Figure 6.52 on page 500. Once again, photocopying or downloading from *www.mkp.com/cod2e.htm* may save time.

6.26 [20] <§6.6> Consider the pipelined datapath in Figure 6.51 on page 499. Can an attempt to flush and an attempt to stall occur simultaneously? If so, do they result in conflicting actions and/or cooperating actions? If there are any cooperating actions, how do they work together? If there are any conflicting actions, which should take priority? Is there a simple change you can make to the datapath to ensure the necessary priority? You may want to consider the following code sequence to help you answer this question:

```
        beq $1,  $2,   TARGET # assume that the branch is taken
        lw  $3,  40($4)
        add $3,  $3,   $3
        sw  $3   40($4)
TARGET: or  $10, $11,  $12
```

6.27 [30] <§6.6> In which stage must the branch decision be made to reduce the branch delay to a single instruction? Redraw the datapath using new hardware that will reduce the branch delay to one cycle.

6.28 [10] <§6.6> One extension of the MIPS instruction set architecture has two new instructions called movn (move if not zero) and movz (move if zero). For example, the instruction

```
movn $8, $11, $4
```

copies the contents of register 11 into register 8, provided that the value in register 4 is nonzero (otherwise it does nothing). The movz instruction is similar but copying takes place only if the register's value is zero. Show how to use the new instructions to put whichever is larger, register 8's value or register 9's value, into register 10. If the values are equal, copy either into register 10. You may use register 1 as an extra register for temporary use. Do not use any conditional branches.

6.29 [10] <§6.6> {Ex. 6.28} The solution to Exercise 6.28 should involve the execution of fewer instructions than would be required using conditional branches. Sometimes, however, rewriting code to use movn and movz rather than conditional branches doesn't reduce the number of instructions executed. Nonetheless, even if the use of movn and movz doesn't reduce the number of instructions executed, it can still make the program faster if it is being executed on a pipelined datapath. Explain why.

6.30 [10] <§6.8> In this exercise, which is similar to the example on page 513, we consider the benefits of performing loop unrolling on code that is executed on the standard MIPS pipeline developed in sections 6.2–6.6. Specifically, consider the following code that has been unrolled but not yet scheduled. In this case, the code has been unrolled once under the assumption that the loop index is a multiple of two (i.e., $s1 is a multiple of eight):

```
Loop:   lw      $t0, 0($s1)
        addu    $t0, $t0, $s2
        sw      $t0, 0($s1)
        lw      $t1, -4($s1)
        addu    $t1, $t1, $s2
        sw      $t1, -4($s1)
        addi    $s1, $s1, -8
        bne     $s1, $zero, Loop
```

First schedule this code for fast execution on the standard MIPS pipeline (assume that it supports addi and addu instructions). Taking into account any necessary stalls, compare the difference in performance between the original unrolled code, which appears on page 485, and your code, which has been unrolled and then scheduled.

6.31 [20] <§6.8> This exercise is similar to Exercise 6.30, except this time the code should be unrolled twice (creating three copies of the code). However, it is not known that the loop index is a multiple of three, and thus you will need to invent a means of ensuring that the code still executes properly. (Hint: Consider adding some code to the beginning or end of the loop that takes care of the cases not handled by the loop.)

6.32 [20] <§6.9> Modifying complex processors such as the PowerPC 604 and the Pentium Pro in order to improve performance involves complex decisions that often can be answered only with the aid of extensive simulation. Assume that technology improvements have increased your "transistor budget" and that you can increase some of the parameters in Figure 6.63 on page 519. What assumptions might cause you to choose specific parameters to improve? How are some of the parameters interrelated?

6.33 [30] <§6.9> New processors are introduced more quickly than new versions of textbooks. To keep your textbook current, investigate some of the latest developments in this area and write a one-page elaboration to insert at the end of section 6.9. You might want to visit the MIPS site via the link at *www.mkp.com/books_catalog/cod/links.htm* as a starting point.

6.34 [1 week] <§§6.4, 6.5> Using the simulator provided with this book, collect statistics on data hazards for a C program (supplied by either the instructor or with the software). You will write a subroutine that is passed the instruction to be executed, and this routine must model the five-stage pipeline in this chapter. Have your program collect the following statistics:

- Number of instructions executed.

- Number of data hazards.

- Number of hazards that result in stalls.

- If the MIPS C compiler that you are using issues nop instructions to avoid hazards, count the number of nop instructions as well.

Assuming that the memory accesses always take 1 clock cycle, calculate the average number of clock cycles per instruction. Classify nop instructions as stalls inserted by software, then subtract them from the number of instructions executed in the CPI calculation.

6.35 [1 month] <§§5.3, 6.3–6.7> If you have access to a simulation system such as Verilog or ViewLogic, first design the single-cycle datapath and control from Chapter 5. Then evolve this design into a pipelined organization, as we did in this chapter. Be sure to run MIPS programs at each step to ensure that your refined design continues to operate correctly.

7

Large and Fast: Exploiting Memory Hierarchy

Ideally one would desire an indefinitely large
memory capacity such that any particular . . .
word would be immediately available. . . .
We are . . . forced to recognize the possibility
of constructing a hierarchy of memories, each
of which has greater capacity than the
preceding but which is less quickly accessible.

A. W. Burks, H. H. Goldstine, and J. von Neumann
Preliminary Discussion of the Logical Design of an Electronic Computing
Instrument, 1946

7.1   **Introduction**   540

7.2   **The Basics of Caches**   545

7.3   **Measuring and Improving Cache Performance**   564

7.4   **Virtual Memory**   579

7.5   **A Common Framework for Memory Hierarchies**   603

7.6   **Real Stuff: The Pentium Pro and PowerPC 604 Memory Hierarchies**   611

7.7   **Fallacies and Pitfalls**   615

7.8   **Concluding Remarks**   618

7.9   **Historical Perspective and Further Reading**   621

7.10   **Key Terms**   627

7.11   **Exercises**   628

The Five Classic Components of a Computer

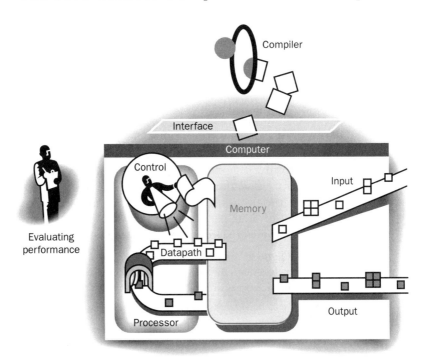

7.1   Introduction

From the earliest days of computing, programmers have wanted unlimited amounts of fast memory. The topics we will look at in this chapter all focus on aiding programmers by creating the illusion of unlimited fast memory. Before we look at how the illusion is actually created, let's consider a simple analogy that illustrates the key principles and mechanisms that we use.

Suppose you were a student writing a term paper on important historical developments in computer hardware. You are sitting at a desk in the engineering or math library with a collection of books that you have pulled from the shelves and are examining. You find that several of the important machines that you need to write about are described in the books you have, but there is nothing about the EDSAC. So, you go back to the shelves and look for an additional book. You find a book on early British computers that covers EDSAC. Once you have a good selection of books on the desk in front of you, there is a good probability that many of the topics you need can be found in them, and you may spend a great deal of time just using the books on the desk without going back to the shelves. Having several books on the desk in front of you saves time compared to having only one book there and constantly having to go back to the shelves to return it and take out another.

The same principle allows us to create the illusion of a large memory that we can access as fast as a very small memory. Just as you did not need to access all the books in the library at once with equal probability, a program does not access all of its code or data at once with equal probability. Otherwise, it would be impossible to make most memory accesses fast and still have large amounts of memory in machines, just as it would be impossible for you to fit all the library books on your desk and still have a chance of finding what you wanted quickly.

This *principle of locality* underlies both the way in which you did your work in the library and the way that programs operate. The principle of locality states that programs access a relatively small portion of their address space at any instant of time, just as you accessed a very small portion of the library's collection. There are two different types of locality:

- *Temporal locality* (locality in time): If an item is referenced, it will tend to be referenced again soon. If you recently brought a book to your desk to look at, you will probably need to look at it again soon.

- *Spatial locality* (locality in space): If an item is referenced, items whose addresses are close by will tend to be referenced soon. For example, when you brought out the book on early computers in England to find out about EDSAC, you also noticed that there was another book shelved next to it about early mechanical computers, so you also brought back that book and, later on, found something useful in that book. Books on the same topic are shelved together in the library to increase spatial locality. We'll see how spatial locality is used in memory hierarchies a little later in this chapter.

Just as accesses to books on the desk naturally exhibit locality, locality in programs arises from simple and natural program structures. For example, most programs contain loops, so instructions and data are likely to be accessed repeatedly, showing high amounts of temporal locality. Since instructions are normally accessed sequentially, programs show high spatial locality. Accesses to data also exhibit a natural spatial locality. For example, accesses to elements of an array or a record will naturally have high degrees of spatial locality.

We take advantage of the principle of locality by implementing the memory of a computer as a *memory hierarchy*. A memory hierarchy consists of multiple levels of memory with different speeds and sizes. The fastest memories are more expensive per bit than the slower memories and thus are usually smaller.

Today, there are three primary technologies used in building memory hierarchies. Main memory is implemented from DRAM (dynamic random access memory), while levels closer to the CPU (caches) use SRAM (static random access memory). DRAM is less costly per bit than SRAM, although it is substantially slower. The price difference arises because DRAM uses significantly less area per bit of memory, and DRAMs thus have larger capacity for the same amount of silicon; the speed difference arises from several factors described in section B.5 of Appendix B. The final technology, used to implement the largest and slowest level in the hierarchy, is magnetic disk. The access time and price per bit vary widely among these technologies, as the table below shows, using typical values for 1997:

Memory technology	Typical access time	$ per MByte in 1997
SRAM	5–25 ns	$100–$250
DRAM	60–120 ns	$5–$10
Magnetic disk	10–20 million ns	$0.10–$0.20

Because of these differences in cost and access time, it is advantageous to build memory as a hierarchy of levels, with the faster memory close to the processor and the slower, less expensive memory below that, as shown in Figure 7.1. The goal is to present the user with as much memory as is available in the cheapest technology, while providing access at the speed offered by the fastest memory.

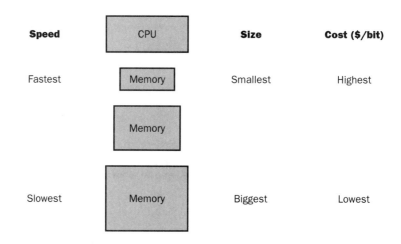

FIGURE 7.1   The basic structure of a memory hierarchy. By implementing the memory system as a hierarchy, the user has the illusion of a memory that is as large as the largest level of the hierarchy, but can be accessed as if it were all built from the fastest memory.

The memory system is organized as a hierarchy: a level closer to the processor is a subset of any level further away, and all the data is stored at the lowest level. By comparison, the books on your desk form a subset of the library you are working in, which is in turn a subset of all the libraries on campus. Furthermore, as we move away from the processor, the levels take progressively longer to access, just as we might encounter in a hierarchy of campus libraries.

A memory hierarchy can consist of multiple levels, but data is copied between only two adjacent levels at a time, so we can focus our attention on just two levels. The upper level—the one closer to the processor—is smaller and faster (since it uses more expensive technology) than the lower level. The minimum unit of information that can be either present or not present in the two-level hierarchy is called a *block*, as shown in Figure 7.2; in our library analogy, a block of information is one book.

If the data requested by the processor appears in some block in the upper level, this is called a *hit* (analogous to your finding the information in one of the books on your desk). If the data is not found in the upper level, the request is called a *miss*. The lower level in the hierarchy is then accessed to retrieve the block containing the requested data. (Continuing our analogy, you get up from your desk and go over to the shelves to look for the desired information.) The *hit rate*, or *hit ratio*, is the fraction of memory accesses found in the upper level; it is often used as a measure of the performance of the memory hierarchy. The *miss rate* (1 – hit rate) is the fraction of memory accesses not found in the upper level.

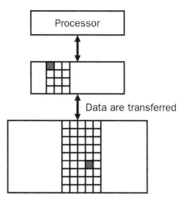

FIGURE 7.2 Every pair of levels in the memory hierarchy can be thought of as having an upper and lower level. Within each level, the unit of information that is present or not is called a *block*. Usually we transfer an entire block when we copy something between levels.

Since performance is the major reason for having a memory hierarchy, the speed of hits and misses is important. *Hit time* is the time to access the upper level of the memory hierarchy, which includes the time needed to determine whether the access is a hit or a miss (that is, the time needed to look through the books on the desk). The *miss penalty* is the time to replace a block in the upper level with the corresponding block from the lower level, plus the time to deliver this block to the processor (or, the time to get another book from the shelves and place it on the desk). Because the upper level is smaller and built using faster memory parts, the hit time will be much smaller than the time to access the next level in the hierarchy, which is the major component of the miss penalty. (The time to examine the books on the desk is much smaller than the time to get up and go look for something in a book on the shelves.)

As we will see in this chapter, the concepts used to build memory systems affect many other aspects of a computer, including how the operating system manages memory and I/O, how compilers generate code, and even how applications use the machine. Of course, because all programs spend much of their time accessing memory, the memory system is necessarily a major factor in determining performance. The reliance on memory hierarchies to achieve performance has meant that programmers, who used to be able to think of memory as a flat, random access storage device, now need to understand how memory hierarchies work to get good performance. We show how important this understanding is with an example in the Fallacies and Pitfalls section.

Since memory systems are so critical to performance, computer designers have devoted a lot of attention to these systems and developed sophisticated mechanisms for improving the performance of the memory system. In this chapter we will see the major conceptual ideas, although many simplifications and abstractions have been used to keep the material manageable in length and complexity. We could easily have written hundreds of pages on memory systems, as a number of recent doctoral theses have demonstrated.

The Big Picture

Programs exhibit both temporal locality, the tendency to reuse recently accessed data items, and spatial locality, the tendency to reference data items that are close to other recently accessed items. Memory hierarchies take advantage of temporal locality by keeping more recently accessed data items closer to the processor. Memory hierarchies take advantage of spatial locality by moving blocks consisting of multiple contiguous words in memory to upper levels of the hierarchy.

A memory hierarchy uses smaller and faster memory technologies close to the processor, as shown in Figure 7.3. Thus accesses that hit in the highest level of the hierarchy can be processed quickly. Accesses that miss go to lower levels of the hierarchy, which are larger but slower. If the hit rate is high enough, the memory hierarchy has an effective access time close to that of the highest (and fastest) level and a size equal to that of the lowest (and largest) level.

In most systems, the memory is a true hierarchy, meaning that data cannot be present in level i unless it is present in level $i + 1$.

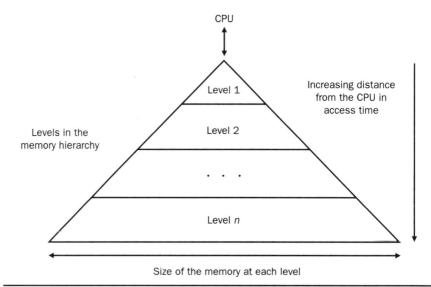

FIGURE 7.3 This diagram shows the structure of a memory hierarchy: as the distance from the CPU increases, so does the size. This structure with the appropriate operating mechanisms allows the CPU to have an access time that is determined primarily by level 1 of the hierarchy and yet have a memory as large as level n. Maintaining this illusion is the subject of this chapter.

7.2   The Basics of Caches

Cache: a safe place for hiding or storing things.

Webster's New World Dictionary of the American Language,
Third College Edition (1988)

In our library example, the desk acted as a cache—a safe place to store things (books) that we needed to examine. *Cache* was the name chosen to represent the level of the memory hierarchy between the CPU and main memory in the first commercial machine to have this extra level. Today, although this remains the dominant use of the word *cache*, the term is also used to refer to any storage managed to take advantage of locality of access. Caches first appeared in research machines in the early 1960s and in production machines later in that same decade; virtually every general-purpose machine built today, from the fastest to the slowest, includes a cache.

In this section, we begin by looking at a very simple cache in which the processor requests are each one word and the blocks also consist of a single word. Figure 7.4 shows such a simple cache, before and after requesting a data item that is not initially in the cache. Before the request, the cache contains a collection of recent references X1, X2, . . . , $Xn - 1$, and the processor requests a word Xn that is not in the cache. This request results in a miss, and the word Xn is brought from memory into cache.

X4
X1
$Xn - 2$
$Xn - 1$
X2
X3

X4
X1
$Xn - 2$
$Xn - 1$
X2
Xn
X3

a. Before the reference to Xn b. After the reference to Xn

FIGURE 7.4   The cache just before and just after a reference to a word Xn that is not initially in the cache. This reference causes a miss that forces the cache to fetch Xn from memory and insert it into the cache.

Looking at the scenario in Figure 7.4, we can see that there are two questions we must answer: How do we know if a data item is in the cache? And, if it is, how do we find it? The answers to these two questions are related. If each word can go in exactly one place in the cache, then we will know how to find the word if it is in the cache. The simplest way to assign a location in the cache for each word in memory is to assign the cache location based on the address of the word in memory. This cache structure is called *direct mapped*, since each memory location is mapped to exactly one location in the cache. The typical mapping between addresses and cache locations for a direct-mapped cache is usually simple. For example, almost all direct-mapped caches use the mapping:

(Block address) modulo (Number of cache blocks in the cache)

This mapping is attractive because if the number of entries in the cache is a power of two, then modulo can be computed simply by using only the low-order $\log_2$ (cache size in blocks) bits of the address; hence the cache may be accessed directly with the low-order bits. For example, Figure 7.5 shows a direct-mapped cache of eight words and the memory addresses between 1_{ten} (00001_{two}) and 29_{ten} (11101_{two}) that map to locations 1_{ten} (001_{two}) and 5_{ten} (101_{two}) in the cache.

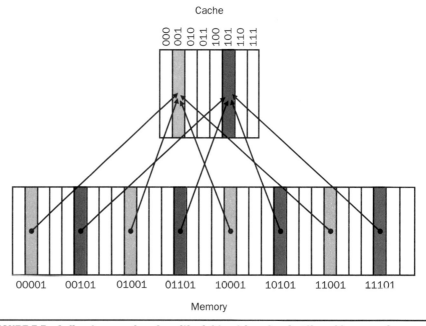

FIGURE 7.5   A direct-mapped cache with eight entries showing the addresses of memory words between 0 and 31 that map to the same cache locations. Because there are eight words in the cache, an address X maps to the cache word X modulo 8. That is, the low-order $\log_2(8) = 3$ bits are used as the cache index. Thus, addresses 00001_{two}, 01001_{two}, 10001_{two}, and 11001_{two} all map to entry 001_{two} of the cache, while addresses 00101_{two}, 01101_{two}, 10101_{two}, and 11101_{two} all map to entry 101_{two} of the cache.

Because each cache location can contain the contents of a number of different memory locations, how do we know whether the data in the cache corresponds to a requested word? That is, how do we know whether a requested word is in the cache or not? We can plan for this by adding a set of *tags* to the cache. The tags contain the address information required to identify whether a word in the cache corresponds to the requested word. The tag needs only to contain the upper portion of the address, corresponding to the bits that are not used as an index into the cache. The reason for this is that the bits corresponding to the index are used to select the unique entry in the cache corresponding to the supplied address, and thus we only need to ensure that the upper portion of the supplied address matches the tag. For example, in Figure 7.5 we need only have 2 of the 5 address bits in the tag, since the lowest 3 bits of the address select the block.

We also need a way to recognize that a cache block does not have valid information. For instance, when a processor starts up, the cache will be empty, and the tag fields will be meaningless. Even after executing many instructions, some of the cache entries may still be empty, as in Figure 7.4. Thus we need to know that the tag should be ignored for such entries. The most common method is to add a *valid bit* to indicate whether an entry contains a valid address. If the bit is not set, there cannot be a match for this block.

For the rest of this section, we will focus on explaining how reads work in a cache and how the cache control works for reads. In general, handling reads is a little simpler than handling writes, since reads do not have to change the contents of the cache. After seeing the basics of how reads work and how cache misses can be handled, we'll examine the cache designs for two real machines and detail how these caches handle writes.

Accessing a Cache

Figure 7.6 shows the contents of an eight-word direct-mapped cache as it responds to a series of requests from the processor. Since there are eight blocks in the cache, the low-order 3 bits of an address give the block number. Here is the action for each reference:

Decimal address of reference	Binary address of reference	Hit or miss in cache	Assigned cache block (where found or placed)
22	10110_{two}	miss (7.5b)	$(10110_{two} \bmod 8) = 110_{two}$
26	11010_{two}	miss (7.5c)	$(11010_{two} \bmod 8) = 010_{two}$
22	10110_{two}	hit	$(10110_{two} \bmod 8) = 110_{two}$
26	11010_{two}	hit	$(11010_{two} \bmod 8) = 010_{two}$
16	10000_{two}	miss (7.5d)	$(10000_{two} \bmod 8) = 000_{two}$
3	00011_{two}	miss (7.5e)	$(00011_{two} \bmod 8) = 011_{two}$
16	10000_{two}	hit	$(10000_{two} \bmod 8) = 000_{two}$
18	10010_{two}	miss (7.5f)	$(10010_{two} \bmod 8) = 010_{two}$

Index	V	Tag	Data
000	N		
001	N		
010	N		
011	N		
100	N		
101	N		
110	N		
111	N		

a. The initial state of the cache after power-on

Index	V	Tag	Data
000	N		
001	N		
010	N		
011	N		
100	N		
101	N		
110	Y	10_{two}	Memory(10110_{two})
111	N		

b. After handling a miss of address (10110_{two})

Index	V	Tag	Data
000	N		
001	N		
010	Y	11_{two}	Memory (11010_{two})
011	N		
100	N		
101	N		
110	Y	10_{two}	Memory (10110_{two})
111	N		

c. After handling a miss of address (11010_{two})

Index	V	Tag	Data
000	Y	10_{two}	Memory (10000_{two})
001	N		
010	Y	11_{two}	Memory (11010_{two})
011	N		
100	N		
101	N		
110	Y	10_{two}	Memory (10110_{two})
111	N		

d. After handling a miss of address (10000_{two})

Index	V	Tag	Data
000	Y	10_{two}	Memory (10000_{two})
001	N		
010	Y	11_{two}	Memory (11010_{two})
011	Y	00_{two}	Memory (00011_{two})
100	N		
101	N		
110	Y	10_{two}	Memory (10110_{two})
111	N		

e. After handling a miss of address (00011_{two})

Index	V	Tag	Data
000	Y	10_{two}	Memory (10000_{two})
001	N		
010	Y	10_{two}	Memory (10010_{two})
011	Y	00_{two}	Memory (00011_{two})
100	N		
101	N		
110	Y	10_{two}	Memory (10110_{two})
111	N		

f. After handling a miss of address (10010_{two})

FIGURE 7.6 The cache contents are shown after each reference request that *misses*, with the index and tag fields shown in binary. The cache is initially empty, with all valid bits (V entry in cache) turned off (N). The processor requests the following addresses: 10110_{two} (miss), 11010_{two} (miss), 10110_{two} (hit), 11010_{two} (hit), 10000_{two} (miss), 00011_{two} (miss), 10000_{two} (hit), and 10010_{two} (miss). The figures show the cache contents after each miss in the sequence has been handled. When address 10010_{two} (18) is referenced, the entry for address 11010_{two} (26) must be replaced, and a reference to 11010_{two} will cause a subsequent miss. The tag field will contain only the upper portion of the address. The full address of a word contained in cache block i with tag field j for this cache is $j \times 8 + i$, or equivalently the concatenation of the tag field j and the index i. For example, in cache f above, index 010 has tag 10 and corresponds to address 10010.

When the word at address 18 (10010_{two}) is brought into cache block 2 (010_{two}), the word at address 26 (11010_{two}), which was in cache block 2 (010_{two}), must be replaced by the newly requested data. This behavior allows a cache to take advantage of temporal locality: recently accessed words replace less recently referenced words. This situation is directly analogous to needing a book from the shelves and having no more space on your desk—some book already on your desk must be returned to the shelves. In a direct-mapped cache, there is only one place to put the newly requested item and hence only one choice of what to replace.

We know where to look in the cache for each possible address: the low-order bits of an address can be used to find the unique cache entry to which the address could map. Figure 7.7 shows how a referenced address is divided into

■ a cache index, which is used to select the block

■ a tag field, which is used to compare with the value of the tag field of the cache

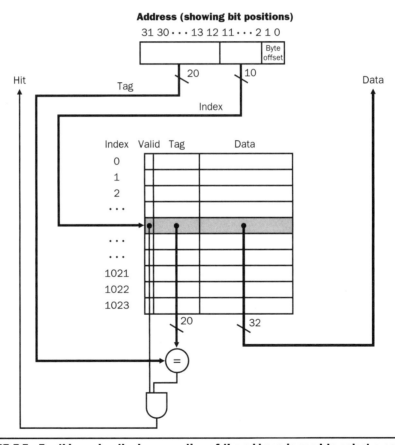

FIGURE 7.7 For this cache, the lower portion of the address is used to select a cache entry consisting of a data word and a tag. The tag from the cache is compared against the upper portion of the address to determine whether the entry in the cache corresponds to the requested address. Because the cache has 2^{10} (or 1024) words, and a block size of 1 word, 10 bits are used to index the cache, leaving $32 - 10 - 2 = 20$ bits to be compared against the tag. If the tag and upper 20 bits of the address are equal and the valid bit is on, then the request hits in the cache, and the word is supplied to the processor. Otherwise, a miss occurs.

Because a given address can appear in exactly one location, the tag need only correspond to the upper portion of the address, which is not used to index the cache. Thus, the index of a cache block, together with the tag contents of that block, uniquely specify the memory address of the word contained in the cache block. Because the index field is used as an address to access the cache and because an n-bit field has 2^n values, the total number of entries in the cache must be a power of two. In the MIPS architecture, the least significant 2 bits of every address specify a byte within a word and are not used to select the word in the cache.

The total number of bits needed for a cache is a function of the cache size and the address size because the cache includes both the storage for the data and for the tags. Assuming the 32-bit byte address, a direct-mapped cache of size 2^n words with one-word (4-byte) blocks will require a tag field whose size is $32 - (n + 2)$ bits, because 2 bits are used for the byte offset and n bits are used for the index. The total number of bits in a direct-mapped cache is $2^n \times (\text{block size} + \text{tag size} + \text{valid field size})$. Since the block size is one word (32 bits) and the address size is 32 bits, the number of bits in such a cache is $2^n \times (32 + (32 - n - 2) + 1) = 2^n \times (63 - n)$.

Bits in a Cache

Example

How many total bits are required for a direct-mapped cache with 64 KB of data and one-word blocks, assuming a 32-bit address?

Answer

We know that 64 KB is 16K words, which is 2^{14} words, and, with a block size of one word, 2^{14} blocks. Each block has 32 bits of data plus a tag, which is $32 - 14 - 2$ bits, plus a valid bit. Thus the total cache size is

$$2^{14} \times (32 + (32 - 14 - 2) + 1) = 2^{14} \times 49 = 784 \times 2^{10} = 784 \text{ Kbits}$$

or 98 KB for a 64-KB cache. For this cache, the total number of bits in the cache is over 1.5 times as many as needed just for the storage of the data.

Handling Cache Misses

Before we look at the cache of a real system, let's see how the control unit deals with cache misses. The control unit must detect a miss and process the miss by fetching the data from memory (or a lower-level cache). If the cache reports a hit, the machine continues using the data as if nothing had happened. Consequently, we can use the same basic control that we developed in

Chapter 5 and enhanced to accommodate pipelining in Chapter 6. The memories in the datapath used in Chapters 5 and 6 are simply replaced by caches.

Modifying the control of a processor to take a hit into account is trivial; misses, however, require some extra work. The basic approach is to stall the CPU, freezing the contents of all the registers. A separate controller handles the cache miss, fetching the data into the cache from memory. Once the data is present, execution is restarted at the cycle that caused the cache miss. The cache miss handling is done with the processor control unit and with a separate controller that initiates the memory access and refills the cache. The processing of a cache miss creates a stall, similar to the pipeline stalls discussed in Chapter 6, as opposed to an interrupt, which would require saving the state of all registers. For a cache miss, we can stall the entire machine, essentially freezing the contents of the temporary and programmer-visible registers, while we wait for memory. In contrast, pipeline stalls, discussed in Chapter 6, are more complex because we must continue executing some instructions while we stall others.

Let's look a little more closely at how instruction misses are handled for either the multicycle or pipelined datapath; the same approach can be easily extended to handle data misses. If an instruction access results in a miss, then the contents of the Instruction register are invalid. To get the proper instruction into the cache, we must be able to instruct the lower level in the memory hierarchy to perform a read. Since the program counter is incremented in the first clock cycle of execution in both the pipelined and multicycle processors, the address of the instruction that generates an instruction cache miss is equal to the value of the program counter minus four. We can compute this value using the ALU, although we may need additional temporary storage in the pipelined implementation. Once we have the address, we need to instruct the main memory to perform a read. We wait for the memory to respond (since the access will take multiple cycles), and then write the word into the cache.

We can now define the steps to be taken on an instruction cache miss:

1. Send the original PC value (current PC – 4) to the memory.

2. Instruct main memory to perform a read and wait for the memory to complete its access.

3. Write the cache entry, putting the data from memory in the data portion of the entry, writing the upper bits of the address (from the ALU) into the tag field, and turning the valid bit on.

4. Restart the instruction execution at the first step, which will refetch the instruction, this time finding it in the cache.

The control of the cache on a data access is essentially identical: on a miss, we simply stall the processor until the memory responds with the data. In the rest of this section we describe two different caches from real machines, and we examine how they handle both reads and writes. In section 7.5, we will describe the handling of writes in more detail.

Elaboration: To reduce the penalty of cache misses, designers employ two techniques, one of which we discuss here and another that we will discuss later. To reduce the number of cycles that a processor is stalled for a cache miss, we can allow a processor to continue executing instructions while the cache miss is handled. This strategy does not help for instruction misses because we cannot fetch new instructions to execute. In the case of data misses, however, we can allow the machine to continue fetching and executing instructions until the loaded word is required. Hence the name for this technique: *stall on use.* While this additional effort may save cycles, it will probably not save very many cycles because the loaded data will likely be needed very shortly and because other instructions will need access to the cache. A more sophisticated technique is used in some modern processors; we describe it in section 7.6.

An Example Cache: The DECStation 3100

The DECStation 3100 was a workstation that used a MIPS R2000 as the processor and a very simple cache implementation. Near the end of the chapter, we will examine the cache design of a more recent computer, but we start with this simple, yet real, example for pedagogical reasons.

This processor has a pipeline similar to that discussed in Chapter 6. When operating at peak speed, the processor requests both an instruction word and a data word on every clock. To satisfy the demands of the pipeline without stalling, separate instruction and data caches are used. Each cache is 64 KB, or 16K words, with a one-word block. Figure 7.8 shows the organization of the DECStation 3100 data cache.

Read requests for the cache are straightforward. Because there are separate data and instruction caches, separate control signals will be needed to read and write each cache. (Remember that we need to write into the instruction cache when a miss occurs.) Thus the steps for a read request to either cache are as follows:

1. Send the address to the appropriate cache. The address comes either from the PC (for an instruction read) or from the ALU (for a data access).

2. If the cache signals hit, the requested word is available on the data lines. If the cache signals miss, we send the address to the main memory. When the memory returns with the data, we write it into the cache.

Writes work somewhat differently. Suppose on a store instruction, we wrote the data into only the data cache (without changing main memory); then, after

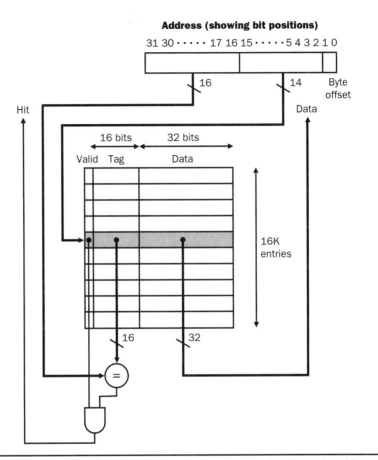

Address (showing bit positions)

31 30 ····· 17 16 15 ····· 5 4 3 2 1 0

16

14

Byte offset

Hit

Data

16 bits   32 bits

Valid   Tag   Data

16K entries

16

32

=

FIGURE 7.8   The caches in the DECStation 3100 each contain 16K blocks with one word per block. This means that the index is 14 bits and that the tag contains 16 bits.

the write into the cache, memory would have a different value from that in the cache. In such a case, the cache and memory are said to be *inconsistent*. The simplest way to keep the main memory and the cache consistent is to always write the data into both the memory and the cache. This scheme, which the DEC-Station 3100 uses, is called *write-through*.

The other key aspect of writes is what occurs on a write miss. Because the data word in the cache is being written by the processor, there is no reason to read a word from memory; it would just be overwritten by the processor. In fact, for this simple cache we can always just write the word into the cache, updating both the tag and data. We do not need to consider whether a write hits or misses in the cache. This observation leads to the following simple scheme for processing writes, used on the DECStation 3100:

1. Index the cache using bits 15–2 of the address.

2. Write bits 31–16 of the address into the tag, write the data word into the data portion, and set the valid bit.

3. Also write the word to main memory using the entire address.

Although this design handles writes very simply, it would not provide very good performance. With a write-through scheme, every write causes the data to be written to main memory. These writes will take a long time and could slow down the machine considerably. In gcc, for example, 13% of the instructions are stores. In the DECStation 3100, the CPI without cache misses for a program like gcc is about 1.2, so spending 10 cycles on every write would lead to a CPI of $1.2 + 10 \times 13\% = 2.5$, reducing performance by more than a factor of two.

One solution to this problem is to use a *write buffer*. A write buffer stores the data while it is waiting to be written to memory. After writing the data into the cache and into the write buffer, the processor can continue execution. When a write to main memory completes, the entry in the write buffer is freed. If the write buffer is full when the processor reaches a write, the processor must stall until there is an empty position in the write buffer. Of course, if the rate at which the memory can complete writes is less than the rate at which the processor is generating writes, no amount of buffering can help because writes are being generated faster than the memory system can accept them.

The rate at which writes are generated may also be *less* than the rate at which the memory can accept them, and yet stalls may still occur. This can happen when the writes occur in bursts. To reduce the occurrence of such stalls, machines usually increase the depth of the write buffer beyond a single entry. For example, the DECStation 3100 write buffer is four words deep. As the difference between the rate at which programs can generate writes and the rate at which the memory system can accept them increases, even deeper write buffers (e.g., 10 entries) are appropriate.

The alternative to a write-through scheme is a scheme called *write-back*. In a write-back scheme, when a write occurs, the new value is written only to the block in the cache. The modified block is written to the lower level of the hierarchy when it is replaced. Write-back schemes can improve performance, especially when processors can generate writes as fast or faster than the writes can be handled by main memory; a write-back scheme is, however, more complex to implement than write-through.

What sort of cache miss rates are attained with a cache structure like that used by the DECStation 3100? Figure 7.9 shows the miss rates for the instruction and data caches for two programs, which we have seen before. The com-

Program	Instruction miss rate	Data miss rate	Effective combined miss rate
gcc	6.1%	2.1%	5.4%
spice	1.2%	1.3%	1.2%

FIGURE 7.9 Instruction and data miss rates for the DECStation 3100 when executing two different programs. The combined miss rate is the effective miss rate seen for the combination of the 64-KB instruction cache and 64-KB data cache. It is obtained by weighting the instruction and data individual miss rates by the frequency of instruction and data references. Remember that data misses include only data reads because writes cannot miss in the DECStation 3100 cache.

bined miss rate is the effective miss rate per reference for each program after accounting for the differing frequency of instruction and data accesses.

Remember that although miss rate is an important characteristic of cache designs, the ultimate measure will be the effect of the memory system on program execution time; we'll see how miss rate and execution time are related shortly. First we must explore how the memory system can take advantage of spatial locality.

Elaboration: A combined cache of the total size equal to the sum of the two split caches will usually have a better hit rate. This higher rate occurs because the combined cache does not rigidly divide the number of entries that may be used by instructions from those that may be used by data. Nonetheless, many machines use a split instruction and data cache to increase the *bandwidth* from the cache.

Here are some measurements for the DECStation 3100 for the program gcc, and for a combined cache whose size is equal to the total of the two caches on the 3100:

- Total cache size: 128 KB
- Split cache effective miss rate: 5.4%
- Combined cache miss rate: 4.8%

The miss rate of the split cache is only slightly worse.

For many systems, the advantage of doubling the cache bandwidth, by supporting both an instruction and data access simultaneously, easily overcomes the disadvantage of a slightly increased miss rate. This observation is another reminder that we cannot use miss rate as the sole measure of cache performance.

Taking Advantage of Spatial Locality

The cache we have described so far, while simple, does nothing to take advantage of spatial locality in requests, since each word is in its own block. As we noted in section 7.1, spatial locality exists naturally in programs. To take advantage of spatial locality, we want to have a cache block that is larger than one word in length. When a miss occurs, we will then fetch multiple words that are adjacent and carry a high probability of being needed shortly.

Figure 7.10 shows a cache that holds 64 KB of data, but with blocks of four words (16 bytes) each. Compared with Figure 7.8 on page 553, which shows the same total size cache with a one-word block, an extra block index field occurs in the address of the cache in Figure 7.10. This block index field is used to control the multiplexor (shown at the bottom of the figure), which selects the requested word from the four words in the indexed block. The total number of tags and valid bits in the cache with a multiword block is smaller because each tag and valid bit is used for four words. This sharing of tags improves the efficiency of memory use in the cache.

How do we find the cache block for a particular address? We can use the same mapping that we used for a cache with a one-word block:

(Block address) modulo (Number of cache blocks)

The block address is simply the word address divided by the number of words in the block (or equivalently, the byte address divided by the number of bytes in the block).

Mapping an Address to a Multiword Cache Block

Example

Consider a cache with 64 blocks and a block size of 16 bytes. What block number does byte address 1200 map to?

Answer

The block is given by

(Block address) modulo (Number of cache blocks)

Where the address of the block is

$$\frac{\text{Byte address}}{\text{Bytes per block}}$$

Notice that this block address is the block containing all addresses between

$$\left\lfloor \frac{\text{Byte address}}{\text{Bytes per block}} \right\rfloor \times \text{Bytes per block}$$

and

$$\left\lfloor \frac{\text{Byte address}}{\text{Bytes per block}} \right\rfloor \times \text{Bytes per block} + (\text{Bytes per block} - 1)$$

Thus, with 16 bytes per block, byte address 1200 is block address

$$\left\lfloor \frac{1200}{16} \right\rfloor = 75$$

which maps to cache block number (75 modulo 64) = 11.

Address (showing bit positions)

31···16 15···4 3 2 1 0

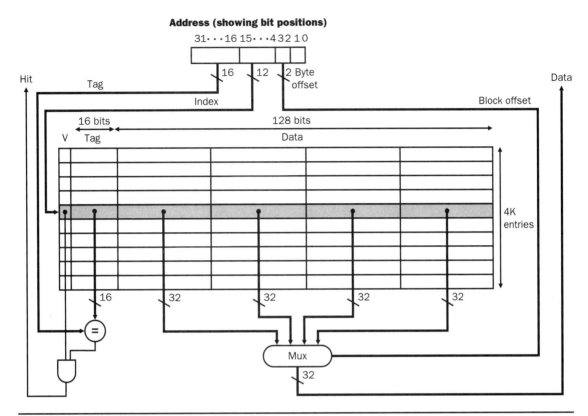

FIGURE 7.10 A 64-KB cache using four-word (16-byte) blocks. The tag field is 16 bits wide and the index field is 12 bits wide, while a 2-bit field (bits 3–2) is used to index the block and select the word from the block using a 4-to-1 multiplexor. In practice, the low-order bits of the address (bits 2 and 3 in this case) are used to enable only those RAMs that contain the desired word, eliminating the need for the multiplexor. Another way to eliminate the multiplexor is to have a large RAM for the data (with the tags stored separately) and use the block offset to supply 2 address bits for the RAM. The RAM must be 32 bits wide and have four times as many words as blocks in the cache.

Read misses are processed the same way for a multiword block as for a single-word block; a miss always brings back the entire block. Write hits and misses, however, must be handled differently than they were in the DECStation 3100 cache. Because the block contains more than a single word, we cannot just write the tag and data. To see why this is true, assume that there are two memory addresses, X and Y, that both map to cache block C, which is a four-word block that currently contains Y. Now consider writing to address X by simply overwriting the data and tag in cache block C. After the write, block C will have the tag for X, but the data portion of block C will contain one word of X and three words of Y!

Program	Block size in words	Instruction miss rate	Data miss rate	Effective combined miss rate
gcc	1	6.1%	2.1%	5.4%
	4	2.0%	1.7%	1.9%
spice	1	1.2%	1.3%	1.2%
	4	0.3%	0.6%	0.4%

FIGURE 7.11 The miss rates for gcc and spice with a cache like that in the DECStation 3100 with a block size of either one word or four words. With the four-word block, we include write misses, which do not incur any penalty for the one-word block and are not included in that case. If write misses were included in both cases, the difference in miss rate would be slightly larger than shown.

We can solve this problem for a write-through cache by writing the data while performing a tag comparison, just as if the request were a read. If the tag of the address and the tag in the cache entry are equal, we have a write hit and can continue. If the tags are unequal, we have a write miss and must fetch the block from memory. After the block is fetched and placed into the cache, we can rewrite the word that caused the miss into the cache block. Unlike the case with a one-word block, write misses with a multiword block will require reading from memory.

The reason for increasing the block size was to take advantage of spatial locality to improve performance. So how does a larger block size affect performance? In general, the miss rate falls when we increase the block size. This trend is easiest to see with an example. Suppose the following byte addresses are requested by a program: 16, ... , 24, ... , 20 and none of these addresses is in the cache. Spatial locality tells us that some pattern of this form is highly probable, although the order of the references may vary. If the cache has a four-word block, then the miss to address 16 will cause the block containing addresses 16, 20, 24, and 28 to be loaded into the cache. Only one miss is encountered for the three references, provided that an intervening reference doesn't bump the block out of the cache. With a one-word block, two additional misses are required because each miss brings in only a single word.

Figure 7.11 shows the miss rates for the programs gcc and spice with one- and four-word blocks. The instruction cache miss rates drop at a rate that is nearly equal to the increase in block size; this larger decrease in the instruction versus data miss rate occurs because the instruction references have better spatial locality.

The miss rate may actually go up if the block size becomes a significant fraction of the cache size because the number of blocks that can be held in the cache will become small, and there will be a great deal of competition for those blocks. As a result, a block will be bumped out of the cache before many of its words are accessed. As Figure 7.12 shows, increasing the block size usually decreases the miss rate. However, the spatial locality among the words in a block decreases with a very large block; consequently, the improvements in the miss rate become smaller—and the miss rate can eventually even increase.

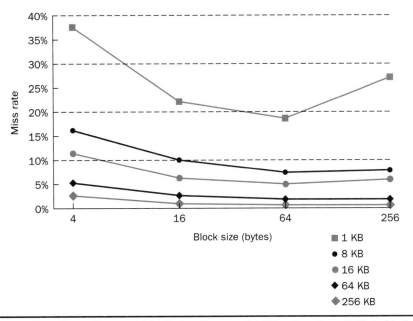

FIGURE 7.12 Miss rate versus block size. For a small 1-KB cache, a large 256-byte block size causes a higher miss rate than the smaller block sizes. This data was collected for a direct-mapped cache using traces (SAVE0) collected by Agarwal for the VAX. More details can be found in A. Agarwal, *Analysis of Cache Performance for Operating Systems and Multiprogramming*, Ph.D. thesis, Stanford Univ., Tech. Rep. No. CSL-TR-87-332 (May 1987).

A more serious problem associated with just increasing the block size is that the cost of a miss increases. The miss penalty is determined by the time required to fetch the block from the next lower level of the hierarchy and load it into the cache. The time to fetch the block has two parts: the latency to the first word and the transfer time for the rest of the block. Clearly, unless we change the memory system, the transfer time—and hence the miss penalty—will increase as the block size grows. Furthermore, the improvement in the miss rate starts to decrease as the blocks become larger. The result is that the increase in the miss penalty overwhelms the decrease in the miss rate for large blocks, and cache performance thus decreases. Of course, if we design the memory to transfer larger blocks more efficiently, we can increase the block size and obtain further improvements in cache performance. We discuss this topic in the next section.

Elaboration: The major disadvantage of increasing the block size is that the cache miss penalty increases. Although it is hard to do anything about the latency component of the miss penalty, we may be able to hide some of the transfer time so that the miss penalty is effectively smaller. The simplest method for doing this, called *early restart*, is simply to resume execution as soon as the requested word of the block is returned, rather than wait for the entire block. Many machines use this technique for instruction access, where it works best. Instruction accesses are largely sequential, so if the memory system can deliver a word every clock cycle, the processor may be able to restart operation when the requested word is returned, with the memory system delivering new instruction words just in time. This technique is usually less effective for data caches because it is likely that the words will be requested from the block in a less predictable way, and the probability that the processor will need another word from a different cache block before the transfer completes is high. If the processor cannot access the data cache because a transfer is ongoing, then it must stall.

An even more sophisticated scheme is to organize the memory so that the requested word is transferred from the memory to the cache first. The remainder of the block is then transferred, starting with the address after the requested word and wrapping around to the beginning of the block. This technique, called *requested word first*, or *critical word first*, can be slightly faster than early restart, but it is limited by the same properties that limit early restart.

Designing the Memory System to Support Caches

Cache misses are satisfied from main memory, which is constructed from DRAMs. In section 7.1, we saw that DRAMs are designed with the primary emphasis on density rather than access time. Although it is difficult to reduce the latency to fetch the first word from memory, we can reduce the miss penalty if we increase the bandwidth from the memory to the cache. This reduction allows larger block sizes to be used while still maintaining a low miss penalty, similar to that for a smaller block.

To understand the impact of different organizations for memory, let's define a set of hypothetical memory access times:

- 1 clock cycle to send the address
- 15 clock cycles for each DRAM access initiated
- 1 clock cycle to send a word of data

If we have a cache block of four words and a one-word-wide bank of DRAMs, the miss penalty would be $1 + 4 \times 15 + 4 \times 1 = 65$ clock cycles. Thus the number of bytes transferred per clock cycle for a single miss would be

$$\frac{4 \times 4}{65} = 0.25$$

Figure 7.13 shows three options for designing the memory system. The first option follows what we have been assuming so far: memory is one word wide, and all accesses are made sequentially. The second option increases the bandwidth to memory by widening the memory and the buses between the processor and memory; this allows parallel access to all the words of the block.

The third option increases the bandwidth by widening the memory but not the interconnection bus. Thus we still pay a cost to transmit each word, but we can avoid paying the cost of the access latency more than once. Let's look at how much these other two options improve the 65-cycle miss penalty that we would see for the first option (Figure 7.13a).

Increasing the width of the memory and the bus will increase the memory bandwidth proportionally, decreasing both the access time and transfer time portions of the miss penalty. With a main memory width of two words, the miss penalty drops from 65 clock cycles to $1 + 2 \times 15 + 2 \times 1 = 33$ clock cycles. With a four-word-wide memory, the miss penalty is just 17 clock cycles. The bandwidth for a single miss is then 0.48 (almost twice as high) bytes per clock cycle for a memory that is two words wide, and 0.94 bytes per clock cycle when the memory is four words wide (almost four times higher). The major costs of this enhancement are the wider bus and the potential increase in cache access time due to the multiplexor and control logic between the CPU and cache.

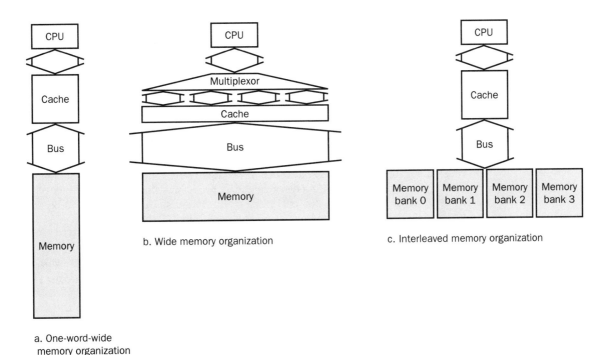

a. One-word-wide memory organization

b. Wide memory organization

c. Interleaved memory organization

FIGURE 7.13 The primary method of achieving higher memory bandwidth is to increase the physical or logical width of the memory system. In this figure, there are two ways in which the memory bandwidth is improved. The simplest design, (a), uses a memory where all components are one word wide; (b) shows a wider memory, bus, and cache; while (c) shows a narrow bus and cache with an interleaved memory. In (b), the logic between the cache and CPU consists of a multiplexor used on reads and control logic to update the appropriate words of the cache on writes.

Instead of making the entire path between the memory and cache wider, the memory chips can be organized in banks to read or write multiple words in one access time rather than reading or writing a single word each time. Each bank could be one word wide so that the width of the bus and the cache need not change, but sending an address to several banks permits them all to read simultaneously. This scheme, which is called *interleaving*, retains the advantage of incurring the full memory latency only once. For example, with four banks, the time to get a four-word block would consist of 1 cycle to transmit the address and read request to the banks, 15 cycles for all four banks to access memory, and 4 cycles to send the four words back to the cache. This yields a miss penalty of $1 + 1 \times 15 + 4 \times 1 = 20$ clock cycles. This is an effective bandwidth per miss of 0.80 bytes per clock, or about three times the bandwidth for the one-word-wide memory and bus. Banks are also valuable on writes. Each bank can write independently, quadrupling the write bandwidth and leading to fewer stalls in a write-through cache. As we will see, there is an alternative strategy for writes that makes interleaving even more attractive.

Elaboration: As capacity per memory chip increases, there are fewer chips in the same-sized memory system. Memory chips are organized to produce a small number of output bits, usually 1 to 16, with 4 and 8 being the most popular in 1997. We describe the organization of a RAM as $d \times w$, where d is the number of addressable locations (the depth) and w is the output (or width of each location). Thus, the most popular 16-Mbit DRAMs are 4M x 4. As memory chip densities grow, the width of a memory chip remains constant (or grows slowly), but the depth increases (see Appendix B for further discussion of DRAMs). Because of this, multiple banks become less attractive, because the minimum memory configuration increases. For example, a 64-MB main memory built using 4-Mbit x 1 chips can be organized into four banks, each 32 bits wide, and holding a total of 128 DRAMs. If we use 16-Mbit x 1 memory chips instead of 4-Mbit x 1 chips, our 64-MB memory can contain only one bank that is 32 bits wide, since the entire memory needs only 32 DRAMs. Of course, four banks could be constructed if we used 4-Mbit x 4 chips rather than 16-Mbit x 1 chips. Likewise, a 64-MB memory with four banks using 64-Mbit chips would require 4-Mbit x 16 DRAMs. This potential requirement for increased width in DRAM chips is the main disadvantage of interleaved memory banks. Another possibility for improving the rate at which we transfer data from the memory to the caches is to take advantage of the structure of DRAMs. DRAMs are logically organized as square arrays, and access time is divided into row access and column access. DRAMs buffer a row of bits inside the DRAM for column access. They also come with optional timing signals that allow repeated accesses to the buffer without a row-access time. One common version of this capability is called *page mode*, which has gone through a series of enhancements, the most recent called EDO (Extended Data Out) RAMs. In page mode, the buffer acts like an SRAM; by changing column address, random bits can be accessed in the buffer until the next row access. This capability changes the access time significantly, since the access time to bits in the row is much lower. For example, the total row and column access times without page mode is about 120 ns; basic page mode provides 60-ns access to data in the page, while EDO mode provides 25-ns access to data in the page. Figure 7.14 shows how the density, cost, and access time of DRAMS have changed over the years.

Year introduced	Chip size	$ per MB	Total access time to a new row/column	Column access time to existing row
1980	64 Kbit	1500	250 ns	150 ns
1983	256 Kbit	500	185 ns	100 ns
1985	1 Mbit	200	135 ns	40 ns
1989	4 Mbit	50	110 ns	40 ns
1992	16 Mbit	15	90 ns	30 ns
1996	64 Mbit	10	60 ns	20 ns

FIGURE 7.14   DRAM size increases by multiples of four approximately once every three years. The improvements in access time have been slower but continuous, and cost almost tracks density improvements, although cost is often affected by other issues, such as availability and demand. Column access time usually determines the time to perform a page mode access. DRAMs are almost always available in narrower configurations initially (e.g., 4 Mbit x 4). Wider configurations (e.g., 1 Mbit x 16) usually track availability of the narrower configuration, and they cost more. Reasons for this are that both the testing cost and package cost for the narrower configuration are slightly cheaper, the narrower configuration is usually the commodity product, and the die size of the narrower configuration is slightly smaller.

The newest development are SDRAMs (synchronous DRAMs). SDRAMs provide for a burst access to data from a series of sequential locations in the DRAM. An SDRAM is supplied with a starting address and a burst length. The data in the burst is transferred under control of a clock signal, which in 1997 can run at up to 100 MHz. The two key advantages of SDRAMs are the use of a clock that eliminates the need to synchronize and the elimination of the need to supply successive addresses in the burst. Together these advantages help lower the time between successive bits from 25 ns for an EDO RAM to 8–10 ns for an SDRAM.

The advantage of these optimizations is that they use the circuitry already largely on the DRAMs, adding little cost to the system while achieving a significant improvement in bandwidth. (The same is true of interleaving.) Furthermore, these DRAM options allow us to increase the bandwidth without incurring system disadvantages in terms of expandability and minimum memory size that are associated with wider memories or interleaving. The internal architecture of DRAMs and how these optimizations are implemented are described in section B.5 of Appendix B.

Summary

We began the previous section by examining the simplest of caches: a direct-mapped cache with a one-word block. In such a cache, both hits and misses are simple, since a word can go in exactly one location and there is a separate tag for every word. To keep the cache and memory consistent, a write-through scheme can be used, so that every write into the cache also causes memory to be updated. The alternative to write-through is a write-back scheme that copies a block back to memory when it is replaced; we'll discuss this scheme further in upcoming sections.

To take advantage of spatial locality, a cache must have a block size larger than one word. The use of a larger block decreases the miss rate and improves the efficiency of the cache by reducing the amount of tag storage relative to the amount of data storage in the cache. Although a larger block size decreases the miss rate, it can also increase the miss penalty. If the miss penalty increased linearly with the block size, larger blocks could easily lead to lower performance. To avoid this, the bandwidth of main memory is increased to transfer cache blocks more efficiently. The two common methods for doing this are making the memory wider and interleaving. In both cases, we reduce the time to fetch the block by minimizing the number of times we must start a new memory access to fetch a block, and, with a wider bus, we can also decrease the time needed to send the block from the memory to the cache.

7.3   Measuring and Improving Cache Performance

In this section, we begin by looking at how to measure and analyze cache performance; we then explore two different techniques for improving cache performance. One focuses on reducing the miss rate by reducing the probability that two different memory blocks will contend for the same cache location. The second technique reduces the miss penalty by adding an additional level to the hierarchy. This technique, called *multilevel caching*, first appeared in high-end machines selling for over $100,000 in 1990, and since then has become common on desktop computers selling for less than $3,000!

CPU time can be divided into the clock cycles that the CPU spends executing the program and the clock cycles that the CPU spends waiting for the memory system. Normally, we assume that the cost of cache accesses that are hits are part of the normal CPU execution cycles. Thus,

$$\text{CPU time} = (\text{CPU execution clock cycles} + \text{Memory-stall clock sycles}) \times \text{Clock cycle time}$$

The memory-stall clock cycles come primarily from cache misses, and we make that assumption here. We also restrict the discussion to a simplified model of the memory system. In real processors, the stalls generated by reads and writes can be quite complex, and accurate performance prediction usually requires very detailed simulations of the processor and memory system.

Memory-stall clock cycles can be defined as the sum of the stall cycles coming from reads plus those coming from writes:

$$\text{Memory-stall clock cycles } = \text{ Read-stall cycles } + \text{ Write-stall cycles}$$

The read-stall cycles can each be defined in terms of the number of read accesses per program, the miss penalty in clock cycles for a read, and the read miss rate:

$$\text{Read-stall cycles } = \frac{\text{Reads}}{\text{Program}} \times \text{Read miss rate} \times \text{Read miss penalty}$$

Writes are more complicated. For a write-through scheme, we have two sources of stalls: write misses, which usually require that we fetch the block before continuing the write (see the elaboration on page 607 for more details on dealing with writes), and write buffer stalls, which occur when the write buffer is full when a write occurs. Thus, the cycles stalled for writes equals the sum of these two:

$$\text{Write-stall cycles} = \left(\frac{\text{Writes}}{\text{Program}} \times \text{Write miss rate} \times \text{Write miss penalty} \right) + \text{Write buffer stalls}$$

Because the write buffer stalls depend on the timing of writes, and not just the frequency, it is not possible to give a simple equation to compute such stalls. Fortunately, in systems with a reasonable write buffer depth (e.g., four or more words) and a memory capable of accepting writes at a rate that significantly exceeds the average write frequency in programs (e.g., by a factor of two), the write buffer stalls will be small, and we can safely ignore them. If a system did not meet these criteria, it would not be well designed; instead the designer should have used either a deeper write buffer or a write-back organization.

Write-back schemes also have potential additional stalls arising from the need to write a cache block back to memory when the block is replaced. We will discuss this more in section 7.5.

In most write-through cache organizations, the read and write miss penalties are the same (the time to fetch the block from memory). If we assume that the write buffer stalls are negligible, we can combine the reads and writes by using a single miss rate and the miss penalty:

$$\text{Memory-stall clock cycles} = \frac{\text{Memory accesses}}{\text{Program}} \times \text{Miss rate} \times \text{Miss penalty}$$

We can also write this as

$$\text{Memory-stall clock cycles} = \frac{\text{Instructions}}{\text{Program}} \times \frac{\text{Misses}}{\text{Instruction}} \times \text{Miss penalty}$$

Let's consider a simple example to help us understand the impact of cache performance on machine performance.

Calculating Cache Performance

Example

Assume an instruction cache miss rate for gcc of 2% and a data cache miss rate of 4%. If a machine has a CPI of 2 without any memory stalls and the miss penalty is 40 cycles for all misses, determine how much faster a machine would run with a perfect cache that never missed. Use the instruction frequencies for gcc from Chapter 4, Figure 4.54, on page 311.

Answer   The number of memory miss cycles for instructions in terms of the Instruction count (I) is

$$\text{Instruction miss cycles} = I \times 2\% \times 40 = 0.80 \times I$$

The frequency of all loads and stores in gcc is 36%. Therefore, we can find the number of memory miss cycles for data references:

$$\text{Data miss cycles} = I \times 36\% \times 4\% \times 40 = 0.56 \times I$$

The total number of memory-stall cycles is 0.80 I + 0.56 I = 1.36 I. This is more than 1 cycle of memory stall per instruction. Accordingly, the CPI with memory stalls is 2 + 1.36 = 3.36. Since there is no change in instruction count or clock rate, the ratio of the CPU execution times is

$$\frac{\text{CPU time with stalls}}{\text{CPU time with perfect cache}} = \frac{I \times \text{CPI}_{stall} \times \text{Clock cycle}}{I \times \text{CPI}_{perfect} \times \text{Clock cycle}}$$

$$= \frac{\text{CPI}_{stall}}{\text{CPI}_{perfect}} = \frac{3.36}{2}$$

The performance with the perfect cache is better by $\frac{3.36}{2} = 1.68$.

What happens if the processor is made faster, but the memory system stays the same? The amount of time spent on memory stalls will take up an increasing fraction of the execution time; Amdahl's law, which we examined in Chapter 2, reminds us of this fact. A few simple examples show how serious this problem can be. Suppose we speed up the machine in the previous example by reducing its CPI from 2 to 1 without changing the clock rate, which might be done with an improved pipeline. The system with cache misses would then have a CPI of 1 + 1.36 = 2.36, and the system with the perfect cache would be

$$\frac{2.36}{1} = 2.36 \text{ times faster}$$

The amount of execution time spent on memory stalls would have risen from

$$\frac{1.36}{3.36} = 41\%$$

to

$$\frac{1.36}{2.36} = 58\%$$

Similarly, increasing the clock rate without changing the memory system also increases the performance lost due to cache misses, as the next example shows.

Cache Performance with Increased Clock Rate

Example

Suppose we increase the performance of the machine in the previous example by doubling its clock rate. Since the main memory speed is unlikely to change, assume that the absolute time to handle a cache miss does not change. How much faster will the machine be with the faster clock, assuming the same miss rate as the previous example?

Answer

Measured in the faster clock cycles, the new miss penalty will be twice as long, or 80 clock cycles. Hence:

Total miss cycles per instruction $= (2\% \times 80) + 36\% \times (4\% \times 80) = 2.75$

Thus the faster machine with cache misses will have a CPI of $2 + 2.75 = 4.75$, compared to a CPI with cache misses of 3.36 for the slower machine.

Using the formula for CPU time from the previous example, we can compute the relative performance as

$$\frac{\text{Performance with fast clock}}{\text{Performance with slow clock}} = \frac{\text{Execution time with slow clock}}{\text{Execution time with fast clock}}$$

$$= \frac{IC \times CPI \times \text{Clock cycle}}{IC \times CPI \times \dfrac{\text{Clock cycle}}{2}}$$

$$= \frac{3.36}{4.75 \times \frac{1}{2}} = 1.41$$

Thus the machine with the faster clock is about 1.4 times faster rather than 2 times faster, which it would have been without the increased effect of cache misses.

As these examples illustrate, relative cache penalties increase as a machine becomes faster. Furthermore, if a machine improves both clock rate and CPI, it suffers a double hit:

1. The lower the CPI, the more pronounced the impact of stall cycles.

2. The main memory system is unlikely to improve as fast as processor cycle time. When calculating CPI, the cache miss penalty is measured in CPU clock cycles needed for a miss. Therefore, if the main memories of two machines have the same absolute access times, a higher CPU clock rate leads to a larger miss penalty.

Thus the importance of cache performance for CPUs with low CPI and high clock rates is greater, and consequently the danger of neglecting cache behavior in assessing the performance of such machines is greater. As we will see in section 7.6, the use of fast, pipelined processors in desktop PCs and workstations has led to the use of sophisticated cache systems even in computers selling for a few thousand dollars.

The previous examples and equations assume that the hit time is not a factor in determining cache performance. Clearly, if the hit time increases, the total time to access a word from the memory system will increase, possibly causing an increase in the processor cycle time. Although we will see additional examples of what can increase hit time shortly, one example is increasing the cache size. A larger cache could clearly have a longer access time, just as if your desk in the library was very large (say, 3 square meters), it would take longer to locate a book on the desk. At some point, the increase in hit time for a larger cache could dominate the improvement in hit rate, leading to a decrease in processor performance.

The next subsection discusses alternative cache organizations that decrease miss rate but may sometimes increase hit time; additional examples appear in the Fallacies and Pitfalls (section 7.7).

Reducing Cache Misses by More Flexible Placement of Blocks

So far, when we place a block in the cache, we have used a simple placement scheme: A block can go in exactly one place in the cache. This placement scheme is called *direct mapped* because there is a direct mapping from any block address in memory to a single location in the upper level of the hierarchy. There are actually a whole range of schemes for placing blocks. At one extreme is direct mapped, where a block can be placed in exactly one location.

At the other extreme is a scheme where a block can be placed in *any* location in the cache. Such a scheme is called *fully associative* because a block in memory may be associated with any entry in the cache. To find a given block in a fully associative cache, all the entries in the cache must be searched because a block can be placed in any one. To make the search practical, it is done in parallel with a comparator associated with each cache entry. These comparators significantly increase the hardware cost, effectively making fully associative placement practical only for caches with small numbers of blocks.

The middle range of designs between direct mapped and fully associative is called *set associative*. In a set-associative cache, there are a fixed number of locations (at least two) where each block can be placed; a set-associative cache with *n* locations for a block is called an *n*-way set-associative cache. An *n*-way set-associative cache consists of a number of sets, each of which consists of *n* blocks. Each block in the memory maps to a unique *set* in the cache given by the index field, and a block can be placed in *any* element of that set. Thus a set-associative placement combines direct-mapped placement and fully associative placement: a block is directly mapped into a set, and then all the blocks in the set are searched for a match.

Remember that in a direct-mapped cache, the position of a memory block is given by

(Block number) modulo (Number of cache blocks)

In a set-associative cache, the set containing a memory block is given by

(Block number) modulo (Number of sets in the cache)

Since the block may be placed in any element of the set, *all the elements of the set* must be searched. In a fully associative cache, the block can go anywhere and *all the blocks in the cache* must be searched. For example, Figure 7.15 shows where block 12 can be placed in a cache with eight blocks total, according to the block placement policy for direct-mapped, two-way set-associative, and fully associative caches.

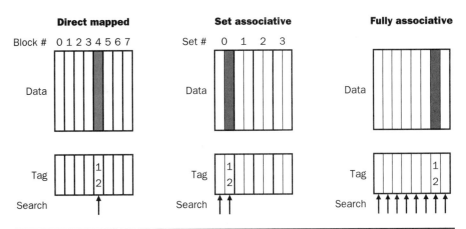

FIGURE 7.15   The location of a memory block whose address is 12 in a cache with eight blocks varies for direct-mapped, set-associative, and fully associative placement. In direct-mapped placement, there is only one cache block where memory block 12 can be found, and that block is given by (12 modulo 8) = 4. In a two-way set-associative cache, there would be four sets, and memory block 12 must be in set (12 mod 4) = 0; the memory block could be in either element of the set. In a fully associative placement, the memory block for block address 12 can appear in any of the eight cache blocks.

We can think of every block placement strategy as a variation on set associativity. A direct-mapped cache is simply a one-way set-associative cache: each cache entry holds one block and forms a set with one element. A fully associative cache with m entries is simply an m-way set-associative cache; it has one set with m blocks, and an entry can reside in any block within that set. Figure 7.16 shows the possible associativity structures for an eight-block cache.

The advantage of increasing the degree of associativity is that it usually decreases the miss rate, as the next example shows. The main disadvantage, which we discuss in more detail shortly, is an increase in the hit time.

One-way set associative (direct mapped)

Block	Tag	Data
0		
1		
2		
3		
4		
5		
6		
7		

Two-way set associative

Set	Tag	Data	Tag	Data
0				
1				
2				
3				

Four-way set associative

Set	Tag	Data	Tag	Data	Tag	Data	Tag	Data
0								
1								

Eight-way set associative (fully associative)

Tag	Data	Tag	Data	Tag	Data	Tag	Data	Tag	Data	Tag	Data	Tag	Data	Tag	Data

FIGURE 7.16 An eight-block cache configured as direct mapped, two-way set associative, four-way set associative, and fully associative. The total size of the cache in blocks is equal to the number of sets times the associativity. Thus, for a fixed cache size, increasing the associativity decreases the number of sets, while increasing the number of elements per set. With eight blocks, an eight-way set-associative cache is the same as a fully associative cache.

Associativity in Caches

Example

There are three small caches, each consisting of four one-word blocks. One cache is fully associative, a second is two-way set associative, and the third is direct mapped. Find the number of misses for each cache organization given the following sequence of block addresses: 0, 8, 0, 6, 8.

Answer

The direct-mapped case is easiest. First, let's determine to which cache block each block address maps:

Block address	Cache block
0	(0 modulo 4) = 0
6	(6 modulo 4) = 2
8	(8 modulo 4) = 0

Now we can fill in the cache contents after each reference, using a blank entry to mean that the block is invalid and a colored entry to show a new entry added to the cache for the associate reference:

Address of memory block accessed	Hit or miss	Contents of cache blocks after reference			
		0	1	2	3
0	miss	Memory[0]			
8	miss	Memory[8]			
0	miss	Memory[0]			
6	miss	Memory[0]		Memory[6]	
8	miss	Memory[8]		Memory[6]	

The direct-mapped cache generates five misses.

The set-associative cache has two sets (with indices 0 and 1) with two elements per set. Let's first determine to which set each block address maps:

Block address	Cache set
0	(0 modulo 2) = 0
6	(6 modulo 2) = 0
8	(8 modulo 2) = 0

Because we have a choice of which entry in a set to replace on a miss, we need a replacement rule. Set-associative caches usually replace the least recently used block within a set; that is, the block that was used furthest in the past is replaced. (We will discuss replacement rules in more detail shortly.) Using this replacement rule, the contents of the set-associative cache after each reference looks like this:

Address of memory block accessed	Hit or miss	Contents of cache blocks after reference			
		Set 0	Set 0	Set 1	Set 1
0	miss	Memory[0]			
8	miss	Memory[0]	Memory[8]		
0	hit	Memory[0]	Memory[8]		
6	miss	Memory[0]	Memory[6]		
8	miss	Memory[8]	Memory[6]		

Notice that when block 6 is referenced, it replaces block 8, since block 8 has been less recently referenced than block 0. The two-way set-associative cache has a total of four misses, one less than the direct-mapped cache.

The fully associative cache has four cache blocks (in a single set); any memory block can be stored in any cache block. The fully associative cache has the best performance, with only three misses:

Address of memory block accessed	Hit or miss	Contents of cache blocks after reference			
		Block 0	Block 1	Block 2	Block 3
0	miss	Memory[0]			
8	miss	Memory[0]	Memory[8]		
0	hit	Memory[0]	Memory[8]		
6	miss	Memory[0]	Memory[8]	Memory[6]	
8	hit	Memory[0]	Memory[8]	Memory[6]	

For this series of references, three misses is the best we can do because three unique block addresses are accessed. Notice that if we had eight blocks in the cache, there would be no replacements in the two-way set-associative cache (check this for yourself), and it would have the same number of misses as the fully associative cache. Similarly, if we had 16 blocks, all three caches would have the same number of misses. This change in miss rate shows us that cache size and associativity are not independent in determining cache performance.

How much of a reduction in the miss rate is achieved by associativity? Figure 7.17 shows the improvement for the programs gcc and spice with a pair of 64-KB caches (split instruction and data) with a four-word block, and associativity ranging from direct mapped to four-way. On gcc, going from one-way to two-way associativity improves the effective combined miss rate by about 20%, but there is no further improvement in going to four-way associativity. The low miss rates for spice leave little opportunity for improvement by increasing associativity.

Locating a Block in the Cache

Now, let's consider the task of finding a block in a cache that is set associative. Just as in a direct-mapped cache, each block in a set-associative cache includes an address tag that gives the block address. The tag of every cache block within the appropriate set is checked to see if it matches the block address from the CPU. Figure 7.18 shows how the address is decomposed. The index value is used to select the set containing the address of interest, and the tags of all the blocks in the set must be searched. Because speed is of the essence, all the tags in the selected set are searched in parallel. As in a fully associative cache, a serial search would make the hit time of a set-associative cache too slow.

If the total size is kept the same, increasing the associativity increases the number of blocks per set, which is the number of simultaneous compares needed to perform the search in parallel: each increase by a factor of two in associativity doubles the number of blocks per set and halves the number of sets. Accordingly, each factor-of-two increase in associativity decreases the size of

Program	Associativity	Instruction miss rate	Data miss rate	Effective combined miss rate
gcc	1	2.0%	1.7%	1.9%
gcc	2	1.6%	1.4%	1.5%
gcc	4	1.6%	1.4%	1.5%
spice	1	0.3%	0.6%	0.4%
spice	2	0.3%	0.6%	0.4%
spice	4	0.3%	0.6%	0.4%

FIGURE 7.17 The miss rates for gcc and spice with a cache like that in the DECStation 3100 but with a block size of four words and associativity varying from one-way to four-way.

Tag	Index	Block Offset

FIGURE 7.18 The three portions of an address in a set-associative or direct-mapped cache. The index is used to select the set, then the tag is used to choose the block by comparison with the blocks in the selected set. The block offset is the address of the desired data within the block.

the index by 1 bit and increases the size of the tag by 1 bit. In a fully associative cache, there is effectively only one set, and all the blocks must be checked in parallel. Thus there is no index, and the entire address, excluding the block off-set, is compared against the tag of every block. In other words, we search the entire cache without any indexing.

In a direct-mapped cache, such as that shown in Figure 7.7 on page 549, only a single comparator is needed, because the entry can be in only one block, and we access the cache simply by indexing. In a four-way set-associative cache, shown in Figure 7.19, four comparators are needed, together with a 4-to-1

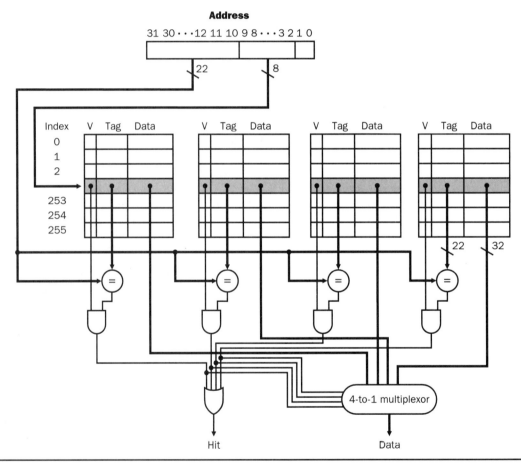

FIGURE 7.19   The implementation of a four-way set-associative cache requires four comparators and a 4-to-1 multiplexor. The comparators determine which element of the selected set (if any) matches the tag. The output of the comparators is used to select the data from one of the four blocks of the indexed set, using a multiplexor with a decoded select signal. In some implementations, the Output enable signals on the data portions of the cache RAMs can be used to select the entry in the set that drives the output. The Output enable signal comes from the comparators, causing the element that matches to drive the data outputs. This organization eliminates the need for the multiplexor.

multiplexor to choose among the four potential members of the selected set. The cache access consists of indexing the appropriate set and then searching the elements of the set. The costs of an associative cache are the extra comparators and any delay imposed by having to do the compare and select from among the elements of the set.

Example

Size of Tags versus Set Associativity

Increasing associativity requires more comparators, as well as more tag bits per cache block. Assuming a cache of 4K blocks and a 32-bit address, find the total number of sets and the total number of tag bits for caches that are direct mapped, two-way and four-way set associative, and fully associative.

Answer

The direct-mapped cache has the same number of sets as blocks, and hence 12 bits of index, since $\log_2(4K) = 12$; hence the total number of tag bits is $(32 - 12) \times 4K = 80$ Kbits.

Each degree of associativity decreases the number of sets by a factor of two and thus decreases the number of bits used to index the cache by one and increases the number of bits in the tag by one. Thus, for a two-way set-associative cache, there are 2K sets, and the total number of tag bits is $(32 - 11) \times 2 \times 2K = 84$ Kbits. For a four-way set-associative cache, the total number of sets is 1K, and the total number of tag bits is $(32 - 10) \times 4 \times 1K = 88$ Kbits.

For a fully associative cache, there is only one set with 4K blocks, and the tag is 32 bits, leading to a total of $32 \times 4K \times 1 = 128K$ tag bits.

The choice among direct-mapped, set-associative, or fully associative mapping in any memory hierarchy will depend on the cost of a miss versus the cost of implementing associativity, both in time and in extra hardware.

Choosing Which Block to Replace

When a miss occurs in a direct-mapped cache, the requested block can go in exactly one position, and the block occupying that position must be replaced. In an associative cache, we have a choice of where to place the requested block, and hence a choice of which block to replace. In a fully associative cache, all blocks are candidates for replacement. In a set-associative cache, we must choose among the blocks in the selected set.

The most commonly used scheme is *least recently used (LRU)*, which we used in the previous example. In an LRU scheme the block replaced is the one that has been unused for the longest time. LRU replacement is implemented by keeping track of when each element in a set was used relative to the other elements in the set. For a two-way set-associative cache, tracking when the two elements were used can be implemented by keeping a single bit in each set and setting the bit to indicate an element whenever that element is referenced. As associativity increases, implementing LRU gets harder; in section 7.5, we will see an alternative scheme for replacement.

Reducing the Miss Penalty Using Multilevel Caches

All modern computers make use of caches. In most cases, these caches are implemented on the same die as the microprocessor that forms the CPU. To further close the gap between the fast clock rates of modern processors and the relatively long time required to access DRAMs, high-performance microprocessors support an additional level of caching. This second-level cache, which often is off-chip in a separate set of SRAMs, is accessed whenever a miss occurs in the primary cache. If the second-level cache contains the desired data, the miss penalty will be the access time of the second-level cache, which will be much less than the access time of main memory. If neither the primary nor secondary cache contains the data, a main memory access is required, and a larger miss penalty is incurred.

How significant is the performance improvement from the use of a secondary cache? The next example shows us.

Performance of Multilevel Caches

Example

Suppose we have a processor with a base CPI of 1.0, assuming all references hit in the primary cache, and a clock rate of 500 MHz. Assume a main memory access time of 200 ns, including all the miss handling. Suppose the miss rate per instruction at the primary cache is 5%. How much faster will the machine be if we add a secondary cache that has a 20-ns access time for either a hit or a miss and is large enough to reduce the miss rate to main memory to 2%?

Answer

The miss penalty to main memory is

$$\frac{200 \text{ ns}}{2\dfrac{\text{ns}}{\text{clock cycle}}} = 100 \text{ clock cycles}$$

The effective CPI with one level of caching is given by

Total CPI = Base CPI + Memory-stall cycles per instruction

For the machine with one level of caching,

Total CPI = 1.0 + Memory-stall cycles per instruction = 1.0 + 5% × 100 = 6.0

With two levels of cache, a miss in the primary (or first-level) cache can either be satisfied in the secondary cache or in main memory. The miss penalty for an access to the second-level cache is

$$\frac{20 \text{ ns}}{2\dfrac{\text{ns}}{\text{clock cycle}}} = 10 \text{ clock cycles}$$

If the miss is satisfied in the secondary cache, then this is the entire miss penalty. If the miss needs to go to main memory, then the total miss penalty is the sum of the secondary cache access time and the main memory access time.

Thus, for a two-level cache, total CPI is the sum of the stall cycles from both levels of cache and the base CPI:

Total CPI = 1 + Primary stalls per instruction
+ Secondary stalls per instruction
= 1 + 5% × 2% × 100 = 3.5

Thus the machine with the secondary cache is faster by

$$\frac{6.0}{3.5} = 1.7$$

Alternatively, we could have computed the stall cycles by summing the stall cycles of those references that hit in the secondary cache ((5% – 2%) × 10 = 0.3) and those references that go to main memory, which must include the cost to access the secondary cache as well as the main memory access time (2% × (10 + 100) = 2.2).

The design considerations for a primary and secondary cache are significantly different because the presence of the other cache changes the optimal choice versus a single-level cache. In particular, a two-level cache structure allows the primary cache to focus on minimizing hit time to yield a shorter clock cycle, while allowing the secondary cache to focus on miss rate to reduce the penalty of long memory access times.

The interaction of the two caches permits such a focus. The miss penalty of the primary cache is significantly reduced by the presence of the secondary cache, allowing the primary to be smaller and have a higher miss rate. For the secondary cache, access time becomes less important with the presence of the primary cache, since the access time of the secondary cache affects the miss penalty of the primary cache, rather than directly affecting the primary cache hit time or the CPU cycle time.

The effect of these changes on the two caches can be seen by comparing each cache to the optimal design for a single level of cache. In comparison to a single-level cache, the primary cache of a multilevel cache is often smaller. Furthermore, the primary cache often uses a smaller block size, to go with the smaller cache size and reduced miss penalty. In comparison, the secondary cache will often be larger than in a single-level cache, since the access time of the secondary cache is less critical. With a larger total size, the secondary cache often will use a larger block size than appropriate with a single-level cache.

Elaboration: There are a number of complications that arise when multilevel caches are used. One of these is that there are now several different types of misses and corresponding miss rates. In the example above, we saw the primary cache miss rate and the *global miss rate*, that is, the fraction of references that missed in all levels. There is also a miss rate for the secondary cache that is given by the ratio of all misses in the secondary cache divided by the number of accesses. This miss rate is called the *local miss rate* of the secondary cache. Because the primary cache filters accesses, especially those with good spatial and temporal locality, the local miss rate of the secondary cache is much higher than the global miss rate. For the example above, we can compute the local miss rate of the secondary cache as: 2%/5% = 40%! Luckily, it is the combined miss rate that dictates how often we must access the main memory! Additional complications arise because the caches will likely have different block sizes to match the larger or smaller total size. Likewise, the associativity of the cache may change. On-chip primary caches are often built with associativity of two to four, while off-chip caches rarely have associativity of greater than two. These changes in block size and associativity introduce complications in the modeling of the caches, which typically means that both levels need to be simulated together to understand the behavior.

Summary

In this section, we focused on three topics: cache performance, using associativity to reduce miss rates, and the use of multilevel cache hierarchies to reduce miss penalties.

Since the total number of cycles spent on a program is the sum of the processor cycles and the memory-stall cycles, the memory system can have a significant effect on program execution time. In fact, as processors get faster (either by lowering CPI or by increasing the clock rate), the relative effect of the memory-stall cycles increases, making a good memory system critical to achieving high performance. The number of memory-stall cycles depends on both the miss rate and the miss penalty. The challenge, as we will see in section 7.5, is to reduce one of these factors without significantly affecting other critical factors in the memory hierarchy.

To reduce the miss rate, we examined the use of associative placement schemes. Such schemes can reduce the miss rate of a cache by allowing more flexible placement of blocks within the cache. Fully associative schemes allow blocks to be placed anywhere, but also require that every block in the cache be searched to satisfy a request. This search is usually implemented by having a comparator per cache block and searching the entries in parallel. The cost of the comparators makes large fully associative caches impractical. Set-associative caches are a practical alternative, since we need only search among the elements of a unique set that is chosen by indexing. Set-associative caches yield an improvement in hit rate but are slightly slower to access, because of the cost of the comparisons and the selection from among the elements of a set. Whether a direct-mapped cache or a set-associative cache yields better performance depends on both the technology and the details of the implementation.

Finally, we looked at multilevel caches as a technique to reduce the miss penalty by allowing a larger secondary cache to handle misses to the primary cache. Second-level caches have become commonplace as designers find that limited silicon and the goals of high clock rates prevent primary caches from becoming large. The secondary cache, which is often 10 or more times larger than the primary cache, catches many accesses that miss in the primary cache. In such cases, the miss penalty is that of the access time to the secondary cache (typically < 10 cycles) versus the access time to memory (typically > 40 cycles). As with associativity, the design trade-offs between size of the secondary cache and its access time depend on a number of aspects of the implementation.

7.4 Virtual Memory

. . . a system has been devised to make the core drum combination appear to the programmer as a single level store, the requisite transfers taking place automatically.

Kilburn et al., "One-level storage systems," 1962

In the previous section, we saw how caches served as a method for providing fast access to recently used portions of a program's code and data. Similarly, the main memory can act as a "cache" for the secondary storage, usually implemented with magnetic disks. This technique is called *virtual memory*. There are two major motivations for virtual memory: to allow efficient and safe sharing of memory among multiple programs and to remove the programming burdens of a small, limited amount of main memory.

Consider a collection of programs running at once on a machine. The total memory required by all the programs may be much larger than the amount of main memory available on the machine, but only a fraction of this memory is actively being used at any point in time. Main memory need contain only the active portions of the many programs, just as a cache contains only the active portion of one program. This allows us to efficiently share the processor as well as the main memory. Of course, to allow multiple programs to share the same memory, we must be able to protect the programs from each other, ensuring that a program can only read and write the portions of main memory that have been assigned to it.

We cannot know which programs will share the memory with other programs when we compile them. In fact, the programs sharing the memory change dynamically while the programs are running. Because of this dynamic interaction, we would like to compile each program into its own *address space*, that is, a separate range of memory locations accessible only to this program. Virtual memory implements the translation of a program's address space to physical addresses. This translation process enforces protection of a program's address space from other programs.

A second motivation for virtual memory is to allow a single user program to exceed the size of primary memory. Formerly, if a program became too large for memory, it was up to the programmer to make it fit. Programmers divided programs into pieces and then identified the pieces that were mutually exclusive. These *overlays* were loaded or unloaded under user program control during execution, with the programmer ensuring that the program never tried to access an overlay that was not loaded and that the overlays loaded never exceeded the total size of the memory. Overlays were traditionally organized as modules, each containing both code and data. Calls between procedures in different modules would lead to overlaying of one module with another.

As you can well imagine, this responsibility was a substantial burden on programmers. Virtual memory, which was invented to relieve programmers of this difficulty, automatically manages the two levels of the memory hierarchy represented by main memory (sometimes called *physical memory* to distinguish it from virtual memory) and secondary storage.

Although the concepts at work in virtual memory and in caches are the same, their differing historical roots have led to the use of different terminology. A virtual memory block is called a *page*, and a virtual memory miss is called a *page fault*. With virtual memory, the CPU produces a *virtual address*, which is translated by a combination of hardware and software to a *physical address*, which in turn can be used to access main memory. Figure 7.20 shows the virtual addressed memory with pages mapped to main memory. This process is called *memory mapping* or *address translation*. Today, the two memory hierarchy levels controlled by virtual memory are DRAMs and magnetic disks (see Chapter 1, pages 19–20). If we return to our library analogy, we can think of a virtual address as the title of a book and a physical address as the location of that book in the library, such as might be given by the Library of Congress call number.

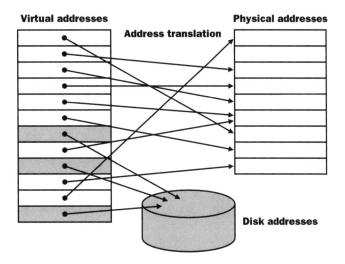

FIGURE 7.20 In virtual memory, blocks of memory (called pages) are mapped from one set of addresses (called virtual addresses) to another set (called physical addresses). The processor generates virtual addresses while the memory is accessed using physical addresses. Both the virtual memory and the physical memory are broken into pages, so that a virtual page is really mapped to a physical page. Of course, it is also possible for a virtual page to be absent from main memory and not be mapped to a physical address, residing instead on disk. Physical pages can be shared by having two virtual addresses point to the same physical address. This capability is used to allow two different programs to share data or code.

Virtual memory also simplifies loading the program for execution by providing *relocation*. Relocation maps the virtual addresses used by a program to different physical addresses before the addresses are used to access memory. This relocation allows us to load the program into any location in main memory. Furthermore, all virtual memory systems in use today relocate the program as a set of fixed-size blocks (pages), thereby eliminating the need to find a contiguous block of memory to allocate to a program; instead, the operating system need only find a sufficient number of pages in main memory. Formerly, relocation problems required special hardware and special support in the operating system; today, virtual memory also provides this function.

In virtual memory, the address is broken into a *virtual page number* and a *page offset*. Figure 7.21 shows the translation of the virtual page number to a *physical page number*. The physical page number constitutes the upper portion of the physical address, while the page offset, which is not changed, constitutes the lower portion. The number of bits in the page offset field determines the page size. The number of pages addressable with the virtual address need not match the number of pages addressable with the physical address. Having a larger number of virtual pages than physical pages is the basis for the illusion of an essentially unbounded amount of virtual memory.

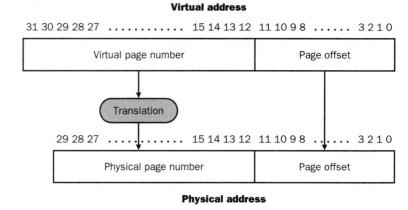

FIGURE 7.21   Mapping from a virtual to a physical address. The page size is 2^{12} = 4 KB. The number of physical pages allowed in memory is 2^{18}, since the physical page number has 18 bits in it. This means that main memory can have at most 1 GB, while the virtual address space is 4 GB.

Many design choices in virtual memory systems are motivated by the high cost of a miss, which in virtual memory is traditionally called a *page fault*. A page fault will take millions of cycles to process. (The table on page 541 shows the relative speeds of main memory and disk.) This enormous miss penalty, dominated by the time to get the first word for typical page sizes, leads to several key decisions in designing virtual memory systems:

- Pages should be large enough to amortize the high access time. Sizes from 4 KB to 16 KB are typical today, with new systems being developed to support 32-KB and 64-KB pages, and 4-KB pages are being phased out.

- Organizations that reduce the page fault rate are attractive. The primary technique used here is to allow fully associative placement of pages.

- Page faults can be handled in software because the overhead will be small compared to the access time to disk. Furthermore, software can afford to use clever algorithms for choosing how to place pages because even small reductions in the miss rate will pay for the cost of such algorithms.

- Using write-through to manage writes in virtual memory will not work, since writes take too long. Instead, virtual memory systems use write-back.

The next few sections address these factors in virtual memory design.

Elaboration: The discussion of virtual memory in this book focuses on paging, which uses fixed-size blocks. There is also a variable-size block scheme called *segmentation*. In segmentation, an address consists of two parts: a segment number and a segment offset. The segment register is mapped to a physical address, and the offset is *added* to find the actual physical address. Because the segment can vary in size, a bounds check is also needed to make sure that the offset is within the segment. The major use of segmentation is to support more powerful methods of protection and sharing in an address space. Most operating system textbooks contain extensive discussions of segmentation compared to paging and of the use of segmentation to logically share the address space. The major disadvantage of segmentation is that it splits the address space into logically separate pieces that must be manipulated as a two-part address: the segment number and the offset. Paging, in contrast, makes the boundary between page number and offset invisible to programmers and compilers.

Segments have also been used as a method to extend the address space without changing the word size of the machine. Such attempts have been unsuccessful because of the awkwardness and performance penalties inherent in a two-part address of which programmers and compilers must be aware.

Many architectures divide the address space into large fixed-size blocks that simplify protection between the operating system and user programs and increase the efficiency of implementing paging. Although these divisions are often called "segments," this mechanism is much simpler than variable block size segmentation and is not visible to user programs; we discuss it in more detail shortly.

Placing a Page and Finding It Again

Because of the incredibly high penalty for a page fault, designers would like to reduce the number of page faults by optimizing the page placement. If we allow a virtual page to be mapped to any physical page, the operating system can then choose to replace any page it wants when a page fault occurs. For example, the operating system can use a sophisticated algorithm and complex data structures, which track page usage, to try to choose a page that will not be needed for a long time. The ability to use a clever and flexible replacement scheme is actually the primary motivation for using fully associative placement of pages. Of course, fully associative placement also reduces the page fault rate.

As we mentioned earlier, the difficulty in using fully associative placement is in locating an entry, since it can be anywhere in the upper level of the hierarchy. A full search is impractical. In virtual memory, we locate pages by using a full table that indexes the memory; this structure is called a *page table*. A page table, which resides in memory, is indexed with the page number from the virtual address and contains the corresponding physical page number. Each program has its own page table, which maps the virtual address space of that program to main memory. In our library analogy, the page table corresponds to a mapping between book titles and library locations. Just as the card catalog may contain entries for books in another library on campus rather than the local branch library, we will see that the page table may contain entries for pages not present in memory. To indicate the location of the page table in memory, the hardware includes a register that points to the start of the page table; we call this the *page table register*. Assume for now that the page table is in a fixed and contiguous area of memory.

Figure 7.22 uses the page table register, the virtual address, and the indicated page table to show how the hardware can form a physical address. A valid bit is used in each page table entry, just as we did in a cache. If the bit is off, the

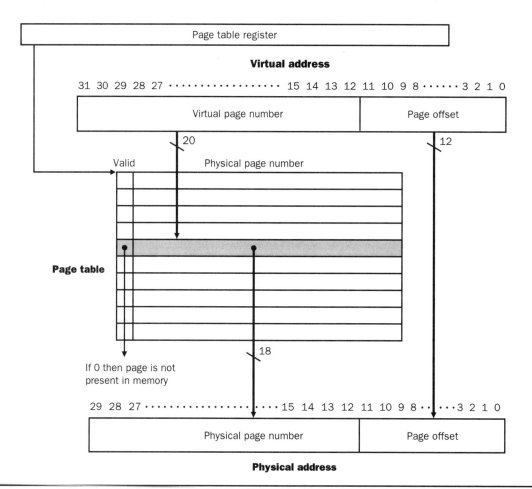

FIGURE 7.22   The page table is indexed with the virtual page number to obtain the corresponding portion of the physical address. The starting address of the page table is given by the page table pointer. In this figure, the page size is 2^{12} bytes, or 4 KB. The virtual address space is 2^{32} bytes, or 4 gigabytes, and the physical address space is 2^{30} bytes, which allows main memory of up to 1 gigabyte. The number of entries in the page table is then 2^{20}, or 1 million entries. The valid bit for each entry indicates whether the mapping is legal. If it is off, then the page is not present in memory. Although the page table entry shown here need only be 19 bits wide, it would typically be rounded up to 32 bits for ease of indexing. The extra bits would be used to store additional information that needs to be kept on a per page basis, such as protection.

page is not present in main memory and a page fault occurs. If the bit is on, the page is valid and the entry contains the physical page number.

Because the page table contains a mapping for every possible virtual page, no tags are required. In cache terminology, the index, which is used to access the page table, consists of the full block address, which is the virtual page number.

Hardware Software Interface

The page table, together with the program counter and the registers, specifies the state of a program. If we want to allow another program to use the CPU, we must save this state. Later, after restoring this state, the program can continue execution. We often refer to this state as a *process*. The process is considered *active* when it is in possession of the CPU; otherwise, it is considered *inactive*. The operating system can make a process active by loading the process's state, including the program counter, which will initiate execution at the value of the saved program counter.

The process's address space, and hence all the data it can access in memory, is defined by its page table, which resides in memory. Rather than save the entire page table, the operating system simply loads the page table register to point to the page table of the process it wants to make active. Each process has its own page table, since different processes use the same virtual addresses. The operating system is responsible for allocating the physical memory and updating the page tables, so that the virtual address spaces of different processes do not collide. As we will see shortly, the use of separate page tables also provides protection of one process from another.

Page Faults

If the valid bit for a virtual page is off, a page fault occurs. The operating system must be given control. This transfer is done with the exception mechanism, the details of which we discuss later in this section. Once the operating system gets control, it must find the page in the next level of the hierarchy (usually magnetic disk) and decide where to place the requested page in main memory.

The virtual address alone does not immediately tell us where the page is on disk. Returning to our library analogy, we cannot find the location of a library book on the shelves just by knowing its title. Instead, we go to the catalog and look up the book, obtaining an address for the location on the shelves, such as the Library of Congress call number. Likewise, in a virtual memory system, we must keep track of the location on disk of each page in the virtual address space.

Because we do not know ahead of time when a page in memory will be chosen to be replaced, the operating system usually creates the space on disk for all the pages of a process when it creates the process. At that time, it also creates a data structure to record where each virtual page is stored on disk. This data structure may be part of the page table or may be an auxiliary data structure indexed in the same way as the page table. Figure 7.23 shows the organization when a single table holds either the physical page number or the disk address.

The operating system also creates a data structure that tracks which processes and which virtual addresses use each physical page. When a page fault occurs, if all the pages in main memory are in use, the operating system must choose a page to replace. Because we want to minimize the number of page faults, most operating systems try to choose a page that they hypothesize will not be needed in the near future. Using the past to predict the future,

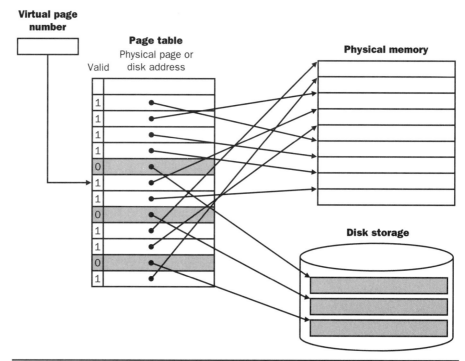

FIGURE 7.23   The page table maps each page in virtual memory to either a page in main memory or a page stored on disk, which is the next level in the hierarchy. The virtual page number is used to index the page table. If the valid bit is on, the page table supplies the physical page number (i.e., the starting address of the page in memory) corresponding to the virtual page. If the valid bit is off, the page currently resides only on disk, at a specified disk address. In many systems, the table of physical page addresses and disk page addresses, while logically one table, is stored in two separate data structures. Dual tables are justified in part because we must keep the disk addresses of all the pages, even if they are currently in main memory. Remember that the pages in main memory and the pages on disk are identical in size.

operating systems follow the least recently used (LRU) replacement scheme, which we mentioned earlier. The operating system searches for the least recently used page, making the assumption that a page that has not been used in a long time is less likely to be needed than a more recently accessed page.

For example, suppose the most recent page references (in order) were 10, 12, 9, 7, 11, 10, and then we referenced page 8, which was not present in memory. The LRU page is page 12; in LRU replacement, we would replace page 12 in main memory with page 8. If the next reference also generated a page fault, we would replace page 9, since it would then be the LRU among the pages present in memory.

> **Hardware Software Interface**
>
> Implementing a completely accurate LRU scheme is too expensive, since it requires updating a data structure on *every* memory reference. Instead, most operating systems approximate LRU by keeping track of which pages have and which pages have not been recently used. To help the operating system estimate the LRU pages, some machines provide a *use bit* or *reference bit*, which is set whenever a page is accessed. The operating system periodically clears the reference bits and later records them so it can determine which pages were touched during a particular time period. With this usage information, the operating system can select a page that is among the least recently referenced (detected by having its reference bit off). If this bit is not provided by the hardware, the operating system must find another way to estimate which pages have been accessed.

Elaboration: With a 32-bit virtual address, 4-KB pages, and 4 bytes per page table entry, we can compute the total page table size:

$$\text{Number of page table entries} = \frac{2^{32}}{2^{12}} = 2^{20}$$

$$\text{Size of page table} = 2^{20} \text{ page table entries} \times 2^2 \frac{\text{bytes}}{\text{page table entry}} = 4 \text{ MB}$$

That is, we would need to use 4 MB of memory for each program in execution at any time. On a machine with tens to hundreds of active programs and a fixed-size page table, most or all of the memory would be tied up in page tables!

A range of techniques are used to reduce the amount of storage required for the page table. The five techniques below aim at reducing the total maximum storage required as well as minimizing the main memory dedicated to page tables:

1. The simplest technique is to keep a bounds register that limits the size of the page table for a given process. If the virtual page number becomes larger than

the contents of the limit register, entries must be added to the page table. This technique allows the page table to grow as a process consumes more space. Thus, the page table will only be large if the process is using many pages of virtual address space. This technique requires that the address space expand in only one direction.

2. Allowing growth in only one direction is not sufficient, since most languages require two areas whose size is expandable: one area holds the stack and the other area holds the heap. Because of this duality, it is convenient to divide the page table and let it grow from the highest address down, as well as from the lowest address up. This means that there will be two separate page tables and two separate limits. The use of two page tables breaks the address space into two segments. The high-order bit of an address usually determines which segment and thus which page table to use for that address. Since the segment is specified by the high-order address bit, each segment can be as large as one-half of the address space. A limit register for each segment specifies the current size of the segment, which grows in units of pages. This type of segmentation is used by many architectures, including the MIPS architecture. Unlike the type of segmentation discussed in the elaboration on page 583, this form of segmentation is invisible to the application program, although not to the operating system. The major disadvantage of this scheme is that it does not work well when the address space is used in a sparse fashion rather than as a contiguous set of virtual addresses.

3. Another approach to reducing the page table size is to apply a hashing function to the virtual address so that the page table data structure need be only the size of the number of *physical* pages in main memory. Such a structure is called an *inverted page table*. Of course, the lookup process is slightly more complex with an inverted page table because we can no longer just index the page table.

4. Multiple levels of page tables can also be used to reduce the total amount of page table storage. The first level maps large fixed-size blocks of virtual address space, perhaps 64 to 256 pages in total. These large blocks are sometimes called segments, and this first-level mapping table is sometimes called a segment table, though the segments are invisible to the user. Each entry in the segment table indicates whether any pages in that segment are allocated and, if so, points to a page table for that segment. Address translation happens by first looking in the segment table, using the highest-order bits of the address. If the segment address is valid, the next set of high-order bits is used to index the page table indicated by the segment table entry. This scheme allows the address space to be used in a sparse fashion (multiple noncontiguous segments can be active) without having to allocate the entire page table. Such schemes are particularly useful with very large address spaces and in software systems that require noncontiguous allocation. The primary disadvantage of this two-level mapping is the more complex process for address translation.

5. To reduce the actual main memory tied up in page tables, most modern systems also allow the page tables to be paged. Although this sounds tricky, it works by using the same basic ideas of virtual memory and simply allowing the page tables to reside in the virtual address space. In addition, there are some small but critical problems, such as a never-ending series of page faults, that must be

avoided. How these problems are overcome is both very detailed and typically highly machine-specific. In brief, these problems are avoided by placing all the page tables in the address space of the operating system and placing at least some of the page tables for the system in a portion of main memory that is physically addressed and is always present and never on disk.

What about Writes?

The difference between the access time to the cache and main memory is tens of cycles, and write-through schemes can be used, although we need a write buffer to hide the latency of the write from the processor. In a virtual memory system, writes to the next level of the hierarchy (disk) take millions of processor clock cycles; therefore, building a write buffer to allow the system to write through to disk would be completely impractical. Instead, virtual memory systems must use write-back, performing the individual writes into the page in memory and copying the page back to disk when it is replaced in the memory. This copying back to the lower level in the hierarchy is the source of the other name for this technique of handling writes, namely *copy back*.

Hardware Software Interface

A write-back scheme has another major advantage in a virtual memory system. Because the disk transfer time is small compared with its access time, copying back an entire page is much more efficient than writing individual words back to the disk. A write-back operation, although more efficient than transferring individual words, is still costly. Thus, we would like to know whether a page *needs* to be copied back when we choose to replace it. To track whether a page has been written since it was read into the memory, a *dirty bit* is added to the page table. The dirty bit is set when the page is first written. If the operating system chooses to replace the page, the dirty bit indicates whether the page needs to be written out before its location in memory can be given to another page.

Making Address Translation Fast: The TLB

Since the page tables are stored in main memory, every memory access by a program can take at least twice as long: one memory access to obtain the physical address and a second access to get the data. The key to improving access performance is to rely on locality of reference to the page table. When a translation for a virtual page number is used, it will probably be needed again in the near future because the references to the words on that page have both temporal and spatial locality.

Accordingly, modern machines include a special cache that keeps track of recently used translations. This special address translation cache is traditionally referred to as a *translation-lookaside buffer (TLB)*. The TLB corresponds to that little piece of paper we typically use to record the location of a set of books we look up in the card catalog; rather than continually searching the entire catalog, we record the location of several books and use the scrap of paper as a cache.

A TLB is a cache that holds only page table mappings. Thus, each tag entry in the TLB holds a portion of the virtual page number, and each data entry of the TLB holds a physical page number. Because we will no longer access the page table on every reference, instead accessing the TLB, the TLB will need to include other bits, such as the reference and the dirty bit. Figure 7.24 shows how the TLB acts as a cache for the page table references.

On every reference, we look up the virtual page number in the TLB. If we get a hit, the physical page number is used to form the address, and the corresponding reference bit is turned on. If the processor is performing a write, the dirty bit is also turned on. If a miss in the TLB occurs, we must determine whether it is a page fault or merely a TLB miss. If the page exists in memory, then the TLB miss indicates only that the translation is missing. In such cases, the CPU can handle the TLB miss by loading the translation from the page table into the TLB and then trying the reference again. If the page is not present in memory, then the TLB miss indicates a true page fault. In this case, the CPU invokes the operating system using an exception. Because the TLB has many fewer entries than the number of pages in main memory, TLB misses will be much more frequent than true page faults.

TLB misses can be handled either in hardware or software. In practice, there is little performance difference between the two approaches because the basic operations that must be performed are the same in either case.

After a TLB miss occurs and the missing translation has been retrieved from the page table, we will need to select a TLB entry to replace. Because the reference and dirty bits are contained in the TLB entry, we need to copy these bits back to the page table entry when we replace an entry. These bits are the only portion of the TLB entry that can be changed. Using a write-back strategy (that is, copying these entries back at miss time rather than whenever they are written) is very efficient, since we expect the TLB miss rate to be small. Some systems use other techniques to approximate the reference and dirty bits, eliminating the need to write into the TLB except to load a new table entry on a miss.

Some typical values for a TLB might be

- TLB size: 32–4,096 entries
- Block size: 1–2 page table entries (typically 4–8 bytes each)
- Hit time: 0.5–1 clock cycle
- Miss penalty: 10–30 clock cycles
- Miss rate: 0.01%–1%

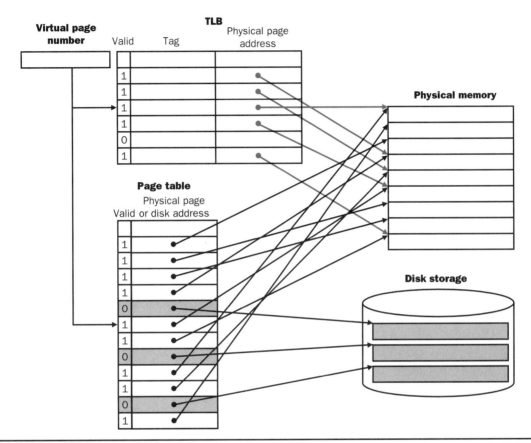

FIGURE 7.24 The TLB acts as a cache on the page table for the entries that map to physical pages only. The TLB contains a subset of the virtual-to-physical page mappings that are in the page table. The TLB mappings are shown in color. Because the TLB is a cache, it must have a tag field. If there is no matching entry in the TLB for a page, the page table must be examined. The page table either supplies a physical page number for the page (which can then be used to build a TLB entry) or indicates that the page resides on disk, in which case a page fault occurs. Since the page table has an entry for every virtual page (it is *not* a cache, in other words), no tag field is needed.

Designers have used a wide variety of associativity in TLBs. Some systems use small, fully associative TLBs because a fully associative mapping has a lower miss rate; furthermore, since the TLB is small, the cost of a fully associative mapping is not too high. Other systems use large TLBs, often with no or small associativity. With a fully associative mapping, choosing the entry to replace becomes tricky since implementing a hardware LRU scheme is too expensive. Furthermore, since TLB misses are much more frequent than page faults and must be handled more cheaply, we cannot afford an expensive software algorithm, as we can for page faults. As a result, many systems provide some support for randomly choosing an entry to replace. We'll examine replacement schemes in a little more detail in section 7.5.

The MIPS R2000 TLB

To see how these ideas work in practice, let's take a closer look at the TLB of the MIPS R2000, which was used in the DECStation 3100. This TLB, while extremely simple, exhibits most of the characteristics in more recent TLBs. The memory system uses 4-KB pages and a 32-bit address space; thus the virtual page number is 20 bits long, as shown in Figure 7.22 on page 584. The physical address is the same size as the virtual address. The TLB contains 64 entries, is fully associative, and is shared between the instruction and data references. Each entry is 64 bits wide and contains a 20-bit tag (which is the virtual page number for that TLB entry), the corresponding physical page number (also 20 bits), a valid bit, a dirty bit, and several other bookkeeping bits.

Figure 7.25 shows the TLB and one of the caches, while Figure 7.26 shows the steps in processing a read or write request. When a TLB miss occurs, the MIPS hardware saves the page number of the reference in a special register and generates an exception. The exception invokes the operating system, which handles the miss in software. To find the physical address for the missing page, the TLB miss routine indexes the page table using the page number of the virtual address and the page table register, which indicates the starting address of the active process page table. Using a special set of system instructions that can update the TLB, the operating system places the physical address from the page table into the TLB. A true page fault occurs if the page table entry does not have a valid physical address. A TLB miss can take as few as 10 cycles, but on average takes about 16 cycles. The hardware maintains an index that indicates the recommended entry to replace; the recommended entry is chosen randomly.

There is an extra complication for write requests: namely, the write access bit in the TLB must be checked. This bit prevents the program from writing into pages for which it has only read access. If the program attempts a write and the write access bit is off, an exception is generated. The write access bit forms part of the protection mechanism, which we discuss shortly.

Integrating Virtual Memory, TLBs, and Caches

Under the best of circumstances, a virtual address is translated by the TLB and sent to the cache where the appropriate data is found, retrieved, and sent back to the CPU. In the worst case, a reference can miss in all three components of the memory hierarchy: the TLB, the page table, and the cache. The following example illustrates these interactions in more detail.

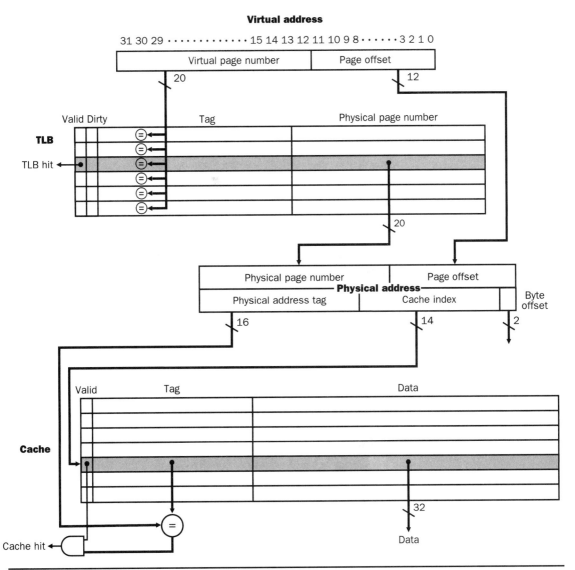

FIGURE 7.25 The TLB and cache implement the process of going from a virtual address to a data item in the DECStation 3100. This figure shows the organization of the TLB and one of the caches in the DECStation 3100. This diagram focuses on a read; Figure 7.26 describes how to handle writes. While the cache is direct mapped, the TLB is fully associative. Implementing a fully associative TLB requires that every TLB tag be compared against theT index value, since the entry of interest can be anywhere in the TLB. If the valid bit of the matching entry is on, the access is a TLB hit, and the page number together with the page offset forms the index that is used to access the cache.

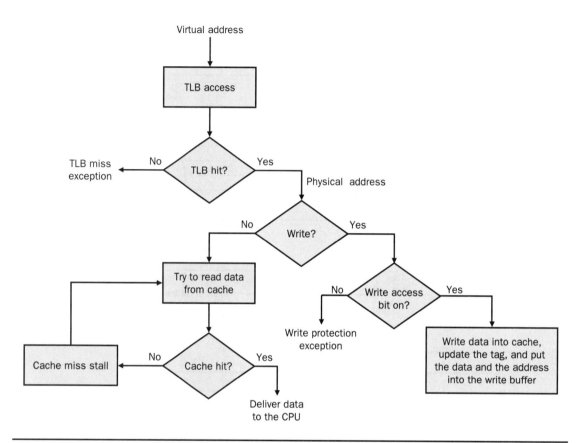

FIGURE 7.26   Processing a read or a write through the DECStation 3100 TLB and cache. If the TLB generates a hit, the cache can be accessed with the resulting physical address. If the operation is a write, the cache entry is overwritten and the data is sent to the write buffer; remember, though, that a cache write miss cannot occur for the DECStation 3100 cache, which uses one-word blocks and a write-through cache. For a read, the cache generates a hit or miss and supplies the data or causes a stall while the data is brought from memory. In actuality, the TLB does not contain a true dirty bit; instead, it uses the write access bit to detect the first write and then set the dirty bit in the page table. Notice that a TLB hit and a cache hit are independent events, and that the cache access is not even tried when a TLB miss occurs. Furthermore, a cache hit can only occur after a TLB hit occurs, which means that the data must be present in memory. The relationship between TLB misses and cache misses is examined further in the exercises at the end of this chapter.

Example

Overall Operation of a Memory Hierarchy

In a memory hierarchy like that of Figure 7.25 that includes a TLB and a cache organized as shown, a memory reference can encounter three different types of misses: a cache miss, a TLB miss, and a page fault. Consider all the combinations of these three events with one or more occurring (seven possibilities). For each possibility, state whether this event can actually occur and under what circumstances.

Answer

Figure 7.27 shows the possible circumstances and whether they can arise in practice or not.

Our virtual memory and cache systems work together as a hierarchy, so that data cannot be in the cache unless it is present in main memory. The operating system plays an important role in maintaining this hierarchy by flushing the contents of any page from the cache, when it decides to migrate that page to disk. At the same time, the OS modifies the page tables and TLB, so that an attempt to access any data on the page will generate a page fault.

Elaboration: Figure 7.27 assumes that all memory addresses are translated to physical addresses before the cache is accessed; Figure 7.25 shows such a memory system organization. In this organization, the cache is *physically indexed* and *physically tagged* (both the cache index and tag are physical, rather than virtual, addresses). In such a system, the amount of time to access memory, assuming a cache hit, must accommodate both a TLB access and a cache access; of course, these accesses can be pipelined.

Cache	TLB	Virtual memory	Possible? If so, under what circumstance?
miss	hit	hit	Possible, although the page table is never really checked if TLB hits.
hit	miss	hit	TLB misses, but entry found in page table; after retry, data is found in cache.
miss	miss	hit	TLB misses, but entry found in page table; after retry, data misses in cache.
miss	miss	miss	TLB misses and is followed by a page fault; after retry, data must miss in cache.
miss	hit	miss	Impossible: cannot have a translation in TLB if page is not present in memory.
hit	hit	miss	Impossible: cannot have a translation in TLB if page is not present in memory.
hit	miss	miss	Impossible: data cannot be allowed in cache if the page is not in memory.

FIGURE 7.27 The possible combinations of events in the TLB, virtual memory system, and cache. Three of these combinations are impossible, and one is possible (TLB hit, virtual memory hit, cache miss) but never detected.

Alternatively, the CPU can index the cache with an address that is completely or partially virtual. This is called a *virtually addressed cache,* and it uses tags that are virtual addresses, hence such a cache is *virtually indexed* and *virtually tagged.* In such caches, the address translation hardware (e.g., the TLB) is unused during the normal cache access, since the cache is accessed with a virtual address that has not been translated to a physical address. When a cache miss occurs, however, the processor needs to translate the address to a physical address so that it can fetch the cache block from main memory.

When the cache is accessed with a virtual address and pages are shared between programs (which may access them with different virtual addresses), there is the possibility of *aliasing.* Aliasing occurs when the same object has two names—in this case, two virtual addresses for the same page. This ambiguity creates a problem because a word on such a page may be cached in two different locations, each corresponding to different virtual addresses. This would allow one program to write the data without the other program being aware that the data had changed. Completely virtually addressed caches introduce either design limitations on the cache and TLB to reduce aliases or require the operating system, and possibly the user, to take steps to ensure that aliases do not occur.

A common compromise between these two design points are caches that are virtually indexed (sometimes using just the page offset portion of the address, which is really a physical address since it is untranslated), but use physical address tags. The cache and the TLB are accessed in parallel, and the physical address tags from the cache are compared against the physical address from the TLB. These designs, which are virtually indexed but physically tagged, attempt to achieve the performance advantages of virtually indexed caches with the architecturally simpler advantages of a physically addressed cache.

Implementing Protection with Virtual Memory

One of the most important functions for virtual memory is to allow sharing of a single main memory by multiple processes, while providing memory protection among these processes and the operating system. The protection mechanism must ensure that although multiple processes are sharing the same main memory, one renegade process cannot write into the address space of another user process or into the operating system either intentionally or unintentionally. For example, if the program that maintains student grades is running on a machine at the same time as the programs of the students in the first programming course, we wouldn't want the errant program of a beginner to write over someone's grades. The write access bit in the TLB can protect a page from being written.

We also want to prevent one process from reading the data of another process. For example, we wouldn't want one student program to read the grades while they were in the processor's memory. Once we begin sharing main memory, we must provide the ability for a process to protect its data from both reading and writing by another process; otherwise, sharing the main memory will be a mixed blessing!

Remember that each process has its own virtual address space. Thus, if the operating system keeps the page tables organized so that the independent virtual pages map to disjoint physical pages, one process will not be able to access another's data. Of course, this also requires that a user process be unable to change the page table mapping. The operating system can assure safety if it prevents the user process from modifying its own page tables. Yet the operating system must be able to modify the page tables. Placing the page tables in the address space of the operating system satisfies both requirements.

Hardware Software Interface

To enable the operating system to implement protection in the virtual memory system, the hardware must provide at least the three basic capabilities summarized below.

1. Support at least two modes that indicate whether the running process is a user process or an operating system process, variously called a *kernel* process, a *supervisor* process, or an *executive* process.

2. Provide a portion of the CPU state that a user process can read but not write. This includes the user/supervisor mode bit, which dictates whether the processor is in user or supervisor mode, the page table pointer, and the TLB. To write these elements the operating system uses special instructions that are only available in supervisor mode.

3. Provide mechanisms whereby the CPU can go from user mode to supervisor mode, and vice versa. The first direction is typically accomplished by a *system call* exception, implemented as a special instruction (*syscall* in the MIPS instruction set) that transfers control to a dedicated location in supervisor code space. As with any other exception, the program counter from the point of the system call is saved, and the CPU is placed in supervisor mode. The return to user mode from the exception, using the *return from exception* (RFE) instruction, will restore the state of the process that generated the exception.

By using these mechanisms and storing the page tables in the operating system's address space, the operating system can change the page tables while preventing a user process from changing them, ensuring that a user process can access only the storage provided to it by the operating system.

When processes want to share information in a limited way, the operating system must assist them, since accessing the information of another process requires changing the page table of the accessing process. The write access bit can be used to restrict the sharing to just read sharing, and, like the rest of the page table, this bit can be changed only by the operating system. To allow another process, say P1, to read a page owned by process P2, P2 would ask the operating system to create a page table entry for a virtual page in P1's address space that points to the same physical page that P2 wants to share. The operating system could use the write protection bit to prevent P1 from writing the data, if that was P2's wish. Any bits that determine the access rights for a page must be included in both the page table and the TLB because the page table is accessed only on a TLB *miss*.

Elaboration: When the operating system decides to change from running process P1 to running process P2 (called a *context switch* or *process switch*), it must ensure that P2 cannot get access to the page tables of P1 because that would compromise protection. If there is no TLB, it suffices to change the page table register to point to P2's page table (rather than to P1's); with a TLB, we must clear the TLB entries that belong to P1—both to protect the data of P1 and to force the TLB to load the entries for P2. If the process switch rate were high, this could be quite inefficient. For example, P2 might load only a few TLB entries before the operating system switched back to P1. Unfortunately, P1 would then find that all its TLB entries were gone and would have to go through TLB misses to reload them. This problem arises because the virtual addresses used by P1 and P2 are the same, and we must clear out the TLB to avoid confusing these addresses.

A common alternative is to extend the virtual address space by adding a *process identifier* or *task identifier*. This small field identifies the currently running process; it is kept in a register loaded by the operating system when it switches processes. The process identifier is concatenated to the tag portion of the TLB, so that a TLB hit occurs only if both the page number *and* the process identifier match. This combination eliminates the need to clear the TLB, except on rare occasions.

Similar problems can occur for a cache, since on a process switch the cache will contain data from the running process. These problems arise in different ways for physically addressed and virtually addressed caches, and a variety of different solutions, such as process identifiers, are used to ensure that a process gets its own data.

Handling Page Faults and TLB Misses

Although the translation of virtual to physical addresses with a TLB is straightforward when we get a TLB hit, handling TLB misses and page faults is more complex. A TLB miss occurs when no entry in the TLB matches a virtual address. A TLB miss can indicate one of two possibilities:

1. The page is present in memory, and we need only create the missing TLB entry.

2. The page is not present in memory, and we need to transfer control to the operating system to deal with a page fault.

How do we know which of these two circumstances has occurred? When we process the TLB miss, we will look for a page table entry to bring into the TLB; if the matching page table entry has a valid bit that is turned off, then the corresponding page is not in memory and we have a page fault, rather than just a TLB miss. If the valid bit is on, we can simply retrieve the physical page number from the page table entry and use it to create the TLB entry. A TLB miss can be handled in software or hardware because it will require only a short sequence of operations to copy a valid page table entry from memory into the TLB.

Handling a page fault requires using the exception mechanism to interrupt the active process, transferring control to the operating system, and later resuming execution of the interrupted process. A page fault will be recognized sometime during the clock cycle used to access memory. To restart the instruction after the page fault is handled, the program counter of the instruction that caused the page fault must be saved. Just as in Chapters 5 and 6, the exception program counter (EPC) is used to hold this value.

In addition, the page fault exception must be asserted by the end of the same clock cycle that the memory access occurs, so that the next clock cycle will begin exception processing rather than continue normal instruction execution. If the page fault was not recognized in this clock cycle, a load instruction could overwrite a register, and this could be disastrous when we try to restart the instruction. For example, consider the instruction lw $1,0($1): the machine must be able to prevent the write-back operation from occurring; otherwise, it could not properly restart the instruction, since the contents of $1 would have been destroyed. A similar complication arises on stores. We must prevent the write into memory from actually completing when there is a page fault; this is usually done by deasserting the write control line to the memory.

Once the process that generated the page fault has been interrupted and the operating system has control, it uses the exception Cause register to diagnose the cause of the exception. Because the exception is a page fault, the operating system knows that extensive processing will be required. Thus it saves the entire state of the active process. This state includes all the general-purpose and floating-point registers, the page table address register, the EPC, and the exception Cause register. The virtual address that caused the fault depends on whether the fault was an instruction or data fault. The address of the instruction that generated the fault is in the EPC. If it was an instruction page fault, the EPC contains the virtual address of the faulting page; otherwise, the faulting virtual address can be computed by examining the instruction (whose address is in the EPC) to find the base register and offset field.

Once the operating system knows the virtual address that caused the page fault, it must complete three steps:

1. Look up the page table entry using the virtual address and find the location of the referenced page on disk.

2. Choose a physical page to replace; if the chosen page is dirty, it must be written out to disk before we can bring a new virtual page into this physical page.

3. Start a read to bring the referenced page from disk into the chosen physical page.

Of course, this last step will take millions of processor clock cycles (so will the second if the replaced page is dirty); accordingly, the operating system will usually select another process to execute in the CPU until the disk access completes. Because the operating system has saved the state of the process, it can freely give control of the processor to another process.

When the read of the page from disk is complete, the operating system can restore the state of the process that originally caused the page fault and execute the instruction that returns from the exception. This instruction will reset the processor from kernel to user mode, as well as restore the program counter. The user process then reexecutes the instruction that faulted, accesses the requested page successfully, and continues execution.

Page fault exceptions that occur for data accesses are difficult to implement because of a combination of three characteristics: they occur in the middle of instructions; the instruction cannot be completed before handling the exception; and, after handling the exception, the instruction must be restarted as if nothing had occurred.

Making instructions *restartable*, so that the exception can be handled and the instruction later continued, is relatively easy in an architecture like the MIPS. Because each instruction writes only one data item and this write occurs at the end of the instruction cycle, we can simply prevent the instruction from completing (by not performing the write) and restart the instruction at the beginning.

For machines with much more complex instructions that may touch many memory locations and write many data items, making instructions restartable is much harder. Processing one instruction may generate a number of page faults in the middle of the instruction. For example, some machines have block move instructions that touch thousands of data words. In such machines, instructions often cannot be restarted from the beginning, as we do for MIPS instructions. Instead, the instruction must be interrupted and later continued midstream in its execution. Resuming an instruction in the middle of its execution usually requires saving some special state, processing the exception, and restoring that special state. Making this work properly requires careful and detailed coordination between the exception-handling code in the operating system and the hardware.

Hardware Software Interface

Between the time we begin executing the exception handler in the operating system and the time that the operating system has saved all the state of the process, the operating system is particularly vulnerable. For example, if another exception occurred when we were processing the first exception in the operating system, the control unit would overwrite the exception program counter, making it impossible to return to the instruction that caused the page fault! We can avoid this disaster by providing the ability to disable and enable exceptions. When an exception first occurs, we set a bit that disables all other exceptions; this could happen at the same time we set the supervisor mode bit. The operating system will then save just enough state to allow it to recover if another exception occurs (namely, the exception program counter and Cause register). The operating system can then reenable exceptions. These steps make sure that exceptions will not cause the processor to lose any state and thereby be unable to restart execution of the interrupting instruction.

Hardware Software Interface

Because the TLB is the subset of the page table that is accessed on every cycle, protection violations are also seen as TLB exceptions. The operating system can handle these with the same basic hardware that it uses to deal with TLB misses and page faults. A special set of values in the Cause register may be used to indicate protection violations (e.g., attempt to perform a write when the write access bit is off), as opposed to a TLB miss. The operating system can access the TLB or page table entry that matched the virtual page so that it can examine the process's access rights and report the appropriate error.

Elaboration: Handling TLB misses in software is analogous to handling page faults: both a TLB miss and a page fault are signaled by the same event in the MIPS R2000 TLB. To speed up processing of a simple TLB miss that will be much more frequent than a true page fault, two different values for the MIPS Cause register are generated by a TLB miss. One setting indicates that there was no matching TLB entry, while another setting indicates that the TLB entry exists but that the page is not present in memory (the TLB valid bit really contains the page table valid bit). On a MIPS R2000/3000 processor, these two events are distinguished. Because the exception for TLB entry missing is much more frequent, the operating system loads the TLB from the page table without examining the entry and restarts the instruction when such an exception occurs. If the entry is invalid, another exception occurs, and the operating system recognizes that a page fault has occurred. This method makes the frequent case of a TLB miss fast, at a slight performance penalty for the infrequent case of a page fault.

Summary

Virtual memory is the name for the level of memory hierarchy that manages caching between the main memory and disk. Virtual memory allows a single program to expand its address space beyond the limits of main memory. More importantly in recent computer systems, virtual memory supports sharing of the main memory among multiple, simultaneously active processes, which together require far more total main memory than exists. To support this sharing, virtual memory also provides mechanisms for memory protection.

Managing the memory hierarchy between main memory and disk is challenging because of the high cost of page faults. Several techniques are used to reduce the miss rate:

1. Blocks, called pages, are made large to take advantage of spatial locality and to reduce the miss rate.

2. The mapping between virtual addresses and physical addresses, which is implemented with a page table, is made fully associative so that a virtual page can be placed anywhere in main memory.

3. The operating system uses techniques, such as LRU and a reference bit, to choose which pages to replace.

Writes to disk are also expensive, so virtual memory uses a write-back scheme and also tracks whether a page is unchanged (with a dirty bit) to avoid writing unchanged pages back to disk.

The virtual memory mechanism also provides address translation from a virtual address used by the program to the physical address space used for accessing memory. This address translation allows protected sharing of the main memory and provides several additional benefits, such as simplifying memory allocation. To ensure that processes are protected from each other requires that only the operating system can change the address translations, which is implemented by preventing user programs from changing the page tables. Controlled sharing of pages among processes can be implemented with the help of the operating system and access bits in the page table that indicate whether the user program has read or write access to a page.

If a CPU had to access a page table resident in memory to translate every access, virtual memory would have too much overhead. Instead, a TLB acts as a cache for translations from the page table. Each address is then translated from a virtual address to a physical address using the translations in the TLB.

Caches, virtual memory, and TLBs all rely on a common set of principles and policies. The next section discusses this common framework.

7.5 A Common Framework for Memory Hierarchies

By now, you've recognized that the different types of memory hierarchies share a great deal in common. Although many of the aspects of memory hierarchies differ quantitatively, many of the policies and features that determine how a hierarchy functions are similar qualitatively. Figure 7.28 shows how some of the quantitative characteristics of memory hierarchies can differ. In the rest of this section, we will discuss the common operational aspects of memory hierarchies and how these determine their behavior. We will examine these policies as a series of four questions that apply between any two levels of a memory hierarchy, although for simplicity we will primarily use terminology for caches.

Question 1: Where Can a Block Be Placed?

We have seen that block placement in the upper level of the hierarchy can use a range of schemes, from direct mapped to set associative to fully associative. As mentioned above, this entire range of schemes can be thought of as variations on a set-associative scheme where the number of sets and the number of blocks per set varies:

Scheme name	Number of sets	Blocks per set
Direct mapped	Number of blocks in cache	1
Set associative	$\dfrac{\text{Number of blocks in cache}}{\text{Associativity}}$	Associativity (typically 2–8)
Fully associative	1	Number of blocks in the cache

Feature	Typical values for caches	Typical values for paged memory	Typical values for a TLB
Total size in blocks	1000–100,000	2000–250,000	32–4,000
Total size in kilobytes	8–8,000	8000–8,000,000	0.25–32
Block size in bytes	16–256	4000–64,000	4–32
Miss penalty in clocks	10–100	1,000,000–10,000,000	10–100
Miss rates	0.1%–10%	0.00001%–0.0001%	0.01%–2%

FIGURE 7.28 The key quantitative design parameters that characterize the three major memory hierarchies in a machine. These are typical values for these levels as of 1997. Although the range of values is wide, this is partially because many of the values that have shifted over time are related; for example, as caches become larger to overcome larger miss penalties, block sizes also grow.

The advantage of increasing the degree of associativity is that it usually decreases the miss rate. The improvement in miss rate comes from reducing misses that compete for the same location. We will examine both of these in more detail shortly. First, let's look at how much improvement is gained. Figure 7.29 shows the data for a workload consisting of the SPEC92 benchmarks with caches of 1 KB to 128 KB, varying from direct mapped to eight-way set associative. The largest gains are obtained in going from direct mapped to two-way

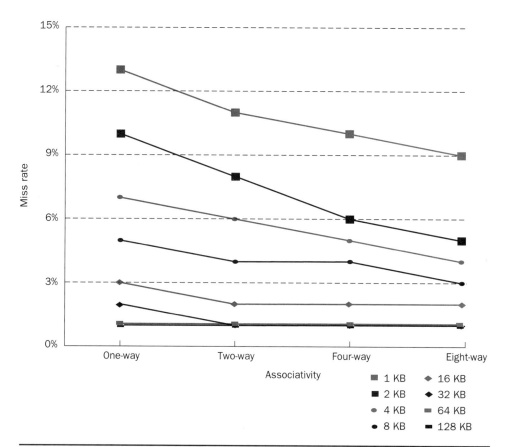

FIGURE 7.29   The miss rates for each of eight cache sizes improve as the associativity increases. While the benefit of going from one-way (direct mapped) to two-way set associative is significant, the benefits of further associativity are smaller (e.g., 8%–16% going from two-way to four-way versus 20%–30% improvement going from one-way to two-way). There is even less improvement in going from four-way to eight-way set associative, which, in turn, comes very close to the miss rates of a fully associative cache. Smaller caches obtain a significantly larger absolute benefit from associativity because the base miss rate of a small cache is larger. This data was generated using the SPEC92 integer and floating-point benchmarks with a 32-byte block size for all caches. This data was collected by Mark Hill and his students and is available online via a link at *www.mkp.com/books_catalog/cod/links.htm.*

set associative, which yields between a 20% and 30% reduction in the miss rate. As cache sizes grow, the relative improvement from associativity is constant or increases slightly; since the overall miss rate of a larger cache is lower, however, the opportunity for improving the miss rate decreases and the absolute improvement in the miss rate from associativity shrinks significantly. The potential disadvantages of associativity, as we mentioned earlier, are increased cost and slower access time.

Question 2: How Is a Block Found?

The choice of how we locate a block depends on the block placement scheme, since that dictates the number of possible locations. We can summarize the schemes as follows:

Associativity	Location method	Comparisons required
Direct mapped	index	1
Set associative	index the set, search among elements	degree of associativity
Full	search all cache entries	size of the cache
	separate lookup table	0

The choice among direct-mapped, set-associative, or fully associative mapping in any memory hierarchy will depend on the cost of a miss versus the cost of implementing associativity, both in time and in extra parts. In general, implementing a high degree of associativity in caches is not worthwhile because the cost in comparators continues to grow, while the miss rate improvements are small. Fully associative caches are prohibitive except for small sizes, where the cost of the comparators is not overwhelming and where the absolute miss rate improvements are greatest.

In virtual memory systems, a separate mapping table (the page table) is kept to index the memory. In addition to the storage required for the table, using an index table requires an extra memory access. The choice of full associativity and the extra table is motivated by four facts:

1. Full associativity is beneficial, since misses are *very* expensive.

2. Full associativity allows software to use sophisticated replacement schemes that are designed to reduce the miss rate. We'll examine these in more detail shortly.

3. The full map can be easily indexed with no extra hardware and no searching required.

4. The large page size means the page table size overhead is relatively small. (The use of a separate lookup table, like a page table for virtual memory, is not practical for a cache because the table would be much larger than a page table and could not be accessed quickly.)

Therefore, virtual memory systems always use fully associative placement.

Set-associative placement is often used for caches and TLBs, where the access combines indexing and the search of a small set. Many recent systems have used direct-mapped caches because of their advantage in access time and simplicity. The advantage in access time occurs because finding the requested block does not depend on a comparison. Such design choices depend on many details of the implementation, such as whether the cache is on-chip or off-chip, the technology used for implementing the cache, and the critical role of cache access time in determining the processor cycle time.

Question 3: Which Block Should Be Replaced on a Cache Miss?

When a miss occurs in an associative cache, we must decide which block to replace. In a fully associative cache, all blocks are candidates for replacement. If the cache is set associative, we must choose among the blocks in the set. Of course, replacement is easy in a direct-mapped cache because there is only one candidate.

We have already mentioned the two primary strategies for replacement in set-associative or fully associative caches:

- *Random:* Candidate blocks are randomly selected, possibly using some hardware assistance.

- *Least recently used (LRU):* The block replaced is the one that has been unused for the longest time.

In practice, LRU is too costly to implement for hierarchies with more than a small degree of associativity (two to four, typically), since tracking the information is costly. Even for four-way set associativity, LRU is often approximated—for example, by keeping track of which of a pair of blocks is LRU (which requires 1 bit), and then tracking which block in each pair is LRU (which requires 1 bit per pair). For larger associativity, LRU is either approximated or random replacement is used. In caches, the replacement algorithm is in hardware, which means that the scheme should be easy to implement. Random replacement is simple to build in hardware, and for a two-way set-associative cache, random replacement has a miss rate about 1.1 times higher than LRU replacement. As the caches become larger, the miss rate for both replacement strategies falls, and the absolute difference becomes small. In fact, random replacement is sometimes better than simple LRU approximations that can be easily implemented in hardware.

In virtual memory, some form of LRU is always approximated since even a tiny reduction in the miss rate can be important when the cost of a miss is enormous. Reference bits or equivalent functionality is often provided to make it easier for the operating system to track a set of less recently used pages. Because misses are so expensive and relatively infrequent, approximating this information primarily in software is acceptable.

Question 4: What Happens on a Write?

A key characteristic of any memory hierarchy is how it deals with writes. We have already seen the two basic options:

- *Write-through*: The information is written to both the block in the cache and to the block in the lower level of the memory hierarchy (main memory for a cache). The caches in section 7.2 used this scheme.

- *Write-back* (also called *copy-back*): The information is written only to the block in the cache. The modified block is written to the lower level of the hierarchy only when it is replaced. Virtual memory systems always use write-back, for the reasons discussed in section 7.4.

Both write-back and write-through have their advantages. The key advantages of write-back are the following.

- Individual words can be written by the processor at the rate that the cache, rather than the memory, can accept them.

- Multiple writes within a block require only one write to the lower level in the hierarchy.

- When blocks are written back, the system can make effective use of a high bandwidth transfer, since the entire block is written.

Write-through has these advantages:

- Misses are simpler and cheaper because they never require a block to be written back to the lower level.

- Write-through is easier to implement than write-back, although to be practical in a high-speed system, a write-through cache will need to use a write buffer.

In virtual memory systems, only a write-back policy is practical because of the long latency of a write to the lower level of the hierarchy (disk). As CPUs continue to increase in performance at a faster rate than DRAM-based main memory, the rate at which writes are generated by a processor will exceed the rate at which the memory system can process them, even allowing for physically and logically wider memories. As a consequence, more and more caches are using or will use a write-back strategy in the future.

Elaboration: Writes introduce several complications into caches that are not present for reads. Here, we discuss two of them: the policy on write misses and efficient implementation of writes in write-back caches.

The Big Picture

While caches, TLBs, and virtual memory may initially look very different, they rely on the same two principles of locality and can be understood by looking at how they deal with four questions:

Question 1: Where can a block be placed?
   Answer: One place (direct mapped), a few places (set associative), or any place (fully associative).

Question 2: How is a block found?
   Answer: There are four methods: indexing (as in a direct-mapped cache), limited search (as in a set-associative cache), full search (as in a fully associative cache), and a separate lookup table (as in a page table).

Question 3: What block is replaced on a miss?
   Answer: Typically, either the least recently used or a random block.

Question 4: How are writes handled?
   Answer: Each level in the hierarchy can use either write-through or write-back.

Consider a miss in a write-through cache. The strategy followed in most write-through cache designs, called *fetch-on-miss*, *fetch-on-write*, or sometimes *allocate-on-miss*, allocates a cache block to the address that missed and fetches the rest of the block into the cache before writing the data and continuing execution. Alternatively, we could either allocate the block in the cache but not fetch the data (called *no-fetch-on-write*), or even not allocate the block (called *no-allocate-on-write*). Another name for these strategies that do not place the written data into the cache is *write-around*, since the data is written around the cache to get to memory. The motivation for these schemes is the observation that sometimes programs write entire blocks of data before reading them. In such cases, the fetch associated with the initial write miss may be eliminated. There are a number of subtle issues involved in implementing these schemes in multiword blocks, including complicating the handling of write hits by requiring mechanisms similar to those used for write-back caches, which we discuss in the next paragraph. Notice that the DEC 3100 cache is a special case, since the one-word block size allows the cache to implement allocate-on-write without having to do a fetch.

Actually implementing stores efficiently in a cache that uses a write-back strategy is more complex than in a write-through cache. In a write-back cache, we must write the block back to memory if the data in the cache is dirty and we have a cache miss. If we simply overwrote the block on a store before we knew whether the store had hit in the cache (as we could for a write-through cache), we would destroy the contents of the block, which is not backed up in memory. A write-through cache can write the data into the cache and read the tag; if the tag mismatches, then a miss occurs. Because the cache is write-through, the overwriting of the block in the cache is irrelevant.

In a write-back cache, because we cannot overwrite the block, stores either require two cycles (a cycle to check for a hit followed by a cycle to actually perform the write) or require an extra buffer, called a *store buffer*, to hold that data—effectively allowing the store to take only one cycle by pipelining it. When a store buffer is used, the processor does the cache lookup and places the data in the store buffer during the normal cache access cycle. Assuming a cache hit, the data is written from the store buffer into the cache on the next unused cache access cycle.

By comparison, in a write-through cache, writes can always be done in one cycle. There are some extra complications with multiword blocks, however, since we cannot simply overwrite the tag when we write the data. Instead, we read the tag and write the data portion of the selected block. If the tag matches the address of the block being written, the processor can continue normally, since the correct block has been updated. If the tag does not match, the processor generates a write miss to fetch the rest of the block corresponding to that address. Because it is always safe to overwrite the data, write hits still take one cycle.

The Three Cs: An Intuitive Model for Understanding the Behavior of Memory Hierarchies

In this section, we look at a model that provides good insight into the sources of misses in a memory hierarchy and how the misses will be affected by changes in the hierarchy. We will explain the ideas in terms of caches, although the ideas carry over directly to any other level in the hierarchy. In this model, all misses are classified into one of three categories (the three Cs):

- *Compulsory misses*: These are cache misses caused by the first access to a block that has never been in the cache. These are also called *cold-start misses*.

- *Capacity misses*: These are cache misses caused when the cache cannot contain all the blocks needed during execution of a program. Capacity misses occur because of blocks being replaced and later retrieved when accessed.

- *Conflict misses*: These are cache misses that occur in set-associative or direct-mapped caches when multiple blocks compete for the same set. Conflict misses are those misses in a direct-mapped or set-associative cache that are eliminated in a fully associative cache of the same size. These cache misses are also called *collision misses*.

Figure 7.30 shows how the miss rate divides into the three sources. These sources of misses can be directly attacked by changing some aspect of the cache design. Since conflict misses arise directly from contention for the same cache block, increasing associativity reduces conflict misses. Associativity, however, may slow access time, leading to lower overall performance.

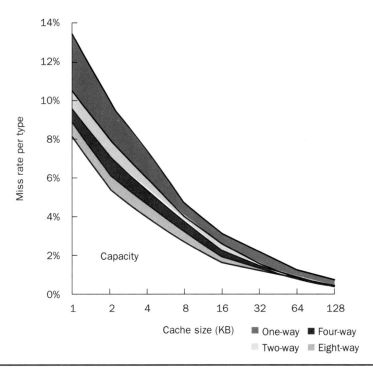

FIGURE 7.30 The miss rate can be broken into three sources of misses. This graph shows the total miss rate and its components for a range of cache sizes. This data is for the SPEC92 integer and floating-point benchmarks and is from the same source as the data in Figure 7.29. The compulsory miss component, which for the long runs seen in the SPEC92 benchmarks and the 32-byte block size is only 0.2%, cannot be seen in this graph. The next component is the capacity miss rate, which depends on cache size. The conflict portion, which depends both on associativity and on cache size, is shown for a range of associativities from one-way to eight-way. In each case, the labeled section corresponds to the increase in the miss rate that occurs when the associativity is changed from the next higher degree to the labeled degree of associativity. For example, the section labeled *two-way* indicates the additional misses arising when the cache has associativity of two rather than four. Thus the difference in the miss rate incurred by a direct-mapped cache versus a fully associative cache of the same size is given by the sum of the sections marked *eight-way, four-way, two-way,* and *one-way.*

Capacity misses can easily be reduced by enlarging the cache; indeed, caches have been growing steadily larger for many years. Of course, when we make the cache larger we must also be careful about increasing the access time, which could lead to lower overall performance.

Because compulsory misses are generated by the first reference to a block, the primary way for the cache system to reduce the number of compulsory misses is to increase the block size. This will reduce the number of references required to touch each block of the program once because the program will consist of fewer cache blocks. Increasing the block size too much can have a negative effect on performance because of the increase in the miss penalty.

The decomposition of misses into the three Cs is a useful qualitative model. In real cache designs, many of the design choices interact, and changing one cache characteristic will often affect several components of the miss rate. Despite such shortcomings, this model is a useful way to gain insight into the performance of cache designs.

 The Big Picture   The challenge in designing memory hierarchies is that every change that potentially improves the miss rate can also negatively affect overall performance, as Figure 7.31 summarizes. This combination of positive and negative effects is what makes the design of a memory hierarchy challenging.

Design change	Effect on miss rate	Possible negative performance effect
Increase size	decreases capacity misses	may increase access time
Increase associativity	decreases miss rate due to conflict misses	may increase access time
Increase block size	decreases miss rate for a wide range of block sizes	may increase miss penalty

FIGURE 7.31   Memory hierarchy design challenges.

7.6   Real Stuff: The Pentium Pro and PowerPC 604 Memory Hierarchies

In this section, we will look at the memory hierarchy in two modern microprocessors: the Intel Pentium Pro (PPro) and the PowerPC (PPC) 604. In 1997, the PPro is used in a variety of high-end PC desktops and servers from a variety of manufacturers, including Dell, DEC, Gateway, HP, Intergraph, and Micron; clock rates range from 150 to 250 MHz. In 1997, the PPC 604 is used in several Apple Macintosh models (7600, 8500, and 9500) and several IBM RS/6000 workstations (41 and 42 series products) at clock rates ranging from 100 to 250 MHz.

Both the PPro and PPC 604 offer support for secondary caches off the main CPU die. The PPro is somewhat unique because it uses a 256-KB or 512-KB secondary cache that is a separate die integrated into the same package, as shown in Figure 7.32. This organization allows a reduced access time to the secondary cache and also reduces the number of pins from the package, since the secondary cache pins remain inside the package. The PPC uses more conventional SRAMs that are separately packaged. The Apple Power Macintosh 7600 and 8500 series use 256-KB secondary caches, while the 9500 series uses a 512-KB secondary cache. The L2 cache organizations are somewhat flexible, with the sizes mentioned here being typical.

Additional Techniques to Reduce Miss Penalties

Both the Pentium Pro and PowerPC 604 have additional optimizations that allow them to reduce the miss penalty. The first of these is the return of the requested word first on a miss, as described in the elaboration on page 559. In addition, the PPC 604 implements optimizations similar to those described on pages 552 and 559, which allow the processor to continue executing instructions during cache misses and to resume execution as soon as the critical word is delivered back to the cache.

The PPro goes a step further than these optimizations, allowing the processor to continue to execute instructions that access the data cache during a cache miss, as opposed to the simpler schemes (early restart and stall on use) that allow only instructions that do not use the data cache to be executed. This technique, called a *nonblocking cache*, is becoming widespread as designers attempt to hide the cache miss latency. The PPro implements both flavors of nonblocking. *Hit under miss* allows additional cache hits during a miss, while *miss under miss* allows multiple outstanding cache misses. The first of these two aims at hiding some of the miss latency with other work, while the second aims at overlapping the latency of two different misses.

FIGURE 7.32   An Intel Pentium Pro showing the secondary cache chip (on the left) packaged together with the processor (on the right). Photo courtesy of Intel.

The Memory Hierarchies of the Pentium Pro and PowerPC 604

The PPro and PPC 604 differ in their address translation, and these differences carry over into the TLB hardware, as shown in Figure 7.33. The PowerPC architecture has a much larger 52-bit virtual address versus the PPro's 32-bit address space.

At the primary cache level, the PPC 604 and PPro differ in size and in the optimizations to reduce the miss penalty, which we discussed earlier. Other than these differences, the primary caches for the two processors are very similar, as shown in Figure 7.34.

Characteristic	Intel Pentium Pro	PowerPC 604
Virtual address	32 bits	52 bits
Physical address	32 bits	32 bits
Page size	4 KB, 4 MB	4 KB, selectable, and 256 MB
TLB organization	A TLB for instructions and a TLB for data Both four-way set associative Pseudo-LRU replacement Instruction TLB: 32 entries Data TLB: 64 entries TLB misses handled in hardware	A TLB for instructions and a TLB for data Both two-way set associative LRU replacement Instruction TLB: 128 entries Data TLB: 128 entries TLB misses handled in hardware

FIGURE 7.33 Address translation and TLB hardware for the Pentium Pro and PowerPC 604. Both machines provide support for large pages, which are used for things like the operating system or mapping a frame buffer. The large-page scheme avoids committing a large number of entries to map a single object that is always present. The PPC 604 also provides a variable page size to enable the use of larger pages (still powers of two).

Characteristic	Intel Pentium Pro	PowerPC 604
Cache organization	Split instruction and data caches	Split instruction and data caches
Cache size	8 KB each for instructions/data	16 KB each for instructions/data
Cache associativity	Four-way set associative	Four-way set associative
Replacement	Approximated LRU replacement	LRU replacement
Block size	32 bytes	32 bytes
Write policy	Write-back	Write-back or write-through

FIGURE 7.34 First-level caches in the Pentium Pro and PowerPC 604. The primary caches in both machines are physically indexed and tagged, like all the other caches we have examined in this chapter; for a discussion of the alternatives, see the elaboration on page 595. The second-level caches for the PPro and PowerPC 604 contain both code and data and are either 256 KB or 512 KB.

The sophisticated memory hierarchies of the PowerPC 604 and Pentium Pro show the significant design effort expended to try to keep the gap between processor cycle times and memory cycle times under control. Future advances in processor pipelines, together with the increased use of multiprocessing (which presents its own problems in memory hierarchies), will provide lots of new challenges for designers.

Elaboration: There are many challenges facing the designers of memory systems for high-performance processors. In this elaboration, we discuss three challenges faced in the PPro and/or PPC 604: supporting multiple memory accesses per clock, taking advantage of nonblocking caches, and efficient implementation of write-back caches.

One of the most significant challenges facing cache designers is to support processors that want to execute more than one memory instruction per clock cycle. For example, the pipeline structure of the Pentium Pro allows both a load and store to be executed on every clock cycle. Multiple requests can be supported in the first-level cache by two different techniques. The cache can be multiported (as our register file is), allowing more than one simultaneous access to the same cache block. Multiporting the cache, however, is often too expensive, since the RAM cells in a multiported memory must be much larger than single-ported cells. Thus this approach is only used for very small caches (tens of entries). The alternative scheme, which is used in the Pentium Pro, is to break the cache into banks and allow multiple, independent accesses (one load and one store), provided the accesses are to two different banks. When a conflict occurs, the load takes priority over the store, since it is most often critical. When such conflicts occur, a buffer for stores allows the processor to avoid stalling, similar to the way a write buffer works.

A second major challenge is integrating and benefiting from the use of nonblocking caches. Obtaining significant performance from nonblocking caches, as in the PPro, requires the use of out-of-order instruction execution, described in the last chapter. Without such a capability, the processor could not hide much of the miss latency, since it would stall for the instruction using the data shortly after detecting the miss. With out-of-order execution, the processor can execute other instructions during the miss time. This ability to continue execution can both hide the miss latency (relying on hit under miss) and find additional misses (relying on miss under miss). To overlap a large fraction of the miss times for two outstanding misses requires a high-bandwidth memory system capable of handling multiple misses in parallel. In desktop systems, the memory may only take small advantage of this capability, but large servers and multiprocessors often have memory systems capable of handling more than one outstanding miss in parallel.

As write-back caches become the norm, implementing them efficiently becomes increasingly important. When we discussed write-through caches, we described the need for write buffers to make such caches practical. Many write-back caches also include write buffers that are used to reduce the miss penalty when a miss requires replacing a dirty block. In such a case, rather than first write out the dirty block to memory and then read the requested block (forcing the processor to stall for two memory access cycles), the dirty block is moved to a write-back buffer associated with the cache, the requested block is read from memory, and execution is resumed (with a stall of only one memory access cycle). The write-back buffer is then written back to memory. Assuming another miss does not occur immediately, this technique halves the miss penalty when a dirty block must be replaced. The Intel PPro uses such write-back buffers for both the primary and secondary caches.

7.7 Fallacies and Pitfalls

As one of the most naturally quantitative aspects of the computer architecture, memory hierarchy would seem to be less vulnerable to fallacies and pitfalls. Not only have there been many fallacies propagated and pitfalls encountered, but some have led to major negative outcomes. We start with a pitfall that often traps students in exercises and exams.

Pitfall: Forgetting to account for byte addressing or the cache block size in simulating a cache.

When simulating a cache (by hand or machine), we need to make sure we account for the effect of byte addressing or multiword blocks in determining which cache block a given address maps into. For example, if we have a 32-byte, direct-mapped cache with a block size of 4 bytes, the byte address 36 maps into block 1 of the cache, since byte address 36 is block address 9 and (9 modulo 8) = 1. On the other hand, if address 36 is a word address, then it maps into block (36 mod 8) = 4. Make sure the problem clearly states the base of the address.

In like fashion, we must account for the block size. Suppose we have a cache with 256 bytes and a block size of 32 bytes. Which block does the byte address 300 fall into? Byte address 300 is block address

$$\left\lfloor \frac{300}{32} \right\rfloor = 9$$

The number of blocks in the cache is

$$\left\lfloor \frac{256}{32} \right\rfloor = 8$$

Block number 9 falls into cache block number (9 modulo 8) = 1.

This mistake catches many people, including authors (in earlier drafts) and instructors who forget whether they intended the addresses to be in words, bytes, or block numbers. Remember this pitfall when you tackle the exercises.

Pitfall: Using miss rate as the only metric for evaluating a memory hierarchy.

As we just discussed, miss rate can be a misleading metric when other cache parameters are ignored. Let's consider a specific example. Suppose that we were running the workload used for the measurements in Figure 7.29 on page 604. Increasing the direct-mapped cache size from 16 KB to 32 KB reduces the miss rate from 3.0% to about 2.0% for a two-way set-associative cache. Suppose the machine with the larger cache has a clock cycle time of 2 ns, while the machine with the smaller cache has a clock cycle time of 1.6 ns, and we assume that the CPI without memory stalls is the same. If the miss penalty to the secondary cache is 20 ns and there are 1.5 memory references per instruction (1 instruction reference and 0.5 data references), the machine with the larger cache is actually slower, despite its superior cache hit rate. To see this, use the following equation:

$$\text{CPU time} = (\text{CPU execution clock cycles} + \text{Memory-stall clock cycles}) \times \text{Clock cycle time}$$

where the memory-stall cycles are given using the equation from page 565:

$$\text{Memory-stall clock cycles} = \frac{\text{Instructions}}{\text{Program}} \times \frac{\text{Misses}}{\text{Instruction}} \times \text{Miss penalty}$$

The term *misses per instruction* combines the instruction and data miss rates into a single term:

$$\frac{\text{Misses}}{\text{Instruction}} = \text{Instruction miss rate} + \left(\text{Data miss rate} \times \frac{\text{Data references}}{\text{Instruction}}\right)$$

For the smaller cache (using I to stand for *instructions per program*),

$$\text{Memory-stall clock cycles} = I \times (3\% \times 1.5) \ \times \left\lceil \frac{\text{Absolute miss penalty}}{\text{Clock cycle time}} \right\rceil$$

$$\text{Memory-stall clock cycles} = I \times 0.045 \times \left\lceil \frac{20}{1.6} \right\rceil = 0.585 \times I$$

For the machine with the larger cache,

$$\text{Memory-stall clock cycles} \ = I \times (2\% \times 1.5) \ \times \left\lceil \frac{\text{Absolute miss penalty}}{\text{Clock cycle time}} \right\rceil$$

$$\text{Memory-stall clock cycles} \ = I \times 0.030 \times \left\lceil \frac{20}{2} \right\rceil = 0.30 \times I$$

Now we can put these pieces into the CPU time equation. Let the CPI without memory stalls be C. Then the number of CPU execution clock cycles is $C \times I$. This leads to the following CPU execution time for the machine with the smaller cache:

$$\text{CPU time} = (\text{CPU execution clock cycles} + \text{Memory-stall clock cycles}) \ \times \text{Clock cycle time}$$

$$\text{CPU time} = ((C \times I) + (0.585 \times I)) \times 1.6 \text{ ns} = (1.6C + 0.936) \times I$$

Now, for the larger cache we obtain

$$\text{CPU time} = ((C \times I) + (0.30 \times I)) \times 2 \text{ ns} = (2C + 0.6) \times I$$

Thus the machine with the larger cache is faster if $(1.6C + 0.936) > (2C + 0.6)$, which is true only if $(C < 0.84)$. So for machines with a pipelined CPI greater than 0.84, the machine with the smaller cache is faster.

Although it seems obvious that focusing on cache miss rate, and ignoring the impact of the cache design on the clock cycle time, would be a mistake, many designers have focused primarily on miss rate in the past, ignoring implications on cycle time.

Pitfall: Ignoring memory system behavior in writing programs or in generating code in a compiler.

This could have easily be written as a fallacy: "Programmers can ignore memory hierarchies in writing code." We illustrate an example that shows this using matrix multiply, but there are many examples we could use.

Here is the inner loop of the version of matrix multiply from Chapter 4:

```
for (i=0; i!=500; i=i+1)
    for (j=0; j!=500; j=j+1)
        for (k=0; k!=500; k=k+1)
            x[i][j] = x[i][j] + y[i][k] * z[k][j];
```

When run with inputs that are 500×500 double precision matrices, the CPU runtime of the above loop on a Silicon Graphics Challenge L containing a MIPS R4000 with a 1-MB secondary cache is 77.2 seconds. If the loop order is changed to k,j,i (so i is innermost), the runtime drops to 44.2 seconds! The only difference is how the program accesses memory and the ensuing effect on the memory hierarchy. Further compiler optimizations using a technique called *blocking* can result in a runtime that is under 10 seconds for this code! This optimization was the basis for the matrix300 results we discussed in Chapter 2.

Pitfall: Extending an address space by adding segments on top of an unsegmented address space.

During the 1970s, many programs grew so large that not all the code and data could be addressed with just a 16-bit address. Machines were then revised to offer 32-bit addresses, either through an unsegmented 32-bit address space (also called a *flat address space*) or by adding 16 bits of segment to the existing 16-bit address. From a marketing point of view, adding segments that were programmer-visible and that forced the programmer and compiler to decompose programs into segments could solve the addressing problem. Unfortunately, there is trouble any time a programming language wants an address that is larger than one segment, such as indices for large arrays, unrestricted pointers, or reference parameters. Moreover, adding segments can turn every address into two words—one for the segment number and one for the segment offset—causing problems in the use of addresses in registers. As this book is being completed, the limits of 32-bit addresses are being reached. Some architectures, such as the MIPS R4000, DEC Alpha, and Sun SPARC, have chosen to support 64-bit flat address spaces. Others, such as HP PA-RISC, are providing an extended address space via segmentation, as a temporary solution. Still other architectures, such as the 80x86, are expected to be replaced by a new 64-bit architecture.

7.8 | Concluding Remarks

The difficulty of building a memory system to keep pace with faster CPUs is underscored by the fact that the raw material for main memory, DRAMs, is essentially the same in the fastest computers as it is in the slowest and cheapest. It is the principle of locality that gives us a chance to overcome the long latency of memory access—and the soundness of this strategy is demonstrated at all levels of the memory hierarchy. Although these levels of the hierarchy look quite different in quantitative terms, they follow similar strategies in their operation and exploit the same properties of locality.

Because CPU speeds continue to increase faster than either DRAM access times or disk access times, memory will increasingly be the factor that limits performance. Processors continue to increase in performance at a spectacular rate, and DRAMs show signs of continuing their fourfold improvement in density every three years. The *access time* of DRAMs, however, is improving at a much slower rate—about 9% per year. Figure 7.35 plots optimistic and pessimistic processor cycle time estimates against the steady 9% annual performance improvement in DRAM speeds. This data includes only the effect of decreasing processor cycle times. Processors have also been reducing the CPI component of performance, leading to more memory access per cycle and a relatively larger penalty for long memory access times.

Recent enhancements in DRAM technology (synchronous DRAMs and related techniques) have led to increases in potential memory bandwidth. This potentially higher memory bandwidth has enabled designers to increase cache block sizes with smaller increases in the miss penalty. In the future, such enhancements and design trade-offs will be critical to limiting the performance loss in the memory system.

Recent Trends

The challenge in designing memory hierarchies to close this growing gap, as we noted in the Big Picture on page 611, is that all the hardware design choices for memory hierarchies have both a positive and negative effect on performance. This means that for each level of the hierarchy there is an opti-

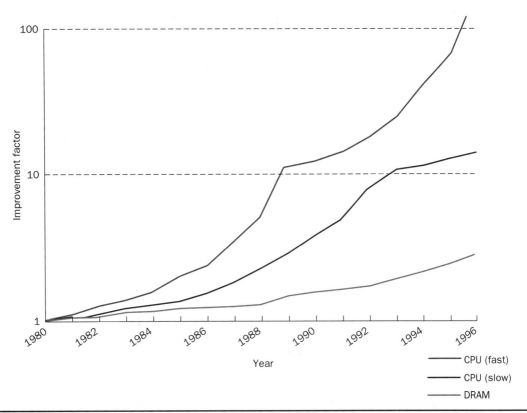

FIGURE 7.35 Using their 1980 performance as a baseline, the access time of DRAMs versus the cycle time of processors is plotted over time. The DRAM baseline is 64 KB in 1980, and the average improvement in access time per year is 9%. Both the fast and slow processor performance lines are based on typical processors produced during this time. The slow processor line shows a 15% improvement per year in cycle time until 1985 and a 25% improvement thereafter. The fast processor line shows a 25% performance improvement per year in clock rate between 1980 and 1985 and 40% per year thereafter. Of course, processor performance has increased by more than just cycle time. Reductions in CPI have yielded an additional factor of 15–20 in performance for the fast CPUs over the period shown in the graph. This reduction in CPI further enlarges the losses due to memory system performance, although the increasing CPI gap may not lead to larger access times for a cache hit. Note that the vertical axis must be on a logarithmic scale to record the size of the processor-DRAM performance gap.

mal performance point, which must include some misses. If this is the case, how can we overcome the growing gap between CPU speeds and lower levels of the hierarchy? This question is currently the topic of much research.

On-chip first-level caches have helped close the gap that was growing between CPU clock cycle time and off-chip SRAM cycle time. To narrow the gap between the small on-chip caches and DRAM, second-level caches became widespread. Today, all mid-range and high-end desktop machines use second-level caches. In fact, high-end servers are using second-level caches of 1–16 MB! Second-level caches also make it possible to more easily use other optimizations for two reasons. First, the design parameters of a second-level cache are different than a first-level cache. For example, because a second-level cache will be much larger, it is possible to use larger block sizes. Second, a second-level cache is not constantly being used by the CPU, as a first-level cache is. This allows us to consider having the second-level cache do something when it is idle that may be useful in preventing future misses; we will see an example of this in just a bit.

Another attempt to reduce the processor-DRAM performance gap is to reassess the interface on the DRAM chips. Several efforts are under way to redesign that interface to offer much higher bandwidth than standard DRAMs, in part by supplying a clock to DRAM chips to synchronize transfers and in part by increasing the number of pins on the DRAMS. These techniques make it easier to justify increasing the block size, since the transfer time component of the miss penalty can be made smaller. Although such DRAMs currently have a price premium (10%–30%, typically), it appears that, at least in some environments, designers are willing to pay these higher costs. A related development has been the use of synchronous SRAMs, which are being used for secondary caches, and which help reduce the time to transfer a block from the secondary to the primary cache. Synchronous SRAMs are becoming the default for secondary caches.

Another possible direction is to seek software help. Efficiently managing the memory hierarchy using a variety of program transformation and hardware facilities is a major focus of research in compilers. Two different ideas are being explored. One idea is to reorganize the program to enhance its spatial and temporal locality. This approach focuses on loop-oriented programs that use large arrays as the major data structure; large linear algebra problems are a typical example. By restructuring the loops that access the arrays, substantially improved locality—and, therefore, cache performance—can be obtained. The example on page 617 showed how effective even a simple change of loop structure could be.

Another direction is to try to use compiler-directed *prefetching*. In prefetching, a block of data is brought into the cache before it is actually referenced. The compiler tries to identify data blocks needed in the future and, using special instructions, tells the memory hierarchy to move the blocks into the cache. When the block is actually referenced, it is found in the cache, rather than causing a cache miss. The use of secondary caches has made prefetching even more attractive, since the secondary cache can be involved in a prefetch, while the primary cache continues to service processor requests.

As we will see in Chapter 9, memory systems are also a central design issue for parallel processors. The growing importance of the memory hierarchy in determining system performance in both uniprocessor and multiprocessor systems means that this important area will continue to be a focus of both designers and researchers for some years to come.

7.9 Historical Perspective and Further Reading

. . . the one single development that put computers on their feet was the invention of a reliable form of memory, namely, the core memory. . . . Its cost was reasonable, it was reliable and, because it was reliable, it could in due course be made large.

Maurice Wilkes,
Memoirs of a Computer Pioneer, 1985

The developments of most of the concepts in this chapter have been driven by revolutionary advances in the technology we use for memory. Before we discuss how memory hierarchies were developed, let's take a brief tour of the development of memory technology. In this section, we focus on the technologies for building main memory and caches; Chapter 8 will provide some of the history of developments in disk technology.

The ENIAC had only a small number of registers (about 20) for its storage and implemented these with the same basic vacuum tube technology that it used for building logic circuitry. However, the vacuum tube technology was far too expensive to be used to build a larger memory capacity. Eckert came up with the idea of developing a new technology based on mercury delay lines. In this technology, electrical signals were converted into vibrations that were sent down a tube of mercury, reaching the other end, where they were read out and recirculated. One mercury delay line could store about 0.5 Kbits. Although these bits were accessed serially, the mercury delay line was about a hundred times more cost-effective than vacuum tube memory. The first known working mercury delay lines were developed at Cambridge for the EDSAC. Figure 7.36 shows the mercury delay lines of the EDSAC, which had 32 tanks and a total of 512 36-bit words.

Despite the tremendous advance offered by the mercury delay lines, they were terribly unreliable and still rather expensive. The breakthrough came with the invention of core memory by J. Forrester at MIT as part of the Whirlwind project, in the early 1950s (see Figure 7.37). Core memory uses a ferrite core, which can be magnetized, and once magnetized, acts as a store (just as a magnetic recording tape stores information). A set of wires running through

FIGURE 7.36   The mercury delay lines in the EDSAC. This technology made it possible to build the first stored-program computer. The young engineer in this photograph is none other than Maurice Wilkes, the lead architect of the EDSAC. Photo courtesy of the Computer Museum, Boston.

the center of the core, which had a dimension of 0.1–1.0 millimeters, make it possible to read the value stored on any ferrite core. The Whirlwind eventually included a core memory with 2048 16-bit words, or a total of 32 Kbits. Core memory was a tremendous advance: It was cheaper, faster, much more reliable, and had higher density. Core memory was so much better than the alternatives that it became the dominant memory technology only a few years after its invention and remained so for nearly 20 years.

The technology that replaced core memory was the same one that we now use both for logic and memory: the integrated circuit. While registers were built out of transistorized memory in the 1960s, and IBM machines used transistorized memory for microcode store and caches in 1970, building main

FIGURE 7.37   A core memory plane from the Whirlwind containing 256 cores arranged in a 16 x 16 array. Core memory was invented for the Whirlwind, which was used for air defense problems, and is now on display at the Smithsonian. (Incidentally, Ken Olsen, the founder and president of Digital for 20 years, built the machine that tested these core memories; it was his first computer.) Photo courtesy of the Computer Museum, Boston.

memory out of transistors remained prohibitive until the development of the integrated circuit. With the integrated circuit, it became possible to build a DRAM (dynamic random access memory—see Appendix B for a description). The first DRAMS were built at Intel in 1970, and the machines using DRAM memories (as a high-speed option to core) came shortly thereafter; they used 1-Kbit DRAMs. In fact, computer folklore says that Intel developed the microprocessor partly to help sell more DRAM. Figure 7.38 shows an early DRAM board. By the late 1970s, core memory became a historical curiosity. Just as core memory technology had allowed a tremendous expansion in memory size, DRAM technology allowed a comparable expansion. In the 1990s, many personal computers have as much memory as the largest machines using core memory ever had.

Nowadays, DRAMs are typically packaged with multiple chips on a little board called SIMM (single inline memory module) or DIMM (dual inline memory module). The SIMM shown in Figure 7.39 contains a total of 1 MB and sells for about $5 in 1997. In 1997, SIMMs and DIMMs are available with up to 64 MB. While DRAMs will remain the dominant memory technology for some time to come, dramatic innovations in the packaging of DRAMs to provide both higher bandwidth and greater density are ongoing.

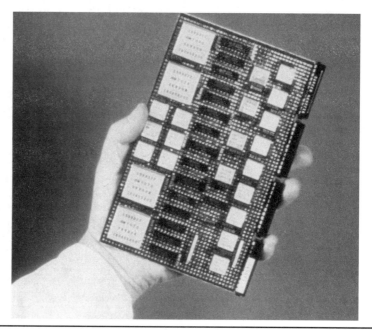

FIGURE 7.38 **An early DRAM board.** This board uses 18-Kbit chips. Photo courtesy of IBM.

FIGURE 7.39 **A 1-MB SIMM, built in 1986, using 1-Mbit chips.** This SIMM, used in a Macintosh, sells for about $5/MB in 1997. In 1997, most main memory is packed in either SIMMs or DIMMs similar to this, though using much higher-density memory chips (16-Mbit or 64-Mbit). Photo courtesy of MIPS Technology, Inc.

The Development of Memory Hierarchies

Although the pioneers of computing foresaw the need for a memory hierarchy and coined the term, the automatic management of two levels was first proposed by Kilburn and his colleagues and demonstrated at the University of Manchester with the Atlas computer, which implemented virtual memory. This was the year *before* the IBM 360 was announced. IBM planned to include virtual memory with the next generation (System/370), but the OS/360 operating system wasn't up to the challenge in 1970. Virtual memory was announced for the 370 family in 1972, and it was for this machine that the term *translation-lookaside buffer* was coined. The only computers today without virtual memory are a few supercomputers, and even they may add this feature in the near future.

The problems of inadequate address space have plagued designers repeatedly. The architects of the PDP-11 identified a small address space as the only architectural mistake that is difficult to recover from. When the PDP-11 was designed, core memory densities were increasing at a very slow rate, and the competition from 100 other minicomputer companies meant that DEC might not have a cost-competitive product if every address had to go through the 16-bit datapath twice. Hence the decision to add just 4 more address bits than the predecessor of the PDP-11. The architects of the IBM 360 were aware of the importance of address size and planned for the architecture to extend to 32 bits of address. Only 24 bits were used in the IBM 360, however, because the low-end 360 models would have been even slower with the larger addresses. Unfortunately, the expansion effort was greatly complicated by programmers who stored extra information in the upper 8 "unused" address bits.

Running out of address space has often been the cause of death for an architecture, while other architectures have managed to make the transition to a larger address space. For example, the PDP-11, a 16-bit machine, was replaced by the 32-bit VAX. The 80386 extended the 80286 architecture from 16 bits to 32 bits. Several recent RISC instruction sets have made the transition from 32-bit addressing to 64-bit addressing by providing a compatible extension of their instruction sets. Intel has announced a plan to develop a new instruction set jointly with HP. This new instruction set will provide 64-bit addressing.

Many of the early ideas in memory hierarchies originated in England. Just a few years after the Atlas paper, Wilkes [1965] published the first paper describing the concept of a cache, calling it a "slave:"

> *The use is discussed of a fast core memory of, say, 32,000 words as slave to a slower core memory of, say, one million words in such a way that in practical cases the effective access time is nearer that of the fast memory than that of the slow memory.*

This two-page paper describes a direct-mapped cache. Although this was the first publication on caches, the first implementation was probably a direct-mapped instruction cache built at the University of Cambridge by Scarrott and described at the 1965 IFIP Congress. It was based on tunnel diode memory, the fastest form of memory available at the time.

Subsequent to that publication, IBM started a project that led to the first commercial machine with a cache, the IBM 360/85. Gibson at IBM recognized that memory-accessing behavior would have a significant impact on performance.

He described how to measure program behavior and cache behavior and showed that the miss rate varies between programs. Using a sample of 20 programs (each with 3 million references—an incredible number for that time), Gibson analyzed the effectiveness of caches using average memory access time as the metric. Conti, Gibson, and Pitkowsky described the resulting performance of the 360/85 in the first paper to use the term *cache* in 1968. Since this early work, it has become clear that caches are one of the most important ideas not only in computer architecture, but in software systems as well. The idea of caching has found applications in operating systems, networking systems, databases, and compilers, to name a few. There are thousands of papers on the topic of caching, and it continues to be an important area of research.

Protection Mechanisms

Architectural support for protection has varied greatly over the past 20 years. In early machines, before virtual memory, protection was very simple at best. In the 1970s, more elaborate mechanisms that supported different protection levels (called *rings*) were invented. In the late 1970s and early 1980s, very elaborate mechanisms for protection were devised and later built; these mechanisms supported a variety of powerful protection schemes that allowed controlled instances of sharing, in such a way that a process could share data while controlling exactly what was done to the data. The most powerful method, called *capabilities*, created a data object that described the access rights to some portion of memory. These capabilities could then be passed to other processes, thus granting access to the object described by the capability. Supporting this sophisticated protection mechanism was both complex and costly because creation, copying, and manipulation of capabilities required a combination of operating system and hardware support. Recent machines all support a simpler protection scheme based on virtual memory, similar to that discussed in section 7.4.

To Probe Further

Conti, C., D. H. Gibson, and S. H. Pitowsky [1968]. "Structural aspects of the System/360 Model 85, part I: General organization," *IBM Systems J.* 7:1, 2–14.

Describes the first commercial machine to use a cache and its resulting performance.

Hennessy, J., and D. Patterson [1996]. Chapter 5 in *Computer Architecture: A Quantitative Approach*, Second edition, Morgan Kaufmann Publishers, San Francisco.

For more in-depth coverage of a variety of topics including protection, improving write performance, virtually addressed caches, multilevel caches, additional latency tolerance mechanisms, and cache coherency.

Kilburn, T., D. B. G. Edwards, M. J. Lanigan, and F. H. Sumner [1962]. "One-level storage system," *IRE Transactions on Electronic Computers* EC-11 (April) 223–35. Also appears in D. P. Siewiorek, C. G. Bell, and A. Newell, *Computer Structures: Principles and Examples*, McGraw-Hill, New York, 135–48, 1982.

This classic paper is the first proposal for virtual memory.

Przybylski, S. A. [1990]. *Cache and Memory Hierarchy Design: A Performance-Directed Approach*, Morgan Kaufmann Publishers, San Francisco.

A thorough exploration of multilevel memory hierarchies and their performance.

Silberschatz, A., and P. Galvin [1994]. *Operating System Concepts*, Addison-Wesley, Reading, MA.

An operating systems textbook with a thorough discussion of virtual memory, processes and process management, and protection issues.

Smith, A. J. [1982]. "Cache memories," *Computing Surveys* 14:3 (September) 473–530.

The classic survey paper on caches. This paper defined the terminology for the field and has served as a reference for many computer designers.

Tanenbaum, A. [1991]. *Operating Systems Principles*, Addison-Wesley, Reading, MA.

An operating system textbook with a good discussion of virtual memory.

Wilkes, M. [1965]. "Slave memories and dynamic storage allocation," *IEEE Trans. Electronic Computers* EC-14:2 (April) 270–71.

The first, classic paper on caches.

7.10 Key Terms

Designers have developed a wide variety of strategies that rely on locality to overcome the gap between processor and main memory, leading to a large amount of terminology to describe these schemes.

address translation or
    mapping
aliasing
block
cache miss
capacity miss
compulsory or cold start miss
conflict or collision miss
context switch
exception or direct-mapped
    cache
fully associative cache
global miss rate
hit rate
hit time
interrupt enable
kernel or supervisor mode

least recently used (LRU)
local miss rate
memory hierarchy
miss penalty
miss rate
multilevel cache
nonblocking cache
page fault
page table
physical address
physically addressed cache
prefetching
protection
reference or use bit
restartable instruction
segmentation
set-associative cache

spatial locality
split cache
system call
tag
temporal locality
three Cs model
translation-lookaside buffer
    (TLB)
valid bit
virtual address
virtual memory
virtually addressed cache
write-back
write buffer
write-through

7.11 Exercises

7.1 [10] <§7.2> Describe the general characteristics of a program that would exhibit very little temporal and spatial locality with regard to data accesses. Provide an example program (pseudocode is fine).

7.2 [10] <§7.2> Describe the general characteristics of a program that would exhibit very high amounts of temporal locality but very little spatial locality with regard to data accesses. Provide an example program (pseudocode is fine).

7.3 [10] <§7.2> Describe the general characteristics of a program that would exhibit very little temporal locality but very high amounts of spatial locality with regard to data accesses. Provide an example program (pseudocode is fine).

7.4 [10] <§7.2> Describe the general characteristics of a program that would exhibit very little temporal and spatial locality with regard to instruction fetches. Provide an example program (pseudocode is fine).

7.5 [10] <§7.2> Describe the general characteristics of a program that would exhibit very high amounts of temporal locality but very little spatial locality with regard to instruction fetches. Provide an example program (pseudocode is fine).

7.6 [10] <§7.2> Describe the general characteristics of a program that would exhibit very little temporal locality but very high amounts of spatial locality with regard to instruction fetches. Provide an example program (pseudocode is fine).

7.7 [10] <§7.2> Here is a series of address references given as word addresses: 1, 4, 8, 5, 20, 17, 19, 56, 9, 11, 4, 43, 5, 6, 9, 17. Assuming a direct-mapped cache with 16 one-word blocks that is initially empty, label each reference in the list as a hit or a miss and show the final contents of the cache.

7.8 [10] <§7.2> Using the series of references given in Exercise 7.7, show the hits and misses and final cache contents for a direct-mapped cache with four-word blocks and a *total size* of 16 words.

7.9 [10] <§7.2> Compute the total number of bits required to implement the cache in Figure 7.10 on page 557. This number is different from the size of the cache, which usually refers to the number of bytes of data stored in the cache. The number of bits needed to implement the cache represents the total amount of memory needed for storing all of the data, tags, and valid bits.

7.10 [10] <§7.2> Find a method to eliminate the AND gate on the valid bit in Figure 7.7 on page 549. (Hint: You need to change the comparison.)

7.11 [10] <§7.2> Consider a memory hierarchy using one of the three organizations for main memory shown in Figure 7.13 on page 561. Assume that the cache block size is 16 words, that the width of organization b of the figure is four words, and that the number of banks in organization c is four. If the main memory latency for a new access is 10 cycles and the transfer time is 1 cycle, what are the miss penalties for each of these organizations?

7.12 [10] <§7.2> {Ex. 7.11} Suppose a processor with a 16-word block size has an effective miss rate per instruction of 0.5%. Assume that the CPI without cache misses is 1.2. Using the memories described in Figure 7.13 on page 561 and Exercise 7.11, how much faster is this processor when using the wide memory than when using narrow or interleaved memories?

7.13 [15] <§7.2> Cache C1 is direct-mapped with 16 one-word blocks. Cache C2 is direct-mapped with 4 four-word blocks. Assume that the miss penalty for C1 is 8 clock cycles and the miss penalty for C2 is 11 clock cycles. Assuming that the caches are initially empty, find a reference string for which C2 has a lower miss rate but spends more cycles on cache misses than C1. Use word addresses.

7.14 [15] <§7.2> For the caches in Exercise 7.13, find a series of references for which C2 has more misses than C1. Use word addresses.

In More Depth

Average Memory Access Time

To capture the fact that the time to access data for both hits and misses affects performance, designers often use average memory access time (AMAT) as a way to examine alternative cache designs. Average memory access time is the average time to access memory considering both hits and misses and the frequency of different accesses; it is equal to the following:

$$AMAT = \text{Time for a hit} + \text{Miss rate} \times \text{Miss penalty}$$

AMAT is useful as a figure of merit for different cache systems.

7.15 [5] <§7.2> Find the AMAT for a machine with a 2-ns clock, a miss penalty of 20 clock cycles, a miss rate of 0.05 misses per instruction, and a cache access time (including hit detection) of 1 clock cycle. Assume that the read and write miss penalties are the same and ignore other write stalls.

7.16 [5] <§7.2> {Ex. 7.15} Suppose we can improve the miss rate to 0.03 misses per reference by doubling the cache size. This causes the cache access time to increase to 1.2 clock cycles. Using the AMAT as a metric, determine if this is a good trade-off.

7.17 [10] <§7.2> [Ex. 7.16} If the cache access time determines the processor's clock cycle time, which is often the case, AMAT may not correctly indicate whether one cache organization is better than another. If the machine's clock cycle time must be changed to match that of a cache, is this a good trade-off? Assume the machines are identical except for the clock rate and the number of cache miss cycles; assume 1.5 references per instruction and a CPI without cache misses of 2. The miss penalty is 20 cycles for both machines.

7.18 [10] <§§7.2, B.5> You have been given 18 32K × 8-bit SRAMs to build an instruction cache for a processor with a 32-bit address. What is the largest size (i.e., the largest size of the data storage area in bytes) direct-mapped instruction cache that you can build with one-word (32-bit) blocks? Show the breakdown of the address into its cache access components (for an example, see Figure 7.8) and describe how the various SRAM chips will be used. (Hint: You may not need all of them.)

7.19 [10] <§§7.2, B.5> This exercise is similar to Exercise 7.18, except that this time you decide to build a direct-mapped cache with four-word blocks as in Figure 7.10. Once again show the breakdown of the address and describe how the chips are used.

7.20 [10] <§7.3> Using the series of references given in Exercise 7.7, show the hits and misses and final cache contents for a two-way set-associative cache with one-word blocks and a *total size* of 16 words. Assume LRU replacement.

7.21 [10] <§7.3> Using the series of references given in Exercise 7.7, show the hits and misses and final cache contents for a fully associative cache with one-word blocks and a *total size* of 16 words. Assume LRU replacement.

7.22 [10] <§7.3> Using the series of references given in Exercise 7.7, show the hits and misses and final cache contents for a fully associative cache with four-word blocks and a *total size* of 16 words. Assume LRU replacement.

7.23 [5] <§7.3> Associativity usually improves the miss ratio, but not always. Give a short series of address references for which a two-way set-associative cache with LRU replacement would experience more misses than a direct-mapped cache of the same size.

7.24 [15] <§7.3> Suppose a computer's address size is k bits (using byte addressing), the cache size is S bytes, the block size is B bytes, and the cache is A-way set-associative. Assume that B is a power of two, so $B = 2^b$. Figure out what the following quantities are in terms of S, B, A, b, and k: the number of sets in the cache, the number of index bits in the address, and the number of bits needed to implement the cache (see Exercise 7.9).

7.25 [10] <§7.3> This exercise concerns caches of unusual sizes. Can you make a fully associative cache containing exactly 3K words of data? How about a set-associative cache or a direct-mapped cache containing exactly 3K words of data? For each of these, describe how or why not. Remember that $1K = 2^{10}$.

7.26 [10] <§7.3> This exercise is similar to Exercise 7.25, except replace 3K with 300. Remember that $300 = 3 * 10^2$.

7.27 [20] <§7.3> Consider three machines with different cache configurations:

- *Cache 1:* Direct-mapped with one-word blocks
- *Cache 2:* Direct-mapped with four-word blocks
- *Cache 3:* Two-way set associative with four-word blocks

The following miss rate measurements have been made:

- *Cache 1:* Instruction miss rate is 4%; data miss rate is 8%.
- *Cache 2:* Instruction miss rate is 2%; data miss rate is 5%.
- *Cache 3:* Instruction miss rate is 2%; data miss rate is 4%.

For these machines, one-half of the instructions contain a data reference. Assume that the cache miss penalty is 6 + Block size in words. The CPI for this workload was measured on a machine with cache 1 and was found to be 2.0. Determine which machine spends the most cycles on cache misses.

7.28 [5] <§7.3> {Ex. 7.27} The cycle times for the machines in Exercise 7.27 are 2 ns for the first and second machines and 2.4 ns for the third machine. Determine which machine is the fastest and which is the slowest.

7.29 [10] <§§7.2, 7.3> The following C program is run (with no optimizations) on a machine with a cache that has four-word (16-byte) blocks and holds 256 bytes of data:

```
int i,j,c,stride,array[256];
...
for (i=0; i<10000; i++)
  for (j=0; j<256; j=j+stride)
  c = array[j]+5;
```

If we consider only the cache activity generated by references to the array and we assume that integers are words, what is the expected miss rate when the cache is direct-mapped and stride = 132? How about if stride = 131? Would either of these change if the cache were two-way set associative?

7.30 [10] <§§7.3, B.5> This exercise is similar to Exercise 7.18, except that this time you decide to build a three-way set-associative cache with one-word blocks. Once again show the breakdown of the address (see Figure 7.19 for an example of a four-way set-associative cache) and describe how the chips are used. Note that each SRAM will only perform a single read per cache access.

7.31 [5] <§§7.2–7.4> Rank each of the possible event combinations appearing in the example on page 595 according to how frequently you think they would occur.

7.32 [15] <§7.4> Consider a virtual memory system with the following properties:

- 40-bit virtual byte address
- 16-KB pages
- 36-bit physical byte address

What is the total size of the page table for each process on this machine, assuming that the valid, protection, dirty, and use bits take a total of 4 bits and that all the virtual pages are in use? (Assume that disk addresses are not stored in the page table.)

7.33 [15] <§7.4> Assume that the virtual memory system of Exercise 7.32 is implemented with a two-way set-associative TLB with a total of 256 TLB entries. Show the virtual-to-physical mapping with a figure like Figure 7.25 on page 593. Make sure to label the width of all fields and signals.

7.34 [15] <§7.3> Assume that the cache for the system described in Exercise 7.32 is two-way set associative and has eight-word blocks and a total size of 16 KB. Show the cache organization and access using the same format as Figure 7.19 on page 574.

7.35 [15] <§7.4> Page tables require fairly large amounts of memory (as described in the elaboration on page 587), even if most of the entries are invalid. One solution is to use a hierarchy of page tables. The virtual page number, as described in Figure 7.21 on page 582, can be broken up into two pieces, a "page table number" and a "page table offset." The page table number can be used to index a first-level page table that provides a physical address for a second-level page table, assuming it resides in memory (if not, a first-level page fault will occur and the page table itself will need to be brought in from disk). The page table offset is used to index into the second-level page table to retrieve the physical page number. One obvious way to arrange such a scheme is to have the second-level page tables occupy exactly one page of memory. Assuming a 32-bit virtual address space with 4-KB pages and 4 bytes per page table entry, how many bytes will each program need to use to store the first-level page table (which must always be in memory)? Provide figures similar to Figures 7.20, 7.21, and 7.22 (pages 581–584) that demonstrate your understanding of this idea.

7.36 [15] <§7.4> Assuming that we use the two-level hierarchical page table described in Exercise 7.35 and that exactly one second-level page table is in memory and exactly half of its entries are valid, how many bytes of memory in our virtual address space actually reside in physical memory? (Hint: The second-level page table occupies exactly one page of physical memory.)

7.37 [10] <§7.4> Some programs, such as complex simulations of weather patterns, are loaded into a computer where they will run, uninterrupted, for long periods of time. Expensive supercomputers are often purchased for these applications. Discuss some of the reasons why virtual memory may or may not be desirable for machines designed for these types of applications. Would a cache be necessary?

7.38 [5] <§§7.5> If all misses are classified into one of three categories—compulsory, capacity, or conflict (as discussed on page 609)—which misses are likely to be reduced when a program is rewritten so as to require less memory? How about if the clock rate of the machine that the program is running on is increased? How about if the associativity of the existing cache is increased?

7.39 [5] <§7.5> The following C program could be used to help construct a cache simulator. Many of the data types have not been defined, but the code accurately describes the actions that take place during a read access to a direct-mapped cache.

```
word ReadDirectMappedCache(address a)
  static Entry cache[CACHE_SIZE_IN_WORDS];
  Entry e = cache[a.index];
  if (e.valid == FALSE !! e.tag != a.tag) {
    e.valid = true;
    e.tag = a.tag;
    e.data = load_from_memory(a);
  }
  return e.data;
```

Your task is to modify this code to produce an accurate description of the actions that take place during a read access to a direct-mapped cache with multiple-word blocks.

7.40 [8] <§7.5> This exercise is similar to Exercise 7.39, except this time write the code for read accesses to an *n*-way set-associative cache with one-word blocks. Note that your code will likely suggest that the comparisons are sequential in nature when in fact they would be performed in parallel by actual hardware.

7.41 [8] <§7.5> {Ex. 7.39} Extend your solution to Exercise 7.39 by including the specification of a new procedure for handling write accesses, assuming a write-through policy. Be sure to consider whether or not your solution for handling read accesses needs to be modified.

7.42 [8] <§7.5> {Ex. 7.39} Extend your solution to Exercise 7.39 by including the specification of a new procedure for handling write accesses, assuming a write-back policy. Be sure to consider whether or not your solution for handling read accesses needs to be modified.

7.43 [8] <§7.5> {Ex. 7.40} This exercise is similar to Exercise 7.41, but this time extend your solution to Exercise 7.40. Assume that the cache uses random replacement.

7.44 [8] <§7.5> {Ex. 7.40} This exercise is similar to Exercise 7.42, but this time extend your solution to Exercise 7.40. Assume that the cache uses random replacement.

7.45 [5] <§§7.7–7.8> Why might a compiler perform the following optimization?

```
/* Before */
for (j = 0; j < 20; j++)
  for (i = 0; i < 200; i++)
   x[i][j] = x[i][j] + 1;
/* After */
for (i = 0; i < 200; i++)
  for (j = 0; j < 20; j++)
   x[i][j] = x[i][j] + 1;
```

7.46 [3 hours] <§7.2> Use a cache simulator to simulate several different cache organizations for the first 1 million references in a trace of gcc. Both dinero (a cache simulator) and the gcc traces are available—see the preface of this book for information on how to obtain them. Assume an instruction cache of 32 KB and a data cache of 32 KB using the same organization. You should choose at least two kinds of associativity and two block sizes. Draw a diagram like that in Figure 7.19 on page 574 that shows the data cache organization with the best hit rate.

7.47 [4 hours] <§§7.2–7.4> We want to use a cache simulator to simulate several different TLB and virtual memory organizations. Use the first 1 million references of gcc for this evaluation. We want to know the TLB miss rate for each of the following TLBs and page sizes:

1. 64-entry TLB with full associativity and 4-KB pages

2. 32-entry TLB with full associativity and 8-KB pages

3. 64-entry TLB with eight-way associativity and 4-KB pages

4. 128-entry TLB with four-way associativity and 4-KB pages

7.48 [1 day] <§7.2> You are commissioned to design a cache for a new system. It has a 32-bit physical byte address and requires separate instruction and data caches. The SRAMs have an access time of 1.5 ns and a size of 32K × 8 bits, and you have a total of 16 SRAMs to use. The miss penalty for the memory system is 8 + 2 × Block size in words. Using set associativity adds 0.2 ns to the cache access time. Using the first 1 million references of gcc, find the best I and D cache organizations, given the available SRAMs.

8

Interfacing
Processors
and Peripherals

*I/O certainly has been lagging
in the last decade.*

Seymour Cray
Public lecture, 1976

8.1   **Introduction**   638

8.2   **I/O Performance Measures: Some Examples from Disk and File Systems**   641

8.3   **Types and Characteristics of I/O Devices**   644

8.4   **Buses: Connecting I/O Devices to Processor and Memory**   655

8.5   **Interfacing I/O Devices to the Memory, Processor, and Operating System**   673

8.6   **Designing an I/O System**   684

8.7   **Real Stuff: A Typical Desktop I/O System**   687

8.8   **Fallacies and Pitfalls**   688

8.9   **Concluding Remarks**   690

8.10   **Historical Perspective and Further Reading**   694

8.11   **Key Terms**   700

8.12   **Exercises**   700

The Five Classic Components of a Computer

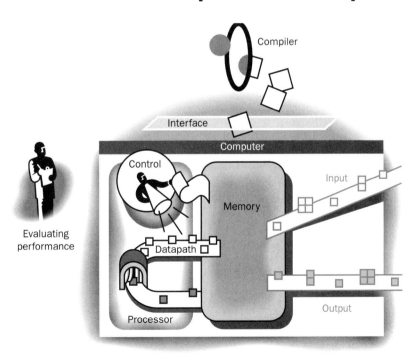

8.1   Introduction

As in processors, many of the characteristics of input/output (I/O) systems are driven by technology. For example, the properties of disk drives affect how the disks should be connected to the processor, as well as how the operating system interacts with the disks. I/O systems, however, differ from processors in several important ways. Although processor designers often focus primarily on performance, designers of I/O systems must consider issues such as expandability and resilience in the face of failure as much as they consider performance. Second, performance in an I/O system is a more complex characteristic than for a processor. For example, with some devices we may care primarily about access latency, while with others throughput is crucial. Furthermore, performance depends on many aspects of the system: the device characteristics, the connection between the device and the rest of the system, the memory hierarchy, and the operating system. Figure 8.1 shows the structure of a system with its I/O. All of the components, from the individual I/O devices to the processor to the system software, will affect the performance of tasks that include I/O.

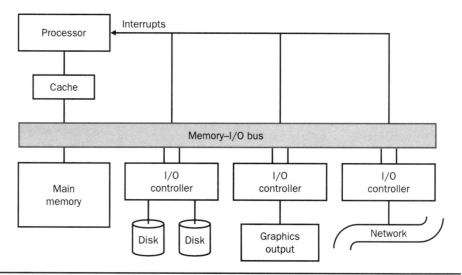

FIGURE 8.1   Typical collection of I/O devices. The connections between the I/O devices, processor, and memory are usually called *buses*. Communication among the devices and the processor use both protocols on the bus and interrupts, as we will see in this chapter.

The difficulties in assessing and designing I/O systems have often relegated I/O to second-class status. Research focuses on processor design; companies present performance using primarily processor-oriented measures; courses in every aspect of computing, from programming to computer architecture, often ignore I/O or give it scanty coverage; and textbooks leave the subject to near the end, making it easier for students and instructors to skip it!

This situation doesn't make sense: imagine how you'd like to use a computer without I/O! Furthermore, in an era when machines, from low-end PCs to the fastest mainframes, and even supercomputers, are being built from the same basic microprocessor technology, I/O capability is often one of the most distinctive features of the machines. Lastly, as the importance of networking and the information infrastructure grows, I/O will play an increasingly important role. Remember that machines interact with people through I/O.

If these concerns are still not convincing, our discussion of Amdahl's law in Chapter 2 should remind us that ignoring I/O is dangerous. A simple example demonstrates this.

Impact of I/O on System Performance

Example Suppose we have a benchmark that executes in 100 seconds of elapsed time, where 90 seconds is CPU time and the rest is I/O time. If CPU time improves by 50% per year for the next five years but I/O time doesn't improve, how much faster will our program run at the end of five years?

Answer We know that

$$\text{Elapsed time} = \text{CPU time} + \text{I/O time}$$
$$100 = 90 + \text{I/O time}$$
$$\text{I/O time} = 10 \text{ seconds}$$

The new CPU times and the resulting elapsed times are computed in the following table:

After n years	CPU time	I/O time	Elapsed time	% I/O time
0	90 seconds	10 seconds	100 seconds	10%
1	$\frac{90}{1.5} = 60$ seconds	10 seconds	70 seconds	14%
2	$\frac{60}{1.5} = 40$ seconds	10 seconds	50 seconds	20%
3	$\frac{40}{1.5} = 27$ seconds	10 seconds	37 seconds	27%
4	$\frac{27}{1.5} = 18$ seconds	10 seconds	28 seconds	36%
5	$\frac{18}{1.5} = 12$ seconds	10 seconds	22 seconds	45%

The improvement in CPU performance over five years is

$$\frac{90}{12} = 7.5$$

However, the improvement in elapsed time is only

$$\frac{100}{22} = 4.5$$

and the I/O time has increased from 10% to 45% of the elapsed time.

How we should assess I/O performance often depends on the application. In some environments, we may care primarily about system throughput. In these cases, I/O bandwidth will be most important. Even I/O bandwidth can be measured in two different ways:

1. How much data can we move through the system in a certain time?

2. How many I/O operations can we do per unit of time?

Which measurement is best may depend on the environment. For example, in many supercomputer applications, most I/O requests are for long streams of data, and transfer bandwidth is the important characteristic. In another environment, we may wish to process a large number of small, unrelated accesses to an I/O device. An example of such an environment might be a tax-processing office of the National Income Tax Service (NITS). NITS mostly cares about processing a large number of forms in a given time; each tax form is stored separately and is fairly small. A system oriented toward large file transfer may be satisfactory, but an I/O system that can support the simultaneous transfer of many small files may be cheaper and faster for processing millions of tax forms.

In other applications, we care primarily about response time, which you will recall is the total elapsed time to accomplish a particular task. If the I/O requests are extremely large, response time will depend heavily on bandwidth, but in many environments most accesses will be small, and the I/O system with the lowest latency per access will deliver the best response time. On single-user machines such as workstations and personal computers, response time is the key performance characteristic.

A large number of applications, especially in the vast commercial market for computing, require both high throughput and short response times. Examples include automatic teller machines (ATMs), airline reservation systems, order entry and inventory tracking systems, file servers, and machines for timesharing. In such environments, we care about both how long each task takes *and* how many tasks we can process in a second. The number of ATM requests you can process per hour doesn't matter if each one takes 15 minutes—you won't have any customers left! Similarly, if you can process each ATM request quickly but can only handle a small number of requests at once, you won't be able to support many ATMs, or the cost of the computer per ATM will be very high.

If I/O is truly important, how should we compare I/O systems? This is a complex question because I/O performance depends on many aspects of the system and different applications stress different aspects of the I/O system. Furthermore, a design can make complex trade-offs between response time and throughput, making it impossible to measure just one aspect in isolation. For example, response time is generally minimized by handling a request as early as possible, while greater throughput can be achieved if we try to handle related requests together. Accordingly, we may increase throughput on a disk by grouping requests that access locations that are close together. Such a policy will increase the response time for some requests, probably leading to a larger variation in response time. Although throughput will be higher, some benchmarks constrain the maximum response time to any request, making such optimizations potentially problematic.

Before discussing the aspects of I/O devices and how they are connected, let's look briefly at some performance measures for I/O systems.

8.2 I/O Performance Measures: Some Examples from Disk and File Systems

Assessment of an I/O system must take into account a variety of factors. Performance is one of these, and in this section, we give some examples of measurements proposed for determining the performance of disk systems. These benchmarks are affected by a variety of system features, including the disk technology, how disks are connected, the memory system, the processor, and the file system provided by the operating system. Overall, the state of benchmarking on the I/O side of computer systems remains quite primitive compared with the extensive activity lately seen in benchmarking processor systems. Perhaps this situation will change as designers realize the importance of I/O and the inadequacy of our techniques to evaluate it.

Before we discuss these benchmarks, we need to address a confusing point about terminology and units. The performance of I/O systems depends on the rate at which the system transfers data. The transfer rate depends on the clock rate, which is typically given in MHz =10^6 cycles per second. The transfer rate is usually quoted in MB/sec. In I/O systems, MBs are measured using base 10 (i.e., 1 MB = 10^6 = 1,000,000 bytes), unlike main memory where base 2 is used (i.e., 1 MB = 2^{20} = 1,048,576). In addition to adding confusion, this difference introduces the need to convert between base 10 (1K = 1000) and base 2 (1K = 1024) because many I/O accesses are for data blocks that have a size that is a power of two. Rather than complicate all our examples by accurately converting one of the two measurements, we make note of this distinction and the fact that treating the two measures as if the units were identical introduces a small error. We illustrate this error in section 8.8.

Supercomputer I/O Benchmarks

Supercomputer I/O is dominated by accesses to large files on magnetic disks. Many supercomputer installations run batch jobs, each of which may last for hours. In these situations, I/O consists of one large read followed by writes to snapshot the state of the computation should the computer crash. As a result, supercomputer I/O in many cases consists more of output than input. The overriding supercomputer I/O measure is data throughput: the number of bytes per second that can be transferred between a supercomputer's main memory and disks during large transfers.

Transaction Processing I/O Benchmarks

Transaction processing (TP) applications involve both a response time requirement and a performance measurement based on throughput. Furthermore, most of the I/O accesses are small. Because of this, TP applications are chiefly concerned with *I/O rate*, measured as the number of disk accesses per second, as opposed to *data rate*, measured as bytes of data per second. TP applications generally involve changes to a large database, with the system meeting some response time requirements as well as gracefully handling certain types of failures. These applications are extremely critical and cost-sensitive. For example, banks normally use TP systems because they are concerned about a range of characteristics. These include making sure transactions aren't lost, handling transactions quickly, and minimizing the cost of processing each transaction. Although reliability in the face of failure is an absolute requirement in such systems, both response time and throughput are critical to building cost-effective systems.

A number of transaction processing benchmarks have been developed. The best-known set of benchmarks is a series developed by the Transaction Processing Council (TPC). The most recent versions of these benchmarks are TPC-C and TPC-D, both of which involve processing of queries against a database. TPC-C involves light- and medium-weight queries based on an order-entry environment, but also typical of the type of transactions needed in a reservation system or online banking system. TPC-D involves complex queries typical of decision support applications.

TPC-C is significantly more sophisticated than the earlier TPC-A and TPC-B benchmarks. It involves nine different types of database records, five different types of transactions, and a model of transaction requests meant to simulate real users generating transactions at terminals. The benchmark specification, including the reporting rules, is 128 pages long! Performance on TPC-C is measured in transactions per minute or second (TPM or TPS) and encompasses a complete system measurement including disk I/O, terminal I/O, and computation. An extensive description of the TPC organization and benchmarks is available via the TPC link at *www.mkp.com/books_catalog/cod/links.htm*.

File System I/O Benchmarks

File systems, which are stored on disks, have a different access pattern. For example, measurements of Unix file systems in an engineering environment have found that 80% of accesses are to files of less than 10 KB and that 90% of all file accesses are to data with sequential addresses on the disk. Furthermore, 67% of the accesses were reads, 27% were writes, and 6% were read-modify-write accesses, which read data, modify it, and then rewrite the same location. Such measurements have led to the creation of synthetic file system benchmarks. One of the most popular of such benchmarks has five phases, using 70 files with a total size of 200 KB:

- *MakeDir*: Constructs a directory subtree that is identical in structure to the given directory subtree
- *Copy*: Copies every file from the source subtree to the target subtree
- *ScanDir*: Recursively traverses a directory subtree and examines the status of every file in it
- *ReadAll*: Scans every byte of every file in a subtree once
- *Make*: Compiles and links all the files in a subtree

As we will see in section 8.6, the design of an I/O system involves knowing what the workload is.

8.3   Types and Characteristics of I/O Devices

I/O devices are incredibly diverse. Three characteristics are useful in organizing this wide variety:

- *Behavior*: Input (read once), output (write only, cannot be read), or storage (can be reread and usually rewritten).

- *Partner*: Either a human or a machine is at the other end of the I/O device, either feeding data on input or reading data on output.

- *Data rate*: The peak rate at which data can be transferred between the I/O device and the main memory or processor. It is useful to know what maximum demand the device may generate.

For example, a keyboard is an *input* device used by a *human* with a *peak data rate* of about 10 bytes per second. Figure 8.2 shows some of the I/O devices connected to computers.

In Chapter 1, we briefly discussed four important and characteristic I/O devices: mice, graphics displays, disks, and networks. We use mice, disks, and networks as examples to illustrate how I/O devices interface to processors and memories, but before we do that it will be useful to discuss these devices in more detail than in Chapter 1.

Device	Behavior	Partner	Data rate (KB/sec)
Keyboard	input	human	0.01
Mouse	input	human	0.02
Voice input	input	human	0.02
Scanner	input	human	400.00
Voice output	output	human	0.60
Line printer	output	human	1.00
Laser printer	output	human	200.00
Graphics display	output	human	60,000.00
Modem	input or output	machine	2.00–8.00
Network/LAN	input or output	machine	500.00–6000.00
Floppy disk	storage	machine	100.00
Optical disk	storage	machine	1000.00
Magnetic tape	storage	machine	2000.00
Magnetic disk	storage	machine	2000.00–10,000.00

FIGURE 8.2   The diversity of I/O devices. I/O devices can be distinguished by whether they serve as input, output, or storage devices; their communication partner (people or other computers); and their peak communication rates. The data rates span six orders of magnitude. Note that a network can be an input or an output device, but cannot be used for storage. Disk sizes, as well as transfer rates for devices, are always quoted in base 10, so that 1 MB = 1,000,000 bytes, and 10 Mbit/sec = 10,000,000 bits/sec.

Mouse

The interface between a mouse and a system can take one of two forms: the mouse either generates a series of pulses when it is moved (using the LED and detector described in Chapter 1 to generate the pulses), or it increments and decrements counters. Figure 8.3 shows how the counters change when the mouse is moved and describes how the interface would operate if it generated pulses instead. The processor can periodically read these counters, or count up the pulses, and determine how far the mouse has moved since it was last examined. The system then moves the cursor on the screen appropriately. This motion appears smooth because the rate at which you can move the mouse is slow compared with the rate at which the processor can read the mouse status and move the cursor on the screen.

Most mice also include one or more buttons, and the system must be able to detect when a button is depressed. By monitoring the status of the button, the system can also differentiate between clicking the button and holding it down. Of course, the mapping between the counters and the button position and what happens on the screen is totally controlled by software. That's why, for example, the rate at which the mouse moves across the screen and the rate at which single and double clicks are recognized can usually be set by the user.

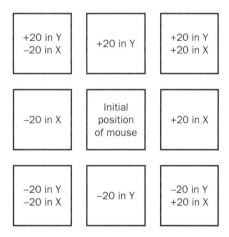

FIGURE 8.3 Moving the mouse in the horizontal direction or vertical direction causes the X or Y counter, respectively, to increment or decrement. Moving it along a diagonal causes both counters to change. Since the ball doesn't move when the mouse is not contacting the surface, it may be picked up and moved without changing the counters. When the mouse uses pulses to communicate its movement, there are four types of pulses: +X, –X, +Y, and –Y. Rather than generate a change in the counter value, the mouse generates the appropriate number of pulses on each of the four pulse signal lines. The value 20 is an arbitrary count that measures how far the mouse has moved.

Similarly, software interpretation of the mouse position means that the cursor doesn't jump completely off the screen when the mouse is moved a long distance in one direction. This method of having the system monitor the status of the mouse by reading signals from it is a common way to interface lower-performance devices to machines; it is called *polling*, and we'll revisit it in section 8.5.

Magnetic Disks

As mentioned in Chapter 1, there are two major types of magnetic disks: floppy disks and hard disks. Both types of disks rely on a rotating platter coated with a magnetic surface and use a moveable read/write head to access the disk. Disk storage is *nonvolatile,* meaning that the data remains even when power is removed. Because the platters in a hard disk are metal (or, recently, glass), they have several significant advantages over floppy disks:

- The hard disk can be larger because it is rigid.

- The hard disk has higher density because it can be controlled more precisely.

- The hard disk has a higher data rate because it spins faster.

- Hard disks can incorporate more than one platter.

For the rest of this section, we will focus on hard disks, and we use the term *magnetic disk* to mean hard disk.

A magnetic disk consists of a collection of platters (1–15), each of which has two recordable disk surfaces, as shown in Figure 8.4. The stack of platters is rotated at 3600 to 7200 RPM and has a diameter from just over an inch to just over 8 inches. Each disk surface is divided into concentric circles, called *tracks*. There are typically 1000 to 5000 tracks per surface. Each track is in turn divided into *sectors* that contain the information; each track may have 64 to 200 sectors, and the sector is the smallest unit that can be read or written. In 1997, sectors are typically 512 bytes in size. The sequence recorded on the magnetic media is a sector number, a gap, the information for that sector including error correction code (see Appendix B, page B-34), a gap, the sector number of the next sector, and so on. Traditionally, all tracks have the same number of sectors and hence the same number of bits.

As we saw in Chapter 1, to read and write information the read/write heads must be moved so that they are over the correct location. The disk heads for each surface are connected together and move in conjunction, so that every head is over the same track of every surface. The term *cylinder* is used to refer to all the tracks under the heads at a given point on all surfaces.

To access data, the operating system must direct the disk through a three-stage process. The first step is to position the head over the proper track. This operation is called a *seek*, and the time to move the head to the desired track is called the *seek time*.

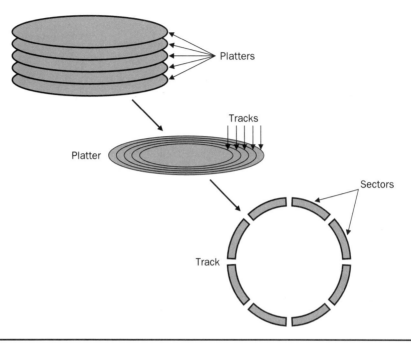

FIGURE 8.4   Disks are organized into platters, tracks, and sectors. Both sides of a platter are coated so that information can be stored on both surfaces. Floppy disks have the same organization, but consist of only one platter.

Disk manufacturers report minimum seek time, maximum seek time, and average seek time in their manuals. The first two are easy to measure, but the average is open to wide interpretation because it depends on the seek distance. The industry has decided to calculate average seek time as the sum of the time for all possible seeks divided by the number of possible seeks. Average seek times are usually advertised as 8 ms to 20 ms, but, depending on the application and scheduling of disk requests, the actual average seek time may be only 25% to 33% of the advertised number, because of locality of disk references. This locality arises both because of successive access to the same file and because the operating system tries to schedule such access together.

Once the head has reached the correct track, we must wait for the desired sector to rotate under the read/write head. This time is called the *rotational latency* or *rotational delay*. The average latency to the desired information is halfway around the disk. Because the disks rotate at 3600 RPM to 7200 RPM, the average rotational latency is between

$$\text{Average rotational latency} = \frac{0.5 \text{ rotation}}{3600 \text{ RPM}} = \frac{0.5 \text{ rotation}}{3600 \text{ RPM} / \left(60 \frac{\text{seconds}}{\text{minute}}\right)}$$

$$= 0.0083 \text{ seconds} = 8.3 \text{ ms}$$

and

$$\text{Average rotational latency} = \frac{0.5 \text{ rotation}}{7200 \text{ RPM}} = \frac{0.5 \text{ rotation}}{7200 \text{ RPM} / \left(60 \frac{\text{seconds}}{\text{minute}}\right)}$$

$$= 0.0042 \text{ seconds} = 4.2 \text{ ms}$$

Smaller diameter disks are attractive because they can spin at higher rates without excessive power consumption, thereby reducing rotational latency.

The last component of a disk access, *transfer time*, is the time to transfer a block of bits, typically a sector. The transfer time is a function of the sector size, the rotation speed, and the recording density of a track. Transfer rates in 1997 are between 2 and 15 MB/sec. The one complication is that most midrange and high-end disks have a built-in cache that stores sectors as they are passed over; transfer rates from the cache are typically higher, and may be up to 40 MB/sec in 1997. Today, most disk transfers are multiple sectors in length.

The detailed control of the disk and the transfer between the disk and the memory is usually handled by a *disk controller*. The controller adds the final component of disk access time, *controller time*, which is the overhead the controller imposes in performing an I/O access. The average time to perform an I/O operation will consist of these four times plus any wait time incurred because other processes are using the disk.

Disk Read Time

Example

What is the average time to read or write a 512-byte sector for a typical disk rotating at 5400 RPM? The advertised average seek time is 12 ms, the transfer rate is 5 MB/sec, and the controller overhead is 2 ms. Assume that the disk is idle so that there is no waiting time.

Answer

Average disk access time is equal to average seek time + average rotational delay + transfer time + controller overhead. Using the advertised average seek time, the answer is

$$12 \text{ ms} + 5.6 \text{ ms} + \frac{0.5 \text{ KB}}{5 \text{ MB/sec}} + 2 \text{ ms} = 12 + 5.6 + 0.1 + 2 = 19.7 \text{ ms}$$

If the measured average seek time is 25% of the advertised average time, the answer is

$$3 \text{ ms} + 5.6 \text{ ms} + 0.1 \text{ ms} + 2 \text{ ms} = 10.7 \text{ ms}$$

Notice that when we consider average measured seek time, as opposed to average advertised seek time, the rotational latency can be the largest component of the access time.

Disk densities have continued to increase for more than 40 years. The impact of this compounded improvement in density and the reduction in physical size of a disk drive has been amazing, as Figure 8.5 shows. The aims of different disk designers have led to a wide variety of drives being available at any particular time. Figure 8.6 shows the characteristics of three different

FIGURE 8.5   Six magnetic disks, varying in diameter from 14 inches down to 1.8 inches.
These disks were introduced over more than a decade ago and hence are not intended to be representative of the best 1998 capacity of disks of these diameters. This photograph does, however, accurately portray their relative physical sizes. The widest disk is the DEC R81, containing four 14-inch diameter platters and storing 456 MB. It was manufactured in 1985. The 8-inch diameter disk comes from Fujitsu, and this 1984 disk stores 130 MB on six platters. The Micropolis RD53 has five 5.25-inch platters and stores 85 MB. The IBM 0361 also has five platters, but these are just 3.5 inches in diameter. This 1988 disk holds 320 MB. In 1997, the most dense 3.5-inch disk has 10 platters and holds 9.1 GB in the same space, yielding an increase in density of about 30 times! The Conner CP 2045 has two 2.5-inch platters containing 40 MB, and was made in 1990. The smallest disk in this photograph is the Integral 1820. This single 1.8-inch platter contains 20 MB and was made in 1992. Photo by Peg Skorpinski.

magnetic disks from a single manufacturer. Large-diameter drives have many more megabytes to amortize the cost of electronics, so the traditional wisdom was that they had the lowest cost per megabyte. But this advantage is offset for the small drives by the much higher sales volume, which lowers manufacturing costs: in 1997, disks cost between $0.10 and $0.20 per megabyte, almost independent of width. The smaller drives also have advantages in power and volume per byte, as Figure 8.6 shows.

Elaboration: Many recent disks have included caches directly in the disk. Such caches allow for fast access to data that was recently read between transfers requested by the CPU. Of course, such capabilities complicate the measurement of disk performance and increase the importance of workload choice. The 5.25-inch Seagate drive shown in Figure 8.6 comes with an integrated cache.

Elaboration: Each track has the same number of bits, and the outer tracks are longer. The outer tracks thus record information at a lower density per inch of track than do tracks closer to the center of the disk. Recording more sectors on the outer tracks than on the inner tracks, called *constant bit density*, is becoming more widespread with

Characteristics	Seagate ST423451	Seagate ST19171	Seagate ST92255
Disk diameter (inches)	5.25	3.50	2.50
Formatted data capacity (MB)	23,200	9100	2250
MTBF (hours)	500,000	1,000,000	300,000
Number of disk surfaces	28	20	10
Rotation speed (RPM)	5400	7200	4500
Internal transfer rate (Mbits/sec)	86–124	80–124	up to 60.8
External interface	Fast SCSI-2 (8–16 bit)	Fast SCSI-2 (8–16 bit)	Fast ATA
External transfer rate (MB/sec)	20–40	20–40	up to 16.6
Minimum seek (track to track) (ms)	0.9	0.6	4
Average seek + rotational delay (ms)	11	9	14
Power/box (watts)	26	13	2.6
MB/watt	892	700	865
Volume (cu. in.)	322	37	8
MB/cu. in.	72	246	273

FIGURE 8.6   Characteristics of three magnetic disks by a single manufacturer. These disks represent the maximum density of the 1997 Seagate product family at each size. The disks shown here either interface to SCSI, a standard I/O bus that we discuss on page 672, or ATA, a standard disk interface for PCs. Compared to the disks shown in the table that appeared in the first edition of this book in 1994, the disks shown above have 25–40 times the MB/watt and 90–450 times the MB/cu. ft.! MTBF stands for mean time before failures—a standard measurement of reliability. The two larger disks contain sector caches that store the contents of sectors as they are passed over. The internal transfer rate is that rate at which bits are read from the disk surface, while the external transfer rate includes that rate at which a sector in the cache that is requested can be transferred. See the link to Seagate at *www.mkp.com/ books_catalog/cod/links.htm* for more information on these drives, as well as some information on modern disk technology.

the advent of intelligent interface standards such as SCSI (see section 8.4). The rate at which an inch of track moves under the head varies: it is faster on the outer tracks. Accordingly, if the number of bits per inch is constant, the rate at which bits must be read or written varies, and the electronics must accommodate this factor when constant bit density is used.

Networks

Networks are the major medium used to communicate between computers. Key characteristics of typical networks include the following:

- *Distance:* 0.01 to 10,000 kilometers
- *Speed:* 0.001 MB/sec to 100 MB/sec
- *Topology:* Bus, ring, star, tree
- *Shared lines:* None (point-to-point) or shared (multidrop)

We'll illustrate these characteristics with three examples.

The RS232 standard provides a 0.3- to 19.2-Kbit/sec *terminal network*. A central computer connects to many terminals over slow but cheap dedicated wires. These point-to-point connections form a star from the central computer, with each terminal ranging from 10 to 100 meters in distance from the computer.

The *local area network* (LAN) is what is commonly meant today when people mention a network, and Ethernet is what most people mean when they mention a LAN. (Ethernet has in fact become such a common term that it is often used as a generic term for LAN.) The basic Ethernet is essentially a 10-Mbit/sec, one-wire bus that has no central control. Messages, or *packets*, are sent over the Ethernet in blocks that vary from 64 bytes to 1518 bytes. Recently, several companies have developed a faster version (usually called Fast Ethernet) that offers rates that are 10 times higher (i.e., 100 Mbit/sec), and a Gigabit Ethernet has been proposed for delivery in 1998.

An Ethernet is essentially a bus with multiple masters and a scheme for determining who gets bus control; we'll discuss how the distributed control is implemented in the exercises. Because the Ethernet is a bus, only one sender can be transmitting at any time; this limits the bandwidth. In practice, this is not usually a problem because the utilization is fairly low. Of course, some LANs become overloaded through poor capacity planning, and response time and throughput can degrade rapidly at higher utilization.

One way in which the limits of the original bus-oriented Ethernet have been overcome is through switched networks. A *switched network* is one in which switches are introduced to reduce the number of hosts per Ethernet segment. In the limit, there is only one host per segment and that host is directly connected to a switch. Switched networks are common in long-haul networks, the next topic, but such networks have recently been popular in local area applications as the use of higher-performance machines and multimedia data has put significant strains on shared Ethernets.

Long-haul networks cover distances of 10 to 10,000 kilometers. The first and most famous long-haul network was the ARPANET (named after its funding agency, the Advanced Research Projects Agency of the U.S. government). It transferred data at 56 Kbits/sec and used point-to-point dedicated lines leased from telephone companies. The host computer talked to an *interface message processor* (IMP), which communicated over the telephone lines. The IMP took information and broke it into 1-Kbit packets, which could take separate paths to the destination node. At each hop, a packet was stored (for recovery in case of failure) and then forwarded to the proper IMP according to the address in the packet. The destination IMP reassembled the packets into a message and then gave it to the host. Most networks today use this *packet-switched* approach, in which packets are individually routed from source to destination.

The ARPANET was the precursor of the Internet. The key to interconnecting different networks was standardizing on a single protocol family, TCP/IP (Transmission Control Protocol/Internet Protocol). The IP portion of the protocol provides for addressing between two hosts on the Internet, but does not guarantee reliable delivery. TCP provides a protocol that can guarantee that all packets are received and that the packets have no transmission errors. These two protocols work together to form a *protocol stack*, where TCP packets are encapsulated in IP packets. The standardization of the TCP/IP packet format is what allows the different hosts and network to communicate.

The bandwidths of networks are probably growing faster than the bandwidth of any other type of device at present. High-speed networks using copper and coaxial cable offer 100 Mbit/sec bandwidths, while optical fiber offers bandwidths up to 1 Gbit/sec. In the future, it appears that Internet-like technologies may be extended up to the 1-Gbit/sec range. These super high-speed networks are likely to be switched rather than using shared links.

Another leader among the emerging network technologies is ATM (Asynchronous Transfer Method). ATM is a scalable network technology (from 155 Mbits/sec to 2.5 Gbits/sec) that originated in long-haul networks switching both voice and data. It is already being deployed in backbone switching applications and, together with Fast Ethernet approaches, is a contender for future desktop connectivity.

The challenge in putting these networks into use lies primarily in building systems that can efficiently interface to these media and sustain these bandwidths between two programs that want to communicate. Meeting this challenge requires that all the pieces of the I/O system, from the operating system to the memory system to the bus to the device interface, be able to accommodate these bandwidths. This is truly a top-to-bottom systems challenge.

Hardware Software Interface

To allow communication across multiple networks with different characteristics, TCP/IP defines a standard packet format. An IP packet, which contains Internet addressing information, encapsulates a TCP packet that contains both address information interpreted by the host and the data being communicated.

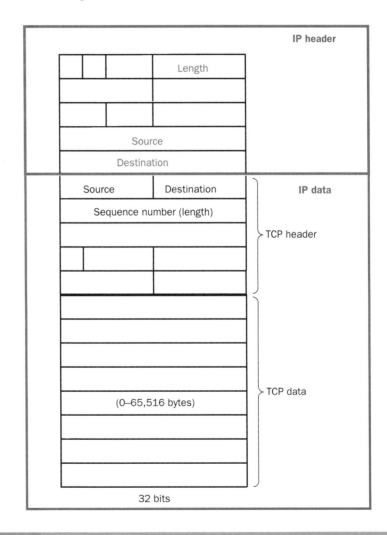

To see the importance of looking at performance from top to bottom, including both hardware and software, consider the following example.

Example

Performance of Two Networks

Example

Consider the following measurements made on a pair of SPARCstation 10s running Solaris 2.3, connected to two different types of networks, and using TCP/IP for communication:

Characteristic	Ethernet	ATM
Bandwidth from node to network	1.125 MB/sec	10 MB/sec
Interconnect latency	15 μs	50 μs
HW latency to/from network	6 μs	6 μs
SW overhead sending to network	200 μs	207 μs
SW overhead receiving from network	241 μs	360 μs

Find the host-to-host latency for a 250-byte message using each network.

Answer

We can estimate the time required as the sum of the fixed latencies plus the time to transmit the message. The time to transmit the message is simply the message length divided by the bandwidth of the network.

The transmission times are

$$\text{Transmission time}_{\text{Ethernet}} = \frac{250 \text{ bytes}}{1.125 \times 10^6 \text{ bytes/sec}} = 222 \text{ μs}$$

$$\text{Transmission time}_{\text{ATM}} = \frac{250 \text{ bytes}}{10 \times 10^6 \text{ bytes/sec}} = 25 \text{ μs}$$

So the transmission time for the ATM network is about a factor of nine lower.

The total latency to send and receive the packet is the sum of the transmission time and the hardware and software overheads:

$$\text{Total time}_{\text{Ethernet}} = 15 + 6 + 200 + 241 + 222 = 684 \text{ μs}$$

$$\text{Total time}_{\text{ATM}} = 50 + 6 + 207 + 360 + 25 = 648 \text{ μs}$$

The end-to-end latency of the Ethrnet is only about 1.06 times higher, even though the transmission time is almost 9 times higher!

8.4 Buses: Connecting I/O Devices to Processor and Memory

In a computer system, the various subsystems must have interfaces to one another. For example, the memory and processor need to communicate, as do the processor and the I/O devices. This is commonly done with a *bus*. A bus is a shared communication link, which uses one set of wires to connect multiple subsystems. The two major advantages of the bus organization are versatility and low cost. By defining a single connection scheme, new devices can easily be added, and peripherals can even be moved between computer systems that use the same kind of bus. Furthermore, buses are cost-effective because a single set of wires is shared in multiple ways.

The major disadvantage of a bus is that it creates a communication bottleneck, possibly limiting the maximum I/O throughput. When I/O must pass through a single bus, the bandwidth of that bus limits the maximum I/O throughput. In commercial systems, where I/O is very frequent, and in supercomputers, where the I/O rates must be very high because the processor performance is high, designing a bus system capable of meeting the demands of the processor as well as connecting large numbers of I/O devices to the machine presents a major challenge.

One reason bus design is so difficult is that the maximum bus speed is largely limited by physical factors: the length of the bus and the number of devices. These physical limits prevent us from running the bus arbitrarily fast. Within these limits, there are a variety of techniques we can use to increase the performance of the bus; however, these techniques may adversely affect other performance metrics. For example, to obtain fast response time for I/O operations, we must minimize the time to perform a bus access by streamlining the communication path. On the other hand, to sustain high I/O data rates, we must maximize the bus bandwidth. The bus bandwidth can be increased by using more buffering and by communicating larger blocks of data, both of which increase the delay to complete the bus access! Clearly, these two goals, fast bus accesses and high bandwidth, can lead to conflicting design requirements. Finally, the need to support a range of devices with widely varying latencies and data transfer rates also makes bus design challenging.

A bus generally contains a set of control lines and a set of data lines. The control lines are used to signal requests and acknowledgments, and to indicate what type of information is on the data lines. The data lines of the bus carry information between the source and the destination. This information may consist of data, complex commands, or addresses. For example, if a disk wants to write some data into memory from a disk sector, the data lines will be used to indicate the address in memory in which to place the data as well as to carry the actual data from the disk. The control lines will be used to indicate what type of information is contained on the data lines of the bus at each point in the transfer. Some buses have two sets of signal lines to separately communicate both data and address in a single bus transmission. In either case, the control lines are used to indicate what the bus contains and to implement the bus protocol. And because the bus is shared, we also need a protocol to decide who uses it next; we will discuss this problem shortly.

Let's consider a typical *bus transaction*. A bus transaction includes two parts: sending the address and receiving or sending the data. Bus transactions are typically defined by what they do to memory. A *read* transaction transfers data *from* memory (to either the processor or an I/O device), and a *write* transaction writes data *to* the memory. Clearly, this terminology is confusing. To avoid this, we'll try to use the terms *input* and *output*, which are always defined from the perspective of the processor: an input operation is inputting data from the device to memory, where the processor can read it, and an output operation is outputting data to a device from memory where the processor wrote it. Figure 8.7 shows the steps in a typical output operation, in which data will be read from memory and sent to the device. Figure 8.8 shows the steps in an input operation where data is read from the device and written to memory. In both figures, the active portions of the bus and memory are shown in color, and a read or write is shown by shading the unit, as we did in Chapter 6. In these figures, we focus on how data is transferred between the I/O device and memory; in section 8.5, we will see how the I/O operation is initiated.

Types of Buses

Buses are traditionally classified as one of three types: *processor-memory buses, I/O buses*, or *backplane buses*. Processor-memory buses are short, generally high speed, and matched to the memory system so as to maximize memory-processor bandwidth. I/O buses, by contrast, can be lengthy, can have many types of devices connected to them, and often have a wide range in the data bandwidth of the devices connected to them. I/O buses do not typically interface directly to the memory but use either a processor-memory or a backplane bus to connect to memory. Backplane buses are designed to allow processors, memory, and I/O devices to coexist on a single bus; they balance the demands of processor-memory communication with the demands of I/O device-memory communication. Backplane buses received their name because they were often built into the *backplane*, an interconnection structure within the chassis; processor, memory, and I/O boards would then plug into the backplane using the bus for communication.

Processor-memory buses are often design-specific, while both I/O buses and backplane buses are frequently reused in different machines. In fact, backplane and I/O buses are often *standard buses* that are used by many different

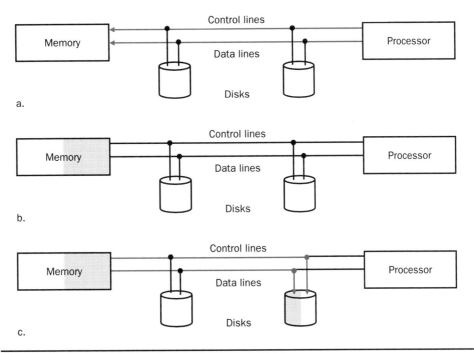

FIGURE 8.7 The three steps of an output operation. In each step, the active participants in the communication are shown in color, with the right side shaded if the device is doing a read and the left side shaded if the device is doing a write. Notice that the data lines of the bus can carry both an address (as in a) and data (as in c). (a) The first step in an output operation initiates a read from memory. The control lines signal a read request to memory, while the data lines contain the address. (b) During the second step in an output operation, memory is accessing the data. (c) In the third and final step in an output operation, memory transfers the data using the data lines of the bus and signals that the data is available to the I/O device using the control lines. The device stores the data as it appears on the bus.

computers manufactured by different companies. By comparison, processor-memory buses are often proprietary, although in many recent machines they may be the backplane bus, and the standard or I/O buses plug into the processor-memory bus. In many recent machines, the distinction among these bus types, especially between backplane buses and processor-memory buses, may be very minor.

During the design phase, the designer of a processor-memory bus knows all the types of devices that must connect to the bus, while the I/O or backplane bus designer must design the bus to handle unknown devices that vary in latency and bandwidth characteristics. Normally, an I/O bus presents a fairly simple and low-level interface to a device, requiring minimal additional electronics to interface to the bus. A backplane bus usually requires additional logic to interface between the bus and a device or between the backplane bus

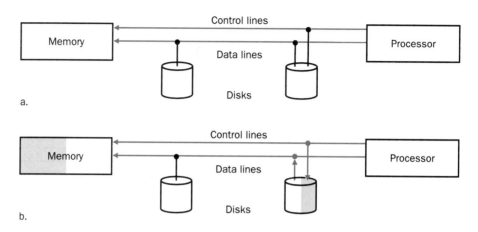

FIGURE 8.8   An input operation takes less active time because the device does not need to wait for memory to access data. As in the previous figure, the active participants in each step in the communication are shown in color, with the right side shaded if the device is doing a read and the left side shaded if the device is doing a write. (a) In the first step in an input operation, the control lines indicate a write request for memory, while the data lines contain the address. (b) The second step in an input operation occurs when the memory is ready and signals the device, which then transfers the data. Typically, the memory will store the data as it receives it. The device need not wait for the store to be completed. In the steps shown, we assume that the device had to wait for memory to indicate its readiness, but this will not be true in some systems that use buffering or have a fast memory system.

and a lower-level I/O bus. A backplane bus offers the cost advantage of a single bus. Figure 8.9 shows a system using a single backplane bus, a system using a processor-memory bus with attached I/O buses, and a system using all three types of buses. Machines with a separate processor-memory bus normally use a bus adapter to connect the I/O bus to the processor-memory bus. Some high-performance, expandable systems use an organization that combines the three buses: the processor-memory bus has one or more bus adapters that interface a standard backplane bus to the processor-memory bus. I/O buses, as well as device controllers, can plug into the backplane bus. The IBM RS/6000 and Silicon Graphics multiprocessors use this type of organization. This organization offers the advantage that the processor-memory bus can be made much faster than a backplane or I/O bus and that the I/O system can be expanded by plugging many I/O controllers or buses into the backplane bus, which will not affect the speed of the processor-memory bus.

Synchronous and Asynchronous Buses

The substantial differences between the circumstances under which a processor-memory bus and an I/O bus or backplane bus are designed lead to two different schemes for communication on the bus: *synchronous* and

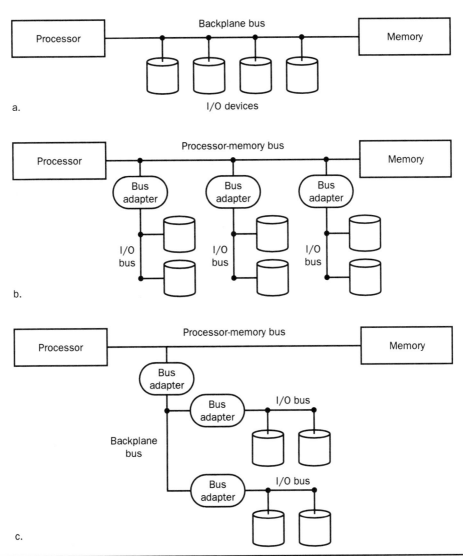

FIGURE 8.9   Many machines use a single backplane bus for both processor-memory and I/O traffic. Some high-performance machines use a separate processor-memory bus that I/O buses plug into. Some systems make use of all three types of buses, organized in a hierarchy. (a) A single bus used for processor-to-memory communication, as well as communication between I/O devices and memory. The bus used in older PCs has this structure. (b) A separate bus is used for processor–memory traffic. To communicate data between memory and I/O devices, the I/O buses interface to the processor-memory bus, using a bus adapter. The bus adapter provides speed matching between the buses. In many recent PCs, the processor-memory bus is a PCI bus (a backplane bus) that has I/O devices that interface directly as well as an I/O bus that plugs into the PCI bus; the latter is a SCSI bus. (c) A separate bus is used for processor-memory traffic. A small number of backplane buses tap into the processor-memory bus. The processor-memory buses interface to the backplane bus. This is usually done with a single-chip controller, such as a SCSI bus controller. An advantage of this organization is the small number of taps into the high-speed processor-memory bus.

asynchronous. If a bus is synchronous, it includes a clock in the control lines and a fixed protocol for communicating that is relative to the clock. For example, for a processor-memory bus performing a read from memory, we might have a protocol that transmits the address and read command on the first clock cycle, using the control lines to indicate the type of request. The memory might then be required to respond with the data word on the fifth clock. This type of protocol can be implemented easily in a small finite state machine. Because the protocol is predetermined and involves little logic, the bus can run very fast and the interface logic will be small. Synchronous buses have two major disadvantages, however. First, every device on the bus must run at the same clock rate. Second, because of clock skew problems, synchronous buses cannot be long if they are fast (see Appendix B for a discussion of clock skew). Processor-memory buses are often synchronous because the devices communicating are close, small in number, and prepared to operate at high clock rates.

An asynchronous bus is not clocked. Because it is not clocked, an asynchronous bus can accommodate a wide variety of devices, and the bus can be lengthened without worrying about clock skew or synchronization problems. To coordinate the transmission of data between sender and receiver, an asynchronous bus uses a *handshaking protocol.* A handshaking protocol consists of a series of steps in which the sender and receiver proceed to the next step only when both parties agree. The protocol is implemented with an additional set of control lines.

A simple example will illustrate how asynchronous buses work. Let's consider a device requesting a word of data from the memory system. Assume that there are three control lines:

1. *ReadReq*: Used to indicate a read request for memory. The address is put on the data lines at the same time.

2. *DataRdy*: Used to indicate that the data word is now ready on the data lines. In an output transaction, the memory will assert this signal since it is providing the data. In an input transaction, an I/O device would assert this signal, since it would provide data. In either case, the data is placed on the data lines at the same time.

3. *Ack*: Used to acknowledge the ReadReq or the DataRdy signal of the other party.

In an asynchronous protocol, the control signals ReadReq and DataRdy are asserted until the other party (the memory or the device) indicates that the control lines have been seen and the data lines have been read; this indication is made by asserting the Ack line. This complete process is called *handshaking.* Figure 8.10 shows how such a protocol operates by depicting the steps in the communication.

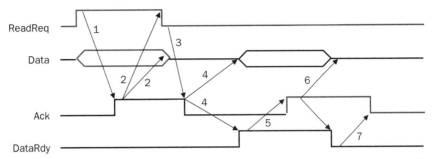

The steps in the protocol begin immediately after the device signals a request by raising ReadReq and putting the address on the Data lines:

1. When memory sees the ReadReq line, it reads the address from the data bus and raises Ack to indicate it has been seen.
2. I/O device sees the Ack line high and releases the ReadReq and data lines.
3. Memory sees that ReadReq is low and drops the Ack line to acknowledge the Readreq signal.
4. This step starts when the memory has the data ready. It places the data from the read request on the data lines and raises DataRdy.
5. The I/O device sees DataRdy, reads the data from the bus, and signals that it has the data by raising Ack.
6. The memory sees the Ack signal, drops DataRdy, and releases the data lines.
7. Finally, the I/O device, seeing DataRdy go low, drops the Ack line, which indicates that the transmission is completed.

A new bus transaction can now begin.

FIGURE 8.10   The asynchronous handshaking protocol consists of seven steps to read a word from memory and receive it in an I/O device. The signals in color are those asserted by the I/O device, while the memory asserts the signals shown in black. The arrows label the seven steps and the event that triggers each step. The symbol showing two lines (high and low) at the same time on the data lines indicates that the data lines have valid data at this point. (The symbol indicates that the data is valid, but the value is not known.)

An asynchronous bus protocol works like a pair of finite state machines that are communicating in such a way that a machine does not proceed until it knows that another machine has reached a certain state; thus the two machines are coordinated.

The handshaking protocol does not solve all the problems of communicating between a sender and receiver that have different clocks. An additional problem arises when we sample an asynchronous signal (such as ReadReq). This problem, called a *synchronization failure,* can lead to unpredictable behavior; it can be overcome with devices called *synchronizers,* which are described in Appendix B.

FSM Control for I/O

Example

Show how the control for an output transaction to an I/O device from memory (as in Figure 8.7) can be implemented as a pair of finite state machines.

Answer

Figure 8.11 shows the two finite state machine controllers that implement the handshaking protocol of Figure 8.10.

If a synchronous bus can be used, it is usually faster than an asynchronous bus because of the overhead required to perform the handshaking. An example demonstrates this.

Performance Analysis of Synchronous versus Asynchronous Buses

Example

We want to compare the maximum bandwidth for a synchronous and an asynchronous bus. The synchronous bus has a clock cycle time of 50 ns, and each bus transmission takes 1 clock cycle. The asynchronous bus requires 40 ns per handshake. The data portion of both buses is 32 bits wide. Find the bandwidth for each bus when performing one-word reads from a 200-ns memory.

Answer

First, the synchronous bus, which has 50-ns bus cycles. The steps and times required for the synchronous bus are as follows:

1. Send the address to memory: 50 ns

2. Read the memory: 200 ns

3. Send the data to the device: 50 ns

Thus, the total time is 300 ns. This yields a maximum bus bandwidth of 4 bytes every 300 ns, or

$$\frac{4 \text{ bytes}}{300 \text{ ns}} = \frac{4 \text{ MB}}{0.3 \text{ seconds}} = 13.3 \frac{\text{MB}}{\text{second}}$$

At first glance, it might appear that the asynchronous bus will be *much* slower, since it will take seven steps, each at least 40 ns, and the step corresponding to the memory access will take 200 ns. If we look carefully at Figure 8.10, we realize that several of the steps can be overlapped with the memory access time. In particular, the memory receives the address at the end of step 1 and does not need to put the data on the bus until the beginning of step 5; steps 2, 3, and 4 can overlap with the memory access time. This leads to the following timing:

Step 1: 40 ns

Steps 2, 3, 4: maximum $(3 \times 40 \text{ ns}, 200 \text{ ns}) = 200$ ns

Steps 5, 6, 7: $3 \times 40 \text{ ns} = 120$ ns

Thus, the total time to perform the transfer is 360 ns, and the maximum bandwidth is

$$\frac{4 \text{ bytes}}{360 \text{ ns}} = \frac{4 \text{ MB}}{0.36 \text{ seconds}} = 11.1 \frac{\text{MB}}{\text{second}}$$

Accordingly, the synchronous bus is only about 20% faster. Of course, to sustain these rates, the device and memory system on the asynchronous bus will need to be fairly fast to accomplish each handshaking step in 40 ns.

Even though a synchronous bus may be faster, the choice between a synchronous and an asynchronous bus has implications not only for data bandwidth but also for an I/O system's capacity in terms of physical distance and the number of devices that can be connected to the bus. Asynchronous buses scale better with technology changes and can support a wider variety of device response speeds. It is for these reasons that I/O buses are often asynchronous, despite the increased overhead.

Increasing the Bus Bandwidth

Although much of the bandwidth of a bus is decided by the choice of a synchronous or asynchronous protocol and the timing characteristics of the bus, several other factors affect the bandwidth that can be attained by a single transfer. The most important of these are the following:

1. *Data bus width*: By increasing the width of the data bus, transfers of multiple words require fewer bus cycles.

2. *Separate versus multiplexed address and data lines*: Our example in Figure 8.8 used the same wires for address and data; including separate lines for addresses will make the performance of writes faster because the address and data can be transmitted in one bus cycle.

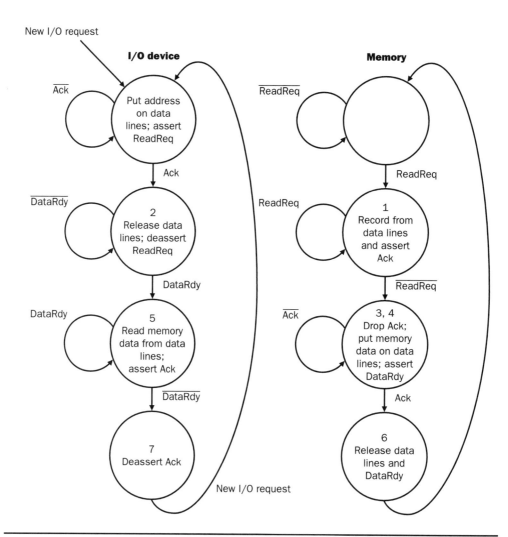

FIGURE 8.11 These finite state machines implement the control for the handshaking protocol illustrated in Figure 8.10. The numbers in each state correspond to the steps shown in Figure 8.10. The first state of the I/O device (upper-left corner) starts the protocol when a new I/O request is generated, just as in Figure 8.10. Each state in the finite state machine effectively records the state of both the device and memory. This is how they stay synchronized during the transaction. After completing a transaction, the I/O side can stay in the last state until a new request needs to be processed.

   3. *Block transfers*: Allowing the bus to transfer multiple words in back-to-back bus cycles without sending an address or releasing the bus will reduce the time needed to transfer a large block.

   Each of these design alternatives will increase the bus performance for a single bus transfer. The cost of implementing one of these enhancements is one or more of the following: more bus lines, increased complexity, or increased response time for requests that may need to wait while a long block transfer occurs.

Performance Analysis of Two Bus Schemes

Example

Suppose we have a system with the following characteristics:

1. A memory and bus system supporting block access of 4 to 16 32-bit words.

2. A 64-bit synchronous bus clocked at 200 MHz, with each 64-bit transfer taking 1 clock cycle, and 1 clock cycle required to send an address to memory.

3. Two clock cycles needed between each bus operation. (Assume the bus is idle before an access.)

4. A memory access time for the first four words of 200 ns; each additional set of four words can be read in 20 ns. Assume that a bus transfer of the most recently read data and a read of the next four words can be overlapped.

Find the sustained bandwidth and the latency for a read of 256 words for transfers that use 4-word blocks and for transfers that use 16-word blocks. Also compute the effective number of bus transactions per second for each case. Recall that a single bus transaction consists of an address transmission followed by data.

Answer

For the 4-word block transfers, each block takes

1. 1 clock cycle that is required to send the address to memory

2. $\dfrac{200 \text{ ns}}{5 \text{ ns/cycle}} = 40$ clock cycles to read memory

3. 2 clock cycles to send the data from the memory

4. 2 idle clock cycles between this transfer and the next

This is a total of 45 cycles, and $256/4 = 64$ transactions are needed, so the entire transfer takes $45 \times 64 = 2880$ clock cycles. Thus the latency is 2880 cycles $\times$ 5 ns/cycle = 14,400 ns. The number of bus transactions per second is

$$64 \text{ transactions} \times \frac{1 \text{ second}}{14,400 \text{ ns}} = 4.44\text{M transactions/second}$$

The bus bandwidth is

$$(256 \times 4) \text{ bytes} \times \frac{1 \text{ second}}{14,400 \text{ ns}} = 71.11 \text{ MB/sec}$$

For the 16-word block transfers, the first block requires

1. 1 clock cycle to send an address to memory

2. 200 ns or 40 cycles to read the first four words in memory

3. 2 cycles to send the data of the block, during which time the read of the four words in the next block is started

4. 2 idle cycles between transfers and during which the read of the next block is completed

Each of the three remaining 4-word blocks requires repeating only the last two steps.

Thus, the total number of cycles for each 16-word block is $1 + 40 + 4 \times (2 + 2) = 57$ cycles, and $256/16 = 16$ transactions are needed, so the entire transfer takes, $57 \times 16 = 912$ cycles. Thus the latency is 912 cycles $\times$ 5 ns/cycle = 4560 ns, which is roughly one-third of the latency for the case with 4-word blocks. The number of bus transactions per second with 16-word blocks is

$$16 \text{ transactions} \times \frac{1 \text{ second}}{4560 \text{ ns}} = 3.51\,\text{M transactions/second}$$

which is lower than the case with 4-word blocks because each transaction takes longer (57 versus 45 cycles).

The bus bandwidth with 16-word blocks is

$$(256 \times 4) \text{ bytes} \times \frac{1 \text{ second}}{4560 \text{ ns}} = 224.56 \text{ MB/second}$$

which is 3.16 times higher than for the 4-word blocks. The advantage of using larger block transfers is clear.

Elaboration: Another method for increasing the effective bus bandwidth when multiple parties want to communicate on the bus is to release the bus when it is not being used for transmitting information. Consider the example of a memory read that we examined in Figure 8.10. What happens to the bus while the memory access is occurring? In this simple protocol, the device and memory continue to hold the bus during the memory access time when no actual transfer is taking place. An alternative protocol, which releases the bus, would operate like this:

1. The device signals the memory and transmits the request and address.

2. After the memory acknowledges the request, both the memory and device release all control lines.

3. The memory access occurs, and the bus is free for other uses during this period.

4. The memory signals the device on the bus to indicate that the data is available.

5. The device receives the data via the bus and signals that it has the data, so the memory system can release the bus.

For the synchronous bus with 16-word transfers in the example above, such a scheme would occupy the bus for only 272 of the 912 cycles required for the complete bus transaction.

This type of protocol is called a *split transaction protocol*. The advantage of such a protocol is that, by freeing the bus during the time data is not being transmitted, the protocol allows another requestor to use the bus. This can improve the effective bus bandwidth for the entire system, if the memory is sophisticated enough to handle multiple overlapping transactions.

With a split transaction, however, the time to complete one transfer is probably increased because the bus must be acquired twice. Split transaction protocols are also more expensive to implement, primarily because of the need to keep track of the other party in a communication. In a split transaction protocol, the memory system must contact the requestor to initiate the reply portion of the bus transaction, so the identity of the requestor must be transmitted and retained by the memory system.

Obtaining Access to the Bus

Now that we have reviewed some of the many design options for buses, we can deal with one of the most important issues in bus design: How is the bus reserved by a device that wishes to use it to communicate? We touched on this question in several of the above discussions, and it is crucial in designing large I/O systems that allow I/O to occur without the processor's continuous and low-level involvement.

Why is a scheme needed for controlling bus access? Without any control, multiple devices desiring to communicate could each try to assert the control and data lines for different transfers! Just as chaos reigns in a classroom when everyone tries to talk at once, multiple devices trying to use the bus simultaneously would result in confusion.

Chaos is avoided by introducing one or more *bus masters* into the system. A bus master controls access to the bus: it must initiate and control all bus requests. The processor must be able to initiate a bus request for memory and thus is always a bus master. The memory is usually a *slave*—since it will respond to read and write requests but never generate its own requests.

The simplest system possible has a single bus master: the processor. Having a single bus master is similar to what normally happens in a classroom—all communication requires the permission of the instructor. In a single-master system, all bus requests must be controlled by the processor. The steps involved in a bus transaction with a single-master bus are shown in Figure 8.12. The major drawback of this approach is that the processor must be involved in every bus transaction. A single sector read from a disk may require the processor to get involved hundreds to thousands of times, depending on the size of each transfer. Because devices have become faster and capable of transferring

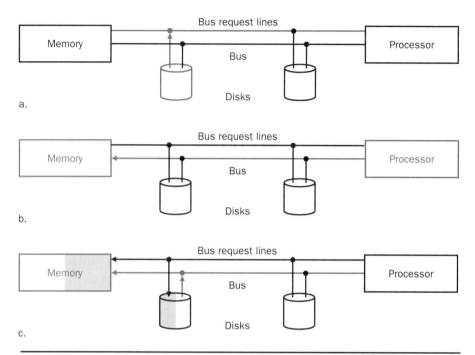

FIGURE 8.12   The initial steps in a bus transaction with a single master (the processor).
A set of bus request lines is used by the device to communicate with the processor, which then
initiates the bus cycle on behalf of the requesting device. The active lines and units are shown in
color in each step. Shading is used to indicate the source of a read (memory) or destination of a
write (the disk). After step c, the bus cycle continues like a normal read transaction, as in Figure
8.7. (a) First, the device generates a bus request to indicate to the processor that the device wants
to use the bus. (b) The processor responds and generates appropriate bus control signals. For
example, if the device wants to perform output from memory, the processor asserts the read
request lines to memory. (c) The processor also notifies the device that its bus request is being
processed; as a result, the device knows it can use the bus and places the address for the request
on the bus.

at much higher bandwidths, involving the processor in every bus transaction
has become less and less attractive.

The alternative scheme is to have multiple bus masters, each of which can
initiate a transfer. If we want to allow several people in a classroom to talk
without the instructor having to recognize each one, we must have a protocol
for deciding who gets to talk next. Similarly, with multiple bus masters, we
must provide a mechanism for arbitrating access to the bus so that it is used in
a cooperative rather than a chaotic way.

Bus Arbitration

Deciding which bus master gets to use the bus next is called *bus arbitration*. There are a wide variety of schemes for bus arbitration; these may involve special hardware or extremely sophisticated bus protocols. In a bus arbitration scheme, a device (or the processor) wanting to use the bus signals a *bus request* and is later *granted* the bus. After a grant, the device can use the bus, later signaling to the arbiter that the bus is no longer required. The arbiter can then grant the bus to another device. Most multiple-master buses have a set of bus lines for performing requests and grants. A bus release line is also needed if each device does not have its own request line. Sometimes the signals used for bus arbitration have physically separate lines, while in other systems the data lines of the bus are used for this function (though this prevents overlapping of arbitration with transfer).

Arbitration schemes usually try to balance two factors in choosing which device to grant the bus. First, each device has a *bus priority*, and the highest-priority device should be serviced first. Second, we would prefer that any device, even one with low priority, never be completely locked out from the bus. This property, called *fairness*, ensures that every device that wants to use the bus is guaranteed to get it eventually. In addition to these factors, more sophisticated schemes aim at reducing the time needed to arbitrate for the bus. Because arbitration time is overhead, which increases the bus access time, it should be reduced and overlapped with bus transfers whenever possible.

Bus arbitration schemes can be divided into four broad classes:

- *Daisy chain arbitration*: In this scheme, the bus grant line is run through the devices from highest priority to lowest (the priorities are determined by the position on the bus). A high-priority device that desires bus access simply intercepts the bus grant signal, not allowing a lower-priority device to see the signal. Figure 8.13 shows how a daisy chain bus is organized. The advantage of a daisy chain bus is simplicity; the disadvantages are that it cannot assure fairness—a low-priority request may be locked out indefinitely—and the use of the daisy chain grant signal also limits the bus speed.

- *Centralized, parallel arbitration*: These schemes use multiple request lines, and the devices independently request the bus. A centralized arbiter chooses from among the devices requesting bus access and notifies the selected device that it is now bus master. The disadvantage of this scheme is that it requires a central arbiter, which may become the bottleneck for bus usage. PCI, a standard backplane bus, uses a central arbitration scheme.

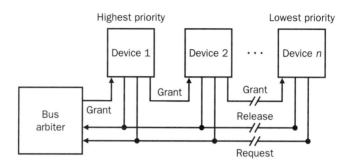

FIGURE 8.13 **A daisy chain bus uses a bus grant line that chains through each device from highest to lowest priority.** If the device has requested bus access, it uses the grant line to determine access has been given to it. Because the grant line is passed on only if a device does not want access, priority is built into the scheme. The name "daisy chain" arises from the structure of the grant line that chains from device to device. The detailed protocol used by a daisy chain is described in the elaboration below.

- *Distributed arbitration by self-selection*: These schemes also use multiple request lines, but the devices requesting bus access determine who will be granted access. Each device wanting bus access places a code indicating its identity on the bus. By examining the bus, the devices can determine the highest-priority device that has made a request. There is no need for a central arbiter; each device determines independently whether it is the high-priority requestor. This scheme, however, does require more lines for request signals. The NuBus, which is the backplane bus in Apple Macintosh IIs, uses this scheme.

- *Distributed arbitration by collision detection*: In this scheme, each device independently requests the bus. Multiple simultaneous requests result in a *collision*. The collision is detected and a scheme for selecting among the colliding parties is used. Ethernets, which use this scheme, are further described in Exercise 8.28 on page 708.

The suitability of different arbitration schemes is determined by a variety of factors, including how expandable the bus must be both in terms of the number of I/O devices and the bus length, how fast the arbitration should be, and what degree of fairness is needed.

Elaboration: The protocol followed by a device on a daisy chain bus is the following:

1. Signal the request line.

2. Wait for a transition on the grant line from low to high, indicating that the bus is being reassigned.

3. Intercept the grant signal, and do not allow lower-priority devices to see it. Stop asserting the request line.

4. Use the bus.

5. Signal that the bus is no longer required by asserting the release line.

By watching for a transition on the grant line, rather than just a level, we prevent the device from taking the bus away from a lower-priority device that believes it has been granted bus access. To improve fairness in a daisy chain scheme, we can simply make the rule that a device that has just used the bus cannot reacquire the bus until it sees the bus request line go low. Since a device will not release the request line until its request is satisfied, all devices will have an opportunity to use the bus before any single device uses it twice. Some bus systems—VME, for example—use multiple daisy chains with a separate set of request and grant lines for each daisy chain and a priority encoder to select from among the multiple requests.

> **The Big Picture**
>
> The different bus characteristics allow the creation of buses optimized for a wide range of different devices, number of devices, and bandwidth demands. Figure 8.14 shows some of the design alternatives we have discussed and what choices might be made in low-cost versus high-performance systems. In general, higher-cost systems use wider and faster buses with more sophisticated protocols—typically a synchronous bus for the reasons we saw in the example on page 662. In contrast, a low-cost system favors a bus that is narrower and does not require intelligence among the devices (hence a single master), and is asynchronous so that low-speed devices can interface inexpensively.

Option	High performance	Low cost
Bus width	separate address and data lines	multiplex address and data lines
Data width	wider is faster (e.g., 32 bits)	narrower is cheaper (e.g., 8 bits)
Transfer size	multiple words require less bus overhead	single-word transfer is simpler
Bus masters	multiple masters (requires arbitration)	single master (no arbitration)
Clocking	synchronous	asynchronous

FIGURE 8.14 The I/O bus characteristics determine the performance of I/O transfers, the number of I/O devices that can be connected, and the cost of connecting devices. Shorter buses can be faster but will not be as expandable. Similarly, wider buses can have higher bandwidth but will be more expensive. Split transaction buses are another way to increase bandwidth at the expense of cost (see the elaboration on page 666).

Bus Standards

Most computers allow users to add additional and even new types of peripherals. The I/O bus serves as a way of expanding the machine and connecting new peripherals. To make this easier, the computer industry has developed several bus standards. The standards serve as a specification for the computer manufacturer and for the peripheral manufacturer. A bus standard ensures the computer designer that peripherals will be available for a new machine, and it ensures the peripheral builder that users will be able to hook up their new equipment.

Machines sometimes become so popular that their I/O buses become de facto standards, as is the case with the IBM PC-AT bus. Once a bus standard is heavily used by peripheral designers, other computer manufacturers incorporate that bus and offer a wide range of peripherals. Sometimes standards are created by groups that are trying to address a common problem. The small computer systems interface (SCSI) and Ethernet are examples of standards that arose from the cooperation of manufacturers. Sanctioning bodies like ANSI or IEEE also create and approve standards. The PCI standard was initiated by Intel and later developed by an industry committee.

Figure 8.15 summarizes the key characteristics of the two dominant bus standards: PCI (a general-purpose backplane bus) and SCSI (an I/O bus). A SCSI bus typically interfaces to a backplane bus or to a processor-memory bus. A SCSI controller coordinates transfers from a device on the I/O bus to the memory via the processor-memory bus. One emerging bus standard is Fibre Channel, proposed as a follow-on to SCSI and based on high-speed point-to-point links, which would be organized as a loop for multiple devices.

Bus bandwidth for a general-purpose bus is not simply a single number. Because of bus overhead, the size of the transfer affects bandwidth significantly. Since the bus usually transfers to or from memory, the speed of the memory also affects the bandwidth.

Buses provide the electrical interconnect among I/O devices, processors, and memory, and also define the lowest-level protocol for communication. Above this basic level, we must define hardware and software protocols for controlling data transfers between I/O devices and memory, and for the processor to specify commands to the I/O devices. These topics are covered in the next section.

Characteristic	PCI	SCSI
Bus type	backplane	I/O
Basic data bus width (signals)	32–64	8–32
Address/data multiplexed?	multiplexed	multiplexed
Number of bus masters	multiple	multiple
Arbitration	centralized, parallel arbitration	self-selection
Clocking	synchronous 33–66 MHz	asynchronous or synchronous (5–10 MHz)
Theoretical peak bandwidth	133–512 MB/sec	5–40 MB/sec
Estimated typical achievable bandwidth for basic bus	80 MB/sec	2.5–40.0 MB/sec (synchronous) or 1.5 MB/sec (asynchronous)
Maximum number of devices	1024 (with multiple bus segments; at most 32 devices/bus segment)	7–31 (bus width – 1)
Maximum bus length	0.5 meter	25 meters
Standard name	PCI	ANSI X3.131

FIGURE 8.15   Key characteristics of two dominant bus standards. Both PCI and SCSI bus standards have been significantly extended. PCI has a double-width version (64 bits vs. 32 bits) and a fast version (66 MHz vs. 33 MHz). The original SCSI bus was asynchronous. Faster, synchronous versions were developed, followed by extensions for a wider bus (16 and 32 bits versus 8, called wide SCSI) and a faster clock (10 MHz, called fast SCSI, vs. 5 MHz for the original synchronous SCSI). Fast, wide SCSI combines the higher clock rate and wider bus. In addition, a 20-MHz version of the SCSI bus (called Ultra) was developed and released in late 1996. The specifications for these standard buses become extremely complex. For example, the PCI standard is 282 pages long, while the SCSI-2 specification, which includes both the faster and wider versions, is over 600 pages long! The SCSI-2 specification, a good overview of SCSI and its development, and the PCI specification are available via links at *www.mkp.com/books_catalog/cod/links.htm.*

8.5   Interfacing I/O Devices to the Memory, Processor, and Operating System

A bus protocol defines how a word or block of data should be communicated on a set of wires. This still leaves several other tasks that must be performed to actually cause data to be transferred from a device and into the memory address space of some user program. This section focuses on these tasks and will answer such questions as the following:

■ How is a user I/O request transformed into a device command and communicated to the device?

■ How is data actually transferred to or from a memory location?

■ What is the role of the operating system?

As we will see when we answer these questions, the operating system plays a major role in handling I/O, acting as the interface between the hardware and the program that requests I/O.

The responsibilities of the operating system arise from three characteristics of I/O systems:

1.   The I/O system is shared by multiple programs using the processor.

2. I/O systems often use interrupts (externally generated exceptions) to communicate information about I/O operations. Because interrupts cause a transfer to kernel or supervisor mode, they must be handled by the operating system (OS).

3. The low-level control of an I/O device is complex because it requires managing a set of concurrent events and because the requirements for correct device control are often very detailed.

Hardware Software Interface

The three characteristics of I/O systems above lead to several different functions the OS must provide:

- The OS guarantees that a user's program accesses only the portions of an I/O device to which the user has rights. For example, the OS must not allow a program to read or write a file on disk if the owner of the file has not granted access to this program. In a system with shared I/O devices, protection could not be provided if user programs could perform I/O directly.

- The OS provides abstractions for accessing devices by supplying routines that handle low-level device operations.

- The OS handles the interrupts generated by I/O devices, just as it handles the exceptions generated by a program.

- The OS tries to provide equitable access to the shared I/O resources, as well as schedule accesses in order to enhance system throughput.

To perform these functions on behalf of user programs, the operating system must be able to communicate with the I/O devices and to prevent the user program from communicating with the I/O devices directly. Three types of communication are required:

1. The OS must be able to give commands to the I/O devices. These commands include not only operations like read and write, but other operations to be done on the device, such as a disk seek.

2. The device must be able to notify the OS when the I/O device has completed an operation or has encountered an error. For example, when a disk has completed a seek, it will notify the OS.

3. Data must be transferred between memory and an I/O device. For example, the block being read on a disk read must be moved from disk to memory.

In the next few sections, we will see how these communications are performed.

Giving Commands to I/O Devices

To give a command to an I/O device, the processor must be able to address the device and to supply one or more command words. Two methods are used to address the device: memory-mapped I/O and special I/O instructions. In memory-mapped I/O, portions of the address space are assigned to I/O devices. Reads and writes to those addresses are interpreted as commands to the I/O device.

For example, a write operation can be used to send data to an I/O device where the data will be interpreted as a command. When the processor places the address and data on the memory bus, the memory system ignores the operation because the address indicates a portion of the memory space used for I/O. The device controller, however, sees the operation, records the data, and transmits it to the device as a command. User programs are prevented from issuing I/O operations directly because the OS does not provide access to the address space assigned to the I/O devices and thus the addresses are protected by the address translation. Memory-mapped I/O can also be used to transmit data by writing or reading to select addresses. The device uses the address to determine the type of command, and the data may be provided by a write or obtained by a read. In any event, the address encodes both the device identity and the type of transmission between processor and device.

Actually performing a read or write of data to fulfill a program request usually requires several separate I/O operations. Furthermore, the processor may have to interrogate the status of the device between individual commands to determine whether the command completed successfully. For example, the DEC LP11 line printer has two I/O device registers—one for status information and one for data to be printed. The Status register contains a *done bit*, set by the printer when it has printed a character, and an *error bit*, indicating that the printer is jammed or out of paper. Each byte of data to be printed is put into the Data register. The processor must then wait until the printer sets the done bit before it can place another character in the buffer. The processor must also check the error bit to determine if a problem has occurred. Each of these operations requires a separate I/O device access.

Elaboration: The alternative to memory-mapped I/O is to use dedicated I/O instructions in the processor. These I/O instructions can specify both the device number and the command word (or the location of the command word in memory). The processor communicates the device address via a set of wires normally included as part of the I/O bus. The actual command can be transmitted over the data lines in the bus. Examples of computers with I/O instructions are the Intel 80x86 and the IBM 370 computers. By making the I/O instructions illegal to execute when not in kernel or supervisor mode, user programs can be prevented from accessing the devices directly.

Communicating with the Processor

The process of periodically checking status bits to see if it is time for the next I/O operation, as in the previous example, is called *polling*. Polling is the simplest way for an I/O device to communicate with the processor. The I/O device simply puts the information in a Status register, and the processor must come and get the information. The processor is totally in control and does all the work.

The disadvantage of polling is that it can waste a lot of processor time because processors are so much faster than I/O devices. The processor may read the Status register many times, only to find that the device has not yet completed a comparatively slow I/O operation, or that the mouse has not budged since the last time it was polled. When the device has completed an operation, we must still read the status to determine whether it was successful.

Polling can be used in several different ways, depending on the I/O device and whether the I/O device can initiate I/O independently. For example, a mouse is an input-only device that initiates I/O independently, when a user moves the mouse or clicks a button. Because a mouse has a low I/O rate, polling is often used to interface to a mouse. Many other I/O devices, such as a floppy disk or a printer, initiate I/O only under control of the operating system. Thus we need only poll such devices when the OS knows that the device is active. As we will see, this allows polling to be used even when the I/O rate is somewhat higher.

Overhead of Polling in an I/O System

Example

Let's determine the impact of polling overhead for three different devices. Assume that the number of clock cycles for a polling operation—including transferring to the polling routine, accessing the device, and restarting the user program—is 400 and that the processor executes with a 500-MHz clock.

Determine the fraction of CPU time consumed for the following three cases, assuming that you poll often enough so that no data is ever lost and assuming that the devices are potentially always busy:

1. The mouse must be polled 30 times per second to ensure that we do not miss any movement made by the user.

2. The floppy disk transfers data to the processor in 16-bit units and has a data rate of 50 KB/sec. No data transfer can be missed.

3. The hard disk transfers data in four-word chunks and can transfer at 4 MB/sec. Again, no transfer can be missed.

Answer First the mouse:

$$\text{Clock cycles per second for polling} = 30 \times 400 = 12{,}000 \text{ cycles per second}$$

$$\text{Fraction of the processor clock cycles consumed} = \frac{12 \times 10^3}{500 \times 10^6} = 0.002\%$$

Polling can clearly be used for the mouse without much performance impact on the processor.

For the floppy disk, the rate at which we must poll is

$$\frac{50 \dfrac{\text{KB}}{\text{second}}}{2 \dfrac{\text{bytes}}{\text{polling access}}} = 25K \frac{\text{polling accesses}}{\text{second}}$$

Thus, we can compute the number of cycles (ignoring the base 2 versus base 10 discrepancy):

$$\text{Cycles per second for polling} = 25K \times 400$$

$$\text{Fraction of the processor consumed} = \frac{10 \times 10^6}{500 \times 10^6} = 2\%$$

This amount of overhead is significant, but might be tolerable in a low-end system with only a few I/O devices like this floppy disk.

In the case of the hard disk, we must poll at a rate equal to the data rate in four-word chunks, which is 250K times per second (4 MB per second/16 bytes per transfer). Thus,

$$\text{Cycles per second for polling} = 250K \times 400$$

Ignoring the discrepancy in bases,

$$\text{Fraction of the processor consumed} = \frac{100 \times 10^6}{500 \times 10^6} = 20\%$$

Thus one-fifth of the processor would be used in just polling the disk. Clearly, polling will probably be unacceptable for a hard disk on this machine.

If we knew that the floppy disk and hard disk were active only 25% of the time and we poll only when the device is active, then the average overhead for polling would be reduced to 0.5% and 5%, respectively. Although this reduces the overhead, notice that once the OS initiates an operation on the device, it must poll continuously since the OS does not know when the device will actually respond and want to initiate a transfer.

The overhead in a polling interface was recognized long ago, leading to the invention of interrupts to notify the processor when an I/O device requires attention from the processor. *Interrupt-driven I/O,* which is used by almost all systems for at least some devices, employs I/O interrupts to indicate to the processor that an I/O device needs attention. When a device wants to notify the processor that it has completed some operation or needs attention, it causes the processor to be interrupted.

An I/O interrupt is just like the exceptions we saw in Chapters 5, 6, and 7, with two important exceptions:

1. An I/O interrupt is asynchronous with respect to the instruction execution. That is, the interrupt is not associated with any instruction and does not prevent the instruction completion. This is very different from either page fault exceptions or exceptions such as arithmetic overflow. Our control unit need only check for a pending I/O interrupt at the time it starts a new instruction.

2. In addition to the fact that an I/O interrupt has occurred, we would like to convey further information such as the identity of the device generating the interrupt. Furthermore, the interrupts represent devices that may have different priorities and whose interrupt requests have different urgencies associated with them.

To communicate information to the processor, such as the identity of the device raising the interrupt, a system can use either vectored interrupts or an exception Cause register. When the interrupt is recognized by the processor, the device can send either the vector address or a status field to place in the Cause register. As a result, when the OS gets control, it knows the identity of the device that caused the interrupt and can immediately interrogate the device. An interrupt mechanism eliminates the need for the processor to poll the device and instead allows the processor to focus on executing programs.

Elaboration: To deal with the different priorities of the I/O devices, most interrupt mechanisms have several levels of priority. These priorities indicate the order in which the processor should process interrupts. Both internally generated exceptions and I/O interrupts have priorities; typically, I/O interrupts have lower priority than internal exceptions. There may be multiple I/O interrupt priorities, with high-speed devices associated with the higher priorities. If the exception mechanism is vectored (see section 5.6), the vector address for a fast device will correspond to the higher-priority interrupt. If a Cause register is used, then the register contents for a faster device are set for the higher-priority interrupt.

Transferring the Data between a Device and Memory

We have seen two different methods that enable a device to communicate with the processor. These two techniques, polling and I/O interrupts, form the basis for two methods of implementing the transfer of data between the I/O device and memory. Both these techniques work best with lower-bandwidth devices, where we are more interested in reducing the cost of the device controller and interface than in providing a high-bandwidth transfer. Both polling and interrupt-driven transfers put the burden of moving data and managing the transfer on the processor. After looking at these two schemes, we will examine a scheme more suitable for higher-performance devices or collections of devices.

We can use the processor to transfer data between a device and memory based on polling. Consider our mouse example. The processor can periodically read the mouse counter values and the position of the mouse buttons. If the position of the mouse or one of its buttons has changed, the operating system can notify the program associated with interpreting the mouse changes.

An alternative mechanism is to make the transfer of data interrupt driven. In this case, the OS would still transfer data in small numbers of bytes from or to the device. But because the I/O operation is interrupt driven, the OS simply works on other tasks while data is being read from or written to the device. When the OS recognizes an interrupt from the device, it reads the status to check for errors. If there are none, the OS can supply the next piece of data, for example, by a sequence of memory-mapped writes. When the last byte of an I/O request has been transmitted and the I/O operation is completed, the OS can inform the program. The processor and OS do all the work in this process, accessing the device and memory for each data item transferred. Let's see how an interrupt-driven I/O interface might work for the floppy disk.

Overhead of Interrupt-Driven I/O

Example

Suppose we have the same hard disk and processor we used in the example on page 676, but we use interrupt-driven I/O. The overhead for each transfer, including the interrupt, is 500 clock cycles. Find the fraction of the processor consumed if the hard disk is only transferring data 5% of the time.

Answer

The interrupt rate when the disk is busy is the same as the polling rate. Hence,

$$\text{Cycles per second for disk} = 250\text{K} \times 500$$

$$= 125 \times 10^6 \text{ cycles per second}$$

$$\text{Fraction of the processor consumed during a transfer} = \frac{125 \times 10^6}{500 \times 10^6} = 25\%$$

Assuming that the disk is only transferring data 5% of the time,

$$\text{Fraction of the processor consumed on average} = 25\% \times 5\% = 1.25\%$$

As we can see, the absence of overhead when an I/O device is not actually transferring is the major advantage of an interrupt-driven interface versus polling.

Interrupt-driven I/O relieves the processor from having to wait for every I/O event, although if we used this method for transferring data from or to a hard disk, the overhead could still be intolerable, since it would consume 25% of the processor when the disk was transferring. For high-bandwidth devices like hard disks, the transfers consist primarily of relatively large blocks of data (hundreds to thousands of bytes). So computer designers invented a mechanism for off-loading the processor and having the device controller transfer data directly to or from the memory without involving the processor. This mechanism is called *direct memory access* (DMA). The interrupt mechanism is still used by the device to communicate with the processor, but only on completion of the I/O transfer or when an error occurs.

DMA is implemented with a specialized controller that transfers data between an I/O device and memory independent of the processor. The DMA controller becomes the bus master and directs the reads or writes between itself and memory. There are three steps in a DMA transfer:

1. The processor sets up the DMA by supplying the identity of the device, the operation to perform on the device, the memory address that is the source or destination of the data to be transferred, and the number of bytes to transfer.

2. The DMA starts the operation on the device and arbitrates for the bus. When the data is available (from the device or memory), it transfers the data. The DMA device supplies the memory address for the read or write. If the request requires more than one transfer on the bus, the DMA unit generates the next memory address and initiates the next transfer. Using this mechanism, a DMA unit can complete an entire transfer, which may be thousands of bytes in length, without bothering the processor. Many DMA controllers contain some memory to allow them to deal flexibly with delays either in transfer or those incurred while waiting to become bus master.

3. Once the DMA transfer is complete, the controller interrupts the processor, which can then determine by interrogating the DMA device or examining memory whether the entire operation completed successfully.

There may be multiple DMA devices in a computer system. For example, in a system with a single processor-memory bus and multiple I/O buses, each I/O bus controller will often contain a DMA processor that handles any transfers between a device on the I/O bus and the memory. Let's see how much of the processor is consumed using DMA to handle our hard-disk example.

Overhead of I/O Using DMA

Example

Suppose we have the same processor and hard disk as our earlier example on page 676. Assume that the initial setup of a DMA transfer takes 1000 clock cycles for the processor, and assume the handling of the interrupt at DMA completion requires 500 clock cycles for the processor. The hard disk has a transfer rate of 4 MB/sec and uses DMA. If the average transfer from the disk is 8 KB, what fraction of the 500-MHz processor is consumed if the disk is actively transferring 100% of the time? Ignore any impact from bus contention between the processor and DMA controller.

Answer

Each DMA transfer takes

$$\frac{8 \text{ KB}}{4 \frac{\text{MB}}{\text{second}}} = 2 \times 10^{-3} \text{ seconds}$$

So if the disk is constantly transferring, it requires

$$\frac{1000 + 500 \frac{\text{cycles}}{\text{transfer}}}{2 \times 10^{-3} \frac{\text{seconds}}{\text{transfer}}} = 750 \times 10^3 \frac{\text{clock cycles}}{\text{second}}$$

Since the processor runs at 500 MHz,

$$\text{Fraction of processor consumed} = \frac{750 \times 10^3}{500 \times 10^6}$$
$$= 1.5 \times 10^{-3} = 0.2\%$$

Unlike either polling or interrupt-driven I/O, DMA can be used to interface a hard disk without consuming all the processor cycles for a single I/O. In addition, the disk will not be actively transferring data most of the time, and this number will be considerably lower. Of course, if the processor is also contending for memory, it will be delayed when the memory is busy doing a DMA transfer. By using caches, the processor can avoid having to access memory most of the time, thereby leaving most of the memory bandwidth free for use by I/O devices.

Elaboration: To further reduce the need to interrupt the processor and occupy it in handling an I/O request that may involve doing several actual operations, the I/O controller can be made more intelligent. Intelligent controllers are often called *I/O processors* (as well as *I/O controllers* or *channel controllers*). These specialized processors basically execute a series of I/O operations, called an *I/O program*. The program may be stored in the I/O processor, or it may be stored in memory and fetched by the I/O processor. When using an I/O processor, the operating system typically sets up an I/O program that indicates the I/O operations to be done as well as the size and transfer address for any reads or writes. The I/O processor then takes the operations from the I/O program and interrupts the processor only when the entire program is completed. DMA processors are essentially special-purpose processors (usually single-chip and nonprogrammable), while I/O processors are often implemented with general-purpose microprocessors, which run a specialized I/O program.

Direct Memory Access and the Memory System

When DMA is incorporated into an I/O system, the relationship between the memory system and processor changes. Without DMA, all accesses to the memory system come from the processor and thus proceed through address translation and cache access as if the processor generated the references. With DMA, there is another path to the memory system—one that does not go through the address translation mechanism or the cache hierarchy. This difference generates some problems in both virtual memory systems and systems with caches. These problems are usually solved with a combination of hardware techniques and software support.

The difficulties in having DMA in a virtual memory system arise because pages have both a physical and a virtual address. DMA also creates problems for systems with caches because there can be two copies of a data item: one in the cache and one in memory. Because the DMA processor issues memory requests directly to the memory rather than through the cache, the value of a memory location seen by the DMA unit and the processor may differ. Consider a read from disk that the DMA unit places directly into memory. If some of the locations into which the DMA writes are in the cache, the processor will receive

Hardware Software Interface

In a system with virtual memory, should DMA work with virtual addresses or physical addresses? The obvious problem with virtual addresses is that the DMA unit will need to translate the virtual addresses to physical addresses. The major problem with the use of a physical address in a DMA transfer is that the transfer cannot easily cross a page boundary. If an I/O request crossed a page boundary, then the memory locations to which it was being transferred would not be contiguous in the physical memory—the memory locations would correspond to multiple virtual pages, each of which could be mapped to any physical page. Consequently, if we use physical addresses, we must constrain all DMA transfers to stay within one page.

One method to allow the system to initiate DMA transfers that cross page boundaries is to make the DMA work on virtual addresses. In such a system, the DMA unit has a small number of map entries that provide virtual-to-physical mapping for a transfer. The operating system provides the mapping when the I/O is initiated. By using this mapping, the DMA unit need not worry about the location of the virtual pages involved in the transfer.

Another technique is for the operating system to break the DMA transfer into a series of transfers, each confined within a single physical page. The transfers are then *chained* together and handed to an I/O processor or intelligent DMA unit that executes the entire sequence of transfers; alternatively, the operating system can individually request the transfers.

Whichever method is used, the operating system must still cooperate by not remapping pages while a DMA transfer involving that page is in progress.

the old value when it does a read. Similarly, if the cache is write-back, the DMA may read a value directly from memory when a newer value is in the cache, and the value has not been written back. This is called the *stale data problem* or *coherency problem*.

We have looked at three different methods for transferring data between an I/O device and memory. In moving from polling to an interrupt-driven to a DMA interface, we shift the burden for managing an I/O operation from the processor to a progressively more intelligent I/O controller. These methods have the advantage of freeing up processor cycles. Their disadvantage is that they increase the cost of the I/O system. Because of this, a given computer system can choose which point along this spectrum is appropriate for the I/O devices connected to it.

> **Hardware Software Interface**
>
> The coherency problem for I/O data is avoided by using one of three major techniques. One approach is to route the I/O activity through the cache. This ensures that reads see the latest value while writes update any data in the cache. Routing all I/O through the cache is expensive and potentially has a large negative performance impact on the processor, since the I/O data is rarely used immediately and may displace useful data that a running program needs. A second choice is to have the OS selectively invalidate the cache for an I/O read or force write-backs to occur for an I/O write (often called cache *flushing*). This approach requires some small amount of hardware support and is probably more efficient if the software can perform the function easily and efficiently. Because this flushing of large parts of the cache need only happen on DMA block accesses, it will be relatively infrequent. The third approach is to provide a hardware mechanism for selectively flushing (or invalidating) cache entries. Hardware invalidation to ensure cache coherence is typical in multiprocessor systems, and the same technique can be used for I/O; we discuss this topic in detail in Chapter 9.

8.6 Designing an I/O System

There are two primary types of specifications that designers encounter in I/O systems: latency constraints and bandwidth constraints. In both cases, knowledge of the traffic pattern affects the design and analysis.

Latency constraints involve ensuring that the latency to complete an I/O operation is bounded by a certain amount. In the simple case, the system may be unloaded, and the designer must ensure that some latency bound is met either because it is critical to the application or because the device must receive certain guaranteed service to prevent errors. Examples of the latter are similar to the analysis we looked at in the previous section. Likewise, determining the latency on an unloaded system is relatively easy, since it involves tracing the path of the I/O operation and summing the individual latencies.

Finding the average latency (or distribution of latency) under a load is a much more complex problem. Such problems are tackled either by queuing theory (when the behavior of the workload requests and I/O service times can be approximated by simple distributions) or by simulation (when the behavior of I/O events is complex). Both topics are beyond the limits of this text.

Designing an I/O system to meet a set of bandwidth constraints given a workload is the other typical problem designers face. Alternatively, the designer may be given a partially configured I/O system and be asked to balance the system to maintain the maximum bandwidth achievable as dictated by the preconfigured portion of the system. This latter design problem is a simplified version of the first.

The general approach to designing such a system is as follows:

1. Find the weakest link in the I/O system, which is the component in the I/O path that will constrain the design. Depending on the workload, this component can be anywhere, including the CPU, the memory system, the backplane bus, the I/O controllers, or the devices. Both the workload and configuration limits may dictate where the weakest link is located.

2. Configure this component to sustain the required bandwidth.

3. Determine the requirements for the rest of the system and configure them to support this bandwidth.

The easiest way to understand this methodology is with an example.

I/O System Design

Example   Consider the following computer system:

- A CPU that sustains 300 million instructions per second and averages 50,000 instructions in the operating system per I/O operation

- A memory backplane bus capable of sustaining a transfer rate of 100 MB/sec

- SCSI-2 controllers with a transfer rate of 20 MB/sec and accommodating up to seven disks

- Disk drives with a read/write bandwidth of 5 MB/sec and an average seek plus rotational latency of 10 ms

If the workload consists of 64-KB reads (where the block is sequential on a track) and the user program needs 100,000 instructions per I/O operation, find the maximum sustainable I/O rate and the number of disks and SCSI controllers required. Assume that the reads can always be done on an idle disk if one exists (i.e., ignore disk conflicts).

Answer
The two fixed components of the system are the memory bus and the CPU. Let's first find the I/O rate that these two components can sustain and determine which of these is the bottleneck. Each I/O takes 100,000 user instructions and 50,000 OS instructions, so

Maximum I/O rate of CPU =

$$\frac{\text{Instruction execution rate}}{\text{Instructions per I/O}} = \frac{300 \times 10^6}{(50 + 100) \times 10^3} = 2000\frac{\text{I/Os}}{\text{second}}$$

Each I/O transfers 64 KB, so

$$\text{Maximum I/O rate of bus} = \frac{\text{Bus bandwidth}}{\text{Bytes per I/O}} = \frac{100 \times 10^6}{64 \times 10^3} = 1562\frac{\text{I/Os}}{\text{second}}$$

The bus is the bottleneck, so we can now configure the rest of the system to perform at the level dictated by the bus, 1562 I/Os per second.

Now, let's determine how many disks we need to be able to accommodate 1562 I/Os per second. To find the number of disks, we first find the time per I/O operation at the disk:

Time per I/O at disk = Seek/rotational time + Transfer time

$$= 10 \text{ ms} + \frac{64 \text{ KB}}{5 \text{ MB/sec}} = 22.8 \text{ ms}$$

This means each disk can complete 43.9 I/Os per second. To saturate the bus requires 1562 I/Os per second, or $1562/43.9 \approx 36$ disks.

To compute the number of SCSI buses, we need to know the average transfer rate per disk, which is given by

$$\text{Transfer rate} = \frac{\text{Transfer size}}{\text{Transfer time}} = \frac{64 \text{KB}}{22.8 \text{ ms}} \approx 2.74 \text{ MB/sec}$$

Assuming the disk accesses are not clustered so that we can use all the bus bandwidth, we can place seven disks per SCSI bus and controller. This means we will need 36/7, or six buses and controllers.

Notice the significant number of simplifying assumptions that are needed to do this example. In practice, many of these simplifications might not hold for critical I/O-intensive applications (such as databases). For this reason, simulation is often the only realistic way to predict the I/O performance of a realistic workload.

8.7 Real Stuff: A Typical Desktop I/O System

The emergence of two dominant standards in the desktop personal computer market has led to an enormous degree of commonality among I/O systems. These two standards are PCI, as a backplane bus, and SCSI or SCSI-2, as an I/O bus. Although systems with older buses (ISA or IDE) continue to ship, such systems have rapidly been replaced on all but the least-expensive, lowest-performance machines. Interestingly, the benefits of a single bus standard, in terms of greater availability of devices and lower cost, have led to the adoption of backplane and I/O bus standards across both the IBM-compatible and Macintosh platforms, and a larger fraction of workstation vendors are also adhering to these standards.

Figure 8.16 shows the I/O system of the Macintosh 7200 series, which is typical of the I/O system of midrange to high-end desktop machines in 1997. PCI is used as the backplane bus, with slower devices sharing a lower-performance bus, such as SCSI.

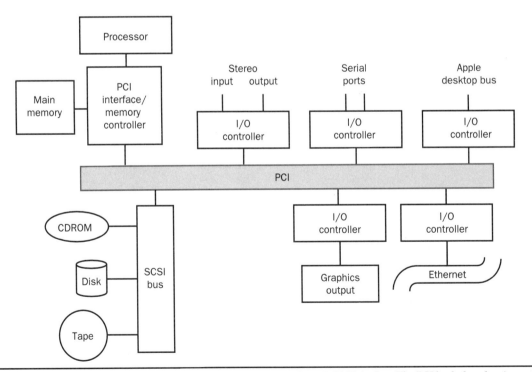

FIGURE 8.16　Organization of the I/O system on the Apple Macintosh 7200 series. The PCI backplane bus is used to interface all devices and interfaces to the processor and memory system. Serial ports provide for connections such as low-speed Appletalk network. The desktop bus provides support for keyboards and mice. In reality, several of the slow I/O devices (audio I/O, serial ports, and the desktop bus) share a single port onto the PCI bus, but we show them separately for simplicity.

Fallacies and Pitfalls

Fallacy: A 100-MB/sec bus can transfer 100 MB of data in 1 second.

Of course, this is only a fallacy when the definition of a megabyte of storage and a megabyte per second of bandwidth do not agree. As we discussed on page 642, I/O bandwidth measures are usually quoted in base 10 (i.e., 1 MB/sec = 10^6 bytes/sec), while 1 MB of data is typically a base 2 measure (i.e., 1 MB = 2^{20} bytes). How significant is this distinction? The time to transfer 100 MB of data on a 100-MB/sec bus is actually

$$\frac{100 \times 2^{20}}{100 \times 10^6} = \frac{1,048,576}{1,000,000} = 1.048576 \approx 1 \text{ second}$$

A similar, but smaller, error is introduced when we treat a kilobyte, meaning either 10^3 or 2^{10} bytes, as equivalent, while a larger error is introduced when we treat a gigabyte, meaning either 10^9 or 2^{20} bytes, as equivalent.

Pitfall: Using the peak transfer rate of a portion of the I/O system to make performance projections or performance comparisons.

Many of the components of an I/O system, from the devices to the controllers to the buses, are specified using their peak bandwidths. In practice, these peak bandwidth measurements are often based on unrealistic assumptions about the system or are unattainable because of other system limitations. For example, in quoting bus performance, the peak transfer rate is often specified using a memory system that is impossible to build.

A PCI bus has a peak bandwidth of about 133 MB/sec. In practice, even for long transfers, it is difficult to sustain more than about 80 MB/sec for realistic memory systems.

Amdahl's law also reminds us that the throughput of an I/O system will be limited by the lowest-performance component in the I/O path.

Fallacy: Magnetic storage is on its last legs and will be replaced shortly.

This is both a fallacy and a pitfall. Such claims have been made constantly for the past 20 years, though the string of failed alternatives in recent years seems to have reduced the level of claims for the death of magnetic storage. Among the unsuccessful candidates proposed to replace magnetic storage have been magnetic bubble memories, optical storage, and photographic storage. None of these systems has matched the combination of characteristics that favor magnetic disks: nonvolatility, low cost, reasonable access time, and high reliability. Magnetic storage technology continues to improve at the same or faster pace it has sustained over the past 25 years. In fact, the rate of density improvement has increased in the last 10 years, and rotational speeds and seek times have also improved significantly in the past few years.

Pitfall: Moving functions from the CPU to the I/O processor, expecting to improve performance without a careful analysis.

There are many examples of this pitfall trapping people, although I/O processors, when properly used, can certainly enhance performance. A frequent instance of this fallacy is the use of intelligent I/O interfaces, which, because of the higher overhead to set up an I/O, can turn out to have worse latency than a processor-directed I/O activity (although if the processor is freed up sufficiently, system throughput may still increase). Frequently, performance falls when the I/O processor has much lower performance than the main processor. Consequently, a small amount of main processor time is replaced with a larger amount of I/O processor time. Workstation designers have seen both these phenomena repeatedly.

A more serious problem can occur when the migration of an I/O feature changes the instruction set architecture or system architecture in a programmer-visible way. This forces all future machines to have to live with a decision that made sense in the past. If CPUs improve in cost/performance more rapidly than the I/O processor (and this will likely be the case), then moving the function may result in a slower machine in the next computer.

The most telling example comes from the IBM 360. It was decided that the performance of the ISAM system, an early database system, would improve if some of the record searching occurred in the disk controller itself. A key field was associated with each record, and the device searched each key as the disk rotated until it found a match. It would then transfer the desired record. This technique requires an extra large gap between records when a key is present.

The speed at which a track can be searched is limited by the speed of the disk and by the number of keys that can be packed on a track. On an IBM 3330 disk, the key is typically 10 characters; the gap is equivalent to 191 characters if there is a key, and 135 characters when no key is present. If we assume that the data is also 10 characters and that the track has nothing else on it, a 13,165-byte track can contain

$$\frac{13,165}{191 + 10 + 10} = 62 \text{ key-data records}$$

The time per key search is

$$\frac{16.7 \text{ ms (1 revolution)}}{62} = 0.27 \text{ ms/key search}$$

In place of this scheme, we could put several key-data pairs in a single block and have smaller interrecord gaps. Assuming that there are 15 key-data pairs per block and that the track has nothing else on it, then

$$\frac{13,165}{135 + 15 \times (10 + 10)} = \frac{13,165}{135 + 300} = 30 \text{ blocks of key-data pairs}$$

The revised performance is then

$$\frac{16.7 \text{ ms (1 revolution)}}{30 \times 15} \approx 0.04 \text{ ms/key search}$$

Of course, the disk-based search would look better if the keys were much longer.

As processors got faster, the CPU time for a search became trivial, while the time for a search using the hardware facility improved very little. While the strategy made early machines faster, programs that use the key search operation in the I/O processor run up to six times slower on today's machines!

8.9 | Concluding Remarks

I/O systems are evaluated on several different characteristics: the variety of I/O devices supported; the maximum number of I/O devices; cost; and performance, measured both in latency and in throughput. These goals lead to widely varying schemes for interfacing I/O devices. In the low end, schemes like buffering and even DMA can be avoided to minimize cost. In midrange systems, buffered DMA is likely to be the dominant transfer mechanism. In the high end, latency and bandwidth may both be important, and cost may be secondary. Multiple paths to I/O devices with limited buffering often characterize high-end I/O systems. Increasing the bandwidth with both more and wider connections eliminates the need for buffering at an increase in cost. Typically, being able to access the data on an I/O device at any time (high availability) becomes more important as systems grow. As a result, redundancy and error correction mechanisms become more and more prevalent as we enlarge the system.

The design of I/O systems is complicated because the limiting factor in I/O system performance can be any of several critical resources in the I/O path, from the operating system to the device. Furthermore, independent requests from different programs interact in the I/O system, making the performance of an I/O request dependent on other activity that occurs at the same time. Lastly, design techniques that improve bandwidth often negatively impact latency, and vice versa. For example, adding buffering usually increases the system cost and also the system bandwidth. But it also increases latency by placing additional hardware between the device and memory. It is this combination of factors, including some that are unpredictable, that makes designing I/O systems and improving their performance challenging not only for architects but also for OS designers and even programmers building I/O-intensive applications.

The Big Picture

The performance of an I/O system, whether measured by bandwidth or latency, depends on all the elements in the path between the device and memory, including the operating system that generates the I/O commands. The bandwidth of the buses, the memory, and the device determine the maximum transfer rate from or to the device. Similarly, the latency depends on the device latency, together with any latency imposed by the memory system or buses. The effective bandwidth and response latency also depend on other I/O requests that may cause contention for some resource in the path. Finally, the operating system is a bottleneck. In some cases, the OS takes a long time to deliver an I/O request from a user program to an I/O device, leading to high latency. In other cases, the operating system effectively limits the I/O bandwidth because of limitations in the number of concurrent I/O operations it can support.

Future Directions in I/O Systems

What does the future hold for I/O systems? The rapidly increasing performance of processors strains I/O systems, whose physical components cannot improve in performance as fast as processors. To hide the growing gap between the speed of processors and the access time to secondary storage (primarily disks), main memory is used as a cache for secondary storage. These *file caches*, which rely on spatial and temporal locality in access to secondary storage, are maintained by the operating system. The use of file caches allows many file accesses to be handled from memory rather than from disk.

Magnetic disks are increasing in capacity quickly, but access time is improving only slowly. One reason for this is that the opportunities for magnetic disks are growing faster in the low end of the market than in the high end, and the low end is driven primarily by the demand for lower cost per megabyte. This market has helped shrink the size of the disk from the 14-inch platters of the mainframe disk to the 1.3-inch disks developed for laptop and palmtop computers. In fact, the dramatic demand for small disks has led to an accelerated rate of improvement in disk density, so that the density of magnetic disks has been growing faster since about 1990 than it ever did! What is surprising is that this period of growth came at a time when a number of people were predicting the end (or at least a reduction in the use) of magnetic disks!

In addition to increases in density, transfer rates have grown rapidly as disks increased in rotational speed and interfaces improved. In addition, virtually every high-performance disk manufactured today includes a track or sector buffer that caches sectors as the read head passes over them.

One major new disk organization that has emerged in the last few years is an array of small and inexpensive disks. The argument for arrays is that since price per megabyte is independent of disk size, potential throughput can be increased by having many disk drives and, hence, many disk heads. Simply spreading data over multiple disks automatically forces accesses to several disks. (While arrays improve throughput, latency is not necessarily reduced.) Adding redundant disks to the array offers the opportunity for the array to discover a failed disk and automatically recover the lost information. Arrays may thus enhance the reliability of a computer system as well as performance. This redundancy has inspired the acronym *RAID* for these arrays: *redundant arrays of inexpensive disks*. A number of computer companies offer RAIDs for their disk subsystems. For example, IBM has both a RAID offering (see the IBM link at *www.mkp.com/books_catalog/cod/links.htm*), as well as a disk subsystem built from the largest disks they manufacture.

The next level of the storage hierarchy below magnetic disks has also yielded extraordinary increases in capacity in the last several years. This increase has come partly from improvements in magnetic recording that also helped disks, but also from a different recording technology, the *helical scan tape*. Found in VCRs, camcorders, and digital audio tapes, helical scan tape records at an angle to the tape rather than parallel, as in longitudinally recorded tapes. The tape still moves at the same speed, but the fast-spinning tape head records bits much more densely—a factor of about 50 to 100 denser than longitudinally recorded tapes. And because the medium was created for consumer products, the improvement in cost per bit over time has been even greater than for traditional magnetic tapes used solely by the computer industry.

Advances in tape capacity are being enhanced by advances on two other fronts: compression and robots. Faster processors have enabled systems to begin using compression to multiply storage capacity. Factors of two to three are common, with compression of 20:1 possible for certain types of data such as images. The second enhancement that is changing the cost-effectiveness of very large online storage is the emergence of inexpensive robots to automatically load and store tapes, offering a new level in the hierarchy between *online* magnetic disks and *offline* magnetic disks on shelves. This *"robo-line"* storage means access to terabytes of information at the delay of tens of seconds, without the intervention of a human operator. Figure 8.17 is a photograph of a tape robot.

Computer networks are also making great strides. Both 100-Mbit Ethernet and switched Ethernet solutions are being used in new networks and in upgrading networks that cannot handle the tremendous explosion in bandwidth created by the use of multimedia and the growing importance of the World Wide Web. ATM represents another potential technology for expanding even further. To support the growth in traffic, the Internet backbones are being switched to optical fiber, which allows a significant increase in bandwidth for long-haul networks.

FIGURE 8.17   The Exabyte EXB-120 holds 116 8-mm helical scan tapes. Each tape holds 10 GB, yielding a total capacity of over a terabyte. The EXB-120 costs about as much as two to four workstations. Photo courtesy of the Exabyte Corporation.

One of the most interesting storage technologies being explored is holography. One research project under way hopes to demonstrate a storage device with terabyte capacity and with transfer rates of 1 Gbit/sec. This would represent about an order of magnitude improvement in both storage size and transfer rate versus the largest disks in 1997. See the pertinent IBM link at *www.mkp.com/books_catalog/cod/links.htm* for a description of this joint academic-industry research activity.

Such advances offer "computing science fiction" scenarios that would have seemed absurd just a few years ago. For example, if all the books in the Library of Congress were converted to ASCII, they would occupy just 10 terabytes (although the pictures might take even more, depending on their number and resolution). Helical scan tapes, tape robots, compression, and high-speed networks could be the building blocks of an electronic library. All the information on all the books in the world would be available at your fingertips for the cost of a large minicomputer. And parallel processing, discussed in the next chapter, will allow this information to be indexed so that all books could be searched by content rather than by title. Electronic libraries would change the lives of anyone with a library card, and the technology to create them is within our grasp.

8.10   Historical Perspective and Further Reading

The history of I/O systems is a fascinating one. Many of the most interesting artifacts of early computers are their I/O devices. Magnetic tape was the first low-cost magnetic storage and today persists as the lowest-cost storage medium. Early tape drives used reel-to-reel technologies and linear recording, which were eventually replaced by tape cartridges and helical recording. As disks became cheaper, tapes were relegated primarily to archival purposes, causing additional focus on density, as opposed to speed, and on large-scale archival technologies such as tape robots.

The earliest random access storage devices were drums and fixed-head disks. A drum had a cylindrical surface coated with a magnetic film. It used a large number of read/write heads positioned over each track on the drum (see Figure 8.18). Drums were relatively high-speed I/O devices often used for virtual memory paging or for creating a file cache to slower-speed devices. Drums, which had no seek time, survived into the 1970s in higher-speed applications, such as paging or use in high-end machines. Eventually improvements in disk speed and the significant cost advantage of disks eliminated drum technology. Large (2 to 3 feet in diameter) single-platter, fixed-head disks were also in use in the 1950s.

In 1956, IBM developed the first disk storage system with both moving heads and multiple disk surfaces in San Jose, helping to seed the development of the magnetic storage industry in the southern end of Silicon Valley. The IBM 305 RAMAC (Random Access Method of Accounting and Control) could store 5 million characters (5 MB) of data on 50 disks, each 24 inches in diameter. The RAMAC is shown in Figure 8.19.

Moving-head disks quickly became the dominant high-speed magnetic storage, though their high cost meant that magnetic tape continued to be used extensively until the 1970s. The next key development for hard disks was the removable hard disk drive developed by IBM in 1962; this made it possible to share the expensive drive electronics and helped disks overtake tapes as the preferred storage medium. Figure 8.20 shows a removable disk drive and the multiplatter disk used in the drive. IBM also invented the floppy disk drive in 1970, originally to hold microcode for the IBM 370 series. Floppy disks became popular with the PC about 10 years later.

The sealed Winchester disk, which was developed by IBM in 1973, completely dominates disk technology today. (All the disks shown in Figure 8.5 on page 649 are Winchester disks.) Winchester disks benefited from two related properties. First, reductions in the cost of the disk electronics made it unnecessary to share the electronics and thus made nonremovable disks economical.

FIGURE 8.18 A magnetic drum made by Digital Development Corporation in the 1960s and used on a CDC machine. The electronics supporting the read/write heads can be seen on the outside of the drum. Photo courtesy of the Computer Museum of America.

Since the disk was fixed and could be in a sealed enclosure, both the environmental and control problems were greatly reduced, allowing significant gains in density. The first disk that IBM shipped had two spindles, each with a 30-MB disk; the moniker "30-30" for the disk led to the name Winchester. Winchester disks grew rapidly in popularity in the 1980s, completely replacing removable disks by the middle of that decade.

Recently, low-cost removable drives have been resurrected for use in back-up and portable locations. These drives typically are available both in floppy

FIGURE 8.19   The RAMAC disk drive from IBM, made in 1956, was the first disk drive with a moving head and the first with multiple platters. The IBM storage technology Web site has a discussion of IBM's major contributions to storage technology. Find the link at *www.mkp.com/books_catalog/cod/links.htm*. Photo courtesy of IBM.

media, storing about 100 MB in 1997, and a removable hard disk format, storing 1–2 GB. These removable disks have lower density and are slower than nonremovable disks, but the removable media are attractive for certain environments.

The 1970s saw the invention of a number of remarkable I/O devices. Perhaps one of the most unusual was a film storage device that stored data optically on small strips of photographic film. These film storage devices could not only read and write film, but actually kept the filmstrips stored in the device (which was about 5 feet by 4 feet by 3 feet), retrieving them mechanically.

The early IBM 360s pioneered many of the ideas that we use in I/O systems today. The 360 was the first machine to make heavy use of DMA, and it introduced the notion of I/O programs that could be interpreted by the device. Chaining of I/O programs was a key feature. The concept of channels introduced in the 360 corresponds to the I/O bus of today.

The trend for high-end machines has been toward use of programmable I/O processors. The original machine to use this concept was the CDC 6600, which used I/O processors called *peripheral processors*.

FIGURE 8.20   This is a DEC disk drive and the removable pack. These disks became popular starting in the mid-1960s and dominated disk technology until Winchester drives in the late 1970s. This drive was made in the mid-1970s; each disk pack in this drive could hold 80 MB. Photo courtesy of the Commercial Computing Museum.

The forerunner of today's workstations and personal computers was the Alto, developed at Xerox Palo Alto Research Center in 1973 [Thacker et al. 1982], shown in Figure 8.21. This machine integrated the needs of the I/O functions into the microcode of the processor. This included support for the bit-mapped graphics display, the disk, and the network. The network for the Alto was the first Ethernet [Metcalfe and Boggs 1976]. The Alto also supported the first laser printer, configured as a print server accessible over the Ethernet. Similarly, disk servers were also built. The mouse, invented earlier by Doug Engelbart of SRI, was a key part of the Alto. The 16-bit processor used a writable control store, which enabled researchers to program in support for the I/O devices. The single microprogrammed engine drove the graphics display, mouse, disks, network, and, when there was nothing else to do, ran the user's program.

While today we associate microprocessors with the personal computer revolution, they were originally developed to meet the demand for special-purpose controllers. Since the invention of the microprocessor, designers have developed many I/O controllers that adapt a microprocessor to a specific task. These include everything from DMA controllers to SCSI controllers to complete Ethernet controllers on a single chip.

FIGURE 8.21   The Xerox Alto. Although never sold as a product, Xerox donated a number of these machines to several major universities as well as using them heavily internally. The use of a mouse, a local area network, and a personal graphics display with a window system were key characteristics of the Alto later broadly adopted by workstation and PC companies. Photo courtesy of the Computer History Center.

The first multivendor bus may have been the PDP-11 Unibus in 1970. DEC encouraged other companies to build devices that would plug into its bus, and many companies did. A more recent example is SCSI (small computer systems interface). This bus, originally called SASI, was invented by Shugart and was later standardized by the IEEE. This open system approach to buses contrasts with proprietary buses using patented interfaces, which companies adopt to forestall competition from plug-compatible vendors. The use of proprietary buses also raises the costs and lowers the availability of I/O devices that plug into proprietary buses because such devices must have an interface designed exclusively for that bus.

Ongoing development in the areas of tape robots (see Figure 8.17 on page 693), head-mounted displays, gloves for complete tactile feedback, and computer screens that you write on with pens are indications that the incredible developments in I/O technology are likely to continue in the future.

To Probe Further

Bashe, C. J., L. R. Johnson, J. H. Palmer, and E. W. Pugh [1986]. *IBM's Early Computers*, MIT Press, Cambridge, MA.

Describes the I/O system architecture and devices in IBM's early computers.

Borrill, P. L. [1986]. "32-bit buses: An objective comparison," *Proc. Buscon 1986 West*, San Jose, CA, 138–45.

A comparison of various 32-bit bus standards.

Chen, P. M., E. K. Lee, G. A. Gibson, R. H. Katz, and D. A. Patterson [1994]. "RAID: High-performance, reliable secondary storage," *ACM Computing Surveys* 26:2 (June) 145–88.

A tutorial covering disk arrays and the advantages of such an organization.

Gray, J., and A. Reuter [1993]. *Transaction Processing: Concepts and Techniques*, Morgan Kaufmann, San Francisco.

A description of transaction processing, including discussions of benchmarking and performance evaluation.

Hennessy, J., and D. Patterson [1995]. *Computer Architecture: A Quantitative Approach*, Second edition, Morgan Kaufmann Publishers, San Francisco, Chapters 6 and 7.

Chapter 6 focuses on I/O devices, including an extensive discussion of RAID technologies and more accurate I/O performance modeling. Chapter 7 focuses on interconnection technologies, including buses and an extensive discussion on networking.

Kahn, R. E. [1972]. "Resource-sharing computer communication networks," *Proc. IEEE* 60:11 (November) 1397–1407.

A classic paper that describes the ARPANET.

Levy, J. V. [1978]. "Buses: The skeleton of computer structures," in *Computer Engineering: A DEC View of Hardware Systems Design*, C. G. Bell, J. C. Mudge, and J. E. McNamara, eds., Digital Press, Bedford, MA.

This is a good overview of key concepts in bus design with some examples from DEC machines.

Metcalfe, R. M., and D. R. Boggs [1976]. "Ethernet: Distributed packet switching for local computer networks," *Comm. ACM* 19:7 (July) 395–404.

Describes the Ethernet network.

Smotherman, M. [1989]. "A sequencing-based taxonomy of I/O systems and review of historical machines," *Computer Architecture News* 17:5 (September) 5–15.

Describes the development of important ideas in I/O.

Thacker, C. P., E. M. McCreight, B. W. Lampson, R. F. Sproull, and D. R. Boggs [1982]. "Alto: A personal computer," in *Computer Structures: Principles and Examples*, D. P. Siewiorek, C. G. Bell, and A. Newell, eds., McGraw-Hill, New York, 549–72.

Describes the Alto—forerunner of workstations as well as the Apple Macintosh.

Key Terms

The wide variety of characteristics present in different I/O devices and the corresponding system techniques for adapting to those devices have introduced a number of new terms, summarized below.

asynchronous bus	distributed arbitration by self-selection	rotation latency or delay
backplane bus	Ethernet	sector
bus arbitration	fairness	seek
bus master	handshaking protocol	slave
bus request	I/O instruction	small computer systems interface (SCSI)
bus transaction	interrupt-driven I/O	split transaction protocol
centralized, parallel arbitration	memory-mapped I/O	synchronous bus
daisy chain arbitration	polling	track
direct memory access (DMA)	processor-memory buses	transaction processing
distributed arbitration by collision detection	redundant arrays of inexpensive disks (RAID)	transfer time

Exercises

8.1 [10] <§§8.1–8.2> Here are two different I/O systems intended for use in transaction processing:

- System A can support 1000 I/O operations per second.
- System B can support 750 I/O operations per second.

The systems use the same processor that executes 50 million instructions per second. Assume that each transaction requires 5 I/O operations and that each I/O operation requires 10,000 instructions. Ignoring response time and assuming that transactions may be arbitrarily overlapped, what is the maximum transaction-per-second rate that each machine can sustain?

8.2 [15] <§§8.1–8.2> {Ex. 8.1} The latency of an I/O operation for the two systems in Exercise 8.1 differs. The latency for an I/O on system A is equal to 20 ms, while for system B the latency is 18 ms for the first 500 I/Os per second and 25 ms per I/O for each I/O between 500 and 750 I/Os per second. In the workload, every 10th transaction depends on the immediately preceding transaction and must wait for its completion. What is the maximum transaction rate that still allows every transaction to complete in 1 second and that does not exceed the I/O bandwidth of the machine? (For simplicity, assume that all transaction requests arrive at the beginning of a 1-second interval.)

8.3 [5] <§8.3> The following simplified diagram shows two potential ways of numbering the sectors of data on a disk (only two tracks are shown and each track has eight sectors). Assuming that typical reads are contiguous (e.g., all 16 sectors are read in order), which way of numbering the sectors will be likely to result in higher performance? Why?

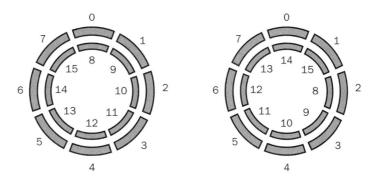

8.4 [5] <§8.3> What size messages would result in ATM outperforming Ethernet by a factor of two, assuming latencies and bandwidths equivalent to those reported in the example on page 654?

8.5 [5] <§8.3> The speed of light is approximately 3×10^8 meters per second, and electrical signals travel at about 50% of this speed in a conductor. When the term *high speed* is applied to a network, it is the bandwidth that is higher, not necessarily the velocity of the electrical signals. How much of a factor is the actual "flight time" for the electrical signals? Consider two computers that are 100 meters apart and two computers that are 5000 kilometers apart. Compare your results to the latencies reported in the example on page 654.

8.6 [5] <§8.3> The number of bytes in transit on a network is defined as the flight time (described in Exercise 8.5) multiplied by the delivered bandwidth. Calculate the number of bytes in transit for the two networks described in Exercise 8.5, assuming a delivered bandwidth of 5 MB/sec.

8.7 [5] <§8.3> A secret government agency simultaneously monitors 100 cellular phone conversations and multiplexes the data onto a network with a bandwidth of 1 MB/sec and an overhead latency of 350 μs per 1-KB message. Calculate the transmission time per message and determine whether there is sufficient bandwidth to support this application. Assume that the phone conversation data consists of 2 bytes sampled at a rate of 4 KHz.

8.8 [10] <§8.3> A program repeatedly performs a three-step process: It reads in a 4-KB block of data from disk, does some processing on that data, and then writes out the result as another 4-KB block elsewhere on the disk. Each block is contiguous and randomly located on a single track on the disk. The disk drive rotates at 7200 RPM, has an average seek time of 8 ms, and has a transfer rate of 20 MB/sec. The controller overhead is 2 ms. No other program is using the disk or processor, and there is no overlapping of disk operation with processing. The processing step takes 20 million clock cycles, and the clock rate is 400 MHz. What is the overall speed of the system in blocks processed per second?

8.9 [10] <§8.3> A transaction processing system utilizes a network and two different message sizes. The transaction request is quite small and consists of a 10-byte message. The transaction response is larger and consists of a 150-byte message. Assume that every transaction consists of a request and a response. Determine which of the two networks described in the example on page 654 would be better for this system.

8.10 [5] <§§8.3, 8.4> Assume that the bus and memory systems described in the example on page 665 are used to handle disk accesses from disks like the one described in the example on page 648. If the I/O is allowed to consume 100% of the bus and memory bandwidth, what is the maximum number of simultaneous disk transfers that can be sustained for the two block sizes?

8.11 [5] <§8.4> The example on page 665 assumed that the memory system took 200 ns to read the first four words, and each additional four words required 20 ns. Redo the example with the assumption that the memory system takes 150 ns to read the first four words and 30 ns to read each additional four words.

8.12 [5] <§8.4> The example on page 665 demonstrates that using larger block sizes results in an increase in the maximum sustained bandwidth that can be achieved. Under what conditions might a designer tend to favor smaller block sizes? Specifically, why would a designer choose a block size of 4 instead of 16 (assuming all of the characteristics are as identified in the example)?

8.13 [15] <§8.4> This question examines in more detail how increasing the block size for bus transactions decreases the total latency required and increases the maximum sustainable bandwidth. In the example on page 665, two different block sizes are considered (4 words and 16 words). Compute the total latency and the maximum bandwidth for all of the possible block sizes (between 4 and 16) and plot your results. Summarize what you learn by looking at your graph.

8.14 [15] <§8.4> This exercise is similar to Exercise 8.13. This time fix the block size at 4 and 16 (as in the example on page 665), but compute latencies and bandwidths for reads of different sizes. Specifically, consider reads of from 4 to 256 words, and use as many data points as you need to construct a meaningful graph. Use your graph to help determine at what point block sizes of 16 result in a reduced latency when compared with block sizes of 4.

8.15 [10] <§8.4> This exercise examines a design alternative to the example on page 665 that may improve the performance of writes. For writes, assume all of the characteristics reported in the example as well as the following:

5. The first four words are written 200 ns after the address is available, and each new write takes 20 ns. Assume a bus transfer of the most recent data to write, and a write of the previous four words can be overlapped.

The performance analysis reported in the example would thus remain unchanged for writes (in actuality, some minor changes might exist due to the need to compute error correction codes, etc., but we'll ignore this). An alternative bus scheme relies on separate 32-bit address and data lines. This will permit an address and data to be transmitted in the same cycle. For this bus alternative, what will the latency of the entire 256-word transfer be? What is the sustained bandwidth? Consider block sizes of four and eight words. When do you think the alternative scheme would be heavily favored?

8.16 <20> <§8.4> Consider an asynchronous bus used to interface an I/O device to the memory system described in the example on page 665. Each I/O request asks for 16 words of data from the memory, which, along with the I/O device, has a 4-word bus. Assume the same type of handshaking protocol as appears in Figure 8.10 on page 661 except that it is extended so that the memory can continue the transaction by sending additional blocks of data until the transaction is complete. Modify Figure 8.10 (both the steps and diagram) to indicate how such a transfer might take place. Assuming that each handshaking step takes 20 ns and memory access takes 60 ns, how long does it take to complete a transfer? What is the maximum sustained bandwidth for this asynchronous bus, and how does it compare to the synchronous bus in the example?

8.17 [15] <§§8.3–8.6> Redo the example on page 685, but instead assume that the reads are random 4-KB reads. You can assume that the reads are always to an idle disk, if one is available.

8.18 [20] <§§8.3–8.6> Here are a variety of building blocks used in an I/O system that has a synchronous processor-memory bus running at 200 MHz and one or more I/O adapters that interface I/O buses to the processor-memory bus.

■ *Memory system:* The memory system has a 32-bit interface and handles four-word transfers. The memory system has separate address and data lines and, for writes to memory, accepts a word every clock cycle for 4 clock cycles and then takes an additional 4 clock cycles before the words have been stored and it can accept another transaction.

■ *DMA interfaces:* The I/O adapters use DMA to transfer the data between the I/O buses and the processor-memory bus. The DMA unit arbitrates for the processor-memory bus and sends/receives four-word blocks from/to the memory system. The DMA controller can accommodate up to eight disks. Initiating a new I/O operation (including the seek and access) takes 1 ms, during which another I/O cannot be initiated by this controller (but outstanding operations can be handled).

■ *I/O bus:* The I/O bus is a synchronous bus with a sustainable bandwidth of 10 MB/sec; each transfer is one word long.

■ *Disks:* The disks have a measured average seek plus rotational latency of 12 ms. The disks have a read/write bandwidth of 5 MB/sec, when they are transferring.

Find the time required to read a 16-KB sector from a disk to memory, assuming that this is the only activity on the bus.

8.19 [15] <§§8.3–8.5> {Ex. 8.18} For the I/O system described in Exercise 8.18, find the maximum instantaneous bandwidth at which data can be transferred from disk to memory using as many disks as needed; how many disks and I/O buses (the minimum of each) do you need to achieve the bandwidth? Since you need only achieve this bandwidth for an instant, latencies need not be considered.

8.20 [20] <§§8.3–8.5> {Ex. 8.18, 8.19} Assume all accesses in the I/O system described in Exercise 8.18 are 4-KB block reads. If there are a total of six I/O buses, six DMA controllers, and 48 disks, find the maximum number of I/Os the system can sustain in steady state assuming that the reads are uniformly distributed to the disks. What is the sustained I/O bandwidth?

8.21 [15] <§§8.3–8.5> {Ex. 8.18, 8.19, 8.20} With the organization in Exercise 8.20, clearly it is possible to saturate the I/O buses because you have six of them at 10 MB/sec and 48 disks at 5 MB/sec. Compute the minimum block size (which should be a power of two) that will saturate the I/O buses. For this block size, how many I/O operations per second can the system perform and what is the I/O bandwidth?

8.22 [15] <§§7.3, 7.5, 8.4, 8.5> Consider a write-back cache used for a processor with a bus and memory system as described in the example on page 665 (assume that writes require the same amount of time as reads). The following performance measurements have been made:

- The cache miss rate is .05 misses per instruction for block sizes of 8 words.

- The cache miss rate is .03 misses per instruction for block sizes of 16 words.

- For either block size, 40% of the misses require a write-back operation, while the other 60% require only a read.

Assuming that the processor is stalled for the duration of a miss (including the write-back time if a write-back is needed), find the number of cycles per instruction that are spent handling cache misses for each block size. (Hint: First compute the miss penalty.)

8.23 [10] <§8.6> Write a paragraph identifying some of the simplifying assumptions that were made in the analysis described in the example on page 681.

8.24 [2 days–1 week] <§8.5, Appendix A> This assignment uses SPIM to build a simple set of I/O routines that will perform I/O to the terminal using polling. First, you need to build two I/O routines, whose C declarations and descriptions are shown below:

```
void print (char *string);
```

The procedure `print` takes a single argument, which is the address of a null-terminated ASCII string. All of the characters of the string except the null-terminating character should be output by `print`. It should print the characters one at a time, waiting for each character to be output before sending the next one. It should not return until all the characters have been output. The procedure `print` should work for strings of any length. This version of `print` should not use interrupts; just test the ready bit of the transmitter control register continuously until the device is ready.

```
char getchar();
```

The procedure `getchar` takes no arguments and returns a character result. If `getchar` waits until a character has been typed on the terminal, then it should return the character's value in $v0 (the result register). Do not use interrupts; simply test the ready bit continuously until a character has arrived.

Write a main program that uses these two procedures to read a line from the terminal, which will be terminated by a carriage return. Then print the entire line to the terminal, including a carriage return and line feed. All your code should obey the conventions in Appendix A for procedure calling, stack usage, and register usage.

8.25 [3 days–1 week] <§8.5, Appendix A> Your assignment is to build an interrupt-driven mechanism for buffered I/O to and from the terminal. (This exercise handles output only; Exercise 8.26 handles input.)

For the output-only portion, there are three parts to the program:

1. A main program, which repeatedly calls procedure `print` to print the string "`I know what I am doing.`"

2. The procedure `print`, which stores the output characters in a buffer shared by it and the interrupt routine.

3. The interrupt routine, which copies characters from the output buffer to the transmitter.

You need to write all three routines. The routine `print` and the interrupt routine should communicate by using a shared circular buffer with space for 32 characters. The `print` procedure should take a string as argument and add the characters of the string to the output buffer one at a time, advancing as soon as there is space in the buffer. Keep in mind that `print` should not manipulate the terminal device registers directly, except to make sure that transmitter interrupts are enabled. Furthermore, `print` should contain additional code to deal with a full output buffer. The main program generates characters much faster than they can be output, so the buffer will quickly fill up. In a real system, if the output buffer fills up, the operating system will stop running the current user's process and switch to a different process. Your program doesn't need to support multiple users, so `print` can take a simpler approach: it just checks the buffer over and over again until eventually it isn't full anymore. The buffer is full when the next position in which `print` wants to insert a character has not been emptied by the interrupt routine.

After writing print, write the interrupt routine called by `print`. Here is a list of things the interrupt routine must do:

1. If the transmitter is not ready, then the interrupt routine should not do anything. (You shouldn't have received an interrupt in the first place if the transmitter isn't ready, but it's a good idea to check anyway.)

2. If the output buffer isn't empty, copy the next character from the output buffer to the Transmitter data register and adjust the buffer pointers.

3. If the output buffer is empty, turn off the interrupt-enable bit in the Transmitter control register. Otherwise, continuous interrupts will occur. Each time it deposits a character in the buffer, `print` will need to turn this bit on.

4. Don't forget that you must save and restore any registers that you use in the interrupt routine, even temporary registers such as register $t0 and register $t1. This is necessary because interrupts can occur at any time

and those registers may be in use at the time of the interrupt. You must save the registers on the stack. The only exceptions to this rule are registers $k0 and $k1, which are reserved for use by interrupt routines; these registers need not be saved and restored. One of these registers can be used to return from the interrupt routine back to the code that was interrupted.

Test your code by writing the main routine that calls `print` to print the string. It should output lines continuously, with each line containing the characters "I know what I am doing."

8.26 [3 days–1 week] <§8.5, Appendix A> {Ex. 8.25} Extend the code you've already written to be able to handle interrupt-driven input. This program should do input in the same way as the previous program did output: by using a buffer to communicate between the routine `getchar` and the interrupt routine. Be aware that `getchar` returns a character from the buffer, waiting in a loop if no characters are present. Similarly, the interrupt routine will add characters as they are typed, discarding characters if the buffer is full when they arrive. For this, an eight-entry buffer should work well.

Use these two routines to read characters from the terminal and to output them to the terminal. Try typing characters rapidly to make sure your program can handle the output or the input buffer filling up. For example, if you type two or three characters rapidly, the output buffer may fill up. However, no output should be lost: the print procedure will simply have to spin for a bit, during which time additional input characters will be buffered in the input buffer. If you type eight or ten characters very rapidly, then the input buffer will probably fill up. When this happens, your interrupt routine will have to discard characters: the program should continue to function, but there won't be any output of the discarded input characters you typed. Once the output catches up with the input, your program should accept input again just as if the input buffer had never filled up.

8.27 [1 day–1 week] <§§8.2–8.4> Take your favorite computer and write programs that achieve the following:

1. Maximum bandwidth from and to a single disk

2. Maximum bandwidth from and to multiple disks

3. The maximum number of 512-byte transactions from and to a single disk

4. The maximum number of 512-byte transactions from and to multiple disks

What is the percentage of the bandwidth that you achieve compared to what the I/O device manufacturer claims? Also, record processor utilization in each case for the programs that are running separately. Next, run all four together and see what percentage of the maximum rates you can achieve. From this, can you determine where the system bottlenecks lie?

In More Depth

Ethernet

An Ethernet is essentially a standard bus with multiple masters (each computer can be a master) and a distributed arbitration scheme using collision detection. Most Ethernets are implemented using coaxial cable as the medium. When a particular node wants to use the bus, it first checks to see whether some other node is using the bus; if not, it places a carrier signal on the bus, and then proceeds to transmit. A complication can arise because the control is distributed and the devices may be physically far apart. As a result, two nodes can both check the Ethernet, find it idle, and begin transmitting at once; this is called a *collision*. A node detects collisions by listening to the network when transmitting to see whether a collision has occurred. A collision is detected when the node finds that what it hears on the Ethernet differs from what it transmitted. When collisions occur, both nodes stop transmitting and delay a random time interval before trying to resume using the network—just as two polite people do when they both start talking at the same time. Consequently, the number of nodes on the network is limited—if too many collisions occur, the performance will be poor. In addition, constraints imposed by the requirement that collisions be detected by all nodes limit the length of the Ethernet and the number of connections to the network. Although this idea sounds like it might not work, it actually works amazingly well and has been central to the enormous growth in the use of local area networks.

8.28 [3 days–1 week] <§§8.3–8.4> Write a program that simulates an Ethernet. Assume the following network system characteristics:

- A transmission bandwidth of 10 Mbits/sec.

- A latency for a signal to travel the entire length of the network and return to its origin of 15 μs. This is also the time required to detect a collision.

Make the following assumptions about the 100 hosts on the network:

- The packet size is 1000 bytes.

- Each host tries to send a packet after T seconds of computation, where T is exponentially distributed with mean M. Note that the host begins its T seconds of computation only after successfully transmitting a packet.

- If a collision is detected, the host waits a random amount of time chosen from an exponential distribution with a mean of 60 μs.

Simulate and plot the sustained bandwidth of the network compared to the mean time between transmission attempts (*M*). Also, plot the average wait time between trying to initiate a transmission and succeeding in initiating it (compared to *M*).

Ethernets actually use an exponential back-off algorithm that increases the mean of the back-off time after successive collisions. Assume that the mean of the distribution from which the host chooses how much to delay is doubled on successive collisions. How well does this work? Is the bandwidth higher than when a single distribution is used? Can the initial mean be lower?

In More Depth

Disk Arrays

As mentioned in section 8.9, one method of organizing disk systems is to use arrays of smaller disks that provide more bandwidth through parallel access. In most disk arrays, all the spindles are synchronized—sector 0 in every disk rotates under the head at the exact same time—and the arms on all the disks are always over the same track. Furthermore, the data are "striped" across the disks in the array, so that consecutive sectors can be read in parallel. Let's explore how such a system might work.

8.29 [20] <§§8.3–8.5> Assume that we have the following two magnetic disk configurations: a single disk and an array of four disks. Each disk has 64 sectors per track, each sector holds 1000 bytes, and the disk revolves at 7200 RPM. Assume that the seek time is 6 ms. The delay of the disk controller is 1 ms per transaction, either for a single disk or for the array. Assume that the performance of the I/O system is limited only by the disks and the controller. Remember that the consecutive sectors on the single disk system will be spread one sector per disk in the array. Compare the performance in I/Os per second of these two disk organizations, assuming that the requests are random reads, half of which are 4 KB and half of which are 16 KB of data from sequential sectors. The sectors may be read in any order; for simplicity, assume that the rotational latency is one-half the revolution time for the single disk read of 16 sectors and the disk array read of 4 sectors. Challenge: Can you work out the actual average rotational latency in these two cases?

8.30 [10] <§§8.3–8.5> {Ex. 8.29} Using the same disk systems as in Exercise 8.29, with the same access patterns, determine the performance in megabytes per second for each system.

9

Multiprocessors

There are finer fish in the sea than have ever been caught.

Irish proverb

9.1 **Introduction** 712

9.2 **Programming Multiprocessors** 714

9.3 **Multiprocessors Connected by a Single Bus** 717

9.4 **Multiprocessors Connected by a Network** 727

9.5 **Clusters** 734

9.6 **Network Topologies** 736

9.7 **Real Stuff: Future Directions for Multiprocessors** 740

9.8 **Fallacies and Pitfalls** 743

9.9 **Concluding Remarks—Evolution versus Revolution in Computer Architecture** 746

9.10 **Historical Perspective and Further Reading** 748

9.11 **Key Terms** 756

9.12 **Exercises** 756

The Five Classic Components of a Computer

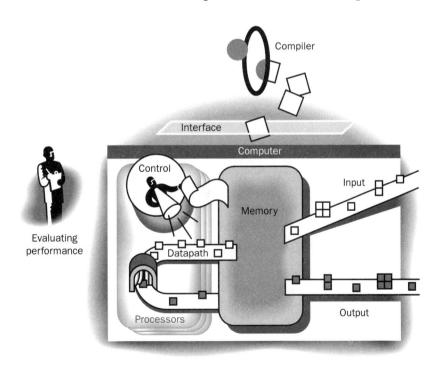

9.1   Introduction

"Over the Mountains
Of the Moon,
Down the Valley of the Shadow,
Ride, boldly ride"
The shade replied,—
"If you seek for Eldorado!"

Edgar Allan Poe, "Eldorado," stanza 4, 1849

Computer architects have always sought the El Dorado of computer design: to create powerful computers simply by connecting many existing smaller ones. This golden vision is the fountainhead of multiprocessors. The customer orders as many processors as the budget allows and receives a commensurate amount of performance. Thus multiprocessors must be scalable: the hardware and software are designed to be sold with a variable number of processors, with some machines varying by a factor of more than 50. Since software is scalable, some multiprocessors can support operation in the presence of broken hardware; that is, if a single processor fails in a multiprocessor with n processors, the system provides continued service with $n - 1$ processors. Finally, multiprocessors may have the highest absolute performance—faster than the fastest uniprocessor.

The good news is that the multiprocessor has established a beachhead. Keeping in mind that the microprocessor is now the most cost-effective processor, it is generally agreed that if you can't handle a timeshared workload on a single-chip processor, then a multiprocessor composed of many single-chip uniprocessors is more effective than building a high-performance uniprocessor from a more exotic technology. Moreover, virtually all current file servers can be ordered with multiple processors, and the database industry has standardized on multiprocessors. Consequently, multiprocessors now embody a significant market.

Commercial multiprocessors usually define high performance as high throughput for independent tasks. This definition is in contrast to running a single task on multiple processors. We use the term *parallel processing program* to refer to a single program that runs on multiple processors simultaneously.

Here are key questions that drive the designs of multiprocessors:

- How do parallel processors share data?
- How do parallel processors coordinate?
- How many processors?

The answers to the first question fall in two main camps. Processors with a *single address space*, sometimes called *shared-memory processors*, offer the programmer a single memory address space that all processors share. Processors communicate through shared variables in memory, with all processors capable of accessing any memory location via loads and stores.

As processors operating in parallel will normally share data, they also need to coordinate when operating on shared data; otherwise, one processor could start working on data before another is finished with it. This coordination is called *synchronization*. When sharing is supported with a single address space, there must be a separate mechanism for synchronization. One approach uses a *lock*: only one processor at a time can acquire the lock, and other processors interested in shared data must wait until the original processor unlocks the variable. Locking is described in section 9.3.

Single address space multiprocessors come in two styles. The first takes the same time to access main memory no matter which processor requests it and no matter which word is asked. Such machines are called *uniform memory access* (*UMA*) multiprocessors or *symmetric multiprocessors* (*SMP*). In the second style, some memory accesses are faster than others depending on which processor asks for which word. Such machines are called *nonuniform memory access* (*NUMA*) multiprocessors. As you might expect, there are more programming challenges to get highest performance from a NUMA multiprocessor than a UMA multiprocessor, but NUMA machines can scale to larger sizes and hence are potentially higher performance.

The alternative model to shared memory for communicating uses *message passing* for communicating among processors. Message passing is required for machines with *private memories*, in contrast to shared memory. As an extreme example, processors in different desktop computers communicate by passing messages over a local area network. Provided the system has routines to *send* and *receive* messages, coordination is built in with message passing since one processor knows when a message is sent and the receiving processor knows when a message arrives. The receiving processor can then send a message back to the sender saying the message has arrived, if the sender needs that confirmation.

One recent phenomenon has been to try to take the extreme example above—computers connected over a local area network—and make it act as a single large multiprocessor. Such *clusters* of computers leverage the switch-based local area networks to provide high bandwidth between computers in the cluster.

In addition to two main communication styles, multiprocessors are constructed in two basic organizations: processors connected by a single bus, and processors connected by a network. The number of processors in the multiprocessor has a lot to do with this choice. We will examine these two styles in detail in sections 9.3 and 9.4.

> **The Big Picture**
>
> Figure 9.1 shows the relationship between the number of processors in a multiprocessor and choice of shared address versus message-passing communication and the choice of bus versus network physical connection. Shared address is further divided between uniform and nonuniform memory access. Although there are many choices for some numbers of processors, for other regions there is widespread agreement.

Category	Choice		Number of processors
Communication model	Message passing		8–256
	Shared address	NUMA	8–256
		UMA	2–64
Physical connection	Network		8–256
	Bus		2–32

FIGURE 9.1 Options in communication style and physical connection for multiprocessors as the number of processors varies. Note that the shared address space is divided into uniform memory access (UMA) and nonuniform memory access (NUMA) machines.

One challenge in writing this book is keeping examples up-to-date when the industry is rapidly changing. We decided that in this chapter we could keep electronic pointers to the real examples available via the World Wide Web. See the section for Chapter 9 at *www.mkp.com/cod2e.htm* to find the latest information on machines that demonstrate these ideas.

Let's start by looking at the general issues in programming multiprocessors.

9.2   Programming Multiprocessors

> *A major concern which is frequently voiced in connection with very fast computing machines . . . is that they will . . . run out of work. . . . It must be considered that . . . [past] problem size was dictated by the speed of the computing machines then available. . . . For faster machines, the same automatic mechanism will exert pressure towards problems of larger size.*
>
> John von Neumann, address presented at IBM seminar
> on scientific computation, November 1949

The bad news is that it remains to be seen how many important applications will run faster on multiprocessors via parallel processing. The obstacle is not the price of the uniprocessor used to compose multiprocessors, the flaws in topologies of interconnection networks, nor the unavailability of appropriate programming languages; the difficulty has been that too few important application programs have been rewritten to complete tasks sooner on multiprocessors. Because it is even harder to find applications that can take advantage of many processors, the challenge is greater for large-scale multiprocessors.

As a result of the programming difficulty, most parallel processing success stories are a result of software wizards developing a parallel subsystem that presents a sequential interface. Examples include databases, file servers, computer-aided design packages, and multiprocessing operating systems.

But why is this so? Why should parallel processing programs be so much harder to develop than sequential programs?

The first reason is that you *must* get good performance and efficiency from the parallel program on a multiprocessor; otherwise you would use a uniprocessor, as programming is easier. In fact, uniprocessor design techniques such as superscalar and out-of-order execution take advantage of instruction-level parallelism, normally without involvement of the programmer. Such innovation reduces the demand for rewriting programs for multiprocessors.

Why is it difficult to write multiprocessor programs that are fast, especially as the number of processors increases? As an analogy, think of the communication overhead for a task done by one person compared to the overhead for a task done by a committee, especially as the size of the committee increases. Although n people may have the potential to finish any task n times faster, the communication overhead for the group may prevent it; n-fold speedup becomes especially unlikely as n increases. (Imagine the change in communication overhead if a committee grows from 10 people to 1000 people to 1,000,000.)

Another reason why it is difficult to write parallel processing programs is that the programmer must know a good deal about the hardware. On a uniprocessor, the high-level language programmer writes the program largely ignoring the underlying machine organization—that's the job of the compiler. But, so far at least, the parallel processing programmer had better know the underlying organization to write programs that are fast and capable of running with a variable number of processors. Moreover, such tailored parallel programs are not portable to other multiprocessors.

Although this second obstacle is beginning to lessen, our discussion in Chapter 2 reveals a third obstacle: Amdahl's law. It reminds us that even small parts of a program must be parallelized to reach their full potential; thus coming close to linear speedup involves discovering new algorithms that are inherently parallel.

Speedup Challenge

Example

Suppose you want to achieve linear speedup with 100 processors. What fraction of the original computation can be sequential?

Answer   Amdahl's law (page 75) says,

Execution time after improvement =

$$\frac{\text{Execution time affected by improvement}}{\text{Amount of improvement}} + \text{Execution time unaffected}$$

Substituting for the goal of linear speedup with 100 processors means the execution time is reduced by 100:

$$\frac{\text{Execution time after improvement}}{100} =$$

$$\frac{\text{Execution time affected by improvement}}{100} + \text{Execution time unaffected}$$

Solving for the unaffected execution time,

$$\text{Execution time unaffected} = \frac{\text{Execution time after improvement}}{100}$$

$$- \frac{\text{Execution time affected by improvement}}{100} = 0$$

Accordingly, to achieve linear speedup with 100 processors, *none* of the original computation can be sequential. Put another way, to get a speedup of 99 from 100 processors means the percentage of the original program that was sequential would have to be 0.01% or less.

Yet there are applications with substantial parallelism.

Speedup Challenge, Bigger Problem

Example   Suppose you want to perform two sums: one is a sum of two scalar variables and one is a matrix sum of a pair of two-dimensional arrays, size 1000 by 1000. What speedup do you get with 1000 processors?

Answer   If we assume performance is a function of the time for an addition, t, then there is 1 addition that does not benefit from parallel processors and 1,000,000 additions that do. If the time before is $1,000,001t$,

Execution time before improvement =

$$\frac{\text{Execution time affected by improvement}}{\text{Amount of improvement}} + \text{Execution time unaffected}$$

$$\text{Execution time before improvement} = \frac{1{,}000{,}000t}{1000} + 1t$$

$$= 1001$$

Speedup is then

$$\text{Speedup} = \frac{1{,}000{,}001}{1001} = 999$$

Even if the sequential portion expanded to 100 sums of scalar variables versus one sum of a pair of 1000 by 1000 arrays, the speedup would still be 909.

9.3 Multiprocessors Connected by a Single Bus

The high performance and low cost of the microprocessor inspired renewed interest in multiprocessors in the 1980s. Several microprocessors can usefully be placed on a common bus for several reasons:

- Each microprocessor is much smaller than a multichip processor, so more processors can be placed on a bus.

- Caches can lower bus traffic.

- Mechanisms were invented to keep caches and memory consistent for multiprocessors, just as caches and memory are kept consistent for I/O, thereby simplifying programming.

Figure 9.2 is a drawing of a generic single-bus multiprocessor, and Figure 9.3 lists the characteristics of some commercial single-bus computers.

Traffic per processor and the bus bandwidth determine the useful number of processors in such a multiprocessor. The caches replicate data in their faster memories both to reduce the latency to the data *and* to reduce the memory traffic on the bus.

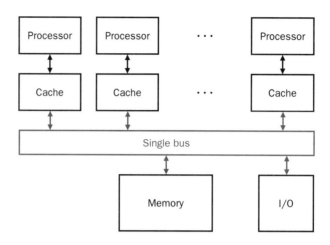

FIGURE 9.2 A single-bus multiprocessor. Typical size is between 2 and 32 processors.

Name	Maximum number of processors	Processor name	Processor clock rate	Maximum memory size/ system	Communi- cations BW/ system
Compaq ProLiant 5000	4	Pentium Pro	200 MHz	2,048 MB	540 MB/sec
Digital AlphaServer 8400	12	Alpha 21164	440 MHz	28,672 MB	2150 MB/sec
HP 9000 K460	4	PA-8000	180 MHz	4,096 MB	960 MB/sec
IBM RS/6000 R40	8	PowerPC 604	112 MHz	2,048 MB	1800 MB/sec
SGI Power Challenge	36	MIPS R10000	195 MHz	16,384 MB	1200 MB/sec
Sun Enterprise 6000	30	UltraSPARC 1	167 MHz	30,720 MB	2600 MB/sec

FIGURE 9.3   Characteristics of multiprocessor computers connected by a single backplane bus that are for sale in 1997. The communication style for these machines is shared memory with uniform memory access times. These machines are generally designed to be used with multiple generations of microprocessors both to allow customers to upgrade their existing machines and to allow companies to amortize their research and development investment. For example, the SGI Power Challenge was first delivered in 1993 with the MIPS R4400 and then again in 1995 with the R8000. Note that the bus and memory system did not change over this time. (See *www.mkp.com/cod2e.htm* for pointers to these and more recent bus-connected multiprocessors.)

Parallel Program (Single Bus)

Example

Suppose we want to sum 100,000 numbers on a single-bus multiprocessor computer. Let's assume we have 10 processors.

Answer

The first step again would be to split the set of numbers into subsets of the same size. We do not allocate the subsets to a different memory, since there is a single memory for this machine; we just give different starting addresses to each processor. Pn is the number of the processor, between 0 and 9. All processors start the program by running a loop that sums their subset of numbers:

```
sum[Pn] = 0;
for (i = 10000*Pn; i < 10000*(Pn+1); i = i + 1)
    sum[Pn] = sum[Pn] + A[i]; /* sum the assigned areas*/
```

This loop uses load instructions to bring the correct subset of numbers to the caches of each processor from the common main memory.

The next step is to add these many partial sums, so we divide to conquer. Half of the processors add pairs of partial sums, then a quarter add pairs of the new partial sums, and so on until we have the single, final sum. We want each processor to have its own version of the loop counter variable i, so we must indicate that it is a "private" variable.

In this example, the two processors must synchronize before the "consumer" processor tries to read the result from the memory location written by the "producer" processor; otherwise, the consumer may read the old value of the data. Here is the code (half is private also):

```
half = 10; /* 10 processors in 1-bus multiprocessor*/
repeat
        synch(); /* wait for partial sum completion*/
        if (half%2 != 0 && Pn == 0)
            sum[0] = sum[0] + sum[half-1];
        half = half/2; /* dividing line on who sums */
        if (Pn < half) sum[Pn] = sum[Pn] + sum[Pn+half];
until (half == 1); /* exit with final sum in Sum[0] */
```

We have used what is called a *barrier synchronization* primitive; processors wait at the barrier until every processor has reached it. Then they proceed. Barrier synchronization allows all processors to rapidly synchronize. This function can be implemented either in software with the lock synchronization primitive, described in section 9.3, or with special hardware that combines each processor "ready" signal into a single global signal that all processors can test.

Recall from Chapter 8 that I/O can experience inconsistencies in the value of data between the version in memory and the version in the cache. This *cache coherency* problem applies to multiprocessors as well as I/O. Unlike I/O, which rarely uses multiple data copies (a situation to be avoided whenever possible), as the second half of the example suggests, multiple processors routinely require copies of the same data in multiple caches. Alternatively, accesses to shared data could be forced always to go around the cache to memory, but that would be too slow and it would require too much bus bandwidth; performance of a multiprocessor program depends on the performance of the system when sharing data.

The protocols to maintain coherency for multiple processors are called *cache coherency protocols*. The next few subsections explain cache coherency protocols and methods of synchronizing processors using cache coherency.

Multiprocessor Cache Coherency

The most popular protocol to maintain cache coherency is called *snooping*. Figure 9.4 shows how caches access memory over a common bus. All cache controllers monitor, or *snoop,* on the bus to determine whether or not they have a copy of the shared block.

Snooping became popular with machines of the 1980s, which used single buses to their main memories. These uniprocessors were extended by adding multiple processors on that bus to give easy access to the shared memory. Caches were then added to improve the performance of each processor, leading to schemes to keep the caches up-to-date by snooping on the information over that shared bus.

Maintaining coherency has two components: reads and writes. Multiple copies are not a problem when reading, but a processor must have exclusive access to write a word. Processors must also have the most recent copy when reading an object, so all processors must get new values after a write. Thus,

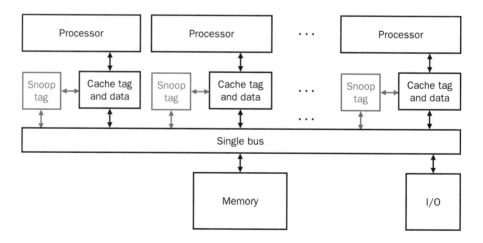

FIGURE 9.4 A single-bus multiprocessor using snooping cache coherency. The extra set of tags, shown in color, are used to handle snoop requests. The tags are duplicated to reduce the demands of snooping on the caches.

snooping protocols must locate all the caches that share an object to be written. The consequence of a write to shared data is either to invalidate all other copies or to update the shared copies with the value being written.

The status bits already in a cache block are expanded for snooping protocols, and that information is used in monitoring bus activities. On a read miss, all caches check to see if they have a copy of the requested block and then take the appropriate action, such as supplying the data to the cache that missed. Similarly, on a write, all caches check to see if they have a copy and then act, either invalidating or updating their copy to the new value.

Since every bus transaction checks cache address tags, you might assume that it interferes with the processor. It would interfere if not for duplicating the address tag portion of the cache (not the whole cache) to get an extra read port for snooping (see Figure 9.4). This way, snooping rarely interferes with the processor's access to the cache. When there is interference, the processor will likely stall because the cache is unavailable.

Snooping protocols are of two types, depending on what happens on a write:

- *Write-invalidate*: The writing processor causes all copies in other caches to be invalidated before changing its local copy; it is then free to update the *local* data until another processor asks for it. The writing processor issues an invalidation signal over the bus, and all caches check to see if they have a copy; if so, they must invalidate the block containing the word. Thus, this scheme allows multiple readers but only a single writer.

- *Write-update*: Rather than invalidate every block that is shared, the writing processor broadcasts the new data over the bus; all copies are then updated with the new value. This scheme, also called *write-broadcast*, continuously broadcasts writes to shared data, while write-invalidate deletes all other copies so that there is only one local copy for subsequent writes.

Write-update is like write-through because all writes go over the bus to update copies of the shared data. Write-invalidate uses the bus only on the *first* write to invalidate the other copies, and hence subsequent writes do not result in bus activity. Consequently, write-invalidate has similar benefits to write-back in terms of reducing demands on bus bandwidth, while write-update has the advantage of making the new values appear in caches sooner, which can reduce latency.

Commercial cache-based multiprocessors use write-back caches because write-back reduces bus traffic and thereby allows more processors on a single bus. To preserve that precious communications bandwidth, all commercial machines also use write-invalidate as the standard protocol.

Measurements to date indicate that shared data has lower spatial and temporal locality than other types of data. Thus shared data misses often dominate cache behavior, even though they may be just 10% to 40% of the data accesses.

> **Hardware Software Interface**
>
> One insight is that block size plays an important role in cache coherency. For example, take the case of snooping on a cache with a block size of eight words, with a single word alternatively written and read by two processors. The protocol that only broadcasts or sends one word has an advantage over a scheme that transfers the full block.
>
> Large blocks can also cause what is called *false sharing*: When two unrelated shared variables are located in the same cache block, the full block is exchanged between processors even though the processors are accessing different variables (see Exercises 9.5 and 9.6). Compiler research is under way to reduce false sharing by allocating highly correlated data to the same cache block and thereby reduce cache miss rates.

Elaboration: In a multiprocessor using cache coherency over a single bus, what happens if two processors try to write to the same shared data word in the same clock cycle? The bus arbiter decides which processor gets the bus first, and this processor will invalidate or update the other processor's copy, depending on the protocol. The second processor then does its write. Bus arbitration forces sequential behavior from writes on different processors, and this explains how writes from different processors to different words in the same block will work correctly.

The policy of when a processor sees a write from another processor is called the *memory consistency model*. The most conservative is called *sequential consistency*: the result of any execution is the same as if the accesses of each processor were kept in order and the accesses among different processors were interleaved. Some machines use more liberal models to achieve higher memory performance.

An Example of a Cache Coherency Protocol

To illustrate the intricacies of a cache coherency protocol, Figure 9.5 shows a finite state transition diagram for a write-invalidation protocol based on a write-back policy. Each cache block is in one of three states:

1. *Read Only*: This cache block is clean (not written) and may be shared.

2. *Read/Write*: This cache block is dirty (written) and may *not* be shared.

3. *Invalid*: This cache block does not have valid data.

The three states of the protocol are duplicated in the figure to show transitions based on processor actions as opposed to transitions based on bus operations. This duplication is done only for purposes of illustration; there is really only one finite state machine per cache, with stimuli coming either from the attached processor or from the bus.

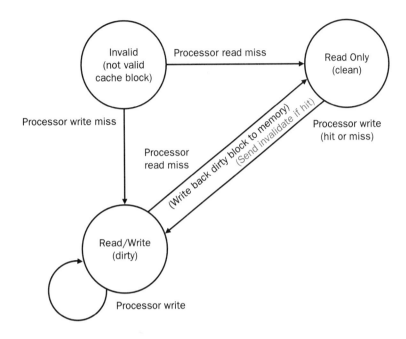

a. Cache state transitions using signals from the processor

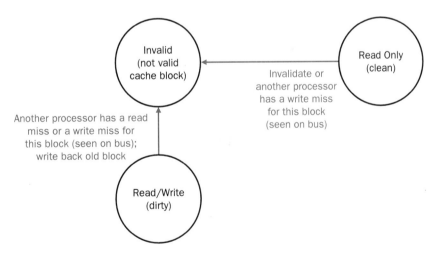

b. Cache state transitions using signals from the bus

FIGURE 9.5 A write-invalidate cache coherency protocol. The upper part of the diagram shows state transitions based on actions of the processor associated with this cache; the lower part shows transitions based on actions of other processors as seen as operations on the bus. There is really only one state machine in a cache, although there are two represented here to clarify when a transition occurs. The black arrows and actions specified in black text would be found in caches without coherency; the colored arrows and actions are added to achieve cache coherency. In contrast to what is shown here, some protocols consider writes to clean data a write miss, so that there is no separate signal for invalidation.

Transitions in the state of a cache block happen on read misses, write misses, or write hits; read hits do not change cache state. Let's start with a read miss. When the processor has a read miss that maps onto a block, it will change the state of that block to Read Only, and then acquire the bus and write back the old block if the block was in the Read/Write state (dirty). All the caches in the other processors monitor the read miss to see if this block is in their cache. If one has a copy and it is in the Read/Write state, then the block is changed to the Invalid state. (Some protocols would change the state to Read Only.) The read miss is then satisfied by reading from memory.

Now let's try writes. To write a block, the processor acquires the bus, sends an invalidate signal, writes into that block, and places it in the Read/Write state. Because other caches monitor the bus, all caches check to see if they have a copy of that block; if they do, they invalidate it.

As you might imagine, there are many variations on cache coherency that are much more complicated than this simple model. The one found on both the Pentium Pro and PowerPC is called *MESI*, a write-invalidate protocol whose name is an acronym for the four states of the protocol: Modified, Exclusive, Shared, Invalid. The Modified state is the same as the Read/Write state in Figure 9.5, and Invalid is the same state too. The Read Only state of Figure 9.5 is divided, depending on whether there are multiple copies (Shared state) or there is just one (Exclusive state). In either case, memory has an up-to-date version of the data. This extra state means that a write to data that is in the Exclusive state does not require an invalidation since there is only one copy of the block. A write to data in the Read Only of Figure 9.5 would require an invalidation, since there may be multiple copies.

Other variations on coherency protocols include whether or not the other caches try to supply the block if they have a copy, whether or not the block must be invalidated on a read miss, as well as whether writes invalidate or update the shared data.

Synchronization Using Coherency

One of the major requirements of a single-bus multiprocessor is to be able to coordinate processes that are working on a common task. Typically, a programmer will use *lock variables* (also known as *semaphores*) to coordinate or synchronize the processes. The challenge for the architect of a multiprocessor is to provide a mechanism to decide which processor gets the lock and to provide the operation that locks a variable. Arbitration is easy for single-bus multiprocessors, since the bus is the only path to memory: the processor that gets the bus locks out all other processors from memory. If the processor and bus provide an *atomic swap operation*, programmers can create locks with the proper semantics. Here the adjective *atomic* means indivisible, so an atomic swap means the processor can both read a location *and* set it to the locked value in the same bus operation, preventing any other processor or I/O device from reading or writing memory until the swap completes.

Figure 9.6 shows a typical procedure for locking a variable using an atomic swap instruction. Assume that 0 means unlocked ("go") and 1 means locked ("stop"). A processor first reads the lock variable to test its state. A processor keeps reading and testing until the value indicates that the lock is unlocked.

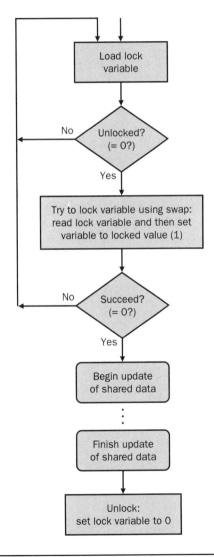

FIGURE 9.6   Steps to acquire a lock or semaphore to synchronize processes and then to release the lock on exit from the key section of code.

The processor then races against all other processors that were similarly *spin waiting* to see who can lock the variable first. All processors use an atomic swap instruction that reads the old value and stores a 1 ("stop") into the lock variable. The single winner will see the 0 ("go"), and the losers will see a 1 that was placed there by the winner. (The losers will continue to write the variable with the locked value of 1, but that doesn't change its value.) The winning processor then executes the code that updates the shared data. When the winner exits, it stores a 0 ("go") into the lock variable, thereby starting the race all over again.

Let's examine how the spin lock scheme of Figure 9.6 works with bus-based cache coherency. One advantage of this algorithm is that it allows processors to spin wait on a local copy of the lock in their caches. This reduces the amount of bus traffic; Figure 9.7 shows the bus and cache operations for multiple processors trying to lock a variable. Once the processor with the lock stores a 0 into the lock, all other caches see that store and invalidate their copy of the lock variable. Then they try to get the new value for the lock of 0. (With write-update cache coherency, the caches would update their copy rather than first invalidate and then load from memory.) This new value starts the race to see who can set the lock first. The winner gets the bus and stores a 1 into the lock; the other caches replace their copy of the lock variable containing 0 with a 1. They read that the variable is already locked and must return to testing and spinning.

This scheme has difficulty scaling up to many processors because of the communication traffic generated when the lock is released.

Step	Processor P0	Processor P1	Processor P2	Bus activity
1	Has lock	Spins, testing if lock = 0	Spins, testing if lock = 0	None
2	Sets lock to 0 and 0 sent over bus	Spins, testing if lock = 0	Spins, testing if lock = 0	Write-invalidate of lock variable from P0
3		Cache miss	Cache miss	Bus decides to service P2 cache miss
4		(Waits while bus busy)	Lock = 0	Cache miss for P2 satisfied
5		Lock = 0	Swap: reads lock and sets to 1	Cache miss for P1 satisfied
6		Swap: reads lock and sets to 1	Value from swap = 0 and 1 sent over bus	Write-invalidate of lock variable from P2
7		Value from swap = 1 and 1 sent over bus	Owns the lock, so can update shared data	Write-invalidate of lock variable from P1
8		Spins, testing if lock = 0		None

FIGURE 9.7 Cache coherency steps and bus traffic for three processors, P0, P1, and P2. This figure assumes write-invalidate coherency. P0 starts with the lock (step 1). P0 exits and unlocks the lock (step 2). P1 and P2 race to see which reads the unlocked value during the swap (steps 3–5). P2 wins and enters the *critical section* (steps 6 and 7), while P1 spins and waits (steps 7 and 8). A critical section is the name for the code between the lock and the unlock.

9.4 Multiprocessors Connected by a Network

Single-bus designs are attractive, but limited because the three desirable bus characteristics are incompatible: high bandwidth, low latency, and long length. There is also a limit to the bandwidth of a single memory module attached to a bus. Thus, a single bus imposes practical constraints on the number of processors that can be connected to it. To date, the largest number of processors connected to a single bus in a commercial computer is 36, and this number seems to be dropping over time.

If the goal is to connect many more processors together, then the computer designer needs to use more than a single bus. Figure 9.8 shows how this can be organized. Note that in Figure 9.2 on page 718, the connection medium—the bus—is between the processors and memory, whereas in Figure 9.8, memory is attached to each processor, and the connection medium—the network—is between these combined nodes. For single-bus systems, the medium is used on every memory access, while in the latter case it is used only for interprocessor communication. Figure 9.9 lists several machines connected via networks.

This brings us to an old debate about the organization of memory in large-scale parallel processors. The debate unfortunately often centers on a false dichotomy: *shared memory* versus *distributed memory*. Shared memory really means a single address space, implying implicit communication with loads

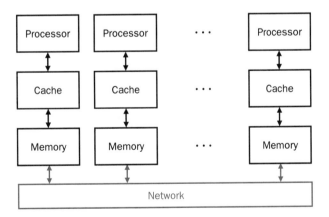

FIGURE 9.8 The organization of a network-connected multiprocessor. Note that, in contrast to Figure 9.2, the multiprocessor connection is no longer between memory and the processor. Multiprocessors have also been built with the network above the memory; the Cray XMP and YMP multiprocessors are perhaps the best-known examples, and the Sun Enterprise 10000 is the most recent example (see Figure 9.9).

and stores. The real opposite of a single address is *multiple private memories*, implying explicit communication with sends and receives.

Distributed memory refers to the physical location of the memory. If physical memory is divided into modules, with some placed near each processor, as in Figure 9.8, then physical memory is distributed. The real opposite of distributed memory is *centralized memory*, where access time to a physical memory location is the same for all processors because every access goes over the interconnect, as in Figure 9.2. This style of machine is sometimes called *dance hall*, with the processors all on one side and the memories all on the other, invoking the image of a school dance with the boys on one side of the floor and the girls on the other. (The Tera Computer is one example; see *www.mkp.com/cod2e.htm* for a pointer to it.)

As we said in section 9.1, single address space versus multiple address spaces, and distributed memory versus centralized memory, are orthogonal issues: multiprocessors can have a single address space and a distributed physical memory. The proper debates concern the pros and cons of a single address space, of explicit communication, and of distributed physical memory.

In machines without a single global address, communication is explicit; the programmer or the compiler must send messages to ship data to another node and must receive messages to accept data from another node.

Name	Maximum number of processors	Processor name	Processor clock rate	Maximum memory size/ system	Communi- cations BW/link	Node	Topology
Cray Research T3E	2048	Alpha 21164	450 MHz	524,288 MB	1200 MB/sec	4-way SMP	3-D torus
HP/Convex Exemplar X-class	64	PA-8000	180 MHz	65,536 MB	980 MB/sec	2-way SMP	8-way crossbar + ring
Sequent NUMA-Q	32	Pentium Pro	200 MHz	131,072 MB	1024 MB/sec	4-way SMP	Ring
SGI Origin2000	128	MIPS R10000	195 MHz	131,072 MB	800 MB/sec	2-way SMP	6-cube
Sun Enterprise 10000	64	UltraSPARC 1	250 MHz	65,536 MB	1600 MB/sec	4-way SMP	16-way crossbar

FIGURE 9.9   Characteristics of multiprocessor computers connected by a network that are for sale in 1997. All these machines have a shared address space with nonuniform memory access time except for the Sun Enterprise 10000, which offers a shared address with uniform memory access time. And all these machines except the Cray Research T3E are cache coherent, with the HP, Sequent, and SGI using directories. The Sun machine uses buses for addresses and a switch for data, so it supports coherency with conventional snooping on the address buses. Communication bandwidth is peak per link, counting all bytes sent including network headers. The bisection bandwidth typically scales with the number of processors. (See *www.mkp.com/cod2e.htm* for pointers to these and more recent network-connected multiprocessors.)

Parallel Program (Message Passing)

Example

Let's try our summing example again for a network-connected multiprocessor with 100 processors using multiple private memories.

Answer

Since this computer has multiple address spaces, the first step is distributing the 100 subsets to each of the local memories. The processor containing the 100,000 numbers sends the subsets to each of the 100 processor-memory nodes.

The next step is to get the sum of each subset. This step is simply a loop that every execution unit follows; read a word from local memory and add it to a local variable:

```
sum = 0;
for (i = 0; i<1000; i = i + 1) /* loop over each array */
  sum = sum + A1[i]; /* sum the local arrays */ limit = 100;
```

The last step is adding these 100 partial sums. The hard part is that each partial sum is located in a different execution unit. Hence, we must use the interconnection network to send partial sums to accumulate the final sum. Rather than sending all the partial sums to a single processor, which would result in sequentially adding the partial sums, we again divide to conquer. First, half of the execution units send their partial sums to the other half of the execution units, where two partial sums are added together. Then one quarter of the execution units (half of the half) send this new partial sum to the other quarter of the execution units (the remaining half of the half) for the next round of sums. This halving, sending, and receiving continues until there is a single sum of all numbers. Let Pn represent the number of the execution unit, send(x,y) be a routine that sends over the interconnection network to execution unit number x the value y, and receive() be a function that accepts a value from the network for this execution unit:

```
half = 100;/* 100 processors */
repeat
  half = (half+1)/2; /* send vs. receive dividing line*/
  if (Pn >= half && Pn < limit) send(Pn - half, sum);
  if (Pn < (limit/2-1)) sum = sum + receive();
  limit = half; /* upper limit of senders */
until (half == 1); /* exit with final sum */
```

This code divides all processors into senders or receivers and each receiving processor gets only one message, so we can presume that a receiving processor will stall until it receives a message. Thus, send and receive can be used as primitives for synchronization as well as for communication, as the processors are aware of the transmission of data.

Addressing in Large-Scale Parallel Processors

Most commercial, large-scale processors use memory that is distributed; otherwise it is either very difficult or very expensive to build a machine that can scale up to scores of processors with scores of memory modules.

The next question facing distributed-memory machines is communication. For the hardware designer, the simplest solution is to offer only send and receive instead of the implicit communication that is possible as part of any load or store. Send and receive also have the advantage of making it easier for the programmer to optimize communication: It's simpler to overlap computation with communication by using explicit sends and receives rather than with implicit loads and stores.

On the other hand, loads and stores normally have much lower communication overhead than do sends and receives. And some applications will have references to remote information that is only occasionally and unpredictably accessed, so it is much more efficient to use an address to remote data when *demanded* rather than to retrieve it in case it *might* be used. Such a machine has *distributed shared memory* (*DSM*).

Hardware Software Interface

Adding a software layer to provide a single address space on top of sends and receives so that communication is possible as part of any load or store is harder, although it is comparable to the virtual memory system already found in most processors (see Chapter 7). In virtual memory, a uniprocessor uses page tables to decide if an address points to data in local memory or on a disk; this translation system might be modified to decide if the address points to local data, to data in another processor's memory, or to disk. Although *shared virtual memory*, as it is called, creates the illusion of shared memory—just as virtual memory creates the illusion of a very large memory—since it invokes the operating system, performance is usually so slow that shared-memory communication must be rare or else most of the time is spent transferring pages.

Caches are important to performance no matter how communication is performed, so we want to allow the shared data to appear in the cache of the processor that owns the data as well as in the processor that requests the data. Thus, the single global address in a network-connected multiprocessor resurrects the issue of cache coherency, since there are multiple copies of the same data with the same address in different processors. Clearly the bus-snooping protocols of section 9.3 won't work here, as there is no single bus on which all memory references are broadcast. Since the designers of the Cray T3E (see Figure 9.9) had no bus to support cache coherency, the T3E has a single address space but it is not cache coherent.

A cache-coherent alternative to bus snooping is *directories*. In directory-based protocols, there is logically a single directory that keeps the state of every block in main memory. Information in the directory can include which caches have copies of the block, whether it is dirty, and so on. Fortunately, directory entries can be distributed so that different requests can go to different memories, thereby reducing contention and allowing a scalable design. Directories retain the characteristic that the sharing status of a block is always in a single known location, making a large-scale parallel processor plausible.

Designers of snooping caches and directories face similar issues; the only difference is the mechanism that detects when there is a write to shared data. Instead of watching the bus to see if there are requests that require that the local cache be updated or invalidated, the directory controller sends explicit commands to each processor that has a copy of the data. Such messages can then be sent over the network. Figure 9.9 shows the characteristics of several directory-based, nonuniform access multiprocessors.

Hardware Software Interface

Note that with a single address space, the data could be placed arbitrarily in memories of different processors. This has two negative performance consequences. The first is that the miss penalty would be much longer because the request must go over the network. The second is that the network bandwidth would be consumed moving data to the proper processors. For programs that have low miss rates, this may not be significant. On the other hand, programs with high miss rates will have much lower performance when data is randomly assigned.

If the programmer or the compiler allocates data to the processor that is likely to use it, then this performance pitfall is removed. Unlike private memory organizations, this allocation only needs to be good, since missing data can still be fetched. Such leniency simplifies the allocation problem.

Another possible solution is to add a second level of coherence to the main memory for every processor. This directory would allow blocks of main memory to migrate, relieving the programmer or the compiler of memory allocation. As long as main memory blocks are not frequently shipped back and forth repeatedly, this scheme may achieve the performance of intelligent allocation of memory at the cost of considerably more hardware complexity. This scheme is called *cache-only memory*. This migration can occur at the page level by the operating system, or we can imagine doing it in hardware.

Figure 9.10 summarizes the coherency options for a single address space.

Since the number of pins per chip is limited, not all processors can be connected directly via a network. This restriction has inspired a whole zoo of topologies for consideration in the design of the network. In section 9.6, we'll look at the characteristics of some of the key alternatives of network designs. But first let's look at another way to connect computers by networks.

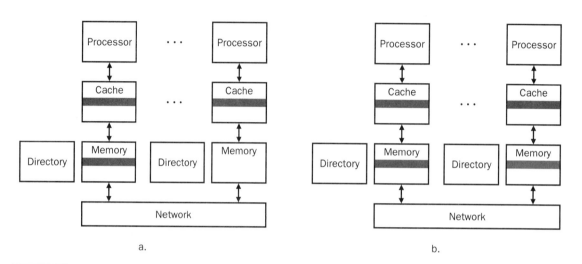

a.   b.

FIGURE 9.10   Options for a single address space in a large-scale parallel processor. The shaded rectangles represent the replicated data. *(a)* Coherence at *cache* level using directories in a network-connected multiprocessor. The original data is in memory, and the copies are replicated only in the caches. *(b)* Coherence at *memory* level using directories in a network-connected multiprocessor. The copies are replicated in remote memory (in color) *and* in the caches. The scheme in *b* is similar to the scheme used in the Kendall Square Research KSR-1. As long as memory is coherent, the data can be safely cached. If the data in a memory is invalidated, then corresponding blocks in the cache must be invalidated as well.

The Big Picture

Figure 9.11 compares cost performance of bus-connected UMA multiprocessors to network-connected NUMA multiprocessors. The network has a smaller initial cost, and then costs scale up somewhat more quickly than the bus-connected machine. Performance for both machines scales linearly until the bus reaches its limit, and then performance is flat no matter how many processors are used. When these two effects are combined, we see that the network-connected NUMA has consistent performance per unit cost, while the bus-connected machine has a "sweet spot" plateau. The plateau suggests that customers need to be more selective with bus-connected than with network-connected multiprocessors, and that bus designers need to be careful to pick a sweet spot that matches the needs of most customers.

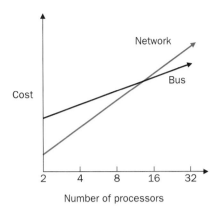

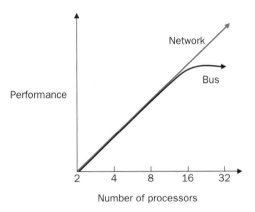

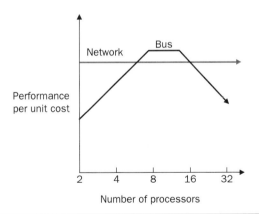

FIGURE 9.11 Cost, performance, and cost/performance of bus-connected and network-connected shared address multiprocessors. The combination of cost and performance suggests a "sweet spot" in 1997 for bus-connected multiprocessors of 8 to 16 processors, shown as a plateau in the cost/performance graph. Network-connected multiprocessors have better cost/performance to the left of the sweet spot because they are less expensive, and better cost/performance to the right of the sweet spot because they have higher performance. A bus designer effectively chooses the sweet spot by the width and the speed of the bus, which determines both the left edge of the plateau (cost) and right edge (scalability).   *(page 733)*

9.5   Clusters

Garry [Kasparov] will win, because the computer cannot improve that much in a single year.

Mike Valvo, expert chess commentator before the match
between Kasparov and Deep Blue, *Techwire*, May 6, 1997

There are many mainframe applications—such as databases, file servers, Web servers, simulations, and multiprogramming/batch processing—amenable to running on more loosely coupled machines than the cache-coherent NUMA machines of the prior section. These applications often need to be highly available, requiring some form of fault tolerance and repairability. Such applications—plus the similarity of the multiprocessor nodes to desktop computers and the emergence of high-bandwidth, switch-based local area networks—suggests that large-scale processing of the future may use *clusters* of off-the-shelf, whole computers. But the most historic example is the victory of the IBM SP2—a cluster of 32 nodes very similar to the RS/6000 workstation with hardware accelerators for chessboard evaluators—over chess champion Kasparov in 1997.

For example, in 1997 a cluster of 100 UltraSPARC desktop computers at UC Berkeley, connected by 160-MB/sec per link Myrinet switches, was used to set world records in database sort—sorting 8.6 GB of data originally on disk in one minute—and in cracking an encrypted message—taking just 3.5 hours to decipher a 40-bit DES key.

The Berkeley cluster above was constructed by the customers using off-the-shelf components, as is often the case. Figure 9.12 shows clusters sold by computer companies such as the IBM SP2. These company-designed clusters are normally sold to provide scalable, highly available systems—that is, systems whose goal is both to scale across a large number of processors, memory, and disks, *and* to be available 24 hours a day, 365 days a year.

One drawback of clusters has been that the cost of administering a cluster of N machines is about the same as the cost of administering N independent machines, while the cost of administering a shared address space multiprocessor with N processors is about the same as administering a single machine.

Another drawback is that clusters are usually connected using the I/O bus of the computer, whereas multiprocessors are usually connected on the memory bus of the computer. The memory bus has higher bandwidth, allowing multiprocessors to drive the network link at higher speed and to have fewer conflicts with I/O traffic on I/O-intensive applications.

Name	Maximum number of processors	Processor name	Processor clock rate	Maximum memory size/ system	Communi- cations BW/link	Node	Maximum number of nodes
HP 9000 EPS21	64	PA-8000	180 MHz	65,536 MB	532 MB/sec	4-way SMP	16
IBM RS/6000 HACMP R40	16	PowerPC 604	112 MHz	4,096 MB	12 MB/sec	8-way SMP	2
IBM RS/6000 SP2	512	Power2 SC	135 MHz	1,048,576 MB	150 MB/sec	16-way node	32
Sun Enterprise Cluster 6000 HA	60	UltraSPARC	167 MHz	61,440 MB	100 MB/sec	30-way SMP	2
Tandem NonSrop Himalaya S70000	4096	MIPS R10000	195 MHz	1,048,576 MB	40 MB/sec	16-way SMP	256

FIGURE 9.12   Characteristics of clusters commercially available in 1997. All but the IBM SP2 are marketed for high-availability applications. The SP2 is used for number-crunching scientific applications and for data mining. (See *www.mkp.com/cod2e.htm* for pointers to these and more recent clusters.)

A final weakness is the division of memory: a cluster of N machines has N independent memories and N copies of the operating system, but a shared address multiprocessor allows a single program to use almost all the memory in the computer. Thus a sequential program in a cluster has $1/N$th the memory available compared to a sequential program in an SMP.

The weakness of separate memories for program size turns out to be a strength in system availability and expandability. Since a cluster consists of independent computers connected through a local area network, it is much easier to replace a machine without bringing down the system in a cluster than in an SMP. Fundamentally, the shared address means that it is difficult to isolate a processor and replace a processor without heroic work by the operating system. Since the cluster software is a layer that runs on top of local operating systems running on each computer, it is much easier to disconnect and replace a broken machine.

Given that clusters are constructed from whole computers and independent, scalable networks, this isolation also makes it easier to expand the system without bringing down the application that runs on top of the cluster. High availability and rapid, incremental expandability make clusters attractive to service providers for the World Wide Web.

Another difference between the two tends to be the price for equivalent computing power for large-scale machines. Since large-scale multiprocessors have small volumes, the extra development costs of large machines must be amortized over few systems, resulting in higher cost to the customer. Since the same switches sold in high volume for small systems can be composed to construct large networks for large clusters, local area network switches have the same economy-of-scale advantages as small computers.

As is often the case with two competing solutions, each side tries to borrow ideas from the other to become more attractive.

On one side of the battle, to combat the high-availability weakness of multiprocessors, hardware designers and operating system developers are trying to offer the ability to run multiple operating systems on portions of the full machine, so that a node can fail or be upgraded without bringing down the whole machine.

On the other side of the battle, since both system administration and memory size limits are approximately linear in the number of independent machines, some are reducing the cluster problems by constructing clusters from small-scale SMPs. For example, a cluster of 32 processors might be constructed from eight four-way SMPs or four eight-way SMPs. Such "hybrid" clusters—sometimes called *clustered, shared memory*—are proving popular with applications that care about cost/performance, availability, and expandability. Indeed, all but one of the commercially provided clusters in Figure 9.12 are based on SMPs.

The next section describes networks used in both clusters and multiprocessors.

9.6   Network Topologies

The straightforward way to connect processor-memory nodes is to have a dedicated communication link between every node. Between the high cost/performance of this *fully connected* network and the low cost/performance of a bus are a set of networks that constitute a wide range of trade-offs in cost/performance. Network costs include the number of switches, the number of links on a switch to connect to the network, the width (number of bits) per link, and length of the links when the network is mapped into a physical machine. For example, on a machine that scales between tens and hundreds of processors, some links may be metal rectangles within a chip that are a few millimeters long, and others may be cables that must stretch several meters from one cabinet to another. Network performance is multifaceted as well. It includes the latency on an unloaded network to send and receive a message, the throughput in terms of the maximum number of messages that can be transmitted in a given time period, delays caused by contention for a portion of the network, and variable performance depending on the pattern of communication. Another obligation of the network may be fault tolerance, since very large systems may be required to operate in the presence of broken components.

Networks are normally drawn as graphs, with each arc of the graph representing a link of the communication network. The processor-memory node is shown as the black square, and the switch is shown as a colored circle. In this section, all links are *bidirectional*; that is, information can flow in either direction. All networks consist of *switches* whose links go to processor-memory nodes and to other switches. The first improvement over a bus is a network that connects a sequence of nodes together:

This topology is called a *ring*. Since some nodes are not directly connected, some messages will have to hop along intermediate nodes until they arrive at the final destination.

Unlike a bus, a ring is capable of many simultaneous transfers. Because there are numerous topologies to choose from, performance metrics are needed to distinguish these designs. Two are popular. The first is *total network bandwidth*, which is the bandwidth of each link multiplied by the number of links. This represents the very best case. For the ring network above with P processors, the total network bandwidth would be P times the bandwidth of one link; the total network bandwidth of a bus is just the bandwidth of that bus, or one times the bandwidth of that link.

To balance this best case, we include another metric that is closer to the worst case: the *bisection bandwidth*. This is calculated by dividing the machine into two parts, each with half the nodes. Then you sum the bandwidth of the links that cross that imaginary dividing line. The bisection bandwidth of a ring is two times the link bandwidth, and it is one times the link bandwidth for the bus. If a single link is as fast as the bus, the ring is only twice as fast as a bus in the worst case, but it is P times faster in the best case.

Since some network topologies are not symmetric, the question arises of where to draw the imaginary line when bisecting the machine. This is a worst-case metric, so the answer is to choose the division that yields the most pessimistic network performance; stated alternatively, calculate all possible bisection bandwidths and pick the smallest. We take this pessimistic view because parallel programs are often limited by the weakest link in the communication chain.

At the other extreme from a ring is a *fully connected network*, where every processor has a bidirectional link to every other processor. For fully connected networks, the total network bandwidth is $(P \times P - 1)/2$, and the bisection bandwidth is $(P/2)^2$.

The tremendous improvement in performance of fully connected networks is offset by the tremendous increase in cost. This inspires engineers to invent new topologies that are between the cost of rings and the performance of fully connected networks. The evaluation of success depends in large part on the nature of the communication in the workload of parallel programs run on the machine.

The number of different topologies that have been discussed in publications would be difficult to count, but the number that have been used in commercial parallel processors is just a handful. Figure 9.13 illustrates two of the popular topologies. Real machines frequently add extra links to these simple topologies to improve performance and reliability.

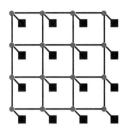   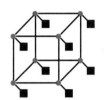

a. 2-D grid or mesh of 16 nodes   b. *n*-cube tree of 8 nodes ($8 = 2^3$ so $n = 3$)

FIGURE 9.13   Network topologies that have appeared in commercial parallel processors. The colored circles represent switches and the black squares represent processor-memory nodes. Even though a switch has many links, generally only one goes to the processor. The Boolean *n*-cube topology is an *n*-dimensional interconnect with 2^n nodes, requiring *n* links per switch (plus one for the processor) and thus *n* nearest-neighbor nodes. Frequently these basic topologies have been supplemented with extra arcs to improve performance and reliability. For example, the switches in the left and right columns of the 2-D grid could be connected through the unused ports on each switch, making four horizontal rings.

An alternative to placing a processor at every node in a network is to leave only the switch at some of these nodes. The switches are smaller than processor-memory-switch nodes, and thus may be packed more densely, thereby lessening distance and increasing performance. Such networks are frequently called *multistage networks* to reflect the multiple steps that a message may travel. Types of multistage networks are as numerous as single-stage networks; Figure 9.14 illustrates two of the popular multistage organizations. A *fully connected* or *crossbar network* allows any node to communicate with any other node in one pass through the network. An *Omega network* uses less hardware than the crossbar network ($2n \log_2 n$ vs. n^2 switches), but contention can occur between messages, depending on the pattern of communication. For example, the Omega network in Figure 9.14 cannot send a message from P0 to P6 at the same time it sends a message from P1 to P7.

Implementing Network Topologies

This simple analysis of all the networks in this section ignores important practical considerations in the construction of a network. The distance of each link affects the cost of communicating at a high clock rate—generally, the longer the distance, the more expensive it is to run at a high clock rate. Shorter distances also make it easier to assign more wires to the link, as the power to drive many wires from a chip is less if the wires are short. Shorter wires are

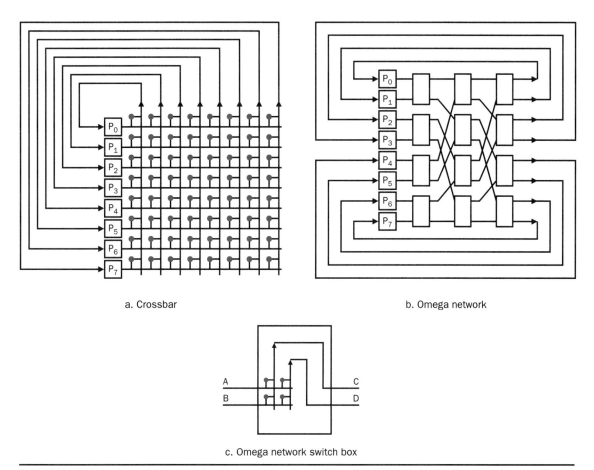

a. Crossbar

b. Omega network

c. Omega network switch box

FIGURE 9.14 Popular multistage network topologies for eight nodes. The switches in these drawings are simpler than in earlier drawings because the links are unidirectional; data comes in at the bottom and exits out the right link. The switch box in c can pass A to C and B to D or B to C and A to D. The crossbar uses n^2 switches, where n is the number of processors, while the Omega network uses $n/2 \log_2 n$ of the large switch boxes, each of which is logically composed of four of the smaller switches. In this case, the crossbar uses 64 switches versus 12 switch boxes, or 48 switches, in the Omega network. The crossbar, however, can support any combination of messages between processors, while the Omega network cannot.

also cheaper than long wires. A final practical limitation is that the three-dimensional drawings must be mapped onto chips and boards that are essentially two-dimensional media. The bottom line is that topologies that appear elegant when sketched on the blackboard may look awkward when constructed from chips, cables, boards, and boxes.

9.7 Real Stuff: Future Directions for Multiprocessors

For over a decade prophets have voiced the contention that the organization of a single computer has reached its limits and that truly significant advances can be made only by interconnection of a multiplicity of computers in such a manner as to permit cooperative solution. . . . Demonstration is made of the continued validity of the single processor approach . . .

Gene Amdahl, "Validity of the single processor approach
to achieving large scale computing capabilities,"
Spring Joint Computer Conference, 1967

Uniprocessor performance is improving at an unprecedented rate, with microprocessors leading the way. Figure 1.20 on page 30 shows that the fastest microprocessors have increased in performance by more than 50% per year every year since 1987. This rapid rate of change does not come free: the estimate of the cost of development of the recent Pentium Pro is $400 million.

Memory capacity has improved at a high rate for a considerably longer time than for processors. Figure 1.14 on page 22 shows that DRAMs have increased their capacity fourfold about every three years. Once again, the tremendous development investment, combined with the low cost of purchasing DRAMs, has led almost all computer manufacturers, including parallel processor companies, to build their memories from DRAMs.

A final technology is the interconnection network. The bandwidth of the interconnection network has improved because of improvements in the speed of logic, improvements in the packaging of parallel processors, and advances in the speed of the physical links. For example, the peak bandwidth per link improved over one decade from 0.5 MB/sec in the Intel iPSC (1986) to 800 MB/sec in the SGI Origin (1996).

Thus the three technologies available to parallel processor designers are fast microprocessors, high-capacity DRAMs, and increasing network bandwidth; interestingly, all are improving at comparable rates.

As mentioned earlier, the rapid change in commercial multiprocessors led us to place the machines that illustrate these ideas on the World Wide Web, so that we could keep the examples from becoming stale. See the section for Chapter 9 at *www.mkp.com/cod2e.htm* to find links to the latest information.

Facts of Life for Large-Scale Parallel Processors

The exciting prospect of building the world's fastest computer is constrained by some facts of life for the parallel processor designer. The first fact of life is that because the nodes are very similar to the core of a desktop computer, the cost of a large-scale parallel processor node is comparable to the cost of a desktop computer.

Most supercomputers cost less than $25,000,000 for processor and memory; since the price of desktop computers has remained between $2500 and $10,000, even if nodes could match desktop computer prices, the largest parallel processors will have no more than 2500 to 10,000 nodes. This estimate does not include the cost of the interconnection network, leading to even fewer nodes. Furthermore, many computers are purchased for scientific applications at a much lower price; thus these machines have far fewer nodes than the practical maximum. Accordingly, while a practical limit of the number of processors is 1000 to 10,000, for many customers and applications, 100 processors will be sufficient.

In 1997, most multiprocessors are in the range of 8 to 16 processors, with the number moving up slowly. If 95% of the machines sold will have less than 100 processors, those 5% of larger machines must carry a larger research and development burden and hence be more expensive per node.

The topology of the interconnection network is important in the construction of a machine that can scale from 100 to 10,000 nodes, and the best topology for 100 to 500 nodes may not be the choice for 1000 to 10,000 nodes. Thus, the topology may vary with the maximum number of nodes and the packaging choices for that machine. The good news is that there are many good interconnection network topologies to choose from; the bad news is that, given these fine alternatives and the importance of the topology to the cost of the machine, there is unlikely to be a single topology that all parallel processor companies will follow.

The second reason for the lesser importance of topologies is that cost-effective fault tolerance is incompatible with topology-dependent algorithms because by definition a broken link or node means that sometimes messages will follow different paths than the programmer would expect from the network topology. Fault tolerance is critical because a machine with 10,000 nodes, each similar to a desktop computer, should have a mean time between failures that is 10,000 times worse than a desktop computer. Thus, with large parallel processors, the question is not *whether* anything is broken at any point in time, but rather *how many* components are broken. Parallel processors must work in the presence of broken network links and broken nodes; hence large parallel processors are not amenable to topology-specific algorithms even if the overhead of communication is reduced.

Hardware Software Interface

The lack of a standard topology is less of an obstacle to portable parallel processor programs than you might first suspect. One reason is that the software overhead to send a message is so large that it masks the effects of the topology. In other words, these overhead costs are so high that the time to send a message to the nearest neighbor node is similar to the time to send to the furthest neighbor. The overhead is high in some cases because the protocols are designed to send large messages, so that sometimes by pipelining them, the latency is seen only once. Other reasons for the high overhead are invoking the operating system on sending or receiving a message and a slow interface between the processor and the network.

Taken in combination, these elements deflate the value of topology-specific algorithms:

- The lack of a standard topology combined with the importance of portable parallel processor programs to the success of the industry

- The high overhead of communication, making the latency virtually the same for messages independent of the distance between nodes

- Operation in the presence of broken links and broken nodes

The Big Picture

A key characteristic of parallel programs is frequency of synchronization and communication. Large-scale parallel machines have distributed physical memory; the higher bandwidth and lower overhead of local memory compared to nonlocal memory strongly rewards parallel processing programmers who utilize locality.

Massive Parallelism

The term *massively parallel* is widely used but rarely defined, but no one would define a computer with less than 100 processors as massively parallel. Even with such a conservative dividing line, parallel processing using more than 100 processors is not yet important in everyday computing. Ideally, we should have a simple model that allows programmers to more easily create portable parallel programs that achieve good performance on real multi-processors *and* that enables researchers to invent new algorithms that will work well on many multiprocessors. Unfortunately, few theoretical models for parallel computation accurately predict performance of current commercial multiprocessors.

One interesting event for massively parallel processors (MPP) is the Accelerated Strategic Computing Initiative (ASCI), a program to accelerate the development of massively parallel supercomputers by ordering a small number of machines costing $50 million to $100 million. A series of ASCI supercomputers will be built, leading up to a 100-teraFLOPS supercomputer by early next century. Figure 9.15 shows the first three ASCI machines. In December 1996, the distributed-memory, message-passing multiprocessor from Intel (ASCI Red) was the first computer to operate at the rate of 1 teraFLOPS (a million MFLOPS).

Name	Number of processors	Processor	Memory size/ system	Communi- cations BW/link	Node	Topology	Peak perfor- mance (tera- FLOPS)	Year
ASCI Red (Intel)	9216	200-MHz Pentium Pro	580,608 MB	800 MB/sec	2-way SMP	two 2-D grids	1.8	1996
ASCI Blue Pacific (IBM RS/6000 SP)	–	successor to Power2 SC	–	–	–	–	3.0	1998
ASCI Blue Mountain (SGI Origin2000)	3072	successor to MIPS R10000	–	–	–	–	3.0	1998

FIGURE 9.15　Characteristics of ASCI supercomputers. All are distributed-memory machines, but only the SGI machine communicates via a shared address and is cache coherent. The costs of the three machines are $46 million, $93 million, and $110 million, respectively. (See *www.mkp.com/cod2e.htm* for pointers to these and more recent MPPs.)

9.8　Fallacies and Pitfalls

Number 9: Quote performance in terms of processor utilization, parallel speedups or MFLOPS per dollar.

David H. Bailey, "Twelve ways to fool the masses when giving performance results on parallel supercomputers,"
Supercomputing Review, 1991

The many assaults on parallel processing have uncovered numerous fallacies and pitfalls. We cover three here.

Pitfall: Measuring performance of parallel processors by linear speedup versus execution time.

"Mortar shot" graphs—plotting performance compared to the number of processors, showing linear speedup, a plateau, and then a falling off—have long been used to judge the success of parallel processors. Although scalability is one facet of a parallel program, it is an indirect measure of performance. The primary question to be asked concerns the power of the processors being scaled: a program that linearly improves performance to equal 100 Intel 8086s may be slower than the sequential version on a single Pentium Pro desktop computer. Be especially careful of floating-point-intensive programs, as processing elements without floating-point hardware assist may scale wonderfully but have poor collective performance.

Measuring results using linear speedup compared to the execution time can mislead the programmer as well as those hearing the performance claims of the programmer. Many programs with poor speedup are faster than programs that show excellent speedup as the number of processors increases.

Comparing execution times is fair only if you are comparing the best algorithms on each machine. (Of course, you can't subtract time for idle processors when evaluating a parallel processor, so CPU time is an inappropriate metric for parallel processors.) Comparing the identical code on two machines may seem fair, but it is not; the parallel program may be slower on a uniprocessor than a sequential version. Sometimes, developing a parallel program will lead to algorithmic improvements, so that comparing the previously best-known sequential program with the parallel code—which seems fair—compares inappropriate algorithms. To reflect this issue, sometimes the terms *relative speedup* (same program) and *true speedup* (best programs) are used.

Fallacy: Amdahl's law doesn't apply to parallel computers.

In 1987, the head of a research organization claimed that Amdahl's law had been broken by a multiprocessor machine. To try to understand the basis of the media reports, let's see the quote that gave us Amdahl's law [1967, p. 483]:

A fairly obvious conclusion which can be drawn at this point is that the effort expended on achieving high parallel processing rates is wasted unless it is accompanied by achievements in sequential processing rates of very nearly the same magnitude.

This statement must still be true; the neglected portion of the program must limit performance. One interpretation of the law leads to the following lemma: portions of every program must be sequential, so there must be an economic upper bound to the number of processors—say, 100. By showing linear speedup with 1000 processors, this lemma is disproved and hence the claim that Amdahl's law was broken.

The approach of the researchers was to change the input to the benchmark: rather than going 1000 times faster, they computed 1000 times more work in comparable time. For their algorithm, the sequential portion of the program was constant, independent of the size of the input, and the rest was fully parallel—hence, linear speedup with 1000 processors. Simply scaling the size of applications, without also scaling floating-point accuracy, the number of iterations, the I/O requirements, and the way applications deal with error may be naive. Many applications will not calculate the correct result if the problem size is increased unwittingly.

We see no reason why Amdahl's law doesn't apply to parallel processors. What this research does point out is the importance of having benchmarks that can grow large enough to demonstrate performance of large-scale parallel processors.

Fallacy: Peak performance tracks observed performance.

One definition of peak performance is "performance that a machine is guaranteed not to exceed." Alas, the supercomputer industry uses this metric in marketing, and its fallacy is being exacerbated with parallel machines. Not only are industry marketers using the nearly unattainable peak performance of a uniprocessor node (see Figure 9.16), but they are then multiplying it by the total number of processors, assuming perfect speedup! Amdahl's law suggests how difficult it is to reach either peak; multiplying the two together also multiplies the sins. Figure 9.17 compares the peak to sustained performance on a benchmark; the 64-processor IBM SP2 achieves only 7% of peak performance. Clearly peak performance does not always track observed performance.

Machine	Peak MFLOPS rating	Harmonic mean MFLOPS of the Perfect Club benchmarks	Percent of peak MFLOPS
Cray X-MP/416	940	14.8	1%
IBM 3090-600S	800	8.3	1%
NEC SX/2	1300	16.6	1%

FIGURE 9.16 Peak performance and harmonic mean of actual performance for the 12 Perfect Club benchmarks. These results are for the programs run unmodified. When tuned by hand, performance of the three machines moves to 24.4, 11.3, and 18.3 MFLOPS, respectively. This is still 2% or less of peak performance.

	Cray YMP (8 processors)		IBM SP2 (64 processors)	
	MFLOPS	**% Peak**	**MFLOPS**	**% Peak**
Peak	2,666	100%	14,636	100%
3D FFT PDE	1,795	67%	1,093	7%

FIGURE 9.17   Peak versus observed performance for Cray YMP and IBM RS/6000 SP2.

Such performance claims can confuse the manufacturer as well as the user of the machine. The danger is that the manufacturer will develop software libraries with success judged as percentage of peak performance measured in megaflops rather than taking less time, or that hardware will be added that increases peak node performance but is difficult to use.

9.9   Concluding Remarks—Evolution versus Revolution in Computer Architecture

The stumbling way in which even the ablest of the scientists in every generation have had to fight through thickets of erroneous observations, misleading generalizations, inadequate formulations, and unconscious prejudice is rarely appreciated by those who obtain their scientific knowledge from textbooks.

James B. Conant, *Science and Common Sense*, 1951

Reading conference and journal articles from the last 30 years can be discouraging; so much effort has been expended with so little impact. Optimistically speaking, these papers act as gravel and, when placed logically together, form the foundation for the next generation of computers. From a more pessimistic point of view, if 90% of the ideas disappeared, no one would notice.

One reason for this predicament is what could be called the "von Neumann syndrome." By hoping to invent a new model of computation that will revolutionize computing, researchers are striving to become the von Neumann of the 21st century. Another reason is taste: researchers often select problems that no one else cares about. Even if important problems are selected, there is frequently a lack of experimental evidence to demonstrate convincingly the value of the solution. Moreover, when important problems are selected and the solutions are demonstrated, the proposed solutions may be too expensive relative to their benefit. Sometimes this expense is measured as straightforward cost/performance—the performance enhancement does not merit the added cost. More often the expense of innovation comes from being too disruptive to computer users.

Figure 9.18 shows what we mean by the *evolution-revolution spectrum* of computer architecture innovation. To the left are ideas that are invisible to the

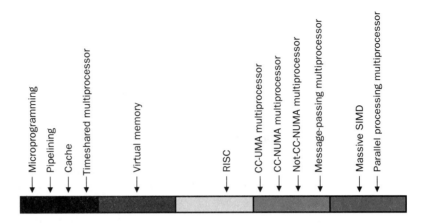

Evolutionary   Revolutionary

FIGURE 9.18   The evolution-revolution spectrum of computer architecture. The first four columns are distinguished from the last column in that applications and operating systems may be ported from other computers rather than written from scratch. For example, RISC is listed in the middle of the spectrum because user compatibility is only at the level of high-level languages (HLLs), while microprogramming allows binary compatibility, and parallel processing multiprocessors require changes to algorithms and extending HLLs. You see several flavors of multiprocessors on this figure. "Timeshared multiprocessor" means multiprocessors justified by running many independent programs at once. "CC-UMA" and "CC-NUMA" mean cache-coherent UMA and NUMA multiprocessors running parallel subsystems such as databases or file servers. "Not-CC-NUMA" means a shared address but *not* cache-coherent NUMA for similar applications. And the same applications are intended for "message passing." "Parallel processing multiprocessor" means a multiprocessor of some flavor sold to accelerate individual programs developed by users. (See section 9.10 to learn about SIMD.)

user (except presumably better cost, better performance, or both); this is the evolutionary end of the spectrum. At the other end are revolutionary architecture ideas. These are the ideas that require new applications from programmers who must learn new programming languages and models of computation, and must invent new data structures and algorithms.

Revolutionary ideas are easier to publish than evolutionary ideas, but to be adopted they must have a much higher payoff. Caches are an example of an evolutionary improvement. Within five years after the first publication about caches, almost every computer company was designing a machine with a cache. The Reduced Instruction Set Computer (RISC) ideas were nearer to the middle of the spectrum, for it took closer to 10 years for most companies to have a RISC product. Examples of revolutionary computer architecture came from several parallel processing companies in the late 1980s. Every program that runs efficiently on those machines was either substantially modified or written especially for it, and programmers needed to learn a new style of programming for it. The obstacles were too large for most of these companies to survive.

Projects that the computer industry ignores may be valuable if they document the lessons learned for future efforts. The sin is not in having a novel architecture that is commercially unsuccessful, but in neglecting to quantitatively evaluate the strengths and weaknesses of the novel ideas. And failures of past research projects do not mean that the ideas are dead forever. Changes in technology may rejuvenate an idea that previously had the wrong trade-offs or rejuvenate an idea that was ahead of the technology.

When contemplating the future—and inventing your own contributions to the field—remember the evolution-revolution spectrum. Acceptance of hardware ideas requires acceptance by software people; therefore, hardware people must learn more about software. And if software people want good machines, they must learn more about hardware to be able to communicate with and thereby influence hardware designers. Also, keep in mind the principles of computer organization found in this book; these will surely guide computers of the future, just as they have guided computers of the past.

9.10   Historical Perspective and Further Reading

As parallelism can appear at many levels, it is useful to categorize the alternatives. In 1966, Flynn proposed a simple model of categorizing computers that is still useful today. Scrutinizing the most constrained component of the machine, he counted the number of parallel instruction and data streams and then labeled the computer with this count:

1. *Single instruction stream, single data stream* (SISD, the uniprocessor)

2. *Single instruction stream, multiple data streams* (SIMD)

3. *Multiple instruction streams, single data stream* (MISD)

4. *Multiple instruction streams, multiple data streams* (MIMD)

Some machines are hybrids of these categories, of course, but this classic model has survived because it is simple, easy to understand, and gives a good first approximation. It is also—perhaps because of its understandability—the most widely used scheme.

Your first question about the model should be, "Single or multiple compared with what?" A machine that adds a 32-bit number in 1 clock cycle would seem to have multiple data streams when compared with a bit-serial computer that takes 32 clock cycles to add. Flynn chose computers popular during that time, the IBM 704 and IBM 7090, as the model of SISD; today, the MIPS implementations in Chapters 5 and 6 would be fine reference points.

Single Instruction Multiple Data Computers

SIMD computers operate on vectors of data. For example, when a single SIMD instruction adds 64 numbers, the SIMD hardware sends 64 data streams to 64 ALUs to form 64 sums within a single clock cycle.

The virtues of SIMD are that all the parallel execution units are synchronized and they all respond to a single instruction that emanates from a single program counter (PC). From a programmer's perspective, this is close to the already familiar SISD. Although every unit will be executing the same instruction, each execution unit has its own address registers, and so each unit can have different data addresses.

The original motivation behind SIMD was to amortize the cost of the control unit over dozens of execution units. Another advantage is the reduced size of program memory—SIMD needs only one copy of the code that is being simultaneously executed, while MIMD may need a copy in every processor. Virtual memory and increasing capacity of DRAM chips have reduced the importance of this advantage.

Real SIMD computers have a mixture of SISD and SIMD instructions. There is typically an SISD host computer to perform sequential operations such as branches or address calculations. The SIMD instructions are broadcast to all the execution units, each with its own set of registers and memory. Execution units rely on interconnection networks to exchange data.

SIMD works best when dealing with arrays in *for* loops. Hence, for massive parallelism to work in SIMD, there must be massive data, or *data parallelism.* SIMD is at its weakest in *case* or *switch* statements, where each execution unit must perform a different operation on its data, depending on what data it has. Execution units with the wrong data are disabled so that units with proper data may continue. Such situations essentially run at $1/n$th performance, where n is the number of cases.

A basic trade-off in SIMD machines is processor performance versus number of processors. The Connection Machine 2 (CM-2), for example, offers 65,536 single-bit-wide processors, while the Illiac IV had 64 64-bit processors. Figure 9.19 lists the characteristics of some well-known SIMD computers.

Surely the best-known SIMD is the Illiac IV (seen in Figure 9.20), perhaps the most infamous of the supercomputer projects. Although successful in pushing several technologies useful in later projects, the Illiac IV failed as a computer. Costs escalated from the $8 million estimated in 1966 to $31 million by 1972, despite the construction of only a quarter of the planned machine. Actual performance was at best 15 MFLOPS compared to initial predictions of 1000 MFLOPS for the full system (see Falk [1976]). Delivered to NASA's Ames Research in 1972, the computer took three more years of engineering before it was operational. For better or worse, computer architects are not easily discouraged; SIMD successors of the Illiac IV include the ICL DAP, Goodyear MPP (Figure 9.21), Thinking Machines CM-1 and CM-2, and Maspar MP-1 and MP-2.

Institution	Name	Maximum no. of proc.	Bits/ proc.	Proc. clock rate (MHz)	Number of FPUs	Maximum memory size/system (MB)	Communications BW/system (MB/sec)	Year
U. Illinois	Illiac IV	64	64	5	64	0.125	2,560	1972
ICL	DAP	4,096	1	5	0	2	2,560	1980
Goodyear	MPP	16,384	1	10	0	2	20,480	1982
Thinking Machines	CM-2	65,536	1	7	2048 (optional)	512	16,384	1987
Maspar	MP-1216	16,384	4	25	0	256 or 1024	23,000	1989

FIGURE 9.19   Characteristics of five SIMD computers. Number of FPUs means number of floating-point units.

FIGURE 9.20   The Illiac IV control unit followed by its 64 processing elements. It was perhaps the most infamous of supercomputers. The project started in 1965 and ran its first real application in 1976. The 64 processors used a 13-MHz clock, and their combined main memory size was 1 MB: 64×16 KB. The Illiac IV was the first machine to teach us that software for parallel machines dominates hardware issues. Photo courtesy of NASA Ames Research Center.

FIGURE 9.21 The Goodyear MPP with 16,384 processors. It was delivered May 2, 1983, to NASA Goddard Space Center and was operational the next day. It was decommissioned on March 1, 1991.

Vector Computers

A related model to SIMD is *vector processing*. It is a well-established architecture and compiler model that was popularized by supercomputers, and is considerably more widely used than SIMD. Vector processors have high-level operations that work on linear arrays of numbers, or vectors. An example vector operation is

$$A = B \times C$$

where A, B, and C are each 64-element vectors of 64-bit floating-point numbers. SIMD has similar instructions; the difference is that vector processors depend on pipelined functional units that typically operate on a few vector elements per clock cycle, while SIMD typically operates on all the elements at once.

Advantages of vector computers over traditional SISD processors include the following:

1. Each result is independent of previous results, which enables deep pipelines and high clock rates.

2. A single vector instruction performs a great deal of work, which means fewer instruction fetches in general, and fewer branch instructions and so fewer mispredicted branches.

3. Vector instructions access memory a block at a time, which allows memory latency to be amortized over, say, 64 elements.

4. Vector instructions access memory with known patterns, which allows multiple memory banks to simultaneously supply operands.

These last two advantages mean that vector processors do not need to rely on high hit rates of data caches to have high performance. They tend to rely on low-latency main memory, often made from SRAM, and have as many as 1024 memory banks to get high memory bandwidth.

To get even higher performance, all vector supercomputers offer multiple processors, a transition to our next topic. Figure 9.22 shows several vector machines.

Elaboration: Although MISD fills out Flynn's classification, it is difficult to envision. A single instruction stream is simpler than multiple instruction streams, but multiple instruction streams with multiple data streams (MIMD) are easier to imagine than multiple instructions with a single data stream (MISD).

While it was conceivable to write 100 different programs for 100 different processors in an MIMD machine, in practice this proved to be impossible. Today MIMD programmers write a single source program and think of the same program running on all processors. This approach is sometimes called *single program multiple data* (*SPMD*).

Name	Vector registers	Elements per vector register	Elements computed per clock cycle	Number of functional units	Processor clock rate	Maximum number of processors	Maximum memory size/system
Cray J90	8	64	1	4	100 MHz	32	8,192 MB
Cray T90	8	128	2	8	455 MHz	32	8,192 MB
Fujitsu VPP300	8–256	64–2048	8	4	140 MHz	16	32,768 MB
NEC SX-4 single node	8 + 8192 scratchpad	256 + variable up to 8K	8	16	125 MHz	32	8,192 MB

FIGURE 9.22   Characteristics of four vector computers that are for sale in 1997. All vector computers in this figure but the Cray T90 use CMOS technology to build the processor. To lower main memory latency (but raise system cost), the T90 uses SRAM instead of DRAM.

Multiple Instruction Multiple Data Computers

It is difficult to distinguish the first MIMD: arguments for the advantages of parallel execution can be traced back to the 19th century [Menabrea 1842]! And even the first computer from the Eckert-Mauchly Corporation had duplicate units, in this case to improve reliability.

Two of the best-documented multiprocessor projects were undertaken in the 1970s at Carnegie-Mellon University. The first of these was C.mmp, which consisted of 16 PDP-11s connected by a crossbar switch to 16 memory units. It was among the first multiprocessors with more than a few processors, and it had a shared-memory programming model. Much of the focus of the research in the C.mmp project was on software, especially in the operating systems area. A later machine, Cm*, was a cluster-based multiprocessor with a distributed memory and a nonuniform access time, which made programming even more of a challenge. The absence of caches and a long remote access latency made data placement critical.

Although very large mainframes were built with multiple processors in the 1970s, multiprocessors did not become highly successful until the 1980s. Bell [1985] suggests the key to success was that the smaller size of the microprocessor allowed the memory bus to replace the interconnection network hardware, and that portable operating systems meant that parallel processor projects no longer required the invention of a new operating system. He distinguishes parallel processors with multiple private addresses by calling them *multicomputers*, reserving the term *multiprocessor* for machines with a single address space.

The first bus-connected multiprocessor with snooping caches was the Synapse N+1 in 1984. The mid-1980s saw an explosion in the development of alternative coherence protocols, and Archibald and Baer [1986] provide a good survey and analysis, as well as references to the original papers. The late 1980s saw the introduction of many commercial bus-connected, snooping-cache architectures, including the Silicon Graphics 4D/240, the Encore Multimax, and the Sequent Symmetry.

In the effort to build large-scale multiprocessors, two different directions were explored: message-passing multicomputers and scalable shared-memory multiprocessors. Although there had been many attempts to build mesh- and hypercube-connected multiprocessors, one of the first machines to successfully bring together all the pieces was the Cosmic Cube, built at Caltech [Seitz 1985]. It introduced important advances in routing and interconnect technology and substantially reduced the cost of the interconnect, which helped make the multicomputer viable. Commercial machines with related architectures included the Intel iPSC 860, the Intel Paragon, and the Thinking Machines CM-5. Alas, the market for such machines proved to be much smaller than hoped, and Intel withdrew from the business (with ASCI Red being their last machine) and Thinking Machines no longer exists. Today this space is mostly clusters, such as the IBM RS/6000 SP2 (Figure 9.23).

FIGURE 9.23 The IBM RS/6000 SP2 with 256 processors. This distributed-memory machine is built using boards from desktop computers largely unchanged plus a custom switch as the interconnect. In contrast to the SP2, most clusters use an off-the-shelf, switched local area network. Photo courtesy of the Lawrence Livermore National Laboratory.

Extending the shared-memory model with scalable cache coherence was done by combining a number of ideas. Directory-based techniques for cache coherence were actually known before snooping cache techniques. In fact, the first cache coherence protocol actually used directories and was implemented in the IBM 3081 in 1976. The idea of distributing directories with the memories to obtain a scalable implementation of cache coherence (now called distributed shared memory or DSM) was the basis for the Stanford DASH multiprocessor; it is considered the forerunner of the NUMA computers in Figure 9.9 on page 728. The Kendall Square Research KSR-1—may it rest in peace—was the first commercial implementation of scalable coherent shared memory. It extended the basic DSM approach to implement a concept called COMA (Cache Only Memory Architecture), which makes the main memory a cache (see Figure 9.10 on page 732).

There is a vast amount of information on multiprocessors: conferences, journal papers, and even books seem to be appearing faster than any single person can absorb the ideas. One good source is the Supercomputing Conference, held annually since 1988. Two major journals, *Journal of Parallel and Distributed Computing* and the *IEEE Transactions on Parallel and Distributed Systems*, contain largely papers on aspects of parallel computing. Textbooks on parallel computing have been written by Almasi and Gottlieb [1989]; Andrews [1991]; Culler, Singh, and Gupta [1998]; and Hwang [1993]. Pfister's book [1995] is one of the few on clusters.

To Probe Further

Almasi, G. S., and A. Gottlieb [1989]. *Highly Parallel Computing*, Benjamin/Cummings, Redwood City, CA.

A textbook covering parallel computers.

Amdahl, G. M. [1967]. "Validity of the single processor approach to achieving large scale computing capabilities," *Proc. AFIPS Spring Joint Computer Conf.*, Atlantic City, NJ, (April) 483–85.

Written in response to the claims of the Illiac IV, this three-page article describes Amdahl's law and gives the classic reply to arguments for abandoning the current form of computing.

Andrews, G. R. [1991]. *Concurrent Programming: Principles and Practice*, Benjamin/Cummings, Redwood City, CA.

A text that gives the principles of parallel programming.

Archibald, J., and J.-L. Baer [1986]. "Cache coherence protocols: Evaluation using a multiprocessor simulation model," *ACM Trans. on Computer Systems* 4:4 (November) 273–98.

Classic survey paper of shared-bus cache coherency protocols.

Arpaci-Dusseau, A., R. Arpaci-Dusseau, D. Culler, J. Hellerstein, and D. Patterson [1997]. "High-performance sorting on networks of workstations," *Proc. ACM SIGMOD/PODS Conference on Management of Data*, Tucson, AZ, May 12–15.

How a world record sort was performed on a cluster, including architecture critique of the workstation and network interface. By April 1, 1997, they pushed the record to 8.6 GB in one minute and 2.2 seconds to sort 100 MB.

Bell, C. G. [1985]. "Multis: A new class of multiprocessor computers," *Science* 228 (April 26) 462–67.

Distinguishes shared address and nonshared address multiprocessors based on microprocessors.

Culler, D. E., and J. P. Singh, with A. Gupta [1998]. *Parallel Computer Architecture*, Morgan Kaufmann, San Francisco.

A new textbook on parallel computers.

Falk, H. [1976]. "Reaching for the Gigaflop," *IEEE Spectrum* 13:10 (October) 65–70.

Chronicles the sad story of the Illiac IV: four times the cost and less than one-tenth the performance of original goals.

Flynn, M. J. [1966]. "Very high-speed computing systems," *Proc. IEEE* 54:12 (December) 1901–09.

Classic article showing SISD/SIMD/MISD/MIMD classifications.

Hord, R. M. [1982]. *The Illiac-IV, the First Supercomputer*, Computer Science Press, Rockville, MD.

A historical accounting of the Illiac IV project.

Hwang, K. [1993]. *Advanced Computer Architecture with Parallel Programming*, McGraw-Hill, New York.

Another textbook covering parallel computers.

Menabrea, L. F. [1842]. "Sketch of the analytical engine invented by Charles Babbage," Bibliothèque Universelle de Genève (October).

Certainly the earliest reference on multiprocessors, this mathematician made this comment while translating papers on Babbage's mechanical computer.

Pfister, G. F. [1995]. *In Search of Clusters: The Coming Battle in Lowly Parallel Computing*, Prentice Hall, Upper Saddle River, NJ.

An entertaining book that advocates clusters and is critical of NUMA multiprocessors.

Seitz, C. [1985]. "The Cosmic Cube," *Comm. ACM* 28:1 (January) 22–31.

A tutorial article on a parallel processor connected via a hypertree. The Cosmic Cube is the ancestor of the Intel supercomputers.

Slotnick, D. L. [1982]. "The conception and development of parallel processors—A personal memoir," *Annals of the History of Computing* 4:1 (January) 20–30.

Recollections of the beginnings of parallel processing by the architect of the Illiac IV.

9.11   Key Terms

These terms reflect the key ideas in the chapter. Check the Glossary for definitions of the terms you do not know.

atomic operation	MESI cache coherency	shared memory
barrier synchronization	protocol	single instruction stream,
cache coherency	message passing	multiple data streams
cluster	multicomputer	(SIMD)
crossbar network	multiple instruction streams,	single instruction stream,
data parallelism	multiple data streams	single data stream (SISD)
directory	(MIMD)	snooping cache coherency
distributed memory	multiprocessor	symmetric multiprocessor
distributed shared memory	multistage network	(SMP)
(DSM)	network bandwidth	synchronization
false sharing	nonuniform memory access	uniform memory access
fully connected network	(NUMA)	(UMA)
lock	parallel processing program	vector processor
main memory coherence	receive message routine	write-broadcast
massively parallel	send message routine	write-invalidate

9.12   Exercises

9.1 [15] <§9.1> Write a one-page article examining your life for ways in which concurrency is present and mutual exclusion is obtained. You may want to consider things such as freeways going from two lanes to one, waiting in lines at different types of businesses, obtaining the attention of your instructor to ask questions, and so on. Try to discover different means and mechanisms that are used for both communication and synchronization. Are there any situations in which you wish a different algorithm were used so that either latency or bandwidth were improved, or perhaps the system were more "fair"?

9.2 [10] <§9.1> Consider the following portions of two different programs running at the same time on two processors in an SMP. Assume that before this code is run, both x and y are 0.

Processor 1:   ...; x := x + 1; y := x + y; ...

Processor 2:   ...; y := x + 1; ...

What are the possible resulting values of x and y, assuming the code is implemented using a load-store architecture? For each possible outcome, explain how x and y might obtain those values. (Hint: You must examine all of the possible interleavings of the assembly language instructions.)

9.3 [10] <§§9.1–9.3> Imagine that all the employees in a huge company have forgotten who runs the company and can only remember whom they work for. Management is considering whether or not to issue one of the following two statements:

- "Today every employee should ask his boss who his boss is, then tomorrow ask that person who *his* boss is, and so forth, until you eventually discover who runs the company."

- "Everyone, please write the name of your boss on a sheet of paper. Find out what name the person on your sheet of paper has on *his* sheet of paper, and tomorrow write that name on your sheet of paper before coming to work. Repeat this process until you discover who runs the company."

Write a paragraph describing the difference between these two statements and the resulting outcomes. Explain the relationship between the two alternatives described above and what you have learned about concurrency and interprocess synchronization and communication.

9.4 [5] <§§9.1–9.3> {Ex. 9.3} Analyze the performance of the two algorithms above. Consider companies containing 100 people, 1000 people, or 10,000 people. Can you think of any ways to improve either of the two algorithms or to accomplish the same task even faster?

9.5 [5] <§9.3> Count the number of transactions on the bus for the following sequence of activities involving shared data. Assume that both processors use write-back caches, write-update cache coherency, and a block size of one word. Assume that all the words in both caches are clean.

Step	Processor	Memory activity	Memory address
1	processor 1	write	100
2	processor 2	write	104
3	processor 1	read	100
4	processor 2	read	104

9.6 [10] <§9.3> False sharing can lead to unnecessary bus traffic and delays. Follow the directions for Exercise 9.5, except change the block size to four words.

9.7 [15] <§9.4> Another possible network topology is a three-dimensional grid. Draw the topology as in Figure 9.13 on page 738 for 64 nodes. What is the bisection bandwidth of this topology?

9.8 [1 week] <§§9.2–9.6> A parallel processor is typically marketed using programs that can scale performance linearly with the number of processors. Port programs written for one parallel processor to the other, and measure their absolute performance and how it changes as you change the number of processors. What changes must be made to improve performance of the ported programs on each machine? What is performance according to each program?

9.9 [1 week] <§§9.2–9.6> Instead of trying to create fair benchmarks, invent programs that make one parallel processor look terrible compared with the others and also programs that always make one look better than others. What are the key performance characteristics of each program and machine?

9.10 [1 week] <§§9.2– 9.6> Parallel processors usually show performance increases as you increase the number of processors, with the ideal being n times speedup for n processors. The goal of this exercise is to create a biased benchmark that gets worse performance as you add processors. For example, one processor on the parallel processor would run the program fastest, two would be slower, four would be slower than two, and so on. What are the key performance characteristics for each organization that give inverse linear speedup?

9.11 [1 week] <§§9.2–9.6> Networked workstations may be considered parallel processors, albeit with slow communication relative to computation. Port parallel processor benchmarks to a network using remote procedure calls for communication. How well do the benchmarks scale on the network versus the parallel processor? What are the practical differences between networked workstations and a commercial parallel processor?

9.12 [1 week] <§§9.2–9.6> *Superlinear* performance improvement means that a program on n processors is more than n times faster than the equivalent uniprocessor. One argument for superlinear speedup is that time spent servicing interrupts or switching contexts is reduced when you have many processors because only one needs service interrupts and there are more processors to be shared by users. Measure the time spent on a workload in handling interrupts or context switching for a uniprocessor versus a parallel processor. This workload may be a mix of independent jobs for a multiprogramming environment or a single large job. Does the argument hold?

9.13 [15] <§9.9> Construct a scenario whereby a truly revolutionary architecture—pick your favorite candidate—will play a significant role. Significant is defined as 10% of the computers sold, 10% of the users, 10% of the money spent on computers, or 10% of some other figure of merit.

9.14 [20] <§§9.1–9.11> This chapter introduced many new vocabulary terms related to the subject of multiprocessors. Some of the exercises in this chapter (e.g., 9.1, 9.3) are based on an analogy in which people are thought of as processors and collections of people as multiprocessors. Write a one-page article exploring this analogy in more detail. For example, are there collections of people who use techniques akin to message passing or shared memories? Can you create analogies for cache coherency protocols, network topologies, or clusters? Try to include at least one vocabulary term from each section of the text.

Assemblers, Linkers, and the SPIM Simulator

James R. Larus
Computer Sciences Department
University of Wisconsin–Madison

*Fear of serious injury cannot alone
justify suppression of free speech
and assembly.*

Louis Brandeis
Whitney v. California, 1927

A.1   **Introduction**   A-3

A.2   **Assemblers**   A-10

A.3   **Linkers**   A-17

A.4   **Loading**   A-19

A.5   **Memory Usage**   A-20

A.6   **Procedure Call Convention**   A-22

A.7   **Exceptions and Interrupts**   A-32

A.8   **Input and Output**   A-36

A.9   **SPIM**   A-38

A.10   **MIPS R2000 Assembly Language**   A-49

A.11   **Concluding Remarks**   A-75

A.12   **Key Terms**   A-76

A.13   **Exercises**   A-76

A.1   Introduction

Encoding instructions as binary numbers is natural and efficient for computers. Humans, however, have a great deal of difficulty understanding and manipulating these numbers. People read and write symbols (words) much better than long sequences of digits. Chapter 3 showed that we need not choose between numbers and words because computer instructions can be represented in many ways. Humans can write and read symbols, and computers can execute the equivalent binary numbers. This appendix describes the process by which a human-readable program is translated into a form that a computer can execute, provides a few hints about writing assembly programs, and explains how to run these programs on SPIM, a simulator that executes MIPS programs. Unix, Windows, and DOS versions of the SPIM simulator are available through *www.mkp.com/cod2e.htm*.

Assembly language is the symbolic representation of a computer's binary encoding—*machine language*. Assembly language is more readable than machine language because it uses symbols instead of bits. The symbols in assembly language name commonly occurring bit patterns, such as opcodes and register specifiers, so people can read and remember them. In addition, assembly language permits programmers to use *labels* to identify and name particular memory words that hold instructions or data.

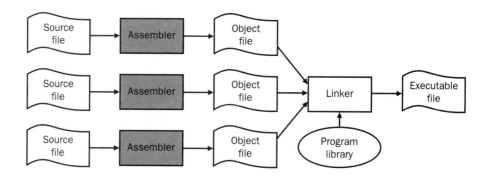

FIGURE A.1   The process that produces an executable file. An assembler translates a file of assembly language into an object file, which is linked with other files and libraries into an executable file.

A tool called an *assembler* translates assembly language into binary instructions. Assemblers provide a friendlier representation than a computer's 0s and 1s that simplifies writing and reading programs. Symbolic names for operations and locations are one facet of this representation. Another facet is programming facilities that increase a program's clarity. For example, *macros*, discussed in section A.2, enable a programmer to extend the assembly language by defining new operations.

An assembler reads a single assembly language *source file* and produces an *object file* containing machine instructions and bookkeeping information that helps combine several object files into a program. Figure A.1 illustrates how a program is built. Most programs consist of several files—also called *modules*—that are written, compiled, and assembled independently. A program may also use prewritten routines supplied in a *program library*. A module typically contains *references* to subroutines and data defined in other modules and in libraries. The code in a module cannot be executed when it contains *unresolved references* to labels in other object files or libraries. Another tool, called a *linker*, combines a collection of object and library files into an *executable file*, which a computer can run.

To see the advantage of assembly language, consider the following sequence of figures, all of which contain a short subroutine that computes and prints the sum of the squares of integers from 0 to 100. Figure A.2 shows the machine language that a MIPS computer executes. With considerable effort, you could use the opcode and instruction format tables in Chapters 3 and 4 to translate the instructions into a symbolic program similar to Figure A.3. This form of the routine is much easier to read because operations and operands are written with symbols, rather than with bit patterns. However, this assembly

```
00100111101111011111111111100000
10101111101111110000000000010100
10101111101001000000000000100000
10101111101001010000000000100100
10101111101000000000000000011000
10101111101000000000000000011100
10001111101011100000000000011100
10001111101110000000000000011000
00000001110011100000000000011001
00100101110010000000000000000001
00101001000000010000000001100101
10101111101010000000000000011100
00000000000000000111100000010010
00000011000011111100100000100001
00010100001000001111111111110111
10101111101110010000000000011000
00111100000000100001000000000000
10001111101001010000000000011000
00001100000100000000000011101100
00100100100001000000010000110000
10001111101111110000000000010100
00100111101111010000000000100000
00000111110000000000000000001000
00000000000000000001000000100001
```

FIGURE A.2   MIPS machine language code for a routine to compute and print the sum of the squares of integers between 0 and 100.

language is still difficult to follow because memory locations are named by their address, rather than by a symbolic label.

Figure A.4 shows assembly language that labels memory addresses with mnemonic names. Most programmers prefer to read and write this form. Names that begin with a period, for example .data and .globl, are *assembler directives* that tell the assembler how to translate a program but do not produce machine instructions. Names followed by a colon, such as str or main, are labels that name the next memory location. This program is as readable as most assembly language programs (except for a glaring lack of comments), but it is still difficult to follow because many simple operations are required to accomplish simple tasks and because assembly language's lack of control flow constructs provides few hints about the program's operation.

By contrast, the C routine in Figure A.5 is both shorter and clearer since variables have mnemonic names and the loop is explicit rather than constructed with branches. (If you are unfamiliar with C, you may wish to look at Web Extension II at *www.mkp.com/cod2e.htm*.) In fact, the C routine is the only one that we wrote. The other forms of the program were produced by a C compiler and assembler.

```
addiu   $29, $29, -32
sw      $31, 20($29)
sw      $4,  32($29)
sw      $5,  36($29)
sw      $0,  24($29)
sw      $0,  28($29)
lw      $14, 28($29)
lw      $24, 24($29)
multu   $14, $14
addiu   $8,  $14, 1
slti    $1,  $8, 101
sw      $8,  28($29)
mflo    $15
addu    $25, $24, $15
bne     $1,  $0, -9
sw      $25, 24($29)
lui     $4,  4096
lw      $5,  24($29)
jal     1048 812
addiu   $4,  $4, 1072
lw      $31, 20($29)
addiu   $29, $29, 32
jr      $31
move    $2,  $0
```

FIGURE A.3 The same routine written in assembly language. However, the code for the routine does not label registers or memory locations nor include comments.

In general, assembly language plays two roles (see Figure A.6). The first role is the output language of compilers. A *compiler* translates a program written in a *high-level language* (such as C or Pascal) into an equivalent program in machine or assembly language. The high-level language is called the *source language,* and the compiler's output is its *target language.*

Assembly language's other role is as a language in which to write programs. This role used to be the dominant one. Today, however, because of larger main memories and better compilers, most programmers write in a high-level language and rarely, if ever, see the instructions that a computer executes. Nevertheless, assembly language is still important to write programs in which speed or size are critical or to exploit hardware features that have no analogues in high-level languages.

Although this appendix focuses on MIPS assembly language, assembly programming on most other machines is very similar. The additional instructions and address modes in CISC machines, such as the VAX (see Web Extension III at *www.mkp.com/cod2e.htm*), can make assembly programs shorter but do not change the process of assembling a program or provide assembly language with the advantages of high-level languages such as type-checking and structured control flow.

```
                        .text
                        .align  2
                        .globl  main
        main:
                        subu    $sp, $sp, 32
                        sw      $ra, 20($sp)
                        sd      $a0, 32($sp)
                        sw      $0,  24($sp)
                        sw      $0,  28($sp)
        loop:
                        lw      $t6, 28($sp)
                        mul     $t7, $t6, $t6
                        lw      $t8, 24($sp)
                        addu    $t9, $t8, $t7
                        sw      $t9, 24($sp)
                        addu    $t0, $t6, 1
                        sw      $t0, 28($sp)
                        ble     $t0, 100, loop
                        la      $a0, str
                        lw      $a1, 24($sp)
                        jal     printf
                        move    $v0, $0
                        lw      $ra, 20($sp)
                        addu    $sp, $sp, 32
                        j       $ra


                        .data
                        .align  0
        str:
                        .asciiz "The sum from 0 .. 100 is %d\n"
```

FIGURE A.4 The same routine written in assembly language with labels, but no comments. The commands that start with periods are assembler directives (see pages A-51–A-53). .text indicates that succeeding lines contain instructions. .data indicates that they contain data. .align n indicates that the items on the succeeding lines should be aligned on a 2^n byte boundary. Hence, .align 2 means the next item should be on a word boundary. .globl main declares that main is a global symbol that should be visible to code stored in other files. Finally, .asciiz stores a null-terminated string in memory.

When to Use Assembly Language

The primary reason to program in assembly language, as opposed to an available high-level language, is that the speed or size of a program is critically important. For example, consider a computer that controls a piece of machinery, such as a car's brakes. A computer that is incorporated in another device, such as a car, is called an *embedded computer*. This type of computer needs to respond rapidly and predictably to events in the outside world. Because a

```
#include <stdio.h>

int
main (int argc, char *argv[])
{
        int i;
        int sum = 0;

        for (i = 0; i <= 100; i = i + 1) sum = sum + i * i;
        printf ("The sum from 0 .. 100 is %d\n", sum);
}
```

FIGURE A.5   The routine written in the C programming language.

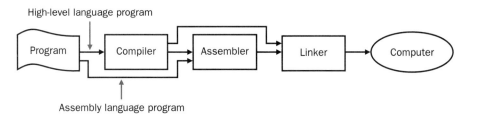

FIGURE A.6   Assembly language either is written by a programmer or is the output of a compiler.

compiler introduces uncertainty about the time cost of operations, programmers may find it difficult to ensure that a high-level language program responds within a definite time interval—say, 1 millisecond after a sensor detects that a tire is skidding. An assembly language programmer, on the other hand, has tight control over which instructions execute. In addition, in embedded applications, reducing a program's size, so that it fits in fewer memory chips, reduces the cost of the embedded computer.

A hybrid approach, in which most of a program is written in a high-level language and time-critical sections are written in assembly language, builds on the strengths of both languages. Programs typically spend most of their time executing a small fraction of the program's source code. This observation is just the principle of locality that underlies caches (see section 7.2 in Chapter 7).

Program profiling measures where a program spends its time and can find the time-critical parts of a program. In many cases, this portion of the program can be made faster with better data structures or algorithms. Sometimes, however, significant performance improvements only come from recoding a critical portion of a program in assembly language.

This improvement is not necessarily an indication that the high-level language's compiler has failed. Compilers typically are better than programmers at producing uniformly high-quality machine code across an entire program. Programmers, however, understand a program's algorithms and behavior at a deeper level than a compiler and can expend considerable effort and ingenuity improving small sections of the program. In particular, programmers often consider several procedures simultaneously while writing their code. Compilers typically compile each procedure in isolation and must follow strict conventions governing the use of registers at procedure boundaries. By retaining commonly used values in registers, even across procedure boundaries, programmers can make a program run faster.

Another major advantage of assembly language is the ability to exploit specialized instructions, for example, string copy or pattern-matching instructions. Compilers, in most cases, cannot determine that a program loop can be replaced by a single instruction. However, the programmer who wrote the loop can replace it easily with a single instruction.

In the future, a programmer's advantage over a compiler is likely to become increasingly difficult to maintain as compilation techniques improve and machines' pipelines increase in complexity (Chapter 6).

The final reason to use assembly language is that no high-level language is available on a particular computer. Many older or specialized computers do not have a compiler, so a programmer's only alternative is assembly language.

Drawbacks of Assembly Language

Assembly language has many disadvantages that strongly argue against its widespread use. Perhaps its major disadvantage is that programs written in assembly language are inherently machine-specific and must be totally rewritten to run on another computer architecture. The rapid evolution of computers discussed in Chapter 1 means that architectures become obsolete. An assembly language program remains tightly bound to its original architecture, even after the computer is eclipsed by new, faster, and more cost-effective machines.

Another disadvantage is that assembly language programs are longer than the equivalent programs written in a high-level language. For example, the C program in Figure A.5 is 11 lines long, while the assembly program in Figure A.4 is 31 lines long. In more complex programs, the ratio of assembly to high-level language (its *expansion factor*) can be much larger than the factor of three in this example. Unfortunately, empirical studies have shown that programmers write roughly the same number of lines of code per day in assembly as in high-level languages. This means that programmers are roughly x times more productive in a high-level language, where x is the assembly language expansion factor.

To compound the problem, longer programs are more difficult to read and understand and they contain more bugs. Assembly language exacerbates the problem because of its complete lack of structure. Common programming idioms, such as *if-then* statements and loops, must be built from branches and jumps. The resulting programs are hard to read because the reader must reconstruct every higher-level construct from its pieces and each instance of a statement may be slightly different. For example, look at Figure A.4 and answer these questions: What type of loop is used? What are its lower and upper bounds?

Elaboration: Compilers can produce machine language directly instead of relying on an assembler. These compilers typically execute much faster than those that invoke an assembler as part of compilation. However, a compiler that generates machine language must perform many tasks that an assembler normally handles, such as resolving addresses and encoding instructions as binary numbers. The trade-off is between compilation speed and compiler simplicity.

Elaboration: Despite these considerations, some embedded applications are written in a high-level language. Many of these applications are large and complex programs that must be extremely reliable. Assembly language programs are longer and more difficult to write and read than high-level language programs. This greatly increases the cost of writing an assembly language program and makes it extremely difficult to verify the correctness of this type of program. In fact, these considerations led the Department of Defense, which pays for many complex embedded systems, to develop Ada, a new high-level language for writing embedded systems.

A.2   Assemblers

An assembler translates a file of assembly language statements into a file of binary machine instructions and binary data. The translation process has two major parts. The first step is to find memory locations with labels so the relationship between symbolic names and addresses is known when instructions are translated. The second step is to translate each assembly statement by combining the numeric equivalents of opcodes, register specifiers, and labels into a legal instruction. As shown in Figure A.1, the assembler produces an output file, called an *object file*, which contains the machine instructions, data, and bookkeeping information.

An object file typically cannot be executed because it references procedures or data in other files. A label is *external* (also called *global*) if the labeled object can be referenced from files other than the one in which it is defined. A label is *local* if the object can be used only within the file in which it is defined. In most assemblers, labels are local by default and must be explicitly declared global. Subroutines and global variables require external labels since they are referenced from many files in a program. Local labels hide names that should not be visible to other modules—for example, static functions in C, which can only be called by other functions in the same file. In addition, compiler-generated names—for example, a name for the instruction at the beginning of a loop—are local so the compiler need not produce unique names in every file.

Local and Global Labels

Example

Consider the program in Figure A.4 on page A-7. The subroutine has an external (global) label `main`. It also contains two local labels—`loop` and `str`—that are only visible with this assembly language file. Finally, the routine also contains an unresolved reference to an external label `printf`, which is the library routine that prints values. Which labels in Figure A.4 could be referenced from another file?

Answer

Only global labels are visible outside of a file, so the only label that could be referenced from another file is `main`.

Since the assembler processes each file in a program individually and in isolation, it only knows the addresses of local labels. The assembler depends on another tool, the linker, to combine a collection of object files and libraries into an executable file by resolving external labels. The assembler assists the linker by providing lists of labels and unresolved references.

However, even local labels present an interesting challenge to an assembler. Unlike names in most high-level languages, assembly labels may be used before they are defined. In the example, in Figure A.4, the label `str` is used by the `la` instruction before it is defined. The possibility of a *forward reference*, like this one, forces an assembler to translate a program in two steps: first find all labels and then produce instructions. In the example, when the assembler sees the `la` instruction, it does not know where the word labeled `str` is located or even whether `str` labels an instruction or datum.

An assembler's first pass reads each line of an assembly file and breaks it into its component pieces. These pieces, which are called *lexemes*, are individual words, numbers, and punctuation characters. For example, the line

```
ble $t0, 100, loop
```

contains 6 lexemes: the opcode ble, the register specifier $t0, a comma, the number 100, a comma, and the symbol loop.

If a line begins with a label, the assembler records in its *symbol table* the name of the label and the address of the memory word that the instruction occupies. The assembler then calculates how many words of memory the instruction on the current line will occupy. By keeping track of the instructions' sizes, the assembler can determine where the next instruction goes. To compute the size of a variable-length instruction, like those on the VAX, an assembler has to examine it in detail. Fixed-length instructions, like those on MIPS, on the other hand, require only a cursory examination. The assembler performs a similar calculation to compute the space required for data statements. When the assembler reaches the end of an assembly file, the symbol table records the location of each label defined in the file.

The assembler uses the information in the symbol table during a second pass over the file, which actually produces machine code. The assembler again examines each line in the file. If the line contains an instruction, the assembler combines the binary representations of its opcode and operands (register specifiers or memory address) into a legal instruction. The process is similar to the one used in section 3.4 in Chapter 3. Instructions and data words that reference an external symbol defined in another file cannot be completely assembled (they are unresolved) since the symbol's address is not in the symbol table. An assembler does not complain about unresolved references since the corresponding label is likely to be defined in another file.

The Big Picture

Assembly language is a programming language. Its principal difference from high-level languages such as BASIC, Java, and C is that assembly language provides only a few, simple types of data and control flow. Assembly language programs do not specify the type of value held in a variable. Instead, a programmer must apply the appropriate operations (e.g., integer or floating-point addition) to a value. In addition, in assembly language, programs must implement all control flow with *go to*s. Both factors make assembly language programming for any machine—MIPS or 80x86—more difficult and error-prone than writing in a high-level language.

Elaboration: If an assembler's speed is important, this two-step process can be done in one pass over the assembly file with a technique known as *backpatching*. In its pass over the file, the assembler builds a (possibly incomplete) binary representation of every instruction. If the instruction references a label that has not yet been defined, the assembler records the label and instruction in a table. When a label is defined, the assembler consults this table to find all instructions that contain a forward reference to the label. The assembler goes back and corrects their binary representation to incorporate the address of the label. Backpatching speeds assembly because the assembler only reads its input once. However, it requires an assembler to hold the entire binary representation of a program in memory so instructions can be backpatched. This requirement can limit the size of programs that can be assembled.

Object File Format

Assemblers produce object files. An object file on Unix contains six distinct sections (see Figure A.7):

- The *object file header* describes the size and position of the other pieces of the file.

- The *text segment* contains the machine language code for routines in the source file. These routines may be unexecutable because of unresolved references.

- The *data segment* contains a binary representation of the data in the source file. The data also may be incomplete because of unresolved references to labels in other files.

- The *relocation information* identifies instructions and data words that depend on absolute addresses. These references must change if portions of the program are moved in memory.

- The *symbol table* associates addresses with external labels in the source file and lists unresolved references.

- The *debugging information* contains a concise description of the way in which the program was compiled, so a debugger can find which instruction addresses correspond to lines in a source file and print the data structures in readable form.

Object file header	Text segment	Data segment	Relocation information	Symbol table	Debugging information

FIGURE A.7 Object file. A Unix assembler produces an object file with six distinct sections.

The assembler produces an object file that contains a binary representation of the program and data and additional information to help link pieces of a program. This relocation information is necessary because the assembler does not know which memory locations a procedure or piece of data will occupy after it is linked with the rest of the program. Procedures and data from a file are stored in a contiguous piece of memory, but the assembler does not know where this memory will be located. The assembler also passes some symbol table entries to the linker. In particular, the assembler must record which external symbols are defined in a file and what unresolved references occur in a file.

Elaboration: For convenience, assemblers assume each file starts at the same address (for example, location 0) with the expectation that the linker will *relocate* the code and data when they are assigned locations in memory. The assembler produces *relocation information*, which contains an entry describing each instruction or data word in the file that references an absolute address. On MIPS, only the subroutine call, load, and store instructions reference absolute addresses. Instructions that use PC-relative addressing, such as branches, need not be relocated.

Additional Facilities

Assemblers provide a variety of convenience features that help make assembler programs short and easier to write, but do not fundamentally change assembly language. For example, *data layout directives* allow a programmer to describe data in a more concise and natural manner than its binary representation.

In Figure A.4, the directive

```
.asciiz "The sum from 0 .. 100 is %d\n"
```

stores characters from the string in memory. Contrast this line with the alternative of writing each character as its ASCII value (Figure 3.15 in Chapter 3 describes the ASCII encoding for characters):

```
.byte 84, 104, 101, 32, 115, 117, 109, 32
.byte 102, 114, 111, 109, 32, 48, 32, 46
.byte 46, 32, 49, 48, 48, 32, 105, 115
.byte 32, 37, 100, 10, 0
```

The .asciiz directive is easier to read because it represents characters as letters, not binary numbers. An assembler can translate characters to their binary representation much faster and more accurately than a human. Data layout directives specify data in a human-readable form that the assembler translates to binary. Other layout directives are described in section A.10 on pages A-51–A-53.

String Directive

Example

Define the sequence of bytes produced by this directive:

```
.asciiz "The quick brown fox jumps over the lazy dog"
```

Answer

```
.byte 84,   104, 101, 32,   113, 117, 105, 99
.byte 107, 32,  98,  114, 111, 119, 110, 32
.byte 102, 111, 120, 32,  106, 117, 109, 112
.byte 115, 32,  111, 118, 101, 114, 32,  116
.byte 104, 101, 32,  108, 97,  122, 121, 32
.byte 100, 111, 103, 0
```

Macros are a pattern-matching and replacement facility that provide a simple mechanism to name a frequently used sequence of instructions. Instead of repeatedly typing the same instructions every time they are used, a programmer invokes the macro and the assembler replaces the macro call with the corresponding sequence of instructions. Macros, like subroutines, permit a programmer to create and name a new abstraction for a common operation. Unlike subroutines, however, macros do not cause a subroutine call and return when the program runs since a macro call is replaced by the macro's body when the program is assembled. After this replacement, the resulting assembly is indistinguishable from the equivalent program written without macros.

Macros

Example

As an example, suppose that a programmer needs to print many numbers. The library routine printf accepts a format string and one or more values to print as its arguments. A programmer could print the integer in register $7 with the following instructions:

```
          .data
int_str: .asciiz"%d"
          .text
          la    $a0, int_str  # Load string address
                              # into first arg
          mov   $a1, $7       # Load value into
                              # second arg
          jal   printf        # Call the printf routine
```

The .data directive tells the assembler to store the string in the program's data segment, and the .text directive tells the assembler to store the instructions in its text segment.

However, printing many numbers in this fashion is tedious and produces a verbose program that is difficult to understand. An alternative is to introduce a macro, print_int, to print an integer:

```
        .data
int_str:.asciiz "%d"
        .text
        .macro  print_int($arg)
        la      $a0, int_str # Load string address into
                             # first arg
        mov     $a1, $arg    # Load macro's parameter
                             # ($arg) into second arg
        jal     printf       # Call the printf routine
        .end_macro
print_int($7)
```

The macro has a *formal parameter*, $arg, that names the argument to the macro. When the macro is expanded, the argument from a call is substituted for the formal parameter throughout the macro's body. Then the assembler replaces the call with the macro's newly expanded body. In the first call on print_int, the argument is $7, so the macro expands to the code

```
la  $a0, int_str
mov $a1, $7
jal printf
```

In a second call on print_int, say, print_int($t0), the argument is $t0, so the macro expands to

```
la  $a0, int_str
mov $a1, $t0
jal printf
```

What does the call print_int($a0) expand to?

Answer

```
la  $a0, int_str
mov $a1, $a0
jal printf
```

This example illustrates a drawback of macros. A programmer who uses this macro must be aware that print_int uses register $a0 and so cannot correctly print the value in that register.

Hardware Software Interface

Some assemblers also implement *pseudoinstructions*, which are instructions provided by an assembler but not implemented in hardware. Chapter 3 contains many examples of how the MIPS assembler synthesizes pseudoinstructions and addressing modes from the spartan MIPS hardware instruction set. For example, section 3.5 in Chapter 3 describes how the assembler synthesizes the blt instruction from two other instructions: slt and bne. By extending the instruction set, the MIPS assembler makes assembly language programming easier without complicating the hardware. Many pseudoinstructions could also be simulated with macros, but the MIPS assembler can generate better code for these instructions because it can use a dedicated register ($at) and is able to optimize the generated code.

Elaboration: Assemblers *conditionally assemble* pieces of code, which permits a programmer to include or exclude groups of instructions when a program is assembled. This feature is particularly useful when several versions of a program differ by a small amount. Rather than keep these programs in separate files—which greatly complicates fixing bugs in the common code—programmers typically merge the versions into a single file. Code particular to one version is conditionally assembled, so it can be excluded when other versions of the program are assembled.

If macros and conditional assembly are useful, why do assemblers for Unix systems rarely, if ever, provide them? One reason is that most programmers on these systems write programs in higher-level languages like C. Most of the assembly code is produced by compilers, which find it more convenient to repeat code rather than define macros. Another reason is that other tools on Unix—such as cpp, the C preprocessor, or m4, a general macro processor—can provide macros and conditional assembly for assembly language programs.

A.3 Linkers

Separate compilation permits a program to be split into pieces that are stored in different files. Each file contains a logically related collection of subroutines and data structures that form a *module* in a larger program. A file can be compiled and assembled independently of other files, so changes to one module do not require recompiling the entire program. As we discussed above, separate compilation necessitates the additional step of linking to combine object files from separate modules and fix their unresolved references.

The tool that merges these files is the *linker* (see Figure A.8). It performs three tasks:

■ Searches the program libraries to find library routines used by the program

■ Determines the memory locations that code from each module will occupy and relocates its instructions by adjusting absolute references

■ Resolves references among files

A linker's first task is to ensure that a program contains no undefined labels. The linker matches the external symbols and unresolved references from a program's files. An external symbol in one file resolves a reference from another file if both refer to a label with the same name. Unmatched references mean a symbol was used, but not defined anywhere in the program.

Unresolved references at this stage in the linking process do not necessarily mean a programmer made a mistake. The program could have referenced a library routine whose code was not in the object files passed to the linker. After matching symbols in the program, the linker searches the system's program libraries to find predefined subroutines and data structures that the program

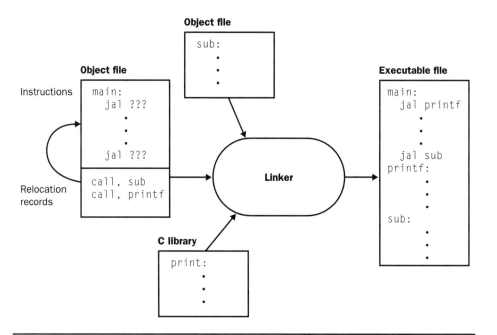

FIGURE A.8   The linker searches a collection of object files and program libraries to find non-local routines used in a program, combines them into a single executable file, and resolves references between routines in different files.

references. The basic libraries contain routines that read and write data, allocate and deallocate memory, and perform numeric operations. Other libraries contain routines to access a database or manipulate terminal windows. A program that references an unresolved symbol that is not in any library is erroneous and cannot be linked. When the program uses a library routine, the linker extracts the routine's code from the library and incorporates it into the program text segment. This new routine, in turn, may depend on other library routines, so the linker continues to fetch other library routines until no external references are unresolved or a routine cannot be found.

If all external references are resolved, the linker next determines the memory locations that each module will occupy. Since the files were assembled in isolation, the assembler could not know where a module's instructions or data will be placed relative to other modules. When the linker places a module in memory, all absolute references must be *relocated* to reflect its true location. Since the linker has relocation information that identifies all relocatable references, it can efficiently find and backpatch these references.

The linker produces an executable file that can run on a computer. Typically, this file has the same format as an object file, except that it contains no unresolved references or relocation information.

A.4   Loading

A program that links without an error can be run. Before being run, the program resides in a file on secondary storage, such as a disk. On Unix systems, the operating system kernel brings a program into memory and starts it running. To start a program, the operating system performs the following steps:

1. Reads the executable file's header to determine the size of the text and data segments.

2. Creates a new address space for the program. This address space is large enough to hold the text and data segments, along with a stack segment (see section A.5).

3. Copies instructions and data from the executable file into the new address space.

4. Copies arguments passed to the program onto the stack.

5. Initializes the machine registers. In general, most registers are cleared, but the stack pointer must be assigned the address of the first free stack location (see section A.5).

6. Jumps to a start-up routine that copies the program's arguments from the stack to registers and calls the program's main routine. If the main routine returns, the start-up routine terminates the program with the exit system call.

A.5   Memory Usage

The next few sections elaborate the description of the MIPS architecture presented earlier in the book. Earlier chapters focused primarily on hardware and its relationship with low-level software. These sections focus primarily on how assembly language programmers use MIPS hardware. These sections describe a set of conventions followed on many MIPS systems. For the most part, the hardware does not impose these conventions. Instead, they represent an agreement among programmers to follow the same set of rules so that software written by different people can work together and make effective use of MIPS hardware.

Systems based on MIPS processors typically divide memory into three parts (see Figure A.9). The first part, near the bottom of the address space (starting at address 400000_{hex}), is the *text segment*, which holds the program's instructions.

The second part, above the text segment, is the *data segment*, which is further divided into two parts. *Static data* (starting at address 10000000_{hex}) contains objects whose size is known to the compiler and whose lifetime—the interval during which a program can access them—is the program's entire execution. For example, in C, global variables are statically allocated since they can be referenced anytime during a program's execution. The linker both assigns static objects to locations in the data segment and resolves references to these objects.

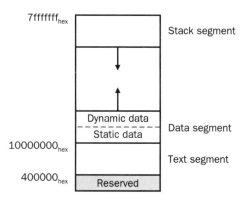

FIGURE A.9   Layout of memory.

Immediately above static data is *dynamic data*. This data, as its name implies, is allocated by the program as it executes. In C programs, the malloc library routine finds and returns a new block of memory. Since a compiler cannot predict how much memory a program will allocate, the operating system expands the dynamic data area to meet demand. As the upward arrow in the figure indicates, malloc expands the dynamic area with the sbrk system call, which causes the operating system to add more pages to the program's virtual address space (see section 7.3 in Chapter 7) immediately above the dynamic data segment.

The third part, the program *stack segment*, resides at the top of the virtual address space (starting at address 7fffffff$_{\text{hex}}$). Like dynamic data, the maximum size of a program's stack is not known in advance. As the program pushes values on the stack, the operating system expands the stack segment down, towards the data segment.

This three-part division of memory is not the only possible one. However, it has two important characteristics: the two dynamically expandable segments are as far apart as possible, and they can grow to use a program's entire address space.

Hardware Software Interface

Because the data segment begins far above the program at address 10000000$_{\text{hex}}$, load and store instructions cannot directly reference data objects with their 16-bit offset fields (see section 3.4 in Chapter 3). For example, to load the word in the data segment at address 10008000$_{\text{hex}}$ into register $v0 requires two instructions:

```
lui   $s0, 0x1000 # 0x1000 means 1000 base 16 or 4096 base 10
lw    $v0, 0x8000($s0) # 0x10000000 + 0x8000 = 0x10008000
```

(The *0x* before a number means that it is a hexadecimal value. For example, 0x8000 is 8000$_{\text{hex}}$ or 32,768$_{\text{ten}}$.)

To avoid repeating the lui instruction at every load and store, MIPS systems typically dedicate a register ($gp) as a *global pointer* to the static data segment. This register contains address 10008000$_{\text{hex}}$, so load and store instructions can use their signed 16-bit offset fields to access the first 64 KB of the static data segment. With this global pointer, we can rewrite the example as a single instruction:

```
lw $v0, 0($gp)
```

Of course, a global pointer register makes addressing locations 10000000$_{\text{hex}}$–10010000$_{\text{hex}}$ faster than other heap locations. The MIPS compiler usually stores *global variables* in this area because these variables have fixed locations and fit better than other global data, such as arrays.

A.6   Procedure Call Convention

Conventions governing the use of registers are necessary when procedures in a program are compiled separately. To compile a particular procedure, a compiler must know which registers it may use and which registers are reserved for other procedures. Rules for using registers are called *register use* or *procedure call conventions*. As the name implies, these rules are, for the most part, conventions followed by software rather than rules enforced by hardware. However, most compilers and programmers try very hard to follow these conventions because violating them causes insidious bugs.

The calling convention described in this section is the one used by the gcc compiler. The native MIPS compiler uses a more complex convention that is slightly faster.

The MIPS CPU contains 32 general-purpose registers that are numbered 0–31. Register $0 always contains the hardwired value 0.

- Registers $at (1), $k0 (26), and $k1 (27) are reserved for the assembler and operating system and should not be used by user programs or compilers.

- Registers $a0–$a3 (4–7) are used to pass the first four arguments to routines (remaining arguments are passed on the stack). Registers $v0 and $v1 (2, 3) are used to return values from functions.

- Registers $t0–$t9 (8–15, 24, 25) are caller-saved registers that are used to hold temporary quantities that need not be preserved across calls (see section 3.6 in Chapter 3).

- Registers $s0–$s7 (16–23) are callee-saved registers that hold long-lived values that should be preserved across calls.

- Register $gp (28) is a global pointer that points to the middle of a 64K block of memory in the static data segment.

- Register $sp (29) is the stack pointer, which points to the first free location on the stack. Register $fp (30) is the frame pointer. The jal instruction writes register $ra (31), the return address from a procedure call. These two registers are explained in the next section.

The two-letter abbreviations and names for these registers—for example $sp for the stack pointer—reflect the registers' intended uses in the procedure call convention. In describing this convention, we will use the names instead of register numbers. The table in Figure A.10 lists the registers and describes their intended uses.

Register name	Number	Usage
$zero	0	constant 0
$at	1	reserved for assembler
$v0	2	expression evaluation and results of a function
$v1	3	expression evaluation and results of a function
$a0	4	argument 1
$a1	5	argument 2
$a2	6	argument 3
$a3	7	argument 4
$t0	8	temporary (not preserved across call)
$t1	9	temporary (not preserved across call)
$t2	10	temporary (not preserved across call)
$t3	11	temporary (not preserved across call)
$t4	12	temporary (not preserved across call)
$t5	13	temporary (not preserved across call)
$t6	14	temporary (not preserved across call)
$t7	15	temporary (not preserved across call)
$s0	16	saved temporary (preserved across call)
$s1	17	saved temporary (preserved across call)
$s2	18	saved temporary (preserved across call)
$s3	19	saved temporary (preserved across call)
$s4	20	saved temporary (preserved across call)
$s5	21	saved temporary (preserved across call)
$s6	22	saved temporary (preserved across call)
$t7	23	saved temporary (preserved across call)
$t8	24	temporary (not preserved across call)
$t9	25	temporary (not preserved across call)
$k0	26	reserved for OS kernel
$k1	27	reserved for OS kernel
$gp	28	pointer to global area
$sp	29	stack pointer
$fp	30	frame pointer
$ra	31	return address (used by function call)

FIGURE A.10   MIPS registers and usage convention.

Procedure Calls

This section describes the steps that occur when one procedure (the *caller*) invokes another procedure (the *callee*). Programmers who write in a high-level language (like C or Pascal) never see the details of how one procedure calls another because the compiler takes care of this low-level bookkeeping. However, assembly language programmers must explicitly implement every procedure call and return.

Most of the bookkeeping associated with a call is centered around a block of memory called a *procedure call frame*. This memory is used for a variety of purposes:

- To hold values passed to a procedure as arguments

- To save registers that a procedure may modify, but which the procedure's caller does not want changed

- To provide space for variables local to a procedure

In most programming languages, procedure calls and returns follow a strict last-in, first-out (LIFO) order, so this memory can be allocated and deallocated on a stack, which is why these blocks of memory are sometimes called *stack frames*.

Figure A.11 shows a typical stack frame. The frame consists of the memory between the frame pointer ($fp), which points to the first word of the frame, and the stack pointer ($sp), which points to the last word the frame. The stack grows down from higher memory addresses, so the frame pointer points above the stack pointer. The executing procedure uses the frame pointer to quickly access values in its stack frame. For example, an argument in the stack frame can be loaded into register $v0 with the instruction

```
lw $v0, 0($fp)
```

A stack frame may be built in many different ways; however, the caller and callee must agree on the sequence of steps. The steps below describe the calling convention used on most MIPS machines. This convention comes into play at three points during a procedure call: immediately before the caller invokes the callee, just as the callee starts executing, and immediately before the callee returns to the caller. In the first part, the caller puts the procedure call arguments in standard places and invokes the callee to do the following:

1. Pass arguments. By convention, the first four arguments are passed in registers $a0–$a3. Any remaining arguments are pushed on the stack and appear at the beginning of the called procedure's stack frame.

2. Save caller-saved registers. The called procedure can use these registers ($a0–$a3 and $t0–$t9) without first saving their value. If the caller expects to use one of these registers after a call, it must save its value before the call.

3. Execute a jal instruction (see section 3.6 of Chapter 3), which jumps to the callee's first instruction and saves the return address in register $ra.

Before a called routine starts running, it must take the following steps to set up its stack frame:

1. Allocate memory for the frame by subtracting the frame's size from the stack pointer.

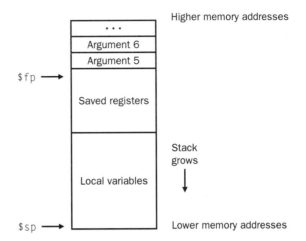

FIGURE A.11   Layout of a stack frame. The frame pointer ($fp) points to the first word in the currently executing procedure's stack frame. The stack pointer ($sp) points to the last word of frame. The first four arguments are passed in registers, so the fifth argument is the first one stored on the stack.

2. Save callee-saved registers in the frame. A callee must save the values in these registers ($s0–$s7, $fp, and $ra) before altering them since the caller expects to find these registers unchanged after the call. Register $fp is saved by every procedure that allocates a new stack frame. However, register $ra only needs to be saved if the callee itself makes a call. The other callee-saved registers that are used also must be saved.

3. Establish the frame pointer by adding the stack frame's size minus four to $sp and storing the sum in register $fp.

Hardware Software Interface

The MIPS register use convention provides callee- and caller-saved registers because both types of registers are advantageous in different circumstances. Callee-saved registers are better used to hold long-lived values, such as variables from a user's program. These registers are only saved during a procedure call if the callee expects to use the register. On the other hand, caller-saved registers are better used to hold short-lived quantities that do not persist across a call, such as immediate values in an address calculation. During a call, the callee can also use these registers for short-lived temporaries.

Finally, the callee returns to the caller by executing the following steps:

1. If the callee is a function that returns a value, place the returned value in register $v0.

2. Restore all callee-saved registers that were saved upon procedure entry.

3. Pop the stack frame by subtracting the frame size from $sp.

4. Return by jumping to the address in register $ra.

Elaboration: A programming language that does not permit recursive procedures—procedures that call themselves either directly or indirectly through a chain of calls—need not allocate frames on a stack. In a nonrecursive language, each procedure's frame may be statically allocated since only one invocation of a procedure can be active at a time. Older versions of Fortran prohibited recursion because statically allocated frames produced faster code on some older machines. However, on load-store architectures like MIPS, stack frames may be just as fast because a frame pointer register points directly to the active stack frame, which permits a single load or store instruction to access values in the frame. In addition, recursion is a valuable programming technique.

Procedure Call Example

As an example, consider the C routine

```
main ()
{
   printf ("The factorial of 10 is %d\n", fact (10));
}

int fact (int n)
{
   if (n < 1)
      return (1);
   else
      return (n * fact (n - 1));
}
```

which computes and prints 10! (the factorial of 10, $10! = 10 \times 9 \times \ldots \times 1$). fact is a recursive routine that computes $n!$ by multiplying n times $(n - 1)!$. The assembly code for this routine illustrates how programs manipulate stack frames.

Upon entry, the routine main creates its stack frame and saves the two callee-saved registers it will modify: $fp and $ra. The frame is larger than required for these two registers because the calling convention requires the minimum size of a stack frame to be 24 bytes. This minimum frame can hold four argument registers ($a0–$a3) and the return address $ra, padded to a double-word boundary (24 bytes). Since main also needs to save $fp, its stack frame must be two words larger (remember: the stack pointer is kept doubleword aligned).

```
        .text
        .globl main
main:
        subu    $sp,$sp,32      # Stack frame is 32 bytes long
        sw      $ra,20($sp)     # Save return address
        sw      $fp,16($sp)     # Save old frame pointer
        addu    $fp,$sp,28      # Set up frame pointer
```

The routine main then calls the factorial routine and passes it the single argument 10. After fact returns, main calls the library routine printf and passes it both a format string and the result returned from fact:

```
        li      $a0,10          # Put argument (10) in $a0
        jal     fact            # Call factorial function

        la      $a0,$LC         # Put format string in $a0
        move    $a1,$v0         # Move fact result to $a1
        jal     printf          # Call the print function
```

Finally, after printing the factorial, main returns. But first, it must restore the registers it saved and pop its stack frame:

```
        lw      $ra,20($sp)     # Restore return address
        lw      $fp,16($sp)     # Restore frame pointer
        addu    $sp,$sp,32      # Pop stack frame
        jr      $ra             # Return to caller

        .rdata
$LC:
        .ascii  "The factorial of 10 is %d\n\000"
```

The factorial routine is similar in structure to main. First, it creates a stack frame and saves the callee-saved registers it will use. In addition to saving $ra and $fp, fact also saves its argument ($a0), which it will use for the recursive call:

```
        .text
fact:
        subu    $sp,$sp,32      # Stack frame is 32 bytes long
        sw      $ra,20($sp)     # Save return address
        sw      $fp,16($sp)     # Save frame pointer
        addu    $fp,$sp,28      # Set up frame pointer
        sw      $a0,0($fp)      # Save argument (n)
```

The heart of the `fact` routine performs the computation from the C program. It tests if the argument is greater than 0. If not, the routine returns the value 1. If the argument is greater than 0, the routine recursively calls itself to compute `fact(n-1)` and multiplies that value times *n*:

```
        lw      $v0,0($fp)      # Load n
        bgtz    $v0,$L2         # Branch if n > 0
        li      $v0,1           # Return 1
        j       $L1             # Jump to code to return

$L2:
        lw      $v1,0($fp)      # Load n
        subu    $v0,$v1,1       # Compute n - 1
        move    $a0,$v0         # Move value to $a0
        jal     fact            # Call factorial function

        lw      $v1,0($fp)      # Load n
        mul     $v0,$v0,$v1     # Compute fact(n-1) * n
```

Finally, the factorial routine restores the callee-saved registers and returns the value in register $v0:

```
$L1:                            # Result is in $v0
        lw      $ra, 20($sp)    # Restore $ra
        lw      $fp, 16($sp)    # Restore $fp
        addu    $sp, $sp, 32    # Pop stack
        j       $ra             # Return to caller
```

Stack in Recursive Procedure

Example

Figure A.12 shows the stack at the call `fact(7)`. `main` runs first, so its frame is deepest on the stack. `main` calls `fact(10)`, whose stack frame is next on the stack. Each invocation recursively invokes `fact` to compute the next-lowest factorial. The stack frames parallel the LIFO order of these calls. What does the stack look like when the call to `fact(10)` returns?

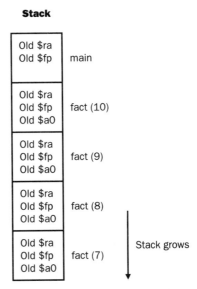

Stack

FIGURE A.12   Stack frames during the call of `fact(7)`.

Answer

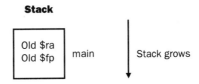

Stack

Elaboration: The difference between the MIPS compiler and the gcc compiler is that the MIPS compiler usually does not use a frame pointer, so this register is available as another callee-saved register, `$s8`. This change saves a couple of instructions in the procedure call and return sequence. However, it complicates code generation because a procedure must access its stack frame with `$sp`, whose value can change during a procedure's execution if values are pushed on the stack.

Another Procedure Call Example

As another example, consider the following routine that computes the `tak` function, which is a widely used benchmark created by Ikuo Takeuchi. This function does not compute anything useful, but is a heavily recursive program that illustrates the MIPS calling convention.

```
int tak (int x, int y, int z)
{
  if (y < x)
    return 1+ tak (tak (x - 1, y, z),
      tak (y - 1, z, x),
      tak (z - 1, x, y));
  else
    return z;
}
int main ()
{
  tak(18, 12, 6);
}
```

The assembly code for this program is below. The tak function first saves its return address in its stack frame and its arguments in callee-saved registers, since the routine may make calls that need to use registers $a0–$a2 and $ra. The function uses callee-saved registers since they hold values that persist over the lifetime of the function, which includes several calls that could potentially modify registers.

```
      .text
      .globl  tak

tak:
      subu    $sp, $sp, 40
      sw      $ra, 32($sp)

      sw      $s0, 16($sp)    # x
      move    $s0, $a0
      sw      $s1, 20($sp)    # y
      move    $s1, $a1
      sw      $s2, 24($sp)    # z
      move    $s2, $a2
      sw      $s3, 28($sp)    # temporary
```

The routine then begins execution by testing if y < x. If not, it branches to label L1, which is below.

```
      bge     $s1, $s0, L1    # if (y < x)
```

If y < x, then it executes the body of the routine, which contains four recursive calls. The first call uses almost the same arguments as its parent:

```
      addu    $a0, $s0, -1
      move    $a1, $s1
      move    $a2, $s2
      jal     tak             # tak (x - 1, y, z)
      move    $s3, $v0
```

Note that the result from the first recursive call is saved in register $s3, so that it can be used latter.

The function now prepares arguments for the second recursive call.

```
addu      $a0, $s1, -1
move      $a1, $s2
move      $a2, $s0
jal       tak          # tak (y - 1, z, x)
```

In the instructions below, the result from this recursive call is saved in register $s0. But, first we need to read, for the last time, the saved value of the first argument from this register.

```
addu      $a0, $s2, -1
move      $a1, $s0
move      $a2, $s1
move      $s0, $v0
jal       tak          # tak (z - 1, x, y)
```

After the three inner recursive calls, we are ready for the final recursive call. After the call, the function's result is in $v0 and control jumps to the function's epilogue.

```
move      $a0, $s3
move      $a1, $s0
move      $a2, $v0
jal       tak          # tak (tak(...), tak(...), tak(...))
j         L2
```

This code at label L1 is the consequent of the *if-then-else* statement. It just moves the value of argument z into the return register and falls into the function epilogue.

```
L1:
   move   $v0, $s2
```

The code below is the function epilogue, which restores the saved registers and returns the function's result to its caller.

```
L2:
   lw       $ra, 32($sp)
   lw       $s0, 16($sp)
   lw       $s1, 20($sp)
   lw       $s2, 24($sp)
   lw       $s3, 28($sp)
   addu     $sp, $sp, 40
   j        $ra
```

The `main` routine calls the `tak` function with its initial arguments, then takes the computed result (7) and prints it using SPIM's system call for printing integers.

```
        .globl  main
main:
        subu    $sp, $sp, 24
        sw      $ra, 16($sp)

        li      $a0, 18
        li      $a1, 12
        li      $a2, 6
        jal     tak                 # tak(18, 12, 6)

        move    $a0, $v0
        li      $v0, 1              # print_int syscall
        syscall

        lw      $ra, 16($sp)
        addu    $sp, $sp, 24
        j       $ra
```

A.7   Exceptions and Interrupts

Section 5.6 of Chapter 5 describes the MIPS exception facility, which responds both to exceptions caused by errors during an instruction's execution and to external interrupts caused by I/O devices. This section describes exception and interrupt handling in more detail. In MIPS processors, a part of the CPU called *coprocessor 0* records the information the software needs to handle exceptions and interrupts. The MIPS simulator SPIM does not implement all of coprocessor 0's registers, since many are not useful in a simulator or are part of the memory system, which SPIM does not implement. However, SPIM does provide the following coprocessor 0 registers:

Register name	Register number	Usage
BadVAddr	8	register containing the memory address at which memory reference occurred
Status	12	interrupt mask and enable bits
Cause	13	exception type and pending interrupt bits
EPC	14	register containing address of instruction that caused exception

These four registers are part of coprocessor 0's register set and are accessed by the `lwc0`, `mfc0`, `mtc0`, and `swc0` instructions. After an exception, register EPC contains the address of the instruction that was executing when the exception occurred. If the instruction made a memory access that caused the exception, register BadVAddr contains the referenced memory location's address. The two other registers contain many fields and are described below.

Figure A.13 shows the Status register fields implemented by the MIPS simulator SPIM. The interrupt mask field contains a bit for each of the five hardware and three software possible interrupt levels. A bit that is 1 allows interrupts at that level. A bit that is 0 disables interrupts at that level. The low 6 bits of the Status register implement a three-deep stack for the kernel/user and interrupt enable bits. The kernel/user bit is 0 if a program was in the kernel when an exception occurred and 1 if it was running in user mode. If the interrupt enable bit is 1, interrupts are allowed. If it is 0, they are disabled. When an interrupt occurs, these 6 bits are shifted left by 2 bits, so the current bits become the previous bits and the previous bits become the old bits (the old bits are discarded). The current bits are both set to 0 so the interrupt handler runs in the kernel with interrupts disabled.

Figure A.14 shows the Cause register fields implemented by SPIM. The five pending interrupt bits correspond to the five interrupt levels. A bit becomes 1 when an interrupt at its level has occurred but has not been serviced. The Exception code register describes the cause of an exception with the following codes:

Number	Name	Description
0	INT	external interrupt
4	ADDRL	address error exception (load or instruction fetch)
5	ADDRS	address error exception (store)
6	IBUS	bus error on instruction fetch
7	DBUS	bus error on data load or store
8	SYSCALL	syscall exception
9	BKPT	breakpoint exception
10	RI	reserved instruction exception
12	OVF	arithmetic overflow exception

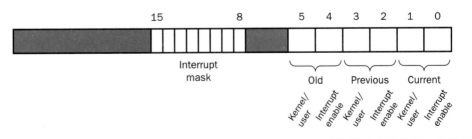

FIGURE A.13   The Status register.

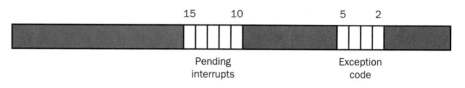

FIGURE A.14 The Cause register. In actual MIPS processors, this register contains additional fields that report: whether the instruction that caused the exception executed in a branch's delay slot, which coprocessor caused the exception, or that a software interrupt is pending.

Exceptions and interrupts cause a MIPS processor to jump to a piece of code, at address 80000080_{hex} (in the kernel, not user address space), called an *interrupt handler*. This code examines the exception's cause and jumps to an appropriate point in the operating system. The operating system responds to an exception either by terminating the process that caused the exception or by performing some action. A process that causes an error, such as executing an unimplemented instruction, is killed by the operating system. On the other hand, exceptions such as page faults are requests from a process to the operating system to perform a service, such as bringing in a page from disk. The operating system processes these requests and resumes the process. The final type of exceptions are interrupts from external devices. These generally cause the operating system to move data to or from an I/O device and resume the interrupted process. The code in the example below is a simple interrupt handler, which invokes a routine to print a message at each exception (but not interrupts). This code is similar to the interrupt handler used by the SPIM simulator, except that it does not print an error message to report an exception.

Interrupt Handler

Example

The interrupt handler first saves registers $a0 and $a1, which it later uses to pass arguments. The interrupt handler cannot store the old values from these registers on the stack, as would an ordinary routine, because the cause of the interrupt might have been a memory reference that used a bad value (such as 0) in the stack pointer. Instead the interrupt handler stores these registers in two memory locations (save0 and save1). If the interrupt routine itself could be interrupted, two locations would not be enough since the second interrupt would overwrite values saved during the first interrupt. However, this simple interrupt handler finishes running before it enables interrupts, so the problem does not arise.

```
.ktext 0x80000080
sw $a0, save0    # Handler is not re-entrant and can't use
sw $a1, save1    # stack to save $a0, $a1
                 # Don't need to save $k0/$k1
```

The interrupt handler then moves the Cause and EPC registers into CPU registers. The Cause and EPC registers are not part of the CPU register set. Instead, they are registers in coprocessor 0, which is the part of the CPU that handles interrupts. The instruction mfc0 $k0, $13 moves coprocessor 0's register 13 (the Cause register) into CPU register $k0. Note that the interrupt handler need not save registers $k0 and $k1 because user programs are not supposed to use these registers. The interrupt handler uses the value from the Cause register to test if the exception was caused by an interrupt (see the preceding table). If so, the exception is ignored. If the exception was not an interrupt, the handler calls print_excp to print a warning message.

```
mfc0    $k0, $13       # Move Cause into $k0
mfc0    $k1, $14       # Move EPC into $k1

sgt     $v0, $k0, 0x44 # Ignore interrupts
bgtz    $v0, done

mov     $a0, $k0       # Move Cause into $a0
mov     $a1, $k1       # Move EPC into $a1
jal     print_excp     # Print exception error message
```

Before returning, the interrupt handler restores registers $a0 and $a1. It then executes the rfe (return from exception) instruction, which restores the previous interrupt mask and kernel/user bits in the Status register. This switches the processor state back to what it was before the exception and prepares to resume program execution. The interrupt handler then returns to the program by jumping to the instruction following the one that caused the exception.

```
done:
        lw    $a0, save0
        lw    $a1, save1
        addiu $k1, $k1, 4 # Do not reexecute
                          # faulting instruction
        rfe               # Restore interrupt state
        jr    $k1


        .kdata
save0:  .word 0
save1:  .word 0
```

Elaboration: On real MIPS processors, the return from an interrupt handler is more complex. The `rfe` instruction must execute in the delay slot of the `jr` instruction (see elaboration on page 444 of Chapter 6) that returns to the user program so that no interrupt-handler instruction executes with the user program's interrupt mask and kernel/user bits. In addition, the interrupt handler cannot always jump to the instruction following EPC. For example, if the instruction that caused the exception was in a branch instruction's delay slot (see Chapter 6), the next instruction may not be the following instruction in memory.

A.8 Input and Output

SPIM simulates one I/O device: a memory-mapped terminal. When a program is running, SPIM connects its own terminal (or a separate console window in the X-window version xspim) to the processor. A MIPS program running on SPIM can read the characters that you type. In addition, if the MIPS program writes characters to the terminal, they appear on SPIM's terminal or console window. One exception to this rule is control-C: this character is not passed to the program, but instead causes SPIM to stop and return to command mode. When the program stops running (for example, because you typed control-C or because the program hit a breakpoint), the terminal is reconnected to spim so you can type SPIM commands. To use memory-mapped I/O (see below), spim or xspim must be started with the -mapped_io flag.

The terminal device consists of two independent units: a *receiver* and a *transmitter*. The receiver reads characters from the keyboard. The transmitter writes characters to the display. The two units are completely independent. This means, for example, that characters typed at the keyboard are not automatically echoed on the display. Instead, a program must explicitly echo a character by reading it from the receiver and writing it to the transmitter.

A program controls the terminal with four memory-mapped device registers, as shown in Figure A.15. "Memory-mapped" means that each register appears as a special memory location. The *Receiver Control register* is at location ffff0000$_{hex}$. Only two of its bits are actually used. Bit 0 is called "ready": if it is 1, it means that a character has arrived from the keyboard but has not yet been read from the Receiver Data register. The ready bit is read-only: writes to it are ignored. The ready bit changes from 0 to 1 when a character is typed at the keyboard, and it changes from 1 to 0 when the character is read from the Receiver Data register.

Bit 1 of the Receiver Control register is the keyboard "interrupt enable." This bit may be both read and written by a program. The interrupt enable is initially 0. If it is set to 1 by a program, the terminal requests an interrupt at level 0 whenever the ready bit is 1. However, for the interrupt to affect the processor,

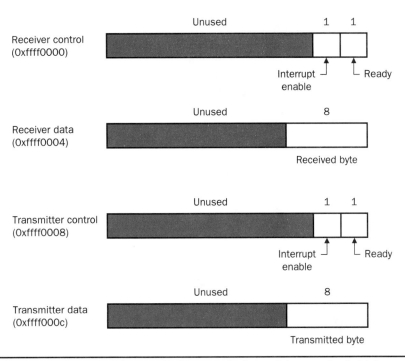

FIGURE A.15 The terminal is controlled by four device registers, each of which appears as a memory location at the given address. Only a few bits of these registers are actually used. The others always read as 0s and are ignored on writes.

interrupts must also be enabled in the Status register (see section A.7). All other bits of the Receiver Control register are unused.

The second terminal device register is the *Receiver Data register* (at address ffff0004$_{hex}$). The low-order 8 bits of this register contain the last character typed at the keyboard. All other bits contain 0s. This register is read-only and changes only when a new character is typed at the keyboard. Reading the Receiver Data register resets the ready bit in the Receiver Control register to 0.

The third terminal device register is the *Transmitter Control register* (at address ffff0008$_{hex}$). Only the low-order 2 bits of this register are used. They behave much like the corresponding bits of the Receiver Control register. Bit 0 is called "ready" and is read-only. If this bit is 1, the transmitter is ready to accept a new character for output. If it is 0, the transmitter is still busy writing the previous character. Bit 1 is "interrupt enable" and is readable and writable. If this bit is set to 1, then the terminal requests an interrupt on level 1 whenever the ready bit is 1.

The final device register is the *Transmitter Data register* (at address ffff000c$_{hex}$). When a value is written into this location, its low-order 8 bits (i.e., an ASCII character as in Figure 3.15 in Chapter 3) are sent to the console. When the Transmitter Data register is written, the ready bit in the Transmitter Control register is reset to 0. This bit stays 0 until enough time has elapsed to transmit the character to the terminal; then the ready bit becomes 1 again. The Transmitter Data register should only be written when the ready bit of the Transmitter Control register is 1. If the transmitter is not ready, writes to the Transmitter Data register are ignored (the write appears to succeed but the character is not output).

Real computers require time to send characters over the serial lines that connect terminals to computers. These time lags are simulated by SPIM. For example, after the transmitter starts to write a character, the transmitter's ready bit becomes 0 for a while. SPIM measures time in instructions executed, not in real clock time. This means that the transmitter does not become ready again until the processor executes a certain number of instructions. If you stop the machine and look at the ready bit, it will not change. However, if you let the machine run, the bit eventually changes back to 1.

A.9   SPIM

SPIM is a software simulator that runs programs written for MIPS R2000/R3000 processors. SPIM's name is just MIPS spelled backwards. SPIM can read and immediately execute assembly language files or (on some systems) MIPS executable files. SPIM is a self-contained system for running MIPS programs. It contains a debugger and provides a few operating system-like services. SPIM is much slower than a real computer (100 or more times). However, its low cost and wide availability cannot be matched by real hardware!

An obvious question is, Why use a simulator when many people have workstations that contain MIPS chips that are significantly faster than SPIM? One reason is that these workstations are not universally available. Another reason is rapid progress toward new and faster computers may render these machines obsolete (see Chapter 1). The current trend is to make computers faster by executing several instructions concurrently. This trend makes architectures more difficult to understand and program. The MIPS architecture may be the epitome of a simple, clean RISC machine.

In addition, simulators can provide a better environment for programming than an actual machine because they can detect more errors and provide more features than an actual computer. For example, SPIM has an X-window interface that works better than most debuggers on the actual machines.

Finally, simulators are a useful tool in studying computers and the programs that run on them. Because they are implemented in software, not silicon, simulators can be easily modified to add new instructions, build new systems such as multiprocessors, or simply to collect data.

Simulation of a Virtual Machine

The MIPS architecture, like that of many RISC computers, is difficult to program directly because of delayed branches, delayed loads, and restricted address modes. This difficulty is tolerable since these computers were designed to be programmed in high-level languages and present an interface appropriate for compilers rather than assembly language programmers. A good part of the programming complexity results from delayed instructions. A *delayed branch* requires two cycles to execute (see elaborations on pages 444 and 502 of Chapter 6). In the second cycle, the instruction immediately following the branch executes. This instruction can perform useful work that normally would have been done before the branch. It can also be a nop (no operation). Similarly, *delayed loads* require two cycles so the instruction immediately following a load cannot use the value loaded from memory (see section 6.2 of Chapter 6).

MIPS wisely chose to hide this complexity by having its assembler implement a *virtual machine*. This virtual computer appears to have nondelayed branches and loads and a richer instruction set than the actual hardware. The assembler *reorganizes* (rearranges) instructions to fill the delay slots. The virtual computer also provides *pseudoinstructions*, which appear as real instructions in assembly language programs. The hardware, however, knows nothing about pseudoinstructions, so the assembler must translate them into equivalent sequences of actual, machine instructions. For example, the MIPS hardware only provides instructions to branch when a register is equal to or not equal to 0. Other conditional branches, such as when one register is greater than another, are synthesized by comparing the two registers and branching when the result of the comparison is true (nonzero).

By default, SPIM simulates the richer virtual machine. However, it can also simulate the bare hardware. Below, we describe the virtual machine and only mention in passing features that do not belong to the actual hardware. In doing so, we follow the convention of MIPS assembly language programmers (and compilers), who routinely use the extended machine. (For a description of the real machines, see Gerry Kane and Joe Heinrich, *MIPS RISC Architecture*, Prentice Hall, Englewood Cliff, NJ, 1992.)

Getting Started with SPIM

The rest of this appendix contains a complete and rather detailed description of SPIM. Many details should never concern you; however, the sheer volume of information can obscure the fact that SPIM is a simple, easy-to-use program. This section contains a quick tutorial on SPIM that should enable you to load, debug, and run simple MIPS programs.

SPIM comes in multiple versions. One version, called `spim`, is a command-line-driven program and requires only an alphanumeric terminal to display it. It operates like most programs of this type: you type a line of text, hit the `return` key, and `spim` executes your command.

A fancier version, called `xspim`, runs in the X-windows environment of the Unix system and therefore requires a bit-mapped display to run it. `xspim`, however, is a much easier program to learn and use because its commands are always visible on the screen and because it continually displays the machine's registers. Another version, `PCspim`, is compatible with Windows 3.1, Windows 95, and Windows NT. The Unix, Windows, and DOS versions of SPIM are available through *www.mkp.com/cod2e.htm*.

Since many people use and prefer `xspim`, this section only discusses that program. If you plan to use any version of `spim`, do not skip this section. Read it first and then look at the "SPIM Command-Line Options" section (starting on page A-44) to see how to accomplish the same thing with `spim` commands. Check *www.mkp.com/cod2e.htm* for more information on using `PCspim`.

To start `xspim`, type `xspim` in response to your system's prompt (%):

```
% xspim
```

On your system, `xspim` may be kept in an unusual place, and you may need to execute a command first to add that place to your search path. Your instructor should tell you how to do this.

When `xspim` starts up, it pops up a large window on your screen (see Figure A.16). The window is divided into five panes:

- The top pane is called the *register display*. It shows the values of all registers in the MIPS CPU and FPU. This display is updated whenever your program stops running.

- The pane below contains the *control buttons* to operate `xspim`. These buttons are discussed below, so we can skip the details for now.

- The next pane, called the *text segments*, displays instructions both from your program and the system code that is loaded automatically when `xspim` starts running. Each instruction is displayed on a line that looks like

```
[0x00400000] 0x8fa40000 lw $4, 0($29)  ; 89: lw $a0, 0($sp)
```

The first number on the line, in square brackets, is the hexadecimal memory address of the instruction. The second number is the instruction's numerical encoding, again displayed as a hexadecimal number. The third item is the instruction's mnemonic description. Everything following the semicolon is the actual line from your assembly file that produced the instruction. The number 89 is the line number in that file. Sometimes nothing is on the line after the semicolon. This means that the instruction was produced by SPIM as part of translating a pseudoinstruction.

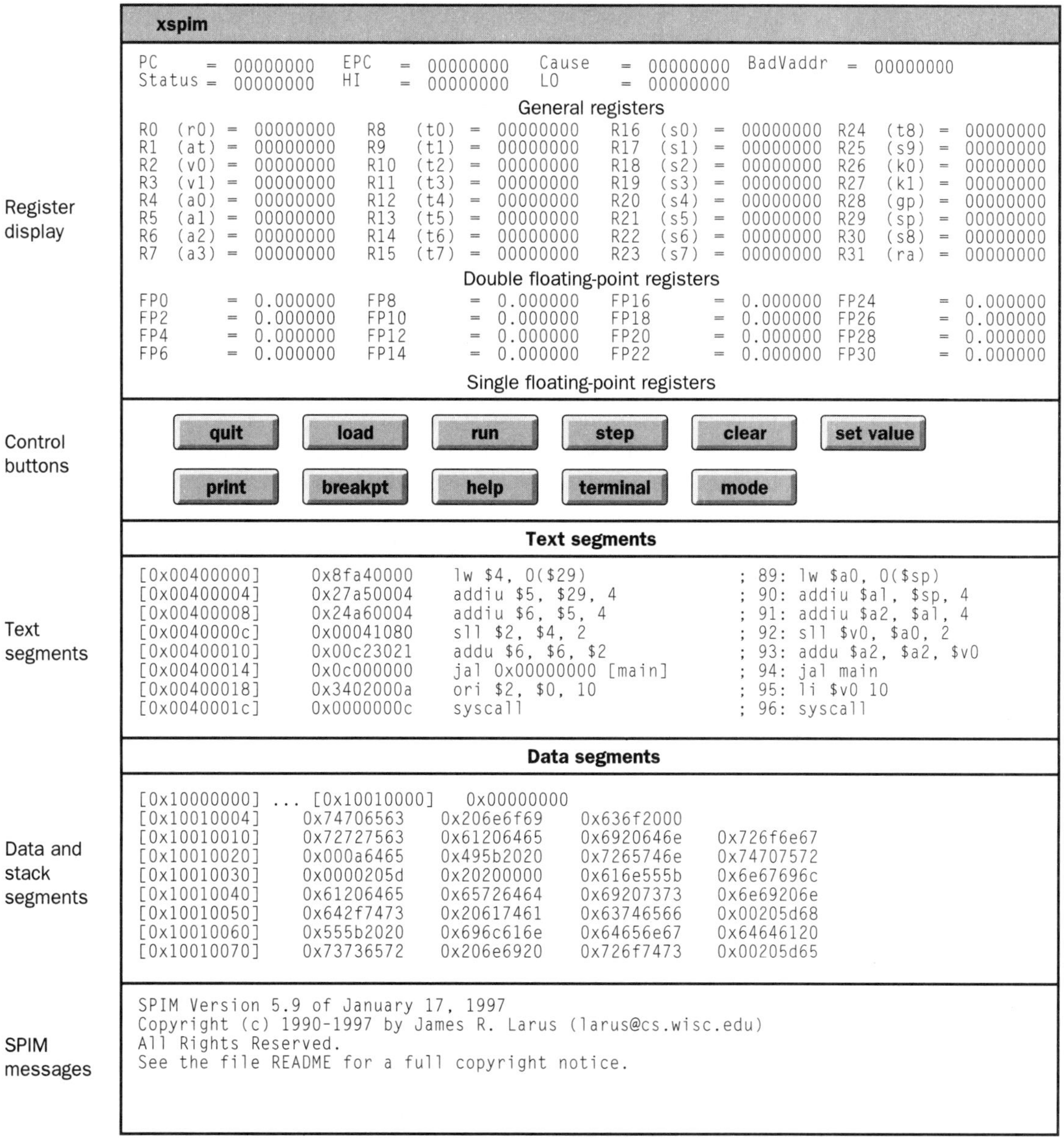

xspim

```
PC     = 00000000   EPC = 00000000   Cause = 00000000   BadVaddr = 00000000
Status = 00000000   HI  = 00000000   LO    = 00000000
                         General registers
R0  (r0) = 00000000   R8  (t0) = 00000000   R16 (s0) = 00000000   R24 (t8) = 00000000
R1  (at) = 00000000   R9  (t1) = 00000000   R17 (s1) = 00000000   R25 (s9) = 00000000
R2  (v0) = 00000000   R10 (t2) = 00000000   R18 (s2) = 00000000   R26 (k0) = 00000000
R3  (v1) = 00000000   R11 (t3) = 00000000   R19 (s3) = 00000000   R27 (k1) = 00000000
R4  (a0) = 00000000   R12 (t4) = 00000000   R20 (s4) = 00000000   R28 (gp) = 00000000
R5  (a1) = 00000000   R13 (t5) = 00000000   R21 (s5) = 00000000   R29 (sp) = 00000000
R6  (a2) = 00000000   R14 (t6) = 00000000   R22 (s6) = 00000000   R30 (s8) = 00000000
R7  (a3) = 00000000   R15 (t7) = 00000000   R23 (s7) = 00000000   R31 (ra) = 00000000
                     Double floating-point registers
FP0  = 0.000000   FP8  = 0.000000   FP16 = 0.000000   FP24 = 0.000000
FP2  = 0.000000   FP10 = 0.000000   FP18 = 0.000000   FP26 = 0.000000
FP4  = 0.000000   FP12 = 0.000000   FP20 = 0.000000   FP28 = 0.000000
FP6  = 0.000000   FP14 = 0.000000   FP22 = 0.000000   FP30 = 0.000000
                      Single floating-point registers
```

Register display

Control buttons

```
 quit     load     run     step    clear   set value

 print   breakpt   help   terminal  mode
```

Text segments

```
[0x00400000]   0x8fa40000   lw $4, 0($29)           ; 89: lw $a0, 0($sp)
[0x00400004]   0x27a50004   addiu $5, $29, 4         ; 90: addiu $a1, $sp, 4
[0x00400008]   0x24a60004   addiu $6, $5, 4          ; 91: addiu $a2, $a1, 4
[0x0040000c]   0x00041080   sll $2, $4, 2            ; 92: sll $v0, $a0, 2
[0x00400010]   0x00c23021   addu $6, $6, $2          ; 93: addu $a2, $a2, $v0
[0x00400014]   0x0c000000   jal 0x00000000 [main]   ; 94: jal main
[0x00400018]   0x3402000a   ori $2, $0, 10           ; 95: li $v0 10
[0x0040001c]   0x0000000c   syscall                  ; 96: syscall
```

Text segments

Data segments

```
[0x10000000] ... [0x10010000]   0x00000000
[0x10010004]   0x74706563   0x206e6f69   0x636f2000
[0x10010010]   0x72727563   0x61206465   0x6920646e   0x726f6e67
[0x10010020]   0x000a6465   0x495b2020   0x7265746e   0x74707572
[0x10010030]   0x0000205d   0x20200000   0x616e555b   0x6e67696c
[0x10010040]   0x61206465   0x65726464   0x69207373   0x6e69206e
[0x10010050]   0x642f7473   0x20617461   0x63374656   0x00205d68
[0x10010060]   0x555b2020   0x696c616e   0x64656e67   0x64646120
[0x10010070]   0x73736572   0x206e6920   0x726f7473   0x00205d65
```

Data and stack segments

SPIM messages

```
SPIM Version 5.9 of January 17, 1997
Copyright (c) 1990-1997 by James R. Larus (larus@cs.wisc.edu)
All Rights Reserved.
See the file README for a full copyright notice.
```

FIGURE A.16 SPIM's X-window interface: xspim.

- The next pane, called the *data and stack segments*, displays the data loaded into your program's memory and the data on the program's stack.

- The bottom pane is the *SPIM messages* that xspim uses to write messages. This is where error messages appear.

Let's see how to load and run a program. The first thing to do is to click on the load button (the second one in the first row of buttons) with the left mouse key. Your click tells xspim to pop up a small prompt window that contains a box and two or three buttons. Move your mouse so the cursor is over the box, and type the name of your file of assembly code. Then click on the button labeled assembly file within that prompt window. If you change your mind, click on the button labeled abort command, and xspim gets rid of the prompt window. When you click on assembly file, xspim gets rid of the prompt window, then loads your program and redraws the screen to display its instructions and data. Now move the mouse to put the cursor over the scrollbar to the left of the text segments, and click the left mouse button on the white part of this scrollbar. A click scrolls the text pane down so you can find all the instructions in your program.

To run your program, click on the run button in xspim's control button pane. It pops up a prompt window with two boxes and two buttons. Most of the time, these boxes contain the correct values to run your program, so you can ignore them and just click on ok. This button tells xspim to run your program. Notice that when your program is running, xspim blanks out the register display pane because the registers are continually changing. You can always tell whether xspim is running by looking at this pane. If you want to stop your program, make sure the mouse cursor is somewhere over xspim's window and type control-C. This causes xspim to pop up a prompt window with two buttons. Before doing anything with this prompt window, you can look at registers and memory to find out what your program was doing. When you understand what happened, you can either continue the program by clicking on continue or stop your program by clicking on abort command.

If your program reads or writes from the terminal, xspim pops up another window called the *console*. All characters that your program writes appear on the console, and everything that you type as input to your program should be typed in this window.

Suppose your program does not do what you expect. What can you do? SPIM has two features that help debug your program. The first, and perhaps the most useful, is single-stepping, which allows you to run your program an instruction at a time. Click on the button labeled step and another prompt window pops up. This prompt window contains two boxes and three buttons. The first box asks for the number of instructions to step every time you click the mouse. Most of the time, the default value of 1 is a good choice. The other box asks for arguments to pass to the program when it starts running. Again, most of the time you can ignore this box because it contains an appropriate value. The button labeled step runs your program for the number of instructions in the top box. If that number is 1, xspim executes the next instruction in your program, updates the display, and returns control to you. The button labeled continue stops single-stepping and continues running your program. Finally, abort command stops single-stepping and leaves your program stopped.

What do you do if your program runs for a long time before the bug arises? You could single-step until you get to the bug, but that can take a long time, and it is easy to get so bored and inattentive that you step past the problem. A better alternative is to use a *breakpoint*, which tells xspim to stop your program immediately before it executes a particular instruction. Click on the button in the second row of buttons marked breakpoints. The xspim program pops up a prompt window with one box and many buttons. Type in this box the address of the instruction at which you want to stop. Or, if the instruction has a global label, you can just type the name of the label. Labeled breakpoints are a particularly convenient way to stop at the first instruction of a procedure. To actually set the breakpoint, click on add. You can then run your program.

When SPIM is about to execute the breakpointed instruction, xspim pops up a prompt with the instruction's address and two buttons. The continue button continues running your program and abort command stops your program. If you want to delete a breakpoint, type in its address and click on delete. Finally, list tells xspim to print (in the bottom pane) a list of all breakpoints that are set.

Single-stepping and setting breakpoints will probably help you find a bug in your program quickly. How do you fix it? Go back to the editor that you used to create your program and change it. To run the program again, you need a fresh copy of SPIM, which you get in two ways. Either you can exit from xspim by clicking on the quit button, or you can clear xspim and reload your program. If you reload your program, you *must* clear the memory, so remnants of your previous program do not interfere with your new program. To do this, click on the button labeled clear. Hold the left mouse key down and a two-item menu will pop up. Move the mouse so the cursor is over the item labeled memory & registers and release the key. This causes xspim to clear its memory and registers and return the processor to the state it was in when xspim first started. You can now load and run your new program.

The other buttons in xspim perform functions that are occasionally useful. When you are more comfortable with xspim, you should look at the description below to see what they do and how they can save you time and effort.

SPIM Command-Line Options

Both Unix versions of SPIM—spim, the terminal version, and xspim, the X version—accept the following command-line options:

-bare	Simulate a bare MIPS machine without pseudoinstructions or the additional addressing modes provided by the assembler. Implies -quiet.
-asm	Simulate the virtual MIPS machine provided by the assembler. This is the default.
-pseudo	Allow the input assembly code to contain pseudoinstructions. This is the default.
-nopseudo	Do not allow pseudoinstructions in the input assembly code.
-notrap	Do not load the standard exception handler and start-up code. This exception handler handles exceptions. When an exception occurs, SPIM jumps to location 80000080_{hex}, which must contain code to service the exception. In addition, this file contains start-up code that invokes the routine main. Without the start-up routine, SPIM begins execution at the instruction labeled __start.
-trap	Load the standard exception handler and start-up code. This is the default.
-noquiet	Print a message when an exception occurs. This is the default.
-quiet	Do not print a message at exceptions.
-nomapped_io	Disable the memory-mapped I/O facility (see section A.8). This is the default.
-mapped_io	Enable the memory-mapped I/O facility (see section A.8). Programs that use SPIM syscalls (see section on "System Calls," page A-48) to read from the terminal *cannot* also use memory-mapped I/O.
-file	Load and execute the assembly code in the file.
-execute	Load and execute the code in the MIPS executable file *a.out*. This command is only available when SPIM runs on a system containing a MIPS processor.

-s <seg> size   Sets the initial size of memory segment *seg* to be *size* bytes.
                The memory segments are named: text, data, stack,
                ktext, and kdata. The text segment contains instruc-
                tions from a program. The data segment holds the pro-
                gram's data. The stack segment holds its runtime stack.
                In addition to running a program, SPIM also executes sys-
                tem code that handles interrupts and exceptions. This code
                resides in a separate part of the address space called the
                kernel. The ktext segment holds this code's instructions,
                and kdata holds its data. There is no kstack segment
                since the system code uses the same stack as the program.
                For example, the pair of arguments -sdata 2000000 starts
                the user data segment at 2,000,000 bytes.

-l <seg> size   Sets the limit on how large memory segment *seg* can grow
                to be *size* bytes. The memory segments that can grow are
                data, stack, and kdata.

Terminal Interface (spim)

The simpler Unix version of SPIM is called spim. It does not require a bit-
mapped display and can be run from any terminal. Although spim may be
more difficult to learn, it operates just like xspim and provides the same functionality.

The spim terminal interface provides the following commands:

exit   Exit the simulator.

read "file"   Read *file* of assembly language into SPIM. If the file has
                already been read into SPIM, the system must be cleared
                (see reinitialize, below) or global labels will be multi-
                ply defined.

load "file"   Synonym for read.

execute "a.out"   Read the MIPS executable file *a.out* into SPIM. This
                command is only available when SPIM runs on a system
                containing a MIPS processor.

run <addr>   Start running a program. If the optional address *addr* is
                provided, the program starts at that address. Otherwise,
                the program starts at the global label __start, which is
                usually the default start-up code that calls the routine at
                the global label main.

step \<N\>   Step the program for *N* (default: 1) instructions. Print instructions as they execute.

continue   Continue program execution without stepping.

print $N   Print register *N*.

print $fN   Print floating point register *N*.

print addr   Print the contents of memory at address *addr*.

print_sym   Print the names and addresses of the global labels known to SPIM. Labels are local by default and become global only when declared in a .globl assembler directive (see "Assember Syntax" section on page A-51).

reinitialize Clear the memory and registers.

breakpoint addr   Set a breakpoint at address *addr*. *addr* can be either a memory address or symbolic label.

delete addr   Delete all breakpoints at address *addr*.

list   List all breakpoints.

.   Rest of line is an assembly instruction that is stored in memory.

\<nl\>   A newline reexecutes previous command.

?   Print a help message.

Most commands can be abbreviated to their unique prefix (e.g., ex, re, l, ru, s, p). More dangerous commands, such as reinitialize, require a longer prefix.

X-Window Interface (xspim)

The tutorial, "Getting Started with SPIM" (page A-39), explains the most common xspim commands. However, xspim has other commands that are occasionally useful. This section provides a complete list of the commands.

The X version of SPIM, xspim, looks different but operates in the same manner as spim. The X-window has five panes (see Figure A.16). The top pane displays the registers. These values are continually updated, except while a program is running.

The next pane contains buttons that control the simulator:

quit   Exit from the simulator.

load   Read a source or executable file into SPIM.

run	Start the program running.
step	Single-step a program.
clear	Reinitialize registers or memory.
set value	Set the value in a register or memory location.
print	Print the value in a register or memory location.
breakpoint	Set or delete a breakpoint or list all breakpoints.
help	Print a help message.
terminal	Raise or hide the console window.
mode	Set SPIM operating modes.

The next two panes display the memory. The top one shows instructions from the user and kernel text segments. (These instructions are real—not pseudo—MIPS instructions. SPIM translates assembler pseudoinstructions into one to three MIPS instructions. Each source instruction appears as a comment on the first instruction into which it is translated.) The first few instructions in the text segment are the default start-up code (__start) that loads argc and argv into registers and invokes the main routine. The lower of these two panes displays the data and stack segments. Both panes are updated as a program executes.

The bottom pane is used to display SPIM messages. It does not display output from a program. When a program reads or writes, its I/O appears in a separate window, called the *console*, which pops up when needed.

Surprising Features

Although SPIM faithfully simulates the MIPS computer, SPIM is a simulator and certain things are not identical to an actual computer. The most obvious differences are that instruction timing and the memory systems are not identical. SPIM does not simulate caches or memory latency, nor does it accurately reflect floating-point operation or multiply and divide instruction delays.

Another surprise (which occurs on the real machine as well) is that a pseudoinstruction expands to several machine instructions. When you single-step or examine memory, the instructions that you see are different from the source program. The correspondence between the two sets of instructions is fairly simple since SPIM does not reorganize instructions to fill delay slots.

Byte Order

Processors can number bytes within a word so the byte with the lowest number is either the leftmost or rightmost one. The convention used by a machine is called its *byte order*. MIPS processors can operate with either *big-endian* or *little-endian* byte order. For example, in a big-endian machine, the directive .byte 0, 1, 2, 3 would result in a memory word containing

Byte #			
0	1	2	3

while in a little-endian machine, the word would contain

Byte #			
3	2	1	0

SPIM operates with both byte orders. SPIM's byte order is the same as the byte order of the underlying machine that runs the simulator. For example, on a DECstation 3100 or Intel 80x86, SPIM is little-endian, while on a Macintosh or Sun SPARC, SPIM is big-endian.

System Calls

SPIM provides a small set of operating-system-like services through the system call (syscall) instruction. To request a service, a program loads the system call code (see Figure A.17) into register $v0 and arguments into registers $a0–$a3 (or $f12 for floating-point values). System calls that return values put their results in register $v0 (or $f0 for floating-point results). For example, the following code prints "the answer = 5":

```
        .data
str:
        .asciiz  "the answer = "
        .text
        li       $v0, 4    # system call code for print_str
        la       $a0, str  # address of string to print
        syscall            # print the string

        li       $v0, 1    # system call code for print_int
        li       $a0, 5    # integer to print
        syscall            # print it
```

The print_int system call is passed an integer and prints it on the console. print_float prints a single floating-point number; print_double prints a double precision number; and print_string is passed a pointer to a null-terminated string, which it writes to the console.

Service	System call code	Arguments	Result
print_int	1	$a0 = integer	
print_float	2	$f12 = float	
print_double	3	$f12 = double	
print_string	4	$a0 = string	
read_int	5		integer (in $v0)
read_float	6		float (in $f0)
read_double	7		double (in $f0)
read_string	8	$a0 = buffer, $a1 = length	
sbrk	9	$a0 = amount	address (in $v0)
exit	10		

FIGURE A.17   System services.

The system calls read_int, read_float, and read_double read an entire line of input up to and including the newline. Characters following the number are ignored. read_string has the same semantics as the Unix library routine fgets. It reads up to $n-1$ characters into a buffer and terminates the string with a null byte. If fewer than $n-1$ characters are on the current line, read_string reads up to and including the newline and again null-terminates the string. *Warning:* Programs that use these syscalls to read from the terminal should not use memory-mapped I/O (see section A.8).

Finally, sbrk returns a pointer to a block of memory containing n additional bytes, and exit stops a program from running.

MIPS R2000 Assembly Language

A MIPS processor consists of an integer processing unit (the CPU) and a collection of coprocessors that perform ancillary tasks or operate on other types of data such as floating-point numbers (see Figure A.18). SPIM simulates two coprocessors. Coprocessor 0 handles exceptions, interrupts, and the virtual memory system. SPIM simulates most of the first two and entirely omits details of the memory system. Coprocessor 1 is the floating-point unit. SPIM simulates most aspects of this unit.

Addressing Modes

MIPS is a load-store architecture, which means that only load and store instructions access memory. Computation instructions operate only on values in registers. The bare machine provides only one memory-addressing mode: c(rx), which uses the sum of the immediate c and register rx as the address. The virtual machine provides the following addressing modes for load and store instructions:

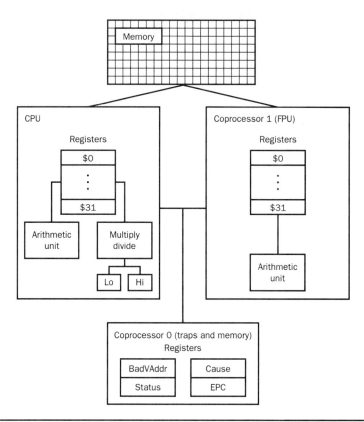

FIGURE A.18   MIPS R2000 CPU and FPU.

Format	Address computation
(register)	contents of register
imm	immediate
imm (register)	immediate + contents of register
label	address of label
label ± imm	address of label + or – immediate
label ± imm (register)	address of label + or – (immediate + contents of register)

Most load and store instructions operate only on aligned data. A quantity is *aligned* if its memory address is a multiple of its size in bytes. Therefore, a half-word object must be stored at even addresses and a full word object must be stored at addresses that are a multiple of four. However, MIPS provides some instructions to manipulate unaligned data (lwl, lwr, swl, and swr).

Elaboration: The MIPS assembler (and SPIM) synthesizes the more complex addressing modes by producing one or more instructions before the load or store to compute a complex address. For example, suppose that the label `table` referred to memory location 0x10000004 and a program contained the instruction

```
ld $a0, table + 4($a1)
```

The assembler would translate this instruction into the instructions

```
lui $at, 4096
addu $at, $at, $a1
lw $a0, 8($at)
```

The first instruction loads the upper bits of the label's address into register `$at`, which the register that the assemble reserves for its own use. The second instruction adds the contents of register `$a1` to the label's partial address. Finally, the load instruction uses the hardware address mode to add the sum of the lower bits of the label's address and the offset from the original instruction to the value in register `$at`.

Assembler Syntax

Comments in assembler files begin with a sharp sign (#). Everything from the sharp sign to the end of the line is ignored.

Identifiers are a sequence of alphanumeric characters, underbars (_), and dots (.) that do not begin with a number. Instruction opcodes are reserved words that *cannot* be used as identifiers. Labels are declared by putting them at the beginning of a line followed by a colon, for example:

```
        .data
item:   .word 1
        .text
        .globl main  # Must be global
main:   lw    $t0, item
```

Numbers are base 10 by default. If they are preceded by *0x*, they are interpreted as hexadecimal. Hence, 256 and 0x100 denote the same value.

Strings are enclosed in doublequotes ("). Special characters in strings follow the C convention:

- newline\n
- tab \t
- quote\"

SPIM supports a subset of the MIPS assembler directives:

.align n   Align the next datum on a 2^n byte boundary. For example, .align 2 aligns the next value on a word boundary. .align 0 turns off automatic alignment of .half, .word, .float, and .double directives until the next .data or .kdata directive.

.ascii str   Store the string *str* in memory, but do not null-terminate it.

.asciiz str   Store the string *str* in memory and null-terminate it.

.byte b1,..., bn   Store the *n* values in successive bytes of memory.

.data <addr>   Subsequent items are stored in the data segment. If the optional argument *addr* is present, subsequent items are stored starting at address *addr*.

.double d1, ..., dn   Store the *n* floating-point double precision numbers in successive memory locations.

.extern sym size   Declare that the datum stored at *sym* is *size* bytes large and is a global label. This directive enables the assembler to store the datum in a portion of the data segment that is efficiently accessed via register $gp.

.float f1,..., fn   Store the *n* floating-point single precision numbers in successive memory locations.

.globl sym   Declare that label *sym* is global and can be referenced from other files.

.half h1, ..., hn   Store the *n* 16-bit quantities in successive memory halfwords.

.kdata <addr>   Subsequent data items are stored in the kernel data segment. If the optional argument *addr* is present, subsequent items are stored starting at address *addr*.

.ktext <addr>   Subsequent items are put in the kernel text segment. In SPIM, these items may only be instructions or words (see the .word directive below). If the optional argument *addr* is present, subsequent items are stored starting at address *addr*.

.set noat and .set at   The first directive prevents SPIM from complaining about subsequent instructions that use register $at. The second directive reenables the warning. Since pseudoinstructions expand into code that uses register $at, programmers must be very careful about leaving values in this register.

.space n   Allocate *n* bytes of space in the current segment (which must be the data segment in SPIM).

.text <addr>   Subsequent items are put in the user text segment. In SPIM, these items may only be instructions or words (see the .word directive below). If the optional argument *addr* is present, subsequent items are stored starting at address *addr*.

> .word w1,..., wn   Store the *n* 32-bit quantities in successive memory words.

SPIM does not distinguish various parts of the data segment (.data, .rdata, and .sdata).

Encoding MIPS Instructions

Figure A.19 explains how a MIPS instruction is encoded in a binary number. Each column contains instruction encodings for a field (a contiguous group of bits) from an instruction. The numbers at the left margin are values for a field. For example, the j opcode has a value of 2 in the opcode field. The text at the top of a column names a field and specifies which bits it occupies in an instruction. For example, the op field is contained in bits 26–31 of an instruction. This field encodes most instructions. However, some groups of instructions use additional fields to distinguish related instructions. For example, the different floating-point instructions are specified by bits 0–5. The arrows from the first column show which opcodes use these additional fields.

Instruction Format

The rest of this appendix describes both the instructions implemented by actual MIPS hardware and the pseudoinstructions provided by the MIPS assembler. The two types of instructions are easily distinguished. Actual instructions depict the fields in their binary representation. For example, in

Addition (with overflow)

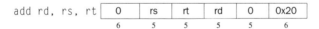

the add instruction consists of six fields. Each field's size in bits is the small number below the field. This instruction begins with 6 bits of 0s. Register specifiers begin with an *r*, so the next field is a 5-bit register specifier called rs. This is the same register that is the second argument in the symbolic assembly at the left of this line. Another common field is imm_{16}, which is a 16-bit immediate number.

Pseudoinstructions follow roughly the same conventions, but omit instruction encoding information. For example:

Multiply (without overflow)

    mul rdest, rsrc1, src2   *pseudoinstruction*

In pseudoinstructions, rdest and rsrc are registers and src2 is either a register or an immediate value. In general, the assembler and SPIM translate a more general form of an instruction (e.g., add $v1, $a0, 0x55) to a specialized form (e.g., addi $v1, $a0, 0x55).

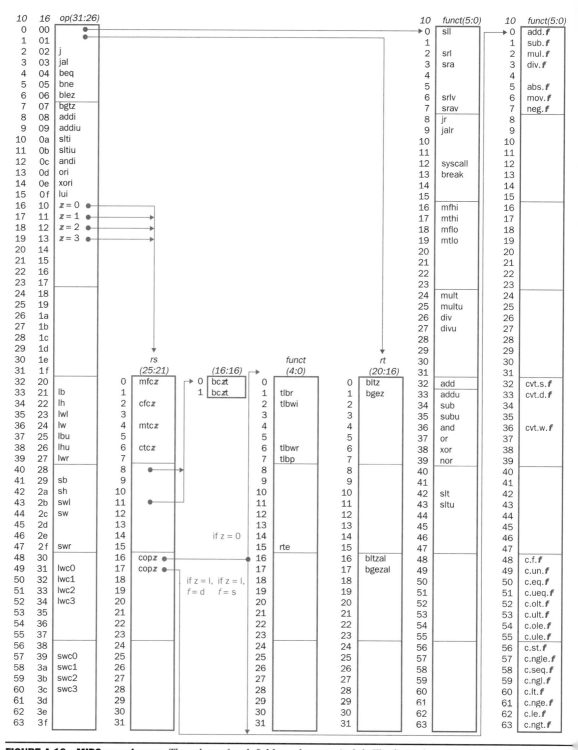

FIGURE A.19 MIPS opcode map. The values of each field are shown to its left. The first column shows the values in base 10 and the second shows base 16 for the op field (bits 31 to 26) in the third column. This op field completely specifies the MIPS operation except for 6 op values: 0, 1, 16, 17, 18, and 19. These operations are determined by other fields, identified by pointers. The last field (funct) uses "*f*" to mean "s" if rs = 16 and op = 17 or "d" if rs = 17 and op = 17. The second field (rs) uses "*z*" to mean "0", "1", "2", or "3" if op = 16, 17, 18, or 19, respectively. If rs = 16, the operation is specified elsewhere: if *z* = 0, the operations are specified in the fourth field (bits 4 to 0); if *z* = 1, then the operations are in the last field with *f* = s. If rs = 17 and *z* = 1, then the operations are in the last field with *f* = d. *(page A-54)*

Arithmetic and Logical Instructions

Absolute value

abs rdest, rsrc   *pseudoinstruction*

Put the absolute value of register rsrc in register rdest.

Addition (with overflow)

add rd, rs, rt

0	rs	rt	rd	0	0x20
6	5	5	5	5	6

Addition (without overflow)

addu rd, rs, rt

0	rs	rt	rd	0	0x21
6	5	5	5	5	6

Put the sum of registers rs and rt into register rd.

Addition immediate (with overflow)

addi rt, rs, imm

8	rs	rt	imm
6	5	5	16

Addition immediate (without overflow)

addiu rt, rs, imm

9	rs	rt	imm
6	5	5	16

Put the sum of register rs and the sign-extended immediate into register rt.

AND

and rd, rs, rt

0	rs	rt	rd	0	0x24
6	5	5	5	5	6

Put the logical AND of registers rs and rt into register rd.

AND immediate

andi rt, rs, imm

0xc	rs	rt	imm
6	5	5	16

Put the logical AND of register rs and the zero-extended immediate into register rt.

Divide (with overflow)

div rs, rt

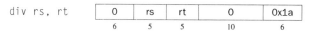

0	rs	rt	0	0x1a
6	5	5	10	6

Divide (without overflow)

divu rs, rt

0	rs	rt	0	0x1b
6	5	5	10	6

Divide register rs by register rt. Leave the quotient in register lo and the remainder in register hi. Note that if an operand is negative, the remainder is unspecified by the MIPS architecture and depends on the convention of the machine on which SPIM is run.

Divide (with overflow)

div rdest, rsrc1, src2   *pseudoinstruction*

Divide (without overflow)

divu rdest, rsrc1, src2   *pseudoinstruction*

Put the quotient of register rsrc1 and src2 into register rdest.

Multiply

mult rs, rt

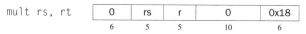

0	rs	r	0	0x18
6	5	5	10	6

Unsigned multiply

multu rs, rt

0	rs	r	0	0x19
6	5	5	10	6

Multiply registers rs and rt. Leave the low-order word of the product in register lo and the high-order word in register hi.

Multiply (without overflow)

mul rdest, rsrc1, src2   *pseudoinstruction*

Multiply (with overflow)

mulo rdest, rsrc1, src2   *pseudoinstruction*

Unsigned multiply (with overflow)

`mulou rdest, rsrc1, src2`   *pseudoinstruction*

Put the product of register `rsrc1` and `src2` into register `rdest`.

Negate value (with overflow)

`neg rdest, rsrc`   *pseudoinstruction*

Negate value (without overflow)

`negu rdest, rsrc`   *pseudoinstruction*

Put the negative of register `rsrc` into register `rdest`.

NOR

`nor rd, rs, rt`

0	rs	rt	rd	0	0x27
6	5	5	5	5	6

Put the logical NOR of registers `rs` and `rt` into register `rd`.

NOT

`not rdest, rsrc`   *pseudoinstruction*

Put the bitwise logical negation of register `rsrc` into register `rdest`.

OR

`or rd, rs, rt`

0	rs	rt	rd	0	0x25
6	5	5	5	5	6

Put the logical OR of registers `rs` and `rd` into register `rt`.

OR immediate

`ori rt, rs, imm`

0xd	rs	rt	imm
6	5	5	16

Put the logical OR of register `rs` and the zero-extended immediate into register `rt`.

Remainder

`rem rdest, rsrc1, rsrc2`   *pseudoinstruction*

Unsigned remainder

```
remu rdest, rsrc1, rsrc2
```
                                        pseudoinstruction

Put the remainder of register `rsrc1` divided by register `rsrc2` into register `rdest`. Note that if an operand is negative, the remainder is unspecified by the MIPS architecture and depends on the convention of the machine on which SPIM is run.

Shift left logical

```
sll rd, rt, shamt
```

0	rs	rt	rd	shamt	0
6	5	5	5	5	6

Shift left logical variable

```
sllv rd, rt, rs
```

0	rs	rt	rd	0	4
6	5	5	5	5	6

Shift right arithmetic

```
sra rd, rt, shamt
```

0	Rs	Rt	Rd	shamt	3
6	5	5	5	5	6

Shift right arithmetic variable

```
srav rd, rt, rs
```

0	rs	rt	rd	0	7
6	5	5	5	5	6

Shift right logical

```
srl rd, rt, shamt
```

0	rs	rt	rd	shamt	2
6	5	5	5	5	6

Shift right logical variable

```
srlv rd, rt, rs
```

0	rs	rt	rd	0	6
6	5	5	5	5	6

Shift register `rt` left (right) by the distance indicated by immediate `sa` or the register `rs` and put the result in register `rd`.

Rotate left

```
rol rdest, rsrc1, rsrc2
```
                                        pseudoinstruction

Rotate right

```
ror rdest, rsrc1, rsrc2          pseudoinstruction
```

Rotate register `rsrc1` left (right) by the distance indicated by `rsrc2` and put the result in register `rdest`.

Subtract (with overflow)

```
sub rd, rs, rt
```

0	rs	rt	rd	0	0x22
6	5	5	5	5	6

Subtract (without overflow)

```
subu rd, rs, rt
```

0	rs	rt	rd	0	0x23
6	5	5	5	5	6

Put the difference of registers `rs` and `rt` into register `rd`.

Exclusive OR

```
xor rd, rs, rt
```

0	rs	rt	rd	0	0x26
6	5	5	5	5	6

Put the logical XOR of registers `rs` and `rt` into register `rd`.

XOR immediate

```
xori rt, rs, imm
```

0xe	rs	rt	Imm
6	5	5	16

Put the logical XOR of register `rs` and the zero-extended immediate into register `rt`.

Constant-Manipulating Instructions

Load upper immediate

```
lui rt, imm
```

0xf	0	rt	imm
6	5	5	16

Load the lower halfword of the immediate `imm` into the upper halfword of register `rt`. The lower bits of the register are set to 0.

Load immediate

```
li rdest, imm                    pseudoinstruction
```

Move the immediate `imm` into register `rdest`.

Comparison Instructions

Set less than

slt rd, rs, rt

0	rs	rt	rd	0	0x2a
6	5	5	5	5	6

Set less than unsigned

sltu rd, rs, rt

0	rs	rt	rd	0	0x2b
6	5	5	5	5	6

Set register rd to 1 if register rs is less than rt, and to 0 otherwise.

Set less than immediate

slti rd, rs, imm

0xa	rs	rd	imm
6	5	5	16

Set less than unsigned immediate

sltiu rd, rs, imm

0xb	rs	rd	imm
6	5	5	16

Set register rd to 1 if register rs is less than the sign-extended immediate, and to 0 otherwise.

Set equal

seq rdest, rsrc1, rsrc2   *pseudoinstruction*

Set register rdest to 1 if register rsrc1 equals rsrc2, and to 0 otherwise.

Set greater than equal

sge rdest, rsrc1, rsrc2   *pseudoinstruction*

Set greater than equal unsigned

sgeu rdest, rsrc1, rsrc2   *pseudoinstruction*

Set register rdest to 1 if register rsrc1 is greater than or equal to rsrc2, and to 0 otherwise.

Set greater than

sgt rdest, rsrc1, rsrc2   *pseudoinstruction*

Set greater than unsigned

sgtu rdest, rsrc1, rsrc2   *pseudoinstruction*

Set register rdest to 1 if register rsrc1 is greater than rsrc2, and to 0 otherwise.

Set less than equal

sle rdest, rsrc1, rsrc2   *pseudoinstruction*

Set less than equal unsigned

sleu rdest, rsrc1, rsrc2   *pseudoinstruction*

Set register rdest to 1 if register rsrc1 is less than or equal to rsrc2, and to 0 otherwise.

Set not equal

sne rdest, rsrc1, rsrc2   *pseudoinstruction*

Set register rdest to 1 if register rsrc1 is not equal to rsrc2, and to 0 otherwise.

Branch Instructions

Branch instructions use a signed 16-bit instruction *offset* field; hence they can jump $2^{15} - 1$ *instructions* (not bytes) forward or 2^{15} instructions backwards. The *jump* instruction contains a 26-bit address field.

In the descriptions below, the offsets are not specified. Instead, the instructions branch to a label. This is the form used in most assembly language programs because the distance between instructions is difficult to calculate when pseudoinstructions expand into several real instructions.

Branch instruction

b label   *pseudoinstruction*

Unconditionally branch to the instruction at the label.

Branch coprocessor *z* true

`bczt label`

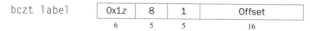

Branch coprocessor *z* false

`bczf label`

Conditionally branch the number of instructions specified by the offset if *z*'s condition flag is true (false). *z* is 0, 1, 2, or 3. The floating-point unit is $z = 1$.

Branch on equal

`beq Rs, Rt, label`

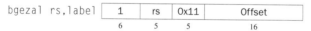

Conditionally branch the number of instructions specified by the offset if register `rs` equals `rt`.

Branch on greater than equal zero

`bgez rs, label`

1	Rs	1	Offset
6	5	5	16

Conditionally branch the number of instructions specified by the offset if register `rs` is greater than or equal to 0.

Branch on greater than equal zero and link

`bgezal rs,label`

1	rs	0x11	Offset
6	5	5	16

Conditionally branch the number of instructions specified by the offset if register `rs` is greater than or equal to 0. Save the address of the next instruction in register 31.

Branch on greater than zero

`bgtz rs, label`

7	rs	0	Offset
6	5	5	16

Conditionally branch the number of instructions specified by the offset if register `rs` is greater than 0.

Branch on less than equal zero

blez rs, label	6	rs	0	Offset
	6	5	5	16

Conditionally branch the number of instructions specified by the offset if register rs is less than or equal to 0.

Branch on less than and link

bltzal rs, label	1	rs	0x10	Offset
	6	5	5	16

Conditionally branch the number of instructions specified by the offset if register rs is less than 0. Save the address of the next instruction in register 31.

Branch on less than zero

bltz rs, label	1	rs	0	Offset
	6	5	5	16

Conditionally branch the number of instructions specified by the offset if register rs is less than 0.

Branch on not equal

bne rs,label	5	rs	rt	Offset
	6	5	5	16

Conditionally branch the number of instructions specified by the offset if register rs is not equal to rt.

Branch on equal zero

beqz rsrc, label   *pseudoinstruction*

Conditionally branch to the instruction at the label if rsrc1 equals 0.

Branch on greater than equal

bge rsrc1,rsrc2, label   *pseudoinstruction*

Branch on greater than equal unsigned

bgeu rsrc1, rsrc2, label   *pseudoinstruction*

Conditionally branch to the instruction at the label if register rsrc1 is greater than or equal to rsrc2.

Branch on greater than

```
bgt rsrc1, src2, label
```
pseudoinstruction

Branch on greater than unsigned

```
bgtu rsrc1, rrc2, label
```
pseudoinstruction

Conditionally branch to the instruction at the label if register rsrc1 is greater than src2.

Branch on less than equal

```
ble rsrc1, src2, label
```
pseudoinstruction

Branch on less than equal unsigned

```
bleu rsrc1, src2, label
```
pseudoinstruction

Conditionally branch to the instruction at the label if register rsrc1 is less than or equal to src2.

Branch on less than

```
blt rsrc1, rsrc2, label
```
pseudoinstruction

Branch on less than unsigned

```
bltu rsrc1, rsrc2, label
```
pseudoinstruction

Conditionally branch to the instruction at the label if register rsrc1 is less than rsrc2.

Branch on not equal zero

```
bnez rsrc, label
```
pseudoinstruction

Conditionally branch to the instruction at the label if register rsrc is not equal to 0.

Jump Instructions

Jump

j target

Unconditionally jump to the instruction at target.

Jump and link

jal target

Unconditionally jump to the instruction at target. Save the address of the next instruction in register rd.

Jump and link register

jalr rs, rd

Unconditionally jump to the instruction whose address is in register rs. Save the address of the next instruction in register rd (which defaults to 31).

Jump register

jr rs

Unconditionally jump to the instruction whose address is in register rs.

Load Instructions

Load address

la rdest, address   *pseudoinstruction*

Load computed *address*—not the contents of the location—into register rdest.

Load byte

lb rt, address

Load unsigned byte

`lbu rt, address` | 0x24 | rs | rt | Offset |

| 6 | 5 | 5 | 16 |

Load the byte at *address* into register `rt`. The byte is sign-extended by `lb`, but not by `lbu`.

Load halfword

`lh rt, address` | 0x21 | rs | rt | Offset |

| 6 | 5 | 5 | 16 |

Load unsigned halfword

`lhu rt, address` | 0x25 | rs | rt | Offset |

| 6 | 5 | 5 | 16 |

Load the 16-bit quantity (halfword) at *address* into register `tt`. The halfword is sign-extended by `lh`, but not by `lhu`.

Load word

`lw rt, address` | 0x23 | rs | rt | Offset |

| 6 | 5 | 5 | 16 |

Load the 32-bit quantity (word) at *address* into register `rt`.

Load word coprocessor

`lwcz rt, address` | 0x3z | rs | rt | Offset |

| 6 | 5 | 5 | 16 |

Load the word at *address* into register `rt` of coprocessor z (0–3). The floating-point unit is z = 1.

Load word left

`lwl rt, address` | 0x22 | rs | rt | Offset |

| 6 | 5 | 5 | 16 |

Load word right

`lwr Rt, address` | 0x23 | Rs | Rt | Offset |

| 6 | 5 | 5 | 16 |

Load the left (right) bytes from the word at the possibly unaligned *address* into register `rt`.

Load doubleword

```
ld rdest, address                    pseudoinstruction
```

Load the 64-bit quantity at *address* into registers `rdest` and `rdest + 1`.

Unaligned load halfword

```
ulh rdest, address                   pseudoinstruction
```

Unaligned load halfword unsigned

```
ulhu rdest, address                  pseudoinstruction
```

Load the 16-bit quantity (halfword) at the possibly unaligned *address* into register `rdest`. The halfword is sign-extended by `ulh`, but not `ulhu`.

Unaligned load word

```
ulw rdest, address                   pseudoinstruction
```

Load the 32-bit quantity (word) at the possibly unaligned *address* into register `rdest`.

Store Instructions

Store byte

```
sb rt, address
```

0x28	rs	rt	Offset
6	5	5	16

Store the low byte from register `rt` at *address*.

Store halfword

```
sh rt, address
```

0x29	rs	rt	Offset
6	5	5	16

Store the low halfword from register `rt` at *address*.

Store word

```
sw rt, address
```

0x2b	rs	rt	Offset
6	5	5	16

Store the word from register `rt` at *address*.

Store word coprocessor

swcz rt, address

0x3(1-z)	rs	rt	Offset
6	5	5	16

Store the word from register rt of coprocessor z at *address*. The floating point unit is z = 1.

Store word left

swl rt, address

0x2a	rs	rt	Offset
6	5	5	16

Store word right

swr rt, address

0x2e	rs	rt	Offset
6	5	5	16

Store the left (right) bytes from register rt at the possibly unaligned *address*.

Store doubleword

sd rsrc, address   *pseudoinstruction*

Store the 64-bit quantity in registers rsrc and rsrc + 1 at *address*.

Unaligned store halfword

ush rsrc, address   *pseudoinstruction*

Store the low halfword from register rsrc at the possibly unaligned *address*.

Unaligned store word

usw rsrc, address   *pseudoinstruction*

Store the word from register rsrc at the possibly unaligned *address*.

Data Movement Instructions

Move

move rdest, rsrc   *pseudoinstruction*

Move register rsrc to rdest.

Move from hi

mfhi rd

0	0	rd	0	0x10
6	10	5	5	6

Move from lo

```
mflo rd
```

0	0	rd	0	0x12
6	10	5	5	6

The multiply and divide unit produces its result in two additional registers, hi and lo. These instructions move values to and from these registers. The multiply, divide, and remainder pseudoinstructions that make this unit appear to operate on the general registers move the result after the computation finishes.

Move the hi (lo) register to register rd.

Move to hi

```
mthi
```

0	rs	0	0x11
6	5	15	6

Move to lo

```
mtlo
```

0	rs	0	0x13
6	5	15	6

Move register Rs to the hi (lo) register.

Move from coprocessor z

```
mfcz rt, rd
```

0x1z	0	rt	rd	0
6	5	5	5	11

Coprocessors have their own register sets. These instructions move values between these registers and the CPU's registers.

Move coprocessor z's register rd to CPU register rt. The floating-point unit is coprocessor z = 1.

Move double from coprocessor 1

```
mfc1.d rdest, frsrc1
```
                                                    pseudoinstruction

Move floating-point registers frsrc1 and frsrc1 + 1 to CPU registers rdest and rdest + 1.

Move to coprocessor z

```
mtcz rd, rt
```

0x1z	4	rt	rd	0
6	5	5	5	11

Move CPU register rt to coprocessor z's register rd.

Floating-Point Instructions

The MIPS has a floating-point coprocessor (numbered 1) that operates on single precision (32-bit) and double precision (64-bit) floating-point numbers. This coprocessor has its own registers, which are numbered $f0–$f31. Because these registers are only 32 bits wide, two of them are required to hold doubles, so only floating-point registers with even numbers can hold double precision values.

Values are moved in or out of these registers one word (32 bits) at a time by lwc1, swc1, mtc1, and mfc1 instructions described above or by the l.s, l.d, s.s, and s.d pseudoinstructions described below. The flag set by floating-point comparison operations is read by the CPU with its bc1t and bc1f instructions.

In the actual instructions below, bits 21–26 are 0 for single precision and 1 for double precision. In the pseudoinstructions below, fdest is a floating-point register (e.g., $f2).

Floating-point absolute value double

abs.d fd, fs
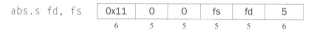

Floating-point absolute value single

abs.s fd, fs

0x11	0	0	fs	fd	5
6	5	5	5	5	6

Compute the absolute value of the floating-point double (single) in register fs and put it in register fd.

Floating-point addition double

add.d fd, fs, ft

Floating-point addition single

add.s fd, fs, ft
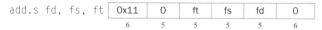

Compute the sum of the floating-point doubles (singles) in registers fs and ft and put it in register fd.

Compare equal double

c.eq.d fs, ft

0x11	1	ft	fs	fd	FC	2
6	5	5	5	5	2	4

Compare equal single

c.eq.s fs, ft

0x11	0	ft	fs	fd	FC	2
6	5	5	5	5	2	4

Compare the floating-point double in register fs against the one in ft and set the floating-point condition flag true if they are equal. Use the bc1t or bc1f instructions to test the value of this flag.

Compare less than equal double

c.le.d fs, ft

0x11	1	ft	fs	0	FC	2
6	5	5	5	5	2	4

Compare less than equal single

c.le.s fs, ft

0x11	0	ft	fs	0	FC	2
6	5	5	5	5	2	4

Compare the floating-point double in register fs against the one in ft and set the floating-point condition flag true if the first is less than or equal to the second. Use the bc1t or bc1f instructions to test the value of this flag.

Compare less than double

c.lt.d fs, ft

0x11	1	ft	fs	0	FC	0xc
6	5	5	5	5	2	4

Compare less than single

c.lt.s fs, ft

0x11	0	ft	fs	0	FC	0xc
6	5	5	5	5	2	4

Compare the floating-point double in register fs against the one in ft and set the condition flag true if the first is less than the second. Use the bc1t or bc1f instructions to test the value of this flag.

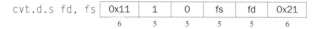

Convert single to double

cvt.d.s fd, fs

0x11	1	0	fs	fd	0x21
6	5	5	5	5	6

Convert integer to double

cvt.d.w fd, fs	0x11	0	0	fs	fd	0x21
	6	5	5	5	5	6

Convert the single precision floating-point number or integer in register fs to a double precision number and put it in register fd.

Convert double to single

cvt.s.d fd, fs	0x11	1	0	Fs	Fd	0x20
	6	5	5	5	5	6

Convert integer to single

cvt.s.w fd, fs	0x11	0	0	fs	fd	0x20
	6	5	5	5	5	6

Convert the double precision floating-point number or integer in register fs to a single precision number and put it in register fd.

Convert double to integer

cvt.w.d fd, fs	0x11	1	0	fs	fd	0x24
	6	5	5	5	5	6

Convert single to integer

cvt.w.s fd, fs	0x11	0	0	fs	fd	0x24
	6	5	5	5	5	6

Convert the double or single precision floating-point number in register fs to an integer and put it in register fd.

Floating-point divide double

div.d fd, fs, ft	0x11	1	ft	fs	fd	3
	6	5	5	5	5	6

Floating-point divide single

div.s fd, fs, ft	0x11	0	ft	fs	fd	3
	6	5	5	5	5	6

Compute the quotient of the floating-point doubles (singles) in registers fs and ft and put it in register fd.

Load floating-point double

```
l.d fdest, address
```
                            pseudoinstruction

Load floating-point single

```
l.s fdest, address
```
                            pseudoinstruction

Load the floating-point double (single) at address into register fdest.

Move floating-point double

```
mov.d fd, fs
```

0x11	1	0	fs	fd	6
6	5	5	5	5	6

Move floating-point single

```
mov.s fd, fs
```

0x11	0	0	fs	fd	6
6	5	5	5	5	6

Move the floating-point double (single) from register fs to register fd.

Floating-point multiply double

```
mul.d fd, fs, ft
```

0x11	1	ft	fs	fd	2
6	5	5	5	5	6

Floating-point multiply single

```
mul.s fd, fs, ft
```

0x11	0	ft	fs	fd	2
6	5	5	5	5	6

Compute the product of the floating-point doubles (singles) in registers fs and ft and put it in register fd.

Negate double

```
neg.d fd, fs
```

0x11	1	ft	fs	fd	7
6	5	5	5	5	6

Negate single

```
neg.s fd, fs
```

0x11	0	ft	fs	fd	7
6	5	5	5	5	6

Negate the floating-point double (single) in register fs and put it in register fd.

Store floating-point double

```
s.d fdest, address
```
　　　　　　　　　　pseudoinstruction

Store floating-point single

```
s.s fdest, address
```
　　　　　　　　　　pseudoinstruction

Store the floating-point double (single) in register `dest` at `address`.

Floating-point subtract double

```
sub.d fd, fs, ft
```

0x11	1	ft	fs	fd	1
6	5	5	5	5	6

Floating-point subtract single

```
sub.s fd, fs, ft
```

0x11	0	ft	fs	fd	1
6	5	5	5	5	6

Compute the difference of the floating-point doubles (singles) in registers `fs` and `ft` and put it in register `fd`.

Exception and Interrupt Instructions

Return from exception

```
rfe
```

0x10	1	0	0x20
6	1	19	6

Restore the Status register.

System call

```
syscall
```

0	0	0xc
6	20	6

Register $v0 contains the number of the system call (see Figure A.17) provided by SPIM.

Break

break

0	code	0xd
6	20	6

Cause exception *code*. Exception 1 is reserved for the debugger.

No operation

nop

0	0	0	0	0	0
6	5	5	5	5	6

Do nothing.

A.11 Concluding Remarks

Programming in assembly language requires a programmer to trade off helpful features of high-level languages—such as data structures, type checking, and control constructs—for complete control over the instructions that a computer executes. External constraints on some applications, such as response time or program size, require a programmer to pay close attention to every instruction. However, the cost of this level of attention is assembly language programs that are longer, more time-consuming to write, and more difficult to maintain than high-level language programs.

Moreover, three trends are reducing the need to write programs in assembly language. The first trend is toward the improvement of compilers. Modern compilers produce code that is typically comparable to the best handwritten code and is sometimes better. The second trend is the introduction of new processors that are not only faster, but in the case of processors that execute multiple instructions simultaneously, also more difficult to program by hand. In addition, the rapid evolution of the modern computer favors high-level language programs that are not tied to a single architecture. Finally, we witness a trend toward increasingly complex applications—characterized by complex graphic interfaces and many more features than their predecessors. Large applications are written by teams of programmers and require the modularity and semantic checking features provided by high-level languages.

To Probe Further

Kane, G., and J. Heinrich [1992]. *MIPS RISC Architecture*, Prentice Hall, Englewood Cliffs, NJ.

The last word on the MIPS instruction set and assembly language programming on these machines.

Aho, A., R. Sethi, and J. Ullman [1985]. *Compilers: Principles, Techniques, and Tools*, Addison-Wesley, Reading, MA.

Slightly dated and lacking in coverage of modern architectures, but still the standard reference on compilers.

A.12   Key Terms

A number of key terms have been introduced in this appendix. Check the Glossary for definitions of terms you are uncertain of.

absolute address	interrupt handler	separate compilation
assembler directive	local label	source language
backpatching	machine language	stack segment
callee-saved register	macros	static data
caller-saved register	procedure call or stack frame	symbol table
data segment	recursive procedures	text segment
external or global label	register-use or procedure-call	unresolved reference
formal parameter	convention	virtual machine
forward reference	relocation information	

A.13   Exercises

A.1 [5] <§A.5> Section A.5 described how memory is partitioned on most MIPS systems. Propose another way of dividing memory that meets the same goals.

A.2 [20] <§A.6> Rewrite the code for fact to use fewer instructions.

A.3 [5] <§A.7> Is it ever safe for a user program to use registers $k0 or $k1?

A.4 [25] <§A.7> Section A.7 contains code for a very simple exception handler. One serious problem with this handler is that it disables interrupts for a long time. This means that interrupts from a fast I/O device may be lost. Write a better exception handler that is interruptable and enables interrupts as quickly as possible.

A.5 [15] <§A.7> The simple exception handler always jumps back to the instruction following the exception. This works fine unless the instruction that causes the exception is in the delay slot of a branch. In that case, the next instruction is the target of the branch. Write a better handler that uses the EPC register to determine which instruction should be executed after the exception.

A.6 [5] <§A.9> Using SPIM, write and test an adding machine program that repeatedly reads in integers and adds them into a running sum. The program should stop when it gets an input that is 0, printing out the sum at that point. Use the SPIM system calls described on pages A-48 and A-49.

A.7 [5] <§A.9> Using SPIM, write and test a program that reads in three integers and prints out the sum of the largest two of the three. Use the SPIM system calls described on pages A-48 and A-49. You can break ties arbitrarily.

A.8 [5] <§A.9> Using SPIM, write and test a program that reads in a positive integer using the SPIM system calls. If the integer is not positive, the program should terminate with the message "Invalid Entry"; otherwise the program should print out the names of the digits of the integers, delimited by exactly one space. For example, if the user entered "728," the output would be "Seven Two Eight."

A.9 [25] <§A.9> Write and test a MIPS assembly language program to compute and print the first 100 prime numbers. A number n is prime if no numbers except 1 and n divide it evenly. You should implement two routines:

- `test_prime (n)`   Return 1 if n is prime and 0 if n is not prime.
- `main ()`   Iterate over the integers, testing if each is prime. Print the first 100 numbers that are prime.

Test your programs by running them on SPIM.

A.10 A.10 [10] <§§A.6, A.9> Using SPIM, write and test a recursive program for solving the classic mathematical recreation, the Towers of Hanoi puzzle. (This will require the use of stack frames to support recursion.) The puzzle consists of three pegs (1, 2, and 3) and n disks (the number n can vary; typical values might be in the range from 1 to 8). Disk 1 is smaller than disk 2, which is in turn smaller than disk 3, and so forth, with disk n being the largest. Initially, all the disks are on peg 1, starting with disk n on the bottom, disk $n - 1$ on top of that, and so forth, up to disk 1 on the top. The goal is to move all the disks to peg 2. You may only move one disk at a time, that is, the top disk from any of the three pegs onto the top of either of the other two pegs. Moreover, there is a constraint: You must not place a larger disk on top of a smaller disk.

The C program on the next page can be used to help write your assembly language program.

```
/* move n smallest disks from start to finish using extra */
void hanoi(int n, int start, int finish, int extra){
  if(n != 0){
    hanoi(n-1, start, extra, finish);
    print_string("Move disk");
    print_int(n);
    print_string("from peg");
    print_int(start);
    print_string("to peg");
    print_int(finish);
    print_string(".\n");
    hanoi(n-1, extra, finish, start);
  }
}
main(){
  int n;
  print_string("Enter number of disks>");
  n = read_int();
  hanoi(n, 1, 2, 3);
  return 0;
}
```

The Basics of
Logic Design

I always loved that word, Boolean.

Claude Shannon
IEEE Spectrum, April 1992
(Shannon's master's thesis showed that the algebra
invented by George Boole in the 1800s could represent the
workings of electrical switches.)

B.1   **Introduction**   B-3

B.2   **Gates, Truth Tables, and Logic Equations**   B-4

B.3   **Combinational Logic**   B-8

B.4   **Clocks**   B-18

B.5   **Memory Elements**   B-21

B.6   **Finite State Machines**   B-35

B.7   **Timing Methodologies**   B-39

B.8   **Concluding Remarks**   B-44

B.9   **Key Terms**   B-45

B.10   **Exercises**   B-45

B.1   Introduction

This appendix provides a brief discussion of the basics of logic design. It does not replace a course in logic design nor will it enable you to design significant working logic systems. If you have little or no exposure to logic design, however, this appendix will provide sufficient background to understand all the material in this book. In addition, if you are looking to understand some of the motivation behind how computers are implemented, this material will serve as a useful introduction. If your curiosity is aroused but not sated by this appendix, the references at the end provide several additional sources of information.

Section B.2 introduces the basic building blocks of logic, namely *gates*. Section B.3 uses these building blocks to construct simple *combinational* logic systems, which contain no memory. If you have had some exposure to logic or digital systems, you will probably be familiar with the material in these first two sections. Section B.4 is a short introduction to the topic of clocking, which is necessary to discuss how memory elements work. Section B.5 introduces memory elements; it describes both the characteristics that are important to understanding how they are used in Chapters 5 and 6, and the background that motivates many of the aspects of memory hierarchy design in Chapter 7. Section B.6 describes the design and use of finite state machines, which are sequential logic blocks. If you intend to read Appendix C, you should thoroughly understand the material in sections B.2 through B.6. But if you intend to read only the material on control in Chapters 5 and 6, you can skim the appendices, but you should have some familiarity with all the material except section B.7. Section B.7 is intended for those who want a deeper understanding of clocking methodologies and timing. It explains the basics of how edge-triggered clocking works, introduces another clocking scheme, and briefly describes the problem of synchronizing asynchronous inputs.

B.2   Gates, Truth Tables, and Logic Equations

The electronics inside a modern computer are *digital*. Digital electronics operate with only two voltage levels of interest: a high voltage and a low voltage. All other voltage values are temporary and occur while transitioning between the values. As mentioned in Chapter 3, this is a key reason why computers use binary numbers, since a binary system matches the underlying abstraction inherent in the electronics. In various logic families, the values and relationships between the two voltage values differ. Thus, rather than refer to the voltage levels, we talk about signals that are (logically) true, or are 1, or are *asserted*; or signals that are (logically) false, or 0, or *deasserted*. The values 0 and 1 are called *complements* or *inverses* of one another.

Logic blocks are categorized as one of two types, depending on whether they contain memory. Blocks without memory are called *combinational*; the output of a combinational block depends only on the current input. In blocks with memory, the outputs can depend on both the inputs and the value stored in memory, which is called the *state* of the logic block. In this section and the next, we will focus only on combinational logic. After introducing different memory elements in section B.5, we will describe how *sequential* logic, which is logic including state, is designed.

Truth Tables

Because a combinational logic block contains no memory, it can be completely specified by defining the values of the outputs for each possible set of input values. Such a description is normally given as a *truth table*. For a logic block with n inputs, there are 2^n entries in the truth table, since there are that many possible combinations of input values. Each entry specifies the value of all the outputs for that particular input combination.

Truth Tables

Example

Consider a logic function with three inputs, A, B, and C, and three outputs, D, E, and F. The function is defined as follows: D is true if at least one input is true, E is true if exactly two inputs are true, and F is true only if all three inputs are true. Show the truth table for this function.

Answer

The truth table will contain $2^3 = 8$ entries. Here it is:

Inputs			Outputs		
A	**B**	**C**	**D**	**E**	**F**
0	0	0	0	0	0
0	0	1	1	0	0
0	1	0	1	0	0
0	1	1	1	1	0
1	0	0	1	0	0
1	0	1	1	1	0
1	1	0	1	1	0
1	1	1	1	0	1

Truth tables can completely describe any combinational logic function; however, they grow in size quickly and may not be easy to understand. Sometimes we want to construct a logic function that will be 0 for many input combinations, and we use a shorthand of specifying only the truth table entries for the nonzero outputs. This approach is used in Chapter 5 and Appendix C.

Boolean Algebra

Another approach is to express the logic function with logic equations. This is done with the use of *Boolean algebra* (named after Boole, a 19th century mathematician). In Boolean algebra, all the variables have the values 0 or 1 and, in typical formulations, there are three operators:

■ The OR operator is written as +, as in $A + B$. The result of an OR operator is 1 if either of the variables is 1. The OR operation is also called a *logical sum*, since its result is 1 if either operand is 1.

■ The AND operator is written as $\cdot$, as in $A \cdot B$. The result of an AND operator is 1 only if both inputs are 1. The AND operator is also called *logical product*, since its result is 1 only if both operands are 1.

- The unary operator NOT, written as $\overline{A}$. The result of a NOT operator is 1 only if the input is 0. Applying the operator NOT to a logical value results in an inversion or negation of the value (i.e., if the input is 0 the output is 1, and vice versa).

There are several laws of Boolean algebra that are helpful in manipulating logic equations.

- Identity law: $A + 0 = A$ and $A \cdot 1 = A$.
- Zero and One laws: $A + 1 = 1$ and $A \cdot 0 = 0$.
- Inverse laws: $A + \overline{A} = 1$ and $A \cdot \overline{A} = 0$.
- Commutative laws: $A + B = B + A$ and $A \cdot B = B \cdot A$.
- Associative laws: $A + (B + C) = (A + B) + C$ and $A \cdot (B \cdot C) = (A \cdot B) \cdot C$.
- Distributive laws: $A \cdot (B + C) = (A \cdot B) + (A \cdot C)$ and $A + (B \cdot C) = (A + B) \cdot (A + C)$.

In addition, there are two other useful laws, called DeMorgan's laws, that are discussed in more depth on page B-46.

Any set of logic functions can be written as a series of equations with an output on the left-hand side of each equation and a formula consisting of variables and the three operators above on the right-hand side.

Logic Equations

Example

Show the logic equations for the logic function described in the previous example.

Answer

Here's the equation for D:

$$D = A + B + C$$

F is equally simple:

$$F = A \cdot B \cdot C$$

E is a little tricky. Think of it in two parts: what must be true for E to be true (two of the three inputs must be true), and what cannot be true (all three cannot be true). Thus we can write E as

$$E = ((A \cdot B) + (A \cdot C) + (B \cdot C)) \cdot (\overline{A \cdot B \cdot C})$$

We can also derive E by realizing that E is true only if exactly two of the inputs are true. Then we can write E as an OR of the three possible terms that have two true inputs and one false input:

$$E = (A \cdot B \cdot \bar{C}) + (A \cdot C \cdot \bar{B}) + (B \cdot C \cdot \bar{A})$$

Proving that these two expressions are equivalent is the task of Exercise B.7.

Gates

Logic blocks are built from *gates* that implement basic logic functions. For example, an AND gate implements the AND function, and an OR gate implements the OR function. Since both AND and OR are commutative and associative, an AND or an OR gate can have multiple inputs, with the output equal to the AND or OR of all the inputs. The logical function NOT is implemented with an inverter that always has a single input. The standard representation of these three logic building blocks is shown in Figure B.1.

Rather than draw inverters explicitly, a common practice is to add "bubbles" to the inputs or output of a gate to cause the logic value on that input line or output line to be inverted. For example, Figure B.2 shows the logic diagram for the function $\bar{A} + B$, using explicit inverters on the left and using bubbled inputs and outputs on the right.

Any logical function can be constructed using AND gates, OR gates, and inversion; several of the exercises give you the opportunity to try implementing some common logic functions with gates. In the next section, we'll see how an implementation of any logic function can be constructed using this knowledge.

FIGURE B.1   Standard drawing for an AND gate, OR gate, and an inverter, shown from left to right. The signals to the left of each symbol are the inputs, while the output appears on the right. The AND and OR gates both have two inputs. Inverters have a single input.

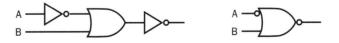

FIGURE B.2   Logic gate implementation of $\overline{\bar{A} + B}$ using explicit inverts on the left and using bubbled inputs and output on the right. This logic function can be simplified to $A \cdot \bar{B}$.

In fact, all logic functions can be constructed with only a single gate type, if that gate is inverting. The two common inverting gates are called NOR and NAND and correspond to inverted OR and AND gates, respectively. NOR and NAND gates are called *universal*, since any logic function can be built using this one gate type. Exercises B.3 and B.4 ask you to prove this fact.

B.3   Combinational Logic

In this section, we look at a couple of basic logic building blocks that we use heavily, and we discuss the design of structured logic that can be automatically implemented from a logic equation or truth table by a translation program. Last, we discuss the notion of an array of logic blocks.

Decoders

Another logic block that we will use in building larger components is a *decoder*. The most common type of decoder has an n-bit input and 2^n outputs, where only one output is asserted for each input combination. This decoder translates the n-bit input into a signal that corresponds to the binary value of the n-bit input. The outputs are thus usually numbered, say, Out0, Out1, . . . , Out$n$. If the value of the input is i, then Out$i$ will be true and all other outputs will be false. Figure B.3 shows a 3-bit decoder and the truth table. This decoder is called a *3-to-8 decoder* since there are 3 inputs and 8 (2^3) outputs. There is also a logic element called an *encoder* that performs the inverse function of a decoder, taking 2^n inputs and producing an n-bit output.

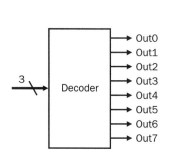

Inputs			Outputs							
I2	I1	I0	Out7	Out6	Out5	Out4	Out3	Out2	Out1	Out0
0	0	0	0	0	0	0	0	0	0	1
0	0	1	0	0	0	0	0	0	1	0
0	1	0	0	0	0	0	0	1	0	0
0	1	1	0	0	0	0	1	0	0	0
1	0	0	0	0	0	1	0	0	0	0
1	0	1	0	0	1	0	0	0	0	0
1	1	0	0	1	0	0	0	0	0	0
1	1	1	1	0	0	0	0	0	0	0

a. A 3-bit decoder

b. The truth table

FIGURE B.3   A 3-bit decoder has 3 inputs, called I2, I1, and I0, and 2^3 = 8 outputs, called Out0 to Out7. Only the output corresponding to the binary value of the input is true, as shown in the truth table. The label 3 on the input to the decoder says that the input signal is 3 bits wide.

Multiplexors

One basic logic function that we saw quite often in Chapters 4, 5, and 6 is the *multiplexor*. A multiplexor might more properly be called a *selector*, since its output is one of the inputs that is selected by a control. Consider the two-input multiplexor. As shown on the left side of Figure B.4, this multiplexor has three inputs: two data values and a selector (or control) value. The selector value determines which of the inputs becomes the output. We can represent the logic function computed by a two-input multiplexor as $C = (A \cdot \overline{S}) + (B \cdot S)$, which is shown in gate form on the right side of Figure B.4.

Multiplexors can be created with an arbitrary number of data inputs. When there are only two inputs, the selector is a single signal that selects one of the inputs if it is true (1) and the other if it is false (0). If there are n data inputs, there will need to be $\lceil \log_2 n \rceil$ selector inputs. In this case, the multiplexor basically consists of three parts:

1. A decoder that generates n signals, each indicating a different input value

2. An array of n AND gates, each combining one of the inputs with a signal from the decoder

3. A single large OR gate that incorporates the outputs of the AND gates

To associate the inputs with selector values, we often label the data inputs numerically (i.e., $0, 1, 2, 3, \ldots, n-1$) and interpret the data selector inputs as a binary number. Sometimes, we make use of a multiplexor with undecoded selector signals.

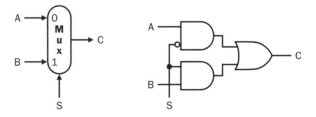

FIGURE B.4 A two-input multiplexor, on the left, and its implementation with gates, on the right. The multiplexor has two data inputs (A and B), which are labeled 0 and 1, and one selector input (S), as well as an output C.

Two-Level Logic and PLAs

As pointed out in the previous section, any logic function can be implemented with only AND, OR, and NOT functions. In fact, a much stronger result is true. Any logic function can be written in a canonical form, where every input is either a true or complemented variable and there are only two levels of gates—one being AND and the other OR—with a possible inversion on the final output. Such a representation is called a *two-level representation* and there are two forms, called *sum of products* and *product of sums*. A sum-of-products representation is a logical sum (OR) of products (terms using the AND operator); a product of sums is just the opposite. In our earlier example, we had two equations for the output E:

$$E = ((A \cdot B) + (A \cdot C) + (B \cdot C)) \cdot (\overline{A \cdot B \cdot C})$$

and

$$E = (A \cdot B \cdot \overline{C}) + (A \cdot C \cdot \overline{B}) + (B \cdot C \cdot \overline{A})$$

This second equation is in a sum-of-products form: it has two levels of logic and the only inversions are on individual variables. The first equation has three levels of logic.

Elaboration: We can also write E as a product of sums:

$$E = (\overline{A} + \overline{B} + C) \lozenge (\overline{A} + \overline{C} + B) \lozenge (\overline{B} + \overline{C} + A)$$

To derive this form, you need to use *DeMorgan's theorems*, which are discussed on page B-46. Exercise B.8 asks you to derive the product-of-sums representation from the sum of products using DeMorgan's theorems.

In this text, we use the more common sum-of-products form. It is easy to see that any logic function can be represented as a sum of products by constructing such a representation from the truth table for the function. Each truth table entry for which the function is true corresponds to a product term. The product term consists of a logical product of all the inputs or the complements of the inputs, depending on whether the entry in the truth table has a 0 or 1 corresponding to this variable. The logic function is the logical sum of the product terms where the function is true. This is more easily seen with an example.

Sum of Products

Example Show the sum-of-products representation for the following truth table.

Inputs			Output
A	**B**	**C**	**D**
0	0	0	0
0	0	1	1
0	1	0	1
0	1	1	0
1	0	0	1
1	0	1	0
1	1	0	0
1	1	1	1

Answer There are four product terms, since the function is true (1) for four different input combinations. These are

$$\bar{A} \cdot \bar{B} \cdot C$$

$$\bar{A} \cdot B \cdot \bar{C}$$

$$A \cdot \bar{B} \cdot \bar{C}$$

$$A \cdot B \cdot C$$

Thus, we can write the function for D as the sum of these terms:

$$D = (\bar{A} \cdot \bar{B} \cdot C) + (\bar{A} \cdot B \cdot \bar{C}) + (A \cdot \bar{B} \cdot \bar{C}) + (A \cdot B \cdot C)$$

Note that only those truth table entries for which the function is true generate terms in the equation.

We can use this relationship between a truth table and a two-level representation to generate a gate-level implementation of any set of logic functions. A set of logic functions corresponds to a truth table with multiple output columns, as we saw in the example on page B-5. Each output column represents a different logic function, which may be directly constructed from the truth table.

The sum-of-products representation corresponds to a common structured-logic implementation called a *programmable logic array* (PLA). A PLA has a set of inputs and corresponding input complements (which can be implemented

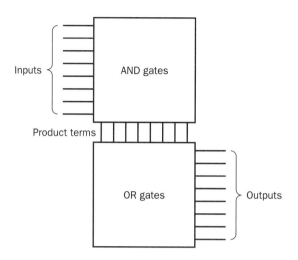

FIGURE B.5   The basic form of a PLA consists of an array of AND gates followed by an array of OR gates. Each entry in the AND gate array is a product term consisting of any number of inputs or inverted inputs. Each entry in the OR gate array is a sum term consisting of any number of these product terms.

with a set of inverters), and two stages of logic. The first stage is an array of AND gates that form a set of product terms (sometimes called *minterms*); each product term can consist of any of the inputs or their complements. The second stage is an array of OR gates, each of which forms a logical sum of any number of the product terms. Figure B.5 shows the basic form of a PLA.

A PLA can directly implement the truth table of a set of logic functions with multiple inputs and outputs. Since each entry where the truth table is true requires a product term, there will be a corresponding row in the PLA. Each output corresponds to a potential row of OR gates in the second stage. The number of OR gates corresponds to the number of truth table entries for which the output is true. The total size of a PLA, such as that shown in Figure B.5, is equal to the sum of the size of the AND gate array (called the *AND plane*) and the size of the OR gate array (called the *OR plane*). Looking at Figure B.5, we can see that the size of the AND gate array is equal to the number of inputs times the number of different product terms, and the size of the OR gate array is the number of outputs times the number of product terms.

A PLA has two characteristics that help make it an efficient way to implement a set of logic functions. First, only the truth table entries that produce a true value for at least one output have any logic gates associated with them. Second, each different product term will have only one entry in the PLA, even if the product term is used in multiple outputs. Let's look at an example.

PLAs

Example

Consider the set of logic functions defined in the example on B-5. Show a PLA implementation of this example.

Answer

Here is the truth table we constructed earlier:

Inputs			Outputs		
A	**B**	**C**	**D**	**E**	**F**
0	0	0	0	0	0
0	0	1	1	0	0
0	1	0	1	0	0
0	1	1	1	1	0
1	0	0	1	0	0
1	0	1	1	1	0
1	1	0	1	1	0
1	1	1	1	0	1

Since there are seven unique product terms with at least one true value in the output section, there will be seven columns in the AND plane. The number of rows in the AND plane is three (since there are three inputs), and there are also three rows in the OR plane (since there are three outputs). Figure B.6 shows the resulting PLA, with the product terms corresponding to the truth table entries from top to bottom.

Rather than drawing all the gates, as we did in Figure B.6, designers often show just the position of AND gates and OR gates. Dots are used on the intersection of a product term signal line and an input line or an output line when a corresponding AND gate or OR gate is required. Figure B.7 shows how the PLA of Figure B.6 would look when drawn in this way. The contents of a PLA are fixed when the PLA is created, although there are also forms of PLA-like structures, called *PALs*, that can be programmed electronically when a designer is ready to use them.

ROMs

Another form of structured logic that can be used to implement a set of logic functions is a *read-only memory* (ROM). A ROM is called a memory because it has a set of locations that can be read; however, the contents of these locations

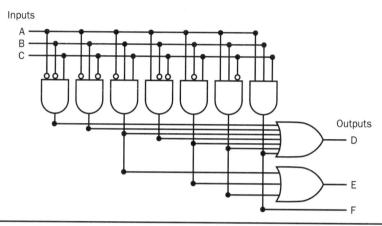

FIGURE B.6   The PLA for implementing the logic function described above.

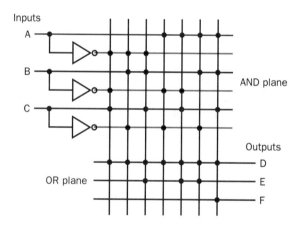

FIGURE B.7   A PLA drawn using dots to indicate the components of the product terms and sum terms in the array. Rather than use inverters on the gates, usually all the inputs are run the width of the AND plane in both true and complement forms. A dot in the AND plane indicates that the input, or its inverse, occurs in the product term. A dot in the OR plane indicates that the corresponding product term appears in the corresponding output.

are fixed, usually at the time the ROM is created. There are also *programmable ROMs* (PROMs) that can be programmed electronically, when a designer knows their contents. There are also erasable PROMs; these devices require a slow erasure process using ultraviolet light, and thus are used as read-only memories, except during the design and debugging process.

A ROM has a set of input address lines and a set of outputs. The number of addressable entries in the ROM determines the number of address lines: if the ROM contains 2^n addressable entries, called the *height*, then there are n input lines. The number of bits in each addressable entry is equal to the number of output bits and is sometimes called the *width* of the ROM. The total number of bits in the ROM is equal to the height times the width. The height and width are sometimes collectively referred to as the *shape* of the ROM.

A ROM can encode a collection of logic functions directly from the truth table. For example, if there are n functions with m inputs, we need a ROM with m address lines (and 2^m entries), with each entry being n bits wide. The entries in the input portion of the truth table represent the addresses of the entries in the ROM, while the contents of the output portion of the truth table constitute the contents of the ROM. If the truth table is organized so that the sequence of entries in the input portion constitute a sequence of binary numbers (as have all the truth tables we have shown so far), then the output portion gives the ROM contents in order as well. In the previous example starting on page B-13, there were three inputs and three outputs. This leads to a ROM with $2^3 = 8$ entries, each 3 bits wide. The contents of those entries in increasing order by address are directly given by the output portion of the truth table that appears on page B-13.

ROMs and PLAs are closely related. A ROM is fully decoded: it contains a full output word for every possible input combination. A PLA is only partially decoded. This means that a ROM will always contain more entries. For the earlier truth table on page B-13, the ROM contains entries for all eight possible inputs, whereas the PLA contains only the seven active product terms. As the number of inputs grows, the number of entries in the ROM grows exponentially. In contrast, for most real logic functions, the number of product terms grows much more slowly (see the examples in Appendix C). This difference makes PLAs generally more efficient for implementing combinational logic functions. ROMs have the advantage of being able to implement any logic function with the matching number of inputs and outputs. This advantage makes it easier to change the ROM contents if the logic function changes, since the size of the ROM need not change.

Don't Cares

Often in implementing some combinational logic, there are situations where we do not care what the value of some output is, either because another output is true or because a subset of the input combinations determines the values of the outputs. Such situations are referred to as *don't cares*. Don't cares are important because they make it easier to optimize the implementation of a logic function.

There are two types of don't cares: output don't cares and input don't cares, both of which can be represented in a truth table. *Output don't cares* arise when we don't care about the value of an output for some input combination. They appear as Xs in the output portion of a truth table. When an output is a don't care for some input combination, the designer or logic optimization program is free to make the output true or false for that input combination. *Input don't cares* arise when an output depends on only some of the inputs, and they are also shown as Xs, though in the input portion of the truth table.

Don't Cares

Example

Consider a logic function with inputs *A*, *B*, and *C* defined as follows:

- If *A* or *C* is true, then output *D* is true, whatever the value of *B*.
- If *A* or *B* is true, then output *E* is true, whatever the value of *C*.
- Output *F* is true if exactly one of the inputs is true, although we don't care about the value of *F*, whenever *D* and *E* are both true.

Show the full truth table for this function and the truth table using don't cares. How many product terms are required in a PLA for each of these?

Answer

Here's the full truth table, without don't cares:

Inputs			Outputs		
A	B	C	D	E	F
0	0	0	0	0	0
0	0	1	1	0	1
0	1	0	0	1	1
0	1	1	1	1	0
1	0	0	1	1	1
1	0	1	1	1	0
1	1	0	1	1	0
1	1	1	1	1	1

This requires seven product terms without optimization. The truth table written with output don't cares looks like

Inputs			Outputs		
A	**B**	**C**	**D**	**E**	**F**
0	0	0	0	0	0
0	0	1	1	0	1
0	1	0	0	1	1
0	1	1	1	1	X
1	0	0	1	1	X
1	0	1	1	1	X
1	1	0	1	1	X
1	1	1	1	1	X

This truth table can be further simplified to yield

Inputs			Outputs		
A	**B**	**C**	**D**	**E**	**F**
0	0	0	0	0	0
0	0	1	1	0	1
0	1	0	0	1	1
X	1	1	1	1	X
1	X	X	1	1	X

This simplified truth table requires a PLA with four minterms, or it can be implemented in discrete gates with one two-input AND gate and three OR gates (two with three inputs and one with two inputs). This compares to the original truth table that had seven minterms and would require four AND gates.

Logic minimization is critical to achieving efficient implementations. One tool useful for hand minimization of random logic is *Karnaugh maps*. Karnaugh maps represent the truth table graphically so that product terms that may be combined are easily seen. Nevertheless, hand optimization of significant logic functions using Karnaugh maps is impractical, both because of the size of the maps and their complexity. Fortunately, the process of logic minimization is highly mechanical and can be performed by design tools. In the process of minimization the tools take advantage of the don't cares, so specifying them is important. The textbook references at the end of this appendix provide further discussion on logic minimization, Karnaugh maps, and the theory behind such minimization algorithms.

Arrays of Logic Elements

Many of the combinational operations to be performed on data have to be done to an entire word (32 bits) of data. Thus we often want to build an array of logic elements, which we can represent simply by showing that a given operation will happen to an entire collection of inputs. For example, we saw on page B-9 what a 1-bit multiplexor looked like, but inside a machine, much of the time we want to select between a pair of *buses*. A bus is a collection of data lines that is treated together as a single logical signal. (The term *bus* is also used to indicate a shared collection of lines with multiple sources and uses, especially in Chapter 8, where I/O buses were discussed.)

For example, in the MIPS instruction set, the result of an instruction that is written into a register can come from one of two sources. A multiplexor is used to choose which of the two buses (each 32 bits wide) will be written into the Result register. The 1-bit multiplexor, which we showed earlier, will need to be replicated 32 times. We indicate that a signal is a bus rather than a single 1-bit line by showing it with a thicker line in a figure. Most buses are 32 bits wide; those that are not are explicitly labeled with their width. When we show a logic unit whose inputs and outputs are buses, this means that the unit must be replicated a sufficient number of times to accommodate the width of the input. Figure B.8 shows how we draw a multiplexor that selects between a pair of 32-bit buses and how this expands in terms of 1-bit-wide multiplexors. Sometimes we need to construct an array of logic elements where the inputs for some elements in the array are outputs from earlier elements. For example, this is how a multibit-wide ALU is constructed. In such cases, we must explicitly show how to create wider arrays, since the individual elements of the array are no longer independent, as they are in the case of a 32-bit-wide multiplexor.

B.4   Clocks

Before we discuss memory elements and sequential logic, it is useful to discuss briefly the topic of clocks. This short section introduces the topic and is similar to the discussion found at the beginning of Chapter 5. More details on clocking and timing methodologies are presented in section B.7.

Clocks are needed in sequential logic to decide when an element that contains state should be updated. A clock is simply a free-running signal with a fixed *cycle time*; the *clock frequency* is simply the inverse of the cycle time. As shown in Figure B.9, the *clock cycle time* or *clock period* is divided into two portions: when the clock is high and when the clock is low. In this text, we use only *edge-triggered clocking*. This means that all state changes occur on a clock edge. We use an edge-triggered methodology because it is simpler to explain. Depending on the technology, it may or may not be the best choice for a clocking methodology.

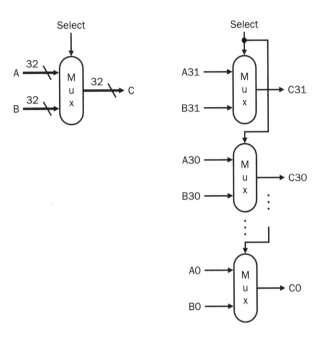

a. A 32-bit wide 2-to-1 multiplexor

b. The 32-bit wide multiplexor is actually an array of 32 1-bit multiplexors

FIGURE B.8 A multiplexor is arrayed 32 times to perform a selection between two 32-bit inputs. Note that there is still only one data selection signal used for all 32-bit multiplexors.

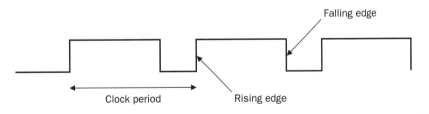

FIGURE B.9 A clock signal oscillates between high and low values. The clock period is the time for one full cycle. In an edge-triggered design, either the rising or falling edge of the clock is active and causes state to be changed.

In an edge-triggered methodology, either the rising edge or the falling edge of the clock is *active* and causes state changes to occur. As we will see in the next section, the state elements in an edge-triggered design are implemented so that the contents of the state elements only change on the active clock edge. The choice of which edge is active is influenced by the implementation technology and does not affect the concepts involved in designing the logic.

The major constraint in a clocked system, also called a *synchronous system*, is that the signals that are written into state elements must be *valid* when the active clock edge occurs. A signal is valid if it is stable (i.e., not changing) and the value will not change again until the inputs change. Since combinational circuits cannot have feedback, if the inputs to a combinational logic unit are not changed, the outputs will eventually become valid. Figure B.10 shows the relationship among the state elements and the combinational logic blocks in a synchronous, sequential logic design. The state elements, whose outputs change only on the clock edge, provide valid inputs to the combinational logic block. To ensure that the values written into the state elements on the active clock edge are valid, the clock must have a long enough period so that all the signals in the combinational logic block stabilize. This constraint sets a lower bound on the length of the clock period. In the rest of this appendix, as well as in Chapters 5 and 6, we usually omit the clock signal, since we are assuming that all state elements are updated on the same clock edge. Some state elements will be written on every clock edge, while others will be written only under certain conditions (such as a register being updated). In such cases, we will have an explicit write signal for that state element. The write signal must still be gated with the clock so that the update occurs only on the clock edge if the write signal is active. We will see how this is done and used in the next section.

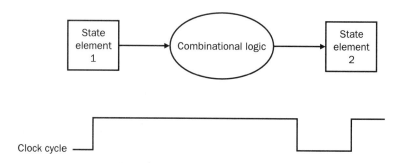

FIGURE B.10   The inputs to a combinational logic block come from a state element, and the outputs are written into a state element. The clock edge determines when the contents of the state elements are updated.

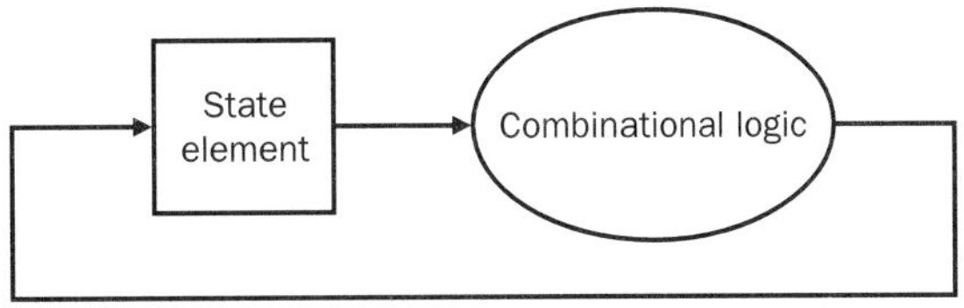

FIGURE B.11 An edge-triggered methodology allows a state element to be read and written in the same clock cycle without creating a race that could lead to undermined data values. Of course, the clock cycle must still be long enough so that the input values are stable when the active clock edge occurs.

One other advantage of an edge-triggered methodology is that it is possible to have a state element that is used as both an input and output to the same combinational logic block, as shown in Figure B.11. In practice, care must be taken to prevent races in such situations and to ensure that the clock period is long enough; this topic is discussed further in section B.7.

Now that we have discussed how clocking is used to update state elements, we can discuss how to construct the state elements.

B.5 Memory Elements

In this section, we discuss the basic principles behind memory elements, starting with flip-flops and latches, moving on to register files, and finally to memories. All memory elements store state: the output from any memory element depends both on the inputs and on the value that has been stored inside the memory element. Thus all logic blocks containing a memory element contain state and are sequential.

The simplest type of memory elements are *unclocked*; that is, they do not have any clock input. Although we only use clocked memory elements in this text, an unclocked latch is the simplest memory element, so let's look at this circuit first. Figure B.12 shows an *S-R latch* (set-reset latch), built from a pair of NOR gates (OR gates with inverted outputs). The outputs Q and $\overline{Q}$ represent the value of the stored state and its complement. When neither S nor R are asserted, the cross-coupled NOR gates act as inverters and store the previous values of Q and $\overline{Q}$. For example, if the output, Q, is true, then the bottom inverter produces a false output (which is $\overline{Q}$), which becomes the input to the top inverter, which produces a true output, which is Q, and so on. If S is asserted then the output Q will be asserted and $\overline{Q}$ will be deasserted, while if R is asserted, then the output $\overline{Q}$ will be asserted and Q will be deasserted. When S and R are both deasserted the last values of Q and $\overline{Q}$ will continue to be stored in the

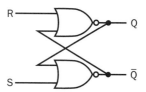

FIGURE B.12   A pair of cross-coupled NOR gates can store an internal value. The value stored on the output Q is recycled by inverting it to obtain $\overline{Q}$ and then inverting $\overline{Q}$ to obtain Q. If either R or $\overline{Q}$ are asserted, Q will be deasserted and vice-versa.

cross-coupled structure. Asserting S and R simultaneously can lead to incorrect operation: depending on how S and R are deasserted, the latch may oscillate or become metastable (this is described in more detail in section B.7).

This cross-coupled structure is the basis for more complex memory elements that allow us to store data signals. These elements contain additional gates used to store signal values and to cause the state to be updated only in conjunction with a clock. The next section shows how these elements are built.

Flip-Flops and Latches

Flip-flops and *latches* are the simplest memory elements. In both flip-flops and latches, the output is equal to the value of the stored state inside the element. Furthermore, unlike the S-R latch described above, all the latches and flip-flops we will use from this point on are clocked, which means they have a clock input and the change of state is triggered by that clock. The difference between a flip-flop and a latch is the point at which the clock causes the state to actually change. In a clocked latch, the state is changed whenever the appropriate inputs change and the clock is asserted, whereas in a flip-flop, the state is changed only on a clock edge. Since throughout this text we use an edge-triggered timing methodology where state is only updated on clock edges, we need only use flip-flops. Flip-flops are often built from latches, so we start by describing the operation of a simple clocked latch and then discuss the operation of a flip-flop constructed from that latch.

For computer applications, the function of both flip-flops and latches is to store a signal. A *D latch* or *D flip-flop* stores the value of its data input signal in the internal memory. Although there are many other types of latches and flip-flops, the D type is the only basic building block that we will need. A D latch has two inputs and two outputs. The inputs are the data value to be stored (called D) and a clock signal (called C) that indicates when the latch should read the value on the D input and store it. The outputs are simply the value of the internal state (Q) and its complement ($\overline{Q}$). When the clock input C is asserted, the latch is said to be *open*, and the value of the output (Q) becomes the value of the input *D*. When the clock input *C* is deasserted, the latch is said to be *closed*, and the value of the output (*Q*) is whatever value was stored the last time the latch was open.

Figure B.13 shows how a D latch can be implemented with two additional gates added to the cross-coupled NOR gates. Since when the latch is open the value of *Q* changes as *D* changes, this structure is sometimes called a *transparent latch*. Figure B.14 shows how this D latch works, assuming that the output *Q* is initially false and that *D* changes first.

As mentioned earlier, we use flip-flops as the basic building block rather than latches. Flip-flops are not transparent: their outputs change *only* on the clock edge. A flip-flop can be built so that it triggers on either the rising (positive) or falling (negative) clock edge; for our designs we can use either type. Figure B.15 shows how a falling-edge D flip-flop is constructed from a pair of D latches. In a D flip-flop, the output is stored when the clock edge occurs. Figure B.16 shows how this flip-flop operates.

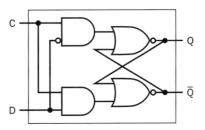

FIGURE B.13   A D latch implemented with NOR gates. A NOR gate acts as an inverter if the other input is 0. Thus, the cross-coupled pair of NOR gates acts to store the state value unless the clock input, *C*, is asserted, in which case the value of input *D* replaces the value of *Q* and is stored. The value of input *D* must be stable when the clock signal *C* changes from asserted to deasserted.

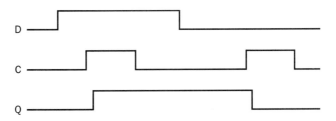

FIGURE B.14   Operation of a D latch assuming the output is initially deasserted. When the clock, *C*, is asserted, the latch is open and the *Q* output immediately assumes the value of the *D* input.

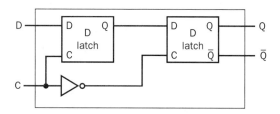

FIGURE B.15   A D flip-flop with a falling-edge trigger. The first latch, called the master, is open and follows the input D when the clock input, C, is asserted. When the clock input, C, falls, the first latch is closed, but the second latch, called the slave, is open and gets its input from the output of the master latch.

Because the D input is sampled on the clock edge, it must be valid for a period of time immediately before and immediately after the clock edge. The minimum time that the input must be valid before the clock edge is called the *set-up time*; the minimum time during which it must be valid after the clock edge is called the *hold time*. Thus the inputs to any flip-flop (or anything built using flip-flops) must be valid during a window that begins at time t_{set-up} before the clock edge and ends at t_{hold} after the clock edge, as shown in Figure B.17. Section B.7 talks about clocking and timing constraints in more detail.

We can use an array of D flip-flops to build a register that can hold a multibit datum, such as a byte or word. We used registers throughout our datapaths in Chapters 5 and 6.

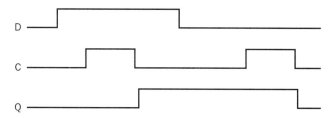

FIGURE B.16   Operation of a D flip-flop with a falling-edge trigger, assuming the output is initially deasserted. When the clock input (C) changes from asserted to deasserted, the Q output stores the value of the D input. Compare this behavior to that of the clocked D latch shown in Figure B.14. In a clocked latch, the stored value and the output, Q, both change whenever C is high, as opposed to only when C transitions.

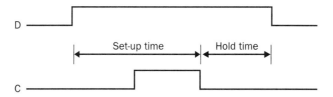

FIGURE B.17   Set-up and hold time requirements for a D flip-flop with a falling-edge trigger. The input must be stable a period of time before the clock edge, as well as after the clock edge. The minimum time the signal must be stable before the clock edge is called the set-up time, while the minimum time the signal must be stable after clock is called the hold time. Failure to meet these minimum requirements can result in a situation where the output of the flip-flop may not even be predictable, as described in section B.7. Hold times are usually either 0 or very small and thus not a cause of worry.

Register Files

One structure that is central to our datapath is a *register file*. A register file consists of a set of registers that can be read and written by supplying a register number to be accessed. A register file can be implemented with a decoder for each read or write port and an array of registers built from D flip-flops. Because reading a register does not change any state, we need only supply a register number as an input, and the only output will be the data contained in that register. For writing a register we will need three inputs: a register number, the data to write, and a clock that controls the writing into the register. In Chapters 5 and 6, we used a register file that has two read ports and one write port. This register file is drawn as shown in Figure B.18. The read ports can be implemented with a pair of multiplexors, each of which is as wide as the number of bits in the register file. Figure B.19 shows the implementation of two register read ports for a 32-bit-wide register file.

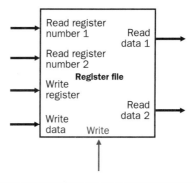

FIGURE B.18   A register file with two read ports and one write port has five inputs and two outputs. The control input Write is shown in color.

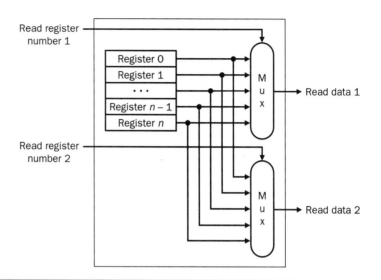

FIGURE B.19   The implementation of two read ports for a register file with _n_ registers can be done with a pair of _n_-to-1 multiplexors each 32 bits wide. The register read number signal is used as the multiplexor selector signal. Figure B.20 shows how the write port is implemented.

Implementing the write port is slightly more complex since we can only change the contents of the designated register. We can do this by using a decoder to generate a signal that can be used to determine which register to write. Figure B.20 shows how to implement the write port for a register file. It is important to remember that the flip-flop changes state only on the clock edge. In Chapters 5 and 6, we hooked up write signals for the register file explicitly and assumed the clock shown in Figure B.20 is attached implicitly.

What happens if the same register is read and written during a clock cycle? Because the write of the register file occurs on the clock edge, the register will be valid during the time it is read, as we saw earlier in Figure B.10. The value returned will be the value written in an earlier clock cycle. If we want a read to return the value currently being written, additional logic in the register file or outside of it is needed. Chapter 6 makes extensive use of such logic.

SRAMs

Registers and register files provide the basic building block for small memories, but larger amounts of memory are built using either _SRAMs_ (static random access memories) or _DRAMs_ (dynamic random access memories). In this section, we discuss SRAMs, which are somewhat simpler, while the next sec-

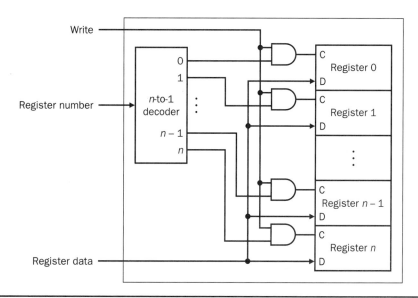

FIGURE B.20 The write port for a register file is implemented with a decoder that is used with the write signal to generate the C input to the registers. All three inputs (the register number, the data, and the write signal) will have set-up and hold-time constraints that ensure that the correct data is written into the register file.

tion discusses DRAMs. SRAMs are simply integrated circuits that are memory arrays with (usually) a single access port that can provide either a read or a write. SRAMs have a fixed access time to any datum, though the read and write access characteristics often differ.

A SRAM chip has a specific configuration in terms of the number of addressable locations, as well as the width of each addressable location. For example, a 256K × 1 SRAM provides 256K entries, each of which is 1 bit wide. Thus it will have 18 address lines (since 256K = 2^{18}), a single data output line, and a single data input line. A 32K × 8 SRAM has the same total number of bits, but will have 15 address lines to address 32K entries each of which holds an 8-bit-wide datum; thus there are eight data output and eight data input lines. As with ROMs, the number of addressable locations is often called the *height*, with the number of bits per unit called the *width*. For a variety of technical reasons, the newest and fastest SRAMs are typically available in narrow configurations: ×1 and ×4. Figure B.21 shows the input and output signals for a 32K × 8 SRAM.

To initiate a read or write access, the Chip select signal must be made active. For reads, we must also activate the Output enable signal that controls whether or not the datum selected by the address is actually driven on the pins. The

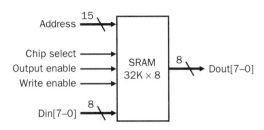

FIGURE B.21   A 32K x 8 SRAM showing the 15 address lines (32K = 2^{15}) and eight data inputs, the three control lines, and the eight data outputs.

Output enable is useful for connecting multiple memories to a single-output bus and using Output enable to determine which memory drives the bus. The SRAM read access time is usually specified as the delay from the time that Output enable is true and the address lines are valid until the time that the data is on the output lines. Typical read access times for SRAMs in 1997 vary from about 5 ns for the fastest CMOS parts to 25-ns parts, which, while slower, are usually cheaper and often denser. The largest SRAMs available in 1997 have over 4 million bits of data.

For writes, we must supply the data to be written and the address, as well as signals to cause the write to occur. When both the Write enable and Chip select are true, the data on the data input lines is written into the cell specified by the address. There are set-up-time and hold-time requirements for the address and data lines, just as there were for D flip-flops and latches. In addition, the Write enable signal is not a clock edge but a pulse with a minimum width requirement. The time to complete a write is specified by the combination of the set-up times, the hold times, and the Write enable pulse width.

Large SRAMs cannot be built in the same way we build a register file because, unlike a register file where a 32-to-1 multiplexor might be practical, the 64K-to-1 multiplexor that would be needed for a 64K × 1 SRAM is totally impractical. Rather than use a giant multiplexor, large memories are implemented with a shared output line, called a *bit line*, which multiple memory cells in the memory array can assert. To allow multiple sources to drive a single line, a *three-state buffer* (or *tri-state buffer*) is used. A three-state buffer has two inputs: a data signal and an Output enable. The single output from a three-state buffer is equal to the asserted or deasserted input signal if the Output enable is asserted, and is otherwise in a *high-impedance state* that allows another three-state buffer whose Output enable is asserted to determine the value of a shared output. Figure B.22 shows a set of three-state buffers wired to form a multiplexor with a decoded input. It is critical that the Output enable of at most one of the three-state buffers be asserted; otherwise, the three-state

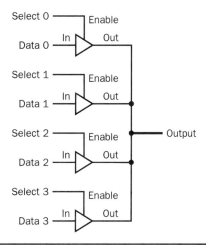

FIGURE B.22 Four three-state buffers are used to form a multiplexor. Only one of the four Select inputs can be asserted. A three-state buffer with a deasserted Output enable, has a high-impedance output that allows a three-state buffer whose Output enable is asserted to drive the shared output line.

buffers may try to set the output line differently. By using three-state buffers in the individual cells of the SRAM, each cell that corresponds to a particular output can share the same output line. The use of a set of distributed three-state buffers is a more efficient implementation than a large centralized multiplexor. The three-state buffers are incorporated into the flip-flops that form the basic cells of the SRAM. Figure B.23 shows how a small 4×2 SRAM might be built, using D latches with an input called Enable that controls the three-state output.

The design in Figure B.23 eliminates the need for an enormous multiplexor; however, it still requires a very large decoder and a correspondingly large number of word lines. For example, in a $16K \times 8$ SRAM, we would need a 14-to-16K decoder and 16K word lines (which are the lines used to enable the individual flip-flops)! To circumvent this problem, large memories are organized as rectangular arrays and use a two-step decoding process. Figure B.24 shows how a $32K \times 8$ SRAM might be organized using a two-step decode. As we will see, the two-level decoding process is quite important in understanding how DRAMs operate.

Recently we have seen the development of both synchronous SRAMs (SSRAMs) and synchronous DRAMs (SDRAMs). The key capability provided by synchronous RAMs is the ability to transfer a *burst* of data from a series of sequential addresses within an array or row. The burst is defined by a starting address, supplied in the usual fashion, and a burst length. The speed advantage of synchronous RAMs comes from the ability to transfer the bits in the

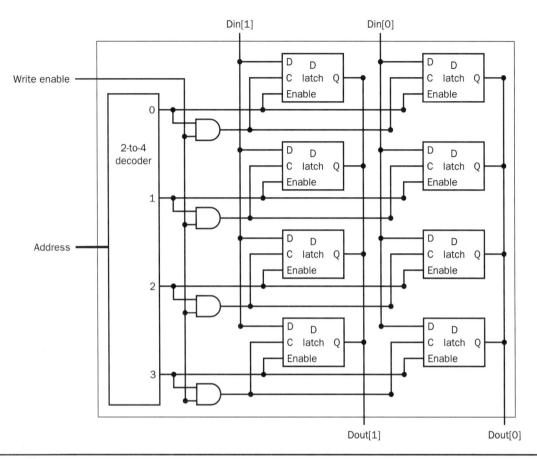

FIGURE B.23   **The basic structure of a 4 × 2 SRAM consists of a decoder that selects which pair of cells to activate.** The activated cells use a three-state output connected to the vertical bit lines that supply the requested data. The address that selects the cell is sent on one of a set of horizontal address lines, called the word lines. For simplicity, the Output enable and Chip select signals have been omitted, but they could easily be added with a few AND gates.

burst without having to specify additional address bits. Instead, a clock is used to transfer the successive bits in the burst. The elimination of the need to specify the address for the transfers within the burst significantly improves the rate for transferring the block of data. Because of this capability, synchronous SRAMs and DRAMs are rapidly becoming the RAMs of choice for building cache-based systems that naturally do block transfers.

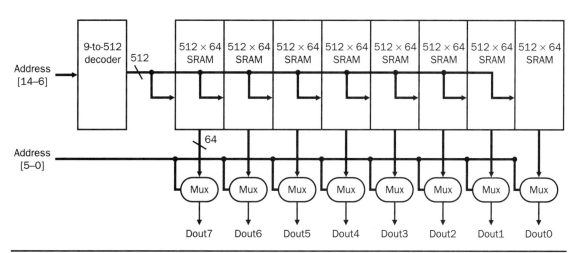

FIGURE B.24   Typical organization of a 32K x 8 SRAM as an array of 512 x 64 arrays. The first decoder generates the addresses for eight 512 × 64 arrays; then a set of multiplexors is used to select 1 bit from each 64-bit-wide array. This is a much easier design than a single-level decode that would need either an enormous decoder (15 to 32K) or a gigantic multiplexor (32K to 1).

DRAMs

In a static RAM (SRAM) the value stored in a cell is kept on a pair of inverting gates, and as long as power is applied, the value can be kept indefinitely. In a dynamic RAM (DRAM), the value kept in a cell is stored as a charge in a capacitor. A single transistor is then used to access this stored charge, either to read the value or to overwrite the charge stored there. Because DRAMs use only a single transistor per bit of storage, they are much denser and cheaper per bit. By comparison, SRAMs require four to six transistors per bit. In DRAMs, the charge is stored on a capacitor, so it cannot be kept indefinitely and must periodically be *refreshed*. That is why this memory structure is called *dynamic*, as opposed to the static storage in an SRAM cell. To refresh the cell, we merely read its contents and write it back. The charge can be kept for several milliseconds, which might correspond to close to a million clock cycles. Today, single-chip memory controllers often handle the refresh function independently of the processor. If every bit had to be read out of the DRAM and then be written back individually, with large DRAMs containing multiple megabytes, we would constantly be refreshing the DRAM, leaving no time for accessing it. Fortunately, DRAMs also use a two-level decoding structure, and this allows us to refresh an entire row (which shares a word line) with a read cycle followed immediately by a write cycle. Typically, refresh operations consume 1% to 2% of the active cycles of the DRAM, leaving the remaining 98% to 99% of the cycles available for reading and writing data.

Elaboration: How does a DRAM read and write the signal stored in a cell? The transistor inside the cell is a switch, called a *pass transistor*, that allows the value stored on the capacitor to be accessed either for reading or writing. Figure B.25 shows how the single-transistor cell looks. The pass transistor acts like a switch: when the signal on the word line is asserted, the switch is open, connecting the capacitor to the bit line. If the operation is a write, then the value to be written is placed on the bit line. If the value is a 1, the capacitor will be charged. If the value is a 0, then the capacitor will be discharged. Reading is slightly more complex, since the DRAM must detect a very small charge stored in the capacitor. Before activating the word line for a read, the bit line is charged to the voltage that is halfway between the low and high voltage. Then, by activating the word line, the charge on the capacitor is read out onto the bit line. This causes the bit line to move slightly towards the high or low direction, and this change is detected with a sense amplifier, which can detect small changes in voltage.

DRAMs use a two-level decoder, as shown in Figure B.26, consisting of a *row access*, followed by a *column access*. The row access chooses one of a number of rows and activates the corresponding word line. The contents of all the columns in the active row are then stored in a set of latches. The column access then selects the data from the column latches. To save pins and reduce the package cost, the same address lines are used for both the row and column address; a pair of signals called RAS (Row Access Strobe) and CAS (Column Access Strobe) are used to signal the DRAM that either a row or column address is being supplied. Refresh is performed by simply reading the columns into the column latches and then writing the same values back. Thus an entire row is refreshed in one cycle. The two-level addressing scheme, combined with the internal circuitry, make DRAM access times much longer (by a factor of 5 to 10) than SRAM access times. In 1997, typical DRAM access times range from 60 to 110 ns. The much lower cost per bit makes DRAM the choice for main memory, while the faster access time makes SRAM the choice for caches.

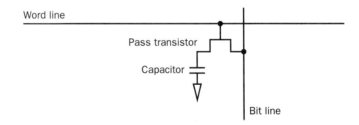

FIGURE B.25   A single-transistor DRAM cell contains a capacitor that stores the cell contents and a transistor used to access the cell.

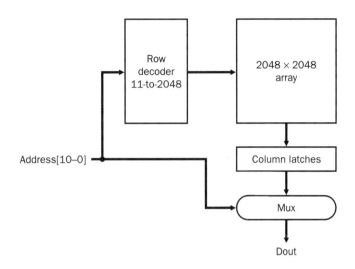

FIGURE B.26   A 4M x 1 DRAM is built with a 2048 x 2048 array. The row access uses 11 bits to select a row, which is then latched in 2048 1-bit latches. A multiplexor chooses the output bit from these 2048 latches. The RAS and CAS signals control whether the address lines are sent to the row decoder or column multiplexor.

You might observe that a 4M × 1 DRAM actually accesses 2048 bits on every row access and then throws away 2047 of those during a column access. DRAM designers have used the internal structure of the DRAM as a way to provide higher bandwidth out of a DRAM. This is done by allowing the column address to change without changing the row address, resulting in an access to other bits in the column latches. *Page-mode* and *static-column-mode* RAMs both provide the ability to access multiple bits out of a row by changing the column address only. (The difference is whether CAS must also be reasserted or not.) *Nibble-mode* RAMs internally generate the next three column addresses, thus providing 4 bits (called a *nibble*) for every row access. EDO (Extended Data Out) represents that latest version in page-mode style RAMs. In 1997, EDO RAMs have become standard for most applications, and provide access times within a row as low as 25 ns. In 1997, SDRAMs are gaining broad acceptance; as stated above, SDRAMs provide even faster access to a series of bits within a row by eliminating the need to specify the column address, instead sequentially transferring all the bits in a burst under the control of a clock signal. As we discussed in Chapter 7, these modes can be used to boost the bandwidth available out of main memory to match the needs of the processor and caches.

Error Correction

Because of the potential for data corruption in large memories, most computer systems use some sort of error-checking code to detect possible corruption of data. One simple code that is heavily used is a *parity code*. In a parity code the number of 1s in a word is counted; the word has odd parity if the number of 1s is odd and even otherwise. When a word is written into memory, the parity bit is also written (1 for odd, 0 for even). Then, when the word is read out, the parity bit is read and checked. If the parity of the memory word and the stored parity bit do not match, an error has occurred. A 1-bit parity scheme can detect at most 1 bit of error in a data item; if there are 2 bits of error, then a 1-bit parity scheme will not detect any errors, since the parity will match the data with two errors. (Actually, a 1-bit parity scheme can detect any odd number of errors; however, the probability of having three errors is much lower than the probability of having two, so, in practice, a 1-bit parity code is limited to detecting a single bit of error.) Of course, a parity code cannot tell which bit in a data item is in error.

A 1-bit parity scheme is an error-detecting code; there are also *error-correcting codes* (ECC) that will detect and allow correction of an error. For large main memories, many systems use a code that allows the detection of up to 2 bits of error and the correction of a single bit of error. These codes work by using more bits to encode the data; for example, the typical codes used for main memories require 7 or 8 bits for every 128 bits of data.

Elaboration: A 1-bit parity code is a *distance-2 code*, which means that if we look at the data plus the parity bit, no 1-bit change is sufficient to generate another legal combination of the data plus parity. For example, if we change a bit in the data, the parity will be wrong, and vice versa. Of course, if we change 2 bits (any 2 data bits or 1 data bit and the parity bit), the parity will match the data and the error cannot be detected. Hence, there is a distance of two between legal combinations of parity and data.

To detect more than one error or correct an error, we need a *distance-3 code*, which has the property that any legal combination of the bits in the error correction code and the data have at least 3 bits differing from any other combination. Suppose we have such a code and we have one error in the data. In that case the code plus data will be 1 bit away from a legal combination and we can correct the data to that legal combination. If we have two errors, we can recognize that there is an error, but we cannot correct the errors. Let's look at an example. Here are the data words and a distance-3 error correction code for a 4-bit data item.

Data	Code bits	Data	Code bits
0000	000	1000	111
0001	011	1001	100
0010	101	1010	010
0011	110	1011	001
0100	110	1100	001
0101	101	1101	010
0110	011	1110	100
0111	000	1111	111

To see how this works, let's choose a data word, say 0110, whose error correction code is 011. Here are the four 1-bit error possibilities for this data: 1110, 0010, 0100, and 0111. Now look at the data item with the same code (011), which is the entry with the value 0001. If the error correction decoder received one of the four possible data words with an error, it would have to choose between correcting to 0110 or 0001. While these four words with error have only 1 bit changed from the correct pattern of 0110, they each have 2 bits that are different from the alternate correction of 0001. Hence the error correction mechanism can easily choose to correct to 0110, since a single error is much lower probability. To see that two errors can be detected, simply notice that all the combinations with 2 bits changed have a different code. The one reuse of the same code is with 3 bits different, but if we correct a 2-bit error, we will correct to the wrong value, since the decoder will assume that only a single error has occurred. If we want to correct 1-bit errors and detect, but not erroneously correct, 2-bit errors, we need a distance-4 code.

Although we distinguished between the code and data in our explanation, in truth, an error correction code treats the combination of code and data as a single word in a larger code (7 bits in this example). Thus it deals with errors in the code bits in the same fashion as errors in the data bits.

While the above example requires $n - 1$ bits for n bits of data, the number of bits required grows slowly, so that for a distance-3 code, a 64-bit word needs 7 bits and a 128-bit word needs 8. This type of code is called a *Hamming code*, after R. Hamming, who described a method for creating such codes.

B.6   Finite State Machines

As we saw earlier, digital logic systems can be classified as combinational or sequential. Sequential systems contain state stored in memory elements internal to the system. Their behavior depends both on the set of inputs supplied and on the contents of the internal memory, or state of the system. Thus a sequential system cannot be described with a truth table. Instead, a sequential system is described as a *finite state machine* (or often just *state machine*). A finite state machine has a set of states and two functions called the *next-state function* and the *output function*. The set of states correspond to all the possible values of the internal storage. Thus, if there are n bits of storage, there are 2^n states. The next-state function is a combinational function that, given the inputs and the current state, determines the next state of the system. The output function produces a set of outputs from the current state and the inputs. Figure B.27 shows this diagrammatically.

The state machines we discuss here and in Chapter 5 are *synchronous*. This means that the state changes together with the clock cycle, and a new state is computed once every clock. Thus, the state elements are updated only on the clock edge. We use this methodology in this section and throughout Chapters

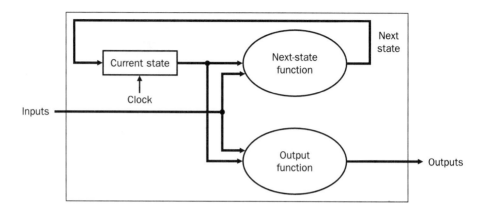

FIGURE B.27   A state machine consists of internal storage that contains the state and two combinational functions: the next-state function and the output function. Often, the output function is restricted to take only the current state as its input; this does not change the capability of a sequential machine, but does affect its internals.

5 and 6, and we do not usually show the clock explicitly. We use state machines throughout Chapters 5 and 6 to control the execution of the processor and the actions of the datapath.

To illustrate how a finite state machine operates and is designed, let's look at a simple and classic example: controlling a traffic light. (Chapters 5 and 6 contain more detailed examples of using finite state machines to control processor execution.) When a finite state machine is used as a controller, the output function is often restricted to depend on just the current state. Such a finite state machine is called a *Moore machine*. This is the type of finite state machine we use throughout this book. If the output function can depend on both the next state and the current input, the machine is called a *Mealy machine*. These two machines are equivalent in their capabilities, and one can be turned into the other mechanically. The basic advantage of a Moore machine is that it can be faster, while a Mealy machine may be smaller, since it may need fewer states than a Moore machine. We discuss this distinction further in Chapter 5 (pages 398–399).

Our example concerns the control of a traffic light at an intersection of a north-south route and an east-west route. For simplicity, we will consider only the green and red lights; adding the yellow light is left for an exercise. We want the lights to cycle no faster than 30 seconds in each direction, so we will use a 0.033-Hz clock so that the machine cycles between states at no faster than once every 30 seconds. There are two output signals.

- *NSlite:* When this signal is asserted, the light on the north-south road is green; when this signal is deasserted the light on the north-south road is red.

- *EWlite:* When this signal is asserted, the light on the east-west road is green; when this signal is deasserted the light on the east-west road is red.

In addition, there are two inputs: NScar and EWcar.

- *NScar:* Indicates that a car is over the detector placed in the roadbed in front of the light on the north-south road (going north or south).

- *EWcar:* Indicates that a car is over the detector placed in the roadbed in front of the light on the east-west road (going east or west).

The traffic light should change from one direction to the other only if a car is waiting to go in the other direction; otherwise, the light should continue to show green in the same direction as the last car that crossed the intersection.

To implement this simple traffic light we need two states:

- *NSgreen:* The traffic light is green in the north-south direction.

- *EWgreen:* The traffic light is green in the east-west direction.

We also need to create the next-state function, which can be specified with a table.

Current state	Inputs		Next state
	NScar	EWcar	
NSgreen	0	0	NSgreen
NSgreen	0	1	EWgreen
NSgreen	1	0	NSgreen
NSgreen	1	1	EWgreen
EWgreen	0	0	EWgreen
EWgreen	0	1	EWgreen
EWgreen	1	0	NSgreen
EWgreen	1	1	NSgreen

Notice that we didn't specify in the algorithm what happens when a car approaches from both directions. In this case, the next-state function given above changes the state to ensure that a steady stream of cars from one direction cannot lock out a car in the other direction.

The finite state machine is completed by specifying the output function:

Current state	Outputs	
	NSlite	EWlite
NSgreen	1	0
EWgreen	0	1

Before we examine how to implement this finite state machine, lets look at a graphical representation, which is often used for finite state machines. In this representation, nodes are used to indicate states. Inside the node we place a list of the outputs that are active for that state. Directed arcs are used to show the next-state function, with labels on the arcs specifying the input condition as logic functions. The graphical representation for this finite state machine is shown in Figure B.28.

A finite state machine can be implemented with a register to hold the current state and a block of combinational logic that computes the next-state function and the output function. Figure B.29 shows how a finite state machine with 4 bits of state, and thus up to 16 states, might look. To implement the finite state machine in this way, we must first assign state numbers to the states. This process is called *state assignment*. For example, we could assign NSgreen to state 0 and EWgreen to state 1. The state register would contain a single bit. The next-state function would be given as

$$\text{NextState} = (\overline{\text{CurrentState} \cdot \text{EWcar}}) + (\text{CurrentState} \cdot \overline{\text{NScar}})$$

where CurrentState is the contents of the state register (0 or 1) and NextState is the output of the next-state function that will be written into the state register at the end of the clock cycle. The output function is also simple:

$$\text{NSlite} = \overline{\text{CurrentState}}$$

$$\text{EWlite} = \text{CurrentState}$$

The combinational logic block is often implemented using structured logic, such as a PLA. A PLA can be constructed automatically from the next-state and output-function tables. In fact, there are computer-aided design (CAD)

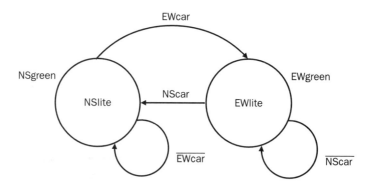

FIGURE B.28 The graphical representation of the two-state traffic light controller. We simplified the logic functions on the state transitions. For example, the transition from NSgreen to EWgreen in the next-state table is $(\text{NScar} \cdot \text{EWcar}) + (\overline{\text{NScar}} \cdot \text{EWcar})$, which is equivalent to EWcar.

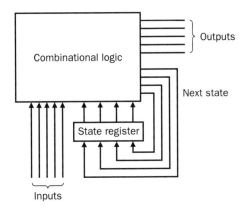

FIGURE B.29 A finite state machine is implemented with a state register that holds the current state and a combinational logic block to compute the next state and output functions. The latter two functions are often split apart and implemented with two separate blocks of logic, which may require fewer gates.

programs that take either a graphical or textual representation of a finite state machine and produce an optimized implementation automatically. In Chapters 5 and 6, finite state machines were used to control processor execution. Appendix C will discuss the detailed implementation of these controllers with both PLAs and ROMs.

B.7 Timing Methodologies

Throughout this appendix and in the rest of the text, we use an edge-triggered timing methodology. This timing methodology has the advantage that it is simpler to explain and understand than a level-triggered methodology. In this section, we explain this timing methodology in a little more detail and also introduce level-sensitive clocking. We conclude this section by briefly discussing the issue of asynchronous signals and synchronizers, an important problem for digital designers.

The purpose of this section is to introduce the major concepts in clocking methodology. The section makes some important simplifying assumptions; if you are interested in understanding timing methodology in more detail, consult one of the references listed at the end of this appendix.

We use an edge-triggered timing methodology because it is simpler to explain and has fewer rules required for correctness. In particular, if we assume that all clocks arrive at the same time, we are guaranteed that a system with edge-triggered registers between blocks of combinational logic can operate correctly without races, if we simply make the clock long enough. A *race* occurs when the contents of a state element depend on the relative speed of different logic elements. In an edge-triggered design, the clock cycle must be long enough to accommodate the path from one flip-flop through the combinational logic to another flip-flop where it must satisfy the set-up time requirement. Figure B.30 shows this requirement for a system using rising edge-triggered flip-flops. In such a system the clock period (or cycle time) must be at least as large as

$$t_{prop} + t_{combinational} + t_{setup}$$

for the worst-case values of these three delays. The simplifying assumption is that the hold-time requirements are satisfied. Satisfying the hold-time requirements in most designs is not a problem, since the propagation time (t_{prop}) is always larger than the hold time for a flip-flop.

One additional complication that must be considered in edge-triggered designs is *clock skew*. Clock skew is the difference in absolute time between when two state elements see a clock edge. Clock skew arises because the clock signal will often use two different paths, with slightly different delays, to reach two different state elements. If the clock skew is large enough, it may be possible for a state element to change and cause the input to another flip-flop to change before the clock edge is seen by the second flip-flop. Figure B.31 illustrates this problem, ignoring set-up time and flip-flop propagation delay. To avoid incorrect operation, the clock period is increased to allow for the maximum clock skew. Thus, the clock period must be longer than

$$t_{prop} + t_{combinational} + t_{setup} + t_{skew}$$

With this constraint on the clock period, the two clocks can also arrive in the opposite order, with the second clock arriving t_{skew} earlier, and the circuit will

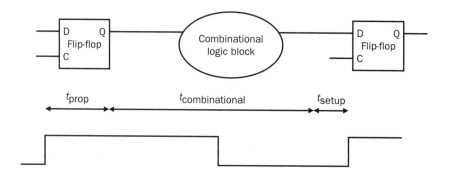

FIGURE B.30   In an edge-triggered design, the clock must be long enough to allow signals to be valid for the required set-up time before the next clock edge. The time for a flip-flop input to propagate to the flip-flip outputs is t_{prop}; the signal then takes $t_{combinational}$ to travel through the combinational logic and must be valid t_{setup} before the next clock edge.

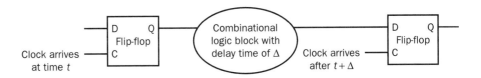

FIGURE B.31   Illustration of how clock skew can cause a race, leading to incorrect operation. Because of the difference in when the two flip-flops see the clock, the signal that is stored into the first flip-flop can race forward and change the input to the second flip-flop before the clock arrives at the second flip-flop.

work correctly. Designers reduce clock skew problems by carefully routing the clock signal to minimize the difference in arrival times. In addition, smart designers also provide some margin by making the clock a little longer than the minimum; this allows for variation in components as well in the power supply. Since clock skew can also affect the hold-time requirements, minimizing the size of the clock skew is important.

Edge-triggered designs have two drawbacks: they require extra logic and they may sometimes be slower. Just looking at the D flip-flop versus the level-sensitive latch that we used to construct the flip-flop shows that edge-triggered design requires more logic. An alternative is to use *level-sensitive clocking*. Because state changes in a level-sensitive methodology are not instantaneous, a level-sensitive scheme is slightly more complex and requires additional care to make it operate correctly.

Level-Sensitive Timing

In a level-sensitive timing methodology, the state changes occur at either high or low levels, but they are not instantaneous as they are in an edge-triggered methodology. Because of the noninstantaneous change in state, races can easily occur. To ensure that a level-sensitive design will also work correctly if the clock is slow enough, designers use *two-phase clocking*. Two-phase clocking is a scheme that makes use of two nonoverlapping clock signals. Since the two clocks, typically called ϕ_1 and ϕ_2, are nonoverlapping, at most one of the clock signals is high at any given time, as shown in Figure B.32. We can use these two clocks to build a system that contains level-sensitive latches but is free from any race conditions, just as the edge-triggered designs were.

One simple way to design such a system is to alternate the use of latches that are open on ϕ_1 with latches that are open on ϕ_2. Because both clocks are not asserted at the same time, a race cannot occur. If the input to a combinational block is a ϕ_1 clock, then its output is latched by a ϕ_2 clock, which is open only during ϕ_2 when the input latch is closed and hence has a valid output. Figure

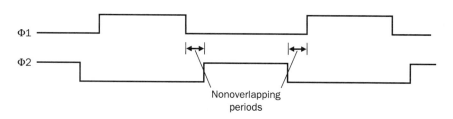

FIGURE B.32   A two-phase clocking scheme showing the cycle of each clock and the non-overlapping periods.

B.33 shows how a system with two-phase timing and alternating latches operates. As in an edge-triggered design, we must pay attention to clock skew, particularly between the two clock phases. By increasing the amount of nonoverlap between the two phases, we can reduce the potential margin of error. Thus the system is guaranteed to operate correctly if each phase is long enough and there is large enough nonoverlap between the phases.

Asynchronous Inputs and Synchronizers

By using a single clock or a two-phase clock, we can eliminate race conditions if clock skew problems are avoided. Unfortunately, it is impractical to make an entire system function with a single clock and still keep the clock skew small. While the CPU may use a single clock, I/O devices will probably have their own clock. In Chapter 8, we showed how an asynchronous device may communicate with the CPU through a series of handshaking steps. To translate the asynchronous input to a synchronous signal that can be used to change the state of a system, we need to use a *synchronizer*, whose inputs are the asynchronous signal and a clock and whose output is a signal synchronous with the input clock.

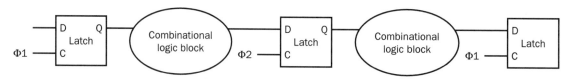

FIGURE B.33   A two-phase timing scheme with alternating latches showing how the system operates on both clock phases. The output of a latch is stable on the opposite phase from its C input. Thus, the first block of combinational inputs has a stable input during ϕ_2 and its output is latched by ϕ_2. The second (rightmost) combinational block operates in just the opposite fashion with stable inputs during ϕ_1. Thus the delays through the combinational blocks determine the minimum time that the respective clocks must be asserted. The size of the nonoverlapping period is determined by the maximum clock skew and the minimum delay of any logic block.

Our first attempt to build a synchronizer uses an edge-triggered D flip-flop, whose *D* input is the asynchronous signal, as shown in Figure B.34. Because we communicate with a handshaking protocol (as we will see in Chapter 8), it does not matter whether we detect the asserted state of the asynchronous signal on one clock or the next, since the signal will be held asserted until it is acknowledged. Thus, you might think that this simple structure is enough to sample the signal accurately, which would be the case except for one small problem.

The problem is a situation called *metastability*. Suppose the asynchronous signal is transitioning between high and low when the clock edge arrives. Clearly, it is not possible to know whether the signal will be latched as high or low. That problem we could live with. Unfortunately, the situation is worse: when the signal that is sampled is not stable for the required set-up and hold times, the flip-flop may go into a *metastable* state. In such a state, the output will not have a legitimate high or low value, but will be in the indeterminate region between them. Furthermore, the flip-flop is not guaranteed to exit this state in any bounded amount of time. Some logic blocks that look at the output of the flip-flop may see its output as 0, while others may see it as 1. This situation is called a *synchronizer failure*. In a purely synchronous system, synchronizer failure can be avoided by ensuring that the set-up and hold times for a flip-flop or latch are always met, but this is impossible when the input is asynchronous. Instead, the only solution possible is to wait long enough before looking at the output of the flip-flop to ensure that its output is stable, and that it has exited the metastable state, if it ever entered it. How long is long enough? Well, the probability that the flip-flop will stay in the metastable state decreases exponentially, so after a very short time the probability that the flip-flop is in the metastable state is very low; however, the probability never reaches 0! So designers wait long enough that the probability of a synchronizer failure is very low, and the time between such failures will be years or even thousands of years. For most flip-flop designs, waiting for a period that is several times longer than the set-up time makes the probability of synchronization failure very low. If the clock rate is longer than the potential metastability period

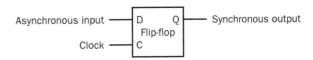

Asynchronous input — D   Q — Synchronous output
                     Flip-flop
Clock — C

FIGURE B.34 A synchronizer built from a D flip-flop is used to sample an asynchronous signal to produce an output that is synchronous with the clock. This "synchronizer" will *not* work properly!

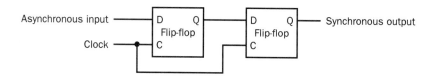

FIGURE B.35   This synchronizer will work correctly if the period of metastability that we wish to guard against is less than the clock period. Although the output of the first flip-flop may be metastable, it will not be seen by any other logic element until the second clock, when the second D flip-flop samples the signal, which by that time should no longer be in a metastable state.

(which is likely), then a safe synchronizer can be built with two D flip-flops, as shown in Figure B.35. If you are interested in reading more about these problems, look into the references.

B.8   Concluding Remarks

This appendix introduces the basics of logic design. If you have digested the material in this appendix, you are ready to tackle the material in Chapters 5 and 6, both of which use the concepts discussed in this appendix extensively.

To Probe Further

There are a number of good texts on logic design. Here are some you might like to look into.

Katz, R. H. [1993]. *Modern Logic Design*, Benjamin/Cummings, Redwood City, CA.

A general text on logic design.

McCluskey, E. J. [1986]. *Logic Design Principles*, Prentice Hall, Englewood Cliffs, NJ.

Contains extensive discussions of hazards, optimization principles, and testability.

Mead, C., and L. Conway [1980]. *Introduction to VLSI Systems*, Addison-Wesley, New York.

Discusses the design of VLSI systems using nMOS technology.

Proser, F. P., and D. E. Winkel [1987]. *The Art of Digital Design*, second edition, Prentice Hall, Englewood Cliffs, NJ.

A general text on logic design.

Wakerly, J. F. [1990]. *Digital Design: Principles and Practices*, Prentice Hall, Englewood Cliffs, NJ.

A general text on logic design.

B.9   Key Terms

This appendix introduces a number of major terms that may be new to you. These key terms are listed below. If you have only browsed this appendix, the key terms should provide a good review. All of these terms are defined in the Glossary at the back of this book.

asserted signal	latch	read-only memory (ROM)
bus	level-sensitive clocking	register file
clock skew	metastability	selector or control value
clocking methodology	minterm or product term	sequential logic
combinational logic	NAND gate	set-up time
D flip-flop	next-state function	state element
deasserted signal	NOR gate	static random access memory
decoder	page mode	(SRAM)
edge-triggered clocking	programmable logic array	sum of products
finite state machine	(PLA)	synchronizer failure
flip-flop	programmable ROM	synchronous system
gate	(PROMs)	
hold time	propagation time	

B.10   Exercises

B.1 [10] <§B.2> Show that there are 2^n entries in a truth table for a function with n inputs.

B.2 [10] <§B.2> One logic function that is used for a variety of purposes (including within adders and to compute parity) is *exclusive OR*. The output of a two-input exclusive-OR function is true only if exactly one of the inputs is true. Show the truth table for a two-input exclusive-OR function and implement this function using AND gates, OR gates, and inverters.

B.3 [15] <§B.2> Prove that the NOR gate is universal by showing how to build the AND, OR, and NOT functions using a two-input NOR gate.

B.4 [15] <§B.2> Prove that the NAND gate is universal by showing how to build the AND, OR, and NOT functions using a two-input NAND gate.

B.5 [15] <§§B.2, B.3> Prove that a two-input multiplexor is also universal by showing how to build the AND, OR, and NOT functions using a multiplexor.

In More Depth

DeMorgan's Theorems

In addition to the basic laws we discussed on pages B-5 and B-6, there are two important theorems, called DeMorgan's theorems, which are

$$\overline{A + B} = \overline{A} \cdot \overline{B} \quad \text{and} \quad \overline{A \cdot B} = \overline{A} + \overline{B}$$

B.6 [10] <§B.2> Prove DeMorgan's theorems with a truth table of the form

A	B	$\overline{A}$	$\overline{B}$	$\overline{A + B}$	$\overline{A} \cdot \overline{B}$	$\overline{A \cdot B}$	$\overline{A} + \overline{B}$
0	0						
0	1						
1	0						
1	1						

B.7 [15] <§B.2> Prove that the two equations for E in the example starting on page B-6 are equivalent by using DeMorgan's theorems and the axioms shown on page B-6.

B.8 [15] <§§B.2–B.3> Derive the product-of-sums representation for E shown on page B-10 starting with the sum-of-products representation. You will need to use DeMorgan's theorems.

B.9 [30] <§§B.2–B.3> Give an algorithm for constructing the sum-of-products representation for an arbitrary logic equation consisting of AND, OR, and NOT. The algorithm should be recursive and should not construct the truth table in the process.

B.10 [5] <§§4.2, B.2, B.3> Assume that X consists of 3 bits, x2 x1 x0. Write four logic functions that are true if and only if

- X contains only one 1
- X contains an even number of 1s
- X when interpreted as an unsigned binary number is less than 3
- X when interpreted as a signed (two's complement) number is less than –1

B.11 [5] <§§4.2, B.2, B.3> {Ex. B.10} Implement the four functions described in Exercise B.10 using a PLA.

B.12 [5] <§§4.2, B.2, B.3> Assume that X consists of 3 bits, x2 x1 x0, and Y consists of 3 bits, y2 y1 y0. Write logic functions that are true if and only if

- X < Y, where X and Y are thought of as unsigned binary numbers

- X < Y, where X and Y are thought of as signed (two's complement) numbers
- X = Y

B.13 [5] <§§B.2, B.3> Show a truth table for a multiplexor (inputs A, B, and S; output C), using don't cares to simplify the table where possible.

B.14 [5] <§§B.2, B.3> Implement a switching network that has two data inputs (A and B), two data outputs (C and D), and a control input (S). If S equals 1, the network is in pass-through mode, and C should equal A, and D should equal B. If S equals 0, the network is in crossing mode, and C should equal B, and D should equal A.

B.15 [10] <§§B.2, B.5> Construct the truth table for a four-input even-parity function (see page B-34 for a description of parity).

B.16 [10] <§§B.2, B.5> Implement the four-input even-parity function with AND and OR gates using bubbled inputs and outputs.

B.17 [10] <§§B.2, B.3, B.5> Implement the four-input even-parity function with a PLA.

B.18 [5] <§B.5> Which of the following two code fragments better describes a D latch? Which better describes a D flip-flop?

```
repeat
  while (clock==low) do
    {} \* nothing *\
  Q = D;
  while (clock==high) do
    {} \* nothing *\
until (power_goes_off)
```

or

```
repeat
  while (clock==high) do
    Q = D
until (the_battery_wears_out)
```

B.19 [5] <§B.5> Quite often, you would expect that given a timing diagram containing a description of changes that take place on a data input D and a clock input C (as in Figures B.14 and B.17 on pages B-23 and B-25, respectively), there would be differences between the output waveforms (Q) for a D latch and a D flip-flop. In a sentence or two, describe the circumstances (e.g., the nature of the inputs) for which there would not be any difference between the two output waveforms.

B.20 [5] <§B.5> Figure B.19 on page B-26 illustrates the implementation of the register file for the MIPS datapath. Pretend that a new register file is to be built, but that there are only two registers and only one read port, and that each register has only 2 bits of data. Redraw Figure B.19 so that every wire in your diagram corresponds to only 1 bit of data (unlike the diagram in Figure B.19, in which some wires are 5 bits and some wires are 32 bits). Redraw the registers using D flip-flops. You do not need to show how to implement a D flip-flop or a multiplexor.

B.21 [10] <§B.6> A friend would like you to build an "electronic eye" for use as a fake security device. The device consists of three lights lined up in a row, controlled by the outputs Left, Middle, and Right, which, if asserted, indicate that a light should be on. Only one light is on at a time, and the light "moves" from left to right and then from right to left, thus scaring away thieves who believe that the device is monitoring their activity. Draw the graphical representation for the finite state machine used to specify the electronic eye. Note that the rate of the eye's movement will be controlled by the clock speed (which should not be too great) and that there are essentially no inputs.

B.22 [10] <§B.6> {Ex. B.21} Assign state numbers to the states of the finite state machine you construct for Exercise B.21 and write a set of logic equations for each of the outputs, including the next state bits.

B.23 [15] <§§B.2, B.5> Construct a 3-bit counter using three D flip-flops and a selection of gates. The inputs should consist of a signal that resets the counter to 0, called *reset*, and a signal to increment the counter, called *inc*. The outputs should be the value of the counter. When the counter has value 7 and is incremented, it should wrap around and become 0.

B.24 [20] <§§B.3, B.5> A *Gray code* is a sequence of binary numbers with the property that no more than 1 bit changes in going from one element of the sequence to another. For example, here is a 3-bit binary Gray code: 000, 001, 011, 010, 110, 111, 101, and 100. Using three D flip-flops and a PLA, construct a 3-bit Gray code counter that has two inputs: *reset*, which sets the counter to 000, and *inc*, which makes the counter go to the next value in the sequence. Note that the code is cyclic, so that the value after 100 in the sequence is 000.

B.25 [25] <§§B.2, B.6> We wish to add a yellow light to our traffic light example on page 36. We will do this by changing the clock to run at 0.25 Hz (a 4-second clock cycle time), which is the duration of a yellow light. To prevent the green and red lights from cycling too fast, we add a 30-second timer. The timer has a single input, called *TimerReset*, which restarts the timer, and a single output, called *TimerSignal*, which indicates that the 30-second period has expired. Also, we must redefine the traffic signals to include yellow. We do this by defining two output signals for each light: green and yellow. If the output NS-green is asserted, the green light is on; if the output NSyellow is asserted, the yellow light is on. If both signals are off, the red light is on. Do *not* assert both the green and yellow signals at the same time, since American drivers will certainly be confused, even if European drivers understand what this means! Draw the graphical representation for the finite state machine for this improved controller. Choose names for the states that are *different* from the names of the outputs.

B.26 [15] <§B.6> Write down the next-state and output-function tables for the traffic light controller described in Exercise B.25.

B.27 [15] <§§B.2, B.6> Assign state numbers to the states in the traffic light example of Exercise B.25 and use the tables of Exercise B.26 to write a set of logic equations for each of the outputs, including the next-state outputs.

B.28 [15] <§§B.3, B.6> Implement the logic equations of Exercise B.27 as a PLA.

Mapping Control to Hardware

A custom format such as this is slave to the architecture of the hardware and the instruction set it serves. The format must strike a proper compromise between ROM size, ROM-output decoding, circuitry size, and machine execution rate.

Jim McKevit et al.
8086 design report, 1977

C.1   **Introduction**   C-3

C.2   **Implementing Combinational Control Units**   C-4

C.3   **Implementing Finite State Machine Control**   C-8

C.4   **Implementing the Next-State Function with a Sequencer**   C-21

C.5   **Translating a Microprogram to Hardware**   C-28

C.6   **Concluding Remarks**   C-31

C.7   **Key Terms**   C-32

C.8   **Exercises**   C-32

C.1   Introduction

Control typically has two parts: a combinational part that lacks state and a sequential control unit that handles sequencing and the main control in a multicycle design. Combinational control units are often used to handle part of the decode and control process. The ALU control in Chapter 5 is such an example. A single-cycle implementation like that in Chapter 5 can also use a combinational controller, since it does not require multiple states. Section C.2 examines the implementation of these two combinational units from the truth tables of Chapter 5.

Since sequential control units are larger and often more complex, there are a wider variety of techniques for implementing a sequential control unit. The usefulness of these techniques depends on the complexity of the control, characteristics such as the average number of next states for any given state, and the implementation technology.

The most straightforward way to implement a sequential control function is with a block of logic that takes as inputs the current state and the opcode field of the Instruction register and produces as outputs the datapath control signals and the value of the next state. The initial representation may be either a finite state diagram or a microprogram. In the latter case, each microinstruction represents a state. In an implementation using a finite state controller, the next-state function will be computed with logic. Section C.3 constructs such an implementation both for a ROM and a PLA.

An alternative method of implementation computes the next-state function by using a counter that increments the current state to determine the next state. When the next state doesn't follow sequentially, other logic is used to determine the state. Section C.4 explores this type of implementation and shows how it can be used for the finite state control created in Chapter 5.

In section C.5, we show how a microprogram representation of sequential control is translated to control logic.

Implementing Combinational Control Units

In this section, we show how the ALU control unit and main control unit for the single clock design are mapped down to the gate level. With modern CAD systems this process is completely mechanical. The examples illustrate how a CAD system takes advantage of the structure of the control function, including the presence of don't-care terms.

Mapping the ALU Control Function to Gates

Figure C.1 shows the truth table for the ALU control function that was developed in section 5.3. A logic block that implements this ALU control function will have three distinct outputs (called Operation2, Operation1, and Operation0), each corresponding to one of the three bits of the ALU control in the last column of Figure C.1. The logic function for each output is constructed by combining all the truth table entries that set that particular output. For example, the low-order bit of the ALU control (Operation0) is set by the last two entries of the truth table in Figure C.1. Thus the truth table for Operation0 will have these two entries.

ALUOp		Funct field						Operation
ALUOp1	ALUOp0	F5	F4	F3	F2	F1	F0	
0	0	X	X	X	X	X	X	010
X	1	X	X	X	X	X	X	110
1	X	X	X	0	0	0	0	010
1	X	X	X	0	0	1	0	110
1	X	X	X	0	1	0	0	000
1	X	X	X	0	1	0	1	001
1	X	X	X	1	0	1	0	111

FIGURE C.1   The truth table for the three ALU control bits (called Operation) as a function of the ALUOp and function code field. This table is the same as that shown Figure 5.15.

Figure C.2 shows the truth tables for each of the three ALU control bits. We have taken advantage of the common structure in each truth table to incorporate additional don't cares. For example, the five lines in the truth table of Figure C.1 that set Operation1 are reduced to just two entries in Figure C.2. A logic minimization program will use the don't-care terms to reduce the number of gates and the number of inputs to each gate in a logic gate realization of these truth tables.

ALUOp		Function code fields					
ALUOp1	ALUOp0	F5	F4	F3	F2	F1	F0
X	1	X	X	X	X	X	X
1	X	X	X	X	X	1	X

a. The truth table for Operation2 = 1 (this table corresponds to the left bit of the Operation field in Figure C.1)

ALUOp		Function code fields					
ALUOp1	ALUOp0	F5	F4	F3	F2	F1	F0
0	X	X	X	X	X	X	X
X	X	X	X	X	0	X	X

b. The truth table for Operation1 = 1

ALUOp		Function code fields					
ALUOp1	ALUOp0	F5	F4	F3	F2	F1	F0
1	X	X	X	X	X	X	1
1	X	X	X	1	X	X	X

c. The truth table for Operation0 = 1

FIGURE C.2 The truth tables for the three ALU control lines. Only the entries for which the output is 1 are shown. The bits in each field are numbered from right to left starting with 0; thus F5 is the most significant bit of the function field, and F0 is the least significant bit. Similarly, the names of the signals corresponding to the 3-bit operation code supplied to the ALU are Operation2, Operation1, and Operation0 (with the last being the least significant bit). Thus the truth table above shows the input combinations for which the ALU control should be 010, 001, 110, or 111 (the combinations 011, 100, and 101 are not used). The ALUOp bits are named ALUOp1 and ALUOp0. The three output values depend on the 2-bit ALUOp field and, when that field is equal to 10, the 6-bit function code in the instruction. Accordingly, when the ALUOp field is not equal to 10, we don't care about the function code value (it is represented by an X). See Appendix B for more background on don't cares.

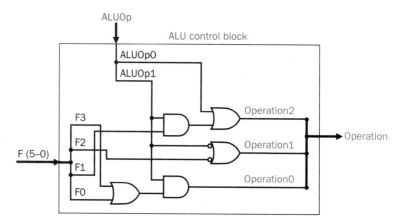

FIGURE C.3   The ALU control block generates the three ALU control bits, based on the function code and ALUOp bits. This logic is generated directly from the truth table in Figure C.2. Only 4 of the 6 bits in the function code are actually needed as inputs, since the upper 2 bits are always don't cares. Let's examine how this logic relates to the truth table of Figure C.2. Consider the Operation2 output, which is generated by two lines in the truth table for Operation2. The second line is the AND of two terms (F1 = 1 and ALUOp1 = 1); the top two-input AND gate corresponds to this term. The other term that causes Operation2 to be asserted is simply ALUOp0. These two terms are combined with an OR gate whose output is Operation2. The outputs Operation0 and Operation1 are derived in similar fashion from the truth table.

From the simplified truth table in Figure C.2, we can generate the logic shown in Figure C.3, which we call the *ALU control block*. This process is straightforward and can be done with a computer-aided design (CAD) program. An example of how the logic gates can be derived from the truth tables is given in the legend to Figure C.3.

This ALU control logic is simple because there are only three outputs, and only a few of the possible input combinations need to be recognized. If a large number of possible ALU function codes had to be transformed into ALU control signals, this simple method would not be efficient. Instead, you could use a decoder, a memory, or a structured array of logic gates. These techniques are described in Appendix B, and we will see examples when we examine the implementation of the multicycle controller in section C.3.

Elaboration: In general, a logic equation and truth table representation of a logic function are equivalent. (We discuss this in further detail in Appendix B.) However, when a truth table only specifies the entries that result in nonzero outputs, it may not completely describe the logic function. A full truth table completely indicates all don't-care entries. For example, the encoding 11 for ALUOp always generates a don't care in the output. Thus a complete truth table would have XXX in the output portion for all entries with 11 in the ALUOp field. These don't-care entries allow us to replace the ALUOp field 10 and 01 with 1X and X1, respectively. Incorporating the don't-care terms and minimizing the logic is both complex and error-prone and, thus, is better left to a program.

Mapping the Main Control Function to Gates

Implementing the main control function with an unstructured collection of gates, as we did for the ALU control, is reasonable because the control function is neither complex nor large, as we can see from the truth table shown in Figure C.4. However, if most of the 64 possible opcodes were used and there were many more control lines, the number of gates would be much larger and each gate could have many more inputs.

Since any function can be computed in two levels of logic, another way to implement a logic function is with a structured two-level logic array. Figure C.5 shows such an implementation. It uses an array of AND gates followed by an array of OR gates. This structure is called a *programmable logic array* (PLA). A PLA is one of the most common ways to implement a control function. We will return to the topic of using structured logic elements to implement control when we implement the finite state controller in the next section.

Control	Signal name	R-format	lw	sw	beq
Inputs	Op5	0	1	1	0
	Op4	0	0	0	0
	Op3	0	0	1	0
	Op2	0	0	0	1
	Op1	0	1	1	0
	Op0	0	1	1	0
Outputs	RegDst	1	0	X	X
	ALUSrc	0	1	1	0
	MemtoReg	0	1	X	X
	RegWrite	1	1	0	0
	MemRead	0	1	0	0
	MemWrite	0	0	1	0
	Branch	0	0	0	1
	ALUOp1	1	0	0	0
	ALUOp0	0	0	0	1

FIGURE C.4   The control function for the simple one-clock implementation is completely specified by this truth table. This table is the same as that shown in Figure 5.27.

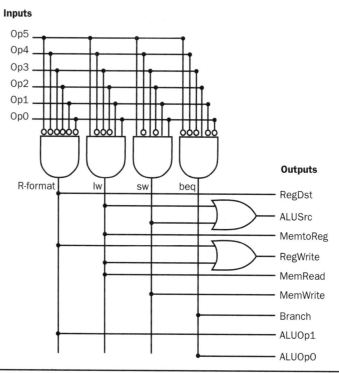

Inputs

Op5
Op4
Op3
Op2
Op1
Op0

Outputs

R-format   lw   sw   beq

RegDst
ALUSrc
MemtoReg
RegWrite
MemRead
MemWrite
Branch
ALUOp1
ALUOp0

FIGURE C.5   The structured implementation of the control function as described by the truth table in Figure C.4. The structure, called a programmable logic array (PLA), uses an array of AND gates followed by an array of OR gates. The inputs to the AND gates are the function inputs and their inverses (bubbles indicate inversion of a signal). The inputs to the OR gates are the outputs of the AND gates (or, as a degenerate case, the function inputs and inverses). The output of the OR gates is the function outputs.

C.3   Implementing Finite State Machine Control

To implement the control as a finite state machine, we must first assign a number to each of the 10 states; any state could use any number, but we will use the sequential numbering for simplicity as we did in Chapter 5. (Figure C.6 is a copy of the finite state diagram from Figure 5.42 on page 396, reproduced for ease of access.) With 10 states we will need 4 bits to encode the state number, and we call these state bits: S3, S2, S1, S0. The current-state number will be stored in a state register, as shown in Figure C.7. If the states are assigned sequentially, state i is encoded using the state bits as the binary

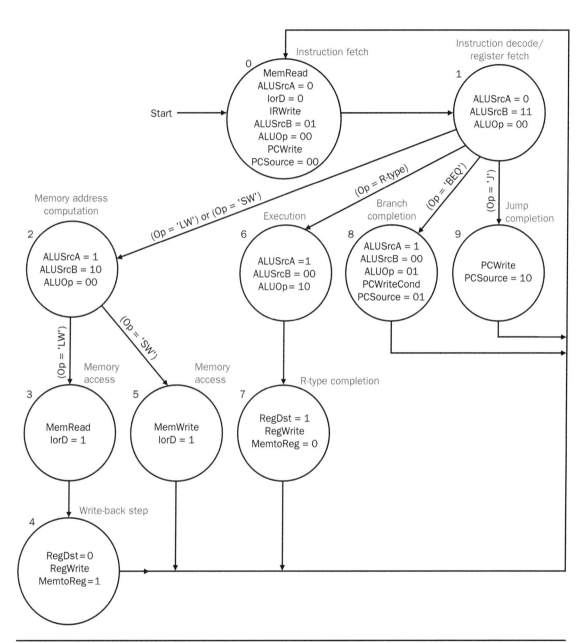

FIGURE C.6 The finite state diagram that was developed in Chapter 5; it is identical to Figure 5.42.

number i. For example, state 6 is encoded as 0110_{two} or S3 = 0, S2 = 1, S1 = 1, S0 = 0, which can also be written as

$$\overline{S3} \cdot S2 \cdot S1 \cdot \overline{S0}$$

The control unit has outputs that specify the next state. These are written into the state register on the clock edge and become the new state at the beginning of the next clock cycle following the active clock edge. We name these outputs NS3, NS2, NS1, NS0. Once we have determined the number of inputs, states, and outputs, we know what the basic outline of the control unit will look like, as we show in Figure C.7.

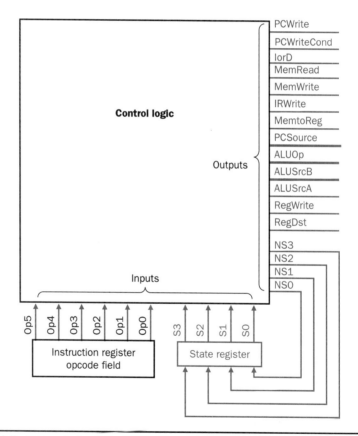

FIGURE C.7   **The control unit for MIPS will consist of some control logic and a register to hold the state.** The state register is written at the active clock edge and is stable during the clock cycle.

The block labeled "control logic" in Figure C.7 is combinational logic. We can think of it as a big table giving the value of the outputs in terms of the inputs. The logic in this block implements the two different parts of the finite state machine. One part is the logic that determines the setting of the datapath control outputs, which depend only on the state bits. The other part of the control logic implements the next-state function; these equations determine the values of the next-state bits based on the current-state bits and the other inputs (the 6-bit opcode).

Figure C.8 shows the logic equations: the top portion showing the outputs, and the bottom portion showing the next-state function. The values in this table were determined from the state diagram in Figure C.6. Whenever a control line is active in a state, that state is entered in the second column of the table. Likewise, the next-state entries are made whenever one state is a successor to another.

Output	Current states	Op
PCWrite	state0 + state9	
PCWriteCond	state8	
IorD	state3 + state5	
MemRead	state0 + state3	
MemWrite	state5	
IRWrite	state0	
MemtoReg	state4	
PCSource1	state9	
PCSource0	state8	
ALUOp1	state6	
ALUOp0	state8	
ALUSrcB1	state1 +state2	
ALUSrcB0	state0 + state1	
ALUSrcA	state2 + state6 + state8	
RegWrite	state4 + state7	
RegDst	state7	
NextState0	state4 + state5 + state7 + state8 + state9	
NextState1	state0	
NextState2	state1	(Op = 'lw') + (Op = 'sw')
NextState3	state2	(Op = 'lw')
NextState4	state3	
NextState5	state2	(Op = 'sw')
NextState6	state1	(Op = 'R-type')
NextState7	state6	
NextState8	state1	(Op = 'beq')
NextState9	state1	(Op = 'jmp')

FIGURE C.8 The logic equations for the control unit shown in a shorthand form. Remember that "+" stands for OR in logic equations. The state inputs and NextState entries outputs must be expanded by using the state encoding. Any blank entry is a don't care.

In Figure C.8 we use the abbreviation state$N$ to stand for current state N. Thus, state$N$ is replaced by the term that encodes the state number N. We use NextState$N$ to stand for the setting of the next-state outputs to N. This output is implemented using the next-state outputs (NS). When NextState$N$ is active, the bits NS[3–0] are set corresponding to the binary version of the value N. Of course, since a given next-state bit is activated in multiple next states, the equation for each state bit will be the OR of the terms that activate that signal. Likewise, when we use a term such as (Op = 'lw'), this corresponds to an AND of the opcode inputs that specifies the encoding of the opcode lw in 6 bits, just as we did for the simple control unit in the previous section of this chapter. Translating the entries in Figure C.8 into logic equations for the outputs is straightforward.

Logic Equations for Next-State Outputs

Example

Give the logic equation for the low-order next-state bit, NS0.

Answer

The next-state bit NS0 should be active whenever the next state has NS0 = 1 in the state encoding. This is true for NextState1, NextState3, NextState5, NextState7, and NextState9. The entries for these states in Figure C.8 supply the conditions when these next-state values should be active. The equation for each of these next states is given below. The first equation states that the next state is 1 if the current state is 0; the current state is 0 if each of the state input bits is 0, which is what the rightmost product term indicates.

$$\text{NextState1} = \text{State0} = \overline{S3} \cdot \overline{S2} \cdot \overline{S1} \cdot \overline{S0}$$

$$\text{NextState3} = \text{State2} \cdot (\text{Op[5-0]} = \text{'lw'})$$
$$= \overline{S3} \cdot \overline{S2} \cdot S1 \cdot \overline{S0} \cdot \text{Op5} \cdot \overline{\text{Op4}} \cdot \overline{\text{Op3}} \cdot \overline{\text{Op2}} \cdot \text{Op1} \cdot \text{Op0}$$

$$\text{NextState5} = \text{State 2} \cdot (\text{Op[5-0]} = \text{'sw'})$$
$$= \overline{S3} \cdot \overline{S2} \cdot S1 \cdot \overline{S0} \cdot \text{Op5} \cdot \overline{\text{Op4}} \cdot \text{Op3} \cdot \overline{\text{Op2}} \cdot \text{Op1} \cdot \text{Op0}$$

$$\text{NextState7} = \text{State6} = \overline{S3} \cdot S2 \cdot S1 \cdot \overline{S0}$$

$$\text{NextState9} = \text{State1} \cdot (\text{Op[5-0]} = \text{'jmp'})$$
$$= \overline{S3} \cdot \overline{S2} \cdot \overline{S1} \cdot S0 \cdot \overline{\text{Op5}} \cdot \overline{\text{Op4}} \cdot \overline{\text{Op3}} \cdot \overline{\text{Op2}} \cdot \text{Op1} \cdot \overline{\text{Op0}}$$

NS0 is the logical sum of all these terms.

As we have seen, the control function can be expressed as a logic equation for each output. This set of logic equations can be implemented in two ways: corresponding to a complete truth table, or corresponding to a two-level logic structure that allows a sparse encoding of the truth table. Before we look at these implementations, let's look at the truth table for the complete control function.

It is simplest if we break the control function defined in Figure C.8 into two parts: the next-state outputs, which may depend on all the inputs, and the control signal outputs, which depend only on the current-state bits. Figure C.9 shows the truth tables for all the datapath control signals. Because these signals actually depend only on the state bits (and not the opcode), each of the entries in a table in Figure C.9 actually represents 64 (= 2^6) entries, with the 6 bits named Op having all possible values; that is, the Op bits are don't-care bits in determining the datapath control outputs. Figure C.10 shows the truth table for the next-state bits NS[3–0], which depend on the state input bits and the instruction bits, which supply the opcode.

Elaboration: There are many opportunities to simplify the control function by observing similarities among two or more control signals and by using the semantics of the implementation. For example, the signals PCWriteCond, PCSource0, and ALUOp0 are all asserted in exactly one state, state 8. These three control signals can be replaced by a single signal.

A ROM Implementation

Probably the simplest way to implement the control function is to encode the truth tables in a read-only memory (ROM). The number of entries in the memory for the truth tables of Figures C.9 and C.10 is equal to all possible values of the inputs (the 6 opcode bits plus the 4 state bits), which is $2^{\# \text{ inputs}} = 2^{10} = 1024$. The inputs to the control unit become the address lines for the ROM, which implements the control logic block that was shown in Figure C.7 on page C-10. The width of each entry (or word in the memory) is 20 bits since there are 16 datapath control outputs and 4 next-state bits. This means the total size of the ROM is $2^{10} \times 20 = 20$ Kbits.

The setting of the bits in a word in the ROM depends on which outputs are active in that word. Before we look at the control words, we need to order the bits within the control input (the address) and output words (the contents), respectively. We will number the bits using the order in Figure C.7 on page C-10, with the next-state bits being the low-order bits of the control *word* and the current-state input bits being the low-order bits of the *address*. This means that the PCWrite output will be the high-order bit (bit 19) of each memory word,

s3	s2	s1	s0
0	0	0	0
1	0	0	1

a. Truth table for PCWrite

s3	s2	s1	s0
1	0	0	0

b. Truth table for PCWriteCond

s3	s2	s1	s0
0	0	1	1
0	1	0	1

c. Truth table for IorD

s3	s2	s1	s0
0	0	0	0
0	0	1	1

d. Truth table for MemRead

s3	s2	s1	s0
0	1	0	1

e. Truth table for MemWrite

s3	s2	s1	s0
0	0	0	0

f. Truth table for IRWrite

s3	s2	s1	s0
0	1	0	0

g. Truth table for MemtoReg

s3	s2	s1	s0
1	0	0	1

h. Truth table for PCSource1

s3	s2	s1	s0
1	0	0	0

i. Truth table for PCSource0

s3	s2	s1	s0
0	1	1	0

j. Truth table for ALUOp1

s3	s2	s1	s0
1	0	0	0

k. Truth table for ALUOp0

s3	s2	s1	s0
0	0	0	1
0	0	1	0

l. Truth table for ALUSrcB1

s3	s2	s1	s0
0	0	0	0
0	0	0	1

m. Truth table for ALUSrcB0

s3	s2	s1	s0
0	0	1	0
0	1	1	0
1	0	0	0

n. Truth table for ALUSrcA

s3	s2	s1	s0
0	1	0	0
0	1	1	1

o. Truth table for RegWrite

s3	s2	s1	s0
0	1	1	1

p. Truth table for RegDst

FIGURE C.9   The truth tables are shown for the 16 datapath control signals that depend only on the current-state input bits, which are shown for each table. Each truth table row corresponds to 64 entries: one for each possible value of the 6 Op bits. Notice that some of the outputs are active under nearly the same circumstances. For example, in the case of PCWriteCond, PCSource0, and ALUOp0, these signals are both active only in state 8 (see (b), (j), and (l)). These three signals could be replaced by one signal. There are other opportunities for reducing the logic needed to implement the control function by taking advantage of further similarities in the truth tables.

Op5	Op4	Op3	Op2	Op1	Op0	S3	S2	S1	S0
0	0	0	0	1	0	0	0	0	1
0	0	0	1	0	0	0	0	0	1

a. The truth table for the NS3 output, active when the next state is 8 or 9. This signal is activated when the current state is 1.

Op5	Op4	Op3	Op2	Op1	Op0	S3	S2	S1	S0
0	0	0	0	0	0	0	0	0	1
1	0	1	0	1	1	0	0	1	0
X	X	X	X	X	X	0	0	1	1
X	X	X	X	X	X	0	1	1	0

b. The truth table for the NS2 output, which is active when the next state is 4, 5, 6, or 7. This situation occurs when the current state is one of 1, 2, 3, or 6.

Op5	Op4	Op3	Op2	Op1	Op0	S3	S2	S1	S0
0	0	0	0	0	0	0	0	0	1
1	0	0	0	1	1	0	0	0	1
1	0	1	0	1	1	0	0	0	1
1	0	0	0	1	1	0	0	1	0
X	X	X	X	X	X	0	1	1	0

c. The truth table for the NS1 output, which is active when the next state is 2, 3, 6, or 7. The next state is one of 2, 3, 6, or 7 only if the current state is one of 1, 2, or 6.

Op5	Op4	Op3	Op2	Op1	Op0	S3	S2	S1	S0
X	X	X	X	X	X	0	0	0	0
1	0	0	0	1	1	0	0	1	0
1	0	1	0	1	1	0	0	1	0
X	X	X	X	X	X	0	1	1	0
0	0	0	0	1	0	0	0	0	1

d. The truth table for the NS0 output, which is active when the next state is 1, 3, 5, 7, or 9. This happens only if the current state is one of 0, 1, 2, or 6.

FIGURE C.10 The four truth tables for the four next-state output bits (NS[3–0]). The next-state outputs depend on the value of Op[5–0], which is the opcode field, and the current state, given by S[3–0]. The entries with X are don't-care terms. Each entry with a don't-care term corresponds to two entries, one with that input at 0 and one with that input at 1. Thus an entry with n don't-care terms actually corresponds to 2^n truth table entries.

and NS0 will be the low-order bit. The high-order address bit will be given by Op5, which is the high-order bit of the instruction, and the low-order address bit will be given by S0.

We can construct the ROM contents by building the entire truth table in a form where each row corresponds to one of the 2^n unique input combinations, and a set of columns indicate which outputs are active for that input combination. We don't have the space here to show all 1024 entries in the truth table.

However, by separating the datapath control and next-state outputs, we do, since the datapath control outputs depend only on the current state. The truth table for the datapath control outputs is shown in Figure C.11. We include only the encodings of the state inputs that are in use (that is, values 0 through 9 corresponding to the 10 states of the state machine).

The truth table in Figure C.11 directly gives the contents of the upper 16 bits of each word in the ROM. The 4-bit input field gives the low-order four address bits of each word, and the column gives the contents of the word at that address.

If we did show a full truth table for the datapath control bits with both the state number and the opcode bits as inputs, the opcode inputs would all be don't cares. When we construct the ROM, we cannot have any don't cares, since the addresses into the ROM must be complete. Thus, the same datapath control outputs will occur many times in the ROM, since this part of the ROM is the same whenever the state bits are identical, independent of the value of the opcode inputs.

Outputs	Input values (S[3–0])									
	0000	0001	0010	0011	0100	0101	0110	0111	1000	1001
PCWrite	1	0	0	0	0	0	0	0	0	1
PCWriteCond	0	0	0	0	0	0	0	0	1	0
IorD	0	0	0	1	0	1	0	0	0	0
MemRead	1	0	0	1	0	0	0	0	0	0
MemWrite	0	0	0	0	0	1	0	0	0	0
IRWrite	1	0	0	0	0	0	0	0	0	0
MemtoReg	0	0	0	0	1	0	0	0	0	0
PCSource1	0	0	0	0	0	0	0	0	0	1
PCSource0	0	0	0	0	0	0	0	0	1	0
ALUOp1	0	0	0	0	0	0	1	0	0	0
ALUOp0	0	0	0	0	0	0	0	0	1	0
ALUSrcB1	0	1	1	0	0	0	0	0	0	0
ALUSrcB0	1	1	0	0	0	0	0	0	0	0
ALUSrcA	0	0	1	0	0	0	1	0	1	0
RegWrite	0	0	0	0	1	0	0	1	0	0
RegDst	0	0	0	0	0	0	0	1	0	0

FIGURE C.11   The truth table for the 16 datapath control outputs, which depend only on the state inputs. The values are determined from Figure C.9. Although there are 16 possible values for the 4-bit state field, only 10 of these are used and are shown here. The 10 possible values are shown at the top; each column shows the setting of the datapath control outputs for the state input value that appears at the top of the column. For example, when the state inputs are 0011 (state 3), the active datapath control outputs are IorD or MemRead.

Control ROM Entries

Example

For what ROM addresses will the bit corresponding to PCWrite, the high bit of the control word, be 1?

Answer

PCWrite is high in states 0 and 9; this corresponds to addresses with the 4 low-order bits being either 0000 or 1001. The bit will be high in the memory word independent of the inputs Op[5–0], so the addresses with the bit high are 000000000, 0000001001, 0000010000, 0000011001, ..., 1111110000, 1111111001. The general form of this is XXXXXX0000 or XXXXXX1001, where XXXXXX is any combination of bits, and corresponds to the 6-bit opcode on which this output does not depend.

We will show the entire contents of the ROM in two parts to make it easier to show. Figure C.12 shows the upper 16 bits of the control word; this comes directly from Figure C.11. These datapath control outputs depend only on the state inputs, and this set of words would be duplicated 64 times in the full ROM, as we discussed above. The entries corresponding to input values 1010 through 1111 are not used, so we do not care what they contain.

Figure C.13 shows the lower 4 bits of the control word corresponding to the next-state outputs. The last column of the table in Figure C.13 corresponds to all the possible values of the opcode that do not match the specified opcodes.

Lower 4 bits of the address	Bits 19–4 of the word
0000	1001010000001000
0001	0000000000011000
0010	0000000000010100
0011	0011000000000000
0100	0000001000000010
0101	0010100000000000
0110	0000000001000100
0111	0000000000000011
1000	0100000010100100
1001	1000000100000000

FIGURE C.12   The contents of the upper 16 bits of the ROM depend only on the state inputs. These values are the same as those in Figure C.11, simply rotated 90°. This set of control words would be duplicated 64 times for every possible value of the upper 6 bits of the address.

In state 0, the next state is always state 1, since the instruction was still being fetched. After state 1, the opcode field must be valid. The table indicates this by the entries marked illegal; we discuss how to deal with these illegal opcodes in section 5.6.

Not only is this representation as two separate tables a more compact way to show the ROM contents, it is also a more efficient way to implement the ROM. The majority of the outputs (16 of 20 bits) depend only on 4 of the 10 inputs. The number of bits in total when the control is implemented as two separate ROMs is $2^4 \times 16 + 2^{10} \times 4 = 256 + 4096 = 4.3$ Kbits, which is about one-fifth of the size of a single ROM, which requires $2^{10} \times 20 = 20$ Kbits. There is some overhead associated with any structured-logic block, but in this case the additional overhead of an extra ROM would be much smaller than the savings from splitting the single ROM.

	Op [5–0]					
Current state S[3–0]	**000000 (R-format)**	**000010 (jmp)**	**000100 (beq)**	**100011 (lw)**	**101011 (sw)**	**Any other value**
0000	0001	0001	0001	0001	0001	0001
0001	0110	1001	1000	0010	0010	illegal
0010	XXXX	XXXX	XXXX	0011	0101	illegal
0011	0100	0100	0100	0100	0100	illegal
0100	0000	0000	0000	0000	0000	illegal
0101	0000	0000	0000	0000	0000	illegal
0110	0111	0111	0111	0111	0111	illegal
0111	0000	0000	0000	0000	0000	illegal
1000	0000	0000	0000	0000	0000	illegal
1001	0000	0000	0000	0000	0000	illegal

FIGURE C.13   This table contains the lower 4 bits of the control word (the NS outputs), which depend on both the state inputs, S[3–0], and the opcode, Op [5–0], which correspond to the instruction opcode. These values can be determined from Figure C.10. The opcode name is shown under the encoding in the heading. The 4 bits of the control word whose address is given by the current-state bits and Op bits are shown in each entry. For example, when the state input bits are 0000, the output is always 0001, independent of the other inputs; when the state is 2, the next state is don't care for three of the inputs, 3 for lw, and 5 for sw. Together with the entries in Figure C.12, this table specifies the contents of the control unit ROM. For example, the word at address 1000110001 is obtained by finding the upper 16 bits in the table in Figure C.12 using only the state input bits (0001) and concatenating the lower 4 bits found by using the entire address (0001 to find the row and 100011 to find the column). The entry from Figure C.12 yields **0000000000011000**, while the appropriate entry in the table immediately above is 0010. Thus the control word at address 1000110001 is **0000000000011000**0010. The column labeled "Any other value" applies only when the Op bits do not match one of the specified opcodes.

Although this ROM encoding of the control function is simple, it is wasteful, even when divided into two pieces. For example, the values of the Instruction register inputs are often not needed to determine the next state. Thus the next-state ROM has many entries that are either duplicated or are don't care. Consider the case when the machine is in state 0: there are 2^6 entries in the ROM (since the opcode field can have any value), and these entries will all have the same contents (namely, the control word 0001). The reason that so much of the ROM is wasted is that the ROM implements the complete truth table, providing the opportunity to have a different output for every combination of the inputs. But most combinations of the inputs either never happen or are redundant!

A PLA Implementation

We can reduce the amount of control storage required at the cost of using more complex address decoding for the control inputs, which will encode only the input combinations that are needed. The logic structure most often used to do this is a programmed logic array (PLA), which we mentioned earlier and illustrated in Figure C.5. In a PLA, each output is the logical OR of one or more minterms. A *minterm*, also called a *product term*, is simply a logical AND of one or more inputs. The inputs can be thought of as the address for indexing the PLA, while the minterms select which of all possible address combinations are interesting. A minterm corresponds to a single entry in a truth table, such as those in Figure C.9 on page C-14, including possible don't-care terms. Each output consists of an OR of these minterms, which exactly corresponds to a complete truth table. However, unlike a ROM, only those truth table entries that produce an active output are needed, and only one copy of each minterm is required, even if the minterm contains don't cares. Figure C.14 shows the PLA that implements this control function.

As we can see from the PLA in Figure C.14, there are 17 unique minterms—10 that depend only on the current state and 7 others that depend on a combination of the Op field and the current-state bits. The total size of the PLA is proportional to (#inputs × #product terms) + (#outputs × #product terms), as we can see symbolically from the figure. This means the total size of the PLA in Figure C.14 is proportional to $(10 \times 17) + (20 \times 17) = 460$. By comparison, the size of a single ROM is proportional to 20 Kbits, and even the two-part ROM has a total of 4.3 Kbits. Because the size of a PLA cell will be only slightly larger than the size of a bit in a ROM, a PLA will be a much more efficient implementation for this control unit.

Of course, just as we split the ROM in two, we could split the PLA in two PLAs: one with four inputs and 10 minterms that generates the 16 control outputs, and one with 10 inputs and 7 minterms that generates the 4 next-state

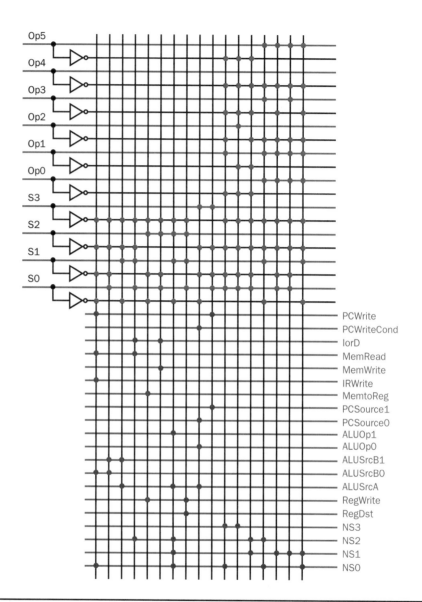

FIGURE C.14   This PLA implements the control function logic for the multicycle implementation. The inputs to the control appear on the left and the outputs on the right. The top half of the figure is the AND plane that computes all the minterms. The minterms are carried to the OR plane on the vertical lines. Each colored dot corresponds to a signal that makes up the minterm carried on that line. The sum terms are computed from these minterms, with each grey dot representing the presence of the intersecting minterm in that sum term. Each output consists of a single sum term.

outputs. The first PLA would have a size proportional to $(4 \times 10) + (10 \times 16) = 200$, and the second PLA would have a size proportional to $(10 \times 7) + (4 \times 7) = 98$. This would yield a total size proportional to 298 PLA cells, about 55% of the size of a single PLA. These two PLAs will be considerably smaller than an implementation using two ROMs. For more details on PLAs and their implementation, as well as the references for books on logic design, see Appendix B.

C.4 Implementing the Next-State Function with a Sequencer

Let's look carefully at the control unit we built in the last section. If you examine the ROMs that implement the control in Figures C.12 and C.13, you can see that much of the logic is used to specify the next-state function. In fact, for the implementation using two separate ROMs, 4096 out of the 4368 bits (94%) correspond to the next-state function! Furthermore, imagine what the control logic would look like if the instruction set had many more different instruction types, some of which required many clocks to implement. There would be many more states in the finite state machine. In some states, we might be branching to a large number of different states depending on the instruction type (as we did in state 1 of the finite state machine in Figure C.6 on page C-9). However, many of the states would proceed in a sequential fashion, just as states 3 and 4 do in Figure C.6.

For example, if we included floating point, we would see a sequence of many states in a row that implement a multicycle floating-point instruction. Alternatively, consider how the control might look for a machine that can have multiple memory operands per instruction. It would require many more states to fetch multiple memory operands. The result of this would be that the control logic will be dominated by the encoding of the next-state function. Furthermore, much of the logic will be devoted to sequences of states with only one path through them that look like states 2 through 4 in Figure C.6. With more instructions, these sequences will consist of many more sequentially numbered states than for our simple subset.

To encode these more complex control functions efficiently, we can use a control unit that has a counter to supply the sequential next state. This counter often eliminates the need to encode the next-state function explicitly in the control unit. As shown in Figure C.15, an adder is used to increment the state, essentially turning it into a counter. The incremented state is always the state that follows in numerical order. However, the finite state machine sometimes "branches." For example, in state 1 of the finite state machine (see Figure C.6 on page C-9), there are four possible next states, only one of which is the sequential next state. Thus, we need to be able to choose between the incremented state and a new state based on the inputs from the Instruction register and

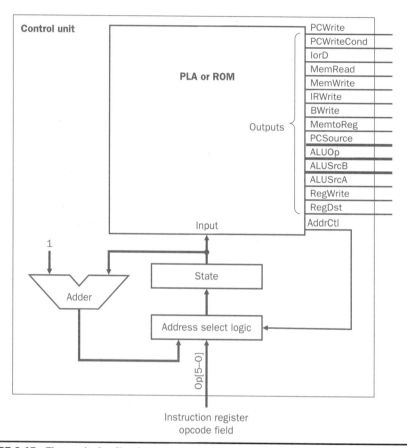

FIGURE C.15   The control unit using an explicit counter to compute the next state. In this control unit, the next state is computed using a counter (at least in some states). By comparison, Figure C.7 on page C-10 encodes the next state in the control logic for every state. In this control unit, the signals labeled *AddrCtl* control how the next state is determined.

the current state. Each control word will include control lines that will determine how the next state is chosen.

It is easy to implement the control output signal portion of the control word, since, if we use the same state numbers, this portion of the control word will look exactly like the ROM contents shown in Figure C.12 on page C-17. However, the method for selecting the next state differs from the next-state function in the finite state machine.

With an explicit counter providing the sequential next state, the control unit logic need only specify how to choose the state when it is not the sequentially following state. There are two methods for doing this. The first is a method we have already seen: namely, the control unit explicitly encodes the next-state function. The difference is that the control unit need only set the next-state lines when the designated next state is not the state that the counter indicates. If the number of states is large and the next-state function that we need to encode is mostly empty, this may not be a good choice, since the resulting control unit will have lots of empty or redundant space. An alternative approach is to use separate external logic to specify the next state when the counter does not specify the state. Many control units, especially those that implement large instruction sets, use this approach, and we will focus on specifying the control externally.

Although the nonsequential next state will come from an external table, the control unit needs to specify when this should occur and how to find that next state. There are two kinds of "branching" that we must implement in the address select logic. First, we must be able to jump to one of a number of states based on the opcode portion of the Instruction register. This operation, called a *dispatch*, is usually implemented by using a set of special ROMS or PLAs included as part of the address selection logic. An additional set of control outputs, which we call AddrCtl, indicates when a dispatch should be done. Looking at the finite state diagram (Figure C.6 on page C-9), we see that there are two states in which we do a branch based on a portion of the opcode. Thus we will need two small dispatch tables. (Alternatively, we could also use a single dispatch table and use the control bits that select the table as address bits that choose which portion of the dispatch table to select the address from.)

The second type of branching that we must implement consists of branching back to state 0, which initiates the execution of the next MIPS instruction. Thus there are four possible ways to choose the next state (three types of branches, plus incrementing the current-state number), which can be encoded in 2 bits. Let's assume that the encoding is as follows:

AddrCtl value	Action
0	Set state to 0
1	Dispatch with ROM 1
2	Dispatch with ROM 2
3	Use the incremented state

If we use this encoding, the address select logic for this control unit can be implemented as shown in Figure C.16.

To complete the control unit, we need only specify the contents of the dispatch ROMs, and the values of the address-control lines for each state. We have already specified the datapath control portion of the control word using the

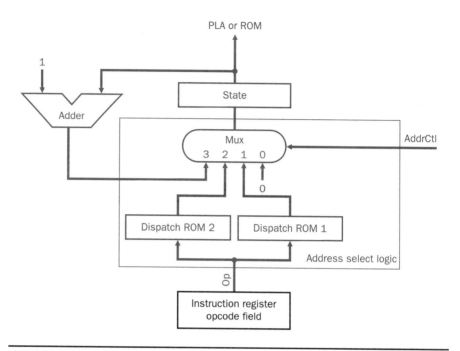

FIGURE C.16   This is the address select logic for the control unit of Figure C.15.

ROM contents of Figure C.12 on page C-17 (or the corresponding portions of the PLA in Figure C.14 on page C-20). The next-state counter and dispatch ROMs take the place of the portion of the control unit that was computing the next state, which was shown in Figure C.13 on page C-18. We are only implementing a portion of the instruction set, so the dispatch ROMs will be largely empty. Figure C.17 shows the entries that must be assigned for this subset. Section 5.6 of Chapter 5 discusses what to do with the entries in the dispatch ROMs that do not correspond to any instruction.

Now we can determine the setting of the address selection lines (AddrCtl) in each control word. The table in Figure C.18 shows how the address control must be set for every state. This information will be used to specify the setting of the AddrCtl field in the control word associated with that state.

The contents of the entire control ROM are shown in Figure C.19. The total storage required for the control is quite small. There are 10 control words, each 18 bits wide, for a total of 180 bits. In addition, the two dispatch tables are 4 bits wide and each has 64 entries, for a total of 512 additional bits. This total of 692 bits beats the implementation that uses two ROMs with the next-state function encoded in the ROMs (which requires 4.3 Kbits).

Dispatch ROM 1		
Op	Opcode name	Value
000000	R-format	0110
000010	jmp	1001
000100	beq	1000
100011	lw	0010
101011	sw	0010

Dispatch ROM 2		
Op	Opcode name	Value
100011	lw	0011
101011	sw	0101

FIGURE C.17 The dispatch ROMs each have 2^6 = 64 entries that are 4 bits wide, since that is the number of bits in the state encoding. This figure only shows the entries in the ROM that are of interest for this subset. The first column in each table indicates the value of Op, which is the address used to access the dispatch ROM. The second column shows the symbolic name of the opcode. The third column indicates the value at that address in the ROM.

State number	Address-control action	Value of AddrCtl
0	Use incremented state	3
1	Use dispatch ROM 1	1
2	Use dispatch ROM 2	2
3	Use incremented state	3
4	Replace state number by 0	0
5	Replace state number by 0	0
6	Use incremented state	3
7	Replace state number by 0	0
8	Replace state number by 0	0
9	Replace state number by 0	0

FIGURE C.18 The values of the address-control lines are set in the control word that corresponds to each state.

State number	Control word bits 17–2	Control word bits 1–0
0	1001010000001000	11
1	0000000000011000	01
2	0000000000010100	10
3	0011000000000000	11
4	0000001000000010	00
5	0010100000000000	00
6	0000000001000100	11
7	0000000000000011	00
8	0100000010100100	00
9	1000000100000000	00

FIGURE C.19 The contents of the control memory for an implementation using an explicit counter. The first column shows the state, while the second shows the datapath control bits, and the last column shows the address-control bits in each control word. Bits 17–2 are identical to those in Figure C.12.

Of course, the dispatch tables are sparse and could be more efficiently implemented with two small PLAs. The control ROM could also be replaced with a PLA.

Optimizing the Control Implementation

We can further reduce the amount of logic in the control unit by two different techniques. The first is *logic minimization*, which uses the structure of the logic equations, including the don't-care terms, to reduce the amount of hardware required. The success of this process depends on how many entries exist in the truth table, and how those entries are related. For example, in this subset, only the lw and sw opcodes have an active value for the signal Op5, so we can replace the two truth table entries that test whether the input is lw or sw by a single test on this bit; similarly we can eliminate several bits used to index the dispatch ROM because this single bit can be used to find lw and sw in the first dispatch ROM. Of course, if the opcode space were less sparse, opportunities for this optimization would be more difficult to locate. However, in choosing the opcodes, the architect can provide additional opportunities by choosing related opcodes for instructions that are likely to share states in the control.

A different sort of optimization can be done by assigning the state numbers in a finite state or microcode implementation to minimize the logic. This optimization, called *state assignment*, tries to choose the state numbers such that the resulting logic equations contain more redundancy and can thus be simplified. Let's consider the case of a finite state machine with an encoded next-state control first, since it allows states to be assigned arbitrarily. For example, notice that in the finite state machine the signal RegWrite is active only in states 4 and 7. If we encoded those states as 8 and 9, rather than 4 and 7, we could rewrite the equation for RegWrite as simply a test on bit S3 (which is only on for states 8 and 9). This renumbering allows us to combine the two truth table entries in part (o) of Figure C.9 on page C-14 and replace them with a single entry, eliminating one term in the control unit. Of course, we would have to renumber the existing states 8 and 9, perhaps as 4 and 7.

The same optimization can be applied in an implementation that uses an explicit program counter, though we are more restricted. Because the next-state number is often computed by incrementing the current-state number, we cannot arbitrarily assign the states. However, if we keep the states where the incremented state is used as the next state in the same order, we can reassign the consecutive states as a block. In an implementation with an explicit next-state counter, state assignment may allow us to simplify the contents of the dispatch ROMs.

If we look again at the control unit in Figure C.15 on page C-22, it looks remarkably like a computer in its own right. The ROM or PLA can be thought of as memory supplying instructions for the datapath. The state can be thought of as an instruction address. Hence the origin of the name *microcode* or *micro-programmed control*. The control words are thought of as *microinstructions* that control the datapath, and the State register is called the *microprogram counter*. Figure C.20 shows a view of the control unit as *microcode*. The next section describes how we map from a microprogram to microcode.

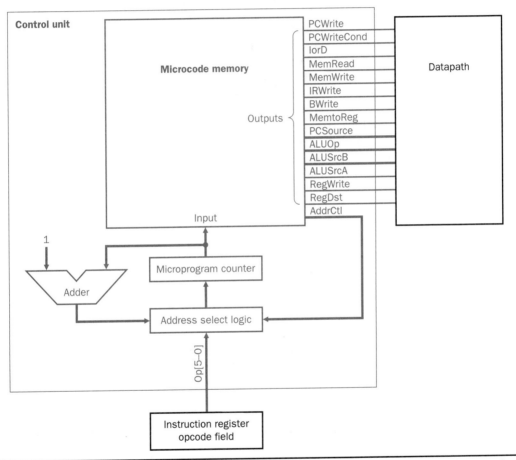

FIGURE C.20 The control unit as a microcode. The use of the word "micro" serves to distinguish between the program counter in the datapath and the microprogram counter, and between the microcode memory and the instruction memory.

C.5   Translating a Microprogram to Hardware

To translate the microprogram of section 5.5 into actual hardware, we need to specify how each field translates into control signals. We can implement the microprogram with either finite state control or a microcode implementation with an explicit sequencer. If we choose a finite state machine, we need to construct the next-state function from the microprogram. Once this function is known, we can map a set of truth table entries for the next-state outputs. In this section, we will show how to translate the microprogram assuming that the next state is specified by a sequencer. From the truth tables we will construct, it would be straightforward to build the next-state function for a finite state machine.

Assuming an explicit sequencer, we need to do two additional tasks to translate the microprogram: assign addresses to the microinstructions and fill in the contents of the dispatch ROMs. This process is essentially the same as the process of translating an assembly language program into machine instructions: the fields of the assembly language or microprogram instruction are translated, and labels on the instructions must be resolved to addresses.

Figure C.21 shows the various values for each microinstruction field that controls the datapath and how these fields are encoded as control signals. If the field corresponding to a signal that affects a unit with state (i.e., Memory, Memory register, ALU destination, or PCWriteControl) is blank, then no control signal should be active. If a field corresponding to a multiplexor control signal or the ALU operation control (i.e., ALUOp, SRC1, or SRC2) is blank, the output is unused, so the associated signals may be set as don't care.

The sequencing field can have four values: Fetch (meaning go to the Fetch state), Dispatch 1, Dispatch 2, and Seq. These four values are encoded to set the 2-bit address control just as they were in Figure C.18 on page C-25: Fetch = 0, Dispatch 1 = 1. Dispatch 2 = 2, Seq = 3. Finally, we need to specify the contents of the dispatch tables to relate the dispatch entries of the sequence field to the symbolic labels in the microprogram. We use the same dispatch tables as we did earlier in Figure C.17 on page C-25.

A microcode assembler would use the encoding of the sequencing field, the contents of the symbolic dispatch tables in Figure C.22, the specification in Figure C.21, and the actual microprogram in Figure 5.46 on page 408 to generate the microinstructions.

Since the microprogram is an abstract representation of the control, there is a great deal of flexibility in how the microprogram is translated. For example, the address assigned to many of the microinstructions can be chosen arbitrarily; the only restrictions are those imposed by the fact that certain microinstruc-

Field name	Value	Signals active	Comment
ALU control	Add	ALUOp = 00	Cause the ALU to add.
	Subt	ALUOp = 01	Cause the ALU to subtract; this implements the compare for branches.
	Func code	ALUOp = 10	Use the instruction's function code to determine ALU control.
SRC1	PC	ALUSrcA = 0	Use the PC as the first ALU input.
	A	ALUSrcA = 1	Register A is the first ALU input.
SRC2	B	ALUSrcB = 00	Register B is the second ALU input.
	4	ALUSrcB = 01	Use 4 as the second ALU input.
	Extend	ALUSrcB = 10	Use output of the sign extension unit as the second ALU input.
	Extshft	ALUSrcB = 11	Use the output of the shift-by-two unit as the second ALU input.
Register control	Read		Read two registers using the rs and rt fields of the IR as the register numbers and putting the data into registers A and B.
	Write ALU	RegWrite, RegDst = 1, MemtoReg = 0	Write a register using the rd field of the IR as the register number and the contents of ALUOut as the data.
	Write MDR	RegWrite, RegDst = 0, MemtoReg = 1	Write a register using the rt field of the IR as the register number and the contents of the MDR as the data.
Memory	Read PC	MemRead, IorD = 0	Read memory using the PC as address; write result into IR (and the MDR).
	Read ALU	MemRead, IorD = 1	Read memory using ALUOut as address; write result into MDR.
	Write ALU	MemWrite, IorD = 1	Write memory using the ALUOut as address, contents of B as the data.
PC write control	ALU	PCSource = 00 PCWrite	Write the output of the ALU into the PC.
	ALUOut-cond	PCSource = 01, PCWriteCond	If the Zero output of the ALU is active, write the PC with the contents of the register ALUOut.
	jump address	PCSource = 10, PCWrite	Write the PC with the jump address from the instruction.
Sequencing	Seq	AddrCtl = 11	Choose the next microinstruction sequentially.
	Fetch	AddrCtl = 00	Go to the first microinstruction to begin a new instruction.
	Dispatch 1	AddrCtl = 01	Dispatch using the ROM 1.
	Dispatch 2	AddrCtl = 10	Dispatch using the ROM 2.

FIGURE C.21 Each microcode field translates to a set of control signals to be set. This table specifies a value for each of the fields that were originally specified in Figure 5.46 on page 408. These 22 different values of the fields specify all the required combinations of the 18 control lines. Control lines that are not set which correspond to actions are 0 by default. Multiplexor control lines are set to 0 if the output matters. If a multiplexor control line is not explicitly set, its output is a don't care and is not used.

tions must occur in sequential order (so that incrementing the State register generates the address of the next instruction). Thus the microcode assembler may reduce the complexity of the control by assigning the microinstructions cleverly.

Microcode dispatch table 1		
Opcode field	Opcode name	Value
000000	R-format	Rformat1
000010	jmp	JUMP1
000100	beq	BEQ1
100011	lw	Mem1
101011	sw	Mem1

Microcode dispatch table 2		
Opcode field	Opcode name	Value
100011	lw	LW2
101011	sw	SW2

FIGURE C.22   The two microcode dispatch ROMs showing the contents in symbolic form and using the labels in the microprogram.

Organizing the Control to Reduce the Logic

For a machine with complex control, there may be a great deal of logic in the control unit. The control ROM or PLA may be very costly. Although our simple implementation had only an 18-bit microinstruction (assuming an explicit sequencer), there have been machines with microinstructions that are hundreds of bits wide. Clearly, a designer would like to reduce the number of microinstructions and the width.

The ideal approach to reducing control store is to first write the complete microprogram in a symbolic notation and then measure how control lines are set in each microinstruction. By taking measurements we are able to recognize control bits that can be encoded into a smaller field. For example, if no more than one of eight lines is set simultaneously in the same microinstruction, then this subset of control lines can be encoded into a 3-bit field ($\log_2 8 = 3$). This change saves 5 bits in every microinstruction and does not hurt CPI, though it does mean the extra hardware cost of a 3-to-8 decoder needed to generate the eight control lines when they are required at the datapath. It may also have some small clock cycle impact, since the decoder is in the signal path. However, shaving 5 bits off control store width will usually overcome the cost of the decoder, and the cycle time impact will probably be small or nonexistent. For example, this technique can be applied to bits 14–9 of the microinstructions in this machine, since only 1 bit of the 7 bits of the control word is ever active (see Figure C.19 on page C-25).

This technique of reducing field width is called *encoding*. To further save space, control lines may be encoded together if they are only occasionally set in the same microinstruction; two microinstructions instead of one are then required when both must be set. As long as this doesn't happen in critical routines, the narrower microinstruction may justify a few extra words of control store.

Microinstructions can be made narrower still if they are broken into different formats and given an opcode or *format field* to distinguish them. The format field gives all the unspecified control lines their default values, so as not to change anything else in the machine, and is similar to the opcode of an instruction in a more powerful instruction set. For example, we could use a different format for microinstructions that did memory accesses from those that did register-register ALU operations, taking advantage of the fact that the memory access control lines are not needed in microinstructions controlling ALU operations.

Reducing hardware costs by using format fields usually has an additional performance cost beyond the requirement for more decoders. A microprogram using a single microinstruction format can specify any combination of operations in a datapath and can take fewer clock cycles than a microprogram made up of restricted microinstructions that cannot perform any combination of operations in a single microinstruction. However, if the full capability of the wider microprogram word is not heavily used, then much of the control store will be wasted, and the machine could be made smaller and faster by restricting the microinstruction capability.

The narrow, but usually longer, approach is often called *vertical microcode*, while the wide but short approach is called *horizontal microcode*. It should be noted that the terms "vertical microcode" and "horizontal microcode" have no universal definition—the designers of the 8086 considered its 21-bit microinstruction to be more horizontal than other single-chip computers of the time. The related terms *maximally encoded* and *minimally encoded* are probably better than vertical and horizontal.

C.6 Concluding Remarks

We began this appendix by looking at how to translate a finite state diagram to an implementation using a finite state machine. We then looked at explicit sequencers that use a different technique for realizing the next-state function. Although large microprograms are often targeted at implementations using this explicit next-state approach, we can also implement a microprogram with a finite state machine. As we saw, both ROM and PLA implementations of the logic functions are possible. The advantages of explicit versus encoded next state and ROM versus PLA implementation are summarized below.

> **The Big Picture**
>
> Independent of whether the control is represented as a finite state diagram or as a microprogram, translation to a hardware control implementation is similar. Each state or microinstruction asserts a set of control outputs and specifies how to choose the next state.
>
> The next-state function may be implemented by either encoding it in a finite state machine or by using an explicit sequencer. The explicit sequencer is more efficient if the number of states is large and there are many sequences of consecutive states without branching.
>
> The control logic may be implemented with either ROMS or PLAs (or even a mix). PLAs are more efficient unless the control function is very dense. ROMs may be appropriate if the control is stored in a separate memory, as opposed to within the same chip as the datapath.

C.7   Key Terms

The most important terms for this appendix are listed here and are defined in the Glossary.

horizontal microcode
logic minimization
maximally encoded
microcode assembler

minimally encoded
next-state counter
next-state outputs
state assignment

state inputs
vertical microcode

C.8   Exercises

C.1 [10] <§C.2> Instead of using 4 state bits to implement the finite state machine in Figure C.6 on page C-9, use 9 state bits, each of which is a 1 only if the finite state machine is in that particular state (e.g., S1 is 1 in state 1, S2 is 1 in state 2, etc.). Redraw the PLA (Figure C.14 on page C-20).

C.2 [5] <§C.3> {Ex. 5.6} How many product terms are required in a PLA that implements the single-cycle datapath for jal, assuming the control additions described in Exercise 5.6 on page 427?

C.3 [5] <§C.3> {Ex. 5.5} How many product terms are required in a PLA that implements the single-cycle datapath and control for addiu, assuming that the control additions you needed were found in Exercise 5.5 on page 427?

C.4 [10] <§C.3> {Ex. 5.27} Determine the number of product terms in a PLA that implements the finite state machine for jal constructed in Exercise 5.27 on page 431. The easiest method to do this is to construct the truth tables for any new outputs or any outputs affected by the addition.

C.5 [10] <§C.3> {Ex. 5.15} Determine the number of product terms in a PLA that implements the finite state machine for addi in Exercise 5.15 on page 429. The easiest way to do this is to construct the additions to the truth tables for addi.

C.6 [20] <§C.4> {Ex. 5.15} Implement the finite state machine of Exercise 5.15 on page 429 using an explicit counter to determine the next state. Fill in the new entries for the additions to Figure C.19 on page C-25. Also, add any entries needed to the dispatch ROMs of Figure C.22 on page C-30.

C.7 [15] <§§C.3–C.6> Determine the size of the PLAs needed to implement the multicycle machine of Chapter 5 assuming that the next-state function is implemented with a counter. Implement the dispatch tables of Figure C.22 on page C-30 using two PLAs, and the contents of the main control unit in Figure C.19 on page C-25 using another PLA. How does the total size of this solution compare to the single PLA solution with the next state encoded? What if the main PLAs for both approaches are split into two separate PLAs by factoring out the next state or address select signals?

Glossary

absolute address A variable's or routine's actual address in memory.

abstraction A model that renders lower-level details of computer systems temporarily invisible in order to facilitate design of sophisticated systems.

activation record *See* procedure frame.

address A value used to delineate the location of a specific data element within a memory array.

address mapping *See* address translation.

address translation Also called address mapping. The process by which a virtual address is mapped to an address used to access memory.

addressing mode One of several addressing regimes delimited by their varied use of operands and/or addresses.

aliasing A situation in which the same object is accessed by two addresses; can occur in virtual memory when there are two virtual addresses for the same physical page.

ALU *See* arithmetic logic unit (ALU).

Amdahl's law A rule stating that the performance enhancement possible with a given improvement is limited by the amount that the improved feature is used.

AND gate Hardware that performs the AND operation on input signals yielding a single signal result.

AND operation An operation that leaves a 1 in the result only if both bits of the operands are 1.

architecture *See* instruction set architecture.

arithmetic logic unit (ALU) Hardware that performs arithmetic and logical operations.

arithmetic mean The average of the execution times that is directly proportional to total execution time.

assembler A program that translates a symbolic version of an instruction into the binary version.

assembler directive An operation that tells the assembler how to translate a program but does not produce machine instructions; always begins with a period.

assembly language A symbolic language that can be translated into binary.

asserted signal A signal that is (logically) true, or 1.

asynchronous bus A bus that uses a handshaking protocol for coordinating usage rather than a clock; can accommodate a wide variety of devices of differing speeds.

atomic operation An operation in which the processor can both read a location and write it in the same bus operation, preventing any other processor or I/O device from reading or writing memory until it completes.

backpatching A method for translating from assembly language to machine instructions in which the assembler builds a (possibly incomplete) binary representation of every instruction in one pass over a program and then returns to fill in previously undefined labels.

backplane bus A bus that is designed to allow processors, memory, and I/O devices to coexist on a single bus.

barrier synchronization A synchronization scheme in which processors wait at the barrier and do not proceed until every processor has reached it.

base addressing Also called displacement addressing. An addressing regime in which the operand is at the memory location whose address is the sum of a register and an address in the instruction.

basic block A sequence of instructions without branches (except possibly at the end) and without branch targets or branch labels (except possibly at the beginning).

biased notation A notation that represents the most negative value by $00 \ldots 000_{two}$ and the most positive value by $11 \ldots 11_{two}$, with 0 typically having the value $10 \ldots 00_{two}$, thereby biasing the number such that the number plus the bias has a nonnegative representation.

binary bit *See* binary digit.

binary digit Also called binary bit. One of the two numbers in base 2, 0 or 1, that are the components of information.

block The minimum unit of information that can be either present or not present in the two-level hierarchy.

Booth's algorithm   An algorithm based on the observation that the ability to both add and subtract allows for multiple ways to compute a product, so that by looking at multiple bits we potentially save arithmetic operations.

branch delay slot   The slot directly after a delayed branch instruction, which in the MIPS architecture is filled by an instruction that does not affect the branch.

branch hazard   Also called control hazard. An occurrence in which the proper instruction cannot execute in the proper clock cycle because the instruction that was fetched is not the one that is needed; that is, the flow of instruction addresses is not what the pipeline expected.

branch history table   *See* branch prediction buffer.

branch not taken   A branch where the branch condition is false and the program counter (PC) becomes the address of the instruction that sequentially follows the branch.

branch prediction   A method of resolving a branch hazard that assumes a given outcome for the branch and proceeds from that assumption rather than waiting to ascertain the actual outcome.

branch prediction buffer   Also called branch history table. A small memory that is indexed by the lower portion of the address of the branch instruction and that contains one or more bits indicating whether the branch was recently taken or not.

branch taken   A branch where the branch condition is satisfied and the program counter (PC) becomes the branch target. All unconditional branches are taken branches.

branch target address   The address specified in a branch, which becomes the new program counter (PC) if the branch is taken. In the MIPS architecture the branch target is given by the sum of the offset field of the instruction and the address of the instruction following the branch.

bubble   *See* pipeline stall.

bus   In logic design, a collection of data lines that is treated together as a single logical signal; also, a shared collection of lines with multiple sources and uses.

bus arbitration   The process of deciding which bus master gets to use a bus next.

bus master   A unit on the bus that can initiate bus requests.

bus request   A signal on the bus requesting access to a bus.

bus transaction   A sequence of bus operations that includes a request and may include a response, either of which may carry data. A transaction is initiated by a single request and may take many individual bus operations.

bypassing   *See* forwarding.

cache coherency   Consistency in the value of data between the versions in the caches of several processors.

cache memory   A small, fast memory that acts as a buffer for a slower, larger memory.

cache miss   A request for data from the cache that cannot be filled because the data is not present in the cache.

callee   A procedure that executes a series of stored instructions based on parameters provided by the caller and then returns control to the caller.

callee-saved register   A register saved by the routine making a procedure call.

caller   The program that instigates a procedure and provides the necessary parameter values.

caller-saved register   A register saved by the routine being called.

capacity miss   A cache miss that occurs because the cache, even with full associativity, cannot contain all the block needed to satisfy the request.

central processor unit (CPU)   Also called processor. The active part of the computer, which contains the datapath and control and which adds numbers, tests numbers, signals I/O devices to activate, and so on.

centralized, parallel arbitration   A bus arbitration scheme that employs multiple request lines by which the devices independently request the bus and that uses a centralized arbiter to choose from the devices requesting bus access and to notify the selected device that it is now bus master.

chip   *See* integrated circuit.

clock   *See* clock cycle.

clock cycle   Also called tick, clock tick, clock period, clock, cycle. The time for one clock period, usually of the processor clock, which runs at a constant rate. The clock cycle is often used to measure the speed at which hardware can perform basic functions.

clock cycles per instruction (CPI)   Average number of clock cycles per instruction for a program or program fragment.

clock period   *See* clock cycle.

clock rate The speed of the processor or system clock measured as the number of clock cycles per second and usually stated in megahertz or millions of clock cycles per second. The clock rate is the inverse of the clock period. Designers refer to the clock cycle time both as the duration of one clock period, measured as seconds per clock cycle (e.g., 2 ns) and as the clock rate, measured as clock cycles per second (e.g., 500 MHz).

clock skew The difference in absolute time between the times when two state elements see a clock edge.

clock tick *See* clock cycle.

clocking methodology The approach used to determine when data is valid and stable relative to the clock.

cluster A set of computers connected over a local area network (LAN) that function as a single large multiprocessor.

cold start miss *See* compulsory miss.

collision miss *See* conflict miss.

combinational logic A logic system whose blocks do not contain memory and hence compute the same output given the same input.

commit unit The unit in a dynamic or out-of-order execution pipeline that decides when it is safe to release the result of an operation to programmer-visible registers and memory.

compiler A program that translates high-level language statements into assembly language statements.

compulsory miss Also called cold start miss. A cache miss caused by the first access to a block that has never been in the cache.

computer generation A classification of computers often based on the implementation technology used in each generation, originally lasting eight to ten years.

conditional branch An instruction that requires the comparison of two values and that allows for a subsequent transfer of control to a new address in the program based on the outcome of the comparison.

conflict miss Also called collision miss. A cache miss that occurs in a set-associative or direct-mapped cache when multiple blocks compete for the same set and that are eliminated in a fully associative cache of the same size.

context switch A changing of the internal state of the processor to allow a different process to use the processor that includes saving the state needed to return to the currently executing process.

control The component of the processor that commands the datapath, memory, and I/O devices according to the instructions of the program.

control hazard *See* branch hazard.

control signal A signal used for multiplexor selection or for directing the operation of a functional unit; contrasts with a data signal, which contains information that is operated on by a functional unit.

control value *See* selector value.

CPI *See* clock cycles per instruction (CPI).

CPU *See* central processor unit (CPU).

CPU execution time Also called CPU time. The actual time the CPU spends computing for a specific task.

CPU time *See* CPU execution time.

crossbar network A network that allows any node to communicate with any other node in one pass through the network.

cycle *See* clock cycle.

D flip-flop A flip-flop with one data input that stores the value of that input signal in the internal memory when the clock edge occurs.

daisy chain arbitration A bus arbitration scheme in which the bus grant line is run through the devices from highest priority to lowest (the priorities are determined by the position on the bus) so that when the bus is requested the highest priority device sees the bus grant signal first.

data dependencies The need for specific data at a given point in a pipeline.

data hazard Also called pipeline data hazard. An occurrence in which a planned instruction cannot execute in the proper clock cycle because data that is needed to execute the instruction is not yet available.

data parallelism Parallelism achieved by having massive data.

data segment The segment of a Unix object or executable file that contains a binary representation of the initialized data used by the program.

data transfer instruction A command that moves data between memory and registers.

datapath The component of the processor that performs arithmetic operations.

datapath element A functional unit used to operate on or hold data within a processor. In the MIPS implementation the datapath elements include the instruction and data memories, the register file, the arithmetic logic unit (ALU), and adders.

deasserted signal A signal that is (logically) false, or 0.

decoder A logic block that has an n-bit input and $2n$ outputs where only one output is asserted for each input combination.

defect A microscopic flaw in a wafer or in patterning steps that can result in the failure of the die containing that defect.

delay *See* rotation latency.

delayed branch A type of branch where the instruction immediately following the branch is always executed, independent of whether the branch condition is true or false.

delayed load A software format that requires load instructions to be followed by an instruction independent of the load.

die The individual rectangular sections that are cut from a wafer, more informally known as chips.

die area The size of a die.

direct-mapped cache A cache structure in which each memory location is mapped to exactly one location in the cache.

direct memory access (DMA) A mechanism that provides a device controller the ability to transfer data directly to or from the memory without involving the processor.

directory A repository for information on the state of every block in main memory, including which caches have copies of the block, whether it is dirty, and so on.

dispatch An operation in a microprogrammed control unit in which the next microinstruction is selected on the basis of one or more fields of a macroinstruction, usually by creating a table containing the addresses of the target microinstructions and indexing the table using a field of the macroinstruction. The dispatch tables are typically implemented in ROM or programmable logic array (PLA). The term *dispatch* is also used in dynamically scheduled processors to refer to the process of sending an instruction to a queue.

displacement addressing *See* base addressing.

distributed arbitration by collision detection A bus arbitration scheme that allows each device to independently request the bus and that uses a scheme for retrying the arbitration when multiple simultaneous requests occur.

distributed arbitration by self-selection A bus arbitration scheme that gives the devices requesting the bus the ability to determine which device gets the bus by having each requester detect whether it should receive the bus allocation.

distributed memory Physical memory that is divided into modules, with some placed near each processor in a multiprocessor.

distributed shared memory (DSM) A memory scheme that uses addresses to access remote data when demanded rather than retrieving the data in case it might be used.

divisor A number that the dividend is divided by; produces the dividend when multiplied by the quotient and added to the remainder.

DMA *See* direct memory access (DMA).

don't-care term An element of a logical function in which the output does not depend on the values of all the inputs. Don't-care terms may be specified in different ways.

double precision A floating-point value represented in two 32-bit words.

DRAM *See* dynamic random access memory (DRAM).

DSM *See* distributed shared memory (DSM).

dynamic pipeline scheduling A form of scheduling that goes past stalls in order to find later instructions to execute while waiting for the stalls to be resolved.

dynamic random access memory (DRAM) Memory that contains the instructions and data of a program while it is running, which allows faster access than accessing a magnetic disk.

edge-triggered clocking A clocking scheme in which all state changes occur on a clock edge.

Ethernet A computer network whose length is limited to about a kilometer. Originally capable of transferring up to 10 million bits per second, newer versions can run up to 100 million bits per second and even 1000 million bits per second. It treats the wire like a bus with multiple masters and uses collision detection and a back-off scheme for handling simultaneous accesses.

exception Also called interrupt. An unscheduled event that disrupts program execution; used to detect overflow.

exception enable Also called interrupt enable. A signal or action that controls whether the process responds to an exception or not; necessary for preventing the occurrence of exceptions during intervals before the processor has safely saved the state needed to restart.

exclusive OR gate Hardware that performs the exclusive OR operation on input signals yielding a single signal result exclusive OR operation; also, an operation that leaves a 1 in the result only if two bits of the operands are unequal.

executable file A functional program in the format of an object file that contains no unresolved references, relocation information, symbol table, or debugging information.

execution time *See* response time.

exponent In the numerical representation system of floating-point arithmetic, the value that is placed in the exponent field.

external label Also called global label. A label referring to an object that can be referenced from files other than the one in which it is defined.

fairness A property of an allocation scheme, such as a bus arbitration protocol, that ensures that no device, even one with low priority, ever be completely locked out from the bus.

false sharing A sharing situation in which two unrelated shared variables are located in the same cache block and the full block is exchanged between processors even though the processors are accessing different variables.

finite state machine A sequential logic function consisting of a set of inputs and outputs, a next-state function that maps the current state and the inputs to a new state, and an output function that maps the current state and possibly the inputs to a set of asserted outputs.

firmware Microcode implemented in a memory structure, typically ROM or RAM.

flip-flop A memory element for which the output is equal to the value of the stored state inside the element and for which the internal state is changed only on a clock edge.

floating point Computer arithmetic that represents numbers in which the binary point is not fixed.

floppy disk A portable form of secondary memory composed of a rotating mylar platter coated with a magnetic recording material.

flush (instructions) To discard instructions in a pipeline, usually due to an unexpected event.

formal parameter A variable that is the argument to a procedure or macro; replaced by that argument once the macro is expanded.

forward reference A label that is used before it is defined.

forwarding Also called bypassing. A method of resolving a data hazard by retrieving the missing data element from internal buffers rather than waiting for it to arrive from programmer-visible registers or memory.

frame pointer A value denoting the location of the saved registers and local variables for a given procedure.

fully associative cache A cache structure in which a block can be placed in any location in the cache.

fully connected network A network that connects processor-memory nodes by supplying a dedicated communication link between every node.

gate A device that implements basic logic functions, such as AND or OR.

general-purpose electronic computer A computer that has not been constructed for one specific function.

general-purpose register (GPR) A register that can be used for addresses or for data with virtually any instruction.

geometric mean $\sqrt[n]{\prod_{i=1}^{n} \text{Execution time ratio}_i}$ A formula useful for summarizing execution times that have been normalized.

gigabyte Traditionally 1,073,741,824 (2^{30}) bytes, although some communications and secondary storage systems have redefined it to mean 1,000,000,000 (10^9) bytes.

global label *See* external label.

global miss rate The fraction of references that miss in all levels of a multilevel cache.

global pointer The register that is reserved for static data.

GPR *See* general-purpose register (GPR).

guard The first of two extra bits kept on the right during intermediate calculations of floating-point numbers; used to improve rounding accuracy.

handshaking protocol A series of steps used to coordinate asynchronous bus transfers in which the sender and receiver proceed to the next step only when both parties agree that the current step has been completed.

hard disk A form of secondary memory composed of rotating metal platters coated with a magnetic recording material.

hardwired control An implementation of finite state machine control typically using programmable logic arrays (PLAs) or collections of PLAs and random logic.

harmonic mean of rates $\text{HM} = \dfrac{n}{\sum_{i=1}^{n} \dfrac{1}{\text{Rate}_i}}$ A summary that tracks execution time when the data is given as rates rather than as a times.

hexadecimal Numbers in base 16.

high-level programming language A portable language such as C, Fortran, or Java composed of English words and algebraic notation that can be translated by a compiler into assembly language.

hit rate The fraction of memory accesses found in a cache.

hit time The time required to access a level of the memory hierarchy, including the time needed to determine whether the access is a hit or a miss.

hold time   The minimum time during which the input must be valid after the clock edge.

horizontal microcode   Use of microinstructions containing many fields that can control the datapath units in parallel and require little additional decoding. The use of many fields makes the microinstructions wider or more horizontal.

immediate addressing   An addressing regime in which the operand is a constant within the instruction itself.

implementation   Hardware that obeys the architecture abstraction.

imprecise exception   *See* imprecise interrupt.

imprecise interrupt   Also called imprecise exception. Interrupts or exceptions in pipelined computers that are not associated with the exact instruction that was the cause of the interrupt or exception.

in-order commit   A commit in which the results of pipelined execution are written to the programmer-visible state in the same order that instructions are fetched.

in-order execution   A conventional pipelined execution, in which all following instructions must wait when an instruction is blocked from executing.

input device   A mechanism through which the computer is fed information, such as the keyboard or mouse.

instruction format   A form of representation of an instruction composed of fields of binary numbers.

instruction latency   The inherent execution time for an instruction.

instruction mix   A measure of the dynamic frequency of instructions across one or many programs.

instruction set   The vocabulary of commands understood by a given architecture.

instruction set architecture   Also called architecture. An abstract interface between the hardware and the lowest level software of a machine that encompasses all the information necessary to write a machine language program that will run correctly, including instructions, registers, memory size, and so on.

integrated circuit   Also called chip. A device combining dozens to millions of transistors.

interrupt   An exception that comes from outside of the processor. (Some architectures use the term *interrupt* for all exceptions.)

interrupt-driven I/O   An I/O scheme that employs interrupts to indicate to the processor that an I/O device needs attention.

interrupt enable   *See* exception enable.

interrupt handler   A piece of code that is run as a result of an exception or an interrupt.

I/O instruction   A dedicated instruction that is used to give a command to an I/O device and that specifies both the device number and the command word (or the location of the command word in memory).

jump address table   Also called jump table. A table of addresses of alternative instruction sequences.

jump-and-link instruction   An instruction that jumps to an address and simultaneously saves the address of the following instruction in a register ($ra in MIPS).

jump table   *See* jump address table.

kernel benchmark   A small, time-intensive code fragment from a real program that is used for performance evaluation.

kernel mode   Also called supervisor mode. A mode indicating that a running process is an operating system process.

kilobyte   1024 (2^{10}) bytes.

LAN   *See* local area network (LAN).

latch   A memory element in which the output is equal to the value of the stored state inside the element and the state is changed whenever the appropriate inputs change and the clock is asserted.

latency (pipeline)   The number of stages in a pipeline or the number of stages between two instructions during execution.

least recently used (LRU)   A replacement scheme in which the block replaced is the one that has been unused for the longest time.

least significant bit   The rightmost bit in a MIPS word.

level-sensitive clocking   A timing methodology in which state changes occur at either high or low clock levels but are not instantaneous, as such changes are in edge-triggered designs.

link editor   *See* linker.

linker   Also called link editor. A systems program that combines independently assembled machine language programs and resolves all undefined labels into an executable file.

load-store machine   Also called register-register machine. An instruction set architecture in which all operations are between registers and data memory may only be accessed via loads or stores.

load-use data hazard   A specific form of data hazard in which the data requested by a load instruction has not yet become available when it is requested.

loader   A systems program that places an object program in main memory so that it is ready to execute.

local area network (LAN)   A network designed to carry data within a geographically confined area, typically within a single building.

local label   A label referring to an object that can be used only within the file in which it is defined.

local miss rate   The fraction of references to one level of a cache that miss; used in multilevel hierarchies.

lock   A synchronization device that allows access to data to only one processor at a time.

logic minimization A technique for reducing the number of gates needed to implement a set of logic functions.

loop unrolling A technique to get more performance from loops that access arrays, in which multiple copies of the loop body are made and instructions from different iterations are scheduled together.

LRU *See* least recently used (LRU).

machine language Binary representation used for communication within a computer system.

macro A pattern-matching and replacement facility that provides a simple mechanism to name a frequently used sequence of instructions.

macroinstruction An instruction in the instruction set architecture being implemented, used to distinguish the instructions visible to the programmer from the microinstructions of a microprogrammed control unit.

magnetic disk A form of nonvolatile secondary memory composed of rotating platters coated with a magnetic recording material.

main memory *See* primary memory.

main-memory coherence Consistency in the value of data in memory in a network-connected multiprocessor.

massively parallel A computer with at least 100 processors.

maximally encoded Use of encoded forms of control that require multiple levels of decode; vertical microcode is maximally encoded.

megabyte Traditionally 1,048,576 (2^{20}) bytes, although some communications and secondary storage systems have redefined it to mean 1,000,000 (10^6) bytes.

megaFLOPS *See* million floating-point operations per second (MFLOPS).

memory The storage area in which programs are kept when they are running and that contains the data needed by the running programs.

memory hierarchy A structure that uses multiple levels of memories; as the distance from the CPU increases, the size of the memories and the access time both increase.

memory-mapped I/O An I/O scheme in which portions of address space are assigned to I/O devices and reads and writes to those addresses are interpreted as commands to the I/O device.

MESI cache coherency protocol A write-invalidate protocol whose name is an acronym for the four states of the protocol: Modified, Exclusive, Shared, Invalid.

message passing Communicating between multiple processors by explicitly sending and receiving information.

metastability A situation that occurs if a signal is sampled when it is not stable for the required set-up and hold times, possibly causing the sampled value to fall in the indeterminate region between a high and low value.

MFLOPS *See* million floating-point operations per second (MFLOPS).

microcode The set of microinstructions that control a processor.

microcode assembler A program that translates microprograms into microinstructions that can be implemented in a ROM or PLA.

microinstruction A representation of control using low-level instructions, each of which asserts a set of control signals that are active on a given clock cycle as well as specifies what microinstruction to execute next.

microprogram A symbolic representation of control in the form of instructions, called microinstructions, that are executed on a simple micromachine.

microprogrammed control A method of specifying control that uses microcode rather than a finite state representation.

million floating-point operations per second (MFLOPS) Also called megaFLOPS. A measurement of program execution speed based on the number of millions of floating-point operations executed per second. MFLOPS is computed as the number of floating-point operations in a program divided by the product of the execution time and 10^6.

million instructions per second (MIPS) A measurement of program execution speed based on the number of millions of instructions. MIPS is computed as the instruction count divided by the product of the execution time and 10^6.

MIMD *See* multiple instruction streams, multiple data streams (MIMD).

minimally encoded Use of an unencoded control format that can directly control a datapath; horizontal microcode is minimally encoded.

minterms Also called product terms. A set of logic inputs joined by conjunction (AND operations); the product terms form the first logic stage of the programmable logic array (PLA).

MIPS *See* million instructions per second (MIPS).

miss penalty The time required to fetch a block into a level of the memory hierarchy from the lower level, including the time to access the block, transmit it from one level to the other, and insert it in the level that experienced the miss.

miss rate The fraction of memory accesses not found in a level of the memory hierarchy.

most significant bit The leftmost bit in a MIPS word.

motherboard A plastic board containing packages of integrated circuits or chips, including processor, cache, memory, and connectors for I/O devices such as networks and disks.

multicomputer Parallel processors with multiple private addresses.

multicycle implementation Also called multiple clock cycle implementation. An implementation in which an instruction is executed in multiple clock cycles.

multilevel cache A memory hierarchy with multiple levels of caches, rather than just a cache and main memory.

multiple clock cycle implementation *See* multicycle implementation.

multiple-instruction issue A procedure in which the instruction fetch unit can send multiple instructions to the next pipeline stage in a single clock cycle.

multiple instruction streams, multiple data streams (MIMD) A computer classification in Flynn's taxonomy referring to computers that use multiple instruction streams and multiple data streams.

multiprocessor Parallel processors with a single shared address.

multistage network A network that supplies a small switch at each node.

NAND gate An inverted AND gate.

network bandwidth Informally, the peak transfer rate of a network; can refer to the speed of a single link or the collective transfer rate of all links in the network.

next-state counter A counter that supplies the sequential next state.

next-state function A combinational function that, given the inputs and the current state, determines the next state of a finite state machine.

next-state output An output of the combinational logic that specifies the next-state number.

nonblocking cache A cache that allows the processor to make references to the cache while the cache is handling an earlier miss.

nonuniform memory access (NUMA) A type of single-address space multiprocessor in which some memory accesses are faster than others depending which processor asks for which word.

nonvolatile memory A form of memory that retains data even in the absence of a power source and that is used to store programs between runs. Magnetic disk is nonvolatile and DRAM is not.

nop An instruction that does no operation to change state.

NOR gate An inverted OR gate.

normalized A number in floating-point notation that has no leading 0s.

NUMA *See* nonuniform memory access (NUMA).

object program A combination of machine language instructions, data, and information needed to place them properly in memory.

opcode The field that denotes the operation and format of an instruction.

operating system Supervising program that manages the resources of a computer for the benefit of the programs that run on that machine.

out-of-order commit A commit in which the results of pipelined execution need not be written to the programmer visible state in the same order that instructions are fetched.

out-of-order execution A situation in pipelined execution when an instruction blocked from executing does not cause the following instructions to wait.

output device A mechanism that conveys the result of a computation to the user.

overflow (floating-point) A situation in which a positive exponent becomes too large to fit in the exponent field.

page fault An event that occurs when an accessed page is not present in main memory.

page mode A mechanism in DRAM that provides the ability to access multiple bits of a row by changing the column address only and, hence, is faster than a normal access cycle that changes row and column addresses.

page table The table containing the virtual to physical address translations in a virtual memory system. The table, which is stored in memory, is typically indexed by the virtual page number; each entry in the table contains the physical page number for that virtual page if the page is currently in memory.

parallel processing program A single program that runs on multiple processors simultaneously.

PC *See* program counter (PC).

PC-relative addressing An addressing regime in which the address is the sum of the program counter (PC) and a constant in the instruction.

personal computer A general-purpose computer designed to be manufactured in high volume and at a cost affordable enough to allow for use in the home.

physical address An address in main memory.

physically addressed cache A cache that is addressed by a physical address.

pipeline data hazard *See* data hazard.

pipeline stall Also called bubble. A stall initiated in order to resolve a hazard.

pipelining An implementation technique in which multiple instructions are overlapped in execution, much like to an assembly line.

pipelining stage A step in executing an instruction that occurs simultaneously with other steps in other instructions and typically lasts one clock cycle.

pixel The smallest individual picture element. Screen are composed of hundreds of thousands to millions of pixels, organized in a matrix.

PLA *See* programmable logic array (PLA).

polling The process of periodically checking the status of an I/O device to determine the need to service the device.

precise exception *See* precise interrupt.

precise interrupt Also called precise exception. An interrupt or exception that is always associated with the correct instruction in pipelined computers.

prefetching A technique in which data blocks needed in the future are brought into the cache early by the use of special instructions that specify the address of the block.

primary memory Also called main memory. Volatile memory used to hold programs while they are running; typically consists of DRAM in today's computers.

procedure A stored subroutine that performs a specific task based on the parameters with which it is provided.

procedure call convention *See* register-use convention.

procedure call frame A block of memory that is used to hold values passed to a procedure as arguments, to save registers that a procedure may modify but that the procedure's caller does not want changed, and to provide space for variables local to a procedure.

procedure frame Also called activation record. The segment of the stack containing a procedure's saved registers and local variables.

processor-memory bus A bus that connects processor and memory and that is short, generally high speed, and matched to the memory system so as to maximize memory-processor bandwidth.

product terms *See* minterms.

program counter (PC) The register containing the address of the instruction in the program being executed

programmable logic array (PLA) A structured-logic element composed of a set of inputs and corresponding input complements and two stages of logic: the first generating product terms of the inputs and input complements and the second generating sum terms of the product terms. Hence, PLAs implement logic functions as a sum of products.

programmable ROM (PROM) A form of read-only memory that can be programmed when a designer knows its contents.

PROM *See* programmable ROM (PROM).

propagation time The time required for an input to a flip-flop to propagate to the outputs of the flip-flop.

protection A set of mechanisms for ensuring that multiple processes sharing the processor, memory, or I/O devices cannot interfere, intentionally or unintentionally, with one another by reading or writing each other's data. These mechanisms also isolate the operating system from a user process.

pseudoinstruction A common variation of assembly language instructions often treated as if it were an instruction in its own right.

quotient The primary result of a division; a number that when multiplied by the divisor and added to the remainder produces the dividend.

RAID *See* redundant arrays of inexpensive disks (RAID).

raster cathode ray tube (CRT) display A display, such as a television set, that scans an image one line at a time, 30 to 75 times per second.

read-only memory (ROM) A memory whose contents are designated at creation time, after which the contents can only be read. ROM is used as structured logic to implement a set of logic functions by using the terms in the logic functions as address inputs and the outputs as bits in each word of the memory.

receive message routine A routine used by a processor in machines with private memories to accept a message from another processor.

recursive procedures Procedures that call themselves either directly or indirectly through a chain of calls.

redundant arrays of inexpensive disks (RAID) An organization of disks that uses an array of small and inexpensive disks so as to increase both performance and reliability.

reference bit Also called use bit. A field that is set whenever a page is accessed and that is used to implement LRU or other replacement schemes.

register addressing A mode of addressing in which the operand is a register.

register file A state element that consists of a set of registers that can be read and written by supplying a register number to be accessed.

register-register machine *See* load-store machine.

register use *See* register-use convention.

register-use convention Also called procedure call convention. A software protocol governing the use of registers by procedures.

relocation information The segment of a Unix object file that identifies instructions and data words that depend on absolute addresses.

remainder The secondary result of a division; a number that when added to the product of the quotient and the divisor produces the dividend.

rename buffer Also called rename register. An extra internal register within processors that is used to hold results while waiting for the commit unit to commit the result to one of the real registers.

rename register *See* rename buffer.

reorder buffer A register that holds instructions in a dynamic pipelined machine whose results have not yet been committed to programmer-visible registers or memory; machines with out-of-order execution and in-order commit will retire an instruction from the reorder buffer only when the instruction has finished execution and all instructions ahead of it have been completed.

reservation station A buffer within a functional unit that holds the operands and the operation.

response time Also called execution time. The total time required for the computer to complete a task, including disk accesses, memory accesses, I/O activities, operating system overhead, CPU execution time, and so on.

restartable instruction An instruction that can resume execution after an exception is resolved without the exception's affecting the result of the instruction.

return address A link to the calling site that allows a procedure to return to the proper address; in MIPS it is stored in register $ra.

ROM *See* read-only memory (ROM).

rotation latency Also called delay. The time required for the desired sector of a disk to rotate under the read/write head; usually assumed to be half the rotation time.

round Method to make the intermediate floating-point result fit the floating-point format; the goal is typically to find the nearest number that can be represented in the format.

scientific notation A notation that renders numbers with a single digit to the left of the decimal point.

SCSI *See* small computer systems interface (SCSI).

secondary memory Nonvolatile memory used to store programs and data between runs; typically consists of magnetic disks in today's computers.

sector One of the segments that make up a track on a magnetic disk; a sector is the smallest amount of information that is read or written on a disk.

seek The process of positioning a read/write head over the proper track on a disk.

segmentation A variable-size address mapping scheme in which an address consists of two parts: a segment number, which is mapped to a physical address, and a segment offset.

selector value Also called control value. The control signal that is used to select one of the input values of a multiplexor as the output of the multiplexor.

semiconductor A substance that does not conduct electricity well.

send message routine A routine used by a processor in machines with private memories to pass to another processor.

separate compilation Splitting a program across many files, each of which can be compiled without knowledge of what is in the other files.

sequential access memory Memory whose access time differs depending on the location of the data being retrieved because data is stored sequentially so that all data must be passed over to access the final bit of information; contrasts with random access memory, in which any bit may be accessed in the same time.

sequential logic A group of logic elements that contain memory and hence whose value depends on the inputs as well as the current contents of the memory.

set-associative cache A cache that has a fixed number of locations (at least two) where each block can be placed.

set-up time The minimum time that the input to a memory device must be valid before the clock edge.

shared memory A memory for a parallel processor with a single address space, implying implicit communication with loads and stores.

sign-extend To increase the size of a data item by replicating the high-order sign bit of the original data item in the high-order bits of the larger, destination data item.

significand In the numerical representation system of floating-point arithmetic, the value in that is placed in the significand field.

silicon A substance found in sand that does not conduct electricity well.

silicon crystal ingot A rod composed of silicon crystal that is between 6 and 12 inches in diameter and about 12 to 24 inches long.

SIMD *See* single instruction stream, multiple data streams (SIMD).

SIMM *See* single in-line memory module (SIMM).

single clock cycle implementation *See* single-cycle implementation.

single-cycle implementation Also called single clock cycle implementation. An implementation in which an instruction is executed in one clock cycle.

single in-line memory module (SIMM) A small printed circuit board containing 4 to 24 DRAM integrated circuits. Today's computers use SIMMs to allow main memory to be upgraded and expanded over time by the customer.

single instruction stream, multiple data streams (SIMD)   A computer classification in Flynn's taxonomy that refers to computers with single instruction streams but multiple data streams and in which a single instruction operates on many data elements at the same time.

single instruction stream, single data stream (SISD)   A computer classification in Flynn's taxonomy that refers to computers with single instruction streams and single data streams. (SISD is the conventional processor covered in the first eight chapters.)

single precision   A floating-point value represented in a single 32-bit word.

SISD   *See* single instruction stream, single data stream (SISD).

slave   A device that responds to read and write requests but does not generate them and hence cannot be a bus master.

small computer systems interface (SCSI)   A bus used as a standard for I/O devices.

SMP   *See* symmetric multiprocessor (SMP).

snooping cache coherency   A method for maintaining cache coherency in which all cache controllers monitor or snoop on the bus to determine whether or not they have a copy of the desired block.

source language   The high-level language in which a program is originally written.

spatial locality   The locality principle stating that if a data location is referenced, data locations with nearby addresses will tend to be referenced soon.

SPEC benchmark   *See* system performance evaluation cooperative (SPEC) benchmark.

speculative execution   A pipelining technique that combines dynamic scheduling with branch prediction.

speedup   The measure of how a machine performs relative to how it previously performed before an enhancement was implemented. Speedup is equal to the ratio of execution time before the enhancement to execution time after the enhancement.

split cache   A scheme in which a level of the memory hierarchy is composed of two independent caches that operate in parallel with each other with one handling instructions and one handling data.

split transaction protocol   A protocol in which the bus is released during a bus transaction while the requester is waiting for the data to be transmitted, which frees the bus for access by another requester.

SRAM   *See* static random access memory (SRAM).

stack   A data structure for spilling registers organized as a last-in-first-out queue.

stack frame   *See* procedure call frame.

stack pointer   A value denoting the most recently allocated address in a stack that shows where registers should be spilled or where old register values can be found.

stack segment   The portion of memory used by a program to hold procedure call frames.

state assignment   A control optimization that works by attempting to choose the state numbers such that the resulting logic equations contain more redundancy and can thus be simplified.

state element   A memory element.

state input   An input to the combinational logic that specifies the current state.

static data   The portion of memory that contains data whose size is known to the compiler and whose lifetime is the program's entire execution.

static random access memory (SRAM)   A memory where data is stored statically (as in flip-flops) rather than dynamically (as in DRAM). SRAMs are faster than DRAMs, but less dense and more expensive per bit.

sticky bit   A bit used in rounding in addition to guard and round that is set whenever there are nonzero bits to the right of the round bit.

stored-program computer   A computer whose instructions are represented as numbers, allowing the same memory to contain instructions and data and thus allowing programs to produce programs.

stored-program concept   The idea that instructions and data of many types can be stored in memory as numbers, leading to the stored program computer.

structural hazard   An occurrence in which a planned instruction cannot execute in the proper clock cycle because the hardware cannot support the combination of instructions that are set to execute in the given clock cycle.

subroutine library   A collection of commonly used programs.

sum of products   A form of logical representation that employs a logical sum (OR) of products (terms joined using the AND operator).

supercomputer   The fastest and most expensive computer, typically used for scientific computation. Supercomputers generally cost between \$1 and \$30 million.

superpipelining   A technique that increases processor speed by lengthening pipelines.

superscalar   An advanced pipelining technique that enables the processor to execute more than one instruction per clock cycle.

superscalar pipelining   A technique that replicates internal components of the computer in order to launch and execute multiple instructions in every pipeline stage.

supervisor mode   *See* kernel mode.

symbol table   A table that matches names of labels to the addresses of the memory words that instructions occupy.

symmetric multiprocessor (SMP)   Also called UMA machine. A multiprocessor in which accesses to main memory take the same amount of time no matter which processor requests the access and no matter which word is asked.

synchronization   The process of coordinating the behavior of two or more processes, which may be running on different processors.

synchronizer failure   A situation in which a flip-flop enters a metastable state and where some logic blocks reading the output of the flip-flop see a 0 while others see a 1.

synchronous bus   A bus that includes a clock in the control lines and a fixed protocol for communicating that is relative to the clock.

synchronous system   A memory system that employs clocks and where data signals are read only when the clock indicates that the signal values are stable.

system call   A special instruction that transfers control from user mode to a dedicated location in supervisor code space, invoking the exception mechanism in the process.

system CPU time   The CPU time spent in the operating system performing tasks on behalf of the program.

system performance evaluation cooperative (SPEC) benchmark   A set of standard CPU-intensive, integer and floating point benchmarks based on real programs.

systems software   Software that provides services that are commonly useful, including operating systems, compilers, and assemblers.

tag   A field in a table used for a memory hierarchy that contains the address information required to identify whether the associated block in the hierarchy corresponds to a requested word.

temporal locality   The principle stating that if a data location is referenced then it will tend to be referenced again soon.

terabyte   Originally 1,099,511,627,776 (2^{40}) bytes, although some communications and secondary storage systems have redefined it to mean 1,000,000,000,000 (10^{12}) bytes.

text segment   The segment of a Unix object file that contains the machine language code for routines in the source file.

three Cs model   A cache model in which all cache misses are classified into one of three categories: compulsory misses, capacity misses, and conflict misses.

tick   *See* clock cycle.

TLB   *See* translation-lookaside buffer (TLB).

track   One of 1000 to 5000 concentric circles that makes up the surface of a magnetic disk.

transaction processing   A type of application that involves handling small short operations (called transactions) that typically require both I/O and computation. Transaction processing applications typically have both response time requirements and a performance measurement based on the throughput of transactions.

transfer time   The time required to transfer a block of bits, typically a sector, during disk access.

transistor   An on/off switch controlled by electricity.

translation-lookaside buffer (TLB)   A cache that keeps track of recently used address mappings to avoid an access to the page table.

ulp   *See* units in the last place (ulp).

UMA   *See* uniform memory access (UMA).

UMA machine   *See* symmetric multiprocessor (SMP).

underflow (floating-point)   A situation in which a negative exponent becomes too large to fit in the exponent field.

uniform memory access (UMA)   Memory access that takes the same amount of time no matter which processor requests the access and no matter which word is asked for.

units in the last place (ulp)   The number of bits in error in the least significant bits of the significand between the actual number and the number that can be prepresented.

unresolved reference   A reference that requires more information from an outside source in order to be complete.

use bit   *See* reference bit.

user CPU time   The CPU time spent in a program itself.

vacuum tube   An electronic component, predecessor of the transistor, that consists of a hollow glass tube about 5 to 10 cm long from which as much air has been removed as possible.

valid bit   A field in the tables of a memory hierarchy that indicates that the associated block in the hierarchy contains valid data.

vector processor   An architecture and compiler model that was popularized by supercomputers in which high-level operations work on linear arrays of numbers.

vector supercomputer   A supercomputer whose instructions operate on vectors of numbers, typically 64 floating-point numbers at a time.

vectored interrupt   An interrupt for which the address to which control is transferred is determined by the cause of the exception.

vertical microcode   Use of microinstructions containing many fewer fields that require additional decoding before being used to control the datapath units. The use of fewer fields makes the microinstructions narrower or more vertical.

very large scale integrated (VLSI) circuit   A device containing tens of thousands to millions of transistors.

virtual address   An address that corresponds to a location in virtual space and is translated by address mapping to a physical address when memory is accessed.

virtual machine   A virtual computer that appears to have nondelayed branches and loads and a richer instruction set than the actual hardware.

virtual memory   A technique that uses main memory as a "cache" for secondary storage.

virtually addressed cache   A cache that is accessed with a virtual address rather than a physical address.

VLSI circuit   *See* very large scale integrated (VLSI) circuit.

volatile memory   Storage, such as DRAM, that only retains data if it is receiving power.

wafer   A slice from a silicon ingot no more than 0.1 inch thick, used to create chips.

weighted arithmetic mean   A summary that tracks the execution time of a workload with weighting factors designed to reflect the presence of the programs in a workload; computed as the sum of the products of weighting factors and execution times.

wide area network   A network extended over hundreds of kilometers which can span a continent.

word   The natural unit of access in a computer, usually a group of 32 bits; corresponds to the size of a register in the MIPS architecture.

workload   A set of programs run on a computer that is either the actual collection of applications run by a user or is constructed from real programs to approximate such a mix. A typical workload specifies both the programs as well as the relative frequencies.

write-back   A scheme that handles writes by updating values only to the block in the cache, then writing the modified block to the lower level of the hierarchy when the block is replaced.

write-broadcast   A snooping protocol scheme in which the writing processor disseminates the new data over the bus, allowing all copies to be updated with the new value.

write buffer   A queue that holds data while the data are waiting to be written to memory.

write-invalidate   A type of snooping protocol in which the writing processor causes all copies in other caches to be invalidated before changing its local copy, which allows it to update the local data until another processor asks for it.

write-through   A scheme in which writes always update both the cache and the memory, ensuring that data is always consistent between the two.

yield   The percentage of good dies from the total number of dies on the wafer.

Index

(comments), A-51
" (double quotes), A-51
_ (underbars), A-51

1-bit adder, 241
  connecting, 234
  illustrated, 232
  input/output specification for, 232
  See also adders
1-bit ALU, 230–234
  31 copies of, 239
  for AND/OR, 231
  with expanded multiplexor, 237, 238
  illustrated, 234, 236
  See also ALU
4-bit adder, 243, 247
8-bit bytes, 112
32-bit ALU, 234–249
  from 31 copies of 1-bit ALU, 239
  final, 240
  illustrated, 235, 240
  tailoring to MIPS, 236–249
  See also ALU
64-bit address extensions, 151
80x86 architecture, 177–185
  32-bit addressing modes, 181
  32-bit subset, 179
  8086, 178, 194, 319
  8087, 178, 302, 319
  80286, 178
  80386, 178
  80486, 178
  addressing modes, 179–181
  arithmetic instructions, 180
  default data size, 180
  double words, 180
  floating point, 302–304
    add operand variations, 304
    instructions, 303

operands, 302
operation classes, 302
performance, 304
history of, 194–195
instruction encoding, 182–183
instruction formats, 184
instruction set, 195, 417, 418
instruction types, 180, 193
integer operations, 180–182
logical instructions, 180
milestones, 178
operations, 183
power, 185
quantity vs. style, 183
registers, 179–180
See also Pentium; Pentium Pro

A

abs.d instruction, A-70
abs pseudoinstruction, A-55
abs.s instruction, A-70
abstractions, 18
  levels of, 242
  principles of, 18
Accelerated Strategic Computing
    Initiative (ASCI), 743
accumulator, 190–191
  architectures, 190–191
  extended, 191
  instructions, compiling assignment
    statement into, 190
  instruction set, 190, 201
  memory-based operand-
    addressing mode, 190
  variables and, 190
ACS project, 527
activation record, 138
active process, 585

Ada language, 222
add.d instruction, 288, A-70
adders
  1-bit, 232, 234, 241
  4-bit, 243, 247
  16-bit, 243, 246
  64-bit, 247
  CarryIn, 232, 235, 241
  carry-lookahead, 242–249
  CarryOut, 232, 233, 241
  carry save, 264, 331, 332
  CDC 6600, 316
  generate, 243
  hardware for carry out signal, 233
  propagate, 243
  ripple carry, 234
  subtraction, 235
  wider, 330
addi instruction, 145, 147, 151, A-55
add instruction, 119, 120, 126, 127,
    137, 151, 438, A-53, A-55
  destination register, 505
  in EX stage, 507, 508
  overflow exception in, 507, 508
  stalls and, 490
  through pipeline, 471–476
add intermediate instruction.
    See addi instruction
addition, 220–225
  binary, 220, 221
  carry save, 332
  floating-point, 280–283
  overflow, 221, 222
  See also arithmetic
addiu instruction, 222, 230, A-55
addresses
  64-bit extensions, 151
  base, 112
  branch target, 349, 386, 407
  byte, 113, 149

addresses *(continued)*
  cache block, 556
  direct-mapped cache, 549, 573
  exception, 412
  jump, 387
  memory, 111, 113, 387
  microinstruction, 401
  physical, 580
  sequential word, 164, 187
  set-associative, 573
  too big, 188
  virtual, 580, 582, 585, 602
addressing
  80x86 modes, 179–180, 181
  base, 151, 152, 181
  in branches, 148–150
  immediate, 151, 152
  indexed, 175
  in jumps, 148–150
  in parallel processors, 730–733
  modes, 151, 152, A-49–A-51
  PC-relative, 148–149, 151, 152
  pseudodirect, 151, 152
  register, 151, 152
  update, 175–176
address space, 580
  flat, 617
  placing page tables in, 597
  process, 585
  single, 713, 732
address translation, 580
add.s instruction, 288, A-70
addu instruction, 222, A-55
Algol 60 programs, 76, 77, 86
aliasing, 596
alignment restriction, 112
Alpha architecture, 425, 520
  Alpha 21264, 516, 522
  design principles, 425
Alto, 696–697, 698
ALU, 230–249, 339
  1-bit, 230–234
  4-bit, using carry lookahead, 246
  32-bit, 234–249
  carry-lookahead and, 241–249
  CMOS, 249
  constructing, 230–249
  as datapath element, 346
  function codes, C-6
  hardware building blocks, 231

input, 387, 413, 481
  for lw/sw instructions, 354
  memory-reference instructions
    use of, 339
  microinstructions, 406
  most significant bit, 237
  multiplexor, 249
  operations in parallel, 511–512
  output, 387, 413
  for R-type instructions, 354
  shared, 378
  signed-immediate input, 488
  symbol, 241
ALU control, 353–356
  3-bit, 354
  bits, 355, 356, C-4
  block, 357–358, C-6
  input, 355
  instruction class and, 354
  lines, 240, C-5
  logic, 466, C-6
  mapping to gates, C-4–C-7
  output, 354
  signals, 392, C-6
  signal settings, 387
  truth table, 355, 356
  unit, 392
  See also ALU; control
ALUOut register, 406
Amdahl's law, 75, 253, 522, 566, 688
  execution time after improvement,
    716
  improvement time, 76
  parallel processors and, 744–745
  speedup, 101, 716
  unaffected execution time, 716
American Standard Code for Infor-
    mation Interchange. *See* ASCII
AND gates, 231, 233, B-7, C-7, C-8
  array, B-12
  illustrated, 231
  output, 382
  See also gates
andi instruction, 227, 230, A-55
and immediate. *See* andi instruction
and instruction, 226–227, 236, 351,
    438, 498, A-55
  stalls and, 490
  through pipeline, 471–476

AND operation, B-5
  1-bit ALU for, 231
  mask, 226
AND plane, B-12, B-13
Apple
  Apple IIC, 41
  Macintosh 7200 series, 687
  Macintosh II, 320
applications, 8
  as benchmarks, 66
  performance metrics and, 54
architectures, 18
  80x86, 177–185
  accumulator, 190–191
  Alpha, 425, 520, 618
  complex, challenges, 417–418
  evolution vs. revolution in,
    746–748
  general-purpose register, 191–192
  Harvard, 35
  high-level-language, 194
  implementation of, 18
  instruction set, 18, 31, 338
  memory-memory, 192
  microarchitectures, 425
  without pipelining, 417
  Power-1, 527
  register-memory, 191, 192
  register-register, 191
  RISC, 194, 425
  System/360, 37
  VAX, 425
  See also Web Extensions I and III;
    MIPS (architecture)
arithmetic
  accurate, 297–298
  computer vs. real world gap, 299
  fallacies and pitfalls, 304–308
  floating point, 275–304, 308
  instructions, 188, A-55–A-59
  See also addition; division;
    multiplication; subtraction
arithmetic logic unit. *See* ALU;
    ALU control
arithmetic mean (AM), 71
  of execution times, 82
  of normalized execution times,
    80–81
  of ratios, 81

standard, 71
weighted, 71, 82
arithmetic right shift, 261
ARPANET, 652
array indices, 171
arrays, 111, 112, 171
 AND gate, B-12
 byte, 143
 clearing with indices, 172
 disk, 709
 flip-flop, B-24
 OR gate, B-12
 pointers vs., 171–174
 setting to all zeros, 171
 variable index, 114–115, 126
ASCII
 binary numbers vs., 212
 character representation, 142
assemblers, 6, A-10–A-17
 addressing mode synthesis, A-51
 backpatching, A-13
 directives, A-5
 first pass, A-12
 function of, A-4, A-10
 microassembler, 402
 microcode, C-28, C-29
 object files, 158, 160, A-4,
  A-10–A-11
 relocation information, A-14
 speed of, A-13
 symbol table, A-12
 syntax, A-51–A-53
assembly language, 6, 157–158, A-3
 advantages, A-4, A-9
 compilers vs., 186
 C program compiled into, 7
 drawbacks, A-9–A-10
 labels and, A-3, A-7
 memory locations, A-5
 object file, 158, A-4
 performance and, 186–187
 programmers, A-8
 programs, 157, A-10, A-12
 roles, A-5–A-6
 routine example, A-6
 source file, A-4
 symbols, A-3
 when to use, A-7–A-9
 See also assemblers; MIPS assembly
  language

asynchronous buses, 660–663
 control lines, 660
 device accommodation, 660
 handshaking protocol, 660, 661
 overhead, 663
 performance analysis, 662–663
 scaling of, 663
 synchronous bus vs., 663
 See also bus(es)
asynchronous inputs, B-42
Atlas computer, 624, 625
ATM (Asynchronous Transfer
  Mode), 652
atomic swap operation, 724
automatic variables, 140, 187
average instruction execution time,
  84
average memory access time
  (AMAT), 629

B

backpatching, A-13
backplane buses, 656–658
 cost advantage, 658
 illustrated, 659
 interface, 657–658
 standard, 656–657
 See also bus(es)
bandwidth
 bisection, 737
 bus, 655, 663–667
 cache, 555
 constraints, 684, 685
 effective, 562
 I/O, 640, 691
 memory, 561
 network, 652
 total network, 737
 write, 562
barrier synchronization, 719
base addressing, 112, 151, 152, 181
base register, 112, 115
basic blocks, 126
bcctr instruction, 420
bclf instruction, 288
bclt instruction, 288
bczf instruction, A-62
bczt instruction, A-62

benchmarks, 66
 applications as, 66
 Dhrystone, 79–80
 file system I/O, 643
 I/O, 641–643
 kernel, 86
 program types for, 66
 selecting, 69
 small, 67, 68
 SPEC, 67, 68, 87–89
 summarizing, 69–70
 supercomputer I/O, 642
 synthetic, 79–80
 transaction processing I/O,
  642–643
 Whetstone, 79
 See also performance
beq instruction, 123, 128, 347, 438,
  A-62
 datapath in operation for, 369
 execution steps, 367
 implementing, 347
 operands, 347
 pipeline impact on, 497
beqz pseudoinstruction, A-63
bge pseudoinstruction, A-63
bgeu pseudoinstruction, A-63
bgezal instruction, A-62
bgez instruction, A-62
bgt pseudoinstruction, A-64
bgtu pseudoinstruction, A-64
bgtz instruction, A-62
biased notation, 220
big-endian byte order, A-48
BINAC, 36
binary addition, 220, 221
binary numbers, 2, 6, 116, 188, 305
 ASCII vs., 212
 to decimal conversion, 214
 hexadecimal conversion table, 218
 multiplication of, 251
 scientific notation for, 275
 sign extension conversion, 216–217
 See also numbers
binary-to-hexadecimal shortcut, 218
bisection bandwidth, 737
bit fields, 227, 229–230
bit line, B-28
bit maps, 13

bits, 5, 116
  dirty, 589
  done, 675
  error, 675
  guard, 297, 334
  least significant, 237
  most significant, 237
  packing/unpacking, 225
  patterns, 299, 308
  quotient, 269
  reference, 587
  round, 297, 298, 334
  shifting, 226
  sign, 213
  sticky, 298, 334
  Sum, 234
  valid, 547
  write access, 597
ble pseudoinstruction, A-64
bleu pseudoinstruction, A-64
blez instruction, A-63
block(s), 542
  addresses, 556
  cache, 550, 555–560
  choosing for replacement, 575–576
  direct mapped placement, 568, 569
  fixed-sized, 583
  flexible placement of, 568–573
  four-word, 557
  fully associative placement, 568,
    569
  index field, 556
  locating, 573–575, 605–606
  location of, 569
  logic, B-7, B-8
  number in cache, 615
  one-word, 556
  placement strategy, 570
  replacement, 606
  set-associative placement, 569
  size of, 558–559, 563–564
  variable-size, 583
  virtual memory, 580
blt pseudoinstruction, A-17, A-64
bltu pseudoinstruction, A-64
bltzal instruction, A-63
bltz instruction, A-63
Bnegate control line, 237

bne instruction, 123, 127, 128, A-63
  address field, 150
  See also conditional branches
bnez pseudoinstruction, A-64
bonding, 23
Boolean algebra, B-5–B-7
  laws, B-6
  operators, B-5–B-6
Boolean *n*-cube network topology,
    738
Booth's algorithm, 259–263
  classifying bit groups and, 260
  multiplier bit values, 263
  with negative multiplier example,
    261, 262
  for positive numbers, 261
  speed and, 264
  tabular form, 263
  two's complement multiplication,
    263
bottleneck, 522
bounds register, 587–588
b pseudoinstruction, A-61
branch condition to count register.
    See bcctr instruction
branch(es)
  addressing in, 148–150
  compiler creation of, 124
  conditional, 123–125, 145–146, 148,
    148–149
  condition of, 350
  datapath, 349, 350, 499
  delayed, 130, 350, 444, 497, 502,
    527, A-39
  delay reduction, 497–498
  delay slot, 502, 503
  distinguishing between types of,
    125
  far away, 150
  finite state machine execution,
    394, 395
  hazards. *See* control hazards
  history buffer, 498
  instructions, A-61–A-64
  at MEM stage, 496
  multicycle design and, 380
  not taken, 349, 444, 496–497
  pipelined, 498

  stalling, 496
  target, 496
  target addresses, 349, 386
  unconditional, 125
branch if equal. *See* beq instruction
branch if not equal. *See* bne
    instruction
branch prediction, 443–444
  1-bit scheme, 501
  2-bit schemes, 501, 502
  accuracy, 501
  assuming branch not taken, 498
  buffer, 498, 501
  dynamic, 444, 498–502
  dynamic scheduling combined
    with, 516
  loops and, 501
  steady-state behavior, 501
  See also branch(es)
break instruction, A-75
breakpoints, A-43
bubble, 442
buffers
  branch history, 498
  branch prediction, 498, 501
  raster refresh, 13
  rename, 517
  reorder, 517
  store, 516, 609
  three-state, B-28, B-29
  translation-lookaside (TLB),
    590–596
  write, 517, 554, 565, 614
  write-back, 614–615
Burkes, Arthur, 34, 122, 312
Burroughs
  B5000, 194
  B5500, 76
bursts, B-29–B-30
bus arbitration, 669–671, 722
  bus priority and, 669
  bus requests and, 669
  centralized, parallel, 669
  daisy chain, 669, 670–671
  distributed by collision detection,
    670
  distributed by self-selection, 670
  fairness, 669, 671
  schemes, 669–670
  single-bus multiprocessor, 724

bus(es), 342, 655–673
  access, 667–668
  advantages, 655
  asynchronous, 660–663
  backplane, 656–658
  bandwidth, 655, 663–667
  block transfers, 664
  bus masters, 667–668
  characteristics, 671
  control lines, 655, 656
  data lines, 655
  data, width, 663
  design difficulty, 655
  disadvantage, 655
  IDE standard, 687
  I/O, 656–658
  ISA standard, 687
  multivendor, 698
  optimizing, 671
  PCI standard, 672, 673, 687
  performance, 663–667
  processor-memory, 656–658
  proprietary, 698
  protocols, 673
  requests, 669
  SCSI standard, 672, 673, 686, 687
  shared, 382
  shorter, 671
  standards, 672–673
  synchronous, 660–663
  types, 656–658
  wider, 671
  See also bus arbitration
bus masters, 667–668
  bus release lines, 669
  multiple, 668
  single, 667–668
bus transactions, 656
  input operation, 656, 658
  output operation, 656, 657
bypassing. See forwarding
byte order, A-47–A-48
  big-endian, A-48
  little-endian, A-48
bytes
  8-bit, 112
  addresses, 113, 149
  array of, 143
  copying, 142
  index, 295

"little end," 113
loading, 142
opcode, 182
storing, 142

C

cache block(s), 555–560
  addresses, 556
  choosing for replacement, 575–576
  increasing size of, 558–559
  index, 550
  locating, 573–575
  miss rates and, 558–559
  multiword, mapping address to, 556
  size, 558–559, 563–564
  spatial locality and, 555
  See also block(s)
cache coherency
  directory-based, 754
  problem, 726
  scalable, 754
  steps, 726
cache coherency protocols, 720–724
  cache block states, 722, 724
  example, 722–724
  MESI, 724
  snooping, 720–721
  variations, 724
  write-invalidate, 721, 723
  write-update, 721, 726
cache memory, 15, 18, 27
  See also cache(s)
cache miss(es), 550–552
  block replacement on, 606
  clock rate and, 567
  control unit and, 550
  direct-mapped, 571
  penalty, 559–560, 565
  penalty reduction, 552
  processing, 551
  processor stall cycles and, 552
  rates, 554–555, 558, 604
  read, 557
  reducing by flexible placement of
    blocks, 568–573
  steps taken in, 551
  write, 558
  See also cache(s); miss(es)

cache-only memory, 731
cache performance, 564–569
  calculation example, 565–566
  direct-mapped, 572
  fully associative, 572
  with increased clock rate, 567
  measuring, 564–566
  multilevel, 576–577
  perfect, 566
  set-associative, 572
cache(s), 545–564
  accessing, 547–550
  associativity in, 571–572
  bandwidth, increasing, 555
  bits in, 550
  combination of events in, 595
  combined, 555
  DECStation 3100 example, 552–555
  design challenges, 614
  direct-mapped, 546, 547–548, 568,
    569, 570, 573
  as evolutionary improvement, 747
  example, before/after references,
    545
  flushing, 684
  fully associative, 568, 570, 579,
    605–606
  history, 545
  location, 546, 547
  magnetic disk, 650
  memory system support, 560–563
  multilevel, 576–578
  nonblocking, 517, 614
  number of blocks in, 615
  perfect, 566
  physically indexed, 595
  physically tagged, 595
  primary, 577, 613
  routing I/O through, 684
  secondary, 576–577, 611–612
  set-associative, 569, 570, 573, 579
  simulating, 615
  snooping, 731
  SPIM simulator and, A-47
  split, 555
  tags, 547, 557
  two-level, 577
  virtually addressed, 596
  virtually indexed, 596
  virtually tagged, 596

cache(s) *(continued)*
  write-back, 554, 563, 607, 609, 614
  write-through, 553, 562, 563, 565,
    607, 614
  See also memory hierarchies
callee, A-23, A-24, A-25
caller, A-23, A-24, A-25
capabilities, 626
capacity misses, 609, 610
CarryIn, 232, 235, 241
  propagate, 243
  specification, 232
  See also 1-bit adder
carry lookahead, 241–249
  fast path, 249
  first level of abstraction, 242–243
  importance of, 248
  levels of abstraction, 242
  plumbing analogy, 244, 245
  ripple carry vs., 248–249
  second level of abstraction,
    243–249
CarryOut, 232, 233, 241
  generate, 243
  specification, 232
  See also 1-bit adder
carry save adder, 264, 331, 332
CAS (Column Access Strobe), B-32
case statement. *See* switch statement
Cause register, 412, 413, 678
  exception collection, 509
  exception recording, 509
  fields implemented by SPIM,
    A-33–A-34
  setting, 415
CDC 6600, 76, 192, 696
  adder, 316
  Algol 60 programs, 76, 77
  photograph, 526
  pipelining, 526
  uniqueness, 526
centralized memory in a multi-
    processor, 728
c.eq.d instruction, A-71
c.eq.s instruction, A-71
chips, 23
  DRAM, 17, 22
  IEEE 754, 319–320

increased capacity of, 562
manufacturing process, 24
memory, 562
motherboard, 13
Pentium, manufacturing, 24–28
SRAM configuration, B-27
clear procedure
  array version, 172
  pointer version of, 173–174
  version comparison, 174
c.le.d instruction, A-71
c.le.s instruction, A-71
clock cycles, 59
  average length, 374
  CPU, 65
  CPU time, 564
  equation, 64
  example, 60–61, 62
  fixed, 375
  for instruction classes, 396, 397
  memory-stall, 564, 565
  multicycle design, 378
  number of, 60, 61
  pipeline stage, 438
  read-stall, 564
  reducing, 60
  for single-cycle machines, 374
  single-cycle pipeline diagrams,
    463–465
  variable, 374–375
  in variable-clock machines, 374
  write-stall, 565
clock cycles per instruction (CPI), 62,
    94, 338
  average number of, 64
  comparing, 66
  computing, 65
  determination of, 338
  example, 62
  implementation and, 338
  for MIPS instruction categories,
    328
  in multicycle CPU, 397
  obtaining, 64
  with one level of caching, 577
  overall, 64
  single-cycle, 371
clock cycle time, 59, 338, B-18
  constraint, B-40

determination, 338
  increasing, 60
clock frequency, B-18
clocking methodology, 341–343
clock period, 59, B-18
clock rate, 59, 60, 78
  cache misses and, 567
  implementation and, 338
  increase, 60, 73
  Pentium, 73
  Pentium Pro, 419
clocks, B-18–B-21
clock skew, B-40
  illustrated, B-41
  reducing, B-41
c.lt.d instruction, A-71
c.lt.s instruction, A-71
clusters, 734–736
  Berkeley, 734
  characteristics of, 735
  drawbacks of, 734
  "hybrid," 736
  IBM SP2, 734
  independent computer, 735
  software, 735
CMOS ALU, 249
Cobol, 8
Cocke, John, 527
code size, 76
coherency
  cache, 720–724
  maintaining, 720
  synchronization with, 724–726
coherency problem, 683
  avoiding, 684
  cache, 720
cold-start misses, 609
collision misses, 609
collisions, 708
Colossus, 35
column access, B-32
column major order, 296
COMA (Cache Only Memory
    Architecture), 754
combinational blocks, B-4
combinational control units, C-4–C-8
  implementing, C-4–C-8
  use of, C-3
  See also control units

combinational elements, 340
combinational logic, 341, 342, 398,
    B-3, B-8–B-18, C-11
    don't cares, B-15–B-17
    function description, B-5
    inputs, B-20
comments, A-51
    # symbol and, A-51
    MIPS assembly language, 107
comparison(s)
    control scheme, 504
    floating-point, 288
    immediate operands and, 146
    instructions, A-60–A-61
    register, 387
compiler(s), 6, 8, 31, A-6, A-9
    assembly language coders vs., 186
    branch/label creation, 124
    C, 186
    C program transformation, 157
    gcc, A-29
    generated instructions, 61
    hazard dependency resolution, 491
    loop replacement, A-9
    machine language without
        assemblers and, A-10
    MIPS, 115, A-29
    optimizations, 66
    programmers vs., A-9
    special-purpose optimizations, 67
compiling
    assignment statement into
        accumulator instructions, 190
    assignment statement into
        memory-memory instruc-
        tions, 192
    assignment statement into stack
        instructions, 193
    assignment with operand in mem-
        ory, 112
    C assignment using registers, 110
    complex C assignment into MIPS,
        109
    floating-point C procedure with
        two-dimensional matrices into
        MIPS, 294–296
    floating-point C program into
        MIPS assembly code, 293
    if statement into conditional
        branch, 123–124

if-then-else into conditional
    branches, 124–125
less than test, 128
with load and store instructions,
    113–114
loops with variable array index,
    126
procedure that doesn't call another
    procedure, 134–135
string copy procedure, 143–144
switch statement using jump
    address table, 129–130
with variable array index, 114–115
while loops, 127
complements, B-4
compulsory misses, 609, 610
computer design
    advances, 5
    cost/performance, 83
    good design demands good
        compromises principle, 118,
        188
    high-performance, 82
    low-cost, 82
    make the common case fast princi-
        ple, 146, 188, 338
    principles, 187–188
    simplicity favors regularity
        principle, 108, 187, 338
    smaller is faster principle, 110, 188
computer(s)
    applications, 4
    in automobiles, 4
    calculators vs., 123
    commercial characteristics of, 43
    commercial development of, 36–41
    communicating to, 21
    components, 16, 31, 53
    cost improvement, 4
    desktop, 10, 741
    economics, 3
    embedded, A-7–A-8
    generations, 42–43
    input devices, 10
    laptop, 4
    minicomputer, 38
    networked, 21
    output devices, 10
    personal, 40–41
    revolution, 3–4

single instruction, 206
supercomputer, 39–40
technology growth, 3
technology performance in, 22
vector, 751–752
computer systems
    decomposability of, 9
    in hierarchical layers, 31
    performance evaluation of, 66
conditional branches, 123, 188
    addressing, 148–149
    compiling if statement into,
        123–124
    compiling if-then-else statement
        into, 124–125
    distinguishing, 125
    on PowerPC, 181
    translating into machine
        language, 145–146
    See also branch(es)
condition codes, 181
conflict misses, 609
constant-manipulating instructions,
    A-59
constants
    32-bit, loading, 147
    inside instruction, 145
    in MIPS assembly language, 134
    operand, 145–147
    too big, 188
context switch, 598
control, 14, 31
    ALU, 353–358, C-4–C-7
    approach tradeoffs, 422–423
    challenge, 410, 421
    in computer organization, 16, 53
    design, 399–400, 421, 422
    exception checking, 413–416
    forwarding, 480
    hardwired, 423, 424
    hazard detection unit, 490
    implementation, 421, 422, 423
    MEM hazard, 483
    microprogrammed, 424, C-27
    multicycle, 390
    optimization, C-26–C-27
    organizing to reduce logic,
        C-30–C-31
    parts of, C-3
    pipelined, 466–476

control (*continued*)
  representations, 421, 422
  scheme comparison, 504
  specification methods, 423
  See also finite state machine(s);
    microprogram(s)
control function, 399
  microprogram, 409
  storing in ROM, 408
control hazard(s), 441–445, 496–509
  delayed decision and, 444
  exceptions, 505–509
  frequency, 496
  predicting branches not taken
    and, 443
  resolution schemes, 496
  solutions, 442
  stalling on conditional branch and,
    442
  See also pipeline hazards;
    pipelining
controller time, 648
control lines
  ALU, 240, C-5
  computing setting of, 363
  EX stage, 466
  for final three stages, 469
  ID stage, 466
  IF stage, 466
  illustrated, 358
  labeling, 466
  MEM stage, 466–468
  multicycle datapath with, 381
  multiplexor, C-29
  Pentium Pro, 418
  setting of, 361
  setting to 0, 496
  single-bit, 359
  WB stage, 468
  See also control
control signals, 359, 412
  1-bit, 384
  2-bit, 384
  ALU settings, 387
  function of, 359
  illustrated, 360
  microinstruction field, 400
  outputs, C-13
  pipelined datapath with, 467

setting, 359
  See also control
control units, 353, 356–371, 399
  address select logic, C-24
  cache misses and, 550
  combinational, C-3, C-4–C-8
  design, 425
  using explicit counter, C-22
  illustrated, 360
  implementation, 356–371,
    389–399, 422
  input, 367
  logic equations, C-11
  as microcode, C-27
  microprogram for, 408
  MIPS, C-10
  multicycle datapath, 382, 383
  output, 367
  small, 354
  specifying with graphical
    representation, 399
  See also control
Coonen, Jerome T., 318
coprocessor 0, A-32, A-49
coprocessor 1, A-49
core instructions, 309, 310, 311
core memory, 621–622, 623
Cosmic Cube, 753
cost/performance design, 83
C programming language, 106
  compilers, 186
  compiling assignment statements
    into, 108
  compiling assignment using-
    registers, 110
  compiling complex assignment
    into MIPS, 109
  loops in, 127
  storage classes, 140
  variables, 140
  See also high-level programming
    languages
CPU (central processor unit), 14,
    A-49
  clock cycles, 65
  execution cycles, 564
  multicycle, CPI in, 397
  performance, 59
  single-cycle, 375–376

system time, 58, 59
  user time, 58, 59
CPU execution time, 58, 60
  clock cycles, 564
  comparing, 373
  measuring, 64
Cray computers, 315
  Cray-1, 39, 40
  multiplier, 316
  overflow, 316
  T90 vector, 320, 516
Cray, Seymour, 39, 40, 315, 526
critical word first, 560
crossbar networks, 738, 739
cross-coupled NOR gates, B-21, B-22
CRT (cathode ray tube) display, 12
  pixels, 12
  refresh rate, 12
  See also graphics display
cvt.d.s instruction, A-71
cvt.d.w instruction, A-72
cvt.s.d instruction, A-72
cvt.s.w instruction, A-72
cvt.w.d instruction, A-72
cvt.w.s instruction, A-72
c.x.d instruction, 288
c.x.s instruction, 288
cylinders, 646

D

daisy chain arbitration, 669
  fairness in, 671
  illustrated, 670
  See also bus arbitration
dance hall organization, 728
data hazard(s), 445–448, 476–496
  complication, 483
  conditions, 479
  datapath modification via
    forwarding, 484
  definition, 485
  detecting, 478, 480–481
  EX, 480
  forwarding and, 476–488
  identified in ID stage, 490
  illustrated, 477
  load-use, 446

MEM, 481
MEM control, 483
 pipeline stalls and, 445
 stalls and, 489–496
 WB stage and, 483
 See also pipeline hazards;
    pipelining
data layout directives, A-14
data misses, 552
data movement instructions,
    A-68–A-69
data parallelism, 749
datapath elements
 ALU, 346
 memory unit, 344
 program counter (PC), 344
 register file, 345, 346
 series operation, 385
 sharing, 351
datapaths, 14, 31
 for beq instruction, 369
 branch, 349, 350, 499
 building, 343–350
 combining, 352
 composing, 351–352
 in computer organization, 16, 53
 control lines, 358
 control scheme, 368
 with controls for handling
    exceptions, 506
 with control unit, 360
 creating, 351–353
 for fetching instructions, 345
 instruction fetch portion, 352, 353
 for jump instruction, 372
 for load/store instructions, 348
 MIPS processor, 421
 multicycle, 382, 383, 385, 417, 421
 with multiplexors, 358
 operation of, 361–367
 Pentium Pro, 418
 performance consequences, 524
 pipelined, 449–466
 for R-type instructions, 346, 347
 single-cycle, 385, 417, 421, 450
 superscalar, 512
 See also datapath elements
data rate, 642, 644
 bus bandwidth and, 655
 keyboard, 644

data segment, A-20–A-21
data selector, 351
data transfer instruction, 111, 188
 base register, 112
 offset, 112, 115
DEC
 8700, 520
 Alpha 21264, 516, 522
 Alpha architecture, 425, 520, 618
 DECStation 3100, 552–555, A-48
 disk drive, 697
 NVAX, 520
 PDP-8, 38
 VAX-11/780, 67
 VAX architecture, 425
decimal numbers, 116
 binary conversion to, 214
 long division with, 265
 multiplication of, 250
 representing, 120, 211
 scientific notation for, 275
 See also numbers
decoders, B-8
 3-to-8, B-8
 column access, B-32
 row access, B-32
 two-level, B-32, B-33
decoding, 392
DECStation 3100, 552–555, A-48
 cache illustration, 553
 cache miss rates, 554–555
 MIPS R2000, 592
 write-back scheme, 554
 write buffer, 554
 write processing, 554
 write-through scheme, 554
dedicated register, 191
delayed branch(es), 130, 350, 444,
    527, A-39
 motivation for, 350
 pipeline, 445
 popularity and, 502
 sequential instruction execution,
    444
 slots, 444
 See also branch(es)
delayed decision, 444
delayed loads, 527, A-39
DeMorgan's theorems, B-6, B-10,
    B-46

denormalized numbers (denorms),
    300, 334
desktop computers, 10
 cost of, 741
 photograph, 10
D flip-flops, B-22, B-24, B-25
Dhrystone benchmark, 79–80, 97, 98
 creation, 79
 optimization distortions, 80
 See also benchmarks
dies, 23
 cost of, 48
 defects, 23, 25
 good, 23
 illustrated, 27
 Pentium, 28
 Pentium Pro, 26, 27, 28
 yield, 23, 48
 See also wafer(s)
DIMMs (dual inline memory
    modules), 623
direct-mapped blocks, 568
 location of, 569
 replacement, 575
 See also block(s)
direct-mapped cache(s), 546, 568, 569
 addresses, 549, 573
 bits in, 550
 choosing, 605
 configuration illustration, 570
 contents, 547–548
 illustrated, 546
 misses, 571, 575
 performance, 572
 tag bits, 575
 See also cache(s)
directory-based multiprocessors, 731
dirty bits, 589
disk arrays, 709
disk controller, 648
dispatch operations, 402, 404, C-23
dispatch ROMs, C-24, C-25, C-26
 filling contents of, C-28
 microcode, C-30
dispatch tables, 402, 408, C-28
displacement addressing, 151
displacements, 180
distributed memory, 728
div.d instruction, 288, A-72

divide algorithms
  first version, 266–268
  second version, 268–269
  third version, 269–271
dividend, 265, 272
div instruction, 273, A-56
division, 265–274
  with decimal numbers, 265
  dividend, 265, 272
  divisor, 265
  first version algorithm, 266–268
  in MIPS, 273
  nonrestoring, 333
  operands, 265
  quotient, 265, 269
  remainder, 266, 272
  restoring, 273, 333
  second version algorithm, 268–269
  signed, 272
  SRT, 297
  terms, 265
  third version algorithm, 269–271
  See also arithmetic
divisor, 265
Divisor register, 266, 269
div pseudoinstruction, A-56
div.s instruction, 288, A-72
divu instruction, 273, A-56
divu pseudoinstruction, A-56
D latches, B-22, B-23
DMA (direct memory access), 680,
      682–684
  chained transfers, 683
  controllers, 680, 681, 697
  devices, multiple, 681
  hard disk interface, 682
  interfaces, 704
  I/O overhead using, 681
  memory system and, 682–684
  processors, 681
  transfer steps, 680–681
  in virtual memory system, 682–683
  writes, 682
done bit, 675
don't cares, B-15–B-17
  example, B-16–B-17
  input, B-16
  output, B-16
  types of, B-16

double precision, 99
  denorm gap, 300
  exponent bias for, 278
  floating-point arithmetic, 277, 294
  MIPS, 277
  registers, 288
  representation example, 279
  S/360, 315
double quotes ("), A-51
double words, 180
DRAM (dynamic random access
      memory), 16–18, 560, 618,
      B-31–B-33
  access time, 20, 541, 576, 618, 619,
      B-32
  capacity history, 49
  capacity increase, 31
  chip capacity, 22
  chips, 17
  cost per megabyte, 20, 541
  growth rule, 22
  history of, 623
  options, 562–563
  packaging, 623
  pass transistor, B-32
  performance gap, reducing, 620
  SDRAMs, 563
  size increase, 563
  speed improvement, 618
  square array organization, 562
  SRAM vs., 541
  synchronous (SDRAM), B-29, B-33
  technology enhancements, 618
  transistors per bit, B-31
  two-level decoding structure, B-31
  See also memory
drums, 694, 695
dynamic branch prediction, 498–502
dynamic data, A-21
dynamic pipelining, 449, 510–511,
      515–517
  branch prediction combined with,
      516
  complexity of, 516
  cost of, 511
  hardware resources, 511
  in-order completion, 516
  motivations, 516
  out-of-order completion, 516

  primary units of, 515
  reservation stations, 515
  See also pipelining

E

early restart, 560
Eckert, J. Presper, 32, 34, 35, 36, 423,
      621
edge-triggered clocking, B-18,
      B-39–B-40
  advantages, B-20–B-21
  clock length and, B-40
  drawbacks, B-41
  falling edge, B-20
  illustrated, B-21
  rising edge, B-20
EDO RAMs, 562, B-33
EDSAC, 33–34, 423, 540
  EDSAC 2, 424
  illustrated, 34
  mercury delay lines, 621, 622
EDVAC, 32–33
  completion of, 34
  paper, 35
Eispack, 314
elapsed time, 58, 59
ELXSI 6400, 320
embedded computers, A-7–A-8
emulation, 424
encoder, B-8
encoding, C-30
ENIAC, 32, 621
  illustrated, 33
  patents, 35
  performance, 83
  size of, 32
EPC register, 412
error bit, 675
error-correcting codes (ECC),
      B-34–B-35
  1-bit, B-34
  distance-3, B-34
  distance-4, B-35
  Hamming, B-35
Ethernet network(s), 21, 651, 708
  coaxial cable medium, 708

collisions, 708
end-to-end latency, 654
exponential back-off algorithm, 709
packets, 651
switched, 651–652, 692
See also network(s)
evolution-revolution spectrum, 746–747
Exception code register, A-33
exception program counter (EPC), 223, 505
copying, 223, 225
jump register and, 225
saving address in, 411
saving PC into, 413
writing into, 413
exception(s), 223, 410–416, A-32–A-36
addresses, 412
arithmetic overflow, 410, 411, 413
cause communication methods, 412
causes of, 507, 509
checking, 413–416
collection in Cause register, 509
control hazard, 505–509
control unit design and, 411
datapath with controls for handling, 506
detecting, 411, 413
finite state machine handling, 416
types of, 413
disabling, 601
handling, 411–413
implementing, 414
imprecise, 509
I/O interrupts vs., 678
multiple, 507
operating system handling of, 411–412
page fault, 599, 600, A-34
in pipelined computers, 507
PowerPC architecture use of, 410
precise, 509
processing, 412
reenabling, 601

routines, 225
support requirements, 411
system call, 597
term use, 410
TLB, 601
types, A-34
undefined instruction, 411, 413
See also interrupt(s)
exclusive OR gates, 249
executable files, 163, A-4, A-19
format, 159
process for producing, A-4
See also linker(s)
execution times, 56, 57
after improvement, 75
arithmetic mean of, 82
average, 71
average instruction, 84
CPU, 58, 60
measurement, 58, 71
miss rates and, 555
normalized, arithmetic mean of, 80–81
number of instructions and, 61
performance and, 58
pipelining and, 449
ratio, 81
of real programs as metric, 83
relative, 70
total, 70–71, 81
validity of, 82
EX/MEM register, 453, 455, 457, 458, 481, 485, 488
expansion factor, A-9
explicit counters, C-22, C-25
exponents
before significand, 278
bias, 278, 283
maximum, 282
negative, 278
of product, 283
EX stage, 474, 475
add instruction in, 507, 508
control fields, changing, 490
control lines, 466
flushing instructions in, 505
hazard, 480
illustrated, 455, 457
instruction label, 486

load instruction in, 453
nop instruction in, 490
operand names, 486
overflow detection, 505
pipeline register during, 480
store instruction, 457
See also pipeline stages
extended accumulator, 191
external labels, A-11

F

fallacies, 29
a 100-MB/sec bus can transfer 100 MB of data in 1 second, 688
Amdahl's law doesn't apply to parallel computers, 744–745
computers use an antiquated method of computation and are running out of steam, 29
floating-point addition is associative, 304–305
geometric mean of execution time ratios is proportional to total execution time, 81–82
hardware-independent metrics predict performance, 76
if there is space in control store, new instructions are free of cost, 420–421
implementing complex instructions with microcode may not be faster than simpler instructions, 419–420
increasing depth of pipelining always increases performance, 521
magnetic storage will be replaced shortly, 688
more powerful instructions mean higher performance, 185
only theoretical mathematicians care about floating-point accuracy, 305–308
peak performance tracks observed performance, 745–746

fallacies *(continued)*
  pipelining ideas can be imple-
    mented independent of
    technology, 520
  pipelining is easy, 520
  synthetic benchmarks predict
    performance, 79–80
  use assembly language for highest
    performance, 186–187
  See also pitfalls
false sharing, 722
fast carry, 249
  using first level of abstraction,
    242–243
  using second level of abstraction,
    243–249
  See also carry lookahead
fetch-on-miss, 607
fetch-on-write, 607
fields of instructions, 117, 154
  I-format, 118, 154
  J-format, 154
  names of, 118
  offset, A-61
  R-format, 154
  See also bit fields
file systems, I/O benchmarks, 643
finite state machine(s), 390,
    B-35–B-39
  for 2-bit prediction scheme, 501
  arcs, 392
  branch instruction execution, 394,
    395
  control, C-8–C-21
    illustration, 396, C-9
    PLA implementation, C-19–C-21
    ROM implementation,
      C-13–C-19
  for controlling memory-reference
    instructions, 392, 393
  with exception detection, 416
  execution steps and, 390
  handshaking protocol control
    implementation, 664
  high-level view of, 391
  implementation, 390, B-38
  implementation with state register,
    B-39
  inputs, B-37
  internal storage, B-35, B-36

I/O control, 662
jump instruction execution, 394,
    395
Mealy machine, 399
Moore machine, 398, 399, B-36
next-state function, B-35, B-36
output function, B-35, B-36, B-37
output signals, B-36–B-37
R-type instruction implemen-
    tation, 394
states, 390, 391
synchronous, B-35
See also control
firmware, 424–425
flat address space, 617
flip-flops, B-22–B-25
  arrays, B-24
  D, B-22, B-24, B-25
  edge-triggered, B-40
  falling-edge, B-23, B-24
  hold time, B-24
  latches vs., B-22
  in metastable state, B-43
  propagation time, B-40
  set-up time, B-24
  See also latches
floating point, 275–304, 308
  accuracy, 282
  addition, 280–283
    arithmetic unit block diagram,
      285
    associative fallacy, 304–305
    binary, 282
    example, 282–283
    illustrated, 284
    steps, 281–282
  binary to decimal conversion, 280
  comparison, 288
  C procedure compilation, 294–296
  decimal unit, 313
  double-precision, 277, 294
  hardware, 313
  IEEE 754 standard, 277, 278
  instructions, 375–376, A-70–A-74
  Intel 8087 coprocessor, 302
  MIPS instructions, 288–297
  MIPS numbers, 276
  multiplication, 283–288
    example, 287–288

    illustrated, 289
    steps, 283, 286
  numbers, 276–280
  operations, 99, 100, 293
  pipelines, 521
  in PowerPC, 301
  precision limitation, 305
  registers, separate, 290, 296
  representation, 276–280
  representation example, 279
  single-precision, 277
  unit, 296
  See also arithmetic
floppy disks, 19
  disadvantages, 646
  See also magnetic disk(s)
flushing instructions, 498, 505
  in EX stage, 505
  in ID stage, 505
  in IF stage, 505
for loops, 127–128, 165, 166, 167–168,
    169
  PowerPC, 177
  variables, 294
  See also loops
format field, C-30
for statement, 166
  See also for loops
Fortran language, 8, 222
forwarding, 445
  control, 480
  data hazards and, 476–488
  dependent store instructions and,
    488
  example, 485–488
  graphical representation, 447
  hazard resolution via, 484
  multiple results and, 448
  multiplexors, 492
  multiplexors, control values, 483
  name origin, 449
  path validity, 446
  pipeline registers before, 482
  pipeline stalls and, 446
  sub instruction and, 485, 486
  with two instructions, 446
forwarding unit, 482, 485, 494
  forwarding data to ALU, 487
  illustrated, 492

forward references, A-11
frame pointer, 138, 139
fully associative block(s), 568
    location, 569
    number of, 572
    replacement, 575
    See also block(s)
fully associative cache(s), 568, 579
    block replacement, 606
    choosing, 605–606
    configuration illustration, 570
    performance, 572
    tag bits, 575
    See also cache(s)
fully connected networks, 736, 737,
    738
function code, 118

G

gate delays, 248
gates, B-3, B-7–B-8
    AND, 231, 233, B-7
    discrete, B-17
    mapping ALU control function to,
        C-4–C-7
    mapping main control function to,
        C-7–C-8
    NAND, B-8
    NOR, B-8
    OR, 231, 233, B-7
gcc program, miss rates, 558, 573
general-purpose registers, 191–192
generate in carry lookahead, 243
    levels, 247–248
    "super," 248
geometric mean
    advantage of, 81
    data series independence, 81
    drawback to, 81–82
    formula, 81
    total execution time and, 81
global pointer, 140
Goldstine, Herman, 32, 34, 122, 312,
    314
Goodyear MPP, 749, 751
go to statement, 123, 130
gradual underflow, 300
graphics display, 12–13

CRT, 12
    gray-scale, 12
    LCD, 12
    raster refresh buffer, 13
Gray code, B-48
guard digits, 297, 334
    rounding with, 297–298
    S/360 double precision and, 315
    shift, 298

H

halfwords, 144
Hamming code, B-35
handshaking, 660
handshaking protocol, 660
    finite state machine implementing
        control for, 664
    functioning of, 661
    illustrated, 661
    split transaction, 667
    See also asynchronous buses
hard disks, 19
    advantages of, 646
    illustrated, 20
    read/write head, 19
    removable, 695
    See also magnetic disk(s)
hardware
    components, 16
    costs, reducing, C-31
    as hierarchical layers, 9
    I/O devices, 10–13
    microprogram translation to, 408,
        C-28–C-31
    motherboard, 13
hardwired control, 423, 424
    characterization, 424
    implementations, 425
    Pentium/Pentium Pro, 425
    See also control
harmonic mean (HM), 100
Harvard architecture, 35
hazard detection unit, 490
    control for, 490
    function, 491
    illustrated, 492
    load-use hazard and, 491
helical scan tape, 692
hexadecimal, 158

binary conversion table, 218
    popularity, 217
high-level programming languages,
    6, A-6
    benefits of, 7–8
    C, 106, 108–110, 140
    Cobol, 8
    computer architectures, 194
    conciseness advantage, 8
    Fortran, 8
    Lisp, 8
    translation hierarchy, 156
high-performance design, 82
hit rate, 542
hits, 542
hit time, 543
holography, 693
horizontal microcode, C-31
HP PA-RISC, 618

I

IBM
    305 RAMAC, 694, 696
    360/65, 625
    360/85, 626
    360/91, 526–527
    704, 748
    7090, 317, 424, 748
    7094, 314–315, 317
    ACS project, 527
    microcode use, 424
    Personal Computer, 40, 191
    Power-1 architecture, 527
    PowerPC, 175–177
    Powerstation 550, 68
    RS/6000, 525, 527, 753, 754
    SHARE, 314, 315
    SP2, 734
    Stretch (7030), 83, 525
    System/360, 37–38, 195, 314, 424,
        625
    System 370, 195, 625
    Winchester disks, 694–695
ID/EX register, 453, 457, 458
ID stage, 472, 473
    branch adder, moving to, 497
    branch execution in, 497
    branch taken determination, 500
    control lines, 466

ID stage (*continued*)
  flushing instructions in, 505
  hazard identification in, 490
  illustrated, 454
  load instruction, 453
  store instruction, 457
  See also pipeline stages
IEEE 754 floating-point standard,
    277, 278, 318
  chips, 319–320
  implementation, 320
  successful parts of, 320
  symbols, 300
  today, 320–321
  See also floating point
IF/ID register, 452, 453, 455, 457, 497,
    498
IF stage, 473
  control lines, 466
  flushing instructions at, 498, 505
  illustrated, 454
  load instruction, 453
  store instruction, 455
  See also pipeline stages
if statement, 123
  compiling into conditional branch,
    123–124
  illustrated options, 125
if-then-else statement, 124–125, 129
Illiac IV, 749, 750
immediate addressing, 151, 152
immediate operands, 145–146
implementation
  80x86 instruction set, 418
  beq instruction, 347
  combinational control unit,
    C-4–C-21
  control, 421, 422, 433
  control unit, 356–371, 389–399
  design principles and, 338
  exception, 414
  finite state machine, 390, 398, B-38,
    B-39
  finite state machine control,
    C-8–C-21
  hardwired control, 425
  instruction set architecture and,
    338
  instruction steps, 339
  jump, 370–371

microcode controller, 409
microprogram, 408–410
MIPS, illustrated, 340
MIPS subset, 343
multicycle, 377–399
next-state function, C-21–C-27
overview, 338–339
Pentium Pro, 416–419
R-format ALU operation, 346
scheme, 351–377
single-cycle, 371–377
imprecise exceptions/interrupts, 509,
    527
inactive process, 585
indexed addressing, 175
  illustrated, 176
  MIPS code, 175
indexes
  cache block, 550
  page table, 583, 584, 585
  variable array, 114–115, 126
index register, 115
inlining procedure, 169
in-order completion, 516
input, 31
  ALU, 387, 413, 481
  ALU control, 355
  asynchronous, B-42
  combinational logic, B-20
  control unit, 367
  devices, 10, 644
  don't cares, B-16
  in I/O, 673–683
  state element, 341
instruction classes
  ALU control and, 354
  branch, 357
  clock cycles for, 396, 397
  execution steps, 382–389
  illustrated, 357
  instruction frequency, 397
  jump, 394
  load and store, 357
  MIPS, 189
  R-type, 357
  sharing datapath elements
    between, 351
  See also instructions
instruction count, 338
  comparing, 66

determination of, 338
measuring, 64
instruction encoding, A-53
  80x86, 182–183, 185
  MIPS, 119, 153
  MIPS floating-point, 292
instruction execution, 382–389
  execution, memory address
    computation, or branch
    completion step, 386–387
  instruction decode and register
    fetch step, 386
  instruction fetch step, 385
  memory access or R-type instruc-
    tion completion step, 388
  memory read completion step,
    388–389
  step summary, 389
instruction formats, 117, 440
  80x86, 184
  designation, 119
  fields, 154
  I-type, 118, 119
  J-type, 148, 149
  R-type, 118, 119, 153, 154
instruction mix, 84, 86
Instruction register (IR), 385
instructions, 5, 104–206
  80x86, 180, 193
  add, 119, 120, 126, 127, 137, 151,
    222, 351, 438, 471–476, A-53,
    A-55
  arithmetic, 188, A-55–A-59
  basic block, 126
  branch, A-61–A-64
  comparison, A-60–A-61
  constant-manipulating, A-59
  constants inside, 145
  core, 309, 310, 311
  data movement, A-68–A-69
  data transfer, 111, 188
  for decision making, 122–131
  decoding, 386
  exception/interrupt, A-74–A-75
  fallacies and pitfalls, 185–187
  fetching, 345, 387
  floating-point, 288–297, A-70–A-74
  flushing, 498, 505
  frequency, 311
  I/O, 675

jump, A-65
as kept on computer, 116
latency, 522
load, 111, 348, A-65–A-67
logical, 329, A-55–A-59
machine, 117
memory-reference, 339
MIPS assembly language, 108, 111,
   117, 150
miss cycles, 566
misses, 551
nop, 478, 485, 490, A-75
numbers for, 6
or, 351, 438, 471–476, A-57
pipelined sequence of, 489
popularity, 188
PowerPC, 176–177
pseudoinstructions. See pseudoinstructions
reducing, 175
relative frequency of, 84
representation of, 106
representing, 116–122
restartable, 600
R-type, 346, 347, 361–363
shift, 226
store, 113, 348, A-67–A-68
string, 182
subtract, 222, 351, 438, 471–476, A-
   59
subsequent, 378
syscall, 597, A-74
undefined, 411, 413
vector, 752
See also specific instruction name;
   instruction execution; instruction sets; microinstruction(s)
instruction set architecture, 18, 31
   implementation and, 338
   maintaining as constant, 31
instruction sets, 106, 422
   80x86, 195, 417, 418
   accumulator, 190, 201
   comparing, 201–202
   computer comparison and, 78
   design principles of, 187–188
   load-store, 202
   memory-memory, 192, 202
   MIPS, 107, 189, 309
   MIPS I, 310

pipelining, 440–441
pipelining complications, 520
pseudo MIPS, 310
register-memory, 192
RISC, 625
stack model, 202
symbolic representation, 116
VAX, 425
integrated circuit(s), 22–24, 622
   cost of, 48
   transistors, 22
   very large-scale (VLSI), 22, 23
Intel
   80x86 microprocessor family,
      177–185
   4004 microprocessor, 38, 39, 194
   8008 microprocessor, 194
   8080 microprocessor, 194
   8088 microprocessor, 194
   instruction set development with
      HP, 625
   iPSC 860, 753
   Paragon, 753
interleaving, 562, 564
interrupt-driven I/O, 678
   overhead, 679–680
   processor in, 680
   See also I/O
interrupt handler, A-34
   example, A-34–A-35
   register moving, A-35
   register storage, A-34
   return from, A-36
interrupt rate, 679
interrupt(s), 223, 410, A-32–A-36
   creation, 411
   imprecise, 509, 527
   Intel 80x86 architecture use of, 410
   I/O, 674, 678
   PowerPC architecture use of, 410
   precise, 509
   term use, 410
   vectored, 412
   See also exception(s)
inverses, B-4
inverted page tables, 588
inverters, 231
I/O
   bandwidth, 640, 691
   controllers, 682, 697

DMA overhead, 681–682
fallacies and pitfalls, 688–690
finite state machine control for, 662
initiation under control, 676
instructions, 675
interrupt-driven, 678, 679–680
memory-mapped, 675
rate, 642
read, 684
routing through cache, 684
throughput, 655
time, 639, 640
write, 684
See also I/O device(s); I/O
   system(s)
I/O benchmarks, 641–643
   file system, 643
   supercomputer, 642
   throughput and, 642
   transaction processing, 642–643
   See also benchmarks
I/O buses, 656–658
   designer, 657
   interface, 657
   standard, 656–657
   See also bus(es)
I/O device(s), 10–13, 644–654
   behavior, 644
   buses and, 655–673
   collection illustration, 638
   communication types, 674
   data rate, 644
   data transfers, 672, 679–682
   diversity of, 644
   giving commands to, 675
   graphics display, 12–13
   interfacing, 673–684
   keyboard, 644
   low-level control, 674
   magnetic disks, 19–20, 646–651
   maximum number of, 690
   mouse, 12, 645–646
   networks, 21, 651–654
   registers, 675
   types of, 644
   See also I/O; I/O system(s)
I/O interrupt(s)
   exceptions vs., 678
   multiple priorities, 678
   priority, 678

I/O performance, 639–640
  aspects, 641
  measures, 641–643
  predicting, 686
  transfer, 671
I/O processors, 682
  moving functions from CPU to, 689
  performance and, 689
  peripheral, 696
  programmable, 696
I/O programs, 682
  chaining, 696
  storage, 682
I/O requests, 640, 673
  large, 641
  performance, 690
I/O system(s), 638–709
  Apple Macintosh 7200 series, 687
  assessment, 641
  bandwidth constraints, 684, 685
  capability, 639
  characteristics, 673–674
  comparing, 641
  design, 638, 667, 690
  design example, 685–686
  designing process, 684–686
  evaluation characteristics, 690
  future directions in, 691–693
  history, 694–695
  interrupt use by, 674
  latency constraints, 684
  performance, 639–640, 691
  polling overhead, 676–677
  shared by multiple programs, 673
  typical, 687
  See also I/O; I/O device(s)
IPC (instructions per clock cycle), 510
isolated 1s, 264
I-type instruction format, 118, 119
  distinguishing, 119
  fields, 118, 154
  See also instruction formats

J

`jal` instruction, 132, 133, 149, 162, A-65
`jalr` instruction, A-65

`j` instruction, 125, 126, 150, A-65
  branch instruction vs., 371
  control and datapath, 372
  instruction format for, 371
Jobs, Steve, 40
`jr` instruction, 129, 130, 133, A-36, A-65
J-type instruction format, 148, 149
  fields, 154
  for `j`/`jal` instructions, 149
  See also instruction formats
jump address tables, 129
  compiling switch statement with, 129–130
  support of, 129
jump-and-link instruction. *See* jal instruction
jump register instruction. *See* jr instruction
jump(s)
  addresses, 387
  addressing, 148–150
  finite state machine execution, 394, 395
  implementing, 370–371
  instructions, A-65
  multicycle design and, 380
  unconditional, 129, 150, 188

K

Kahan, William, 317, 319
Karnaugh maps, B-17
kernels, 86–87

L

labels, A-3, A-7
  branch, 126
  compiler creation of, 124
  declaring, A-51
  external, A-11
  local, A-11
  names of, A-12
`la` pseudoinstruction, A-65
large-scale parallel processor(s), 730–733
  caches, 730

directory-based protocols, 731
  realities, 741–742
  shared virtual memory, 730
  single address space options, 732
  See also multiprocessor(s)
latches, B-22–B-23
  closed, B-23
  D, B-22, B-23
  flip-flops vs., B-22
  open, B-22
  S-R, B-21, B-22
  transparent, B-23
  See also flip-flops
latency, 522, 562
  constraints, 684
  response, 691
law of diminishing returns, 75
`lb` instruction, 142, 144, 214, A-65
`lbu` instruction, 214, A-66
LCDs (liquid crystal displays), 12
`ld` pseudoinstruction, A-67
`l.d` pseudoinstruction, A-73
leaf procedures, 136
least recently used (LRU) scheme, 576, 587
  approximation, 606
  implementing, 587
least significant bit, 237
  of multiplier, 252
  of significands, 298
less than test, 128
level-sensitive clocking, B-41
`lh` instruction, A-66
`lhu` instruction, A-66
libraries
  program, A-4
  subroutine, 8
link editors. *See* linker(s)
linker(s), 159–162, A-4, A-17–A-19
  absolute references and, 159
  address field updating, 162
  executable file, 159, 163, A-19
  function, 159, A-18
  steps, 159
  task illustration, A-18
Linpack, 86, 314
`li` pseudoinstruction, A-59
Lisp, 8
little-endian byte order, A-48
Livermore Loops, 86

load byte unsigned. *See* lbu instruction
loading, A-19–A-20
load instructions, 111, A-65–A-67
    bug, 458
    data addresses for, 124
    datapath for, 348
    delayed, 527, A-39
    implementation units, 348
    list of, A-65–A-67
    microinstructions for, 405
    operation of, 368
    pipelining walkthrough, 453–455
    signed, 214
    steps, 363
load-store machine(s), 191
    examples, 192
    instruction set, 202
load upper intermediate instruction. *See* lui instruction
load word. *See* lw instruction
local area networks (LANs), 21, 651
    message passing over, 713
    See also network(s)
locality
    principle, 540
    spatial, 540–541, 555–560
    temporal, 540, 541
    types of, 540–541
local labels, A-11
lock variables, 724, 725
logic, 339–341
    combinational, 341, 342, 398, B-3
    designing, 340
    elements, 340
    sequential components, 341
    state elements, 340
logical instructions, 329, A-55–A-59
logical operations, 225–230
logic blocks, B-7, B-8
logic minimization, C-26
long-haul networks, 652
long instruction word (LIW), 528
LOOP instruction, 420
loops, 125–128
    branch prediction and, 501
    in C language, 127
    compiling with variable array index, 126

for loops, 127–128, 165, 166, 167–168, 169, 294
    scheduling, 514
    while, 127
loop unrolling, 513
    code, 514
    for superscalar pipelines, 513–514
low-cost design, 82
l.s pseudoinstruction, A-73
lui instruction, 146, 147, A-59
    effect of, 146
    function of, 146
lwc1 instruction, 288, 294
lwc2 instruction, A-66
lw instruction, 111, 119, 137, 438, A-66
    ALU for, 354
    compiling example with, 113–114
    identification, 120
    through pipeline, 471–476
lwl instruction, A-66
lwr instruction, A-66

M

machine code, 117, 154
machine language, 117
    branch offset in, 149
    decoding, 151–154
    MIPS, 121, 131, A-5
    MIPS floating-point, 291
    symbolic representation of, 147
    translation into, 119–120
macro(s), A-15–A-16
    calls, A-15
    example, A-15–A-16
    formal parameters, A-16
    use, A-17
magnetic disk(s), 646–651
    access times, 20, 648
    caches, 650
    capacity, 691
    characteristics, 650
    controller time, 648
    cost per megabyte, 20, 650, 691
    cylinders, 646
    densities, 649
    diameter variations, 649–650

disk controller, 648
fallacy and pitfall, 688
floppy, 19, 646
hard, 19, 646
    main memory vs., 20
    in memory hierarchy, 541
    offline, 692
    online, 692
    platters, 646, 647
    RAID, 692
    read time, 648–649
    rotational latency, 647–648
    sectors, 646, 647
    seek times, 646, 647, 649
    tracks, 646, 647
    transfer time, 648, 691
    See also I/O device(s)
main memory, 19, 580
    magnetic disks vs., 20
    miss penalty, 576
    page table, 588
    speed of, 74
    See also memory
Mark-I, 33, 35
Mark-II, 35
Mark-III, 35
Mark-IV, 35
mask, 226
massive parallelism, 742–743
    ASCI, 743
    SIMD, 749
Mauchly, John, 32, 34, 35, 36, 423
maximally encoded, C-31
Mealy machine, 399
memory, 13, 31
    access, 388, 517, 544
    average, access time (AMAT), 629
    bandwidth, 561
    cache, 15, 18, 27
    cache-only, 731
    centralized, 728
    chips, 562
    clocked elements, B-21
    contents of, 111
    core, 621–622, 623
    data segment, A-21–A-22
    distributed, 728
    DRAM, 16–18, 541, 560, 562–563, 618

memory *(continued)*
  elements, B-21
  fallacies and pitfalls, 615–617
  fastest, 541
  I/O device data transfer and,
    679–682
  layout, A-20
  magnetic disk, 541
  main, 19, 541, 580
  motherboard, 13
  multiple private, 728
  nonvolatile, 19
  one-word-wide, 562
  operands, 112, 441
  output, 392
  physical, 580
  primary, 19
  private, 713
  read completion, 388
  ROM, 398, 401, 424, B-13–B-15
  secondary, 19
  shared, 727–728
  SRAM, 541
  stack segment, A-21
  technology, 5
  text segment, A-21
  unclocked elements, B-21
  units, 373, 378
  usage, A-20–A-21
  virtual, 579–603
  width increase, 561
memory addresses, 111, 113, 387
  calculation, 392, 393
  illustrated, 111, 113
  MIPS, 113
memory consistency model, 722
memory data register (MDR), 388
memory hierarchies, 5, 541
  blocks, 542
  caches, 545–564
  common framework for, 603–611
  data, 542
  design challenges, 611, 618–619
  development of, 624–626
  elements of, 541
  hit rate, 542
  hits, 542
  hit time, 543
  importance of, 621

  levels in, 542
  lower level, 542, 543
  magnetic disks in, 541
  managing, 602
  memory technologies, 544
  misses, 542
  miss penalty, 543
  miss rate, 542
  overall operation of, 595
  Pentium Pro, 611–614
  performance and, 543
  PowerPC, 611–614
  protection mechanisms, 626
  quantitative design parameters,
    603
  reliance on, 543
  spatial locality and, 541, 544
  structure diagram, 544
  structure illustration, 542
  technologies for, 541
  temporal locality and, 541
  three Cs model, 609–611
  upper level, 542, 543
  virtual memory, 579–603
  write options, 607
memory-mapped I/O, 675
memory mapping, 580
memory-memory machine, 192
  add instruction, 202
  instruction set, 192, 201
memory-reference instructions, 339
  finite state machine for controlling,
    392, 393
  microprogram for, 405
memory-stall clock cycles, 564, 565
  number of, 578
  from reads/writes, 564
memory systems
  cache support, 560–563
  design options, 561
MEM stage, 475
  branches at, 496
  control fields, changing, 490
  control lines, 466–468
  hazard, 481
  hazard control, 483
  illustrated, 456, 459
  load instruction, 455
  operand names and, 486

  pipeline register during, 480
  store instruction, 457
  See also pipeline stages
MEM/WB register, 455, 458, 485, 488
MESI protocol, 724
message passing
  over LANs, 713
  parallel program example, 729
  private memory machines and, 713
metastability, B-43, B-44
metrics, 60–66
  for different applications, 54
  formula, 60
  hardware-independent, 76
  MFLOPS as, 99–100
  MIPS as, 76–79
  See also performance
`mfc` instruction, 223
`mfc1.d` pseudoinstruction, A-69
`mfcz` instruction, A-69
`mfhi` instruction, 264, A-68
`mflo` instruction, 264, A-69
MFLOPS, 84, 86
  dependability, 99
  formula, 99
  normalized, 100
  as performance metric, 99–100
  rating, 99–100
microarchitectures, 425
microassembler, 402
microcode, C-27
  advantages/disadvantages, 419
  assembler, C-28, C-29
  controller, 409
  control unit as, C-27
  dispatch ROMs, C-30
  fetch time, 419
  field translation, C-29
  horizontal, C-31
  IBM use of, 424
  storage, 409
  vertical, C-31
microinstructions, 399–400, C-27
  addresses, 401
  ALU control field, 401
  ALU operation, 406
  for datapath control, 409
  executing, 400
  fields, 400, 401
  field values, 403

format definition, 400–402
label field, 403, 404
load for, 405
Memory field, 401, 403
PCWrite control field, 401, 403
Register control field, 401, 403
sequences, 404
Sequencing field, 401, 402, 403, 404
SRC1 field, 401, 403
SRC2 field, 401, 403
store for, 406
symbolic labels, 402
target, 402
See also microcode; micro-
    program(s)
microprocessor(s), 41, 712
cost-effectiveness, 712
Intel 4004, 38, 39
popular, 41
speedup challenge, 715–717
success, 42
VLSI, 42
See also processors
Microprocessor without Interlocked
    Pipelined Stages (Stanford
    MIPS), 527
microprogrammed control, 424, C-27
microprogramming, 389, 399–410
benefits of, 420
popularity, 425
microprogram(s)
branch sequence, 407
for control unit, 408
counter, 409, C-27
creating, 402–408
firmware, 424–425
format, 400
implementing, 408–410
jump sequence, 407
main control function, 409
for memory-reference
    instructions, 405
for R-type instructions, 406
sequencers, 424
symbolic representation, 400
as text representation of finite state
    machine, 408
translating into hardware, 408,
    C-28–C-31
See also control; microinstructions

MIMD, 748, 753–754
minicomputers, 38
minimally encoded, C-31
minterms, B-12, C-19
MIPS (architecture), 107
addressing, 145–155
addressing modes summary, 151,
    152
compilers, 115, A-29
floating-point
    instruction encoding, 292
    machine language, 291
    numbers, 276
    operands, 291
implementation, 340
instruction classes, 189
instruction encoding, 119, 153
instruction formats, 440
instruction frequency, 311
instruction set, 107, 189, 309
machine language, 121, 131, 141,
    151–154, A-5
memory addresses, 113
memory allocation, 160
multiply in, 264
opcode map, A-54
operands, 116, 121, 131, 141, 155,
    219, 224, 228, 274
overflow detection, 223
processor, 109
register convention, 140
registers, 115
    access time, 115
    number of, 109–110
    size of, 109
relative, 85
words, 211
MIPS assembly language, 107, 116,
    121, 131, 141, 155, 219, 224,
    228, 274
C loop code, 126
comments, 107
compiling complex C assignment
    into, 109
constants in, 134
C translation to, 108
floating-point, 291
machine language translation, 119
sort procedure version, 170
structures, 108, 116

summary, 108
symbolic representation of, 110
MIPS I, 309, 310
MIPS instructions, 108, 111, 150
length of, 440
translation into machine
    instruction, 117
MIPS M/2000, 520, 521
MIPS (million instructions per
    second)
1-MIPS machine, 85
computation, 79
equation, 77
as machine comparison
    measurement, 78
native, 77
peak, 84
as performance measure, 78–79
MIPS R2000, A-49–A-75
CPU, A-50
FPU, A-50
page faults/TLB misses and,
    601–602
TLB, 592
MIPS R4000, 618
MISD, 748, 752
miss(es), 542
cache, 550–552, 559–560, 567
capacity, 609, 610
cold-start, 609
collision, 609
compulsory, 609, 610
conflict, 609
cycles, 567
data, 552
decomposition, 611
instruction, 551
per instruction, 616
read, 557
TLB, 590, 591, 592, 595, 598–602
write, 558
See also page fault(s)
miss penalty, 543
block size and, 560
cache, 559–560
calculations, 560
increase in, 559
latency component of, 559
to main memory, 576
read, 565

miss penalty *(continued)*
  reducing, 560, 612
  reducing with multilevel caches,
      576–578
  write, 565
  See also miss(es)
miss rates, 542
  block size and, 558–559
  cache, 554–555
  for cache sizes, 604
  combined, 554–555
  DECStation 3100, 554–555
  effective, 555
  execution time and, 555
  gcc program, 558, 573
  improvement in, 604
  increased, disadvantages of, 555
  miss sources and, 609–610
  as only metric, 615–617
  reducing, 579, 602
  spice program, 558, 573
  split cache, 555
  See also miss(es)
module(s), A-4, A-17
  changes to, A-17
  references, A-4
  See also program(s)
Moore machine, 398, 399, B-36
most significant bit, 237
motherboard, 13
  chips, 13
  closeup, 17
  components, 13
  heat sinks, 17
  illustrated, 14
  memory, 13
  processor, 14
Motorola
  68000, 183, 195
  68881, 320
  PowerPC, 175–177
mouse, 11, 645–646
  buttons, 645
  mechanical version, 11
  position interpretation, 646
  X/Y counters, 645
  See also I/O device(s)
mov.d instruction, A-73
move pseudoinstruction, A-68
mov.s instruction, A-73

MSI (medium-scale integration), 424
mtcz instruction, A-69
mthi instruction, A-69
mtlo instruction, A-69
mul.d instruction, 288, A-73
mulo pseudoinstruction, A-56
mulou pseudoinstruction, A-57
mul pseudoinstruction, A-56
mul.s instruction, 288, A-73
multicomputers, 753
multicycle control, finite state
      machine method, 390
multicycle implementation, 377–399
  advantages, 377
  branch support, 380
  clock cycle, 378
  control definition, 389–399
  with control lines, 381
  control unit, 382, 383
  datapath, 382, 383, 385, 417, 421
  functional units, 377
  high-level view of, 378
  instruction execution, 382–389
  jump support, 380
  MIPS datapath, 380
  performance consequences, 524
  pipelined control vs., 504
  single-cycle vs., 377, 504
  temporary registers, 378–379
multilevel cache(s), 564, 576–578
  cache interaction, 577
  performance of, 576–577
  primary cache, 577
  secondary cache, 577
  See also cache(s)
mult instruction, 264, A-56
multiple-clock-cycle pipeline
      diagrams, 461
  illustrated, 462
  instruction execution, 477
  traditional, 462
  of two instructions, 462
  uses of, 461
  See also pipeline diagrams
multiple instruction streams,
      multiple data streams
      (MIMD), 748, 753–754
multiple instruction streams, single
      data stream (MISD), 748, 752
multiplexor(s), 351, B-9, B-18, B-19

2:1, 488
  control, 361, 390
  control lines, C-29
  control signals, 359
  creating, B-9
  datapath combining with, 352
  expanded, 237, 238
  forwarding, 483, 492
  illustrated, 231, B-9
  parts, B-9
  two-input, B-9
multiplicand, 250
  Booth's algorithm and, 260
  fixed relative to product, 254
  shifting left, 252, 263
multiplication, 250–264
  of binary numbers, 251
  of decimal numbers, 250
  floating-point, 283–288
  in MIPS, 264
  multiplicand, 250, 252, 254, 260,
      263
  multiplier, 250, 252, 260, 263, 264
  signed, 257, 264
  of significands, 286, 287
  terms, 250
  See also arithmetic
multiplication algorithms
  first version, 251–254
  second version, 254–256
  third version, 256–257, 258
multiplication hardware
  first version, 251
  second version, 254
  third version, 257
multiplier, 250
  bit values of, 263
  Booth's algorithm and, 260
  least significant bit of, 252
  two's complement representation
      of, 264
Multiplier register, 251, 254
multiprocessor(s), 710–759
  bus-connected, 753
  cache-based, 721
  design drivers, 712
  directory-based, 731
  fallacies and pitfalls, 743–746
  future directions, 740–743

hypercube-connected, 753
large-scale, 715
memory capacity, 740
network, 727–733
NUMA, 713, 732
number of processors in, 714
on common bus, 717
programming, 714–717
single address space, 713
single bus, 717–726
size of, 741
SMP, 713
Stanford DASH, 754
synchronization, 713
UMA, 713, 732
See also processors
multistage network topologies, 738,
   739
`multiu` instruction, 264, A-56

N

NAND gates, B-8
negation shortcut, 216
`neg.d` instruction, A-73
`neg` pseudoinstruction, A-57
`neg.s` instruction, A-73
`negu` pseudoinstruction, A-57
nested procedures, 136–138
Network Computer (NC), 193
network-connected multiproces-
   sor(s), 727–733
   characteristics, 728
   cost/performance, 733
   medium scale, 727
   organization, 727
   See also multiprocessor(s)
network(s), 21, 651–654
   advantages, 21
   ARPANET, 652
   bandwidth, 652
   characteristics, 651
   crossbar, 738, 739
   Ethernet, 21, 651
   fully connected, 736, 737, 738
   interconnection, 736-739
   local area (LANs), 21, 651, 713
   long-haul, 652
   multistage, 738

Omega, 738, 739
packet-switched, 652
performance, 654, 736
protocol stacks, 652
switches, 736–737
wide area (WANs), 21
network topologies, 736–739
   Boolean *n*-cube, 738
   crossbar, 738, 739
   illustrated, 738
   implementing, 738–739
   importance of, 741
   link distance, 738
   multistage, 738
   Omega, 738, 739
   ring, 737
Newton's iteration, 296
next-state counters, C-24
next-state function, 390, B-35, B-36,
   C-32
next-state outputs (NS), C-12
   bits, truth tables for, C-15
   logic equations for, C-12
   truth table, C-18
nibble-mode RAMs, B-33
no-allocate-on-write, 608
no-fetch-on-write, 608
nonblocking caches, 517
nonuniform memory access
   (NUMA) multiprocessors,
   713, 732
nonvolatile memory, 19, 646
`nop` instruction, 478, 485, 490, A-75
   in EX stage, 490
   use example, 478
NOR gates, B-8
   cross-coupled, B-21, B-22
   See also gates
`nor` instruction, 329, A-57
normalized numbers, 275
NOT operator, B-6
`not` pseudoinstruction, A-57
numbers
   biased, 285
   binary, 2, 6, 116, 188, 212, 305
   decimal, 116, 120, 211
   denormalized, 300, 334
   floating-point, 276–280
   hexadecimal, 158, 217
   normalized, 275

in real world, 299
representation of, 212
signed, 210–220
two's complement, 120, 213
unsigned, 210–220

O

object file(s), 158, 160, A-4,
   A-10–A-11
   components, 158, A-10
   execution, A-11
   format, A-13–A-14
   illustrated, A-13
   sections, A-13
   See also assemblers
observed performance, 745–746
offset, 112, 115
   branch, 149
   segment, 583
Omega network, 738, 739
one's complement representation,
   219–220, 235
   negative of, 219
   two's complement vs., 220
opcode, 118
   80x86, 182
   map for MIPS, A-54
operands, 109–116
   constant, 145–147
   division, 265
   first register source, 118
   immediate, 145–147
   intermediate, moving, 253
   memory, 112, 441
   MIPS, 116, 121, 131, 155, 219, 224,
   228, 274
   MIPS floating-point, 291
   register destination, 118
   second register source, 118
   subtraction and, 221
operating systems, 8
   context switch, 598
   I/O device communication with,
   673–674
   page fault steps, 599–600
   performance and, 59
   in virtual memory protection
   implementation, 597

operations
  add, 220–225
  AND, 226–227, B-5
  dispatch, 402, 404
  floating-point, 99, 100, 293
  logical, 225–230
  multiplication, 250–264
  nor, 329
  NOT, B-6
  OR, 227, B-5
  subtraction, 220–225
  xor, 329
optical compact disks (CDs), 19
OR gates, 231, 233, B-7, C-7, C-8
  array, B-12
  exclusive, 249
  illustrated, 231
  output, 382
  two levels of, 249
  See also gates
ori instruction, 227, 230, A-57
or immediate. See ori instruction
or instruction, 351, 438, A-57
  through pipeline, 471–476
  stalls and, 490
OR operation, 227, 236, B-5
  1-bit ALU for, 231
  exclusive, 498
OR plane, B-12, B-13
out-of-order completion, 516
output, 31
  ALU, 387, 413
  ALU control, 354
  AND gate, 382
  buffer, 706
  in computer organization, 16, 53
  control signal, C-13
  control unit, 367
  devices, 10
  don't cares, B-16
  function, B-35, B-36, B-37
  in I/O, 673–683
  memory, 392
  OR gate, 382
  register file, 345
  state element, 341, B-20
overflow, 212, 214, 308
  addition, 221, 222
  checking, 281, 282

Cray computer, 316
  detection, 222, 223, 249, 413
  exceptions, 410, 411, 413, 505–509
  exponent, 276
  EX stage detection, 505
  handling, 222
  predefined action in response to,
    411
  subtraction, 221, 222
  testing and, 223
  thresholds, 315
  trapping on, 223
  See also exception(s)
overlays, 580

P

packet-switched networks, 652
page fault(s), 580, 585–589, A-34
  exceptions, 599, 600
  handling, 598–602
  instruction, 599
  occurrence of, 585, 586
  operating system steps, 599–600
  penalty, 583
  rate, 582
  signaling, 601
  virtual address causing, 599
  See also miss(es); virtual memory
page mode, 562
page offset, 581
page(s), 580
  addressable, 581
  LRU, 587
  number of, 581
  physical, 588
  size, 582
  tracking, 589
  See also virtual memory
page table(s), 583, 585, 605
  contents, 585
  entries, 583–584
  indexing, 583, 584, 585
  inverted, 588
  main memory, 588
  placing in address space of
    operating system, 597
  references, 590

register, 584
  segment, 588
  size computation, 587
  size, reducing, 588
  storage, 589
  storage, reducing, 587–589
  TLB and, 590, 591
  two, 588
  in virtual memory organization,
    586
  See also virtual memory
PALs, B-13
parallel processing programs, 712,
    715
  frequency of synchronization in,
    742
  message passing example, 729
  single-bus multiprocessor
    example, 718–719
  speedup challenge, 715–717
  writing, 715
parallel processors
  Amdahl's law and, 744–745
  large-scale, 730–733, 741–742
  performance measurement, 744
partial products, 332
PCI bus
  peak bandwidth, 688
  realistic transfer speeds, 688
  standard, 672, 673, 687
  See also bus(es)
PC-relative addressing, 148–149,
    151, 152
PDP-11, 698, 753
peak MIPS, 84
peak performance, 745–746
  observed performance vs., 746
  percentage of, 746
  unattainable, 745
  See also performance
Pentium chip manufacturing, 24–28
  dies, 26, 27, 28
  pins, 28
  wafer, 24, 25
Pentium processor(s), 178
  bugs, 306–308
  floating-point divide algorithm,
    305–306
  hardwired control, 425

implementation, 416–419
instructions executed per clock
cycle, 418
pipelining, 417
See also 80x86 architecture
Pentium Pro processor(s), 178
address translation, 613
clock rates, 419
comparison, 74
control lines, 418
datapaths, 418
hardwired control, 425
implementation, 418–419
instructions executed per clock
cycle, 418
memory hierarchy, 611–614
miss penalties, reducing, 612
performance increase, 73
pipeline organization, 517–519
pipelining, 417, 517–519
primary cache, 613
secondary cache support, 611–612
SPECfp95 ratings, 74
SPECint95 ratings, 73
TLB hardware, 613
See also 80x86 architecture
performance, 52–102
airplane, 55
assembly language and, 186–187
assessing, 54
bus, 663–667
cache, 564–569
code sequence example, 64–65
comparing, 69–71
components, 63
CPU, 59
defining, 55–58
determination methods, 55–58
equation, 62–63
evaluation programs, 66–69
execution time and, 58
fallacies and pitfalls, 75–82
growth rate, 29
improvement rate, 30
improving, 29, 60–61
I/O request, 690
I/O system, 639–640, 691
kernels and, 86–87
key factors affecting, 63
maximizing, 56

measurement reproducibility, 69
memory hierarchies and, 543
metrics, 54, 60–66
network, 654, 736
observed, 745–746
operating systems and, 59
original measurement of, 84
parallel processor, measuring, 744
peak, 745–746
pipelined, 438
prediction accuracy, 76
ratios, 97
relative, 57, 70
single-cycle, 373–375
subtlety of, 55
summarizing, 69–71, 82, 87
system, 59
workstation increase, 30
See also benchmarks
peripheral processors, 696
personal computers, 40–41
Alto, 696–697
Apple, 40
IBM, 40
See also computer(s)
physical addresses, 580, 582
physical memory, 580, 586
physical page number, 581
pipelined branches, 498
pipelined control, 466–476
goals of, 503
overview, 492
performance, 504
single-cycle/multicycle control vs.,
504
specifying, 466
pipelined datapaths, 449–466
control line meanings and, 469
with control signals, 467
with control signals connected to
pipeline registers, 470
final, 523
with five stages, 460
illustrated, 452, 523
modification to resolve hazards via
forwarding, 484
See also pipeline stages
pipelined dependencies, 477
classifying, 479
compiler resolution of, 491

detection, 479
illustrated, 477
latency and, 522
between pipeline registers, 480,
481
pipelined execution
data flow in, 451
illustrated, 451
labeled, 471–476
pipeline diagrams, 446, 461–465
multiple-clock-cycle, 461, 462
single-clock-cycle, 461, 463–465
pipelined performance, 514
improvement of, 440
single cycle performance vs., 438,
439
throughput increase and, 440, 449,
514, 522
See also performance
pipeline hazards, 441–448
control, 441–445, 496–509
data, 445–448
structural, 441, 458
pipeline register(s), 452
before forwarding, 482
dependencies, 480
pipeline(s)
bubble insertion in, 490
depth, 521
exceptions and, 507
five-stage, 449–450
floating-point, 521
graphical representation, 446,
461–465
impact on branch instruction, 497
instruction sequence, 489
longer, 522
Pentium Pro, 517–519
PowerPC 604, 517–519
stall insertion into, 491
See also pipelining
pipeline stages, 436
clock cycle, 438
control lines and, 466–469
EX, 453, 455, 457
ID, 453, 454, 457
IF, 453, 454, 456
list of, 450
load instruction, 453–455
MEM, 455, 456, 457, 459

pipeline stages (continued)
  store instruction, 455–458
  WB, 453, 455, 456, 458, 459
pipeline stalls, 442
  avoiding with reordered code,
    447–448
  branch, 496
  data hazards and, 445, 489–496
  examples of, 490
  forwarding and, 446
  illustrated, 442
  insertion, 491
  need for, 447
  on branch performance, 442
  unexpected, 491
  See also pipeline hazards
pipelining, 416–417, 436–536
  advances in, 525–528
  architectures without, 417
  CDC 6600, 526
  dynamic, 449, 510–511, 515–517
  first processor with, 417
  instruction execution time and, 449
  instruction set complications, 520
  instruction sets, 440–441
  laundry analogy, 436, 437
  load instruction walkthrough,
    453–455
  MIPS instruction set, 441
  overview, 436–449
  paradox, 436
  parallelism exploitation, 448
  Pentium/Pentium Pro, 417
  speedup formula, 438
  static, 516
  store instruction walkthrough,
    455–458
  subtlety of, 520
  superpipelining, 510
  superscalar, 418, 449, 510, 511–514
  See also pipeline(s)
pitfalls, 29
  expecting performance improve-
    ment of one aspect to increase
    performance by proportional
    amount, 75–76
  extending address space by adding
    segments on top of unseg-

mented address space,
  617–618
failure to consider instruction set
  design can adversely impact
  pipelining, 520–521
forgetting byte addressing or cache
  block size in cache simulation,
  615
forgetting sequential word
  addresses in machines with
  byte addressing do not differ
  by one, 187
ignoring memory system behavior
  in writing programs, 617
ignoring progress of hardware
  when planning a new
  machine, 29
measuring performance of
  parallel processors by linear
  speedup vs. execution time,
  744
MIPS instruction addiu sign-
  extends its 16-bit immediate
  field, 305
moving functions from CPU to
  I/O processor, expecting to
  improve performance,
  689–690
using arithmetic mean of normalized execution times to predict
  performance, 80–81
using MIPS as performance metric,
  76–79
using miss rate as only metric for
  evaluating memory hierarchy,
  615–617
using peak transfer rate to make
  performance projections or
  performance comparisons, 688
using pointers to automatic variables outside defining procedure, 187
  See also fallacies
pixels, 12
PLA (programmable logic array),
  398, 401, B-11–B-13, C-7, C-8
  characteristics, B-12
  contents, B-13
  example, B-13

finite state machine control
  implementation, C-19–C-21
  form illustration, B-12
  illustrated, B-14
  inputs, B-11–B-12
  microcode storage, 409
  microinstruction generation, 419
  minterms, C-19
  product terms, C-19
  ROM vs., B-15
  splitting, C-19–C-21
  total size of, B-12, C-19
platters, 646
  illustrated, 647
  See also magnetic disk(s)
pointers
  arrays vs., 171–174
  to automatic variables, 187
  frame, 138, 139
  global, 140
  stack, 133, 135, 138
  for zeroing arrays, 173–174
polling, 646, 676–678
  disadvantage of, 676
  overhead, 676–677
  rate, 679
  use methods, 676
postbytes, 182–183
PowerPC, 175–177
  address translation, 613
  conditional branches on, 181
  exceptions/interrupts and, 410
  floating point in, 301
  indexed addressing, 175
  for loops, 177
  memory hierarchy, 611–614
  miss penalties, reducing, 612
  multiply-add instruction, 301
  pipeline organization, 518–519
  pipelines, 517-519
  primary cache, 613
  secondary cache support, 611–612
  SRAMs, 612
  TLB hardware, 613
  unique instructions, 176–177
  update addressing, 175–176
precise exceptions/interrupts, 509
prediction. See branch prediction
prefetching, 620

primary cache, 577, 613
primary memory, 19
private memories, 713
procedure call(s), A-22–A-32
  callee, A-23, A-24, A-25
  caller, A-23, A-24, A-25
  conventions, A-22–A-23
  examples, A-26–A-32
  frame, A-24
  last in, first-out (LIFO) order, A-24
  recursive, A-29–A-32
  stack allocation, 139
  stacks and, 134
  what is preserved across, 138
procedure(s), 132–142
  compiling, that don't call other
    procedure(s), 134–135
  extra parameters and, 139
  frame, 138
  inlining, 169
  jumping to, 133
  leaf, 136
  nested, 136–138
  print, 705, 706
  program execution steps, 132
  recursive, 136–137, 204, A-26,
    A-28–A-29
  register allocation, 132
  registers needed for, 133–135
  See also procedure call(s)
process, 585
  active, 585
  address space, 585
  identifier, 598
  inactive, 585
  switch, 598
processor-memory bus(es), 656–658
  design-specific, 656, 657
  See also bus(es)
processors, 14
  in computer organization, 16, 53
  DMA, 681
  inside, 15
  Intel 80x86, 177–185, 194
  I/O, 682, 689
  Java, 425
  key technologies for, 31
  MIPS, 109
  parallelism, 31

Pentium, 178, 416–419
Pentium Pro, 178, 418–419
peripheral, 696
shared-memory, 713
  with single address space, 713
See also control; datapath(s);
  microprocessor(s);
  multiprocessor(s)
product, 250
  normalized, 287
  partial, 332
  rounding, 288
  shifting right, 254
  for signed numbers, 257
  sign of, 286
  terms, C-19
  unnormalized, 286
  See also multiplication
product of sums representation, B-10
Product register, 253, 254, 256, 260,
  261
program counter (PC), 133
  branch target, 404
  incrementing, 362, 380, 385, 412
  reading into, 385
  sequential, 404
  single-cycle control and, 380
  write signals, 380
  write control, 393–394
  writing from, 385
program library, A-4
programmable ROMs (PROMs), B-14
programmers, A-8–A-9
  compilers vs., A-9
  improved productivity of, 8
program(s)
  assembly language, 157, A-10
  expansion factor, A-9
  memory sharing, 580
  modules, A-4, A-17
  profiling measures, A-8
  starting, 156–163
  translation hierarchy, 156
propagate, 243
  levels, 247–248
  "super," 247
protocols
  bus, 673
  cache coherency, 720–724

  handshaking, 660, 661, 664
  snooping, 720–721
  split transaction, 667
  TCP/IP, 652, 653
  write-invalidate, 721, 723, 724
  write-update, 721, 726
protocol stacks, 652
pseudodirect addressing, 151, 152
pseudoinstructions, 157, 196, A-17,
  A-39
  identifying, A-53
  SPIM translation of, A-47
  *See also specific pseudoinstruction
    name;* instructions
pseudo MIPS, 309, 310

Q

quotient, 265
  bit, 269
  See also division
Quotient register, 266

R

R3000-based machine, 84
RAID (redundant arrays of
  inexpensive disks), 692
RAM, 424
  EDO, 562, B-33
  nibble-mode, B-33
  page-mode, B-33
  static-column-mode, B-33
  See also DRAM (dynamic random
    access memory); SRAM
    (static random access
    memory)
RAMAC disk, 694, 696
RAS (Row Access Strobe), B-32
raster refresh buffer, 13
read misses, 557
read-stall clock cycles, 564
read/write head, 19
reals, 275
  examples of, 275
  scientific notation for, 276
receiver, A-36
Receiver Control register, A-36, A-37

Receiver Data register, A-36, A-37
recursive procedure(s), 136–137, 204,
 A-26
 example, A-29–A-32
 iteration and, 204
 stack in, A-28–A-29
 values, A-26
 See also procedure call(s);
  procedure(s)
reduced instruction set computer.
 See RISC architecture
reel-to-reel technologies, 694
reference bit, 587
references, A-4
 external, A-19
 forward, A-11
 unresolved, A-4
refresh rate, 12
register addressing, 151, 152
register file, 345, 373, 392, B-25–B-26
 accesses, 385, 386
 contents, B-25
 copy of, 516
 as datapath element, 346
 hardware file, 478
 illustrated, B-25
 outputs, 345
 reading, 364
 read port implementation, B-26
 write port implementation, B-26,
  B-27
 writing into, 388
register-memory machines, 191, 192
register number, 345, 388
 specifying, 345
 WB stage and, 458
register-register machines, 191
registers, 109
 80x86, 179–180
 access time, 115
 base, 112, 115
 bounds, 587–588
 callee-saved, A-25, A-30
 caller-saved, A-25
 Cause, 412, 413, 415, 509, 678,
  A-33–A-34
 compiling C assignment using, 110
 coprocessor 0, A-32
 counter, 177
 in data transfer instruction, 115

dedicated, 191
 destination, 119
 double precision, 288
 EPC, 223, 412
 Exception code, A-33
 fetching, 386
 floating-point, 185, 290, 296
 general-purpose, 191–192
 Hi, 264
 index, 115
 Instruction (IR), 385
 integer, 185
 I/O device, 675
 jump, 129, 130
 Lo, 264
 mapping names, 116
 MIPS convention, 140
 number of, 109–110
 page table, 584
 pipeline, 452, 480
 preserving in sort procedure,
  168–169
 procedure calling allocation, 132
 for procedures, 133–135
 program counter, 133
 rename, 517
 reserved, 225
 rules for using, A-22–A-32
 single precision, 288
 size of, 109
 special-purpose, 191
 spilling, 115, 133, 135
 temporary, 110, 115, 135, 378
 usage conventions, A-23, A-25
 variable association with, 112
relative MIPS, 85
relative performance, 57, 70
relative speedup, 744
relocation, 581, A-14
Remainder register, 266, 269, 271
remainders, 266
 calculating, 272
 shifting to left, 268
 sign of, 272
 See also division
removable media, 695
rem pseudoinstruction, A-57
remu pseudoinstruction, A-58
rename buffers, 517
reorder buffer, 517

requested word first, 560
reservation stations, 515
response time, 56, 58
 example, 56
 minimizing, 56
 See also performance; throughput
restoring division, 273, 333
return address, 132–133
return from exception (RFE)
  instruction, 597, A-36, A-74
ring network topology, 737
rings, 626
ripple carry adder, 234
 carry lookahead vs., 248–249
 illustrated, 331
 See also adders
RISC architecture, 194, 425, 625, 747
 See also Web Extension I
rol pseudoinstruction, A-58
ROMs (read-only memories), 398,
  401, 424, B-13–B-15
 control entries, C-17
 dispatch, C-24, C-25, C-26
 finite state machine control
  implementation, C-13–C-19
 height, B-15
 microcode storage, 409
 PLA vs., B-15
 programmable (PROM), B-14
 shape, B-15
 speed, 422
 storing control function in, 408
 width, B-15
 See also memory
ror pseudoinstruction, A-59
rotational latency, 647–648
round bit, 297, 298, 334
rounding
 accuracy, 282
 always round down, 300
 always round up, 300
 extra bits, 298
 with guard digits, 297–298
 modes, 297, 300
 product, 288
 round to nearest even, 300
 truncate, 300
 worst case for, 298
row access, B-32
row major order, 296

R-type instruction format, 118, 119,
153, 154
ALU and, 354
ALU operation implementation,
346
distinguishing, 119
fields, 154
shamt field, 226
See also instruction formats
R-type instructions
completion step, 388
datapath, 346, 347
execution steps, 361–363
first phase of, 362
fourth phase in, 366
implemented with two-state finite
state machine, 394
microprogram sequence for, 406
second phase in, 364
third phase in, 365

S

sb instruction, 142, 144, A-67
Scaled Index addressing mode, 181
scientific notation, 275
binary numbers in, 275
decimal numbers in, 275
for reals, 276
SCSI bus
controllers, 697
invention, 698
standard, 672, 673, 686, 687
See also bus(es)
SDM (Systems Development
Multitasking) benchmarks, 88
sd pseudoinstruction, A-68
s.d pseudoinstruction, A-74
SDRAMS (synchronous DRAMs),
563
secondary caches, 577, 611–612
secondary memory, 19
sectors, 646
illustrated, 647
See also magnetic disk(s)
seek time, 646
average, 647
measured average, 649

reporting, 647
See also magnetic disk(s)
segmentation, 583
segments, 588
adding, 617
data, A-20–A-21
number, 583
offset, 583
page table, 588
stack, A-21
text, A-20
uses of, 583
segment tables, 588
semaphores, 724, 725
semiconductors, 23
seq pseudoinstruction, A-60
sequencers
microprogram, 424
next-state function implementation with, C-21–C-27
sequencing function, 408–409
sequential consistency, 722
sequential word addresses, 164, 187
set-associative blocks
location of, 569
replacement, 575
set associative cache(s), 569, 579
addresses, 573
block replacement, 606
choosing, 605
configuration illustration, 570
contents, 572
four-way, implementation, 574
least recently used block
replacement, 572
performance, 572
tag size and, 575
See also cache(s)
set on less than instruction. *See* slt
instruction
SFS (System-level File Server)
benchmarks, 88
sge pseudoinstruction, A-60
sgeu pseudoinstruction, A-60
sgt pseudoinstruction, A-61
sgtu pseudoinstruction, A-61
shared bus(es), 382
drawbacks, 382
uses, 382
See also bus(es)

shared memory, 727–728
distributed, 754
processors, 713
virtual, 730
See also memory
shift, 226
amount, 226
arithmetic right, 261
guard digit, 298
instructions, 226
left, 252, 262, 305
right, 254, 305
sh instructions, A-67
sign and magnitude representation,
212, 276
sign bit, 213
signed numbers, 210–220
addi/slti and, 230
division with, 272
multiplication with, 257
product for, 257
unsigned vs., 214, 215
See also numbers
sign extension, 214, 216–217
significands
addition, 281
exponents before, 278
least significant bits of, 298
multiplication, 286, 287
silicon, 23, 31
SIMMs (single inline memory
modules), 17, 623
photograph, 624
size of, 623
See also memory
single-bus multiprocessor(s),
717–726
arbitration, 724
cache coherency protocols, 720–724
characteristics, 718
illustrated, 718
limitations, 727
medium, 727
parallel program, 718–719
with snooping cache coherency,
720
traffic per processor, 717
See also multiprocessor(s)

single-clock-cycle pipeline
diagrams, 461, 463–465
uses of, 461
See also pipeline diagrams
single-cycle design, 371–377
clock cycle in, 374
CPI, 371
cycle time, 376
datapath, 385, 417, 421, 450
inefficiency, 377
instruction execution, 451
multicycle/pipelined control
comparison, 504
multicycle vs., 377
penalty, 375
single-cycle performance, 373–375
consequences, 524
with floating-point instructions,
375–376
pipelined performance vs., 438,
439
single instruction stream, multiple
data streams (SIMD), 748
characteristics, 750
instructions, 749
massive parallelism in, 749
motivation behind, 749
trade-off, 749
virtues, 749
single instruction stream, single data
stream (SISD), 748
single-precision floating-point
arithmetic, 277
binary representation, 279
exponent bias, 278
general representation, 279
maximum exponent, 282
registers, 288
single program multiple data
(SPMD), 752
sle pseudoinstruction, A-61
sleu pseudoinstruction, A-61
sll instruction, 226, A-58
sllv instruction, A-58
slti instruction, A-60
slt instruction, 128, 236, 438, A-60
sltiu instruction, 230, A-60
sltu instruction, A-60

small computer systems interface.
See SCSI bus
sne pseudoinstruction, A-61
snooping caches, 731
snooping protocols, 720–721
write-invalidate, 721
write-update, 721
software
applications, 8
as hierarchical layers, 9
performance, improving, 54
portable numerical, 314
systems, 8
source files, A-4
source language, A-6
spatial locality, 540–541, 544, 555–560
cache blocks and, 555
memory hierarchies and, 541, 544
taking advantage of, 555–560
See also locality
SPEC89 benchmarks, 68, 88
SPEC92 benchmarks, 88, 604, 610
SPEC95 benchmarks, 71–74
descriptions, 72
list of, 72
SPECfp95, 71, 72, 73, 74
SPECint95, 71, 72, 73
SPEC benchmarks, 67
processor suite, 67
ratio, 71
running of, 72
SDM, 88
SFS, 88
SPECbase, 88
SPECfp, 88
SPEChpc96 suite, 88
SPECint, 88
system description, 69
See also benchmarks
special-purpose register, 191
speculative execution, 516
speedup, 101
relative, 744
true, 744
spilling registers, 115, 133
data structure, 133
reducing, 135
SPIM simulator, A-3, A-38–A-49

assembler directive subset
support, A-51–A-53
byte order, A-47–A-48
caches and, A-47
Cause register fields implemented
by, A-33–A-34
command abbreviations, A-46
command-line options, A-44–A-45
commands, A-36, A-45–A-46
components, A-38
console, A-47
coprocessor 0 registers, A-32
coprocessor simulation, A-49
debugger, A-38
getting started with, A-39–A-43
memory latency and, A-47
pseudoinstruction translation,
A-47
running, A-45
speed, A-38
spim, A-40, A-45–A-46
syscall instruction, A-48–A-49
system services, A-48–A-49
terminal, A-36
usefulness, A-38
versions, A-40
xspim, A-40–A-43, A-46–A-47
spin waiting, 726
split transaction protocol, 667
sra instruction, A-58
SRAM (static random access
memory), 541, B-27–B-31
access time, 541
chip configuration, B-27
cost per megabyte, 541
DRAM vs., 541
height, B-27
large, B-28
organization of, B-31
PowerPC, 612
structure illustration, B-30
synchronous (SSRAM), B-29
width, B-27
See also memory
srav instruction, A-58
S-R latch, B-21, B-22
srl instruction, 226, A-58
srlv instruction, A-58
SRT division, 297

s.s pseudoinstruction, A-74
stack frames, A-24, A-27
  build methods, A-24
  contents of, A-24, A-25
  layout, A-25
  in recursive procedures,
    A-28–A-29
stack model, 193, 202
stack pointer, 133
  adding to, 133
  changing, 138
  values of, 135
stacks, 133
  allocation, 139
  "growing," 133
  pop, 133, 135, 137
  preservation, 138
  procedure calls and, 134
  procedure frame, 138
  push, 133
  values of, 135
  See also procedure(s)
stack segment, A-21
stale data problem, 683
stall on use, 552
Stanford DASH multiprocessor, 754
state assignment, B-38, C-26
state element(s), 340
  combinational logic and, 342
  edge-triggered methodology, 343
  inputs, 341
  on clock edges, B-20
  outputs, 341, B-20
  valid, B-20
State register, C-29
static-column-mode RAM, B-33
static data, A-20
static pipelining, 516
static variables, 140
Status register, 675, A-33
sticky bit, 298, 334
store buffer, 516, 609
stored-program concept, 121–122
  illustrated, 122
  invention of, 122
  principles, 187
store instructions, 113, A-67–A-68
  data addresses for, 124
  datapath for, 348

implementation units, 348
list of, A-67–A-68
microinstruction for, 406
pipelining walkthrough, 455–458
store word. *See* sw instruction
strength reduction, 264
Stretch (IBM 7030), 83, 535
string(s)
  C, how to use, 143–144
  copy procedure, 143–144
  double quotes (") and, A-51
  instructions, 182
  representation choices, 143
structural hazards, 441, 458
sub.d instruction, 288, A-74
sub instruction, 222, 351, 438,
    471–476, A-59
  forwarding and, 485, 486
  through pipeline, 471–476
subroutine libraries, 8
sub.s instruction, 288, A-74
subtraction, 220–225
  adder, 235
  binary, 220
  negative number from positive
    number, 222
  overflow, 221, 222
  same sign operands, 221
  See also arithmetic
subu instruction, 222, A-59
summarizing performance, 69–71, 82,
    87
sum of products representation, B-10
  equation, B-10
  example, B-11
Sun SPARC, 618, A-48
supercomputers, 39–40
  ASCI, 743
  cost of, 741
  I/O benchmarks, 642
  vector, 752
  See also computer(s)
superpipelining, 510
superscalar, 418, 449, 510, 511–514
  code scheduling, 513
  datapath, 512
  DEC Alpha 21264, 516
  development, 527
  effectiveness limit, 512

laundry analogy, 510
LIW design vs., 528
loop unrolling for, 513–514
machines, 510
MIPS, 511–514
pipeline operation, 511
throughput increase, 514
wider, 514
See also pipelining
swc1 instruction, 288, 294
swcz instruction, A-68
sw instruction, 113, 119, 134, 392, 438,
    A-67
  ALU for, 354
  compiling example with, 113–114
  identification, 120
switch statement, 129–130
  compiling with jump address
    table, 129–130
  jumping to exit, 130
swl instruction, A-68
swr instruction, A-68
symbol table, 158, A-12
symmetric multiprocessors (SMP),
    713
Synapse N+1, 753
synchronization, 713
  barrier, 719
  with coherency, 724–726
  failure, 661
  frequency of, 742
synchronizers, 661, B-42–B-44
  from D flip-flop, B-43
  failure, B-43
  metastability and, B-43, B-44
synchronous buses, 660–663
  asynchronous bus vs., 663
  bandwidth, 667
  clock, 660
  performance analysis, 662–663
  See also bus(es)
synchronous DRAMs (SDRAMs),
    B-29, B-33
synchronous SRAMs (SSRAMs), B-29
synchronous system, B-20
synthetic benchmarks, 79–80
  Dhrystone, 79–80
  drawbacks of, 79–80
  Whetstone, 79
  See also benchmarks

`syscall` instruction, 597, A-74
System/360, 37–38, 424, 625
   double precision, 315
   guard digits and, 315
   models, 37
   price/performance, 37
   single precision words, 314
system call exception, 597
system calls, A-48–A-49
system CPU time, 58, 59
system performance, 59
System Performance Evaluation
      Cooperative. *See* SPEC
      benchmarks
systems software, 8

T

tags, 547, 557
   checking, 573
   direct-mapped caches and, 575
   fully associative caches and, 575
   size vs. set associativity, 575
   storage, reducing, 564
   TLB, 593
target language, A-6
task identifier, 598
TCP/IP (Transmission Control
      Protocol/Internet Protocol),
      652, 653
temporal locality, 540, 541, 544
temporary registers, 110, 115, 135
   finite state machine implemen-
      tation, 398
   multicycle implementation,
      378–379
   with write control, 385
tests
   equality, 127
   inequality, 127
   less than, 128
text segment, A-20
Thinking Machines CM-5, 753
three-state buffers, B-28, B-29
throughput, 56
   example, 56
   I/O, 655
   I/O benchmarks and, 642
   pipelining increase of, 440, 449,
      514, 522

superscalar increase of, 514
   See also response time
timing methodologies, B-39–B-44
   edge-triggered, B-39–B-41
   level-sensitive, B-41–B-42
   two-phase, B-41, B-42
Tomasulo's algorithm, 526
total network bandwidth, 737
tracks, 646
   bits, 650
   illustrated, 647
   outer, 650, 651
   sectors, 646, 647
   See also magnetic disk(s)
Transaction Processing Council
      (TPC), 643
transaction processing (TP) I/O
      benchmarks, 642–643
   TPC-C, 643
   TPC-D, 643
   See also benchmarks
transfer rate, 642
transfer time, 648
transistors, 22
   number increase of, 22
   pass, B-32
translation hierarchy, 156
translation-lookaside buffer (TLB),
      590–596, 625
   associativity in, 591
   as cache, 602
   combination of events in, 595
   contents, 590
   DECStation 3100, 593, 594
   entries, 590, 598
   exceptions, 601
   hits, 594
   integration, 593–596
   MIPS R2000, 592
   miss(es), 590, 591, 592, 595
      handling, 598–602
      indication, 598
      occurrence of, 598
      processing, 599
      signaling, 601
   page tables and, 590, 591
   Pentium Pro, 613
   PowerPC, 613
   tags, 593
   updating, 592
   values, 590

in virtual memory organization,
      591
   write access bit, 596
transmitter, A-36
transparent latches, B-23
true speedup, 744
truth tables, 389, B-4–B-5
   for ALU control bits, 355, 356, C-4
   control function, C-7
   for datapath control outputs, C-16
   example, B-5
   for next-state output bits, C-15
   optimizing, 356
   with output don't cares, B-17
   single-cycle implementation con-
      trol function, 370
   two-level representation relation-
      ship, B-11
two-level mapping, 588
two-level representation, B-10
   forms, B-10
   truth table relationship, B-11
two-phase clocking, B-41
   designing, B-41–B-42
   illustrated, B-42
two's complement representation,
      120, 213
   advantage of, 213
   binary integer arithmetic, 308
   binary-to-hexadecimal shortcut,
      218
   Booth's algorithm and, 263
   complement of, 219
   negation shortcut, 216
   negative number, 213
   overflow detection, 222
   sign extension shortcut, 217

U

`ulh` pseudoinstruction, A-67
`ulhu` pseudoinstruction, A-67
ulp (units in the last place), 298
`ulw` pseudoinstruction, A-67
unconditional branches, 125
   jumps, 150
   See also branch(es)
unconditional jumps, 129, 150, 188
undefined instructions, 411
   detection of, 413
   See also exception(s)

underbars (_), A-51
underflow, 277, 308
  checking, 281, 282
  gradual, 300
  thresholds, 315
  See also overflow
Unicode, 144
uniform memory access (UMA)
    multiprocessors, 713, 732
UNIVAC I, 36
unsigned numbers, 210–220
  andi/ori and, 230
  signed vs., 214, 215
  See also numbers
update addressing, 175–176
  illustrated, 176
  MIPS code, 176
use bit, 587
user CPU time, 58, 59
ush pseudoinstruction, A-68
usw pseudoinstruction, A-68

V

valid bit, 547
variable array index
  compiling loops with, 126
  compiling with, 114–115
variable clock example, 374–376
variables
  accumulators and, 190
  automatic, 140, 187
  lock, 724, 725
  for loop, 294
  static, 140
VAX architecture, 425
  instruction set, 425
  VAX-11/780, 67, 85
  See also Web Extension III
vector computer(s), 751–752
  advantages, 751–752
  characteristics, 752
  supercomputers, 752
vectored interrupts, 412
vector instructions, 752
vertical microcode, C-31

very large-scale integrated circuits
    (VLSI), 22, 23
  components of, 23
  microprocessors, 42
very long instruction word (VLIW),
    528
virtual addresses, 585
  32-bit, 587
  causing page faults, 599
  fast translation of, 589–591
  mapping from, 582
  space, 585, 597, 598
  translation of, 580
virtually addressed cache, 596
virtual memory, 579–603
  address, 181
  blocks, 580
  combination of events in, 595
  DMA and, 682–683
  fully associative placement, 606
  illustration, 581
  implementing protection with,
    596–598
  motivation for, 579–580
  page faults, 580
  pages, 580
  protection function, 596–598
  relocation, 581
  shared, 730
  systems, 581, 606
  translation process, 580, 602
  write-back, 589
  See also virtual addresses
virtual page number, 581, 584
von Neumann computer, 33
von Neumann, John, 32, 34, 35, 122,
    312, 314
von Neumann syndrome, 746

W

wafer(s), 23
  cost, 25
  defects, 23, 25
  dicing, 23
  illustrated, 25, 26

yield, 23, 48
  See also dies
wall-clock time, 58
WB stage, 453, 476
  control fields, changing, 490
  control lines, 468
  data hazard and, 483
  illustrated, 456, 459
  load instruction, 455
  operand names and, 486
  register number and, 458
  store instruction, 458
  See also pipeline stages
weighted arithmetic mean, 71, 82
weighting factor, 71
Whetstone benchmark, 79
  performance, 86
  See also benchmarks
while loops, 127
Whirlwind project, 35, 623
wide area networks (WANs), 21
Wilkes, Maurice, 33, 312, 423
Winchester disks, 694–695
words
  double, 180
  field definition within, 227
  MIPS, 211
  representation of, 210
  sequential addresses of, 164, 187
workload, 66, 70
  measurement, 82
  relative execution times of, 70
Wozniak, Steve, 40
write-back buffers, 614–615
write-back cache(s), 554, 563
  advantages, 607
  in cache-based multiprocessors,
    721
  implementing, 614
  stalls, 565
  stores, 609
  in virtual memory, 589
  See also cache(s)
write buffer, 516, 554, 614
  DECStation 3100, 554
  depth, 565
  stalls, 565

write-invalidate protocol, 721
   illustrated, 723
   MESI, 724
   See also cache coherency protocols
write-stall clock cycles, 565
write-through cache(s), 553, 562, 563
   advantages, 607
   misses, 607
   organization, 565
   write buffers, 614
   writes, 609
   See also cache(s)
write-update protocol, 721, 726

X

xori instruction, A-59
xor operation, 329, A-59
xspim, A-40
   assembly file button, A-42
   breakpoints and, A-43
   breakpoints button, A-43, A-47
   clear button, A-43, A-47
   command-line options, A-44–A-45
   console window, A-42, A-47
   continue button, A-42, A-43
   control buttons, A-46–A-47
   help button, A-47
   interface, A-41
   load button, A-42, A-46
   mode button, A-47
   print button, A-47
   quit button, A-43, A-46
   run button, A-42, A-47
   set value button, A-47
   starting, A-40
   step button, A-42, A-43, A-47
   terminal button, A-47
   window panes, A-40, A-42
   See also SPIM simulator

Z

Zuse, Konrad, 35, 312